CHABOT COLLEGE - HAYWARD
D0217831
Not to be taken from this room

international encyclopedia of men and masculinities

international encyclopedia of men and masculinities

edited by

michael flood
judith kegan gardiner
bob pease
keith pringle

LONDON AND NEW YORK

First published 2007
by Routledge
2 Park Square, Milton Park, Abingdon, Oxon OX14 4RN

Simultaneously published in the USA and Canada
by Routledge
270 Madison Avenue, New York, NY 10016

Routledge is an imprint of the Taylor & Francis Group, an informa business

Typeset in Bembo and Helvetica by
Taylor & Francis Books
Printed and bound in Great Britain by
MPG Books Ltd, Bodmin

British Library Cataloguing in Publication Data
A calalogue record for this book is available from the British Library

Library of Congress Cataloging-in-Publication Data
A catalog record for this book has been requested

ISBN 978-0-415-33343-6 (hbk)
ISBN 978-0-203-41306-7 (ebk)

contents

introduction

The Routledge *International Encyclopedia of Men and Masculinities* is a key reference guide to theoretical and empirical research about men, masculinities, and masculinity studies around the world. It reflects multidisciplinary perspectives in the social sciences, humanities and, to a lesser extent, the sciences, and in such fields as popular culture, feminist, women's, gender and sexuality studies. Its information is current, accessible and informed by contemporary global scholarship so as to be useful to a broad range of readers. The encyclopedia is designed to be an essential resource for teaching, an invaluable companion to independent study, and a solid starting point for wider exploration.

There is now a well-established wide-ranging scholarship on men and masculinities that offers an increasingly diverse and sophisticated theorization of men and gender relations. The Routledge *International Encyclopedia of Men and Masculinities* (hereafter *IEMM*) reflects and extends this scholarship. Its essays document the organization of masculinities in specific milieux and locales, from schools and workplaces to families or prisons. They investigate the intersections of masculinity with other axes of social differentiation such as race, class, sexuality, age, disability and nation. They examine the construction of masculinities in myriad representations and discourses, from popular films to historical texts, scholarly disciplines and the professions, and explore key aspects of men's material practices, including those associated with gender inequalities. They draw on and engage with contemporary theorizing in feminist, queer, critical race and other scholarship.

IEMM is the first general volume on men and masculinities with a truly international scope. While it features scholarship from Western and/or English-speaking nations in North America, the United Kingdom and the Pacific, it also internationalizes the critical study of men and masculinities to include Latin America, Africa, Asia, Continental Europe and the Nordic countries where significant research about men and masculinities is occurring.

Like the fields of women's studies and gender studies with which it is typically associated, contemporary scholarship on men and gender draws on the theoretical frameworks and tools of such disciplines as sociology, psychology, history, education, literary and cultural studies, anthropology, law, social and community work, religious studies, health and therapy, philosophy of science, political science, economics, criminal justice and philosophy. Each of these fields has been compelled, in addressing gender as a significant category of analysis, to reflect on men's relations to gender, such that, following the insights of feminist scholarship in the past several decades, men and masculinities are subject to critical scrutiny in every discipline across the humanities and social sciences and in some sciences as well. *IEMM* guides students and researchers to key concepts, frameworks and theorists in the field across – and between – these diverse disciplines, thus assisting in the synthesis and integration of the field. It also features essays that metacritically analyse the disciplines from the perspective of masculinity studies.

IEMM also provides succinct and precise guides to issues such as men's health, boys' education, fathering, and men's violence, that are relevant for policy-makers, health professionals, social workers, community workers and students. In other words, this encyclopedia includes a significant focus on work with men and/or boys, whether through therapeutic engagements with particular groups of boys or men or large-scale attempts to mobilize men in communities and activist movements.

IEMM is the key reference work for undergraduate and postgraduate studies of men and masculinities in gender studies, women's studies and in the newly emerging field of critical studies on men. It is also intended to be used as a key reference for the study of men in other social science and humanities courses. Beyond a university readership, *IEMM* can be used by researchers, policy analysts, activists and welfare practitioners who are involved in transforming the social relations of gender. The encyclopedia will inform anti-violence work, counter-sexist education in schools, men's health promotion, and practice with men in the human services, providing an invaluable resource for such work.

The state of scholarship on men and gender

There is nothing new in conducting research on men. Indeed, doing so has been the standard fare of much of traditional academic practice. Historically, much of academic scholarship has been in a sense 'men's studies', in studying men while positioning this as constituting generic human experience. In the past four decades, however, profound social, political and academic shifts have made visible and subjected to critical analysis a number of dominant social categories, including those of maleness or masculinity. Feminism, lesbian, gay and queer politics, as well as the politics of racism and of ethnicity, have challenged dominant social formations of masculinity and contested the social relations of gender and sexuality.

Such developments have been accompanied by new scholarship. The academic destabilization of dominant constructions of men and manhood began in earnest in the mid-1970s, particularly in North America. 'Men's Studies' emerged as an academic discipline, distinctive because of how it studied rather than what, in examining men and masculinities as historically and culturally variable and as politically problematic. Scholarship on men under the name 'Men's Studies' was widely criticized in the late 1980s and early 1990s for its failure to develop a feminist-informed and critical scholarship. At the same time, many feminist and pro-feminist scholars writing on men and masculinities have attempted to develop scholarship that collaborates with academic feminism rather than colonizing it, that is informed rather than ignorant of feminist scholarship, and that furthers progressive social change. Such scholarship is described in various ways, including 'critical scholarship on men and masculinities' and 'masculinity studies'. While some scholarship uses feminist theory to do masculinity studies, others explore men and masculinity in order to revise and reinvigorate feminist and gender theory. Entries in the *IEMM* take up and analyse key terms and concepts, which assume altered shapes in the context of masculinity studies. And as the entries in *IEMM* attest, scholars both engage with and critique a wide variety of other academic disciplines in examining men and gender.

The development of the field of masculinity studies has accelerated since the mid-1990s in four ways.

First, diverse academic journals were launched, such as *Men and Masculinities* (1998), *Psychology of Men & Masculinity* (2000), and the *International Journal of Men's Health* (2002).

More recently, journals focused on particular areas of scholarship and practice have emerged, including the *International Journal of Men's Health*, the *Journal of Men's Health and Gender*, *Fathering* and the *Journal of Men, Masculinities and Spirituality*.

Second, the first readers, handbooks and encyclopedias in masculinity studies were published: Whitehead and Barrett's *The Masculinities Reader* (2001), Adams and Savran's *The Masculinity Studies Reader* (2002), Carroll's *American Masculinities: A Historical Encyclopedia* (2003), Kimmel and Aronson's *Men and Masculinities* (2003) and Kimmel, Hearn and Connell's *Handbook of Studies on Men and Masculinities* (2005). These complement early readers such as Kimmel and Messner's *Men's Lives*, first published in 1989 and frequently revised.

Third, texts focused on men and gender have proliferated. The last decade has seen the publication of scholarly works on men and masculinities in particular nations or regions, including the Middle East, South Asia, the Caribbean, Africa, China and Japan, the Nordic countries and Europe more generally. Academic texts focused on men and gender in relation to particular domains, practices and issues have flourished, as have books and manuals focused on working with boys and men in gender-related work in the human services, community sectors and government, whether as husbands and fathers, sexual partners, perpetrators or victims of violence and crime, students, workers or policy-makers and practitioners.

Fourth, and more generally, the publication of works on men and gender has intensified, with at least 200 new books published in the field since 1998, as the online Men's Bibliography attests. The Routledge *IEMM* highlights the contributions and delineates the debates within this expanding scholarship.

Entries and entry selection

The Routledge *International Encyclopedia of Men and Masculinities* contains 353 free-standing entries written from their individual perspectives by eminent scholars in their fields. Entries are organized alphabetically for general ease of access but also listed thematically at the front of the encyclopedia for the convenience of readers with specific areas of interest.

As the thematic list of entries indicates, some entries focus on gendered processes (such as ageing), practices (such as fathering, violence or work), institutions (such as military organizations or religions), relations (such as friendship or kinship relations) or representations (such as those in film, literature or pornography). The general 'Theory' cluster of entries includes both entries describing the insights regarding men and masculinities contributed by particular theoretical and disciplinary perspectives and also entries centred on key concepts in the field.

The cluster 'Cultural formations' features entries organized into three areas. Six entries address regions that together cover the entire globe, examining cultural formations of manhood in each. Six 'formation' entries address colonial, imperialist, diasporic and migrant masculinities. The third area includes entries on cultural formations for which there is scholarship and entries on terms or concepts significant in culturally specific formations of masculinity. (Of course, in a sense all terms and concepts in masculinity studies are culturally specific, in that they are grounded in particular social locations and histories.) The cluster 'Histories and historical formations' offers entries covering the various historical epochs, histories of regions around the globe, and further entries with a historical focus.

Entries in the cluster 'Masculinity politics' address groups, movements and mobilizations in which men's positions in gender relations and the meanings of masculinities are at issue. Finally, the cluster 'Working with men and boys' offers entries exploring work with particular groups of boys or men, or in particular contexts, or using particular approaches.

The list of entries was produced through several processes. We drew on our own expertise to generate potential entry terms, and we collected words and phrases from the indexes of various key texts in masculinity studies. We invited suggestions for entries from sixteen Consultant Editors in Australia, Canada, Finland, Japan, Hong Kong, Poland, South Africa, the UK and the USA. And we included suggestions from actual and potential authors themselves. We then sorted through the resulting list of potential entries for relevance and coherence. The list has been further refined and modified as the project has proceeded.

In this process, perhaps the most significant challenge was to produce a truly international volume on men and masculinities. Although social formations and social processes related to men and gender exist around the world, scholarship on these is very unevenly distributed, and Western and/or English-language scholarship is both over-represented and over-influential. In addition, all four of the co-editors of this encyclopedia originally derive from English-speaking countries, and the volume is primarily addressed to readers of English. *IEMM* does reflect a now wide-ranging international examination of men and masculinities. Its authors have endeavoured to reflect on the international and cross-cultural dimensions of their topics and to locate the scholarship they describe. Nevertheless, *IEMM* still represents the dominance of 'English-speaking analyses' in this field. Consequently, the editors hope readers will see the encyclopedia as one further stage in the ongoing struggle to create truly international and cross-cultural dialogues on the topic of men and masculinities.

We chose not to include biographical entries for individual scholars. Selecting who to feature or omit would have been a difficult and problematic exercise, and we did not wish to highlight 'the great men (and women) of masculinity studies' rather than the empirical and theoretical contributions they have made. Nevertheless, we acknowledge that critical reflection on the social locations and speaking positions of oneself and other knowledge producers is a desirable element of progressive academic practice, perhaps especially for members of privileged social categories.

how to use this book

The Routledge *International Encyclopedia of Men and Masculinities* is composed of 353 free-standing entries, divided into short, medium and longer essays of 400–2,250 words in length, comprising 400,000 words in total. The encyclopedia offers a comprehensive guide to the current state of scholarship about men, masculinities and gender around the world.

IEMM's A–Z format makes this scholarship easily accessible. Cross-referencing in the form of 'See also' lists at the end of most entries refers the reader to other related entries. Each article contains a list of references, including sources cited by the writer as well as additional items that may interest the reader. A thorough, analytical index complements the accessibility of the entries, easing the reader's entry into the wealth of information provided. A thematic list of entries is also included to assist readers with research in particular subjects.

A total of 260 authors have contributed to this encyclopedia. They are based in Australia, Canada, Colombia, Cyprus, Denmark, Finland, Germany, Hong Kong, Hungary, India, Indonesia, Ireland, Israel, Japan, the Netherlands, New Zealand, Norway, Poland, Romania, South Africa, Spain, Sweden, Thailand, the United Kingdom, the USA and Zimbabwe. The expertise of a wide-ranging group of contributors provides the reader with an effective overview of the diverse scholarship on men and masculinities under way around the globe.

acknowledgements

This volume could not have reached completion without the support and assistance of many people. Gerard Greenway at Routledge first proposed the project and assisted the Volume Editors with much of the early developmental work. Jamie Ehrlich assisted us with overall administration throughout much of the process of commissioning and editing entries. Kate Aker, also at Routledge, then managed the final stages.

The Consultant Editors have been an invaluable source of advice and support. Our thanks go, finally, to the authors on whose contributions this encyclopedia rests. We deeply appreciate the wealth of expertise and wide variety of approaches they bring to *IEMM*. We are grateful to have learned so much from our authors over the course of this project.

consultant editors

contributors

James Eli Adams
Cornell University, USA

Rebecca G. Adams
University of North Carolina, Greensboro, USA

Hossein Adibi
Queensland University of Technology, Australia

Patricia A. Adler
University of Colorado, USA

Peter Adler
Keystone Centre, Colorado, USA

Samuel Adu-Poku
Youngstown State University, USA

Stuart C. Aitken
San Diego State University, USA

Claire Alexander
London School of Economics, UK

Fred Alford
University of Maryland, USA

Katherine R. Allen
Virginia Polytechnic, USA

Tammy L. Anderson
University of Delaware, USA

Tomoko Aoyama
University of Queensland, Australia

Brian Attebery
Idaho State University, USA

Andrew Austin
University of Wisconsin-Green Bay, USA

Robert John Balfour
University of KwaZulu-Natal, South Africa

Edward Read Barton
Michigan State University, USA

John Beebe
C.G. Jung Institute of San Francisco, USA
University of California, San Francisco, USA

James K. Beggan
University of Louisville, USA

John Beynon
University of Glamorgan, UK

Elizabeth Bishop
New York Public Library, USA

Chris Borst
University of Toronto, Canada

Leo Braudy
University of Southern California, USA

Susannah Bredenkamp
University of Alberta, Canada

Harry Brod
University of Northern Iowa, USA

Heather Brook
Flinders University, Australia

David Buchbinder
Curtin University of Technology, Australia

Brian Burtch
Simon Fraser University, USA

Gerald R. Butters
Aurora University, USA

Mihri Inal Cakir
USA

Darcey Callison
York University, Canada

Lucy M. Candib
University of Massachussetts Medical School, USA

Terrell Carver
University of Bristol, UK

Jachinson W. Chan
University of California, Santa Barbara (1994–2000), USA

Radhika Chopra
University of Delhi, India

Alastair Christie
University College Cork, Ireland

Kenneth Clatterbaugh
University of Washington, USA

Frances Cleaver
University of Bradford, UK

Sam V. Cochran
University of Iowa, USA

Richard Collier
University of Newcastle upon Tyne, UK

David Collinson
Lancaster University, UK

Margaret Collinson
Lancaster University, UK

Raewyn Connell
University of Sydney, Australia

John P. Corr
McMaster University, Canada

Malcolm Cowburn
University of Sheffield, UK

Gillian Cowlishaw
University of Technology Sydney, Australia

Barbara Creed
University of Melbourne, Australia

Martin Crotty
University of Queensland, Australia

Philip Culbertson
University of Auckland, New Zealand

Romit Dasgupta
University of Western Australia, Australia

Kevin G. Davison
The National University of Ireland, Ireland

Sandra Dema
Universidad de Oviedo, Spain

Jed Diamond
MenAlive, California, USA

Capitolina Diaz
Universidad de Oviedo, Spain

Mario Di Gangi
City University of New York, USA

Toby L. Ditz
Johns Hopkins University, USA

Andrea Doucet
Carleton University, Canada

Gary W. Dowsett
La Trobe University, Australia

Peter Drucker
International Institute for Research and Education, The Netherlands

Murray Drummond
University of South Australia, Australia

Matthew R. Dudgeon
Emory University, USA

Dean Durber
Curtin University of Technology, Australia

Tim Edwards
University of Leicester, UK

Andrew Elfenbein
University of Minnesota, Twin Cities, USA

Maria Eriksson
Uppsala University, Sweden

Marianne A. Ferber
University of Illinois at Urbana-Champaign, USA

Murray Fisher
University of Sydney, Australia

Stephen Fisher
Chisolm Institute, Australia

Michael Flood
La Trobe University, Australia

Martin Foreman
Thailand

Greg Forter
University of South Carolina, USA

Christopher E. Forth
Australian National University, Australia

Thomas W. Gallant
York University, Canada

Judith Kegan Gardiner
University of Illinois at Chicago, USA

Joseph Gelfer
Victoria University of Wellington, Australia

James Gifford
University of Victoria, Canada

Rob Gilbert
James Cook University, Australia

James M. Glass
University of Maryland, USA

Iklim Göksel
University of Illinois at Chicago, USA

Gloria González-López
University of Texas at Austin, USA

Patricia Adair Gowaty
University of Georgia, USA

Naomi Graetz
Ben Gurion University of the Negev, Israel

Mark Graham
Stockholm University, Sweden

Colin Green
The George Washington University, USA

Gabriele Griffin
University of York, UK

Hollis Griffin
Northwestern University, USA

Michael Groneberg
Université Fribourg, Switzerland

Scott William Gust
Bowling Green State University, USA

Matthew C. Gutmann
Brown University, USA

Dawn Hadley
University of Sheffield, UK

Jill M. Harbison
University of Louisville, USA

Ken Harland
University of Ulster, UK

Caro Harper
Syracuse University, USA

Glenn P. Harvey
University of New England, Australia

Andrea Hasenbank
University of Alberta, Canada

Helen Hatchell
Murdoch University, Australia

Brian Heaphy
University of Manchester, UK

Jeff Hearn
Linköping University, Sweden
Svenska Handelshögskolan, Finland
University of Huddersfield, UK

Karla A. Henderson
North Carolina State University, USA

Peter Hennen
Ohio State University at Newark, USA

Gregory M. Herek
University of California, Davis, USA

Ray Hibbins
Griffith University, Australia

Paul Higate
University of Bristol, UK

John Hoberman
University of Texas at Austin, USA

Brendan Hokowhitu
University of Otago, New Zealand

Shane Hopkinson
Central Queensland University, Australia

Richard Howson
University of Wollongong, Australia

Susan Hunt
Santa Monica College, USA

Mark Hunter
University of Toronto at Scarborough, Canada

Mark Hussey
Pace University, USA

David Iacuone
RMIT University, Australia

Marcia C. Inhorn
University of Michigan, USA

Kimio Ito
Osaka University, Japan

Gavin Ivey
University of the Witwatersrand at Johannesburg, South Africa

David Jackson
Nottinghamshire Men' Health Group, UK

William A. Jellison
Colgate University, USA

Thomas Johansson
University of Gothenburg, Sweden

Waldo E. Johnson, Jr
University of Chicago at Illinois, USA

Terry Jones
Elderhood Institute, West Linn, Oregon, USA

Vernon Jones
Red Barnet, Save the Children Fund, Denmark

Bruce Kapferer
University of Bergen, Norway

Mary Jane Kehily
The Open University, UK

Michael Kehler
University of Western Ontario, Canada

Deborah Kerfoot
University of Keele, UK

Marjorie Kibby
University of Newcastle, Australia

Angela Kiire
University of Bradford, UK

Michael Kimmel
State University of New York at Stony Brook, USA

Björn Krondorfer
St. Mary's College of Maryland, USA

Terry A. Kupers
The Wright Institute, Berkeley, California, USA

John C. Landreau
The College of New Jersey, USA

Thomas Laqueur
University of California at Berkeley, USA

Helen Leslie
New Zealand Agency for International Development (NZAID), New Zealand

David Leverenz
University of Florida, USA

Donald P. Levy
University of Connecticut, USA

Ellen Lewin
University of Iowa, USA

Sonya Lipsett-Rivera
Carleton University, Canada

Jørgen Lorentzen
University of Oslo, Norway

Kam Louie
Hong Kong University, Hong Kong

Scott A. Lukas
Lake Tahoe College, USA

Ami Lynch
The George Washington University, USA

Dawn Lyon
University of Essex, UK

Carole McCann
University of Maryland, Baltimore County, USA

Melanie McCarry
University of Bristol, UK

Sara I. McClelland
The City University of New York, USA

Sam McCready
University of Ulster, UK

Fiona McDermott
University of Melbourne, Australia

Tara MacDonald
McGill University, Canada

Jim McKay
University of Queensland, Australia

Shaun K. McLaughlin
University of British Columbia, Canada

Mark McLelland
University of Wollongong, Australia

Anthony McMahon

James Mahalik
Boston College, USA

Jason L. Mallory
Estrella Mountain Community College, USA

Susan Marine
Harvard University, USA

William Marsiglio
University of Florida, USA

Brian Martin
Williams College, USA

Shelley Martin
University of Louisiana at Lafayette, USA

Wayne Martino
University of Western Ontario, Canada

Amade M'charek
University of Amsterdam, The Netherlands

Robert Meadows
University of Surrey, UK

Jonathan M. Metzl
University of Michigan, USA

Stephan F. Miescher
University of California, Santa Barbara, USA

Martin Mills
University of Queensland, Australia

Victor Minichiello
University of New England, Australia

Lee Clark Mitchell
Princeton University, USA

Daniel Monterescu
Central European University, Hungary

Julie Mooney-Somers
University of Western Sydney, Australia

Clive Moore
University of Queensland, Australia

Samantha A. Morgan-Curtis
Tennessee State University, USA

Robert Morrell
University of Natal, South Africa

Michaela Mudure
Babes-Bolyai University, Romania

Ursula Müller
Universität Bielefeld, Germany

Peter F. Murphy
Murray State University, USA

Linzi Murrie
Southern Cross University, Australia

Henri Myrtinnen
INSIST/KEPA, Indonesia

Joane Nagel
University of Kansas, USA

Stuart Newman
University of Sydney, Australia

Hertta Niemi
Swedish School of Economics and Business Administration (HANKEN), Sweden

Jade M. Nobbs
Curtin University, Australia

Robert A. Nye
Oregon State University, USA

Patrick O'Leary
University of South Australia, Australia

Elżbieta H. Oleksy
University of Lodz, Poland

Andrea O'Reilly
York University, Canada

Caroline Osella
University of London, UK

Filippo Osella
University of Sussex, UK

Nelly Oudshoorn
University of Twente, The Netherlands

Marc Ouellette
McMaster University, Canada

Elizabeth Ozanne
University of Melbourne, Australia

Gilad Padva
University of Tel Aviv, Israel

Andrew Parker
University of Warwick, UK

Wendy Parkin
University of Huddersfield, UK

Rob Pattman
University of Kwa-Zulu Natal, South Africa

Dean Peacock
Sonke Gender Justice, South Africa

Bob Pease
Deakin University, Australia

Andreas G. Philaretou
Cyprus College, Cyprus

Lisbeth Pike
Edith Cowan University, Australia

David Plummer
University of West Indies, Jamaica

Scott Poynting
University of Western Sydney, Australia

Lisa S. Price
Canada

Keith Pringle
Mälardalen University College University, Sweden

Paul M. Pulé
Murdoch University, Australia

Najat Rahman
University of Montreal, Canada

Gillian Ranson
University of Calgary, Canada

Sarah L. Rasmusson
University of Illinois at Urbana-Champaign, USA

Gayatri Reddy
University of Illinois at Chicago, USA

Elizabeth Renfro
California State University, Chico, USA

Emma Renold
Cardiff University, UK

Amy Richlin
University of California at Los Angeles, USA

Damien W. Riggs
University of Adelaide, Australia

Sally Robinson
Texas A&M University, USA

Victoria Robinson
University of Sheffield, UK

Warren Rosenberg
Wabash College, USA

Marlon B. Ross
University of Virginia, USA

John Rowan
UK

Helen I. Safa
University of Florida, USA

Thomas J. Scheff
University of California at Santa Barbara, USA

Richard Schmitt
Brown University, USA

Toni Schofield
University of Sydney, Australia

Michael Schwalbe
North Carolina State University, USA

Samuel R. Schwartz
University of Arizona, USA

Chris Shelley
University of British Columbia, Canada

Margrethe Silberschmidt
Institute of Public Health, Copenhagen, Denmark

Andrew Singleton
Monash University, Australia

Mrinalini Sinha
Penn State University, USA

Andrew Smiler
State University of New York at Oswego, USA

Royce W. Smith
Wichita State University, USA

Tyson Smith
State University of New York at Stony Brook, USA

Katherine V. Snyder
University of California at Berkeley, USA

Andrew Spicer
University of the West of England, UK

Sanjay Srivastava
Deakin University, Australia

Derek Stanovsky
Appalachian State University, USA

Kathleen Starck
Osnabrück University, Germany

Todd Starkweather
University of Illinois at Chicago, USA

Harry Stecopoulos
University of Iowa, USA

Lara M. Stepleman
Medical College of Georgia, USA

James P. Sterba
University of Notre Dame, USA

Heather Streets
Washington State University, USA

Barbara Sullivan
University of Queensland, Austraiia

Nikki Sullivan
Macquarie University, Australia

Claude Summers
University of Michigan at Dearborn, USA

Raymond Suttner
University of South Africa, South Africa

Nicholas L. Syrett
University of Northen Colorado, USA

Calvin Thomas
Georgia State University, USA

Manuel Torres
University of Delaware, USA

Michael Uebel
University of Texas at Austin, USA

Koji Ueno
Florida State University, USA

Nancy van Styvendale
University of Alberta, Canda

Nicole Vitellone
Liverpool University, UK

Mara Viveros Vigoya
Universidad Nacional de Colombia, Colombia

Ben Wadham
Flinders University, Australia

Vandana Wadhwa
University of Akron, USA

Maurice O. Wallace
Duke University, USA

Chris Walton
Lancaster University, UK

Joan Wardrop
Curtin University of Technology, Australia

Elyssa D. Warkentin
University of Alberta, Canada

John T. Warren
Southern Illinois University, USA

Linda D. Wayne
University of Minnesota, USA

Marcus B. Weaver-Hightower
University of North Dakota, USA

Stephen M. Whitehead
Keele University, UK

Liz Wilson
Miami University of Ohio, USA

Michelle M. Wright
Macalester College, USA

thematic list of entries

All entries are assumed to be focused on questions of men and gender. For example, the entry 'Science' refers to '*Men and masculinity in* science'.

Entries vary from 2,250 words, substantial essays (marked with ★) on major topics, to shorter essays of 1,000 words on important topics, to 400-word entries on concepts and terms.

Some entries are listed under more than one heading.

Pederasty
Penetration
Phallocentrism
Pimps and traffickers
Playboys
Procreation
Prostitutes, men as
Prostitution
Radical Faeries
Reproductive issues and technologies
Sadism
Semen anxiety
Sexual anxiety
Sexuality*
Sexually transmitted infections
Sodomy
Tantric and Taoist sexualities
Viagra
Virility

Fatherhood

Fatherhood, Fathering*
Fatherhood, gay
Fatherhood, single
Fatherhood, stepfathers
Fatherhood, teenage
Fatherhood and paid work
Fatherhood and violence

Violence and crime

Aggression
Armies
Bullying
Child abuse*
Child pornography
Commercial sexual exploitation of children
Crime, criminality and law*
Domestic violence*
Duelling
Elder abuse
Fatherhood and violence
Honour killings
Hunting
Lynching
Rape
Self-harm
Sexual violence*
Terrorism*
Torture
Violence*
Violence, men as victims of
Violence, organisational and collective*
Violence, workplace
Violence, sport
War*
Working with perpetrators or offenders
Working with victims and survivors

Health

Demography
Depression
Disability
Drugs, addiction, and abuse
Health, occupational
Health and illness, men's*
HIV/AIDS
Impotence and sexual dysfunction
Infertility
Karôshi
Menopause, male
Men's health studies
Risk-taking
Sexually transmitted infections
Suicide

Work, class and economic relations

Class, work and masculinity*
Domestic labour
Leisure
Men in women's/feminised occupations
Men working with children
Occupational segregation
Organisations, gendered
Unions/organised labour movements
Violence, workplace*

INSTITUTIONS

Academia
Criminal justice system
Education
Families*
Family law
Fraternities
Gangs
Marriage
Medicine
Military institutions
Police
Prisons

BODIES

REPRESENTATIONS

Arts

Literature

Miscellaneous categories

THEORY

Theoretical and disciplinary perspectives on men and masculinities

Key concepts in the field

FORMS OF MASCULINITY

CULTURAL FORMATIONS

Regions

Formations

Further scholarship and categories

HISTORIES AND HISTORICAL FORMATIONS

Periods/epochs

Regions

Further entries

MASCULINITY POLITICS

WORKING WITH MEN AND BOYS

alphabetical list of entries

ACADEMIA

'Academia' is the academic world of colleges and universities, institutions of post-secondary education usually comprised of faculty, administration and students. Those who are 'in academia', also known as academics, administer or teach at the college level. Until the later nineteenth century in most countries, the ranks of academia were comprised almost exclusively of men; to this day, men constitute the majority of academics.

Academia is etymologically derived from the Greek Academy, founded in Athens in the fourth century BCE for the purposes of educating both men and women in philosophy, science and mathematics. The present system of academia is more recognisable as a descendant of the first European universities founded during the late twelfth and early thirteenth centuries in Bologna and Paris, respectively. Universities throughout the world owe their form and function to this European system of academia, often through direct colonisation by European nations but also through the conscious adaptation of European models of the university (Rüegg 1992).

Although the education of students remains a chief academic concern, those in academia are also charged with the production of knowledge in the sciences, humanities and social sciences. Academics, then, are not just teachers of post-secondary education but also researchers, scientists, scholars and writers.

Feminists have criticised the academy for its overt sexism and also for its hierarchy and methods of pedagogy, both of which have been cited as particularly masculine in orientation. In terms of overt sexism, much evidence suggests not only that male students are given preferential treatment and male academics remunerated more substantially and promoted more frequently, but also that those disciplines generally considered masculine (the sciences, mathematics and engineering) are often accorded more prestige and funding than those considered more traditionally feminine (the arts and humanities). The critique of masculinity as inherent in this form of the academy argues that women and men typically learn and interact in different ways, men through hierarchy, women through cooperation. Because the academy originated as an exclusively masculine domain, it continues to employ those operational practices that favour the masculine (see Martínez Alemán and Renn 2002).

References and further reading

Martínez Alemán, A. and Renn, K. (eds) (2002) *Women in Higher Education*, Santa Barbara, CA: ABC-CLIO.

Rüegg, W. (ed.) (1992) *A History of the University in Europe*, 4 vols, Cambridge and New York: Cambridge University Press.

Stone, L. (ed.) (1974) *The University in Society*, 2 vols, Princeton, NJ: Princeton University Press.

NICHOLAS L. SYRETT

ADVENTURE LITERATURE

The literary genre of the adventure tale, defined broadly as a group of narratives that emphasises 'the primacy of action as opposed to the primacy of feeling' (Richards 1989: 2), is historically associated with a male readership. Although there are several antecedents, the adventure genre proper is usually considered to have been inaugurated in 1719 with the publication of Daniel Defoe's castaway novel *Robinson Crusoe*. The genre was immediately popular and has remained so.

An adventure narrative is characterised by a central male protagonist who typically leaves his home to face the unknown caused by forces beyond his control, undergoing hardship and danger with stoic goodwill in his quest to attain independence. As Green argues in his pioneering study of the 'Great Tradition' of adventure literature, this quest is almost always set against a backdrop of Western imperial conquest; it includes contact with a racial 'other' usually depicted as inferior and savage. Further, the primary emotional thrust of the genre is towards triumph (Green 1979: 82). It is no coincidence that the genre reached its height of popularity in the last decades of the nineteenth century – the simultaneous height of the British Empire.

A representative sample of British adventure novels begins with *Robinson Crusoe* and its depiction of a master–servant relationship and includes the re-imaginings of that novel that dot the eighteenth century. Victorian examples include *Treasure Island* (Stevenson 1883), *King Solomon's Mines* (Haggard 1885), and several of the longer works of Arthur Conan Doyle, all of which variously depict facets of British imperial conquest. In the twentieth century, the media of adventure shift from print to television and film. The genre moves from texts like *Kim* (Kipling 1901) and *Tarzan of the Apes* (Burroughs 1914), to filmed versions of earlier adventure literature and more contemporary original narratives that reinterpret the genre in light of the century-long decline of Western imperialism.

British colonies, too, exhibit their own adventure traditions, incorporating their geographic specificities into the framework of the genre and often focusing on the colonisation of Aboriginal lands and cultures. In Canada, survival stories like *The Young Fur Traders* (Ballantyne 1856) and later the novels and stories of Jack London were read widely, and in Australia books like *The Secret of the Australian Desert* (Favenc 1896) were equally popular. American adventure stories, meanwhile, often incorporate the history of the settlement of the western states or the Civil War. In Mark Twain's *Huckleberry Finn* (1885), the boy hero's quest to free a slave expanded physical journey into a national moral quest.

The adventure genre became, in the nineteenth century, a staple of boys' reading. With increasing education and ever-rising literacy rates among the working classes throughout the Victorian era, a new market for cheap publications opened up, and boys' adventure books and magazines flooded the market. Called 'penny dreadfuls', these stories drew on the sensational tradition of the Gothic novel. Popular titles included *The Boy Highwayman*, *The Boy Pirate* and *The Boy King of the Outlaws*, and magazines included *The Bad Boy's Paper* and *Wild Boys of London*. These publications appropriated many aspects of traditional adventure literature (including, usually, the imperial discourse), but refused to conform to dominant Victorian ideals of socially acceptable behaviour. This led to reactionary concerns about the 'corruption' of working-class boys, and upper- and middle-class fears about a coming generation of unruly, possibly criminal young men. In response, the end of the century ushered in a new respectability in mass-published boys' literature: the Religious Tract Society began publishing the successful *Boy's Own Paper* in 1879, and many others took advantage of the lucrative market and followed suit.

Recognised by many social institutions as an effective tool of entertainment and instruction, these books positioned their young readers as potential heroes and simultaneously conducted a subtle didactic campaign to shape masculine identities in service of nation and empire, to instil dominant values, and to provide wholesome role models (Richards 1989: 3). The well-known *Tom Brown's School Days* (Hughes 1857) casts the schoolboy as a heroic figure, while other texts simply insert boy heroes into pre-existing narratives (often with titles like *The Boy Crusoe*). As Bristow argues, there are inevitably embedded in these stories elements 'which would take the boy into areas of history and geography that placed him at the top of the racial ladder and at the helm of all the world' (1991: 21). Indeed, Baden-Powell's influential and continually popular manifesto on proper conduct for boys, *Scouting for Boys* (1908) makes these expectations overt and recommends that boys model themselves after literary adventure heroes. Boy adventure stories, most critics agree, strive to produce imperial men.

Academic study of the adventure literature genre began in the 1980s. It has focused from the beginning on images of imperialism within the texts, as well as their dissemination and reception. Postcolonialism has facilitated studies of the representation of colonised cultures in the texts. Attention has also been paid to the complicated interactions of class, gender and race that occur in many of the narratives, as well as the marginal role of girls and women in the genre (although a parallel stream of girls' adventure literature evolved in the late nineteenth and twentieth centuries). Finally, postmodern cultural scholars have considered the ways in which adventure texts are 'used' by subordinate cultures to produce meanings of resistance and self-determination at odds with the texts' overt significations.

References and further reading

Bristow, J. (1991) *Empire Boys*, London: HarperCollins.

Dunae, P. (1979) 'Penny dreadfuls', *Victorian Studies*, 22: 133–50.

Green, M. (1979) *Dreams of Adventure, Deeds of Empire*, New York: Basic Books.

Phillips, R. (1997) *Mapping Men and Empire*, London: Routledge.

Reynolds, K. (1990) *Girls Only?* New York: Harvester Wheatsheaf.

Richards, J. (ed.) (1989) *Imperialism and Juvenile Literature*, Manchester: Manchester University Press.

ELYSSA D. WARKENTIN

ADVERTISING

Advertising is a form of mass media designed to promote a specific product, service, or idea on behalf of a business or organisation. Advertisers ordinarily use such media as television, radio, print (magazines, newspapers and billboards), sponsorship of cultural and sporting events, and the internet. Today advertisers also use settings less obvious than billboards and TV commercials, such as sidewalks, movies and school buses. Guerrilla marketing tactics like 'product placement' – where the intended audience is unaware that they have been exposed to an advertisement, while the desired impression of the product remains – are increasingly common.

In the early twentieth century, advertising in the US was primarily directed towards women because they were responsible for most consumer purchases, the exception being 'big ticket' products like cars and major appliances (O'Barr 2006). Ads oriented towards men were straightforward and usually included an image and description of the product's function, price and location. After World War II, however, industries increasingly courted the adult male consumer, and then with the advent of youth culture, teens and young adults.

Today, advertisements regularly play on consumers' anxieties and emotions. As Galbraith presciently argued, advertising's main function is to create desires that previously did not exist (Galbraith 1971: 149). A standard ploy is to make the consumer feel as though the product will remedy a specific insecurity. Ad designers prey on a modern culture obsessed with self-enhancement, youth, body image and gender identity – a favoured theme aimed at both men and women (Barthel 1988, 1990; Goffman 1976). However, advertising's ubiquitous presence also creates a more sceptical and desensitised audience. Men, in particular, tend to believe that they are less susceptible to marketing ploys (Elliot and Elliot 2005).

In mainstream Western advertisements, men are usually portrayed in active, authoritative and important roles. Common themes are the provider father, the strong athlete, the socially successful hunk and the wealthy, in-control businessman. Men are represented in more television advertisements than women, with the exception of health and beauty products (Ganahl *et al.* 2003). Global research concludes that commercials in Latin America use similar storylines and depictions of men (Medrado *et al.* 2001).

In voice-overs, male narrators are usually employed to convey greater authority. Research from Brazil found that 86 per cent of commercials had male narrators (Medrado *et al.* 2001). While women are still more frequently depicted as sex objects, ads increasingly show men as sex objects. Idealised male figures are now employed for many fashion, health and beauty products – including erectile dysfunction or impotence remedies. Although marketers deliberately evoke both insecurity and relief, it is a delicate balance. A pitch that overly induces shame will not likely succeed for men (Irvine 2006).

Ads portraying men as sex objects face challenges because the 'male gaze' is traditionally directed at women, and appearance is supposedly less of a man's concern. Ads commonly address this dilemma by depicting a 'masculine' character with overt heterosexual desires. For example, grooming product commercials equate shaving with high speed racing or rocket ships and conclude with a sexy woman caressing the adventurer's shaven cheek.

In the ongoing tension between consumer resistance and advertising appeal, advertisers sometimes embrace images that contrast with traditional male ideals. One instance is the recent trend towards rejoinder ads celebrating ordinary guys who sit around, delight in TV and fattening foods, and seem utterly unconcerned with their appearance. This depiction – which resembles the average male body type far more than most ads for women match real female bodies – suggests that not only is the ideal body unattainable for most men (Elliot and Elliot 2005), but also rebelling against it can be 'cool'. Very few female-oriented ads, in contrast, depict women who stray far from the sexualised, thin body ideal.

Several recent ad campaigns for men court viewers by playing upon a threatened sense of manhood. The pitches portray men's behaviour and 'needs' as opposed to the demands of women or gender non-conforming men (gays, wimps, etc.). For example, a Burger King ad called the 'Manthem', first aired in 2006, features hungry men taking a city by storm while holding big hamburgers and singing 'I Am Man!', a parody of Helen Reddy's 'I Am Woman'. The ad included men burning their underwear (a wink to supposed 'bra burning' in the 1960s women's liberation movement) and flipping a mini-van over a highway overpass (a rebellion against domesticity). These over-the-top ads use comedy to handle the irony of portraying men as a constituency group with unmet needs (Smith 2005).

A thirty-something white, middle-class heterosexual male remains the standard version of 'man' in popular culture, although many advertisers seek to capitalise on the variety of masculine identities. Awareness of various 'masculinities' allows advertisers to cater to specific male demographics. Sophisticated techniques like data mining help identify (and subsequently create) niche consumption desires. Additionally, hyper-specialised media outlets enable advertisers to target precise demographics. For example, advertisers began designing ads for gay men and airing them on gay-oriented cable television channels like Here TV and Logo.

References and further reading

Barthel, D. (1988) *Putting on Appearances: Gender and Advertising*, Philadelphia, PA: Temple University Press.

—— (1990) 'A consumer and a gentleman', *Public Culture*, 2 (2): 129–34.

Elliot, R. and Elliot, C. (2005) 'Idealized images of the male body in advertising', *Journal of Marketing Communications*, 11 (1): 3–19.

Galbraith, J.K. [1958] (1971) *The Affluent Society*, 2nd edn, Boston, MA: Houghton Mifflin.

Ganahl, D.J., Prinsen, T.J. and Netzley, S.B. (2003) 'A content analysis of prime time commercials', *Sex Roles*, 49: 545–51.

Goffman, E. (1976) *Gender Advertisements*, New York: Harper and Row.

Irvine, J.M. (2006) 'Selling Viagra', *Contexts*, 5 (2): 39–44.

Medrado, B., Lyra, J. and Monteiro, M. (2001) 'Masculinities in Brazil' in B. Pease and K. Pringle (eds) *A Man's World*, New York: Zed Books, pp. 163–76.

O'Barr, W. (2006) 'Representations of masculinity and femininity in advertising', *Advertising and Society Review*, 7 (2); available online at http://muse.jhu.edu/journals/asr/indexb.html (accessed 14 September 2006).

Smith, T. (2005) 'Pumping irony', *Advertising and Society Review*, 6 (3); available online at http://muse.jhu.edu/journals/asr/indexb.html (accessed 14 September 2006).

See also: culture and representation

TYSON SMITH

AESTHETICS

'Aesthetics' is from the Greek *aistheta*, 'things perceptible by the senses', and *aisthetes*, 'one who perceives'. Aesthetics is related to criticism of the beautiful and the theory of taste, usually in criticism of art. An aesthete is a person devoted to the beautiful in art and aestheticism is the point of view that art is self-sufficient (*l'art pour l'art*). 'Beauty', 'sensibility' and 'looking' are therefore central terms connected to aesthetics.

Aesthetics was a central part of Antique philosophy, but became unpopular with Bacon, Descartes and Spinoza in the Age of Reason in the seventeenth century. We could say that seventeenth-century rationality strengthened the split between the rational man and the emotional and sensible woman which can be traced back through Aquinas to the Greece of Plato and Aristotle. This dualism became even more important in the bourgeoisie period. Romanticism brought a reaction against rationalism in the late eighteenth and nineteenth centuries and opened up space for a masculine sensibility among artists. This new sensibility developed into an aestheticism practised by decadents and dandies. The Danish Herman Bang and the Irish Oscar Wilde became well-known figures of masculine aestheticism. 'Life is a work of art' was their principle. The hero of this programme was Des Esseintes, the main character of J.K. Huysmans' novel *A Rebours* (1884), who seeks to create an entirely artificial life.

In the last few decades, masculinity and aesthetics have again become an issue. Calvin Klein's campaigns from the mid-1980s, with beautiful naked men advertising underwear, were a starting point (see Bordo 1999). Men were not there to desire but to be desired. Since the mid-1980s the commercial aspects of masculine aesthetics have flourished and opened up a new arena for masculinity, often called 'new man' or known by the more urban stylish nickname 'Metrosexual'. But masculine aesthetics have also opened up flexible and diversified masculinities against the rigidity of patriarchal and rational masculinity. Playfulness, beauty and sensibility have become a new part of manhood, for heterosexual as well as for homosexual men.

References and further reading

Bordo, S. (1999) *The Male Body*, New York: Farrar, Straus and Giroux.

Huysmans, J.K. [1884] (1982) *Against Nature* (*A Rebours*), Harmondsworth: Penguin Books.

JØRGEN LORENTZEN

AFFIRMATIVE ACTION

Affirmative action is a political tool used to prevent or challenge social inequality for those groups in a position of inferiority, both as a consequence of discrimination being suffered and as a result of past discrimination whose effects are still present. Its aim is to promote processes to allow social groups suffering from discrimination to achieve equality. Affirmative action measures are dependent and temporary in nature since they exist only in so far and as long as the discrimination persists against the group for which they are intended. The United States was the first Western country to implement these measures and to do so with the greatest force. However, it should not be forgotten that such policies were in use long ago in India to help certain castes, such as the untouchables, isolated communities and those marginalised socially and educationally.

Policies of affirmative action have been put into practice in different countries to encourage women, ethnic minorities, disabled people and other discriminated groups to take part in politics, the labour market and education. Recently these measures have begun to be applied to reconciling family and employment issues. Some measures are exclusively addressed to men, such as paternity leave or fathers' extended leave of absence for child care.

However, affirmative action policies are not free from controversy. An important social debate has arisen with regard to their suitability, legitimacy and fairness. For instance, different groups within the feminist and men's movements have taken part in these debates: some argue that the measures constitute a form of inverted discrimination as they are prejudicial against men who themselves have not committed discriminatory acts. In defence of the measures, they are argued as offering compensation and reparation for the effects of a long-standing and ingrained discrimination: they are necessary to transform an unjust social order that harms not only those for whom affirmative action is intended but also the whole society.

References and further reading

Bacchi, C.L. (1996) *The Politics of Affirmative Action: Women, Equality and Category Politics*, London: Sage.

Dema, S. (2000) *A la igualdad por la desigualdad: La acción positiva como estrategia para combatir la discriminación de las mujeres* (To Equality through Inequality. Positive Action as Strategy to Overcome Discrimination against Women), Oviedo: KRK Ediciones.

Diaz, C. (2006) 'Acción Positiva', in C. Torres, S. Giner and E. Lamo de Espinosa (eds) *Diccionario de Sociologia* (Dictionary of Sociology), Madrid: Alianza.

Rosenfeld, M. (1991) *Affirmative Action and Justice. A Philosophical and Constitutional Inquiry*, New Haven, CT and London: Yale University Press.

SANDRA DEMA
CAPITOLINA DIAZ

AFRICAN–AMERICAN MASCULINITIES

African–American masculinities encompasses the range of acts and attitudes associated with the diversity of African–American men's unique self-expression from slavery to the present.

Denying that its captives were even human, American slavery also deprived slaves of the power and privileges of man- and womanhood traditionally afforded to free white persons in early American society. The specific struggle of African–American men to reclaim black humanity by demonstrating visible signs of comparably masculine traits and behaviours has been ongoing ever since, and chronically difficult. However trying the historical obstinacy of white American men to grant to African–American men equal social and political status, the greater difficulty of black men's struggles in America remains the improbability of their ever fully realising the idealised model of American manhood. For that model, white recognises and congratulates itself precisely for not being black. The pluralisation of African–American masculinity into African–American masculinities thus represents the multiplication of attempts to escape from this quandary which naturalises masculinity to white men.

The history of African–American masculinities in the United States must have had its beginnings in New England during the revolutionary period when a free black man named Prince Hall and fourteen other free black men of Boston enlisted in the Ancient and Accepted Order of Freemasons. Initiated by a lodge of Irish Freemasons at Bunker Hill, Massachusetts, the new inductees joined the ranks of the colonies' most distinguished white men. They had hoped that their induction would affirm their equal manliness, but the refusal of the colonies' white Freemasons to officially recognise Provisional African Lodge No. 1 dashed their hopes immediately. The immense efforts African Lodge No. 1 made (and makes still) to be universally recognised as legitimate Freemasons established the general theme of black masculine pride and prejudice distinguishing the history of African–American masculinities in the US to the present.

Until the 1980s and early 1990s little attention was paid to the peculiarities of African–American masculinity. Up to then, with modest exceptions, only the leanest scholarly space was given to black masculinity because it was regarded as only a minor variation on white American middle-class masculinity. The years 1994 and 1995, however, marked an important shift. New writing by Wideman, cultural critic Mercer, filmmaker Julien and curator-critic Golden put black men and masculinities in a new light. Golden's brilliant curating of the 'Black Male' exhibition at the Whitney Museum of American Art in 1994 and her editing of the exhibition catalogue, *Black Male*, made for the defining events of that year. One year later, the O.J. Simpson murder trial and the Million Man March on Washington added ever wider attention to the discourse and, with the 'Black Male' events, inaugurated the present era of interest in African–American males and masculinity. This period's greatest concern, perhaps, has been the wide and consistent demonisation of African–American males in the public sphere.

A whole racist repertoire of historical black male stereotypes has helped demonise African–American men in the public eye. The most pervasive stereotypes have portrayed African–American men as alternately idle and uneducable, or constitutionally criminal and licentious. Stock character types from literature and early popular culture, like Sambo, Jumping Jim Crow and Stowe's Uncle Tom, exemplify the former class while historical figures such as Turner, boxing champion Johnson and Wright's Bigger Thomas variously evoke the incorrigibility of the latter. Against this long sweep of stereotypes, over 150 years of agitation for black enlistment and an integrated military; for the right to vote, hold office and serve jury duty; for jobs, education and civil rights – all worked to counteract the historical power of those damnable images. Still, stereotype analysis is not the whole of African–American masculinities studies. The contemporaneous advancement of black feminist theory in the 1980s and 1990s, and of sexuality studies not much later, yielded new insights into the sexual politics and desires of normative African–American masculinity. As feminism generally, and black feminism in particular, came to comprehend and lay bare the ways 'woman' was invoked to serve male authority and empowerment, the implications of what it had come to mean to be a 'man' in the first place were brought under irrevocable and rigorous scrutiny.

By the end of the twentieth century, as gender was becoming universally understood as a social construction and the 'natural' differences between the sexes a gross exaggeration, thinking about African–American masculinity had evolved dramatically. No longer exclusively imagined by a singular expression of black masculinity, nor even solely associated with black males uniquely, 'African–American masculinities' signifies a repertoire of enactments of African–American masculinity including not only enactments of black male power over black women and over sexual minorities, male and female, but anxious enactments vexed by race, region, class, age and sexuality as well. Sometimes, new African–American masculinities emerge from the liberating exercise of black men's own critical self-interrogations. African–American women, performing a genus of African–American masculinity, may produce new masculinities too. In all their forms, African–American masculinities tell a story greater than their most representative group.

References and further reading

Bederman, G. (1995) *Manliness and Civilization*, Chicago, IL: University of Chicago Press.

Carby, H. (1998) *Race Man*, Cambridge, MA: Harvard University Press.

Golden, T. (ed.) (1994) *Black Male*, New York: Whitney Museum of American Art.

Harper, P. (1996) *Are We Not Men?* New York: Oxford University Press.

Hine, D. and Jenkins, E. (eds) (1999) *A Question of Manhood*, 2 vols, Bloomington, IN: Indiana University Press.

Mercer, K. (1994) *Welcome to the Jungle*, New York: Routledge.

Mercer, K. and Julien, I. (1998) 'Race, sexual politics and black masculinity', in R. Chapman and J. Rutherford (eds) *Male Order*, London: Lawrence and Wishart.

Staples, R. (1982) *Black Masculinity*, San Francisco, CA: The Black Scholar.

Wallace, M.O. [1979] (1990) *Black Macho and the Myth of the Superwoman*, London: Verso.

—— (2002) *Constructing the Black Masculine*, Durham: Duke University Press.

Wideman, J. (1995) *Fatheralong*, New York: Vintage.

See also: critical race studies; female masculinity; fraternities; lynching; military masculinities; queer masculinities; race and ethnicity; racialised masculinity politics; racism

MAURICE O. WALLACE

AFRICAN NATIONALISM

The discourse and practices surrounding masculinities in African nationalism are complex. It is impossible to do justice to their local diversity and any overview can only be partial. Purporting to cover an entire continent, one inevitably privileges some phenomena and neglects others. Furthermore, many of the nationalisms mentioned here changed over time.

African nationalism has taken diverse forms and passed through distinct phases. The moment of origin of nationalism may be disputed or in fact be quite different in various parts of the continent. This divergence in origins relates to the weight placed on early resistance to conquest or precolonial kingdoms and varies within movements. This essay is therefore conditional and may apply broadly in some cases and only with extensive qualification in others.

All nationalisms are profoundly gendered concepts, presupposing as they do a project that is performed in the public domain, an area of activity supposedly reserved for men. Consequently, the precursors to most nationalist movements, often warriors, are primarily men. Even where women act as warriors, they sometimes signify that this is a male role through referring to themselves 'wearing trousers' and thereby taunt their menfolk (Suttner, 2005). Or in some pre-colonial situations women warriors had to adopt certain masculinist practices, such as taking of 'wives'. Manthatisi, of the Tlokwa, mother of the regent who was then still a boy, while a very powerful ruler and war leader, had nevertheless to lead in accordance with the predominant masculinist norms.

Nationalist movements tend to be dominated by men, at least among the leadership. In many cases women were not allowed to be members until late, if at all. The entire famous pantheon of African nationalist leaders is men – Mandela, Cabral, Nyerere, Nkrumah, Lumumba, and so on. This apparently confirms the occupation of public space as the place where men play out politics. Yet in most if not all parts of the continent, women did enter the public space and were important components of the nationalist or less formal resistance movements. In some cases de jure non-membership coexisted with de facto exercise of those rights. But more importantly, women entered the public space, even when denied membership of nationalist movements and where the discourse may have depicted the future nation as male.

Similarly, the discourse of African nationalism tends to be suffused with male idioms – emasculation of a nation, recovery of manhood, a virile nation and similar phrases. At one level this discourse excludes women in that the nation appears to be conceived as a male affair and to relate in its primary emphasis to reversing emasculation.

However, this discourse must be read in relation to important qualifying factors. Denial of manhood was not an imaginary crisis as one finds depicted in Western discourse, but a reality. Men were infantilised and called 'boys' no matter what their age. It was a characteristic feature of colonial rule that the encounter between colonial ruler and native peoples infantilised the natives – men and also women.

Even in the discourse of colonial rulers one finds a connection made between this notion of a child race and the need to continue to rule them, as constituting a sacred trust of civilisation, tutelage or similar terms. The restoration of manhood therefore responded to both a denial of manhood and also the denial of freedom through colonial overlordship.

That the discourse is masculinist cannot be read as necessarily signifying denial of rights for women. This discourse is heavily linked to overrule by foreigners or whites in the case of South Africa and, whether or not the men willed it, their womenfolk were not content to be marginalised.

In many nationalist struggles of the continent women have been important players. Funimile Ransome Kuti of Nigeria was one such woman. In certain situations, women have been crucial players in armed struggle and even in apparently conventional domestic roles; in providing food and shelter, they have been crucial in fulfilling logistical elements of a war effort.

The involvement of women as active combatants in more recent guerrilla movements was mediated by the way in which men related to them as comrades in arms. In many cases male camaraderie and other resentments prevented such female combatants contributing as equals towards their own liberation as women. But the reactions of male soldiers were not uniform, and in some cases men like the assassinated African National Congress military and political leader, Chris Hani, never left the guerrilla camps without raising gender issues and asserting the rights of women.

The manifestation of masculinities in the course of nationalist struggles affects also the way one understands key gender-related concepts, like patriarchy. One of its connotations is male protection of women and children. In the colonial and apartheid context, such protection did in some respects connote conventional patriarchal notions. But it also carried specific meanings arising from the unique dangers caused by repression against the nationalist movements. Police harassment and arrest of mothers and daughters evoked real fears of what would happen to them, if they were not protected by their fathers or husbands. Situations where men were not able to do this manifested not only a denial of a patriarchal right but also a denial of manhood resulting from colonial oppression.

The formation of African masculinities in African nationalism was therefore framed by the colonial relationship, which saw their infantilisation as tied to political submission. It was also conditioned by the assertion of women's rights in the public sphere in a variety of forms. Masculinity formation in these nationalisms cannot simply be characterised through categories having supposedly universal meanings. What emerges is that there were patriarchies and feminisms and masculinities, taking different forms in different contexts. The processes around masculinity formation and its relation to gender equality are still unfolding in both the African and global context. The outcomes cannot be pre-ordained.

Reference and further reading

Suttner, R. (2005). 'Masculinities in the illegal ANC-led liberation movement', *Kleio*, 37: 71–106.

See also: cultural formations, Africa; history, Africa

RAYMOND SUTTNER

AGE AND AGEING

The physical deterioration of one's body is an inevitable part of the ageing process. However, the ageist cultural and societal attitudes that often accompany ageing are not. The way in which Western culture both marginalises and stigmatises ageing individuals is a socially constructed phenomenon. Noteworthy is the way in which some cultures view and utilise the experiences of aged individuals in their community. Indigenous cultures such as that of the Australian Aboriginals, for example, revere their elders, and in particular their male elders, as people from whom they can seek counsel and guidance. Contemporary Western society arguably devalues the experiences and capabilities of older people at the expense of championing youth. This becomes increasingly evident where employment is concerned, with most large companies and corporations investing heavily in youth policies possibly seeking new and contemporary methods of business acumen. The result is the obvious identification of acceptance of youth over older individuals who may have gained a wealth of experience.

Given that the workplace is an area which men have established as being a significant site for the social construction of masculinity, including masculine identity, retirement plays a major role in defining men as they age. Retirement clearly denotes that a specific productive period of a man's life, where he is often a financial provider for the family, is over. It is also a period in which feelings associated with self-worth and identity are strong. One of the first things that men engage in when meeting new male peers is to develop a system of hierarchy. That is, they will often shake hands and say, 'What do you do?' Therefore, early periods of retirement can be problematic for some men as they no longer 'do' anything specifically that defines their existence, other than being retired.

Understanding men in ageing is important. Significantly, research on men and masculinities in general does not have a long history. There is still so much that needs to be explored regarding men's lives and constructions of masculinities throughout the life course. Even more significant is the dearth of information on ageing men and masculinities, which in turn renders this aspect of men's lives even less understood. As Thompson and Whearty (2004) claim, research addressing later life masculinities is in its infancy. Further, they go on to state that older men's masculinities remain hazy and need to be outlined. Davidson (2004) adds weight to this argument by identifying that while there has been a growth in sociological research on men and masculinities, the lives of older men have been conspicuously absent. These are important claims and indeed provide justification for the lack of understanding surrounding older men's lives.

Arguably, as the research indicates, there are a number of key issues that ageing men must confront. Significantly, because ageing is constructed as much socially as it is physiologically, these issues are 'fluid' in the sense that they have capacity to change over time and with circumstances. As has already been noted, retirement plays a significant role in the ageing process for men. This is particularly so for males born in an era where men constructed their masculine identity on work and being financial providers for the family. For the majority of ageing men in contemporary Western culture it is possible to contend that this is still the case (Kaye and Crittenden 2005). However, it is arguable that the 'Babyboomer' generation may impact this notion significantly as it has been identified that this generation of males with higher income, higher levels of education, less debt and more transient views of culture are less likely to put such emphasis on retirement than those that have come before them. Further, it is a generation that has experienced feminism in action and therefore has a greater understanding of women's involvement in the workforce and their contribution to household income generation. Quite possibly the transition to retirement may be less traumatic for Babyboomer males because of their experiences and understanding of feminist issues that have the capacity to impact males.

Socialisation is an important component in an individual's health and wellbeing. It is commonly cited that women have far more confidantes than men and that their social support network casts its net further (Krause and Keith 1989; Scott and Wenger 1995). The result is that, when faced with a crisis, women have the ability to call upon a number of different people to seek advice and provide direction, thus assisting in the maintenance of positive emotional and mental health. This appears not to be the case for most men. Additionally, as men age it is claimed that their social network diminishes, in stark contrast to women's, and that ageing men are more comfortable with such an occurrence (Kaye and Crittenden 2005). Further, they take solace in seeking the primary, almost sole, companionship of their wife or partner. This is reflected in Thompson and Whearty's (2004) claims suggesting that older men's social support networks reflect the importance of a few significant people rather than many acquaintances. They go on to identify that older men do not continue to engage in replacing lost peripheral acquaintances as these do not have the desired intimacy. As a consequence, it is argued that as men age their social contacts diminish at the expense of attempting to seek companionship and time that is emotionally rewarding. However, herein lies a problem for aged men who become widowed or divorced. Davidson (2004) confirms such a claim by identifying that older lone men are particularly likely to experience social isolation. Similarly Kaye and Crittenden (2005) concur in so far as highlighting that when an older man loses his spouse he loses a close confidante as well as an important component of his social support network.

While it might be argued that the reduction in social support can have deleterious effects on ageing men, it might also be claimed that for many men this change in emphasis to a more complicit form of masculinity, in which intimacy and nurturing is championed, is beneficial to the ageing male's masculine identity. Ageing men have been identified to provide close friends and individuals from younger generations with life experiences through grandparenting, role modelling and mentoring as well as volunteering (Adams 1994; Erikson *et al.* 1994).

Body size and musculature play a significant role in the construction of a man's masculine identity (Drummond 2005b). Indeed, a greater amount of emphasis is being placed on males to live up to a certain masculine archetype based on body shape, size and muscularity. As men age, the physiological processes that underpin muscle size take effect to begin the muscular atrophy: that is, the reduction of musculature. Therefore it is inevitable that ageing men will lose muscle size and, with it, will lose muscle strength. There are several resultant occurrences. As men have been socially constructed to look up to a certain body ideal, any deviation from the archetype can have negative implications for ageing men in the short term (Drummond 2003). However, more significant is the loss of associated strength. Historically, strength has been a signifier of masculinity. One only has to invite younger males to discuss meanings of masculinity and the response generally revolves around strength. Sometimes it relates to character, but mostly it relates to physicality (Drummond 2005b). Therefore, it is particularly difficult for ageing men to come to terms with the changing nature of their bodies and not being able to 'do' the physical acts that they once could perform as younger men. As one older man stated in Drummond's 2003 research:

> When I was ill for ten months, I used to be more physically fit and stronger, and I will never get it back like I used to. It makes me feel terrible, absolutely terrible. I could never understand my father-in-law, who used to be a boxer and was pretty fit, and he used to complain that he couldn't take a lid off a jar and he would get very upset that he physically could not do these things. And that was really upsetting. And that's the way I feel. I have physically lost things that my body just can't do.
>
> (Drummond 2003: 191)

Coming to terms with physical, emotional and social change throughout the life course is the cornerstone of positive mental health for both men and women. In terms of men and their masculine identity, while the reduction in physical strength may be an impacting factor it does not have to be, nor does it appear to be, a long-term concern. Most men develop a sense of understanding of the broad physiological deterioration that takes place with ageing. However, in the event of having to challenge their physicality, many ageing men express an initial surprise that their bodies cannot 'do' what they once could 'do'. An immediate sense of loss often occurs as a realisation is established that they no longer have certain physical capabilities. Significantly, it is these physical capabilities that often provided them with a sense of masculine identity. It was also these physical capabilities that enabled them to use their bodies in gendered, masculinised ways, such as getting up on the roof to clean the gutters or opening lids on jars for their female partners (Drummond 2003).

Importantly, as men age they do come to terms with the physical limitations that age bestows upon them. Further, ageing men realise that both musculature and strength diminish, along with flexibility and other physiological parameters. Once these men identify that masculinity does not need to be displayed through bodily physicality, there appears to be a sense of contentment with respect to the ageing process. One might contend that through the ageing process masculinity is no longer an extrinsically oriented phenomenon that occurs via the body, but rather an intrinsic one based on other qualities.

Ageing men have a wealth of expertise, knowledge and life experiences to pass on to future generations, both males and females alike. Too often, when discussing aspects of age and ageing relating to men we can focus on the negative aspects. It is important to recognise the attributes of older males and their potential to influence the ways masculinity(ies) is socially constructed in contemporary culture. Because of ageist attitudes it is easy to disregard the voices of older males and render their perspectives as antiquated. However, life experiences have the potential to impact cultures in profound ways. Currently in Australia there is a resurgence associated with honouring war veterans, and in particular the ANZACs (Australian and New Zealand Army Corps) who served in the First and Second World Wars. While women also served their country, it is the stories of the 'diggers' (male veterans) that are capturing the attention of the younger generation. It was not long ago that the cancellation of the ANZAC Day marches was being considered for lack of numbers, both in terms of the veterans marching and the onlookers honouring the veterans. However, over the past decade, culturally Australia has come to identify the importance of what these ageing men have to say and how their experiences will add depth and breadth to the future generations of Australians. It is on ANZAC Day that Australians embrace their ageing men who fought for their country and that they identify with the ethos that underpinned their reasoning to defend the nation. It is arguable that there is evidence of such understanding being sustained longer than the day itself. However, it must become culturally embedded rather than a mere token gesture.

Significantly, individuals are now living longer than ever before. Both men's and women's life expectancies are steadily increasing thanks to a number of factors which largely relate to health promotion, public health and medicines. However, with increased life expectancy comes the need for quality of life as well. Sexual intimacy is a part of quality of life for men of all ages. Importantly, the new medications that have been developed to assist in positive sexual functioning have provided interesting debate on ageing and sexual practice. Perhaps the most significant factor to emerge for the production of the new medications is the heightened awareness of sexuality in the lives of older people. Further, the attention this topic has received in mainstream media has desensitised it to the point where older men are beginning to feel less intimidated in discussing such concerns as sexual dysfunction with health practitioners. Until recently, sexual dysfunction in men, generally termed 'impotency', was frowned upon as something that was less than masculine, and possibly even feminine. Sexual virility among males has been a strong signifier of masculinity across many cultures throughout the world, and continues to be so.

The ageing process for men does not have to be a turbulent one. Old age can provide men with an opportunity to explore aspects of their lives with the addition of experience and wisdom, arguably something they did not have as younger males. Most men develop a family unity and spend a good deal of their time nurturing and raising children while simultaneously working and forging careers. The middle years of a man's life can be hectic and unwavering as a consequence of work and family commitments. The years beyond retirement, and when the children have become adults, provide men with an opportunity to reflect and use their experiences wisely. This is a time when they can become a little more selfish and enjoy the lives they have made for themselves.

References and further reading

Adams, R.G. (1994) 'Older men's friendship patterns', in E. Thompson (ed.) *Older Men's Lives*, Thousand Oaks, CA: Sage, pp. 159–77.

Davidson, K. (2004) 'Why can't a man be more like a woman? Marital status and social networking of older men', *Journal of Men's Studies*, 13 (1): 25–43.

Drummond, M. (2003) 'Retired men, retired bodies', *International Journal of Men's Health*, 2 (3): 183–99.

—— (2005a) 'Men's bodies: listening to the voices of young gay men', *Men and Masculinities*, 7 (3): 270–90.

—— (2005b) 'Men's bodies and the meaning of masculinity', paper published in the Ian Potter Museum of Art Masculinities Symposium proceedings; available at www.artmuseum.unimelb.edu.au/events_transcripts.aspx?type=Symposium&typetitle=Masculinities:%20Gender,%20Art%20and%20Popular%20Culture

Erikson, E., Kivnick, H.Q. and Erickson, J.M. (1994) *Vital Involvement in Old Age: The Experience of Old Age in Our Time*, New York: William Morrow.

Kaye, L. and Crittenden, J. (2005) 'Principles of clinical practice with older men', *Journal of Sociology and Social Welfare*, XXXII (1): 99–123.

Krause, N. and Keith, V. (1989) 'Gender differences in social support among older adults', *Sex Roles*, 21: 609–28

Scott, A. and Wenger, G.C. (1995) 'Gender and social support networks in later life', in S. Arber and J. Ginn (eds) *Connecting Gender and Ageing: A Sociological Approach*, Buckingham: Open University Press, pp. 58–172.

Thompson, E. and Whearty, P. (2004) 'Older men's social participation: the importance masculinity ideology', *Journal of Men's Studies*, 13 (1): 5–24.

See also: ageism; bodybuilding; mid-life crisis; muscles and muscularity; retirement; working with older men

MURRAY DRUMMOND

AGEISM

Although there is considerable diversity among ageing men in different societies, with an increasing split between affluent early retirers and low-paid men, many older men are shaped by an ageist discourse to be socially excluded, diminished and largely invisible.

Ageism is a relational construct created through the othering and dehumanising of older men. The relatively dominant discourse of young, active, virile masculinities is constructed through the unequal and relational othering of ageing and disabled masculinities. Everything that is threatening and disruptive to the internal composure of the dominant discourse, such as physical and psychological changes and the processes of growing old and dying, is split off and projected outside itself on to a severely restricted version of ageing masculinities.

There are three main types of ageism encountered in older men's lives: cultural ageism, institutional ageism and the professionalisation of ageism.

Cultural ageism focuses on the undervaluing of older men's lives through taken-for-granted representations and narratives. Men are assumed inevitably to lose their human resilience or to become men of a limited and inferior kind as they age.

Western myths and stereotypes of 'grumpy old men', often depicted on film and television as moaning, angry, messy or miserable, make it extremely difficult to get to grips with the more varied and unexpected lives of ageing men. These myths often render invisible the hidden realities of, for example: the relatively unseen worlds of respected black elders; the daily caring routines of older male spouses looking after ill partners; the active campaigning of some men in their seventies and eighties for better pension rights; active grandparenting; and the rich social networks of many older gay men.

The ways societies are organised, in terms of work, health, welfare, retirement and pensions, often lead to some older men being categorised as worn out and old-fashioned. At the level of government policies and legislation, institutional ageism is sometimes experienced as age discrimination in work practices through imposed age limits. These limits can also give rise to increasing levels of medical neglect in the lives of older men.

Institutional ageism can also be seen as structured dependency arising from pension policies, health and welfare legislation, and the traditional stages of life-course narratives regulating our ways of thinking about childhood, the working years and the constructed differences between those stages and an inevitably declining old age.

Ageism has been professionalised through the distancing of some health workers from their own ageing processes and from older men. Health professionals may adopt patronising expectations and relations in working with ageing men, speak for them without consultation, or take decisions for them in ways that silence ageing men. Some academic gerontologists have over-emphasised decay and deterioration at the expense of viewing older men as active subjects.

See also: age and ageing; mid-life crisis; retirement; working with older men

DAVID JACKSON

AGENCY

Agency is a term used by poststructuralist, feminist and postcolonial theories to denote self-actualised power, usually of the individual, or 'subject'. The term is most commonly deployed in discourses that critique patriarchal, capitalist, Western and/or white hegemonic structures, ranging from the formal disciplining powers of the state to corporate influence over economies and media, to the informal practices of macro- and micro-societies. Most specifically, these discourses ask whether individuals, especially socioeconomic minorities, can resist and/or accurately represent themselves in dominant discourses and practices.

Within Western philosophy and poststructuralist theory, agency is tied to the 'subject', i.e. a self-conscious, rational human being who is (implicitly or explicitly) usually white, male and the owner of property. In the early 1800s, G.W.F. Hegel argued that the subject, or individual, is distinguished from all others by the Will to Power – i.e. the ability to manifest his ideas into reality. By the late nineteenth century, Hegel's arguments were increasingly tied to colonialist discourse, as the emerging American and Western European democracies defended their military invasions and domination as the inevitable will of a nation of subjects who could and would impose their will on those incapable of self-determination.

The question of agency is now debated within the arena of language and racial, sexual or gender privilege. In *Black Skin, White Masks*, Martiniquan theorist Frantz Fanon argues that black men cannot speak from a position of authority within colonialist discourse and only violent resistance will grant them agency. Post-World War II feminists like Betty Friedan argued that in patriarchal societies, agency is synonymous with masculinity. African–American feminists such as bell hooks reject this view, arguing that white feminists fail to acknowledge their agency in racial privilege. Post-structural theorist Gayatri Spivak believes that agency is located in the act of speaking, or self-representation, but other postcolonial and African Diasporic discourses disagree on whether the marginalised subject can or will achieve agency through speech or action.

References and further reading

Fanon, F. (1957) *Black Skin, White Masks*, New York: Grove Press.

Friedan, B. (1963) *The Feminine Mystique*, New York: W.W. Norton.

Hegel, G.W.F. (1970) *The Philosophy of Right*, Cambridge: Cambridge University Press.

hooks, b. (1981) *Ain't I a Woman? Black Women and Feminism*, Boston, MA: South End Press.

Spivak, G.C. (1994) 'Can the subaltern speak?' in P. William and L. Chrisman (eds) *Colonial Discourse and Postcolonial Theory*, New York: Columbia University Press.

MICHELLE M. WRIGHT

AGGRESSION

At this time there is no generally accepted theory of the cause of violent aggression. The emotional/relational configuration in hypermasculinity is one possibility. Because of the virtual invisibility of the emotional/relational world in modern societies, it is seldom considered, even by experts.

Four emotions seem central: 'the vulnerable emotions' (grief, fear and shame) on the one hand, and anger on the other. The relational component is the absence of close bonds. Suppression of vulnerable emotions, acting out anger, and isolation give rise to the silence/violence pattern: meeting threats to self or to group with either silence or violence.

Two of many possible instances illustrate both the individual and the collective pattern: the massacre of civilians at My Lai, Vietnam, ordered and assisted by Lt William Calley, and the monstrous aggression by the Germans under Hitler. The biographical material for Calley suggests no close bonds and frequent failure and shame that went unacknowledged. Hitler's biographies provide many examples: hiding vulnerable emotions, anger tantrums and absence of bonds. The silence/violence pattern results in aggression directly through leaders and also indirectly, when the collective pattern is the basis of group support for aggressive leaders. The majority of Calley's company and Hitler's nation supported the aggression of their leader.

Erving Goffman's discussion (1967) of 'character contests' implies that masculine men have 'character'. A man with character who is under stress is not going to cry like a woman or child. Social occasions are seen as opportunities for one to test one's own character compared to the other person's. The hypermasculine pattern promotes competition rather than bonding. Men's loyalty to each other in competitive attitudes does not constitute a secure bond, since it requires suppressing a vital part of self, their own cooperativeness.

Goffman sees hypermasculine control of emotions as a virtue. But this pattern can be seen as a flaw leading to aggression or to passive acceptance of slaughter. This report from World War I describes the destruction of a British brigade as it moved towards German lines:

> They advanced in line after line, dressed as if on parade and not a man shirked going through the extremely heavy barrage ...

> not a man wavered, broke the ranks, or attempted to come back. I have never seen such a magnificent display of gallantry, discipline and determination.
>
> (Koenigsberg 2005)

As with Goffman, this episode was viewed as virtuous, but it actually is a vice, suggesting a lethal addiction to the cult of masculinity.

The absence of secure bonds with others seems crucial in creating violent aggression both at the individual and collective levels (widespread alienation). For example, males who go 'postal', killing many others, have been loners. In modern societies, the great majority of men have sealed over their vulnerable emotions, and a large minority act out anger. Yet not all of them are aggressive. Complete isolation triggers violence when it occurs in those who have repressed their vulnerable emotions and act out anger.

Silence/violence and hypermasculinity

Boys learn that showing vulnerable feelings (grief, fear and shame) are seen as signs of weakness. At first merely to protect themselves, boys begin suppressing these feelings and acting out anger. Most boys learn to hide their feelings in emotionless talk, withdrawal or silence, or to cover them behind a display of hostility. Vulnerable feelings are first hidden from others and then, after many repetitions, from self. In this latter stage, behaviour becomes compulsive. When hypermasculine men face what they construe to be threatening situations, they are compulsively silent or enraged.

In close relationships, men show more silence/violence than women. With their partners, most men talk less freely than women about feelings and the relationship. This may be the reason they are more likely to show anger: they seem to be backed up on feelings, and sense that only anger is allowed them. Although women are as verbally aggressive as men, they attack physically less often, and then usually only a single individual close to them. The pattern of multiple killings, including strangers, is almost entirely limited to men.

Numbing out fear, particularly, makes men dangerous. Fear is an innate signal of danger with survival value. When a car heads towards us, we have an automatic fear response. Much faster than thought, this reaction increases our chance of survival. When fear, grief and shame are repressed, the likelihood of an aggressive rather than problem-solving approach to individual and collective tension is heightened. Volkan (2004) has shown how transgenerational transmission of emotional trauma can lead to unending conflict between groups.

Repression of emotions leads to a vicious circle. One represses emotions to avoid painful feelings. At first the painful feelings have their origins in the reactions of others. In order to avoid pain, we learn to repress emotions that lead to rejection. After many curtailments, repression becomes habitual and out of consciousness. In this way, avoidance leads to avoidance in a self-perpetuating loop. At the collective level, men admire leaders who display their own swaggering style of shooting first and negotiating later, if at all.

Newman (2004) collected information about 'postal' episodes between 1974 to 2002. She found twenty-seven shootings involving twenty-nine boys. (There were two shooters in two episodes.) None of the boys seemed to have a single secure bond. Even the cases in which two boys acted together may support my thesis, since their relationship seems to be engulfed (self-estranged), rather than a secure bond. In these cases, as in group aggression, alienation from self or others and suppression of feelings lead to hypermasculine silence/violence.

References and further reading

Goffman, E. (1967) 'Where the action is', in E. Goffman, *Interaction Ritual*, New York: Anchor, pp. 149–270.

Koenigsberg, R.A. (2005) 'Virility and slaughter', available at http://home.earthlink.net/~libraryofsocialscience/online_pubs.htm

Newman, K. (2004) *Rampage*, New York: Basic Books.
Scheff, T. (2005) *Goffman's Legacy*, Boulder, CO: Paradigm.
Volkan, V. (2004) *Blind Trust*, Charlottesville, VA: Pitchstone.

See also: domestic violence; rape; sexual violence; violence

THOMAS J. SCHEFF

ANDROGYNY

Androgyny (male and female in one, both sexes in one person) is often put forward as the answer to patriarchal consciousness. One argument is that certain qualities which have been called feminine are really Yin qualities, which are culturally associated with women, but can be found both in women and men. Certain qualities which have been called masculine are Yang qualities, which are attributed socially to men, but can be found both in men and women. All that is wrong is that these two sets of qualities have become too separated and specialised. If we could encourage men to develop their Yin qualities, and women to develop their Yang qualities, we would achieve a good psychologically balanced androgyny.

Ancient Chinese texts on Yin and Yang did not associate these with the feminine or masculine. We can then abandon the notion that this is traditional wisdom.

Contemporary Jungians have written a great deal about masculine and feminine qualities and their relating. Harding (1971) is as typical as any when she says that the essential feminine qualities are emotion and relatedness, which are personal in character, and the essential masculine qualities are thinking, impersonality and spirit, leading to a concern for justice, logic and a cause. This, of course, is essentialist thinking, and the move towards androgyny for man is seen as a move towards accepting more of the qualities regarded as feminine and questioning the qualities regarded as masculine.

But to be any use, the concept would have to offer us a true maleness and a true femaleness not contaminated by social stereotyping. Because of the all-pervasive influence of patriarchy, we have no idea of what males or females are really like under all the conditioning. Feminists have wrestled with language and culture to try and discover what being a female might be – some of the bravest and most exciting efforts in this direction being by Mary Daly. And it is worth noticing that in her striking book *Gyn/Ecology* she says: 'Experience proved that this word [androgyny] which we now recognise as expressing pseudo wholeness in its combination of distorted gender descriptions, failed and betrayed our thought' (Daly 1979: 387).

This is the key to understanding why the usual idea of androgyny won't do. For it is an attempt to repair the distortions of one patriarchal position by using material from the opposite distortion of another. The appeal to androgyny is a way of avoiding many of the real and painful difficulties of redefining ourselves against the grain. Masculinity and femininity are fatally flawed concepts, culturally loaded, patriarchally based, unusable except as names of harmful stereotypes. Maleness and femaleness bear no definite cultural meanings other than those we build, discover, choose, co-create and explore. In changing patriarchal consciousness, men have to meet the challenge at the social, unconscious and spiritual levels (Rowan 1997).

References and further reading

Daly, M. (1979) *Gyn/Ecology*, Boston, MA: Beacon Press.
Harding, E. (1971) *Women's Mysteries*, London: Rider.
Rowan, J. (1997) *Healing the Male Psyche: Therapy as Initiation*, London: Routledge.

JOHN ROWAN

ANTHROPOLOGY

Anthropology has always involved men talking to men about men. Until recently, however, very few within the discipline of the 'study of man' had truly examined men as men. Although in the past three decades the study of gender and sexuality comprises one of the most important new bodies of theoretical and empirical work in the discipline of anthropology overall, gender/sexuality studies are still often equated with women's studies.

It is the new examinations of men as engendered and engendering subjects that encompass the anthropology of men and masculinities today. There are at least four distinct ways that anthropologists define and use the concept of masculinity and the related notions of male identity, manhood, manliness and men's roles. Marking the fluidity of these concepts, and frequently the regrettable lack of theoretical rigour in approaching this issue, most anthropologists writing on this subject employ more than one of these concepts.

The first concept of masculinity holds that it is, by definition, anything that men think and do. The second is that masculinity is anything men think and do to be men. The third is that some men are inherently or by ascription considered more manly than other men. The final manner of approaching masculinities emphasises the general and central importance of male–female relations, so that masculinity is considered anything that women are not.

In the anthropological literature on masculinity to date much attention has been paid to how men in different cultural contexts perform their own and others' manhood. Thus Herzfeld (1985) writes of the importance to men in a village on Crete of distinguishing between being a good man and being good at being a man, because here it is the performative excellence of manliness that counts for far more than merely being born male.

In his ethnographic study of 'a masculine subculture' among the Sambia in New Guinea, Herdt (1994) seeks to present how men view themselves as male persons, their ritual traditions, their females and the cosmos. The path to understanding Sambia masculinity, Herdt argues, therefore lies in paying close attention to Sambia male idioms: that is, what these men say about themselves as men. Further, in exploring male initiations among the Sambia, Herdt accentuates what he calls 'an intense, phallic masculinity' such that the issue is not one of males striving for masculinity versus femininity but rather for a particular kind of masculinity that is, by its nature, only available to men to achieve. Nonetheless, Herdt writes that 'the public dogma' of men among the Sambia is that maleness itself emerges from femaleness.

In the first major study of manhood in anthropology Brandes (1980) describes how male identities develop in relation to women. In this examination of folklore and men in rural Andalusia, Brandes argues that even if women are not physically present with men while working or drinking, and even if not reflected in men's conscious thoughts, women's 'presence' is a significant factor in men's own subjective understanding of what it means to be men. Discussing changing gender identities in working-class Mexico City, Gutmann (1996) also argues that most men during most of their lives view male identities in comparison to female identities.

Insufficient attention has actually been paid to men-as-men in anthropology, and much of what anthropologists have written about masculinity must be inferred from research on women and by a process of extrapolation from studies on other topics.

In addition to utilising different conceptual frameworks, two distinct topical approaches are evident in the anthropological study of masculinity: some studies mainly treat 'men only' issues, events and locations like male initiation, men's cults, men's houses, bars and sex between men. Other studies include descriptions and analysis of women as integral to the broader study of manhood and masculinity. Exemplary of the first type is the widely read survey by Gilmore (1990). This study, functionalist in orientation, insists on widespread if not necessarily universal male imagery in the world and on an underlying archetypal and 'deep structure' of masculinity cross-culturally and transhistorically. The other approach has been to document the ambiguous and fluid nature of masculinity within particular spatial and temporal contexts and document that there exists no unitary man's point of view.

Among the topics anthropologists have recently studied in relation to men and manhood are same-sex sex; divisions of household labour; family, kinship and friendship ties; the body; and contests over power. In the absence of systematic theorisation of masculinity, most studies of men-as-men in anthropology focus on only one or two of these topics, while by default they have created myriad and contradictory categories and definitions of men.

From early interest in sexual drives (those of natives and anthropologist alike), male authority (and how it may reside in men other than the father) and the Oedipal complex, anthropologists have played a not insignificant role in the development and popularisation of 'native' definitions and distinctions regarding masculinity, femininity, homosexuality, and more. To what extent the views expressed have represented those of men, women or anthropologist – or a combination of all these – is in retrospect far from clear. Early feminist anthropological studies in the 1970s, the earliest approaches to studying masculinity, tended to depict an overly dichotomised world in which men were men and women were women, and women contributed as little to 'making' men as men did to 'making' women. Unlike these initial feminist studies of women in anthropology, however, which sought to address in part women's previous 'invisibility' in the canon, men have never been invisible in ethnography or anthropological theories of 'mankind'.

Two of the most important areas of theoretical work on men and masculinities in anthropology concern same-sex sex, or sex between men (MSM), and the relation of women to men and masculinities.

The erotic component to male bonding and rivalry is clearly demonstrated in many new studies on same-sex sex. Many studies in the anthropology of masculinity have as a central component the reporting and analysis of some kind of sexual relations, attractions and fantasies between males. Of great importance theoretically is the fact that the term 'homosexuality' is increasingly out of favour, seen as too culturally narrow in meaning and implication.

Try as we might to describe and champion a vast diversity of masculinities and femininities in Latin America, there is no mistaking the fact that dichotomous dualities, for instance those positing active and passive men who have sex with other men, recur with what may be for some a frustrating regularity. Nor is the blessed distinction between sex and gender – that is, between bodies and culture – still found to be nearly as useful as many scholars in gender studies once presumed and hoped. As Parker shows (1999), while retaining useful elements, the active/passive taxonomy can miss as much as it captures with respect to changing norms and actual sexual practices. With both so-called political passivity and sexual passivity there is evidently more at play than is perhaps immediately apparent; both forms of assumed passivity represent territories that remain to be more fully charted. Clearly one obstacle that must be overcome in studying sexual passivity in Latin America is the notion that passivity is the mirror opposite of activity.

To reverse decades of male anthropologists rather exclusively interviewing and describing male informants, feminist anthropologists placed greater emphasis beginning in the 1970s on women and so-called 'women's worlds'. In good measure this was a question of 'discovering' the women so notoriously absent (or 'disappeared') in earlier ethnographies. Only in the 1980s did men systematically begin exploring men as engendered and engendering persons. Yet ironically most ethnographic studies of manhood have made insufficient use of feminist contributions to our knowledge of gender and sexuality and have failed to engage sufficiently in the important debates within this discourse. In part this illustrates what Lutz (1995) calls the 'masculinisation of theory', here through the evasion of what is considered theoretically unworthy.

How to incorporate the opinions and experiences of women with respect to men and masculinity is an important concern. Some anthropologists have argued that, as men, they are severely limited in their ability to work with women. Gutmann (1997) argues that ethnographic investigations of men and masculinity must include research on women's ideas about and experiences with men. More than a simple statistical assertion that increasing one's sample size will sometimes increase one's understanding of a subject, and more than providing a supplement to ethnographic work with men on masculinity through adding women's voices and distinct experiences to those of men, the issue is even more that masculinities develop and transform and have little meaning except in relation to women and female identities and practices in all their similar diversity and complexity.

The recurrent theme in much anthropological writing on masculinity is that, 'according to the natives', men are made and women are born: the thorough critique of this view has been very influential in feminist anthropology, but unfortunately too little considered by anthropologists for whom women are largely irrelevant to constructions of masculinity. It seems worth asking, however, if bias might not enter into some ethnographers' accounts. This is a methodological issue, and even more a conceptual one, because although it is a mistake to assume too much similarity from one cultural context to another, conclusions regarding the impossibility of a male ethnographer compiling any useful information about women, much less from women about men, seem to merit further attention. Whether or not women and men absent themselves from the other's presence during rituals, for example, women and men do regularly interact at other times, and they profoundly affect each other's lives and identities. We must not confuse formal roles and definitions with daily life.

Important strides have been made in studying women in a variety of cultural contexts. Corresponding studies of masculinities still lag far behind. This does not mean that ethnographies of men should be viewed, understood or utilised primarily as a complement to women's studies. Rather, they must be developed and nurtured as integral to understanding the ambiguous relationship between multigendered differences and similarities, equalities and inequalities. As with the study of ethnicity, one can never study one gender without studying others.

In any discussion of masculinity there are potential problems involved, especially if the topic is reduced to possession of male genitalia, or still worse if it is regarded as 'for men only'. The present review is intended to counter such typologising, which is in many ways arbitrary and artificial. This essay has not, I trust, been read in any sense as representing 'men's turn' at the scholarly tables of gender inquiry. Rather, my purpose has been to describe studies of men-as-men in the field within the context of a multigendered puzzle.

Anthropologists of various subjects will recognise the taken-for-granted nature of men and manhood in much work to date. A quick perusal of the indexes to most ethnographies shows that 'women' exist as a category while 'men' are far more rarely listed. Masculinity is either ignored or it is considered so much the norm that a separate inventory is unnecessary. Then, too, 'gender' often means women and not men.

Between the performative modes in which manhood is emphasised and the attempt to invent modern hurdles for achieving manhood status lie a variety of qualities and characterisations that anthropologists have labelled masculine and manly. Contrary to the assertion that men are made while women are born (albeit 'in the natives' point of view') is the understanding that men are often the defenders of 'nature' and 'the natural order of things', while women are the ones instigating change in gender relations and much else. This is part and parcel of the contradictions, inequalities and ambiguities of gender relations, ideologies and practices in all their myriad facets and manifestations that themselves prove central to the process of engendered social transformations.

References and further reading

Blackwood, E. (2005) 'Wedding bell blues', *American Ethnologist*, 32 (1): 3–19.
Brandes, S. (1980) *Metaphors of Masculinity*, Philadelphia, PA: University of Pennsylvania Press.
Connell, R. (1995) *Masculinities*, Berkeley, CA: University of California Press.
Delaney, C. (1991) *The Seed and the Soil*, Berkeley, CA: University of California Press.
Elliston, D. (2004) 'A passion for the nation', *American Ethnologist*, 31(4): 606–30.
Gilmore, D. (1990) *Manhood in the Making*, New Haven, CT: Yale University Press.
Gutmann, M. (1996) *The Meanings of Macho*, Berkeley, CA: University of California Press.
—— (1997) 'The ethnographic (g)ambit', *American Ethnologist*, 24 (4): 833–55.
Herdt, G. (1994) *Guardians of the Flutes: Idioms of Masculinity*, Chicago, IL: University of Chicago Press.
Herzfeld, M. (1985) *The Poetics of Manhood*, Princeton, NJ: Princeton University Press.
Lancaster, R. (1992) *Life is Hard*, Berkeley, CA: University of California Press.
Lutz, C. (1995) 'The gender of theory', in R. Behar and D.A. Gordon (eds) *Women Writing Culture*, Berkeley, CA: University of California Press, pp. 249–66.
Nanda, S. (1990) *Neither Man Nor Woman: The Hijras of India*, Belmont, CA: Wadsworth.
Parker, R. (1999) *Beneath the Equator*, New York: Routledge.
Tuzin, D. (1997) *The Cassowary's Revenge*, Chicago, IL: University of Chicago Press.

MATTHEW C. GUTMANN

ANTI-FEMINISM

Anti-feminism in its various forms denies one or more of three general principles that underlie feminist theory. All forms of feminism accept as fairly evident the following principles. First, the social arrangements among men and women are neither natural nor divinely determined. Second, the social arrangements among men and women favour men. And third, there are collective actions that can and should be taken in order to transform these arrangements into more just or equitable arrangements.

The denial of the first principle is central to many anti-feminisms. Many sociobiologists, for example, argue that the arrangements among men and women are biologically grounded and that efforts to transform society will fail because it is an effort to go against nature. Thus, Steven Goldberg argues that patriarchy is inevitable given the biological differences between men and women. Religious conservatives, while they may admit that things might be different, argue that attempts to change the social order will invite divine punishment, perhaps in the form of unhappiness or domestic dysfunction. Much of the Promise Keepers' rhetoric is premised on the idea that God has ordained men to be head of the family. Some classical conservatives argue that the traditional roles of men and women are what they are because they allow for the most optimal functioning of society. And, in some cases, they also deny the second general principle that social arrangements actually favour men.

Even men who claim to be profeminist may fall into denying one of the three general principles. Liberal profeminist men sometimes seem to argue that men are not socially advantaged by their place in society but instead that men are equally oppressed or degraded by the social roles that they play. They come close to denying the second principle. Men's rights defenders go even further in finding that men are actually disadvantaged relative to women in society. Thus Herb Goldberg argues that men cannot be considered top dog when they are subject to high disease rates from stress and higher successful suicide rates.

References and further reading

Gilder, G. (1986) *Men and Marriage*, London: Pelican.
Goldberg, H. (1976) *The Hazards of Being Male*, New York: Signet.

Goldberg, S. (1993) *Why Men Rule*, Chicago, IL: Open Court.
Hicks, R. (1993) *The Masculine Journey*, Colorado Springs, CO: Navpress.

See also: fathers' rights; men's rights

KENNETH CLATTERBAUGH

APHRODISIACS

Aphrodisiacs are most commonly understood as substances which cause or increase sexual desire. The United States Food and Drug Administration (FDA) report on Aphrodisiacs (1996) concludes that there is no proof that any substance has an effect on human sexual desire. However, as Peter Taberner's (1985) exhaustive study, *Aphrodisiacs*, indicates, the myths are stronger than the science. Etymologically, the name derives from Aphrodite, the Greek counterpart of Venus. Aphrodite was born from the sea, which contributes to the folklore surrounding the arousal-inducing powers of many types of seafood. Several items, most notably mandrake root, rhinoceros horn and ginseng (whose name literally means 'man root') have gained their reputations solely on the basis of the 'law of similarity': that is, shapes which may resemble a penis. Similarly, the penises of animals – for example, the tiger for its ability to copulate several times per hour and the elephant, rhinoceros and bear for sheer size – purportedly imbue male consumers with an incumbent potency.

Exotic, luxurious and unfamiliar foods have been attributed with aphrodisiacal powers through myth, mistranslation and misunderstanding. The *Oxford English Dictionary* records references as early as 1753 to tomatoes as 'love apples'. For example, this mistranslation of the French for 'Moorish apple' finds its way into James Joyce's classic novel *Ulysses*, along with the more familiar oysters. Passionfruit's name is often taken to refer to its extraordinary powers and not its more pristine origin as having been discovered on the Christian holy day, Passion Sunday. Perhaps the most infamous and persistent aphrodisiac is so-called 'Spanish Fly', which was described by Hippocrates as a remedy for several conditions. The substance is produced by crushing dried blister beetles. The males of the species secrete cantharidin and give it to the females as part of the mating ritual. However, it is a poison which does in fact cause severe urinary tract swelling and only 10 mg is a fatal dose. Nevertheless, in Roman times Emperor Nero's wife allegedly laced the food of her guests with the powder. In 1772 the notorious Marquis de Sade gave aniseed sweets laced with cantharidin to some prostitutes, hoping to make them lusty, but instead it poisoned them.

The facts and the fictions about aphrodisiacs invoke several simultaneous and often contradictory masculinist discourses, including the millennia-old nature–culture debate. Perhaps the most pernicious among these is the perceived difference between treatments for males and females, both in the type of treatment and in the motivation for it. Underlying the predominance of aphrodisiacs and performance enhancers is the assumption of both perpetual feminine receptivity and several versions of a phallic inferiority complex. This point is underscored by the development of the Cybersuit by Internet pornography retailer Vivid Video. The neoprene suits cover the body entirely and have carefully placed stimulators – thirty-six for the female, only twenty-seven for the male – for simulated copulation. The French film *Thomas in Love* (2000) portrays a comic but dystopic view of one man's dependence on technology for his pleasure.

Significantly, the FDA differentiates between sexual performance and sexual appetite: that is, between erectile dysfunction and sexual arousal disorder. Contemporary performance-enhancing drugs are sought as correctives for either erectile dysfunction (formerly impotence) and/or sexual arousal disorder. Recently, several drugs – most famously Viagra, but also Cialis, Levitra and PT-141 – have been introduced to correct erectile dysfunction by relaxing smooth muscle tissue and dilating the major artery in the penis. In popular discourses, these drugs are de facto aphrodisiacs since their primary function is that of helping men achieve and maintain an erection. The difference lies in the bases of the two maladies: sexual arousal disorder is catalogued in the *DSM-IV*; erectile dysfunction is not. Thus, sexual arousal disorder reinscribes the feminisation of mental illness and the medicalisation of femininity, as well as the myths of frigidity and/or the hysterical woman, while associating masculinity with the practice of medicine and of science. The emphasis on phallic performance underscores the perpetuation of phallocentrism in popular discourses and the continued privileging of penetrative sexual acts over other forms of intercourse.

Similarly, the Western, scientific approach serves as another site for the feminisation and infantilisation of Asian cultures while simultaneously exnominating the imbrication of sex (and sexuality) with prevailing politics, especially with respect to China. In these discourses, the West is superior morally, politically and evolutionarily. Asian cultures, like women, are characterised as more attuned to nature and more likely to subscribe to superstitions, as Elferink (2000) describes in his research into Aztec and Inca aphrodisiacal practices. The ultimate triumph occurs in the tendency to punish nations which traffic in the parts of endangered animals through economic sanctions, often with North America's Indigenous peoples stereotypically portrayed as providers of poached animal parts. Not only is the (white) Westerner again rescuing primitive peoples, but in the revised discourse the technological modulation of the sexual urge mirrors the supposed dispassionate masculine reserve of late capitalism and its ideological foundations.

References and further reading

American Psychiatric Association (1994) *Diagnostic and Statistical Manual of Mental Disorders* (*DSM-IV*), Washington, DC: American Psychiatric Association.

Elferink, J.G. (2000) 'Aphrodisiac use in pre-Columbian Aztec and Inca cultures', *Journal of the History of Sexuality*, 9 (1–2): 25–40.

Haraway, D.J. (1991) *Simians, Cyborgs, and Women: The Reinvention of Nature*, New York: Routledge.

Joyce, J. (2000) *Ulysses*, London: Penguin Books.

Lewis, N. (1995) 'Aphrodisiacs I have known', *Granta*, 52: 99–109.

Nordenburg, T. (1996) 'Looking for a libido lift? The facts about aphrodisiacs', US Food and Drug Administration, 25 January, available at http://vm.cfsm.fda.gov/~dms/fdaphrod.html

Renders, P.-P. (director) (2000) *Thomas in Love*, Toronto: Seville Pictures.

Taberner, P.V. (1985) *Aphrodisiacs: The Science and the Myth*, Philadelphia, PA: University of Pennsylvania Press.

Vivid Video (1999) 'Cybersuit', 18 April and 2 November, available at http://www.vividvideo.com/cyber/cyber.html

See also: Viagra

MARC OUELLETTE

ARCHETYPES

In 1919 Jung introduced the term 'archetype'. The archetype is seen as a purely formal skeletal concept, which is then fleshed out with imagery, ideas, motifs and so on. The archetypal pattern is inherited but the content is variable, subject to environmental and historical changes. From 1946 onwards, Jung made a sharp distinction between archetype and archetypal image. He refers to the archetype as an unknowable nucleus that 'never was conscious and never will be . . . it was, and still is, only interpreted' (*CW* 9i: para 266).

But before we settle for this, let us look at another view: Let us then imagine archetypes as the deepest patterns of psychic functioning, the roots of the soul governing the perspectives we have of ourselves and the world. They are the axiomatic, self-evident images to which psychic life and our theories about it ever return. (Hillman 1989: 23–4).

We do not look for biological explanations, which perhaps could be seen as a reductionist way of going on, but rather trust to the mythopoetic mind itself as its own explanation. Singer (1990) speaks of 'the archetypal matrix in which we are all embedded', and this is perhaps more like it – archetypes are not things which we have, but more like a sort of home in which we partake.

But it is not only gods and goddesses who can be perceived and treated in this way: there are many archetypes, and today there are a number of writers who are treating them as important. For example, Moore and Gillette (1990) have written at length about the importance of the four archetypes King, Warrior, Magician and Lover for understanding men, the maturity in men. Carol Pearson (1991) has given us a great deal of information and help in tackling twelve archetypes: the Innocent, the Orphan, the Seeker, the Lover, the Warrior, the Caregiver, the Destroyer, the Creator, the Magician, the Ruler, the Sage and the Fool. She has even devised a questionnaire which enables people to discover which archetypes are dominant in their lives at a given moment, and which archetypes have something to do with the Shadow – that aspect of ourselves which we like least and may disown altogether. And more recently Caroline Myss (2003) has been talking about eighty archetypes which may be important in therapy.

References and further reading

Hillman, J. (1989) *The Essential James Hillman: A Blue Fire*, introduced and edited by T. Moore in collaboration with the author, London: Routledge.

Jung, C.G. (1968) *The Archetypes and the Collective Unconscious*, in *Complete Works* (*CW*), Vol. 9i, 2nd edition, London: Routledge.

Moore, R. and Gillette, D. (1990) *King Warrior Magician Lover*, San Francisco, CA: Harper.

Myss, C. (2003) *Archetype Cards Guidebook*, Carlsbad, CA: Hay House.

Pearson, C. (1991) *Awakening the Heroes Within*, College Park, MD: Meristem Publishing.

Singer, J. (1990) *Seeing Through the Visible World*, London: Unwin Hyman.

See also: mythopoetic movement; psychoanalysis; spirituality

JOHN ROWAN

ARMIES

Armies have a central place in human societies. Their role changes across cultures but one element remains relatively universal, the relationship between political systems and armies – the state and the military. The vocation of soldiering is deeply embedded in secular Western thought (Feld 1977: 13) and is considered by different key Western thinkers as one element in the evolution of rational bureaucratic civilisations. Armies are constituted through the hegemonic masculine logic of us and them defined in opposition to the civilian communities they are commissioned to protect.

A paradox thus marks the army in Western civilised societies: the contradiction of adopting violent and destructive forces in order to protect liberal cultural values of fraternity, liberty and equality.

Armies and their core business, war and violence, are literally and symbolically masculinist practices. Symbolically, the acts of invasion, killing and violation are masculinist. They represent the practices of control, domination and authoritarianism. Armies institutionalise hegemonic masculinity within its ranks yet also authorise this cultural phenomenon in broader society. The adversarial and competitive character of armies and soldiering is evident in other enclaves of society including the warfare of sport or the 'dog eat dog' world of corporate life, the adversarial character of law, the gratuitously violent temperament of popular film and the highly competitive disposition of politics. The life of the soldier is characterised by these attributes including stoicism, phallocentricity, the domination of weaker individuals and aspiration to heroic achievement (Hopton 2003: 112).

Literally, it is and has been men who have been the leaders and statesmen who controlled the decision and resources for engaging in war, men who are the military leaders and men who are the soldiers who do the fighting and killing. Armies around the world are predominantly populated by men, although women play an increasing part in military service. Boys become men in the military. The relationship between boys' organisations and boys' public (private) schools is clear. The Boy Scouts, the Boys' Brigade, School Cadets and the military-like character of boys-only elite schools all demonstrate the links between militarism, the liberal democratic state and military masculinities outside the armed forces. However, armies have changed significantly over the past twenty or so years, incrementally allowing women to serve in greater numbers and in positions with proximity to the traditionally male bastion of frontline combat.

Armies are the principal agency of state-sanctioned violence. They are an expression of the male-dominated rule of law that characterises Western societies. Soldiers and their armies are structurally located as the principal guardians of the liberal democratic state. The army is the protector of Reason, Order and the expression of disciplined, rational rule. Armies are the primary force saving humans and their societies from disintegration into the Hobbesian ideal of individualistic and impulsive gratification. The Utopian vision of the mastery of culture over nature is realised by the armed force: the protectors of democracy, the colonisers of new lands, the defenders of the common good. Property, law, polity and community are established through the army, which is understood in many ways as the final barrier to disorder and chaos. Armies are thus the sanctuary of men, the home of the disciplined guardian, the embodiment of Reason and the Enlightenment vision of linear progress and civil, political and technological advancement.

Armies are also highly bureaucratised and impersonal institutions. They express the Weberian ideal of bureaucracy characterised by reliability, precision, routine, discipline, predictability, order and regimentation. Obedience to authority and submission to tradition are key aspects of armies. These are masculinist in that they reflect total authority, singularity of purpose and the total embodiment of masculinist rationality. Armies foster and cultivate the disciplined rational man. The army bureaucracy displays a hierarchical authority structure, a monolithic body of regulations and a highly specialised division of labour. The formal culture of masculinity is supported by an equally authoritative body of regulations governing the way soldiers should behave in the company of other soldiers. Thus fraternity, male bonding and mateship are significant aspects of armies that perpetuate and protect the elite hegemonic masculinity that expresses the contemporary aspirations of the military force.

In 1991, 40,000 North American women were stationed with other soldiers in Saudi Arabia for the Gulf War operation against Saddam Hussein in Iraq. Over the past twenty years the debate over women serving in frontline capacity within armies has developed into reality. The inclusion of women in armies has significantly changed their masculinist character. Alongside the inclusion of women has been the incorporation of various measures of bureaucratic equality, namely equal opportunity legislation and anti-sexual harassment regulations. Broadly speaking, the development of the idea of 'peacekeeping' also demonstrates this movement, away from the primary function of control and conquer to the role of protection and guardianship. These bureaucratic measures and operational imperatives have been articulated as encouraging the effeminisation of the military and the impotency of soldiering while at the same time providing some kind of organisational framework for female soldiers to exist within the military. The imperative of peacekeeping significantly challenges the traditionally masculinist character of warfare also.

Contemporary armies are thus located within an interesting paradox. On the one hand, they seek to demonstrate the epitome of civilisation, tolerance and equality, yet on the other they seek to maintain an organisation whose primary function is to kill and colonise. This paradox challenges the hegemonic masculinist practices of autonomy, independence and the opacity of military culture by introducing measures that scrutinise and constrain an organisation which is marked by its discrete separation from broader society and its intimate relationship with the nation-state.

References and further reading

Feld, M.D. (1977) *The Structure of Violence: Armed Forces as Social Systems*, London: Sage.

Hearn, J. (2003) 'Foreword: On men, women, militarism and the military', in P.R. Higate (ed.) *Military Masculinities: Identity and the State*, London: Westport, pp. xi–xv.

Hockey, J. (1986) *Squaddies: Portrait of a Subculture*, London: University of Exeter Press.

Hopton, J. (2003) 'The state and military masculinity' in P.R. Higate (ed.) *Military Masculinities: Identity and the State*, London: Westport, pp. 111–23.

See also: military institutions; military masculinities; war

BEN WADHAM

ART

Locating ideologies and constructions of manhood and masculinity within art (painting, mixed media, performance art, etc.), as well as in its production and reception, requires interrupting traditional interpretive discourses maintained by patriarchal art histories. These histories are largely concerned with evaluating art for its aesthetic values and formal qualities. They propagate notions like the masterpiece, the canon and the genius. While these values, qualities and ideas continue to remain ripe for reinterpretation, we must also situate art in larger societal, historical and ideological contexts in order to fully understand how it both passively mirrors and actively contributes to cultural formations like gender. Feminist art historians, for example, continue to question why women have often been excluded from established art institutions, why contributions by women artists are often ignored or made the exception to putative male superiority in creating art, and why women's bodies are often appropriated, idealised and sometimes distorted by male artists in order to gratify voyeuristic desires and perpetuate myths of femininity that rely on a limited set of types: the virgin, the mother, the goddess, the whore.

Unhinging the myths that protect and stabilise normative masculinity, especially as they are reflected in and produced by art, requires asking questions similar in their intent (dislodging patriarchy and demystifying gender), but modified to accommodate: (1) the different ways in which males are depicted throughout the history of art (in relation to women and other men); (2) the different statuses that male artists occupy with respect to female and male artists in different eras, cultures and nations; and (3) the dynamics of the male gaze as it exists within works of art and as it beholds art.

A few key projects in the 1990s have begun the task of categorising and interpreting the diverse range of male types in Western painting. For example, Abigail Solomon-Godeau's *Male Trouble* traces two specific types of males that come to the fore of neoclassical French painting during and after the French Revolution. Linking these images directly with the nation's political events and social climate, Solomon-Godeau argues that ideal manhood is expressed in French painting during this period either in the form of 'hypervirile, martial' images of men or in the form of 'androgynous, unconscious, menaced, expiring, dead, or otherwise disempowered male protagonists' (Solomon-Godeau 1997: 45, 7). Jacques-Louis David's *The Oath of the Horatti* (1785) and *The Death of Joseph Bara* (1794) exemplify these types. In the former, strong warriors are actively posed in straight lines and painted in bright colours, opposite the mourning, huddled, passive women on the right of the composition, providing a clear dichotomy between the masculine and the feminine. Yet in *The Death of Joseph Bara*, the boy martyr is highly feminised and androgynous, which might signal a conscious disruption of that dichotomy. But Solomon-Godeau interprets these practically opposite portrayals of men as serving the same purpose: these types of 'feminised masculinities' were substituted for the 'eroticised femininity deemed inimical to republican and civic values' (11), the same femininity that was also commonly associated with the old aristocratic order. In the paintings of this era, one can trace how art performs an important symbolic function in which male anxieties can be resolved in the secure and safe space of artifice.

In a similar project, Joseph Kestner's *Masculinities in Victorian Painting* outlines five recurring male types in late nineteenth-century British painting: the classical hero, the gallant knight, the challenged paterfamilias, the valiant soldier and the male nude. These types not only existed in themselves but were often portrayed in homosocial spaces, among other men, a portrayal that mirrored the homosocial Victorian art world, which continued to be populated primarily by men who controlled the academies, galleries and exhibitions, as well as art journalism and art education. This meant that images of men were created and viewed primarily by men, thus establishing a quarantined and sanitised space that effectively dealt with the threat posed by women artists and women viewers who might interpret masculinity otherwise. The classical hero, for example, venerated throughout a culture which sought to 'Hellenise' itself, performed a range of functions: it provided a traditional paradigm of male heroism (Hercules was a common subject) that also resonated with the increased identification of masculinity as embodied and visible. Likewise, representations of mythological stories like Perseus rescuing Andromeda from Medusa or Apollo's attempted rape of Daphne were images that, by calling upon ancient patriarchal standards of maleness, provided models clearly differentiating men's and women's roles. Such differentiation quelled male anxieties during a period in which industrialisation was transforming social structures, women were gaining new forms of autonomy, and the British Empire was facing rebellion and unrest in its colonies.

Although the classical hero, gallant knight and male nude harked back to eras that Victorians perceived as providing stable models of masculinity, the Victorian era (like many others) was not able to contain the inevitable contradictions, fantasies and outright falsities inherent in patriarchal masculinity. Just as the androgynous boy provided a tenuous substitute for erotic femininity in late eighteenth-century French painting, one which betrayed its role in consolidating male power by opening up the possibility of homoerotic desire, there exist within many different eras, schools and traditions of painting those images that imperfectly align with the status quo. For example, paintings of wounded soldiers or challenged fathers render problematic the pretensions of otherwise hegemonic portrayals of manhood and masculinity. Norman Bryson's study of the French painter Theodore Gericault's paintings of wounded soldiers provides evidence that not every artist was completely deferential to normative types. Gericault's *Charging Chasseur* (1812), for example, is fundamentally different from other grandiose portrayals of Napoleonic conquest because it separates the soldier from the battlefield and strips away any possibility for heroic action, emitting an aura of failed and uncertain masculinity. The paintings are not only an allegory for the 'failure of the Napoleonic adventure', but also expose the rift between what Bryson describes as the ideal 'imago' of masculinity and actual male bodies. Even Gericault's more conventional soldier portraits of men in full military regalia reveal how masculinity is not inherent to the male body but is produced by either idealising the male form or adorning it with signs of maleness that are as shifting and contingent as are fashions.

Categorising male types and their aberrations in painting is not the only method for unveiling the mostly complicit relationship between patriarchal masculinities and their representations in art. The film theorist Laura Mulvey developed a theory of the gaze that many art critics apply to the politics and psychology of how art is viewed. Mulvey maintains that films are constructed according to the power and erotics of the male gaze upon women, denying them any agency beyond their status as sex objects. While this model may apply to paintings whose primary subject is women, the theory seems limited when considering that before the nineteenth century, male bodies were the primary subject for paintings of all genres. Additionally, since the art world, even into the twentieth century, has been chiefly populated by male interests – consisting mostly of male artists, subjects and viewers – the politics of the gaze perhaps needs to be reconsidered. Solomon-Godeau notes that 'few studies have focused . . . on the dynamics of the male gaze in relation to male bodies', and questions how a theory of the gaze can explain, for instance, why 'passive, disempowered or feminised male bodies were produced for male spectators' (1997: 9). Bryson asks similar questions of the 'underdeveloped' theory of the gaze and suggests a complication of the theory: 'Male subjectivity cannot be considered as simply voyeuristic in its visual expressions, and we need to recognise the process of assuming male identification and subject positions as an extremely complex negotiation, one that opens . . . directly onto the field of history' (1994: 258). Yet other theorists such as Michael Hatt warn that the male gaze upon the male body often serves the same power structures that benefit from the male gaze upon the female body. In fact, if masculinity is a set of learned characteristics, many of which are projected on to the body (via clothes, poses, physical culture, etc.) 'a visual exchange between men' becomes essential in conveying and maintaining the continuity of gender norms (Hatt 1993: 63). Nevertheless, since the male gaze upon the male body always leaves open the possibility for the transgressive eroticisation of the subject (especially in the case of male nudes), a more complex theory of the male gaze that is able to adapt to different combinations of viewers and subjects seems necessary.

Beyond art's subject matter and its viewer lies another equally important place for investigating the nexus of art and masculinity – the artist him- (and in some cases her-) self. The status of the male artist radically fluctuates depending on time and place, and much artwork produced by men directly reflects their own confidence or anxiety about being an artist. One painter whose work several art historians and critics have debated in this regard is the late nineteenth-century American painter Thomas Eakins. Paintings like *The Gross Clinic* (1875), *The Swimming Hole* (1885), *Salutat* (1898) and other portrayals of male athletes all depict male bodies in specifically homosocial spaces, depictions that made his critics nervous at times for their thinly veiled eroticisations of the male body. But what is also interesting about Eakins is how his paintings reflect the internal conflicts he faced about being an artist in a society growing suspicious of an art world perceived as being overly influenced by European aestheticism, a movement often degraded in the US for its 'effeminacy' and 'degeneracy'. In *Man Made*, Martin Berger argues that Eakins fashions his own definition of masculinity through his work in response to his anxiety over his tenuous status as an artist in a country preoccupied with associating manhood with labour and business. While some critics question the extent to which Eakins sought to challenge hegemonic masculinity, given that his paintings often idealise men and male bodies (just as centuries of classical and neoclassical painting had), others argue that Eakins's paintings consistently crossed boundaries that separated what was acceptable from what was not in terms of portraying the male nude (Hatt 1993: 68). One might contrast Eakins with one of his contemporaries, Winslow Homer, who more readily adapted his role as artist to conventional manhood. The perception of Homer as businessman and individualist made viewing his depictions of man and nature unthreatening to those who viewed, bought and eventually canonised his work (Burns 1996: 216–17).

Modernist art is also interpretable as a movement obsessed with the role of the male artist in society, a role that many modernists constructed as 'virile', 'primitive' and individualist – hence, inherently male and decidedly anti-feminine. Lisa Tickner argues that paintings like Wyndham Lewis's *Self Portrait as a Tyro* (1920–1) evince a carefully projected image of manhood that is, unlike the advanced techniques that characterise modernist painting, rather unadvanced. Even though many modernist male artists were anti-bourgeois and willing to reject certain prescriptions for manhood, they ultimately did not challenge patriarchal power structures in the art world or beyond. One method especially conducive to interpreting modernist art from the perspective of masculinity is to reconsider not only how men are depicted, but also how men paint women. Carol Duncan, for example, provides a useful model for this type of investigation in her commentary on Picasso's *Les Demoiselles d'Avignon* (1906–7). She argues that the painting's female subjects – amalgams of primal, hypersexualised femininities – reveal as much about the emptiness of masculinities supported by the reduction and simplicity of the feminine as they reveal about stereotypical representations of women alone (1993: 97). Masculinity in art, then, is readable not only in how men represent themselves, but in how they represent women; the subject becomes even more complex and interesting when considering how manhood and masculinity are potentially complicated by women artists as well.

References and further reading

Berger, M. (2000) *Man Made*, Berkeley, CA: University of California Press.

Bryson, N. (1994) 'Gericault and masculinity', in N. Bryson, M.A. Holly and K. Moxey (eds) *Visual Culture*, Hanover, NH: Wesleyan University Press, pp. 228–59.

Burns, S. (1996) *Inventing the Modern Artist*, New Haven, CT: Yale University Press.

Duncan, C. (1993) *The Aesthetics of Power*, Cambridge: Cambridge University Press.

Golden, T. (ed.) (1994) *Black Male*, New York: Whitney Museum.

Hatt, M. (1993) 'Muscles, morals, mind', in K. Adler and M. Pointon (eds) *The Body Imaged*, Cambridge: Cambridge University Press, pp. 57–70.

Jones, A. (1994) 'Dis/playing the phallus', *Art History*, 17 (4): 546–84.

Kent, S. and Morreau, J. (1985) *Women's Images of Men*, London: Writers and Readers.

Kestner, J. (1995) *Masculinities in Victorian Painting*, Aldershot: Scolar Press.

Lubin, D. (1997) 'A manly art', in K. Martinez and K. Ames (eds) *The Material Culture of Gender, the Gender of Material Culture*, Hanover, NH: University Press of New England, pp. 365–92.

Melosh, B. (1991) *Engendering Culture*, Washington, DC: Smithsonian Institution.

Perry, G. (1999) *Gender and Art*, New Haven, CT: Yale University Press.

Solomon-Godeau, A. (1997) *Male Trouble*, New York: Thames and Hudson.

Tickner, L. (1994) 'Men's work?' in N. Bryson, M.A. Holly and K. Moxey (eds) *Visual Culture*, Hanover, NH: Wesleyan University Press, pp. 42–82.

See also: aesthetics; culture and representation; elite culture; literature; photography; poetry; sculpture; theatre and performance studies

SAMUEL R. SCHWARTZ

ASIAN–AMERICAN MASCULINITIES

The subject of Asian–American masculinities was popularised in the 1970s by the editors of the literary anthology *Aieeeee!* The ensuing discussions generated by the objectives of the anthology have led to a deeper understanding of the different ways in which Asian–American masculinities are perceived in disciplines such as history, sociology, psychology and cultural studies.

The editors of *Aieeeee!* identified the need for readers to re-focus on literary texts that depicted a broad spectrum of Asian–American issues in order to counter the one-dimensional representations of Asian men in more popular literary texts, such as Maxine Hong Kingston's work, as well as popular images from the media. This lively debate among some Asian–American groups would surface in the public's consciousness when *The Joy Luck Club* and *M. Butterfly* were made into feature-length films.

The crux of the debate centred on the power of representations. The lack of diverse and complex representations of Asian–American men has had a significant impact on Asian–American men in terms of how they perceive and construct their masculine identities. Without multi-dimensional representations of Asian–American men, the theorisation of Asian–American masculinities is limited to the critique of controlling images in the media and the exclusion of Asian–American men from mainstream representations.

In light of the continual marginalisation of Asian–American men in textual and media representations, the arguments become clearer and more complex at the same time. On the one hand, there are those who believe that the way to confront the problem of stereotypical portrayals is to focus on heterosexual and 'macho' representations of Asian–American men. On the other hand, some believe that an exploration of non-mainstream representations of Asian–American men will serve to show the diversity and uniqueness of Asian–American masculinities.

The remasculinisation of Asian–American images has been criticised by feminist scholars who point out that any remasculinisation project would entail an affirmation of a patriarchal order. The replication of a normative heterosexuality would mean conforming to a sexual/gender hierarchy that marginalises other sexual and gender identities among Asian Americans. The opposing project would be to challenge and critique patriarchal hierarchies to explore the complexity of Asian–American men. Representations of gay men, for example, could challenge a normative and hegemonic sexual order. Unfortunately, non-heterosexual images of Asian–American men would also reinforce the stereotypical notion that Asian–American men are effeminate. The cyclical nature of the issues reveals the conflicted position Asian–American men occupy in the larger cultural and social American landscape. Due to the lack of representational power of Asian–American men, almost any significant model of masculinity would be critiqued as representative and stereotypical.

The problem for those who study Asian–American men's issues is that representations of Asian–American men are so few and scarce that when Asian Americans are represented or recognised, they become a stereotype by default. When an international star such as Bruce Lee made a name for himself in Hollywood, he broke one stereotype and created another. Asian–American men were no longer weak, emasculated and effeminate but hypermasculine and powerful. However, Bruce Lee also became the stereotypical Kung Fu hero that continues today with Jacky Chan and Jet Li.

When some Asian–American students gained recognition as good students, the model minority myth gained national prominence. Asian–American students were then expected to live up to exceedingly high academic standards. Even positive images of studious Asian–American students are problematic, though, because the pressure to succeed and the expectations to do well are so powerful that other opportunities for Asian Americans are deemed unattainable. Asian–American men are not supposed to be athletic, artistic or creative.

The irony is that even positive stereotypes have negative consequences for those who do not fit the mode. Countering negative stereotypes (the patriarchal Asian father, the triad member, the businessman, the sexual deviant, the nerd, the evil dictator) with positive stereotypes (model minority, martial arts hero) creates more one-dimensional models of masculine identities for Asian–American men. The danger of stereotypes is that they are too easily dismissed as inconsequential and yet they do have a significant impact on how Asian–American men are perceived. For example, they perpetuate social and cultural prejudice and discrimination: Asian–American men are perceived as less sexually attractive, athletic and creative than their Caucasian counterparts.

One of the first steps in understanding the complexity of Asian–American masculinities is to recognise that the category Asian includes Americans from China, Taiwan, Japan, Thailand, Philippines, India, Pakistan, Singapore, Korea, Vietnam, Hmong, Cambodia, and so on. In short, Asia must be acknowledged as a diverse region that includes all Asian countries, and even within these countries there are regional differences in terms of how Asian men define and shape their masculine identities. Religious, historical, economic, political and cultural backgrounds also affect the ways in which masculinities are constructed. Inter-racial marriages have also produced Asian–American men of mixed ancestry. Even Asian–American men from the same family are distinct in terms of their generations. A first-generation immigrant Asian–American man is very different from his second-generation or third-generation American offspring. American men of Asian descent are so diverse that this group defies categorisation

The formulation of unique models of masculinity should be based on multiple points of view. The exploration of differences among Asian–American men may yield a more meaningful understanding of how masculinities are framed.

References and further reading

Chan, J. (2001) *Chinese American Masculinities: From Fu Manchu to Bruce Lee*, New York: Routledge.

Eng, D.L. (2001) *Racial Castration: Managing Masculinity in Asian America*, Durham, NC: Duke University Press.

Han, S. (2000) 'Asian–American gay men's (dis)-claim on masculinity', in P.M. Nardi (ed.) *Gay Masculinities*, Thousand Oaks, CA: Sage (Research on Men and Masculinities Series).

JACHINSON W. CHAN

AUSTRALIAN MASCULINITIES

Australia has traditionally been depicted as 'man's country'. Iconic figures from the nation's history have always been white males – the convict, the free settler, the bushman, the Anzac soldier, the surf lifesaver, the sportsman and the suburban provider. Australian art, television programming, films, literature, museums, public statues and parades all continue to code Australia as 'male'.

There is substantial social reality underlying this imaging. Males predominated among the early British settlers, causing population imbalances that were most marked in rural areas, and men also dominated activities associated with nation-building, such as gold-seeking, exploring, land-clearing and fighting. Feminist history has recently highlighted the extent of women's contributions, but public memory and much academic history still privileges the masculine contribution.

This masculine pre-eminence, however, should not suggest consensus. The convict origins and intensely working-class nature of the Australian colonies generated an immediate divide between bond and free conceptions of masculinity, while the nation's relatively open, liberal and dynamic nature has allowed challenges and challengers to flourish. The nature of Australian masculinity and its dominance has always been contested.

In the early colonial period, from 1788 through to the mid-nineteenth century, free settlers attempted to elevate more refined, genteel and distinctly middle-class notions of masculinity over those of the convicts, emancipists and Indigenous people. Convict mores emphasising physical hardiness and aggression were regarded with scorn, while the emancipists were viewed as scarcely better as their characters remained forever tarnished. Indigenous Australians were regarded as barbarous savages and then as a dying 'other' who were not part of the new nation that emerged in 1901. Never fully incorporated into the nation until the 1960s, their masculinity was not part of the dominant image.

Also worth considering with regard to the early colonial period, yet largely unacknowledged by Australian historians, is that both modern and traditional understandings of sexuality and gender were transferred to the colonies, where they continued to compete, often with extra intensity because of both colonial social mobility and the predominance of lower-class males in the colonies. The divide between heterosexuality and homosexuality and the idea of separate gender spheres became ascendant in Australia as elsewhere, but only after a long struggle against older and less rigid gender and sexual patterns.

In the second half of the nineteenth century, middle-class and working-class masculinities appear to have moved closer together, without the distance that separated British classes. Late nineteenth- and early twentieth-century innovations such as universal secular education and compulsory military training, aided by the growth of pedagogic juvenile literature and youth groups such as the Boy Scouts, sought to define masculinity with little or no reference to class. Parallel to this development was the emergence of a nationalist artistic and literary imagery that celebrated and romanticised rugged and egalitarian masculinity, predominantly through the figure of the bushman, despite the fact that almost all Australians live in towns and cities.

Male privilege, however, was challenged in the 1890s through a vigorous women's movement. Women won the franchise, and masculine dominance was weakened by female assertiveness in areas such as divorce law reform and birth control. There are also counter-currents that remain largely ignored, such as questioning of the socio-sexual nature of male mateship and close male bonding in rural areas, suggesting that homoeroticism is a more prominent part of Australian masculinity than usually supposed. In the first half of the twentieth century Australian masculinity was more deliberately socially engineered, particularly in regard to service to the nation. This is clear in the creation of a dominant heterosexual masculinity through the Anzac legend, the Citizens' Military Forces, strong gendering in education and a variety of measures directed at ensuring the eugenic and social health of the nation. Australian involvement in the First and Second World Wars, and deliberate government adoption of military male imagery, supported by organisations such as the Returned Servicemen's League, helped to create the dominant twentieth-century male image of a tough reliable patriot who stuck by his 'mates' or male comrades. In the early decades of the twentieth century, time for leisure accompanied work and family life, and once more masculine imaging came to the fore, through sports such as football and cricket, and through a new Australian fascination with the beach, which spawned another icon, the male lifesaver.

As well as their civic responsibilities, men also had the duty of working and providing for wives and families. Women were not part of the national projection: they were primarily home-makers, wives and mothers, a role that was not seriously challenged until after the 1940s.

The demographics of Australia altered after the 1940s, from essentially British origins to encompass millions of migrants from Continental Europe and, from the 1970s, from Asia. In the 1960s and 1970s dissident social movements such as second wave feminism and gay liberation began to undermine the dominant masculinity. Women entered the workforce in greater numbers, took control of their own fertility, and demanded a voice in politics, changing forever the male preserve. While unreconstructed males, fond of 'footy', pub culture and submissive wives, can still be found, over the last thirty years there has been a major realignment of gender and sexual identities that has left a less dominant singular masculinity and moved towards recognising multiple masculinities, inclusive of multicultural values and more liberated attitudes in family life and relationships.

The male imagery associated with Australian bush legend is still evident in the media personas of Paul Hogan or Russell Crowe, but is now countered by women such as Kylie Minogue, Cate Blanchett and Elle McPherson. Sydney's gay and lesbian Mardi Gras, meanwhile, attracts a larger crowd than its Anzac Day marches, if not the same level of national veneration, and homosexual law reform in Australia has been largely completed. Australian masculinity is now multifaceted and a long way not only from its British convict and settler origins, but also from the hegemonic masculine formations in the first half of the twentieth century.

References and further reading

Connell, R. (1995) *Masculinities*, Sydney: Allen and Unwin.

Crotty, M. (2001) *Making the Australian Male: Middle-class Masculinity*, Melbourne: Melbourne University Press.

Moore, C. and Saunders, K. (eds) (1998) 'Australian masculinities: men and their histories', *Journal of Australian Studies*, Special Issue, 56.

See also: mateship

CLIVE MOORE
MARTIN CROTTY

BACHELORS AND BACHELORHOOD

Bachelors and bachelorhood have been long associated in the popular imagination with the 1950s Hugh Hefner-style playboy: consumer of luxury goods, hedonistic swinger, hyper-sexualised harbinger of the Sexual Revolution. Yet the conjectural etymology of the word 'bachelor' – *bas chevalier*, meaning a young knight who served an older knight – dates back as far as the fourteenth century. Only in the mid-eighteenth century, however, did the current primary meaning of 'bachelor' arise: an unmarried man of marriageable age.

A variety of demographic and social shifts, including declines in marriage rates and uneven regional distributions of single men, contributed to the perception of bachelors and bachelorhood as problematic in developed countries during the late nineteenth and twentieth centuries. Bachelor communities arose, for example, in US and Canadian Chinatowns as a result of restrictive immigration policies. Bachelor subcultures centred around men's residences such as boarding houses, the YMCA and men's clubs, and sites of male sociability including cafés, saloons and pool halls. Many married men participated in these bachelor subcultures, suggesting that bachelorhood was blamed, then as now, for the extra-domestic values and practices associated with homosocial or 'sporting male' subcultures.

In cultures that valued the religious celibacy of monks or priests, or in ones like Orthodox Judaism that regarded unmarried men as immature, bachelorhood had other connotations, but in Britain and North America elderly bachelors were seen as deficient in the performance of manhood. Bachelors were imagined as selfishly spending their money and as dangerously dissipating their sexual energy to prostitutes, same-sex partners and masturbation. One form of deviance linked to consorting with prostitutes, both female and male, was *the* paradigmatic turn-of-the-twentieth-century perversion: homosexuality. Not all bachelors were considered homosexuals, although 'bachelor' came increasingly to be used as a slur against gay men or as an insider's codeword. Whether as a specific type of sexual deviant or as a more generalised locus of trouble, the bachelor disrupted the proper regulation that defined home economics, as well as the boundaries that ostensibly separated the private and public spheres, throughout the nineteenth and twentieth centuries.

References and further reading

Chudacoff, H. (2000) *The Age of the Bachelor*, Princeton, NJ: Princeton University Press.

Gilfoyle, T. (1992) *City of Eros*, New York: Norton.

Snyder, K. (1999) *Bachelors, Manhood, and the Novel, 1850–1920*, Cambridge: Cambridge University Press.

KATHERINE V. SNYDER

BERDACHE

Berdaches are Native North Americans whose gender identities share the traits of both men and women, yet remain distinct from these identities. Generally understood by anthropologists and ethnohistorians to occupy a 'third gender' role within their respective tribes, berdaches are morphological males whose gender is not determined by their anatomical sex, which scholars often depict as fixed. Less commonly reported and studied, female-bodied berdaches also exist, although alternative terms such as 'cross-gender females' and 'warrior women' are used to designate this 'fourth gender'. Berdaches are occasionally defined as individuals who 'cross over' to the gender role of the 'opposite sex'; however, most researchers agree that this definition reifies the Euro-American gender binary and obscures Native gender diversity.

While most scholarship in English explores the berdache in a North American context, the term 'berdache' was first used in the Americas by Spanish explorers in contact with Amerindians. Colonial, anthropological and ethnohistorical sources offer differing accounts of this figure: records beginning in the sixteenth century depict berdaches as morally reprehensible, cross-dressing sodomites; mid-twentieth-century anthropologists define the role as one of 'institutionalised homosexuality', a sanctioned status for gender 'deviants'; and late twentieth-century specialists situate the identity either as the natural expression of an individual's 'spirit' (Williams 1986) or the product of social imperatives (Trexler 1995). Since the 1970s, most scholars have agreed on a core set of traits that constitute berdache identity: specialised work roles, gender difference, spiritual sanction and same-sex relations (Roscoe 1998). Although berdaches usually form sexual relationships with non-berdaches of the same sex, critics caution against the assumption of berdache 'homosexuality', noting the non-Native roots of this category and suggesting that berdache behaviour might more accurately be defined as 'heterogender'.

Scholars emphasise the importance of using tribal names, such as *nadle* (Navajo) and *winkte* (Lakota), to refer to distinct berdache identities. Subject to much critical scrutiny for its colonial etymology and pejorative connotations, 'berdache' has been largely replaced with 'Two-Spirit', a pantribal, panhistorical term referring to Native North Americans whose genders and sexualities both incorporate and exceed the berdache designation (Jacobs *et al.* 1997).

References and further reading

Jacobs, S., Thomas, W. and Lang S. (eds) (1997) *Two-Spirit People*, Urbana and Chicago. IL: University of Illinois Press.

Roscoe, W. (1998) *Changing Ones*, New York: St Martin's Press.

Trexler, R. (1995) *Sex and Conquest*, Ithaca, NY: Cornell University Press.

Williams, W. [1986] (1992) *The Spirit and the Flesh*, Boston, MA: Beacon.

NANCY VAN STYVENDALE

BILDUNGSROMAN

The term 'bildungsroman' describes a type of novel that narrates the development of a single, usually male, main character. Goethe's *Wilhelm Meister's Apprenticeship* (1795) is widely recognised as the first bildungsroman, which relates a young man's quest to find his place in the changing world of eighteenth-century Germany. Goethe's novel proved hugely influential, and as a result the bildungsroman became one of the most popular genres of nineteenth-century fiction. It continues to inform representations of individual development today, as its seminal representation of the personality as something dynamic and susceptible of growth underpins a wide array of contemporary discourses, ranging from psychology and education through to romantic fiction, feature film, biography and self-help literature.

The bildungsroman emerged as a combination of various European narrative traditions, including the picaresque (the travel and adventure tale), the novel of education and the novel of religious introspection. The result is a novel whose protagonist forms himself through interaction with his environment, and who learns in the course of the story to find his place in the world (Shaffner 1984; Moretti 1987).

Some scholars argue the bildungsroman constitutes a key site for the construction of modern masculine identity (Minden 1997; Mosse 1996). By presupposing a male protagonist, the bildungsroman reinforces the connection between masculinity and the autonomous, self-determining individual articulated in liberal and Enlightenment thought. It also reinforces the ideology of separate spheres: while the masculine protagonist develops in the modern public sphere, subordinate female characters remain static, confined to the reproductive, private sphere.

The increased presence of marginal voices – in particular feminist, postcolonial and queer – in contemporary literature has significantly challenged the masculine, eurocentric idea of development so central to the bildungsroman. As a result, contemporary literature tends rather to privilege an image of the subject as unstable, fragmented and without an ultimate goal or aim. The bildungsroman nevertheless remains hugely influential in Western culture, due to the ongoing appeal of many classic nineteenth-century examples (such as *David Copperfield*) and the ubiquity of concepts of personal development in popular culture (as in the Harry Potter saga, for instance) and everyday life.

References and further reading

Goethe, J.W. von [1795] (1824) *Wilhelm Meister's Apprenticeship and Travels*, London: Chapman and Hall.

Minden, M. (1997) *The German Bildungsroman: Incest and Inheritance*, Cambridge: Cambridge University Press.

Moretti, F. (1987) *The Way of the World: The Bildungsroman in European Culture*, London: Verso.

Mosse, G.L. (1996) *The Image of Man: The Creation of Modern Masculinity*, New York and Oxford: Oxford University Press.

Shaffner, R.P. (1984) *The Apprenticeship Novel: A Study of the Bildungsroman as a Regulative Type in Western Literature*, New York: Peter Lang.

See also: history, modernity; literature; novel, the

JADE M. NOBBS

BIOLOGY

The field of biology is currently delivering a broad repertoire of explanatory tools for identity, behaviour and social configurations. After the Second World War, while physicists were celebrated as hero scientists, biology was condemned for its connections to eugenics, Nazi medical experiments and bad science (Keller 1992; Kevles 1985). Since the late twentieth century, however, biology has regained public confidence with the powerful Human Genome Project (Kevles and Hood 1992). Nowadays biology has found strong allies in technology, industry and politics and contributes to public discussion of such social issues as health and disease, behaviour, identity and kinship. Given the place of biology in contemporary society, the question of what is a man or a woman is often assumed to be a question that only biology can answer, and a central public debate concerns the distinction between, or roles of, what are thought of as the separate realms of 'nature' and of 'nurture'. This debate structures but confuses much current discussion of gender.

Although the biology of 'Man' had been virtually non-existent until the twentieth century, men have been both the objects and the subjects of biology, especially as deviancies to the prime subject: Man. As many scholars have shown, this prime subject was not so much linked to nature, biological processes or the flesh, but to culture, reason and the mind. Moreover, twentieth-century biology was less interested in individuals and their innate qualities than in clusters of individuals (social groups) and the relations between them. Biology, and most problematically so in its eugenic variant, had been preoccupied with delivering biological answers for the (racial, sexual and class) ordering of societies (Haraway 1989). It had focused its attention to otherness, the alleged threat to the social order and the masculinity of the centre (Duster 2003). In biological research racial differences, criminal or violent behaviour, and sexual reproductive success or deviancies had been the subjects of choice while studying men (Kevles 1985). Men of colour or members of lower classes were enrolled as objects in biological studies of various kinds. Brain masses were measured to establish the human chain of being (Gould 1981), IQ studies were studied to explain poverty and social status (Lewontin *et al.* 1984); phrenology and hereditary studies aimed at criminal behaviour and violence were studied preferably among (black) prisoners (Kevles 1985; Duster 2003); sexual behaviour, reproductive success and sexual deviancies (such as homo- or bi-sexuality) were conducted preferably among the lower classes (Kevles 1985). Thus although men have been objects of biology contributing to the inscription of deviancy among social groups, man and masculinity had not been put on the research table of nineteenth- and early twentieth-century biology.

From deviancies to dominance

In a different branch of late twentieth-century biology, 'Man' the prime subject had been contrasted to the animal kingdom. For example, during the 1970s and 1980s sociobiological studies of animal behaviour had become powerful legitimating tools for male dominance. Studies of ant colonies or primate apes have figured as laboratory controlled experiments where the biology and behaviour of males could be studied in ways that would enlighten our understanding of men in society. Such studies have been both hailed (in the fields of biology and psychology) and criticised (especially by feminists) because they contributed to the legitimisation of male violence and aggression. Violence, aggression, territoriality and dominance were explained as communication strategies, contributing to evolutionary success, and as guarantees for the future existence of a population or a species (Haraway 1991). A classical socio-biological study, Dawkins's (1979) *The Selfish Gene*, borrows from cybernetics and computer science to establish the chain of command in such communication and to argue that genes have a life of their own aiming at diversity in the gene pool and at competition between different genotypes. In this context, genes ('the replicators') are eager to reproduce and use human bodies as vehicles to safeguard their future existence. Although men, or humans for that matter, do not enter the scene until the last chapter of Dawkins's book, the message is crystal clear: the nature of masculinity is gene-driven, and dominance, competition and violence are goods in themselves. This understanding of masculinity had prevailed in popular science books by the end of the twentieth century.

From deviancies to differences

Biological knowledge and discourse are powerful. They tend to travel more easily to the rest of society than, say, knowledge about electrons. It is for this reason that feminist scholars have insisted on an engagement with biology. The stakes in biological knowledge have been high. In contrast to 'Man', biology has quite a lot to say about 'woman'. Whereas men have been conceived of as non-biological, i.e. rational and detached, etc., in dominant social and biological discourse women have been considered biology-driven, i.e. emotional, attached, and so forth. This dichotomy has contributed to women's association with nature and related domains, such as the household or child care, whereas men were placed outside of nature in the public sphere.

Feminist scholars have participated strongly in the so-called 'nature–nurture' debate and argued that scientists claiming to study biological sex-differences had actually been inscribing social phenomena on to the biological. The introduction of the concept of gender in the 1980s found a warm welcome in feminist science studies. Juxtaposed against the biological (sex), this cultural concept (gender) provided feminists with a powerful tool to study inequalities between men and women and concepts of femininity and masculinity and to intervene in processes of domination. During the 1980s and 1990s gender became the category of choice, and sex its stable yet not so relevant referent. Feminist scholars, such as Haraway (1991) and Mol (2002) argued that biological sex was too important to be left to biologists for study and too complex to be reduced to one thing. Influenced by the constructivist turn in science studies, Haraway, Mol and others have insisted on a view of science as a cultural practice. Since scientific practice is heterogeneous, its objects of study are multiple by nature, be this biological sex, man, woman, the body or race. Others, especially feminist women of colour, have raised similar questions about the unified subject of feminist politics, namely woman. They have argued that woman may be a variety of different things or positions depending on where you are in the world. If woman is multiple, what about man (Connell 1995)? Important here is that biological sex has changed from a stable reference out there in nature to a fluid subject, intricately connected to scientific work and technology (M'charek 2005). Biology is plural, and so are masculinities and femininities.

Rather than a mere critique of biology as a form of ideology, the constructivist turn has contributed to taking biological knowledge and practice seriously. For biology (and science in general) as a field has contributed to our understanding of ourselves, and it has delivered technologies that are intimately connected to our daily lives and identities. The constructivist turn has thus contributed to strands of research that are interested in how biology produces differences, knowing that these differences are not lying out there in nature, waiting for scientists to reveal them. Sex differences are material cultural products that matter in serious ways. For example in her study of the male pill, Oudshoorn (2002) shows that in contrast to the expectations of scientists and industry, men were actually eager to take a hormonal contraceptive. Moreover, men would welcome an effective alternative to the condom if only to alleviate the burden for their female partners. Oudshoorn shows that the medical field was not equipped to provide this care for men. Whereas women with questions concerning contraception would be referred to a gynaecologist, no such discipline existed for men, indicating a lack of knowledge about the male reproductive system. Although men did see urologists, these professionals did not want to be involved in the clinical trials for the male pill. Their core business was improving men's sexual performance and not anything that might jeopardise this, such as hormonal contraceptives. The study of the male pill shows that in order to produce future users of the male pill, different masculinities had to be fashioned both in biological and clinical research and outside. Thus taking biology seriously allows us to go beyond one male nature (which lies in hormones, genes, cortex, skeletons, gonads, etc.) and to see a variety of differences that biology helps produce.

Y-man?

By the end of the twentieth century biology had predominantly become the biology of the gene. The launch of the Human Genome Project (HGP) and the completion of that genome (the first human genetic map) in June 2000 contributed substantially to this 'genetic revolution'. Whereas genetics and heredity had been an anathema outside medical practice, nowadays genes for virtually anything are being announced, varying from maleness and homosexuality to violence or language capability (Sykes 2003). In practice, scientists would acknowledge that any behaviour is much more complex than an identification of a gene, yet the message widely received is that the answer is there in biology – even better, in the genetic code. The most exciting result of the HGP and its technologies is the insight that the DNA is a huge landscape. Based on similarities and differences in the DNA, this allows for an endless clustering of individuals. Genetic differences are less a matter of DNA than matters of technologies. The difference between one population and the other, or one individual and the other, depends on the technologies applied and on the part of the DNA that is being studied (M'charek 2005).

Let us take a step back to view what is considered the ultimate identifier of masculinity in genetics, the Y-chromosome. This chromosome was 'discovered' in 1959. At that time the paradigm of biological research was: 'more is better'. Similar to attempts aimed at finding evidence for more brain mass in males (Gould 1981), biologists expected to find more chromosomes in men (Kevles 1985). Yet scientists ended up finding that one of the smallest chromosomes seemed to demarcate the difference between the sexes. Ever since, the genetic difference between females and males has been represented as XX–XY. Presence of the Y-chromosome seemed to make man. However, research in the 1990s shows that it is not so much the Y-chromosome as a specific gene that is involved in sex determination, the SRY-gene. This gene is usually found on the Y-chromosome, but its functioning depends on genes located on the X-chromosome. In some cases it is even located on the X-chromosome. Does this mean that the biology of sex differences is determined and understood? If we take man to be more than a bag of genes, we are still left with complexities that resist general or universal claims. For, in addition to genes, hormones, minerals, gonads, brains, breasts, diets, metabolic processes and so on, also matter. However, these biological 'objects' or mechanisms do not add up to a full picture of what a man is (see also Mol 2002). More often than not, they may conflict as they cluster individuals in different categories. One could say that the more knowledge biology produces about maleness, the further away we move from a unified signifier of masculinity.

References and further reading

Connell, R. (1995) *Masculinities*, Berkeley, CA: University of California Press.

Dawkins, R. (1979) *The Selfish Gene*, Oxford: Oxford University Press.

Duster, T. (2003) *Backdoor to Eugenics*, New York, London: Routledge.

Gould, S.J. (1981) *The Mismeasure of Man*, New York: Norton.

Haraway, D. [1989] (1992) *Primate Visions*, London, New York: Verso.

—— (1991) *Simians, Cyborgs, and Women*, London: Free Association.

Keller, E.F. (1992) *Secrets of Life, Secrets of Death*, New York: Routledge and Kegan Paul.

Kevles, D.J. (1985) *In the Name of Eugenics*, Cambridge, MA: Harvard University Press.

Kevles, D.J. and Hood, L. (1992) *The Code of Codes*, Cambridge, MA: Harvard University Press.

Lewontin, R.C., Rose, S. and Kamin, L.J. (1984) *Not in Our Genes*, New York: Pantheon.

M'charek, A. (2005) *The Human Genome Diversity Project*, Cambridge: Cambridge University Press.

Mol, A. (2002) *The Body Multiple*, Durham, NC: Duke University Press.

Oudshoorn, N. (2002) *The Male Pill*, Durham, NC: Duke University Press.

Sykes, B. [2003] (2004) *Adam's Curse*, New York, London: Norton.

See also: bodies and biology, male

AMADE M'CHAREK

BISEXUALITY

Bisexuality is central to masculinity in terms of impacting culture-specific gender roles and identities and their ties to sexual practices, thoughts and desires (Diamond 1993; Herdt 1985). Bisexuality has been historically underexplored in contrast to heterosexuality and homosexuality, though its ties to identity politics are similar. In part, this is due to the gay and lesbian rights movement, where bisexuality has been seen by some as an apolitical position and, with its tendency to destabilise polarities of sexuality, as a challenge to hard-won identities (Armstrong 1995; Weiss 2003). Likewise, from the perspective of homophobia, bisexuality is easily seen as contiguous with homosexuality.

Bisexuality is also subject to a range of flexible definitions, which generally acknowledge that sexual practices, desires and self-identifications can change over time. Despite attempts to explain bisexuality as a transitional stage between homosexuality and heterosexuality (Stokes *et al.* 1997; Armstrong 1995), bisexuality continues to develop as an accepted identity, and especially so in the growth of queer theory and queer masculinities in the late 1990s (Burrill 2002). However, the tendency in literary studies to regard bisexual authors and texts with depictions of bisexual practices or desires as within gay and lesbian studies indicates the difficulties that persist in accepting bisexuality as a viable identity.

If viewing bisexuality as a transitional identity implies that bisexuality as such does not exist, the opposite position is to see it as ubiquitous: all humans are bisexual. The psychoanalyst Sigmund Freud was among the earliest researchers to posit bisexuality as a normal disposition, which is repressed during maturation. Alfred Kinsey made this point more forcefully for male sexuality when he developed the still controversial Kinsey Scale (Kinsey [1948] 1998). The Kinsey Scale uses a variety of measures including fantasies, thoughts, dreams, emotional feelings and frequency of sexual activity to place an individual in a gradation between homosexuality and heterosexuality based on actual experiences and psychological reactions. More recently, psychiatrist Fritz Klein adjusted this scale to include such factors as Past History, Present History, Present Feelings and Future Inclination: this is the Klein Sexual Orientation Grid (KSOG) (Klein [1978] 2004). The KSOG is popular because it recognises the potential for change over time and for disagreement between current sexual practices and self-identification. The effect of these ways of conceptualising bisexuality is to destabilise any binary notions of sexual identity; instead, this conceptualisation introduces an unstable continuum of sexual practices and desires from which it is difficult to derive a discrete and stable homosexual or heterosexual identity. Kinsey's study also challenged the perceived preponderance of heteronormativity, asserting that 46 per cent of men had responded erotically or were sexually active with both men and women.

The approach developed from Freud through Kinsey and Klein introduces further complexities: the potential flexibility of sexual practices over time and the difficulties surrounding discrete identities that are based on a combination of practices, desires, fantasy, circumstances and involuntary response. The Kinsey Scale explicitly considers both sexual activities and feelings. It then follows that given the potential for repression, denial and conflict between social identities, bisexuality as a concept creates potential difficulties for reliable and stable sexual identities of any kind (Hansen 1985): since sexual practices, fantasies and self-identification are all subject to change over time and through the effects of repression and suppression, each factor is insufficient for creating a stable sexual identity.

More recently, several theorists based in queer theory have proposed a view of sexuality not based on stable identities. This view potentially conflicts with the struggle for recognition of the legitimacy of gay and lesbian identities. Such arguments have moved from the purely academic to more mainstream publications by such authors as Bert Archer ([1999] 2000) and Frank Browning ([1996] 1998).

Common questions surrounding bisexuality include the possibility of infidelity (Matteson 1985), promiscuity, sexually transmitted infections, sexually transmitted diseases such as HIV/AIDS, hedonistic bisexuality, and so forth. Because bisexuals have been a traditionally under-researched group, it is difficult to give definitive responses to such questions, and this difficulty is compounded by the variable nature and definitions of bisexuality.

References and further reading

Archer, B. [1999] (2000) *The End of Gay (and the Death of Heterosexuality)*, Toronto: Doubleday Canada.

Armstrong, E. (1995) 'Traitors to the cause?' in N. Tucker, L. Highleyman and R. Kaplan (eds) *Bisexual Politics*, New York: Harrington Park.
Browning, F. [1996] (1998) *A Queer Geography*, New York: Noonday.
Burrill, K.G. (2002) 'Queering bisexuality', *Journal of Bisexuality*, 2 (2–3): 95–105.
Diamond, M. (1993) 'Homosexuality and bisexuality in different populations', *Archives of Sexual Behavior*, 22 (4): 291–310.
Hansen, E.A. (1985) 'Bisexuality reconsidered', *Journal of Homosexuality*, 11 (1–2): 1–6.
Herdt, G.H. (1985) 'A comment on cultural attributes and fluidity of bisexuality', *Journal of Homosexuality*, 11 (1–2): 53–61.
Kinsey, A.C. [1948] (1998) *Sexual Behavior in the Human Male*, Bloomington, IN: Indiana University Press.
Klein, F. [1978] (2004) *The Bisexual Option*, Binghamton, NY: Haworth Press.
Matteson, D.R. (1985) 'Bisexual men in marriage', *Journal of Homosexuality*, 11 (1–2): 149–71.
Stokes, J.P., Damon, W. and McKirnen, D.J. (1997) 'Predictors of movement toward homosexuality', *The Journal of Sex Research*, 34 (3): 304–12.
Weiss, J.T. (2003) 'GL vs BT: the archaeology of biphobia and transphobia within the US gay and lesbian community', *Journal of Bisexuality*, 3 (3–4): 25–55.

See also: men who have sex with men; sexuality

JAMES GIFFORD

BODIES AND BIOLOGY, MALE

Bodies and male biology are intricately interwoven with the way masculinities are understood and practised. Male biology is commonly defined by physical characteristics, external sexual organs and chromosomal composition. Biological males are classified chromosomally as XY and females as XX. Biological characteristics associated with maleness are located on the Y chromosome. Locating maleness chromosomally allows for a distinction to be made between biological sex (male/female) and other socially constructed differences such as gender (men/women). Yet this distinction is habitually collapsed with the assumption that biological sex differences are stable categories that exceed human subjectivities and are therefore able to dictate the 'acceptable' boundaries and definitions of gender.

Biology, however, is less reliable, stable and predictable than is ordinarily assumed. There are always anomalies, mutations, inconsistencies and change in nature. For example, some people have the physical characteristics and working sexual organs of a biological female, but possess the chromosomal karyotype XXY. Similarly, there are people who are biologically and physically male, but are chromosomally XYY. The possibility for biological change and diversity challenges the uniqueness of the Y chromosome as exclusively male and the root communicator of maleness.

Despite chromosomal variations, physical and biological traits are commonly relied on to identify maleness because so much of masculinity is conveyed by the physical presence of the body. The body can be understood as a social and cultural text upon which gender, race, class, sexuality and other differences are marked and displayed (Scott and Morgan 1993). For some the male body can be aggressive and threatening, while for others it may be kind and pleasurable. Individual bodies are disciplined into particular social and cultural practices that rely on specific contexts and continually change over time (Foucault 1977): that is, the hegemonic masculinity of a stonemason in ancient Mesopotamia is different from the masculine ideals of a business executive in the early twenty-first century. Furthermore, the same executive may enact masculinity differently on the sports field than he would at his child's daycare, and might engage a different masculinity with his male partner.

Regardless of context and cultural expectations, gender has been theorised as a performative act (Butler 1990). The performativity of gender habitually employs the body to present the variety of ways gender might be displayed. The way one sits, walks, holds one's hands, dresses, throws a ball and speaks conveys a gendered message. Because hegemonic masculinity is continually being renegotiated, particular ways of performing masculinity are given greater social and cultural value over others. Many people spend a great deal of time and energy attempting to 'measure up' to bodily hegemonic expressions of masculinity in order to achieve some of the social privileges it promises.

A part of hegemonic masculinity also includes identifying the 'gay' person, sometimes based on the way the body text is read as 'inappropriately' gendered, and employing homophobia to enforce hetero-reality through harassment (Smith 1998). The systemic collusion with hegemonic masculinity occurs through individual gendered practices as well as through public institutions, such as schools, which assist in the shaping of the body and masculinity (Davison 2000). Popular cinema and television also commonly feature mimetic performances of hegemonic masculine bodily ideals, and in many post-industrialised countries people participate in regular fitness routines to remain closer to the contemporary bodily standard of masculinity.

In the West in the 1980s, public gymnasiums and weight rooms were relatively uncommon. Yet by the early 1990s the body-conscious culture grew, and fitness centres became more popular to both women and men of all ages. While an unhealthy subservience to feminine body ideals produced a growth of body image and eating disorders in young women, by the late 1990s sociological, psychological and medical research found that hegemonic masculinity also created some unhealthy body image 'side effects' in men and boys. Some men have developed anorexia or bulimia, and even more men and boys have developed 'reverse anorexia' or 'bigorexia' (Pope *et al.* 2000). When measuring up to the cosmetic demands of hegemonic masculinity or competing in sport, many men and boys actively construct a hypermasculine physique through weight-training (Messner and Sabo 1994). Yet, despite working out in the gym for several hours per day and subsequently gaining muscle mass, some boys and men continue to see themselves as thin or unmuscular. The dissatisfaction with the shape of the physical body can lead some men and boys to excessive exercising, extended weight training, extreme dieting, anabolic steroids and an unhealthy relationship towards the body and self (Davison 2000; Pope *et al.* 2000). The disconnection between the physical body and the psychic construct among those afflicted with reverse anorexia arises from gendered expectations and the social focus on the muscular body as a desired physical shape.

Since the late 1980s, the emphasis on the display of male bodies has saturated the media, popular culture, pornography, advertising, sport and even children's entertainment. For example, toy 'action figures' have become hypermasculine, featuring musculature that would only be possible for humans to emulate through the use of steroids (Pope *et al.* 2000). The objectification and commodification of male bodies, not unlike the historical objectification of female bodies, has demanded a greater degree of conformity to gender ideals as performed by the body. Magazines that address men's health, fashion and entertainment, for example, focus on the visual presentation of masculinity as a mirror of hegemonic standards; at the same time, they fuel insecurities about the body and gender by advertising a variety of muscle-enhancing and weight gain supplements, erectile dysfunction aids and hair loss 'cures'. Built on men's anxieties about their bodies and their masculine performances, the hegemonic muscular body has become a fetishised and unrealistic ideal.

Since philosopher René Descartes in the seventeenth century argued for the separation of the mind and the body, attempts to regulate and discipline the body demonstrate both the ability of individual control and symbolic control of the broader environment. Some elements of the body's ordinary functioning – for example, aging, illness and dying – commonly resist human intervention and control. Yet many people still attempt to push the limits of the body through cosmetic plastic surgery and diverse implants. Some undergo facial surgery to disguise aging; others have pectoral, calf or gluteal implants in order to make the body appear more 'fit' or muscular. Both of these examples illustrate how the social and cultural demands masculinity can impose put stress upon the physical body and can even extend the assumed limits of the body.

Since the late twentieth century in many post-industrial countries, there has been a renewed focus on individualising the body, transgressing tidy categories, by marking it with tattoos, piercings, branding and scarification (Atkinson 2004; Favazza 1996). Some see this as an attempt to hold on to control of the body's significance at a time when technological advancements and new computer-mediated communications seem to have marginalised the physical body as simply flesh, or 'meat'. Radical body modifications may represent a further fetishisation of bodies when the cultural significance of the body is waning, 'disappearing' or being replaced by cybernetic technologies that combine human bodies with machines (i.e. artificial organs and limbs) (Kroker and Kroker 1993).

The mass production and distribution of personal computers since the 1990s has changed the way people communicate. While the physical body does not disappear when engaged with computer-mediated communication, the distance between the physical body and social communication events is widened, which allows for a shift in the degree to which gender performances are body dependent (Davison 2003). Textual communication is also gendered, of course, but the absence of the physical body in a chat room, e-mail or even telephone conversation can offer some people freedom from the way their biological body positions them socially in the world. For example, female-to-male transsexuals may find computer-mediated communication allows them to 'pass' as masculine more often than if both physical bodies are present for the communication exchange.

Because gender is often tested on the physical body, it has also been the instrument for renegotiating hegemonic masculinity. Some gay men transgress masculinity and assumptions about 'appropriate' male bodies by impersonating conventional femininity in drag queen performances. Furthermore, women have appropriated masculinities from the assumed exclusivity of male bodies through performing as drag kings (Halberstam 1998). Such performances mock and parody masculinities, and in so doing weaken the authority of dominant and repressive masculinities that are often assumed to be 'naturally' the domain of a small group of men (Volcano and Halberstam 1999).

Transsexuals and transgender people offer an additional challenge to the way bodies and male biology are implicated in the forms through which masculinities are understood and performed (Holliday and Hassard 2001). Medical and psychiatric definitions of gender identity have recognised that masculinities do not always correspond to a biologically male body. Some people may be masculine and not biologically male, while others may be feminine and remain biologically male. Because social and cultural traditions regarding gender have assumed that male bodies convey masculinities and female bodies convey femininities, some people have chosen to undergo sex reassignment surgery to radically rearrange their physical body to match their gender in a traditional configuration. Transgender people, on the other hand, use their bodies to demonstrate that gender and biology need not line up in traditional ways.

Male bodies and male biology, cross culturally, are markers of masculinity. However, there is great diversity in how masculinities are layered and folded across bodies and male biology. As cultures, identities and technologies continue to shift, within national boundaries and outside them, hegemonic masculinities are renegotiated and may become less reliant on biologically male bodies. This need not lead to the obsolescence of the physical body, but rather to a rearrangement and retheorisation of the categories that have been assumed to be inevitable and inalterable (Frank 1997). Bodies and male biology have historically transmitted very specific gendered information about 'appropriate' ways to be gendered that has excluded some men and most women. Rethinking the foundations of biological sex and the limitations of the physical body may enable gender articulations that are more inclusive and equitable.

References and further reading

Atkinson, M. (2004) 'Figuring out body modification cultures', *Health*, 8 (3): 273–86.

Butler, J. (1990) *Gender Trouble*, New York: Routledge.

Davison, K. (2000) 'Boys' bodies', *The Journal of Men's Studies*, 8 (2): 255–66.

—— (2003) 'Body talk and masculinities', unpublished doctoral dissertation, University of South Australia, Adelaide.

Favazza, A.R. (1996) *Bodies Under Siege*, Baltimore, MD: Johns Hopkins University Press.

Foucault, M. (1977) *Discipline and Punish*, New York: Pantheon.

Frank, B. (1997) 'Masculinity meets postmodernism', *Canadian Folklore Canadien*, 19 (1): 15–33.

Halberstam, J. (1998) *Female Masculinity*, Durham, NC: Duke University Press.

Holliday, R. and Hassard, J. (eds) (2001) *Contested Bodies*, New York: Routledge.

Kroker, A. and Kroker, M. (1993) *The Last Sex*, New York: St Martin's Press.

Messner, M. and Sabo, D. (1994) *Sex, Violence and Power in Sports*, Freedom, CA: Crossing Press.

Pope, H.G., Phillips, K.A. and Olivardia, R. (2000) *The Adonis Complex*, New York: Free Press.

Scott, S. and Morgan, D. (eds) (1993) *Body Matters*, London: Falmer.

Smith, G.W. (1998) 'The ideology of "fag"', *The Sociology Quarterly*, 39 (2): 309–35.

Volcano, D. and Halberstam, J. (1999) *The Drag King Book*, London: Serpent's Tail.

See also: body image; bodybuilding; hegemonic masculinity; muscles and muscularity; transgender

KEVIN G. DAVISON

BODY IMAGE

Body image is a high-stakes issue in this postmodern world where movies, television, art and other media are central in shaping cultural notions of 'proper' masculinity. The role of the mediated body image in installing a hegemonic masculinity has dire consequences for real men who consume, internalise and naturalise these images. The 1990s saw the ongoing cinematic revival of a narrative tradition that has as its purpose the establishment of an ideal body image and standard of masculinity. This narrative pattern, epitomised by the D.H. Lawrence novel *Lady Chatterley's Lover* (1929), places male characters coded as intellectual, cultured and/or upper-class in opposition to male characters associated with the body – coded as working-class or 'of the earth'. This mind/body dichotomy is formed around the contested site of the female body – a beautiful, intelligent woman who is desired by both the 'mind' and 'body men'. Although the desired woman is initially attached to a mind man in some way (married, engaged, etc.), the casting, narrative development and visual presentation of the male characters privilege the body man. The principal strategy for establishing the body man's narrative superiority is to have him awaken the desired woman's sexuality in a way that the mind man cannot (Lehman and Hunt 1999a).

The pattern has two repeating aspects: the love-making style of the body man and his body image itself. Love-making in most of these films normalises an athletic, vigorous, 'do-it-all-night' sex style (*Legends of the Fall* (1994), *End of the Affair* (1999)), with the body men (played by actors such as Brad Pitt, Jude Law and Jon Bon Jovi) performing masterfully upon first-time intercourse with the desired woman, often under implausibly difficult circumstances (*Titanic* (1997), *Enemy at the Gates* (2001)). The normalisation of what might be called the 'good pounding' sex style precludes imaginative or alternative sexual scenarios that may be more pleasurable.

Since the penetration model is the privileged sex style in these films, the penis is inextricably linked with the preferred performance. Interestingly, the mind/body films frequently include full frontal male nudity, always associated with the body men (*At Play *in the Field of the Lords* (1991), *The Piano* (1993), *Sirens* (1994), *Angels and Insects* (1995), *The Governess* (1997), *Box of Moon Light* (1996), *Lawn Dogs* (1997)). In all cases, actors' penises conform to a type that is conventional in various modes of representation: it is visibly impressive when flaccid – hanging over the scrotum, in contrast to being retracted above it. This normalisation of the full, 'hanging down' penis excludes a range of male body types from representation, promoting a highly limited image of what is needed for 'good sex': one that does not match the actual bodies of many men who are small or even retracted when flaccid but fully adequate when erect.

A disturbing aspect of all the body man/mind man films is that the female characters, often coded as intelligent and feminist, easily succumb to the allure of the body man and the style of sex his body offers them, implying that this is what all women want and need to be truly satisfied. The enticing notion of an erotics of intelligence suggested in films such as *The Governess* and *Angels and Insects* is notably absent. Key films of the pattern also raise the issue of anti-intellectualism *vis-à-vis* representations of the Jewish male body and masculinity. In such films as *Enemy at the Gates*, the sexually humiliated mind man is Jewish, denigrating while perpetuating the cultural stereotype of the intellectual Jew (Lehman and Hunt 2006). On the other hand, the elevation of the body man's masculinity raises important issues of socio-economic class in that the body men are frequently depicted as manual labourers (handymen, gardeners, mechanics, house painters) and are thus empowered in the narrative in ways that are not available to their referents in American society.

Current work on race and ethnicity offers a rich opportunity for further exploration of masculinity. Disturbing stereotypes emerge if we map race and sexuality issues over the mind man/body man paradigm: the body man is linked to the well-endowed, hypersexual black man; the mind man to the under-sexed Asian man with a small penis who is a poor lover but a good student and a successful professional (hooks 2004; Poulson-Bryant 2005; Fung 1991). These body images in film can create painful, difficult problems for men of colour much as the standardised representation of the flaccid penis as long, full and visually impressive can create similar problems for men with small or retracted penises.

A partial list of post-millennial films in the mind/body pattern (and transmutations of it) includes: *The Tailor of Panama* (2001), *Nowhere in Africa* (2001), *Sweet Home Alabama* (2002), *The Notebook* (2004) and *The Woodlanders* (2005).

References and further reading

Fung, R. (1991) 'Looking for my penis', in Bad Object-Choices (ed.) *How Do I Look?* Seattle, WA: Bay Press.

hooks, b. (2004) *We Real Cool*, New York: Routledge.

Lehman, P. (1993) *Running Scared*, Philadelphia, PA: Temple University Press.

Lehman, P. and Hunt, S. (1999a) 'Something and someone else', in K. Sandler, K. Studlar and G. Studlar (eds) *Titanic*, New Brunswick, NJ: Rutgers University Press, pp. 89–107.

—— (1999b) 'From casual to melodramatic', *Framework*, 40: 69–84.

—— (2002a) 'The inner man', in M. Pomerance (ed.) *Enfant Terrible*, New York: New York University Press, pp. 195–209.

—— (2002b) 'Passion and a passion for learning in *The Governess*', *Jump Cut* 45 (online).

—— (2002c) 'Severed heads and severed genitals', *Framework*, 43: 161–73.

—— (forthcoming 2007) *The Naked and the Dead*, in *Sunshine and Enemy at the Gates*.

Poulson-Bryant, S. (2005) *Hung*, New York: Doubleday.

See also: bodies and biology, male; bodybuilding; muscles and muscularity

SUSAN HUNT

BODYBUILDING

Bodybuilding, which is grounded in the bodily, muscular, aesthetic, is often central to discussions of the construction of muscular masculine males (Drummond 1996). This is largely due to the historical nexus between muscularity, strength and masculinity. Historically muscles have played a significant role in the construction of men's masculinity, and men's engagement in muscle-building activities has had a long history (Dutton 1995). Noteworthy is that bodybuilding is mostly a Western cultural phenomenon with the majority of participants being male.

Bodybuilding is a contentious activity. Some people view it as a sport, while others regard it as a pastime, or as a leisure and recreation activity (Drummond 2002). However, those who engage in serious bodybuilding are often perceived (and labelled) by many as being narcissistic, self-indulgent individuals with a penchant for vanity (Klein 1993). Irrespective of the arguments surrounding its sporting status, elite-level bodybuilding is an intense activity that requires devotion and commitment. Committed participants, regardless of whether they compete or not, identify themselves as bodybuilders and spend many hours in a gymnasium each day undertaking heavy and repetitious lifting regimes. Not only do the participants make a commitment to the physical act of bodybuilding, most commit to living the life of a bodybuilder which is underpinned by a subcultural ethos based on accruing muscularity and size as the foremost component of one's life.

While the sport may be legitimated by its competitive elements, it is the judges who ultimately determine a bodybuilder's ability. Unlike other judged sports such as gymnastics and diving, where physical aesthetics are supposedly not a criterion of judgment, bodybuilders are conscious of how their bodies appear. Therefore, the aesthetic appearance of the body, based on a set of arbitrary standards, is the vehicle through which success or failure is represented.

References and further reading

Drummond, M. (1996) 'The social construction of masculinity as it relates to sport: an investigation into the lives of elite level athletes competing in individually oriented masculinised sports', unpublished doctoral thesis, Edith Cowan University, Perth, Western Australia.

—— (2002) 'Masculinity and self-identity in elite triathlon, bodybuilding and surf lifesaving', in D. Hemphill and C. Symons (eds) *Gender, Sexuality and Sport: A Dangerous Mix*, NSW: Walla Walla Press, pp. 39–48.

Dutton, K.R. (1995) *The Perfectible Body: The Western Ideal of Physical Development*, St Leonards, NSW: Allen and Unwin.

Klein, A. (1993) *Little Big Men: Bodybuilding Subculture and Gender Construction*, Albany, NY: State University of New York Press.

See also: bodies and biology, male; body image; muscles and muscularity

MURRAY DRUMMOND

BOYS AND BOYHOOD

Sociopolitical perspectives on boys and boyhood have been very useful in highlighting the importance of culture and historical context in how boys learn to define and negotiate their masculinities. For example, the framework for theorising masculinities provided by Connell has led to important insights and research being conducted into the impact of hegemonic heterosexual masculinities in boys' lives, with its implications for developing a deeper understanding about gender and experiences of boyhood that move beyond the limits of sex-role socialisation theories. Carrigan *et al.* (1987) offered a critique of sex-role theory that provided the foundation for developing an alternative conceptual framework for gender theorising. This spoke to the dynamics of power and the sexual politics implicated in gender relations and argued for the need to address issues of interrelated factors such as class and sexual orientation. While sex-role theory offered a limited and static view of identity formation, the new sociology provided a more fruitful analysis of the complexities and contradictions involved in negotiating gender and relations of what Connell (1995) termed hegemonic, complicit and subordinated masculinities. This theoretical perspective has been instrumental in producing more nuanced analyses of the experiences of boyhood, particularly in relation to documenting the interplay and dynamics of masculinities in boys' lives.

However, while there has been an explosion of studies into boys and masculinities in the last decade, this has been accompanied by what might best be termed a neo-liberal and neo-conservative political agenda that has impacted on and continues to impact significantly on social and educational policy. This has had major implications for establishing and authorising certain truths about boys and men as the 'new disadvantaged' who have suffered as a result of feminism and the feminising influences of women. This is represented by the media in terms of a 'moral panic' and a 'masculinity crisis', which Lingard and Douglas (1999) claim is driven by a recuperative 'masculinity politics'. This anti-feminist politics of backlash has been manifested most significantly in terms which invoke essentialised notions of boys and of boyhood as a rite of passage thwarted by the absent father and, more broadly, by men's absence as role models in boys' lives. For example, Biddulph (1995) claims that boys with absent fathers are more likely to use violence, get into trouble, do poorly at school and join a teenage gang.

Hoff Sommers (2000) also reiterates the need for fathers to help boys become apparently *proper* or *normal* men and stresses the 'misery' that is caused for boys by those in schools who deny what is natural or in boys' nature:

> It is obvious that a boy wants his father to help him become a man, and belonging to the culture of manhood is important to almost every boy. To impugn his desire to become 'one of the boys' is to deny that a boy's biology determines much of what he prefers and is attracted to.
>
> (Hoff Sommers 2000)

Unfortunately, by denying the nature of boys, education theorists can cause them much misery.

Flood (2000) claims that while feminist reform agendas were committed to critiquing sex-role expectations defined for girls and to expanding their skills beyond the limits imposed by traditional femininities, this has not been the case for boys and men. He draws attention to the problematic tendency or failure to address the impact of hegemonic masculinities on boys' lives in much of the populist literature and that driven by a neo-conservative and backlash agenda. Within the limits imposed by such political frameworks, Flood (2000: 4) argues that boys 'are still universally encouraged to purge themselves of any hint of softness or femininity':

> In contrast to the new situation that prevails for girls, many male role models in the world of athletics and the media continue to support stereotypes of masculinity. It is no wonder, then, that males grow up attuned to and comfortable expressing themselves with violence.

This tendency to invoke gender polarisation, and hence to assert that boys are essentially different from girls, as a basis for recuperating or reinstating dominant forms of masculinity, has a long history. As Petersen (1998) has illustrated, this reflects a deep anxiety about the status of masculinity under threat by the perceived gains made by women at certain historical points in time. For example, he claims that following the rise of liberal democracy and the accompanying threat posed by the increasing demands of women for equal rights, male political philosophers began to support a political ideology of sex role differences as grounded in the biological sexed body.

Sexton (1969), a sociologist who set out to study the impact of the feminisation of boys and men in the 1960s, represents a response to the feminisation of schooling and men/boys that parallels the resurgence of a 'masculinity crisis' that characterises much of the moral panic about boys and boyhood in the past decade. As Petersen has illustrated, these sorts of responses need to be contextualised within historically specific milieux of social change in which challenges or threats to the established male order are manifested though an intensification of anxiety surrounding the expression and/or definition of 'proper' masculinity. This moral concern about the feminisation, and hence the emasculation, of boys and men, as it is expressed by Sexton, needs to be understood as a response to broader social changes of the time in terms of the impact of the second wave feminism and gay/lesbian rights/activism within the context of the sexual revolution and its impact on the changing roles of men and women in society. For example, Sexton equates feminisation with female dominance over boys, claiming that it occurs 'as males fall under the dominance of women who have been consigned to home and school' (Sexton 1969: 18). In fact, for Sexton, women – both mothers and female teachers – emerge as potential figures of fear and loathing in their capacity to castrate and hence emasculate men and boys. This, she stresses, has particular devastating psychological and emotional consequences for both boys and male teachers, particularly within feminising contexts such as school that threaten 'normal masculine growth'. Sexton argues that the school enforces a form of passive conformity, which is equated with femininity and conflicts with the *natural* expression of *healthy* masculinity. This results in rebellion and anti-social behaviour, she argues, leading boys to be cast as 'outsiders and misfits'.

This discourse about the inimical effects of the feminisation of boys resonates with current concerns about boys and boyhood, in which introducing more male role models and boy-friendly curricula in schools is seen as a panacea for addressing their educational and social needs (see Martino *et al.* 2004, for a critique of these approaches). Set against the tide of such recuperative masculinist approaches, however, is a body of research literature which continues to highlight a more nuanced analysis of power relations and differences amongst boys (Mac an Ghaill 1994; Gilbert and Gilbert 1998; Archer 2003). Martino and Pallotta-Chiarolli (2003) in their book *So What's a Boy?* focus on a range of different boys' experiences in Australian schools to foreground how relations of masculinity and gender impact on their lives. The aim of such research is to problematise the ways in which adolescent boys, from diverse backgrounds and locations, negotiate and perform their masculinities, both at school and in the wider society (see also Martino and Pallotta-Chiarolli 2005). Set against a critique of moral panic about the status of all boys as the 'new disadvantaged', the emphasis is on those boys who are positioned on the margins in terms of their cultural backgrounds, sexuality, indigeneity, disability and socio-economic status. They negotiate social systems of identification that are often grounded in hierarchical and dichotomous classifications. These social relations impact on their relationships and attitudes to schooling in very significant ways. However, in providing the perspectives of a diverse range of boys positioned on the margins, the concern is to foreground the various ways in which some of these boys also invest in particular versions of masculinity to compensate for their inferiorised positioning – at the bottom of the social hierarchy – by other boys at school. Such hierarchical power relations also impact on and are actively negotiated by white Anglo-Australian middle socio-economic status boys.

Such scholarship provides further insights into the intra-group dynamics governing boys' social practices of masculinity and experiences of boyhood at school. For example, 'cool' dominant white boys in this Australian study used a variety of strategies to maintain their position at the top of the social hierarchy. They played a major role in assigning and policing the inclusion and exclusion of other boys' membership into groups. Many of these criteria were classified into neat hierarchical binaries such as being thin or fat, being 'sporty' or 'nerdy', having a 'big dick' or 'small dick', or being seen with popular girls or unpopular girls. However, many other boys actively challenged and questioned these normalising practices and policing techniques which circumscribed their experiences of boyhood and schooling. Boys from all backgrounds questioned the limits imposed by normative constructions of gendered relations of power, with some highlighting the significant role played by adult men and particularly their fathers in trying to enforce a particular version of masculinity built on a rejection of certain forms of emotionality read as weakness.

Boys themselves may offer sophisticated accounts of the multiple social relations which shape and constitute gender and sexual relations in schools. For example, in Martino and Pallotta-Chiarolli's (2003) interviews, an Italo-Australian boy describes the hierarchical power relations that are inflected by homophobia and heterosexism and which cut across class, ethnic and racial boundaries. He draws attention to the pecking order of ethnicities at a single-sex Catholic boys' school where the Asian boys were positioned at the bottom of the social ladder, but were only too ready to taunt him in homophobic ways on the basis of his sexuality. This boy also talks about other Italian boys who were unable to reconcile 'being Italian' and 'being gay', given that his particular expression of straight-acting masculinity confounded their stereotypes of the gay male as essentially effeminate.

Such boyhood experiences highlight the significance of critical theoretical frameworks that examine the complexities and intersections of masculinity, sexuality, class, geographical location and ethnicity in boys' lives. In addition, by including the voices of those boys who are marginalised and who are also willing to interrogate hegemonic constructions of masculinity, such research foregrounds the extent to which 'masculinity', as a set of social practices, is governed by historically and culturally specific norms for determining what are to count as legitimate expressions or experiences of boyhood.

Such literature represents an attempt to elaborate a theoretical framework that builds on that provided by Connell by drawing on theorists such as Foucault, Anzaldua and Minh-ha. These theorists provide useful conceptual frameworks for placing boys and boyhood under a particular kind of investigation. They enable a focus on analysing normalisation, surveillance and regulation in all boys' lives, while directing particular attention to those positioned on the margins or borderlands. Given the tendency to homogenise boys, and hence the consequent failure of the media and much current educational policy to engage with more nuanced and complex understandings of boyhood and what it means to be a boy, research which provides the perspectives of those boys positioned at the margins has much to offer. In addition, such research represents a commitment to a transformative social agenda committed to fostering gender justice.

References and further reading

Archer, L. (2003) *'Race', Masculinity and Schooling*, Buckingham: Open University Press.

Biddulph, S. (1995) *Manhood*, Sydney: Finch Publishing.

Carrigan, T., Connell, B. and Lee, J. (1987) 'Toward a new sociology of masculinity', in H. Brod (ed.) *The Making of Masculinities*, Boston, MA: Allen and Unwin.

Connell, R. (1995) *Masculinities*, Sydney: Allen and Unwin.

Flood, C. (2000) 'Safe boys, safe schools', *WEEA Digest*, November: 4–7.

Gilbert, P. and Gilbert, R. (1998) *Masculinity Goes to School*, Sydney: Allen and Unwin.

Hoff Sommers, C. (2000) 'The war against boys', *The Atlantic Monthly*, 285 (5): 59–74, available at http://www.deltabravo.net/custody/waronboys.php

Lingard, R. and Douglas, P. (1999) *Men Engaging Feminisms*, Buckingham: Open University Press.

Mac an Ghaill, M. (1994) *The Making of Men*, Buckingham: Open University Press.

Martino, W. and Pallotta-Chiarolli, M. (2003) *So What's a Boy?* Maidenhead: Open University Press.

—— (2005) *'Being Normal is the Only Thing to Be'*, Sydney: UNSW Press.

Martino, W., Mills, M. and Lingard, B. (2004) 'Issues in boys' education', *Gender and Education*, 16 (4): 435–54.

Petersen, A. (1998) *Unmasking the Masculine*, London, Thousand Oaks, CA, New Delhi: Sage.
Sexton, P. (1969) *The Feminized Male*, New York: Random House.

See also: male youth cultures; young men

WAYNE MARTINO

BROTHERS

Brotherhood refers to a wide variety of sibling relationships and fraternal associations, notably in religious, ethnic, humanist, homosocial and military contexts.

In the Judeo-Christian tradition, Cain and Abel represent the primordial brother relationship and the cultural origins of sibling rivalry. Cain's murder of Abel in the Old Testament (Torah) establishes a recurring dynamic of fraternal antagonism, repeated between Jacob and Esau, and Joseph and his jealous brothers. The Greco-Roman tradition echoes these ancient models of fraternal enmity, from Remus and Romulus, the fratricidal founders of Rome, to Oedipus' sons Eteocles and Polynices, who killed one another over the throne of Thebes.

In many fratricidal relationships, fraternal competition for parental love and approval becomes a deadly struggle for dynastic succession and political power. This is true of Shakespeare's numerous warring brothers, such as the fratricidal Claudius in *Hamlet* and the tyrannical Richard in *Richard III*. For half-brothers, such as Edgar and Edmund in Shakespeare's *King Lear* or Ivan and Smerdiakov in Dostoyevsky's *The Brothers Karamazov*, the risks of fraternal violence are even greater, as contested legitimacy leads to paternal rejection and fraternal hatred. Elsewhere, the political dynamics of brotherhood have led to a cooperative sharing of power. Napoléon placed three of his brothers on European thrones: Joseph (Naples and Spain), Louis (Holland) and Jérôme (Westphalia). In twentieth-century America, brothers have played an important role in presidential politics, from the fraternal dynasty of John, Robert and Edward Kennedy, to the colourful antics of Jimmy Carter's brother Billy and Bill Clinton's brother Roger, to the leadership of Florida Governor Jeb Bush during his state's controversial voting scandal and the contested election of his brother George W. Bush.

While some scholars look to the competition theories of the political economist Malthus and the evolutionary biologist Darwin to explain sibling rivalry, others cite the evolutionary theorist Hamilton's rule on biological altruism as an explanation of sibling affection, cooperation and collaboration. Early psychoanalytic theory understood sibling rivalry as an important developmental stage: Freud and Adler explained fraternal competition as an Oedipal or dethronement complex; Levy popularised the term 'sibling rivalry'; and Klein examined sibling love, affection, incest and violence.

Contrary to sibling rivalry, many brothers demonstrate great affection to their brothers and sisters in the face of mutual suffering, as in the protective relationships between Hector and Paris in Homer's *Iliad,* Orestes and Electra in Sophocles' *Oresteia*, and Laertes and Ophelia in Shakespeare's *Hamlet*. Troubled but benevolent brothers also figure prominently in Maupassant's *Pierre and Jean*, Steinbeck's *Of Mice and Men*, O'Neill's *Long Day's Journey Into Night* and Miller's *Death of a Salesman*. In addition, brotherly collaboration and inspiration have produced countless social contributions to: literature and philosophy (Henry and William James, Edmond and Jules Goncourt, Jacob and Wilhelm Grimm); technology (Wright Brothers); entertainment (Ringling Brothers), comedy (Marx, Belushi and Wayans Brothers), music (Gershwin, Gibb and Jackson Brothers), film (Lumière, Warner, Coen, Wachowski and Farrelly Brothers) and business (Lazard, Lehman and Salomon Brothers).

Twins represent a uniquely intimate form of brotherhood. In ancient mythology, Cain and Abel, Remus and Romulus, and Eteocles and Polynices were all twins, as were Castor and Pollux, who became the twin stars

Gemini. Identical (one egg or monozygotic), fraternal (two eggs or dizygotic) and conjoined twins (or Siamese twins, after Eng and Chang Bunker, the famous conjoined brothers from Thailand) are often characterised as indistinguishable pairs or polar opposites, a mirrored double or an inverse other. In Shakespeare's *As You Like It*, *Twelfth Night* and *The Comedy of Errors*, as well as in the fiction of Twain, Dumas, Carroll, Arundhati Roy and Zadie Smith, twins demonstrate the comic effects and mortal dangers of mistaken identity and symbolise what the intellectuals Benjamin, Baudrillard and Schwartz have identified as a popular fascination with the copy, clone and replica.

Brotherhood itself is symbolically replicated in countless homosocial or fraternal associations, such as monastic religious orders (Franciscans, Dominicans, Buddhists), ethnic and political movements (Black Panthers) and fraternal organisations (college fraternities, Masons, Shriners). While brotherhood has often been invoked by humanists, such as Montaigne, Schiller and Whitman, in their call for universal peace, fraternity has also been used to describe military camaraderie in war. The military origins of fraternity can be traced back to the ancient race of warriors described by Plutarch and Plato as the 'Sacred Band of Thebes' or 'Army of Lovers' and to the Greco-Roman soldiers in Homer's *Iliad* and Virgil's *Aeneid*. During the French Revolution, citizen-soldiers swore fraternal military oaths and thus introduced brotherly devotion into the national republican slogan, *Liberté, égalité, fraternité* (Liberty, Equality, Fraternity). And Shakespeare's celebrated description of English soldiers in *Henry V* as a 'band of brothers' has been repeatedly used by historians (Ambrose 1999), poets (Owen) and fraternal war films (*The Fighting Sullivans*, *Saving Private Ryan*, *Band of Brothers*) to describe soldiers during the First and Second World Wars. In both literal and symbolic contexts, brotherhood continues to represent intimacy and enmity, affection and violence.

References and further reading

Adler, A. [1921] (1999) *The Neurotic Constitution*, London: Routledge.

Ambrose, S. (1999) *Band of Brothers*, New York: Simon and Schuster.

Baudrillard, J. [1983] (1994) *Simulacra and Simulation*, Ann Arbor, MI: University of Michigan Press.

Benjamin, W. [1936] (1999) *Illuminations*, London: Pimlico.

Coles, P. (2003) *The Importance of Sibling Relationships in Psychoanalysis*, London: Karnac.

Freud, S. [1916–17] (1989) *Introductory Lectures on Psychoanalysis*, New York: Norton.

Klein, M. [1932] (1997) *The Psychoanalysis of Children*, New York: Vintage.

Levy, D. (1937) *Studies in Sibling Rivalry*, New York: American Orthopsychiatry Association.

Mitchell, J. (2003) *Siblings*, Cambridge: Polity.

Mock, D. (2004) *More than Kin and Less than Kind*, Cambridge, MA: Belknap/Harvard University Press.

Sanders, R. (2004) *Sibling Relationships*, New York: Palgrave Macmillan.

Schwartz, H. (1996) *The Culture of the Copy*, New York: Zone.

See also: men's relations with men

BRIAN MARTIN

BULLYING

Bullying is repeated verbally or physically abusive behaviour in the context of an unequal power relationship. Most discussions about bullying have been located in school settings. However, there has been a more recent trend to use the term to describe a range of workplace interactions. This entry will focus on debates and concepts primarily in relation to schools, although they have broader applicability.

The use of the bullying label to describe certain anti-social behaviour among youth is problematic as it tends to minimise or downplay the significance of the abuse. For example, actions resulting in physical harm between children or adolescents in the schoolyard may be labelled bullying and the perpetrator cautioned by a teacher. Were the same injurious actions to occur between adults in a public setting, they would be called assault and might well result in criminal charges.

Most research on and programmes to address bullying tend to be gender blind, arguing that perpetrators are of both sexes. However, while both girls and boys bully there are differences in style. Boys tend to use verbal and physical intimidation whereas girls employ tactics like teasing, gossiping or social exclusion. There are also clear gender differences in incidence. In one of the most comprehensive studies undertaken, Rigby (1996) found that 69 per cent of boys said the aggressor was male. However, girls suffered from male and female bullies at an equal rate – 24 per cent. The figure for girl to boy aggression was significantly low with only 4 per cent of boys saying they were always bullied by a girl. These results also need to be considered in light of the greater reluctance of boys to admit to being bullied.

Explanations for bullying in schools can be broadly described as gendered or non-gendered. One of the most common non-gendered explanations is that the behaviour is due to individual characteristics or 'the bullying or deviant personality'. There is little evidence to support the notion that bullies tend to have low self-esteem or are struggling academically. In fact studies now indicate that bullies often have higher than average self-esteem (Olweus 1993) and verbal ability, consistent with the notion of a hierarchy of masculinities. That is, feeling powerful by intimidating others (both verbally and physically) makes the perpetrator 'feel good'. It is also false to suggest that the physical strength of an individual is implicated in abuse. Sometimes it is the most well-built boys who are considered targets.

Another questionable concept is that bullies are individuals who have difficulty in containing or controlling their angry impulses. This is the assumption of a number of programmes designed to teach anger management. This misses the point that bullying is primarily instrumental behaviour designed to intimidate and control, rather than an expressive outburst. In fact such programmes run the risk of increasing a bully's repertoire of skills in harming their victims by providing them with a new set of concepts that can be used to excuse their behaviour.

Individualistic explanations also focus on the personal characteristics of the victim. Rigby (2002) suggests that victims tend to be introverted, have low self-esteem and lack social skills. This approach is of concern where it leads to interventions designed to bully-proof victims by improving assertiveness, thus effectively holding victims partially responsible for their abuse. A similar trend has been seen in debates about domestic violence. People commonly ask why women who experience domestic violence do not simply leave, or family therapists may hold to a family systems model that sees all members contributing to a dysfunctional dynamic.

Other approaches acknowledge the gendered character of bullying behaviour, although they vary in their recognition and analysis of the social foundations of bullying. Gendered explanations include conservative essentialist and social learning approaches on the one hand and critical examinations of the social construction of gender on the other. Essentialist accounts that acknowledge the predominance of male aggression argue that brain or hormonal differences or social evolution lead to boys' bullying behaviour. This 'boys will be boys' approach has been effectively countered by many writers. Social learning presents boys' bullying as a learnt activity stemming from pressures to conform to expectations of what it means to be a real man. While social learning accounts move away from biological determinism, they are limited by their dependence on sex role theory and their concomitant failure to recognise power relations, the perpetrator's agency or the notion of masculinity as performance.

A more accurate and useful explanation for bullying refocuses on the importance of gender and draws on the idea of the social construction of masculinities (Connell 1995; Gilbert and Gilbert 1998). In a school it is often necessary to assert or defend one's male status. This is done by a boy distancing himself from and denigrating anything perceived as female and, by extension, gay. Boys perceived as soft or feminine will be targeted for abuse as a way for the bully to assert his manhood to his peer spectators. This is the same dynamic that operates in the instance of sexual harassment and homophobic put-downs or attacks (Duncan 1999).

Rather than simply implicating parents (particularly fathers), individual teachers, the mass media or broader socio-cultural trends for this gender regime, writers such as Gilbert and Gilbert (1998) and Mac an Ghaill (1994) have pointed to the ways in which the very structure and culture of schools actively reproduce gender relations that support male aggression. For example, some boys with athletic ability may be implicitly supported by the school in bullying on and off the sports field as a demonstration of competitive achievement. For working-class boys, bullying behaviour often represents the demonstration of toughness and hypermasculinity, in a context where they are unlikely to excel in the academic arenas celebrated in many schools.

Similar dynamics of intra-male power, homophobia and sexual power may be visible in bullying in other contexts such as workplaces, the military and executive boardrooms.

References and further reading

Connell, R. (1995) *Masculinities*, Sydney: Allen and Unwin.

Duncan, N. (1999) *Sexual Bullying*, London: Routledge.

Gilbert, R. and Gilbert, P. (1998) *Masculinity Goes to School*, Sydney: Allen and Unwin.

Mac an Ghaill, M. (1994) *The Making of Men*, Buckingham: Open University Press.

Olweus, D. (1993) *Bullying in Schools*, Cambridge, MA: Blackwell.

Rigby, K. (1996) *Bullying in Schools and What to Do About It*, Melbourne: ACER.

—— (2002) *New Perspectives on Bullying*, London: Jessica Kingsley.

Skelton, C. (2001) *Schooling the Boys*, Buckingham: Open University Press.

See also: violence; violence, workplace

STEPHEN FISHER

C

CAMP

Characterised by parody, incongruity, exaggeration, theatricality and humour – to name but a few of its defining qualities – camp is variously described as a subculture sensibility, a collector's aesthetic, a gay survival strategy and a mode of political critique that questions dominant aesthetic conventions and cultural categories. While the debate continues as to whether camp is a quality of certain objects and people, or whether it exists only in the eye of the 'campy' beholder, critics agree that camp depends for its meaning upon an audience: it is a performance, a stylised re-presentation of the 'normal', a spectacular refusal of invisibility. As Susan Sontag asserts, 'camp sees everything in quotation marks' (1964: 280).

Although camp is generally understood as a product of the mid-twentieth-century Anglo-American gay community, Mark Booth (1983) locates the roots of this sensibility in seventeenth-century France, a period well known for its artifice and pageantry, the most elaborate articulation of which can be observed in the 'camp Eden' of Louis XIV's Versailles. The camp taste for wit, decadence and social satire has also been found in the Aesthetic movement of the late nineteenth century, and playwright Oscar Wilde is often cited as an exemplary camp persona.

When theorised as an outgrowth of homosexual oppression, camp is the 'secret code' through which gay people of the pre-Stonewall (1969) era not only expressed their identities but also flouted, through satiric representation, the conventions of heteronormative society. Gays who were required to hide their sexuality and 'pass' as straight supposedly developed an ironic attachment to the notion of life-as-theatre and being-as-role; this notion is epitomised in the drag queen, the pre-eminent symbol of camp. Central to the drag queen identity is the mimicry of gender roles, which dismantles the assumption of gender as biological fact and speaks to the imitative, performative quality of all camp: through its parodic repetitions, camp highlights the constructedness of 'natural' categories of being. Although many theorists invest camp with political potential, others underline the possibility of its conservatism, asking if it in fact depends upon and thus reinforces the normative values and identities it seems to question.

References and further reading

Bergman, D. (ed.) (1993) *Camp Grounds*, Amherst, MA: Massachusetts University Press.

Booth, M. (1983) *Camp*, London, Melbourne and New York: Quartet.

Sontag, S. (1964) 'Notes on "camp"', in S. Sontag, *Against Interpretation*, New York: Farrar, Straus and Giroux, pp. 275–92.

See also: homosexuality; identity; oppression; sexuality

NANCY VAN STYVENDALE

CASTRATION

I remember my own castration quite clearly. It did involve a 'cut', but the castration of which I speak had nothing to do with real genitalia, something to do with speaking, and everything to do with a severed relationship to – everything itself. Four years old, unselfconsciously at play in a small backyard, I suddenly withdrew from myself in my own perception, looked down at myself as if from above, and heard myself being put into words, thinking: 'No, you're not all that – you're only that.'

As psychoanalysis would parse this sentence: no (my own little echo of the prohibitory 'no of the father'), you're not all that ('that' being 'everything', the mythical plenitude of primary narcissism's nostalgia), you're only that (image of small boy's body translated into even smaller pronoun, signifier constitutively exiled from its signified). In short, in other words, I remember being shortened, diminished to a word, to 'that' shrunken residue of an 'I' that must be spoken but cannot complete itself by designating itself in any statement, that comes into linguistic being only at the cost of losing 'everything', being cut off from the oceanic 'all that'. Identifying myself in language, I lost myself in it like an object – and it hurt like hell, I have to tell you.

But why regard this abrupt recognition of being not all, this small sacrifice of being to meaning, as a sexual dismemberment? Why call this memory/event castration? There are splendid reasons not to; however, for psychoanalysis, castration is the correct word because of the way this alienating sense of losing/being lost (from) 'everything' gets mapped on to an interpretation of the female body as castrated ('not all'), the mother's 'lack' allegorising the 'incomplete' condition of the word as the presence of the absence of the thing. For psychoanalysis, literal castration is so rare as to be relatively unimportant. Castration anxiety, however, is for Freud the necessary condition for the normative resolution of the Oedipus complex for boys, while symbolic castration is for Lacan the universal condition of anyone who speaks. Subject of/to language/desire, I am castrated because I say so, because language, desire and subjectivity are all 'not all', all 'no-thing', so that . . .

But here I break off, consenting to castration, leaving that sentence as incomplete as any 'I' must be.

References and further reading

Fink, B. (1995) *The Lacanian Subject*, Princeton, NJ: Princeton University Press.
Taylor, G. (2002) *Castration*, New York: Routledge.

See also: psychoanalysis

CALVIN THOMAS

CHILD ABUSE

The issue of child abuse is centrally relevant to men and boys in terms of both those who perpetrate child abuse and those who are subject to it. Men and boys as perpetrators of child abuse is a welfare topic that, in many countries, has been difficult to place on policy, research or public agendas. In countries where it has reached one or more of those agendas, it still invariably creates heated debate. This resistance to acknowledging the issue may itself be significant – as is the international pattern of that resistance. For gendered aspects of the social dynamics which contribute to child abuse have tended to receive considerably more research attention – and also a degree of policy and welfare practice attention – in some countries of the world which might be described as 'English-speaking' (e.g. Australia, Canada, New Zealand, United Kingdom, United States) than elsewhere. Indeed, such a relative lack of attention even applies to the Nordic countries. This is somewhat surprising given that the Nordic societies emphasise gender as a high-profile societal issue; and in general possess relatively advanced welfare provision – certainly compared to the United States and the United Kingdom, two countries in the world where the issue of men committing child abuse has received the most serious attention.

This state of affairs is especially surprising in the case of child sexual abuse, where existing research evidence on the gender dynamics involved is now considerable in a number of 'Western' countries and rather consistent over both time and space. For almost all the evidence suggests that the large majority of perpetrators are men and boys (see below for further details). Moreover, despite a relative lack of research on this issue in the Nordic countries, there are still some significant indications that such abuse may be at considerable levels there (Lundgren *et al.* 2001). Since a similar pattern of research and recognition/non-recognition can be found in relation to the issue of men's violence to women, some commentators have suggested that there may be particular cultural barriers to the recognition of gendered violence in the Nordic countries and, by contrast, some relatively facilitative cultural factors in countries such as the United States and the United Kingdom (Pringle 2005).

However, as noted, even in those countries where the issue of men as perpetrators of child abuse is taken seriously – such as the United Kingdom and United States – there is still heated controversy about it publicly, professionally, academically and in terms of policy. Although the reasons for this are complex, one factor may be that this topic has clear implications for the issue of men as active carers of children which is being promoted vigorously by many 'Western' governments. There is certainly a real policy tension between the legitimate desire to promote men as active carers and the legitimate need to respond to the strong evidence (regarding child sexual abuse) that men and boys pose a greater statistical threat to children than women and girls – even though it is clearly a minority of men and boys who engage in such activities. So, there may be a tendency among certain researchers, policy-makers and professionals to deny the gendered aspect of the problem as a way of resolving that tension. An alternative viewpoint (Pringle 1998) is that these policy tensions can be managed creatively.

Child sexual abuse creates the most controversy even though research understanding about its dynamics is clearer than for other forms of child abuse. Despite warnings from some commentators that the levels of child sexual abuse committed by women may be underestimated (Elliott 1993), the vast majority of surveys across the world over the last twenty years suggest that men and boys perpetrate about 90 per cent of child sexual abuse: with a slightly lower figure for abuse by non-adults – a category which may account for as much as a quarter to a third of all child sexual abuse.

Most prevalence surveys, unlike clinic-based studies, also reveal little or no correlation between child sexual abuse and the class, ethnicity or sexuality of perpetrators: the most significant correlate is the gender of the perpetrator. The feminist view that the dynamics underpinning child sexual abuse are closely associated with the social construction of dominant forms of masculinity rests on this fact and its globally widespread incidence (Finkelhor 1991). Researching the size of the problem involves difficult methodological issues such as choice of definition. The large prevalence survey by Kelly *et al.* (1991) used a range of definitions with various degrees of breadth. Prevalence ranged from 1 in 2 to 1 in 5 for girls and 1 in 6 to 1 in 14 for boys: thus even the narrow definitions revealed very significant levels of abuse. Given the large gender imbalance among perpetrators and the extent of the problem, it is hard to escape such a feminist analysis. However, some commentators sympathetic to that perspective suggest that one must also take into account a series of other power relations, in addition to gender, which 'intersect' with or 'mutually constitute' one another (Pringle 2005), such as those associated with dimensions of age, sexuality, disability and ethnicity. For instance, the commercial sexual exploitation by West European men of children from other countries and from within minority ethnic groups could be interpreted as the outcome of interconnecting power relations associated with age, gender, sexuality, ethnicity – and perhaps class.

Other forms of child abuse tend to offer a less clear picture of the gendered dimensions involved. If we take physical abuse, women seem to constitute at least 30 per cent of abusers of children and the figure rises to at least 50 per cent for emotional abuse – a category that is particularly difficult to define. In contrast, as some commentators suggest (Parton 1989), several other contextual factors may have to be taken into account in assessing these gender balances. First, one needs to recognise that, given the general care-taking patterns in most societies, the amount of contact between women and children is generally much larger than that for children and men. Second, one must consider the gendered power dynamics operating within the lives of some of those women who abuse children – where they are placed, for instance, in terms of their relationships with men.

The oppression of women by men and linkages to child abuse also figure largely in another body of important research which focuses on the way children are affected by witnessing violence to mothers – a phenomenon which some therapists and researchers would define as abuse in itself. Moreover, there is now a considerable body of international research, largely (but not exclusively) from the US and the UK, which has demonstrated that there is a significant overlap between men who are abusive to their partners and men who abuse their children physically and/or sexually (Hester *et al.* 2000). Such findings have important implications for the way child protection services for children and services for abused women are organised: in particular, how far there is systematic co-ordination between both sets of services (where they exist); and how far men's history of violence to partners is taken into account when decisions are made about what in some countries is known as child contact and residence or access and custody. In an increasing number of countries the legal systems are incorporating these kinds of findings into their operations – New Zealand being perhaps the most significant and creative example. On the other hand, in many countries where these issues are being considered, such as Britain and Sweden, difficulties with the system still continue (Eriksson and Hester 2001) – and in other countries, such as Denmark (Hester 2005), the legal protection for women and children in these situations seems to be deteriorating. Some feminist and profeminist commentators contextualise this research more broadly by emphasising the close connections in practice between all forms of what they would regard as men's violence, including child abuse, violence to women, war, pornography and prostitution (Cowburn and Pringle 2001).

Gender also, of course, enters into the question of who is abused. Once again, child sexual abuse throws up some especially important issues relating to men and boys. On the one hand, it is certainly the case that all research evidence over a considerable period of time confirms that the majority of children sexually abused are girls (Kelly *et al.* 1991). On the other hand, research from the 1990s has shown higher levels of abuse to boys than was found in previous studies. Although one cannot be sure how far this represents a change in the pattern of abusing or a change in attitudes about revealing such abuse, many commentators place more emphasis on the second of these possibilities. It does remain clear from studies that child sexual abuse of boys is mainly committed by men rather than women – even though the difference between the genders in terms of who abuses boys seems to be slightly less than is the case for abuse of girls. Moreover, some evidence suggests a greater tendency for boys to be abused outside family networks than is the case for girls.

'Treatment' programmes for abusers of children have been developed in a number of countries – most especially in the 'English-speaking' world. Controversy has particularly attached to those programmes dealing with child sexual abuse – which are mainly directed towards men and boys. Research on the effectiveness of such programmes is conflicting, though considerable agreement exists that they may be helpful in assisting some people to maintain more control over their behaviour. However, dispute remains about the effectiveness of different approaches: for instance, many feminist and profeminist researchers have been critical of programmes which do not explicitly address issues of power, both gendered and otherwise. Moreover, there are profound methodological problems in assessing effectiveness – not least the difficulty of knowing whether those who have received 'treatment' commit abuse again. The topic of effectiveness is also relevant in debates about how much funding should be devoted to services for child abusers and how much to those who have been abused, with feminist and profeminist commentators emphasising that services for abusers should not be financed at the direct expense of services for those who have been abused.

Finally, this leads to the question of prevention. Some commentators have suggested that if societies are serious about dealing with the issue of child abuse, then they must address it in concerted national – perhaps international – educational programmes. As regards physical abuse, the example of countries such as Sweden suggests that this kind of an approach can be extremely successful given a suitable cultural context. As regards child sexual abuse, no country in the world – and that includes the Nordic countries – has attempted such a concerted and broad societal campaign. Given the degree to which the practices of men and boys are involved in that form of abuse, it is hard to see how any such national project could avoid addressing directly the issue of power relations and men, which is perhaps why massive national educational campaigns are significant by their absence. However, the relative success of more locally focused campaigns across various parts of the world such as those in the United Kingdom by the Zero Tolerance Trust or Operation Kvinnofrid (Operation Women's Peace) in the Stockholm area of Sweden – both of which made explicit links between various forms of men's violence, including violence to women and children – suggests it could be done – if there was the political will. So far, no government in the world has really met this challenge. Many feminists and profeminists would suggest that this once again brings us back to the ever-present issue of men's power.

References and further reading

Cowburn, M. and Pringle, K. (2001) 'Pornography and men's practices', *Journal of Sexual Aggression*, 6: 52–66.

Elliott, M. (ed.) (1993) *Female Sexual Abuse of Children: The Ultimate Taboo*, Harlow: Longman.

Eriksson, M. and Hester, M. (2001) 'Violent men as good enough fathers? A look at England and Sweden', *Violence Against Women: European Perspectives on Violence Against Women*, Special Issue, 7 (7): 779–99.

Finkelhor, D. (1991) 'The scope of the problem', in K. Murray and D.A. Gough (eds) *Intervening in Child Sexual Abuse*, Edinburgh: Scottish Academic Press, pp. 9–17.

Hester, M. (2005) 'Children, abuse and parental contact in Denmark', in M. Eriksson, M. Hester, S. Keskinen and K. Pringle (eds) *Tackling Men's Violence in Families – Nordic Issues and Dilemmas*, Bristol: Policy Press.

Hester, M., Pearson, C. and Harwin, N. (2000) *Making an Impact: Children and Domestic Violence. A Reader*, London: Jessica Kingsley.

Kelly, L., Regan, L. and Burton, S. (1991) *An Exploratory Study of the Prevalence of Sexual Abuse in a Sample of 16–21 Year Olds*, London: Polytechnic of North London.

Lundgren, E., Heimer, G., Westerstrand, J. and Kalliokoski, A.-M. (2001) *Slagen Dam: Mans Vald mot Kvinnor I Jamstallda Sverige – en Omfangsundersokning* (English version: The Captured Queen: Men's Violence Against Women in Gender-Equal Sweden – a Prevalence Survey), Uppsala: Fritzes Offentliga.

Parton, C. (1989) 'Women, gender oppression and child abuse', in Violence Against Children Study Group (eds) *Taking Child Abuse Seriously*, London: Unwin Hyman, pp. 41–62.

Pringle, K. (1998) 'Men and childcare: policy and practice', in J. Popay, J. Hearn and J. Edwards (eds) *Men, Gender Divisions and Welfare*, London: Routledge, pp. 312–36.

—— (2005) 'Neglected issues in Swedish child protection policy and practice: age, ethnicity and gender', in M. Eriksson, M. Hester, S. Keskinen and K. Pringle (eds) *Tackling Men's Violence in Families – Nordic Issues and Dilemmas*, Bristol: Policy Press.

See also: child pornography; commercial sexual exploitation of children; domestic violence; fatherhood, fathering; fatherhood and violence

KEITH PRINGLE

CHILD CUSTODY

Child custody is a legal term which has been used to describe the legal and practical relationship between a parent and child, notably in proceedings involving dissolution of marriage or other proceedings where the residence and care of children are concerned. In most jurisdictions custody has been determined by the 'best interests of the child'. In some instances (for example in England and Wales) the term 'custody' itself is no longer used, having been replaced by the making of 'contact' and 'residence' orders. Questions of masculinity have become increasingly central to debates around custody/contact. The legal status, responsibilities and rights of men who are fathers – married or unmarried, cohabiting or separated, biological or social in nature – is a topic with a long, well-documented history. There has occurred internationally, however, a heightening of concern around post-divorce/separation contact and child custody, in particular in the light of a 'new welfarism' in the field of family law (Smart 1997). An increasingly vocal, visible and organised fathers' rights movement has been credited with influencing perceptions of the politics of family justice in this area (Boyd 2003). Fathers, it is argued, have become the 'new victims' of custody laws. Although child custody has secured a high public visibility across Western societies, a presumption of joint or 50:50 custody has been unequivocally rejected by some governments (as, for example, in the UK: Parental Separation 2004). Key arguments advanced by fathers' rights campaigners have been questioned; the assumption, for example, that the majority of men are equal carers; the belief that a '50:50' shared parenting split is, in the vast majority of cases at least, ever workable in material and practical terms (Kaganas 2002). Critics note the conceptual ambiguity of the 'meaningful relationship' sought by some men in child custody debates. Concern has also been expressed over the consequences for women and children of the enforcement of court orders of the kind sought by some fathers' rights groups. Several academic commentators suggest that it is the needs and choices of women and children which have, if anything, been marginalised by this growing focus on fatherhood within the law relating to custody (Boyd 2003; Kaganas and Day Sclater 2004).

References and further reading

Boyd, S. (2003) *Child Custody, Law and Women's Work*, Oxford: Oxford University Press.

Kaganas, F. (2002) 'Shared parenting – a 70% solution?' *Child and Family Law Quarterly*, 14 (4): 365–79.

Kaganas, F. and Day Sclater, S. (2004) 'Contact disputes: narrative constructions of "good parents"', *Feminist Legal Studies*, 12 (1): 1–27.

Lord Chancellor's Advisory Board on Family Law, Children Act Sub-Committee (2002) *Making Contact Work*, London: HMSO.

Parental Separation (2004) *Parental Separation: Children's Needs and Parents' Responsibilities*, London: HMSO.

Smart, C. (1997) 'Wishful thinking and harmful tinkering? Sociological reflections on family policy', *Journal of Social Policy*, 26 (3): 1–21.

See also: divorce and separation; family law; fathers' rights

RICHARD COLLIER

CHILD PORNOGRAPHY

Child pornography is increasingly being conceptualised as a form of child sexual abuse and exploitation (Healy 1996). The production of child pornography is instrumental in the sexual abuse of children. Child pornography records the sexual abuse of a child and can also be used to perpetuate further abuse (Itzin 1997).

The advent and widespread use of the internet and new computer technologies (e.g. digital cameras, e-mail and web-cams) has radically altered patterns of consumption, production and distribution, blurring the boundaries between amateur and commercial, producer and consumer, national and international. There is a growing body of research documenting how child pornography is used for sexual stimulation, grooming, entrapment, blackmail and commercial gain. Less, however, is known about the wider patterns of child pornography consumption, particularly among those unknown to the police, and about child sex offenders' use of the internet (Renold and Creighton 2003).

While reports from police operations record and publish the volume of child pornography images on the internet, they do not indicate the numbers of children abused, or provide an adequate understanding of how child pornography is part of a cycle of sexual exploitation. Taylor and Quayle (2003), however, suggest that the age of children, particularly girls, is decreasing, with around half aged between nine and twelve. These findings raise a commonly neglected issue within child pornography literature, the need to recognise that 'child pornography' is not a separate genre by or for 'paedophiles'. Rather, it is embedded within a wider context in which the cultural ideal of beauty is youth. Indeed, the ubiquity of images sexualising children (especially girls) and infantilising women's bodies produces a paradox in which the sexual exploitation of children is both abhorrent and desirable (Renold 2005).

There has been very little examination of the full and long-term impact on children who are abused in the making of child pornography, their coping strategies and the support they do or do not receive. How images are used to identify children during the legal process and the effect of using images to prompt disclosure of abuse are also under-researched (Carr 2003).

References and further reading

Carr, J. (2003) *Child Pornography, Child Abuse and the Internet*, London: Barnardos.

Healy, M.A. (1996) *Child Pornography: An International Perspective*, Stockholm: World Congress Against Commercial Sexual Exploitation of Children.

Itzin, C. (1997) 'Pornography and the organisation of intrafamilial and extrafamilial child sexual abuse: developing a conceptual model', *Child Abuse Review*, 6: 94–106.

Jenkins, Philip (2001) *Beyond Tolerance: Child Pornography on the Internet*, New York and London: New York University Press.

Renold, E. (2005) *Girls, Boys and Junior Sexualities*, London: RoutledgeFalmer.

Renold, E. and Creighton, S. with Atkinson, C. and Carr, J. (2003) *Images of Abuse: A Review of the Evidence on Child Pornography*, London: NSPCC.

Taylor M. and Quayle, E. (2003) *Child Pornography*, Hove: Brunner-Routledge.

See also: commercial sexual exploitation of children; pornography

EMMA RENOLD

CHILDHOOD STUDIES

In his groundbreaking work on the history of childhood as a social institution, Ariés (1960) argued that childhood, as a separate and specific period in an individual's life is a 'modern' invention, socially and culturally constituted, and not a natural occurrence unaffected by time and space. It was not until the 1980s that this insight started to guide both empirical and theoretical work within the social sciences on a broader scale. Since then the so-called 'new social studies of childhood' has grown rapidly, and today it forms a well-established, expanding and interdisciplinary part of academia, not least in the English-speaking world. However, so far, scholars writing on men and masculinities have not made use of this theoretical body to any great extent.

The main critique aimed at previous and current mainstream research on childhood concerns explicit or implicit constructions of children, adults and child–adult relations where adulthood is the norm and children are portrayed as dependent and unfinished beings, not yet fully human: as half-developed (as in developmental psychology) or half-socialised (as in socialisation theory) passive victims of the adult world. In contrast, writers within the new social studies of childhood claim that children should be treated analytically as social actors among other social actors. They claim, further, that children and childhood ought to be dealt with as key issues for research, and not just as, for example, childhood as a transition period on the path to adulthood or children as future citizens or adults' past. The everyday experience of children actually living in the social world as 'a child' is a topic in its own right. Finally, it is argued that researchers need to involve children directly as actors/informants in research more often than has been the practice so far, since children have unique perspectives on their own situation and participation in social life.

The theoretical and conceptual frameworks developed within the new social studies of childhood aim at explaining and deconstructing everyday discourses about children and childhood. This concerns both the longstanding constructions of, for example, the 'evil child' and the 'innocent child', and perhaps most notably notions grounded in developmental psychology and socialisation theory that still permeate contemporary scholarship: the 'naturally developing child' and 'socially developing child' respectively (James *et al.* 1998).

To map the theoretical development up to the late 1990s, three central researchers in the field, James, Jenks and Prout (1998), use key sociological dichotomies to categorise different perspectives on children and childhood. Through looking at the ways in which various writers deal with the issues of structure and agency, identity and difference, continuity and change, the global and the local, James and her colleagues identify four dominant discourses. The first they call 'the social structural child'. In this approach, childhood is viewed as a constant and recognisable component of all social structures, across space and time. The child bears a unit of analysis – of its own kind – and is thus comparable to other units that constitute the social system studied. In approaches marked by this discourse, childhood is claimed as a universal, global and generalisable category, an enduring (though changing) feature of any society. The second discourse, 'the minority group child', is 'an embodiment of the empirical and politicised version of the "social structural child"' (James *et al.* 1998: 210). Although childhood is also constructed here as a universal experience, the focus is on the way children are structurally differentiated within societies and how they experience power differently from adults. In particular, power in its institutionalised and legitimated forms tends to be scrutinised. The third discourse is named 'the socially constructed child'. With this category, James and her colleagues point both to radical relativist and deconstructive approaches and to time as a critical dimension in understanding childhood as historically contingent. Here, multiple conceptions of childhood are in focus, and the child is a local rather than global phenomenon: particular – not universal. The fourth discourse is 'the tribal child'. In parallel with the argument about the minority group child, the tribal child is described as the politicised version of the previous discourse, the socially constructed child. However, here children's agency and independence from the adult world are emphasised. According to this discourse, children's cultures ought to be regarded as self-maintaining systems of signs, symbols and rituals guiding the way of life of children in particular socio-historical settings (James *et al.* 1998). These worlds are unfamiliar to adults: they need to be revealed through research.

Although this broad framework certainly captures tendencies and patterns of diversity within the field, a lot more could of course be said about the various theoretical debates that have been and are ongoing within the new social studies of childhood. For example, one current debate concerns the conceptualisation of age as a structural phenomenon. While some scholars support the use of the concept of generation when discussing childhood as a social and structural condition (e.g. Alanen 2001), others argue that the multiple meanings of the term 'generation' in current social research – including family/kinship relations, cohorts and historical periods – make it less precise and applicable than concepts like 'life phase' or 'age category' (see Närvänen and Näsman 2004). Another debate concerns theoretical, methodological and ethical issues associated with children's involvement in research (see e.g. Christensen and Mayall 2001). Researchers struggle with the tension between the notion that children ought to be able to participate in research on their own premises and the insight that child informants suffer a multiple structural disadvantage due to their subordinate positions in both researcher–researched and child–adult relations. Scholars query the extent to which the conceptualisation of children as social actors requires that actual children are involved as informants, and, further, how the ambition to use a 'bottom-up' approach and take children's own perspectives seriously is negotiated when faced with the researchers' task of interpreting children's accounts, self-presentations and narratives.

In a review of a recently published series of seven volumes on childhood, collecting contributions from key researchers in a range of countries, Haavind identifies three main strategies of analysis: sensitive explorations of subjective positionings and processes of negotiating meanings and social relationships; detection and reconstruction of universalistic notions of the child, highlighting diversity across varied and culturally embedded life modes for different children; and finally the reflection upon social change and how such changes may affect what childhood is about in a particular setting (Haavind 2005). However, as Haavind points out, although children's diversity and analytical sensitivity to social relationships are key perspectives, this book series tends to make gender neutral and thereby renders it invisible (Haavind 2005). This can be regarded as one example of a broader pattern within the new social studies on childhood. Even though gender has been a central dimension for some of the key researchers in the field, such as Thorne (1993), so far childhood scholars in general cannot be said to engage deeply with gender studies – including studies on men and masculinities.

Similarly, scholars within the studies on men and masculinities have not profited fully from the new social studies of childhood. They have mainly focused upon children and young people – and especially boys and young men – as gendered, rather than using the theoretical development within childhood studies to look at how gender – including masculinity – is 'aged' (age-marked). Connell's publication on 'men' and 'boys' is a case in point (2000). Here, a theoretical perspective previously developed to understand the position of men (gendered adults) and multiple forms of masculinities (gendered adulthoods) is used to talk about boys and young men as well, without any further discussion about the implications of meanings of age or of age-related power. The work to develop an integrated age and gender theory on the positions and practices of boys and young men, as well as different forms of 'boyhood' and 'young masculinities', can therefore be said to be only at an early stage.

There are of course exceptions to this pattern. Attempts have been made, for example, to look at the relationship between men and children as a relationship where age- and gender power become intertwined (e.g. Pringle 1995, 2005). One example of such integrated approaches is Collier's discussion about developments within family law and fathers' rights movements like the Fathers 4 Justice in the United Kingdom (Collier 2005). In this work Collier draws upon research on shifts in relation to childhood as a social institution and argues that these shifts are of considerable significance for the discourses and practices in relation to fathers' rights in contemporary Western societies. According to this perspective, we need to understand changes in meanings of age to make sense of shifting meanings of gender, including masculinities and the position of men as adults and parents in relation to children. Another example is my own work on Swedish social workers' approaches to violent fathers (Eriksson 2005). This empirical material demonstrates two different constructions of parenthood. One model is gender complementary and one is explicitly gender neutral, but implicitly gendered since the social workers use motherhood as the standard for good parenthood. To understand this gendering of parenthood it is necessary to recognise that notions of motherhood are intimately connected with constructions of children (cf. 'the developing child' of developmental psychology discussed above): to understand why motherhood is implicitly used as the standard for fathers, we need to recognise meanings of age.

Given current developments within both childhood studies and studies of men and masculinities, the separation of these academic fields is likely to be modified. This is partly due to the growing body of empirical research calling for more elaborate conceptual frameworks, such as research on both girls and boys, young women and men in school settings or in relation to crime. Furthermore, and perhaps more importantly, a debate on 'diversity', 'intersectionality' and the 'doing of difference' is ongoing in both fields (see e.g. Messerschmidt 1998; Pringle and Pease 2001; Thorne 2004). This fact points to new possibilities for dialogue between childhood studies and the study of men and masculinities and to new ways of theorising the relationship between 'childhood' and 'men'.

References and further reading

Alanen, L. (2001) 'Exploration in generational analyses', in L. Alanen and B. Mayall (eds) *Conceptualizing Child–Adult Relations*, London: Routledge.

Ariés, P. (1960) *L'enfant et la vie familiale sous l'ancien régime*, Paris: Plon (English version (1962) *Centuries of Childhood*, London: Cape).

Christensen, P. and Mayall, B. (eds) (2001) *Research with Children*, London: Falmer.

Collier, R. (2005) 'Fathers 4 Justice, law and the new politics of fatherhood', *Child and Family Law Quarterly*, 17 (4): 511–33.

Connell, R.W. (2000) *The Men and the Boys*, Cambridge: Polity.

Eriksson, M. (2005) 'A visible or invisible child?' in M. Eriksson, M. Hester, S. Keskinen and K. Pringle (eds) *Tackling Men's Violence in Families*, Bristol: Policy.

Haavind, H. (2005) 'Towards a multifaceted understanding of children as social participants', *Childhood*, 12 (1): 139–52.

James, A., Jenks, C. and Prout, A. (1998) *Theorizing Childhood*, Cambridge: Polity.

Messerschmidt, J.W. (1998) 'Men victimizing men', in L.H. Bowker (ed.) *Masculinities and Violence*, Thousand Oaks, London, New Delhi: Sage.

Närvänen, A.-L. and Näsman, E. (2004) 'Childhood as generation or life-phase?' *Young*, 12 (1): 71–91.

Pringle, K. (1995) *Men, Masculinities and Social Welfare*, London: UCL Press.

—— (2005) 'Neglected issues in Swedish child protection policy and practice', in M. Eriksson, M. Hester, S. Keskinen and K. Pringle (eds) *Tackling Men's Violence in Families*, Bristol: Policy.

Pringle, K. and Pease, B. (2001) 'Afterword', in B. Pease and K. Pringle (eds) *A Man's World?* London: Zed Books.

Thorne, B. (1993) *Gender Play*, New Brunswick, NJ: Rutgers University Press.

—— (2004) 'Theorizing age and other differences', *Childhood*, 11 (4): 403–8.

See also: family law; fathers' rights

MARIA ERIKSSON

CHINESE MASCULINITIES

Although many would argue that gender relations and questions of masculinity and femininity are universal, a cursory look at Chinese literary and media representations of men suggests that there are specific features in Chinese masculinity that are unique. In terms of models at least, Chinese men do not conform to the stereotypes that are dominant in Western popular discourses of masculinity. Indeed, while images may or may not reflect reality, the prima facie evidence suggests that Chinese masculinity is different from masculinity in other cultures and therefore deserves special consideration. This is especially true since Chinese sexuality has often been described in the West mainly in terms of Taoist bedroom techniques and exotica such as bound feet, and the very few studies of Chinese men focus on the non-mainstream aspects such as homosexuality (Xiaomingxiong 1997). As recently as 2000, when in China itself there were many magazines and books that focused on men, one of the very few scholarly books in English that exclusively dealt with 'mainstream' masculinity described men as feeling psychologically 'besieged' (Zhong 2000) and thus not quite 'normal'.

Notions of Chinese masculinity, like all other gender constructs, have changed and continue to do so. Variations are not only temporal, but also spatial, since 'Chinese' as a concept encompasses many ethnic groups spread over a wide geographical area. 'Minority' groups such as the Mongolian in the north and the Miao in the south have very different conceptions of the make-up of a 'real man'. Here, 'Chinese' is taken to refer mostly to the Han, who are the dominant ethnic group in China. Even for this group, there have been dramatic changes in ideas of 'manliness' across the lengthy Chinese past. Van Gulik notes the changing ideals of masculine beauty over the dynasties and relates them to the fluctuating importance of physical activities. For instance, it was fashionable for the men of the Tang period (AD 618 – 907) to grow beards and moustaches. They also cultivated bodily strength and practised military arts. By the Ming and Qing dynasties (1368 – 1911), however, brute strength and body hair were considered more characteristic of barbarians. The ideal young man was depicted as hypersensitive and physically frail (Van Gulik 1974). Difficult as it is to pinpoint essential gender characteristics that belong to Chinese men, defining male sexuality is equally complex.

In discussions of Chinese sexuality, the most obvious and most commonly invoked paradigm is *yin–yang* philosophy. Under this paradigm, femininity and masculinity are placed in a dichotomous relationship whereby *yin* is female and *yang* is male. This binary relationship applies not just to sex and gender, but to all things in the universe, so that the male–female dyad has its counterparts in light–dark, sun–moon, fire–water and so on. *Yin* and *yang* essences are regarded as being in constant interaction, where *yin* merges with *yang* and vice versa in an endless dynamism. Thus, 'real men' are supposed to have more *yang* essence than effeminate men, and strong women can have a surplus of *yang*. This suggests that every man and woman embodies both *yin* and *yang* essences at any given moment, and that the two sexes exchange sexual essences during sexual intercourse. Although it seems neat and simple, the all-encompassing nature of the *yin–yang* dyad renders it ineffective as an explanatory and descriptive tool for Chinese masculinities.

There is, however, a paradigm that applies to Chinese masculinity alone: the binary opposition between *wen*, the mental or civil, and *wu*, the physical or martial (Louie 2002). This *wen–wu* dyad is particularly relevant to understanding masculinity because it invokes the authority of both the scholar and the soldier and avoids the tendency towards the emphasis placed on both sexes found in the *yin–yang* binary. Chinese masculinity can be theorised as comprising both *wen* and *wu*, so that a scholar is considered to be no less masculine than a soldier. Indeed, at certain points in history the ideal man was expected to embody a balance of *wen* and *wu*. At other times only one or the other was expected, but importantly *either* was considered acceptably manly. By contrast, women cannot be productively discussed in terms of *wen* or *wu*, because both these aspects of official social life were denied women to varying degrees over the broad sweep of the Chinese past.

Of course, this does not imply that women did not excel in literary, martial or other accomplishments. It only demonstrates that the social constructions and practices of 'manhood' were policed by very powerful forces. Most significantly, this was officially displayed in the men-only civil service examinations (the *wenju*) and military service examinations (*wuju*). Thus, the term for the model of a successful man, *wenren* – literally '*wen* people' – can only be translated as 'cultured men'. It was assumed that women who achieved excellence in *wen* were abnormal. And they probably were, given the social situation in traditional China. Despite its exclusive nature, *wen–wu* for centuries unambiguously showed that ideal masculinity was not innate, but something that was to be achieved, so that, provided one was a man, it was an ideal that was theoretically attainable by all.

In recent decades, the dominance of American media has meant that Anglophone values are becoming increasingly commonplace in China. For example, in contrast to the traditional Chinese disdain shown to men with financial wealth but no *wen–wu* accomplishments, businessmen and entrepreneurs are now considered highly desirable. Glossy magazines that are spin-offs of those in the West such as *Men's Health* promote a jet-set lifestyle that only a few decades ago would have been denounced as corrupt and depraved. Along with this 'modern' masculinity whereby superficial appearances such as having accessories such as brand-name electronic gadgets are considered manly, some traditional customs such as having 'concubines' have made a comeback. Though illegal, it is considered both right and proper for wealthy men to keep a 'second wife', especially if the men are from Hong Kong and Taiwan and the women from Mainland China. In short, ideas about masculinity and masculine practices are changing rapidly. While some features are more 'modern' and 'global', some traditional characteristics have had a strong revival.

References and further reading

Louie, K. (2002) *Theorising Chinese Masculinity: Society and Gender in China*, Cambridge: Cambridge University Press.

Van Gulik, R.H. (1974) *Sexual Life in Ancient China*, Leiden: E.J. Brill.

Xiaomingxiong (1997) *Zhongguo tongxingai shilu* (History of Homosexuality in China), revised edn, Hong Kong: Rosa Winkel Press.

Zhong Xueping (2000) *Masculinity Besieged? Issues of Modern and Male Subjectivity in Chinese Literature of the Late Twentieth Century*, London: Duke University Press.

KAM LOUIE

CHRISTIAN MEN'S MOVEMENTS

Christian men's movements include various approaches within the Church to address a perceived crisis in masculinity. While historically Christianity has been a 'men's club', modern writers in this field are generally not males writing about Christianity, but Christian males writing about the interface between masculinity and religious identity, as part of the unfolding concern to address gender and sexuality's effect upon Christian faith and practice.

Clatterbaugh's (1997) taxonomy describes the Promise Keepers as the only significant Christian men's movement, but in fact there are several men's movements within Christianity. Some are anti-feminist, others are profeminist. Some, working out of sex role theory, assume masculinity to be either essentialist or deeply archetypal. Others, working out of social construction and postmodernism, argue that masculinity is performative, unstable and cued by culture, family and experience. The movements have no common approach to theology and spirituality, and no agreed-upon goal.

Evangelical Christian men's movements arose out of panic that women were co-opting the sacred (Kirkley 1996). The first development, from the mid-1800s in England, was known as Muscular Christianity (Hall 1994). Next, the American Freethought movement (1880–1920) characterised churches as feminised, weak and irrational. Men and Religion Forward (from World War I to the 1950s) coined the slogan 'More Men for Religion, More Religion for Men'. The fourth movement was spearheaded by evangelist Billy Sunday, who prayed, 'Lord, save us from off-handed, flabby-cheeked, brittle-boned, weak-kneed, thin-skinned, pliable, plastic, spineless, effeminate, ossified three-karat Christianity' (*Trenton Evening Times*, 6 January 1916). The most recent manifestation of this moralistic and conservative movement is the Promise Keepers, arguing for men to reclaim their rightful position as God-fearing fathers and husbands, guarding the family against feminism and moral crisis (see Bartkowski 2004).

Closer to the middle range between evangelicalism and liberalism lie the Christian reworkings of mythopoetics. Sanford (1981) is a typical example, reading the stories of biblical men as archetypal myths. However, most contemporary work by masculinity-focused scholars of religion takes a more deconstructive approach to the Bible. While many feminists dismiss the Bible as irredeemably patriarchal, some male authors are working to find more room in the text for non-hegemonic masculinities. Culbertson (1992), for example, employs his experience as a biblical scholar and counsellor to re-examine the psychology of five male characters in Scripture.

Boyd (1995) identifies six barriers that prevent white Christian men from embracing intimacy with the multiplicity of God's creation: classism, anti-Semitism, racism, homophobia, sexism and femiphobia. This list can be completed by adding men's obsession with work as identity, disappointments with biological fathers (and father gods), tolerance of violence, body unconsciousness and emotional deadness.

A growing number of Christian men write about spirituality, both critically and autobiographically. The male body is reclaimed as a positive part of a religious identity, so that the threats of impotence, disease, aging and homophobia are turned into spiritual resources. Rather than denigrating men's erotic nature, the sexual body is understood as a source of theologies of intimacy with humans and the divine. These writings usually shun the privileging of hegemonic masculinity in order to engage otherness in the form of race, class and sexual orientation. Instead, new forms of masculine spirituality are located in relationality, shared power, the aesthetics of the body, creativity, ritual and the living out of social justice through quiet service (see Culbertson 2002).

In biblical studies, theology and spirituality, Christian male writers usually build upon gender studies, feminist theory and criticism, the secular men's movement, gay liberation and disciplines including psychology, sociology and anthropology. However, Staley (2003) regrets the inability of so many scholars of men's studies in Christianity to connect their work with the 'real world' that every man faces. So far, the academic end of the Christian men's movement has only begun to find its transformative offering to those who struggle with masculinities in the workaday world.

Some Christian writers understand gay spirituality as a theology from the margins, defining itself by difference, otherness and intimacy. Sexuality is often conceived as an act of sacramental Eros and gay spirituality as an act of political protest. Gay men's studies walk a fine line between mainstream integration and resistance to Christian scriptural and theological heterosexism. Others have divided gay men's spirituality into four types: the apologetic (the reasoned defence of homosexuality), the therapeutic ('coming-out' as a spiritual journey), the ecological (liberation theology and right relation) and the autobiographical (Boisvert 2000). This typology must be expanded to include the growing repertoire of transgressive and queer theologies and spiritualities, and Christian support for those living with HIV and AIDS (Goss 2002).

Non-white writers in Christian men's studies have been slower to develop. Struggling against the racism that is endemic to hegemonic masculinity, African–American writers such as Kasimu Baker-Fletcher have only begun to find their voice, partially since the 1995 Million Man March.

Some Christian men's movements are critical of masculinities' invisibility in the Christian tradition; others of the erosion of masculine authority and identity in Christian practice. Yet in their diversity, all re-envision new ways for men to engage the Christian heritage, broadly defined.

References and further reading

Baker-Fletcher, G.K. (1998) *Black Religion after the Million Man March*, Maryknoll, NY: Orbis.

Bartkowski, J. (2004) *The Promise Keepers*, New Brunswick, NJ: Rutgers University Press.

Boisvert, D. (2000) *Out on Holy Ground*, Cleveland, OH: Pilgrim.

Boyd, S. (1995) *The Men We Long to Be*, San Francisco, CA: HarperSanFrancisco.

Clatterbaugh, K. (1997) *Contemporary Perspectives on Masculinity*, Boulder, CO: Westview.

Culbertson, P. (1992) *New Adam*, Minneapolis, MN: Fortress.

—— (ed.) (2002) *The Spirituality of Men*, Minneapolis, MN: Fortress.

Goss, R. (2002) *Queering Christ*, Cleveland, OH: Pilgrim.

Hall, D. (ed.) (1994) *Muscular Christianity*, Cambridge: Cambridge University Press.

Kirkley, E. (1996) 'Is it manly to be Christian? The debate in Victorian and modern America', in S. Boyd, M. Longwood and M. Muesse (eds) *Redeeming Men*, Louisville, KY: Westminster/John Knox, pp. 80–8.

Sanford, J. (1981) *The Man Who Wrestled with God*, New York: Paulist Press.

Staley, J. (2003) 'Manhood and New Testament studies after September 11', in S. Moore and J. Anderson (eds) *New Testament Masculinities*, Atlanta, GA: SBL, pp. 329–35.

See also: spirituality; world religions, Christianity

PHILIP CULBERTSON

CIRCUMCISION

Male circumcision is one of the world's most common and controversial surgical procedures. The 'official story' told by circumcising cultures describes ostensible benefits to the circumcised as its justification, but anthropological explanations tend to analyse its meaning for the circumcisers, while psychoanalytic explanations invoke intergenerational psychodynamics to explain the rite, paradigmatically father–son relationships and Oedipal anxieties. Thus Judaism and Islam cite putative spiritual benefits as justification, while modern secular culture, especially in the United States, whose males have by far the highest rate of the surgery performed on them (estimates range from 70 to 95 per cent), cites putative medical benefits.

Circumcision separates the foreskin (prepuce) from the shaft of the penis. While this is commonly performed in the West shortly after birth, many cultures circumcise at or around puberty. Circumcision is a quintessential male initiation rite, performed on young males by older men to initiate them into a male community. The term 'female circumcision' is a euphemism for a much more severe procedure of female genital mutilation, often involving the complete removal of the clitoris.

Passing from Judaism into Islam as biblically based, though actually older, practised in ancient Egypt and elsewhere, circumcision is replaced by baptism in Christianity. God says to Abraham in the key text:

> I will make you exceedingly fertile, and make nations of you . . . Such shall be the covenant between Me and you and your offspring to follow which you shall keep: every male among you shall be circumcised. You shall circumcise the flesh of your foreskin, and that shall be the sign of the covenant between Me and you. And throughout the generations, every male among you shall be circumcised at the age of eight days.
>
> (Genesis 17: 6, 10–11, Jewish Publication Society translation)

One strand of ancient rabbinic interpretation saw circumcision, linked to fertility in the text, as God demanding of men that they join in furthering God's creation, described in Genesis as acts of separation which establish clear demarcations, conferring form on formlessness. The more dominant interpretive strain of early rabbinic Judaism linked circumcision to blood sacrifice, emphasising not the foreskin's separation from the penile shaft but the drawing of blood in its removal. Here circumcisional male genital bleeding, created and controlled by men, is contrasted with female menstrual bleeding, natural and uncontrolled. In contemporary Lacanian terms, circumcision emerges as the literal inscription of the phallus on to the penis, marking the erection of patriarchy.

Medieval Judaism saw the meaning of circumcision change to desexualisation, demonstrating that men could rise above their animal nature and subjugate their sexual impulses to their will (i.e. sublimate their sexual urges into religious ones, in modern Freudian terms). Maimonides, the pre-eminent Jewish philosopher and also court physician to the twelfth-century Egyptian Muslim Sultan Saladin, very influentially embraced the importance of circumcision because he believed it lessened sexual arousal and sensitivity in men.

For many Jews circumcision marks a male as a Jew, though theologically Jewish identity is inherited, traditionally from one's mother, or acquired through conversion. Those who practise Islamic circumcision base it not on any passage in the Qur'an but on what is understood to have been the practice and teaching of Muhammed.

Medical circumcision emerged as a common practice in the United States and Britain in the later Victorian period. The neonatal surgical procedure marked middle- and upper-class whites as 'modern', where birthing practices became medicalised into the hands of male doctors in hospitals rather than female midwives in homes, and as distinct from lower-class and 'darker' immigrants who did not have access to 'modern' ways and generally did not circumcise. The regulation of sexuality emerged as a great cultural concern in this period, and the belief that circumcision inhibited sexuality made it an important part of major moral crusades against masturbation and what were seen as other sexual excesses.

Psychoanalytic theory interprets circumcision as sublimation of castration anxiety, as the son's symbolic separation from the mother and subjugation to the father. Anthropologists interpret it as the father's symbolic sacrifice to and identification with the group, taming the son's nascent rebelliousness. It is interpreted as both masculinising, enforcing gender differentiation by raising the physical and symbolic prominence of the penis/phallus, and feminising, the cut and bleeding bringing the male closer to the female, diminishing penile/phallic physical and symbolic presence.

In the twentieth century and at present, greatly disputed claims have been made that circumcision lessens the incidence of infections, sexually transmitted diseases and penile cancer. Major medical associations have in recent years taken positions against routine neonatal circumcision, on the grounds that such benefits, even if existent, are minimal and do not warrant the attendant risks and injury of surgery. Earlier theories that newborns feel circumcisional pain minimally or not at all are no longer accepted by the medical community, and therefore arguments based on this view now carry less currency.

Recent years have seen an increase in organisations and individuals opposing circumcision as unjustified surgical mutilation, inflicting trauma without the infant patient's consent. Some advocate reversing the effects of the procedure, either surgically or through techniques to stretch the remaining skin.

References and further reading

Barth, L.M. (ed.) (1990) *Berit Mila in the Reform Context*, USA: Berit Mila Board of Reform Judaism.

Gollaher, D.L. (2000) *Circumcision*, New York: Basic Books.

Hirji, H., Charlton, R. and Sarmah, S. (2005) 'Male circumcision', *The Journal of Men's Health and Gender*, 2 (1): 21–30.

Hoffman, L.A. (1996) *Covenant of Blood*, Chicago, IL: University of Chicago Press.

Kimmel, M.S. (2005) *'The Kindest Un-Cut': The Gender of Desire*, Albany, NY: State University of New York Press.
Knights, B. (2004) 'Men from the boys', *Literature and History*, 13 (1): 25–42.
Mark, E.W. (ed.) (2003) *The Covenant of Circumcision*, Hanover, NH: Brandeis University Press.

HARRY BROD

CLASS, WORK AND MASCULINITY

The workplace is an important site for the reproduction of men's masculine power and status. As entrepreneurs, owners, executives, managers, trade unionists and employees, men have both produced and been shaped by the organisations that now predominate in contemporary societies. While masculinity has fundamentally influenced the nature of the workplace, organisations also significantly impact on men, their power, cultures and identities. Hence, work, organisation and masculinity often co-exist in complex, mutually reinforcing and sometimes contradictory relationships.

Yet within the literature these dialectical interrelations are frequently neglected. Organisational researchers often talk about work without critically examining men or masculinity in any explicit way. Writers on gender and/or men sometimes underestimate the impact of organisations as both the medium and outcome of masculine cultures, identities and practices. However, there is now increasing interest in critically examining men and masculinities and the multiple conditions, processes and consequences of their continued dominance in organisations.

'Men' and 'masculinity' at 'work'

Feminist studies highlight the embeddedness of masculine assumptions in organisational structures, cultures and practices. They reveal the significance of paid work as a central source of masculine authority. For many men, employment provides the interrelated economic and symbolic benefits of financial rewards, skills, careers, power and status. Research suggests that masculinity can be embedded in formal organisational practices (e.g. recruitment and promotion) through to more informal, cultural dynamics (e.g. the social construction of skill and workplace friendship). Central to men's valorisation of 'work' is also a close identification with machinery and technology. Masculine dynamics at work can also be reproduced through men's sexuality and the sexual harassment of women. DiTomaso (1989) argued that men often engage in a type of workplace power play in which they use sexuality to subordinate women. Kimmel (1993) highlights men's homophobia and their fear of other men as key factors shaping the dominant definition of masculinity.

Feminist writers also emphasise men's dominance in the home and how this can reinforce their power in employment. For men, 'work' still refers primarily to the organisational, to employment and to what happens in 'public'. Arguing that unpaid (and often invisible) domestic labour also constitutes important work, feminists suggest that women continue to be responsible for most housework and that men benefit significantly from these domestic labours.

Many feminists use the concept of 'patriarchy' to examine men's power in employment and at home. Others criticise this concept for being too monolithic, ahistorical, biologically overdetermined and dismissive of women's resistance, difference and agency. Some notions of patriarchy have also been criticised for neglecting inequalities and differences between men, particularly those based on class, hierarchy and status as well as ethnicity, age and other aspects of diversity.

Partly as a result of these criticisms there has been increasing interest in 'multiple masculinities' (discussed elsewhere in this volume). Suffice it to say here that the concept of multiple masculinities helps us to appreciate the gendered nature of workplace power and inequality between men as well the ways in which organisations can be saturated with masculinities that subordinate women. There are many different kinds of workplaces, occupations, industries and sectors that may constitute important sites for the reproduction of multiple forms of masculinity.

Class and status inequalities constitute important factors cutting across relations between men and sustaining different masculine workplace cultures. By no means the only difference or inequality between men, class nevertheless remains important as a medium of gendered power and identity within contemporary organisations. For example, the institutionalised distinction in Western societies between mental and manual work frequently results in some men enjoying unequal access to various workplace rewards such as pensions, holidays, job security and company stocks and shares as well as experiencing very different levels of danger at work.

Many of the most illuminating studies of men and masculinity in organisations focus on working-class masculinities. Cockburn's (1983) study of UK printers reveals how the 'hot-metal' manual skills of linotype compositors have historically been protected as the exclusive province of men. Willis (1977) describes how working-class lads construct a highly masculine school counter-culture through which they resist authority and 'celebrate' the so-called 'freedom' and 'independence' of manual work. Their valorisation of working-class masculinity leads 'the lads' directly into manual labour. Only later do they realise the reality of class subordination after reaching the factory with no educational qualifications and little chance of escape.

Collinson (1992) shows how men manual workers are often treated as 'second-class citizens' and how they consequently redefine their sense of masculine dignity and respect through shop-floor counter-cultures. He found that workers elevated themselves (and negated others) through specifically masculine values of being a family breadwinner, 'practical', 'productive', 'having common-sense' and being 'able to swear when you like' and 'give and take a joke like a man'. The informal shop-floor interaction between men manual workers was often highly aggressive, sexist and derogatory, humorous yet insulting, playful but degrading. New members were teased incessantly and their masculinity tested to see whether they were 'man enough' to take the insults couched in the humour of 'piss taking' and the embarrassment of highly explicit sexual references.

These studies reveal how masculine working-class cultures often symbolically invert the values and meanings of class society, but in ways that unintentionally reinforce the status quo. They illustrate how counter-cultures typically emphasise workers' perceived 'honesty', 'independence' and 'authenticity' as confirmation of manhood and opposition to management. In many cases rejecting even the very idea of promotion because it would compromise their sense of masculine 'freedom', men manual workers often insist that this would require them to become conforming 'yes men'.

Other studies suggest that 'white-collar' occupations may also be shaped by masculine values, albeit ones that are typically less aggressive and sexual than those found in shop-floor settings. Research reveals that middle-class, male-dominated professions like doctors, academics and computer specialists can all be characterised by such masculine cultures. For example, Pearce (1995) graphically describes US attorneys' 'Rambo litigator' style of courtroom intimidation. Until the late nineteenth century, clerical employment tended to be the preserve of men. With the expansion of bureaucracies and the introduction of typewriters, much clerical employment became 'sex-typed' as 'women's work'. Feminisation led to clerical work being downgraded and undervalued, associated with 'homemaker' tasks within the workplace. By contrast, male white-collar workers are typically employed in well-paid positions with higher levels of discretion and remuneration, often reflecting their status as 'organizational breadwinners' (Collinson *et al.* 1990).

Particular masculinities can also pervade senior leadership and managerial positions.

Only relatively recently has men's numerical and cultural domination of leadership and management become a serious topic of concern. Yet a closer analysis reveals innumerable ways in which management and leadership implicate 'men' and 'masculinities' (Roper 1993). This applies in the construction of dominant models of leadership and management, in leadership styles and practices, in the language of management and leadership, in management cultures and so on (Collinson and Hearn 1996).

An early analysis by Kanter (1977) argued that scientific management, with its emphasis on rationality and efficiency, is infused with an irreducibly 'masculine ethic'. She also suggested that Human Relations theory still rests on the image of the rational/masculine manager as 'the man who could control his emotions whereas workers could not' (ibid.: 24). Certainly there is a strong link between management's concern with control over labour and men's preoccupation with control over women. This preoccupation can be expressed and reproduced through various masculine discourses such as: authoritarianism; paternalism; entrepreneurialism; informalism and careerism (Collinson and Hearn 1994).

By no means completely cohesive, leadership and management in organisations can also be characterised by highly competitive processes and internal struggles over power, career and interfunctional rivalries, all of which can take highly masculine forms. For example, the division between line and personnel managers is often reinforced by stereotyped assumptions of the line manager as 'producer', 'provider' and 'breadwinner' for the organisation and the HRM/personnel manager as dependent, domestic and organisational 'welfare worker'.

Multiple masculinities, multiple workplaces, multiple selves

This focus on multiple masculinities facilitates the development of a more nuanced conception of patriarchy which acknowledges the differentiated nature of workplace masculinities, the variation between different types of organisations and the shifting ways in which these may be perceived and experienced. Recent poststructuralist perspectives develop this approach by exploring the additional importance of 'identity work' for understanding the reproduction of masculine workplace cultures. They suggest that gendered subjectivity is a specific, historical product, embedded in prevailing power relations that is ambiguous, fragmentary, discontinuous, multiple, sometimes fundamentally non-rational and frequently contradictory (Collinson 2003).

Research in this area highlights the way in which men often seem preoccupied with the maintenance of various masculine selves. Men workers frequently engage in identity work as part of their desire to secure respect and dignity in conditions of its erosion (Barrett 1996). Their search to sustain coherent identities often draws upon a whole variety of organisational resources and appears to be an ongoing, never-ending project. Typically, it seems, men's gender identities are constructed, compared and evaluated by self and others according to a whole variety of criteria within the workplace. Like all identities, masculine selves constantly have to be negotiated and reconstructed in routine social interaction both in the workplace and elsewhere, typically through simultaneous processes of identification and differentiation.

On the one hand, men often seem to collaborate, cooperate and identify with one another in ways that reinforce a shared unity between them; but on the other hand, these same masculinities can simultaneously be characterised by conflict, competition and self-differentiation in ways that intensify the differences and divisions between men. Given these deep-seated tensions, ambiguities and contradictions, the unities that exist between men should not be overstated. They are often more precarious than superficial appearances suggest. Indeed, this tendency to become preoccupied with seeking to secure clearly defined and coherent masculine selves may in itself be inherently paradoxical, likely to reinforce, rather than resolve, men's deep-seated sense of insecurity.

Conclusion

Organisations constitute an important site for the reproduction of men's patriarchal power and status. Men's power can be reproduced through multiple masculinities and masculine selves within patriarchal workplace dynamics. By highlighting the diversity of men's workplace power and status, analyses can begin to make sense of the multiple, shifting but tenacious nature of gendered power regimes as they are embedded in diverse workplace structures, cultures and practices. They can begin to examine the dynamic, shifting and often contradictory organisational relations through which men's differences and similarities are reproduced in particular practices and power asymmetries. The possibility of a challenge to men's taken-for-granted dominant masculinities could facilitate the emergence of less coercive and less divisive organisational structures, cultures and practices, a fundamental rethinking of the social organisation of the domestic division of labour and a transformation of 'men' at 'work'.

Several issues require further work. The conceptualisation of 'masculinity/ies' needs clarification. How do the ideological, discursive and symbolic features of masculinities interrelate with economic, material and physical aspects? The ways in which masculinities interact with other elements of power, culture and subjectivity in organisations needs greater consideration. In what ways and with what consequences are multiple masculinities embedded in other workplace practices, such as control, consent, compliance and resistance? We need to know more about how other inequalities and differences (e.g. ethnicity, race, nationality, religion and age) are intertwined with those of masculinity, work and organisation. This in turn raises important questions about the gendered nature of globalisation, global restructuring, transnational corporations (Kimmel *et al.* 2005) and about international cultural differences between men and masculinities, particularly in non-Western contexts (Pease and Pringle 2001). Finally, while recognising a multiplicity of possible masculinities and workplace sites, analyses also need to retain a focus upon the asymmetrical nature of gendered power relations and subjectivities. This emphasis upon men and masculinities should not become a new means of forgetting, excluding or subordinating women.

References and further reading

Barrett, F. (1996) 'The organizational construction of hegemonic masculinity: the case of the US Navy', *Gender, Work and Organization*, 3 (3): 129–42.

Cockburn, C. (1983) *Brothers*, London: Pluto Press.

Collinson, D.L. (1992) *Managing the Shopfloor: Subjectivity, Masculinity and Workplace Culture*, Berlin: Walter de Gruyter.

—— (2003) 'Identities and insecurities: selves at work', *Organization*, 10 (3): 527–47.

Collinson, D.L. and Hearn, J. (1994) 'Naming men as men: implications for work, organization and management', *Gender, Work and Organization*, 1 (1): 2–22.

Collinson, D.L. and Hearn, J. (eds) (1996) *Men as Managers, Managers as Men*, London: Sage.

Collinson, D.L., Knights, D. and Collinson, M. (1990) *Managing to Discriminate*, London: Routledge.

DiTomaso, N. (1989) 'Sexuality in the workplace: discrimination and harassment', in J. Hearn, D. Sheppard, P. Tancred-Sheriff and G. Burrell (eds) *The Sexuality of Organization*, London: Sage, pp. 71–90.

Kanter, R.M. (1977) *Men and Women of the Corporation*, New York: Basic Books.

Kimmel, M. (1993) 'Masculinity as homophobia: fear, shame, and silence in the construction of gender identity', in H. Brod and M. Kaufman (eds), *Theorizing Masculinities*, Newbury Park, CA, and London: Sage, pp. 119–41.

Kimmel, M., Hearn, J. and Connell, R. (eds) (2005) *Handbook of Studies on Men and Masculinities*, London: Sage.

Pearce, J. (1995) *Gender Trials*, Berkeley, CA: University of California Press.

Pease, B. and Pringle, K. (eds) (2001) *A Man's World*, London: Zed Books.

Roper, M. (1993) *Masculinity and the British Organization Man, 1945 to the Present*, Milton Keynes: Open University Press.
Willis, P. (1977) *Learning to Labour*, London: Saxon House.

DAVID COLLINSON

COLONIAL AND IMPERIAL MASCULINITIES

The modern world is in large part a product of imperialism and colonialism; these, in turn have shaped, and been shaped by, modern notions of gender, both masculinities and femininities. This phenomenon, which R. Connell has called 'globalizing masculinities', has had profound repercussions on imperial metropolitan as well as on colonial and semi-colonial societies around the world (Connell 1998).

However, beyond this connection between masculinity and imperialism, it is impossible to make any overarching generalisations about its multiple manifestations. Masculinity by its very nature is neither a monolithic nor even a stable category of analysis; not only are there multiple masculinities that are themselves constantly subject to change, but masculinity itself is produced in relation to several other categories, and it acquires meaning only in specific socio-historical contexts. The workings of empires are also immensely varied; our generalisations about the nature of modern empires, for example, are largely based on European overseas empires rather than on the contemporaneous multinational and contiguous empires in Europe and elsewhere (Austro-Hungarian, Ottoman, Chinese and Russian). Yet there is also now a vast and rich body of scholarship that has opened up some broad themes for explorations of masculinity and imperialism. These may be summarised as follows: the gendering of the imperial and colonial enterprise as masculine; imperialism as constitutive of masculinities in both imperial and colonial societies; and the ideological significance of masculinity for colonialism as well as for anti-colonial nationalisms.

The European overseas empires were largely European male preserves. To be sure, scholars have done much to make visible the role of European women in the overseas empires; but throughout the history of empires European men greatly outnumbered European women. This was equally true of the administrative colonies as of the colonies of European settlement. For example, from the total numbers of people who emigrated to the colonies from Britain over the course of the nineteenth century, men outnumbered women by far. Yet this numerical preponderance of men over women tells us little by itself about the gendered nature of these empires or about imperialism as a masculinist enterprise. Evidence for the latter comes instead from such things as the equation between imperialism and manliness made in the popular imagination as well as from the compacts made between European and indigenous men that frequently underwrote the stability of imperial regimes.

The most popular representations of overseas imperial adventures portrayed empire as a test of metropolitan masculinity; and support for empires was presented typically as vindication of a virile manhood. This was especially true of particular historical moments, such as during the period of 'high imperialism' in the late nineteenth century, which affected the US as much as it did Europe. For example, advocates of an overseas imperial role for the US during the Spanish–American and Philippines–American wars drummed up support for their cause by appeals to the ideals of a threatened manliness; by contrast, anti-imperialist opponents were portrayed as akin to 'old ladies' (Hoganson 1998). Behind the heavily gendered rhetoric of this 'New Imperialism', as several scholars have demonstrated, was also an underlying anxiety about a perceived crisis of metropolitan masculinity: a result of a variety of developments, including shifting patterns of work and challenges from an organised women's movement. The masculinisation of empire certainly helped sustain popular support for empire at home, but whether certain ideals of manliness actually drove the push towards empire remains a more contentious claim. Likewise, imperialism was also manifested in the colonies in a variety of masculinist ways. The loss of power that it entailed in the colonies was frequently expressed and experienced in specifically masculine terms. Furthermore, imperial regimes that had concerns for their own political stability ended up compromising with a variety of indigenous patriarchies. For all the talk of colonialism's benevolent paternalism towards indigenous women, empires frequently paid for their stability by underwriting the patriarchal authority of indigenous men over indigenous women. This patriarchal compromise between men was as true of overseas empires as of the multinational and contiguous empires in Europe and elsewhere. The masculinist nature of the modern-day imperial enterprise was thus a multifaceted affair based both on representations and practices of imperialism.

The constitutive impact of imperialism on the making of various masculinities, as well as of modern gender ideologies per se, has provided a second major theme in the explorations of masculinity and imperialism. The scholarship on the early modern period has been especially suggestive in pointing to the constitutive impact of empire and of overseas explorations on the making of our modern absolutist and binary ways of thinking about gender in Europe. Take the example of the South Sea voyages of Captain James Cook (between 1768 and 1780) that were widely reported in metropolitan literary, scientific and religious establishments of the time. The encounter of Captain Cook and his men with the Pacific islanders produced 'mutual confusions' about gender and sexual practices: initially at least, European social typologies of gender and sexual practices were destabilised in the encounter with the customs and practices of the Pacific islanders. This initial confusion and instability, however, was only recast subsequently by evangelical moralists to portray an absolute 'difference'; this, in turn, produced by the late Georgian period new (and more rigid) ways of thinking about gender and sexuality in the metropole itself (Wilson 2003). The more fluid gender orders of the earlier period were calcified into more rigid ways of thinking in the process of constituting national and racial 'difference' in the wake of European overseas expansion.

The implications of imperialism on the making of metropolitan masculinities have received considerable attention. Even though imperialism in its various stages, from conquest to pacification, gave rise correspondingly to differing ideals of metropolitan masculinity, it created a climate where particular traits, such as independence and physical prowess, acquired considerable prominence as ideals of metropolitan manhood. The empire produced a cult of both real and fictional 'soldier heroes' who influenced how masculinity was represented and experienced in the metropole. Their influence in Europe went beyond the imperial powers themselves; nineteenth-century Germans may have lagged behind in acquiring an overseas empire, but through the imaginative labour of 'colonial fantasies' they too shared in the imperial remaking of metropolitan masculinities (Zantop 1997). The empire also provided an opportunity for individuals to remake themselves as 'men'. Theodore Roosevelt is only the most famous example. His reinvention of himself from a somewhat 'effete' and 'weakling' New Yorker into a symbol of US imperial masculinity was capped by his exploits as a 'Rough Rider' during the Spanish–American and Philippines–American wars. Even marginalised groups, whether African–American men in the US who took up the 'black man's burden' or the lower-middle-class male office clerks in Britain who became the backbone of the 'jingoists' during the South African wars, often thought that they could redeem their threatened masculinity by turning to empire (Mitchell 1999; Tosh 2005). The empire provided a means for scores of men to fulfil their expectations of masculinity; while some sought refuge in the empire from domesticity, others found in it the means to establish the kind of family life made increasingly difficult at home. Empire may have meant different things to different men, but it played an important role in forging metropolitan masculinities.

In the colonies too imperialism served both to constitute and reconstitute gender relations as well as the ideals and expectations of masculinity. Take, for example, the British colonial interventions in the matrilineal *tharavadu* (households) in colonial Malabar in India. Whereas the basis for the distribution of power within the household was initially based on age rather than gender, the colonial state's policies created gender differences within the household by singling out the eldest male as the household head (Arunima 2003). Likewise, British slave emancipation in the Western Cape of South Africa was informed by European bourgeois ideologies of gender and family. The project of emancipation was shaped by the view of ostensibly 'liberating the family' so that free African men could take up their 'proper' roles as fathers and as heads of households and free African women could, as wives and mothers, be brought under the natural authority of the male head of the family (Scully 1997). The gendered regimes imposed by colonial policies and practices thus played a significant role in the making of 'men' in the first place. Yet the imposition of new gender regimes did not mean that older gender systems disappeared completely. In Nigeria, where biological sex had not always corresponded to ideological gender, Igbo women until the 1920s continued to play a variety of roles usually considered the monopoly of men and to be classified as 'males' in certain situations (Amadiume 1987). These residual 'female masculinities' remain as reminders of the gender revolution that was wrought in the wake of imperialism and colonialism.

The colonial relations of domination and subordination – captured in the racist language of white men and black 'boys' – provided the general backdrop for the articulation of different masculinities in the colonies. Yet the impact of colonialism for men in the colonies was uneven. Colonialism undermined as well as shored up existing gender, generation, class and other hierarchies in the colonies, thereby closing some and opening up other avenues of advancement for men both as men and as members of particular groups. This was manifested in a variety of tensions between classes, generations, regions, religions, ethnicities, and so on. The economic and political imperatives of colonialism sometimes also produced radically new contexts for the articulation of masculinities in the colonies. For example, the recruitment of men for the gold mines in South Africa created artificial single-sex labour camps. The same-sex mine marriages contracted by men under these conditions were a form of resistance to the proletarianisation imposed by mine work (Moodie 1994). Indigenous resistance along with colonial imperatives provided the conditions in which men and masculinities were shaped in the colonies.

The politics of masculinity also worked as an ideology of power in both colonialism and anticolonial nationalism. 'Colonial masculinity' – a politics that informed both colonisers and colonised – illustrates the multiple ways in which masculinity cemented relations of power in the colonies (Sinha 1995). It constituted a hierarchy of masculinities: in which an elite 'white' masculinity presided above both loyal-but-simple 'martial' or 'manly' races and clever-but-treacherous feminised or effeminate native men. The self-definition of white imperial masculinity also included the benevolent protection of women. The supposed protection of 'Oriental' women not only justified various colonial interventions, but was also used against the transferring of political rights to indigenous men. Above all, however, the most dramatic show of white imperial masculinity in the colonies followed the real or imagined threat to white women from the alleged assaults of native men. Even rumours of attacks on white women – as, for example, during the Rebellion of 1857–8 in India – produced a call to arms to white men to avenge the 'honour' of the English race. Brutal acts of vengeance in the colonies reverberated back 'at home' to transform existing understandings of metropolitan masculinity (Hall 1992). The anticolonial movements also often demonstrated a preoccupation with claiming masculinity (Gouda 1999; White 1990). These both appropriated and contested colonial gender norms through masculinities that were militarised and self-disciplined. Sometimes this even took the form of demanding the right to control/protect 'their' women from foreigners and foreign influence with ambiguous consequences for women. In the famous case of M.K. Gandhi, however, the politics of anticolonialism produced a deliberately softer, gentler and almost androgynous masculinity. Masculinity as an ideological mechanism of power has worked to cement multiple relations of power, whether between nations, between men, or between men and women.

References and further reading

Amadiume, I. (1987) *Male Daughters, Female Husbands*, London: Zed Books.

Arunima, G. (2003) *There Comes Papa*, New Delhi: Orient Longman.

Connell, R.W. (1998) 'Masculinities and globalization', *Men and Masculinities*, 1 (1): 3–23.

Gouda, F. (1999) 'Gender and "hyper-masculinity" as post-colonial modernity during the Indonesian struggle for independence, 1945–49', in A. Burton (ed.) *Gender, Sexuality, and Colonial Modernities*, London and New York: Routledge, pp. 161–74.

Hall, C. (1992) 'Competing masculinities', in C. Hall, *White, Male, and Middle Class*, New York: Routledge, pp. 255–95.

Hoganson, K.L. (1998) *Fighting for American Manhood*, New Haven, CT: Yale University Press.

Mitchell, M. (1999) 'The black man's burden', *International Review of Social History*, 44: 77–99.

Moodie, D.T. with V. Ndatshe (1994) *Going for Gold*, Berkeley and Los Angeles, CA: University of California Press.

Scully, P. (1997) *Liberating the Family?* Portsmouth, NH: Heinemann.

Sinha, M. (1995) *Colonial Masculinity*, Manchester: Manchester University Press.

Tosh, J. (2005) *Manliness and Masculinities in Nineteenth-Century Britain*, London: Pearson Longman.

White, L. (1990) 'Separating the men from the boys', *International Journal of African Studies*, 23 (1): 1–25.

Wilson, K. (2003) *The Island Race*, London and New York, Routledge.

Zantop, S. (1997) *Colonial Fantasies*, Durham, NC: Duke University Press.

MRINALINI SINHA

COMICS

Comic book superheroes have served as icons of masculinity for generations. They provided boys with fantasies of amazing transformations from scorned 98-pound weaklings to super strong men that females adored, often shown in the magazines' ads.

The superhero genre was inaugurated by Superman in Action Comics #1 (1938), created by Siegel and Shuster, Jewish teenagers from Cleveland, Ohio. The industry's early writers, artists and publishers were often Jewish men, excluded from the more lucrative creative and advertising industries then developing, expressing themselves through these tales of men who appeared ordinary but had secret identities as powerful champions of justice.

The poles of this superhero universe were defined by Superman and Batman, introduced in Detective Comics #27 (1939). Superman was a sky god buoyed by lofty ideals, Batman a dark avenger of the night. While Superman became increasingly powerful and nearly invulnerable, Batman's specialty came to be his abilities to both dispense and recover from a beating.

After their popularity peaked in the 1940s, when American GIs went off to war with the latest adventures of their favourite comic book heroes folded into their pockets, comic books declined in the 1950s, partly because they were condemned by a Congressional investigation as a leading cause of juvenile delinquency and moral degeneracy, and partly because the heroes had lost their dastardly wartime villains, often portrayed in racist caricatures.

Comic books were reinvigorated by the 1960s Marvel Comics characters, including Spider-Man, the Fantastic Four, the X-Men, the Hulk, etc., who had more 'realistic' personalities, particularly sensitive to teenage male angst. In the 1980s superhero comic books took a darker turn, becoming more narratively gritty and graphically violent. Comic book publications have recently again suffered decline, not because mainstream culture rejects them, as in the 1950s, but rather because comic book superheroes have now been thoroughly absorbed into that culture, inspiring major new films, television shows, books and video games. Other aspects of comic books have morphed into more 'respectable' graphic novels, such as Spiegelman's *Maus* which, along with Chabon's novel *The Amazing Adventures of Kavalier and Clay*, both Pulitzer Prize winners, returns the genre to its Jewish immigrant roots.

References and further reading

Chabon, M. (2000) *The Amazing Adventures of Kavalier and Clay*, New York: Random House.
Jones, G. (2004) *Men of Tomorrow*, New York: Basic.
Spiegelman, A. (1993) *Maus*, New York: Pantheon.
Wright, B. (2001) *Comic Book Nation*, Baltimore, MD: Johns Hopkins University Press.

HARRY BROD

COMMERCIAL SEXUAL EXPLOITATION OF CHILDREN

This term describes criminal practices that demean, degrade and threaten the physical and psychosocial integrity of children. There are three primary and interrelated forms of commercial sexual exploitation (CSE) of children: prostitution, pornography and trafficking for sexual purposes. Other forms of exploitation include child sex tourism, child marriage and forced marriage. The vast majority of perpetrators of these forms of exploitation are men and teenage boys. Women may sexually exploit children in sex tourism or gain economically as third-party exploiters in coercing children into prostitution or trafficking.

Various international conventions and protocols have recognised the need to protect children from CSE. Articles 34 and 35 of the UN Convention on the Rights of the Child deal specifically with sexual exploitation and trafficking. The UN Optional Protocol to the Convention on the Rights of the Child was specifically implemented to strengthen the protection of children from CSE.

Two world congresses, Stockholm 1996 and Yokohama 2001, have allowed governments, inter- and non-governmental organisations and other stakeholders to discuss the commercial sexual exploitation of children. These congresses resulted in two documents aimed at implementing international cooperation and national action plans as means of combating this global problem, with 122 governments signing the Stockholm Agenda for Action. The Yokohama Global Commitment was an affirmation of the commitments made in Stockholm but many governments still had not implemented the Agenda for Action and progress has been slow in implementing national legislation to protect children.

The terminology used to describe the commercial sexual exploitation of children has been criticised by some children's rights organisations. For example, the terms 'child pornography' and 'child prostitution' imply a degree of consent or responsibility and may oversimplify what is a very complex social problem. The term 'child abuse images' could be a more constructive way of describing the phenomenon of children being exploited in the production and distribution of images showing the sexual abuse of children (Save the Children 2005). There have also been heated discussions about the term 'commercial sexual exploitation'. Some commentators would rather use the term 'sexual exploitation of children' as a holistic means of describing all forms of sexual abuse and exploitation of children instead of on commercial aspects of the abuse.

References and further reading

Davidson, J.O. (2005) *Children in the Global Sex Trade*, Cambridge: Polity.

Save the Children Europe Group (2005) Position paper regarding online images of sexual abuse and other Internet-related sexual exploitation of children.

See also: child abuse; prostitution

VERNON JONES

COMPLICIT MASCULINITY

Complicit masculinity is the benefit men derive from hegemonic or dominant masculinity without actually participating in dominant behaviours. These men neither explicitly support nor condemn the forms of masculinity that provide them with advantages. The proportion of men who fit the dominant forms of masculinity in a society is far less than the proportion who profit from such behaviours. The latter group may be called 'slacker versions of hegemonic masculinity' (Connell 1995: 79). They may receive higher salaries, more prestigious careers and positions of public office through images of hegemonic masculinity that advance and justify all men's position in society.

According to Connell, masculinity is never truly fixed; there are many masculinities within each society (1995). Also, men can occupy more than one form of masculinity throughout their lifetime. The dominant or hegemonic form of masculinity in a society is defined in relation to these other masculinities. Hegemonic masculinity in American and European societies encompasses such characteristics as being hard, inexpressive, independent, non-emotional and goal-oriented. Complicit masculinity allows many men to reap the rewards from the subordination of other masculinities as well as of women in a given society.

Race and class privilege affects men's ability to exhibit complicit forms of masculinity. Messerschmidt (1994) illustrates how middle-class boys through their accumulated cultural capital are able to prove their masculinity more easily than working-class boys. Middle-class boys are able to reflect dominant forms of masculinity within a society without having fully to conform behaviourally. Working-class boys, in contrast, are more likely to develop oppositional forms of masculinity.

The institutionalised and pervasive nature of hegemonic masculinity symbolises culturally valued forms of maleness while simultaneously providing gains to males who do not openly deviate from such characteristics. Complicit masculinity illustrates the varied forms of masculinity co-existing within a society and demonstrates their social construction (Connell 1995; Messerschmidt 1994).

References and further reading

Connell, R. (1995) *Masculinities*, Berkeley, CA: University of California Press.

Messerschmidt, J. (1994) 'Schooling, masculinities and youth crime by white boys', in T. Newburn and E. Stanko (eds) *Men, Masculinities and Crime: Just Boys Doing Business*, London: Routledge.

MANUEL TORRES

CONDOMS

While in the contemporary period condoms are considered to play a key role in preventing HIV and STI transmissions, this cultural object is also considered to stigmatise certain social groups and threaten normative gender identities, especially for white heterosexual men. For instance, post-AIDS the object of the condom in the discourse of safer (hetero)sex is understood to inscribe heterosexual women's bodies as risky and contaminating while simultaneously positioning heterosexual men as free from such corporeal internalisations (Waldby 1996). Moreover, for heterosexual men, condom use is often seen as a curtailment of the male sex drive and as a threat to the constitution of a heterosexual male body-image (see Kimmel and Levine 1992; Segal 1990; Patton 1994; Waldby 1996).

Vitellone (2000, 2002) highlights how these understandings of the object of the condom as signifying 'the other' in AIDS heterosexual culture are also pervasive in empirical studies of safer heterosex practice. In addressing these empirical findings Vitellone (2002), however, calls into question the dominant interpretation of the condom as concerning the figuring of women's bodies as contaminating and an 'absent,' 'invisible' and 'unmarked' heterosexual male body. Such research findings, she suggests, are illustrative not of the constitution of 'the other' but of the configuration of a masculine self-image and a heterosexual self-identity, one that takes place through the prosthetic object of the condom (Vitellone 2002). Vitellone further suggests that interpretations of the condom as curtailing the male sex drive and threatening a masculine self-identity (for heterosexual men) take for granted the way in which the object of the condom is itself constitutive of hydraulic male sexuality (Vitellone 2000).

References and further reading

Kimmel, M.S. and Levine, M.P. (1992) 'Men and AIDS', in M.S. Kimmel and M.A. Messner (eds) *Men's Lives*, New York: Macmillan, pp. 318–29.

Patton, C. (1994) *Last Served? Gendering the HIV Pandemic*, London: Taylor & Francis.

Segal, L. (1990) *Slow Motion, Changing Masculinities, Changing Men*, Piscataway, NJ: Rutgers University Press.

Vitellone, N. (2000) 'Condoms and the making of "Testosterone Man": a cultural analysis of the male sex drive in AIDS research on safer heterosex', *Men and Masculinities*, 3 (2): 152–67.

—— (2002) 'Condoms and the making of sexual difference in AIDS culture', *Body and Society*, 8 (3): 71–94.

Waldby, C. (1996) *AIDS and the Body Politic*, London and New York: Routledge.

See also: contraception, male; HIV/AIDS; sexuality

NICOLE VITELLONE

CONSUMPTION

Consumption, defined as the purchase and/or use of consumer goods, has a stronger association with femininity than masculinity, especially since the rise of industrialisation and the separation of home and work along gendered lines, particularly for the middle classes. Veblen's study of the rise of conspicuous consumption, for example, highlighted the role of women in this process (Veblen 1925). In contrast, the 1980s witnessed increasing interest in masculinity and consumption. Unprecedented developments in that decade include the rise of designer fashion for men, related markets for cosmetics and grooming products specifically targeted to men, style magazines aimed directly at men as consumers, advertising campaigns that eroticised the male body, and the wider construction of men as objects of consumer desire across the media.

From this masculinity scholars have developed certain themes: first, the impact of men's consumption upon sexual politics (Chapman and Rutherford 1988); second, the significance of visual codes around masculinity where men are encouraged to engage with other men as consumers of style (Mort 1996; Nixon 1996); and third, the wider question of the reconstruction of masculinity through the practices of consumption (Edwards 1997).

However, the separation of masculinity from consumption is false given the historical legacy of associating masculinity with certain modes of consumption, including cars, technology, sports activities and drinking. Further, the role of men in more 'feminine' forms of consumption has a number of precedents, whether in the form of the dandy, the flâneur or the aristocrat. In addition, men's consumption in today's world varies considerably according to wide social divisions of age, income and geography. As a result, the contemporary reconstruction of masculinity through consumption is neither new nor as widespread as is commonly supposed. Much concern remains about masculinity's association with sexuality, and undermining the boundaries between masculine and feminine, straight and gay in relation to consumption continues to provoke anxiety.

References and further reading

Chapman, R. and Rutherford, J. (eds) (1988) *Male Order*, London: Lawrence and Wishart.
Edwards, T. (1997) *Men in the Mirror*, London: Cassell.
Mort, F. (1996) *Cultures of Consumption*, London: Routledge.
Nixon, S. (1996) *Hard Looks*, London: UCL Press.
Veblen, T. [1925] (1934) *The Theory of the Leisure Class*, New York: The Modern Library.

See also: body image; culture and representation

TIM EDWARDS

CONTRACEPTION, MALE

Since the Second World War, thirteen new contraceptives for women have been developed, including the contraceptive pill. This is in sharp contrast to contraceptives for men. The major methods of contraception available to men (condom, withdrawal and periodic abstinence) do not differ from those available to men over 400 years ago, with only one exception: sterilisation techniques, an irreversible contraceptive method (Clarke 1998; Tone 2001). The 'Contraceptive Revolution' thus remained largely restricted to female methods. Because of the innovation in female contraceptive methods – including the hormonal contraceptive pill, intrauterine devices (IUDs) and hormonal methods such as Norplant – women's methods have come to predominate as practices of family planning. Female sterilisation, oral contraceptives and IUDs account for the majority of contraceptive methods currently in use (Lissner 1992).

The gender gap in contraceptives was first challenged in the late 1960s and early 1970s. As in the case of the pill for women, the request for developing new male contraceptives came from outside the scientific community. In this case, social pressures came from two different sides: feminists in the Western industrialised world and Southern governments, most notably in China and India. Feminists demanded that men share the responsibilities and health hazards of contraception, whereas governmental agencies urged the inclusion of 'the forgotten 50 per cent of family planning' as a target for contraceptive development (Oudshoorn 2003). Although research in male reproduction and the development of new male contraceptives has increased due to these pressures, the pill's 'male twin' has not yet appeared on the market.

The delay in the development of new contraceptives for men is usually explained by referring to biological and technical constraints. Biomedical scientists and journalists encourage us to assume that techniques to intervene in male reproductive bodies have not proliferated because the male reproductive system is by nature more resistant to intervention than that of women. Biological explanations are, however, inadequate to understand the slow pace of development of male contraceptives. Whereas contraceptive drugs development usually covers a period of approximately fifteen years, the development of male hormonal contraceptives has already taken more than three decades. Most importantly, the technical feasibility of hormonal contraceptives for men had already been demonstrated as early as the late 1970s. The delay in the development of new contraceptives for men can thus not be explained by technical constraints but is caused by social and cultural processes (Oudshoorn 2003).

First, the slow pace of development can be understood in the social context of the specific infrastructures in which this technological innovation takes place. Until the late 1990s, pharmaceutical firms had shown hardly any interest in male contraceptive research and development (R&D) because of stringent drug regulatory requirements, liability issues related to safety concerns, and a reluctant market. The advocates of new male contraceptives thus had to create an alternative R&D network to compensate for the pharmaceutical industry's reluctance to participate in the development of this new technology. Because of the resistance of industry, international public-sector agencies and most notably the World Health Organization (WHO) became the major actors in promoting and coordinating R&D for male contraceptive technologies. They created networks of academic centres with the expertise, skills and facilities to synthesise new hormonal compounds and to conduct clinical trials. Although these networks were successful in mobilising resources to overcome major barriers to male contraceptive development, they could not rely on any previous experience or routines in such a collaborative endeavour. It is therefore not surprising to notice that most activities, including collaborative efforts to synthesise and test hormonal compounds, were very time-consuming. The history shows that persistence prevails. Eventually, the results of these alternative networks convinced the pharmaceutical industry of the technical feasibility of male hormonal contraceptives. In the late 1990s, two European pharmaceutical firms, Organon in the Netherlands and Schering in Germany, decided to start a joint effort to develop hormonal contraceptives for men (Oudshoorn 2003). Representatives of Organon now expect to have a product on the market within seven years.

Second, the delay in male contraceptive development can be ascribed to cultural constraints. Ever since the idea of a male contraceptive pill or injection was first articulated, many scientists, clinicians, journalists, feminists and pharmaceutical entrepreneurs have questioned whether men or women would accept a new male contraceptive if it were available. The predominance of modern contraceptive drugs for women has disciplined men and women to delegate responsibilities for contraception largely to women. Consequently, contraceptive use came to be excluded from hegemonic masculinity. The successful development of new contraceptives for men therefore depends to a great extent on changing cultural ideas about reproductive responsibility. In the last two decades, the advocates of new contraceptives for men have worked hard to accomplish the cultural feasibility of this technology-in-the-making. Reproductive scientists and feminists have promoted the view that men are willing to share responsibilities for contraception with their partners. Family planning clinics, which used to be almost exclusively women spaces, have developed new services for men. Social scientists and reproductive scientists have conducted acceptability studies among both men and women, articulating positive attitudes towards the new technology. These studies have played an important role in convincing industry of the cultural feasibility of the new technology. And, last but not least, many men have taken the step of participating in the clinical trials of the new technology (Oudshoorn 2003). The major conclusion to be drawn from this history is that the development of the new contraceptives for men is ultimately a story as much about the design of masculinities as it is about the development of safe and effective technologies.

References and further reading

Clarke, A. (1998) *Disciplining Reproduction*, Chicago. IL: Chicago University Press.

Lissner, E.A. (1992) 'Frontiers in nonhormone male contraceptive research', in H.B. Holmes (ed.) *Issues in Reproductive Technology*, New York: Garland.

Oudshoorn, N. (2003) *The Male Pill*, Durham, NC and London: Duke University Press.

Tone, A. (2001) *Devices and Desires*, New York: Hill and Wang.

See also: bodies and biology, male; condoms; feminism; hegemonic masculinity; reproductive issues and technologies

NELLY OUDSHOORN

COUNSELLING AND THERAPY

Based on the way they are socialised by a patriarchal culture in a 'macho', hypermasculine way, Euro-American men are reluctant to ask for help or directions. Many men have different relational and coping styles than women. Traditional men are reluctant to seek therapy because it does not fit within their conception of what it means to be a man, how they define their masculinity. These 'traditional' men have been observed to be difficult to engage in therapy, often being described as resistant, unworkable and unfeeling in therapeutic settings. With patriarchal hegemonic masculinity (Real 1997; Connell 1987), seeking or asking for therapeutic assistance can be humiliating, feel like losing control and raise a man's fear of intimacy. Thus many men are less likely to seek or benefit from therapists who use traditional emotional-focused psychotherapy.

Proponents of men's therapy believe that the mental health community has failed to recognise men's special needs and therefore failed to create therapeutic alliances with men and failed to see the 'connection between men's problematic behaviours and their psychic pain' (Brooks and Good 2001: 13).

Traditional men's lives are shaped by rigid gender roles, which cause them to feel they must follow a prescribed male script to be considered a man. It includes such traits as yielding to the external pressures for men to project a masculine image, otherwise to be accused of being feminine, staying in control at all costs and holding in all emotions except anger. Further examples are that men are raised to work and to be the provider, even when living in a society where they no longer have the sole provider role for the family while they may, on the other hand, now share more with child care and household chores.

Recognising that men are gendered individuals with distinctive needs, a new approach to therapy for men is evolving (Meth and Pasick 1990), a new psychology of men (Brooks 1998). With this new gender-sensitive approach, which is sensitive to issues like how little control most men actually have over their lives, the standard of being a man is changing. There are now many opportunities to design therapeutic modalities for different populations of men and their various masculinities (Lucas 2000), 'more gender aware, gender sensitive, and gender fair' therapeutic approaches, which call for therapists to consider women's and men's cultural and gender contexts in developing interventions (Brooks and Good 2001: 13, citations omitted).

Part of the dynamic of therapy involves the therapist pushing for change and emotional healing. Scher (1981) states therapists have a professional responsibility to serve their clients by encouraging changes that will result in emotional healing. One way for therapists to fulfil that responsibility is to do their own emotional healing work so that they may understand their clients better. Another way is to be aware of the opportunities for personal development through their own participation in the contemporary men's movement and men's studies activities (Paterik 1995). Therapists have found that 'their participation in [their mythopoetic] support groups ... helped them individually [in their own growth and transformation] as well to become better therapists' (Barton 2003: 181). In addition they can refer their clients to mythopoetic men's movement activities and men's studies activities that would be of value to their clients and that could provide an adjunct to psychotherapy (Barton 2000).

The mythopoetic men's movement believes that men should be seen as having a special gendered culture. It advocates that men who counsel men receive diversity training and practise the experiential mythopoetic work needed for experiencing, feeling and learning recognition of men's psychic pain and men's gendered contexts. When men's experiences are understood in a gendered, cross-cultural counselling context, therapeutic bonds will be easier to establish. Therapists will be much more empathetic and compassionate towards men, and men will be more eager to use and engage in psychotherapy (Brooks and Good 2001).

References and further reading

Barton, E.R. (ed.) (2000) *Mythopoetic Perspectives of Men's Healing Work*, Westport, CT: Bergin and Garvey.

—— (2003) 'A qualitative exploration of participation in men's peer mutual support groups', unpublished doctoral dissertation, Michigan State University.

Brooks, G.R. (1998) *A New Psychotherapy for Traditional Men*, San Francisco, CA: Jossey-Bass.
Brooks, G.R. and Good, G.E. (2001) *The New Handbook of Psychotherapy and Counseling with Men*, San Francisco, CA: Jossey-Bass.
Connell, R.W. (1987) *Gender and Power*, Stanford, CA: Stanford University Press.
Lucas, R.T. (2000) 'The use of myth and quasi-myth in therapy', in E.R. Barton (ed.) *Mythopoetic Perspectives of Men's Healing Work*, Westport, CT: Bergin and Garvey, pp. 121–9.
Meth, R.L. and Pasick, R.S. (1990) *Men in Therapy*, New York: Guilford.
O'Neil, J. and Egan, J. (1992) 'Men's gender role transitions over the life span', *Journal of Mental Health Counseling*, 14 (3): 305–24.
Paterik, R.C. (1995) 'The correlation of men's studies involvement and gender role development among counseling psychologists', unpublished doctoral dissertation, Texas Woman's University.
Real, T. (1997) *I Don't Want to Talk About It*, New York: Scribner.
Scher, M. (1981) 'Men in hiding', *Personnel and Guidance Journal*, 59: 199–202.

See also: recovery and self-help; working with men

EDWARD READ BARTON

CRIME, CRIMINALITY AND LAW

The issue of masculinity has become centrally relevant to the study of crime, law and criminal justice, informing a growing number of studies in the field. The relationship between men, masculinities and crime has, since the mid-1990s, assumed an increasing prominence both within academic criminology internationally (Carlen and Jefferson 1996; Maguire *et al.* 1997) and in relation to a series of debates about the substance and direction of criminal justice policies and practices. The starting point for this 'masculinity turn' (Collier 1998) rests on a paradox at the heart of the discipline of criminology. Criminologists of diverse persuasions have long recognised sex-status, along with youth, to be one of the strongest predictors of criminal involvement. The vast majority of conversations and debates about criminal justice have, historically, been largely about the actions of men. The now well-established feminist critique which emerged in the 1970s was focused on the way in which the sex-specificity of crime has been conceptualised. Criminology has been flawed in (at least) two senses. First, it has failed to account, in anything like an adequate manner, for the nature of women's offending and the treatment of women within criminal justice systems. And, second, it has failed to address the 'gender of crime': the masculinity or maleness of crime, the crimes of men *as men* (that is, as gendered beings: Walklate 1995: 169).

Addressing the crimes of women has been the concern of a now considerable body of feminist scholarship (see, for example, Naffine 1997). Explicitly addressing the interconnections between masculinity and crime – from a perspective informed by the feminist critique – is a project of more recent origin. Following the publication of James Messerschmidt's text *Masculinities and Crime: Critique and Reconceptualization of Theory* (1993, see also 1997), a growing number of books, articles and research projects have sought to explore the relationship between men and crime via recourse to the idea that the gender of men is interlinked to, is a cause of or is in some other way associated with crime and criminality (Newburn and Stanko 1994). What is seen as uniting men is, relative to women, their overwhelming propensity towards criminality, as testified to across jurisdictions by official criminal statistics, victimisation and self-report studies, as well as everyday lived experience. Adequately addressing the fact that crime is almost always committed by men has become a litmus test for the viability of the discipline and for criminal justice systems internationally in seeking to control crime. For, if we cannot explain the cross-cultural gender ratio of crime, if criminology cannot address its own 'generalisability problem' (do theories designed to account for men's offending necessarily apply to women?), what does this tell us about governmental attempts to deal with crime? And what does it say about men?

To give no more than a flavour of the body of work which has taken place in the area of criminal justice, the concept of masculinity has been utilised in studies of topics as diverse as: the dynamics of 'cop culture' and strategies aimed at challenging sex discrimination within criminal justice systems; persistent offending, the dynamics of urban disorder and the relation between crime, multiple deprivation and 'family breakdown'; delinquency, schooling and educational underachievement; victims and the fear of crime; men in prison and the interconnections of race, ethnicity and crime; environmental crime, drug use and media representations of crime; white-collar crime; and, in greater volume perhaps than any other topic, the seemingly intractable problem of men's violences against women, children and other men.

To extrapolate unity to such a wide-ranging literature is difficult. Yet it is possible to identify some recurring themes within these attempts to unpack the interconnections of masculinity, crime and criminal justice. It has been argued, in particular, that the shifting experience of crime across late-modern societies is a phenomenon bound up with the idea of masculine crisis, emblematic of wider concerns and anxieties around the meaning of social, economic, cultural and political change. Recent literature on masculinities and crime rejects the functionalist, positivist and broadly sex-role framework which had marked earlier engagements. It has sought, rather, to focus on what has been termed the 'accomplishment' of masculinity through the 'doing' of crime.

The concept of hegemonic masculinity has been central to these studies of crime and criminal justice; and, in the work of James Messerschmidt, the potential implications of R. Connell's work (1995) received their most thought-out and sophisticated development in the field of crime. Drawing on diverse influences, Messerschmidt argues that men exist in different positions in relation to the dominant hierarchies of gender, race, class and sexuality; and, as a result, their resources for the accomplishment of masculinity vary. It is when these class and race relations combine to reduce conventional opportunities that crime is seen as a ready replacement, a potential solution for men in their struggle to become (to be) masculine. As Messerschmidt puts it, crime is a behavioural response to the particular conditions and situations in which we participate.

Rightly heralded as an extremely important advance in understanding masculinity, crime and criminal justice, this attempt to integrate the complexities of race, class, gender and sexuality has nonetheless been subject to criticism. In particular, it has been argued, it is marked by a failure to engage with the subjectivity of individual men: the question, that is, of why some men 'turn to' crime and others do not. Most crime is committed by highly specific sub-groups of the category 'men', men who are themselves often the principal victims of crime (Hall 2002). The masculine social subject deployed by Messerschmidt relates in a distinctly deterministic way to the cultural norms of hegemonic masculinity (whatever these may be). To account for the complex diversity of crime in terms of men accomplishing their gender identity is itself questionable. Is it the case that all crime is to be explained in this way? Or only some crime? Masculinity is depicted as both primary and underlying cause (or source) of a social effect (crime), a particular 'gendered' criminal justice system; and, simultaneously, as something which results from (after all, it is accomplished through) recourse to crime. As Walklate (1995) observes, not only does this reflect a failure to resolve fully the tendency towards universalism, it can also be read as tautological. Most men, regardless of their socio-economic group, 'do' a masculine gender without resorting to (at least certain) crimes. Yet it is difficult to see in Messerschmidt's structured action theory any account of why this should be the case; or, importantly, how individual life-history and biography impact on any such 'choice'.

It is this latter issue which has concerned those writers who have sought to develop a 'psycho-social' approach to masculinities, crime and criminal justice (see, for example, Jefferson 1994, 1996). This work focuses on the tensions between the social and psychic processes which are seen to inform men's experience of masculinity. In an attempt to take the psychic dimensions of men's subjectivity seriously, research into diverse aspects of crime and criminal justice practice has sought to explore how men come to invest – whether consciously and unconsciously – in empowering social discourses around masculinity. By integrating questions of individual biography and life-history, it is argued, a handle is given on the important question, noted above, of why some men do, and others do not, engage in certain crimes.

While this has been an advance politically on the (always, already) empowered masculine subject implicit in much other work on men and crime, certain questions remain. It is difficult to see, for example, how the kinds of psycho-social readings produced in this area can ever be tested or proven in any meaningful way. Or are we left, ultimately, with a wholly semiotic account, one in which only the trained psychologist, counsellor or academic expert will be able to ascertain what is 'really' behind an individual's actions? As Hood-Williams (2001) notes, it is very difficult to maintain that psychoanalysis – as deployed, for example, in the work of Jefferson – is just one of many 'discourses of subjectivication' and, at the same time, that the claims it is making are grounded in real, historically specific and irreducible psychological processes. The implications in terms of policy and practice are similarly uncertain.

The wider interrogation of masculinity in crime and criminal justice studies, as in law, echoes developments within sociology. And, as in other fields of study, feminist and queer perspectives arguably remain marginal (Groombridge 1999). Both the structured action and psycho-social approaches discussed above engage – in different ways – with the question of how ideas of masculinity become problematised at particular historical moments and social contexts. Yet both approaches stand in an uneasy relation to some essentialist conceptualisations of masculinity itself – whether it is in the tendency of structured action theory to depict a mechanistic relation between masculinity, culture and crime or in the psycho-social grounding of gender difference in psychic processes.

It is open to question, ultimately, how adequate the concept of masculinity itself is when seeking to explain, understand or otherwise account for the crimes of men and the masculinism of global criminal justice systems. By the mid-1990s masculinity, crime and criminal justice was a topic described as an area in which much more work needed to be done. A decade on, it would appear that the vast majority of writing on crime continues to associate sex/gender with aspects of the still-pervasive 'Woman question' – albeit in an ostensibly pro-feminist form. Whatever limitations and unanswered questions remain, the study of masculinity, crime and criminal justice has progressed. In another sense, however, crime and criminal justice remains a story of 'boys doing business' as usual (Newburn and Stanko 1994).

References and further reading

Carlen, P. and Jefferson, J. (1996) *British Journal of Criminology*, Special Issue, 'Masculinities and crime', 33 (6).

Collier, R. (1998) *Masculinities, Crime and Criminology*, London: Sage.

Connell, R. (1995) *Masculinities*, Cambridge: Polity.

Groombridge, N. (1999) 'Perverse criminologies: the closet of Doctor Lombroso', *Social and Legal Studies*, 8 (4): 529–48.

Hall, S. (2002) 'Daubing the drudges of fury: men, violence and the piety of the "hegemonic masculinity" thesis', *Theoretical Criminology*, 6 (1): 35–61.

Hood-Williams, J. (2001) 'Gender, masculinities and crime: from structures to psyches', *Theoretical Criminology*, 5 (1): 37–60.

Jefferson, T. (1994) 'Theorizing masculine subjectivity', in T. Newburn and E.E. Stanko (eds) *Just Boys Doing Business? Men. Masculinities and Crime*, London: Routledge, pp. 10–31.

—— (1996) 'Introduction', in T. Jefferson and P. Carlen (eds) *British Journal of Criminology*, 35 (1): 1337–47.
—— (1997) 'Masculinities and crime', in M. Maguire, R. Morgan and R. Reiner (eds) *The Oxford Handbook of Criminology*, 2nd edn, Oxford: Clarendon Press, pp. 535–57.
Maguire, M., Morgan, R. and Reiner, R. [1994] (1997) *The Oxford Handbook of Criminology*, 2nd edn, Oxford: Clarendon Press.
Messerschmidt, J.W. (1993) *Masculinities and Crime: Critique and Reconceptualization of Theory*, Lanham, MD: Rowman and Littlefield.
—— (1997) *Crime as Structured Action: Gender, Race, Class and Crime*, Thousand Oaks, CA: Sage.
Naffine, N. (1997) *Feminism and Criminology*, Cambridge: Polity.
Newburn, T. and Stanko, E.E. (eds) (1994) *Just Boys Doing Business? Men, Masculinities and Crime*, London: Routledge.
Walklate, S. (1995) *Gender and Crime: An Introduction*, Hemel Hempstead: Prentice Hall/Harvester Wheatsheaf.

See also: criminal justice system; criminology; prisons; working with men in prison

RICHARD COLLIER

CRIMINAL JUSTICE SYSTEM

The criminal justice system refers to the use of law enforcement and police, the courts and the prison industry to address crime in society systematically. Criminology tends to focus exclusively on men (Friedman 1993: 423), and this fact is also reflected in social policies that commonly target more men than women. In many societies, a 'get tough on crime' policy reflects the ideology of retribution – a masculinised approach that includes physical violence, psychological humiliation and permanent stigma being attached to offenders (Beckett and Sasson 1999).

Studies indicate a 'cult of masculinity' within policing culture in the United States and the United Kingdom (Smith and Gray 1985). Some female and gay police officers feel unable to conform to this culture, which incites aggressiveness and toughness in its officers (Herbert 1997). This culture also results in enforcement policies that rely heavily on violence to deal with suspects. Because, in the United States, this culture uses profiling measures to locate suspects, males, African Americans and Hispanic Americans are disproportionately arrested in comparison with other groups.

The judicial systems of many industrialised nations reflect a competitive approach to crime that assesses the actions of offenders and the harms committed in terms of victors and losers. In the United States, harsh sentences – including the death penalty and mandatory long sentences for repeat offenders – further stress a masculinised judicial system. In contrast, legal systems of some African societies strive to solve problems more broadly, restoring peace across the community and among offenders and victims.

In terms of prisons, many societies use correctional approaches that stress retribution over rehabilitation, thus decreasing the offender's ability to be reintegrated into society. Torture, sexual humiliation and threats of death – illustrated in the United States' Abu Ghraib prison in Iraq – are common in prisons worldwide. Interpersonal violence, collective violence (including prison gangs), rape and institutionalised homosexuality are also prevalent in prisons.

References and further reading

Beckett, K. and Sasson, T. (1999) *The Politics of Injustice*, Thousand Oaks, CA: Pine Forge.
Friedman, L.W. (1993) *Crime and Punishment in American History*, New York: Basic.
Herbert, S. (1997) *Policing Space*, Minneapolis, MN: University of Minnesota Press.
Smith, D. and Gray, J. (1985) *Police and People in London*, Aldershot: Grower.

See also: crime, criminality and law; criminology; police; prisons

SCOTT A. LUKAS

CRIMINOLOGY

Criminology is the systemic study of the 'nature, extent, cause, and control of law-breaking behavior' (Lanier and Henry 1998:

2). For hundreds of years, criminologists have sought to explain the disproportional numbers of crimes committed by men as compared to women.

The earliest theory of criminology is the demonic perspective. The demonic perspective focuses on supernaturalism (possession) to explain crime as well as administer punishment. During the Salem witch trials of the 1600s in colonial America, numerous individuals were accused of witchcraft, and a disproportionate number of those accused were women. One theory of this disparity suggests that men used the witchcraft allegation to quell the growing political and social interests that women expressed in their communities (Erikson 1966). Others argue that those who fell outside the social order, including women who rejected heterosexual marriage and gay men, were punished (Pfohl 1994: 38). In today's world, the demonic perspective is used by evangelical leaders to explain events of mass violence like 9/11, and gays and lesbians are often targeted for their transgressive lifestyles. Similarly, demonic possession has been claimed by male serial killers including David Berkowitz.

The second major criminological theory, the classical perspective, emerged in the eighteenth century as a response to the arbitrary and unscientific demonic perspective. Associated with Beccaria and Bentham, it focused on philosophical concepts of the social contract and free will: individuals would be protected from injustices committed by the state or other citizens and, in return, they would exercise good judgment, according to their free will, and not commit crime. Many of the administrative justice concepts of the classical perspective, including Beccaria's (1963), formed the basis of the human rights principles expressed in the US Constitution (Lanier and Henry 1998: 67). Classical theory sought less to explain why crime occurred and more to administer forms of justice that would protect all equally under the law. A current application of the classical perspective, known as rational choice theory, extends the focus on free will and analyses why people commit crimes. This theory addresses choice structuring – the idea that people will engage in criminal acts if their net gain will outweigh their risks and potential losses – and initially emphasised the criminality of men; once women achieved greater social and economic rights, their rationality led them to commit crimes similar to those of men (Adler 1975).

In the nineteenth century, biological or pathological theory used positivism, purported empirical testing and biological determinism to suggest that crime was the result of biological or psychological predispositions. This theory is the first major criminological perspective to focus on males as the primary source of crime in society, and it focused on inherent biological abnormalities as explanations of why men committed crime. Biological criminologists argued that certain body types were associated with certain forms of crime (Pfohl 1994: 108). Later works, including *The Female Offender* (Lombroso and Ferrero 1900), focused on the rare case of female criminality and suggested that female criminals were those who exhibited excessive male characteristics. As biological explanations of crime waned, psychological theories influenced by the work of Freud analysed the internal conflicts of the mind that resulted from childhood traumas in the offender (Lanier and Henry 1998: 115). Contemporary pathological theories combine biological and psychological elements and target both male and female offenders. Testosterone is often cited as a physiological precondition that causes men to commit more crimes than women, particularly rape (Booth and Osgood 1993), while female physiology, including menstruation and menopause, has been used to explain the rare incidence of female offence (Pollak 1950).

The learning perspective is the first of a series of criminological theories that emphasises the nature of an individual's involvement in social relations. Sutherland relativised previous theories of crime and said that 'any person can be trained to adopt and follow' patterns of crime and deviance (1934: 51).

According to Sutherland's 'differential association' concept, the frequency of interactions with criminal offenders, the prestige of criminals and the duration of contact between offenders and potential offenders are all factors in an individual's likelihood to engage in criminal lifestyles (Pfohl 1994: 302–3). Sutherland also emphasised that concomitant with the development of criminal behaviours in social groups, 'rough and tough' attitudes increased the individual's propensity to internalise criminal attitudes. Studies of the gang phenomenon present the influence of older male role models as a primary factor in younger males' likelihood to join gangs and commit criminal activities (Cloward and Ohlin 1960).

A second social theory of criminology is social control theory. This theory analyses why some individuals engage in criminal behaviour and why others do not, and its analytical frame includes inner controls (including morality and conscience) and outer controls (including social control agents like police, teachers and parents). Social control theory has been used to explain the prevalence of crime committed by males, and many criminologists have emphasised that males are more likely to engage in crime because they have been socialised to rely on masculine traits like aggressiveness and toughness to resolve interpersonal conflict (Messerschmidt 1993). Additionally, other criminologists suggest that failed social bonds early in life, and broken ones later, lead to males choosing criminal over lawful behaviour (Lanier and Henry 1998: 159).

Labelling theory is a contemporary perspective that analyses how self-concept affects an individual's decision to commit crime. A number of influential studies argue that crime and deviance are the result of the interaction of offenders and those who respond to social violations and, more specifically, the nature of categorisation (or labelling) that is used to identify some individuals as criminal and others as law-abiding (Erikson 1966; Goffman 1963). The power of one individual to label another is key to labelling theory. In terms of identity and self-concept leading to the commission of crime, sociologists have emphasised that masculinity plays a major role in the socialisation of boys and thus leads to the prevalence of male offenders (Parsons 1964). Boys' self-concept is often tied to the acting out of socially accepted masculine roles, and in some cases a boy's gender can become a master status, essentially defining the essence of his personality (ibid.: 33). Such powerful labels, including 'he is just a tough guy', can lead a boy to accept the labels imposed on him and actually engage in the criminal behaviours that society is attempting to abate. Collier has called for the reappraisal of masculinity as it relates to criminology (1998). Particularly, criminologists need to address the complexity of masculinity – as cultural and political phenomenon – and analyse the ways in which theories of crime focus on limited and over-determined concepts of maleness.

Another major variety of criminological theories analyses how crime develops as a result of large-scale or macro social conditions. The first of these perspectives is social disorganisation theory, and it is associated with the Chicago School of Sociology. Members of the school identified major and rapid forms of social change, including immigration, upheavals like warfare and economic depression, and technological changes, as the primary factors in producing crime. Using ecological models of explanation, social disorganisation theory identified specific zones of crime, and these typically were found in transitional zones of the city. Shaw and McKay studied the nature of juvenile delinquency among boys in early twentieth-century Chicago and concluded that delinquency was most common in the inner city.

Strain theory, derived by Merton from Durkheim's concept of anomie, focuses on crime resulting from discrepancies between socially constructed goals and the availability of means of achieving such goals. This criminological perspective emphasises that there is an inherent flaw in the nature of society – unattainable aspirations – and this leads people to pursue success and achievement by any means necessary. Money and autonomy are common goals that are connected to the value systems of capitalist nations, and when these goals are unmet, individuals may resort to socially deviant ways of achieving them. Strain theory is applicable to the understanding of males and crime, especially as the male emphasis on status and respect can result in the promulgation of criminal activity. Some current organisations, including Advocates for Youth in the United States, have directly addressed strain theory and masculinity by developing peer discussion groups focused on self-esteem and awareness.

Another major perspective in contemporary criminology includes conflict and radical theory. These theories are founded on the work of Marx; they suggest that the cause of crime is found in the 'conflict that stems from the inequalities produced by capitalist society' (Lanier and Henry 1998: 236). Conflict and radical approaches analyse the ways in which capitalism's economic and cultural systems produce a criminogenic society, one that is prone to crime. One explanation for the high percentage of males who commit crime is that males' greater economic and social power, resulting from the gendered nature of capitalism, puts them in positions to commit crime. Conversely, women occupy positions of less prominence and are less able to participate in criminal activity. When men do commit crimes, they often do so to maintain the systems of exploitation common to capitalism. According to conflict and radical criminology, crime is systemic: it allows the powerful members of society to maintain their control of economic and cultural resources. One recent example of elite corporate deviance in the United States, the Enron case in which insiders gained huge profits from manipulating energy supplies while consumers suffered blackouts, illustrates the extent to which property crimes are connected to the exploitative elements of capitalism. Though a majority of the Enron criminals were male, some conflict and radical criminologists argue that if women were in the same positions of corporate power, they would commit similar crimes since the economic system produces crime regardless of the sex of the offenders. A recent extension of Marxist criminology, Marxist feminism, focuses on the ways in which men maintain exploitative relations within capitalism. For example, they claim that rape in capitalist societies illustrates the idea that crime is connected to the problems associated with capitalism: men rape not for sexual pleasure but for maintaining control within other spheres of society (Lanier and Henry 1998: 275).

A final strain of criminological theory is referred to as critical criminology. The first critical approach is anarchist criminology. According to anarchist criminologists, men are the unwitting victims of the power dynamics of criminal justice systems. Most commonly, they are the ones committing crime, administering its punishment and often its victims. Closely aligned with this approach is abolitionist criminology. According to abolitionist criminologists, 'punishment is never justified' (Lanier and Henry 1998: 287), and many call for the complete abandonment of traditional forms of criminal justice, including penology. As opposed to the masculinised model of justice that is common to most industrialised societies, the abolitionist approach focuses on restorative systems of justice that reduce pain rather than inflict it. A third critical criminological strain, peacemaking criminology, argues for a similar alteration of masculinised criminal justice systems. Peacemaking criminology opposes concepts like 'the war on drugs' and analyses the unjust nature of criminal justice policy, including boot camps, degradation punishment and the death penalty. In each of these examples, males are victimising other males through systems of retribution that perpetuate the violence they ostensibly seek to eliminate. Finally, feminist criminological theory addresses the unique statuses afforded to women in society and within the criminal justice system. According to some feminist criminologists, the disproportionate number of male offenders in many societies means that women face the harms of patriarchal society, including the physical, psychological and social vulnerability associated with crime. Feminist theorists have also written that many areas of the criminal justice system, including rape and pornography policy, are biased against women. Many have also addressed the erasure of women from criminology – both as victims and as offenders – and suggest the need to develop more comprehensively gendered scholarship and more equity for those scholars within the field (Lanier and Henry 1998: 269). Many criminologists have called for a more explicit focus on masculinity in its relationship to the theories of crime and criminal justice practices of society. Some criminological theories have not emphasised masculinity as a multifaceted and socially complex phenomenon while others have de-emphasised the status of men as victims within crime (Newburn and Stanko 1994).

References and further reading

Adler, F. (1975) *Sisters in Crime*, New York: McGraw-Hill.

Beccaria, C. (1963) *On Crimes and Punishment*, Indianapolis, IN: Bobbs-Merrill.

Booth, A. and Osgood, D.W. (1993) 'The influence of testosterone on deviance in adulthood', *Criminology*, 31 (1): 93–117.

Cloward, R. and Ohlin, L. (1960) *Delinquency and Opportunity*, Glencoe, IL: Free Press.

Collier, R. (1998) *Masculinities, Crime and Criminology*, London: Sage.

Erikson, K. (1966) *Wayward Puritans*, New York: Wiley.

Goffman, E. (1963) *Stigma*, New York: Simon and Schuster.

Lanier, M. and Henry, S. (1998) *Essential Criminology*, Boulder, CO: Westview.

Lombroso, C. and Ferrero, W. (1900) *The Female Offender*, New York: D. Appleton.

Messerschmidt, J.W. (1993) *Masculinities and Crime*, Lanham, MD: Rowman and Littlefield.

Newburn, T. and Stanko, E. (1994) 'When men are victims', in T. Newburn and E. Stanko, *Just Boys Doing Business: Men, Masculinities and Crime*, London: Routledge.

Parsons, T. (1964) *Social Structure and Personality*, New York: Free Press.

Pfohl, S. (1994) *Images of Deviance and Social Control*, 2nd edn, New York: McGraw-Hill.

Pollak, O. (1950) *The Criminality of Women*, Philadelphia, PA: University of Pennsylvania Press.

Sutherland, E. (1934) *Principles of Criminology*, Philadelphia, PA: Lippincott.

See also: crime, criminality and law; criminal justice system: working with men in prison

SCOTT A. LUKAS

CRISIS IN MASCULINITY

Beginning in the late 1990s, discussions of a crisis in masculinity began to appear in both popular and academic discourse in the United States and Britain. In books like Faludi's *Stiffed* stories about individuals' waning economic and social power became stories about the attrition of specifically male power and privilege. Feminism was often seen as contributing to this erosion, and many commentators saw the crisis in masculinity as a 'feminisation' of men. Feminist scholars took a different tack, arguing that if masculinity was in fact 'in crisis', it was not necessarily the case that male power suffered. Modleski warned that 'we need to consider the extent to which male power is actually consolidated through cycles of crisis and resolution, whereby men ultimately deal with the threat of female power by incorporating it' (Modleski 1991: 7; see also Robinson 2000). Other scholars have been more sympathetic to the idea that men as a group have recently suffered from a gradual but steady erosion of both actual male power and the symbolic power of a traditional concept of masculinity (see Pfeil 1995). Activist groups in the US and Britain have developed around their alarm at a crisis in masculinity: for example, groups that lobby for fathers' rights and less explicitly political groups that aim to recoup a more traditional masculinity. Some groups and accounts of the crisis in masculinity are openly hostile to feminism as causing the crisis, while others applaud feminism for bringing the masculinity crisis to public notice. In the early twenty-first century, the discourse of masculinity crisis is diminishing as the growing inequities of economic restructuring affect women as much as men. Heartfield, for example, argues that British scholars have mistaken the crisis in the working class for a crisis of masculinity. The perception of a crisis in masculinity depends on the stability of a concept of masculinity, and it has now become increasingly difficult to find that stability.

References and further reading

Faludi, S. (1999) *Stiffed*, New York: William Morrow.

Heartfield, J. (2002) 'There is no masculinity crisis', *Genders*, 35, available at http://www.genders.org/g35/g35_heartfield.html

Modleski, T. (1991) *Feminism without Women*, New York and London: Routledge.

Pfeil, F. (1995) *White Guys*, New London and New York: Verso.

Robinson, S. (2000) *Marked Men*, New York: Columbia University Press.

SALLY ROBINSON

CRISIS TENDENCIES

The term 'crisis tendencies', coined by Jürgen Habermas (1975), describes inherent, structural tensions and inequalities in social systems that lead to social crisis. Habermas' focus was late capitalism. Connell (1995), though, applies the concept of crisis tendencies to masculinity studies to describe the tendency of a gender order towards crisis. He also makes an important distinction between crisis tendencies in gender orders and the common use of 'crisis in masculinity'. That is, whereas a gender order is a coherent social system, masculinity is merely a configuration within that system, so masculinity only shows the symptoms of the gender order's crisis tendencies.

For Connell, three structures inherent in a gender order make it tend towards crisis: power relations, production relations and relations of cathexis (or sexual desire). The first, power relations, demonstrates the most visible evidence of crisis tendencies, notably women's struggles for economic, political and public policy equality – along with men's reactions to these. Crises stemming from production relations, second, are evidenced by still other institutional changes as women struggle for labour rights and more women join the workforce. The final structure, relations of cathexis, shows signs of crisis resulting from the increasing social acceptance of women's desire and non-heterosexual sexuality.

The impact on men and masculinity from these crisis tendencies is highly variable. One result can be the production of crisis discourses, like moral panics over boys' education seen in works like Sommers' *The War Against Boys* (2000). Crises of masculinity can also produce violence, like domestic violence (e.g. Faludi 1999) or terrorism (e.g. Weaver-Hightower 2002), in contexts where men's economic or civil prospects appear diminished or challenged. Not all responses to crisis, however, are retrogressive. Crisis tendencies can also push some men towards profeminist and progressive positions, like, for example, the Men's League for Woman Suffrage at the turn of the twentieth century in the United States (see Kimmel 1996).

References and further reading

Connell, R. (1995) *Masculinities*, Berkeley, CA: University of California Press.

Faludi, S. (1999) *Stiffed: The Betrayal of the American Man*, New York: William Morrow.

Habermas, J. [1973] (1975) *Legitimation Crisis*, Boston, MA: Beacon.

Kimmel, M.S. (1996) *Manhood in America*, New York: Free Press.

Sommers, C.H. (2000) *The War against Boys*, New York: Simon and Schuster.

Weaver-Hightower, M.B. (2002) 'The gender of terror and heroes? What educators might teach about men and masculinity after September 11, 2001', *Teachers College Record*, available at http://www.tcrecord.org

See also: crisis in masculinity; domestic violence; education; feminism; gender; heterosexuality; power relations; terrorism

MARCUS B. WEAVER-HIGHTOWER

CRITICAL RACE STUDIES

Critical race studies, as an approach to understanding how racism is structured through social institutions such as the law, has now a considerable history within academia. From what started as a critique of the racialised assumptions that inform the legal profession (and national laws more broadly), critical race studies has grown through its engagement with feminist critiques of racism and race privilege, and through the recent development of the field of critical whiteness studies (e.g. see essays in Delago 1995). Critical race studies continues to inform the ways in which laws are developed in response to the growing recognition of racism as systemic within Western nations, as well as being used to examine how race informs areas such as public policy, academic research and everyday interactions.

In a similar way, studies of masculinities have sought to examine how Western nations prioritise the experiences and values of men, and in particular white middle-class heterosexual men. The privileges that men hold under heteropatriarchy are thus examined as sites for elaborating how such privilege comes at the expense of a wide range of people. Thus, much like critical race studies, the study of masculinities examines the intersections of privilege and oppression, and is engaged in developing an account of masculinity and heteropatriarchy that moves beyond simply examining individual men's privileges (though obviously this is an important point as well) to looking at the systemic oppressions that result from the prioritisation of particular normative accounts of gender.

In this regard, Connell (cited in Flood 2002: 208) raises an important point about analyses of masculinities: namely, that it is important to emphasise

> the relationship between the two meanings of masculinity as cultural ideal and as patriarchal gender practice. [Connell] cautions that the most visible bearers of hegemonic masculinity are not always the most powerful people, and individual holders of power do not necessarily conform to hegemonic patterns in their own lives.

This point demonstrates the importance of employing critical race studies in conjunction with studies of masculinities in order to explore how men experience differential relations to power under heteropatriarchy, and how these differences may be played out in relation to discourses of race.

In order to demonstrate these points, the remainder of this entry provides a practical elaboration of how we may look at intersections of power and oppression. There exists a long history of literature that examines hierarchies of either gender or race (e.g. Greer 1970; Hollinsworth 1998), and there is also a body of literature that examines how particular (white heterosexual) men and women benefit from race privilege (e.g. Schloesser 2002). However, there is little research that explores how the privilege of white men and women is mediated by discourses of sexuality, and little research that examines the ways in which non-heterosexual white men and women are also complicit with white hegemony (Běrubě 2001 and Nicoll 2001 being notable exceptions). This is in part the result of a long history of identity politics, particularly in the context of lesbian and gay rights, whereby much writing and activism has focused on singular 'aspects' of identity in order to secure equality. While this has resulted in many important outcomes, it has also had the effect of silencing the privileges that white lesbians and gay men (for example) may hold as white people.

The following sections focus on the example of race relations in Australia and their location within the realities of colonisation and dispossession. By exploring some of the privileges and oppressions that white gay men have experienced under the law, attention is drawn to the ways in which race mediates rights. As a result, this brief exploration of sexuality in Australia through the lens of both critical race studies and studies of masculinities contributes to a growing recognition of the need for an examination of identities and experiences as multiple and contingent.

Possessive investments: the law as a gendered and racialised practice

This section provides a brief account of some of the laws that existed in regard to sodomy in colonial Australia. This account focuses in particular on three aspects of what Moreton-Robinson (2004) has termed 'possessive investments in whiteness', namely: (a) the normative gendered assumptions that informed colonial law; (b) the varying constructions of sexuality that circulated within colonial Australia; and (c) the shifts in power dynamics that encouraged white colonisers to accept as necessary the denial of Indigenous sovereignty.

As feminist scholars have continued to elaborate, the law is a priori designed to protect the status quo under heteropatriarchy (e.g. Smith 1993). This fact is explicitly evident in early colonial laws in Australia, which were premised on the assumption that only white men had the necessary faculties (i.e. rationality) required to access and decide law practices (an assumption that has again been asserted in the Yorta Yorta land rights claim; see Moreton-Robinson 2004). The law thus held only limited control over the lives of white men, as opposed to the laws that governed the rights of white women, and the laws that controlled the movement, rights and indeed lives of Indigenous people. While it is true that white men's access to the law was mediated by their status in regard to class and sexual preference, this does not negate the fact that all white men stood to benefit from the normative assumptions of patriarchal law. An example of this comes from a case of sodomy in 1855 presented by Connors (1994: 98–9). In the case the complainant testified that the defendant had 'attempt[ed] to commit an unnatural crime'. Connors suggests, however, that 'it seems likely that [the complainant and defendant] had had a homosexual relationship', and that the fight between them was a matter of jealousy. The intervention of the law thus only came on the invitation of the complainant: both men (as white men) were otherwise relatively free from the incursion of the law upon their lives. In other words, unless they were 'caught' engaging in sodomy, or brought accusations against one another, white men were presumed to be heterosexual, and thus entitled to full sanction by the law. Thus as Aldrich (2003: 238) suggests, the statistics on white men convicted on accounts of sodomy 'do not give evidence of a particularly vicious campaign against homosexuals'. This relative leniency may be contrasted with the sustained campaign of violence that was mounted against Indigenous people, and which continues to be evidenced in the laws and public policy that deny Indigenous sovereignty.

Changes in colonial law brought about a range of outcomes for men who engaged in homosexual practices. Some examples of these include (a) 1828: men convicted of sodomy ceased to lose their property rights; (b) 1883: the death penalty was removed as a punishment for sodomy; and (c) 1860: the increasing introduction of the category 'homosexual' as a means to understanding homosexual practices within the law. These shifts in the law, while often accompanied by a relatively greater or lesser level of prosecutions for sodomy (or for lesser offences such as 'indecent exposure with a male', see Fogarty 1992), translated into a shift from a 'power based on discipline to one transfigured into normalization' (Stoler 1995: 89). Thus the construction of the category 'homosexual', and its recognition within law courts, alongside the growing rights of white women, meant that white men and women, regardless of sexuality, were provided with examples of how to 'approximate the norm' (Aldrich 2003). As suggested in the following section, these 'aspirational practices' thus allowed homosexual white men an increased freedom in determining their status within colonial Australia, one that was dependent upon the acceptance of normative ideals.

'Aspirational practices': shoring up the nation

The previous section, in regard to the racialisation of colonial law, provides a framework within which to understand how a range of 'aspirational practices' were used to encourage white homosexual men and white women in general to invest in the 'logic of possession'. While these practices may not have been the explicit intention of the law, they were founded on the possessive logic of the patriarchal white nation, whereby individuals are constructed as either objects or subjects of the legal gaze. Amendments to sodomy laws thus produced 'the sodomite' (and later 'the homosexual') as an agentic subject, which was directly contrasted with the construction of white and Indigenous women (and at times, Indigenous men) as being objects of white men's 'uncontrollable lust' (Fogarty 1992).

The amendment of sodomy laws in 1828 to allow convicted men to retain their property and property rights was founded on a possessive logic, whereby white men (albeit mediated by class and 'convict status') were a priori entitled to own land. Thus while men who were convicted may have had less symbolic capital, it still benefited both them and the white nation to recognise their status as citizens (particularly those of wealth). The following example demonstrates how possessive investments were managed in regard to convictions of sodomy.

In the case mentioned earlier, the defendant ended up escaping prosecution for sodomy, as the complainant failed to appear in court. However, the defendant was still subjected to scrutiny by the court as a result of the accusation. As Connors (1994: 99) reports, 'since [the defendant] was a ticket-of-leave holder, the mere allegation of attempted sodomy was damaging and the crown solicitor directed that he be returned to the bench of magistrates to decide the fate of his ticket'. A ticket of leave entitled a convict to work and live within a given area before their term had expired, and it also entitled them to own property. This again demonstrates how colonial law operated through a possessive logic, whereby it was beneficial for the law to be lenient in order to grant white men (regardless of their sexual acts) the right to own land. The granting of rights to (some) men convicted of crimes such as sodomy served a purpose for the white nation: it allowed more white people access to land ownership, and thus encouraged an investment in such ownership on the terms set by the white nation (which was anxious to refute Indigenous sovereignty).

These contradictory applications of the law (whereby white men were at times convicted of sodomy, but at the same time they were granted clemency in the form of a ticket of leave, or were allowed to maintain property rights following conviction) can be reconciled if viewed as constructing a range of 'aspirational practices'. These practices served to reinforce a series of hierarchies, within which homosexual white men could gain access (or 'aspire') to traditionally hetero-patriarchal institutions. Such aspirational practices not only outlined for homosexual men how to access certain privileges, but also directed the white heterosexual majority on how to 'stay white' (i.e. how to maintain their privileges). This racialisation of property rights thus encouraged all white people to adopt normative white values in relation to ownership, and to do so via the disavowal of Indigenous sovereignty.

Conclusions

From the starting point of critical race studies and the study of masculinities, herein are outlined some of the ways in which the study of race in conjunction with the study of gender and sexuality may contribute to the destabilisation of white hegemony. Exploring the complex ways in which privilege and oppression intersect may thus allow for a more nuanced understanding of race privilege, and the ways it is propped up by particular investments in patriarchal white sovereignty.

Understanding identities as multiple sites (rather than as singular) is one of the critical tools that race and gender studies have contributed to understandings of oppression. Exploring histories of complicity and resistance need not entail 'pointing the finger', or seeking to allocate blame per se. Rather, by researching intersections we may further our understanding of the ways in which racism and (hetero)sexism operate through social institutions that privilege certain groups over others. Critical race studies is thus one framework through which we may better understand these institutions, and challenge their authority in regard to privilege and oppression.

References and further reading

Aldrich, R. (2003) *Colonialism and Homosexuality*, London: Routledge.

Běrubě, A. (2001) 'How gay stays white and what kind of white it stays', in B.B. Rasmussen, E. Klinenberg, I.J. Nexica and M. Wray (eds) *The Making and Unmaking of Whiteness*, Durham, NC: Duke University Press, pp. 234–65.

Connors, L. (1994) 'Two opposed traditions: male popular culture and the criminal justice system in early Queensland', in R. Aldrich (ed.) *Gay Perspectives 2*, Sydney: University of Sydney Press, pp. 83–114.

Delago, R. (ed.) (1995) *Critical Race Theory: The Cutting Edge*, Philadelphia, PA: Temple University Press.

Flood, M. (2002) 'Between men and masculinity', in S. Pearce and V. Muller (eds) *Manning the Next Millennium: Studies in Masculinities*, Chicago, IL: Black Swan Press.

Fogarty, W.J. (1992) '"Certain habits": The development of the concept of the male homosexual in New South Wales law, 1788–1900', in R. Aldrich and G. Wotherspoon (eds) *Gay Perspectives*, Sydney: University of Sydney Press, pp. 59–76.

Greer, G. (1970) *The Female Eunuch*, London: HarperCollins.

Hollinsworth, D. (1998) *Race and Racism in Australia*, Katoomba: Social Science Press.

Moreton-Robinson, A. (2004) 'The possessive logic of patriarchal white sovereignty: the High Court and the Yorta Yorta decision', *Borderlands e-journal*, 3, available at http://www.borderlandsejournal.adelaide.edu.au/vol3no2_2004/moreton_possessive.htm

Nicoll, F. (2001) *From Diggers to Drag Queens*, Annandale, MN: Pluto.

Schloesser, P. (2002) *The Fair Sex*, New York: New York University Press.

Smith, P. (1993) *Feminist Jurisprudence*, Oxford: Oxford University Press.

Stoler, A.L. (1995) *Race and the Education of Desire*, Durham, NC: Duke University Press.

See also: race and ethnicity

DAMIEN W. RIGGS

CUCKOLDRY

A derisive name for the husband of an unfaithful wife, 'cuckold' derives from analogy with the female cuckoo, whose practice of laying eggs in another bird's nest was associated with infidelity. Cuckolds populate Medieval and Renaissance European art and literature, as well as church court records in cases of sexual slander, as Laura Gowing has demonstrated.

Much scholarship on cuckoldry focuses on its widespread appearance as a sign of inadequate masculinity (and its attendant anxieties) in sixteenth- and seventeenth-century theatre. Shakespeare scholar Coppélia Kahn demonstrates that the concept of cuckoldry intertwines three patriarchal ideologies: the belief in women's lustfulness; the double standard that disproportionately condemns female promiscuity; the dependence of a husband's honour on his wife's chastity. Using psychoanalytic theory, Kahn suggests that the traditional joke about the cuckold's horns reveals the presence of a psychological displacement: emasculated and figuratively reduced to a state of stupid animality by his wife, the cuckold sprouts shamefully visible phallic symbols on his head.

Katherine Maus and Bruce Boehrer explore the social and sexual dilemmas of cuckoldry as presented on the English Renaissance stage. Maus argues that through acts of theatrical voyeurism – witnessing or graphically imagining the scene of his sexual betrayal – the cuckold compensates for his emasculation through pride in his superior discernment. Yet once publicly exposed as a cuckold, he becomes a ridiculed, feminised spectacle himself. According to Boehrer, in Renaissance plays influenced by Ovid's *Amores* the cuckold fails to control not only his wife's but also his own sexual desires, hence exposing masculinity itself as an unattainable ideal.

Defining cuckoldry as a sexual act performed by a man on another man, Eve Sedgwick argues that heterosexual relations in the Restoration play *The Country Wife* primarily advance the formation of homosocial bonds. The successful cuckolder is a young aristocratic male who achieves masculinity by establishing sexual dominance over other men.

References and further reading

Boehrer, B. (2001) 'Ovid and the dilemma of the cuckold in English Renaissance drama', in G. Stanovukovic (ed.) *Ovid and the Renaissance Body*, Toronto: University of Toronto Press, pp. 171–88.

Gowing, L. (1996) *Domestic Dangers*, Oxford: Oxford University Press.

Kahn, C. (1981) *Man's Estate*, Berkeley, CA: University of California Press.

Maus, K.E. (1987) 'Horns of dilemma: jealousy, gender, and spectatorship in English Renaissance drama', *ELH*, 54: 561–83.

Sedgwick, E.K. (1985) *Between Men*, New York: Columbia University Press.

MARIO DI GANGI

CULTURAL FORMATIONS, AFRICA

In Africa, issues of masculinity and varying forms of masculinities have surfaced during recent years. The relationship between masculinity, gender and sexuality is increasingly addressed, prompted by the need to understand the impact of social change, many forms of violence, the HIV/AIDS pandemic, and how a colonial past, patriarchal cultural structures and different knowledge systems create masculine identities and sexualities (Lahouchine and Morrell 2005).

Inspired by Western feminism, gender and gender inequality have figured overwhelmingly on the research and 'development' agenda in Africa since the 1970s. Gender concepts have been forced into gender research in Africa, and gender largely appears as analytical shorthand for women's subordination within conjugal relationships (Cornwall 2005). Extensive enquiries were made into women's lives – not into men's lives. With African societies being strongly patriarchal, men are seen as drawing on the 'patriarchal dividend' (cf. Connell 1995), and as having access to privileges that women do not have. Focus, therefore, has been on the negative impact of patriarchal ideologies and on how these ideologies have caused gender inequality. From the presumption of an oppositional hierarchy between the categories women and men, and of men as the problem, the gender myths of contemporary gender and development continue to sustain interventions that seek to reshape African gender identities – just as in colonial times (Cornwall 2005).

In spite of contradictory images and different strands in the gender literature, with one portraying the African woman as the victim of male oppression and the other as the self-reliant agent who poses threat to normative conjugal relations, the first image dominates the gender and the development agenda. Images of men have been equally polarised, with men being portrayed either as powerful dominant figures, colluding with colonial or post-colonial institutions to deepen women's subordination or as rather useless characters that women can do without – yet at the same time treated as a unified homogeneous category.

However, reading African lives through this lens may misconstrue women's agency and overlook the realities of men's lives. Although the main axis of patriarchal power is still the overall subordination of women, a singular notion of patriarchy is inadequate to capture existing complexities (Cornwall 2005). Much recent work, though, continues to rely on static and unproblematised notions of patriarchy that overlook the fundamental changes in most African nations during the last century.

In order to understand masculinities in Africa, Lahouchine and Morrell (2005) suggest three necessary steps: first, a geopolitical approach that does not assume homogeneity or uniformity but that, in spite of vast differences, diversity and inequality, does recognise particular experiences of colonialism and development that have had profound effect on the wealth of the continent's people; second, an analytical framework that involves theories of masculinities, identifies power inequalities among men, and recognises that all men do not have the same opportunities or life trajectories; third, specific analyses of gender in Africa.

The geopolitical step

Very few attempts have been made to analyse in gendered terms how the legacy of colonialisation, globalisation and race have affected men's lives and produced complex forms of male identity. As a result of the European colonisation of Africa, men and women were confronted with collapsing traditional structures, new unstable situations, new social roles, contradicting norms and values and economic hardship. While research on women since the 1970s accumulated deep insights into the implications of socio-economic change, poverty and increasing workloads for African women, similar insights on men were not documented. In attempts to make African women's work visible, some analyses represented African rural men as doing very little (Whitehead 2000). Boserup's important observation (1980) that the change in women's work has been less radical than that in men's work was never pursued.

Throughout sub-Saharan Africa, missionaries and labour recruiters were catalysts for transforming men's gendered relationships and identities. Missionaries and administrators worked through churches, schools and workplaces, explicitly or implicitly propagating their own ideal of domesticity and men's place in households and marriages. As they intervened in politics, religion, legal systems, agricultural regimes and labour markets, European actors worked to remake men. Of particular importance was colonial administrators' encouragement of cash cropping and labour migration, because of which men became less able to control their wives than previously (Cornwall 2005; Lindsay and Miescher 2003; Silberschmidt 2001). Although colonial ideology sought to create male breadwinners, colonial practices had different results: when men were forced to migrate, when men's areas of responsibility were eliminated by the colonial powers, or when men's economic opportunities diminished, and women became heads of household and earned money as well. Men's changed role – or lack of role – had a strong impact on their masculinity, sexuality and the relations between genders.

Theories of masculinities

Masculinity is composed of elements, identities and behaviours that are not always coherent. They may be competing, contradictory and mutually undermining; they may have multiple and ambiguous meanings according to context, culture and time (Connell 1995). Ideologies of masculinity, like those of femininity, are culturally and historically constructed, their meanings continually contested and always in the process of being renegotiated in the context of existing power relations. While Western gender theories should be handled with care and perhaps revised in order to understand gender relations and categories of men and masculinity in Africa, all men do have access to the 'patriarchal dividend', i.e. the power that being a man gives them to choose and exercise power over women and sometimes over other men. Connell's distinction (1995) between hegemonic and subordinate masculinities opens up the possibility of examining subordinate masculinities and the ways in which some men may experience stigmatisation and marginalisation. Whereas in the West this examination has mainly focused on men stigmatised because of their sexual orientation, in Africa the psychological and economic effects of colonialisation have occupied the centre stage. This analysis has revealed that while men are predominantly the beneficiaries where gender inequities exist, not all men benefit to the same degree – indeed, some men do not benefit at all. Many pay heavy costs for the general supremacy of men in a patriarchal gender order that ignores their own vulnerability. Consequently, theories of patriarchy that consign men to stereotypical gender roles (as victimisers and exploiters of women) ignore men as gendered subjects and are neither sensitive nor appropriate tools for analysis.

Gender in present Africa

While colonialism has been perceived as an assault on African masculinity, African women and men were not simply subjects created by colonial gender discourse. They were actively engaged in reconfiguring their own identities. However, the contradictions that emerged during the colonial era between the realities of women's contributions to household provisioning and the inability of most men to sustain dependent wives still continue in post-colonial Africa. Therefore, defining gender roles and relations in terms of notions of patriarchy or of the different functions that men and women fulfil in response to gender norms fails to recognise the complexity, mobility and negotiated nature of contemporary gender roles and relations.

Poverty in most rural and urban contexts is massive and has caused economic hardship for both men and women. However, men and women have often responded differently to the economic crisis. While many men have withdrawn from their traditional responsibilities as head of household, women have been forced to take on new roles. Thus, structurally subordinate women have aggressively responded to the challenges of economic hardship. In this process, they have started to challenge men, their social value and their position as heads of household. Such challenges pose serious threats to men's honour, reputation and masculinity, and conflicts of interests embedded in gender relations become more visible. Although the main axis of patriarchal power is still the overall subordination of women, material conditions often undermine the normative order of patriarchy. With most men retaining a patriarchal ideology bereft of its legitimising activities, men's authority has come under threat and so have their identity and self-esteem. For patriarchy does not mean that men have only privileges. Men also have many responsibilities. The irony of the patriarchal system resides precisely in the fact that male authority has a material base while male responsibility is normatively constituted. This has made men's roles and identities confusing and contradictory (Silberschmidt 2001).

Persisting patriarchal structures and stereotyped notions of gender hide the increasing disempowerment of many men in both rural and urban contexts (ibid.). Caught between discursive domains that create variant images of masculinity, from responsible provider to insatiable lover, becoming a man is fraught with complications. Accused by wives of being useless and passed over by girlfriends for lacking satisfactory economic potency, men find themselves with diminishing control (Silberschmidt 2005; Lindsay and Miescher 2003; Silberschmidt, 2001). With the close link between masculinity and sexuality, male identity and self-esteem seem to have become increasingly linked to sexual manifestations – often acted out in violence and sexual aggressiveness. Consequently, multi-partnered/extra-marital and casual sexual relations are often fundamental to bolstering male self-esteem (Silberschmidt 2005, 2001).

Studies by Caldwell and collaborators (1989) have been influential for discussions of African systems of sexuality and male sexual behaviour in debates around AIDS. However, the proposed models have been severely criticised for emphasising African sexuality as permissive, if not promiscuous, and for overlooking values and morality surrounding manhood and sexuality (Heald 1999). While morality as well as respectability is central for male sexual behaviour and men's earning powers remain central in constructions of masculinity worldwide, most notions of masculinity are closely associated with virility, sexuality, potency, fertility and male honour (Cornwall and Lindisfarne 1994). This conjunction offers crucial new insights into issues of gender and sexuality; it has extensive theoretical and policy implications in terms of the HIV/AIDS epidemic (Silberschmidt 2005). However, just as men are missed as a target group in 'gendered' development initiatives (Chant and Gutman 2000), men are also omitted as active agents in combating HIV/AIDS – even if men have been identified as key actors in reducing HIV transmission (UNAIDS 2000). Men have been blamed and held responsible for women's deteriorating health because of culturally condoned male sexual behaviours, whereas men's prominent sexual and reproductive roles have not been clearly recognised. The AIDS pandemic, though, has promoted a debate about gender. Paradoxically, despite the severity of its destructive power, AIDS may serve as a leveller of conflicting gender interests, transforming gender relations and encouraging alliance-building and new ideas of masculinity (Cornwall 2005; Baylies and Bujra 2000).

In conclusion, the emerging studies of men and masculinities contribute to an understanding of how African masculinities, African male bodies, subjectivities and experiences are constituted in specific historical, cultural and social contexts. They underline that African masculinities are not uniform and monolithic, and masculine behaviour in Africa is not static. Instead they suggest the possible emergence of new, perhaps less violent and less oppressive ways of being masculine.

References and further reading

Baylies, C. and Bujra, J. (2000) *Aids, Sexuality and Gender in Africa*, London: Routledge.

Boserup, E. (1980) 'African women in production and household', in C. Presvelou, S. Spijkiers-Zwart, H. Weenmann and B.V. Zonen (eds) *The Household, Women and Agricultural Development*, Wageningen: H. Weenmann and B.V. Zonen, pp. 237–47.

Caldwell, J.C., Caldwell, P. and Quiggin, P. (1989) 'The social context of AIDS in sub-Saharan Africa', *Population and Development Review*, 15: 185–234.

Chant, S. and Gutman, M. (2000) *Mainstreaming Men into Gender and Development*, Oxford: Oxfam.

Connell, R. (1995) *Masculinities*, Cambridge: Polity.

Cornwall, A. (2005) 'Introduction', in A. Cornwall (ed.) *Readings in Gender in Africa*, Bloomington, IN and Oxford: Indiana University Press and James Curry, pp. 2–20.

Cornwall, A. and Lindisfarne, N. (1994) 'Dislocating masculinity', in A. Cornwall and N. Lindisfarne (eds) *Dislocating Masculinity*, London: Routledge, pp. 11–47.

Heald, S. (1999) *Manhood and Morality*, London and New York: Routledge.

Lahouchine, O. and Morrell, R. (eds) (2005) *African Masculinities*, New York and South Africa: Palgrave Macmillan and KwaZulu-Natal Press.

Lindsay, L.A. and Miescher, S. F. (eds) (2003) *Men and Masculinities in Modern Africa*, Portsmouth: Heinemann.

Silberschmidt, M. (2001) 'Disempowerment of men in rural and urban East Africa', *World Development*, 29 (4): 657–71.

—— (2005) 'Poverty, male disempowerment, and sexuality', in O. Lahouchine and R. Morrell (eds) *African Masculinities*, New York and South Africa: Palgrave Macmillan and KwaZulu-Natal Press.

UNAIDS (2000) *Men Make a Difference*, Geneva: UNAIDS.

Whitehead, A. (2000) 'Continuities and discontinuities in political constructions of the working man in rural sub-Saharan Africa', *European Journal of Development Research*, 12 (2): 23–53.

MARGRETHE SILBERSCHMIDT

CULTURAL FORMATIONS, ASIA AND PACIFIC

Interest in constructions of masculinities in the richly diverse Asia-Pacific region has grown enormously since 2000. This interest has been catalysed by the influence on Asian male and female international students of exposure to diverse representations and practices of masculinities; Asian feminist critiques of gender inequalities and exploitation of female migrant labour; critiques of epistemological and ontological biases in applying Western ideas in the East; changing economies in

Asia affecting employment, household labour, consumer behaviour, technology and popular culture; transnationalism and globalisation. Influential Chinese and Indian diasporas have also had significant economic, political and cultural impacts.

While prior theoretical work and empirical studies have been dominated by Western academics, Chinese and Japanese academics and to a lesser extent Indian academics are developing more culturally sensitive concepts of male gender identity and questioning comparative studies that use purportedly universal concepts.

In China and Japan, contradictions between the political structure in the former and economic recession in the latter and global economic changes and consumerism destabilised the status and power of men as well as constructions of masculinity. Such fluctuations have also been experienced in Korea and Taiwan. Lu (1993) points to the misogynistic discourse of Chinese literature in the 1980s, especially among male authors who sought masculinity by asserting their individuality and nostalgic longings for cultural authority while protesting Communism's ostensibly egalitarian ideology. Similarly, Zhong (2000: 15) argues that post-Mao Chinese literature and culture deplored a lack of 'masculine' identity and expressed men's desire for rebellion. In the People's Republic of China, Brownell and Wasserstrom (2002: 33) suggest that market reforms have created an atmosphere of anxiety for men who no longer understand the standards for success for proving masculinity. Incursions of the global marketplace have made local benchmarks of masculinity less predictable. Litzinger (2002: 417) warns that representations of masculine and feminine ethnic subjects in China are characterised by shifting meanings, unstable power relations and inherent contradictions. In Japan, economic recession undercut the masculine stereotype of the salaryman, stripping men's benefits of lifetime employment, promotion by seniority and company unionism (Roberson and Suzuki 2003: 9).

Louie (2002) provides a comprehensive historical and social constructionist account of masculinity in China. Discarding the old *yin–yang* binary, Louie proposes instead an opposition between *wen* (the mental and civic) and *wu* (the physical or martial). The *wen–wu* paradigm invokes two forms of Chinese masculinity: the scholar's and the soldier's. Louie contends that throughout Chinese history the ideal man would be expected to embody a balance of *wen* and *wu* (2002: 11).

Traditionally, *wen* masculinity was characterised by literary excellence, civilised behaviour, general education and genteel qualities associated with artistic pursuits of classical scholars. *Wu* qualities included powerful physique, fearlessness and fighting skills. The meanings associated with these qualities changed over time. Communism and Western capitalism, especially exposure to Western media, cinema and the Internet, provide other models of manliness. Although economic success was traditionally given little emphasis, over time the accumulation of business skills and success in the marketplace have taken on new significance. The place of sexuality and sexual performance in the *wen–wu* binary has also changed, as have attitudes to women, and all these attitudes vary according to ethnicities and social class. Increasing movement of Chinese males to the West for education has introduced Western concepts of maleness, whereas the increasing popularity of martial arts films in the West has changed the images of Chinese manly valour (Louie 2002: 13), thus indicating the mutual influences of globalisation on masculinities.

In a comparison to white American males, Chua and Fujino (1999) classify the masculinity of Asian–American males as 'flexible' masculinity. These males, unlike their white American counterparts, do not oppose their masculinity to their femininity. They engage more with their offspring and with housework. In contrast, recently arrived Asian migrants emphasise the traditional masculine values of patriarchal China where males value being sole providers and protectors of their families.

In contrast, Chinese male migrants to Australia were ambivalent about their spouse's working despite the duration of settlement (Hibbins 2003). Where Chinese males were unemployed, they felt pressures from kin and loss of status and power.

In Western academic literature the Asian male 'other' has been seen as emasculated, feminised and infantilised. Stereotypes that appeared during the gold rushes in North America and Australia depict Chinese males as inscrutable, sexually bizarre and a threat to the employment of Caucasian women. Fung describes Western stereotypes of the Asian man as either an 'egghead/wimp' or 'the kung fu master/ninja/samurai', sometimes dangerous, sometimes friendly, but always characterised by a desexualised Zen asceticism (cited in Tasker 1997: 328). Similar Western stereotypes of Japanese males appeared during World War II. Such depictions focused on physical characteristics like body size, colour of hair and eye shape and to a lesser extent on sexuality.

The extent to which Asian men have lived up (or down) to the stereotypes has been debated in the literature. Ayres' film *China Dolls* (1997) documents Chinese gay men who try to whiten their skin and develop more muscular bodies. They initially prefer prestigious Caucasian partners but eventually recognise the diversities of gay masculinities among both Chinese and Caucasian men. The 'nerd' stereotype has also been recently aimed at Asian males who are academically inclined and work in the information technology and engineering professions.

Discussions surrounding hegemonic or dominant variants of masculinities within ethnic groups as well as between ethnic groups pervade the identity literature. For example, in Australia dominant males are stereotypically sport-loving, beer-swilling, well-muscled, heterosexual, homophobic and ready to brag about women they have 'conquered'.

Recent depictions of Asian masculinities have been influenced by changing economic contexts in Japan and China and particularly among Asian male migrants in the diaspora in North America, Australia and the Pacific. Such representations focus on the increasing importance of financial success and consumerism. Louie argues that such worldly possessions would have been perceived as vulgar and even barbarian in traditional Confucian constructions of *wen* masculinity. Fluctuating economic circumstances in Asia have been associated with debates about 'the sick man of Asia'. With Japan's economic ascent during the late 1980s and early 1990s, the 'salaryman' became prominent, and economic success measured masculine dominance. With economic recession, uncertainty and vulnerability entered debates about Asian masculinity. During this decline in Japan, Asia experienced the economic rise of mainland China, the rise and fall of Hong Kong and Taiwan. Family, kin, marriage are now accompanied by economic success as measures of masculine dominance. With increasing divorce rates, economic recession and greater emphasis on the upwardly mobile young executive, traditional measures of dominance for middle-aged Japanese males are uncertain.

While comparative studies are methodologically useful, they also give insights into difference and constructions of the 'other'. More importantly, however, they show the hazards of false universalism where Asian masculinity(ies) and Asian/Pacific cultural formations omit nuanced differences between ethnic groups. When 'Asian' is seen collectively, ethnic minority differences are ignored. This blindness is as epistemologically and ontologically dangerous as omitting considerations of the intersections of gender, ethnicity, sexuality and class.

Attitudes to sexuality and particularly homosexuality and public displays of physicality have changed, particularly in mainland China. Homosexuality was practised traditionally in China. Only with the growth of communism in the PRC and Christianity in Hong Kong has homophobia emerged and male homosexuality been stigmatised. Louie (2002: 245) suggests that Chinese sexuality is less a site of struggle than in the West. Further, Louie (2002: 158) argues that whereas *wen* men made love to women, *wu* heroes regarded women as obstacles to true brotherhood and only made love (Platonic or otherwise) to their sworn brothers. Because traditional values stress the importance of marriage, family and kin, in both China and Japan many gay males are married.

Most gay males in Japan and China don't 'come out' in the Western sense. In discussing the importance of the Internet for homosexual cruising, McLelland (2003: 72) suggests that coming out for Japanese men is more a coming to terms with homosexual desire. He also refers to the difficulties of the Japanese language in expressing Western notions of 'coming out' and to the Japanese media's conflation of homosexuality, transgender and cross-dressing (McLelland 2000). In both China and Japan, self-disclosure by gay men is limited to very close friends. Chinese gay male migrants in Australia report needing to be circumspect regarding public disclosure, social milieux and locales for fear of local homophobic practices (Hibbins 2005). As in Korea, gay men in Japan are considered more 'feminine' than straight men, best suited to lives in the entertainment world and as best friends for women; however, such stereotypes flatten the diversity among gay males, who fall along a continuum from those who manifest hypermasculine qualities to those who appear more 'feminine' (McLelland 2003: 74).

Altman (2001: 93) reports that even the most politically aware gay Malaysians insist that there is no need to come out to their family because lovers are accepted by the family, although the harshness of sharia law may also be a factor in Malaysian discretion. The examples of Fiji and Indonesia point to the problems associated with ethnicity and generational differences faced by Indian and Chinese males in their respective diasporas in the Asia Pacific region. In Fiji, for example, Indian families cannot own land even though traditionally their families were farm labourers. Indians experienced racism and discrimination in Fiji, and many migrated to Australia. The Indians who remained, like the Chinese in Indonesia, moved into small commercial businesses where they face an uncertain future. Males are vulnerable in these cases where traditional markers of masculinity are uncertain. Young educated males in Samoa also face an uncertain future where unemployment is high, as are risk behaviour, rates of crime, depression rates and suicide. Samoa today seems far removed from the idyllic islands portrayed in the groundbreaking work of Margaret Mead as a culture of gentle permissiveness, free of tensions and anxieties. Other scholarship, in contrast, depicts Samoan culture as rigid, hierarchical, puritanical and watchful. Samoa is typical of many island nations in the Pacific where there are clashes between the older males and tradition and younger males influenced by consumerism depicted on Western television. Samoan young people migrate in large numbers to the USA, New Zealand or Australia to avoid conflicts with elders, especially male chiefs, often fuelled by alcohol. In both Fiji and Samoa the sport of rugby union is popular and seen as a rite of passage by males who can make it into national teams. Some have called it a 'second faith' in islands that are strongly influenced by Christianity.

The emerging cultural studies, historical and social scientific literature on male gender identity in Asia and the Pacific has introduced the need for culturally sensitive concepts and methodologies. This literature is spotty. In particular there is little research work on ethnic minorities, marginalised groups and indigenous peoples. Wasserstrom and Brownell (2002: 441) suggest there is a need for more work on gender in local and regional identities in China, and for more work that places gender within the context of the larger regions of East Asian and Asia. Louie's works satisfy this in part, but the cross-currents between gender in Japan, South Korea, Hong Kong, Taiwan and mainland China need to be explored. Further, consideration of the intersections of gender, sexuality, ethnicity and social class in studies of constructions of masculinities in the Asia/Pacific area is needed. This region is undergoing massive sociocultural transformation against the background of globalisation and transnationalism that has unpredictable outcomes for male identity formation.

References and further reading

Altman, D. (2001) *Global Sex*, Crows Nest, NSW: Allen and Unwin.

Brownell, S. and Wasserstrom, J.N. (eds) (2002) *Chinese Feminisms, Chinese Masculinities: A Reader*, Berkeley, CA: University of California Press.

Chua, P. and Fujino, D.C. (1999) 'Negotiating new Asian-American masculinities', *Journal of Men's Studies*, 7 (3): 391–413.

Connell, R. (2003) 'Australian masculinities', in S. Tomsen and M. Donaldson (eds) *Male Trouble*, North Melbourne: Pluto, pp. 9–21.

Fung, R. (1995) 'Burdens of representation, burdens of responsibility', in M. Berger, B. Wallis and S. Watson (eds) *Constructing Masculinity*, New York: Routledge, pp. 291–8.

Hibbins, R. (2003) 'Male gender identities among Chinese male migrants', in K. Louie and M. Low (eds) *Asian Masculinities*, London: Routledge Curzon, pp. 197–214.

—— (2005) 'Migration and gender identity among Chinese skilled male migrants in Australia', *Geoforum*, 36: 167–80.

Litzinger, R. (2002) 'Tradition and the gender of civility' in S. Brownell and J.N. Wasserstrom (eds) *Chinese Feminisms, Chinese Masculinities: A Reader*, Berkeley, CA: University of California Press, pp. 412–34.

Louie, K. (2002) *Theorising Chinese Masculinity*, Cambridge: Cambridge University Press.

Louie, K. and Low, M. (eds) (2003) *Asian Masculinities*, London: Routledge Curzon.

Lu, T. (ed.) (1993) *Gender and Sexuality in Twentieth Century Chinese Literature and Society*, Albany, NY: State University of New York Press.

McLelland, M.J. (2000) *Male Homosexuality in Modern Japan*, Surrey: Curzon.

—— (2003) 'Gay men, masculinity and the media in Japan' in K. Louie and M. Low (eds) *Asian Masculinities*, London: Routledge Curzon, pp. 59–78.

Roberson, J. and Suzuki, N. (eds) (2003) *Men and Masculinities in Contemporary Japan*, London: RoutledgeCurzon.

Tasker, Y. (1997) 'Fists of fury', in H. Stecopoulos and M. Uebel (eds) *Race and the Subject of Masculinities*, Durham, NC: Duke University Press, pp. 315–36.

Wasserstrom, J.N. and Brownell, S. (2002) 'Afterword', in S. Brownell and J.N. Wasserstrom (eds) *Chinese Feminisms, Chinese Masculinities: A Reader*, Berkeley, CA: University of California Press, pp. 435–45.

Zhong, X. (2000) *Masculinity Besieged?* Durham, NC: Duke University Press.

RAY HIBBINS

CULTURAL FORMATIONS, EUROPE

The notion of culture has been deployed in many ways within European contexts, often to explain 'other' cultures as well as European ones. These include: characterising the social life of nation-states as supposedly 'gender-neutral', even though it is men who are often foregrounded, and explaining and justifying men's actions, especially men's negative actions, such as violence to women. In all such uses, we can ask: whose culture is being invoked, and how are these references gendered, implicitly or explicitly, in relation to men and masculinities? More precisely, do 'national' or 'regional cultures' in fact refer to (certain) men's cultures?

This entry focuses on the position and impact of men in the context of changing societal and cultural dynamics within Europe, especially within the EU (Hearn and Pringle 2006). The analysis builds on earlier work on women's gendered relations to culture(s) in European contexts. Our broadly sociological perspective regards 'cultures' as relatively stable, but nevertheless contested, dynamic configurations of beliefs and practices. Here we seek to rectify the relative neglect and yet gradually growing analysis of gendered economic, political, cultural, welfare and state regimes in central and Eastern Europe. A similar relative neglect applies to the southern regions of Europe compared with the greater attention paid to northern and western regions.

There are many complex ways in which gendered power relations associated with dominant forms of masculinity are entering the processes whereby the EU, its member states and associated countries are seeking to redefine what is 'Europe' and what it is to be 'European'. The part played by gender relations, specifically those associated with masculinities, within these processes has largely been kept invisible in both policy and academia.

Research attention in northern, southern and western Europe has focused far more on 'the problems that men endure' compared to the attention devoted to 'the problems that men create'. The EU's own research and policy approach to men's practices has largely mirrored this imbalance in concerning itself far more with issues such as reducing limitations on men as carers and improving men's working conditions and health, rather than on topics such as men's violences to women and children.

While some shifts are occurring in the EU's approach, EU policy and research priorities still remain tilted in favour of the 'problems that men endure'. Even the attention of the EU to the trafficking of women, pornography and the sexual exploitation of children betrays these priorities. In the past that attention largely focused on the activities of EU citizens (mainly men) outside the territory of the EU – typically in parts of central and Eastern Europe and south and east Asia. This emphasis obscured the systematic abuse and exploitation of women and children within the EU-15 (Pringle 1998). Now that some countries in central and Eastern Europe are themselves EU members, the development of EU policy on these issues is of considerable interest.

In the past, the EU and its member states frequently separated the issue of trafficking women and children from prostitution and pornography; moreover, policy debate around trafficking has often been dealt with in the broader context of policies on inward migration. This association, even confusion, in policy terms, along with the allied topic of racism, demonstrates how power relations associated with dominant forms of masculinity enter into the processes that construct the idea of 'Europe'. Racism is widespread throughout Europe, even if its precise configurations vary from one cultural context to another. Yet the issue of dominant forms of masculinity is remarkably absent in debates on racism in Europe; the relative silence about men's practices and racism in European academic and policy debate is particularly noteworthy. Often central to the issues of racism in Europe and how EU member states treat migrants are questions about what is 'Europe', who is 'European' and who is 'more European' – who is 'other'? Such questions may often be partly about 'whose masculinity' is 'purer' or 'superior'. Yet both the pre-2004 member states of the EU and the European Commission itself have largely avoided confronting those highly gendered issues in their policies to combat racism and address migration. The part played by power relations associated with dominant forms of masculinity in the processes of 'Europe creation' – including both pre-2004 and newer member states – has thus been disguised and ignored.

In recent years the position of Muslims has become especially problematic for many in the Christian White western supposed 'centre(s)' – even though Muslims comprise a large and long-established set of communities in some regions of 'Europe'. As with other taken-for-granted dominant 'centres' (Hearn 1996), Europe or Europeans rarely deconstruct themselves in reference to the discourses of 'elsewhere' further east: the Orient, Asia, Africa and so on. However, transnational collective memories on a European scale are becoming more clearly articulated, whether in terms of the Holocaust, the EU as a legal entity, 'parliamentary democracy' or difference from other powers and continents. Paradoxically, at the cultural level, Europe is both affirming a coherent identity in relation to 'others' and blurring its own divisions of 'east' and 'west'.

Historically, European nation-states have developed differently, establishing differing civil societies and so forming and re-forming different men, masculinities and men's practices. Within the rapidly changing and gendered configurations of Europe there are multiple variations and, moreover, complications and contradictions. Some clear differences exist in recent political history between the following: the countries of the EU-15; those of western Europe outside the EU (Iceland, Norway, Switzerland); those ten countries that joined the EU-25 in 2004; those awaiting accession; and those not in the accession process. These last three categories include both those that were previously communist regimes and those that were not – so giving eight different geopolitical locations (see Pringle *et al.* 2006).

However, there remains a danger of over-generalising about men's practices within the complex context of political, economic and social restructurings. In considering regional comparisons, it is important to minimise 'western European-centrism' so as not to make western European nation-states or welfare states the reference point against which to compare experiences and outcomes elsewhere in Europe. A recent World Economic Forum Report (Lopez-Claros and Zahidi 2005) concluded that the five Nordic countries lead in woman's empowerment, in terms of economic, political, educational and health and well-being measures. Yet, at the same time, major dominations of men persist in these countries, for example in business, violence, the military, academia and religion (Hearn 2002; Pringle 2005; Balkmar and Pringle 2006; Hearn and Pringle 2006). Similarly, while Trifiletti (1999) offers a thoroughly persuasive feminist analysis of gender relations within the welfare structures of southern Europe, she cautions against over-simplistic assessments using purely north-west European frames of reference.

Furthermore, various contradictions persist, both within gender relations and between gender relations and other social relations; these are major barriers to generalisation. Different trajectories in, say, economic, religious or cultural power are part of the production not just of complications but of contradictions in gender relations around men and masculinities. Gender relations, both dominant and subordinated gender relations, may intersect and contradict social relations of other forms.

A first set of contradictions, and indeed a further antagonism to over-generalisation, concerns the multiple and complex impacts of social changes from beyond societies. Analysis of gender, men and women requires a long-term comparative historical analysis of how cultural meanings of gender have been constituted, stabilised and destabilised in specific settings. National histories represent extremely rich yet still under-researched potential archives for the investigation of the construction of men's relations to gender orders (Novikova *et al.* 2003; Novikova 2006). Dominance remains a key dimension of social structures in previously subject European countries whose gender relations have historically been part of diverse European imperial configurations often with associated large-scale inequalities. Most states and cultures of central and Eastern Europe, together with their perceived European identity, have been historically shaped by forces of exclusion and marginalisation, as well as by shared peripherality to various and differing historical political blocs: the German, Russian, British, Austro-Hungarian and Ottoman empires.

Over the last two decades, labour and gender inequalities have been restructured across Europe in interdependent, often contradictory, ways through the interplay of quite different political economic systems – most obviously, the previously socialist or Soviet system and the developing capitalist, often neo-liberal system. This has involved changing forms of transnational economic restructurings, labour migration and domestic service across altered borders, with gender hierarchies, including those among men, produced and maintained in relation to transnational circuits of labour mobilisation and capital accumulation. Transnational (trans-European) labour migration, with its gender hierarchies, confronts welfare policies. These have been the contexts for producing gender equality policies and gender mainstreaming within national and supranational agendas of Europe and the EU. In central and Eastern Europe, they intersect with and may contradict post-socialist reformist agendas, with national machineries defusing gender challenges. These issues of men and masculinities in east-central Europe, the Baltic states and the countries of the New Independent Commonwealth need to be contextualised within such regional and national developments, and similarly with the way the gendering of cultures and nations has 'organised' variable routes into modern formations of nation-state and citizenship. In such postcolonial contexts some categories of men have benefited markedly, whether through a reinforcement of traditional family authority or economic success, while others, for example ex-military, minority ethnic and unemployed men, have experienced major destabilising changes in their lives.

Looking to the future, great gender uncertainty and contradictions continue. The pattern of alliances around the Iraq War and contested debates on the European Constitution and the EU budget may suggest new cleavages between east and west, 'Old Europe' and 'New Europe'. Possible inter-societal divisions may be accompanied by growing polarisation among men within some national societies, with tendencies towards greater marginalisation of the poor and greater accumulation for the rich. How far dominant power relations can be subverted in transformation by the rapidly changing societies of central and Eastern Europe will be crucial for the well-being of all living there, especially women and children, but also men.

Even more complex questions apply to rapidly changing, economic, political, cultural and gendered configurations in Turkey, the Balkans, the Middle East, the huge Asian expanses of the Russian Federation and the Central Asian Republics, and their often ambiguous relations to 'Europe' or the rest of Europe. There are also growing attempts to redefine Europe, politically and economically, in different ways, in relation to China and Africa. Meanwhile, intersections of state militarism and non-state terrorism, both heavily dominated by men, are not only being brought to the streets and subways of Europe – Moscow, Madrid, London, elsewhere – but are also ways of defining 'the West'/'Europe' and 'the East', and producing 'Europe' as a new collective actor in foreign policy, as well as the ongoing production of 'others'.

References and further reading

Balkmar, D. and Pringle, K. (2006) *Sweden National Reports on Men's Practices – Reports on Research, Statistical Information, Law and Policy, EU FP6 CAHRV*, Stockholm: Centre for Gender Studies, University of Stockholm.

Hearn, J. (1996) 'Deconstructing the dominant', *Organization*, 3 (4): 611–26.

—— (2002) 'Nation, state and welfare', in B. Pease and K. Pringle (eds) *A Man's World*, London: Zed Books, pp. 85–102.

—— (2003) 'Men: power, challenges of power and the "big picture" of globalisation', in I. Novikova and D. Kambourov (eds) *Men and Masculinities in the Global World*, Helsinki: Kikimora, Aleksantteri Institute, pp. 45–74.

Hearn, J. and Pringle, K., with Critical Studies on Men in Europe (CROME) (2006) *European Perspectives on Men and Masculinities*, Houndmills: Palgrave Macmillan.

Lopez-Claros, A. and Zahidi, S. (2005) *Women's Empowerment*, Geneva: World Economic Forum. Available at http://www.weforum.org/pdf/Global_Competitiveness_Reports/Reports/gender_gap.pdf

Novikova, I., Pringle, K., Oleksy, E. and Hearn, J. (2003) '"Men", Europe and postsocialism', in I. Novikova and D. Kambourov (eds) *Men and Masculinities in the Global World*, Helsinki: Kikimora Publishers, Aleksantteri Institute, pp. 75–102.

Pringle, K. (1998) *Children and Social Welfare in Europe*, Buckingham: Open University Press.

—— (2005) 'Neglected issues in Swedish child protection policy and practice', in M. Eriksson, M. Hester, S. Keskinen and K. Pringle (eds) *Tackling Men's Violences in Families – Nordic Issues and Dilemmas*, Bristol: Policy Press, pp. 155–71.

Pringle, K., Hearn, J. Ferguson, H., Kambourov, D., Kolga, (2006) *Men and Masculinities in Europe*, London: Whiting and Birch.

Trifiletti, R. (1999) 'Southern European welfare regimes and the worsening position of women', *Journal of European Social Policy*, 9: 49–64.

JEFF HEARN
KEITH PRINGLE

CULTURAL FORMATIONS, LATIN AMERICA

Beginning in the 1990s, numerous studies of men and masculinities in Latin America began to make significant conceptual and substantive contributions to the field overall. Despite the vast area covered – with hundreds of millions of people, more than twenty countries and over 100 languages spoken – in the 1990s scholarly research on hombres and homens in Latin America became integrated into gender studies as a whole.

Scholarship on men and masculinities in Latin America was initiated and developed in good measure by feminist women as an outgrowth of their previous work in the 1970s on women's oppression and feminist movements. In contrast to the English-speaking world, in Latin America the field was thus seen from the beginning as an integral part of gender studies and the struggle against gender inequalities. The study of masculinities in Latin America also emerged from practical efforts to understand and combat AIDS. In this respect, the study of AIDS illustrates another noteworthy feature of the study of masculinities in Latin America: that social problems and their solutions are of enduring significance in academic scholarship.

There is a tendency in research on masculinities in Latin America to oversimplify supposed common traits found among men generally in the region as a whole and to equate manliness with particular national or regional qualities, as if distinctions among men within the region mattered little and as if women were not also active participants in the creation and transformation of cultural traits in general. The tension between generalising for Latin American men overall and emphasising cultural diversity between men continues to provoke debate and controversy. Similarly, the impact on the region of gender stereotypes about the region that emanate elsewhere is a reflection of the conceptualisation outside Latin America of a solitary Latin American mestizo male. Other men – black and Indian men and men who have sex with other men, for example – have been largely ignored and/or misrepresented.

Many initial studies of masculinities in Latin America were conducted by anthropologists, historians, psychologists, sociologists and researchers in public health. Although some disciplines, area concentrations and interests have been better represented than others in the field, feminist studies on the relationship of men to gender inequality and attention to AIDS and same-sex sex have been consistent concerns within the emerging scholarship on men and masculinities throughout Latin America.

In the 1990s, several North Americans wrote excellent ethnographies and histories in English of men and masculinities in Latin America. During the same period there was a simultaneous boom in research on this subject written in Spanish and Portuguese in Latin America. But very few of these Spanish and Portuguese studies were translated into English, and for this reason many English-only scholars have not had access to the investigations and conclusions of their Latin American colleagues.

By the end of the 1980s in social science scholarship in Latin America generally, renewed attention was paid to questions of daily life, emotions and feelings and gender relations. As the working class became less central to much scholarship on the region, the so-called new social movements – among them the feminist movement – opened the way for new theoretical conceptions and new social concerns.

Theories of hegemonic and marginal masculinities have been adapted to specific local conditions in studies throughout the region, and more recently concepts developed in queer theory have helped researchers frame certain aspects of their investigations relating to subordinate forms of masculinity. Among the important studies of masculinity and the body in Latin America have been those by Leal (1995) and Viveros (2002). Leal, for example, notes that gaucho identity is strongly linked to masculine identity and described cultural expressions of the former such as myths, enchantments and seduction magic, verbal duels and representations of death.

Among the areas of research that have been developed in the study of masculinity in Latin America, some of the most promising have focused on questions of family divisions of labour, parenting and housework; homosociality in friendship and social spaces; masculine identity construction; reproductive health issues concerning same-sex sex, active and passive sexuality, AIDS and male reproductive rights; ethnicity and masculinity among indigenous, Afro-Latino and mestizo populations; class and work; and the infamous matter of machismo (see Gutmann 1996, 2003).

With respect to ethnicity and race, for instance, in Latin American societies it has become necessary to think about the various ways in which masculine identities are constructed in various social sectors, ethnic groups and sociocultural contexts. Although still too few in number, studies already conducted on ethnicity, race and masculinity in Latin America have drawn important conclusions and indicate several new areas for future research regarding the importance of recognising multiple masculinities across ethnic and racial lines, as well as the fact that there are no essential 'Latin' masculinities that cross all these lines. Just as it is important to recognise multiple masculinities across ethnic and racial lines, it is also necessary to understand that there is no essential black, gaucho or indigenous masculinity in Latin America.

Of the many specific topics of significant discussion and disagreement in the study of men and masculinities in Latin America at the beginning of the twenty-first century, we would highlight three. One, as indicated above, is the subject of same-sex sex. By the late 1990s, most scholars carefully avoided simplistic employment of the term 'homosexual' to refer to men who have sex with other men in the region, and many began to question the dichotomous representation of active and passive participants in same-sex sex as poorly representative of the realities of these men's lives. Work on Brazil and Mexico has been especially fruitful in developing these distinctions. Parker (1999) in Brazil and Núñez (1994) in Mexico have shown that the active–passive dichotomy with which previous scholars have characterised same-sex sex in those countries can miss as much as it captures with respect to changing norms and actual sexual practices.

Another topic of controversy in the region has related to understanding change and resilience, and more specifically how much men have changed in recent years. One area of research has been new forms of masculine domination and contradictions between modern discourses and so-called traditional practices. More generally, there has been considerable debate regarding diverse factors involved in change, such as political movements, modernisation efforts with respect to education, reproductive health and changing employment patterns.

Finally, in a general sense it is important to note certain general differences evident in studies conducted from, in contrast to those about, Latin America. Scholars from Latin America often are especially concerned with developing and adapting theories for the complex conditions pertaining in different parts of the region, and they have shown themselves more reticent to adopt wholesale theories of hegemonic masculinity, for example, that initially emerged from distinct European and US historical and cultural contexts. It goes without saying that sweeping generalisations about 'Latin American men' or 'Latin American machismo', for example – stereotypes as often as not grounded in the colonial imaginary and European notions of modernity – are encountered far more in the studies written by scholars writing outside than by researchers writing from within the region.

The study of men as engendered and engendering beings in Latin America has since its onset adopted a more unambiguous critical feminist lens for understanding men-as-men within general paradigms delineating power and inequality. The 'me-tooism' which developed in parallel in certain wings of men's studies in North America and Europe has been far less influential in Latin America. With respect to announcements of the death of antiquated masculinity, one need not adopt the view that there is a new man who has surfaced from the Argentine pampas to the shallows of the Rio Grande River, nor claim that challenges to men and masculinity are novel phenomena of our contemporary age, in order to recognise that men and women throughout Latin America have been grappling with what seem to many to be new ideas and relationships related to their masculine identities.

Despite differences of class, ethnic group, region and generation, Latin America is still seen by many as constituting in some palpable sense a coherent area of historical and cultural commonalties with respect to certain aspects of gender and sexuality. That is, despite the real and unanimous acknowledgement of the profound impact of globalisation on sexualities throughout Latin America, there is still simultaneously the deep-seated sense that these global influences were still filtered through particular, local, Latin American contexts. For this reason, in order to understand men and masculinities in the region, we are compelled to seek more than simply the Latin versions of global trends and transformations.

Although we find pan-Latin frameworks altogether inaccurate, we are compelled nonetheless to ask how sexualities in Latin America are part of global processes of change, those transformations underway since the late twentieth century which carry profound implications for sexualities in the Latin Americas. Parker (1999) and Olavarría (2003), for example, demonstrate the relationship between changing masculinities and economic changes evident in neoliberal programmes on reproductive health, the growing number of women working outside the home for money, and the expansion of international sex markets.

Brennan (2004) documents how Europeans travel to the north coast of the Dominican Republic to live out their racialised fantasies among Dominican and Haitian women. Politically men and masculinities in Latin America have been affected in dramatic ways by feminist projects in the region and globally, by urban movements for social services in which women have often played a significant role and men have been challenged by women's independence and initiative (see Fuller 2001; Gutmann 1996), by general trends towards democratisation that have raised new issues of cultural citizenship including with respect to gender differences (see Viveros 2002; Gutmann 2003), and by AIDS activism in many countries of the region, including the important correlation between social development and social networks for gay communities and the resulting reduction of risk in sexual behaviour (see Parker 1999).

Demographically, mass access to modern forms of contraception and the consequent fall in birth rates has tested gender/sexuality identities, behaviour and roles in intimate and associational ways, while the fact that girls' attendance rates at school have risen more quickly than boys' has had obvious implications in numerous ways, including the training and qualifications of women and men for various sectors of employment. The shift from more uniformly differentiated divisions of household labour in the countryside to situations which have given rise to greater fluidity in gender employment patterns as a result of modernisation and urbanisation has accordingly had dramatic consequences for men and women as they have become more thoroughly incorporated into wage labour relations.

Research is needed in several areas relating to men and masculinity in Latin America. As mentioned, the relationship between ethnicity, race and masculinity in the region is an important topic for future work. Another concerns various aspects of masculinity and violence, from state-sponsored wars to domestic abuse to questions of criminality. Despite recent work on reproductive health, additional studies on issues as diverse as AIDS and vasectomies are necessary. Although some histories of masculinity in Latin America have appeared in English, we need to better distinguish between genuinely more novel identities and social relations involving men and women and those sometimes too casually termed 'traditional'. More generally, there is some urgency to bring gender analysis into areas of research involving men but in which men have not been treated as engendered and engendering beings themselves, such as the displaced of Colombia, Mexican migrants in the United States, and the political hierarchies throughout the continent.

References and further reading

Brennan, D. (2004) *What's Love Got to Do with It?* Durham, NC: Duke University Press.

Chant, S. (2002) *Gender in Latin America*, New Brunswick, NJ: Rutgers University Press.

Fuller, N. (2001) *Masculinidades*, Lima: Pontificia Universidad Católica del Perú.

Gutmann, M.C. (1996) *The Meanings of Macho*, Berkeley, CA: University of California Press.

—— (ed.) (2003) *Changing Men and Masculinities in Latin America*, Durham, NC: Duke University Press.

Lancaster, R.N. (1992) *Life is Hard*, Berkeley, CA: University of California Press.

Leal, O.F. (ed.) (1995) *Corpo e Significado*, Porto Alegre, Brazil: Editora da Universidade.

Limón, J. (1994) *Dancing with the Devil: Society*, Madison, WI: University of Wisconsin Press.

Núñez Noriega, G. (1994) *Sexo entre varones*, Mexico City: UNAM/Porrúa/El Colegio de Sonora.

Olavarría, J. (ed.) (2003) *Varones adolescentes*, Santiago: FLACSO.

Parker, R. (1999) *Beneath the Equator*, New York: Routledge.

Ramírez, R. (1999) *What It Means to Be a Man*, New Brunswick, NJ: Rutgers University Press.

Salzinger, L. (2003) *Genders in Production*, Berkeley, CA: University of California Press.

Viveros Vigoya, M. (2002) *De quebradores y cumplidores*, Bogotá: Universidad Nacional de Colombia.

Viveros Vigoya, M., Olavarría, J. and Fuller, N. (2001) *Hombres e identidades de género*, Bogotá: Universidad Nacional de Colombia.

MATTHEW C. GUTMANN
MARA VIVEROS VIGOYA

CULTURAL FORMATIONS, MIDDLE EAST

Images of Middle Eastern masculinities and manhood often fall victim to Orientalist stereotypical representations of the region. These discourses locate Middle Eastern men within a monolithic system of patriarchy that depicts them as victimising women. However, masculinity is an unstable gender category that is in constant flux in the Middle East. Models of manhood and masculinity take form under the political, social and economic forces unique to each country in the region. As in other parts of the world, the introduction of global mass media images and Western popular culture to the area over the years has played and continues to play an important role in shaping men's understandings and experiences with masculinities. The dynamics of global market economies in the region equally construct multiple masculinities and assign men different roles. While some men enjoy the pleasures of driving luxurious cars, eating at fast-food restaurants and shopping at malls, others struggle with the challenges of class segregation and unequal distributions of wealth. In most areas of the Middle East men suffer the disadvantages of illiteracy, unemployment, social and economic insecurities just as women do (Mernissi 1987).

Generational, class and regional differences among men challenge any notions of a homogeneous patriarchal arrangement in the Middle East. Ethnographic research conducted in the area reveals that an array of social movements such as industrialisation, urbanisation and globalisation constitutes Middle Eastern men's lives. Therefore, the rich notions of manhood and masculinity that operate in Middle Eastern societies find expression in a series of discursive and non-discursive practices. Meanings associated with manhood and masculinity are constantly negotiated and contested. They are used in manifold ways and are enmeshed in the competing definitions of what it means to be a man.

One of the idealised versions of masculinity finds expression in notions of honour and women's virginity. In many countries of the Middle East the virginity of a woman is highly valued, and a man's honour is strictly tied to it (Mernissi 1987). An ethnographic study conducted among the Duranni Pashtuns of Afghanistan points to the ways in which masculine identities are constructed in relation to notions of honour (Lindisfarne 1994). In a context where honour entails moral strength of character, rationality and responsibility, honourable men are considered to be those who ensure that women in their families preserve their virginities. Thus, a man's masculine capabilities are weakened if his daughter, sister or other female family member loses her virginity prematurely or inappropriately. *Izzat* (honour) in north India, Bangladesh and Pakistan is heard in men's talk of conflict, rivalry and struggle. Honourable men are considered to be those who make a good name for themselves (Mandelbaum 1988). In many parts of the Middle East, men may also commit and justify the murder of women in the name of honour.

Although wedding-night defloration (the removal of a woman's virginity) celebrates men's ability at penetrative sex and defines successful ways of being a man, it also marks subordinate masculinities. Subordinate masculinities emerge when a bride proves to be unchaste or a groom fails to deflower her. Colonisation in some regions of the Middle East has played a crucial role in causing a man's honour to be equated with his ability to protect the motherland. Notions of protection and honour as belonging to men's domain are explored by Najmabadi in the context of Iranian modernity (1987). Najmabadi describes the ways in which the homeland (*vatan*) is a gendered notion, imagined as a female beloved that needs to be protected by men. As Iran came to represent the female body, a man's failure to defend his country against foreign intrusion meant the loss of his honour.

An exploration of the notions of honour and pride is also found in Gilmore's *Manhood in the Making*, which examines images of manhood in the Islamic Mediterranean. Ideals of manhood in the region entail protecting one's family from harm. A man's reputation, respectability and dignity are closely linked to his ability to undertake this responsibility. Gilmore refers to Bourdieu's ethnography among the Kabyles of Algeria and in Morocco where men's readiness to confront and fight for their kinsmen and family represents true manhood (1990: 47). Furthermore, according to Hildred Geertz's study of manly pride or *rajula* in Morocco, masculinity entails autonomy and independence from women (in Gilmore 1990: 50). Parallel to the idea of asserting one's manhood by means of distancing oneself from women, Gilmore reports Crapanzano's examination of Moroccan folklore in which falling under the spell of a female jinn represents masculine fear of woman (1990: 50).

Recently, idealised versions of manhood within discourses on nationalism were defined in Turkey through the highly acclaimed 2004 Cola Turka soft drink commercial series. When the Ülker group was ready to launch the diet version of the soft drink, it found itself undecided about whether to name the soft drink 'Cola Turka light' or 'Cola Turka diet', since public debates revealed that many people questioned the appropriateness of coupling Cola Turka with the word 'light'. Many expressed concern that 'Cola Turka light' implied a light Turk and that a Turk, especially a Turkish man, could never be light.

Physical traits also construct images of manliness and are projected by the moustache in the region. For example, in Turkey a bushy moustache is the trademark of the strong Turkish macho man. A recent manifestation of this image is found in the Cola Turka commercial series in which a man taking a sip of Cola Turka instantly grows a thick bushy moustache (for a discussion of moustaches in the Middle East, see Daoud 2000). In stark contrast to the bushy moustache that projects strength and power, a thin moustache conveys a different version of masculinity – an Islamic identity – among groups of Muslim men in both Turkey and the Middle East. Equally, growing a beard is also representative of one's religious identity among devout Muslim men.

The male population in the Middle East is predominantly Muslim, and teachings of Islamic rule impact notions of manhood and masculinity. The region is witness to rising Islamic fundamentalism and religiously based social movements that impact gender categories. In contexts where Islamic fundamentalist narratives dominate, Islamic jihad and martyrdom articulate ideals of Islamist masculinity that are associated with warfare and the will to fight against the West. In the Israeli context, notions of masculinity are implicated in discourses of struggle and fight that position men as possessors of power. Berlovitz looks at Israeli nationalism as a male enterprise that endows men with leadership, planning and training during the building process of the state of Israel (2000).

The practice of male circumcision also reproduces ideas of dominant masculinity. The practice is an event that celebrates the male genitalia. In most areas of the Middle East, male circumcision is a celebration of entry to manhood from boyhood. Usually, the experience of circumcision carries with it the pride of becoming a true man and shapes men's conceptions of self (Bouhdiba and Khal 2000; Bilu 2000).

Links between masculinity, virility and fertility have been studied in countries such as Egypt and Lebanon where qualities of virility and fertility are associated with strength and power. Inhorn's study reveals that men who are infertile in Cairo, Egypt and Beirut, Lebanon, are considered to have failed in conforming to ideals of manhood and are associated with emasculation (Inhorn 2004). The centrality of penetration marks sexuality and notions of masculinity in some areas in the region. In contexts where sexual relations are understood as relations of power, the male penetrator's same-sex activity is not defined as homosexuality but rather as hypermasculinity (Tapınç 1992).

Middle Eastern societies usually identify the public sphere as mainly men's domain. Public spaces are sites where men are expected to assert their manhood and perform their masculinities. In particular, coffee houses are men's localities where they engage in political debates, drink tea and coffee and play backgammon. Although gender segregation is declining in major cities in the region where both men and women occupy public spaces, the idea that men belong outside the domestic sphere persists.

Local instabilities of gender result because of the globalised nature of gender (Connell 1998). Connell defines these instabilities as forces that disrupt local understandings of gender, that construct new spaces that allow women to enter public spheres, and that produce gay politics in metropolitan areas. Such instabilities can be observed in the Middle East especially as transnational corporations, global markets and information technologies make their way into the region. For example, Kandiyoti points to the paradoxical structure of Turkish society, which plays a crucial role in the construction of masculinities (1997). In a context where the male transvestite and the bearded Islamic militant occupy the same public spaces and where a popular transsexual singer voices a desire to become a good Muslim woman (Abu-Lughod 1998), gender hierarchies and images of masculinity become increasingly unstable.

Instabilities in a range of social and cultural contexts incite a desire for control and complicate masculine practices in myriad ways. Tribal customs and cultural traditions extend to both the agricultural and urban communities where notions of masculinity are both essentialised and reformulated.

References and further reading

Abu-Lughod, L. (1998) 'Feminist longings and postcolonial conditions', in L. Abu-Lughod (ed.) *Remaking Women*, Princeton, NJ: Princeton University Press.

Berlowitz, Y. (2000) 'No home at home', in B. Shoshan (ed.) *Discourse on Gender/Gendered Discourse in the Middle East*, Westport, CT and London: Praeger.

Bilu, Y. (2000) 'Circumcision, the first haircut and the Torah', in M. Ghoussoub and E. Sinclair-Webb (eds) *Imagined Masculinities*, London: Saqi.

Bouhdiba, A. and Khal, A. (2000) 'Festivities of violence', in M. Ghoussoub and E. Sinclair-Webb (eds) *Imagined Masculinities*, London: Saqi.

Connell, R. (1998) 'Masculinities and globalization', *Men and Masculinities*, 1 (1): 3–23.

Daoud, H. (2000) 'Those two heavy wings of manhood', in M. Ghoussoub and E. Sinclair-Webb (eds) *Imagined Masculinities*, London: Saqi.

Gilmore, D. (1990) *Manhood in the Making*, New Haven, CT and London: Yale University Press.

Inhorn, M.C. (2004) 'Middle Eastern masculinities in the age of new reproductive technologies', *Medical Anthropology Quarterly*, 18 (2): 162–82.

Kandiyoti, D. (1997) 'Gendering the modern', in S. Bozdogan and R. Kasaba (eds) *Rethinking Modernity and National Identity in Turkey*, Seattle, WA: University of Washington Press.

Lindisfarne, N. (1994) 'Variant masculinities, variant virginities', in A. Cornwall and N. Lindisfarne (eds) *Dislocating Masculinity*, London: Routledge.

Mandelbaum, D. (1988) *Women's Seclusion and Men's Honor*, Tucson, AZ: Arizona University Press.

Mernissi, F. (1987) *Beyond the Veil*, Bloomington and Indianapolis, IN: Indiana University Press.

Najmabadi, A. (1997) 'The erotic Vatan [homeland] as beloved and mother', *Comparative Studies in Society and History*, 39: 442–67.

Tapınç, H. (1992) 'Masculinity, femininity, and Turkish male homosexuality', in K. Plummer (ed.) *Modern Homosexualities*, London and New York: Routledge.

IKLIM GÖKSEL

CULTURAL FORMATIONS, NORTH AMERICA

The extraordinary diversity of masculine identities and popular culture in the United States, Mexico, Canada and Québec cannot be easily summarised. Detailed discussions of many North American masculine identities (including African, Asian, Mexican, European, First Nation, Jewish and Queer North Americans) and their representation in popular culture (such as radio, television, film, music, sports, journalism, advertising and fashion) can be found throughout this volume.

One approach to understanding such diversity is to examine popular cultural archetypes of North American masculinity, including the American cowboy, Mexican ranchero, Canadian Mountie and Québecois woodsman. Long before the creation of the North American Free Trade Agreement (NAFTA) in 1994, these popular icons of North American manhood moved as frequently across national borders and landscapes as they did through the popular media of radio, television and film. While these popular archetypes cannot encompass all the cultural formations of North American masculinities, they serve as powerful metaphors for both the positive and negative stereotypes of North American men in popular culture.

United States

The American cowboy has been idealised as a fearless frontiersman and legendary loner, whose rugged individualism and confidence embody the spirit of American self-reliance celebrated by de Tocqueville, Emerson and Turner. However, the cowboy has also been criticised for his role in western colonial expansion, vigilante violence and the genocidal massacre of Native Americans. Rooted in the nineteenth century, these opposing sides of cowboy culture can be seen throughout American history: from Columbus's explorations, to Washington and Jefferson's leadership; from Crockett and Boone's adventures, to Lewis and Clark's discoveries; from Patton and Eisenhower's military campaigns, to Kennedy's conquest of space; from Johnson and Nixon's Vietnam aggression, to Reagan's Cold War confrontations and George W. Bush's militarism following the attacks on the World Trade Center on 9/11. The deeply rooted American belief in cowboy justice, courage and action has alternately led to struggles for social justice and acts of great violence.

The cowboy is ubiquitous in American popular culture. Giants of popular fiction (Cooper, Grey, L'Amour), Wild West entertainment (Buffalo Bill, Autry, Rogers), the musical stage (Copeland, Rodgers and Hammerstein), country music (Williams, Brooks, Travis) and television (*The Lone Ranger, Bonanza, Lonesome Dove, Deadwood*) have celebrated cowboy courage and manhood. Hollywood has produced hundreds of cinematic Westerns in which actors from Wayne and Henry Fonda to Eastwood and Costner have portrayed such cowboy legends as Billy the Kid, Jesse James and Wyatt Earp.

In radio, television and cinema, cowboys inspired other popular icons of American masculinity, such as superheroes, gangsters, soldiers and athletes, who replicated the cowboy culture of physical prowess, outlaw violence and self-made success. While superheroes like Tarzan, Superman and Batman always saved the day, pop idols from Elvis to Sinatra and movie stars from Bogart to Redford moved seamlessly between these masculine genres, exuding movie macho as western cowboys, city gangsters, battlefield soldiers and baseball players. These masculine models were later reinvented in the action-hero, who transported cowboy culture to modern and futurist landscapes with even greater violence and muscularity. Action-heroes such as Bronson, Willis, Stallone and Schwarzenegger popularised the genre and served as a bridge between an earlier generation of outlaws played by Cagney and Brando and the later generation of action-heroes played by 'The Rock' (Dwayne Johnson) and Vin Diesel.

For some, the action-hero's popularity reflects a crisis in late twentieth-century American masculinity. As industrial labour markets downsized, outsourced and transformed America into a service economy, many men demonstrated a need for expressions of muscular masculinity in popular culture: from the exponential growth of the American football, baseball and basketball industries; to the expansion of fitness, gym and weekend-warrior culture; to the swelling of male muscularity in fashion photography, magazines and even toys. While this shift from labour to leisure masculinity has produced new popular pleasures, many argue that it has also contributed to the increased anxieties and frustration seen in urban gang violence, steroid and drug use, and the violent crimes of McVeigh in Oklahoma (1995), the Unabomber Kaczynski in Montana (1978–95) and the Columbine High School massacre in Colorado (1999). Grounded in similar scenarios of frustrated masculinity, action-hero bravado and western vigilante violence, these grisly crimes represent the legacy of cowboy culture gone terribly wrong.

Hollywood Westerns also overemphasise white cowboy bravery and overlook the ethnic diversity of the nineteenth-century American West, in which Native American resistance, Latino exploration, African–American ranching and Asian–American labour played central roles. While Hollywood Westerns underscore First Nation defeats (Wounded Knee, 1890), they minimise Native American victories (Little Big Horn, 1876), legends (Geronimo, Sitting Bull, Crazy Horse) and the great humiliation and slaughter of the Apache, Cheyenne, Lakota and Navajo nations. The same exclusions and discrimination can be seen throughout popular culture representations of American masculinity.

African–American men are often demonised in popular culture, despite their extraordinary contributions to television (Cosby), film (Poitier, Spike Lee), comedy (Pryor, Murphy), sports (Jackie Robinson, Jesse Owens) and music (Cole, Charles). Rap and hip-hop artists such as Public Enemy are often blamed for promoting the very urban violence that their music openly condemns. Specious media coverage of the Rodney King beatings and LA Riots (1991–2), the murder of gangsta rapper Tupac Shakur (1996) and the criminal trials of O.J. Simpson (1995) and Michael Jackson (2005) demonstrate the persistently racist depiction of African–American men in popular culture as criminally violent. Despite a long history of marginalisation, the demographic growth of the Latino population in the United States – especially in the Mexican, Cuban and Puerto Rican communities – has translated into the expansion of Spanish-speaking television (Telemundo, Univisión) and the popularity of Latino athletes (Martínez, De La Hoya), musicians (Santana, Ricky Martin), comedians (Rodriguez, Leguizamo), television actors (Arnaz, Olmos, Bratt, Smits) and film stars (Elizondo, Bernal, Del Toro). Once stigmatised by the wars in Japan, Korea and Vietnam, and caricatured by the yellow-face film characters Fu Manchu and Charlie Chan, Asian–American men from Soo and Morita to B.D. Wong have made enormous contributions to popular culture. In both television and film, a new generation of Asian–American action-heroes, from Cain to Keanu Reeves, emulates the virile masculinity of the Hong Kong action-heroes Bruce Lee, Jackie Chan and Chow Yun-Fat. Despite the historical brutalities and exclusions of anti-Semitism, Jewish American filmmakers (Spielberg), television comedians (Seinfeld, Sandler), actors (Kirk and Michael Douglas), athletes (Koufax, Greenberg) and composers (Berlin, Sondheim) have shaped and revolutionised all aspects of American popular culture. While homophobic cinema has caricatured American gay men as criminal (*Rope,* 1948), effeminate (*Tea and Sympathy*, 1956) and pathological (*Silence of the Lambs*, 1991), queer men from Fierstein to RuPaul continue to challenge gay invisibility and heterocentrism in television (*Will and Grace*, *Queer as Folk*), film (*Torch Song Trilogy*, 1988; *Philadelphia*, 1993), music (Mercury), sports (Louganis) and fashion (Tom Ford).

Mexico

Although Mexican masculinities are examined in greater detail elsewhere in this volume, it is important to note the analogous cowboy tradition in Mexican popular culture. While the legendary Zoro comes out of the Spanish gentry class of *caballeros*, Mexican cowboy *rancheros*, *vaqueros*, or *charros* were composed of indigenous men or biracial *mestizos*, whose courage and labour contributed to the European exploration and settlement of Mexico, Texas and the American Southwest. Rooted in the indigenous masculinity of the ancient Mayas and Aztecs and infused with both the masculine courage and ruthless violence of the Spanish conquistadors Cortés and Alvarado, the Mexican cowboy's leadership presages the later tradition of the Mexican revolutionary, from Pancho Villa to Emiliano Zapata and Subcomandante Marcos. Popularised by such cinematic legends as Elizondo, Brando and Banderas, these outlaw revolutionaries have become icons of Mexican manhood. Elsewhere overlooked or demonised in Hollywood Westerns, the Mexican *vaquero* can be credited with the introduction of Mexican macho, music, language and folklore into Anglo-American popular culture. Given their common linguistic and cultural ties, Latino communities throughout North America continue to share a passion for modern Mexican, Californian and Texan (Tejano) music, television and film.

Canada

Despite Canada's distinct history, Canadian popular culture shares much with American representations of masculinity. This has as much to do with the extensive work of Canadians in the American entertainment and sports industries as with the countries' common Anglophone language. Canada's ethnic and regional diversity includes masculine identities ranging from Asian, African, Latino, European and Native Canadians, to Maritime fishermen, prairie farmers, northern loggers, western cattlemen and Arctic hunters. Canada's early explorers and pioneers loom large in the popular imagination as icons of masculine courage and perseverance in the face of harsh northern landscapes: from the ancient Inuit migrations to North America, to Ericsson's Viking voyage to Labrador and Newfoundland (c. 1000), Hudson's pursuit of the Northwest Passage (1610) and Mackenzie's pioneering voyage to the Pacific (1793).

Canadian cattlemen played a central role in the European exploration and exploitation of the Native peoples and territories of the Canadian West, from Manitoba, Saskatchewan and Alberta, to British Columbia, Yukon and the Northwest Territories. In addition to the cowboy, the Royal Canadian Mounted Police (RCMP) have been celebrated and parodied as icons of Canadian masculinity. Founded during the nineteenth century to bring public order to the Northwest, the mounted police oversaw frontier forts and settlements, policed the whiskey trade, transcontinental railroad and Klondike Gold Rush and engineered the acquisition of the western frontier from the Cree, Sioux, Blackfoot and Inuit peoples. 'Mounties' (RCMP officers) have been widely mythologised and lampooned in Anglophone popular culture, from the dozens of early Hollywood Mountie films or 'Northerns' (*McGuire of the Mounted*, *Rose Marie*) and popular television series *Sergeant Preston of the Yukon* and *Due South*, to the cinematic spoof *Dudley Do-Right* (1999), starring the Canadian Frasier as a Mountie who 'always gets his man'.

In this tradition of northern comedy, many Canadian men (Akroyd, Michael J. Fox, McCormack, Myers, Short, Carrey) have gained the reputation as brilliant comic actors. Other Canadian men loom large in pop music (Adams), broadcast journalism (Jennings), television (Shatner, Priestley) and filmmaking (Cameron, Cronenberg, Egoyan, Sutherland). In a nation famous for its winters, Canadian athletes have played out a range of masculinities on the ice from the graceful figure skating of Browning and Stojko to the aggressive athleticism of the hockey legends Orr and Gretzky.

Québec

Because of Québec's unique Francophone identity, Québecois masculinity is culturally and historically distinct from its North American neighbours. The spirit of exploration exemplified by Cartier's discovery of New France (1534) and Champlain's foundation of Québec (1608) echoes the masculine courage and enterprise of Columbus and Cortés to the south. But many of the most colourful icons of North American masculinity – which were later borrowed by American or Canadian men – find their origins in the popular culture and folklore of Québec. Unlike the cowboy tradition in Mexico, Canada and the United States, Québecois frontier masculinity is located in the figures of its *coureurs des bois* (woodsmen), *bûcherons* (loggers) and *trappeurs* (trappers), who pitted their muscular strength against the harsh natural climate. The early colonisation, economic development and national identity of Québec were built on the forest labour of these men, whose stories have been broadly celebrated in Québecois culture. In such popular fiction, radio, television and film as Hémon's *Maria Chapdelaine* (1916), Guèvremont's *Le Survenant* (*The Outlander*, 1945) and Jutra's *Mon Oncle Antoine* (*My Uncle Antoine*, 1971), the hardships and humiliations of agricultural and industrial labour are contrasted with the romantic and heroic masculinity of Québecois woodsmen. It is thus not surprising that the popular legend of Paul Bunyan, who is perhaps the most famous icon of the North American lumberjack, finds its origins in the timberlands of Québec.

Like these woodsmen who battled snow in northern logging camps, other Québecois men pitted their masculine strength in athletic competition on ice. Later exported to its North American and Nordic European neighbours, hockey was invented and formalised in Montréal and many of its greatest players hail from Québec, including Lemieux, Richard and Lafleur. Elsewhere, the popular novels, plays and films of Tremblay, Bouchard and Arcand analyse the role of the clergy, working class and gay community in constructing Québecois manhood.

Much of Québec's most important cultural production has been inspired by its pursuit of national sovereignty. As in Mexico, the figure of the revolutionary looms large in the Québecois popular imagination. The masculine courage and leadership of the nineteenth-century *Patriotes* Rebellion (1837–8) and its leaders de Lorimier and Papineau have been cinematically fêted by filmmakers Falardeau and Brault. From the Quiet Revolution of the 1960s to the independence movement of the 1980s, 1990s and beyond, the Québecois struggle against Anglophone exploitation and assimilation has been chronicled in the popular music of Vigneault, Charlebois and Boucher. In Québecois popular culture, noted federalist leaders such as the Canadian Prime Minister Trudeau are often criticised as collaborators, while legendary sovereignty leaders such as the Québecois Prime Minister Lévesque are often lauded as visionaries for what many believe is the inevitable future of an independent and Francophone Québec.

References and further reading

Basso, M., McCall, L. and Garceau, D. (eds) (2001) *Across the Great Divide*, New York: Routledge.

Berger, M., Wallis, B. and Watson, S. (eds) (1995) *Constructing Masculinity*, New York: Routledge.

Bobo, J., Hudley, C. and Michel, C. (eds) (2004) *The Black Studies Reader*, New York: Routledge.

Emerson, R.W. [1841] (2005) 'Self-reliance,' in D. Robinson (ed.) *The Spiritual Emerson*, Boston, MA: Beacon.

Grace, S. (2002) *Canada and the Idea of North*, Montréal: McGill-Queen's University Press.

Habell-Pallán, M. and Romero, M. (eds) (2002) *Latino/A Popular Culture*, New York: New York University Press.

Horrocks, R. (1995) *Male Myths and Icons*, New York: St Martin's.

Jenkins, H., McPherson, T. and Shattuc, J. (eds) (2002) *Hop on Pop*, Durham, NC: Duke University Press.

Kimmel, M. (2005) *The History of Men*, Albany, NY: SUNY Press.

Lee, R. (1999) *Orientals*, Philadelphia, PA: Temple University Press.

Neal, M. (2002) *Soul Babies*, New York: Routledge.

Tatum, C. (2001) *Chicano Popular Culture*, Tucson, AZ: University of Arizona Press.

Tétu de Labsade, F. (1990) *Le Québec*, Montréal: Boréal.

Tocqueville, A. de [1835–40] (2004) *Democracy in America*, New York: Penguin.

Turner, F.J. [1893] (1996) *The Frontier in American History*, New York: Dover.

BRIAN MARTIN

CULTURAL STUDIES

Sometimes misunderstood as a subset of anthropology – or, indeed, more specifically of comparative anthropology – cultural studies originated at the Centre for Contemporary Cultural Studies, founded in 1964 in Great Britain, at the University of Birmingham. In 1972 the Centre published the first issue of *Working Papers in Cultural Studies*, in which the aims and parameters of 'cultural studies' began to be defined. The key figures at this early moment in the history of cultural studies were Richard Hoggart, Raymond Williams and Stuart Hall, whose work has remained influential, and whose Marxist approach has continued to provide a key theoretical underpinning for the cultural analyses of many scholars working in the field.

Cultural studies came to be 'exported' internationally, and developed in particular and characteristic ways in North America, Australia, Europe (especially France) and South-East Asia. In this expansion and transfer of the field, cultural studies, in its earlier years chiefly an intellectual tradition in Britain, in time became a discipline, with a particular (but not necessarily fixed) array of theoretical underpinnings and analytical practices, and even a profession – it is now possible to seek employment at a university in the area of cultural studies.

As a field of inquiry, cultural studies occupies a unique place in the general schema of intellectual and analytical practice and history. Culture is not only the object of inquiry in cultural studies, it is also the context for both the specific objects (texts) under analysis and the analytical practices brought to bear on those objects. Therefore, to perform cultural analysis the practitioner of cultural studies must use a range of methods of analysis and inquiry available, in order, as it were, to triangulate observation of cultural texts and practices. As an intellectual field, then, cultural studies is in fact cross- or inter-disciplinary, drawing on a wide range of other intellectual, academic and professional fields, including sociology, history, psychology, film and television studies, literary theory, philosophy, gender theory, anthropology and marketing theory.

It is necessary first to understand the difference between *society* and *culture*, as cultural studies defines these. *Society* and *the social* refer to the way a particular population/community is structured, in terms of class and division of labour, say, in relation to a history of its structuring and its means of sustaining itself. Such terms as 'agrarian society', 'urban society', 'industrial society' thus encode a set of analytical terms and assumptions about how adults and children, men and women, hunters and gatherers, workers and owners of the means of production, etc., may be defined and given roles in the organisation and dynamics of the community.

Culture and *the cultural*, by contrast, refer less, in the context of cultural studies, to particular activities – such as the high-cultural interest in literature or opera, the popular-cultural interest in football or rock-and-roll music, or what we might call the folk-cultural interest in weaving and folksong (though *culture* and *the cultural* include all of these activities) – than to an understanding that 'culture' is concerned with meaning: how it is enabled and made, by whom, for whom, and in what context. The activities listed above require that meaning be attributed to or made out of them, otherwise we cannot understand what 'literature', 'football' or 'weaving' even are, let alone how they differ from each other both in terms of the activity involved and of the ways that activity might be valued or hierarchised.

Cultural studies, then, is primarily concerned with the meaning-making systems in any given culture at any given historical moment, and with who has access to them as a meaning-maker, whether in the sense of producing something with meaning, or receiving something with meaning. It is thus concerned also with groupings or communities within the larger social structure – with the cultures of family, for instance, or of age-cohorts, or of interest groups. In this sense, therefore, cultural studies is also concerned with a cultural politics – with which social or cultural group or groups dominate the meaning-making system, how other groups may be ranged around that domination, and how particular kinds of meaning may be encouraged and advantaged over others.

Accordingly, in cultural studies any artefact – a book or a painting, or, more abstractly, a pattern of behaviour, an activity or a context such as a building or a quarter of the city – has the status of text: that is, it has been deliberately (if not always consciously) produced, and therefore has meaning, making it available to analysis or reading. Such a reading may be undertaken by means of a variety of techniques or practices, ranging from semiotics (which looks at the material sign systems used and how these systems and individual signs function meaningfully in a given cultural context) to the theory of discourse developed by the French philosopher Michel Foucault (see below).

The implication of this is that, as users/readers of the culture and its artefacts, we can never access the reality of culture directly: it is always mediated to us by its multiple and various texts. That is, texts are representations of the objects, persons, events and practices described – even when wholly 'factual' – and thence also of the culture itself. A corollary of this is that the meaning of cultural texts is always multiple and fluid, since the text is always situated at the nexus of various cultural activities, needs or assumptions about meaning. Indeed, Jean Baudrillard, an important theorist in cultural studies, goes so far as to say that we now exist in a culture that is not only mediated to us through representations but, via communication modes such as film, television and the internet, is also so heavily 'media-ted' that we cannot access reality at all. Instead, we live in a hyperreality (a 'beyond-reality') created for us by the media, advertising and other forms of electronic communication, and it is this that has become our 'reality'. As a result, we must deal with what Baudrillard calls 'simulacra', simulations of the real, rather than the real itself.

While the Baudrillardian approach would seem to suggest that cultural studies is at home only in analyses or readings of contemporary texts delivered via contemporary media, this is not in fact the case. Michel Foucault, another significant figure in the development of cultural studies, especially in the last couple of decades of the twentieth century, approaches culture by means of what he calls an 'archaeology of knowledge': that is, understanding texts, ideas and practices at any given historical moment in relation to their positioning within a broader context of contemporaneous texts, ideas and practices. That is, particular cultural preoccupations or topics are produced out of a discursive formation that in turn regulates how people in the culture at a given historical moment are enabled to 'think' ideas or meanings. Foucault forages far and wide within specific 'bands' of history in order to demonstrate how particular ways of thinking and behaving did not occur either naturally or eccentrically, but rather were produced out of and governed by certain discursive factors operating at that time.

Thus, for instance, in the highly influential first volume of his three-volume *History of Sexuality* (the final fourth volume remains incomplete after his death in 1984), Foucault argues that our common assumption that the nineteenth century – and especially Britain under Queen Victoria – manifested an unusual prudishness with regard to sex and sexuality is mistaken, and that, to the contrary, a discourse emerged in the late eighteenth and through the nineteenth century that did nothing but encourage talk about sex, though often this took place within legal, medico-pathological and psychological discursive formations, and functioned to control the social subject or individual by categorisation and response to that categorisation. So, for example, in an often-quoted passage, Foucault observes that the category of 'the homosexual' emerges first in the nineteenth century, and signifies not a theological category of sinners of the flesh (as it did prior to the eighteenth century), but rather a discursive object that could be measured, tested, analysed and given a personal history and a particular value (Foucault 1978: 43). (For a Foucauldian reading of men's fashion, see Nixon 1997.)

The study of men, masculinities and male sexualities developed in the 1970s in Britain (Andrew Tolson's *The Limits of Masculinity* was published in 1977), chiefly in the disciplinary areas of sociology and psychology. The attention paid to the topic by scholars working in cultural studies dates from the mid-1980s (Eve Kosofsky Sedgwick's important contribution, *Between Men: English Literature and Male Homosocial Desire* was published in 1985), and today includes, in addition to the exploration of formal texts such as literature and film, the examination of significant cultural events and moments, and the cultural responses of all kinds to these.

Cultural studies is a field in constant movement, both in terms of its objects of analysis and its theoretical approaches. The danger for the student of cultural studies is an unconsidered and unsystematic use of a variety of theories and approaches that may not be self-consistent. However, at its best cultural studies offers insights precisely because of the richness and variety of its approaches, insights that discipline-specific analyses might overlook.

References and further reading

Adams, R. and Savran, D. (eds) (2002) *The Masculinity Studies Reader*, Malden, MA, and Oxford: Blackwell.

Barker, C. (2000) *Cultural Studies*, London: Sage.

Beynon, J. (2002) *Masculinities and Culture*, Buckingham and Philadelphia, PA: Open University Press.

Buchbinder, D. (1998) *Performance Anxieties*, St Leonards, NSW: Allen and Unwin.

Du Gay, P., Hall, S., Janes, L., McKay, H. and Negus, K. (1997) *Doing Cultural Studies*, London: Sage.

Foucault, M. [1976] (1978) *The History of Sexuality*, vol. 1, New York: Vintage.

Hartley, J. (2002) *Communication, Cultural and Media Studies*, London and New York: Routledge.
Johnson, R., Chambers, D., Raghuram, P. and Tincknell, E. (2004) *The Practice of Cultural Studies*, London: Sage.
Lehman, P. (ed.) (2001) *Masculinity*, New York and London: Routledge.
Lewis, J. (2002) *Cultural Studies*, London: Sage.
Nixon, S. (1997) 'Exhibiting masculinity', in S. Hall (ed.) *Representation*, London: Sage, pp. 291–330.
Sardar, Z. and Van Loon, B. (1997) *Cultural Studies for Beginners*, Cambridge: Icon.
Schirato, T. and Yell, S. (2000) *Communication and Cultural Literacy*, Crows Nest, NSW: Allen and Unwin.
Sedgwick, E.K. (1985) *Between Men*, New York: Columbia University Press.
Tolson, A. (1977) *The Limits of Masculinity*, London: Tavistock.

DAVID BUCHBINDER

CULTURE AND REPRESENTATION

Representations are discourses of imagined and rendered connections that may influence opinion or action, or effect change. They include, but are not limited to, texts, visualisations, music and landscapes. Culture is about shared ways of living and is linked to representations through meanings expressed in the material and symbolic practices of everyday life.

Representations are cultural artefacts, and culture is produced through processes that are understood as representable or non-representable. Non-representable processes are related primarily to emotions. There are great difficulties in simultaneously describing cultures, representations and masculinities because each has real effects on the others. Cultures are experienced and understood through our bodies. It follows that the production of culture also produces certain kinds of embodiment. An abstraction of this kind makes sense only if 'bodies' are understood not only as the physical 'embodiment' of certain kinds of people but also as a culturally constructed set of representations about what bodies are appropriate for men and women. To a large degree, the representations of popular culture are geared towards identifying what it is, and what it means, to be a man or a woman (Mitchell 2000: 171). These meanings are constantly negotiated, contested and resisted through lived experiences. Popular representations such as television, radio, advertising, video-games, public service announcements, poetry, stories, books and web-pages are particularly powerful forums for displaying cultural ideals about masculinity.

Steve Neale observed in 1983 that representations of masculinity had rarely been studied (see Neale 1993). In the last couple of decades, there has been an explosion of interest in the ways men are represented in popular culture. Prior to this, masculinity was not considered a problematic or troubling category. Contemporary interest is sparked by feminist theory, queer theory, cultural studies, media studies and, more recently, poststructuralist theory. A powerful initiator of this work came from feminist study of film.

In 1975, Laura Mulvey rocked the world of film studies with an article that used psychoanalytic theory as a political weapon. The thrust of her attack focused on a larger political unconscious that created meaning through visual representations. Mulvey (1975: 8) suggested that many mainstream movies are reinforced by 'patterns of fascination already existing in and at work within the individual subject and the social formations that have molded them'. Hollywood cinema, she claimed, reified an important aspect of Western culture wherein the audience looked, the male character looked and the female character was looked at. Her constitution of the *male gaze* not only as a filmic reality but also as part of a patriarchal unconscious furthered the 1970s feminist elaboration of woman as object of desire. Mulvey's male gaze characterises masculinity as active and powerful both in the narrative action of male characters and the political unconscious of male filmmakers and male viewers. For Mulvey and her followers, the power of Hollywood representations is opened up through psychoanalytic theory. For example, this theory positions all portrayals of bodily mutilation as gender-linked to male fears of castration. Evidence from science fiction's cybernetic implants to the draping of human flesh over Terminators to slasher-film representations of spewing innards and gushing blood demonstrates the preoccupation with violent transgressing of male bodies.

Henry Giroux (1995) characterises the representation of male violence in Hollywood action cinema and in video-games as 'ritualistic'. In cinema, it is commonly accompanied with male action heroes such as Arnold Schwarzenegger, Bruce Willis and Mel Gibson. Violence of this type is dramatic and visceral, serving primarily for entertainment. At the same time, Giroux argues, the focus on human/alien, good guy/bad guy divisions serves to represent violence in sexual and racial terms. Alternatively, the representation of aggression in movies like *Boys Don't Cry* (1999) is 'symbolic violence' because it connects on-screen brutality to real human problems (in this case, cross-dressing and homophobia) and therefore serves more as critical engagement than as entertainment. Finally, Giroux argues that representations of 'hyperreal violence' in movies like Tarantino's *Pulp Fiction* (1994) reduce brutality to an aesthetic that isolates male contexts from larger social contexts.

What does the spectator get out of representations of violence, and how does this relationship connect to gender? In her classic discussion of the slasher film, Carol Clover's (1989) concern is how to explain the appeal to a large male audience of a film genre that invariably features a female victim-hero (such as Sigourney Weaver's character in the *Alien* series or Jamie Lee Curtis in the *Halloween* series). Clover characterises these women as 'Final Girl' and notes that men's ease at engaging with them is indicative of cross-gender representations. The Final Girl's unfemininity is marked by her abilities with 'the active investigating gaze normally reserved for males' (Clover 1989: 93). According to Clover (1989: 94), the association between Final Girl and the monster is a 'shared masculinity, materialised in all those phallic symbols – and it is also a shared femininity, materialised in what comes next: the castration, literal or symbolic, of the killer in her hands'.

Neale (1993) points in an important direction here: if power is attained through representing men as perpetrators and sadists, what kind of power lies in the portrayal of men as objects of desire? He opens a space in Mulvey's thesis to argue that the elements she considers in relation to representations of women can and should be considered in relation to images of men. His point is not to detract from critiques that the spectorial gaze of mainstream cinema is implicitly male, but to note that the erotic elements that relate male images to spectators are constantly repressed and denied: 'women are a problem, a source of anxiety, of obsessive enquiry; men are not. Where women are investigated, men are not' (Neale 1993: 19). To investigate masculine representations is to set aside norms, to embrace contradictions, and to dig deeper into what is disavowed in patriarchal contexts.

Robert Hanke (1992) argues that to understand the relations between representations of masculinity and Western culture, we need to understand the relations between hegemonic, conservative and subordinate masculinities. Hegemonic masculinity – premised on the subordination of women and other minorities and focused on a dominant male Anglo-European white culture – is frequently articulated in representations of men. Many action films, Westerns, sport telecasts, beer commercials and comic book heroes represent this form of masculinity. Conservative masculinities are represented by books, advertisements, television shows and movies that suggest a less macho and sexist narrative of middle-class professional men. This image, suggested by American television shows such as *Seinfeld* and *Frasier*, is a mythic expression of the cultural ascendancy of the professional/managerial class. Subordinated masculinities are elaborated in representations of groups of men who are marginalised within the hegemonic culture. Hanke argues, as an example, that gay men are often negatively stereotyped as subversives, superficial or victims of ridicule.

Delgado and Stefancic (1995: 210) argue that African-American men historically are portrayed as 'criminal, lascivious, irresponsible, and not particularly smart'. The colonial depiction of black males as bestial and brutish, to their portrayal as childlike buffoons in D.W. Griffith's *Birth of a Nation* (1915) led Heidi Nast (2000) to connect cultural representations with infantilisation and 'unconscious' colonial violence and racism. Media images have historically played on fears of the sexual violation of white women by animalistic black males. Racist images of black men give society permission to perpetuate discrimination and injustice. Nast notes that this discrimination takes material forms such as the creation of a barrier between whites and blacks from 1900 to 1930 through Chicago's famous elevated railway.

Suzanne Hatty (2000: 165) argues that the issue of self-representation has assumed an urgency in the black community, as suggested, for example, in the work of film director Spike Lee or the so-called 'pornography' of photographer Robert Mapplethorpe in his depiction of black male bodies. In her writing on the latter, Kobena Mercer (1994: 173) argues that Mapplethorpe staged taboo sexual and racial imagery to say something about how white people look at black male bodies as different, excessive and hypersexual. Other problematic agendas foment from popular representations of naked bodies. Kelly Karrell (2003), for example, observes that working-class men in the film *The Full Monty* (1997) became convenient metaphors for an invigorated post-imperial national identity that preserved the oppression of British class divisions.

Representations of men as active, virile, commanding and dominant predominate in Western media through the 1960s. The idea of a 'new man' (which closely relates to Hanke's conservative masculinity described above) refers to the emergence of new representations of masculinity in Western society during the 1970s and 1980s. This development reacts to critiques of chauvinism and sexism by the women's movement and gay rights activism and also creates an important cultural response to social change through representations focused on domesticity, non-competitiveness and gentleness as well as self-confidence. Representations turned to a more heterosexual 'new man' during the 1990s in magazines such as *GQ* (*Gentleman's Quarterly*) and *FHM* (*For Him Magazine*) as suggested by a format that is highly visual but also ironic and cynical (Jackson *et al.* 2001).

Hegemonic masculinities hold sway through a variety of representational strategies, including portraying feminised masculinities, black bestiality and negative or humorous stereotypes of working-class masculinities. They work through both the exclusion and the inclusion of subordinated masculinities, 'thus supporting and maintaining a gender hierarchy among men that justifies and legitimises the oppression of gay men' (Hanke 1992: 196) and other minorities. The overall cultural effect of these processes of representation is to gloss over any real questioning of power relations, gender inequities, work relations and sexual and racial politics. Through changing representations, there is a shift in the cultural meanings of masculinity without any shift in dominant social and spatial material arrangements. This notion of stasis is disputed by Katie Willis (2005), who argues that while national representations of masculinity in Latin America still focus on 'the macho', men's performances as *men* vary significantly across space. Clearly there are important geographies as well as histories of the representations and performances of masculinity.

Engagement with video-game and musical representations is complex because different forms of interaction and performance offset static theories of spectatorship. Portable game- and music-players, Blackberries and mobile telephones enable texts, visualisations, music and other cultural representations to be accessed in relative privacy, even when in public places. Such discretion enables the possibility of subversive communities such as the production of queer spaces as well as the possibility of advertising and coercion by corporate interests. That video-game representations incite subversion and aggression is contested by data that show a sharp decline in aggravated assault among teenage boys in the late 1990s at precisely the same time that some of the most violent games (e.g. Mortal Kombat) appeared on the market.

Recent writing on embodied, emotional contexts for masculinities and their relations to empowering difference and enabling social transformations opened the door for a reappraisal of the uses of representational theory and its relations to culture. The core criticism of representations is their lack of connection to the material world. However, Deleuze (1986), in particular, claims their uselessness for understanding the embodied affects that are deeply part of culture. Deleuzian post-structural theory suggests a new set of relations with the material world, one that challenges static representations of identity that, in turn, facilitate a caricature of men embedded in a form of power that is always about the construction of dominant hierarchies (Aitken 2006). In contrast, the call to understand emotional bodies and images is certainly a call for the fluidity of male subjectivity, and it is also a call to understand the relationships among representations, masculinities and places and contexts.

References and further reading

Aitken, S.C. (2006) 'Leading men to violence and creating spaces for their emotions', *Gender, Place and Culture*, 13 (5): 491–507.

Clover, C. (1989) 'Her body, himself: gender in the slasher film', in J. Donald (ed.) *Fantasy and the Cinema*, London: British Film Industry, pp. 91–133.

Delgado, R. and Stefancic, J. (1995) 'Minority men, misery, and the marketplace of ideas', in M. Berger, B. Wallis and S. Watson (eds) *Constructing Masculinity*, New York and London: Routledge, pp. 210–20.

Deleuze, G. (1986) *Cinema 1*, translated by H. Tomlinson and B. Habberjam, London: Athlone.

Farrell, K. (2003) 'Naked nation', *Men and Masculinities*, 6 (2): 119–35.

Giroux, H. (1995) '*Pulp Fiction* and the culture of violence', *Harvard Educational Review*, 65 (2): 299–314.

Hanke, R. (1992) 'Redesigning men', in S. Craig (ed.) *Men, Masculinity, and the Media*, Newbury Park, CA: Sage, pp. 185–98.

Hatty, S. (2000) *Masculinities, Violence and Culture*, Thousand Oaks, CA: Sage.

Jackson, P., Stevenson, N. and Brooks, K. (2001) *Making Sense of Men's Magazines*, Malden, MA: Blackwell.

Mercer, K. (1994) *Welcome to the Jungle*, New York and London: Routledge.

Mitchell, D. (2000) *Cultural Geography*, Oxford: Blackwell.

Mulvey, L. (1975) 'Visual pleasure and narrative cinema', *Screen*, 23 (5): 72–9.

Nast, H. (2000) 'Mapping the "unconscious"', *Annals of the Association of American Geographers*, 90 (2): 215–55.

Neale, S. (1993) 'Prologue', in S. Cohan and I. Hark (eds) *Screening the Male*, New York and London: Routledge, pp. 9–20.

Willis, K. (2005) 'Latin American urban masculinities: going beyond "the Macho"', in B. van Hoven and K. Hörschelmann (eds) *Spaces of Masculinities*, New York and London: Routledge, pp. 97–110.

See also: art

STUART C. AITKEN

CYBERSPACE AND THE INTERNET

The internet's origins in science and military applications meant that for many years it was a male-dominated space, consistent with the traditional alignment of masculinity and technology. The internet has now penetrated every aspect of modern life, from learning and locating information to communication, shopping and recreation. For those with internet access, increasing experience in the online environment leads to a growing use of the internet for the serious business of life, such as work-related tasks, financial transactions, serious communication and seeking important information (Horrigan and Rainie 2002: 2). The wide range of functions for which the internet can now be used has meant that where there are high levels of internet usage, the proportion of women online is closer to the proportion of men online. In 2003, 65 per cent of American men were using the internet, compared with 61 per cent of American women.

There are a number of cognitive factors that influence internet usage: familiarity with technology, self-efficacy and attitudes that predict behaviour (Jackson *et al.* 2001: 367–8). With the increasing use of the internet at work and at home, men and women are becoming equally familiar with the technology. Where self-efficacy is a belief that one's actions will lead to desirable outcomes, males may feel more self-efficacious with regard to computer technology than females. Research on gendered attitudes to computers suggests that women have less favourable attitudes to computers than men (Mitra *et al.* 2001). These cognitive factors may be why men and women seem to use the internet in quite different ways. High proportions of female internet users go online to look for health or religious information, while a large percentage of male users are looking for news, or financial, sport or political information (Madden and Rainie 2003). Email is overwhelmingly the most popular use of the internet, and females tend to use email more than males, consistent with women's stronger motivation for interpersonal communication (Morahan-Martin 1998).

Men with internet access tend to get their news from the internet. While women may log on to find out more about an event they have heard about elsewhere, men are more likely to log on to get the news in the first place, checking online sources to find out what is happening in the world. Regardless of gender, however, wealthier and more educated internet users are more likely to go online for news. Getting financial information and completing financial transactions online are also activities that seem to be highly correlated with being male, high-income and well-educated. Researching stocks, getting share prices, and buying and selling stocks and bonds online is primarily the province of well-to-do, educated men. Men also seem to use the internet more for searching for information about products and services. Browsing for information on large ticket items such as computers, electrical goods and cars often takes place at work. However, when it comes to buying products, the gender gap disappears, with equal numbers of men and women reporting that they have purchased items over the internet. Men, though, are more likely to participate in online auctions. When it comes to using the internet for leisure pursuits – looking for information about books and films, hobby interests and leisure activities; playing games; taking part in chat rooms; and listening to or downloading music – slightly more men are doing so than women. The biggest demographic difference here, however, is age rather than gender, with young people using the internet for leisure pursuits far more than older generations (The PEW Project 2000). Not surprisingly, males make up the majority of visitors to sports sites, where they constitute over 60 per cent of visitors, and to 'adult' sites. A national Australian survey found that 16.5 per cent of men and 2.4 per cent of women had visited an internet sex site on purpose in the previous year (Richters *et al.* 2003: 185).

The simple statistics of gendered internet use disguise the complexity of the mutual shaping of gender and the internet, as the range of uses to which the internet is put impacts upon both how gender is experienced and how the internet develops to accommodate nascent uses. An analysis of the everyday uses of the internet shows that technology is as multidimensional as gender, and both are experienced 'in complex and contradictory ways' (Van Zoonan 2002: 6).

The internet does seem to invite people to experiment in ways that they otherwise might not. The internet's accessibility, affordability and anonymity facilitate activities that may be more problematic off-line. First there is an appearance of personal security – users log on from the comfortable space of their home or office. Then there is a perception of privacy – once you have created a screen name and online persona, it is easy to believe that the real you is effectively disguised. And there is an appearance that the online environment is ephemeral, as sites are exited, messages deleted and texts disappear from the screen. While these perceptions might not be accurate, they do make possible experiences that are restricted off-line by the obvious absence of anonymity, security and erasure. For example, it seems as though online gay chat rooms primarily attract younger men, men who do not identify as gay, and men who live outside the major cities (Tikkanen and Ross 2000: 614).

Research into internet sex finds that women are more likely to spend time flirting or having 'cybersex' with others in sexually oriented chat rooms, while men are drawn to porn web sites (Cooper *et al.* 2000). However, in interactive online sex forums, men are encouraged to participate in erotic displays and performances. In providing 'a space where men can explore the erotic pleasures of sexualised display', these forums 'augment the development of male sexual identities that incorporate passivity and vulnerability' (Kibby and Costello 1999: 364). While the internet offers a range of sex- and sexuality-related information and opportunities that can significantly enhance human welfare and quality of life, it also offers problematic pornographic materials, allows sexual offenders to recruit victims, provides a convenient environment for cyberstalkers and sexual harassers, and enables infidelity and adultery (Barak and King 2000: 518).

Most cyberstalking perpetrators are male, and the majority of victims are female. While stalking also is an off-line phenomenon, the online environment facilitates the gathering of information on the target and enables a range of ways to communicate with them. The internet also makes possible third-party stalking, where others are induced to stalk or harass the victim through communications which purport to come from the victim (Adam 2002: 136), or present the victim in such a way as to invite contact (Kibby 1997).

Online relationships can, however, be an effective 'practice ground for learning and exploring sexuality and relationships' (Levine 2000: 572). Online, relationships flourish insulated from the irritating minutiae of everyday life, as cyberspace provides a playground where all people can feel sexually desired, and no particular type of relationship is valued above others. For many, the skills developed online are applied to face-to-face relationships; however, for some the attraction to virtual relationships may become uncontrollable. Whether cybersexual addiction (compulsive use of online pornography) and cyber-relationship addiction (pathological involvement in online relationships) are internet addictions or uses of the internet to satisfy sex-related addictions is open to debate; however, it is agreed that the internet 'may provide an alternative reality to the user and allow them feelings of immersion and anonymity which may lead to an altered state of consciousness' (Griffiths 2000: 539). This alternative reality might be as addictive as drugs, with similar effects.

As the internet becomes as much a consumer route as an information highway, gender differences in attitudes towards e-commerce become more apparent. Researchers see an 'easy fit between men's buying concerns and the Internet environment' (Dittmar *et al.* 2004: 443) as 'functional motives become even more important on-line than in conventional buying, and psychological motivations, especially social experiential concerns, become less important' (Dittmar *et al.* 2004: 440). Men are unlikely to be deterred from online shopping by the lack of social contact, and it could be that men expect that the internet will allow them to avoid those aspects of conventional shopping that they see as negative. In addition, the increased functionality of online purchasing is likely to attract men.

Those looking at the internet as it developed saw the new technology as profoundly liberating, opening up outlets for the people at the margins of society to tell their own stories. Because posting information on the Web is so individual, inexpensive and immediate, internet enthusiasts believed that it would virtually eliminate barriers to self-publishing. It was thought that the internet would democratise the flow of information, replacing top-down dependence on traditional news and media organisations with bottom-up sharing among individuals. While there has not been a wholesale revolution, weblogs have broken key news stories with significant political and economic effects. For example, Beldar Blog was able to force the resignation of long-esteemed newsman Dan Rather of CBS, by revealing that the documents cited in a *60 Minutes* story, which suggested lapses in President Bush's military record, could not be authenticated. Weblogs are the fastest growing type of online publishing, eclipsing the personal homepage. There are three basic types of weblogs: 'filters', which are primarily links to links to world events and external comment; 'journals', which are the blogger's thoughts or descriptions of their day-to-day life; and 'knowledge-logs', which are repositories of information and observations on a particular content area (Herring, Scheidt, Bonus and Wright 2004). Teenage girls seem to produce most journal-type blogs, but all other categories are dominated by adult males (Herring, Kouper, Scheidt and Wright 2004).

A good deal of the public debate surrounding the potential harmful effects of the internet concerns children's access to pornography. Research which examines how children and technology come together in diverse communities of practice is in its infancy, but there is widespread concern over the efficiency of filtering software and the long-term effect of the internet's delivery of pornography on a scale and breadth previously unimaginable. File-sharing networks, in particular, can lead to a tremendous amount of intentional and inadvertent exposure of children and young people to pornography and other adult sexual media. This exposure must have a considerable impact on the development of sexuality, sexual attitudes, moral values and gendered practices.

Cyberspace might not have turned out to be the democratic whole-earth community envisioned by Rheingold (1993), but the internet is enabling people to overcome the previous communication boundaries of time, place and cost as well as inhibition, custom and proscription, to connect with new individuals and groups, experiences and information. The experience of cyberspace is gendered, and its gender relations are an extension of those in the off-line world. However, the internet does appear to facilitate the softening of gender boundaries in some areas, and the increasing range of gendered activities online is shaping the way in which cyberspace develops.

References and further reading

Adam, A. (2002) 'Cyberstalking and Internet pornography: gender and the gaze', *Ethics and Information Technology*, 4: 133–42.

Cooper, A., Delmonico, D.L. and Burg, R. (2000) 'Cybersex users, abusers, and compulsives: new findings and implications', *Sexual Addiction and Compulsivity: The Journal of Treatment and Prevention*, 7: 1–25.

Dittmar, H., Long, K. and Meek, R. (2004) 'Buying on the Internet: gender differences in on-line and conventional buying motivation', *Sex Roles*, 50: 423–44.

Greenfield, P.M. (2004) 'Inadvertent exposure to pornography on the Internet: implications of peer-to-peer file-sharing networks for child development and families', *Applied Developmental Psychology*, 25: 741–50.

Griffiths, M. (2000) 'Excessive Internet use: implications for sexual behavior', *CyberPsychology and Behavior*, 3 (4, August): 537–52.

Herring, S.C., Kouper, I., Scheidt, L.A. and Wright, E. (2004) 'Women and children last: the discursive construction of weblogs', in L. Gurak, S. Antonijevic, L. Johnson, C. Ratliff and J. Reyman (eds) *Into the Blogosphere: Rhetoric, Community, and Culture of Weblogs*, available at http://blog.lib.umn.edu/blogosphere/

Herring, S.C., Scheidt, L.A., Bonus, S. and Wright, E. (2004) 'Bridging the gap: a genre analysis of weblogs', *Proceedings of the Thirty-seventh Hawaii*

International Conference on System Sciences (HICSS-37), Los Alamitos: IEEE Press; available at http://www.blogninja.com/DDGDD04.doc

Horrigan, J.B. and Rainie, L. (2002) 'Getting serious online', *Pew Internet and American Life Project*, available at http://www.pewinternet.org/

Jackson, L.A., Ervin, K.S., Gardner, P.D. and Schmitt, N. (2001) 'Gender and the Internet: women communicating and men searching', *Sex Roles*, 44 (5–6): 363–79.

Kibby, M. (1997) 'Babes on the web: sex, identity and the home page', *Media International Australia*, 84 (May): 39–45.

Kibby, M. and Costello, B. (1999) 'Displaying the phallus: masculinity and the performance of sexuality on the Internet', *Men and Masculinities*, V1 (4, April): 352–64.

Levine, D. (2000) 'Virtual attraction: what rocks your boat?' *Cyberpsychology and Behavior*, 3 (4): 565–73.

Madden, M. and Rainie, L. (2003) 'America's online pursuits', *Pew Internet and American Life Project*, available at http://www.pewinternet.org/

Mitra, A., LaFrance, B. and McCullough, S. (2001) 'Differences in attitudes between women and men toward computerization', *Journal of Educational Computing Research*, 25 (3): 227–44.

Morahan-Martin, J. (1998) 'Males, females and the Internet', in J. Gackenbach (ed.) *Psychology and the Internet*, San Diego, CA: Academic Press, pp. 169–98.

Rheingold, H. (1993) *The Virtual Community: Homesteading on the Electronic Frontier*, Reading, MA: Addison-Wesley.

Richters, J., Grulich, A.E., de Visser, R.O., Smith, A.M.A. and Rissel, C.E. (2003) 'Autoerotic, esoteric and other sexual practices engaged in by a representative sample of adults', *Australian and New Zealand Journal of Public Health*, 27: 180–90.

The PEW Project (2000) *The Internet Life Report: Tracking Life Online*, at http://www.pewinternet.org/pdfs/Report1.pdf

Tikkanen, R. and Ross, M.W. (2000) 'Looking for sexual compatibility: experiences among Swedish men in visiting Internet gay chat rooms', *Cyberpsychology and Behavior*, 3: 605–16.

Van Zoonan, L. (2002) 'Gendering the Internet: claims, controversies and cultures', *European Journal of Communication*, 17 (1): 5–23.

MARJORIE KIBBY

D

DANCE

As an area of research, masculinity and dance remains under-examined, due in part to the overwhelming Western notion that men don't dance and to the homophobic assumption that men who do dance are gay. Scholarly research has primarily utilised feminist methodology, performance studies and queer theory to examine the construction of power and gender on stage and in social dances and the meaning of the body within social and ritual contexts. Questioning Western notions about men who dance, Burt (1995) outlines the biases that dominate masculinity within the practice of Western theatrical twentieth-century dance. Also, Cohan (1993) and Dyer (2002) have written important essays on entertainment and danced masculinity in popular culture.

Men have danced throughout history as a form of communication and pleasure within the cultural boundaries that define their masculinity. In early history a man's physical abilities and stature were demonstrated in danced rituals that included warrior, hunting, healing and fertility rites. Today, in many nations, traditional male dances have been transformed into entertainments for tourists, creating the illusion of a masculine 'otherness' that contributes to the 'imperialistic stereotypes' that Said outlines as 'the hegemony of Orientalism' (Said 1979: 329). However, in certain areas of Guyana, India, Bali and other societies, male dancers continue to perform important roles in the ritual and spiritual functions that have been a part of their cultures for generations.

In Europe, the height of the male dancer's prestige was in the Baroque court of Louis XIV (1638–1715), who used dance as a means of propaganda to establish his divine right to rule. This artificial court system required that men establish their nobility in daily public dance lessons, numerous weekly balls and performances in ballet spectacles. In this era a well-turned-out leg, an open chest, a smooth turn of the wrist and the skill to physically demonstrate musical innuendo symbolised a man's breeding, his harmonious relationship with nature, his stature at court, his potential as a lover and his integrity as a business partner. Also, the technique and coordination of Baroque dance was understood to mirror the arts of war (fencing and horsemanship), so dancing also demonstrated a man's skill as a warrior.

By the mid-1700s women dominated theatrical dance, and ballet became a peep show for men to gaze at women's legs and to find mistresses from the chorus of underprivileged female dancers. The Western notion that dancing is a female activity developed with the rise of the Romantic Ballet (1832), coinciding with the Industrial Revolution and the emerging middle class's construction of male and female identity. Burt outlines this development and interprets the homophobia that accompanies the expressive male body on display in Western theatrical dance throughout the twentieth century.

The eighteenth-century male ballet dancer found a home in the Danish Ballet of August Bournonville (1805–1889) and Mauris Petipa's (1818–1910) choreography for the Imperial Russian Ballet. Vaslov Nijinsky (1889–1950) is the most famous – and infamous – dancer to train in the Russian tradition and was one of the rare dance artists who possessed both a remarkable physical technique and the ability to fully inhabit the roles he performed. Critics wrote that when Nijinsky leaped he seemingly stayed in the air until he wanted to land and that the cells of his body appeared to reshape his body with each role he performed. It is speculated that Nijinsky's schizophrenia, which was eventually diagnosed, may have facilitated his ability to lose himself in his dancing.

Although Nijinsky's relationship with ballet impresario Serge Diaghilev (1872 – 1929) is the first publicised and most popular homosexual affiliation in ballet, today all Western theatrical male dancers must cope with the homophobic assumptions that accompany their career. In Hollywood, Fred Astaire and Gene Kelly overcame the assumptions that male dancers are homosexual by making their dancing about difficult physical accomplishments, sports, teaching and courting women. Bill 'Bojangles' Robinson (1878–1949) and other black dancers in early Hollywood needed to overcome deep-seated racism within the movie industry and the general audience. Hollywood's early image of the black male dancer was derived from minstrel shows, a complicated mix of black men parodying white men parodying black dancers parodying European social dances. The Nicholas Brothers' thirty films made them among the most admired Hollywood tap dancers, who established their masculine identity by creating athletic tap dance spectacle, jumping over each other and landing in the splits as they travelled down a flight of stairs, or dancing incredibly fast unison combinations.

By the time John Travolta danced in *Saturday Night Fever* (1979), male dancing had all but disappeared from Hollywood, due in part to the feminist movement and gay liberation's probing questions about the construction of gender. In response to these questions, Travolta's solo became an affirmation of his character's heterosexuality by subverting the gaze into a performance of his sexual potential. Gregory Hines and Mikhail Baryshnikov's performance in *White Nights* (1985) is one of the very few examples of a male relationship expressed in dance. Recent films such as *The Full Monty* (1997) and *Billy Elliot* (2000) assert heterosexual normative assumptions about the men who are forced to dance as a last-ditch effort to escape the dead-end existence of the UK's labour culture.

Challenging the assumption that men don't dance, choreographers such as Bill T. Jones, Mark Morris and Lloyd Newson have created work that clearly demonstrates that dance is a site for the expression and examination of masculinity.

References and further reading

Burt, R. (1995) *The Male Dancer*, New York: Routledge.

Cohan, S.R. (1993) 'Feminizing the song and dance man', in S. Cohan and I.R. Hark, *Screening the Male*, New York: Routledge, pp. 46–69.

—— (2000) *Art, Dance, and the Body in French Culture of the Ancient Régime*, Cambridge: Cambridge University Press.

Dyer, R. (2002) *Only Entertainment*, 2nd edn, New York: Routledge.

Said, E. (1979) *Orientalism*, New York: Vintage Books.

DARCEY CALLISON

DANDY, THE

A prominent social and literary figure of the past two centuries, the dandy expresses detachment from or disdain for the dominant social order by means of stylised costume and demeanour. Although the figure derives from earlier models of aristocratic masculinity, such as the courtier and the fop, the dandy comes to prominence in the nineteenth century as a being who affronts both aristocratic power and newly ascendant bourgeois values through an aestheticising of life itself. The single most influential dandy was George 'Beau' Brummel (1778–1840), whose hyper-fastidious elegance famously rebuked more slovenly aristocratic display in Regency Britain. Brummel became immensely influential in France, where Barbey D'Aurevilly's *Du Dandysme* (1845) and the writings of Baudelaire celebrated the dandy as an elite sensibility devoted to the pleasures of artifice, a being who resisted all appeals to nature and utility. As such, the dandy has been closely affiliated with avant-garde writing and art. In Britain, dandyism retreated under the force of Victorian social decorum until its spectacular resurgence in the late-century career of Oscar Wilde.

In Wilde's career, the dandy became closely bound up not only with the rise of aestheticism and 'decadence', but with the construction of gay identity. The dandy has retained this association in a host of contexts, from film and cabaret to the novels of Proust and Evelyn Waugh. But as an icon of resistance to social norms, the dandy has always eluded easy categories of both gender and sexuality. The dandy threatens normative masculinity through his resistance to action and his cultivation of sensibility and self-display. Yet the Wildean dandy jostles with other popular versions of the figure ('Jim Dandy') that body forth flamboyant heterosexuality. This ambiguity has led some critics to argue that the dandy is both fundamentally 'queer' and an emblem of the inherent instability and indeterminacy of gender itself.

References and further reading

Adams, J.E. (1995) *Dandies and Desert Saints*, Ithaca, NY and London: Cornell University Press.

Barbey D'Aurevilly, J. [1845] (1986) *Du Dandysme et de George Brummel*, Paris: Balland.

Feldman, J. (1993) *Gender on the Divide*, Ithaca, NY and London: Cornell University Press.

Moers, E. [1960] (1978) *The Dandy*, Lincoln, NE: Nebraska University Press.

Stanton, D. (1980) *The Aristocrat as Art*, New York: Columbia University Press.

JAMES ELI ADAMS

DEMOCRATIC MANHOOD

'Democratic manhood' describes a type of masculinity and a vision of a political future. Democratic manhood synthesises two apparently antithetical traditions. Whereas democracy is usually understood to mean equality, manhood refers to hierarchies of domination and inequality: to the inequalities between women and men, as well as those among men.

Developed by Michael Kimmel, among others, in *Manhood in America* (1996, 2005), the concept of democratic manhood includes a historical critique of the methods men in the United States have used to ground their masculinity in the public sphere and in a homosocially competitive marketplace. In a nation of supposedly 'self-made men', American men have sought to prove their masculinity (1) through the exclusion of others (women, non-whites, non-native-born immigrants, gay men); (2) by gaining self-control (over one's body and its physical expression); and (3) by escape (seeking one's manhood at sea, in the army, in the woods, or in some other environment in which men test each other).

Since the nineteenth century, American men have tried – and failed – to prove their manhood in these ways. Thus, there has been an incessant 'crisis' of masculinity for successive generations. However powerful and strong they become, men remain haunted by fears of weakness and softness. Manhood becomes a relentless test.

Proving manhood by excluding others has also failed, leaving the in-group uncertain and their criteria unstable. Nor has running away from society securely demonstrated manhood.

Kimmel argues that manhood cannot be retrieved by reasserting traditional privilege, nor by retreats to all-male island hideaways. He proposes a new definition of masculinity,

> a definition that is more about the character of men's hearts and souls than about the size of their biceps or their wallets. A definition that is capable of embracing differences among men and enabling other men to feel secure and confident rather than just

> excluding them; a definition that centres around standing up for justice and equality instead of running away from commitment and engagement.
>
> (1996: 333)

Democratic manhood means a gender politics of inclusion, of standing up against injustice based on difference. Some men have embraced feminism, gay liberation and multiculturalism to provide a blueprint for this reconstruction of masculinity.

References and further reading

Kimmel, M. (1996) *Manhood in America*, New York: Free Press; 2nd edn 2005, Oxford University Press.

MICHAEL KIMMEL

DEMOGRAPHY

This social science employs mathematical techniques to describe and analyse human populations. Practices of demographic quantification contribute fundamental techniques to modern governments. Censuses enumerate identity categories (gender/race/ethnicity/religion) as they map populations on to territory (Appadurai 1996). Vital statistics – annual tabulations of births, deaths, marriages and migrations – track national wealth and power. Population models demonstrate the mathematical regularities observed in censuses and vital statistics, producing patterns by which nations can be compared. The resulting numbers, charts and graphs become population 'facts' that obscure the social relations they represent and the complex calculations by which they are produced.

The discipline traces its origin to political economist and clergyman Malthus, who quantified and mapped the modern facts of population in 1798. Malthusian logic hinges on the differential mathematics underlying population and resources growth: a powerful 'instinct to propagation' leads inexorably to 'superabundant growth' by which population may double every twenty-five years. The growth potential of material resources (food and space) is more limited, increasing only when new land is cultivated. Thus, population will always outgrow resources, leading to high death rates through misery, war, famine, or reduced fertility caused by sexual vice. The capacity for reason, by which man might see the economic benefit of limiting his progeny, offers the only hope.

Malthus's principle is unmistakably bourgeois and masculine: population replicates the boom and bust of capitalist business cycles. The instinct of propagation is specifically cast as men's heterosexual desire; and delayed marriage along with abstinence offers the only virtuous 'habits with regard to the sex' (women). Malthus's survey of worldwide population trends ranks the known races/nations on a scale that measures civilisation by mortality rates, sexual mores and agricultural productivity. With a predictably bourgeois orientalism, he disparages the prospects for rational moral restraint in areas outside of Europe and among the European poor.

In the Cold War era, demographers modernised Malthusian logic in demographic transition theory. In this version, high fertility rates constitute the principal threat to economic growth in developing nations. The theory describes as normal the process of population change which purportedly began in Europe during Malthus's time (Szreter 1993). That is, the urbanisation and industrialisation associated with economic progress trigger a decline in the high mortality and fertility rates characteristic of traditional societies. Mortality drops almost automatically with rising living standards, but fertility decline requires deliberate effort and lags behind, producing rapid population growth. When fertility declines sufficiently, the stable low-growth population patterns of modern societies emerge. Predicated on this logic, demographers concluded that the patterns seen in developing nations during the 1950s were abnormal. Earlier colonialist interventions produced a premature decline in mortality, but customs governing family life in traditional cultures responded very slowly to the declining value of large families. Thus, demographers argued, governments had to actively promote the small family norm and deliberate fertility control if they were to restore the normal process of economic modernisation.

The interventions needed to decrease fertility hinge on modernising gender relations. However, although demographers became champions of deliberate fertility control, they have had a 'troubled relationship to feminism' (Greenhalgh 1996). Reflecting the tenets of sex-role theory, modern gender relations demographers described men and women as complementary personalities in male-dominated nuclear families. These normative sex roles govern contemporary demographic measurement practices, which authorise surveillance and biomedical interventions into women's reproductive lives.

The controversy over missing women provides a ready example. In the 1980s, demographers worried about high and increasing ratios of males to females born in the world's two largest populations, China and India, where birth records record more boys born than girls. Estimates made in the 1990s ranged as high as 100 million missing women worldwide (Hartmann 1995). These calculations rely on formulaic East–West comparisons: Centuries of birth records from Western nations are said to demonstrate that the 'normal', 'biological' sex ratio at birth (SRB) is nearly equal (105–6 males per 100 females, with the slight male advantage dismissed as compensation for their greater rates of fatal birth defects). If equality is nature's norm, then social inequality and differential treatment of women becomes the favoured explanation for less than 50 per cent girls in birth cohorts. The near equal Western sex ratios at birth and women's low mortality rates reflect their social equality, while higher sex ratios and female mortality rates in China and India are said to reflect women's poor treatment and a traditional son-preference. Widely available techniques of sex-selective abortion supplement purportedly traditional practices of abandonment and infanticide. Influenced by demographic theory, both nations have pursued aggressive fertility decline policies (e.g. India's sterilisation programmes of the 1970s and China's one-child policy in the 1990s). Those policies may have exacerbated son-preference and produced practices aimed at reducing girls' numbers. Yet deliberate misreporting of sex in censuses and under-reporting of girls in birth registries can also account for the statistical discrepancies (Greenhalgh 2001; Hartmann 1995). While debate will continue about whether girls and women are missing from 'the social landscape' or just from the data (Greenhalgh 2001), the terms of the debate reflect the continuing tangle of gender and orientalism by which Western population practices become the global standard.

References and further reading

Appadurai, A. (1996) *Modernity at Large*, Minneapolis, MN: Minnesota University Press.

Duden, B. (1992) 'Population', in W. Sachs (ed.) *The Development Dictionary*, London: Zed Books, pp. 146–57.

Greene, R. (1999) *Malthusian Worlds*. Boulder, CO: Westview.

Greenhalgh, S. (1996) 'The social construction of population science', *Comparative Studies of Society and History*, 5: 26–66.

—— (2001) 'Fresh winds in Beijing', *Signs*, 26: 847–87.

Greenhalgh, S. and Li, J. (1995) 'Engendering reproductive policy and practice in peasant China', *Signs*, 20: 601–41.

Hartmann, B. (1995) *Reproductive Rights and Wrongs*, Boston, MA: South End.

Malthus, T. [1798] (1992) *An Essay on the Principle of Population*, ed. D. Winch. Cambridge: Cambridge University Press.

Riedmann, A. (1993) *Science that Colonizes*, Philadelphia, PA: Temple University Press.

Riley, N. and McCarthy, J. (2003) *Demography in the Age of the Postmodern*, Cambridge: Cambridge University Press.

Szreter, S. (1993) 'The idea of demographic transition and the study of fertility', *Population and Development Review*, 19: 659–701.

CAROLE MCCANN

DEPRESSION

Depression is the most common of all mental disorders. Almost one in four persons will be diagnosed with depression at some point in their lives. Of special note to scholars who study men and masculinity is the consistent discrepancy between men and women in rates of depression. The most recent epidemiological data available indicates that women are almost twice as likely to experience a depressive episode over the course of a lifetime as are men.

Notwithstanding these rates of depression, in the United States alone it is estimated that at least 6 million men suffer with depression each year. To further compound the seriousness of the problem of undiagnosed and untreated depression in men, the rates of suicide are significantly elevated in men when compared with women. For all ages and races, men commit suicide more frequently than women.

Researchers have begun to uncover important relations between the effects of traditional gender role socialisation, masculinity ideologies and elevated risk for depression in men. Traditional masculine values that pertain to restricting emotional expressiveness and avoiding seeking help have been found to be associated with elevated risk for depression. Moreover, problems such as alcohol and drug abuse, domestic violence and problems with anger and aggression also appear to be closely related to depression in men.

In addition to these important empirical findings, several proposals have been made that call for an expansion of how social scientists and mental health professionals view depression. This expansion argues for recognition of the gendered nature of the concept of depression and for a re-evaluation of the widely accepted standardised criteria used to diagnose depression codified in the *Diagnostic and Statistical Manual of Mental Disorders* of the American Psychiatric Association. Expanded criteria for diagnosing depression in men would recognise how men are socialised to suppress or hide the traditional symptoms of depression such as depressed mood, sadness and crying. Expanded criteria would take into account the potential co-occurrence of alcohol and substance abuse, anger and violence in men's depressive episodes.

References and further reading

Cochran, S.V. and Rabinowitz, F.E. (2000) *Men and Depression: Clinical and Empirical Perspectives*, San Diego, CA: Academic Press.

Pollack, W.S. (1998) 'Mourning, melancholia, and masculinity', in W.S. Pollack and R. Levant (eds) *New Psychotherapy for Men*, New York: Wiley, pp. 147–66.

Real, T. (1998) *I Don't Want to Talk about It*, New York: Fireside, Simon and Schuster.

See also: age and ageing; aggression; domestic violence; drugs, addiction and abuse; health and illness, men's; suicide

SAM V. COCHRAN

DETECTIVE NOVEL, CRIME FICTION

Portrayals of masculinity in Anglo-American crime fiction can be divided into four categories. The first three correspond roughly to three subtypes of the genre: the analytical detective story, the hardboiled detective story and the psychological crime thriller. The fourth extends these trends in contemporary crime fiction. Taken together, the categories reveal the varied and historically shifting relations between male identity and a genre that has often been seen as intrinsically masculinist.

The analytical detective story was invented by Poe in 1841 with 'The murders in the Rue Morgue'. It is distinguished by a detective who remains morally and emotionally unimplicated in the world under investigation. That detective is sometimes a woman, as in the case of Christie's Miss Marple. More common are such figures as Poe's Dupin and Conan Doyle's Holmes – figures who embody a Victorian ideal of manliness that was central to US and British societies in the late nineteenth century. That ideal entailed the expression of a purportedly innate male aggressiveness that was central to success in the capitalist workplace. The ideal also required, however, that men control their violent passions in the name of developing the compassion necessary to authentic civic virtue.

The analytical detective offered a specific resolution of this tension. The sleuthing enterprise, as imagined in these stories, requires an aggression that is at once controlled and already civically virtuous. Analytic detectives sublimate their directly aggressive impulses into a battle of wits with the criminal. The defining feature of their detecting, accordingly, is the intellectual labour, transcending the body and its passions, required to solve the crime and bring the criminal to justice. These are, in short, 'armchair detectives', their victories achieved through analytic reason rather than through physical acts of courage or aggression.

Hardboiled fiction can be read as a reaction against this version of the detective. Due in part to social transformations at the turn of the twentieth century, the upper-class gentility of the analytic detective story became by the late 1920s and 1930s increasingly inadequate for resolving contemporary manhood's contradictions. 'Masculinity' emerged now as the radical antithesis of 'femininity', as a quality cleansed of any soft or feminine taint. Hardboiled fiction thus took as its task the courting yet vanquishing of feminising dangers.

Several modifications followed from this shift. Unlike the analytical detective, the 'dick' in Hammett and Chandler is a professional ('dick' is slang for 'detective', with obvious connotations); his detective work is paid labour, predicated on economic exchange rather than on intellectual detachment. This exchange functions as a gateway to erotic temptations, emotional entanglements and physical vulnerabilities from which the analytical sleuth was protected. The interest of the hardboiled story thus lies less in the ultimate solution of a mystery than in the detective's successful navigation of a violence to which he is subject yet surmounts, and a seduction that tempts him but that he resists.

In navigating these dangers, the detective is drawn into a universe starkly different from that of Poe or Conan Doyle. Crime is not here deviant or aberrant; it is constitutive and practically universal. Far from affirming the social order's goodness, hardboiled fiction insists upon its toxicity – a toxicity embodied over and again in a *femme fatale* who threatens the detective's 'discrete sense of selfhood' (Marling 1982: 67). At its best, this treatment gives rise to the wounded lyricism of Hammett's Spade or Chandler's Marlow. At its worst, it offers a readymade generic formula for the sadistic misogyny of a Spillane.

The third subspecies of crime fiction emerged simultaneously with the hardboiled form and in response to identical social pressures. Critics have called it the psychological crime thriller in order to emphasise two points: it diminishes, eliminates or pathologises the figure of the detective; and its interest lies primarily in the psychological effects of crime on the criminal. These transformations enabled such writers as Cain, Thomson, Highsmith and (in France) Simenon to explore how men might *embrace* the feminine threats to selfhood that the hardboiled form parries. For the books' male protagonists, this is hardly good news. Their encounters with the feminine lead directly to their psychological dismantling. They are forced to acknowledge that the feminine criminality they try to externalise is internal to themselves, and the result is a destruction that takes the form either of literal death or of a psychotic rupture in which the female-criminal other is shown to 'inhabit' the masculine self.

Contemporary crime fiction encompasses while extending these traditions. Not only can one find, in the early twenty-first century, examples of all the subspecies described so far, but the genre has also spawned such mutations as the police procedural, the medical-forensic thriller and the psychologist-detective novel. This subgeneric multiplication has been accompanied by a greater openness to countercultural voices. Authors of crime fiction now include African Americans (Mosley,

Neely), heterosexual women (Grafton, Rendell), gay men (Hansen), lesbians (Wilson) and writers from Latin America (Fonseca, Boullosa), Africa (McCall Smith, Dow) and the Caribbean (Chamoiseau). Such shifts are not without precedent. Crime fiction migrated by the late nineteenth century to places as varied as Brazil, Mexico, Italy, Sweden and Russia. It had from early on such female practitioners as Christie and Sayers. And the African American Himes's brilliant hardboiled novels date from the 1950s and 1960s. The contemporary moment is unique, however, for two reasons. First, it boasts unprecedented numbers of women, blacks, gay men, lesbians and postcolonial authors who adapt the genre to their concerns; and second, even white male authors now grapple habitually with the legacy of social movements that challenge their hegemony, especially those of feminism, civil rights and the struggle against colonialism.

References and further reading

Forter, G. (2000) *Murdering Masculinities*, New York: New York University Press.

Irons, G. (ed.) (1995) *Feminism in Women's Detective Fiction*, Toronto: University of Toronto Press.

Marling, W. (1982) 'The Hammett succubus', *Clues*, 3: 66–75.

Reddy, M.T. (2003) *Traces, Codes, and Clues*, New Brunswick, NJ: Rutgers University Press.

See also: culture and representation; hegemonic masculinity; literature

GREG FORTER

DEVELOPMENT

'Development' is a politically loaded term, heavy with meaning and associated with contentious ideas about growth, modernisation, power and social transformation. As a concept that was constructed in the industrialised north, it is the subject matter of ongoing debates over the meaning of progress in poor southern countries. It is more than just an idea, however. Development is an aspiration to be worked towards – a process that is inextricably interventionist in nature which encapsulates the need to take action and effect change.

The promotion of gender-equal societies has become an increasingly significant part of that process. This trend has corresponded with the widespread acknowledgement that, more often than not, gender difference amounts to gender inequality. As a result, gender-conscious language now pervades development literature and gender equality is explicitly promoted through the Millennium Development Goals.

The difficulty is that men appear to be missing from much gender and development policy and practice. The field has been dominated by a focus on ending men's privilege and women's subordination. Early approaches to gender in development were aimed at rectifying the so-called 'feminisation' of poverty through the provision of women's welfare, measures to increase women's visibility in projects and programmes, and the promotion of the productive potential of women as a means of securing the more effective delivery of development. Later, development theorists began to direct their attention to the social structures and processes that shape gender norms. The change of terminology from Women in Development (WID) to Gender and Development (GAD) represented a shift towards recognising the need to analyse social relationships between men and women and to be more aware of factors such as class, age and personal agency in these. Despite this shift in emphasis, however, there remains little recognition in much development policy of the need to analyse and understand the lives of men as well as women.

With a few notable exceptions, men are rarely explicitly mentioned in gender policy documents. Where men do appear, they are generally seen as obstacles to women's development: men must surrender their positions of dominance for women to become empowered. The superiority of women as hard-working, reliable, trustworthy, socially responsible, caring and co-operative is often asserted; while men on the other hand are frequently portrayed as lazy, violent, promiscuous and irresponsible drunkards.

Why then, focus on men? Emerging critiques of policy argue for special attention to be paid to men and masculinities in development, as follows.

Gender is relational. It concerns the relationships between men and women which are subject to negotiation in both private and public spheres. To focus analysis on women only is inadequate: a better understanding of men's perceptions and positions and the scope for changing these, is essential. For example, development initiatives that involve men in reproductive and sexual health decision-making need to recognise men and women's differing constructions of sexuality, as well as building their capacity to negotiate mutually agreed practices (Doyle in Cleaver 2002).

Equality and social justice. Men as well as women may be disadvantaged by social and economic structures; they both have the right to live life free from poverty and repression. Empowerment processes should enable women *and men* to be liberated from the confines of gender-stereotyped roles.

Gendered vulnerabilities. Stereotyping men as the oppressors and women as the oppressed is considered unhelpful. Evidence from several studies suggests that while women in general may face greater social and economic disadvantages, men are not always the winners and that generalising about their situation risks overlooking gender-specific inequities and vulnerabilities, such as the damaging health effects of certain 'masculine' labour roles or social practices.

Crises of masculinity. It is suggested that changes in the economy, social structures and household composition are resulting in 'crises of masculinity' in many parts of the world. The 'demasculinising' effects of poverty and of economic and social change may be eroding men's traditional roles as providers and limiting the availability of alternative, meaningful roles for men in families and communities.

Strategic gendered partnerships. There is a strong argument that if gender-equitable change is to be achieved in households, communities and organisations, then men are needed as allies and partners. This links to concerns about the need to mainstream gender issues in development policy to ensure that they are not sidelined or underfunded as 'women's issues'.

As with many other development activities, questions of how to track and evaluate changes in gender relationships prove difficult. Indeed, the whole emerging area of men and development is a challenging one and the critical scholarship is still limited. Nevertheless, a number of recurring themes can be identified.

Dominant masculinities

Attention is drawn to the fact that understanding the power dimensions of gender relations requires consideration of the hierarchies that exist both between men and women and between men and other men. Connell (2000) suggests that not all men benefit equally from the institutions of patriarchy and that some forms of masculinity are culturally elevated, in certain times and places, above others. For example, in certain African communities, elderly men may exert greater social power and political position than younger men (Bujra in Cleaver 2002).

There is reflection on the different cultural concepts of manliness and the variety and complexity of ways of 'being a man'. Additionally, there is a need to consider class, race and age in understanding men's and women's lives, and the ways in which they relate to each other (White 1999; Nye 2005). Questions also arise about the extent to which dominant masculinities and gender relations are bound up with historical relations of economic and political domination, particularly with the workings of imperialism and capitalism.

Empowerment

A recognition of the potential of the wider social and economic structures of society to oppress both men and women raises questions of the limitations of development projects and their ability to promote empowerment. Research on micro-credit projects for women offers contradictory evidence variously illustrating the empowering effects of credit on some women (more control over household finances), the disempowering effects (men threatened by such changes resort to domestic violence), the potential of gendered partnerships achieved through household negotiation (men and women agreeing on the use of credit to the benefit of the household) and the severe limitations of such interventions (the money gained is small in quantity and does little to address structural poverty) (Osmani 1998; Goetz and Gupta 1996).

Personal, sexual and family issues

The importance of an awareness of changing needs and priorities over life courses is strongly emphasised here. As with much development activity, there is a strong concentration on reproductively and economically active young people and adults, to the neglect of older men and their concerns (Varley and Blasco 2000).

Development interventions projects and research emphasise the importance of men's roles in relation to employment and the ability to provide for families. This has become an area of crisis as structural reform of economies results in the widespread loss of formal sector jobs, while processes of globalisation in some places lead to the 'feminisation' of the workforce. The inability of men to fulfil the 'breadwinner' role may lead to considerable insecurity and frustration, often translated into violence. A further concern is that, where men do fulfil their roles in conditions of extreme economic pressure, the time, effort and responsibility involved may render them vulnerable to poor health.

Poverty is seen as a serious obstacle to the ability to be a good father; for example, poor men express anxiety above the circumstances which push them to send young children to work (Jackson 1998). Additionally economic stress, poor self-esteem and traditional ideas about gender roles have been linked to domestic violence, and addressing this has become a key concern of current development activities

Sex and sexuality play a large part in discussions of men and masculinity. Greig (in White 1999) has pointed out that masculinity is deeply implicated in the harm men experience in their lives and cause in the lives of others. This observation is particularly relevant in the area of HIV transmission. Much debate speculates about how far sexuality and relationships are the appropriate focus of development issues, and how to involve men in discussing these. Several projects and studies emphasise that it is far easier to get men involved in reflecting upon such issues when the focus is child health and well-being rather than sex and sexuality per se.

Gender and working lives

The concept of the excessive labour burden of women, their 'triple role' in productive, reproductive and community work, has been queried on several grounds. First, the dominance of time studies showing women's greater burden of work is questioned. While most acknowledge the usefulness of these studies in making visible domestic work, their oversimplified application has led to the assertion that men are lazy and do little work. Time studies are shown to be problematic in their methodology and to incompletely record male domestic labour and other activities related to building social capital. They have also been criticised for their lack of attention to other dimensions of work such as effort and intensity. Jackson suggests that when these dimensions are taken into account gender inequities in work burden may not be as marked (Jackson 1998).

A common question raised concerns as to how gendered divisions of labour come about. Is there anything inherently 'male' about men's work, or essentially 'female' about women's work (MacInnes 1998)? The fluidity in roles and the scope for shifting these, especially in light of the negative impact that globalisation processes may have on both poor men and poor women, suggest that gendered divisions of labour are far from 'natural'. This has implications for rethinking development policy which specifically targets women, for example, as responsible for children's health and education.

The role of the state

The role of state action in creating masculinities, or creating the conditions for changing gender relations, is emphasised in a number of academic studies. For example, Dolan and Kandirikirira (writing respectively about Uganda and Namibia) both link state action (or inaction) to the creation of distorted and damaging forms of masculinity, often expressed in violence. Morrell (2001), however, draws on recent South African experience to show how the state may be a positive agent for change. There is an emerging strand of thought which emphasises the need to see societal-level violence and domestic violence as intrinsically linked through gendered socialisation, experiences of fear and weakness, and the ubiquitous 'warrior discourse' through which ways of 'being a man' are defined (Vijayan in Cleaver 2002).

Gender analysis and development practice

Several writers note the difficulty gender analysis poses to development practice when it strays into the 'private' realm. Indeed, it is claimed that development agencies prefer to tackle the less contentious and public dimensions of gender (promoting women's involvement, etc.) rather than becoming embroiled in the personal politics of intimate relationships.

There is a set of questions about whose voices and experiences are reflected in a focus on men and masculinities. These are particularly significant given the widespread adoption of participatory processes in development interventions, though well-meaning, participatory approaches may be driven by gendered interests and may actually exclude or marginalise the least powerful (Cornwall 2003).

The question of whether women can promote a gendered approach to development which embraces men as partners mirrors previous questions of 'Can men be feminists?' Pearson (2000) suggests that it is a cause for concern that few 'mainstream' male development policy-makers seem interested in the subject. It has been argued that in order to mainstream gender concerns, it is necessary to involve men in development agencies more closely with the shaping of gender-related policy and practice. Indeed, some development agencies stress the need to foster an organisational culture which promotes equitable participation and distribution of power between men and women in the organisation. However, the problem of the 'patriarchal culture' of development organisations (Chant and Gutmann 2000) may result in the marginalising of gender concerns as peripheral 'women's issues'.

References and further reading

Chant, S. and Gutmann, M. (2000) *Mainstreaming Men, Gender and Development: Debates, Reflections and Experiences*, Oxfam Working Paper, Oxford: Oxfam.

Cleaver, F. (ed.) (2002) *Masculinities Matter! Men, Gender and Development*, London: Zed Books.

Connell, R. (2000) *The Men and the Boys*, Cambridge: Polity Press.

Cornwall, A. (2000) 'Men, masculinities and development: politics, policies and practice', *IDS Bulletin*, 31 (2 April): 1–6.

—— (2003) 'Whose voices? Whose choices? Reflections on gender and participatory development', *World Development*, 31 (8): 1325–42.

Goetz, A. and Gupta, S. (1996) 'Who takes the credit? Gender, power and control over loan use in rural credit programmes in Bangladesh', *World Development*, 24 (1): 45–64.

Jackson, C. (1998) 'Gender, irrigation and environment: arguing for agency', *Agriculture and Human Values*, 15 (4): 313–24.

MacInnes, J. (1998) 'Capitalist development: creator of masculinity and destroyer of patriarchy?' Men, Masculinities and Gender Relations in Development Seminar, available at http://www.brad.ac.uk/acad/dppc/gender.html

Morrell, R. (ed.) (2001) *Changing Men in Southern Africa*, London: Zed Books.

Nye, R.A. (2005) 'Locating masculinity: some recent work on men', *Signs: Journal of Women in Culture and Society*, 30 (3): 1937–62.

Osmani, L. (1998) 'The Grameen Bank experiment: empowerment of women through credit', in H. Afshar (ed.) *Women and Empowerment: Illustrations from the Third World*, Basingstoke: Macmillan, pp. 67–85.

Pearson, R. (2000) 'Masculinities and gender analysis', *The British Council Network Newsletter*, 21 (November), The British Council, Manchester, pp. 2–3.

Varley, A. and Blasco, M. (2000) 'Exiled to the home: masculinity and ageing in urban Mexico', *European Journal of Development Research*, 12 (2, December): 115–38.

White, S. (1999) 'The politics of the personal: seminar report', Men Masculinities and Gender Relations in Development Seminar, available at http://www.brad.ac.uk/acad/dppc/gender.html

FRANCES CLEAVER
ANGELA KIIRE

DIASPORIC AND MIGRANT MASCULINITIES

Acts of migration frequently unsettle assumptions about gender. Highly regulated, naturalised codes of masculinity are revealed to be heavily coded performances when expressions of gender from one culture violate the social expectations of a new country or cultural space. Fashionably masculine hair or clothing styles from one culture, for instance, may be considered non-conformist or even effeminate in another. Lapses in the gendered translation of cultures can be extremely stressful on the level of everyday experience, but they can also offer the opportunity for a conscious reconsideration of imbalances in the gendered structures of ordinary lives.

The condition of diaspora, in which a displaced community transplants cultural practices to a new host country with different cultural practices, offers an ideal forum for exploring the all-pervasiveness of gender in culture. People in diaspora often experience these differences as a clash, as if two cultures could be sturdy static entities. By highlighting how gender and other cultural differences are negotiated, however, people in diaspora embody the way that gender and other aspects of culture are actually a matter of dynamic, ongoing meaning-making, representation and interpretation. The idea of diaspora as cultural narrative, not essential identity, was introduced by Stuart Hall in 'Cultural identity and diaspora' (1990).

Gender in dislocation

Daniel Coleman, in *Masculine Migrations* (1998), offers the metaphor of a straw in water or a sound wave in air to introduce the idea of cross-cultural gender refraction. Just as a straw appears to bend as it enters liquid or a sound wave appears to change pitch as it moves from cool to warm air, masculinities and femininities are vulnerable to distortion as they shift from one cultural medium to another. This is not to say that codes of masculinity and femininity become totally unrecognisable as they relocate across cultures, only that migrating performances of gender, evidenced, for example, in clothing styles, family narratives and body language, reveal themselves as historically, geographically and culturally specific, not universal. Because patriarchal advantage understands itself as natural and universal in most places in the world, it is important to denaturalise gender relations and expose the particularities of their constructions.

Coleman's analysis of gendered dislocation in masculine migrant narratives is heavily influenced by the theoretical work of psychoanalytic/queer theorist Judith Butler. Butler stresses that, though taken as absolute, gender is an effect of persistent, overlapping representations. These representative acts do not 'reveal' whether a person 'has' masculinity or femininity, but instead actually produce and regulate masculine and feminine identities. The importance of meaning-making and regulation in gender practice is made particularly clear in moments of dislocated masculinity and femininity.

Butler, particularly in her 1990 text *Gender Trouble*, emphasises the idea of gender as a strictly enforced, overlapping series of performative moments which can be accidentally or deliberately misperformed for political, cultural, or ideological ends. For instance, if a man who has migrated to Canada wraps his lower body in a skirt-like garment, his performance can take on significantly different meanings depending on details and context.

If the migrant is a Scot and his 'skirt' is a wool tartan kilt, matched with a tuxedo jacket on his wedding day (a common sight in Canada), then he is confirming and reproducing several overlapping ideologies about migration, cultural heritage and gender. The wedding-day kilt also reinforces dominant notions about race and, possibly, sexuality. Whatever the Scottish migrant's individual inspiration in choosing that dress, he is likely to be interpreted as embodying and reinforcing: (a) the Canadian passion for social, apolitical multiculturalism; (b) the masculine mythology of rugged, dignified Highlander physicality (especially if he jokes loudly about following the legendary tradition of not wearing underwear); (c) Canadian militarism (for some Canadian regiments, the kilt is still part of formal military wear); (d) an Anglo-Saxon Protestant racial-religious heritage; (e) the patrilineage coded in the tartan; and, if he is marrying a woman, (f) the promise of cultural continuation through potential reproduction.

This faithful reinscription of multiple ideologies would not occur if the details of the performance were slightly different. The act of a man wrapping his lower body in cloth would signify with less patriotism and, arguably, less masculinity if the man was not a white migrant and was merely walking down the street in a bright sarong. At best, such a transcultural performance of masculinity might be interpreted as contributing to Canadian multiculturalism, albeit signifying in a less familiar way than in the instance of the Scottish kilt. The sarong would fail to evoke the interlocking institutions of religious, racial and cultural 'heritage' that the kilt seamlessly reinforces in a Canadian context. By not producing the other interlocking masculinised ideologies, the bright sarong could also, by default, evoke some of the femininity of a Canadian woman's skirt, even if not directly mistaken for it. In its potential proximity to the feminine skirt, the sarong could be interpreted as being a *threat* to, or at least in defiance of, dominant masculinity, naturalised heterosexuality, patriotism and culture at large.

While individual crises of gender are liable to occur in migration, consistent ruptures in gender practice are sometimes clearer in instances of collective ethnic relocation. A particularly useful concept for understanding the problems, compromises and negotiations of gender-in-motion is 'diaspora'.

Diaspora defined

The term 'diaspora' comes from an ancient Greek term meaning 'to sow over' or 'to scatter around'. As Robin Cohen points out in *Global Diasporas* (1997), there is a fundamental tension in the etymology of 'diaspora'. The term first appeared in ancient Greek as a way of describing the practice of imperial expansion and territorial absorption. Later, however, in the Greek translation of the Christian Bible, the term described the traumatic exile of the Jewish population as a refugee community. Cohen makes passing reference to the patriarchal overtones of colonial 'seed scattering' in the term's history, but he is otherwise silent about the negotiations and compromises that the diasporic condition demands of gendered identities.

Despite its silence on the topic of gender, Cohen's text is significant for its recognition of how the term 'diaspora' eventually expanded to include, along with victimised and colonising collectivities, ethnic groups displaced for reasons of labour, trade and culture. Many studies of diaspora throughout the 1990s tend to overlook the gendered politics of how diasporas manage to exist, how transplanted cultures are sustained and reproduced by men and women who understand themselves through renegotiated versions of masculinity and femininity.

Diaspora and gendered labour

Sometimes diasporas are formed with stark gender imbalances because host countries pass migration laws that attempt to satisfy specific labour needs while restricting the reproduction of immigrant culture. Gender imbalances in diasporas also occur in instances of illegal labour migration, as can be seen with female domestic workers in the United States and the trafficking of women for prostitution across both post-Communist Eastern Europe and South Asia at the end of the twentieth century and start of the twenty-first century.

The creation of some labour diasporas demonstrates the interdependence of identity categories such as 'race' and 'gender'. Historically, governments have regulated particular kinds of labour to enforce racist ideologies. For example, in need of workers to build the Canadian Pacific Railway in the late nineteenth century, the Canadian government encouraged the migration of Chinese men because they would work with explosives and heavy rocks, doing the hardest work for the least pay. After the railway was completed in 1885, however, the government sought to cut off the development of a Chinese presence by imposing an expensive racialised head tax that severely limited the men's ability to bring their wives and children to join them. The Canadian government's need for 'expendable' male labour and their conflicting desire to restrict the reproduction of migrant culture effectively created what is commonly referred to as a 'bachelor society'. When the threat of Chinese-Canadian culture thoroughly outweighed the government's need for imported male labour, the government imposed the migration-halting Chinese Exclusion Act in 1923 (in effect until 1947).

As well as being racialised and ethnicised, diasporic masculinities and femininities are also organised around class positions, as happened when the Canadian government introduced the 1955 Domestic Scheme. This plan encouraged women from Jamaica, Trinidad and Barbados to become domestic labourers in the homes of affluent Canadians. A condition of the women's immigration was that the workers were required to live with the families for whom they worked for at least a year before applying for citizenship. Whereas many of these women were subordinate to men in their home cultures and clearly subordinate to the Canadian families for whom they worked, the women's newfound access to work and legal immigration destabilised the patriarchal organisation of social relations in diaspora.

Women labourers in this position often became the primary, if not sole, providers of financial resources for their families in the Caribbean and also became a gateway for the legal immigration of Caribbean men. Austin Clarke's novel *The Meeting Point* (1967) represents in detail how diasporic masculinity could become increasingly blustery, anxious and fragile as the men sought to preserve pride while depending heavily on women.

Armine Ishkanian, in 'Mobile motherhood: Armenian women's labour migration in the post-Soviet period' (2002), describes the gendered re-evaluation of status that happens in certain illegal diasporas. As described above, the migrant female worker is likely to be disempowered in the complex reorganisation of gender, class and racial/ethnic status. Ishkanian points out that the work of domestic cleaning carries connotations of lower-class status in both the USA and Armenia. Despite these disadvantages, the female Armenian diasporic worker has experienced increased status in her diasporic community and her country of origin at the expense of dependent migrating men in diaspora and non-migrating, unemployed women at home.

Gender and diasporic youth

In *Schooling, Diaspora, and Gender* (2001), Georgina Tsolidis gives a detailed examination of the complexities that diasporic teenagers face as they attempt to balance the differently ethnicised and gendered expectations coming from parents, extended family and community on the one hand and public institutions, teachers and mainstream-culture peers on the other. Tsolidis studies the way in which the children of immigrants in multicultural Australia work with the restrictions, but also the unexpected freedoms and pleasures, that come with inheriting transcultural gender ideologies.

Tsolidis looks at performances of both masculinity and femininity as she studies pressures to protect the reputations of diasporic youth. Focusing on a Greek community in Australia, Tsolidis points out that females were particularly subject to policing by parents and the censuring gossip of older women; male youth were in a contradictory bind of being both subject to diasporic scrutiny and also expected to contribute to the chaperoning of the females. The parents' expectation that teenage males were chaperoning teenage females was reinforced, paradoxically, whether the boys openly agreed to watch protectively over the girls or whether they disagreed and rebelliously invited the girls to socialise with them outside of the home.

The patriarchal fear of tarnished young female reputation is not specific to diaspora, but it can be heightened because of generalised feelings of disempowerment and cultural exclusion. Although the male teenagers in the study complained of racial discrimination, they experienced greater social freedom than their female counterparts. The males could share in mainstream Australian masculinity through sport and other social activities, as well as socialising with female Australian peers and enjoying later curfews than diasporic females. A pattern emerged in Tsolidis's study wherein the diasporic boys' compliance in 'protecting' the girls increased in proportion to the degree of racism that they had personally experienced. Tsolidis writes that while the diasporic girls did not like this oppressive arrangement, they coped with it by reinforcing their sense of ethnic community in making cross-cultural clothing choices, idolising foreign musicians and using languages other than English in the classroom, all of which distinctly combined performances of ethnicity with teenage femininity.

Tsolidis draws attention to the levels of agency that diasporic females and males discover in what is, in many ways, a system of rigidly patriarchal gender relations. She analyses one girl's narrative of her semi-arranged marriage to a young man from her home country of Turkey. The teenager's Australian teachers viewed the traditional wedding as archaic, patriarchal and life-limiting. Tsolidis, however, found that the young diasporic woman was able to flex a good deal of agency in the selection of a groom, purchase of a house and rapid establishment of a small business. Tsolidis concludes that, though it may appear that masculine privilege dominates in apparent collisions of culture, sometimes transplanted tradition helps diasporic youth reach thoughtful and progressive cultural compromises that draw on the best of different cultural practices.

References and further reading

Butler, J. (1990) *Gender Trouble*, London: Routledge.

Clarke, A. [1967] (1988) *The Meeting Point*, Toronto: Vintage.

Cohen, R. (1997) *Global Diasporas*, Seattle, WA: University of Washington Press.

Coleman, D. (1998) *Masculine Migrations*, Toronto: University of Toronto Press.

Ember, M., Ember, C.R. and Skoggard, I. (eds) (2004) *Encyclopedia of Diasporas*, vols 1 and 2, New York: Kluwer Academic.

Hall, S. (1990) 'Cultural identity and diaspora', in J. Rutherford (ed.) *Identity: Community, Culture, Difference*, London: Lawrence and Wishart, pp. 222–37.

Ishkanian, A. (2002) 'Mobile motherhood', *Diaspora*, 11 (3): 383–415.

Tsolidis, G. (2001) *Schooling, Diaspora, and Gender*, Buckingham: Open University Press.

See also: agency; Chinese masculinities; class, work and masculinity; global masculinities; history, colonisation; honour; race and ethnicity

JOHN P. CORR

DISABILITY

A disability is a physical or mental impairment that substantially limits one or more major life activities (Americans with Disabilities Act (ADA) 1990) and which may be congenital or the result of an illness or injury. Disability rights activists and theorists have argued for understanding disability as a linguistic or socio-political category, not a medico-legal one. Everyone, if they live long enough, will encounter a degree of physical or mental impairment, a reality which has caused disability theorists to speak of the temporarily abled, rather than the 'able-bodied' (Davis 1995). A relational model of disability sees impairment as a result of the relationship between individuals and the environment, produced by architectural, economic and other barriers. Deafness is not a disability in a community which uses sign language, while stairs, but not ramps, produce an impairment for someone using a wheelchair. These circumstances challenge the self-evidence of disability as a physical condition and highlight its instability and contextuality.

Within the applied fields of education, medicine and social services, the disability rights movement has argued for the complete integration of 'special education' and for seeing disability as a variable in dealing with client needs, rather than a defining characteristic. Within academia, disability studies is a growing field, with theorists such as Lennard Davis and Rosemarie Thomson calling for the inclusion of a theoretical perspective on disability within history, psychology, women's studies, literature, philosophy and anthropology.

Disability has historically been defined as a lack of economic productivity (Davis 1995). Under the ADA definition of disability, a history of employability has been interpreted in the courts as proof that people are not disabled, and therefore not protected by anti-discrimination legislation. Sixty-nine per cent of Americans who have disabilities are unemployed (Davis 1995), and when they do work they earn less than the 'abled' population. The loss in income is greater for disabled men than for disabled women due to the fact that men generally earn more than women. However, disabled men continue to earn more than disabled women. (Gerschick 2000). Davis describes the relationship between disability and poverty, noting the lack of medical care and greater likelihood of job-related injuries among working-class populations. The majority of new incidences of quadriplegia and paraplegia are due to gunshot wounds and occur among young urban working-class men, who are also more likely to sustain injuries in car accidents, at war or from contact sports than other groups. Shakespeare (1999) notes that other behaviours traditionally associated with masculinity, such as excessive consumption, recklessness and risk-taking also contribute towards disability through illness and injury.

Men with disabilities have often been represented as not really men/masculine (Hahn 1997). Shakespeare finds that men with lifelong physical disabilities are unwilling, or feel unable, to live up to ideals of masculinity which centre on strength or authority and therefore experience and live gender in ways that may not fit stereotypes of masculinity. He also finds that disabled men who are unable to have intercourse may feel asexual and argues that this is due to an over-emphasis on the importance of penetrative sex as the only valid sexuality for men (1999). However, disabled men are four times more likely than disabled women to marry, and four times less likely to get divorced if they develop a disability while married (Gerschick 2000).

A postcolonial definition of disability applies especially to the deaf community, which can be seen as an ethnic group with its own language, carrying genetic information that is passed down from generation to generation

(Davis 1995). Activism and theory by the deaf community calls for an understanding of deafness as a culture, not an impairment, and a recognition of ASL (American Sign Language) as a legitimate language in academic curricula. Verena Keck cautions against using Western medical categories in cross-cultural studies of disability. Her analysis of the Yupno of Papua New Guinea finds a system already in place for naming and understanding disability, in the use of the terms *kadim* (referring to behavioural criteria) and *ngamu* (referring to social and mental criteria) which designate 'disabilities', but which are not mutually exclusive as applied to individuals in the culture. The factors that influence the development of disability cross-culturally also differ from those in Western contexts. In Western cultures, disability as a consequence of aging is more often experienced and reported by women than men, and marriage reduces the negative effects of aging for both parties, although men experience a greater health benefit. In India, however, men are less likely to become disabled as they age, but women experience greater health benefits from marriage (Sengupta and Agree 2002).

References and further reading

Davis, L. (1995) *Enforcing Normalcy*, New York: Verso.

—— (2002) *Bending Over Backwards*, New York: New York University Press.

Garland-Thomson, R. (1997) *Extraordinary Bodies*, New York: Columbia University Press.

Gerschick, T.J. (2000) 'Toward a theory of disability and gender', *Signs*, 25 (4): 1263–8.

Hahn, H. (1997) 'Advertising the acceptably employable image', in Lennard David (ed.) *The Disability Studies Reader*, London: Routledge, pp. 172–86.

Keck, V. (1999) 'Colder than cool', *Anthropology and Medicine*, 6 (2): 261–83.

Linton, S. (1998) *Claiming Disability*, New York: New York University Press.

McRuer, R. (2002) 'Compulsory able-bodiedness and queer/disabled existence', in S.L. Snyder, B.J. Brueggemann and R. Garland-Thomson (eds) *Disability Studies*, New York: Modern Language Association of America, pp. 88–99.

Norden, M.F. (1994) *The Cinema of Isolation*, New Brunswick, NJ: Rutgers University Press.

Sengupta, M. and Agree, E.M. (2002) 'Gender and disability among older adults in North and South India', *Journal of Cross-Cultural Gerontology*, 17: 313–36.

Shakespeare, T. (1999) 'The sexual politics of disabled masculinity', *Sexuality and Disability*, 17 (1): 53–64.

Smith, B.J. and Hutchison, B. (eds) (2004) *Gendering Disability*, New Brunswick, NJ: Rutgers University Press.

See also: bodies and biology, male; health and illness, men's

SUSANNAH BREDENKAMP

DIVORCE AND SEPARATION

Divorce and separation have long been sites of contestation and struggle. There are signs, however, that the nature of these struggles may be changing across jurisdictions, in particular in the area of post-divorce/separation contact and child custody. In this process questions of masculinity are becoming increasingly prominent.

Divorce, Kaganas and Day Sclater have argued, obliges parents to position themselves in relation to a range of often competing discourses (legal, welfare, therapeutic and, more recently, human rights) and to find ways of living alongside them (2004). There has emerged since the 1980s – notably, although not exclusively, in the UK, Canada, Australia and the United States – a move towards a 'new welfare discourse' in the field of divorce (Sclater and Piper 1999). In marked contrast to earlier ideas of the post-marriage 'clean break', children are being conceptualised as vulnerable and divorce and separation are seen as particularly damaging, for the individuals concerned, for children and for society. Located within the context of a political refocusing, across Western societies, on issues of citizenship and ideas of (divorcing) responsibly (Reece 2003), there has occurred in the UK context a clear and determined attempt to effect social engineering in the area of the family by changing the very nature of post-divorce family life (Smart and Neale 1999). In this process, a repositioning of men and masculinity has been seen as a central element. Ideas of 'good' fatherhood have been reconstructed, reconstituted, remade in the legal regulation of post-divorce family life.

What constitutes 'good enough' post-divorce parenting is not, and has never been, universally agreed struggles over meaning and desired norms around gender. The welfare discourse has involved a model of child welfare that places co-operative parenting and contact with the non-resident parent at the centre of children's well-being: a non-resident parent who is, in the majority of cases, the father. The new paradigm of divorce has positioned men and women in different ways as, variously, the good, responsible (or irresponsible) subjects of divorce. It is in this context that questions around masculinity have themselves become a recurring theme within the growing body of international research on post-divorce separation life, not least in work concerned with fathers' rights agendas and the rise of 'gender neutral' (Fineman 1995) family law. The findings of therapeutic, psychological and sociological research have been drawn on so as to suggest a qualitative, as well as quantitative, shift in men's physical and emotional relationship to children and child care in the post-divorce/separation context, as well as in men's own self-identification around ideas of 'family life'. This rests on a number of assumptions about fathers as respectable and socially 'safe' subjects (Collier 1995); as sharers of responsibilities, active participants in paid employment, child care and domestic labour.

These developments have not been without critics. A growing research base has questioned what this means for parents who divorce – and, in particular, the impact of the 'new contact culture' on mothers. Research suggests that the new divorce ideal has impacted on the practices of the courts, lawyers, family welfare professionals and parents. There has emerged in case law the figure of the 'implacably hostile', bad, selfish mother. It is assumed that fatherhood and 'what men do' is revealed as problematic at the point of divorce or separation. However, Smart and Neale (1999) point to the disjuncture between an equality rhetoric and the continuing (gendered) realities of parenting both during subsisting relationships and after divorce/separation. Others note a marginalisation of men's violences in mediation practice and the new pressures placed on women to agree to contact arrangements.

It is unsurprising that both men and women should frame the meaning of divorce disputes in terms of a 'battle of the sexes'. Parenting remains a profoundly gendered activity. It does appear, however, that men display a greater propensity to evoke a rights discourse within the process of separation; and, in turn, to engage in what has been termed a distinctive 'masculinised discourse' of divorce (Arendell 1995). The very form of the protests of fathers' rights groups in the area of divorce can be seen to be distinctively masculine in nature: public displays of physical endeavour, outward projects of an inner anger. Aspects of the new divorce correlate with this tendency for men to relate to a rights-based framework. The good father would and should 'fight for' his children, given the messages conveyed within the new contact culture. The 'bad mother', in failing her children, further necessitates the presence of the father, if necessary by recourse to law.

The experience of divorce and separation is shaped by the distinctive 'gendered lives' of men and women. Questions of gender difference continue to frame and mediate many aspects of the social experience of marriage and divorce. Law's prescriptions towards consensus, however, would appear to clash in a number of respects with the emotional imperatives driving this engagement, not least in relation to the complex issue of conflict (Day Sclater 1999). Men appear to be caught in a double-bind between discourses of provider/breadwinner and carer/nurturer; dealing with feelings of loss and vulnerability by recourse to appeals to discourses of equity, justice and rights. Ultimately, Day Sclater argues, perhaps real change in this area will require that parents of whatever gender engage with these questions of emotion and find better ways of dealing with the vulnerabilities that divorce and separation throw up.

References and further reading

Arendell, T. (1995) *Fathers and Divorce*, London: Sage.

Collier, R. (1995) *Masculinity, Law and the Family*, London: Routledge.

Day Sclater, S. (1999) *Divorce: A Psycho-social Study*, Aldershot: Ashgate.

Fineman, M. (1995) *The Neutered Mother*, New York: Routledge.

Giddens, A. (1992) *The Transformations of Intimacy*, Cambridge: Polity.

Kaganas, F. and Day Sclater, S. (2004) 'Contact disputes: narrative constructions of "good parents"', *Feminist Legal Studies*, 12 (1): 1–27.

Reece, H. (2003) *Divorcing Responsibly*, Oxford: Hart.

Sclater, S. and Piper, C. (eds) (1999) *Undercurrents of Divorce*, Aldershot: Ashgate.

Smart, C. and Neale, B. (1999) *Family Fragments*, Cambridge: Polity.

See also: child custody; family law; fathers' rights

RICHARD COLLIER

DOMESTIC LABOUR

Domestic labour is work pertaining to the household, home, or family, typically including such activities as cleaning, tidying, shopping, cooking and household management, as well as the physical and emotional care of household members. Under the 'separate spheres' ideology of social life, which constructs distinct domains of competence for men and women, domestic labour falls largely to women in the private sphere of the home. This dichotomous model of sex categories became dominant in Europe during the nineteenth century; at the same time industrial production introduced a material division between the factory, as the site of productive work, and the home, as the site of reproductive work. This sexual division of domestic labour mirrors the industrial division and mechanisation of industrial labour. Domestic labour continues to be an issue of debate in feminist discourse, as well as in development theory.

In Marxist terms, the home is the centre of social relations and reproduction, providing the necessary support to external productive economic activity. Domestic labour, by transforming commodities of food, fuel, clothing into a consumable form, is essential to the physical reproduction of the worker. Its unpaid status creates additional surplus labour for the capitalist. As such, Engels identifies the family as the molecule of bourgeois society and applies class structures to its analysis. He advocates the abolition of the monogamous family as the economic unit of society and the accession of women into the public sphere in order to achieve social equality.

During the 1970s, Marxist feminists took up the debate surrounding domestic labour at the point of intersection between the personal and the political. They argued the public and productive value of housework and proposed wages for work done in the home. However, critics (Malos 1980) asserted that paid housework would not necessarily end its exploitative character but merely couch it in a different form. From the 1960s onward, advances in technology were expected to end heavy domestic labour. However, every advance in the mechanisation of household tasks has generally been accompanied by an attendant increase in the caring role and social demands placed on women in the home (Le Feuvre 2003). Rubin (1975) asserts that domestication arises only under specific social-economic relations and identifies sexism as a product of capitalism's profit motive; therefore, the only solution is the overturning of the capitalist mode of production.

At the end of the twentieth century and the beginning of the twenty-first, the debate around domestic labour shifted to the ethics of employing outside workers in the home. In many cases, offloading difficult or time-consuming tasks on to lower-class or immigrant workers, usually women, provides greater professional and personal freedom to women of greater means while leaving the sexual division of labour intact. However, even those who earn enough to delegate some tasks to other, employed, persons continue to perform the role of domestic management. Indeed, women tend to use their own earnings to remunerate these hired workers, revealing the extent to which women are considered, and consider themselves, solely responsible for domestic work and childcare. Migrant workers from developing countries are vulnerable to exploitation in this limited sphere of work through the dynamics of the personal relationship between employer and employee and the private nature of labour performed in the home. The existence of markets for domestic labour depends on inequalities of race/ethnicity, class and gender; but critics (Meagher 2002) suggest that if those concerned with social justice were to stop employing domestic workers, they would likely inflict economic harm on themselves and those they employ in the short term.

Many scholars and journalists argue that domestic labour is now being 'transformed', with men participating more, women doing less, and with outside help being utilised more often. They identify a 'lagged adaptation' in men, as those born after 1965 have only ever known a society characterised by the impact of second-wave feminism and women's greater involvement in the workforce. However, sociological studies (Singleton and Maher 2004) show that discourses about gender and equality have yet to be fully translated into practice. Women continue to shoulder more of the burden of domestic labour despite the rhetoric of positive change among young people and the recognition among young couples that labour in the home should be shared equally. The analysis of men's participation in domestic labour is largely related to the dimension of 'mental burden': that is, the management and coordination of timetables and needs in order to maintain the functions of the household. This aspect of domestic labour continues to fall almost exclusively on women, regardless of more egalitarian sharing of physical tasks between men and women. As such, a new dichotomy emerges within the home between female domestic managers and compliant male 'helpers'. The self-assessments of men and women regarding domestic labour likely reflect the gender value system of Western society, in which change is more often idealised than realised.

References and further reading

Anderson, B. (2001) 'Just another job?' *Gender and Development*, 9 (2): 25–33.

Engels, F. [1884] (2001) *The Origin of the Family: Private Property and the State*, Seattle, WA: University Press of the Pacific.

Friedan, B. [1963] (2001) *The Feminine Mystique*, New York: Norton.

Le Feuvre, N. (2003) 'Women, work and employment in Europe', Women in the European Union project, Christina Institute for Women's Studies, University of Helsinki, available at http://www.helsinki.fi/science/xantippa/wee/wee22.html

Malos, E. (ed.) (1980) *The Politics of Housework*, London: Allison and Busby.

Marx, K. [1932] (1998) *The German Ideology*, Buffalo, NY: Prometheus.

Meagher, G. (2002) 'Is it wrong to pay for housework?' *Hypatia*, 17 (2): 52–66.

Rubin, G. (1975) 'The traffic in women,' in R. Reiter (ed.) *Toward an Anthropology of Women*, London: Monthly Review, pp. 157–210.

Singleton, A. and Maher, J.M. (2004) 'The 'New Man' is in the house', *Journal of Men's Studies*, 12 (3): 227–40.

Sullivan, O. (2000) 'The division of domestic labour', *Sociology*, 34 (3): 447–56.

See also: class, work and masculinity

ANDREA HASENBANK

DOMESTIC VIOLENCE

Domestic violence (DV) is a term that has entered popular vocabularies; however, it is a contested term with various conflicting meanings. In the West, the most commonly accepted definition is that domestic violence refers to violence and/or abuse (physical, mental, sexual, financial) between adults who are in an intimate or sexual relationship with each other or have been in the past. The term may also include children's subjection to or witnessing of violence/abuse by family members and violence/abuse between other family members. There are debates regarding the overlap between domestic violence and sexual violence or rape, and while rape and sexual violence occur between intimates and non-intimates, both rape and sexual violence can be part of DV. DV affects women and men of all ages, classes, cultures, ethnic, racial and cultural heritages; although it may take different forms in different contexts. For instance, in India it is often experienced as dowry-related violence. There is also no evidence that DV occurs to a greater or lesser extent in any particular cultural or racial group.

A consistent and recurrent research finding in the West is that the majority of victims are women and the vast majority of the perpetrators are men (Hague and Malos 2005). Most Western studies concentrate on DV in heterosexual relationships and omit other types of DV where perpetrators are women (such as mothers-in-law or lesbian partners) or where it is linked to children. This entry also focuses on heterosexual adult DV unless otherwise stated.

Historical background

Since the 1970s there has been a worldwide movement of women (and latterly of men) campaigning against DV and demanding state intervention and support. It was principally women/feminist activists of the 1970s who made male violence a public concern and reconceptualised DV as the systematic exercise of power and control (Kelly and Radford 1996). In addition to local government initiatives, governments around the globe have started to formally recognise the prevalence and incidence of DV, and numerous declarations and strategies have been ratified. The 1995 Beijing World Conference on Women and the resulting 1995 Platform for Action prioritised DV and committed governments to take action on violence against women and on women's disadvantage in general. Such institutional positions publicly recognise the relationship between structural gender inequality and interpersonal gendered abuse.

Incidence and prevalence

Issues of methodology make global comparisons of domestic violence problematic. Comparative studies illustrate the problems inherent in the diverse cultural terms and meanings attached to different issues (Hester and Gangoli 2005). However, DV is now recognised as a form of violence against women that has a similar pattern across the globe. Whether in countries in the West or in the developing world, between one in five and one in three women will experience DV at some point in their lives. Statistics from the UK show that one in four women will at some point in their lives experience domestic violence, and every week two women are murdered by their current or former partner. While domestic violence has the highest rate of repeat victimisation, concurrently it is the least likely violent crime to be reported to the police (UK Home Office 2003). DV presents not only a serious health threat but also a very substantial economic cost. Walby (2004) argues that DV is estimated to cost £22.9 billion per year in the UK (England and Wales) and $67 billion per year in the US, with a further $127 on rape.

Not only are there difficulties in developing meaningful transnational comparative data, but there are also more fundamental problems in collating data. For instance, while many countries now have specific legislation allowing for civil and criminal remedies to deal with DV, the statistics generally reflect only those incidents resulting in physical harm and do not, therefore, include other forms of non-physical violence or abuse such as emotional, sexual, psychological or financial control. This suggests that all official data underrepresent the problem (Kelly and Radford 1996).

Explanatory models

Broadly, the theoretical understanding of DV can be separated into three basic schemata: individualised, sociological and feminist.

Psychological accounts of domestic violence present individualistic explanations, including psychological or biological abnormalities of the perpetrator and/or victim. There are many criticisms of this individualised approach, for it can pathologise both the victims and the offenders. By individualising DV, a psychological approach cannot identify why more men than women abuse their partners. Following a psychological analysis, 'interventions' can lead to counselling therapy, recommended for both the abuser and the abused. Furthermore, locating the problem in internal, psychological 'disorders' exonerates perpetrators from their abusive behaviours and does not recognise the deliberate and controlled nature of DV.

Walker (1983) argued that abused women develop a 'battered woman syndrome' in which women victims of DV present specific characteristics. Many activists and practitioners advocate this model because it acknowledges the psychological trauma resulting from abuse. The syndrome has been used as a legal defence where abused women have assaulted their violent partners. However, this approach has significant limitations as it pathologises women, raising questions about abused women's capabilities in caring for themselves and their children.

Sociological analyses replaced a focus on individual psychopathology with an explanation of DV grounded in socio-structural organisations and societal cultural norms and values. For sociologists it is the impact of external pressures, primarily those relating to age, sex, position in the socio-economic structure, and race and ethnicity (Gelles 1993) that lead to tension in the home culminating in violence and abuse. While there are many different models within the sociological framework, the most influential is the Family Violence approach, in which the family and its internal relations are the central focus of analyses (Gelles 1993).

The most controversial aspect of this model concerns the methodology used to obtain its data and the decontextualised understanding of violence on which this is based. In an attempt to quantify the levels of DV, Straus *et al.* (1979) developed the Conflict Tactics Scales (CTS) which measure the amount and type of violence used in interpersonal relationships. Criticisms of the CTS led to modifications, and Straus and colleagues developed the CTSII, in which they added questions relating to sexualised violence and differentiations in violence, particularly in relation to injuries sustained. Findings from the CTS and CTSII suggested that husbands and wives were equally responsible for committing violence and that DV is symmetrical and could therefore be understood as 'mutual combat'.

A central challenge was that in quantifying the level of violence the CTSII did not account for the fact that men often underestimate the extent of their violent behaviour and women overestimate, therefore skewing the results (Dobash and Dobash 1992). Another significant criticism is that the CTS/CTSII disregards issues relating to the *motives*, *intentions* and *consequences* of the violence because it treats all violent acts as a single category, such that a beating leading to hospitalisation is in the same category as a push (Johnson 1998). Furthermore, it does not account for violence committed in self-defence and cannot quantify non-physical abuse such as coercive emotional control.

Just as there are various sociological and individualistic approaches, there are also differences within feminist analyses. However, most feminist models share a focus on gendered power relations and argue that male violence is a manifestation of power and male gender role behaviour sanctioned by patriarchal ideology (Pence and McDonnell 2000). Feminist analysis also involves an understanding of the private/public division and the centrality of the patriarchal family (Dobash and Dobash 1979). It is now widely documented that almost universally, from childhood to adulthood, women are most at risk in their own homes and from men known to them, such as partners or ex-partners, relatives and acquaintances (McCarry 2003). Furthermore, feminists argue that the different manifestations of male violence against women and children have shared origins, dynamics and impacts. In around 30 per cent of cases children are present while DV is being perpetrated: where there is DV in the household, children are more likely to experience some form of child abuse, either sexual, physical or both (Alexander *et al.* 2005).

Feminists argue that while psychological problems may be contributory factors, they are not always strictly causal. Unlike the sociological model, the feminist critique argues that inequalities of power and resources in heterosexual interpersonal relations reflect the wider differential access to power between women and men, both within the home and in the wider public sphere. Thus, instead of conceptualising DV as 'mutual combat' or a 'conflict tactic', the feminist analysis conceptualises it as coercive control (Yllo 1993). Furthermore, current feminist theory recognises that gender relations intersect with other relations of race, class, ethnicity, etc.

One criticism of the feminist model is that it overemphasises power relations based on gender. However, the Indian Women's Movement, for example, also utilises a male power and control model, and this model is also relevant to explain the abuse of women by other women (Gangoli 2006). Thus, the feminist model can be applied in diverse cultural contexts and to explain women's abuse of partners and domestic violence in same-sex relationships.

Prevention and treatment

Safe houses, refuges or hostels, outreach work and telephone helplines are regarded as essential crisis interventions for women experiencing DV, and in some countries these now have state funding. However, it is often the case that even where there is a political commitment to eradicating DV there remains a financial shortfall.

The explanatory model used for understanding DV determines the intervention employed; in some cases, women are referred to safe houses, or for medical intervention, or for counselling. In other cases women are held responsible for the abuse perpetrated against them, and it is 'justified' by arguing that these women have transgressed 'appropriate' gender role behaviour according to proscribed (patriarchal) cultural norms. Perpetrators may be dealt with punitively through the criminal justice system or through civil legislation, or referred for medical intervention or anger management or counselling. Usually they do not receive any sanction at all. Thus, even though some countries are now prioritising DV prevention as opposed to crisis intervention, not enough is being done because women still face the continued risk of injury, abuse and death from male partners and ex-partners.

References and further reading

Alexander, H., Macdonald, E. and Paton, S. (2005) 'Raising the issue of domestic abuse in Scotland', *Children and Society*, 19 (3): 187–98.

Dobash, R.E. and Dobash, R.P. (1979) *Violence Against Wives*, Somerset: Free Press.

—— (1992) *Women, Violence and Social Change*, London: Routledge.

Dobash, R.E. and Dobash, R.P. and Gangoli, G. (2006) *Indian Feminisms*, Aldershot: Ashgate.

Gelles, R. (1993) 'Through a sociological lens', in R.J. Gelles and D.R. Loseke (eds) *Current Controversies on Family Violence*, London: Sage, pp. 31–46.

Hague, G. and Malos, E. (2005) *Domestic Violence*, 3rd edn, Cheltenham: New Clarion.

Hester, M. and Gangoli, G. (2005) 'Comparison and collaboration', in T. Skinner, M. Hester and E. Malos (eds) *Researching Gender Violence*, Devon: Willan, pp. 105–24.

Home Office [UK] (2003) *Domestic Violence and Violence Against Women*, http://www.homeoffice.gov.uk/crimpol/crimreduc/domviolence/index.html (and see Home Office Research and Statistics, Home Office: London for full British

Crime Survey statistics: http://www.homeoffice.gov.uk/rds/index.htm).
Johnson, H. (1998) 'Rethinking survey research on violence against women', in R.E. Dobash and R.F. Dobash (eds) *Rethinking Violence Against Women*, London: Sage, pp. 23–51.
Kelly, L. and Radford, J. (1996) '"Nothing really happened"', in M. Hester, L. Kelly and J. Radford (eds) *Women, Violence and Male Power*, Buckingham: Open University Press, pp. 19–33.
McCarry, M. (2003) 'The connection between masculinity and domestic violence', unpublished PhD thesis, University of Bristol.
Pence, E.L. and McDonnell, C. (2000) 'Developing policies and protocols in Duluth, Minnesota', in J. Hanmer and C. Itzin, with S. Quaid and D. Wigglesworth (eds) *Home Truths about Domestic Violence*, London: Routledge, pp. 249–68.
Straus, M.A., Gelles, R.J. and Steinmetz, S. (1979) *Behind Closed Doors*, London: Sage.
Walby, S. (2004) *The Cost of Domestic Violence*, London: Department of Trade and Industry Women and Equality Unit, available at http://www.womenandequalityunit.gov.uk/research/cost_of_dv_Report_sept04.pdf
Walker, L.E. (1983) 'The Battered Woman Syndrome Study' in D. Finkelhor, R.J. Gelles, G.T. Hotaling and M.A. Straus (eds) *The Dark Side of Families*, London: Sage, pp. 31–48.
Yllo, K. (1993) 'Through a feminist lens', in R.J. Gelles and D.R. Loseke (eds) *Current Controversies on Family Violence*, London: Sage, pp. 47–62.

See also: aggression; child abuse; elder abuse; fatherhood and violence; honour killings; rape; sexual violence; violence; working with perpetrators or offenders; working with victims and survivors

MELANIE MCCARRY

DRAG AND CROSS-DRESSING

Drag involves wearing clothing usually associated with the opposite sex. In virtually every culture, gender identity is signalled by dress and clothing (as well as other aspects of appearance such as hair and bodily comportment). Women can cross-dress and perform as 'drag kings' but are not the focus of this entry. Drag and cross-dressing must not be confused with sexual orientation; they are ways of performing gender rather than sexuality. Nor should they be confused with third-gender status in many cultures, such as the *berdaches*, *hijras* or Samoan *fa'afefine*.

Drag has a long history. Across cultures, women's roles in the theatre often were played by men. Shakespearean plays and Japanese kabuki, for example, forbade women from performing (Senelick 1992). Cross-dressers, also known as transvestites, are men who appear either publicly or privately in women's clothes. In public, they usually attempt to 'pass' as a woman, including adopting feminine mannerisms. Why men cross-dress is controversial. The *DSM-IV* (2000) pathologises such behaviour, under the heading of 'Transvestic fetishism or gender identity disorder'. Historians of gender behaviour would disagree with this aetiology, understanding cross-dressing as a normal part of the male gender repertoire.

Drag describes a sort of 'parody' of female dress and behaviour; those who present in drag are called drag queens. Drag is commonly associated with the gay male community, where queens sing or mime songs by popular female performers. Drag queens usually cue the audience that they are male, either by the outrageous character of their dress and performance, or by retaining some signal of their true identity, such as a beard (Schacht 2002).

What holds cross-dressing and drag together as categories is the concept that gender is 'performed' according to cultural and social scripts (Tyler 2003). Thus cross-dressing and drag often can be understood as intentional subversions, transgressive acts, designed to undermine both heterosexism and hegemonic masculinity.

References and further reading

Butler, J. (1990) *Gender Trouble*, New York: Routledge.
Culbertson, P. (2005) 'Mothers and their golden sons', in C.K. Robertson (ed.) *Sex and Religion*, New York: Peter Lang, pp. 205–34.
Diagnostic and Statistical Manual of Mental Disorders (2000) 4th edn, text revision (*DSM-IV-TR*), Washington, DC: American Psychiatric Association.

Schacht, S. (2002) 'Four renditions of doing female drag', *Gendered Sexualities*, 6: 157–80.
Senelick, L. (ed.) (1992) *Gender in Performance*, Hanover, NH: University Press of New England.
Tyler, C.-A. (2003) *Female Impersonation*, New York: Routledge.

See also: transgender; transsexual

PHILIP CULBERTSON

DRESS, FASHION AND CLOTHING

Men's fashion and clothing integrate erotics and politics, sexual expression and moral values, conforming and dissenting social codes of physique and visibility. Men's clothing, almost always differentiated from women's clothing, reflects hierarchical gender division. They are interrelated with a cultural construction of sexuality, 'class', occupation, ethnicity and life style. For centuries, men's fashion in the West was dictated by the ruling classes, as seen in classic portraits of European aristocrats. Their clothing in the sixteenth century, for example, consisted of a doublet with breeches and hose and sometimes a jerkin or a cloak, made of a variety of fabrics, often leather, and reflecting protective military attire. In seventeenth-century England, new moralisation led to King Charles II approving a less extravagant form of dress and substituting vests for doublets. However, he soon reverted to more colourful fabrics (Tarrant 1996).

Trousers, a nowadays essential item of men's clothing, were invented at the beginning of the nineteenth century. They were initially considered undignified for evening wear, but gradually became accepted for both day and evening. By the late nineteenth century, with the arrival of the tuxedo from America, British evening dress relaxed, and the young men of this period, termed Dandies, Swells or Decadents, delighted in outrageous clothes. Oscar Wilde and his friends appeared at the premiere of his play *Lady Windermere's Fan* in 1892 with green carnations in their buttonholes, which to Wilde symbolised a subtle artistic temperament; others saw moral decadence and homosexuality (Mosse 1994).

Mainstream Western menswear was also gradually changing. The increasing popularity of sports such as golf in the twentieth century, demanding clothes that allowed free arm movement, probably speeded the acceptance of knitwear. Although suits continued to be worn for formal occasions, the tweed sports jacket with grey flannel trousers became standard informal wear. The 1950s saw young men wishing to dress differently than their fathers. Teddy Boys, inspired by the Edwardian Dandy, combined a long jacket with velvet collar, drain-pipe trousers and string tie (Tarrant 1996), while the Rockers went for leather jackets, tight T-shirts and fitted jeans.

Departing from formality and neutral colours, men's clothing in the 1960s and 1970s took a step towards women's fashion, integrating fantasy and bright colours. Underwear, shirts, jackets and tennis attire all allowed a free play of colour combinations (Lipovetsky 2002). As the complexities of men's dress and tailoring increased, gendered differences in dress remained rigid, although more subtle (Craik 1994; Edwards 1997; Finkelstein 1991; Hollander 1994). Edwards (1997) suggests that the apparently gender-neutral pair of jeans exemplifies how even the same item of clothing can be used to add to gender difference through fit alone: Levi's tight-fitting 501 jeans in the 1980s, like the tight Speedo swimsuit of the 1970s (and its 'comeback' in the early 2000s), situated the man at the centre of an erotic spectacle, with clothes covering but emphasising the genitals and glorifying the penis as a phallus, symbolising male dominance. In contrast, a skirt worn by a Western man was perceived as a deviant image. For example, in the 1970s David Bowie was the first singer to project a blatantly transvestite image, with frocks, eye makeup, extravagant red wigs and jewellery (Crane 2000).

The fashion pages in men's glossy life-style magazines showed off the new man in the mid-1980s, followed in the 1990s by the muscular-but-sensitive, well-built-but-neat 'Metrosexual' of the early twenty-first century. This man is represented in fashion as smooth, sportive, virile, super-sexy, young and mostly 'white'. Neither the new man nor the Metrosexual transgresses rigid Western codes of gender performance. In the mid-1990s, Jean-Paul Gaultier daringly presented skirt-pants for men, striving to prove that men would not lose their masculinity if they wore skirts rather than trousers (McDowell 2000).

Openly gay men had begun to express sexual flexibility and gender-bending in the late nineteenth and early twentieth centuries, wearing flamboyant shirts and trousers. After 'Gay Liberation' began in New York with the Stonewall uprising in 1969, gay culture became more visible, diverse and proud. The emergent gay lifestyle of the 1970s was an attempt to acquire a sense of community through consumption (Bronski 1998), by dressing in different fashions, according to diverse subcultural identifications, from an effeminate style to masculine attire as manifested in the Village People's 'macho' look (muscular body, hairy chest, moustache and jeans); sadomasochistic costumes (leather trousers, chains, rubber masks and metal accessories); and men-in-uniforms (policemen, soldiers, sailors, etc.), in addition to 'camp', 'drag' queens and 'cross-dressers' (Padva 2000).

The gay clubber's fashion of the 1990s and 2000s (tight T-shirts, colourful buttoned shirts with lace and gold embroidery, gaudy synthetic fur coats, stylish haircuts) has been rapidly adopted by many straight men, as had been the previously gay-identified earrings, body piercing, dyed hair, skin-care products, depilation and hair transplants, and low-waist jeans, which signify the well-kept, sophisticated urban man in the assimilating age of 'globalisation', whatever his sexual orientation. Consequently, there is no longer a distinct gay men's dress, fashion or clothing.

References and further reading

Bronski, M. (1998) *The Pleasure Principle*, New York: St Martin's Press.

Craik, J. (1994) *The Face of Fashion*, London: Routledge.

Crane, D. (2000) *Fashion and Its Social Agendas*, Chicago, IL and London: Chicago University Press.

Edwards, T. (1997) *Men in the Mirror*, London and Herndon, VA: Cassell.

Finkelstein, J. (1991) *The Fashioned Self*, London: Polity.

Hollander, A. (1994) *Sex and Suits*, New York: Knopf.

Lipovetsky, G. (2002) *The Empire of Fashion*, Princeton, PA: Princeton University Press.

McDowell, C. (2000) *Jean Paul Gaultier*, London: Cassell.

Mosse, G. (1994) 'Masculinity and the decadence', in R. Porter and T. Mikulas (eds) *Sexual Knowledge, Sexual Science*, Cambridge: Cambridge University Press, pp. 251–66.

Padva, G. (2000) '*Priscilla* fights back', *Journal of Communication Inquiry*, 24 (2): 216–43.

Tarrant, N. (1996) *The Development of Costume*, London and New York: Routledge.

See also: culture and representation

GILAD PADVA

DRUGS, ADDICTION AND ABUSE

By the early twenty-first century, drug abuse and dependence have been called public health, social, criminal and economic problems across the globe. Most nations have experienced undesirable rates of drug abuse historically and continue to do so presently. Despite the important differences between nations regarding which drugs are abused and the policies designed to address them, they share remarkable consistencies. One of the most prominent is the gendered nature of the problem.

Information about the extent and prevalence of drug use, abuse and dependence across the globe reveals that men's rates are higher than women's in most nations (United Nations 2004). For example, 90 per cent of all illicit drug use in India is by males. Heroin, cocaine and marijuana use by them is higher in Ireland, Australia, France, Switzerland and all of Asia. Amphetamine-type stimulants and ecstasy use are also consistently higher among males in most nations, although women abuse minor tranquillisers more than men do.

Rates are similar in the US, which has publicly available information on drug abuse and dependence on licit and illicit drugs by gender. Billions of dollars are allocated annually to track drug use by such US data sets as the National Survey of Drug Abuse and Health (NSDAH) and DAWN (Drug Abuse Warning Network). This information can serve as a proxy in understanding the scope and nature of male drug abuse and dependence more globally. The most recent general population study of drug use and abuse in the US (OAS 2004a) shows that male use, abuse and dependence to all illicit substances (except crack cocaine) as well as tobacco and alcohol is significantly higher than that of females. In general, males use more drugs more often and for longer periods of time.

Males also encounter more health-related drug and alcohol problems than females in the US, an issue for which few other nations have comparable data. For example, using emergency department hospital mentions of licit and illicit drugs in metropolitan areas in the US, DAWN reports that men more often visit emergency rooms for health conditions (e.g. overdose) directly related to illicit drugs, such as cocaine, heroin, marijuana, stimulants, hallucinogens and ecstasy than do women (OAS 2004b). Furthermore, men are at higher risk than women of becoming dependent on drugs and alcohol as they age (OAS 2004a).

Why are men's rates and levels consistently higher than women's (despite some growth) across nation and time? Is there something about being a man or masculine that affects this disparity? Little information is available to answer these questions, although historically the study of drug abuse was conducted largely on men and by men. However, it did not link masculinity to explanations of drug-related phenomena but opted instead for more generic conceptual models.

Feminist challenges to the scientific method in the last quarter of the twentieth century called attention to androcentric bias in this research, especially in the US. They criticised over-reliance on the male subject and gender-neutral models in understanding women's experiences with drugs. Consequently, women began studying women drug abusers and addicts, often using gender-oriented frameworks that tied patriarchal social organisation and feminine role performance to women's drug abuse and addiction. Subsequent research showed that women's experience was different from men's in many ways. Moreover, this research inadvertently showed that men's drug abuse and addiction were also likely to be gendered. Unfortunately, a gendered understanding of men's experience received little attention and continues to be neglected today. The drugs discourse globally lacks knowledge about how social and cultural constructs and practices of masculinity affect men's experience with drug abuse and addiction.

Literature searches reveal a persistent absence of gender-based explanations for men's drug abuse. Articles pertaining to drug use and abuse among men who have sex with men were most prominent. Most – but not all – were situated in the US and focused on the public health aspects of club drug use and disease prevalence (e.g. HIV) from gay male socialising (e.g. circuit party attendance). Few employed a gender-based (i.e. masculinity) framework. More consulted the sexualities or public health literatures to understand the problem.

Men's alcohol consumption in relation to sexual assault and violence is another common topic. Again, most of these studies were US based and examined male college students rather than males in general. Within the literature on men, alcohol and assault, there was, however, a greater utilisation of gendered frameworks, including a small literature on how masculinity (e.g. power demands and risk taking, etc.) affected drinking habits and assault.

Other studies compared mental and physical health outcomes among men and women drug abusers or their success in treatment programmes. Few of these articles employed gender-based frameworks, as did some concerning gender-based treatment programming. Gendered frameworks were most often utilised by scholars working outside of the US in places such as the UK and Europe.

Globally, men's rates of drug abuse, dependence and related social and public health problems continue to surpass those of women. The dominance of men in this regard should alert scholars and policy-makers throughout the world that drug abuse and dependence is gendered. Consequently, efforts to improve our understanding of and success in remedying it must consider social and cultural constructions of masculinity. Moreover, the unequal focus on special sub-groups of males prevents adequate attention to the larger population of male drug abusers. A richer and more comprehensive understanding of male drug abuse and dependence in the general population, using gender-based conceptual frameworks, must be forthcoming.

References and further reading

CORK online database of substance abuse research, at http://www.projectcork.org/database_search/

Office of Applied Studies (OAS) (2004a) *Overview of Findings from the 2003 National Survey on Drug Use and Health*, Rockville, MD: US Department of Health and Human Services.

—— (2004b) *Drug Abuse Warning Network, 2003: Interim National Estimates of Drug Department Emergency Visits*, Rockville, MD: US Department of Health and Human Services.

United Nations (2004) *World Drug Report*, Vienna: United Nations.

See also: health and illness, men's

TAMMY L. ANDERSON

DUELLING

The duel in Western civilisation evolved from various forms of knightly combat and from the 'judicial' duel, which could determine the guilt or innocence of noble individuals. By the sixteenth century the duel had become private and had lost its juridical dimension, but it retained the capacity to measure a man's courage and his social worthiness. The duel's elaborate procedures served as a useful defence of aristocratic prerogative, but knowledge of duelling rituals was insufficient if a man did not otherwise possess the wealth, the social connections, or the kinship networks that allowed him to lay claim to honourable status.

State-building monarchies in England and France endured duelling epidemics in the seventeenth century as noblemen resisted efforts to reduce their autonomy from above by engaging in murderous encounters with their peers. A man's courage, skill and status claims were on display in duels; however, the right to duel was never judged according to some common standard of manliness, but by narrow social and legal criteria that trumped any other evaluation of a man's personal qualities. A man suffered social derogation if he refused a legitimate challenge, but the outcome of duels mattered less than a man's gentlemanly comportment *in extremis*.

These aspects of the duel endured until the twentieth century in France, Italy, Germany, Spain and the Habsburg lands. The duel was both less dangerous and more democratic in the modern era. Social and professional qualifications remained, but the honour that men defended was increasingly more a category of political rights and civil autonomy than of class privilege. However, judgments about duellers now included a broader range of personal qualities than appraisal of courage alone. A man's financial or sexual history, the quality of his personal or political loyalties, his family life and other aspects of his identity were now aspects of his honourable selfhood. By the end of the nineteenth century a modern notion of masculinity that subsumed character, behaviour and inner dispositions into a gendered body had emerged in duelling discourse as a tacit standard of honourability.

References and further reading

Frevert, U. (1995) *Men of Honour*, translated by Anthony Williams, Cambridge: Polity.

Kiernan, V.G. (1988) *The Duel in European History*, Oxford: Oxford University Press.

Nye, R.A. (1993) *Masculinity and Male Codes of Honor in Modern France*, New York: Oxford University Press.

ROBERT A. NYE

EAST EUROPEAN MASCULINITIES

As the history of Eastern Europe (east of Vienna and west of the Urals) has been scarred by numerous invasions and imperial expansions, an important feature of East European masculinities is their identification with local ethnic and national values.

At the beginning of the Middle Ages, shrewd politicians and hereditary rulers, sometimes advised by female relatives, saw political advantages in the new religion of Christianity and imposed with the sword the religion of love and turning the other cheek. Vladimir the grand duke of Kiev, Boris of Bulgaria, Stephen of Hungary, Mindaugas of Lithuania and Boleslav I of Bohemia are emblematic of this hegemonic masculinity of the founders.

Later, during the prolonged Middle Ages, the invasions of the Mongols and Turks as well as the rise of some regional powers (Poland, Hungary, Russia) favoured the construction of a masculine ideal relying on a strictly gendered division of responsibilities: men led armies and fought enemies, while women stayed home and raised boys to become soldiers. Stephan the Great in Moldova (see Pecican 2005), Michael the Brave in Wallachia, Ivan the Terrible in Russia, Gediminas in Lithuania, Bogan Khmelnytsky in Ukraine, John Sobiesky in Poland, Janos Hunyadi in Hungary and Skanderbeg in Albania proved their force by defeating enemies, inseminating women both in and out of wedlock, and expecting the offspring of their people to die with them, for them and the country. From the perspective of these domineering masculinities, women were merely the passive receptacles of biological and political power, a real or symbolic territory for conquest and subjection. Motherhood, its protective impulses suppressed, was just an appendage to patriarchal power.

During 1848–1921, revolutionary and nationalist movements led to the collapse of the three empires in Eastern Europe: the Ottoman, the Austrian and the Tsarist. A new type of masculinity appeared, influenced by romantic and nationalist ideals. The ideal nationalist was a man who had studied abroad, become imbued with the ideals of Western modernity and envisaged his nation as a modern structure that eradicated all feudal remains. The Romanians Nicolae Balcescu and Alexandru Ioan Cuza, the Poles Adam Miczkiewick and Josef Pilsudski, the Hungarian Lajos Kossuth and the Czech Tomas Masaryk represented these new masculinities. Men were the active, political, future-oriented element of the emerging nations, justifying their nationalism as rightful protection against exterior threats. The nation was the erotic for these men, and their 'good' nationalism was fully justified as small nations' rightful protection against exterior impositions. Meanwhile, women continued to serve as the men's inert source and essence, as reproductive vessels of population and tradition.

The appearance of Communist regimes in the twentieth century led to the emergence of other masculinities. The sexuality of the Communist male activists was sublimated into their dedication to the Revolution and efforts to build a new society (Ostrovsky 1952). Women were just disquieting comrades who might deter them from their noble task. When the Communist ideology consolidated, the Party became the great patron of society and emasculated the whole society, not only its male activists. Men and women in the private space of their homes banded together against the oppressive Party, but inside the domestic space the old gendered hierarchies continued. Although both men and women were breadwinners, men expected women to nurture and pamper them in the privacy of their homes. Domestic violence was often the outlet for these spoiled and, at the same time, frustrated men, who could not act in the public space dominated by the Party nor within the hierarchical Party structure.

In the successive Fascist and Communist dictatorships of the 1940s and 1950s, an interesting East European masculinity developed. For example, Sergiu Malagamba (1913–78) was a famous jazz player from Bessarabia (Soviet Moldova) who lived most of his life in Romania. He became famous for his exuberant music, and his exuberant dandy 'Malagambist' dress became immensely popular among urban young men as a revolt against the dreary, monotonous dress code imposed by the totalitarian regimes.

The fall of the Communist international system after the 1989 revolutions as well as the implosion of the Communist federal entities (Yugoslavia, the Soviet Union) led to a restructuring of masculinities. Many men who had worked in the inefficient Communist factories could no longer maintain their position as family providers. Recurring national failures to be accepted in the European Union, as well as the obsessive mimicry of 'European' values, led to disappointment and frustration, which men experienced as an emasculation of their nations. The tension produced by these new realities erupted in the compensatory infliction of sexual violation on the internal Other: women and other ethnic groups. The dramatic increase, after 1990, of sexual violence, racism, xenophobia, anti-Roma feelings and attitudes, and ethnic conflicts in former Yugoslavia and the former Soviet Union are relevant to this evolution of East European masculinities.

In this context, the dominant ideology denies that masculinity is culture-specific and context-bound. Instead, an essentialist perspective on masculinity as a monolithic value hides the gendered hierarchies in culture and the aggressive androcentric core of East European societies. Furthermore, most East European cultures express considerable anxiety about admitting definitions of masculinity that do not rely on heterosexuality. A current definition of masculinity in this area supposes that man must desire and lead woman. Exceptions (Negoitescu 1994) are few and notable.

References and further reading

Babeti, A. (2005) *Dandysmul*, Iasi: Polirom.

Borenstein, E. (2000) *Men Without Women*, Durham, NC: Duke University Press.

Clements, B.E., Friedman, R. and Healey, D. (eds) (2002) *Russian Masculinities in History and Culture*, Houndmills, New York: Palgrave.

Cockburn, C. and Zarkov, D. (eds) (2002) *The Post-War Moment*, London: Lawrence and Wishart.

Feischmidt, M. (1997) *Women and Men in East European Transition*, Cluj-Napoca: Editura Fundatiei pentru Studii Europene.

Negoitescu, I. (1994) *Straja dragonilor*, Cluj-Napoca: Biblioteca Apostrof.

Ostrovsky, N. [1932–4] (1952) *How the Steel Was Tempered*, Moscow: Foreign Languages Publishing House.

Pecican, O. (2005) *Sange si trandafiri*, Chisinau: Cartier.

Seidler, V.J. (ed.) (1991) *Achilles Heel Reader*, London: Routledge.

MICHAELA MUDURE

ECOLOGY AND ENVIRONMENTAL STUDIES

Rarely are inquiries into masculinities and other-than-human nature viewed together. The former explore violence, race, sex and the experiences of men's lives, making little if any mention of environmental ethics (Allister 2004: 9). The latter offer philosophical and scientific studies that almost entirely fail to acknowledge gender identity and the ethics they infuse.

For profeminist scholars, the hegemonisation of Western masculinities has been selective and socially sanctioned. Masculine hegemony is driven by 'malestream' ethics. These ethics produce individuals and conceptual frameworks that daringly respond to critiques of their power and authority with all the resources at their disposal, from organised repression of activists through to denigrating homophobia. These ethics are consequently referred to as *ethics of daring*. Ethics of daring are directed towards inequality (manifesting hierarchical power and control). The traits that these masculinist hegemonies express are rational, reductionist, emotionless (except for anger and aggression), powerful, controlling, confident, conceited, selfish, outspoken, strong, competitive, virile, objective, chivalrous and condescending expressions of the self. These traits feature on both the personal and political level. In addition to subordinating inferiorised groups of men and masculinities such as gays and queers, ethics of daring at best instigate an attitude of stewardship over subordinated groups as the only expression of caring that hegemonically masculine identities can exhibit. At their worst, these ethics terrorise people and the planet with war and tyranny.

Ethics of daring inferiorise other-than-human nature and women. In contrast, the ethics that drive a feminised 'ability-to-care' for and be 'cared-for-by' wider natural phenomena have been noted (Warren 2000: 108). These ethics of caring are reflective of a 'fuller', 'wider' and 'deeper' human experience and favour love, friendship, trust, compassion, consideration, reciprocity and co-operation between human and other-than-human life (Noddings 1984: 3–6). These ethics of caring are directed towards equality (manifesting a communitarian temperament). These ethics permit easier, deeper and more effective access to fuller flourishing of the self. They also complement social and environmental justice agendas since caring for the wider biota supports developmental policies and practices that meet the needs of current and future generations of humans and non-humans. Therefore, ethics of caring encourage the concurrent mainstreaming of social equanimity, environmental preservation and economic prosperity.

That depression, drug and alcohol abuse, violence and suicide are predominantly male ailments is no coincidence. Such is the price paid for hegemonisation. Contemporary Western social experiences attest that when these ethics are combined with social and ecological devastation, being a 'real man' is detrimental to personal, interpersonal, physiological, social, ecological and spiritual health. The utilitarian bias of hegemonic masculinities creates a forum for bolstering the ego-self at the expense of the other-than-human world. Proving one's manhood or salving personal insecurities by conquering physical nature is not an uncommon occurrence in the West. Hegemonic masculinities produce unhealthy masculine praxes. These praxes support *Logos* (the ancient Greek word for divine reason associated with a masculine tendency towards hostile motivation) while shunning *Eros* (also Cupid, the most beautiful of ancient Greek masculine deities, god of passion, fertility, sexual love and desire). Hegemonic masculine (and men's) identities harbour an imbalance between head and heart. Hegemonic masculinities seek fulfilment through rational and pragmatic means. Such identities are destructive to self, society and planet when isolated from erotic encounters between self and human/other-than-human others. Hegemonic masculine identities have succeeded in permeating both the personal and political realms of modern Western society and are most readily internalised by men, but find expression in women also.

Social and environmental justice movements have rightly identified hegemonic masculinities as centrally complicit in perpetrating social and environmental woes. But heaping blame on all men and masculine identities is misguided. While receiving privileges from the hegemony in private and public ways, the majority of men and masculinities are not hegemonic and may not support hegemonic sustainability. In examining the collective and discursive structuring of masculinities, individual hegemonic men need to be held accountable for gendered inequalities and privileges. But to effectively deconstruct hegemonic masculine identities and reconstruct identities that are socially and environmentally just requires expressions of empathetic compassion and caring even towards these most brazen of foes. The primary focus of a deconstructive analysis would be better directed towards the ways in which hegemonic masculine identities are internalised, rather than individual men per se. This strategy could avoid ongoing conflict between hegemonic and dissenting individuals within social and environmental discourses. In practical terms this requires a softening of boundaries between the conceptual frameworks within masculinities and environmental discourses. The intention is to make the spectrum of social and environmental justice concerns more central to the masculinities discourse, and to bring the spectrum of masculinities concerns to the environmental discourse, concurrently. An 'ecologisation' of the masculinities discourse is needed. To clarify, the term 'ecologised' implies the need for an alternative modus vivendi to the hegemonic identities that permits interpenetration of self-identity with ecological (indeed universal) wholeness. An alternative modus operandi is also suggested where hegemonic conceptual frameworks within the masculinities discourse are permeated with environmental wisdom.

Ecological feminism may be a crucial guide through this 'ecologisation' of the masculinities discourse and introduction of masculinities concerns into environmentalism. Beyond gendered social divisions and power differentials dwells a dominion-free and inclusive concept of fairness and respect, where the oppression of women and nature is eliminated (Warren 2000: 187–9). But differences in power relations between the masculinities (and men's) and feminist (and women's) discourses make it impossible to replicate ecological feminism when attempting to ecologise the masculinities discourse. Panpsychism takes the ecologisation process beyond gendered identities by awakening feminised ethics that encourage a letting-go into landscape, and enables the hearts of both men and women to grow full with desire and in so doing re-enters the enchantment of the self (Mathews 2003: 20). Panpsychism is an eroticised and loving approach to self-identity in the context of wider-nature, is less prone to defensiveness, and combines the 'psychoenergetic rhythms [of the self] with those of others to create new rhythms, new patterns or tracks in the wider field' of planetary (and universal) beingness (ibid.: 138). Panpsychism willingly engages in an 'orchestrated dance of mutualism' between the Many individuated or individuating human selves that this planet supports with those other-than-human others that represent universal Oneness. Panpsychist virtues are sensual, instinctual, intuitive and spontaneous self-expressions that value relationship over individuation, without obscuring the latter. They are not, however, preconscious, unevolved (as in archaic) and unreflective, nor are they devoid of rationality. Drawing both feminist and masculinities discourses closer to this 'trans-gendered' (as in 'beyond-gendered') expression of fuller-humanness may allow caring to become reflex for both men and women as well as all permutations of gender identity. This seems a worthy ethical objective, but to reach an effective Panpsychism requires the re-enchantment of the masculinities discourse first. To do otherwise is to leapfrog over foundational epistemological territory on the masculinities end of social theory.

Unlike feminism, the masculinities discourse is not currently 'ecologised'. I introduce an 'ecomasculinity' personal praxis to encourage relationship building between these conceptual frameworks. To achieve strengthened relationships requires the acceptance of conceptual differences throughout the discourse. To achieve acceptance requires the virtues of patience, understanding, humility, trust, loving-kindness, empathy and compassion. To achieve these virtues requires the personal internalisation of an ethics of caring. 'Ecomasculinity' offers a path towards this internalisation, doing so by emphasising relationality and points of convergence between the conceptual frameworks within the masculinities discourse. That said, 'ecomasculinity' is Leftist leaning and profeminist; looking beyond the limitations of masculine (and men's) hegemony by assuming that some important contributions to the masculinities discourse are uniquely present on the Right, and are therefore worthy of consideration. For example, an emphasis on family cohesion is taken to be fundamentally benevolent, but in desperate need of a broader definition of 'family' to reach beyond nuclear heteronormitivity. One of the key aims of 'ecomasculinity' is to renegotiate individuated self-identification away from the isolated self-righteousness of an ethics of daring, and encourage synergistic engagements conducive to ethics of caring throughout the masculinities discourse. In this way 'ecomasculinity' is metaphorically ecologised, and works towards freeing masculine identities (and men) from the isolation that ethics of daring instil.

Unto itself, 'ecomasculinity' runs the risk of avoiding important socio-political insights. An alternative modus operandi is also needed, whereby environmental concerns are included in the masculinities discourse. To politically ecologise the masculinities discourse requires an ecological masculinism politics. Ecological masculinism extends the ecological metaphor to a theoretical praxis of socially and environmentally just considerations, beginning with three crucial axioms. First, hegemonic masculinities are complicit in the decline of social and environmental health. Second, 'ecomasculinity' reinforces individuation; a complementary and more holistic theoretical approach is therefore also needed since metaphors do not automatically embrace global social or ecological justice on systemic levels. Third, calls for greater social and environmental justice require long-term systemic alterations if the problems that persist between humans and wider nature are to be effectively resolved. These concerns can best emerge through rigorous deconstructions and reconstructions of masculine identities on the systemic level. An ecological masculinism politics offers such a possibility.

Ecological masculinism gives consideration to a variety of social and environmental discourses beyond ecological feminism. They are: feminist critiques of sociobiology, deep ecology, social ecology, ecopsychology, the Gaia hypothesis, inclusionality theory, systems thinking and bioregionalism. When examined in combination with ecofeminism, these environmentalisms offer a wealth of ecological wisdom. Feminist critiques of sociobiology note the biological determinism that pervades sociobiology, suggesting that traditional interpretations of evolutionary theory are patriarchal and erroneously lean on physiological and evolutionary arguments to force females into roles of passive and nurturing mothers (Hrdy 1999: xiv). Deep ecology aims to reconcile the burgeoning ecological crises, which it views to be products of anthropocentric humanism, and advocates for the realisation of a deeper and expanded self-consciousness that gives rise to an 'ecological self' whose intimate connection with other-than-human nature acknowledges the intrinsic value of all life (Naess 1989: 11). Social ecology seeks the creation of ecologically benign societies that function on decentralised libertarian ideals and works towards building 'rounded' human communities that prioritise the resolution of deep-seated social problems while also addressing the ecological future of the planet (Bookchin 1993: 354). Where ecology illuminates the relationships between organisms 'out there', psychology explores dysfunctions of the mind 'in here' which, when combined through ecopsychology, unifies this outer/inner division by arguing that nature critically determines human physical, mental and emotional wellbeing (Roszak *et al.* 1995: 4). The Gaia hypothesis offers a scientific study of the interactions between the atmosphere, lithosphere and hydrosphere, noting that living macrosystems are comprised of tightly coupled living subsystems that help the planet function like a single self-regulating organism (Lovelock 1979: 119–23). The Gaia hypothesis also substantiates cryptic and anthropomorphic agitations of the malestream by using scientifically valid evidence to suggest that assaults upon the planet's ecological integrity can be replaced with a reverence for the earth's unique emergent properties (Sahtouris 1989: 19–28). Inclusionality theory views all living and nonliving entities as 'dynamic inclusions' by noting the complex couplings between inner individuals and outer collectives through reciprocal perceptions of the self imbedded in nature (Rayner 2003: 10). Systems-thinking juxtaposes open systems against closed systems, using physics to prove that life on earth is adaptively self-organising, internally teleological and therefore self-sustaining, rather than entropic (Bertalanffy 1950: 23). Bioregionalism is both a scholarly and community-based movement that examines human interactions with distinct geographical areas. This movement supports adaptive and inhabitory human attitudes by acknowledging the interplay between inanimate and animate aspects of a bioregion, which thereby reveal the 'natural' characteristics of a specific place. From a bioregional perspective, people's presence within living systems becomes integral (Berg and Dasmann 1978: 217–20). Similarly, the various positionalities within the environmental discourse are less discrete than their theories imply. These environmentalisms are united in positing the interpenetrating aspects of human: other-than-human nature relationships. They trail behind ecological feminism in failing to deconstruct the intersection between masculine gender identity and ecological concerns. Each of these disciplines formulates unique insights into the human: other-than-human nature relationship; they also support a shift towards long-term ecological sustainability. They avoid contributing constructive environmental commentary to the masculinities discourse. An ecological masculinism politics is offered here to address this need.

Ecological masculinism is not autoic, rational or pragmatic, nor is it self-righteous or allured by a wealth/power/control dynamic. Ecological masculinism does not offer a single path for all existing masculinities to tread, nor does it applaud one particular political position while denigrating others. Ecological masculinism is, then, a politicised meta-narrative that draws on the aforementioned environmentalism to help imbue masculine identities with environmental ethics. Ecological masculinism examines the personal implications of an ecologisation process through 'ecomasculinity' and does so similarly on the political level through the aforementioned environmentalism. Ecological masculinism calls for ongoing critical analyses of hegemonic masculine ethics, noting that they are self, societally and planetarily suicidal. Ecological masculinism does not aim to subvert masculine hegemonies, but rather invites hegemonic individuals and identities to flex with others in the direction of longer-term social and ecological sustainability. Ecological masculinism is therefore an invitation to dialogue across existing boundaries between the masculinities and environmental discourses, aiming to inject the synergistic wisdom of various environmentalisms into personal praxes of masculinities discourse and masculinities nuances into environmentalism.

Ecological masculinism prepares the masculinities discourse for Mathews' Panpsychism. Through an 'ecomasculinity' embedded in an ecological masculinism, the head (Logos) and the heart (Eros) are invited to dance in harmony, supporting each other in charting a course towards the fullest expressions of socially and environmentally sensitive masculine identities and praxes.

References and further reading

Allister, M. (ed.) (2004) *Ecoman: New Perspectives on Masculinity and Nature*, Charlottesville, VI: University of Virginia Press.

Berg, P. and Dasmann, R. (1978) 'Reinhabiting California', in P. Berg (ed.) *Reinhabiting a Separate Country: A Bioregional Anthology of Northern California*, San Francisco, CA: Planet Drum.

Bertalanffy, L. von [1950] (1969) 'The theory of open and closed systems in physics and biology', *Science*, 111: 23–9.

Bookchin, M. (1993) 'What is social ecology?' in M. Zimmerman, J.B. Callicott, G. Sessions, K.J. Warren and J. Clark (eds) *Environmental Philosophy*, Englewood Cliffs, CO: Prentice Hall, pp. 354–73.

Connell, R. (1987) *Gender and Power: Society, the Person and Sexual Politics*, Cambridge: Polity Press.

Hrdy, S. (1999) *Mother Nature: Natural Selection and the Female of the Species*, London: Chatto and Windus.

Lovelock, J. (1979) *Gaia: A New Look at Life on Earth*, Oxford: Oxford University Press.

Mathews, F. (2003) *For Love of Matter: A Contemporary Panpsychism*, Albany, NY: State University of New York Press.

Naess, A. (1989) *Ecology, Community and Lifestyle*, Cambridge: Cambridge University Press.

Noddings, N. (1984) *Caring: A Female Approach to Ethics and Moral Education*, Berkeley, CA: University of California Press.

Rayner, A.D.M. (2003) 'Inclusionality – an immersive philosophy of environmental relationships', in A. Winnett and A. Warhurst (eds) *Towards an Environment Research Agenda: A Second Selection of Papers*, Basingstoke: Palgrave Macmillan, pp. 5–19.

Roszak, T., Gomes, M.E. and Kanner, A.D. (1995) *Ecopsychology: Restoring the Earth, Healing the Mind*, San Francisco, CA: Sierra Club Books.

Sahtouris, E. (1989) *Gaia: The Human Journey from Chaos to Cosmos*, New York: Pocket Books.

Warren, K. (2000) *Ecofeminist Philosophy: A Western Perspective on What It Is and Why It Matters*, Lanham, MD: Rowman and Littlefield.

PAUL M. PULÉ

ECONOMICS

This essay offers a feminist critique of economics, which has been and remains a men's field. This is true in part because it is still dominated by men. The proportion of PhDs awarded to women rose from 5 per cent in 1949–50 to only 29 per cent in 2000–1 (US Department of Education 2002: Table 255). It is also true, however, because most members of the profession see economics as a one-dimensional story of sustained progress guided only by self-evident facts and logic. There have, of course, been many critics, male as well as female, of this 'masculinist' view, but feminist economists stand out because they offer a fundamental and comprehensive critique of this unrealistic approach. Their concerns go beyond the objections raised by 'feminist empiricists' who focus on inequities facing women and try to break down remaining barriers against women in the economics profession but do not challenge the conventional economic paradigm.

Contrary to the widespread perception that feminist economists are critical of the mainstream of the profession because it is too objective, most feminists find fault with the discipline as currently practised because it is not objective enough. Like the mythical Procrustes, who mutilated people to make them fit his bed, most economists ignore the complexities of the real world and pretend that reality conforms to their elegant but one-dimensional models. An early volume that brought together a number of path-breaking essays that demonstrate this point is Marianne A. Ferber and Julie A. Nelson's (1993) *Beyond Economic Man*, followed ten years later by Ferber and Nelson (2003) *Feminist Economics Today*. The papers in these volumes offer incisive critiques of crucial aspects of the dominant neoclassical school they consider unrealistic or misguided. A number of these are summarised below.

Rebecca Blank's (1993: 134) explanation of why she has considerable sympathy for the feminist approach, although she finds 'the economic model of choice-based behavior an extremely powerful and useful analytic tool' sets the stage for an explanation of the fundamental difference between feminist and conventional economics. As she so aptly puts it, 'Too often during a seminar or a conversation with a colleague, I've suddenly realised with surprise, "He really believes all this stuff about individuals constantly making fully informed and rational choices accounting for all expected lifetime costs and benefits"' (p. 133).

Julie A. Nelson (1993) raised the most basic question of whether economics is the study of choice, as most economists would have it, or of 'provisioning', as Adam Smith, 'the father of economics', proposed. Nelson makes a strong case that, in order to be useful, economics needs to be concerned with the creation and distribution of the necessities and conveniences of life, rather than merely with 'the mathematical theory of individual choice' (p. 34). Unlike standard economics, provisioning does not focus exclusively on market production, the traditional domain of men, but also on housework, the traditional domain of women, which facilitates consumption. Both are essential for sustaining human life.

Another crucial issue raised by Paula England (1993) and Julie A. Nelson (2003) is whether the 'separative' models of the individual and of the firm are realistic. England, focusing on the individual, notes that three of the most basic assumptions underlying traditional economic theory are that interpersonal utility comparisons are impossible, tastes are exogenous and unchanging, and an individual's utility is independent of the utility of others. She, however, points out that these assumptions flow from an unrealistic model of human nature that assumes individuals are wholly autonomous, impervious to social influences and so devoid of sufficient emotional connections as to make empathy with others impossible.

Nelson extends England's analysis to business organisations which are variously regarded by most economists as fully bounded entities only interested in maximising profits but also, inconsistently, as being entirely at the mercy of inexorable market forces beyond their control. Neither of these views can explain such events as one lone securities trader bringing down Barings Bank, which in turn set off the Asian financial crisis of 1995, or the 2002 crash of Enron, one of the ostensibly most successful giant US corporations. Nelson's explanation is that these entities involve real people who form social as well as economic relationships and have only a passing resemblance to the corporation of the theorists.

Paula England and Nancy Folbre (2003) turn their attention to the much-neglected issue of care work and the fact that women have long been disadvantaged because it has been their responsibility. Even today, when women's labour force participation in economically advanced countries ranges from almost 65 per cent (in Japan) to about 75 per cent (in the Scandinavian countries), the care of children, the elderly and the infirm continues to be largely their responsibility. Further, they do by far most of the paid work that now replaces some of the services family members used to perform. Thus, while less than 20 per cent of architects, clergy, dentists and engineers are women, more than 90 per cent of registered nurses and preschool as well as elementary school teachers are fenale. It is also the case that mothers who are employed earn considerably less than other women, and workers in predominantly female occupations earn considerably less than other workers with comparable qualifications.

Neoclassical economists argue that this is because homemakers, and particularly mothers, expend more energy on household work than people without 'family responsibilities' and hence do not perform as well in their paid job, but no one has even attempted to provide proof of such a connection. Similarly, these economists claim that male-dominated occupations are more highly rewarded because they are more demanding, more stressful or more dangerous. Alternatively, they claim it is because they make more valuable contributions. But does anyone really believe that plumbers or construction workers are under more strain or at greater risk than nurses, who are responsible for human lives and are exposed to health risks every day they spend on the job? And do investment brokers or advertising executives make greater contributions than grade school and kindergarten teachers who help our children to become successful and responsible adults?

Women's greater commitment to family is also frequently used to explain their slow progress in climbing the ladder within organisations. According to a report by Catalyst on Fortune 500 companies, in 1999 only 12 per cent of all corporate officers and 5 per cent of top-level executives were women; and women held just 3 per cent of top-earner spots comprised of the five highest-paid executives in the company. Similarly, women comprise almost 60 per cent of instructors but fewer than 20 per cent of full professors at academic institutions; and the situation is worse at the prestigious research universities.

Myra H. Strober (2003) addresses another important issue when she expresses serious reservations about the emphasis most economists place on the role of training students in skills that increase their value in the workplace and tend to ignore the importance of education that can help young people to achieve their human potential and to be responsible members of society. This is in stark contrast to some economists who go so far as to argue that it is irrational for people to take the time to vote when they are not likely to reap any direct, concrete rewards.

Finally, unlike the authors discussed so far, Nancy Folbre (1993) focuses on the different views of feminists and socialists. She emphasises that like Friedrich Engels most of them considered their brand of socialism, which was concerned with the exploitation of the industrial proletariat, 'scientific', but branded those who were concerned with gender inequality as 'utopian'. Yet Folbre argues persuasively that such socialists as August Bebel, Robert Owen and William Thompson were no less scientific for being sympathetic to feminism. They criticised competitive individualism, called for social cooperation and invoked the categories of right and wrong. Foreshadowing criticisms by modern feminists of Gary Becker, who assumes that a family necessarily has a 'head' (presumably the man) who is entirely benevolent, Thompson and Bebel also disparaged the assumption that men are self-interested in their dealings with other men but altruistic in their dealings with women. Further, while Folbre does not mention the debate between Clara Zetkin who recurrently urged the USSR during its early days to provide the services they had promised women to make lives easier, and Vladimir I. Lenin, who continued to respond that they would do so as soon as more urgent needs were taken care of, this dispute provides additional evidence that from the revolution till the fall of the Soviet Empire women's issues were never taken seriously by 'mainstream socialists', just as has been true of most classical and neoclassical economists, from Adam Smith and Alfred Marshall to Milton Friedman and Paul Samuelson. The scant attention paid to women and women's issues in introductory economics texts, discussed by Ferber and Nelson (2003), provides evidence that this continues to be the case.

Feminist economists also raise questions about many tenets of neoclassical economics not specifically mentioned above, from the almost universally accepted premise that more is better than less (is it really better to have more cars on the road?), the implicit assumption that externalities tend to be relatively minor (is pollution inconsequential as compared to the production of goods people often buy because they are heavily advertised?) and the contention that a dollar's worth of different goods always has equal value (does a $100,000 addition to a $1,000,000 mansion provide as much satisfaction to its tenants as a $100,000 house to a previously homeless family?).

Similarly, feminists challenge other implicit assumptions of laissez-faire economics. Among these is the notion that everyone has an equal opportunity to succeed. This is obviously not true as long as people are born with different capabilities and raised in environments not equally conducive to achieving their full potential. Hence, feminists question the basic tenet that distribution according to contribution, which can lead to great wealth for some and dire poverty for others, is fair. Finally, they are critical of the failure of producers to bear the cost of exhausting natural resources and polluting the environment. These concerns lead feminists and other dissidents to the heretical conclusion that a smaller output more equally distributed, within and among nations, would most likely improve overall wellbeing.

In sum, this essay emphasises the contrast between what may be broadly characterised as 'masculinist' and feminist economics. However, as already noted, not all men subscribe to the former, nor do all women subscribe to the latter. In other words, the difference is not categorical, and certainly not merely determined by biology. Rather, women who have been acculturated to be caring and concerned about the welfare of others, especially children and the helpless, tend to have different priorities than men who are expected to be tough and ambitious. Thus, mainstream economists, male and female, emphasise maximising income, while feminist economists, again both male and female, stress the importance of distributive justice and are more concerned with quality of life rather than merely quantity of output.

References and further reading

Becker, G.S. (1981) *A Treatise on the Family*, Cambridge, MA: Harvard University Press.

Blank, R.M. (1993) 'What should mainstream economists learn from feminist theory?' in M.A. Ferber and J.A. Nelson (eds) *Beyond Economic Man: Feminist Theory and Economics*, Chicago, IL: University of Chicago Press, pp. 133–43.

England, P. (1993) 'The separative self', in M.A. Ferber and J.A. Nelson (eds) *Beyond Economic Man: Feminist Theory and Economics*, Chicago, IL: University of Chicago Press, pp. 37–53.

—— (2003) 'Separative and soluble selves', in M.A. Ferber and J.A. Nelson (eds) *Feminist Economics Today. Beyond Economic Man*, Chicago, IL: University of Chicago Press, pp. 33–60.

England, P. and Folbre, N. (2003) 'Contracting for care', in M.A. Ferber and J.A. Nelson (eds) *Feminist Economics Today*, Chicago, IL: University of Chicago Press, pp. 61–80.

Ferber, M.A. and Nelson, J.A. (eds) (1993) *Beyond Economic Man: Feminist Theory and Economics*, Chicago, IL: University of Chicago Press.

Ferber, M.A. and Nelson, J.A. (eds) (2003) 'Introduction', in M.A. Ferber and J.A. Nelson (eds) *Feminist Economics Today*, Chicago, IL: University of Chicago Press, pp. 1–31.

Folbre, N. (1993) 'Socialism, feminist and scientific', in M.A. Ferber and J.A. Nelson (eds) *Beyond Economic Man: Feminist Theory and Economics*, Chicago, IL: University of Chicago Press, pp. 94–110.

Lenin, V.I. (1975) 'A great beginning. On the heroism of workers in the rear', reprinted in R.C. Tucker, *The Lenin Anthology*, New York: W.W. Norton.

Nelson, J.A. (1993) '"The study of choice or the study of provisioning?" Gender and the definition of economics', in M.A. Ferber and J.A. Nelson (eds) *Beyond Economic Man: Feminist Theory and Economics*, Chicago, IL: University of Chicago Press, pp. 23–36.

Report of the Committee on the Status of Women in the Economics Profession (2003) *American Economic Review*, 93 (2, May): 513–20.

Strober, M.H. (2003) 'The application of mainstream economics constructs to education: a feminist analysis', in M.A. Ferber and J.A. Nelson (eds) *Feminist Economics Today: Beyond Economic Man*, Chicago, IL: University of Chicago Press, pp. 157–74.

US Department of Education National Center for Education Statistics (2002) *Digest of Education Statistics*, Washington, DC: US Department of Education.

Zetkin, C. (1975) 'Dialogue with Clara Zetkin', reprinted in Robert C. Tucker, *The Lenin Anthology*, New York: W.W. Norton.

MARIANNE A. FERBER

EDUCATION

Education has traditionally been a selection mechanism for reproducing the dominant social and economic role of men in society.

However, there is now a concern in many education systems that boys are not succeeding in school as much as they should. This conclusion is usually based on comparisons with the performance of girls, though some have questioned whether this is an adequate explanation for the recent prominence of debates about the education of boys (Griffin 2000).

Emphases on boys' education in policy and research have arisen particularly from concerns about boys' disruptive behaviour in the classroom, their reluctance to engage in such 'feminine' activities as literature and the arts, and, almost universally in Western countries, lower literacy achievement and school retention rates.

Literacy in particular has received much attention, where international studies show that boys' literacy performance is on average lower than that of girls, although boys perform better on mathematical literacy. These traditional patterns are problematic as they reflect and reproduce stereotypically narrow curriculum choices by many boys and girls. In the case of boys, these outcomes are seen as incompatible with employment trends towards professional, service and culture industries which require a more literate workforce.

Explanations of these problems are varied (Weaver-Hightower 2003). Some have argued that they are biological, though this argument fails to explain historical and cultural differences. Others accuse educators of ignoring the needs of boys in favour of promoting equity for girls, or blame 'feminised' pedagogies, curricula and female-dominated teaching. Avoiding gender essentialism, a more balanced approach recognises the varied needs of different boys arising from the construction of masculine identities and how these relate to the cultures of schooling (Gilbert and Gilbert 1998). This has led to increasing recognition of the intersections between the construction of masculinities and the experience of other forms of identity and difference, especially race and sexuality (Lesko 2000; Martino and Meyenn 2001).

References and further reading

Gilbert, R. and Gilbert, P. (1998) *Masculinity Goes to School*, Sydney: Allen and Unwin.

Griffin, C. (2000) 'Discourses of crisis and loss: analysing the "boys' underachievement" debate', *Journal of Youth Studies*, 3: 167–88.

Lesko, N. (ed.) (2000) *Masculinities at School*, Thousand Oaks, CA: Sage.

Martino, W. and Meyenn, B. (eds) (2001) *What About the Boys?* Buckingham: Open University Press.

Weaver-Hightower, M. (2003) 'The "boy turn" in research on gender and education', *Review of Educational Research*, 73: 471–98.

See also: boys and boyhood

ROB GILBERT

EFFEMINACY

Dating from early seventeenth-century Europe, use of this term has allowed class battles to shift from the private turf of financial conflicts to the social terrain of sex/gender expression. Although a gendered term, 'effeminacy' originally referred to class affectation and an aristocratic over-delicacy of manners in men. The meaning of the term began to change during the later eighteenth century as the authority of the aristocracy eroded. Reinterpreted by the new bourgeois class, the airs and adornments of the upper class took on a negative taint, and the effeminate label was used to suggest a failure of masculine power.

The older notion of effeminacy as affectation carried into the late nineteenth-century dandyism of a dwindling aristocratic class, while its use as a derogatory label was applied by sexologists and criminal anthropologists to describe a problematic lack of masculinity. These new social sciences redefined effeminacy as improper sex/gender expression, which was held to be symptomatic of hereditary sexual degeneration. As if to ensure the end of aristocratic pretensions, sexologists medicalised effeminacy as a form of sexual aberration just as dandy and author Oscar Wilde was sentenced to prison for the supposed crime of sexual inversion.

Aligning hypermasculinity with war, counter-culture movements of the 1960s reclaimed effeminacy when men grew their hair and donned, robes and beads. At the same time, Newton points out, gay men struggled to throw off the stigmatising label of effeminacy and distanced themselves from the more feminine drag queen and trans communities. Thirty years later the queer movement again reclaimed effeminacy in an attempt to replace the restrictive masculine/feminine dichotomy with a continuum of possible gender expressions.

The class/gender concept of effeminacy is mainly Western, but this does not mean that men in other societies have not taken on gender expressions that are otherwise assumed to belong to women. Although these gender expressions can seem 'feminine' to Western eyes, they may instead signify a variety of alternative meanings including spiritual distinction or a third category of gender. Even cultures that consider gender transgression unacceptable may allow festivals or special holidays where the expression of male effeminacy is tolerated or even encouraged.

References and further reading

Newton, E. (1972) *Mother Camp*, Englewood Cliffs, NJ: Prentice-Hall.

LINDA D. WAYNE

EGALITARIANISM

Egalitarianism covers those beliefs and practices that are opposed to all forms of social, economic, political and religious hierarchy, ranking or stratification that do not admit of the essential equality of human beings usually rooted in the natural order of things. Throughout historical time there are numerous different kinds of egalitarian thought and practice. These are usually to be found among small-scale societies outside state systems or operate as small communities, often religious, apart from the mainstream. Clastres (1987) demonstrates egalitarianism as a positive moral value in many societies (Native American groups are his main examples) deeply antagonistic to state hierarchies or their very idea. Major civilisational religions such as Buddhism, Christianity and Islam have strong moral egalitarian themes contesting the inegalitarianism around them.

As a whole, modern egalitarianism is rooted in strong notions of the autonomous individual whose essential freedom is denied by society. Many populist movements of a strong nationalist kind reflect egalitarian sentiments of an individualist kind from fascist to democratic. Dumont (1980, 1986) has argued, not without criticism, that egalitarianism in modern Western societies, founded in individualism, paradoxically contains the germs of gross social inequality and racism. Thus the stress on communal or community equality, a refusal of difference, results in exclusionary practices. The main examples are Nazi Germany and South Africa under apartheid.

One principle in modern egalitarianism is the assertion that similarity of interest is founded in fundamental biological/natural characteristics that are independent of social construction. The social groups that form on such a basis are believed to be 'natural' societies and, as such, to be strongly bonded because they are constituted by no external social and political coercion. They are often regarded as having a natural moral authority or worth. Much male bonding, from youth gangs to the military, to the male-centred mateship of Australian nationalism, expresses such aspects.

Egalitarianism is in many ways the major force of modernity. Potentially liberating as representations of it may be in movements of gender equality or in processes of democratisation, these are nonetheless prone to generating forms of inequality and social and moral oppression that they are intended to subvert.

References and further reading

Clastres, P. (1987) *Society Against the State*, New York: Zone Books.

Dumont, L. (1980) *Homo Hierarchicus*, Chicago, IL: Chicago University Press.

—— (1986) *Individualism*, Chicago, IL: Chicago University Press.
Kapferer, B. (1998) *Legends of People, Myths of State*, Washington, DC: Smithsonian Institution Press.

BRUCE KAPFERER

ELDER ABUSE

Elder abuse, first discussed as 'granny battering' (Baker 1975; Burston 1975) during the mid-1970s, remained marginal to discussions of gender until the 1990s, not least because it concerned one of the least powerful social groups – elderly people. Increasing debates from the mid-1980s onwards about demographic shifts in Western populations (in particular declining birth rates; rising longevity; the growing elderly population – see Arber and Ginn 1991) and about related public policy issues (the shift to 'care in the community' and, more recently, the pensions crisis) forced greater engagement with the (mal)treatment of the elderly. Elder abuse may involve acts of omission or commission; it may be physical, emotional, material, sexual; it may entail neglect of various kinds and/or the social isolation or abandonment of the elderly person. Often it has multiple dimensions. Factors such as the degree of economic and physical dependency of the abused person; the particular traits and histories of both abuser and abused including intra-familial cycles of violence; histories of drug and alcohol abuse; and overburdening of staff in residential homes all play a role.

Elder abuse does not readily fit the pattern of other forms of violence identified in feminist discourse since both victims and perpetrators are likely to be female. The vast majority of those over seventy-four years old in Western cultures are female, frequently but not inevitably cared for in the home and in institutional settings, by other females. Since both conventional femininity and caring are culturally constructed as nurturing, the notion of the abusing female carer remains a conundrum. Whereas early research (e.g. Lau and Kosberg 1979) identified the abuser in familial settings as a middle-aged daughter, later research (e.g. Ogg and Bennett 1991) suggested a male (son, husband) with a history of mental illness and/or alcohol abuse as the typical abuser. This research by and large reproduced conventional heteronormative perceptions of gender roles and took little account of the shifts in relational and familial patterns that have begun to occupy research since the mid-1990s.

As in other contexts, so with regard to elder abuse: it has been difficult to acknowledge that such abuse frequently involves same-sex relationships which may be, but are not inevitably, intergenerational. There is no significant research to date on elder abuse in same-sex relationships, particularly between men. It is, however, clear that household configurations in Western cultures are changing, and that men are increasingly required to care for elderly people, both women and men. The resultant shifts in gender roles need investigation. Given the demographic changes in Western culture predicted over the next twenty years, we can anticipate a rise in elder abuse and the need to research same-sex interactions, both within a homosexual and within a heterosexual frame, more thoroughly.

References and further reading

Arber, S. and Ginn, J. (1991) *Gender and Later Life: A Sociological Analysis of Resources and Constraints*, London: Sage.
Baker, A.A. (1975) 'Granny battering', *Modern Geriatrics*, 5 (8): 20–4.
Burston, G.R. (1975) 'Granny battering', *British Medical Journal*, 3: 592.
Lau, E. and Kosberg, J.I. (1979) 'Abuse of the elderly by informal care providers', *Ageing*, 229–300 (September–October): 10–15.
Ogg, J. and Bennett, G. (1991) 'Elder abuse: providing answers to some of the questions', *Geriatric Medicine*, October: 15–16.

See also: domestic violence; sexual violence; violence; violence, men as victims of

GABRIELE GRIFFIN

ELDERS

Older persons in the West could often enter retirement taking on roles such as mentor, conservationist, storyteller and source of blessing. Most of us, however, don't have models for how to utilise the expanded life span that is available in the twenty-first century in a way that is generative and nourishing to others and Earth. We lose ourselves in work for most of our adult lives. Like our fathers, many of us, both men and women who have had careers, have been emotionally distant from our children and have lost touch with our spirit centre. We are not skilled in nurturing our spirit.

Men of all ages share a hunger for spiritual and emotional growth. Many of us missed the nurturing only a father can bring. In men's gatherings one is reminded about the archetype of the *elder*. Often, older men present for weekends come to be known as the elders in organisations such as the Mankind Project and Boys to Men. They try to fill a vacuum left after two centuries of diminishing credibility for older people. The elders of pre-industrial communities had been more available to the young because they were less mobile and often aged in the same community in which they were born. The prejudice in contemporary Western culture about aging, combined with an increasing divorce rate, has separated children from their grandparents. With industrialisation came an increasing lack of respect for older mentors who could not teach survival in factories that did not exist when they were learning a trade. The young could survive the demands of the factory better than the old. With immigration and the separation of older people from their ancestral homes, men turned increasingly to their peers for support and training. Older people used to teach youngsters their skills and offered the magic of presence that came with being in a mentor's energy field. People in the West have submitted to a bias against older people that has discouraged us from embracing the role of elder.

Modernised Western culture in particular would benefit greatly if older people would venture into an exploration of the potential of elder-like expression, the second half of life adventure in celebrating long life, passing on a legacy and advocacy for the young. An elder is a steward of life, both human life and the life of our planet. An elder seeks to affirm life by embracing the ancient archetype of the elder within the soul and psyche.

Elders foster consensus rather than conflict and competition. They energise themselves through use of the tools of wisdom: meditation, contemplation and listening. They accept their mortality and honour their body, which they understand is slowly in depletion. With this knowledge they model taking care of themselves, an uncommon trait for North American males. Most of all, the persons who embrace the role of elder make themselves available to younger people, to the family and to the community. They have confidence in the fruits of long life experience and want to seed the future by sharing with the young.

The task of those who are curious about the elder role is less about becoming an elder than about going within oneself to stir elder energy and growing from adulthood into elderhood. The affirmation by the elder that is an active commitment to assist us in obtaining our dream is the blessing of the celebrant quality of elderhood. When the elder stands up for the beauty of Earth and does what he can to deepen and maintain this beauty, he is demonstrating the earthkeeper quality of elderhood. When the elder shares his wisdom he is a mentor. When he arranges to leave the legacy of his story he is a wisdomkeeper.

Any person inclined to serve society in the second half of life is embracing a key aspect of elderhood. Because few elder models exist, Western people assume that the second half of life means resting, declining in health, becoming useless. An elder's depletion is only physical, however. Elders address old age by reaping what has been sown rather than whining about reduced strength. The process of becoming more elder-like requires reviewing the decline of older people's credibility over the past few centuries and considering the concept of elder as a victim of progress. This leads to the personal work of confronting the bias towards aging, embracing the reality of our mortality, forgiving those who have harmed us and deciding if one is ready to give back to the community. This could lead to 'action elderhood' not because the world needs aged activists but because elder expression is known to the world by its works.

The elder is often a spiritual person who believes that he exists for a reason. His search for the reason is what I call the spiritual journey. This journey takes action elders where they can serve others, empower and bless others. At the same time, elders honour the reality that each day brings them closer to death than they were when they were 'action youths'. Action elderhood moves the heart more than the legs. Elders glean the energy they need from contemplative activity. The older they get, the more they become acquainted with their spiritual centre.

The biggest demand for action elderhood is inside your personal sphere of influence – family, community, church and workplace. It is likely that most of the people inside your sphere will not expect action elderhood from you. Therefore, the aspiring elder should move into action in small ways at first, developing the ancient male roles of provider, protector and teacher gradually. The process might begin with increasing your accessibility and then moving to some minor community advocacy work. No matter how elder-like we presently are in our extended family, this is where we are probably going to find the most opportunity for action elderhood.

References and further reading

Jones, T. (2001) *The Elder Within*, West Linn, OR: Elderhood Institute.

Miller, R.S. and Schachter-Shalomi, Z. (1995) *From Age-Ing to Sage-Ing*, New York: Warner Books.

See also: age and ageing; retirement; rites of passage

TERRY JONES

ELITE CULTURE

'Elite culture' is a term which loosely refers to particular ways of doing things among members of elite groupings. There is no singular elite and therefore no singular elite culture. There are many specific ways of doing things associated with 'religious', 'corporate' or 'military' elites among others, in different settings and at different historical times. Indeed, in their worldwide survey Shore and Nugent (2002) emphasise the diversity of ways in which elites operate. This is relevant for what takes place within a single setting as well as across national or cultural divides.

Notwithstanding this multiplicity, interconnections between elites across fields, most notably between business and government in national or regional contexts, and more recently internationally (facilitated by globalisation), mean that there are some shared cultural styles. Furthermore, there is some evidence of a trend towards universal cultural practices within a single field. Connell (1998) developed the concept of transatlantic business masculinities to refer to a dominant form of masculinity derived from politicians and business executives who operate in global markets and transnational corporations. In life-history research with Australian businessmen, Connell and Wood (2005) found some support for this hypothesis alongside evidence of older styles of what they call 'bourgeois masculinity'.

Interconnections across key fields of power are widely recognised, for instance in everyday references to the 'British Establishment' (Shore and Nugent 2002). Elite cultures are created and sustained through a variety of institutions and largely homosocial (Kanter 1977) social and cultural practices, including education, sport and gentlemen's clubs and societies, resulting in powerful networks and friendships (e.g. Kadushin 1995). Considerable research has demonstrated the significance of education in the reproduction of elites. For example, in Britain this is secured through the public school system, and in France through the system of *grandes écoles*. Watching, discussing and playing sport (especially rugby and golf) and participation in gentlemen's clubs and societies also teaches valued styles of 'manly' behaviour and offers a semiotics for the practice of leadership.

References and further reading

Connell, R. (1998) 'Masculinities and globalization', *Men and Masculinities*, 1 (1): 3–23.

Connell, R. and Wood, J. (2005) 'Globalization and business masculinities', *Men and Masculinities*, 7 (4): 347–64.

Kadushin, C. (1995) 'Friendship among the French financial elite', *American Sociological Review*, 60 (2): 202–21.

Kanter, R.M. (1977) *Women and Men of the Corporation*, New York: Basic Books.

Shore, C. and Nugent, S. (eds) (2002) *Elite Cultures, Anthropological Perspectives*, London and New York: Routledge.

See also: culture and representation

DAWN LYON

EMASCULATION

Webster's gives two definitions of the word: to castrate; and to deprive of masculine strength or vigour. It is the second definition that interests us here. Other expressions for losing masculine strength include weakening of masculinity, effeminate and being unmanly. Emasculation is normally used as a negative characterisation of other men for not being masculine enough, but institutions and organisations may also be seen to be 'emasculated' if they are stripped of their powers and authority. In both cases, masculinity is equated with power. Emasculation changes historically and culturally. In nineteenth-century Europe, drinking and gambling were the main reason for emasculation. Since the turn of the century emasculation has increasingly been associated with feminisation, illustrated in terms like 'girly', 'pussy' and 'sissy'. The 'danger' of emasculation has also been connected to the lack of men in pedagogical institutions. The concern is that boys are growing up without masculine role models. Today there is an ongoing debate about boyhood, sometimes called a moral panic (see Martino and Meyenn 2001).

Another way of using emasculation can be found in Sigmund Freud's Schreber-analysis. Schreber is talking about emasculation (*Entmannung*) in the traditional negative way, but also in a positive way, which is unusual. Schreber wants to seduce God and by that save the world, but as a man he does not have the sensibility to seduce. By an act of *Entmannung* and transforming into a woman, Schreber think he is able to seduce God and save the world. Emasculation has become a positive strategy to create a better world. In this way we could think of emasculation in a positive way as changing and criticising traditional and patriarchal masculinity for lack of emotionality.

Emasculation is also connected to George Mosse's term 'countertype' (1996). Countertypes are contradictory to ideal masculinity, and in Mosse's study countertypes are exemplified with people who are Jewish or homosexual. Related to emasculation is also the term 'unmanly', a term used as an analytical tool in today's Nordic studies of masculinities (Liliequist 1999). Instead of trying to define or categorise masculinities, a study of unmanliness brings perspectives on the limits, borders and risk of masculinity. Instead of locating hegemonic masculinity, a perspective centred on the unmanly looks for the threat to hegemonic positions, and thereby places a focus on dynamics and changes in the culture of masculinities.

References and further reading

Freud, S. [1911] (1958) *The Case of Schreber*, in *The Standard Edition of the Complete Psychological Works of Sigmund Freud*, Vol. 12, London: Hogarth Press.

Liliequist, J. (1999) 'Från niding till sprätt: En studie i det svenska omanlighetsbegreppets historia från vikingatid till sent 1700-tal', in Ann-Marie Berggren (ed.) *Manligt och omanligt i ett historiskt*, Report 99:4, Stockholm: Forskningsrådsnämnden.

Martino, W. and Meyenn, B. (eds) (2001) *What About the Boys?* Philadelphia, PA: Open University Press.
Mosse, G. (1996) *The Image of Man*, Oxford: Oxford University Press.

JØRGEN LORENTZEN

EMOTIONS

At the end of the twentieth century, the predominant view within Western cultures of men's relationship with emotions was characterised by terms such as 'the inexpressive male' and 'restrictive emotionality'. In self-report studies, men typically reported a lower frequency and intensity of experience of both positive emotions, such as love, affection and joy, and negative emotions, such as embarrassment, fear and sadness, than did women. Men reported lower levels of positive and negative emotional expressiveness than women; crying much less frequently; and no greater frequency of experience, expression or suppression of anger (Kring 2000). However, men did report that their anger involved aggression towards others more than women's did. Men's accounts of their emotional selves varied only slightly from observational studies and those examining cultural beliefs and stereotypes. Men used no fewer emotion terms in naturalistic talk or in recounting emotional experiences than women, but they were observed and believed to verbally communicate their feelings less than women. The only exception was that men were believed to express their anger vocally, through facial expressions and behaviour (Brody and Hall 2004). So strong were these beliefs and stereotypes that Robinson *et al.* (1998) termed it the 'gender heuristic': men were believed to experience and express more socially desirable self-oriented emotions, such as pride, and more socially undesirable other-oriented emotions, such as anger, than women.

These accounts of men's patterns of emotional response resulted in the adoption of a deficit model, wherein men were assumed not to express the emotions they experienced. Men were supposed to be internalisers; their emotional experiences found expression only as physiological arousal rather than through speech or behaviour, resulting in a litany of personally, relationally and socially undesirable consequences, including drink and drug abuse, dangerous driving, violent outbursts, loneliness, depression and psychophysiological disorders such as headaches, backaches and ulcers (Goldberg 1976). At its extreme, this approach pathologised men's purported inability to express their emotions verbally as 'normative male alexithymia' (Levant 1998). Given the personal and social ills that were supposed to follow from men's emotional inexpressivity, men's emotional lives became a primary location of efforts towards change in sexual politics: by changing the way men expressed their emotions, they might change both their selves and their societies for the better (Petersen 1998).

To believe that men's patterns of emotional responding can change is, however, to theorise emotions differently from much of mainstream psychology. This research typically follows Darwin (1872) in conceptualising emotions as essential, as differing patterns of physiological and expressive responses to differing environmental stimuli, which must, in order to become cross-culturally prevalent through inheritance, serve some beneficial adaptive function (Buss 1995). However, the literature on biological differences, in areas such as cerebral lateralisation and testosterone levels, regularly concludes that the findings are inconclusive and even that the direction of causality between biological differences and differences in emotional expressiveness is uncertain (Brody 1999). Reported differences between men and women in emotional expressivity cannot be accounted for by recourse to biology or evolution alone.

In the absence of overwhelming biological or evolutionary proof regarding men's emotional patterns, theorists turned to sociocultural accounts. For Seidler (1994), the post-Enlightenment epistemologies of mind, reason and objectivity provided for a version of masculinity into which men, in order to occupy dominant positions at personal, social and cultural levels, were forced to fit. By doing so, men devalued the embodied, the emotional and the subjective, both in themselves and in others. Through this estrangement from their own essential masculine emotional selves, men did violence to their selves and fell victims to culturally prescribed standards of masculinity. Such an account, by ascribing to men the status of victims, was highly compatible with the Men's Liberation movement of the 1970s and 1980s and clearly identified the object requiring change as the hegemonic post-Enlightenment version of masculinity.

However, such accounts of men's relationship with emotions were challenged at the start of the twenty-first century by more dynamic accounts of the role played by emotions in the politics of everyday life (Shields 2005). There were ways by which men and women could publicly express emotions that were considered 'manly'. 'Manly emotion' was characterised by the subtle communication of a powerful emotional experience held under equally powerful control. Such an emotional display evidenced individuals' authenticity, their essential humanity, while at the same time evidencing their capacity to exercise self-control and to act within reason, all celebrated characteristics within Western cultures. The association of the masculine with the rational and the feminine with the emotional began to collapse. Attention was turned from how performances of masculinity, specifically the devaluing of emotional experience and expression, ensured and perpetuated male dominance to how particular performances of emotion, in particular relational and social contexts, could confer power and authority on individuals, regardless of gender.

References and further reading

Brody, L.R. (1999) *Gender, Emotion and the Family*, Cambridge, MA: Harvard University Press.

Brody, L.R. and Hall, J.A. (2004) 'Gender, emotion and expression', in M. Lewis and J.M. Haviland-Jones (eds) *Handbook of Emotions*, 2nd edn, New York: Guilford, pp. 338–49.

Buss, D.M. (1995) 'Psychological sex differences', *American Psychologist*, 50 (3): 164–8.

Darwin, C. (1872) *The Expression of Emotions in Man and Animals*, London: John Murray.

Goldberg, H. (1976) *The Hazards of Being Male*, New York: Signet.

Kring, A.M. (2000) 'Gender and anger', in A.H. Fischer (ed.) *Gender and Emotion*, Cambridge: Cambridge University Press, pp. 211–31.

Levant, R.F. (1998) 'Desperately seeking language', in W.S. Pollack and R.F. Levant (eds) *New Psychotherapy for Men*, New York: John Wiley, pp. 35–56.

Petersen, A. (1998) *Unmasking the Masculine*, London: Sage.

Robinson, M.D., Johnson, J.T. and Shields, S.A. (1998) 'The gender heuristic and the database', *Basic and Applied Social Psychology*, 20: 206–19.

Seidler, V.J. (1994) *Unreasonable Men*, London: Routledge.

Shields, S.A. (2005) 'The politics of emotions in everyday life', *Review of General Psychology*, 9 (1): 3–15.

See also: essentialism; hegemonic masculinity; intimacy; love; methods, methodology and research; psychology; sociobiology

CHRIS WALTON

EPISTEMOLOGY

Epistemology is concerned with the nature, scope and limits of knowledge (Klein 1998). As Baber (1994) writes, this is not to suggest that epistemology has knowledge per se as its principal focus. Rather, it is concerned with *how we know* (Williams 2003) and the grounds for believing something. For example, traditional empiricism's epistemological stance states that perception and the testing of prediction can justify claims to knowledge of the world. Thus, for Hume when one billiard ball hits another, what is observed is simply two balls moving (Hollis 1994: 48). Causation becomes nothing more than being able to say that in similar situations the same event can be observed. Alternatively, rationalism suggests that reflective reason enables a move beyond what the senses can discover. Descartes, for example, believed that from intuition alone he could ascertain that he was a 'thing which thinks', allowing him to be certain of his statement *cogito ergo sum* ('I think therefore I am': Hollis 1994).

However, the traditional discussion of epistemic justification (Baber 1994) and what should or should not be believed, found within schools of thought such as empiricism and rationalism, have been criticised as a result of their prioritising of the objective, detached observer and embodiment of male norms (ibid.). Feminist epistemologies argue that these dominant modes of social inquiry disembody knowledge (Flood 1997) and ignore the intrinsic relationship between *how we know* and gender. In this respect, feminist epistemologies appear to be closely aligned to epistemological Pragmatism, which suggests that theory governs experience and experience governs theory (Hollis 1994).

As well as fundamental debate existing between epistemological schools of thought, differences also exist within them. Sandra Harding (1986) suggests that, within feminist epistemological discussion, debates have given rise to three basic schools of thought: feminist empiricism, standpoint feminism and Postmodern Feminism. As with any typology, there is an element of simplification within Harding's discussion and it is tacitly accepted that cases will exist which do not fit easily into one of the mutually exclusive 'types'. Despite this, the typology remains widely referred to (Smart 1995) and will be discussed briefly here.

Feminist empiricism rests upon the assumption that what passes for science is not objective, as it claims, but in fact relates to the world as perceived by men (Smart 1995: 40). Ontologically, this does not negate the possibility that objective facts do exist, but rather suggests that the questions science has traditionally asked, and its biases, superstitions and ignorance, have excluded women and the interests of women (Smart 1995: 40; Harding 1997: 166).

For Feminist empiricism, tighter adherence to the methodological norms of scientific research can eliminate prejudices (Harding 1997: 166) and eradicate the socially constructed connection between gender and knowing. As Harding (1997) states, this is not to suggest that feminist empiricism is completely consistent with traditional Empiricist answers to *how we know*. Feminist empiricism argues that women or feminists (both male and female) are more likely to produce unbiased claims, thus negating the traditional Empiricist claim that the social identity of the observer is irrelevant to the 'goodness' of results.

With standpoint feminism (Harding 1998), *how we know* becomes less involved with empirical methods and more to do with position. Standpoint feminism suggests that women's experiences are epistemologically privileged and provide less distorted knowledge claims (Harding 1997). This approach owes much to the writings of Hegel, Marx, Engels and Lukacs and stresses that, through their status as 'oppressed', women can offer a 'less false' view of reality. To achieve a feminist standpoint, then, one must engage in the struggles necessary to see social life from the point of view of disdained activity and not the partial and perverse view of the 'ruling gender' (Harding 1997: 169).

Although Haraway develops an account of epistemology in opposition to the Feminist Standpoint positions it does incorporate key elements of a standpoint strategy (Haraway 1991: 194). Haraway (ibid.) calls for 'situated and embodied knowledges' and 'knowledge claims' which can be called into account. What is meant here is that there is a need to acknowledge the choices involved with where we are situated and an acceptance of the way in which a situation affects representations. Further to this, there is a need to see things from other (numerous) perspectives. This is not to suggest that relativism, which states that all points of view are equally valid, should be embraced. For Haraway (ibid.), relativism equates to being nowhere while stating that you are everywhere. Relativism, like totalisation, denies the influence of location and 'partial perspectives'. It is a 'god-trick', in that it promises vision from everywhere and nowhere.

In this respect, Haraway's work can also be seen as a criticism of some Postmodern Feminism. Postmodernism is often underpinned by the core assumption that we have now discovered that nothing can be known with any certainty (Giddens 1990). There is a rejection of the notion of a single, true reality (Smart 1995) which can be gleaned through empirical methods or awareness of position. *How we know*, then, almost becomes a redundant question, and instead the focus is pushed on to relativism and pluralism.

Although Postmodern Feminism is a problematic label because of diversity within those who are said to fall within it (Smart 1995), it can be seen to share elements of these core assumptions. Postmodern Feminism began with the demise of 'sisterhood' and a refusal of the Marxist theories which underpinned standpoint feminism. The recognition of differences in class, race, sexuality and so on among women forced feminism to look for other ways of thinking which did not subjugate other subjectivities (Smart 1995: 45). The focus turned to knowledges, the deconstruction of Truth claims and the analysis of the relations between power and Truth claims (Smart 1995). Issues of importance became why some epistemologies are prioritised above others and the power effects that these claims may have.

Feminist epistemological writings raise important methodological questions relating to men as researchers and research subjects. For example, if *how we know* is related to gender, what does each feminist epistemology mean for men's knowledge and knowledge of men? With reference to men as objects of research, Campbell (2003) suggests that feminist epistemologies do not necessarily wish to ghettoise into an 'all-woman camp'. Men's experiences should not be ignored wholesale but should be subjected to rigorous and critical analysis. There is a need to be aware that men's accounts may become confessions or alibis, obscuring the real sources of gender inequality and power (Morgan 1992; Jackson 1990) and that an exclusive concern with subjective accounts offered by men may deflect attention away from power and reproduce sexist regimes of truth (Flood 1997: 4).

Feminist empiricism believes that men and women can gain feminist subjectivities (Harding 1998) as both can conduct 'good science'. As Harding writes (ibid.), just as Thomas Kuhn points to the importance of scientific communities in producing the best environment for the growth of 'good science', Feminist Empiricists have suggested that membership of a feminist community may be beneficial to men (and women). Indeed, despite the starting premise that women are less likely to produce biased claims, for some Feminist Empiricists women and men have nothing distinctive to contribute as feminist thinkers. The goal is, simply, to become the 'rational man' advocated and championed by the Enlightenment (Harding 1998: 177–8).

Standpoint Feminists also offer men a way to gain feminist subjectivities. Marx and Engels, whose work underpins a large proportion of Standpoint discussion, were not proletarians and yet purported to think from proletarian positions (Harding 1986). Similarly, men can begin their thought in women's lives, although how, exactly, is problematic (Harding 1998). For Flood, men's anti-patriarchal standpoint *is* possible because the ontology of privileged groups is not completely determining. Men can 'reinvent' themselves as 'Other' and adopt 'traitorous' (Kimmel 1994) social locations and identities (Flood 1997: 3). However, this involves more than simply will or moral conviction. A change in 'lived reality' is required, which for Flood (ibid.) involves adopting the status of 'outsider within'.

The ontologies of dominant groups provide resources for this change in 'lived reality'. Men, themselves, can be subject to 'misnamings' and 'silences' because of their status as gay, bisexual, working-class, disabled or 'non-white'. As Calasanti argues, although hegemonic masculinities (Connell 1995) may be the ideal, many men are powerless because of their relationships with other men (Calasanti 2003: 16). Critical reflection on their own subjection to domination and their own temporary experience of 'otherness', can enable men to find points of contact with women (Flood 1997: 3–4).

This difference is also said to point towards locations where men can develop and access distinctive forms of feminist knowledges (Harding 1998: 185). As Harding (1998) suggests, men who have learned to think through feminist theories can examine the gap between how their lives are shaped by their feminist concerns and how dominant ideologies shape men's lives. Likewise, masculinity discourses are heavily linked to public domains and, as such, a men's feminist standpoint could, it is suggested, contribute to understandings of the models of gender linked to these discourses (Harding 1998: 187).

In relation to the final feminist epistemology discussed here, Postmodern Feminism suggests that feminist claims are more plausible only insofar as they are grounded in solidarity between fractured identities and the politics they create (Harding 1986: 28). For Pease (1996: 2000) men can also destabilise their identities as heterosexual men: creating solidarity with women (and others) on the basis of a respect for difference. The usage of difference here is not meant to reflect the mythopoetic concern with the 'naturalness' of male/female distinctions but rather recognises differences as being related to the body as discursively constituted (Mills and Lingard 1997).

Similarly, Whitehead (2002) suggests that more men are now prepared to critically reflect on themselves as masculine subjects in a postmodern world and engage in ways of being more closely aligned to feminism. Yet the modernist feminist understanding of men as oppressors does not necessarily sit alongside the postmodern/poststructuralist view that there is no founding subject, merely a fragmented, differentiated, discursive self (Whitehead 2002: 224). In essence, conflict can arise between postmodern refusal of essentialist 'categories', such as men and women, and structural views of power relations and the influences these may have on *how we know*.

However, Whitehead (2002) believes that the self-reflexivity, required by feminist empiricism, standpoint feminism and postmodern Feminism, is still absent for a large proportion of men. Kahane (1998) is also less optimistic about the possibility of male feminist knowledge. He agrees with the notions that men can draw upon feminist insights to reinterpret their lives, but is more pessimistic about the likelihood of this happening. Male feminism is an identity rife with contradictions and only in a transformed world, Kahane argues, will male feminism be anything more than an oxymoron. Thus epilogue becomes prologue and this entry returns to questions of *how we (can) know*: questions which necessarily need contemplating when investigating men or when being a male investigator.

References and further reading

Baber, H. (1994) 'The market for feminist epistemology', *Monist*, 77 (4): 403–24.

Calasanti, T. (2003) 'Masculinities and care work in old age', in S. Arber, K. Davidson and J. Ginn (eds) *Gender and Ageing: Changing Roles and Relationships*, Maidenhead: Open University Press.

Campbell, E. (2003) 'Interviewing men in uniform: a feminist approach?' *International Journal of Social Research Methodology, Theory and Practice*, 6 (4): pp. 285–304.

Connell, R. (1995) *Masculinities*, Cambridge: Polity.

Flood, M. (1997) 'Doing research on men and as men: politics and problems', paper to conference 'Masculinities: Renegotiating Genders', University of Wollongong, 20 June (available from Michael Flood; see www.mensbiblio.xyonline.net).

Giddens, A. (1990) *The Consequences of Modernity*, Cambridge: Polity.

Harding, S. (1986) *The Science Question in Feminism*, Ithaca, NY: Cornell University Press.

—— (1997) 'Is there a feminist method?' in S. Kemp and S. Squires (eds) *Feminisms*, Oxford: Oxford University Press.

—— (1998) 'Can men be the subject of feminist thought?' in T. Digby (ed.) *Men Doing Feminism*, London: Routledge.

Haraway, D. (1991) *Simians, Cyborgs and Women: The Reinvention of Nature*, London: Routledge.
Hollis, M. (1994) *The Philosophy of Social Science: An Introduction*, Cambridge: Cambridge University Press.
Jackson, D. (1990) *Unmasking Masculinity: A Critical Autobiography*, London: Unwin Hyman.
Kahane, D.J. (1998) 'Male feminism as oxymoron', in T. Digby (ed.) *Men Doing Feminism*, London: Routledge.
Kimmel, M.S. (1994) 'Who's afraid of men doing feminism?' in T. Digby (ed.) *Men Doing Feminism*, London: Routledge.
Klein, P.D. (1998) 'Epistemology', in E. Craig (ed.) *Routledge Encyclopedia of Philosophy*, London: Routledge.
Mills, M. and Lingard, B. (1997) 'Masculinity politics, myths and boys' schooling: a review essay', *British Journal of Educational Studies*, 45 (3): 276–92.
Morgan, D. (1992) *Discovering Men*, London: Routledge.
Pease, B. (1996) 'Pro-feminist politics', *XY, Men, Sex, Politics*, 6 (3, Spring).
—— (2000) *Recreating Men: Postmodern Masculinity Politics*, London: Sage.
Smart, C. (1995) *Law, Crime and Sexuality: Essays in Feminism*, London: Sage.
Whitehead, S.M. (2002) *Men and Masculinities: Key Themes and New Directions*, Cambridge: Polity.
Williams, S. (2003) 'Beyond meaning, discourse and the empirical world: critical realist reflections on health', *Social Theory and Health*, 1 (1): 42–71.

ROBERT MEADOWS

ESSENTIALISM

For Aristotle, to define something was to describe its inherent natural characteristics or essences. For 'man', this defining characteristic was reason, a quality in which women were said to be deficient. In the twentieth century, postmodernist thinkers criticised this way of thinking, claiming that essentialism arose from modernist desires to order and classify and that it assumes solidarity, sameness and unity among a particular group. While such classification may be strategic and political, essentialism is seen as problematic due to the way it excludes those outside the group and privileges those inside it.

Essentialism implies that differences between assumed static categories, say, man/woman or black/white, reduce to a binary of superior versus inferior. Failure to recognise the plurality of differences and other intersecting axes of diversity such as gender, race, class, sexuality and ability within any category, promotes the experiences of one group at the expense of others. For example, in addressing concerns about boys' academic underachievement, analysis regularly assumes that 'boys' are being disadvantaged by contrasting and positioning them against the achievements of 'girls', rather than examining the divisions between boys themselves that may contribute to gendered disparities in literacy and learning.

Unity within essentialised categories is habitually presumed to be a natural fact grounded in biology. This naturalisation of difference makes inequities difficult to question and divides insider from outsider knowledge.

Essentialism is also employed strategically to create political categories to counter social inequities. For example, to identify as African American involves locating oneself as a part of a group based on a shared experience of exclusion and difference in order to highlight social injustice.

Anti-essentialists argue it is naïve to assume that people in a group will always share the same experiences because categories always leak. However, critiquing such identity categories can be seen to threaten activism by dissolving the unity that grounds the group's political position.

The tension between essentialist subject positions in the postmodern condition of fractured and multiple subjectivities may be addressed by acknowledging the contextual and contingent nature of identity and applying a critical gaze to all identities, even if fictitious.

References and further reading

Alcoff, L. (1991) 'The problem of speaking for others', *Cultural Critique*, Winter: 5–32.
Butler, J. (1990) *Gender Trouble*, London: Routledge.
Fuss, D. (1989) *Essentially Speaking*, London: Routledge.
Segal, L. (1990) *Slow Motion*, London: Virago.

Trinh, M.-H. (1992) *Framer Framed*, London: Routledge.

See also: biology; bodies and byology, male

KEVIN G. DAVISON

ETHNOGRAPHY

Over the past three and a half decades ethnography has increasingly been used as a methodology for qualitative researchers engaged in educational research, although it has a long and more comprehensive history within the fields of anthropology and sociology (Atkinson *et al.* 2001). In its most distinctive form the ethnographic researcher participates in the daily lives of a group of people for an extended period of time. S/he observes what happens, listens to what is said, poses questions and collects as much data as necessary to illuminate issues that frame the research study. The private moments of the culture, group or people under study are rendered public, and readers of ethnographic research are assumed to understand the representation by the ethnographer of events and the actors who participated. This particular version of ethnography has added a degree of complexity and richness to the evolving field of men and masculinities research, with the past two decades witnessing a considerable rise in ethnographic research aimed at capturing and providing a micro-level analysis of masculinities.

In 2002, some twenty-five years after his landmark ethnographic research describing boys and schooling, Willis addressed the American Education Research Association. He spoke of the 'lads and earoles' from his well-known study *Learning to Labour* (1977). In its time his work provided a major shift in the way researchers examined male youth identities, uncovering and teasing out the complex relations that shaped the world of disaffected working-class English males and their views of schooling and its relation to their anticipated adult lives. Since then many others have used ethnography to uncover the complex relations of masculinities within school settings (Foley 1990; Mac an Ghaill 1994; Connell 1995; Kehler 2004; Skelton 2001). Mac an Ghaill (1994), for example, explored the interplay of schooling, sexuality and masculinity. His work centred on inferring meanings by understanding the context, through participation in the life of the students and teachers. This kind of inquiry allowed him to more deeply understand the cultural production of different versions of masculinity. Connell (1995) highlighted the constant struggle for dominance in which certain types of masculine groups engage, and, conversely, the versions of masculinity that are oppressed in this struggle. Theoretically, Connell moves beyond naming groups of people and instead raises important questions for how patterns of gender practice are examined and recorded. She provides a useful conceptual development by unsettling past rigid and linear notions of gender and in its place points to relationships between bodies and social practice in a way that compels researchers and ethnographers in particular to acknowledge the historicity of gender and the fundamental way masculinities are processes or what he refers to as 'gender projects' located in particular times and places.

Ethnography redefined

Since Willis's 1977 seminal ethnographic research on masculinities, however, the field of ethnography itself has undergone substantive changes or so-called 'turns'. The emergence of postmodern and poststructuralist influences in qualitative research has reshaped the face of ethnography and caused a shift from more traditional ethnographic accounts like that of Willis to more textual narratives. Such a shift has called into question the nature of core concepts in ethnographic research such as 'culture', 'identity', 'representation' and 'authority'. From bounded, static and accepted notions of these concepts, ethnography in a poststructuralist research world has increasingly come to view these concepts as permeable and unstable, fluid and contingent. Ethnography, it is posited, can only describe and illuminate 'partial truths and fictions' (Britzman 2000: 28). Let us examine very briefly these four central elements of ethnography and how they have been reframed since the 1990s.

Culture, characterised as a coherent and bounded way of living (Eisenhart 2001), was once a widely accepted anthropological definition. Postmodernism and poststructuralism have highlighted that we can no longer conceive of social groups of people with a culture that is clearly delineated and similarly meaningful for all of its participants. Individuals and the groups to which they belong are shaped by multiple and at times competing cultural influences. We may need to think of culture more as a performance or production constituted by discourses, practices, materials and meanings that can be likened to sources of knowledge upon which individuals may draw to shape their identity.

Identity in the postmodern world should be viewed as a multi-layered, often contradictory construct, formed at intersections in particular times and spaces. It is rarely permanent, stable or uniform within any individual or group of individuals, but rather a construct that points to the fluidity and multiplicity of identities. If ethnography is to capture even the partial truths of the phenomena under investigation and maintain the integrity, multiplicity and contradictory voices emerging from the participants, ethnography admittedly becomes an even 'messier' research undertaking but with considerable potential to produce complex and rich understandings of the daily lives of men.

The permeability and temporality of culture and identity raise methodological and ethical issues for a researcher regarding 'who' and 'what' is represented in any ethnographic study and on what authority any such representations rest. If culture and identity are diffuse for those who are researched, then the same must hold for those researching. The representations of the ethnographer and her/his authority should be read with a questioning stance and should be viewed as a production of the ethnographer's own subjectivities and biography. Postmodernist and poststructuralist ethnography necessitates an explication and legitimising of the ethnographer's role in the study and of how biography and cultural productions have shaped her/his representation of self and of others. The role of the omnipotent and omniscient ethnographer conveying a realist and objective description would seem to be a relic of the past and inconsistent with the notion of ethnography as a textual narrative of subjectivities and biographies.

Implications for masculinities research

This broader debate regarding the characteristics and principles that should frame good ethnographic research has found a particular resonance among researchers undertaking the study of boys and men. In a similar vein to poststructuralist notions of culture as being fragmented and particularistic in time and space, so ideals of masculinity have been shown to be historically and contextually dependent (Weaver-Hightower 2003). The existence of multiple masculinities has affirmed the notion that masculine identities are also fluid and permeable and thus changeable. Masculine identities as constructs that are multi-layered, intersecting with constructs of race, class, religion and sexuality, have also been advanced by many ethnographers in this field. The cacophony of voices and richly diverse experiences conveyed through a more nuanced analysis of the everyday interactions of men have deepened the kind of textured lives previously absent or 'unauthored' in ethnographic studies of men. These nuanced analyses by fe/male researchers have presented their own epistemological and methodological complications, similar to the broader complexities and problematics on representation and authority that poststructuralist thought has accentuated.

With regard to the reflexive role of the ethnographer in masculinities studies, Mac an Ghaill (1994) has noted that many male ethnographers of young men's lives in school settings have scarcely acknowledged the tacit male knowledges and understandings that have underpinned the thoughts, speech and actions of their male participants. These implicit notions, critics note, must be made more explicit, more visible, so that the consumer of an ethnographer's work might have a greater repertoire of possible readings of the representation of data. This critique is merited given the emphasis accorded by poststructuralists to the role that subjectivities and biographies may play in the representation of an ethnographer's work. It would thus seem beneficial for ethnographic research on men and masculinities to be consciously multi-voiced and multi-centred, explicit about the ways our own desires as fe/male researchers have shaped the texts we create. We must be clear about how and when we listen to participants, to ourselves as researchers, and ultimately to developing an 'ethnographic portrayal' of participants that will 'more likely treat them with integrity than as products of our own constructions' (Quantz and O'Connor 1988: 107).

This call for greater reflexivity has been echoed by feminist researchers who have noted the need for a clearer and more explicit positioning of male ethnographers in the research process itself. Using Parker's 1974 study entitled *View From the Boys* as one example, feminist writer Skelton (1998) has highlighted how the author associated himself with many of the 'laddish' modes of masculinity he investigated in order to access and illuminate issues of masculinity in his male participants. Skelton notes that Parker did not seem aware of a particular 'macho' standpoint he brought to his research as a result of his association with his participants. Although this association may have given him access to issues of masculinity that many women feminist researchers have found impenetrable, his lack of reflection on the power and privilege garnered from his role as a male ethnographer is troubling. Notions of how power and privilege are constructed and utilised have been central to ethnographic studies on men and masculinities, and Skelton aptly notes that an active and explicit engagement with these notions can bridge ethnographic work on masculinities to issues raised by feminists in other gender equity research.

Challenges and directions for ethnographic research on masculinities

From the voices of the lads and earoles, the hallway hangers and Brothers, to the more recent voices of young men resisting counter-hegemonic masculinities, ethnographic studies have added considerable depth and richness to the once fragmented and partial stories of boys and young men. Yet, despite its ability to unearth the complexities of gender and its role in schooling, Connell (2000) has called attention to the limiting nature of ethnographic studies on men and masculinities. A majority of the ethnographic studies on young men have addressed micro-level units of analysis, whether they are reactions to school curriculum, playground interactions, conversations or use of texts. Connell has argued that researchers on men and masculinities look beyond the micro or local, and begin to focus on the construction and expression of masculinities around larger social forces such as globalisation. His call has been echoed by Foley (1990), Mac an Ghaill (1994) and Nayak (2003), who argue that young men's gendered identities cannot be fully understood within the microcosm of school alone. Rather, a deeper, more fully textured analysis of masculinities is better drawn by considering young men's complex relations within a network of family, peers, geo-political locales and changing work practices in an increasingly de-industrialised global labour market.

In light of the challenge to move ethnographic research beyond the local or micro-level of analysis, coupled with the post-structuralist admonition to consider identities as made up of multiple cultural productions that emanate from multiple sites, the methodological issues that accompany this movement in research are unquestionably perplexing. Are conventional ethnographic data collection tools adequate or appropriate to track phenomena that could be wide-ranging and diffuse? How might a researcher with limited means undertake ethnographic work that is beyond the local? Is ethnography the most appropriate method when a researcher seeks to investigate the formation of masculinities on a more macro or global level? The call for a move beyond the local may also have implications for the ongoing tension between ethnographic research that seeks primarily and unabashedly to understand and illuminate issues of social relevance and studies that legitimate the poststructuralist angst over ethnography that serves an understanding of self as much as the phenomena of others. These are some of the questions and challenges that may shape the debate among ethnographic scholars of masculinities in years to come.

References and further reading

Atkinson, P., Coffey, A., Delamont, S., Lofland, J. and Lofland, L. (eds) (2001) *Handbook of Ethnography*, London: Sage.

Britzman, D. (2000) 'The question of belief', in E. St Pierre and W.S. Pillow (eds) *Working the Ruins*, New York: Routledge, pp. 27–40.

Connell, R. (2000) *The Men and the Boys*, Berkeley, CA: University of California Press.

—— (1995) *Masculinities*, Berkeley, CA: University of California Press.

Eisenhart, M. (2001) 'Educational ethnography past, present and future', *Educational Researcher*, 8: 16–27.

Epstein, D. (1997) 'Boyz' own stories', *Gender and Education*, 9: 105–15.

Foley, D. (1990) *Learning Capitalist Culture*, Philadelphia, PA: University of Pennsylvania Press.

Kehler, M.D. (2004) 'Masculinities and resistance', *Taboo*, 8 (1): 97–113.

Mac an Ghaill, M. (1994) *The Making of Men*, Buckingham: Open University Press.

Nayak, A. (2003) 'Boyz to men', *Educational Review*, 55: 147–59.

Parker, H.J. (1974) *View from the Boys*, Newton Abbot: David and Charles.

Quantz, R. and O'Connor, T. (1988) 'Writing critical ethnography', *Educational Theory*, 38: 95–109.

Skelton, C. (1998) 'Feminism and research into masculinities and schooling', *Gender and Education*, 10: 217–27.

—— (2001) *Schooling the Boys: Masculinities and Primary Education*, Buckingham and Philadelphia, PA: Open University Press.

Weaver-Hightower, M. (2003) 'The "boy turn" in research on gender and education', *Review of Educational Research*, 73: 471–98.

Willis, P. (1977) *Learning to Labour*, Aldershot: Saxon House.

MICHAEL KEHLER
COLIN GREEN

FAMILIES

Families are unities formed by groups of persons who are connected closely by blood or affinity. It may be argued that families are the first, and perhaps most significant, arenas within which masculinities are constructed, and fathers are often the first and most influential role models for sons. While families are an important context for the construction of maleness, outcomes are not uniform, and they are not uncontested. What is clear is that there are important connections between family forms, fathering and the construction of diverse forms of manhood. It is now seen as vitally important to reflect upon how men's identities are learned in relation to fathers and mothers, elders and children, and how those identities are shaped by the produced and occupied spaces of families and households.

The formal academic study of families is relatively recent, coming to conscious attention in the late nineteenth century when rapid economic and spatial reorganisation precipitated swift social change. A large part of that change was the construction of new family forms. The etymological root of the term 'family' comes from the Latin word *famulus,* meaning servant. When the term was first used in English in the fifteenth century, it described a unity among a household's domestic servants. Gradually the term broadened to include the whole household and, then, in the middle of the seventeenth century, it narrowed to define a group of people related by blood ties. Acceptance of apprentices, servants and live-in staff as 'family' became much rarer in Western society through the eighteenth and nineteenth centuries as the control of the means of production moved away from the private sphere. New models of fatherhood at this time moved men away from their role as the family overseer that is suggested in early European and American family structures (Demos 1970), although men still had patriarchal authority and continued taking on the role of family disciplinarian. Of course, the idea of a monolithic family form predominating in any time period, or different family forms existing in different places (e.g. extended families in the global south and nuclear families in the global north) is as problematic as suggesting that men play singular roles in families. In actuality, there are myriad different kinds of families through time and across space. The key is to understand the complex roles that men play in diverse families.

Feminists argue that from the beginning of the industrial era a male-dominated system of control strengthened along with a growing spatial separation between private, domestic spheres of reproduction and public spheres of production. Within this framework, the history of the familial domestic sphere needs to be understood in terms of men's and women's struggles around control over the means of production and subsistence. This argument, which focuses on the reciprocal relationship between the development of capitalism as an oppressive economic system, and the creation of the modern family form as an oppressive social system, differs from the work of more conservative family historians such as Gottlieb (1993) who suggest that the family is a natural unit of biological and social reproduction that is largely impervious to larger economic and political transformations. Alternatively, following feminist arguments, a number of contemporary poststructural and critical theorists argue that the family, if understood as an existent, unchanging and monolithic form, and especially when coupled with terms such as 'family values', is the fundamental political vehicle for the creation and maintenance of patriarchy as a system that subordinates women, children and some men.

The construction of modern family forms as irrepressibly subservient to larger political, economic and social structures, and as different from traditional or 'extended' family forms, gained institutional legitimacy with George Peter Murdoch's (1949: 1) use of the term 'nuclear family' to describe 'a social group characterised by common residence, economic cooperation, and reproduction ... [i]t includes adults of both sexes, at least two of whom maintain a socially approved sexual relationship, and one or more children'. Through the 1950s, common wisdom on the nuclear family restricted one part of the adult complement (most often a male) to waged labour and the other (most often a female) to domestic and child-rearing activities. Deniz Kandiyoti (1988) characterises a problematic 'patriarchal bargain' within this nuclear family form where women seek men's economic support and protection in return for domestic services and subordination.

Men are also constrained by the gender roles and relations prescribed within the patriarchal bargain. In particular, with the beginning of the industrial revolution, the father figure was increasingly distanced from the emotional heart of family life. His image became associated with the office, the factory and other places of waged labour that are spatially distinct from the home environment and the rearing of children (Aitken 1998: 61).

With fathers over the last century in Western society spending more and more time away from their families, researchers sought a clearer understanding of how this change reflects on ideas of manhood and fatherhood. Even at the beginning of the industrial revolution, the terms 'manhood' and 'fatherhood' were rarely conflated in the same sense that womanhood was defined in association with motherhood. The term 'mothering' refers not only to an activity but also to a gender, and many people find it difficult to comprehend any other approach to parenting. As a consequence, the work and emotions of fathering are much less understood than those of mothering. Men in households who are solely responsible for childcare often refer to themselves as 'Mr Mom' or 'house-husbands', reflecting and refracting their identities from the norms of mother and housewife (Aitken 2000). A further issue relating to the seeming 'female' context of mothering focuses on fifty years of research exposing a great deal of abuse within families, often perpetrated by men. While women can be violent and abusive, some argue that male aggression makes fathers problematic childcarers, and so encouraging men to be more involved in families may put children at risk.

Frank Furstenberg (1988) famously speculated on the roles of men in families as ideologically polarised between 'good dads' and 'bad dads', and focused especially on the so-called 'dead-beat dad' issue that was engaging policy debates in the United States in the 1980s. Because of the increased externalisation of women's roles beyond the family since World War II and their increased waged labour since the 1960s, Furstenberg argued that men increasingly opted out of the 'family wage earner and good provider' role. A man's earning abilities established his authority in the home, but a movement 'from ascription to achievement' during the nineteenth century 'signaled a profound erosion in the roles of men in families' (Furstenberg 1988: 196).

By the end of the twentieth century, a rigid structural division of gender roles in Western families suggested a precariousness in the larger social system because neither men nor women could uphold their end of the patriarchal bargain. At the same time, statistics confirmed that women were increasingly taking on the dual roles of family earner and domestic caretaker.

Since Furstenberg's suggestion, researchers have argued that the contexts of men in families are much more complex. Some suggest that the intricate structural forces implied by Furstenberg do not necessarily give fathers clear choices between retreating from responsibility or participating in the family. Others argue that there is an evolving respected role for men in families as nurturers and carers. From the mid-1980s onwards, proponents of a new, domesticated model of manhood produced optimistic figures suggesting that men were spending more time with domestic and childrearing responsibilities (Lamb 1997).

Thomas Laqueur (1992) raised concerns about how little was written about 'the new public man in private' and by what he saw as a return to naturalism in legal debates over the child custody rights of mothers. The naturalism that concerned Laqueur is indicated by arguments suggesting that motherhood is a biological fact and, as such, is ontologically a different category from fatherhood, which is an idea. He argues, instead, for a labour theory of parenting in which emotional work counts. Moral rights and commitments are born from familial connectedness, which begs for fuller understanding of the emotional basis of men's and women's work in families. From the perspective of Laqueur's labour theory of parenting, the fact of fatherhood is based upon the work that goes into emotional and moral connections.

It may be argued that the father figure has evolved in Western society from the distant breadwinner of the nineteenth century, through the genial dad and sex role model of most of the last century to today's father as equal coparent. Susan Faludi (1999) notes that for many men, life in families is now harder work than life in paid employment. Awkward spaces and uneasy fits are created as men grapple with contradictions between the rational and egalitarian basis of shared responsibilities on the one hand, and the irrationality and emotion of the day-to-day work of childcare on the other (Aitken 2005: 229).

Since Judith Stacey's (1990) seminal work on the complexities of families as ideological, symbolic and emotional constructs, a picture of difference and diversity has emerged that makes it difficult to articulate any one family form as predominant. Diversity of, and within, families raises issues of men's identities and place in families. The concept of diverse families has opened space in which diverse fatherhoods can be discussed. In the same way that we cannot talk about one masculinity, so we cannot talk about one form of fatherhood. Hawkins and Dollahite (1997) introduce the term 'generative fathering' to argue that previous research on fathers is flawed because it fails to accommodate men's desires and abilities to care for the next generation. Other work focuses on the caring practices of lone-parent fathers (e.g. Winchester 1999).

Despite the growing literature espousing the value of a new domesticated father, the conduct of fathering (what men actually do in families) has been much slower to change. Skelton and Valentine (2005) point out that the lack of change in the conduct of fathering is very evident in fathers' reactions to their sons coming out as gay. In short, the culture of the new nurturing, caring father is often absent when hegemonic, heterosexual masculinity is challenged. They argue that masculine homophobia damages important familial relationships, whereas fatherhoods built upon caring and nurturing masculinities create the space for negotiation, acceptance and rewarding relationships. Even with measurable changes in the practices of fathering, alternative fatherhoods are still far from being adequately recognised and conceptualised.

Masculinity is a gendered project that takes place through an individual life course, through symbolic practices and in sites where gender is learnt. Families constitute an important formative site. Contemporary work on masculinities and families moves beneath, around and through specific notions of masculinity and fatherhood by focusing on the gendered spatial and historical complexity of social production, consumption and reproduction. What emerged through the twentieth century was a strict division of gender roles that was precarious from the start because it gave fathers a choice that is apparently not afforded mothers. The empirical literature is clear that fathers in contemporary Western society spend more time with their children than ever before and feel free to be more affectionate with them, and they also, more often than before, simply walk out of their families. Thus, although large-scale structural forces are widening the gap between men and families, forces at the individual level sometimes work in the direction of closing the gap. There are emotional geographies here that are gaining further academic attention from both the perspective of global economic restructuring and changes in local community and familial space.

References and further reading

Aitken, S.C. (1998) *Family Fantasies and Community Space*, New Brunswick, NJ: Rutgers University Press.

—— (2000) 'Fathering and faltering', *Environment and Planning* A, 32 (4): 581–98.

—— (2005) 'The awkward spaces of fathering', in B. van Hoven and K. Hoerschelmann (eds) *Spaces of Masculinity*, New York and London: Routledge, pp. 222–37.

Demos, J. (1970) *A Little Commonwealth*, New York: Oxford University Press.

Faludi, S. (1999) *Stiffed*, New York: William Morrow.

Furstenberg, F. (1988) 'Good dads – bad dads', in A.J. Cherlin (ed.) *The Changing American Family and Public Policy*, Washington, DC: Urban Institute, pp. 193–218.

Gottlieb, B. (1993) *The Family in the Western World*, New York: Oxford University Press.

Hawkins, A.J. and Dollahite, D.C. (eds) (1997) *Generative Fathering*, Thousand Oaks, CA: Sage.

Kandiyoti, D. (1988) 'Bargaining with patriarchy', *Gender and Society*, 2: 274–90.

Lamb, M. (ed.) (1997) *The Father's Role in Child Development*, 3rd edn, New York: John Wiley and Sons.

Laqueur, T.W. (1992) 'The facts of fatherhood', in B. Thorne and M. Yalom (eds) *Rethinking the Family*, Boston, MA: Northeastern University Press, pp. 140–54.

Murdoch, G.P. (1949) *Social Structure*, New York: Free Press.

Skelton, T. and Valentine, G. (2005) 'Exploring notions of masculinity and fatherhood', in B. van Hoven and K. Hoerschelmann (eds) *Spaces of Masculinity*, New York and London: Routledge, pp. 207–21.

Stacey, J. (1990) *Brave New Families*, Berkeley and Los Angeles, CA: University of California Press.

Winchester, H. (1999) 'Lone fathers and the scales of justice', *Journal of Interdisciplinary Gender Studies*, 4 (2): 81.

See also: fatherhood, fathering

STUART C. AITKEN

FAMILY LAW

Family law, a sub-field of legal studies and practice, has in many respects been at the forefront of the analysis of masculinity within legal scholarship. Across a range of studies, research has explored how law has been involved in the construction or reproduction of ideas about men, women and (heteronormative) 'family life' via reference to the concept of masculinity. For some the attempt to deconstruct the relationship between hegemonic masculinity and law has been part of an engagement with the hidden gender of law itself. Within recent work, attention has shifted to the ways in which family law can itself be seen to exemplify broader questions about the analytical limits of the concept of masculinity within a context of formal (legal) equality (Collier 2003).

The concept of masculinity has been extensively deployed in studies of institutions and practices relating to aspects of law and legal regulation concerning families; in accounts, for example, of the work of solicitors, barristers and judges; the administration of criminal and civil justice; and in studies of legal education, law schools and legal curricula. Within this work a heteronormative definition of family life has been historically enmeshed with a range of gendered beliefs. The 'masculinism' of legal institutions and practice is evident in the systematic benchmarking of women against a normative figure – an individual understood to be gender-neutral with regard to those commitments and 'inevitable dependencies' relating to the private familial domain (Fineman 1995; Smart 1984). Within later work the focus of analysis turned, increasingly, to the inherent 'maleness' of patriarchal legal systems, methods and reasoning. By the mid/late 1980s, however, feminist scholarship drawing in particular on developments around postmodernism sought to question the discursive construction of the subject 'Woman' in legal texts and practices; and, increasingly, feminist and pro-feminist scholars turned their attention to men and masculinity. Carol Smart's influential book *Feminism and the Power of Law* encapsulates aspects of this shift in its discussion of how 'both law and masculinity are constituted in discourse' (Smart 1989).

Legal studies has opened out to analysis the plurality and contingency of those discourses which speak of men and masculinities across diverse institutional and cultural contexts (Collier 1995). It has unpacked the ways in which ideas about men have been constructed in family law at particular historical moments (O'Donovan 1993). In laws concerning marriage and divorce, assumptions have been made about a natural sexual 'fit' between the bodies of women and men, with notions of male (hetero)sexual activity and female passivity informing the legal determination, historically, of what does, and does not, constitute a valid marriage. In accounts of men as 'respectable' and socially safe familial subjects, meanwhile, an ideal of the liberal rational individual has been deployed in such a way as to depict a figure constituted as male in ways dependent on a separation from other men and, crucially, on a hierarchical difference from women.

Recent work has sought to explore how the bodies of men have been constructed and understood within law (Sheldon 1999). Men's subjectivity has appeared bound up with historically specific ideas about heterosexuality, parenthood and family practices; assumptions about the nature of men's physical and emotional relationship to children, childcare and ideas of dependency (Collier 2001). Engagements with masculinity in family law also embrace concerns with the political and cultural ramifications of a crisis of masculinity. Across diverse cultural artefacts bearing on policy and practice relating to law and the family, concerns and anxieties around what is (or is not) happening *to* men and 'their' masculinity/ies have assumed a powerful, symbolic significance.

Increasingly, concerns about how to *change* men's practices and attitudes appear bound up within debates about law reform. Whether in relation to work–life balance, the promotion of 'good enough' post-divorce/separation parenting or the provision of child support, questions of gender equity have placed issues of masculinity at centre stage. There has occurred a further questioning of the way in which masculinity mediates men's experiences of the family justice process, with research speaking of the emergence of a distinctive 'masculinised discourse' of divorce, of men adopting 'masculine' subject positions; a normative masculinity correlating with the tendency of men to relate to, and appeal in their engagement with the legal process in terms of a right-based framework. Internationally, meanwhile, an increasingly high-profile fathers' rights movement has argued that it is *men*, and not women, who have become the 'new victims' of family law.

While family law remains an analytically contested terrain (Diduck 2003), a rethinking of the male (gendered) subject(s) of family law has become a central theme within wider debates about the future direction and politics of feminist legal scholarship. However, across diverse areas of family law and policy, gender-neutral norms and assumptions are still being applied to what remain, in many cases, profoundly gendered areas of social life. What is revealing about present struggles in this area is how much of the rhetoric in conversations about men, masculinities and family law takes the form of attempts to bolster and reaffirm traditional social relations in the face of the challenges posed by economic and cultural change and by feminism.

References and further reading

Collier, R. (1995) *Masculinity, Law and the Family*, London: Routledge.

—— (2001) 'A hard time to be a father? Law, policy and family practices', *Journal of Law and Society*, 28: 520.

—— (2003) 'Reflections on the relationship between law and masculinities: rethinking the "man question in legal studies"', *Current Legal Problems*, 56: 345–402.

Diduck, A. (2003) *Law's Families*, London: Butterworth.

Fineman, M. (1995) *The Neutered Mother, the Sexual Family and Other Twentieth Century Tragedies*, New York: Routledge.

O'Donovan, K. (1993) *Family Law Matters*, London: Pluto.

Sheldon, S. (1999) 'Reconceiving masculinity: imagining men's reproductive bodies in law', *Journal of Law and Society*, 26: 129.

Smart, C. (1984) *The Ties that Bind: Law, Marriage and the Reproduction of Patriarchal Relations*, London: Routledge and Kegan Paul.

—— (1989) *Feminism and the Power of Law*, London: Routledge.

See also: child custody; divorce and separation

RICHARD COLLIER

FASCISM AND NAZISM

The social chaos of Europe after 1918 brought about totalitarian regimes such as Fascism and Nazism in Italy and Germany. According to Italian historian De Felice (1975), it is most instructive to regard 'Fascist movements' and 'Fascist regimes' separately. During the movement period, Fascism and Nazism had extremely anti-establishment and violent trends. Even while strongly criticising liberal and democratic political regimes, they also opposed socialist alternatives, insisting on 'the third way' (Mussolini), neither capitalism nor socialism. Although Italy was one of the victor countries of the First World War, it had suffered from a crushed sense of territorial ambition, called a 'mutilated victory', while in Germany – a loser of the war – there were feelings of gloom and humiliation imposed by the Treaty of Versailles. By presenting themselves as the political powers that could solve the social and political chaos of the post-war period, Fascists and Nazis attracted the middle classes and farmers who had been left in an unstable situation, and thus seized political victory.

However, once these originally anti-establishment Fascists and Nazis came into power, under the charismatic dictatorships of Mussolini and Hitler they cooperated with the established military and industrial powers and oppressed dissidents. At the same time, in order to gain the trust and support of the citizens in rallying for war, they promoted propaganda through the education system and mass media, and various 'voluntary' organisations from each generation and class.

Several elements permeate both the movement and regime periods of Fascism and Nazism. One is the expression of ferocity and emphasis on power, the will of authority and militarism – through the glorification and admiration of 'manliness'. Mosse (1996) reports that the First World War united nationalism and masculinity more strongly than ever before. The Fascist and Nazi movements, products of the social chaos brought about by the First World War, offered compensation for the sentiments of dissatisfaction felt by the soldiers returning home through their emphasis on masculinity combined with nationalism. They emphasised the spirit of sacrifice and bravery tempting fate on the battlefield, on the one hand, and violence and cruelty, on the other. This type of masculinity was evident in the violent, destructive activities of the all-male Fascist Blackshirt squads, as well as in the behaviour of the Nazi SA stormtroopers in the streets. In fact, after seizing power, Mussolini in 1926 promoted Fascism as 'the reinstitution of masculinity as an opposition to the dregs of the old, democratic, liberal Italy'. The Fascist and Nazi movements, as well as the process of their seizure of power, are precisely a Masculine Revolution (Ito 1984).

This emphasis on masculinity continued throughout the regime period. In Italy, the philosophy of the 'new men' was born, based on Nietzsche's idea of the 'overman'. This philosophy actually involved the misinterpretation of Nietzsche's idea, but copied his negation of old morals and systems. Compared to Nietzsche's anti-Christian stance, the philosophy of the Fascist 'new men' was strongly tied to Catholic tradition. This glorification of masculinity applied to both the strength of the mind and the toughness of the body. The encouragement of physical education, training and sports was one of the most important cultural policies of Fascism.

The Nazis also encouraged displays of masculinity as supports for the regime. Theweleit (1987) stresses the importance of masculine fantasies within Germany from the end of the First World War through the time of the Nazis. In particular, the Nazis, even more than the Italian Fascists, glorified masculine Aryan characteristics of physical beauty and toughness in their racial vilification of Jews and the Roma people as weak and ugly.

The ideology of Fascist and Nazi masculinity depended on a sharp division between men and the 'opposite' sex (De Grazia 1992). The differences between men and women were propagated repetitively as official ideology. For example, Italy's 1937 *Women's Yearbook* stated that

> Fascism, as a theoretic principle, is trying to bring women back to the fundamental duties of a child-bearer, to the duties of housework. Also, it is trying to bring men back to the fundamental status of a husband, and it is trying to bring back the household to its role as an educational, social function.

The public ideology of Nazism is similar. The idea of 'women back in the home' was tied to population policy in preparation for the war and became a common slogan for the Fascist and the Nazi regimes alike.

The Masculine Revolution composed by the Fascist and Nazi movements flaunted male supremacy in the glorification of war and violence, authoritarianism and power. In addition, by organising society along thoroughly divided gender roles, it created a male-only world that excluded women. Moreover, it facilitated homosocial or homoerotic, as well as homosexual, relations between men. In fact, according to Mosse (1988), homosexuals were never the target of attacks during the Nazi movement period. However, after the purge of Rohm's SA stormtroopers in Germany, the oppression of homosexuals quickly progressed. Although not as much as in Germany, in Italy too legal regulations were enforced with regard to homosexuals. It is here that homophobia's importance in forming and maintaining masculine identity of masculinity can be seen, as well as the pathological trend of the Fascist and Nazi regimes as they tried to forcibly and morally unite their citizens under the mantle of 'Pure Empire'. While 'normal' masculinity – that is, the glorification of homosocial or homoerotic relations between males – was being promoted, homosexuality was being oppressed as a 'heresy' of masculinity and punished with policies comparable to those on race discrimination under the totalitarian regimes.

References and further reading

De Felice, R. (1975) *Intervista sul fascismo*, Roma-Bari: Laterza.

De Grazia, V. (1992) *How Fascism Ruled Women*, Berkeley, CA: University of California Press.

Ito, K. [1984] (1993) 'The rise and fall of masculine', in K. Ito, *Otokorasisa-no-yukue* (Direction for Masculinities), Tokyo: Shinyo-sha.

Mosse, G.L. (1988) *Nationalism and Sexuality*, Madison, WI: University of Wisconsin Press.

—— (1996) *The Image of Man*, Oxford: Oxford University Press.

Theweleit, K. (1987) *Male Fantasies*, Minneapolis, MN: University of Minnesota Press.

KIMIO ITO

FATHER–DAUGHTER RELATIONSHIPS

Compared with the other parent–child relationships, namely father–son, mother–son or mother–daughter relationships, the father–daughter pair has attracted only limited attention. This relative neglect derives primarily from the weak position of the daughter in patriarchal society, combined with the traditional lack of recognition of the significance of fatherhood or fathering as opposed to the widely acknowledged importance of motherhood and mothering. The topic engages a number of research fields, including psychoanalytical, psychological, psychiatric, literary, anthropological and feminist studies.

Given the privileged position of the son in the patriarchal family, it is hardly surprising to note the tendency to focus on the parent–son relationship, especially its implications for the son's psychological, sexual, social and emotional development. No one would question the influence of Freud's theory of the Oedipus complex, not only in psychoanalysis but also in many different fields throughout the twentieth century, but the Electra complex (a term rejected by Freud) has not entered into the public domain. Freud saw the difference between male and female versions of the Oedipus complex in terms of the effects of the castration complex. Whereas the fear of castration in the boy leads to the development of his super-ego, the girl, according to Freud (Young-Bruehl 1990: 326–7), 'acknowledges the fact of her castration, and with it too, the superiority of the male', and hence develops 'penis envy'. Thus, according to Freud, castration does not destroy but creates the female Oedipus complex. This view and its phallocentrism have attracted much controversy and criticism.

Although the focus of Freudian theory is the father's role in the sexual development of the daughter, feminist critics have examined the father–daughter relationship in the context of the patriarchal institution, often employing the Lacanian notions of the 'name of the father' and the 'law of the father' in their analysis. The symbolic father as the law not only prohibits, oversees and controls but also (re)presents logic, order, structure, language and culture. With this new interest in the linguistic and textual significance of the symbolic father, feminist thinkers such as Luce Irigary and Hélène Cixous proposed new readings of the father–daughter relationship in texts, including those texts produced by the 'fathers' of psychoanalysis, Freud and Lacan. Instead of a phallocentric view of the daughter as castrated, they focused on and celebrated the daughter's desire.

In the last quarter of the twentieth century analysis expanded to include a much wider variety of both textual and actual father–daughter relationships, going beyond Greek mythology and Western fairy tales; a number of texts, modern and classic, and written by men and women, have been examined. This analysis goes far beyond simple accusation of patriarchal repression and oppression and often includes discussions of the revolt of daughters. Reis (1995), for instance, examines the lives of four women writers, Emily Dickinson, H.D., Sylvia Plath and Anaïs Nin, and traces the ways in which they developed strategies to transform themselves 'from father's daughter to creative woman'. Using the myth of Saturn, the melancholic father who devours his children, Reis describes how his daughters develop from inside the father's belly through social contacts and negotiation to the 'New Earth'.

Although most studies available in English deal with Western literature, research in other cultures has also begun. Copeland and Ramirez-Christensen (2001), for instance, explore the father–daughter plot in the lives and literature of Japanese women writers from the tenth to the twentieth century, revealing that the daughter's revolt against the 'law of the father' is evident not only in the overtly iconoclastic texts of modern times but also in tales and memoirs of earlier eras. There is also a surge of research interest in representations of diasporic (e.g. Chinese-American) father–daughter relationships in films and literature.

Besides (re)reading and interpreting, feminist researchers have been engaged in compiling both written and oral accounts of father–daughter relationships. These are narrated mostly from the daughters' point of view; researchers note the need for further study to document the fathers' side of the stories. In compiling daughters' reflections upon their fathers, Owen recognises 'a problematic bond, full of ambivalences and longings' (1983: 11), with recurring themes such as the daughter's loyalty, her need to please the father, and her later recognition of the mother's significance. Alongside these recurrent themes, Owen emphasises the wide variety of subjects and forms that daughters adopt in telling their stories.

Although there is a clear move to recognise the active and creative power of the daughter, the last part of the twentieth century also witnessed notable development in studies and reports on child abuse, including incest committed against daughters by their biological, step- and other surrogate fathers. As Herman (2000: 3) points out, the subject of incest is 'entirely enmeshed not only in myth and folklore, but also in ideology': feminist understanding of the mechanisms of oppression, abuse and exploitation of women has released the subject from long-standing bias and suppression and helped the victims of the crime.

References and further reading

Boose, L.E. and Flowers, B.S. (eds) (1989) *Daughters and Fathers*, Baltimore, MD: Johns Hopkins University Press.

Copeland, R. and Ramirez-Christensen, E. (eds) (2001) *The Father–Daughter Plot*, Honolulu, HI: University of Hawaii Press.

Gallop, J. (1982) *Feminism and Psychoanalysis*, London: Macmillan.

Herman, J.L. (2000) *Father–Daughter Incest*, Cambridge, MA: Harvard University Press.

Lacan, J. (1977) *Écrits: A Selection*, London: Tavistock.

Leonard, L.S. (1982) *The Wounded Woman*, Boston, MA and London: Shambhala.

Owen, U. (ed.) (1983) *Fathers: Reflections by Daughters*, London: Virago.

Reis, P. (1995) *Daughters of Saturn*, New York: Continuum.

Sharpe, S. (1994) *Fathers and Daughters*, London: Routledge.

Ward, E. (1984) *Father–Daughter Rape*, London: The Women's Press.

Yaeger, P. and Kowaleski-Wallace, B. (eds) (1989) *Refiguring the Father*, Carbondale, IL: Southern Illinois University Press.

Young-Bruehl, E. (ed.) (1990) *Freud on Women*, London: Hogarth.

See also: families; fatherhood, fathering

TOMOKO AOYAMA

FATHER–SON RELATIONSHIPS

Freudian psychoanalysis places the Greek Oedipal myth, dramatised by Sophocles, as a timeless and universal frame to define father–son relations. Erotic longing for the mother, a key narrative element in the myth, creates feelings of violence and aggression towards the father and in Freudian psychoanalysis was at the root of male experience and the formation of male identity. The Oedipal Complex privileges the attrition of rivalry as a key mode in father–son relations, simultaneously making male experience the exemplar for identity formation and canonising one interpretation as common to all cultures.

Cultural anthropologists, folklorists and psychoanalysts have challenged the Freudian claim to the universality of the Oedipal Complex and argued that support and love are equally central to the father–son relation. The prodigal son myth (in the parables of the Gospel of Luke, for example) emphasises the merciful father pardoning the rebel son. The benign father appears in Korean folktale encouraging and offering protection for his son's journey into manhood. Mead's anthropological study of non-Western societies (1935) contested the view that competition is the key element in every boy's experience of growing up.

Disputes notwithstanding, the pre-eminence of the Oedipal Complex remains significant through it appears in different forms. A.K.

Ramanujam's post-modern understanding (1999) interprets the castration complex of the Oedipus myth in South Asia as a reversal. In Indian mythic renditions, the father, Shiva, kills his son, Ganesh, whom he sees entering his wife's chamber but then restores him to life by placing an elephant head on his body. Others, particularly Courtright (1999) and Obeyesekere (1999), interpret the symbolism of the flaccid elephant trunk as a castration of the son's sexuality by the jealous father.

Jokes and humour also dwell on the oedipal theme. In the southernmost Andalusian province of Spain explored by Brandes (1980), jokes focus on filial awe and anxiety about the father's phallic superiority linked to hierarchic notions of male power. Mocking the son's inability to measure up to the father's genitals, jokes transgress the extreme codes of modesty between fathers and sons and counter the injunctions that restrain fathers from exposing their genitals to their sons. On the other hand, rebellion is expressed in ridiculing the potency and sexual prowess of the father, comparing his anatomy unfavourably with animal genitalia or his inability to satisfy the mother.

The emphasis on the biological link in myth and humour provides a powerful paradigm for non-kinship contexts. In north India, for example, employers commonly extend the term for son to workers. Owners of family businesses in pre-industrial England treated certain categories of employees as sons and included them in their households, especially if the young men were children of friends or distant kin. While inheritance was restricted by blood or kin ties, business and craft skills were passed on to unrelated young men. Authority and concern are simultaneous in fictive kinship relations and unrelated older and younger men follow the idioms of father–son relations in their dealings with each other.

The father as a critical role model is important in studies of juvenile delinquency that assume the necessity of the authoritative presence and active involvement of fathers in the lives and socialisation of sons. Criminology creates the Absent Father–Delinquent Son as a new dyad in the landscape of modern post-industrial society. These assumptions place women-headed households as a major factor in the increasing delinquency of young boys growing up without clear male role models or paternal authority to curb them.

Violence and fatherhood had a particular resonance in Nazi Germany and the subsequent historiography of the father–son relation. The links between the Nazi state, the discourse of the Fatherland and the political cadres of young men produced a political configuration of the father–son relation that was no longer confined to the domestic domain but entered the public arena of violent political action. Dying for the fatherland or cleansing the nation-as-family of pollution by non-Aryan blood became expressive of the loyal son fulfilling his duty towards his Fatherland.

Subsequent critiques of Germany's Nazi past had to deal with the vexed question of fathers who may have been part of the Nazi political regimes. Student revolts and civil disobedience movements in 1968 were a rejection by young men of their fathers' complicity in Nazi fascist violence. Adorno (1969) drew parallels between the 'fatherless society' of Nazi Germany, where the state assumed the father's role, and the totalitarian socialist state of East Germany. The state entered the family and displaced the breadwinner role of fathers and the childrearing functions of the family, and created what Adorno referred to as a family without fathers that was responsible for right-wing voting patterns backed by the violence of young men.

References and further reading

Adorno, T.W., Frenkel-Brunswik, E. and Levinson, D.J. [1950] (1969) *The Authoritarian Personality*, New York: W.W. Norton.

Brandes, S. (1980) *Metaphors of Masculinity: Sex and Status in Andalusian Folklore*, Philadelphia, PA: University of Pennsylvania Press (American Folk Lore Society, New Series).

Courtright, P. (1999) *Fathers and Sons*, Ganesa, NY: Oxford University Press.

Mead, M. [1935] (1963) *Sex and Temperament in Three Primitive Societies*, New York: Morrow Quill Paperbacks.

Obeyesekere, G. (1999) 'Further steps in relativization: the Indian Oedipus revisited', in T.G. Vaidyanathan and J. Kripal (eds) *Vishnu on Freud's Desk: A Reader in Psychoanalysis and Hinduism*, Delhi: Oxford University Press, pp. 147–162.

Ramanujam, A.K. (1999) 'The Indian Oedipus', in T.G. Vaidyanathan and J. Kripal (eds) *Vishnu on Freud's Desk: A Reader in Psychoanalysis and Hinduism*, Delhi: Oxford University Press, pp. 109–36.

Vaidyanathan, T.G. and Kripal, J. (eds) (1999) *Vishnu on Freud's Desk: A Reader in Psychoanalysis and Hinduism*. Delhi: Oxford University Press.

See also: families; fatherhood, fathering

RADHIKA CHOPRA

FATHERHOOD, FATHERING

From the 1970s to the early twenty-first century, scholarship on fathering/fatherhood has gone from being relatively ignored to a burgeoning field of theoretical and empirical research. This proliferation of interest has arisen partly out of the profound recent social changes in women's and men's lives, particularly within North America, Scandinavia, Australia and New Zealand, and much of Europe; such changes include men's declining wages, increasing male unemployment, sustained growth in women's labour force participation, rise in divorce rates, the decline of the nuclear family, and changing ideologies associated with men's and women's roles and identities. At the same time, increased social alarm on the issue of fatherless families and an interest in how enhanced personal development can be positive and 'generative' for involved fathers as well as for their children and partners has led researchers of all political and theoretical stripes towards understanding fathering/fatherhood.

Research on fathering was initially very focused on the experiences of white middle-class men. Since the 1990s, however, scholarship on fathering/fatherhood has become increasingly multidisciplinary, cross-cultural and diverse in terms of theoretical underpinnings, methodological approaches and samples of fathers being studied. It is thus no longer possible to speak of fathering or fatherhood as monolithic concepts or experiences. In the same way that feminist scholars pointed out that mothering differs as experience and institution, this also applies to our understandings of fathering and fatherhood: fathering refers to how men perceive, live out and enact practices of fathering while doing so within the larger political, social, cultural, symbolic, ideological and discursive institutions of fatherhood. Recent scholarship highlights how class, ethnicity, sexualities, age, culture, ability/disability and household form influence the ways in which fathering is understood, experienced and enacted. Research conducted in the early years of the twenty-first century has questioned seemingly commonplace concepts and experiences, such as 'deadbeat dads' (Mandell 2002), unmarried or nonresidential fathers (Waller 2002), stepdads (Marsiglio 2004), gay fatherhood (McGarry 2003) and stay-at-home fathers and primary caregiving fathers (Doucet 2006).

The subject area of fathering/fatherhood is one of the most ideologically charged areas of study within the larger fields of masculinities and gender relations. Seemingly straightforward topics such as gender equality in parenting or fathering involvement have taken on politically charged objectives and ensuing ideological and policy tensions. While feminist scholars and activists have long highlighted the social and personal costs of women's disproportionate responsibility for children, they also have a long history of focusing on how *not* caring has affected men. From very different theoretical and political perspectives, men's rights and fathers' rights groups have argued similarly about the imbalances between women and men in relation to breadwinning and caring, and these groups have proliferated since the 1980s. While raising important issues for men, these fathers' rights advocates also introduce political tensions within fathering advocacy in that some of them are explicitly anti-feminist, anti-woman or even misogynist.

Significant theoretical differences are also present in scholarship and policy work that promotes active fathering, particularly with regard to the ways in which gender differences are either highlighted or downplayed in parenting. For example, some fathers' rights movements have taken up discourses of equality and gender-neutral parenting to reinforce their claims in child custody cases for greater access to children (see Boyd 2003). On the other hand, fathers' rights organisations, such as the Promise Keepers and sections of the Fatherhood Responsibility Movement, assert a more 'masculine' kind of fathering which emphasises purportedly natural differences between women and men and the view that fathers should be primary breadwinners and mothers, primary caregivers. Some fathers' groups, which Coltrane calls 'moral entrepreneurs', promote active fathering to bolster a narrow model of the family that promotes the moral superiority of heterosexual married couples, decries divorce and asserts that men are the natural heads of households (Coltrane 2001).

Feminist theoretical and policy positions also vary in relation to fathering. On the one hand, a large body of feminist research calls for active fathering as a means to equalise gender relations in domestic life and to enable mothers to participate more equally in the labour market and in society more generally. Beginning in the 1970s, this scholarship has focused on investigating and analysing time–budget studies and the division of tasks and responsibilities between mothers and fathers. This research has been underpinned by the views that gender equality between mothers and fathers is desirable and possible and that mothering and fathering are interchangeable identities and practices (e.g. Deutsch 1999). Others have questioned the possibility of achieving equality in domestic life. They argue for spaces and contexts where gender differences can be present and where gendered embodiment can matter, and they advocate an approach that straddles both equality and differences in domestic and community parenting while also investigating where differences turn into disadvantages (Doucet 2006). Another strand of feminist thinking on fathering is found in the work of scholars and policy advocates who focus on gender differences that emerge as critically important in divorce and child custody cases; these authors maintain that gender differences arise in parenting out of dominant social patterns of caring between women and men (Boyd 2003). In addition to varied positions concerning what involved fathering should look like and what it means politically and ideologically, there are also divergent understandings of just *how* involved fathers actually are. Some argue that much of the evidence of the new father is more fiction than reality, the 'new man' has not yet appeared, and that women still take on the lion's share of care giving across the globe (McMahon 1999). On the other hand, many argue that today's fathers are more involved in their children's lives than fathers of previous generations, with significant increases in the time allotted to fathering as well as more equal gender balance of childcare tasks. Nevertheless, there is a resounding consensus across a broad range of literature since the 1980s that there remains a persistent connection between women and the *responsibility* for children and for domestic and community life even where women have equal participation in paid employment.

As fathering research has become even more established across the social sciences, it has also become apparent that fathering can only be understood through recognising the intricate connections between mothering and fathering and how these co-exist as both collective and individual experiences and as social institutions (Dowd 2000). At the level of experience, many scholars have highlighted how mothers and fathers co-create gender differences and thus partake in processes of 'doing gender' in childcare and housework. Scholars point out that greater research is still needed across nations and cultures on the complex gendered negotiations in parenting and domestic life (Hearn *et al.* 2002). For example, a growing body of scholarship shows how mothers may resist greater fathering involvement through maternal gatekeeping, wherein women's beliefs and behaviours impede men's participation in caring for children (Allen and Hawkins 1999).

In addition to these issues, the vast literature on gendered divisions of labour has drawn attention to key obstacles to greater fatherhood involvement, including: the role of work in fathers' lives; parental modelling after one's own father; gender ideologies or discourses of fatherhood, gender differences in the creation and maintaining of community parenting networks, and effects of male embodiment on fathering. On the other hand, fathering involvement can be dramatically improved through family-friendly policies aimed specifically at men (Hobson 2002). Parental leave policies, for example, have encouraged fathers of infants and young children to take time off to care for their children. Nordic countries, notably Sweden and Norway and, more recently, Iceland, have innovated ways of encouraging leave by fathers; two such measures are 'daddy days' (leave reserved exclusively for fathers, as is the case in Sweden and Norway) and the equal (nine-month) division of parental leave periods between mother, father and then both parents dividing the final three months at their own discretion (e.g. Iceland). Parental leave is still taken up mainly by women, both in terms of numbers of women in comparison to men and the amount of time taken. While mothers continue to take more leave than fathers in all countries, however, allocating leave entitlement specifically to fathers does lead to an increase in fathers' take-up of leave from work to care for their infants.

Fathers' active adoption of caregiving raises the interesting question of what happens to masculinities when men engage in female-dominated and feminine-defined activities such as childcare. Until recently, the issue of fatherhood has been dealt with rather sparsely in key works on masculinities, with attention mainly given to how hegemonic masculinity is reproduced as fathers push their boys to concentrate on sports or tutor them in breadwinning. The link between masculinities and caring is important, since hegemonic masculinity is largely associated with the devaluation of the feminine while caring is often equated with feminine practice. Fathering can become incorporated into hegemonic masculinity (Brandth and Kvande 1998) or, alternatively, a *complicit* relationship exists such that fathers express support for equal parenting while also maintaining more traditional divisions of labour (see Plantin *et al.* 2003). Still others argue that involved fathering neither reproduces nor challenges hegemonic masculinity but creates new forms of masculinity that incorporate varied aspects of femininities (Doucet 2006).

Research on fathering experiences and the changing social institution of fatherhood continues to grow through national and international research initiatives, conferences, websites and publications. Regarding the social institution of fatherhood, research is still needed on the interplay between fathering and masculinities and how this plays out for varied groups of fathers such as gay fathers, fathers of different ages (e.g. teen fathers, mid-life fathers) and with children of each gender at different ages, and fathers living in different household formations (i.e. fathers who are single, non-residential or living in blended families).

References and further reading

Allen, S.M. and Hawkins, A.J. (1999) 'Maternal gatekeeping', *Journal of Marriage and the Family*, 61: 199–212.

Boyd, S.B. (2003) *Child Custody, Law and Women's Work*, Don Mills, Ontario: Oxford University Press.

Brandth B. and Kvande, E. (1998) 'Masculinity and child care', *Sociological Review*, 46: 293–313.

Coltrane, S. (2001) '"Marketing the marriage solution": 2001 Presidential Address to the Pacific Sociological Association', *Sociological Perspectives*, 44: 387–418.

Deutsch, F.M. (1999) *Halving It All*, Cambridge, MA: Harvard University Press.
Doucet, A. (2006) *Do Men Mother?* Toronto: University of Toronto Press.
Dowd, N.E. (2000) *Redefining Fatherhood*, New York: New York University Press.
Hearn, J., Pringle, K., Müller, U., Oleksy, E., Lattu, E. *et al.* (2002) 'Critical studies on men in ten European countries: (1)', *Men and Masculinities*, 4: 380–408.
Hobson, B. (2002) *Making Men into Fathers*, Cambridge: Cambridge University Press.
McGarry, K. (2003) *Fatherhood for Gay Men*, New York: Haworth
McMahon, A. (1999) *Taking Care of Men*, Cambridge: Cambridge University Press.
Mandell, D. (2002) *Deadbeat Dads*, Toronto: University of Toronto Press.
Marsiglio, W. (2004) *Stepdads*, Boulder, CO: Rowman and Littlefield.
Plantin, L., Månsson, S.-A. and Kearney, J. (2003) 'Talking and doing fatherhood', *Fathering*, 1: 3–26.
Waller, M.M. (2002) *My Baby's Father*, Ithaca, NY and London: Cornell University Press.

See also: child custody; divorce and separation; families; fatherhood, gay; fatherhood, single; fatherhood, stepfathers; fatherhood, teenage; fatherhood and paid work; heterosexuality; homophobia and heterosexism; husbands; marriage; men's relations with women

ANDREA DOUCET

FATHERHOOD, GAY

Gay men may become fathers in a number of ways. Those who had children in prior heterosexual unions may face struggles over custody and visitation, sometimes exacerbated by fears surrounding HIV/AIDS. But since the 1990s, gay men increasingly have sought fatherhood outside of heterosexual unions. Some may serve as fathers to children through informal or extra-legal arrangements, permanently or for periods of time, while others may collaborate with a woman or a lesbian couple to father children, usually using alternative insemination. Others foster or adopt children through public agencies, often accepting children defined as 'hard to place' – i.e. older, non-white or mixed-race, and/or with physical or mental disabilities. Still other gay fathers use private domestic adoption to locate pregnant women willing to choose them as adoptive parents for their babies. Other gay men adopt children internationally, though only a few countries consider 'unmarried' men as applicants and many seek to exclude gays (or lesbians) from the adoption process. Finally, some gay men work with specialised surrogacy agencies, typically using both egg donors and gestational surrogates. Surrogacy is the most expensive route to parenthood, with high medical expenses and fees to agencies, attorneys and surrogates; surrogacy also presents a higher likelihood of multiple births because of *in vitro* fertilisation.

In most jurisdictions in the United States, gay couples who become parents together, or who wish to gain recognition for their families, must begin with just one of the men having the status of legal parent and the second father adopting afterwards. Regulation of these legal procedures varies widely, though at this writing only one state (Florida) absolutely bans all adoptions by gay men or lesbians. But other states and local jurisdictions have obstacles in place that make the establishment of gay-father headed families more difficult and costly.

Because conventional definitions of homosexuality preclude fatherhood, most writing on gay fathers focuses on the formerly married. More recently, struggles over gay family issues have made gay men's desires to form families more visible, and research has begun on fathers and their families.

References and further reading

Benkov, L. (1994) *Reinventing the Family*, New York: Crown.
Bozett, F.W. (1987) 'Gay fathers', in Frederick W. Bozett (ed.) *Gay and Lesbian Parents*, New York, Westport, CT, and London: Praeger, pp. 3–22.
Green, J. (1999) *The Velveteen Father*, New York: Villard.
Mallon, G.P. (2004) *Gay Men Choosing Parenthood*, New York: Columbia University Press.

See also: fatherhood, fathering

ELLEN LEWIN

FATHERHOOD, SINGLE

This is a term used primarily to describe fathers who have residential day-to-day care and responsibility for their children, usually as a result of separation or divorce. Single-father families (SFF) are less common than single-mother families, arguably as a consequence of courts traditionally awarding custody or residency to mothers. SFF are increasingly part of the social fabric of contemporary Western society (e.g. USA, Europe, Australia); they are less prevalent in cultures or societies that adhere to more traditional gender roles.

Numbers of SFF have increased rapidly over the past decade as fathers have argued for their legal rights and demonstrated their capabilities as residential parents. Concurrently, there has been gradual acceptance in Western society of the notion of 'stay-at-home dads', as social norms including expectations that fathers will be involved in the care and rearing of their children, increased flexibility in the workplace and other changes have facilitated a diversity of parenting arrangements.

Despite their growth in numbers, overall SFF still represent a very small portion of single-parent households. For example, only 2 per cent of Australian children aged from birth to seventeen live with a lone father, and it has been difficult to collect demographically representative data about them. Consequently, until relatively recently, SFF have been largely ignored by researchers, therapists and lawmakers. Therefore, very little is known about the functioning and dynamics of these families either from the fathers' perspective or in terms of outcomes for the children. However, research has consistently demonstrated that fathers are capable of raising healthy, well-adjusted children of both sexes and of providing supportive and nurturing home environments comparable to those provided by single mothers.

Contemporary scholarship on SFF explores social constructionist frameworks of fathering, outcomes for their children and adolescents, the impact of demographic characteristics, particularly economic factors such as child support, and diversity within SFF populations.

References and further reading

Downey, D., Ainsworth-Darnell, J. and Dufor, M. (1998) 'Sex of parent and children's wellbeing in single parent households', *Journal of Marriage and the Family*, 60 (November): 878–93.

Grief, G. (1995) 'Single fathers with custody following separation and divorce', *Marriage and Family Review*, 20 (1–2): 213–31.

See also: child custody; divorce and separation; family law; fatherhood, fathering; fathers'right

LISBETH PIKE

FATHERHOOD, STEPFATHERS

Men's status as stepfathers and their socially constructed bonds with stepchildren occur outside the legal and biological domains associated with formal paternity. Men become and express themselves as stepfathers in numerous ways and in diverse family arrangements (Marsiglio 2004a). Although marriage to the stepchild's mother is often perceived as the key marker for stepfatherhood, those who cohabit with the birth mother can also be perceived as stepfathers or 'social fathers'. As a result of marriage, divorce, remarriage and childbearing patterns during the past thirty to forty years in many Western societies, men increasingly are engaged in stepfathering for some period of time.

In the United States, stepfathers who are married to women with children or cohabit with mothers tend to have less education and lower incomes than biological fathers living with their children. Stepfathers are more likely to be divorced compared to men who are not stepfathers. Many men who are stepfathers also have their own offspring, though most of these children do not live with them. Even though loyalty conflicts may arise through having both stepchildren and biological children, stepfathers who have their own offspring tend to have better relationships with stepchildren than childless men. This pattern appears to be most evident when stepfathers' biological children live with them.

Unlike the typical biological father, stepfathers must grapple with a complex process whereby they attempt to join and expand a pre-existing family including, at minimum, a birth mother and her child. When stepfathers socially construct family ties they often engage in affinity-seeking and affinity-maintaining strategies in order to have stepchildren accept and like them. Stepfathers' relationship with stepchildren can be influenced by characteristics of the mother, child and biological father (Marsiglio 1995; McDonald and DeMaris 2002).

Some stepfathers orient to stepchildren in ways similar to the father–child relationship (Marsiglio 2004b). A form of paternal claiming occurs when stepfathers express a readiness to nurture, provide for, protect and see a child as their own. This intriguing social psychological process sometimes highlights stepfathers' and fathers' competing experiences and interests. Although stepfathers may perceive themselves as having a fatherly identity and presence in a child's life, and others may reciprocate this image, stepfathers do not have the same legal rights as fathers. On average, children experience more positive outcomes when raised by a resident biological father, but many stepfathers contribute positively to stepchildren's well-being (Hofferth and Anderson 2003; White and Gilbreth 2001).

References and further reading

Hofferth, S.L. and Anderson, K.G. (2003) 'Are all dads equal? Biology versus marriage as a basis for parental investment', *Journal of Marriage and Family*, 65: 213–32.

McDonald, W.L. and DeMaris, A. (2002) 'Stepfather–stepchild relationship quality. The stepfather's demand for conformity and the biological father's involvement', *Journal of Family Issues*, 23: 121–37.

Marsiglio, W. (1995) 'Stepfathers with minor children living at home: parenting perceptions and relationship quality', in W. Marsiglio (ed.) *Fatherhood: Contemporary Theories, Research, and Social Policy*, Thousand Oaks, CA: Sage, pp. 78–101.

—— (2004a) 'When stepfathers claim stepchildren: a conceptual analysis', *Journal of Marriage and Family*, 66: 22–39.

—— (2004b) *Stepdads: Stories of Love, Hope, and Repair*, Boulder, CO: Rowman and Littlefield.

White, L. and Gilbreth, J.G. (2001) 'When children have two fathers: effects of relationships with stepfathers and noncustodial fathers on adolescent outcomes', *Journal of Marriage and Family*, 63: 155–67.

See also: fatherhood, fathering

WILLIAM MARSIGLIO

FATHERHOOD, TEENAGE

Teenage fatherhood can be understood as the role that young men who become fathers should play in the lives of their children. But the concept is neither simple nor uncontested. It reflects historical concern about dangerous youth (cf. Thrasher 1927) and hence contains a strong normative element. Periodically in the twentieth century, the fear that young men pose a danger to society was expressed. Indicators of the problem included involvement in crime, gang activities, substance abuse, school dropout and teenage fatherhood. The public eye often identified minority and working-class youth as being particularly threatening or at risk. In this context, teenage fatherhood is understood to be undesirable, an indication of young men doing what they are not supposed to do, and even a cause for their misdoings. This being the case, much of the policy and research work on fatherhood has ignored teenage fathers and fatherhood or confronted them as a problem.

There are a number of difficulties with this approach. Historically, the age at which men become fathers has varied over time. While in recent times the age of first fatherhood is being delayed, in many cultures and in the past it was not uncommon for men in their teens to become fathers. Culturally, the relevance of age to fathering varies. In much of the developed world, the phenomenon of a middle-class teenager becoming a father is unwelcome, though often not as unwelcome as a teenage girl becoming pregnant. In this context, teenage fatherhood deviates from the cultural ideal of masculinity. In the developing world, and indeed among some minorities in the developed world, such stigma is not universally present. This variation is reflected in the wide range of definitions given to the terms 'teenager' and 'youth'. Researchers undertaking quantitative work in the United States, for example, define teen fatherhood as 'becoming a biological parent before age 20' (Xie *et al.* 2001: 493) or as 'a father or an acknowledged father-to-be (who is) under the age of twenty-one years' (Hendricks *et al.* 1984: 183). The definitional gap is much more dramatic in developing contexts, where statistics on fathers are often unavailable. In South Africa, the National Youth Commission Act of 1996 defines youth as 'all people between the ages of 14 and 35'.

Where teen fatherhood carries no stigma it is more likely that young men will become fathers. However, even where there is stigma in the majority culture, young men may purposefully become fathers in situations where fathering a child is considered a valued element of male identity. Certain groups of young men are more likely to become young fathers than others. In the US, studies using the data from the National Survey of Families and Households and National Longitudinal Survey of Youth show that young men who become fathers are more likely to be African-American and working class with disrupted family backgrounds. They are likely to have experienced problems with education, substance abuse and the law. There is a danger in reading such findings unproblematically into the field of masculinity. When this has occurred, it has been argued that teen fathers are irresponsible, neglectful and uncaring. In fact, much research shows that many young fathers desire contact with their children and maintain such contact, even though the bulk of responsibility is taken on by the mother. A major reason given for the failure to realise the fatherhood role is a lack of economic resources.

Where fatherhood is unconditionally valued, taking on the fatherhood role is encouraged. Here there is a close connection between manhood and fatherhood. In the South American context, this is captured in the phrase 'When the child arrives, the father is born' (Olavarria 2003: 343). Yet even in these contexts, teen fatherhood may be an arena of struggle. Since the role of fatherhood imposes responsibilities and obligations which are socially sanctioned and policed, young men seeking to escape their obligations will be hounded and may in turn reject the fatherhood role and/or deny paternity. Fatherhood requires men to take responsibility for their children, which in turn presupposes material, social and psychological resources. Teenage fathers frequently lack the necessary resources to discharge this role fully and thus are likely to constitute an unstable social group unless provided with support.

References and further reading

Hendricks, L.E., Montgomery, T.A. and Fullilove, R.E. (1984) 'Educational achievement and locus of control among black adolescent fathers', *Journal of Negro Education*, 53 (2): 182–8.

Olavarria, J. (2003) 'Men at home?' in M.C. Guttman (ed.) *Changing Men and Masculinities in Latin America*, Durham, NC: Duke University Press, pp. 333–50.

Stouthamer-Loeber, M. and Wei, E.H. (1998) 'The precursors of young fatherhood and its effects on delinquency of teenage males', *Journal of Adolescent Health*, 22: 56–65.

Thrasher, F.M. (1927) *The Gang*, Chicago, IL: University of Chicago Press.

Xie, H., Cairns, B.D. and Cairns, R.B. (2001) 'Predicting teen motherhood and teen fatherhood', *Social Development*, 10 (4): 488–509.

See also: fatherhood, fathering

ROBERT MORRELL

FATHERHOOD AND PAID WORK

Fatherhood and paid work are connected in a way that is both empirical and ideological. In industrialised countries, the ideological linkage is often traced back to the effects of industrialisation itself. As this economic form gradually replaced agricultural economies from the early nineteenth century onwards, so the basis of family financial support shifted to wages earned in industrial workplaces, separated from the homes and family holdings of an earlier era. As men came to dominate this new waged workforce, workplaces came to be constructed symbolically as the domain of men, while homes – and the daily care of children – were the symbolic domain of women. One consequence of this 'separate spheres' ideology was to construct men's paid work as the most important means by which they discharged their family responsibilities.

The ideological linkage of fathers with breadwinning has persisted even in the face of demographic changes that have seen increasing numbers of mothers entering paid employment and sharing breadwinning responsibilities with fathers. For example, in 2003 some 60 per cent of US married couples with children were dual-earner couples (US Bureau of Labor Statistics 2004). The proportions are similar in other industrial economies. But in spite of these significant changes, men continue to be viewed, and to view themselves, as being ultimately responsible for the family's financial support (Townsend 2002; Wilkie 1993). Research also indicates that the identification of fathers with financial support has a moral dimension, closely linked to understandings of appropriate masculinity (Doucet 2001).

The expectation that it is men's responsibility to provide for their families may also be reflected at a national policy level. For example, both Britain and the United States have policies requiring fathers to pay child support after family breakdown. In contrast, Scandinavian welfare states like Sweden and Norway, characterised by greater social acceptance of the dual-earning family, have enacted policies (like shared parental leave) designed to promote fathers' involvement in families outside of their responsibilities as breadwinners (Hobson 2002).

Even in countries like the United States where there is little support at the policy level to encourage fathers to become more involved with the caring, as well as the financial support of their children, the cultural image of the 'new father' is growing in significance (LaRossa 1988). This new father is an emotionally available, hands-on caregiver from the moment of his child's birth (Pleck 1987). But whether or not this new image reflects a shift in the way many fathers engage with their children, the expectation does not seem to be waning that they will continue to work, on a full-time basis, to support their families financially.

Expectations about fathers and paid work are inflected by class and race in industrialised economies. For example, a common strategy in dual-earning working-class families in the US is to have parents work alternating shifts, so that outside childcare is minimised. This positions fathers to share both caregiving and financial support with their partners on a much more equal basis – even though the father may still be seen as the breadwinner (Deutsch and Saxon 1998). Among middle-class families, though, there may be more of a lag between the 'new father' culture and the actual conduct of fatherhood (LaRossa 1988). And in elite professions, as Coltrane (2004) points out, gendered expectations still prevail.

If fathers are slower to assume domestic responsibility than mothers have been to take up paid work, entrenched organisational expectations about men as workers may be at least partly responsible. The influx of women into paid employment has led to greater awareness of the need for work/family balance, since women, unlike men, are assumed to have family responsibilities that are not discharged by financial provision. But though 'family-friendly' policies like parental leave or flexible schedules may be couched in gender-neutral terms, men have been slow to take them up, and they may face negative workplace reaction if they do so (Rapoport and Bailyn 1996; Hochschild 1997).

Christiansen and Palkovitz (2001) argue that providing is a legitimate and important form of paternal involvement in families, one that is often overlooked or poorly conceptualised in research. At the same time, the durability of the ideological connection between fatherhood and breadwinning is striking, given the extent to which, in the majority of families, financial support is shared with mothers. Bernard ([1981] 1995) offers another perspective, commenting that while in practice men's good-provider role may be on its way out, the responsibilities of the role have attenuated far faster than have its 'prerogatives and privileges' (Bernard [1981] 1995: 161).

References and further reading

Bernard, J. [1981] (1995) 'The good-provider role', in M. Kimmel and M. Messner (eds) *Men's Lives*, 3rd edn, Boston, MA: Allyn and Bacon, pp. 149–63.

Christiansen, S. and Palkovitz, R. (2001) 'Why the "good provider" role still matters', *Journal of Family Issues*, 22: 64–106.

Coltrane, S. (2004) 'Elite careers and family commitment', *Annals of the American Academy of Political and Social Science*, 596: 214–20.

Deutsch, F. and Saxon, S. (1998) 'Traditional ideologies, non-traditional lives', *Sex Roles*, 38: 331–62.

Doucet, A. (2001) 'You see the need perhaps more clearly than I have', *Journal of Family Issues*, 22: 328–57.

Hobson, B. (ed.) (2002) *Making Men into Fathers*, Cambridge: Cambridge University Press.

Hochschild, A. (1997) *The Time Bind*, New York: Metropolitan Books.

LaRossa, R. (1988) 'Fatherhood and social change', *Family Relations*, 37: 451–8.

Pleck, J. (1987) 'American fathering in historical perspective', in M. Kimmel (ed.) *Changing Men*, Newbury Park, CA: Sage, pp. 83–95.

Rapoport, R. and Bailyn, L. (1996) *Rethinking Life and Work*, Darby, PA: Diane.

Townsend, N. (2002) *The Package Deal*, Philadelphia, PA: Temple University Press.

US Bureau of Labor Statistics (2004) *Employment Characteristics of Families Summary*, available at http://www.bls.gov/CPS (accessed 27 April 2005).

Wilkie, J. (1993) 'Changes in US men's attitudes toward the family provider role, 1972–89', *Gender and Society*, 7: 261–79.

See also: fatherhood, fathering

GILLIAN RANSON

FATHERHOOD AND VIOLENCE

For more than a decade there has been a significant growth in the international study of fatherhood. However, until now very little research has focused directly on the relationship between fatherhood and violence, and very few structured interventions with violent men as fathers and/or parents have been documented. This gap in knowledge particularly concerns white/Western fathers. Studies on fatherhood and the practices of fathers – both as co-parents and as parents to children – have typically focused on 'ordinary' or 'new' (heterosexual) fathers. The issue of violence has not been a main concern. In addition, there has been a lack of focus on men as parents in studies of men's violence in close relationships, including violence to women. This is in spite of the growing body of research documenting a clear link between men's violence to women and men's psychological, physical and sexual violence to the children living in the family (see Eriksson *et al.* 2005). Exceptions to this overall pattern are mainly some studies on (non-white) fathers' violence that is carried out in the name of 'honour', and on the post-separation safety of women/mothers and children.

However, the literature on the violence of fathers has been growing. The existing studies of fathers who are violent to women suggest that such fathers tend to construct fatherhood in terms of rights to children and that they may be more concerned with maintaining control over their children than with nurturing them (see Peled 2000). They may, for example, be more likely to fight for custody or not pay child or spousal support than non-abusive men. In addition to being directly abusive, fathers who are violent to women tend to be under-involved and neglectful parents, usually in combination with periods of rigid and authoritarian involvement; they may undermine the mother; be self-centred and expect that children should meet their needs; be manipulative, and expect the rewards and public status of being fathers without the difficulties and sacrifices that are involved in parenting (Bancroft and Silverman 2002). Although there are differences among violent fathers, even those with greater awareness of the impact of their violence may be teaching violence to their children. In addition, post-separation or divorce violence by fathers towards children may be linked specifically to childcare activities (Harne 2003).

The emerging literature on the relationship between fatherhood and violence increasingly addresses the implications for practice concerning a number of areas: support to and recovery of women/mothers and children, both boys and girls (e.g. Bancroft and Silverman 2002; Peled 2000); work with violent men (e.g. Råkil 2006); and the issues of safety and risk in custody, contact and living arrangements after separation and divorce (e.g. Eriksson *et al.* 2005; Jaffe *et al.* 2003).

However, there is still a major need for future work on this topic, both empirically and theoretically. There is a lack of in-depth knowledge about the subjectivities and identity projects of violent fathers, and about the relationship between fatherhood and violence based upon the voices of fathers themselves. Furthermore, differences in the 'doing' of violent fatherhood, in the outcomes for women/mothers and children and in the possibilities for change, must be explored and explained more thoroughly. Here, previous work on masculinities offers some possibilities. Future studies also need to engage with the debates about intersecting power relations. In understanding fathers' approaches to children, it is especially important that the dimensions of age and generation, together with insights from childhood studies, should be taken into account.

Interventions with violent fathers, whether as family law assessments or work with perpetrators, must be documented and evaluated systematically. However, intervention cannot be the only context for research. There is still very little knowledge developed from an everyday life perspective. Furthermore, there is a great need for studies of the implications for the relationship between fatherhood and violence of institutional and cultural contexts. For example, in large parts of the 'Western' world new forms of hegemonic masculinity are currently developing – and being an involved and caring father seems to be becoming a central feature. What might such developments mean for the practices and identity projects of fathers post-separation/divorce?

Finally, judging from current studies, some conceptual issues regarding the practices of fathers need to be addressed. First, it is not always clear what the relationship is between the explicitly gendered concept of *fathering* and *parenting* defined as adults' child-centred care for minor children. The study of gender and parenthood should engage with child–adult relations as well as notions of children and children's interests and needs. Second, the identity work of fathers, the subjective experience of fathering, and parenting as adults' child-centred care for minor children, cannot be presumed to be identical. These forms of practices must be explored empirically. In the context of violent fathers, the relationship between them is crucial for the safety and well-being of both children and co-parents.

References and further reading

Bancroft, L. and Silverman, J.G. (2002) *The Batterer as Parent. Addressing the Impact of Domestic Violence on Family Dynamics*, Thousand Oaks, CA, London, New Delhi: Sage.

Eriksson, M., Hester, M., Keskinen, S. and Pringle, K. (eds) (2005) *Tackling Men's Violence in Families. Nordic Issues and Dilemmas*, Bristol: Policy Press.

Harne, L. (2003) 'Childcare, violence and fathering – are violent fathers who look after their children likely to be less abusive?' in R.C.A. Klein and B. Wallner (eds) *Gender, Conflict, and Violence*, Wien: Studien Verlag.

Jaffe, P., Lemon, N. and Poisson, S. (2003) *Child Custody and Domestic Violence. A Call for Safety and Accountability*, Thousand Oaks, CA, London, New Delhi: Sage.

Peled, E. (2000) 'Parenting by men who abuse women: issues and dilemmas', *British Journal of Social Work*, 30 (1): 25–36.

Råkil, M. (2006) 'Are men who use violence against their partners and children good enough fathers? The need for an integrated child perspective in the treatment work with the men', in C. Humphreys and N. Stanley (eds) *Domestic Violence and Child Protection: Directions for Good Practice*, London, Jessica Kingsley.

See also: child abuse; domestic violence; fatherhood, fathering; sexual violence; violence

MARIA ERIKSSON

FATHERS' RIGHTS

'Fathers' rights' refers to organised groups or networks of fathers who act in support of the collective interests of fathers, especially separated fathers whose children do not reside with them. Fathers' rights (hereafter 'FR') groups are active particularly in lobbying for changes in family law.

FR is defined by the claim that fathers are deprived of their 'rights' and subjected to systematic discrimination as men and fathers, in a system biased towards women and dominated by feminists. FR groups overlap with men's rights groups and both represent an organised backlash to feminism. While other networks also promote fathers' involvement in families, the FR movement is distinguished by its anti-feminist discourse of men or fathers as victims. At the same time, FR perspectives do have a wide currency across the political spectrum.

FR groups have emerged in most Western countries over the past three decades (Collier and Sheldon 2006), in the context of profound shifts in gender, intimate and familial relations. More men are living separately from their biological children, fathering outside of marriage, having parenting relationships with children who are not biologically theirs, and being custodial single fathers. Cultural definitions of fatherhood also have changed. The notion of the nurturing and highly involved father now exerts a powerful influence on popular perceptions. However, the culture of fatherhood has changed much faster than the conduct (Flood 2003).

Two experiences particularly bring men into FR groups. First, many heterosexual men experience considerable emotional difficulties in the wake of separation and divorce. FR groups are characterised by anger and blame towards ex-partners and the 'system', and such themes are relatively common among men who have undergone separation (Lehr and MacMillan 2001). While some men respond to divorce by making a priority of relationships with their children, others withdraw from parental and financial involvement (Arendell 1995). Second, separated fathers often are dissatisfied with their lack of contact with their children. While most children's living arrangements are finalised without the need for a Family Court order, over time many non-resident fathers have increasingly distant relationships with their children.

While FR groups purport to act on behalf of separated fathers, many in fact stifle their healing processes, constrain their parenting involvements and directly compromise the wellbeing of children themselves.

Some men do find solace and support in FR groups. At the same time, many groups offer their members subject positions based only in victimhood, and centred on hostility towards and blame of the legal system and their ex-partners. Such approaches fix men in positions of anger and hostility.

While many of the individual men in FR groups do desire greater involvement with their children, FR advocates have done little to foster fathers' positive involvement in children's lives, whether before or after separation and divorce. The FR movement focuses on gaining an equality concerned with fathers' 'rights' and status rather than the actual care of children (Rhoades 2000).

In their public rhetoric throughout the 1990s, Australian FR groups had emphasised issues of 'rights' and discrimination, but by the early twenty-first century their rhetorical strategies focused on the need for 'equal parenting', emphasising that this is what is best or children. However, they continue to ignore actual gendered divisions of labour in families prior to separation, and give no attention to the practical realities of shared care after separation. Some FR groups seem more concerned with re-establishing paternal authority and fathers' decision-making related to their children's and ex-partners' lives than with actual involvements with children (Stacey 1998).

FR groups have neglected the primary obstacle to fathers' involvement with children after separation, their lack of involvement *before* separation (Flood 2003). Groups in Australia and the US have focused on achieving a rebuttable presumption of joint child custody or residence in family law, but the lack of such a presumption is not a significant barrier to men's involvement in post-divorce fathering. The parents to whom a presumption of joint residence would apply are least able to set up shared parenting arrangements, because of conflict, violence and lack of social and material resources.

FR groups have attempted to force parental contact on to children regardless of children's own desires and regardless of potentially negative effects on children's wellbeing. The influence of FR agendas in family law has meant that fathers' contact with children is privileged over children's safety from violence, and children now face a greater requirement to have contact with abusive or violent parents. By depicting women as parasitical, mendacious and vindictive (Kaye and Tolmie 1998b), FR groups have intensified interparental conflict, with negative impacts on children's wellbeing. They have worked to reduce the obligations of non-resident fathers to provide child support, leaving children and their resident parents with fewer financial and material resources. At the same time, aspects of the existing child support system have imposed unjust financial penalties on some non-resident parents.

FR groups have been able to increase community acceptance of several myths: that women routinely make false accusations of child abuse or domestic violence to gain advantage in family law proceedings and to arbitrarily deny their ex-partners' access to the children, and that domestic violence is gender-equal. The FR movement has sought to wind back the protections available to victims of domestic violence, and to increase the protections available to alleged perpetrators.

References and further reading

Arendell, T. (1995) *Fathers and Divorce*, London: Sage.

Collier, R. and Sheldon, S. (eds) (2006) *Fathers' Rights Activism and Law Reform in Comparative Perspective*, Oxford: Hart.

Flood, M. (2003) *Fatherhood and Fatherlessness*, Discussion Paper No. 59, Canberra: Australia Institute.

—— (2004) 'Backlash', in S.E. Rossi (ed.) *The Battle and Backlash Rage On*, Philadelphia, PA: Xlibris, pp. 261–78.

Kaye, M. and Tolmie, J. (1998a) 'Fathers' rights groups in Australia and their engagement with issues of family law', *Australian Journal of Family Law*, 12 (1): 19–67.

—— (1998b) 'Discoursing dads', *Melbourne University Law Review*, 22: 162–94.

Lehr, R., and MacMillan, P. (2001) 'The psychological and emotional impact of divorce', *Families in Society*, 82 (4): 373–82.

Rhoades, H. (2000) 'Posing as reform: the case of the Family Law Reform Act', *Australian Journal of Family Law*, 14: 142–59.

Smart, C. (2004) 'Equal shares', *Critical Social Policy*, 24 (4): 484–503.

Stacey, J. (1998) 'Dada-ism in the 1990s: getting past baby talk about fatherlessness', in C.R. Daniels (ed.) *Lost Fathers: The Politics of Fatherlessness*, London: Macmillan, pp. 51–84.

See also: fatherhood, fathering; masculinity politics; men's movement; men's rights

MICHAEL FLOOD

FEMALE MASCULINITY

'Female masculinity' refers to traditionally masculine traits of character or appearance occurring in biological women. *Female Masculinity*

(1998) is a book by American cultural theorist Judith Halberstam that describes masculine-gendered types in non-male bodies, including the anatomically mixed androgyne, the sexually aggressive tribade, the melancholic female invert, the female husband, the gallant lesbian stone butch, the female-to-male transsexual, and the costumed drag king. These historically specific figures, Halberstam argues, validate contemporary queer theory, especially Judith Butler's 'performative' theory of gender (1990), to show that gender is not natural but socially constructed. These female masculinities vary in qualities of body, psychological characteristics, sexual orientation, fantasies and desires, dress and comportment, and degree of permanence. They disrupt conventional associations between masculinity, male bodies and power. Halberstam believes that studying female masculinities reveals the operations of hegemonic male masculinity, unmasks its claims to naturalness, demonstrates alternative and often desirable forms of social power for women, and disrupts the gender binary.

Masculine women are recorded throughout history. Often the masculine woman is an exceptional mythic or heroic figure, an Amazon, saint or a warrior queen like the fifteenth-century French warrior peasant Joan of Arc or Queen Elizabeth I of England. Maxine Hong Kingston's Asian–American novel, *The Woman Warrior* (1976), elaborates the Chinese legend of the transvestite warrior Fa Mu Lan. A more common figure is the romping tomboy, like the heroine of Louisa May Alcott's popular *Little Women* (1868). On the other hand, ordinary adult women taking on masculine traits or indicating desire for other women have been severely censured in many societies.

In some African cultures, the 'female husband' may be a culturally sanctioned woman who officially marries another woman in order to have access to her children and to maintain property within her lineage. This arrangement may also provide both partners with emotional closeness, heterosexual freedom, freedom from male interference, and sometimes sexual relations with one another.

References and further reading

Alcott, L.M. [1868] (1994) *Little Women*, Oxford and New York: Oxford University Press.

Butler, J. [1990] (1999) *Gender Trouble*, London and New York: Routledge.

Halberstam, J. (1998) *Female Masculinity*, Durham, NC, and London: Duke University Press.

Kingston, M.H. (1976) *The Woman Warrior*, New York: Alfred A. Knopf.

Njambi, W.N. and O'Brien, W.E. (2000) 'Revisiting "woman–woman marriage": notes on Gikuyu women', *NWSA Journal*, 12 (1): 1–23.

JUDITH KEGAN GARDINER

FEMINISM

Being a feminist means more than just articulating a particular literary theory or cultural critique. Feminism requires change; it demands that we live our lives differently as women and as men. Feminist masculinities embrace the core idea that the personal is political. At the centre of the relationships men (and women) create resides a power dynamic. When men (especially straight white men) come to an awareness of their sense of privilege and their assumption of entitlement, they can begin to create more egalitarian relationships. Women's equality is one crucial aspect of this quest. Another important component is a feminist interrogation of men and masculinities. The former, men's active involvement in the campaign for women's rights, predates both the development of feminism as a radical political philosophy and the application of that perspective to men's roles in general.

The relation between the sexes has engendered, historically, a critique by men of women's persistently unequal situation. Prescriptiveness concerning women – their roles in marriage, their educability, their sexuality, their 'beauty' and their sphere of activity – informs these 'pro-women' tracts. In their writings, these male authors question whether women differ from the writer's own sex, whether it is natural or just that they should occupy their present status, and how they might be released from the worst effects of restrictions placed upon them.

Men supporting women's rights have often done so in dialogue with female advocates beginning at least with Christine de Pizan in the early fifteenth century and continuing through today. The earliest male defenders are found in late-fifth and early-fourth century BCE Greece, however, with Aristophanes' *Lysistrata* (411 BCE) and Plato's *Republic* (380 BCE). In both of these works, women assume roles of equality with men in the context of important political decisions and in educational opportunities. In the Medieval period, Chaucer writes his ambiguously proto-feminist 'Wife of Bath's Tale', with its defence of women against misogyny and an advocacy of women's autonomy, and he and Boccaccio compile 'catalogues' of famous women in history.

After Chaucer, probably the earliest familiar male supporter of women's rights is Agrippa, who in 1509 argues against the misogynist interpretations of women's capacities, roles and rights. Several important works by men follow closely upon Agrippa's treatise: Tilney revives the discussion of friendship within marriage, and Poulain de la Barre provides the first truly radical, uncompromising and profoundly effective defence of women's equality at all levels of society.

The eighteenth century was a particularly rich period for pro-women writings by men, encompassing a host of well-known French thinkers from Diderot and Montesquieu to d'Holbach and Condorcet, such American writers as Paine and Rush, and the German von Hippel. While the French writers argued on behalf of the rights of women on such issues as birth control and constitutional rights, von Hippel opposes vigorously the dominant ideology of the time: that women are irrational, unreasonable (or without reason altogether) and emotional.

In the nineteenth century, with the rise in Europe of liberalism, Marxism and anarchism, feminism emerges as a radical political theory and movement. Mill and Engels presented arguments in favour of women's rights, while in America Douglass and Garrison were early advocates of a woman's right to vote.

The early years of the twentieth century, the period of 'First Wave Feminism', were a time dominated by such political demands as equal pay and a focus on anti-war and anti-fascist activism. First wave feminists endorsed the vote for women, equal opportunities in the professions, access to higher education and the elimination of restrictions within marriage. In Britain, Russell critiqued the repressive nature of conventional sexual morality, while Montagu argued against women's inferiority.

In her book *The Second Sex* (1949), Beauvoir provides a crucial transition to what becomes the radical feminism of the 1960s and 1970s. Beauvoir's identification of woman as Other helped articulate an understanding of the female as alienated from her humanity due to the objectification of woman intrinsic to patriarchy. Following closely on Beauvoir's history of women's oppression, and in the context of this decade of radical political engagement and change across all areas of society, men started asking, 'What does it mean to be a man in patriarchal society?' From feminism men gained insights into their own dehumanised lives, thus coming to the realisation that manhood may not be all that healthy for men.

In the context of the New Left, the US Civil Rights movement, opposition to the war in Vietnam, and leftist men's own sexism, the Women's Liberation Movement emerged. Feminists expanded their struggle to address personal and individual issues, out of which came the crucial insight that 'the personal is political'. The realisation that who we are as individuals constitutes a political construction, coupled with the creation of consciousness-raising groups, inspired a crucial change in the relationship between feminism and men. For men, feminism became more a critical perspective through which they could scrutinise masculinity and less a call for them to act solely as advocates for women's causes (though the latter remains an important component of the 'profeminist men's movement').

Beginning in the 1960s, men start to apply feminism to an examination of their own lives as men in a patriarchal society. While many of these analyses evoked reactionary answers, and (at least in the US) several remained liberal at best, out of these initial engagements a more radical position emerged, especially from the UK. Men were not alone in this feminist analysis of masculinities. Several women contributed invaluable insights into the discourse of 'men's studies', 'feminist masculinities' and the 'male condition', and in this dialogue with women the investigation of what it means to be a man in patriarchal society became more subtle.

The 1970s was a rich period for the emergence of a feminist analysis of masculinities. In the US, Sawyer's 'On male liberation', published originally in *Liberation* magazine (1970), and Wittman's 'A gay manifesto' introduce the two divergent, though sometimes overlapping concerns: that of male heterosexual liberation on the one hand and gay liberation on the other.

Following closely on Sawyer's essay came Snodgrass's helpful anthology, *For Men Against Sexism* (1977). The essays in Snodgrass's collection represent some of the more radical work being done by men in the first half of the 1970s. In 'Toward gender justice', for example, Stoltenberg locates male bonding and men's need to oppress women as much in gay men's liberation as in the heterosexual male community.

Later in the decade, Pleck contributed to the emerging anti-sexist men's movement. His interest in the world of men's work, where most American men, far from being power wielders, find themselves relatively powerless, inspired subsequent scholarship, as did his analysis of the psychological reasons why American males seek power over women.

The work of Tolson, a British Marxist, represents one of the marked differences between the more liberal and at times psychologising focus of the American contribution and the more political, overtly socialist analysis of British writers. In *The Limits of Masculinity* (1977), Tolson applies a Marxist analysis to his personal struggle against sexism. For Tolson, ideology, institutional boundaries and accepted rules of behaviour structure social consciousness. Seidler, another important British intellectual and activist, was an early member of the editorial collective for *Achilles Heel*, a journal that focused on positive conceptions of masculinity with an emphasis on the ways men can change in response to the challenge of feminism.

Other early radical works include Hoch's *White Hero Black Beast* (1979), in which masculinity is seen as an interracial competition for women that rests on a fear of impotence and homosexuality, while positing the inevitable victory of the white hero over the black beast. In *Holy Virility* (1983), Reynaud, a French intellectual, addresses the fundamental question of what being a 'man' within patriarchy means and how power can be redistributed between the sexes.

In the mid-1980s, Connell co-authored a ground-breaking essay, 'Toward a new sociology of masculinity', that both reviews the 'Books on Men' period of the men's movement and stresses the absence in most of these early works of any attempt to engage the relationship of heterosexual men's liberation with gay men's liberation. In contrast to these previous works, Connell *et al.* introduce their innovative (though contested) concept of hegemonic masculinity.

Kimmel, one of the major voices in the American profeminist men's movement spanning the past three decades, has published extensively on the subject of men and masculinity and helped to organise profeminist men in the National Organization for Men Against Sexism (NOMAS). In an oft printed essay, 'Masculinity as homophobia', for example, Kimmel sees masculinity as a historical construction defined 'in opposition to a set of "others" – racial minorities, sexual minorities, and, above all, women'.

In addition to writing about feminist masculinities, men have been active in anti-sexist groups and organisations. Founded in 1975,

NOMAS represents the oldest and certainly most active profeminist men's group in the United States (and has links to several international organisations). Promoting the cause of gender equality and social justice for everyone, NOMAS rests on the principles of profeminism, gay-affirmation, anti-racism and enhancing the lives of men. To realise these principles, profeminist men are active on a number of fronts: they participate in Gay Pride parades; are active in men's anti-rape organisations; work in prisons; offer workshops on fathering, on 'gender training' (for workers/managers), and on sexual harassment.

These initiatives are by no means limited to the US. The White Ribbon Campaign, for example, that began in Montreal in 1991 after the massacre of fourteen women, spread to the US, Europe, Africa, Latin America and Australia, becoming 'the first large-scale male protest against violence in the world' (Flood 2001: 1). Today, international campaigns on the part of men's groups to end men's violence against women exist in India, the Republic of Trinidad and Tobago, Central America, Nicaragua, Brazil and Australia. In addition, European profeminist networks have been established in Austria, Belgium, Denmark, Finland, France, Germany, Greece, Ireland, Italy, Norway, Spain, Sweden to name just a few. In Japan, as Connell points out in *The Men and the Boys*, a media debate about men's liberation arose in the mid-1990s that spawned the foundation of a men's centre and a national debate on change. Out of these international programmes has come a burgeoning interest in global masculinities.

With the realisation that patriarchy and masculine domination are neither singular nor universal, profeminist men see masculinities as 'under constant revision, negotiation and movement' (Whitehead 2002: 5). Indeed, men and masculinities exist in particular historical contexts and are thus defined by certain dominant characteristics and assumptions.

At the same time, though, the identification of male roles that represent a marginal masculinity, one that challenges the seemingly hegemonic definition of manhood during any given historical period, represents the potential for disruption that Butler refers to as a 'subversive bodily act' and Whitehead describes as a 'masculine-oriented performativity'. These masculine improvisations can undermine traditional masculine roles while at the same time reinforcing them. This dialectic of masculine performance provides a rich area for problematising a seemingly hegemonic masculinity.

One example of how this dialectic can be interrogated with radical implications is apparent in the way high-speed computer access affects our perceptions of masculinities. Adult video-conferencing sites where men present sexualised bodies as objects of the gaze through an interactive medium, for example, raise questions about how men construct a masculine subjectivity and a male sexual identity that is both an affirmational community performance and an individual erotic display.

As we move into the twenty-first century, other sub-fields of feminist masculinity studies begin to emerge. A focus on the language men use when they talk about themselves as men has been an important area of exploration, for example. By exposing the subtleties of the discourse of male bonding we may be able to alter the way men live as men through changing their habits of speech.

One concern remains central, however: because many men are forced to comply with macho standards of performance, standards frequently reinforced in modern literature and culture, they experience their power and sexuality as heavy burdens. By adopting a model of sexuality and social relations informed deeply by a feminist perspective and thus neither hierarchical nor exploitative, men can begin to construct alternative relationships among themselves as well as with women. Feminist masculinities offer a way to engage these issues and strive to attain these changed relationships.

References and further reading

Butler, J. (1990) *Gender Trouble*, New York: Routledge.
Connell, R. (2000) *The Men and the Boys*, Berkeley, CA: University of California Press.
Flood, M. (2001) 'Men's collective anti-violence activism and the struggle for gender justice', *Development*, 44 (3): 42–7.
Gardiner, J.K. (ed.) (2002) *Masculinity Studies and Feminist Theory*, New York: Columbia University Press.
Kimmel, M.S. and Mosmiller, T.E. (eds) (1992) *Against the Tide*, Boston, MA: Beacon.
Murphy, P.F. (2001) *Studs, Tools and the Family Jewels*, Madison, WI: University of Wisconsin Press.
—— (ed.) (2004) *Feminism and Masculinities*, Oxford: Oxford University Press.
Seidler, V. (1994) *Unreasonable Men*, London: Routledge.
Whitehead, S. (2002) *Men and Masculinities*, Cambridge: Polity.

See also: feminist theory; homophobia and heterosexism; men's; movement; profeminism

PETER F. MURPHY

FEMINIST THEORY

Masculinity studies developed in conjunction with feminist theories, and feminist theories developed in response to male dominance in society. Thus men and masculinity are central to feminist theories.

Theories aid action by helping actors conceptualise issues, problems and approaches. Feminist theories, in all their considerable diversity, conceptualise gender as a category of analysis and assert, explain, protest and attempt to remedy women's subordination to men. Theories suggest which questions are worth asking. Feminist theories ask new questions about men, women and the relations between them, examining conditions previously not noticed or considered obvious or unchangeable – like why women want to be mothers or how rape functions in a society. Feminist theories seek what benefits women, then ask which women, which benefits and who decides. Feminist theories analyse existing gender arrangements and the forces that uphold them, then imagine better alternatives and strategies to reach them.

Feminist theories generally claim that societies, not simply biology, divide people into the categories of women and men; that women as a category are systematically disadvantaged in relation to the category of men; that this disadvantage is changeable by human action; and that people should strive for gender justice, which will benefit both women and men. All these beliefs have direct corollaries for men and masculinities: that is, they dispute claims of intrinsic male and masculine superiority to women and to femininity, on the one hand, and also assertions of male victimisation, on the other. They contest the authorities that proclaim male superiority or victimisation, often by attacking the bias or inaccuracy of traditional authorities or interpretations of nature or divine will. Feminist theories do not presume that men are a unified group. They do see the category of men as materially and ideologically advantaged by male status, although individual men may hold marginal or devalued positions among other men, or they may uphold women's rights in alliance with women or against men's group interests.

Although it is still common to distinguish between the biological sexes of human males and females and the culturally constructed genders of masculine and feminine, current feminist theories question these binary distinctions. Current feminist theories use the concept of gender as a way of understanding the pervasive, world-wide differential distribution of power, status and resources. For example, Enloe claims, 'security, moral satisfaction, progress, civilisation – all are gendered' (Enloe 2004: 304). Feminist theories today see the power relations between the genders as always affected by and affecting other hierarchical social categories, like those of nationality, ethnicity, 'race', age, ability, status, sexuality and economic class. Furthermore, they understand gender as a basic and significant part of most individuals' self-concepts, identity structures and fantasies, and as shaped by and shaping cultural representations of men and women, the divine and the natural world. Current feminist theories do not presuppose that there must be only two sexes or two genders in all societies or that genders must be conceived in opposition to one another. They do not assume that masculine or feminine gender aligns smoothly with sexual orientation or with a person's self-labelling as male or female.

Feminist theories have developed in relation to the cultures and historical periods in which women have found themselves. Prior to organised feminism, some women and men argued against male dominance. These earliest statements were often ambivalent about women's capacities in relation to men's. Explicit feminist theory begins with the response to the European Enlightenment in the eighteenth century. In the pioneering document, 'A vindication of the rights of woman' (1792), Wollstonecraft in England claimed that if women were educated equally with men, their apparent emotional weakness and intellectual inferiority would disappear. In the United States, Stanton imitated the rhetoric of the Declaration of Independence to assert the equality of women with men as humans and as citizens entitled to 'life, liberty, and the pursuit of happiness' despite the 'repeated injuries and usurpations on the part of man toward woman' (Stanton in Kolmar and Bartkowski, 2005: 71–2). The foremost English male theorist of women's equality and rights in the nineteenth century, John Stuart Mill, formulated his ideas on 'The subjection of women' (1869) in dialogue with his partner Harriet Taylor. These early feminist statements posited a generic human rationality in all individuals and then asserted that women should have the same access to the rights accruing to such individuals as men already did, although of course not all men had these rights either.

The argument that women are equal to men in reason and therefore entitled to equal rights remains a part of feminist theorising into the present. Conferences affiliated with the United Nations use this theoretical approach. For example, the 1995 Beijing Declaration and Platform for Action claims that women's equality is necessary 'to advance the goals of equality, development and peace for all women everywhere in the interest of all humanity' and that 'women's rights are human rights' ('Beijing' in Kolmar and Bartkowski 2005: 521–2). This tradition of liberal feminism upholds women's rights equally with men's to national citizenship and political participation, access to education, jobs and professions, and representation in cultural forms.

Some authors oppose such 'equality' or 'sameness' feminist theories, which assert that women are fundamentally like men in the factors that define humanity and confer rights, to 'sexual difference' theories, which emphasise women's distinctive capacities and experiences, including childbearing and susceptibility to vaginal rape. However, this distinction is too schematic to describe feminist theories well, and many sets of labels have been used to describe various strands of feminist theory. Feminist theories generally recognise women's commonalities with many men and particularly with the oppressions of marginalised men, and they recognise significant differences between men's and women's typical experiences as well as significant differences among women. Beauvoir's pioneering book *The Second Sex* (1949) argues that 'one is not born, but rather becomes, a woman': that is, that the category of women is socially constructed, not the inevitable outcome of biology (Beavoir in Kolmar and Bartkowski 2005: 184). Beauvoir assumes that reason, will and projects to transcend one's immediate circumstances are available to both men and women, and therefore argues for potential equality and reciprocity between women and men. However, she also details the ways in which women are differently situated than men and describes the specific attitudes, behaviours and experiences that typically develop in wives, mothers, mistresses and young and old women in comparison with men at the same stages of life.

The focus on women as mothers and sexual objects informs much feminist theory that highlights women's differences from men and the dominance that men exert over women through controlling women's bodies, sexuality, reproduction and labour power. Proponents of what is sometimes called 'radical feminism' see the gender division as basic to all other social divisions. It is this group that is most commonly accused of male-bashing, since it holds that the basic inequality in society is that of men dominating women. For these theorists, masculinity produces crime, war and other forms of violence, while its apparently more rational forms may appear in the guise of the corrupt judge, the biased scientist or masculinist law. For some radical feminists, penetrative heterosexual intercourse is so implicated in male dominance that women should avoid it. American theorist MacKinnon argues that pornography is a significant factor in male violence because through pornography men learn to become aroused by images of submissive and violated women. According to MacKinnon, 'sexuality is the set of practices that inscribes gender as unequal in social life' (MacKinnon 2005: 275). MacKinnon claims that 'the movement for the liberation of women . . . is first practice, then theory' (MacKinnon 2005: 23) and has put her theories into practice through the delineation of sexual harassment law and attempts to outlaw pornography.

Such theories are attentive to masculine violence against women both in domestic forms, like wife-beating, and also in institutionalised forms like rape during the Bosnian war or the sexual abuse of Korean 'comfort women' by the Japanese during the Second World War. Although holders of these 'radical feminist' viewpoints recognise that some men ally with women and that others, including homosexual men, may be largely excluded from male privilege, they tend to see masculinity as antithetical to rather than constitutive of humanity. Radical feminists claim that prevailing standards of law and ethics are based on a masculine model that is not universal, not fair and not humane. Thus, for instance, defining pregnancy as an illness would not make sense if the normative human were a woman, and defining citizenship in terms of military service would be seen as biased in favour of violent rather than non-violent modes of conflict resolution.

Seeking to understand women's acceptance of an unequal gender order, psychoanalytic feminist theorists like Dinnerstein (*Mermaid and the Minotaur*, 1976) and Chodorow (*Reproduction of Mothering*, 1978) found in mother-dominated childrearing a universal cause of male dominance. Helpless infants cared for chiefly by women come to associate women with dangerous power and later seek to control it by controlling women, while also associating women with life-giving nurturance. This leads both men and women to feel ambivalent about female authority and to expect instinctual satisfactions from the bodies of women that they don't expect from men. These theories polarise nurturant, empathic femininity against an autonomous but rigid masculinity that reinforces misogyny but that also makes men the agents of potential transformation for the entire gender order: if men shared equally in childrearing, then the unconscious causes of sexism would disappear.

Since the 1990s, new trends have been prominent in feminist theory. Poststructuralist theories stressing performance often explain cultural formations, while theories of globalisation place gender in contexts of changing world economic, political and cultural structures, structures of representation, new technologies and media. Feminist theorists also aspire to intersectional analyses that relate gender to other social categories like 'race', sexuality, social class and nationality.

The performative theory of gender outlined by Butler (*Gender Trouble*, 1990) has been enormously influential in explaining how gender is persistently produced through repetitive human actions, like habitual ways of walking or dressing, yet malleable. The example of male drag, of men imitating femininity, represents not an imitation of gender but the way all gender operates. This theory does not focus specifically on women and has proved useful to masculinity and queer theories and to feminist disability studies, which describe, for instance, how spinal cord injuries affect the injured person's performances of masculinity or femininity. Moreover, the sexual division of labour, even the creation of two distinct and opposing sexes, and the subjection of women all depend on compulsory heterosexuality, in which the categories men and women need to be made socially central and antithetical. Butler claims that such contemporary phenomena as the intersexed movement and transsexuals both challenge societies' commitments to maintaining 'a natural dimorphism' (Butler 2004: 6).

Globalisation theories arise from a global feminist movement that is anti-imperialist, anti-masculinist, environmentalist and engaged with the meaning of new technologies from the internet to sexual reassignment surgery. Earlier socialist, materialist feminist theories looked to Marx and Engels' contention that class oppressions begin in the family and focused on such issues as the division of labour and women's unpaid housework and carework. Now Moghadam says that feminists seek to 'reinvent globalisation' from 'a *project of markets* to a *project of peoples*' (Moghadam 2005: 199). Global feminist theories see the men and women of developing countries and marginalised sectors within developed countries as oppressed and exploited by neo-imperialism and multinational capital in gendered ways. Thus global feminist theories call for 'coalition work' between first world women and women of the rest of the world, and also with men in progressive movements, while critiquing hegemonic masculinity as a bulwark of reactionary ideologies (Bulbeck 1998: 221). One example of a global feminist organisation generating new theories in response to current situations is Women Living under Muslim Laws (WLUML), founded in 1984. It focuses on 'the three themes of fundamentalisms, militarisation, and their impact on women's lives, and sexuality', while 'violence against women' is central to all of its projects. Like other contemporary feminist theorists, WLUML recognises that women's struggles are interconnected and complementary, and it therefore has a commitment to international solidarity (WLUML 2005).

At present there are many areas of convergence among feminist, queer, gender and masculinity theories, all of which will benefit from empirical studies and political practices to assess the theories' usefulness as guides for progressive social change. In the twenty-first century, feminism is one of the world's forces seeking greater equality among people, an end to dominations of all sorts, and a more just allocation of natural and human resources. At the same time, other social forces, chiefly multinational capitalism, neo-colonialisms, imperialisms and religious fundamentalisms, are increasing inequalities among people and exacerbating women's poverty and violence against women. Contemporary feminist theories attempt to analyse the resulting contradictions and suggest potential solutions.

References and further reading

Bulbeck, C. (1998) *Re-Orienting Western Feminisms*, Cambridge: Cambridge University Press.

Butler, J. (2004) *Undoing Gender*, New York and London: Routledge.

Enloe, C. (2004) *The Curious Feminist*, Berkeley, CA: University of California Press.

Gardiner, J.K. (ed.) (2002) *Masculinity Studies and Feminist Theory*, New York: Columbia University Press.

Kolmar, W.K. and Bartkowski, F. (eds) (2005) *Feminist Theory*, 2nd edn, Boston, MA: McGraw Hill.

MacKinnon, C.A. (2005) *Women's Lives, Men's Laws*, Cambridge, MA, and London: Belknap/Harvard University Press.

Moghadam, V.M. (2005) *Globalizing Women*, Baltimore, MD and London: Johns Hopkins University Press.

Murphy, P.F. (ed.) (2004) *Feminism and Masculinities*, Oxford: Oxford University Press.

Women Living under Muslim Laws (WLUML) (2005) at http://www.wluml.org/

See also: Marxism; postmodernism

JUDITH KEGAN GARDINER

FILM

Masculinity in film considers the representation of masculine characters in feature films, the personae of male stars and the marketing and publicity of those images.

The way males are represented in feature films has always been an issue for film studies because it is impossible to write about genre or stardom without considering male figures and their actions. But the genuine emergence, after occasional precursors, of a specific concern with masculinity may be dated from the appearance of an influential collection of essays, *Screening the Male* (ed. Cohan and Hark) in 1993, swiftly followed by two edited by Pat Kirkham and Janet Thumim, *You Tarzan* (1993) and *Me Jane* (1995), written by male and female academics respectively. These anthologies demonstrated the range and variety of masculinities occurring in both popular and 'art house' cinema and the necessity to subject these masculinities to close textual scrutiny as even apparently straightforward, taken-for-granted images revealed a surprising complexity. In doing so, these essays broke with the assumptions of earlier feminist analysis that tended to conceive masculinity as monolithic and self-confident, by revealing masculinity to be performative (socially and culturally constructed), fragile and often neurotic or paranoid. They also revealed how closely studies of masculinity and stardom are interwoven as the bodies, looks, performances and personae of male stars are central to how masculinity is represented.

Screening the Male's preoccupation with American cinema was reflected in several subsequent book-length studies, which subjected aspects of Hollywood's construction of masculinity to rigorous and detailed scrutiny. Gaylyn Studlar's *This Mad Masquerade* (1996) focused on contrasting stars – John Barrymore, Lon Chaney, Douglas Fairbanks and Rudolph Valentino – to demonstrate how they condensed and made available some of the sharply conflicting ideologies that characterised the 1920s 'Jazz Age'. Studies of genres included Frank Krutnik's *In a Lonely Street* (1991), an exploration of *film noir*, which has often been seen as the privileged site for portrayals of weak, corrupt or paranoid males, and Yvonne Tasker's *Spectacular Bodies* (1993), which focused on action genres and images of the hypermasculinised body-built male such as Arnold Schwarzenegger and Sylvester Stallone. There were also period studies, including Steven Cohan's *Masked Men* (1997), which scrutinised images of masculinity in the Fifties across a range of contrasting stars and genres situated within their wider cultural context.

The attention to Hollywood was inevitable and proper – the global presence of American popular cinema makes its representations of masculinity enormously influential – but, as with studies of genre, there was a tendency to conceive of American masculinities as an (albeit plural) norm. This has been challenged by studies of British and European cinema, which have demonstrated the national specificity of images of masculinity and the necessity to understand how those images work within particular cultures. Andrew Spicer's *Typical Men* (2001) used the concept of competing cultural types (such as the gentleman, the rebel and the damaged man) to map postwar British cinema's complex and conflicting constructions of masculinity; other essays focused on a post-Thatcher 'crisis' of masculinity in Nineties' British films. Phil Powrie's *French Cinema in the 1980s* (1997) located a similar crisis in French cinema of the 1980s, the result of the destabilisation of traditional male attitudes and assumptions without anything to replace them. Other studies focused on Spanish, Soviet and Italian cinema, notably Jacqueline Reich's *Beyond the Latin Lover* (2004), which revealed that beneath the conventional image of Marcello Mastroianni as the consummate Latin Lover lurked the *inetto* (the inept man), an anti-heroic figure, passive, sexually indifferent and alienated, expressing the contradictions and problems in postwar Italian society. *The Trouble with Men* (2004) underlined this increasing attention to European masculinity by devoting the majority of its essays to that topic, ranging over a number of countries and periods.

Several essays focused on the abject male body or explored homosexual images, a reflection of the emergence of gay and queer studies which can be dated from Richard Dyer's *Now You See It* (1990), a wide-ranging analysis of gay and lesbian cinema that was influential and inspiring. Other previously marginalised concerns in film studies, including black, Asian and Third World cinemas, have also become firmly established topics, generating studies of masculinity which include Kyung Hyun Kim's *The Remasculinization of Korean Cinema* (2004) charting the shifting filmic masculinities in a country experiencing profound social and cultural change.

The range and specificity of these studies shows the increasing importance of masculinity on film and how far its study has evolved from an earlier ahistorical, over-determinist psychoanalytical approach. The works cited here are characterised by their sophisticated use of theory, a nuanced attention to the complexities of masculine representations on film, and their determination to situate those representations within their social, political, cultural and historical contexts. These include the operations of the film industry itself – the ways in which studios, producers, directors, stars and marketing departments attempt to control or influence how males are depicted, as well as the external pressures of official interventions and agendas (including censorship) which reflect broader ideologies. Much work remains to be done, not only encompassing other national cinemas and periods and stars, but also giving increased attention to the complex and highly problematic reception of masculinity by cinema audiences.

References and further reading

Cohan, S. (1997) *Masked Men*, Bloomington, IN: Indiana University Press.

Cohan, S. and Hark, I.R. (eds) (1993) *Screening the Male*, London: Routledge.

Dyer, R. (1990) *Now You See It*, London: Routledge.

Kim, K.H. (2004) *The Remasculinization of Korean Cinema*, Durham, NC: Duke University Press.

Kirkham, P. and Thumim, J. (eds) (1993) *You Tarzan*, London: Lawrence and Wishart.

—— (eds) (1995) *Me Jane*, London: Lawrence and Wishart.

Powrie, P. (1997) *French Cinema in the 1980s*, Oxford: Clarendon.

Powrie, P., Davies, A. and Babington, B. (eds) (2004) *The Trouble with Men*, London: Wallflower.

Reich, J. (2004) *Beyond the Latin Lover*, Bloomington, IN: Indiana University Press.

Spicer, A. (2001) *Typical Men*, London: I.B. Tauris.

Studlar, G. (1996) *This Mad Masquerade*, New York: Columbia University Press.

Tasker, Y. (1993) *Spectacular Bodies*, London: Routledge.

ANDREW SPICER

FOOTBALL

Football is a competitive and highly commercialised sport played out in various forms at both amateur and professional levels. Prefixes include: Association, American and Australian. As the most established variety, Association Football (soccer) has long since been identified with a hyper-masculine, working-class Englishness (Critcher 1979). Viewed either in terms of its occupational or its social characteristics, football is a strictly gendered affair. Its relational dynamics, its working practices, its commercial ventures are replete with images of maleness.

Like other modern-day sports (e.g. rugby), football was codified within the all-male English public schools of the mid-nineteenth century; a time (in Britain at least) when sporting practice was regarded as a training ground for the development of moral character, physical health and military and colonial pre-eminence (Mangan 1981). The key protagonist here was Thomas Arnold of Rugby School, whose beliefs in the combined benefits of religious purity and physical exertion (subsequently termed 'muscular Christianity') transformed pre-industrial (folk) football into a more regulated and ordered activity whilst also serving to re-validate masculine norms amidst the perceived feminisation of a rapidly changing society (Crossett 1990). In turn, football established its own formal playing code and governing organisation. The Football Association (FA) was formed in the 1860s, at the same time as the Rugby Football Union, each body framing the rules, regulations and procedures that were to shape their respective sports.

English professional football is a social setting that openly despises deviation from heterosexual orientation on the part of its participants, embracing and manifesting an aggressive, almost virulent conception of masculinity alongside a sharp-edged and highly sexist humour. Despite the global influences that have changed the way in which football has been organised and played out in recent years, and the affluent circumstances of its top stars, its embedded sense of working-class 'manliness' remains pervasive (Cashmore and Parker 2003).

References and further reading

Cashmore, E. and Parker, A. (2003) '"One David Beckham ... ?" Celebrity, masculinity and the socceratti', *Sociology of Sport Journal*, 20 (3): 214–32.

Critcher, C. (1979) 'Football since the war', in J. Clarke, C. Critcher and R. Johnson (eds) *Working Class Culture*, London: Hutchinson, pp. 161–84.

Crossett, T. (1990) 'Masculinity, sexuality and the development of early modern sport', in M.A. Messner and D.F. Sabo (eds) *Sport, Men and the Gender Order*, Champaign, IL: Human Kinetics Press, pp. 45–54.

Mangan, J.A. (1981) *Athleticism in the Victorian and Edwardian Public Schools*, Cambridge: Cambridge University Press.

See also: sport, athletes and athletic training; sports literature, sportscasting; violence, sport

ANDREW PARKER

FRATERNITIES

Fraternities are exclusive all-male clubs to promote socialising and 'brotherhood' among college students and to form networks to aid alumni after graduation. Most fraternities employ either two or three Greek letters as a name. The oldest fraternity in the United States, for instance, is called Kappa Alpha (KA); others include Chi Phi (CΦ), Delta Kappa Epsilon (ΔKE), and Alpha Delta Phi (AΔΦ). Originating in the United States (but with chapters in Canada and the Philippines as well), most fraternities are 'nationals': they have numerous chapters on different college campuses all belonging to the same national organisation. Each also has a coordinating national office. Some fraternities are 'locals', in that they do not have affiliated chapters at other schools. Most fraternities employ ritual and secrecy to solemnise the bonds that unite the 'brothers'; an initiation ceremony whereby pledgers become brothers is the most obvious example of this phenomenon. Since their founding, men in fraternities have been concerned with their masculinity; the regulation of membership is one method whereby they have established themselves as the pinnacle of masculinity on many college campuses.

Fraternities were founded in 1825 at Union College in Schenectady, New York, and modelled themselves in part after ritualistic fraternal organisations like the Freemasons, an organisation that had its roots in Europe, as well as Phi Beta Kappa, an academic honour society originally founded as a college literary and debate club in Virginia in 1776. Fraternities developed as a means for young men to socialise with each other outside the purview of the faculty who taught and supervised them. They allowed students to assert a manly sense of independence in the face of faculty regulation and served as a venue for debating the current issues and literature that were not addressed by college curricula. Because fraternities were outlawed on most college campuses and seen as sacrilegious by their ministerial faculty, fraternities soon became the bastions of wealthy students who were not training for the ministry. By the second half of the nineteenth century, wealth had become one of the prime criteria for membership.

Fraternities also valued good looks and athletic success as they selected their members. All of these criteria were evaluated in gendered terms as being particularly manly (Syrett 2005).

By the late nineteenth and early twentieth centuries, as the children of immigrants as well as small numbers of African Americans began to arrive on campuses that had been almost exclusively white, male and Protestant until that point, fraternities solidified the boundaries of their membership (and their manhood), enacting strict regulations that forbade the initiation of any man who was not white and Protestant. As a result, the first Jewish fraternity (Pi Lambda Phi) was founded in 1895 at Yale, the first Catholic fraternity (Phi Kappa Sigma) in 1889 at Brown, the first black fraternity (Alpha Phi Alpha) in 1906 at Cornell, and the first fraternity for Chinese students (Rho Psi) in 1916, also at Cornell. While emphasising many of the same ideals of masculinity as the predominantly white fraternities – good looks, wealth and athletic success – these organisations enrolled men that the others excluded (see Sanua 2003 and Horowitz 1987).

By the 1920s, fraternities had assumed the form on college campuses that they still occupy today. During this first era of mass education and increasing coeducation, enrolment in colleges and in fraternities boomed. Many colleges and universities relied upon fraternities (and their female counterparts, sororities) to supply housing and social programming for undergraduates (Turk 2004; Fass 1977). Those who were asked to join were generally the most popular students on campus. As dating replaced home-based and parent-supervised forms of courtship, men from the top fraternities dated women from the top sororities in unsupervised outings. Most people on campus were well aware of how such a hierarchy was constituted: as the most exclusive organisations on campus, fraternities largely controlled the social scene. As standards for sexual behaviour became more permissive – and, not incidentally, as women asserted more power on campus – fraternity men incorporated sexual success into their enactment of masculinity. The man who was most popular with his female classmates and was able to go furthest sexually gained the most approbation from his fraternity brothers. This trend continued throughout the twentieth century, gaining greater momentum during and after the sexual revolution of the 1960s, which only increased the pressure upon fraternity men to achieve sexual success with their classmates (Syrett 2005).

In more recent years, college administrators have criticised fraternities for their dangerous hazing initiation rites and binge drinking, both of which serve as tests of masculinity and loyalty for brothers (Nuwer 1999). Feminists have criticised many fraternities' emphasis upon hypersexuality and its consequences for the construction of masculinity, particularly in relation to rape and coercive sexual relations. In so doing, they have noted a number of interrelated phenomena in which many fraternity men engage: group viewing of pornography, gang rapes, mandatory sexual history reporting, homoerotic hazing and virulent homophobia (Sanday 1990). In tandem with the rise of 'the homosexual' as an identity category, the intimacy and affection fostered through brotherhood has led many fraternity men to disavow the possibility of homosexuality among their ranks by enacting a homophobic and sexually exploitative masculinity (Syrett 2005).

References and further reading

Fass, P. (1977) *The Damned and the Beautiful*, New York: Oxford University Press.

Horowitz, H.L. (1987) *Campus Life*, New York: Knopf.

James, A.W. (2000) 'The college social fraternity antidiscrimination debate, 1945–1949', *The Historian*, 62 (2): 303–24.

Nuwer, H. (1999) *Wrongs of Passage*, Indianapolis, IN: Indiana University Press.

Sanday, P.R. (1990) *Fraternity Gang Rape*, New York: New York University Press.

Sanua, M. (2003) *Going Greek*, Detroit, MI: Wayne State University Press.

Schwartz, M.D. and DeKeseredy, W.S. (1997) *Sexual Assault on the College Campus*, Thousand Oaks, CA: Sage.
Syrett, N.L. (2005) 'The company he keeps: white college fraternities, masculinity, and power, 1825–1975', PhD dissertation, University of Michigan.
Turk, D.B. (2004) *Bound by a Mighty Vow*, New York: New York University Press.

See also: men's relations with men

NICHOLAS L. SYRETT

FRATRIARCHY

Fratriarchy is a fusion of 'patriarchy' and 'fraternity' and involves the rule of brotherhoods or fraternities, as opposed to patriarchy's rule of fathers. Fratriarchy in its marriage to patriarchy forms androcracy, rule by men (Remy 1990). Remy proposes that it is a mode of male domination, based on the self-interest of the association of men itself (Remy 1990). Fratriarchy is placed, alongside patriarchy, in the 'men's hut', the place of male power which rigidly excludes women.

Others see fratriarchy as the public form of patriarchy, a form of competitive bonding that keeps things in the family of men (Hearn 1992). Thus, the relationship between patriarchy and fratriarchy is overlapping and asymmetrical. Hearn, for instance, describes bureaucracies as mixtures of patriarchal and fratriarchal organisations, where men meet in fratriarchies, but relate through patriarchal hierarchies (Hearn 1992).

Fratriarchy's 'competitive bonding' is based on a fictitious kinship in brotherhoods or fraternities. These can be found for example in male pub culture, hooliganism, bookmakers, college fraternities, political institutions, managerial boards, sporting teams, working men's clubs, the army, street gangs, scientific societies, boarding schools, or marauding youths during a war. Often there are rites of passage and initiation ceremonies involved and rightful membership needs to be proven time and again. Collinson (1995) and Lyman (1987) give examples of the pressures of the fraternal bond's joke culture, where rule-governed aggression is used to test the individual's 'coolness'. Other examples are drinking contests (see English 'lager louts' in Remy (1990) or gang rapes, which Hood (1995) analyses as adolescent male-bonding rituals). She points out that the boys in question had learned that to be masculine means to dominate others through sex and violence, i.e. to exert the rule of the brothers. Remy (1990: 45) adds the notion of deviance when he states that '[fratriarchy] reflects the demand of a group of lads to have the "freedom" to do as they please'.

References and further reading

Collinson, D.L. (1995) '"Engineering humour": masculinity, joking and conflict in shop-floor relations', in M. Kimmel and M. Messner (eds) *Men's Lives*, New York: Macmillan, pp. 164–75.
Hearn, J. (1992) *Men in the Public Eye*, London: Routledge.
Hood, J.C. (1995) '"Let's get a girl": male bonding rituals in America', in M. Kimmel and M. Messner (eds) *Men's Lives*, New York: Macmillan, pp. 307–11.
Lyman, P. (1987) 'The fraternal bond as a joking relationship', in M. Kimmel (ed.) *Changing Men*, Newbury Park, CA: Sage, pp. 148–63.
Remy, J. (1990) 'Patriarchy and fratriarchy as forms of androcracy', in J. Hearn and D. Morgan (eds) *Men, Masculinities and Social Theory*, London: Unwin Hyman, pp. 43–54.

See also: men's relations with men

KATHLEEN STARCK

FRIENDSHIP

There are at least two ways in which friendship relates to masculinity. First, men bring masculinity to their friendships. In other words, men's unique ways of acting, thinking and feeling influence how men develop friendships and interact with friends. Second, men individually and collectively develop and maintain masculinity in their friendships. As a consequence, friendships influence other aspects of men's lives such as family and work.

Our focus in this essay is on the former perspective – how men express masculinity in their friendships. Ethnographers have studied male friendships in a variety of specific contexts, such as Whyte's (1943) description of the friendship among a group of working-class Italian American men in *Street Corner Society*, Liebow's (1967) account of the relationships among the unemployed African-American men who spent time at *Tally's Corner*, and Duneier's (1994) portrayal of the interracial friendships among the retired working-class men in Chicago who ate regularly at the Valois Restaurant where *Slim's Table* was located. In this essay, however, we draw primarily on other social scientific studies, which were designed to make generalisations about men's friendships. Most of these studies included both men and women and attempted to identify gender differences in specific aspects of friendships. Many researchers limited their study scope to same-sex friendships in part because both men's and women's friendship networks tend to be gender homogeneous. Therefore, we focus on men's friendships with other men, although we briefly discuss men's experiences in cross-sex friendships.

Size of men's friendship networks

Network size is the most fundamental characteristic of friendship structure. Although findings are not completely consistent across studies, men seem to have larger friendship networks than women. For example, using a national sample of Canadian adults, de Vries (1991) reported that men have a greater number of close friends but fewer kin members in their personal networks, compared to women.

As men move from middle to later stages of life course, their friendship networks change in size. In de Vries' (1991) study, women's friendship networks start to increase when children leave home and continue to increase gradually throughout the later part of the life course. In contrast, men experience an increase right after launching children but then a decrease throughout the rest of the later life course. This shrinkage experienced by older men most likely results from their declining opportunities to make friends at work. Women, in contrast, experience a reduction in household obligations, which provides them with more opportunities to develop and maintain friendships. It is also possible that men's friendship networks shrink in late stages of life course due to their fading desire to engage in social activities and make new friends.

Interactive aspects of men's friendships

Consistent with the findings on network size, many studies have found that during middle adulthood, men have more frequent face-to-face contact with their friends than women do, although men do not call or write to friends as frequently as women. When they are older adults, however, men have less frequent contact with friends than women. Retirement may reduce men's opportunities to engage in friendship activities as well as reducing their network size. The diminishing contact with friends may also be attributed to what men do with their friends. Men's friendships are maintained through joint activities, in contrast to women's friendships maintained through confiding. This emphasis on shared activities among men becomes even more pronounced when men are older adults. Therefore, it may be more difficult for men to participate in joint activities than for women to continue confiding.

Men's friendship activities tend to take place in certain situational contexts. In his study of Toronto residents, Wellman (1992) noted that men engage in friendship activities in dyads or small groups. Contrasting his data to the findings reported before his, Wellman also argued that the context of men's friendships has moved from public places to private homes, and married men's friendships are now managed by their wives.

Among various types of friendship activities, talk is the most frequently studied.

Compared to women, men disclose their personal information and feelings to friends less frequently. Furthermore, men discuss topics such as sports, business and politics with friends, whereas women talk to friends about relational and personal matters. These conversation patterns are consistent with emotional aspects of men's friendships; men are less emotionally intimate with friendships than women (Wright and Scanlon 1991).

A few factors contribute to this gender difference. First, men do not think, to the same extent women do, that self-disclosure contributes to intimacy in friendships. In addition, the competitiveness in men's friendships discourages them from disclosing personal information, so they can maintain their power in the relationships. Men also tend to think that their friends would not respond positively to or reciprocate self-disclosure.

One needs to be cautious about how to interpret men's lower level of self-disclosure because most previous studies relied on men's (and women's) self-reporting of self-disclosure. In a qualitative study, Walker (1995) observed that men do disclose their personal information to their friends and share feelings, but they tend to underestimate this feminine aspect of their friendships. In this way, men can maintain their image of friendships that are consistent with their gender expectations. Walker's argument is consistent with the findings of other studies; men do confide in friends and trust their friends.

Cross-sex friendships

So far we have discussed patterns of men's friendships with other men, as compared to women's friendships with other women. Although the friendship literature has traditionally focused on same-sex friendships, researchers have recently begun to examine the prevalence and characteristics of opposite-sex friendships (Monsour 2001).

Both men's and women's friendship networks increase in sex homogeneity during young adulthood and maintain it during most of their adulthood. The gender composition of men's friendships is more likely to be affected by stage of the life course, however. For example, the proportion of female friends in men's friendship networks increases in late life stages, whereas women maintain high sex homogeneity in their friendship networks. This increasing sex heterogeneity in older men's friendship networks may result from their greater need for support particularly from female friends as well as men's shorter life span, which reduces the number of potential male friends within the age group.

As described above, men and women approach friendships differently, and these differences create problems in cross-sex friendships. For example, McWilliams and Howard (1993) argued that men assume women to be social and communal due to their stereotypes of women, and women perceive male friends as instrumental and competitive. These stereotypes may create an impression that men and women pull their opposite-sex friendships in different directions – men wanting the friendships to be instrumental and hierarchical and women wanting the friendships to be emotionally intimate. In addition, cross-sex friendships may have a greater risk of creating imbalance in social support exchange, compared to same-sex friendships. In the above-mentioned Toronto study by Wellman (1992), for example, men received emotional support from both male and female friends, whereas women receive emotional support mostly from their female friends. Despite these difficulties, cross-sex friendships have some unique benefits for both men and women. For example, cross-sex friendships provide men with opportunities to learn how to develop emotionality.

Cross-cultural differences

Owing to the very small number of cross-cultural studies, little is known about how men's friendship patterns vary across countries. An exception is Bruckner and Knaup's (1993) analysis of friendship patterns in five countries, including the US, Great Britain, Germany, Italy and Hungary. The study showed that gender variations are much smaller than cultural variations in terms of network size, composition and frequency of visiting. Moreover, not many culture-specific gender differences were found. Theoretically, however, one would expect some cultural variations in men's friendships patterns or culture-specific gender differences. Men's social positions, relative to women's, vary considerably across cultures, and those structural differences are likely to influence how men and women develop and maintain friendships. Perhaps a comparison between Western and non-Western countries is necessary to demonstrate such cultural differences. Although some friendship research has been conducted in non-Western countries, these studies have not included examinations of gender differences.

Future research

Previous friendship studies have generated considerable knowledge, but there are still some limitations in the current literature. First, very few studies included more than one age group in the samples or examined changes in friendships over time. Consequently, little is known about how men's friendships change over time and over the life course. Related to this issue, there are many studies that examine college students only. These studies often make implicit assumptions that gender differences among college students apply to non-college populations and other age groups. The assumption has rarely been tested. Second, the current literature provides information on how men's friendships differ from women's, but it tells little about how friendships vary across different groups of men, although there are some excellent exceptions, which describe friendship patterns among gay men (Nardi 1992a), African-American men (Franklin 1992) and working- versus middle-class men (Walker 1995). Third, researchers frequently fail to develop explanations for the gender differences that they report. In future studies, it will be important to identify how men's friendship patterns result from the social positions they occupy within society, from their psychological dispositions, and from the interplay between these two aspects of gender (see Adams *et al.* 2004, for an example of a framework which can guide such studies).

Finally, as some authors have pointed out (e.g., Adams and Berggren 2004; Nardi 1992b), the friendship literature has been feminised or is lacking topics important to the understanding of men's friendships. That is, researchers tend to examine gender differences in aspects of friendships that are more common among women (e.g. satisfaction, intimacy). To understand men's friendships fully, we need to formulate research questions differently. Instead of relying on concepts of friendship characteristics repeatedly used in the current literature, researchers first need to identify what processes and structures may characterise men's friendships and then test whether they distinguish men's friendships from women's.

References and further reading

Adams, R.G. and Berggren, J.M. (2004) 'The influence of female scholars on the literature on older adult friendship', presented at the Meetings of the International Association of Relationship Researchers, Madison, WI, 22–25 July.

Adams, R.G., Ueno, K. and Blieszner, R. (2004) 'The Adams–Blieszner–Ueno integrative conceptual framework for friendship research', unpublished manuscript.

Bruckner, E. and Knaup, K. (1993) 'Women's and men's friendships in comparative perspective', *European Sociological Review*, 9: 249–66.

de Vries, B. (1991) 'Friendship and kinship patterns over the life course', *Caring Communities Proceedings of the Symposium on Social Supports*, Statistics Canada, Catalogue No. 89–514, pp. 99–107.

Duneier, M. (1994) *Slim's Table*, Chicago, IL: University of Chicago Press.

Franklin, C.W. (1992) 'Hey, home – yo, bro', in P.M. Nardi (ed.) *Men's Friendships*, Newbury Park, CA: Sage, pp. 201–14.

Liebow, E. (1967) *Tally's Corner*, Boston, MA: Little Brown.

McWilliams, S. and Howard, J.A. (1993) 'Solidarity and hierarchy in cross-sex friendships', *Journal of Social Issues*, 49: 191–202.
Monsour, M. (2001) *Women and Men as Friends*, Mahwah, NJ: Lawrence Erlbaum.
Nardi, P.M. (1992a) 'Sex, friendships, and gender roles amongst gay men', in P.M. Nardi (ed.) *Men's Friendships*, Newbury Park, CA: Sage, pp. 173–85.
—— (1992b) 'Seamless souls', in P.M. Nardi (ed.) *Men's Friendships*, Newbury Park, CA: Sage, pp. 1–14.
Walker, K. (1995) 'Always there for me', *Sociological Forum*, 10: 273–96.
Wellman, B. (1992) 'Men in networks', in P.M. Nardi (ed.) *Men's Friendships*, Newbury Park, CA: Sage, pp. 74–114.
Whyte, W.F. (1943) *Street Corner Society*, Chicago, IL: University of Chicago Press.
Wright, P.H. and Scanlon, M.B. (1991) 'Gender role orientations and friendship', *Sex Roles*, 24: 551–66.

See also: intimacy; maleship; men's relations with men

KOJI UENO
REBECCA G. ADAMS

G

GANGS

The idea of 'the gang', both in the academic and popular imagination, is an essentially masculine one, conjuring up often over-romanticised notions of collective male solidarities, belonging and struggle. Although there has been evidence of the existence and rising significance of 'girl gangs' (Campbell 1984), it is estimated that in the US women constitute around 10 per cent of 'gang' membership (and this is likely to be even lower elsewhere), often joining for shorter periods of time and occupying secondary status, with minimal involvement in gang activities (Spergel 1995).

Maleness is then a key definitional feature of 'the gang', along with age and socio-economic, ethnic or racial minority status. 'Gangs' are usually associated with 'youth' (aged sixteen to twenty-five), although this category has been stretched to include individuals as young as ten or twelve and as old as thirty years or above. 'Gangs' can be found across different parts of the world, from the United States to Europe, South America to South Africa, Australia to China (Klein 1995). They are also found among a range of racial and ethnic groups – for example, in America the focus has been on Irish, African–American, (East and South-East) Asian and Hispanic 'gangs'; in the UK on 'Yardies' and (South) Asian 'gangs'; across northern Europe on Turkish, Moroccan and Pakistani 'gangs'. However, what constitutes a 'gang' varies widely in terms of definition from country to country, between ethnic groups, or between different institutions working with 'gangs'. This makes conceptual clarity and comparison very problematic, since 'gangs' take very different shapes in different national, ethnic or local contexts.

The dominant arena for research on 'gangs' is the United States, and it is from this work that key definitive criteria are usually drawn. Although at its broadest, the term 'gang' has been viewed as synonymous with 'group', the term has been used more usually and specifically to refer to young men in urban and public spaces. The public, everyday, 'street' nature of 'the gang' is what distinguishes it from other forms of male group identity, such as football 'firms', fraternities, clubs, mobs or highly focused groupings such as skinheads or motorcycle gangs (although these latter two exclusions are contentious, cf. Spergel 1995).

Sociological research on 'gangs' finds its roots in work of the Chicago School in early twentieth-century America. The most famous of these is Thrasher's 1927 study *The Gang*, which examined 1,313 juvenile gangs in Chicago. The primary explanation of this 'social ecological' approach was that in environments characterised by marginalisation and social disorganisation, 'gangs' served to bolster self-esteem and provide an important source of social support in the transitional period between childhood and adulthood. In these classic approaches, the 'gang' has a range of key features. It is associated with processes of urban migration, and arises in areas of weak social organisation. The gang is defined through its exclusion from full participation in mainstream society, and is often linked to minority status. It has boundaries formed through competition for control over territory and an internal, hierarchical structure with clearly defined roles and loyalty reinforced through conflict. Finally, the gang is a locus for identity production, with distinct subcultural features (name, rituals, dress and language).

Increasingly, however, from the post-war period onwards, many gang researchers have insisted on an additional feature – that of criminal activity and delinquency – as an essential element of 'gang' development (Klein 1995; Spergel 1995). Studies which emerged in the 1950s and 1960s shifted 'gang' research away from the sociology of youth into criminology (Katz and Jackson Jacobs 2003). These studies saw 'gangs' as groups of individuals who come together around a set of deviant values and lifestyles in which violence and crime are central (Cloward and Ohlin 1960; Cohen 1955; Matza 1964). 'Gangs' were understood as a reaction to the failure to accommodate middle-class norms and values – what is known as 'strain theory'. This failure is compounded by the blocking of opportunities for marginalised young men to achieve mainstream success, leading them to retreat to an exaggerated (and illusory) performance of masculine strength signalled through violence (Yablonsky 1962).

Since the 1970s, these more quantitative and theoretically oriented accounts of 'the gang' have been replaced with a proliferation of qualitative empirical studies that have explored the diversity of 'gang' life and experience. On the one hand, the proliferation of 'gangs' throughout the 1990s has been linked to the growth of organised crime, particularly around drugs distribution, and has become an increasing focus of criminal justice policy and social control. On the other hand, empirical studies of 'gangs' across the globe have pointed to the wide variety of ways in how 'gangs' are formed and operate, and have contested any clear meaning to the term. Some researchers have argued that it is this breadth and complexity that is the primary significance of 'the gang' (Horowitz 1990; Jankowski 1991), while others have argued that this renders the concept useless as an explanatory framework (Klein 1995; Spergel 1995).

References and further reading

Campbell, A. (1984) *The Girls in the Gang*, Oxford: Blackwell.

Cloward, R.A. and Ohlin, L.E. (1960) *Delinquency and Opportunity: A Theory of Delinquent Gangs*, Glencoe, IL: Free Press.

Cohen, A. (1955) *Delinquent Boys: The Culture of the Gang*, Glencoe, IL: Free Press.

Horowitz, R. (1990) 'Sociological perspectives on gangs: conflicting definitions and concepts', in A.P. Goldstein and C.R. Huff (eds) *Gangs in America*, Champaign, IL: Research Press, pp. 37–54.

Jankowski, M.S. (1991) *Islands in the Stream: Gangs and American Urban Society*, Berkeley, CA: University of California Press.

Katz, J. and Jackson Jacobs, C. (2003) 'The criminologists' gang', in C. Sumner (ed.) *The Blackwell Companion to Criminology*, Oxford: Blackwell, pp. 91–124.

Klein, M. (1995) *The American Street Gang: Its Nature, Prevalence and Control*, New York and Oxford: Oxford University Press.

Matza, D. (1964) *Delinquency and Drift*, New York: John Wiley.

Spergel, I.A. (1995) *The Youth Gang Problem: A Community Approach*, New York and Oxford: Oxford University Press.

Thrasher, F. (1927) *The Gang*, Chicago, IL: University of Chicago Press.

Yablonsky, L. (1962) *The Violent Gang*, New York: Macmillan.

See also: crime; criminality, the law; violence

CLAIRE ALEXANDER

GAY AND LESBIAN STUDIES

In the behavioural and social sciences, gay and lesbian studies refers to theory and empirical inquiry that addresses the experiences and development of lesbian and gay people. In the past decade, it has also come to include scholarship on bisexual individuals. Most of this work has been conducted in the fields of sociology, psychology, anthropology and gender studies, but significant contributions have also come from other academic fields, including political science and economics.

Research conducted under the umbrella of gay and lesbian studies incorporates a variety of techniques, both qualitative (e.g. structured interviews, focus groups) and quantitative (e.g. survey questionnaires, laboratory experiments). Because many sexual minority individuals are reluctant to disclose their sexual orientation to researchers, probability samples are difficult to obtain, and consequently most empirical research has utilised convenience samples of volunteers recruited through gay community venues. The extent to which these individuals represent the entire sexual minority population is unknown.

Although research in gay and lesbian studies is diverse, one of its main objectives is to gain a better understanding of human sexuality and gender, including the power dynamics involved. Research has been particularly helpful in accurately documenting conditions in society (e.g., economic discrimination, commitment in same-sex relationships) and refuting the stereotypes used to justify discrimination, thus improving the lives of non-heterosexual individuals. Research in this area explores numerous topics including the nature, prevalence and origins of sexual orientations; how sexual identity is defined and develops; sexual prejudice and its effects on the well-being of sexual minorities; and intimate relationships among people of the same sex.

Prevalence and origins of sexual orientations

Sexual orientation can be defined as an enduring pattern or disposition to experience sexual, affectional or romantic attractions primarily to men, to women, or to both. It also refers to an individual's sense of personal and social identity based on those attractions, behaviours expressing them, and membership in a community of others who share them. Even though the concept of sexual orientation applies to both heterosexuality and homosexuality, early work on sexuality emphasised those who deviated from a heterosexual norm, thereby focusing research on homosexuality. However, recent theorising and empirical work recognise the importance of studying all sexual orientations.

Throughout the twentieth century, sexuality research was dominated by a medical model that pathologised non-procreative sexual behaviours. Early empirical research and theoretical models emphasised preventing and curing non-heterosexual sexual expression. In the early 1950s, however, the view that homosexuality is pathological was increasingly challenged. Kinsey's studies of male and female sexuality showed that homosexual behaviour was much more common in American society than previously assumed (see Morin 1977). Ford and Beach documented non-heterosexual behaviour across species and in different human cultures. In 1957, Hooker's landmark study reported no differences in psychological functioning between gay and heterosexual men.

Research exploring the origins of sexual orientation has a long history that has relied variously on psychodynamic, learning, ethological, hormonal and genetic models, among others. Current debates about the roots of homosexuality and heterosexuality often pit biological against social explanations. Biological arguments have attempted to document linkages between adult sexual orientation and birth order, sibling sexual orientation, specific brain structures (e.g. in the hypothalamus) and patterns of hormonal response, among other factors. By contrast, proponents of social constructionism have argued that sexual orientation and its component identities are entirely products of culture, with the meaning, experiences, and consequences attached to sexual attractions and behaviours created by social consensus within individual societies. According to this view, in cultures that have defined categories for sexual orientation, people learn what it means to be heterosexual and homosexual by adopting the sexual scripts of those around them. Empirical studies conducted to date have not yielded conclusive evidence that sexual orientation is determined by any particular factor or factors. It is possible that future research will ultimately reveal multiple pathways to adult sexual orientation.

Understanding sexual identity

Homosexuality has many dimensions, including (a) sexual attraction and desire for people of the same sex; (b) sexual behaviour with members of the same sex; (c) personal identities based on one's homosexuality; (d) intimate same-sex relationships and families based on them; and (e) membership in communities based on shared sexual orientation. Thus, homosexuality specifically and sexual orientation generally are operationally defined in varied ways. Definition and measurement concerns include how to accurately assess sexual orientation (e.g. through emotional desire or sexual behaviour) and whether sexual orientation is a single bipolar (heterosexuality vs homosexuality) construct or comprises multiple attributes that can vary independently.

The meanings attached to sexual behaviour vary across time and cultures. Historically, for example, in Greece and Rome, male same-sex relationships helped maintain power and status; in China, adult–youth homoerotic relations occurred principally among the male elite; and two women married to the same man in northern Africa and the Middle East may have developed intimate, sexual relationships with each other as well. Furthermore, cross-culturally, in various New Guinea societies, male adolescents are expected to engage in sexual behaviour with older boys and men as part of their development into manhood; in the African culture of Lesotho, older women ('mummies') develop intimate, sometimes sexual, relationships with younger women ('babies') to help prepare the latter for their future husband; and in many indigenous North American cultures, revered 'two-spirits', were viewed as blessed to be a third sex (man-woman) and took on social and sexual roles contrary to their biological sex. In contemporary Western societies, sexual and affectional preferences and behaviour have come to define identity, especially for individuals who do not fit the heterosexual norm. However, even in contemporary Western societies, considerable variability exists among gay men and lesbians in the development and understanding of their sexual identity. The ways in which sexual behaviour and identity are expressed are greatly influenced by cultural expectations of heterosexuality and the stigma surrounding non-heterosexual manifestations of sexuality.

Sexual prejudice and its effects

Although society's attitudes towards lesbians, gay men and bisexuals have become more tolerant recently, substantial numbers of heterosexuals continue to express antigay hostility and believe that sexual minorities should be treated differently from heterosexuals by some of society's major institutions. For example, most American adults oppose discrimination against gay men and lesbians in employment and housing but are unwilling to allow same-sex couples to adopt children or legally marry. Violence against sexual minorities continues to be widespread. These individual attitudes are reflected in society's institutions, many of which exclude or denigrate sexual minority individuals and communities.

As a consequence of living in an often hostile social environment, lesbian, gay and bisexual individuals are routinely exposed to a variety of stressors not experienced by heterosexuals. Such stressors range from violence and discrimination based on one's sexual orientation to experiences of subtle avoidance and ostracism. Although most gay men, lesbians and bisexuals cope effectively with these challenges and remain psychologically healthy, experiencing minority stress creates problems for some sexual minority individuals. It may manifest in heightened levels of depression, anxiety, and substance abuse and other self-destructive behaviours. However, involvement with and support from the gay and lesbian community can help reduce the detrimental effects of minority stress.

To avoid the consequences of societal stigma, many lesbian, gay and bisexual individuals conceal their sexual orientation from others. Even though hiding one's sexual orientation can be logistically difficult (especially for sexual minority individuals who violate gender roles) and can create psychological distress, it can also offer protection from violence, discrimination and rejection. Consequently, most lesbian, gay and bisexual individuals find they must develop skills for managing the reactions of others during social interactions and must continually assess the costs and benefits of disclosure in new situations and settings.

Lesbian, gay or bisexual individuals may choose to disclose or conceal depending upon the environmental context (e.g. social vs workplace setting) and audience (e.g. close friends vs acquaintances). For example, they may choose to disclose in order to reduce the stress that comes with concealment, to improve intimacy in an interpersonal relationship, to resolve an existing or anticipated problem or issue (e.g. continually explaining why one is not married), or to bring about social or political change by educating others. In addition, sometimes disclosures may occur spontaneously or via a third party. Other individuals may conceal their sexual orientation for many of the same reasons (e.g. to protect an interpersonal relationship; for political or social reasons) or to avoid violence and negative social sanctions. However, many scholars, activists and health care professionals believe that disclosure of one's sexual orientation fosters a healthy gay or lesbian identity and can help to reduce anti-gay prejudice. Heterosexuals who have personal contact with an openly gay person (e.g. a close friend, a family member) tend to be more tolerant and accepting of gay men and lesbians.

Lesbian and gay male couples

Empirical research on gay and lesbian couples in the United States first burgeoned in the early 1980s. Findings from this research indicate that many gay men and lesbians successfully form stable, long-lasting, committed relationships whose psychological and social characteristics closely resemble those of heterosexuals. Although heterosexual and homosexual couples alike manifest substantial variability, they overlap considerably on such factors as the level of intimacy, equity and satisfaction within the relationship.

An emerging field of inquiry in gay and lesbian studies addresses gay and lesbian parenting and families. Increasing numbers of gay male and lesbian couples are adopting children, bearing them through donor insemination or surrogate mothering, or raising children from prior heterosexual marriages. Research in this area has found no reliable differences between children raised by lesbians or gay men versus heterosexual parents in terms of psychological (e.g. self-esteem), emotional (e.g. anxiety, depression), behavioural (e.g. conduct problems) and social (e.g. friendships) well-being. Nor does empirical research suggest that having a gay or lesbian parent has a harmful effect on children's sexual identity, gender identity or social gender role development.

Although their relationship dynamics are similar to those of heterosexual couples, gay and lesbian couples may experience more problems because of societal stigma. These challenges may include difficulty in finding relationship partners, lack of legal and institutional recognition of their relationship, and issues concerning whether or not both partners have disclosed their sexual orientation to others. However, research suggests that social and family support can help to reduce this strain on gay and lesbian relationships.

References and further reading

Bohan, J.S. (1996) *Psychology and Sexual Orientation*, New York: Routledge.
D'Augelli, A.R. and Patterson, C.J. (eds) (1995) *Lesbian, Gay, and Bisexual Identities over the Lifespan*, New York: Oxford University Press.
Foucault, M. (1990) *The History of Sexuality, Vol. 1*, trans. R. Hurley, New York: Vintage.
Garnets, L.D. and Kimmel, D.C. (eds) (2003) *Psychological Perspectives on Lesbian, Gay, and Bisexual Experiences*, 2nd edn, New York: Columbia University Press.
Greene, B. and Herek, G.M. (eds) (1994) *Lesbian and Gay Psychology*, Thousand Oaks, CA: Sage.
Herdt, G. (1997) *Same Sex, Different Cultures*, Boulder, CO: Westview.
Herek, G.M. (ed.) (1998) *Stigma and Sexual Orientation*, Thousand Oaks, CA: Sage.
—— (2004) 'Beyond "homophobia"', *Sexuality Research and Social Policy*, I: 6–24.
Herek, G.M. and Berrill, K.T. (eds) (1992) *Hate Crimes*, Newbury Park, CA: Sage.
Kimmel, M.S. (1997) 'Masculinity as homophobia', in M.M. Gergen and S.N. Davis (eds) *Toward a New Psychology of Gender*, New York: Routledge, pp. 225–42.
Kurdek, L.A. (2004) 'Are gay and lesbian cohabiting couples really different from heterosexual married couples?' *Journal of Marriage and Family*, 66: 880–900.
Meyer, I.H. (2003) 'Prejudice, social stress, and mental health in lesbian, gay, and bisexual populations', *Psychological Bulletin*, 129: 674–97.
Morin, S.F. (1977) 'Heterosexual bias in psychological research on lesbianism and male homosexuality', *American Psychologist*, 32: 629–37.
Sandfort, T.G.M., Schuyf, J., Duyvendak, J.W. and Weeks, J. (eds) (2000) *Lesbian and Gay Studies*, London: Sage.
Tolman, D.L. and Diamond, L.M. (2001) 'Desegregating sexuality research', *Annual Review of Sex Research*, 12: 33–74.

See also: bisexuality; drag and cross-dressing; gay masculinities; homophobia and heterosexism; homosexuality; queer theory; social construction

WILLIAM A. JELLISON
GREGORY M. HEREK

GAY LIBERATION

Gay Liberation describes a new social movement that emerged in the USA initially and then swept the Western world from the late 1960s onwards. Deriving much of its early framework from the Black and Women's Liberation movements, and borrowing from the anti-psychiatry and existing sexual reform movements, Gay Liberation initially sought to free human sexuality, particularly between people of the same sex, from regulation, persecution, pathologisation and stigmatisation. The agenda soon became to reform criminal and civil laws that treated homosexual men (and women where applicable) and their sexual behaviour as illegal or open to prosecution, and to remove human sexual expression from the professional gaze of science, which had relegated it to the realms of biological disease, mental illness or social deviancy. This agenda was preceded by, and drew on, forms of social unrest and civil protest developed in response to the Cold War and in opposition to the Vietnam War, and from the struggles after 1945 by developing countries to free themselves from Western colonialism. Hence, 'liberation' was the term adopted. Finally, the counterculture of the 1960s offered tactics (the 'Zap') and cultural resources (fashion, the arts, popular music) to carry protest to new heights of representation (e.g. the 'kiss-in') and performance (e.g. the 'gender fuck') (Richmond and Noguera 1973).

These forces produced among homosexual men and women a determination to resist *oppression*, as the opposing forces (e.g. the state, the Church, modern medicine) were characterised (Altman 1972). The birth of Gay Liberation involved street riots in New York on 27 June 1969, when gay men, lesbians, street hustlers and 'queens' (drag artists, transsexual and cross-dressing men) found a local bar again raided by police. It was the day of Hollywood star, chanteuse and gay icon Judy Garland's funeral. Rather than submit to brutality and arrest, the saddened patrons of the Stonewall Bar in the West Village rioted. Four days of civil unrest followed with calls to end such persecution. The Stonewall Rebellion subsequently led to a mammoth re-appraisal of the situation of gay men and lesbians in a radical set of demands for social and legal change, and the elevation of homosexual interests, desires and practices to a revolutionary cry for liberation: 'Get your laws off our bodies!', 'Two, four, six, eight: gay is just as good as straight!', 'It takes balls to be a fairy!' Existing civil rights organisations such as the Homosexual Law Reform Societies in Britain and Australia, the Mattachine Society, and the Daughters of Bilitis in the US found their cautious lobbying style overtaken by radical forms of protest. Sexual revolution seemed not only necessary but imminent.

Various homophile rights movements had existed for over a hundred years in the West, and had achieved some success (e.g. the UK had legalised sex between men in private in 1967) (Weeks 1977). Gay Liberation quickly moved from the arguments of civil equality to radical positions influenced by the New Left, socialist theory and politics, and feminism. This was not surprising, as in many countries university students, already seeking other social change, provided Gay Liberation with an intelligentsia, developing new theory, linking various radical ideologies (e.g. Marxism and sexual liberation in critiques of Patriarchy and the 'capitalist family'), and challenging existing frameworks of deviancy and medically pathologised sexuality (Foucault 1978). Gay Liberation demanded an end to all sexual categories and the freedom for all people to pursue and enjoy same sex pleasures and desires. The claim that sexuality could be the site of liberation from many oppressions formed a radical break with an agenda of civil equality and eventually led to a schism between more radical arms of the gay liberation movement and the progressive reform arms.

Notions of 'gay pride' used the inverted pink triangle (with which the Nazis marked homosexuals in concentration camps) as a symbol of freedom. The rapid development of a world-wide network of print media, publishers, conferences and national and international organisations revealed the power of the idea of sexual liberation, and provided momentum for the rapid reappraisal of sexuality that has proceeded undaunted ever since. All this activity influenced various academic disciplines in rethinking human sexuality, in recovering the history of gay and lesbian lives, in positioning the homosexual at the centre of art and literature, in rethinking modern medicine, particularly psychiatry and psychology, and in linking sexuality to analyses of power and inequality that have been advanced since the 1960s (Plummer 1981; Greenberg 1988). This activism and the flourishing literary, artistic and cultural work made visible and audible in a way never seen before the 'love that dare not speak its name'.

What is left? The term is rarely used now, and if used invokes only the past. Presently, 'gay community' serves to describe the various collectivities of gay men around the world. Many reforms have been achieved to varying degrees, although the postcolonial legacy still dogs many developing countries. The advent of the HIV pandemic in the early 1980s left scars on gay men's lives and robbed communities of many leaders, artists, intellectuals and activists. It forced an engagement with the public health systems and required a different type of politics accommodating the state. Sexuality became less a revolutionary act and more a form of individual comportment: a 'good' gay man practised safer sex and thereby helped stop the epidemic. Sexual freedom for all became civil equality before the law for homosexual sex and relationships, and placed homosexuality on a par with heterosexuality, rather than pursuing for all an unbounded sexual expression – universal liberation became a minority lifestyle.

References and further reading

Altman, D. (1972) *Homosexual: Liberation and Oppression*, Sydney: Angus and Robertson.

Foucault, M. (1978) *The History of Sexuality, Volume 1 – An Introduction*, Harmondsworth: Penguin.

Greenberg, D.F. (1988) *The Construction of Homosexuality*, Chicago, IL: University of Chicago Press.

Plummer, K. (ed.) (1981) *The Making of the Modern Homosexual*, London: Hutchinson.

Richmond, Len and Noguera, G. (eds) (1973) *The Gay Liberation Book*, San Francisco, CA: Ramparts Press.

Weeks, J. (1977) *Coming Out*, London: Quartet Books.

GARY W. DOWSETT

GAY LITERATURE

Although the study of gay literature has only recently been recognised as an academic specialty, gay literature itself – defined as the representation in a wide variety of literary and subliterary genres of same-sex love and desire – is neither a new phenomenon nor an esoteric one. Indeed, the earliest surviving example of gay literature, the Sumerian epic *Gilgamesh*, a poem structured around the eponymous hero's love for another man, predates the Hebrew Bible and the Homeric epics, which themselves offer examples of same-sex love and desire.

Notwithstanding the fact that open discussion of homosexuality was severely limited from the twelfth century of the Christian era until the second half of the twentieth century, gay literature contains not only works that have been marginalised because of their subject matter, but also a surprisingly large number of texts by authors as firmly entrenched in the canon of Western literature as Virgil, Horace, Ovid, Michelangelo, Shakespeare, Marlowe, Gray, Whitman, Balzac, Tennyson, Goethe, Wilde, Rimbaud, Verlaine, Gide, Proust, Hopkins, Housman, Gogol, Kuzmin, Mann, Lorca, Genet, Cavafy, Forster, Auden and Williams, among many others. Moreover, gay literature is plentiful not only in the Classical and modern European languages, but also in Asian and Middle Eastern languages as well.

Gay literature encompasses both works in which same-sex desire is explicitly evoked or thematised and also works in which same-sex attraction is implicit. That is, it includes texts written by openly gay authors about gay characters living within a gay subculture – such as Holleran's *The Dancer from the Dance* or Kramer's *Faggots*, and works in which homosexual discovery is the explicit subject, such as Forster's *Maurice* or Baldwin's *Giovanni's Room*, and texts that protest the abuse and discrimination suffered by homosexuals, such as Wilde's *De Profundis* or Isherwood's *A Single Man* – but it includes as well works written by presumably heterosexual authors about relationships that could not have been acknowledged as homosexual when they were written, such as Tennyson's homoerotic elegy *In Memoriam*.

Gay literature also includes texts in which homosexual themes are encoded or disguised (such as Byron's 'To Thyrza', which pretends to be addressed to a woman, but was actually inspired by love for a young man) and works that are particularly susceptible to gay readings (such as Melville's *Moby Dick* or Hughes's 'Young Sailor'). Even works that present homosocial relationships (i.e. non-sexual bonding between members of the same sex) may qualify as gay literature, especially when, as in those depicted in the novels of James or Lawrence, they include a significant amount of homoeroticism. Finally, gay literature also includes texts exploring 'platonic' love, in which same-sex sexual feelings are repressed, and apologias, such as Symonds's *A Problem in Modern Ethics* or Gide's *Corydon*, in which same-sex love is defended.

Crucial to studying the representation of homosexuality as a transcultural and transhistorical phenomenon is the recognition that sexualities are socially constructed and vary from era to era. While homoerotic desire and behaviour have been documented in every conceivable kind of society, what vary are the meanings accorded to them from time to time and place to place. In every society there are undoubtedly individuals who are predominantly attracted to members of their own sex, but the extent to which that sexual attraction functions as a defining characteristic of these individuals' personal and social identities varies considerably from culture to culture, and it is important not to interpret earlier representations of sexuality in contemporary terms unmediated by historical understanding.

However, to recognise that each culture, by means not fully understood, constructs its own sexualities, should not obscure the fact that love and sex are universal human emotions and preoccupations. Nor should the recognition of the differences between the construction of sexualities in earlier eras and in our own entail the dismissal of the significant similarities and continuities between those constructions.

For example, modern North American and western European male homosexuality, which is predominantly androphiliac (that is, between adults), egalitarian and socially disdained, is in many respects different from ancient Greek male homosexuality, which was predominantly pederastic, asymmetrical in power and socially valorised. But awareness of those differences should not obviate the similarities that link the two distinct historical constructs or cause us to ignore the enormous influence that the classical Greek literature of homosexuality exerted on later gay literature. Ancient Greek literature and art provided readers, writers and artists of subsequent centuries a pantheon of heroes, a catalogue of images and a set of references by which same-sex desire could be encoded into their own representations and through which they could interpret their own experiences.

The most significant context that shaped gay literature created during most of the Christian era is the hostility directed towards homosexuality, which was construed almost exclusively in terms of crime and sickness and nearly always shadowed by religious and social disapproval. This homophobia, which attempted to render homosexuality literally 'unspeakable', affected the production of gay literature in manifold ways, including the need to employ codes and disguises and to publish anonymously and pseudonymously, as well as the practice of self-censorship by gay authors.

Although gay literature has frequently been dismissed and denigrated, it is actually rich and central. Preoccupied with such themes as self-knowledge, the relationship of the individual to society, the contemplation of forbidden beauty, the experience of otherness, the pain of exclusion, the yearning for union, the need to escape moralistic strictures, the dilemma of the divided self, and the joy of discovery, gay literature is both universal in its concerns and a significant part of world literature.

References and further reading

Crompton, L. (2003) *Homosexuality and Civilization*, Cambridge, MA: Harvard University Press.

Greenberg, D.F. (2000) *The Social Construction of Homosexuality*, Chicago, IL: University of Chicago Press.

Malinowski, S. (1994) *Gay and Lesbian Literature*, Detroit, MI: St James Press.

Summers, C. (2002) *The Gay and Lesbian Literary Heritage*, revised edn, New York: Routledge.

Woods, G. (1998) *A History of Gay Literature*, New Haven, CT and London: Yale University Press.

See also: gay and lesbian studies; homoeroticism; homophobia and heterosexism; homosexuality; men's relations with men; queer theory

CLAUDE SUMMERS

GAY MASCULINITIES

The appearance of distinctly gay masculinities came in the wake of advances made by the homosexual liberation movement of the 1950s and 1960s. Its successor, gay liberation, was less defensive than the earlier homosexual activism and had considerable success in wresting definitions of same-sex sexuality out of the hands of the medical and psychiatric professions. The term 'gay' was widely adopted in Western countries in part because it did not have the medical associations of homosexual and neither did it carry the stigma of gender non-conformity associated with words such as 'queer', 'pansy' or 'fairy'. To be gay no longer automatically implied or demanded rejection of many elements of conventional masculinities. Gay male relationships also underwent changes and became increasingly egalitarian rather than organised around differences of age, class or gender roles.

One of the earliest and most visible forms of gay masculinity was the clone style of the 1970s consisting of short hair, a moustache or short beard, tight jeans to emphasise the bottom and crotch, a heavy belt, working men's boots, and a flannel shirt or tightly fitting T-shirt to emphasise the chest and arms (Levine 1988). The rejection of femininity also extended to sexual behaviour which did not always have to conform to a model based on gendered roles of active top or passive bottom. The latter role was masculinised in phrases like 'Take it like a man!' Yet, despite its initial visibility, the clone style was never more than one expression of gay masculinity and nowadays is largely confined to North America and older gay men. In terms of appearance and style, gay masculinities today display at least as much variation as heterosexual masculinities (Cole 2000).

A major difference between earlier homosexual masculinities and gay masculinities lay in the insistence on the need to 'come out' as gay. This entailed openly stating and embracing a core sexual identity based on same-sex attraction. The existence of urban commercial infrastructure also made it possible to come out into a social milieu. In most larger Western cities, white, gay-identified men enjoy access to a wide range of organisations such as gay bikers, clubs for leather and fetish devotees, and sports clubs, through to gay hikers and ramblers to opera lovers, devotees of drag, and literary groups. These cater to most tastes and many are less concerned with emphasising conventional masculinity.

Given that gay masculinities are associated with urban centres and commercial entertainment, the inaccurate assumption that gay men are all hedonistic and wealthy has been encouraged. The increasing visibility of gay men and their concentration in larger cities to specific neighbourhoods – especially but not exclusively in North America – also encouraged the view that gay men (and lesbians) constitute a distinct minority. The minoritarian view has also been promoted by opponents of gay rights who exaggerate the distinction between a gay minority and heterosexual majority.

The vulnerability of a minority definition became apparent with the onslaught of the AIDS epidemic in the 1980s. If gay men constitute a clearly defined minority, then a disease that affected them disproportionately was not perceived as a threat to the heterosexual population and some governments were slow to respond to the threat that HIV posed. Because gay masculinities were built first and foremost on a sexual identity, HIV struck at the very core of that identity. Yet, however devastating the impact of AIDS, the response to it from within the gay male community, including political protests and mobilisation, safe-sex campaigns and voluntary support groups, showed that gay male communities were more resilient than purely commercial sexual subcultures.

Just what kinds of masculinity ought to be encouraged within the gay community is the object of considerable discussion. There has long been a tension within gay male cultures between the emphasis on masculinity and sexuality (evident in the clone style) and the equation of gay men with a 'feminine' interest in consumption, fashion and taste that distinguishes them from heterosexual men, an equation that the commercial urban gay scene has done much to reinforce. The latter stereotype has recently been revived in the pervasive media image of the gay consumer and the belief among advertisers and business that a distinct and wealthy gay male consumer niche exists in urban centres (Chasin 2000).

Yet there has long been dissatisfaction with the more consumerist aspects of urban gay male culture. Young urban professionals with disposable incomes are the targets of many gay male publications. Indeed, class differences have always marked gay masculinities as with all other masculinities. Differences in wealth determine access to commercial venues and also which parts of the gay scene, and which of the gay masculinities found there, are most attractive and accessible. For example, the skinhead style in the UK (with or without right-wing ideological baggage) has existed since the 1960s, but became very visible in the 1980s. More recently in the UK the 'scally' style, based on the eroticisation of sportswear and training clothes and its emphasis on tough working-class masculinity, has also emerged. Such styles can be seen as protests, or at least alternatives, to the more commercial and consumer-oriented sectors of the gay urban scene.

Gay critics have also pointed to the marginalisation of feminine men within gay subcultures that began in the 1970s as part of the reaction against the feminine stereotype of the male homosexual. Other men object to the almost exclusive focus on youth and physical beauty in many gay publications and to the segregation along racial and ethnic lines that is noticeable in some countries and cities. (For a variety of critical opinions, see Simpson 1996.)

Politically conservative gay men have criticised what they see as the overemphasis on the sexuality of gay men who, they argue, are basically no different from their heterosexual counterparts except in the gender of their sexual object choice. By placing less emphasis on sex, they argue that an assimilationist strategy is possible and desirable (e.g. Bawer 1993). More recently, the demand for gay marriage has highlighted the division among gay men between those who see it as a fundamental and necessary right and those who view it as succumbing to heterosexist demands for sexual conformity. It is dissatisfaction with the more assimilationist position that partly underlies the appearance of queer masculinities among younger men.

As these debates have proceeded in Western countries, the term 'gay' has spread to other parts of the world where its key assumptions that sexual identity and sexual behaviour coincide and its status as a 'modern' and more 'advanced' form of sexual identity have been variously embraced, reworked or challenged (Manalansan 20003; Binnie 2004).

The divisions that exist between gay men in Western countries clearly reflect social cleavages and forms of inequality that affect all men regardless of their sexual orientation. The debates surrounding them also point to the dynamism of gay masculinities. The development of gay male subcultures has been rapid and all the indications are that the proliferation of gay masculinities is likely to continue. One consequence is that the boundaries between young gay men and their heterosexual peers in terms of fashion, tastes and consumer behaviour, and socialising are becoming increasingly blurred, even if they have by no means disappeared entirely.

References and further reading

Bawer. B. (1993) *A Place at the Table. The Gay Individual in American Society*, New York: Simon and Schuster.

Binnie, J. (2004) *The Globalization of Sexuality*, London: Sage.

Chasin, A. (2000) *Selling Out: The Gay and Lesbian Movement Goes to Market*, New York: Palgrave.

Cole, S. (2000) *Don We Now Our Gay Apparel: Gay Men's Dress in the Twentieth Century*, Oxford: Berg.

Herdt, G. (ed.) *Gay Culture in America: Essays from the Field*, Boston, MA: Beacon Press.

Levine, M. (1988) *Gay Macho: The Life and Death of the Homosexual Clone*, New York: New York University Press.

Manalansan, M. (2003) *Global Divas: Filipino Gay Men in the Diaspora*, Durham, NC, and London: Duke University Press.

Nardi. P. (1999) *Gay Men's Friendships: Invincible Communities*, Chicago, IL: Chicago University Press.

—— (2000) *Gay Masculinities*, Thousand Oaks, CA: Sage.

Simpson, M. (ed.) (1996) *Anti-Gay*, London: Freedom Editions.

See also: fatherhood, gay; Gay Liberation; homophobia and heterosexism; homosexuality; queer theory; working with gay men

MARK GRAHAM

GENDER

The concept of gender relates to the relationships between men and women, and to the way members of society are divided into the two groups based on their assigned biological sex at birth. These groups are allocated different gendered attributes and social roles which affect all features of social life. The concept of gender embodies cultural attributes and definitions relating to masculinity and femininity as well as the sexual division of labour (Bradley 1999). Gender thus refers to cultural specific patterns of behaviour which are identified as masculine or feminine. It is socially constructed and differs across social classes, cultural and ethnic groups within the same society, as well as from one society to another. Gender also relates to ways in which different life chances and life choices are assigned within different social groups. Representational practices based on gender define and possess a power to establish *normal* behaviours (Weedon 1997). Children, as members of a society, learn what it is to be masculine and what it is to be feminine from an early age. Through inherent beliefs, boys are praised for *male* achievements and girls for *girlness*, to the extent that language also becomes more *masculine* or *feminine*. Gendered discourses influence ways in which males and females behave, feel, think, play and dress. Gendered expectations are subsequently fulfilled. The gendered nature of individuals is further intensified by the gendered nature of social institutions, such as the family, education system and the workplace (see for example Kimmel 2000). Thus gender is socially constructed through a process which continues to shape males and females throughout life depending on their assigned sex at birth.

The concept of gender functions as a crucial tool for analysing ways in which males and females are socially constructed (Oakley 1997). While males and females may be biologically different, cultural traits of femininity and masculinity are often treated by society as opposites. The fluidity and political power of differences relating to sex and gender effectively disappears so that sex means gender and gender means sex. Biological differences are frequently linked to the construction of gender inequality. However, it is gender inequality that strengthens observable gender differences in attitudes and behaviour (Kimmel 2000). Central to the gender inequality question is the public (masculine) versus the private (feminine) debate and where domestic responsibility persists in the hindrance of access to the public spheres for females.

Discourses are gendered if it is suggested that males and females do things differently. The gender difference discourse maintains essentialist thinking which advocates assigned gendered attributes as natural (Sunderland 2004). This discourse retains a commonsense status through which the world is viewed and is often used to justify rather than explain perceived masculine behaviour, such as the *natural* boisterous behaviour of boys. Gendered cultural patterns inevitably lead to gendered power relations, situating some groups into superior positions and others into subordinate positions as everyday practices are engaged with (Bradley 1999). Thus a focus on differences reinforces dominant binary discourses which continue to marginalise specific groups, such as females, nonwhites and working classes. Power needs also to be linked with agency whereby power functions in a different manner at different sites. Agency offers us explanations of asymmetries of power (Bradley 1999). Different gendered powers can be identified in different sites, with a tendency for masculine power to be situated in public arenas, and feminine power in private arenas. Advantages that men generally lay claim to, or the 'patriarchal dividend' (Connell 1998), remain prevalent in society. However, it is important to recognise that advantages are relational and not *all* men have access to this patriarchal dividend to the same extent. Thus, not all men are equally powerful and, similarly, not all women are equally oppressed.

Although we are all multipositioned in variable degrees at different times, there appears to be an inevitability in the way binary pairs are or have been constructed: male/female, white/black, us/them. Binary pairs become so fundamental to our way of thinking that we often do not even realise that we are using them in our understanding of the world. The inevitability of binary opposites may be reinforced because we learn to see binaries as part of an apparently unconstructed absolute truth (Davies 1997). In our society, a person belongs to one of the categories of the binary pair male/female. The privilege of the first, more dominant term is dependent on the 'otherness' of the subordinate term (Davies 1997). Through binary opposition, political issues allow identification of *others* to become the source of societal problems. Hierarchically arranged binary categories are often constructed unconsciously or unintentionally through the processes of language. In this way, oppositions are created out of what are only differences and these gender differences construct masculinity and femininity as a binary opposition. Indeed, the binary nature of gender maintains stable gender identities, often defined hierarchically, at the expense of, for example, gay people (Butler 1990). However, each time binary oppositions like male/female are reinforced as part of a *natural* state, so too other binary opposites are reinforced, like powerful/powerless, truth/untruth. Thus it is important to deconstruct this fictitious opposition and to deconstruct, as it has also been described, this 'violent hierarchy' (Sunderland 2004).

The masculine/feminine dichotomy and the question as to how and why an individual needs to belong to a category is challenged within feminist poststructuralism to enable differences within a range of any particular elected category to exist without the inevitability of binary opposites, and without the need to be categorised in limiting positions (Davies 1997). A general feminist theoretical recognition of the idea of diversity within categories continually eludes many ethnographers in respect of issues relating to masculinities, resulting in suggestions for a need to move beyond these theoretical dichotomies which have been fictitiously conceived (Conway-Long 1994). Feminisms have highlighted the diversities among females, but it is also important to recognise diversities among different groups of males and that binary opposites operate within masculinity. Feminism offers men positions to be more 'free' (Kimmel 2000). Biological essentialism often results in the binary nature of gender being accepted as *natural*, with a hegemonic form of masculinity considered the norm for males. In multicultural Western countries, such as Australia, the United Kingdom and the United States of America, white males often retain a power through reinforcement of hegemonic masculinity. Males who do not easily fit a hegemonic masculine framework are often revealed as disadvantaged. Indeed, when heterosexuality is seen as the only option for 'real men' then positions such as homosexuality become seen as 'abnormal' (Buchbinder 1994). Heterosexuality and homosexuality thus operate as binary opposites with disadvantages intensified by a lack of easily accessible alternatives to hegemonic heterosexual masculinities discourses.

Gender difference discourses which focus on masculine/feminine dichotomy and embrace views of essentialised differences are disadvantageous to both females and males. Females fluctuate between different discourses: for example, new discourses that suggest they can succeed in what are perceived as masculine arenas and old discourses that they retain the main responsibility for domestic arrangements. Males similarly fluctuate between different discourses, such as new discourses that incorporate tenets of gender equity and old discourses that housework is still a feminine job. The gender difference discourse is particularly not emancipatory for females and distracts attention from evidence that women are still the second-class sex (Sunderland 2004). Females continue to experience lower salaries, lower status jobs, lower paid work, and remain responsible for most of the housework. Women's achievements are often negated or ignored, giving an appearance of continually having to start from scratch rather than building on previous achievements.

The schooling system is a significant site where social constructs such as gender are constructed. Although schools need to redress such issues, essentialised notions are nevertheless often reproduced (Kimmel 2000). For example, although Australia purports to strive for equality, when it was perceived that females might be succeeding in high-status *masculine* subjects in the 1990s and early 2000s, projects were set up in order to address the educational needs of boys at school. Such government policies and actions reinforce socially constructed attributes, definitions and hierarchical nature of masculinity and femininity. Popular media in other countries such as the United Kingdom and the United States of America also attributed blame to girls for succeeding at the expense of boys. The 'poor boys discourse' is a gendered discourse with a familiar and international theme which links closely to the men's movement argument and to the 'boys will be boys' discourse and can be seen to generate gender difference discourses as well as their associated hierarchical nature. Hegemonic masculinity discourses with their compulsory heterosexuality practices somehow justify misogynist and homophobic behaviour and absolve males from the need to strive academically (Sunderland 2004).

Gender is often coded to mean women (as 'race' is often coded to mean black), so that men's spaces are often depicted as neutral or ungendered (Pettman 1992). Pretence to neutrality benefits specific groups of males through identification of feminine and masculine roles where these roles exist in binary opposition to each other. Classification by gender affects our lives and makes it impossible to be 'gender neutral' (Bordo 1990) in our society. Although masculinity and femininity are constructed culturally, they become constant locations of political struggle over meanings that have actual life effects for males and females (Jordan and Weedon 1995). The socially constructed categories of 'women' and 'men' homogenise females and males while they disguise their association with ethnic and social class identities (Pettman 1992) and effectively reinforce their links with femininity and masculinity. Gender issues relate to both males and females and contradictions should be seen as an indication of political differences. Groups who are already privileged or prejudiced by gender and also ethnicity and social class are further advantaged or disadvantaged through being positioned within or opposite power-linked categories such as male, white and 'us'. However, variables along social constructs potentially provide multiple positionings. Through feminist deconstruction, binary opposites are metaphysically transformed to become multiples (Davies 1997). Feminist poststructuralism offers us ways in which to deconstruct the social concept of gender and to perceive and access multiple possibilities of gender, masculinity and femininity. Binary opposites are frequently seen as fixed unchanging categories, but if seen metaphysically these categories become part of a range of possibilities leading to a multiplicity of potential gender identities. The academic use of the terms 'masculinities' and 'femininities' has become fairly common as the world entered the twenty-first century.

It remains important to examine the construction of gender in order to deconstruct the ideals of both masculinity and femininity and the ways in which these are persistently normalised. By complicating our understanding of gender, it is possible to address and incorporate other influences in the construction of gendered social positions, such as ethnicity, socio-economic status and sexuality (Collins *et al.* 2000). At the beginning of the twenty-first century, attitudes of males and females have changed to incorporate the understanding that there should not be gender inequalities for males and females. However, behaviour remains gendered – for example, school students continue to choose gender-typical subjects (see, for example, Collins *et al.* 2000). The inevitability of a male/female binary opposition can be challenged through understanding the fluid and discursive nature of the social construction of gender. Although gender is often linked to biological characteristics, it is a social construct and like femininity and masculinity is linked to learned behaviours. There is a need not only to problematise gender, but also to acknowledge that gender is inclusive of males as well as females. Masculinity is not natural and fixed. Male heterosexuality is a dominant but unstable category. Social discursive practices have the effect of contradictory positionings for males which highlight the fractured and fragile nature of identity construction for males (Mac an Ghaill 1994). Although males are not generally oppressed or exploited by sexism, they may still suffer as a consequence. Gender may not necessarily be the most significant component of a male's identity, but it will have a relational influence with other social constructs like 'race'/ethnicity, social class and sexuality.

References and further reading

Bordo, S. (1990) 'Feminism, postmodernism, and gender-scepticism', in L. Nicholson (ed.) *Feminism/Postmodernism*, New York: Routledge, pp. 133–56.

Bradley, H. (1999) *Gender and Power in the Workplace*, New York: St Martin's Press.

Buchbinder, D. (1994) *Masculinities and Identities*, Melbourne: Melbourne University Press.

Butler, J. (1990) *Gender Trouble*, London: Routledge.

Collins, C., Kenway, J. and McLeod, J. (2000) *Factors Influencing the Educational Performance of Males and Females in School and Their Initial Destinations after Leaving School*, Canberra: Commonwealth Department of Education, Training and Youth Affairs.

Connell, R. (1998) 'Gender politics for men', in S. Schacht and D. Ewing (eds) *Feminism and Men*, New York: New York University Press, pp. 225–36.

Conway-Long, D. (1994) 'Ethnographies and masculinities', in H. Brod and M. Kaufman (eds) *Theorizing Masculinities*, Thousand Oaks, CA: Sage, pp. 61–81.

Davies, B. (1997) 'Constructing and deconstructing masculinities through critical literacy', *Gender and Education*, 9 (1): 9–30.

Jordan, G. and Weedon, C. (1995) *Cultural Politics*, Oxford: Blackwell.

Kimmel, M. (2000) *The Gendered Society*, Oxford: Oxford University Press.

Mac an Ghaill, M. (1994) *The Making of Men*, Buckingham: Open University Press.

Oakley, A. (1997) 'A brief history of gender', in A. Oakley and J. Mitchell (eds) *Who's Afraid of Feminism?* London: Penguin Books, pp. 29–55.

Pettman, J. (1992) *Living in the Margins*, Sydney: Allen and Unwin.

Sunderland, J. (2004) *Gendered Discourses*, New York: Palgrave Macmillan.

Weedon, C. (1997) *Feminist Practice and Poststructuralist Theory*, 2nd edn, Oxford: Blackwell.

HELEN HATCHELL

GENDER ORDER

The term 'gender order' refers to the patterning of gender at the level of an entire society. In any particular society, there are systematic ways of creating social women and men and ordering the patterns of relations among and between them (Matthews 1984). Every society has a gender order, which may take a variety of forms. The term 'patriarchy' is not equivalent to the term 'gender order', but names a particular type of gender order whose content or form is characterised by dominant males' authority over women and other men (Matthews 1984). It is not logically necessary that gender orders be hierarchical or oppressive, although most if not all are and have been. The social organisation of gender relations intersects with, is modified by, and itself modifies other axes of social differentiation and meaning. Modern gender orders have been formed by intersecting processes of industrialisation, urbanisation and globalisation (Connell 1995).

'Gender order' is one of several terms used by Connell and other scholars to describe the social organisation of gender relations at different levels of social life. 'Gender order' refers to the current state of a macro-politics of gender; it is described through a structural inventory of an entire society. 'Gender regimes' refer to the pattering of gender in given institutions, including clearly boundaried formal institutions such as schools or workplaces, large sprawling ones such as the state, and informal milieux such as the street (Connell 1987).

Such formulations assume neither that the patterning of gender is static, nor that it is produced in deterministic ways. Connell (1995) emphasises that masculinity and femininity are configurations of gender practice or, more precisely, processes of configuring practice through time. Although specific forms of social organisation in a particular gender order or gender regime do impose constraints on men's and women's agency and practice, they are only maintained by practice and may be changed by practice (Connell 1987). Moreover, patterns of gender at the level of a society do not determine patterns of gender at more local levels. Relations between and among gender orders and gender regimes may be complementary or abrasive, and these different fields may be internally differentiated, in flux or contradictory.

References and further reading

Connell, R. (1987) *Gender and Power*, Sydney: Allen and Unwin.

—— (1995) *Masculinities*, Sydney: Allen and Unwin.

Matthews, J.J. (1984) *Good and Mad Women*, Sydney: Allen and Unwin.

See also: patriarchy

MICHAEL FLOOD

GENDER RELATIONS

'Gender relations' refers to the circumstances in which lesbian, gay, heterosexual, bisexual and transgender individuals interrelate and the political, social and epistemological contexts of their relationships. Because of gender socialisation, many societies exhibit strained gender relations, and they can cause psychological harm in individuals as well as lead to abuse and violence within intimate relationships. Contemporary theorists of gender and masculinity have analysed the foundations of strained gender relations and have suggested approaches to improving the relationships among different gender groups.

One approach involves the analysis of positionality or the consideration of the ways in which individuals are subjected to different social forces as a result of their gender. By understanding the positionality of the subaltern or marginalised individual, the person in the greater position of power can work to alleviate negative social forces. John Stoltenberg and Men Against Pornography developed the Pose Workshop to address the ways in which gender relations are impacted by the negativity of pornography (1994). Many contemporary feminist analyses of gender emphasise that for gender relations to be improved, men must confront sexism in their lives; in short, they should implement a 'feminist masculinity' (hooks 2000: 70).

The complexities of contemporary masculinity have led to strained relations among the genders, including those among men. Susan Faludi has argued that the combination of being labelled as an aggressor and being given mixed signals about one's masculinity leads to a crisis of identity among males (2000). Some contemporary constructions of masculinity identify the ideal male as one who acts alone and who moves outside the boundaries of traditional social relations (Gibson 1994). As hooks has written, it has been difficult for some activists to realise that the problem of sexism 'did not just lie with men' (2000: 67). In the contemporary, globalised world, representatives of all gender groups must work together to create relationships that stress acceptance, equality and understanding.

References and further reading

Faludi, S. (2000) *Stiffed*, New York: Perennial.
Gibson, J.W. (1994) *Warrior Dreams*, New York: Hill and Wang.
hooks, b. (2000) *Feminism is for Everybody*, Cambridge, MA: South End.
Stoltenberg, J. (1994) *What Makes Pornography Sexy?* Minneapolis, MN: Milkweed Editions.

See also: father–daughter relationships; men's relations with men; men's relations with women; working with boys; working with men

SCOTT A. LUKAS

GENDER ROLE STRAIN

Joseph Pleck developed the idea of gender role strain in *The Myth of Masculinity* (Pleck 1981) by applying the ideas of role strain from sociology and social psychology to the experiences of gender role socialisation. The construct of gender role strain is a broad one encompassing an array of ideas including that (a) gender role norms are contradictory and inconsistent; (b) large numbers of individuals violate gender role norms; (c) violating gender role norms leads to condemnation and negative psychological consequences; (d) some of society's prescribed gender role norms are psychologically dysfunctional; and (e) violating gender role norms has more severe consequences for males than females.

Pleck further organised the phenomena of gender role strain into three categories.

Gender role *discrepancy strain* reflects the low self-esteem, stress and negative reactions from others due to the individual's failure to fulfil masculine or feminine ideals. Richard Eisler and his colleagues operationalised discrepancy strain via the Masculine and Feminine Gender Role Stress Scales and reported gender role stress to relate to a variety of negative psychological and physical health consequences (Eisler 1995).

Gender role *trauma strain* is described as the negative side effects of experiencing the harshness of certain aspects of gender role socialisation. Experiences such as hazing from sports teams, military training or warfare, and intense shaming from the social environment for acting in 'feminine' ways represent some examples of trauma strain for boys and men.

Gender role *dysfunction strain* is the idea that many of society's ideals of masculinity and femininity can be dysfunctional for the individual, families or society. Examples of dysfunction strain include men meeting the societal standard of being tough and aggressive through violence, or women meeting the Western standard of thinness through eating disorder behaviours. Research on men tends to support the idea that men endorsing traditional societal standards for masculine gender roles may be vulnerable to an array of presenting concerns (Mahalik *et al.* 2003).

References and further reading

Eisler, R.M. (1995) 'The relationship between masculine gender role stress and men's health risk: the validation of a construct', in R.F. Levant and W.S. Pollack (eds) *The New Psychology of Men*, New York: Basic Books, pp. 207–28.
Mahalik, J.R., Good, G.E. and Carlson, M. (2003) 'Masculinity scripts, presenting concerns and help-seeking: implications for practice and training', *Professional Psychology: Theory, Research and Practice*, 34: 123–31.
Pleck, J.H. (1981) *The Myth of Masculinity*, Cambridge, MA: MIT Press.

See also: sex role theory

JAMES MAHALIK

GENIUS

A genius is a man or woman whose original abilities seem so extraordinary as to transcend rational explanation. The concept of genius has a long history, going back to the classical period, when a genius was a local god for a person or household. In time, the term lost its associations with religion to become a general term for the distinctive character of a given entity. The history of the concept took a marked turn in the eighteenth century when it was connected to originality. An original genius had not merely a distinctive set of characteristics but also the god-like power to invent something out of nothing. The concept of the original genius quickly gained huge cultural significance and popularity, so that 'genius' became the preferred name for any exceptionally promising creator.

With the rise of this concept came an interest in the genius's particular characteristics. First, the genius was usually understood to be male; women created children, but men created works of genius. If genius was attributed to a woman, she was usually understood to have masculinised herself in some way. Second, geniuses were usually seen as social misfits, evident most prominently in their unsuitability for marriage. Geniuses tended to be either bachelors or bad husbands. Third, geniuses, though male, combined traits stereotypically understood to be masculine and feminine. This combination meant that geniuses, though usually male, were not quite manly: traits that might be regarded as inappropriate in ordinary men, such as homosexuality or addiction, became acceptable or at least excusable in a genius. Such associations led to various attempts to distinguish between more and less culturally approved aspects of genius. The twentieth-century educational category of the gifted child, for example, was developed to protect the child from the supposedly worrying associations of genius. Nevertheless, the older myth of genius that links it to socially unmanly behaviours retains its fascination in scholarship and popular culture.

References and further reading

Battersby, C. (1989) *Gender and Genius*, Bloomington, IN: Indiana University Press.

Elfenbein, A. (1999) *Romantic Genius*, New York: Columbia University Press.

Lombroso, C. (1891) *The Man of Genius*, London: W. Scott.

Murray, P. (ed.) (1989) *Genius*, Oxford: Basil Blackwell.

Pickover, C. (1998) *Strange Brains and Genius*, New York: Plenum.

Young, E. [1759] (1966) *Conjectures on Original Composition*, Leeds: Scolar.

See also: intellectuals

ANDREW ELFENBEIN

GEOGRAPHY

Foundational to contemporary human geography is the belief that social relations are always spatial relations and that social practice and identities are geographically constructed phenomena. According to one prominent theorist, Massey (1994), space is best seen as a web of interconnected relations that stretch across multiple scales – for instance, the local, national and global. Up until the 1970s, a positivist epistemology predominated within the discipline. But from this decade radical geographers such as Massey and Harvey drew on Marxist theory to argue that space was actively produced through class and (in the case of Massey) gender contestations and structures. Further important theoretical influences on geographers in the 1980s and 1990s included structuration theory (through the work of Giddens), feminist theory and poststructuralism.

Early writings on masculinities did not explicitly consider questions of place and space; these works tended to be rooted in the disciplines of sociology, history and anthropology (for example, Connell 1987). Nevertheless, premised on the constructiveness of sexuality, empirical studies soon demonstrated the diverse historical and geographical contexts in which men became men. One well-known comparative study, crossing seven societies, was Gilmore's (1990) *Manhood in the Making*. Although criticised for downplaying the existence of multiple masculinities within societies, this study was typical in the way in which it used 'local' ethnographic data to draw conclusions about men and masculinities at the scale of the 'ethnic group', 'nation' or 'society'.

In the 1980s and particularly the 1990s, a growing number of studies within human geography addressed the topic of masculinities. This trend was underpinned by a more vocal critique of male bias within the discipline and the related emergence of feminist geography. Other masculinities studies also took on a more geographical slant as they sought to engage with 'globalisation', a concept perhaps most forcefully problematised within the discipline of geography.

Masculine geographers and the production of knowledge

Professionalised in the nineteenth century, founders of the discipline of geography drew inspiration from the heroic adventures of male explorers (Domosh 1991). In her pivotal book, *Feminism and Geography*, Rose (1993) drew attention to the deeply entrenched 'masculinism' in the discipline, a dynamic reflected in the undervaluing of feminist perspectives and research and the long-standing authority of men. Work by feminist geographers such as Rose and Domosh also illustrated how a detached, rational, masculine viewpoint fashioned geographical concepts such as 'a sense of place' and 'time-geography'.

Postcolonial studies, a field that emerged with the 'cultural turn' in the 1980s, also sought to deconstruct dominant spatialised discourses, especially those encompassing colonised spaces (for the influence of postcolonial theory on a prominent geographer, see Gregory 1994). One of the foundational texts of this field, Said's (1976) *Orientalism*, shows how the West feminised the Orient, rendering it disposed to Western dominance. Building on this, McClintock (1995) argued that colonial discourses positioned the colonised world as what she called the 'porno-tropics'; she also explores everyday interactions between coloniser and colonised to demonstrate the importance of sexuality to the inner workings of the colonial project. Colonialism, she argues, was simultaneously moulded by and constitutive of racialised and gendered representations of space.

If these studies are premised on the deconstruction of masculine representations of space, other scholars have questioned the spatialised production of knowledge *about* masculinities. Berg and Longhurst (2003) note that knowledge on masculinities is being produced in a wide range of places but that research outside of the West tends to be viewed as 'case studies' rather than as theoretical contributions; it is Western-based journals that claim authority over theoretical innovations on the subject. There is therefore a geographical hierarchy to the production of knowledge, including on men and masculinities.

One large node of masculinity studies, not strongly reflected in the theoretical literature and a good example of this point, is situated in Africa. The Africanist masculinities literature has followed a distinct trajectory, moulded by recognition of the continent's colonial past and, more recently, the contemporary AIDS pandemic (see Morrell 1998). Writings that engage with the racialised nature of the colonial project question some common underpinnings of the broader masculinities literature. A number of Africanist scholars, for instance, have argued that there is rarely one single African masculinity that is 'hegemonic' – a widely used concept within the masculinities literature (Morrell 1998). In South Africa white masculinity exercised its hegemony in 'white' areas but not in 'native reserves'. The geographical de-centring of masculinity studies, with significant nodes of research in areas such as Africa and Latin America, therefore offers a potential for reconstituting mainstream theory.

Feminist geography and masculinities

In the 1980s and 1990s, masculinities became a prominent topic within feminist geography, reflecting a broader move within gender studies away from simply the study of women. In an early contribution, Peter Jackson (1991) drew on the paradigm of 'cultural materialism' to stress the spaces in which masculinities are contested; he called for theoretically informed historical *and* geographical work on men and the production of masculinities. A number of subsequent accounts of masculinities and space appeared in the journal *Gender, Place, and Culture*, which was launched in 1994. This literature forefronted the spaces in which masculinities are constructed, the importance of movement to masculinities and, more broadly, the socio-spatial power dynamics through which gendered practices and discourses are produced.

In the 1990s, the study of masculinities became more integrated with feminist geography and its prevailing set of conceptual categories. One of the leading writers on gender and geography, McDowell, organised her recent study of spaces of gender, including masculinities, through the concept of scale, i.e. different *types* of places such as the home, community, workplace, public and nation state (McDowell 1999). In one chapter, for instance, McDowell discusses a community-based masculinity, showing how it emerged from shared male camaraderie in a company town; in another, she explores the scale of work, giving an example of how men maintain their privileges and salaries through appropriating technology.

A further related field addresses the 'geographies of sexuality'. A central aim of masculinity studies has been to critique the naturalness of, and power dynamics underpinning, compulsory heterosexuality. Written in 1995, Bell and Valentine's *Mapping Desire* demonstrates the importance of space to the production of non-hegemonic masculinities as well as struggles against normative sexualities. Contained within the volume are contributions on topics that include the heterosexualisation of the workplace, queer politics, and surveillance and sexuality.

Connecting the local to the global

Geographers, stressing the rootedness of social practice in place, have been among the most vociferous critics of a globalisation literature that can often oversimplify complex spatial processes (see, for instance, Katz 2004). Most do not refute there having been substantial changes in the flows of people and goods over the last few decades. Nevertheless, they tend to emphasise the concrete sites and institutions driving 'globalisation' and demonstrate how the 'local' is always simultaneously constitutive of other scales, including the global. Through a conceptual vocabulary that includes place and space, scale, interconnections and situated practices and identities, geographers challenge implicit assumptions about cultural and economic homogenisation.

Pointing to the powerful influences of geopolitical struggles, multinational corporations, labour migration and transnational media on men, Connell (2000) has recently argued that masculinity studies must now engage more explicitly with questions of 'globalisation'. This interest in global masculinities is potentially a quite radical shift from the scale of the 'nation' or 'ethnic group' upon which founding ethnographies and theories of masculinities were based. In her recent book *The Men and the Boys*, Connell (2000) notes global processes that have transformed or are transforming masculinities: imperialism, global divisions of labour, global models of love, and a global media. New forms of gender relations always articulate with and never simply sweep aside the old, and she points to four globalising masculinities for further research: masculinities of conquest and settlement, masculinities of empire, masculinities of postcolonialism and masculinities of neo-liberalism.

Katz's (2004) ethnography *Growing Up Global* is an example of a book from a geographer that partially takes up this challenge. The book chronicles changes to children's everyday lives in Sudan and New York through long-term ethnographic research. Katz's study vividly demonstrates connections between a changing global political economy, greater mobility and new cultural influences and the way in which these are intertwined with gendered understandings of growing up – although she does not specifically study young men and masculinities. Katz positions this work as a 'critical ethnography of globalisation' – a field in which geographers are playing a leading role.

The centring of global health pandemics, especially HIV/AIDS, in the Global South is a further dynamic fostering greater research on masculinities, health and global change. Twenty-five million people in Africa are living with HIV or AIDS and, in this continent, largely marginalised from international investment, the political economy of unemployment and social divisions greatly affects sexuality and health (for instance, Hunter 2004).

Within recent anthropological work, a strong related theme is transnational movements. Bao's (2005) recent book demonstrates important changes to male identity as men moved from China to Thailand and to the US. She shows how Chinese-born men who move to Thailand conform to the Chinese ideal of masculinity – a reliable breadwinner – while embracing aspects of the Thai ideal of masculinity, especially the notion of being a virile womaniser. Her argument is that the reworking of feminine and masculine identities constitutes a central part of the cultural struggles within transnational spaces. As these studies suggest, probing the ways in which gender relations are constructed through movement and reconfiguring spatial interconnections is a fertile terrain upon which geography and masculinity studies may come together in the future.

References and further reading

Bao, J. (2005) *Marital Acts*, Honolulu, HI: University of Hawaii Press.

Bell, D. and Valentine, G. (eds) (1995) *Mapping Desire*, New York: Routledge.

Berg, L. and Longhurst, R. (2003) 'Placing masculinities and geography', *Gender, Place and Culture*, 10 (4): 351–60.

Connell, R. (1987) *Gender and Power: Society, the Person and Sexual Politics*, Cambridge, MA: Blackwell.

—— (2000) *The Men and the Boys*, Berkeley, CA: University of California Press.

Domosh, M. (1991) 'Towards a feminist historiography of geography', *Transactions of the Institute of British Geographers*, 16 (1): 94–104.

Gregory, D. (1994) *Geographical Imaginations*, Cambridge, MA: Blackwell.

Hunter, M. (2004) 'Masculinities, multiple-partners and AIDS in KwaZulu-Natal', *Transformation*, 54: 123–53.

Jackson, P. (1991) 'The cultural politics of masculinity', *Transactions of the Institute of British Geographers*, 16 (2): 199–213.

Katz, C. (2004) *Growing Up Global*, Minneapolis, MN: University of Minnesota Press.

McClintock, A. (1995) *Imperial Leather*, New York: Routledge.

McDowell, L. (1999) *Gender, Identity and Place*, Cambridge: Polity.

Massey, D. (1994) *Space, Place and Gender*, Cambridge: Polity.

Morrell, R. (1998) 'Of boys and men', *Journal of Southern African Studies*, 24 (4): 605–31.

Rose, G. (1993) *Feminism and Geography*, Minneapolis, MN: University of Minnesota Press.

MARK HUNTER

GLOBAL MASCULINITIES

The study of 'global masculinities' can mean two things. It can mean investigating the different forms of masculinity around the world, each seen in an ethnographic perspective. This cross-cultural exploration has been an important contribution to modern thinking about men and masculinity. It has powerfully reinforced the critique of monolithic, 'essentialist' visions of an eternal, unchanging masculinity. Cross-cultural investigation has given concrete detail to the idea that there are many different patterns of masculinity in the world, each to be understood in a local context. This concept directs our attention to cultural tradition and the diverse character of established masculinities.

Alternatively, 'global masculinities' can mean the patterns of masculinity constructed in global forums, or under the influence of global processes. This idea has become prominent since social sciences began to emphasise the idea of 'globalisation', understood either as homogenisation on a world scale or as the subordination of national and local societies to the forces of the world economy. It is certainly true that individual lives are powerfully influenced by geopolitical struggles, imperialism and colonialism, global markets, multinational corporations, labour migration and transnational media. This concept directs our attention to emerging patterns of gender relations and the possible appearance of new masculinities.

There is now some convergence between these two concepts. Recent research has explored the interplay between local constructions of masculinities and men's lives, and global processes. What emerges is not a simple subordination of the local to the global but a vigorous process of negotiation and interpretation, in which even poor people in marginalised communities may play an active role (Gutmann 2002).

To understand masculinities on a world scale we must recognise the constitution of a world gender order (Connell 2002). This may be defined as the structure of relationships that interconnect the gender regimes of institutions, and the gender orders of local societies, on a world scale.

This gender order is an aspect of a larger reality: global society. The creation of global society is itself a complex field of debate, easily misunderstood. Current discussions of 'globalisation' often picture an irresistible process sweeping across the world, driven by new technologies, producing vast unfettered global markets, world music, global advertising and world news in which all participate on equal terms. In reality, however, the global economy is highly unequal, and the degree of economic and cultural homogenisation is often exaggerated.

The historical processes that produced global society were, from the start, gendered. Colonial conquest and settlement were carried out by gender-segregated forces. In colonial societies new gender divisions of labour were produced in plantation economies and colonial cities. During the second half of the twentieth century, the growth of a post-colonial world economy saw gender divisions of labour changing again, with the labour demands of the 'global factory'. This period saw the further spread of gendered violence alongside Western military technology.

Imperial conquest, neo-colonialism and the current world systems of power, investment, trade and communication, have brought very diverse societies into contact with each other, including their gender orders. For instance, in the eastern Mediterranean region, over the last two centuries the military and economic power of the European empires, the United States and international capital has resulted in particularly violent and disruptive interaction with this part of the Islamic world.

Effects of such forces on local gender orders are well illustrated by Morrell's (2001) analysis of contemporary South Africa. The transition from apartheid has created an extraordinary social landscape. In a context of reintegration into the global polity and economy, rising unemployment, continuing violence and a growing HIV/AIDS epidemic, there are attempts to reconstitute rival patriarchies in different ethnic groups. These attempts clash with agendas for the modernisation of masculinity, with South African feminism and the new government's 'human rights' discourse. Some of these ideas, in turn, are challenged by arguments for 'African philosophy' and for policies based in indigenous communal traditions, which would de-emphasise gender divisions.

The other great dynamic of change in gender relations is the creation of new arenas beyond individual countries and regions. The most important of the new arenas are transnational corporations, the international state, global markets and globally operating mass media.

All of these arenas are gendered. Transnational corporations typically have a strong gender division of labour, and a strongly masculinised management culture. The institutions of diplomacy and war, the principal means by which sovereign states have related to each other, are heavily masculinised. United Nations agencies, the European Union and a range of other international agencies have been set up to transcend these old arrangements. They too are gendered, mainly run by men, though with more cultural complexity than multinational corporations (Gierycz 1999).

Multinational media corporations circulate film, video, music and news on a very large scale. There are also more decentralised media (post, telegraph, telephone, fax, the Internet, the Web). All contain gender arrangements and circulate gender meanings. International markets – capital, commodity, service and labour markets – have an increasing 'reach' into local economies, and they too are often strongly gender-structured.

World politics is now increasingly organised around the needs of transnational capital and the creation of global markets. De-regulation of the economy, in a corporate world, places strategic power in the hands of particular groups of men – managers and entrepreneurs. Wajcman's (1999) study of multinational corporations based in Britain shows that even where women have entered management they do so on men's terms, conforming to the masculinised culture and practices of the managerial elite.

Direct research on business masculinities gives partly contradictory indications. Donaldson's (2003) study, based on biographical sources about the very rich, emphasises emotional isolation and a deliberate toughening of boys in the course of growing up; a sense of social distance, material abundance combined with a sense of entitlement and superiority. Hooper's (2001) study of the imagery of masculinity in international business and politics suggests a break from old-style patriarchal business masculinity, and its replacement by a more technocratic pattern that emphasises a cooperative, teamwork-based style of management. Connell and Wood (2005) document similar practice among some executives of international businesses in Australia. It is likely that a variety of masculinities co-exist in international business, as they do in many other social contexts, with local struggles for dominance.

The re-shaping of local masculinities is likely to be uneven. Taga's (2001) case studies of young Japanese middle-class men show this very clearly. Under cultural pressure from women to move away from 'traditional' Japanese patriarchal masculinity, men do not all produce the same response. Indeed, Taga identifies four contrasting patterns of response, ranging from rejection of change to transformation of identity.

It is characteristic of modernity that the world of 'work' is culturally defined as men's realm. But if capitalist development changed masculinities by linking gender identity with waged work, this same process makes masculinities vulnerable. The global economy is turbulent, marked by economic downturns as well as booms, regional decline as well as regional growth. Mass unemployment will undermine masculinities identified with 'work'. This situation is now very common – as a result of both the decline of former industrial areas such as northern England, and the rural–urban migration that has created huge under-employed workforces in cities like New Delhi, Sao Paulo and Mexico City. We can reasonably regard this as a major dynamic of change in contemporary masculinities. Even the Japanese 'salaryman' is vulnerable. As the security provided by the Japanese corporate world declined in the 1990s, there has been more satire and anxiety around this pattern of masculinity. The new image of the 'salaryman escaping' has appeared in Japanese media discussions (Dasgupta 2000).

The colonial and postcolonial world has tended to break down systems of patriarchy based on the extreme subordination and isolation of women, in the name of modernisation and women's rights (Kandiyoti 1994). Most men now, at least formally, accept women's presence in the public realm. At the same time, the process of development has produced in most postcolonial societies a public realm where men continue to hold the great majority of top positions in government, business and civil society. State institutions have seen important challenges to this dominance, by women's movements demanding equal opportunity in employment, childcare facilities, anti-discrimination laws, etc. But under neo-liberalism, state institutions tend to shrink, and power shifts to the market and the corporations. In this realm, the power of men remains largely undisturbed.

In anti-colonial and postcolonial struggles, the remaking of masculinity may be closely associated with violence. This can be seen for instance in the Palestinian resistance to Israeli occupation of the West Bank (Peteet 1994). Here the violence of the occupation and the resistance have changed the conditions in which masculinity is constructed. Older men lose authority over the process; rather, leadership moves into the hands of young men. Beatings and imprisonment by the occupying forces become a rite of passage for Palestinian youth. The personal trauma involved in anti-colonial struggles – small-scale, intimate warfare with a racial or religious dimension, with one's 'civilian' communities all around and in reach of the weapons – should not be under-estimated.

Patterns of emotional attachment are also subject to reconstruction by global social forces. Under colonialism, Christian missionaries often intervened against indigenous sexual customs. In the postcolonial world, the growth of individualism, and the disruption of communities by migration, has changed customary patterns of family formation. Concepts of 'romantic love' not only influence young women, they also affect young men. It is change in the arena of emotional relations that seems to underlie the discontent with masculinity among younger urban men in Chile, in a study by Valdés and Olavarría (1998). Their discontent does not involve a basic critique of the hegemonic model of masculinity, but takes the form of a sense of imprisonment in unchanging family roles.

Sexuality and emotional relationships may also be sites where larger social tensions are registered. Ghoussoub (2000) points to such a process in Egypt, where rumours about impotence-causing chemicals, and a burst of popularity for medieval sex manuals, would seem to be signs of a larger cultural disturbance about masculinity. Ghoussoub notes that the recent increase in women's status in Arab societies has posed dilemmas for men whose identities are still based in traditional conceptions of gender.

Complexity has also emerged in homosexual identities. A North American style of gay identity, as the main alternative to heterosexual masculinity, has now circulated globally. This process is often criticised as a form of cultural imperialism. But as Altman (2001) observes, on the basis of experience in South-East Asia, the 'globalisation of sexual identities' does not simply displace local models. Rather, they interact in extremely complex ways, generating some entirely new identities, and with many opportunities for code-switching.

However the problem is conceptualised, it is clear that the study of global masculinities involves extremely complex processes of change, in directions that are still far from clear. There is certainly no sweeping imposition of 'Western' masculinities on the rest of the world. Yet men in the majority world are unavoidably affected by the contemporary patterns of globalisation, for better and for worse.

References and further reading

Altman, D. (2001) *Global Sex*, Chicago, IL: University of Chicago Press.

Connell, R. (2002) *Gender*, Cambridge: Polity Press.

Connell, R. and Wood, J. (2005) 'Globalization and business masculinities', *Men and Masculinities*, 7 (4): 347–64.

Dasgupta, R. (2000) 'Performing masculinities? The "salaryman" at work and play', *Japanese Studies*, 20 (2): 189–200.

Donaldson, M. (2003) 'Studying up: the masculinity of the hegemonic', in S. Tomsen and

M. Donaldson (eds) *Male Trouble*, Melbourne: Pluto, pp. 156–79.
Ghoussoub, M. (2000) 'Chewing gum, insatiable women and foreign enemies: male fears and the Arab media', in M. Ghoussoub and E. Sinclair-Webb (eds) *Imagined Masculinities*, London, Saqi Books, pp. 227–35.
Gierycz, D. (1999) 'Women in decision-making: can we change the status quo?' in I. Breines, D. Gierycz and B. Reardon (eds) *Towards a Women's Agenda for a Culture of Peace*, Paris: UNESCO, pp. 19–32.
Gutmann, M.C. (2002) *The Romance of Democracy*, Berkeley, CA: University of California Press.
Hooper, C. (2001) *Manly States: Masculinities, International Relations, and Gender Politics*, New York: Columbia University Press.
Kandiyoti, D. (1994) 'The paradoxes of masculinity: some thoughts on segregated societies', in A. Cornwall and N. Lindisfarne (ed.) *Dislocating Masculinity*, London: Routledge, pp. 197–213.
Morrell, R. (ed.) (2001) *Changing Men in Southern Africa*, Pietermaritzburg: University of Natal Press.
Peteet, J. (1994) 'Male gender and rituals of resistance in the Palestinian intifada: a cultural politics of violence', *American Ethnologist*, 21 (1): 31–49.
Taga F. (2001) *Dansei no Jendâ Keisei: 'Otoko-Rashisa' no Yuragi no Naka de* (The Gender Formation of Men: Uncertain Masculinity), Tokyo, Tôyôkan Shuppan-sha.
Valdés, T. and Olavarría, J. (1998) 'Ser Hombre en Santiago de Chile: A Pesar de Todo, un Mismo Modelo', in T. Valdés and J. Olavarría (eds) *Masculinidades y Equidad de Género en América Latina*, Santiago: FLACSO/UNFPA, pp. 12–36.
Wajcman, J. (1999) *Managing Like a Man*, Sydney: Allen and Unwin.

See also: colonial and imperial masculinities; diaspotic and migrant masculinities; indigenous and First Nations masculinities; postcolonial masculinities

RAEWYN CONNELL

GLOBALISATION

Globalisation generally refers to recent transformations in governance and economy, manifested in the growing significance of multinational corporations, global markets, international institutions and mass communication. Some critics, however, criticise the conception of globalisation as unprecedented change of 'integration and interdependence', drawing precisely on earlier historical precedents (Pease and Pringle 2001: 9).

Masculinity scholars like Connell and Kimmel, who consider globalisation as inevitably gendered, call for taking gender into account in the work on globalisation. They furthermore signal the need to refocus research on masculinities beyond local and comparative studies (Connell 2001: 373). Pease and Pringle, alternatively, insist on examining local men's practices in a transnational context (Pease and Pringle 2001: 4).

Transnational business masculinity has often been identified by proponents of globalisation as a new phenomenon, as the current hegemonic form that reinforces gender disparities, characterised as 'egocentric' with 'conditional loyalties', 'a declining sense of responsibility for others' and 'a growing tendency to commodify relations with women' (Connell 2001: 370). As corporations are increasingly unregulated, the tendency has been to privilege men in all aspects of work (Kimmel 2000: 3). Moreover, economic reform through neo-liberal movements has weakened social programmes, including childcare services and anti-discrimination acts, to the detriment of women and the historically disadvantaged.

Globalisation has disrupted local and regional cultures. Its effects can be seen in widespread cultural homogenisation. Such disruption extends to local gender arrangements and articulations of identity, and it has often been met with the reassertion of more orthodox gender practices and ideals.

Gender in turn constitutes an important aspect of the resistance to globalisation. Oppositional movements highlight how global integration produces migration, loss of local authority, disappearance of customs and local institutions; therefore, 'efforts to reclaim economic autonomy, to reassert political control, and revive traditional domestic arrangements thus take on the veneer of restoring manhood' (Kimmel 2000: 4).

References and further reading

Connell, R. (2001) 'Masculinity politics on a world scale', in S.M. Whitehead and F.J. Barrett (eds) *The Masculinities Reader*, Cambridge: Polity, pp. 369–73.

Connell, R. and Wood, J. (2005) 'Globalization and business masculinities', *Men and Masculinities*, 7 (4): 347–64.

Kimmel, M. (2000) 'Global masculinities', *Gender Policy Review*, November: 1–5.

Pease, B. and Pringle, K. (2001) 'Introduction', in R. Pease and K. Pringle (eds) *A Man's World?* London: Zed Books, pp. 1–17.

See also: International Relations

NAJAT RAHMAN

GUN LOBBY

The term 'gun lobby' (or gun rights/pro-gun lobby) refers in the technical sense collectively to political pressure groups which oppose legislation that might curtail the production, purchase, import/export, ownership and use of guns. While this theoretically covers a range of pro-arms groups, including industry lobbyists, it usually refers to groups advocating on behalf of the private ownership of small arms and light weapons (SALW), ranging from collectors' items and hunting weapons to handguns and assault rifles. The most vociferous groups are in traditionally pro-gun societies with the political space necessary for lobbying for the 'right' to own weapons – even those that are expressly designed for military and police use.

By far the most powerful organisation in this respect, with enormous lobbying power both within and outside the USA, is the National Rifle Association (NRA), with over 4 million members. The NRA has been at the forefront to counter attempts to control firearms in the USA and has also brought its influence to bear in international trade negotiations and efforts to counter the spread of SALW (Small Arms Survey 2002).

The ideology of the gun lobby reflects a 'gun culture' with a mostly conservative view of the world, stressing a patriarchal masculinity (Kimmel and Mahler 2003) in which the armed male head of the household needs his weapon to protect himself and his family against outside intruders and potentially against a tyrannical government.

Though it is not explicitly stated, much of the subtext of this worldview is based on explicitly sexist as well as latently racist and class-based paranoia. It is a vision of the white man violently protecting himself, his property and his family with his weapons against the threat of the 'racially other' and/or socio-economically underprivileged. Gun lobbyists also must ward off the 'feminising' threat posed by 'liberals', and these political opponents are regularly derided in misogynist and homophobic terms, with slogans like 'Gun Free South Africa – Suck My Glock' (Kirsten 2002). These processes can be seen as being linked to both overt and implied sexual and gender connotations attached to firearms (Myrttinen 2003).

As the gun lobby wishes to gain widespread political support, these tendencies have usually been repressed in official pronouncements and increased efforts are being made to reach out to non-white, female and gay gun owners.

References and further reading

Kimmel, M. and Mahler, M. (2003) 'Adolescent masculinity, homophobia and violence', *American Behavioral Scientist*, 46 (10): 1439–58.

Kirsten, A. (2002) 'White men with weapons', in V. Farr and K. Gebrewold (eds) *Gender Perspectives on Small Arms and Light Weapons*, Bonn: BICC.

Myrttinen, H. (2003) 'Disarming masculinities', *Disarmament Forum*, 4, UNIDIR: Geneva.

Small Arms Survey (2002) *Small Arms Survey 2002*, Geneva: Small Arms Survey.

See also: masculinity politics; military masculinities

HENRI MYRTTINEN

HAIR

Men's body hair is a relatively neglected subject in the sociology of the body literature. Hair, in the male body sites, like face, chest and head, is an important part of the discursive and material construction of masculine subjectivities. From a gendered perspective, 'real' men are traditionally perceived as hairy men as well as large, hard and strong. Beards, moustaches and a conspicuous display of chest hair are all symbolic signs of dominant manhood in Western societies.

Hairiness in many men becomes gendered through its demonstration of distance from femininity and smooth men or hairless men. Indeed, the 'shame' of hairlessness plays a part in the policing of acceptable boundaries between different hierarchies of men and boys, whether among boys going through puberty or older men losing head hair.

Men and body hair is an area of considerable, gendered ambivalence as well as being historically differentiated. As gender relations have shifted so there have also been changes in men's relations to body hair. At times of insecurity about traditional masculinities, men's body hair has often been seen as a symbolic object of masculine reassurance.

The rigidity of the old, masculine/feminine binary has started to give way to more multiple and fluid masculine identities and related forms of body hair, such as long, hippy hair, male ponytails, dyed hair and decorative effects like dreadlocks and the plaiting of men's hair in some Afro-Caribbean cultures. The fixity of the conventional equation ('real' man equals hairy man) has been unsettled by many men's new interests (often powerfully influenced by gay culture) in fashion, body enhancement and body-focused narcissism. Some male athletes, bodybuilders, models and others have luxuriated in the clean lines of smooth, muscled bodies and turned away from excessive body hair by using depilation. In others, baldness has been rescued from the negative association of masculine inadequacy by actors like Yul Brynner and Telly Savalas, while in gay male 'bear' cultures it is large, hairy male bodies that are eroticised.

In a global context there is a much greater diversity associated with men's body hair. The Wodobe men of the Sahara see physical beauty as the foundation of their masculinity while the Karo men of Ethiopia (Gerschick 2004) use elaborate hair designs (ochre-coloured hair buns) as masculine symbols.

References and further reading

Gerschick, T. (2004) 'Masculinity and degrees of bodily normativity in western culture', in M. Kimmel, J. Hearn and R. Connell (eds) *Handbook of Studies on Men and Masculinities*, Thousand Oaks, CA: Sage.

See also: body image; metrosexual

DAVID JACKSON

HEALTH, OCCUPATIONAL

Within working-class settings, occupational health and safety is embedded in the culture of masculinity. Workers' attitudes and practices regarding occupational safety are conditioned by this cultural construct. For example, Watson (1990) discovered that for some male timber-mill workers, taking risks was regarded as an important part of being a 'real man'. In his research on the timber industry in the Australian state of New South Wales, Watson examined a group of timber workers who earned a living from chopping down trees. Watson noted that the timber workers valued the practical experience gained from manual labour, possessed a strong manual work ethic and gained pride from the risky nature of their occupation (Watson 1990: xix–xx).

For the male fellers and log haulers, chopping down trees was a job that required great bravery because the occupation involved high risks. As far as the workers were concerned, this was a job that only men were capable of doing (Williams 1993: 65).

In another example, Beynon (1973) studied social relations at Ford's car manufacturing plant in Liverpool circa 1960. He was interested in exploring how the employees experienced work on the assembly line, how they viewed their own place in the world and how they made sense of political forces that influenced their lives.

Beynon found that young men's deliberate bravado created dangerous situations. In the late 1960s, the Halewood plant was forced to lower the minimum age of recruitment to eighteen, which resulted in the employment of many youngsters. As is the case among many young people, they often participated in practical jokes. The adolescents constantly pulled the safety wire on the assembly line and on one shift, production was stopped on thirty-six occasions. The young 'lads' also manufactured 'Bostik bombs' (an explosive device made out of flammable glues) and hurled them into nearby dumpsters. The resulting explosion produced flames twenty feet high. Someone could easily have been killed by this practice (Beynon 1973: 139).

Haas (1977) also found that working-class masculinity gave rise to special occupational safety considerations when he conducted research on a construction site in the US. Haas was interested in studying an occupational group within the construction industry known as the 'high-steel workers'. They are responsible for installing the skeletal steel foundations of buildings.

Haas was filled with an overwhelming anxiety in the first days of the nine months he would spend as a participant-observer on a twenty-one-storey office building. He took out a US $50,000 accident policy to protect his family from the possibility of his death. He was baffled by the apparent lack of fear these workers demonstrated when working on the high-steel beams and columns. When traversing the narrow metal walkways, a sudden lapse in a tradesman's concentration could result in death (Haas 1977: 149).

He suspected that they developed a shared perspective for dealing with the fears of working under such dangerous conditions. Extensive research led him to the following hypothesis: the collective way in which the tradesmen dealt with *fear* was to treat it as though it did not exist. Each worker, feeling that they were more afraid than the next, would secretly live out their fears (Haas 1977: 153). High-steel workers could not express their feelings of anxiety to their co-workers. This would lead their co-workers to question their trustworthiness, which is a requisite for such a dangerous occupation. This working situation is one where the actions of an individual can affect the wellbeing of other workers.

More importantly, Haas's research is an example of a particular set of hegemonic values. Manliness was defined in relation to being fearless. Indeed, the workers contributed to the maintenance of the hegemonic structure. Workers who did not display these masculine attributes were ridiculed and generally disliked.

There was a shared belief that a fearful steel worker was an untrustworthy worker. Apprentices were often warned by established tradesmen about being careful who they trusted (Haas 1977: 154). This was part of the process whereby apprentices came to learn the shared perspective of the high-steel workers.

The high-steel workers' desire to conceal their anxieties and their need to appear fearless in front of their fellow workers caused many workers to deliberately flaunt the situation by taking risks. They showed off by volunteering for the most dangerous assignments (Haas 1977: 157).

Applebaum (1981) observed similar behaviour among a group of construction workers. His ethnographic research took place on commercial buildings and other projects like highways. In the course of his study, he examined many themes including job autonomy, hazardous work conditions, job satisfaction and the role of unions. Applebaum's central thesis is that because most tradesmen use their own tools, they have control over the work process and therefore have a substantial amount of autonomy and independence over their working lives.

Applebaum comments about a tradesman he calls Dan L. This man recalled the time when he first started working as a surveyor. One of his first jobs was over the Niagara river gorge, 368 feet above the river. On the first occasion on which Dan L had to walk out on to the steel, everyone was watching him to see how he would react. They knew he was scared, but they just wanted to test his reactions in order to determine whether he was a trustworthy worker (Applebaum 1981: 85–7).

References and further reading

Applebaum, H. (1981) *Royal Blue: The Culture of Construction Workers*, New York: Holt, Rinehart and Winston.

Beynon, H. (1973) *Working for Ford*, London: Penguin Books.

Cherry, M. (1974) *On High Steel*, New York: Quadrangle Press.

Germov, J. (1999) 'Class, health inequality, and social justice', in J. Germov (ed.) *Second Opinion: An Introduction to Health Sociology*, Melbourne: Oxford University Press, pp. 20–38.

Haas, J. (1977) 'Learning real feelings: a study of high steel ironworkers' reactions to fear and danger', *Sociology of Work and Occupations*, 4 (2): 147–71.

Iacuone, D. (2005) '"Real men are tough guys": hegemonic masculinity and safety in the construction industry', *Journal of Men's Studies*, 13 (2): 247–66.

Riemer, J. (1979) *Hard Hats: The Work World of Construction Workers*, Beverly Hills, CA: Sage.

Watson, I. (1990) *Fighting Over Forests*, Sydney: Allen and Unwin.

See also: health and illness, men's; masculinity/masculinities

DAVID IACUONE

HEALTH AND ILLNESS, MEN'S

Men's health has emerged as an important public concern that demands new types of health services and a larger share of public resources. In the process, the meaning of 'men's health' has been generally accepted as self-evident. It involves the health concerns of men and boys, as distinct from those of women and girls. This essay suggests that this common-sense understanding is ill-founded and limited in its capacity to serve as a conceptual basis for the development of effective policy and action to address the health problems of men. It over-simplifies and misrepresents the issues that are involved. A more sound theoretical foundation is required.

Since the 1990s, 'men's health' discourse has spread through various channels but public policy and popular media have been especially influential. The conceptual bedrock of this discourse is the idea that sex difference, or the bodily 'reproductive distinction' between men and women (Connell 2002: 10), creates two gender-based public health constituencies. Men's health is constructed by a contrast with 'women's health' (Schofield *et al.* 2000: 248). From this perspective, women's health is usually understood as a sex-based aggregate of statistical indicators related to women's reproductive pathologies, to their health service use, and to their mortality, morbidity, disability and 'lifestyle' practices (such as cigarette and alcohol consumption). Men's health is, correspondingly, constituted by the same indicators but in relation to men as a sex-based category. If the magnitudes between the two are different or unequal then so, too, are the health statuses of men and women. It is the margins of difference in the measurements between the two categories that indicate the presence of what is understood as a gender-specific health issue. Conversely, the absence of any significant difference suggests a gender-neutral health outcome and, therefore, no cause for 'gender-specific' public action (Schofield 2002: 34).

The development of men's health discourse and of the social movement that has advanced it, then, has depended heavily on the representation of men and their health in terms of men as a sex that, in aggregate, experiences less favourable rates than women on a significant range of health indicators. Such a representation has served as a foundation for the public claim that men as a sex experience specific health difficulties that require a sex-specific public response.

The evolving discipline of 'gender-specific medicine' has lent unexpected support to this approach with its use of the term 'gender' when it refers to sex differences. This new biomedical field has emerged in the context of a critique of biomedical research as having been insensitive to 'gender'. Practitioners and researchers within 'gender-specific medicine' suggest that biomedical research has generally proceeded on the basis that women are 'small men' and, therefore, have not needed to be included (Legato 2004). They argue that, by contrast, the biomedical research that they conduct and which informs the field is based on the inclusion of both sexes. They say that the results of this work show irrefutably small but significant 'gender differences' in the patterns of physiological functioning and disease among men and women, from heart attack symptoms to neurological responses (Legato 2004). Yet, as a review of this text on the subject published in a well-respected biomedical journal states, the principal mission of 'gender-specific medicine' is to advance knowledge of *sex differences* in systems medicine (Miller 2005).

This is not to suggest that men's health discourse promotes a crude biological reductionism in relation to its conceptualisation of men. On the contrary, men's health discourse, especially its public policy proponents, has embraced social understandings of men to indicate that the sex-based category 'men' (human bodies with male reproductive characteristics) is *also* constituted by a 'male role' or masculine practices that are *socially* determined. These are distinguished by their contrast with the 'female role' and feminine practices. Just as this approach imagines human embodiment as dimorphic, so too does it represent the social practices of human beings as taking 'the shape of a dichotomy between all-women and all-men' (Connell 2002: 36). It advances a match between embodiment and culture. These dichotomous hybrids constitute what men's health discourse understands as gender. Despite its incorporation of 'the social' in its representation of men and women, it still views gender as a matter of two distinct, and mutually exclusive, categories of people.

One of the distinctive features of men's health discourse, then, is its insistence that men have a collective interest and identity that is produced by its differentiation from the 'other sex' (Schofield 2004: 26). However, within men's health policy, the idea of a collective interest among men in relation to their health goes hand-in-hand with the idea of a *plurality* of interests among them. Although all men might appear to be the subject of men's health discourse, the discourse also emphasises ways in which men's health disadvantage is *not* generalised among men (Courtenay 2002: 6). Particular groups of men are often identified as bearing a particular burden: indigenous men, men from non-English speaking backgrounds, African–American men (in the United States), men with disabilities, gay men, men of low socio-economic status, and rural men. This creates some tension in the dominant formulation of men's health (Schofield *et al.* 2000: 249). On the one hand, to the extent that there is a shared or collective interest in men's health, all men as a whole have comparable or worse health than women as a whole. Yet on the other hand, while there are differences among men, only certain groups of men have comparable or worse health than women as a whole. Clearly, both are not tenable. Such a representation is conceptually contradictory. If it is the social disadvantage of *some* men that produces the rates of health differences between men and women, then to what extent is 'men's health' sex-specific at all? (Schofield *et al.* 2000: 248).

The emphasis on sex differences in men's health discourse is also associated with a further significant limitation. This involves the *evidence* that has been used to support their existence. The authors of a study commissioned by the Australian government to examine a range of issues associated with men's health, including sex differences in health, concluded that *there is no evidence that the differences exceed the similarities in health* (Connell *et al.* 1999). Clearly, a vast international literature on sex differences in health exists, as official statistics and extensive project-based research shows. Indeed, an extraordinary diversity characterises the health conditions for which these differences are examined. Typical examples are mortality, average life expectancy, chronic illness, injury and disability from accidents, suicide and substance abuse. But they also include 'diet and weight-control practices ... snake bites, dog attacks, and infections from eating with chopsticks' (Schofield *et al.* 2000: 249).

Yet, as the report from the Australian study explains,

> a finding of sex difference need not imply a difference between *all* men and *all* women. In fact, it usually does not. Quite small differences among a minority of the population may produce statistically significant differences in overall rates or averages.
>
> (cited in Schofield *et al.* 2000: 249)

Further, as the report also points out, 'in many research reports ... men and boys have *similar* averages or rates to women and girls; in other studies, men and boys have *better* averages or rates than women and girls' (cited in Schofield *et al.* 2000: 250). As the report stressed, however, this is not to trivialise or dismiss the serious health trouble that *some groups* of men are in, especially indigenous men, working-class men, men from non-English speaking backgrounds, some gay men and some rural men. However, men as a whole are not worse off than women.

The meaning of men's health that prevails in most men's health discourse, then, is characterised by significant flaws in conceptualisation and in the use of empirical evidence. There are no grounds – apart from those associated with men's reproductive biology – for advancing the idea that men as a whole share a set of health needs and that these disadvantage them *vis-à-vis* women as a whole. There are certainly *groups* of men with *pressing* health needs but these are generally related to factors associated with men's class, their indigeneity and, for some, their ethnicity and homosexuality.

Advancing a dynamic gender approach to men's heath

As the preceding has argued, the limitations evident in common understandings of men's health derive from thinking that imagines gender as two mutually exclusive categories of human beings. It proffers a static view, and one in which gender is basically a *noun* that refers to sex-differentiated characteristics, including behaviour. A more fruitful approach suggested here proposes an understanding of gender as dynamic social practice that demands the dissolution of the match between sex-based, dimorphic human embodiment and culture.

This does not mean that bodies do not count, especially in relation to the 'reproductive distinction' between them. On the contrary, this bodily distinction is vital. But from a dynamic perspective, the singularly most significant concern is how this distinction is brought into play in such a way that it comes to be one of the most potent forces in shaping who gets to participate in which social practices, how, and with what kinds of material and symbolic consequences, including health outcomes (Schofield 2004: 36). In other words, a dynamic approach of the kind offered here is concerned with gender as a principle of embodied social organisation, and one that has significant implications for the social distribution and exercise of power and its consequences (Ferree *et al.* 1998; Alsop *et al.* 2002; Connell 2002). By comparison with its categoricalist and static counterpart, it also has greater analytical or explanatory power in understanding men and their health.

This can be illustrated in relation to the health problem of occupational disability and fatality among men in 'blue-collar' work. According to official statistics, the highest rates of mortality and impairment generated by employment occur among men, especially those in hazardous occupations. This health problem is usually represented as a simple correlation between the greatest magnitudes of death and disability incurred in employment, and the category 'men'. Often, the correlation involves the category 'men by occupation'. The indicators of death and impairment in the workplace, however, are not explained by such a correlation. The dynamic approach, by contrast, would suggest that the greater burden of employment fatality and disability that is disproportionately incurred by working-class men is attributable to the greater participation by working men in hazardous and injurious jobs compared with their female partners, wives, sisters and daughters. In short, working-class employment has been organised in relation to, and constituted by, social practices in which the reproductive distinction between bodies has been central. Working-class men historically have tended to occupy more of the available jobs, especially full time, and have participated across a wider range of occupations than their female counterparts. Unfortunately, their greater and more diverse employment has gone hand-in-hand with more exposure to injurious and fatal work (Waldron 1995).

One of the most influential factors responsible for such an outcome has been the adoption by both management and unions of aggressively exclusionary approaches to women's employment in these hazardous jobs. This *gendering* of employment has seen a thoroughgoing masculinisation of such work and men's greater assumption of bodily damage in doing it. The lethal and hazardous effects of class in the workplace, in other words, have been *gendered*.

From a dynamic approach to gender and its emphasis on social practice, the mobilisation of the bodily reproductive distinction is not understood as being confined only to producing a division between men and women. It also operates *among* men with consequent gendered health effects. The realm of sexual practice, for example, is one in which a division in the kinds and frequencies of sexual experience does not apply only to women and men. It is also played out among men through the structure of sexual desire and embodied sexual practice. This has been most clearly demonstrated among homosexual men where a reproductive distinction in sexual desire and practice has been accompanied by a differentiated pattern of morbidity and mortality associated with HIV-AIDS (Dowsett 1996). In this way, homosexual men's sexual practice can be understood as gendered, including the health consequences generated by it. Such an understanding provides a practical basis for health interventions to address a men's health issue of global proportions. It contrasts significantly with a crude, sex-based binary approach, the main contribution of which appears to be the tabulation of human health and illness conditions by sex.

Conclusion

Constituencies of men worldwide face enormous health challenges. Addressing and redressing them requires more than simplistic formulations that are conceptually incoherent and politically divisive, especially in relation to women. Effective political action demands the formulation and implementation of public health policy that is informed by thinking and evidence that represents men's poor health, and the processes responsible for it, in terms of a critically reasoned and dynamic approach to gender.

References and further reading

Alsop, R., Fitzsimons, A. and Lennon, K. (2002) *Theorising Gender*, Cambridge: Polity Press.
Connell, R. (2002) *Gender*, Cambridge: Polity Press.
Connell, R., Schofield, T., Walker, L. and Wood, J.F. (1999) *Men's Health: A Research Agenda and Background Report*, Canberra: Commonwealth Department of Health and Aged Care.
Courtenay, W. (2002) 'A global perspective on the field of men's health: an editorial', *International Journal of Men's Health*, 1 (1): 1–13.
Dowsett, G. (1996) *Practicing Desire: Homosexual Sex in the Era of AIDS*, Stanford, CA: Stanford University Press.
Ferree, M., Lorber, J. and Hess, B.B. (eds) (1998) *Revisioning Gender*, London: Sage.
Legato, M.J. (ed.) (2004) *Principles of Gender-Specific Medicine, Vol. 1 and Vol. 2*, New York: Elsevier Academic Press.
Miller, V.M. (2005) 'Book review: *Principles of Gender-Specific Medicine, Vol. 1 and Vol. 2*', *The Physiologist*, 48: 2.
Schofield, T. (2002) 'What does "gender and health" mean?' *Health Sociology Review*, 11 (1 and 2): 29–38.
—— (2004) *Boutique Health? Gender and Equity in Health Policy*, Australian Health Policy Institute Commissioned Paper Series 2004/08, Sydney: Australian Health Policy Institute at the University of Sydney.
Schofield, T., Connell, R., Walker, L. and Wood, J.F. (2000) 'Understanding men's health and illness: a gender-relations approach to policy, research, and practice', *Journal of American College Health*, 48 (May): 247–56.
Waldron, I. (1995) 'Contributions of changing gender differences in behavior and social roles to changing gender differences in mortality', in D. Sabo and D.F. Gordon (eds) *Men's Health and Illness*, Newbury Park, CA: Sage, pp. 22–45.

TONI SCHOFIELD

HEGEMONIC MASCULINITY

Developed in the 1980s (Carrigan *et al.* 1985) to provide a relational and socially constructed conception of men and masculinities, the term 'hegemonic masculinity' describes the hierarchical interaction between multiple masculinities and explains how some men make it appear normal and necessary that they dominate most women and other men (Connell 1987).

Hegemonic masculinity describes: (1) a position in the system of gender relations; (2) the system itself; and (3) the current ideology that serves to reproduce masculine domination. Connell demonstrates the essentialistic, ahistorical and normative liabilities in previous men's studies scholarship. In the concept of hegemonic masculinity Connell joins the constructivist view of 'doing gender' (West and Zimmerman 1987) with insights drawn from feminist scholars who described the ways in which gender relations shape social structures (Hartsock 1983).

Connell seeks to explain: (1) how some men succeed in making it appear normal, natural and necessary for them to enjoy power over other men and most women; (2) why it is that so many men and women participate willingly in their own oppression; and (3) how resistance to hegemonic masculinity can promote gender justice.

Connell posits four types of masculinities, more as positions in relation to one another than as personality types: hegemonic, complicit, subordinated and marginalised. The hegemonic position is the currently accepted male ideal within a particular culture at a particular time. As such, the hegemonic male is an ideal-type (Weber 1946). Connell notes that this image changes over time and place as well as being subject to contestation within a particular culture.

Most men fall within the second category, complicit. These men accept and participate in the system of hegemonic masculinity so as to (1) enjoy the material, physical and symbolic benefits of the subordination of women, (2) through fantasy experience the sense of hegemony and learn to take pleasure in it, and (3) avoid subordination.

The relations among the four positions are hierarchical. A man in the subordinated position suffers that fate despite appearing to possess the physical attributes necessary to aspire to hegemony. Men run the risk of subordination when they do not practise gender consistent with the hegemonic system and ideology. Marginalised men are those who cannot even aspire to hegemony, most often men of colour and men with disabilities.

The second manner in which Connell uses 'hegemonic masculinity' is to describe the current system of gender relations: current 'configurations of practice' organise social relations and structures to the overall benefit of men in relation to women and of some men in relation to other men. Connell stresses that these configurations of practice take place across four dimensions: power, the division of labour, cathexis or emotional relations and the symbolic. Connell's argument is that hegemonic masculinity as a system becomes built into social institutions so as to make it appear normal and natural for men's superordinate position to be maintained.

The third usage of hegemonic masculinity, as an ideology, provides the justification through which patriarchy is legitimated and maintained. As an ideology hegemonic masculinity structures the manner in which all people experience and thereby know their world, although those experiences vary as both men and women are differentially situated by race, class and sexuality. This ideology, referred to as hegemonic complicity, can be measured across four dimensions: ideal-type masculinity, hierarchical ranking of self and others, subordination of women and the subordination of woman-like behaviour (Levy 2005). The first dimension, ideal-type masculinity, is the belief that there is a single type of masculinity that is appropriate. Different men or groups of men and women can posit a different ideal-type, contesting the definition of that type, but the underlying belief in a single ideal-type typifies this dimension.

Hierarchical ranking of oneself and others is perhaps the least studied component of hegemonic masculinity as an ideology. Previous scholars (Lewis 1978) spoke of competition as a restrictive component of masculinity or as a barrier to meaningful interaction. This conceptualisation fails to capture the ever-present intra-psychic dimension of active hierarchic assessment. Hierarchical ranking is a process in which men compare themselves and others actively and incessantly to their general or contextual ideal-type.

Subordination of women and anyone or any trait perceived to be woman-like includes overt and covert sexism as well as homophobia. Although some would argue that both overt sexism and homophobia have been in decline, the lingering or residual effects, often in the form of beliefs about men, women and sexuality, are quite active.

The three dimensions of hegemonic masculinity as a position, a system and an ideology can be theoretically separated while their interaction and interconnections are still recognised. Those who criticise the concept of hegemonic masculinity for confusion, reification or elitism (Demetriou 2001; Lorber 1998; Martin 1998; Whitehead 1999) need to recognise its multiple usages.

References and further reading

Carrigan, T., Connell, R. and Lee, J. (1985) 'Toward a new sociology of masculinity', *Theory and Society*, 14: 551–604.

Connell, R. (1987) *Gender and Power*, Stanford, CA: Stanford University Press.

Demetriou, D.Z. (2001) 'Connell's concept of hegemonic masculinity: a critique', *Theory and Society*, 30: 337–61.
Hartsock, N. (1983) *Sex and Power*, New York: Longman.
Levy, D.P. (2005) 'Hegemonic complicity, friendship and comradeship', *Journal of Men's Studies*, 13 (2): 199–225.
Lewis, R.A. (1978) 'Emotional intimacy among men', *Journal of Social Issues*, 34: 108–21.
Lorber, J. (1998) 'Symposium on R. Connell's *Masculinities*', *Gender and Society*, 12: 469–72.
Martin, P.Y. (1998) 'Symposium on R. Connell's *Masculinities*', *Gender and Society*, 12: 472–4.
Weber, M. (1946) *Essays in Sociology*, edited by H.H. Gerth, Oxford: Oxford University Press.
West, C. and Zimmerman, D.H. (1987) 'Doing gender', *Gender and Society*, 1: 125–51.
Whitehead, S. (1999) 'Hegemonic masculinity revisited', *Gender, Work and Organization*, 6: 58–62.

See also: masculinity/masculinities; sex role theory

DONALD P. LEVY

HEROES

A hero is a figure to look up to and admire. Heroes are brave and often have superhuman powers. The hero embodies traits typically associated with masculinity, such as physical strength, intelligence and fortitude. Heroes appear in some of our earliest written works, including *Gilgamesh*, *Beowulf* and the Greco/Roman tales of Perseus and Hercules. Traditionally, and in Aristotle's eyes, the tragic hero has a flaw so that, while inspirational, he also has a quality that can bring him low and make him more like us. We see this characteristic in Achilles (invulnerable except for his heel) and Samson (strong until his hair is cut). In modern times, the tragic weakness can be seen in Superman's kryptonite, Spider-Man's neuroses and Edward Norton's alter ego Brad Pitt in *Fight Club*.

Joseph Campbell (1949) originally described the hero's journey as consisting of four stages: separation, initiation, return and recognition. Campbell found similarities between the heroes of literature and the figures of great religions. Moses, for instance, is separated from his family and initiated by his realisation of his own Judaism and the Pharaoh's evil. Ultimately, he returns to Judaism and is recognised as a prophet. In a similar manner, Superman is separated from his world when his father sends him to Earth in a rocket. He is initiated by the Kents, a typical American couple, to accept his role as protector of humanity. His return manifests itself in his assumption of the Superman identity. Recognition comes in the form of approbation from a grateful public. Campbell asserted that the story of the hero is a universal and played out in all forms of media, including popular fiction and film.

In the United States, the availability of cheap newsprint led to the dawn of pop culture in the late nineteenth century and celebrated contemporary figures like William F. (Buffalo Bill) Cody and Davy Crockett. The heroes' quite impressive accomplishments were obscured by the fiction created around them. It is doubtful, for example, that Davy Crockett 'kilt him a bar when he was only three' but interesting to note how this story resembles the legend of Hercules strangling two serpents in his crib.

If the cowboy was America's version of the knight in shining armour, the detectives of the hard-boiled school were the knights of the city. The two most famous detectives were Philip Marlowe and Sam Spade, created by Raymond Chandler and Dashiell Hammett, respectively. They were hardly role models, living lonely lives full of drink, cigarettes, murder and cheap women, but they were motivated by a strict, if non-traditional, moral code. Sam Spade was motivated to find his partner's killer. Philip Marlowe would turn in his best friend if it was the right thing to do. These characters, often referred to as anti-heroes because they practised what they individually considered 'justice' rather than necessarily following the law, grew out of the malaise that stemmed from America's post World War I collective realisation that war was not a great adventure but rather a terrible, ugly business. Mickey Spillane took the violence of the private detective to an extreme degree in his ultra-violent satyr Mike Hammer. His character evolved into the 1980s Reagan-era heroes of Rambo and *Die Hard*'s John McClane.

In the 1930s, the hero pulps – magazines that centred on the adventures of a single character – were an important step in the development of the hero because they reinvented the idea of a main character with greater than normal powers. The obsessively and perfectly trained Doc Savage and the mysterious and elusive detective The Shadow eventually gave birth to the comic book hero and the modern pop culture phenomenon of the superhero in movies and toy stores.

Probably the first true superhero was Superman, created in 1938 by two teenage boys who had grown up steeped in popular culture. Other superhero icons include Batman and Spider-Man. Most superheroes possess powers granted to them by scientific or supernatural forces. Whereas some superheroes gain their powers by accident, such as through the bite of a radioactive spider, others are destined for greatness as a consequence of being born on an alien planet. Despite such exotic imaginary origins, superheroes are a uniquely American creation. Although American audiences do not seem drawn to heroes created in other countries, the United States has exported a huge selection of superheroes, especially through movies and television.

One of the earliest women superheroes was Wonder Woman, an Amazon princess who came to the United States during World War II because of her love for an American soldier. However, many women comic book superheroes, such as Supergirl and Batgirl, were uninspired copies of their male counterparts. As a result of the feminist movement, a new genre of female hero has emerged (Inness 1998). One of the earliest examples was Emma Peel from the British television show *The Avengers* (herself a refinement of the previous, less approachable *Avengers* character Cathy Gale, who more clearly resembled the untouchable Amazons of mythology). Although not superhuman, she was a karate-trained secret agent. Other examples of tough women heroes include Ellen Ripley (the only survivor in the film *Alien*), Xena and Captain Janeway, the first woman starship commander in the long-running *Star Trek* franchise. Buffy the Vampire Slayer has proven to be a popular heroine who has also attracted a great deal of attention among scholars and post-pubescents. Because heroism is not considered part of the stereotypic role for women, female heroes often have to navigate between toughness and femininity. As counterpoints, female heroes challenge societal conventions about heroic behaviour as an exclusively masculine domain.

References and further reading

Campbell, J. (1949) *The Hero with a Thousand Faces*, Princeton, NJ: Princeton University Press.

Feiffer, J. (1965) *The Great Comic Book Heroes*, New York: Dial.

Hamilton, E. (1942) *Mythology*, Boston, MA: Little, Brown.

Inness, S.A. (1998) *Tough Girls*, Philadelphia, PA: University of Pennsylvania Press.

See also: culture and representation

SHAUN K. MCLAUGHLIN
JAMES K. BEGGAN

HETEROSEXUALITY

The issue of how masculinity and heterosexuality are conceptually connected has a historical location in feminist theorising around these terms. Feminist theorists and activists have highlighted heterosexuality's role in reproducing women's subordination through a focus on a diversity of issues such as: domestic violence, child abuse, representations of sexuality, sexual relationships and practices, domestic life and the labour contract in marriage, among other issues (see Richardson 1997). Heterosexuality has been described as institution, practice, experience and identity. The notion of heterosexuality as an institution, as something which has become 'institutionalised', refers in part to its 'invisibility' according to Holland *et al.* (1996: 144). Furthermore, heterosexuality is institutionalised through state-sanctioned marriage and family law, powerful cultural discourses of sex and love, and everyday practices which privilege heterosexuality as the unspoken norm. It has also been argued that institutionalised heterosexuality frames all sexuality and that heterosexuality is an institution which encompasses much more than sexual desire or sexual acts.

As well as highlighting how heterosexuality as social practice constitutes gender, feminist critiques also identify the prevailing belief in the 'naturalness' of heterosexuality as an important reason why outdated, oppressive beliefs and practices persist. When social institutions are seen as the outcome of 'natural drives', resistance to change is harder to overcome. Further, it is within heterosexual relations that traditional forms of masculinity and femininity are reproduced. Holland *et al.*, in their study of young women's and men's sexuality in the context of AIDS, consider accounts of first heterosexual experiences and conclude that 'we are arguing that heterosexuality is not a balanced (or even unbalanced) institutionalisation of masculinity-and-femininity, it is masculinity' (1996: 145). It is within this context that young women's femininity is constructed within heterosexuality and within male territory, territory which is seen to exist only with female collusion and consent.

Feminist theorising has raised pressing questions about the relationship between changing femininities and masculinities and the 'decision' to form heterosexual relationships. It has asked whether new gender identities produce different patterns of relationships, which in turn become sites of change where new heterosexual masculinities and femininities are reinvented, or stabilised, and where women's agency and the potential for more democratic heterosexual relationships are recognised (Hockey *et al.* 2002).

Masculinity studies and the theorising of heterosexuality and masculinity

Feminist theorising on heterosexuality and how heterosexuality connects to power, gender roles, identities and masculinities has informed other theorists' attempts to conceptualise heterosexuality and masculinity. These theorists, such as those from the new men's studies or critical studies of men and masculinities, have started to theorise masculinity in relationship to heterosexuality in new ways. This has been on diverse topics and from a variety of perspectives. These men include male academics who embrace postmodernism, queer theory and psychoanalysis, as well as anti-sexist men involved in both the men's movement and academia (see Seidler 1992) and those who are anti-feminist (Jukes 1993). Jukes has argued that men are dominated by an urge to both conquer and dominate women and that heterosexual desires are compromised by the need to penetrate women and impregnate them. The penis is seen to be a rock of stability to which most men turn under stress. The bottom line, he argues, is that men's abusiveness, violence and power are not within men's control and are seen as inherent to their natures. Those sympathetic to feminism share a social constructionist view of gender, masculinities and heterosexuality, rejecting the essentialising, deterministic viewpoint held by Jukes.

Seidler (1992), on the other hand, feels it is important for men writing about sexuality, that heterosexual men are seen to engage with both feminism and gay liberation movements and do so from both personal experience and theoretical standpoints. He asserts that even though heterosexuality functions as an oppressive norm within patriarchal society, heterosexuality itself should not be renounced. Heterosexuality could be seen as a political choice and men could learn to accept and celebrate their heterosexuality.

Men crucially have to face their own fear of intimacy, recognising how little they know about their own sexuality and how estranged men are from their bodies, which they use in instrumental ways.

It has also been argued that popular, gendered assumptions about 'men's emotional inarticulacy' are reflected in the lack of sociological attention to the emotional dimensions of men's experiences of heterosexuality. Theorists such as Seidler (1992) have stressed that men have had to deal with the consequences of their emotional alienation from themselves, and highlighted their painful struggle for a suitable 'emotional language'. The 'wounded' emotionally inarticulate male may be asked now to take more emotional responsibility for himself and others, but despite this, others feel that men are still silent about their own sexuality as opposed to the objects of their desire. Nonetheless, theorists such as Connell (2000) have recently asserted that a consideration of emotional relations in the context of masculinity is a fundamental new direction in theory and research.

Heterosexuality has also been theorised in relation to class (see Connell 2000) and race. For example, it has been argued that black men can alienate black women, especially feminists, through performing in aggressive or misogynistic ways, which, though possibly enabling for them, reinforce racialised heterosexual images (see Whitehead 2002).

Though a variety of perspectives exist for analysing masculinity and heterosexuality, there has been little engagement with particular perspectives, for instance queer. As well, popular culture, through men's magazines and the media, can be seen to sidetrack any discussion on masculinity and heterosexuality into the personal, offering individual solutions to men's sexual and emotional problems. This can be at the expense of stressing structural constraints or issues of power and inequality. The problem here also can be that heterosexuality is often implicit in debates as a taken-for-granted substrate, not explicitly identified and addressed in terms of identity or practice. Heterosexual men's lack of confidence in their own bodies, in the context of issues such as relationship problems or cosmetic surgery, can be raised, but not in terms of the implications for women.

Hegemonic masculinities

A number of theorists have closely linked hegemonic masculinities to heterosexuality which is seen to have consequences for diverse groups of women and men in different ways. Mac an Ghaill (1996) asserts that theorists have explored the ways in which dominant definitions of heterosexual masculinity are affirmed and authenticated within social and cultural arenas, where ideologies, discourses, representations and material practices, for instance, systematically privilege men and boys. In the late 1970s and early 1980s, an emphasis on men's violence as systematic and central to male domination, and a growing critique of normative heterosexuality and masculine sexuality as fundamentally implicated in this, was asserted (see Hearn 1998.) More recently, there has been a growing complexity in feminist accounts of power and violence in heterosexuality, as exemplified, for instance, in the work of theorists such as Stevi Jackson (1999). Heterosexual men have been seen to be entrenched in a defence of patriarchy, but some, like Connell (2000), have also found reasons why it is in men's interests to question the institution of heterosexuality and their part in upholding this and patriarchal relations.

The concept of masculism recognises hierarchical forms of masculinity as powerful and privileged in different settings and contexts, including the way heterosexual men are advantaged (see Whitehead 2002 and Carrigan *et al.* 1985). As well, hegemonic masculinity can be seen as the way dominant male sexual practices are used to generate a naturalised view of the world that is so embedded in dominant culture that it appears as 'common sense'. Furthermore, hegemonic masculinities are premised on masculinity being defined as femininity's opposite, and within this context heterosexuality is the unchallenged, often essentialised norm which upholds this hegemony (see Connell 2000). Connell also argues that men have different relationships to heterosexuality. Subordinate masculinities, such as the categories of effeminate or unassertive heterosexuals, may not be part of a dominant masculinity. There has been much discussion and problematising of the notion of counter-hegemonic masculinities (see Connell 2000; Whitehead 2002).

Specific issues that have had sustained critical interest specifically in relation to hegemonic masculinities and heterosexuality have been, for instance, education, sport, violence, intimacy, the emotions and relationships.

In education, where hegemonic forms of masculinity cultivated in a school environment are implicated with regimes of compulsory heterosexuality, masculinity can be seen to be constructed as the necessary counterpart to heterosexuality, and so anything that does not fit into this pairing up of masculinity and heterosexuality becomes a point of difference. In environments where young straight males are exploring the boundaries of their sexuality, it becomes necessary to assert their masculinity, and so their heteronormativity (see Mac an Ghaill 1996).

With reference to sport and heterosexual, homophobic, hegemonic masculinities, these issues have been theorised in relation to wrestling, athletics, nationalism, sport and sexuality, football and more non-traditional extreme sports, among others (see McKay *et al.* 2000).

Heterosexuality and gender

The connection between heterosexuality and gender has received much attention: from the assertion that heterosexuality is not primarily experienced as a sexual identity, but as something inherent in being human, to the view that within the ideologies of patriarchal structures, heterosexuality has been structured as the normative gender.

A definition of masculinity as a category maintained by making strict polar distinctions of gender and sexuality is reflected in the idea of the heterosexual matrix. This can be conceived of as the cultural demand for heterosexuality creating the need for clear markers of gender so that sexual partners can be 'correctly chosen'. This process epitomises how gender is used to maintain heterosexuality (see Brod and Kaufman 1994).

However, historical perspectives have conceptualised masculinity and its connection to heterosexuality in different ways, allowing us to see the historical construction of both the terms and the identities men adopt. For example, they have problematised the idea of exclusive sexual interest in women as the desideratum of normal masculinity, in which heterosexuality is seen as a distinct identity.

Theorists have also considered how masculinities and heterosexuality connect to homosexuality and homophobia. If, to prove their masculinity, men must display a coherent heterosexuality, then men must distance themselves from homosexuality through homophobic behaviour, which can be seen not as much to do with others' sexuality as a means to display their own heterosexual masculinity (Alsop *et al.* 2002).

Feminist critique

In their diverse responses to theorising heterosexuality and masculinity, male theorists have varied in their relation to feminist theory and feminism as a political movement. Some have acknowledged the debt male theorists owe to feminism, while others have rejected feminist insights or stereotyped particular feminist positions such as radical feminism. Feminists have critiqued these attempts to reflect on how heterosexuality and masculinity are interconnected. Robinson (1996) asks if men's attempts to theorise these issues reflect men's diverse experiences, consider power imbalances, or have an empathic relationship to feminist theory. From another perspective, feminism has been seen, by some feminists and male theorists, to have created a 'heterophobia' where women and men cannot relate to each other any more, because claims of sexual harassment have created such a climate of fear. However, most feminists and those writing on men, masculinity and heterosexuality from a new men's studies/critical studies of men and masculinity background have argued differently. Though power issues need to be central, a questioning of the links between masculinity, heterosexuality, gender and domination allows for a reconfiguration of masculinity, heterosexuality and gender relations.

References and further reading

Alsop, R., Fitzsimons, A. and Lennon, K. (eds) (2002) *Theorizing Gender*, Cambridge: Polity.
Brod, H. and Kaufman, M. (eds) (1994) *Theorizing Masculinities*, Thousand Oaks, CA: Sage.
Carrigan, T., Connell, R. and Lee, J. (1985) 'Towards a new sociology of masculinity', *Theory and Society*, 14 (5): 551–604.
Connell, R. (2000) *The Men and the Boys*, London: Polity.
Edwards, T. (1994) *Erotics and Politics: Gay Male Sexuality, Masculinity and Feminism*, London: Routledge.
Hearn, J. (1998) *The Violences of Men*, London: Sage.
Hockey, J., Robinson, V. and Meah, A. (2002) 'For better or worse?": heterosexuality reinvented', *Sociological Research Online*, 7 (2), available at http://www.socresonline.org.uk/7/2/hockey.html
Holland, J., Ramazanoglu, C. and Thomson, R. (1996) 'In the same boat? The gendered (in)experience of first heterosex', in D. Richardson (ed.) *Theorising Heterosexuality*, Buckingham: Open University Press.
Jackson, S. (1999) *Heterosexuality in Question*, London: Sage.
Jukes, A. (1993) *Why Men Hate Women*, London: Free Association Press.
Mac an Ghaill, M. (ed.) (1996) *Understanding Masculinities*, Buckingham: Open University Press.
McKay, J., Messner, M. and Sabo, D. (eds) (2000) *Masculinities, Gender Relations and Sport*, London: Sage.
Richardson, D. (1997) 'Sexuality and feminism', in V. Robinson and D. Richardson (eds) *Introducing Women's Studies: Feminist Theory and Practice*, London: Macmillan.
Robinson, V. (1996) 'Heterosexuality and masculinity: theorising male power or the male wounded psyche?' in D. Richardson (ed.) *Theorising Heterosexuality*, London: Open University Press.
Seidler, V. (1992) *Men, Sex and Relationships: Writings from Achilles Heel*, London: Routledge.
Whitehead, Stephen M. (2002) *Men and Masculinities: Key Themes and New Directions*, Cambridge: Polity.

See also: domestic violence; education; emotions; feminist theory; friendship; gay masculinities; homophobia and heterosexism; homosexuality; intimacy; marriage; men's relations with women; sexual violence

VICTORIA ROBINSON

HIJRAS

The word *hijra* is a masculine noun, widely translated as either 'eunuch' or 'hermaphrodite' (intersexed). The popular understanding of *hijras* as 'the third sex of India' is predicated on a model of intersexuality – most typically, a *male* model whereby *hijras* are commonly represented as sexually anomalous or impotent men who lack desire for women. This is most dramatically embodied in the (ideal but not always actualised) imperative to emasculate oneself, i.e. sacrifice one's genitalia to the Hindu goddess Bedhraj Mata, in return for the divine power to bless or curse with fertility/infertility – an act interpreted as a 'rebirth' from male to *hijra*. As vehicles of this divine (asexual) power, *hijras* perform at births and marriages and at Bedhraj Mata's temple, although currently many *hijras* also work as sex workers.

Whether *hijras* are 'born' or 'made', their identity is primarily envisioned in terms of lost virility; they are 'men minus men' (O'Flaherty 1980) who perform many aspects of female-gendered identity: wearing women's clothes, embodying 'feminine' performative gestures and attributes, and adopting women's names. However, *hijras* are also 'not women', their inability to bear children being the most significant factor in this understanding.

While *hijras* are the most identifiable 'alternative' sex/gender in India, they locate themselves within a larger spectrum of non-normative sex/gender configurations, their *kothi* 'family', which includes, among others, self-identified gay men. Within this family, *hijras* differentiate themselves as deserving of greater respect for their complex, nationwide kinship structure, their (idealised) renunciation of sexual desire/practice, and their highly visible modes of self-presentation, including their distinctive speech and dress.

Given the wide diversity of sex/gender configurations, the national census data that only codes for 'men' and 'women', and *hijras*' migratory lifestyles, current estimates of *hijra* numbers are notoriously ambiguous, ranging from 50,000 to over 2 million, mostly in urban locales.

References and further reading

Cohen, L. (1995) 'The pleasures of castrations', in P. Abramson and S. Pinkerton (eds) *Sexual Nature, Sexual Culture*, Chicago, IL: University of Chicago Press.

Hall, K. (1997) 'Go suck your husband's sugarcane', in A. Livia and K. Hall (eds) *Queerly Phrased*, New York: Oxford University Press.

Jaffrey, Z. (1996) *The Invisibles*, New York: Pantheon.

Nanda, S. (1999) *Neither Man Nor Woman*, 2nd edn, New York: Wadsworth.

O'Flaherty, W. (1980) *Women, Androgynes, and Other Mythical Beasts*, Chicago, IL: University of Chicago Press.

Reddy, G. (2005) *With Respect to Sex*, Chicago, IL: University of Chicago Press.

See also: Indian masculinities

GAYATRI REDDY

HISTORY, AFRICA

Although Africa's historiography contains much information about African men and, at least implicitly, about masculinities, only in the late 1990s did historians start studying the construction of masculinities. Building on the insights of feminist scholarship that had introduced gender as an analytical category, historians set out to explore African men as gendered social subjects and unpack changing meanings of masculinity.

Many scholars have commented on the fluidity and multiplicity of gender in African societies, articulated with age, seniority, wealth and ritual authority (Hodgson and McCurdy 2001; Cole *et al.* 2006). This applies to masculinity. There are not only a diversity of men and a plurality of masculinity in any African society, but ideologies of masculinity (like those of femininity) are also subject to historical change. Historical transformations, such as the introduction of capitalism, the abolition of slavery and the slave trade, colonialism, wage labour and cash cropping, migration and urbanisation, as well as the spread of Islam, Christianity and Western education, had an impact on understandings of masculinity while these transformations were being shaped by gender as well. Inspired by Connell (1995), historians of southern Africa have embraced the model that one form of masculinity is hegemonic in terms of power and masculine privilege, while others remain subordinate (Morrell 1998a, 2001a). Other scholars have critiqued Connell's approach, since it does not recognise situations, like those in (post)colonial Africa, where competing notions of masculinity, of local and foreign origins, coexisted without any one of them becoming hegemonic. Instead scholars have asked: which forms of masculinity were most contested? How did individual actors engage with a multiplicity of masculinities? How did age, class or generation intersect with notions of masculinity? What were the continuities and changes in a gender order?

Three perspectives help study African masculinities: a focus on discourse, on practice and on formations of identities and subjectivity. Discourses – produced by institutions and individuals – express cultural ideals and expectations of those considered masculine. Understandings of masculinity are revealed by social practice, situated within historical contexts; they are also reflected in individual experience (Lindsay and Miescher 2003).

The historiography of masculinity has concentrated on West and southern Africa since the late nineteenth century (Morrell 1998a, 2001a; Lindsay and Miescher 2003; Ouzgane and Morrell 2005). Scholars have paid less attention to the ideologies and practices of masculinity in pre-colonial African societies, although there is rich evidence about gender flexibility and its ability to transcend sex. In Igbo societies 'female husbands' and 'male daughters' took up responsibilities and status of positions usually reserved for men (Amadiume 1987). The enduring figure of the African 'big man' was crucial in the process of state formation. In West and Central Africa, ambitious men enlarged their households with women and men, some of them slaves, to pursue political and material goals. This 'wealth in people' enabled them to establish polities. Big men, instrumental in the operations of the Atlantic slave trade, paradoxically sold slaves to Europeans in order to purchase imported goods for attracting additional followers (Lindsay and Miescher 2003). In eighteenth-century Asante, the creation of a centralised kingdom corresponded with a shift in gender relations. Women lost access to spiritual and political power because of militarisation and the introduction of the male warrior ideal (Akyeampong and Obeng 1995). Big men became associated with a title granted by the Asante ruler for their generosity and display of wealth. Upon their death, the state appropriated their riches. By the end of the nineteenth century, the big-man status no longer referred to men acting on behalf of the Asante state but to an emerging class of traders who accumulated fortunes dealing in kola and rubber. Still big men faced the expectation to share their wealth (Miescher 2005).

Colonial conquest challenged the social position of senior African men, affecting ideas of masculinity. In Ovamboland, northern Namibia, the co-existence of two dominant masculinities, one based on fatherhood, the other on elite status, predated colonial rule. A political centralisation led to the formation of 'supermasculinity' among elite men who controlled cattle and clients. Young men used new opportunities like access to missions and migrant labour as alternative routes to manhood. Migrants reduced their economic dependence on fathers for access to cattle and marriage without calling into question the ideology of fatherhood in terms of affection and deference (McKittrick 2003). Challenges to established orders could also come from women. In the Nsukka Division of northern Igboland, Nigeria, Ahebi Ugbabe refused to be sacrificed to the goddess Ohe. Instead she fled to neighbouring Igalaland, taking up work as a prostitute and trader. She only returned after having established close relations with the British colonial rulers who valued her as an interlocutor. By 1918 she was appointed as the only female warrant chief and also acquired the *Eze* (king's) title. But when she attempted to sponsor her own masquerade, the spiritual prerogative of (biological) Igbo men, Ahebi was stopped by male elders. The British declined to support her ambition for full manhood, instead siding with Nsukka's gerontocratic elite. This case not only corrects the argument that colonial rule undermined Igbo gender flexibility but also demonstrates its continuity and limits. Although Ahebi skilfully seized Igbo opportunities of female masculinity as headman, warrant chief and husband, she was prevented from carrying gender transformation too far (Achebe 2003).

Colonial programmes for re-making individual African men through schools, churches, mission societies and work places have received much scholarly attention. In nineteenth-century Ghana, the Basel Mission founded separate communities with distinct gender rules and established educational institutions to transform male converts into a new kind of men: monogamous husbands who privileged their children over their matrilineage and who were devoted to their work and church communities as loyal colonial subjects. Life histories show how a group of men dealt with competing notions of masculinity, those promoted by the Presbyterian Church and those dominant in their hometowns. None of these became hegemonic. Rather the men created their own synthesis by aspiring to Akan ideals of senior masculinity and big-man status while also drawing on missionary teachings (Miescher 2005). Across colonial Africa, men's access to wage labour became the key to marriage and adulthood. Among Nigerian railway men, steady pay cheques changed gender identities. Railway employees took on more domestic expenses like food and school fees. During labour disputes they deployed the notion of a male breadwinner and demanded family allowances. Still, in personal pursuits railway men continued to embrace the big-man ideal, although in a colonial economy access to money had replaced older strategies, like wealth in people, in reaching this goal (Lindsay 2003). Coal miners in southeastern Nigeria experienced the treatment by their employers as emasculating. Miners, called 'boy' by European employers, challenged their infantilisation at work by drawing strength from their positions as senior men in home villages (Brown 2003).

These processes were more pronounced and violent in South Africa, where a British imperial masculinity had arrived in the nineteenth century. While this 'settler masculinity' – promoted in the military, family, schools, sports and leisure clubs – became hegemonic, other masculinities, Afrikaner and African, changed. In the cities and townships, an emerging 'black masculinity', characterised by violence, distinguished itself from the older 'African masculinity' of the countryside and labour reserves (Morrell 1998b, 2001b).

In late nineteenth-century Natal violence was prevalent among Indian indentured labourers toiling in sugar plantations and living in single-sex compounds. Those who married brought compound violence into their domestic lives, which were further complicated by sharing crowded quarters with unmarried men. Denied entry into the white settler society, Indian men developed a form of 'indentured masculinity' which reflected the harsh conditions and violence they lived under (Vahed 2005). In the exclusively male environment of gold mines, violence was ubiquitous underground. Both black and white miners shared a notion of masculinity that celebrated physical strength and courage. Different forms of sports – rugby for white Afrikaners, stick fighting for blacks from the Transkei – served as sites of male socialisation. Interpersonal, often violent conflicts dominated the miners' everyday lives. White supervisors, 'shift-bosses', used beatings of African subordinates to maintain the racial hierarchy. Black miners considered the lack of respect for their own seniority emasculating and humiliating. One of them told the 1913 Crown Mines commission, 'We are not children, we are men' (Breckenridge 1998: 682). Migration to the mines led to intergenerational struggles. Because of a rural economy devastated by drought and rinderpest, Zulu men were forced to migrate to earn bridewealth. Upon returning home they often defied elders' authority in disregard of local norms (Carton 2000).

By the 1950s, as a result of proletarianisation, Zulu and other African male age-cohorts had transformed into urban gangs, leading to the emergence of an urban black masculinity which featured work as central to its identity with little upward social mobility (Morrell 1998b). Youth gangs, which offered a sense of belonging, acted against the Apartheid state, Europeans, other gangs, elders and especially women in urban and rural areas (Mager 1998; Glaser 1998). Yet these were not the only images of masculinity. Popular print media promoted other models of masculinity. They constructed urban black men, like urban whites, as modern autonomous individuals, detached from kin and domestic spaces. In the early 1950s, *Drum* magazine –

read widely across Anglophone Africa – featured successful male athletes within their family and community settings; advertisements depicted men as breadwinners, foregrounding responsibilities as fathers, husbands and sons. By the 1960s, these representations had changed. *Drum* presented men as inhabiting public spaces, revealing nothing about their domestic lives. These changes reflected Apartheid pass laws and forced removals that led to a reduction in the number of urban men living with their families (Clowes 2005).

Resistance against colonialism intersected with ideas about masculinity. In Asante the queen mother Yaa Asantewaa appropriated senior masculinity and led the 1900 uprising against the British. Half a century later, during a crisis in Ghana's nationalist movement, Asante's young men failed to rework notions of senior masculinity because, as social juniors, they lacked Asantewaa's royal pedigree and connections to religious power (Obeng 2003). In Kenya the autobiographies of former Mau Mau fighters reveal that during their 1950s uprising they were concerned not only about reclaiming land appropriated by settlers but also about masculinity. Worries about domestic lives, about being fathers, husbands and lovers, were part of their political struggles. Literate fighters sought companionate marriage, similar to the idea of a 'respectable' family promoted by colonial officials to stabilise a skilled African work force. Yet illiterate fighters, the so-called Kenya Riigi, had different ideas of gender: they banned rank among themselves, as well as conjugal relationships. In rehabilitation camps, British officials used a gendered strategy to reconstruct former male fighters through domestic work, thereby dissolving the two male genders (White 2003). Other scholars have studied connections between masculinity and modernities. Maasai people of Kenya coined the notion of *ormeek* (modern) masculinity for those who attended school and broke with the nomadic life style. Since the 1970s, *ormeek* men, originally considered effeminate and subordinate, have become socially valued and dominant at the expense of older norms (Hodgson 2003).

Since the 1980s, economic decline and reform attempts like structural adjustment programmes dictated by the World Bank had consequences for masculinities. In southwestern Nigeria many women consider unemployed young men as 'useless' when they fail to meet financial expectations as lovers and potential husbands (Cornwall 2003). Similarly, in Dar es Salaam, Tanzania, men feel disempowered, as poverty threatens their patriarchal authority, leading to more casual sex and spread of HIV/AIDS (Silberschmidt 2005). Economic difficulties have led not only to women asserting their independence but also to a contestation of dominant masculinity ideals. New notions are emerging within the fast changing postcolonial world. Some men have embraced alternative forms of masculinity, like those actively seeking gender equity within the new South Africa (Morrell 2005), or those producing African gay identities (Louw in Morrell 2001; Epprecht 1998; Gevisser and Cameron 1995). Masculinities promise to transform further as Africa becomes more connected to a wider world through globalisation and the Internet. Yet ideologies and practices of masculinity will continue to blend innovations with powerful continuities.

References and further reading

Achebe, N. (2003) '"And she became a man": King Ahebi Ugbabe in the history of Enugu-Ezike, Nsukka Division, 1880–1948', in L.A. Lindsay and S.F. Miescher (eds) *Men and Masculinities in Modern Africa*, Portsmouth, NH: Heinemann.

Akyeampong, E. and Obeng, P. (1995) 'Spirituality, gender, and power in Asante history', *International Journal of African Historical Studies*, 28: 481–508.

Amadiume, I. (1987) *Male Daughters, Female Husbands*, London: Zed Books.

Breckenridge, K. (1998) 'The allure of violence: men, race and masculinity on the South African goldmines, 1900–1950', *Journal of Southern African Studies*, 24 (4): 669–94.

Brown, C.A. (2003) 'A "man" in the village is a "boy" in the workplace: colonial racism, worker militance, and Igbo notions of masculinity in the Nigerian coal industry, 1930–1945', in L.A. Lindsay and S.F. Miescher (eds) *Men and Masculinities in Modern Africa*, Portsmouth, NH: Heinemann.

Carton, B. (2000) *Blood from Your Children*, Charlottesville, VI: University Press of Virginia.

Clowes, L. (2005) 'To be a man: changing constructions of manhood in *Drum* magazine 1951–65', in L. Ouzgane and R. Morrell (eds) *African Masculinities*, New York: Palgrave, pp. 89–108.

Cole, C.M., Manuh, T. and Miescher, S.F. (eds) (2006) *Africa after Gender?* Bloomington, IN: Indiana University Press.

Connell, R. (1995) *Masculinities*, Berkeley, CA: University of California Press.

Cornwall, A.A. (2003) 'To be a man is more than a day's work: shifting ideals of masculinity in Ado-Odo, S.W. Nigeria', in L.A. Lindsay and S.F. Miescher (eds) *Men and Masculinities in Modern Africa*, Portsmouth, NH: Heinemann.

Epprecht, M. (1998) 'The "unsaying" of indigenous homosexualities in Zimbabwe: mapping a blindspot in an African masculinity', *Journal of Southern African Studies*, 24: 631–52.

Gevisser, M. and Cameron, E. (eds) (1995) *Defiant Desire*, New York: Routledge.

Glaser, C. (1998) 'Swines, hazels and the Dirty Dozen: masculinity, territoriality and the youth gangs of Soweto, 1960–1976', *Journal of Southern African Studies*, 24 (4): 719–36.

Hodgson, D.L. (2003) 'Being Maasai men: modernity and the production of Maasai masculinities', in L.A. Lindsay and S.F. Miescher (eds) *Men and Masculinities in Modern Africa*, Portsmouth, NH: Heinemann.

Hodgson, D.L. and McCurdy, S.A. (eds) (2001) *Wicked Women and the Reconfiguration of Gender in Africa*, Portsmouth, NH: Heinemann.

Lindsay, L.A. (2003) *Working with Gender*, Portsmouth, NH: Heinemann.

Lindsay, L.A. and Miescher, S.F. (eds) (2003) *Men and Masculinities in Modern Africa*, Portsmouth, NH: Heinemann.

Louw, R. (2001) 'Mkhumbane and new traditions of (un)African same-sex weddings', in R. Morrell (ed.) *Changing Men in Southern Africa*, London: Zed Books, pp. 287–96.

McKittrick, M. (2003) 'Forsaking their fathers? Colonialism, Christianity, and coming of age in Ovamboland, North Namibia', in L.A. Lindsay and S.F. Miescher (eds) *Men and Masculinities in Modern Africa*, Portsmouth, NH: Heinemann.

Mager, A. (1998) 'Youth organisations and the construction of masculine identities in the Ciskei and Transkei, 1945–1960', *Journal of Southern African Studies*, 24 (4): 653–68.

Miescher, S.F. (2005) *Making Men in Ghana*, Bloomington, IN: Indiana University Press.

Morrell, R. (ed.) (1998a) 'Masculinities in southern Africa', Special Issue of *Journal of Southern African Studies*, 24.

—— (1998b) 'Of boys and men', *Journal of Southern African Studies*, 24: 605–30.

—— (ed.) (2001a) *Changing Men in Southern Africa*, London: Zed Books.

—— (2001b) *From Boys to Gentlemen*, Pretoria: UNISA.

—— (2005) 'Men, movements, and gender transformation in South Africa', in L. Ouzgane and R. Morrell (eds) *African Masculinities*, New York: Palgrave, pp. 271–88.

Obeng, P. (2003) 'Gendered nationalism: forms of masculinity in modern Asante, Ghana', in L.A. Lindsay and S.F. Miescher (eds) *Men and Masculinities in Modern Africa*, Portsmouth, NH: Heinemann.

Ouzgane, L. and Morrell, R. (eds) (2005) *African Masculinities*, New York: Palgrave.

Silberschmidt, M. (2005) 'Poverty, male disempowerment, and male sexuality: rethinking men and masculinities in urban and rural East Africa', in L. Ouzgane and R. Morrell (eds) *African Masculinities*, New York: Palgrave, pp. 189–204.

Vahed, G. (2005) 'Indentured masculinity in colonial Natal, 1860–1910', in L. Ouzgane and R. Morrell (eds) *African Masculinities*, New York: Palgrave, pp. 239–56.

White, L. (2003) 'Matrimony and rebellion: masculinity in Mau Mau', in L.A. Lindsay and S.F. Miescher (eds) *Men and Masculinities in Modern Africa*, Portsmouth, NH: Heinemann.

See also: colonial and imperial masculinities; cultural formations, Africa; history, modernity; postcolonial masculinities

STEPHAN F. MIESCHER

HISTORY, ANCIENT MEDITERRANEAN CIVILISATIONS

The history of masculinity in the ancient Mediterranean might be understood as a history of two competing paradigms. In one, associated with Greece and Rome, masculinity is precarious, the male body as apt to be penetrated as to penetrate. In the other, associated with Semitic cultures, masculinity is a given. In actuality, the ancient Mediterranean was a hodgepodge of interrelated cultures, in many of which each of these paradigms can be amply attested; there were multiple paradigms, class and urban/rural location being major factors; influence came from the north as well as the east. Still, by around 500 CE, the Semitic paradigm had come to predominate throughout the former Roman Empire – from Ireland to Turkey, from southern Germany to North Africa – and the Greco-Roman paradigm had been suppressed.

Sources pose a problem, since we have few personal documents and must depend on literary, legal and medical texts, which have a marked elite bias, and on visual imagery (Dover 1989; Clarke 1998). Lower-class values appear in graffiti; in everyday documents written on clay, papyrus or wood tablets; and in curses inscribed on sheets of lead foil.

Cultural evidence for Egypt and the Near East goes back to 3200 BCE, and the range of cultures in the ancient Mediterranean was wide. Evidence concerning gender among most ancient cultures is limited to archaeological data (bones, grave goods) and to ethnographic accounts by hostile cultures (e.g. Greek and Roman accounts of Africans, Celts, Armenians, Germans). On masculinity in pharaonic Egypt, see Meskell (1999); on Mesopotamia, see Leick (1994).

Greeks

Our knowledge of Greek ideas about masculinity begins with Homer's *Iliad* and *Odyssey*, composed in the Greek Dark Age (1100–776 BCE) but describing Bronze Age culture (3500–1100 BCE). Other Bronze Age evidence comes from the Linear B tablets – largely household records – which indicate role titles like 'king' and 'war leader', and from the wall paintings of Crete and the Aegean islands and the grave goods of Mycenae, which show men fighting, hunting and leaping over the backs of bulls. Homer's warriors are obsessed with their *kleos* (fame), and live to rule their men well, give respected counsel, exchange gifts (including women), support their allies, and above all fight and die gloriously in battle. Homer's Hector is a faithful husband and father; Odysseus, if markedly unfaithful, in the end returns to home and much-loved wife. Homeric men are known by a patronymic (name meaning 'son of X'), and the *Odyssey* is as much the tale of the coming to manhood of Odysseus's son Telemachus as it is of Odysseus's return. That Achilles, hero of the *Iliad*, and his companion Patroclus were lovers is not clear in the *Iliad* and became a common claim only much later, in the Classical period (Halperin 1990).

The Archaic period in Greece (776–479 BCE) is better attested. Here in the developing city-states of Greece, the Aegean islands and the coast of Asia Minor, we see a still aristocratic culture through more everyday texts: love poems, hymns, laws (Hubbard 2003). Male poets like Alcaeus and Anacreon sing the praises of beloveds both male and female; satiric poets like Archilochus mock cowardly soldiers and threaten their enemies with scathing abuse. The warrior culture of Sparta, with its harsh gender-segregated training of young men, is much admired, though not much copied. Masculine competition is channelled into athletics; the games at Olympia, Nemea, Delphi and Corinth date to 776 BCE, and served as another means through which aristocratic young men could achieve the deathless fame offered by poets like Pindar.

In this period we first see clearly the sex/gender system sometimes known as 'Greek love'; the Greeks called it *paiderastia*, 'love of boys', hence the current scholarly term 'pederasty' (Dover 1989). Adult males, characterised in vase paintings of this and later periods as tall and bearded, court male adolescents, characterised as beardless and either short and childlike or tall and muscular. The vases show couples mostly naked and occasionally having intercourse, usually in the 'intercrural' position (adult male faces youth and rubs penis between youth's thighs). Pederastic graffiti from the island of Thera apparently boast of anal sex with boys. Adult males were also expected to marry and beget children, and frequented female prostitutes. Citizen boys were expected to put up with the sex for the sake of the training and role-modelling provided by their adult lovers. Not all Greeks accepted this system, calling it 'unnatural'. Meanwhile, as seen in the Classical period (fifth to fourth centuries BCE) in the comedies of Aristophanes, males past adolescence who enjoyed being penetrated were stigmatised as *cinaedi* (fags).

The Classical period is best attested in Athens, which is thus often wrongly taken to be normative. Athenian male citizens belonged to *demes*, family/neighbourhood groups, into which their sons would be initiated in their late teens. Citizen males served as soldiers and in local government – the famed democracy – which during this period ruled an oppressive empire, punishing uncooperative subject cities by killing the adult males and selling the women and children into slavery (standard practice for all ancient Mediterranean cultures, including the Jews). Athenians were litigious, and we learn much about gender roles through court speeches (Roisman 2005). Aischines' speech *Against Timarchus* (346–345 BCE) accuses him, in exhaustive detail, of prostituting himself (Dover 1989; Winkler 1990). Athenian men's behaviour resembles that of modern Greek men in pastoral cultures, where manhood is vigorously contested within a zero-sum system (Halperin 1990; Winkler 1990). An Athenian adult male would also be the *kyrios* (lord) of his household, with power over his wife's sexuality, her ability to leave the house, and her finances. Such control was less absolute in other Greek city-states.

Greeks viewed all non-Greek-speaking peoples as barbarians, and this attitude accompanied the conquests of Alexander in the mid-4th century BCE. By 300 BCE, Greek-speaking cultures were established in Egypt (centred on Alexandria, Montserrat 1996) and Syria (centred on Antioch), where the jostling of Greek and Semitic sexual norms is well documented.

Romans

Roman culture overlaps chronologically with Greek; the city traditionally dates from 753 BCE. Roman myths told that the city was founded by twins, Romulus and Remus, and that Romulus killed Remus in the process. This fratricide became central to the Roman self-image after their Republic disintegrated into civil war (132–131 BCE). The Romans were ancestor-worshippers, always looking to the past for a model, and what Roman writers saw in their earliest past was a series of 'hard men' – stern, honest farmers who served their state bravely as soldiers, statesmen and fathers. The peninsula of Italy was widely multicultural, but these Roman soldier-farmers, by the mid-Republic (146 BCE), had forced not only most of their neighbours under Roman rule but most of the Mediterranean as well.

Like Athens, Rome was a slave state and derived many slaves from conquest. Unlike the Athenians, Roman writers associated pederasty closely with this process, designating young male slaves as the appropriate sex partners of adult male Roman citizens, but putting adolescent male Roman citizens legally off limits. The slave's body thus became a primary locus of sexual stigma – especially problematic since Roman house slaves, unlike Greek slaves, were often freed. As in Greece, prostitution in Rome was tied to conquest and slavery. The plays of Plautus (c. 200 BCE) are the earliest extant Roman texts; performed during and after the second war against Carthage, they are full of soldiers, pimps, and sex slaves male and female. The main characters are often young citizen men in love with a slave prostitute, their grumpy fathers, and their devoted and clever male slaves. Plautus and the other (lost) writers of Roman comedy all were reportedly prisoners of war or soldiers, and comic actors were probably male slaves as well. The *cinaedus* reappears here as a male sex slave and dancer (Williams 1999). Historians have questioned whether pederasty was indigenous to Rome or borrowed from the Greeks, but it is attested as early in Roman history as we have texts.

Marriage and the family were central to Roman culture, as seen in the earliest Roman law code, the Twelve Tables (450 BCE). The family was dominated by the *paterfamilias*, the oldest living ascendant, who had the right of life and death over those in his power. His adult male descendants, until his death, could technically own nothing, and respect for parents was a basic Roman virtue. Roman legends show that men were expected to control their emotions (Barton 2001). But historical anecdotes suggest they rarely did; Roman public life was full of yelling, spitting and taunting. A form of verbal duelling is attested for Roman males from the time of Plautus on: opponents confronted each other and took turns chanting rhythmic insults. Accusations included greed, thievery, dirtiness, slave status and openness to sexual penetration, both oral and anal. Again, post-adolescent males who desired to be penetrated were stigmatised, here subject to civil disabilities as well as to ridicule (Richlin 1993).

The phallus pervaded Roman culture. Citizen boys wore a phallic amulet, the *fascinum*; walls, shop signs, paving stones, jewellery and armour bore phallic decorations, and Roman armies took the phallus with them. Like the Greeks, the Romans sometimes pictured their empire as raped – an accurate reflection of the experiences of war captives. Roman writers associate effeminacy with Greece and the Near East, crude hypermasculinity with northern Europe. Rape jokes constitute a major part of Roman humour, and the ithyphallic god Priapus appears in the poetry of Catullus (d. 55 BCE) and remains popular in literature and home decor thereafter (Richlin 1992).

Like the Athenians, upper-class Roman males enacted their masculinity in the courtroom. Rhetorical training was the standard Mediterranean preparation for manhood from about 450 BCE through the Middle Ages. In the Republic, this training aimed at getting a young man into public office. When rule by emperors replaced the Republic (31 BCE), this goal became empty, causing a major shift in the meaning of Roman manhood. Rhetorical competition became an end in itself, as seen in the institution of the rhetorical school and its stars, who grew rich entertaining crowds (Gleason 1995). The African rhetorician Fronto rose to tutor the future emperor Marcus Aurelius; their correspondence describes a pederastic relationship from both sides (Richlin 2006).

This period also sees the rise of Christianity, along with a general rise in the practice of *askesis* – a regimen of diet and exercise for the good of the spirit (Perkins 1995). Men could now compete not just in oratory but in self-deprivation, and with the invention of monasticism in the third century CE, many men retired into the Egyptian and Syrian deserts. A misogyny always present in Greek and Roman cultures now takes on a Judeo-Christian edge, while writers going back to Philo of Alexandria (c. 49 CE) begin to lump together all same-sex relations as wicked, so that pederasty looks as bad as the *cinaedus*. Where philosophers going back to the Athenians Plato (c. 429–347 BCE) and Zeno (335–263 BCE) had endorsed pederasty as conducive to knowledge of the good, Paul launched a long Christian campaign to eradicate all homosexual intercourse (Gaca 2003). By the fourth century CE, pederasty was disappearing from view; there is no more pederastic love poetry after Nemesianus (c. 290 CE), only invective against *cinaedi*. This was probably expedited by the Council of Elvira (305 CE), at which pederastic intercourse was made punishable by excommunication (Boswell 1990). Pederasty probably continued among aristocratic subcultures in the old Roman cities of the fallen Western Empire, as well as in Byzantium, which continued as a self-defined Roman culture until 1453. But it's hard to find anyone willing to go on record.

Jews

The Jewish cultures of the Hebrew Bible were contemporary with Archaic and Classical Greek cultures. Biblical masculinity resembles that of the Greek pastoral cultures discussed above (Moore 2001). Rabbinical schools grew up in the second century CE, though their ideas would not become normative until later periods. The rabbis, themselves participants in an all-male culture that featured study and dispute, had much to say about sex and gender, both male and female (Boyarin 1993; Satlow 1995). They place a higher value on sex with women, which for them meant marital sex, than do the Greeks or Romans; they set up minimum requirements for the number of times per month a man should have sex with his wife. Sex between males they generally find wrong and disturbing, associating it with their non-Jewish neighbours. Greek-influenced rabbis living in Alexandria and Jerusalem; however, differ here from rabbis in Babylon. It seems likely that Paul's attitudes towards sexuality stem from Jewish thought (Boyarin 1993; Gaca 2003), though Paul achieved a punitive system undreamt of by the rabbis.

References and further reading

Barton, C. (2001) *Roman Honor*, Berkeley, CA: University of California Press.

Boswell, J. (1990) *Christianity, Social Tolerance, and Homosexuality*, Chicago, IL: University of Chicago Press.

Boyarin, D. (1993) *Carnal Israel*, Berkeley, CA: University of California Press.

Clarke, J. (1998) *Looking at Lovemaking*, Berkeley, CA: University of California Press.

Dover, K. (1989) *Greek Homosexuality*, Cambridge, MA: Harvard University Press.

Gaca, K. (2003) *The Making of Fornication*, Berkeley, CA: University of California Press.

Gleason, M. (1995) *Making Men*, Princeton, NJ: Princeton University Press.

Halperin, D. (1990) *One Hundred Years of Homosexuality*, New York: Routledge.

Hubbard, T. (ed.) (2003) *Homosexuality in Greece and Rome*, Berkeley, CA: University of California Press.

Leick, G. (1994) *Sex and Eroticism in Mesopotamian Literature*, London: Routledge.

Meskell, L. (1999) *Archaeologies of Social Life*, Oxford: Blackwell.

Montserrat, D. (1996) *Sex and Society in Graeco-Roman Egypt*, London: Kegan Paul.

Moore, S. (2001) *God's Beauty Parlor*, Stanford, CA: Stanford University Press.

Perkins, J. (1995) *The Suffering Self*, London: Routledge.

Richlin, A. (1992) *The Garden of Priapus*, New York: Oxford University Press.

—— (1993) 'Not before homosexuality', *Journal of the History of Sexuality*, 3: 523–73.

—— (2006) *Marcus Aurelius in Love*, Chicago, IL: Chicago University Press.

Roisman, J. (2005) *The Rhetoric of Manhood*, Berkeley, CA: University of California Press.

Satlow, M. (1995) *Tasting the Dish*, Atlanta, GA: Scholars Press.

Williams, C. (1999) *Homosexuality and the Roman Man*, Oxford: Oxford University Press.

Winkler, J. (1990) *The Constraints of Desire*, New York: Routledge.

See also: history, European Middle Ages; world religions, Christianity; world religions, Judaism

AMY RICHLIN

HISTORY, COLONISATION

Colonisation is as old as culture itself. From the Roman Empire to the European invasion of the New World, throughout history cultures have sought to colonise other cultures, for either wealth, natural resources or the sheer prestige of empire. Insofar as colonisation has generally been transacted by and between men, it has always been linked to the performance and legitimation of masculinity. This can be illustrated in a number of ways. For instance, there is the construction of colonised territories as 'feminine': desirable, passive and open to foreign penetration. Also, colonisation is often played out as a struggle between competing masculinities in which women feature as objects of male rivalry. The stable identity of the male coloniser depends heavily upon the marginalisation of the colonised male. Thus the history of colonisation provides a particularly fertile ground for exploring the ways in which masculinity is constructed in and through processes of cultural differentiation and domination.

Exploration and discovery

While colonisation is ubiquitous throughout history, this essay restricts itself to the era of colonisation most germane to the construction of contemporary masculinities: that is, the period starting from the voyages of exploration in the fifteenth and sixteenth centuries through to the colonial scramble of the nineteenth century. During this period of time, the major European powers– Portugal, Spain, France, Britain and Holland – progressively drew the whole world into a comprehensive network of trade routes, settlements, colonies, trading posts and fortresses that encompassed North and South America, the Caribbean, India, East and South-East Asia, the Antipodes, the Pacific Islands and Africa. There is scarcely a region in the globe that went unaffected by the modern era of colonial expansion.

The 'masculinity' of this process can be traced to the gendered nature of the maritime and military apparatuses that were the chief means of searching out and acquiring new territories. Women were excluded from the fields of military and maritime endeavour on the basis of their social inferiority: these were fields of male honour and prowess, and to allow women to enter them would be to upset the established order of things (Creighton and Norling 1996: ix). Seafaring and colonial conquest was, then, by its very culture a male business, and as such it incorporated into its practices all the tensions and contradictions of male subjectivity. In her book *Imperial Leather*, McClintock argues that the voyages of exploration and discovery were framed by fantasies of projection and disavowal that constructed the New World as a sexual fantasy-land waiting to be penetrated and mastered by the male coloniser (1995: 22). Myths about El Dorado, Arcadia and the original Eden lying beyond the great sea all formed part of this male fantasy, as they constructed the unknown continents as a reflection of the male coloniser's desire for power and mastery over the 'Other'.

McClintock also argues that the construction of the imperial project as male fantasy is underpinned by the fact that in the Old World women were themselves a dominated population and thus provided a ready metaphor for conceptualising and naturalising the process of maritime colonisation (1995: 24). We can see this in popular iconography equating exotic territories with images of nubile, receptive women: in van der Straet's famous 1600 painting depicting Vespucci's discovery of the New World, the male explorer stands bold and erect before a naked, reclining female figure (Hall 1992: 303). The Pacific Islands that Cook explored in the eighteenth century were persistently associated with the naked bodies of Polynesian women whom many commentators compared to 'nymphs' (Hall 1992: 302). The Middle East and northern Africa were associated with the pleasures of the harem and the mysterious, veiled sexuality of Arab women (Said 1978: 188–90). Similar imagery can be adduced for almost any territory coveted by the appropriating gaze of colonial desire. Indeed, the association between the bodies of women and the colonial territory became so ingrained that by the time Haggard penned the colonial adventure novel *King Solomon's Mines* in the late nineteenth century, the accompanying map showing the course of our hero's adventure bears a remarkable likeness to a map of the female anatomy. Here, the body of woman and the colonised territory are merged into a single naturalised figure, a significant index of the confluence between masculinity and imperialism (McClintock 1995: 1–4).

Settlement

The association between sexual domination and imperial domination also had a literal counterpart in the appropriation and exploitation of indigenous women by the European coloniser. The voluptuous descriptions that travellers gave of nubile Polynesians, lascivious Africans and coy geishas were not merely innocent rhapsodies: they articulate the way in which indigenous women were fetishised as sexual objects and often exploited for their sexual services. This is an inherent feature of the colonial project in many instances, exacerbated by the scarcity of European women in the seafaring and early colonial worlds.

However, the exchange of indigenous women also formed an integral part of negotiations between early explorer-settlers and the indigenous populations they encountered in the New World. This draws attention to the fact that the colonised lands were not 'virgin territories' but had organised societies which – like those of Europe – were strongly patriarchal. In most of the tribal societies encountered in the colonial world, women circulated as objects of exchange, articulating and reinforcing power relations and alliances between men. When the European men arrived, then, they often found local leaders and chieftains who were willing to trade women for the exotic merchandise – tools, weapons, silver, tobacco, alcohol, gunpowder, horses, etc. – of these strange new arrivals from the other side of the world. However, such negotiations were delicate matters, and often the settlers failed to understand the bonds of ongoing reciprocity that such exchanges entailed in indigenous cultures (Reynolds 1990: 71). The arrogance of many settlers and freebooters often incited violent reprisals from the native populations, which in turn led colonial authorities to wage war on the local tribes. The imperiousness of the male coloniser was also embodied in the way in which, while indigenous women were treated as objects of exchange in the colonial context, white women were not considered part of the bargaining process (Dixon 1995: 45–61; Hall 1992: 284–5; Sinha 1995: 11). Thus, through the simultaneous exploitation of native women and the protective cloistering of European women, the coloniser sought to establish dominance over the local indigenous patriarchy.

What develops in the colonial context, then, is a struggle between two competing patriarchal systems, two forms of masculine authority vying for control of the means of sexual exchange, sovereignty over the land, and the right to legislate and administer the law. The settlers' imposition of their own (rather hypocritical) sexual values without respect for indigenous sexual customs reinforced their overriding of other aspects of indigenous culture: customs relating to the land and sacred sites, rituals and ceremonies, attitudes towards property. The key to colonial domination was breaking the power of the tribal patriarchs, undermining their customs through the introduction of the market system and private land ownership, and generally disrupting the traditional means of economic and sexual circulation.

Of course, military force was an ever-present option. Early colonial settlers lived in a state of perpetual tension with native populations, and pre-emptive violence was often sanctioned by colonial authorities as being in the interests of the general order. Official proclamations justifying – even inciting – settler violence against indigenous populations were commonplace in the British colonies, as Robinson and York (1997: 78) and Dixon (1995: 50) demonstrate. And in the wake of the mutinies of native populations in India and Jamaica in the second half of the nineteenth century, colonial authorities became increasingly sensitive to signs of native resistance and determined to protect their interests through authoritarian means.

In this way, colonisation was played out as a form of male rivalry between competing colonial and indigenous masculinities. However, given the more advanced technology and greater resources of the colonial powers, the native populations often fought a losing battle. Nevertheless, such conflicts took their toll on settler populations and helped shape imperial ideologies of 'race', which saw the conflict between settler and indigenous cultures as the result of evolutionary laws, the struggle for racial supremacy, the 'survival of the fittest'. As a result, Western masculinity in the colonial context was increasingly defined in terms of the imperial ideal of the white conqueror and bringer of civilisation, the rough, brazen frontiersman who took up the historical load of the 'white man's burden', the mission to subdue savagery and spread light into the darkest regions of the globe. Such ideas would become central to colonies which would later become nationalised, such as South Africa, Australia and North America, which defined national identity and national manhood through eugenic concepts of white racial purity and superiority, legislated in policies of racial segregation and exclusion. In postcolonial settler societies, only white men were 'real men' (Bhabha 1994: 85–92; Sinha 1995: 15).

Scramble for territory

However, male rivalry in the colonial context was not limited to conflict between the male coloniser and his indigenous counterpart. It also operated between competing colonial powers, who often trod upon one another's toes in the scramble for colonial territories. Spain, France and Britain tussled over the Americas; the Portuguese, Dutch and British fought over control of the East Indies trade; Portugal, France, Germany, Britain and Holland all converged upon Africa. The drive for colonies was propelled and structured by the perceived need on the part of European nations to compete for limited resources in the New World. Possession of colonies by one European power encouraged other countries to follow suit in order to attain a similar position of imperial power and prestige. Within a century of Spain's voyages of discovery to the New World, Britain and France launched similar expeditions with a view to colonisation. Thus, in the scramble for colonies that takes place from the sixteenth century onwards, we can observe the invidious process of masculine rivalry writ large: 'my empire's bigger than yours.'

It is important to note the way in which, within this structure of colonial rivalry, the colonies themselves are constituted as 'passive', feminised objects to be wrangled over by the 'masculine' powers of imperial Europe. This evinces a triangulated structure of desire similar to that which Sedgwick analyses in her book *Between Men* (1985), where masculine identity is constructed in and through homosocial rivalry between men for a desirable 'feminine' object. Here, of course, the object of desire is the colonial territory itself, often figured analogically or metaphorically as a woman: passive, desirable, able to be penetrated and mastered by the male coloniser. Just as rivalry between the coloniser and colonised is played out across the bodies of women (both indigenous and non-indigenous), so too rivalry between colonial powers is played out across the bodies of territories and peoples constituted as feminised, open to (white) male penetration and possession. Colonisation demonstrates the extent to which masculinity relies for its definition upon something posited as radically exterior to it, whether it be the exotic landscapes of imperial legend, the strange culture and customs of indigenous peoples, the 'foreign' bodies of women and other races, or the empty, uncivilised spaces of empire waiting to be tamed by the colonial male.

Such images were central to the construction of masculinity during the era of colonial expansion, and they continue to inform the construction of masculinity today, insofar as the material and symbolic legacy of the colonial era remains an integral part of postcolonial identity politics.

References and further reading

Bhabha, H.K. (1994) 'Of mimicry and man', in H.K. Bhabha, *The Location of Culture*, London and New York: Routledge, pp. 85–92.

Creighton, M.S. and Norling, L. (eds) (1996) *Iron Men and Wooden Women*, Baltimore, MD and London: Johns Hopkins University Press.

Dixon, R. (1995) *Writing the Colonial Adventure*, Melbourne: Cambridge University Press.

Hall, C. (1992) *White, Male and Middle-Class*, Cambridge: Polity.

Hall, S. (1992) 'The West and the rest', in S. Hall and B. Gieben (eds) *Formations of Modernity*, Cambridge and Oxford: Polity, pp. 275–331.

McClintock, A. (1995) *Imperial Leather*, New York: Routledge.

Reynolds, H. (1990) *The Other Side of the Frontier*, Ringwood, Victoria: Penguin.

Robinson, F. and York, B. (1997) *The Black Resistance*, Camberwell, Victoria: Widescope.

Said, E. (1978) *Orientalism*, London and New York: Penguin.

Sedgwick, E.K. (1985) *Between Men*, New York: Columbia University Press.

Sinha, M. (1995) *Colonial Masculinity*, Manchester and New York: Manchester University Press.

See also: colonial and imperial masculinities; diasporic and migrant masculinities; global masculinities; globalisation; Indigenous and First Nation masculinities; postcolonial masculinities

JADE M. NOBBS

HISTORY, EUROPE, EARLY MODERN TO 1917

The idea of what it meant to be a 'man' and the cultural constructions of masculinity in Europe underwent a profound transformation over the two hundred years from the early eighteenth century to the First World War. At the beginning of the period, masculinity was manifested in many forms, and those behaviours that constituted 'proper' male activities were highly varied. Over the course of the eighteenth and nineteenth centuries these underwent a series of changes that, by the end of the First World War, produced a more uniform idea of masculinity that was based on a duality between domesticity and patriotic manhood. The pace and pattern of homogenisation, however, varied across time, space and social class.

Being a man in early modern Europe was contingent upon a person's status, age and sexual behaviour. Inherited from the Middle Ages was the idea, based on the writings of the ancient medical writer Galen, that male and female were biologically of the same essence and that sexual difference was based on behaviour. People obviously knew that men and women were physically different, but they believed that there was a spectrum of gendered beings, with men at one end and women at the other and a host of others – celibates, eunuchs, hermaphrodites, etc. – in between. For them, sex was based more on behaviour than on biology. While the physical nature of sex was seen as a spectrum rather than as a simple bipolar opposition between male and female, this does not mean that there was equality. On the contrary, as with so much else in the pre-modern world, the spectrum was arranged hierarchically with the 'true' man at the top. And the proper behaviour that defined a man was highly dependent on status and age. Indeed, so diverse were the culturally constructed expectations of what constituted acceptable male behaviour that scholars refer to multiple masculinities during this period.

Early modern society was highly stratified, and power and authority were keyed to a person's place in the social scheme. Cutting across all social groupings, however, was the idea and reality of patriarchy. Patriarchy now tends to refer generally to the rule of men over women, but in the past it connoted, as the root meaning of the word – father-rule – suggests, the legal and practical dominance of the male head of a household over all its members. A man achieved his rightful place in society when he married and established his own household as a locus of reproduction and production. His paramount goal thereafter was to ensure its economic viability and the perpetuation of his lineage, ideally through the siring and proper rearing of sons. The cultural idea for men was to exert and maintain total control over their households. Men's lives revolved around their households not just metaphorically but physically as well. For the overwhelming majority of men, their working as well as their home life took place in the house or in adjacent premises. Male householders spent their lives alongside their wives, children and servants, while male servants lived in the houses of their masters. There were, of course, places like taverns and alehouses where men socialised, but even these domains of homosociality often had a significant female presence. To the extent that we can speak of 'separate spheres' in the early modern period, it involved the separation not of men from women but of people from different social strata.

Certain forms of masculine behaviour cut across status boundaries. The most important of these was violence. Rooted in an ethos of honour, men were supposed to respond aggressively and violently to any challenge to their name, reputation or authority. Physical force was routinely deployed within plebeian households against wives, children, and servants – both male and female – to maintain 'proper order'. Among artisans, it was expected that masters would beat their apprentices. Men of the upper orders of society settled their differences over honour with recourse to the duel. Among nobles and plebeian men, then, violence was the first order response to any slight, perceived or real, to a man's reputation. Since almost all men were armed with bladed implements and weapons, it should occasion no surprise that the rates of interpersonal violence in the early modern period were very high and far exceeded what they are now. In sum, at that time masculinity and violence were intimately and integrally related.

This situation, however, was changing. The first factor in the development of a different conception of masculinity was related to the scientific revolution and the supplanting of the Galenic model of sexual difference. Advances in biology led to the creation of the 'two sex' model. In this view, male and female were envisioned as separate and distinct polar opposites, each with its own essence. Gender difference from this time on was seen as being rooted in biological difference. This created a bi-polar opposition between men and women and naturalised what were previously seen as culturally constructed modes of behaviour. Masculinity and femininity were canonised and essentialised: one was the essence of manhood, and the other of womanhood; everything else was unnatural and deviant. This ideology would help shape the development of masculinity during the eighteenth and nineteenth centuries.

A second development that ushered in changes in masculinity was the decoupling of violence from manhood. This move occurred first among the upper orders of society through what noted sociologist Norbert Elias referred to as the 'civilising process'. Elias argued that the culture of honour that predominated in early modern Europe was prone to violence precisely because honour and violence were causally connected. Men of honour fought, and they fought over honour. For him and for the historians who have followed his lead, the aristocratic duel was a perfect manifestation of this connection. He argued further that the rise of a culture of civility and then later of a 'bureaucratic ethos' during the nineteenth century supplanted the ethic of honour, and that alternative mechanisms of dispute resolution arose. The age of the noble duel waned as the connection between masculinity and violence was severed. Encouraging this development further was the move by centralising European states to exert a monopoly over legitimate violence by, among other things, outlawing the carrying of lethal arms in public. These developments applied primarily to the upper echelons of society; violence persisted as a crucial element of plebeian and working-class masculinity till much later, and the duel itself re-emerged sporadically among the non-aristocrats until the twentieth century. Nonetheless, the severing of violence from masculinity was well underway by the end of the eighteenth century.

The effects of the next transformative process leading to the emergence of a new masculinity began to be felt towards the end of the eighteenth century and early in the nineteenth in northwestern Europe and later elsewhere. It was related to industrialisation, the growth of cities and the concomitant development of a modern class structure, and especially the emergence of a middle class. Industrialisation, urbanisation and the development of a modern capitalist economy profoundly affected the lifeways of men from all classes, but of no group more than the class created by these developments: the bourgeoisie. Since this class dominated nineteenth-century society, middle-class masculinity eventually came to dominate the lives of upper- and working-class men as well, and at the heart of bourgeois masculinity was domesticity. Men's lives still centred on the care, sustenance and perpetuation of their households but in quite different ways than earlier. Domestic life and work were now spatially separate. The home was no longer where men worked. It was now where they sought privacy, comfort and solace from the pressures of the workplace. The ties that bound the members of the bourgeois household together were to be based on affection and mutual respect, not utilitarian need as in the past. Reinforcing the values of masculine domesticity was Evangelicalism, so much so that some even refer to 'Evangelical masculinity'. To be sure, men still participated in homosocial activities outside of the home (clubs and associations), and violence still occurred, but both had been profoundly changed. The venues and the nature of bourgeois homosociality, for example, were transformed, and acceptable middle-class male violence became restricted to only a few highly ritualised and stylised forms, like the duel, but even these would vanish before long. The 'new' masculinity founded on an ideology of domestic manhood had arrived and flourished.

The beliefs, practices and values of the older tradition, however, persisted longer among the working class and the peasantry, but eventually change would come to them as well. The rise of the factory and the move to the city divorced home and work, just as it had for the middle class, and so altered social and economic relations between household members. Among the working class, these developments reinforced older patterns of male behaviour, like violence and homosociality in pubs, taverns and wineshops. During the nineteenth century, states established a number of institutions and deployed numerous initiatives the goals of which were to 'civilise' working men by inculcating in them the cultural values associated with the new masculinity, like self-control, restraint, discipline and respect for order. The strict work regime in the factory, for example, created an environment in which all of those behaviours were required and enforced daily; when trade unions came to accept them, it also gave them legitimacy in the eyes of working-class men. By the middle of the nineteenth century, industrial unrest focused on issues related to hours and wages and not on the general working environment. Indeed, when working-men's associations went on strike to get a living wage that would support a family, it signified that they had internalised the middle-class vision of domesticity, predicated on the separation between work and home. Mass public education helped to inculcate impressionable young boys with these values. The spread of Evangelicalism and other religious movements, some of which specifically focused on the working class, contributed to this process as well.

The state did its part by passing laws that criminalised many of the behaviours that had been essential elements of traditional masculinity and by founding institutions of public order to enforce these laws and punish their transgressors. The military came to play an increasingly important role in this process not only by reinforcing the values of discipline, order and obedience but also by providing a venue where aggression and violence were not merely acceptable but laudable. In many ways, the military was especially crucial in this process by becoming the repository of martial masculinity and deploying it on behalf of the nation. Some of those elements that had once been defining elements of an individual's manhood became essentialised characteristics of the nation while simultaneously creating what has been referred to as patriotic manhood. There was then a transfer of key aspects of traditional masculinity – honour, aggression, violence, etc. – from the individual to the nation. This masculinisation of nationalism also became implicated in the social discourse of imperialism, especially from the 1870s onward. The white's man burden of empire building was precisely that: a task undertaken by European white men. At least, that was how it was portrayed in the popular press of the day.

By the time Europe stood on the brink of war in 1914, a new masculinity had developed that was quite different from what had existed two hundred years earlier. Through a variety of processes, the multiple masculinities that had characterised early modern society had been transformed and homogenised. In their place stood what scholars refer to as the new or modern masculinity. This novel ideology, though unitary in form, had a dual nature. On the one side was domestic manhood and on the other was patriotic manhood. In their home life, men were to be providers and nurturers, and their behaviour was to be determined by values like respect, courtesy, obedience and charity. When acting on behalf of their homeland, however, another set of values and codes of behaviour – rooted in older forms of masculinity that privileged honour, aggression and violence – determined how real men comported themselves.

References and further reading

Burrus, V. (2000) *'Begotten, Not Made'*, Stanford, CA: Stanford University Press.

Elias, N. (1987) *Power and Civility*, New York: Pantheon.

Foyster, E.A. (1999) *Manhood in Early Modern England*, London: Longman.

Gallant, T.W. (2000) 'Honor, masculinity, and ritual knife-fighting in nineteenth century Greece', *American Historical Review*, 105: 359–82.

Gilmore, D.D. (1990) *Manhood in the Making*, New Haven, CT: Yale University Press.

Hadley, D. (1999) *Masculinity in Medieval Europe*, London: Longman.

Long, K.P. (2002) *High Anxiety*, Kirksville, MO: Truman State University Press.

Nagel, J. (1998) 'Masculinity and nationalism', *Ethnic and Racial Studies*, 21: 252–70.

Roper, M. and Tosh, J. (1991) *Manful Assertion*, London: Routledge.

Shepard, A. (2003) *Meanings of Manhood in Early Modern England*, Oxford: Oxford University Press.

Spierenburg, P. (ed.) (1998) *Men and Violence*, Columbus, OH: Ohio State University Press.

Streets, H. (2004) *Martial Races*, Manchester: Manchester University Press.

Tosh, J. (1999) *A Man's Place*, New Haven, CT: Yale University Press.

—— (2005) *Manliness and Masculinities in 19th-century Britain*, London: Longman.

Wiener, M.J. (2004) *Men of Blood*, Cambridge: Cambridge University Press.

See also: duelling; honour

THOMAS W. GALLANT

HISTORY, EUROPEAN MIDDLE AGES

The study of masculinity in the Middle Ages (c. 400–1500) has developed as an important field within medieval studies since the 1990s and emerged out of a long tradition of gender studies that focused overwhelmingly on women. Early studies were greatly influenced by research into masculinities in other disciplines, such as sociology, cultural studies and psychoanalysis, and emphasised issues that had already been articulated in these disciplines, such as the plurality of masculine identities, masculine anxieties, the concepts of hegemonic and subordinate masculinities and the notion of masculinity periodically being in crisis.

The study of medieval masculinities has been dominated by examination of the experiences of men in religious contexts. Medieval documentary and literary sources reveal that men who entered monastic communities or the priesthood encountered considerable anxieties about the renunciation of their secular masculine attributes, in particular the capacity to fight or have sexual intercourse. It was expected that monks and priests should not marry or have sexual relations, but it was only in the eleventh century that this became widely and explicitly enforced. The sexual self-denial required of early medieval monks extended to exercising control over nocturnal emission of semen. While some scholars have interpreted such prescriptions as evidence of male sexual anxiety, others have related discussion of bodily control to the language of early medieval politics, in which a successful ruler was one who could exercise physical self-control. So powerful was the rhetoric of sexual renunciation in the early Middle Ages that men of the secular elite are sometimes described in contemporary chronicles and biographies as experiencing anxiety about sexual activity.

By the eleventh century the enforcement of celibacy contributed to a climate of theological debate about the roles of men, and this debate was also encouraged by broader social changes, such as population expansion and the growth of towns and universities. The traditional social order, typically characterised as consisting of 'those who pray, those who fight and those who toil', could not easily incorporate the social classes that emerged from these new professional and economic opportunities. Moreover, within this transformed society it was far more difficult to maintain traditional ideological means of subordinating women, given that new social and economic opportunities did not depend upon such typically masculine attributes as martial ability, while the end of clerical marriage resulted in increased numbers of single women who could not be subordinated through the institution of marriage. Some scholars have accordingly regarded the eleventh and twelfth centuries as a period in which a crisis was precipitated in the gender system of medieval society. The struggle of celibate religious men to establish their masculinity without recourse to secular masculine behaviour has also prompted debate about whether priests should be regarded as a different form of masculinity from that of lay masculinity or, alternatively, as a third gender. The activities in which priests were not meant to engage – for example, sexual intercourse, drinking and fighting – typically formed the basis of legal cases against them and featured strongly in literary depictions of priestly behaviour. It is debatable whether this reflects high levels of transgression or whether these were plausible-sounding accusations for a sceptical laity to levy. The language of battle was often employed by religious men writing about their struggles with celibacy and may have offered a symbolic means of retaining some aspects of secular masculine characteristics.

Many studies of medieval masculinity have focused on men who differed from the secular norm. Eunuchs, for example, were an integral part of the Byzantine empire (fourth to fifteenth centuries AD), playing important roles in the imperial household and administration. They were obviously different from other men as they lacked testicles following castration, and, since this typically occurred prior to puberty, eunuchs also usually lacked beards and had high-pitched voices. On the basis of these physical characteristics, contemporaries frequently likened eunuchs to women, but it is also apparent that the perceived effeminacy of eunuchs was based on considerable stereotyping, for example through claims that they preferred sex with men, that they were unable to control their sexual passions, a charge often levied at women, and that they lacked courage and martial skills. It has been argued that these stereotypes were an important means by which other Byzantine men maintained a distinction from eunuchs; such stereotypes also played a part in the western European perception of the Byzantine empire and its people as a whole as effeminate.

Another group that differed from the norm and that have attracted the attention of modern scholarship are those men who engaged in homosexual sex. Medieval writers did not categorise men as homosexuals; rather, they regarded homosexual sexual relations as simply one of a range of sexual relations that a man might enter into. Homosexual relations were rarely condemned more vociferously than any other form of what was perceived as transgressive sexual behaviour, such as adultery, bestiality and clerical marriage. Caution must be exercised in interpreting physical intimacy between men in medieval chronicles and literature as being indicative of latent homosexual desire. Touching, embracing, kissing and bed-sharing, for example, were all metaphors for close social bonds of fidelity and friendship, and were rarely indicative of sexual desire; the relationships are now considered to have been homosocial rather than homosexual. In epic and Romance literature, physical contact between characters was often deployed as a means of externalising emotions of friendship and loyalty, as the poets did not have a well-developed language of introspection. Misunderstanding of these literary *topoi*, which were also often employed by chroniclers, has encouraged the labelling as homosexual of such historical figures as King Richard I of England (ruled 1189–99) who shared a bed with King Philip I of France (ruled 1180–1223). The medieval language of male love and friendship was commonly borrowed from Classical, such as Cicero's (c.103–43 BC) *de Amicitia* (On Friendship), in which true friendship is depicted as being possible only between good and virtuous men. Monastic letter collections of the eleventh and twelfth centuries contain some very intense and passionate expressions of love and friendship between men, but these are primarily demonstrations of Classical learning and intended as public statements of political networking rather than expressions of intimate relations. Medieval writing that was intended to have homoerotic connotations was rarely ambiguous, and was, again, influenced by Classical models of homoerotic poetry.

Medieval medical notions of maleness were also heavily influenced by Classical authors, particularly from the late eleventh century when the Crusades brought western European scholars back into contact with Classical works that had been lost to the West for centuries but preserved in Arabic scholarship. There was no consensus in medieval medical literature about the workings of the body, but most medieval medical authors were influenced by Classical medicine in believing that greater heat enabled males to grow beards, develop external genitalia and produce semen; although there was a strain of medical thought influenced by Galen (AD 129–200) that believed in the existence of female sperm as a necessary component of conception. Male foetuses were believed to have been created when there was greater heat in the sperm, in the testicles of the father or in the uterus of the mother. Males were also widely regarded as more complete versions of humans than females, an idea influenced by the work of Aristotle (384–322 BC). Capacity to have sexual intercourse and to father children was an important quality of medieval masculinity, and impotence was one of the few grounds on which a woman could be divorced from her husband. Hermaphrodism presented challenges to the binary norms of maleness and femaleness, but although they were condemned by some authors, many writers accepted hermaphrodites as long as they chose a single sexual persona, which it was expected would be determined by whichever sexual 'member' was predominant.

Appropriate dress was also considered an essential component of masculine identity. For a man to wear the clothes of a woman was widely regarded as a sin. Conversely, female cross-dressing as a man, when in the pursuit, in particular, of spiritual fulfilment through, for example, entering a monastery or a desire to achieve sanctity was broadly acceptable. Dress and hairstyles were common foci of complaint and ridicule in circumstances where men were deemed to be troublemakers. For example, anti-clerical rhetoric often likened clerical dress to female clothing, while longer hairstyles for secular men, especially at courts with a reputation for disreputable behaviour, were liable to be criticised as effeminate.

The study of medieval men has largely focused on elite men. The full range of attributes expected of adult aristocratic men were acquired during the course of infancy and adolescence, and it was not uncommon for such men to spend time in other households as part of the process of training as an adult male, during which time training in aggression and violence was commonplace. Medieval poetic depictions of aristocratic men and of chivalric culture indicate that there was a cultural perception that such men should not only be militarily successful, but should also be physically robust and dress well, have at least one close and reliable male comrade in arms and be capable of impressing women. Among the urban classes it was not uncommon for young men to spend time training as an apprentice in the household of another; the lack of adult, civic masculinity that this dependence on another man implied seems to have given rise to a desire for apprentices to prove themselves men, in particular through violence, rape and sporting contests. The study of peasant men has attracted less attention, in part because of the more limited written sources for this class. Peasant men and women typically undertook different activities, with men's work more commonly based outside of the household. Within Christian societies, labouring on the land was valorised through the biblical model of Adam, offering a more positive role model than Eve, the cause of the fall of mankind, for peasant women.

Archaeological evidence has illuminated gender roles and relations, particularly in the early medieval period when burials in many regions of Europe were accompanied by grave goods: the graves of men frequently contained weapons, in contrast to female graves which contained jewellery. Not all individuals were accorded these gendered assemblages and it has accordingly been suggested that those whose deaths caused the greatest disruptions to their families, that is those of child-bearing and marriageable age, were accorded the most elaborate funerary provision. Although the styles of grave goods varied across Europe, nonetheless the association of weaponry with the burials of males, even sometimes for those males too young, old or physically incapacitated to fight, reveals the strong and widespread association of maleness with martial ability. Such associations outlasted the abandonment of grave goods (the seventh and eighth centuries in most parts of western Europe, the tenth century in Scandinavia, and later in Eastern Europe), and across Europe many later medieval funerary monuments depicted males with weapons.

The distinctions between the gender roles of men and women were usually very clear in medieval society, yet in some contexts, in particular when women were absent, men drew on typically feminine characteristics as part of their public persona. For example, in twelfth-century monastic contexts, in particular among the Cistercians, monks and abbots described themselves and also Jesus as female figures, in particular as mothers, or using feminine terms. This was another development of the aforementioned period of ecclesiastical reform, and was a means by which religious men could depict their possession of qualities normally regarded as feminine. What was regarded as appropriate masculine behaviour varied across medieval Europe and over time. Nonetheless, it is striking in an era without mass media that certain expectations of men were widely found. It is undoubtedly the case that religious beliefs played an important part in informing expectations of male behaviour. In particular, the main religions of medieval Europe shared a suspicion of women and frequently a belief in their inherent sinfulness. While it has been argued that theological misogyny was merely a rhetorical game, it is nonetheless apparent that negative beliefs about women were widely disseminated within religious spheres, and that this was an important context within which masculine identity was constructed throughout the Middle Ages.

References and further reading

Bynum, C.W. (1982) *Jesus as Mother*, Berkeley, CA: University of California Press.
Cadden, J. (1993) *Meanings of Sex Difference in the Middle Ages*, Cambridge: Cambridge University Press.
Cohen, J. and Wheeler, B. (eds) (1997) *Becoming Male in the Middle Ages*, New York: Garland.
Cullum, P. and Lewis, K. (eds) (2004) *Holiness and Masculinity in the Middle Ages*, Cardiff: University of Wales Press
Elliott, D. (1997) 'Pollution, illusion and masculine disarray: nocturnal emissions and the sexuality of the clergy', in K. Lochrie, P. McCracken and J. Schultz (eds) *Constructing Medieval Sexuality*, Minneapolis, MN: Minnesota University Press, pp. 1–23.
Hadley, D.M. (ed.) (1999) *Masculinity in Medieval Europe*, London: Longman.
Hotchkiss, V. (1996) *Clothes Make the Man*, New York: Garland.
Karras, R. (2002) *From Boys to Men*, Philadelphia, PA: Pennsylvania University Press.
Lees, C. (ed.) *Medieval Masculinities*, Minneapolis, MN: Minnesota University Press.
Murray, J. (ed.) (1999) *Conflicted Identities and Multiple Masculinities*, New York: Garland.

See also: divorce and separation; dress, fashion and clothing; elite culture; fatherhood, fathering; hair; history, ancient Mediterranean civilisations; homoeroticism; homosexuality; men who have sex with men; men's relations with men; semen anxiety; sport, athletes and athletic training

DAWN HADLEY

HISTORY, INDUSTRIALISATION

Industrialisation ushered in a radical new sexual division of labour in Western society and thereby changed gender roles and the definition of masculinity and femininity. Industrialisation converted small-scale household producers into wage labour, necessitating a separation of home and workplace, and the growing differentiation of gender roles. Women were to remain in the home, tending to the children and household chores, while men became the principal breadwinners. Women's restriction to the home largely explained their legal, social and ideological subordination as male hegemony increased.

Stages in British industrialisation

Britain was the first country to industrialise, and the way in which this process affected various classes has been well documented. Because of their important role in pre-industrial home production, working-class women never found employment and femininity incompatible, and even when confined to the home as wives and mothers strove to add to the family income. Middle-class women, on the other hand, did not massively enter paid employment until white-collar jobs commensurate with their status opened up.

In the earliest stages of industrialisation in the mid-nineteenth century, when light industry such as textiles predominated, all family members worked in the mills, sometimes as a family group. Families who had engaged in home production moved to the cities. The wages of the family formed a common fund, and parents tried to keep wage-earning children at home as long as possible, even if it meant taking care of a daughter's illegitimate child (Tilly and Scott 1978). Children and their mother traded off work roles, with the mother stopping paid employment as soon as the children were old enough to work, sometimes as young as ten. Even when married women remained at home, they did piecework for garment production and/or took in lodgers. Though men were the primary wage earners, mothers managed household expenditures and kept in touch with relatives, who could help out in an emergency.

The move towards heavy industry in the early twentieth century accentuated male employment and the role of the male breadwinner. The image of women at home came to be seen as a sign of prosperity, and a man whose wife worked was stigmatised. Single women worked, however, including middle-class women as jobs opened up in clerical work and teaching, which fitted their status. Married women generally did not work for wages, and even professional women faced a marriage bar instituted by employers. Men's wages increased, particularly when unions demanded a 'family wage' that would support an entire family. Families were motivated to have fewer children, who were now more financially dependent and required longer schooling. But the better-off families still had more than one wage earner.

An increase in consumer goods and in the demand for women workers in the growing service industry in the early twentieth century gradually encouraged married women to join the labour force, in what Tilly and Scott term 'the family consumer economy'. Mothers worked instead of children, but were still paid as supplementary wage earners. The entrance of married women into full-time paid employment was the biggest challenge to the man's role as breadwinner, because it reduced women's financial dependence and made them question their subordinate role in the family and society. Women began to press for rights like maternity leave and day care centres, which would reduce their disadvantages to men in full-time employment.

Racial and ethnic differences in wage employment in the US

Industrialisation in the US started with the first textile mills in Lowell, Massachusetts, in the 1820s and 1830s (Tilly 1993: 27) and was marked by sharp regional differences as well as racial and ethnic diversity. The European middle-class notion of the male breadwinner was imposed on these subordinate populations, but with little success in cases where the man could not earn a sufficient wage to support his family, as among African Americans and many first-generation immigrants. Only white men were able to earn a family wage, and resisted the entrance of African-American men into wage employment. Black married women always worked, initially in domestic service and after World War II in manufacturing and white-collar jobs. This led black women to reject the white feminist notion of the family as the centre of women's oppression.

Until 1930, men and single white women predominated in manufacturing employment, while married white women were governed by a cult of domesticity that confined women to the home. Protective legislation for women reinforced their domestic role and hastened the process of occupational segregation by gender, which continues to this day. As Tilly (1993) observes, occupational segregation reduced competition between men and women for the same jobs and restricted women to lower-level jobs at lower wages.

Domesticity declined with the massive entrance of white married women into the labour force after World War II to meet an increasing demand for women in clerical and other white-collar employment. Starting in 1970, the decline in male wages and increases in male unemployment reinforced the need for a dual wage-earner family. Manufacturing employment gradually declined as it faced foreign competition and was transferred abroad, starting with female-dominated sectors like the garment industry, but de-industrialisation later reached heavy industry in which white men predominated, such as steel and automobiles. White men continue to monopolise high-level managerial and professional employment, while African Americans and Latino(a)s are concentrated in the growing service sector. Despite the increasing percentage of white women in high-level jobs, gender and ethnic employment hierarchies persist and can now be seen within each racial and ethnic group, as well as among women (Amott and Matthai 1991).

As in Europe, the massive entrance of married women into the labour force struck a fundamental blow to the notion of the male breadwinner. In all racial/ethnic groups, there has been a decline in married couple households and an increase in female-headed households, especially among African Americans and Latino/as. The declining ability of men to fulfil their roles as principal breadwinner encouraged lone mothers to raise children on their own, whether as divorced or as unwed mothers.

Industrialisation in developing countries: the case of the Hispanic Caribbean

The process of industrialisation outlined above differed considerably in developing countries, which lacked the capital and technology found in Europe and in the US. Developing countries could supply an abundant quantity of cheap labour, sought by metropolitan companies as wages and social benefits increased at home. Puerto Rico in the 1950s became one of the first sources of offshore employment for the US garment industry, aided by both the federal and island government. While US unions objected initially, they reached a compromise in which these new Puerto Rican workers were compelled to join unions to find a job (Safa 1995: 62).

In larger independent countries with more resources, like Argentina, Brazil and Mexico, the move towards heavy industry received strong state support under a programme of import substitution industrialisation (ISI). ISI, which started in World War II, was designed to reduce these countries' dependence on the US and Europe for manufactured goods by domestically manufacturing consumer goods like automobiles and refrigerators. ISI in Latin America also privileged male workers, because of its emphasis on heavy industry and its conscious effort to increase wages in order to promote an internal domestic market capable of purchasing the consumer goods produced. The weak development of this internal market, lack of sophisticated technology, and the debt crisis which hit Latin America in the 1980s spelled an end to ISI, as countries were again forced to open their markets to cheaper manufactured goods produced elsewhere. Now many of these larger countries, and especially Mexico through its Border Industrialisation programme, have embarked on export-led industrialisation, which offers cheap labour to US and European industries that have transferred their manufacturing abroad.

The move towards export manufacturing in Latin America, supported by US government programmes like the Caribbean Basin Initiative and NAFTA, sharply reduced wages in order to be competitive internationally. Export manufacturing initially relied heavily on young female labour because women were cheaper and more skilled in the garment and electronics industries, which dominated the early stages. As in developed countries, women also sought employment to add to the family income as men's wages declined and unemployment grew. The family wage for male labour was never firmly established in Latin America, with the possible exception of some highly skilled men in heavy industry.

Export-led industrialisation became the preferred development strategy in the Caribbean because of the small size of these countries, which precluded the development of an internal market. The Caribbean has relied on exports since colonial days, principally sugar, which became highly mechanised in its processing in the twentieth century. Men predominated as both cane cutters and mill workers, but in the 1930s two-thirds of Puerto Rico's manufacturing workers were women, principally employed in home needlework for US industry. Staying at home enabled these women to carry on with their domestic routine, and they did not think of themselves as principal breadwinners, even when their meagre wages were the principal source of income (Baerga 1993).

The collapse of the sugar economy in the Caribbean led to widespread male unemployment and wage declines, necessitating an increase in women's employment to maintain household incomes. Migration from the West Indies, Puerto Rico and later the Dominican Republic also grew, initially among men but now including both sexes and whole families. Remittances from relatives living abroad have become an increasingly important source of family income in all of the Caribbean. Men were angered at the loss of their former economic hegemony and ridiculed women factory workers as promiscuous and irresponsible (Safa 2002). But studies have shown that many of these women are supporting entire families on their meagre wages, particularly as female-headed households have grown. With growing economic independence, women are no longer willing to tolerate male abuse or negligence, nor are they willing to marry men whom they know can never be secure sources of support.

West Indian women have long relied on their own resources for family support, working in agriculture, as hagglers, and now in new offshore industries. As among women of colour in the US, the notion of dependence on a male breadwinner never took hold. In the Hispanic Caribbean, Catholicism combined with a strong tradition of confining women to the home did bring about greater female dependence on men. But this is now waning, as women are forced to become more financially independent, notably married women.

There are many interesting parallels between these Caribbean working-class households and Tilly and Scott's description of the household in the early stages of industrialisation in Britain. All working members contribute to a common fund, and pregnant unwed daughters are expected to remain within the household with their children. Pregnancy strengthens the mother–child tie, and mothers often look after their daughters' children while the daughters work. Adult kin may be incorporated as wage earners as part of an extended family survival strategy (Safa 1995).

It has been argued (Safa 1999) that these extended female-headed households are not simply a result of the current economic crisis in the Caribbean but correspond to a much older family pattern in which consanguineal kin are more important than the marital bond. Similar patterns have been found among African–American families in the US prior to the 1950s, when industrialisation, geographic dispersal and the growth of the welfare state have weakened extended kin ties (Safa 2005).

De-industrialisation in developed and developing countries

Both the Caribbean and other developing areas as well as developed countries like the United States and western Europe are now undergoing de-industrialisation. This is particularly true of high-wage areas like Puerto Rico, but all developing countries are suffering from competition from cheap labour in Asia, particularly China. Puerto Rico is now a post-industrial economy heavily dependent on federal transfers to sustain an increasingly impoverished population.

De-industrialisation has resulted in economic collapse and large-scale migration from the Caribbean and within the US from older industrial centres to newer cities in the West and South. Export-led industrialisation depressed wages not only in developing areas, but also among industrial workers in the US and elsewhere, from which these companies fled. Women did not replace men in male-designated jobs, but the entire economy shifted away from manufacturing towards service and high-tech jobs.

Under de-industrialisation, it is doubtful that the myth of the male breadwinner can be resurrected. But it continues to shape state policy, employer preferences and union practices.

References and further reading

Amott, T. and Matthaei, J. (1991) *Race, Gender and Work*, Boston, MA: South End.

Baerga, M. (ed.) (1993) 'El género y la construcción social de la marginalidad del trabajo femenino en la industria de la confección de ropa', in *Género y Trabajo*, San Juan: Editorial de la Universidad de Puerto Rico.
Safa, H.I. (1995) *The Myth of the Male Breadwinner*, Boulder, CO: Westview.
—— (1999) 'Female headed households in the Caribbean', *Latino(a) Research Review*, 4 (1–2).
—— (2002) 'Questioning globalization', *Journal of Developing Societies*, 18 (2–3): 11–31; reprinted in C. Menjívar (ed.) (2003) *Through the Eyes of Women*, Ontario: De Sitter.
—— (2005) 'Welfare reform, racism and single motherhood in the Americas', in F. Harrison (ed.) *Resisting Racism and Xenophobia*, Walnut Creek, CA: Altamira Press, pp. 105–22.
Tilly, L. (1993) *Industrialization and Gender Inequality*, Washington, DC: American Historical Association.
Tilly, L. and Scott, J. (1978) *Women, Work and Family*, New York: Holt, Rinehart and Winston.

HELEN I. SAFA

HISTORY, LATIN AMERICA

Whether true or not, Latin America has often been considered a region steeped in machismo. Latin American masculinity comes from a long history that begins with indigenous warrior culture, proceeds through the culture of honour imported from Europe, and includes nationalist glorification of male heroes.

Although Latin American cultures were shaped on a base indigenous culture, not much has been written about masculinity among the original inhabitants except for the Aztecs. Among the Aztecs, masculinity was very much associated with being a warrior. It was especially connected to successfully capturing other warriors for sacrifice, which allowed advancement within society and up to the noble classes. War was chronic in Aztec society and always present in the culture.

Midwives welcomed Aztec boys into the world with a war cry and presented them with toy weapons. Young boys shouted the name of the male baby in the streets in a way reminiscent of a victory. Clearly a large part of their identity as men was defined from birth as associated with war. There were also physical markers reserved for boys that prepared them for their roles as men. Shortly after birth, all boys had their lips pierced in preparation for taking a warrior's lip plug. At the warrior festival of Toxcatl, priests slashed all boys, even infants, on their stomachs, chests and arms in order to demonstrate their dedication to the Aztecs' principal god. Male hair also changed according to age and warrior status. As boys began their military training, they grew a longer strand of hair that was removed upon taking a prisoner. Men who failed to take a captive in war after many campaigns were humiliated by having their hair shaved off the crown of their head. After this ritual shaming, they would only be allowed base employment.

As adults, Aztec men engaged in a profession during most of the year and then periodically joined in military campaigns. All were very much aware that although combat could bring glory, it could end up with death on the battlefield or on a sacrificial stone in some neighbouring city. If successful, an Aztec male could marry, and with greater success, he would wear the symbols of his valour. The emperor gave men who captured five or more opponents on the battlefield clothes and jewellery that represented their valour. Such men, wearing red capes, eagle claws, yellow or blue lip-plugs, elaborate headdresses, impressed everyone they met in the streets. These men were expected to be assertive, loud braggarts, but stoicism in the face of possible death was also admired. To be a man in Aztec society, as in many indigenous societies, was intimately tied to success in warfare. This fundamental basis of their identity as men ended with the Iberian conquest.

The feats of small bands of Spanish and Portuguese men who defeated large indigenous empires provide us with many stories of individual prowess and supply us with another similar brand of masculinity. Although many scholars have successfully challenged the notion of European superiority in these conquests, at the time, Iberian men undoubtedly sensed that their military achievements imparted upon them a kind of hypermasculinity. Indeed, while Iberian men took on the role of conquerors with the attendant honours, part of the process of colonisation entailed a feminisation of indigenous males. Spanish chroniclers showed a marked interest in locating homosexuality among indigenous cultures, along with cannibalism, in order to confirm to themselves that Europeans were superior men and justifiably the conquerors of these decadent civilisations.

Within the colonies that developed out of the process of conquest and colonisation, masculinity was very much influenced by the ideas of honour imported from the Mediterranean. These codes of honour assigned both women and men certain roles that were interdependent but also contradictory. For example, men derived some of their status as men from their position as patriarch and especially by ensuring the virginity and chastity of the women in their household. But, as men of the larger community, they also achieved status by seducing the women of other men's households. In some cases, as Socolow (1980) shows, men raped the wives or lovers of men who had insulted them or incurred their enmity.

On an ideal level, honour was something that belonged only to the elites of Latin America. However, new research has shown that plebeians adopted the ideas of honour, which were as important to slaves and servants as to elites. Plebeian men asserted their control over women in their entourage and exerted a domination over any women – whether they were married or not – whom they supported financially. Stern (1995) has shown that the position of patriarch was not an automatic attribute for men. In fact, it was a negotiated role. Women recognised this elusive quality and would appeal to various patriarchs as it suited them. Thus men could not count on being recognised as patriarchs but had to earn that right.

Men as patriarchs had authority over the servants and slaves who were part of their domestic setting. They exerted their superiority over such social inferiors but also drew from this relationship some of their honour. So masculinity was asserted in a hierarchical manner with the greatest honour or status to those with rank in society but also by control over households and social inferiors.

The ranks of different men could be defined in tangible ways: for example, by the way they dressed, whether they wore a sword or rode a horse. Rank also was lived out by the bodily language of submission: people who were socially lower in rank doffed their hats, bowed their heads and their upper bodies, and made way for those who were their betters. Male etiquette instructed young men on the complex dance of respect and submission. Men had to judge their position relative to all men they met and thus decide whether they had to dismount to greet someone in the street, make way for another while walking through town, meet them at the door of their house or at the top of the staircase, and even choose which chair in any room appropriately conveyed their ranking among those present.

Plebeian men also learned the intricacies of social hierarchy. Lower-class men had their own ways of structuring rank within their social circles according to age, wealth and a kind of intangible masculine quality. Their ways of dealing with each other can be discerned through some of the explosions of masculine anger that were recorded in the court records of the period. Johnson (1999) notes that Argentine plebeian men were quick to take offence for perceived insults that could in other circumstances be affectionate gestures. He tells of an incident when one man reached over to another to pull a wood chip out of the first's beard, but the touching of facial hair provoked a brutal attack that led to a death. Other incidents that Johnson recounts seem similar to those that Stern mentions for Mexico in which jokes could be misperceived and lead to an unleashing of rage that was often fatal. There were many unwritten rules of male sociability that governed plebeian male everyday life. Chambers (1999) found that male codes of conduct privileged hospitality and generosity. In late eighteenth-century Peru, for example, an honourable man could not refuse a drink and then was obliged to buy the next round. Places of intense sociability like the tavern or family gatherings provided the plebeian equivalent of the kind of setting in which upper-class men determined their social place and acted within the limits and parameters of that position.

In many ways, the wars of independence and the nations that emerged from those bloody confrontations did not change the social landscape very much. Social change was much slower than political transformations. But the way in which masculinity was defined began to alter with independence and an emphasis on the new category of citizen. Men's honour became less associated with being the head or patriarch of a family and more with the fact that they had served their nation as soldiers. Male status and honour was increasingly associated with military rank but also with the related notions of the work ethic. The army tried to instil the kinds of mentality that privileged hard work over swagger. Peter Beattie (1991) shows how Brazilian officials had to transform the status of soldier from dishonourable criminal to one who exuded masculinity. The prevailing idea of the masculine also began to stress the importance of financially supporting family members rather than simply having authority over them. Wives began to assert their rights as mothers in opposition to those husbands whom they asserted were bad fathers. The ideology of men's inherent and natural authority was beginning to be eroded as the ethos of male social responsibility was being imposed.

In many parts of nineteenth-century Latin America, caudillos emerged as political leaders. These were men who ruled with an iron fist but largely with great popular support and the assistance of a private army. Chasteen (1995) demonstrates that caudillos appealed to the masses largely because of their charisma derived from their hypermasculinity. In his study of Aparicio and Gumercindo Saravia, he shows how the two brothers inspired their followers at least in part because they displayed all the traditional skills of the gaucho. They were excellent horsemen, fierce with knives and great seducers of women. Their appeal was to a more traditional machismo, one that harked back to the colonial period and contrasted with the kind of masculine ideal – good breadwinner, loyal soldier – that Latin American elites were trying to impose.

In contrast, elites in nineteenth-century Latin America were discovering a new kind of masculine pursuit – the duel. The duel was not common in the colonial period because upper-class men, unlike their counterparts in Europe, preferred to use litigation to resolve insults and affronts. But as members of newly independent nations, they looked to Europe as model and adopted many practices in the pursuit of modernity. By the 1860s, reports of deaths caused by duelling men began to be common in all parts of Latin America.

The twentieth century was marked by revolutions and insurrections. Many of these movements' leaders derived their popularity not just from their political ideas but also because they represented a new kind of hero. In some senses, the fascination that Latin Americans had with the caudillo did not really fade after the nineteenth century but rather transformed into a new male archetype – the revolutionary hero. Such figures as Zapata of the Mexican Revolution and Guevara, who fought in the Cuban Revolution, had many of the same qualities that characterised the Saravia brothers.

The twentieth century also meant major changes in the ways in which Latin Americans lived. The population converted from a highly rural distribution to a predominantly urban pattern, and at the same time work and education patterns changed. As women began to get access to higher education, they took on jobs that were previously considered the preserve of men. Professions such as school teachers, dentists and pharmacists were taken over by women because they were acceptable for women, but this transformation meant that these jobs became feminised. Women were invading formerly male preserves all over, taking jobs as secretaries, sales clerks and in factories, and as a result the work spaces reserved for men, although still existing, had to be more clearly defined and limited. The entry of women into these work spaces caused considerable anxiety for many men. Their notions of the protection of female virtue had been attenuated but were not extinct. Thus, even the socialist party in Argentina argued about female and child labour, in regards not so much to their work conditions but to the protection of their chastity.

Men in Latin America no longer derive their masculine identity from being warriors but rather from a complex mixture of sexual norms and the ethics of being a good patriarch and citizen. Their sometimes contradictory impulses derive from their history.

References and further reading

Beattie, P. (1991) 'The house, the street, and the barracks', *Hispanic American Historical Review*, 76: 439–73.

Chambers, S.(1999) *From Subjects to Citizens*, University Park, PA: Pennsylvania State University Press.

Chasteen, J. (1995) *Heroes on Horseback*, Albuquerque, NM: University of New Mexico Press.

Clendinnen, I. (1991) *Aztecs*, Cambridge: Cambridge University Press.

Johnson, L. (1999) 'Dangerous words, provocative gestures, and violent acts', in L. Johnson and S. Lipsett-Rivera, *The Faces of Honor*, Albuquerque, NM: University of New Mexico Press, pp. 127–51.

Johnson, L. and Lipsett-Rivera, S. (eds) (1999) *The Faces of Honor*, Albuquerque, NM: University of New Mexico Press.

Joyce, R. (2000) 'Girling the girl and boying the boy', *World Archaeology*, 31: 473–83.

Lipsett-Rivera, S. (2001) 'Marriage and family relations in Mexico during the transition from colony to nation', in V. Uribe-Uran (ed.) *State and Society in Spanish America during the Age of Revolution*, Wilmington, DE: Scholarly Resources.

Parker, D. (2001) 'Law, honor, and impunity in Spanish America', *Law and History Review*, 19: 311–41.

Socolow, S. (1980) 'Women and crime', *Journal of Latin American Studies*, 12: 39–54.

Stern, S. (1995) *The Secret History of Gender*, Chapel Hill, NC: University of North Carolina Press.

SONYA LIPSETT-RIVERA

HISTORY, MIDDLE EAST

Globalisation and growing cultural influences of the West are creating new conflicts and challenges in the Middle East. In a post 9/11/2001 environment, Western popular cultures depict the Muslim male from this region as an existential threat. Yet Middle Eastern Islam is in the grip of powerful changes. The quest to renew Islam includes resistance to Western influences, and raises challenges for Muslim masculinities in relation to global hegemonic masculinities.

The Middle East is the most ancient region of human civilisation. At around 10,000 BCE farming first developed in the area called the Fertile Crescent. The emergence of plough agriculture, requiring muscular effort to guide the plough and use large animals, about 3000 BCE is thought to have initiated a patriarchal social structure throughout the Middle East (Ehrenberg 1989).

The Middle East also became the birthplace of the three monotheist world religions of Judaism, Christianity and Islam. A millennium prior to these religions, Mithraism was the dominant religion of the region. Mithra, a male god, was worshipped only by men in Mithraic shrines. Mithraism spread to Europe, and the ancient Romans and Greeks considered Mithra not only as a sun god but also as the god of kings and warriors and hence the god of war. Mithraism influenced Judaism, Zoroastrianism, Christianity and later on Islam in the region (Cumont 1956).

The social structure of patriarchy as its legacy has survived through these religions up to the present time. Documents from Mesopotamia in the second millennium BCE provide considerable detail relating to laws of personal status. The male was the virtual owner of his family. He could sell his wife and children or pawn them as security for debt (Ehrenberg 1989).

From the seventh century AD, Islam became the dominant religion of the region. Muslim men formed the religious hierarchy and excluded women from attending mosques. The division of labour was predominantly based on gender. The economy in the traditional Islamic cities revolved around the bazaar, where all merchants, shopkeepers, traders and service providers were men. Muslim men not only took control of the domain of politics but also dominated the economy.

In the pre-modern era, the Middle East became part of the Ottoman, then the Safavid empires. The Ottoman Empire existed from 1299 to 1923. During the sixteenth and seventeenth centuries its territory, in addition to the Middle East, included Anatolia, parts of North Africa, and much of southeastern Europe to the Caucasus. The Safavid Empire lasted from 1501 to 1722. It covered Iran and parts of Turkey and Georgia. Iran became the only Shiite government in the entire Muslim world during that time. Shiism revitalised *Shahadat* (martyrdom), a concept that has been monopolised by Islamist men to secure a place in Paradise by sacrificing their lives to defend Islam. This concept dates back to the early development of Islam, particularly the short-lived government of Ali and the Battle of Karbala in 680 CE. After the Fourth Caliph Ali was assassinated, Hussein, his son, tried to regain power from Caliph Yazid but was killed in the Battle of Karbala in 680 CE. Ali as the 'warrior' persona and Hussein as 'martyr' represent two different masculinity types in Shiite Islam (Gerami 2005). This perspective sees Hussein as a positive role model of courage and resistance against tyranny and is celebrated during *Ashura*, a Shiite day of mourning. This custom has been integrated into the construction of Islamist masculinity within Shiite communities globally.

During the late nineteenth century and in response to modernism, Islamic modernists, such as Jamal al-Deen Asadabadi, developed new ideas, one being a discourse of Islamic orthodoxy, and claimed a monopoly of legitimate religious expression. Other contending concepts were secular discourses and religious ideologies resulting from European interventions which began to powerfully invade the cultural landscape of Islamic countries (Moaddel 2005: 19).

A global Western imagery of masculinity emerged in this era. The invasion of Islamic countries by Western colonial powers intensified the language of 'rape of the motherland' by a penetrating foreign force (Ahmed 1992). Thus, with colonialism, men's protecting women's honour became a symbol of national honour. This created serious challenges to local masculinities as men's honour was threatened and called upon to protect the motherland (Gerami 2005).

During the early twentieth century, masculinities in Middle Eastern societies progressed from diffused ethnic, tribal, rural and urban masculinities to a national masculinity of independence movements, and then to the diverse masculinities of contemporary times. National media experimented with a variety of masculinity models including peasant, working-class and ethnic masculinities. However, the dominant prototype remained shaped by such strong nationalistic figures as Ataturk in Turkey, Rezah Shah in Iran and Nassir in Egypt. In Iran, Rezah Shah banned the women's veil and barred men from wearing ethnic, religious or tribal clothing.

By 1916, under the secret Sykes–Picot agreement, the French and British divided up the Middle East, with the Balfour declaration of 1917 leading to the establishment of the State of Israel in 1948. Modern-day divisions based on the above agreements became embedded in the collective memories of people in the region, leading to the clash of domestic masculinity with global hegemonic masculinity observable among Palestinians today. The occupation of land previously deemed theirs created a crisis for Palestinian masculinities. The only way, some Islamist men believed, to defend the motherland has been to sacrifice their lives under the banner of *Intifada* (Palestinian uprising). These measures are one response of Islamist young men, and even boys, to chronic feelings of guilt, shame and humiliation by Israel and the West. This process has become a dominant discourse shaping the masculinity of young Palestinians and Israeli men through military institutions.

An analysis of army institutions and regional wars offers a view of male hegemonic practices. Peteet (2000) examines *Intifadas* where the masculine identity of Palestinian males is closely linked to resistance against the far greater powers wielded by the Israeli defence forces.

Kaplan (2000) identifies the extent to which military service in the Israeli army inculcates versions of exemplary masculinity that are inextricably bound up with Zionism or ideas about Israeli rights to biblical lands, and with the status and recognition of manhood in triumph over Palestinians. In hegemonic Islamist masculinity, however, youth obtain their venerated manhood through acts of sacrifice in the name of country, faith and honour (Sinclair-Web 2000).

Islamist fundamentalist movements generating Islamist masculinity enact a retroactive ideology by establishing what is claimed as an earlier 'pure' Islamic society of Shariah. Since the 1950s, this fundamentalism has spread across the Middle East led by people such as Ayatollah Khomeini from Iran, al-Banna and Qutb from Egypt, Maududi from Pakistan, as-Siba'i and Abbasi Madani, Shaikh Nahnah and Belhaj from Algeria. These leaders rejected Western influences and insisted on unconditional loyalty to their visions of Islam. Pan-Arab nationalism co-existed with fundamentalist movements and redrawn state borders to become a compelling force of cultural change and masculine identity in virtually all Arab countries during the 1950s.

In Iran, the nationalistic movement failed and parliamentary politics ended with a coup in 1953. From the 1960s onward, with the establishment of a new political party called the Freedom Movement (*Nehzate Azadi*), cultural shifts away from secularism and to moderate, then radical, Islamism occurred. These orientations were based on different readings of the Qur'an. Religious opposition attacked the Shah as anti-Islamic and a promoter of decadent Western culture. A distinctive feature of the opposition was the emergence of Islamist masculinity and the rise of a clergy-centred Islamic discourse and ideology.

Islamist masculinity is embedded within cultural institutions in the Middle East conditioned by a patriarchal society that exercises control over women, particularly through the practices associated with honour and shame. Another feature of patriarchy is the social desirability of male children to carry the family name. Family-centred societies consider it tragic if male lineage dies out. Patriarchy is also sustained by male circumcision. This is a practice where masculinity is explicitly and usually publicly affirmed. Male circumcision is prevalent in Muslim and Jewish societies and assumed to be a religious duty, yet evidence suggests cultural origins (Kassamali 1998). Hoffman (1996: 44) claims that in patriarchy it is the duty of the father to circumcise his son, 'a practice reflecting the extension of the creation of the son by the father'.

Islamist masculinity discourse is founded on the principles of *Jihad* and *Shahadat*. Most modern-day Muslims regard *jihad* as a personal struggle and distinguish it from warfare (Esposito 2003: 38), whereas the West identifies warfare *Jihad* as the prototype of Islamist masculinity. The concept of *Shahadat* (martyrdom) derived from Shiite Islam implies a personal and a public level of engagement to protect Islam or an Islamic nation (Gerami 2005).

However, masculinity as a social construct may take a variety of forms in the Middle East. Some are tolerated by the larger society, while others may incur serious consequences. Among the latter is homosexuality. During Islamic history, homosexuality has always been regarded as a 'deviant' sexual practice against 'real' heterosexual masculinity. This belief operates at many levels and has produced severe social sanctions. However, at the present time in Iran, the practice of sex change provides a contrast to homosexual intolerance in Islam. The Islamic Republic of Iran is the world leader for sex change operations. These operations are legal in Iran for anyone who can afford the cost and satisfy interviewers that they meet necessary psychological criteria (Guardian Unlimited 2005). These two examples indicate deviant masculinity is a fluid concept within the Islamic framework that is subject to different interpretations and sanctions in different times and places.

The major prototypes of contemporary Middle Eastern Muslim masculinities are based on class locations and economic structures. For example, in Iran the new upper class is made up of top-level Shiite religious clergy who by and large are strong supporters of fundamentalism and patriarchy.

In the twenty-first-century Middle East, economic and cultural forces of globalisation combined with demographics will strongly influence reconstruction of masculinity and gender roles in this region. The median age in the Middle East region is approximately twenty-one years (Gerami 2005), while 60 per cent of the 70 million population of Iran is aged less than thirty-five years (Farr 1999). Of the 3 million unemployed people in Iran, urban lower- or middle-class families are overrepresented and current trends point to increases in unemployment in the future (Salehi-Esfahani and Taheripour 2002). The identities of young Middle Eastern university-educated males are challenged because of social pressures to conform to Middle Eastern constructs of masculinity associated with providing income as breadwinner.

The oppressed people (*mostazaafin*) in the Middle East are encountering two major and opposing counter-currents: Islamic fundamentalism and cultural liberalism. Middle East governments may provide some assistance for segments of this population but are unable to provide all these men with stable employment around which familiar models of masculinity are organised.

The new professional middle class faces different challenges. Engaged in professional activities with meaningful employment, men in this group strive to secure university places for their children while facing blocked or limited political participation. Their education, professional activities and connections with the Western world condition them to be potential supporters of cultural liberalism and strong advocates for gender equality (Adibi 1980).

In the twenty-first century, more female than male students are entering universities in Muslim countries such as Iran, Turkey and Egypt. Yet university education has failed to deliver them secure lives; as a result, demand grows for migration to Western countries. It is within this context that Muslim fluid masculinities are re-forming within the social structures of class, patriarchy, culture, economic structure, religion and politics.

For the future, the constriction of Muslim identities in the Middle East is likely to be primarily affected by men's social class. While political change may take place rapidly, attitudes towards gender equality are changing more slowly. Social factors leading to intensification of the growing disparity among social classes will hinder the progress towards gender equality and may lead to unfortunate consequences.

References and further reading

Adibi, H. (1980) *Iranian New Middle Class*, Tehran: Jameah.

Ahmed, L. (1992) *Women and Gender in Islam*, New Haven, CT: Yale University Press.

Cumont, F. (1956) *The Mysteries of Mithra*, translated T.J. McCormack, New York: Dover.

Ehrenberg, M. (1989) *Women in Prehistory*, Norman, OK: University of Oklahoma Press.
Esposito, J. (2003) *Unhappy War*, New York: Oxford University Press.
Farr, G. (1999) *Modern Iran*, Boston, MA: McGraw-Hill College.
Gerami, S. (2005) 'Islamist masculinity and Muslim masculinities', in M.S. Kimmel, J. Hearn and R. Connell (eds) *Handbook of Studies on Men and Masculinities*, London: Sage, pp. 448–57.
Guardian Unlimited (2005) 'A fatwa for freedom', 27 July, available at http://www.guardian.co.uk/g2/story/0,3604,1536658,00.html
Hoffman, L. (1996) *Covenant of Blood*, Chicago, IL: University of Chicago Press.
Kaplan, D. (2000) 'The military as a second bar mitzvah', in M. Ghoussoub and E. Sinclair-Web (eds) *Imagined Masculinities*, London: Saqi.
Kassamali, N. (1998) 'When modernity confronts traditional practices', in H.L. Bodman and N. Tohidi (eds) *Women in Muslim Societies*, London: Lynne Rienner, pp. 39–61.
Moaddel, M. (2005) *Islamic Modernism, Nationalism and Fundamentalism*, Chicago, IL: University of Chicago Press.
Peteet, J. (2000) 'Male gender and rituals of resistance in the Palestinian intifada', in M. Ghoussoub and E. Sinclair-Web (eds) *Imagined Masculinities*, London: Saqi.
Salehi-Esfahani, H. and Taheripour, F. (2002) 'Hidden public expenditures and the economy in Iran', *International Journal of Middle East Studies*, 34: 691–718.
Sinclair-Web, E. (2000) 'Introduction', in M. Ghoussoub and E. Sinclair-Web (eds) *Imagined Masculinities*, London: Saqi.

HOSSEIN ADIBI

HISTORY, MODERNITY

The history of masculinity in the Western world has been indelibly marked by what is commonly referred to as 'modernity', a complex and interrelated cluster of social, political, cultural and economic developments that has characterised Western societies since the decline of the feudal era. Although some scholars have treated the Western conception of history as a 'grand narrative' of the white, bourgeois and masculinist exploitation of nature, women, sexual 'deviants' and indigenous populations, the material and psychological conditions of modernity have also generated a counter-narrative that depicts the march of modern 'civilisation' as a steady drift towards over-refinement, cerebrality, luxury and sedentary living that diminishes rather than bolsters many traditional masculine ideals. To the extent that these conditions of modernity challenge the physical basis for male privilege, this counter-narrative presents modernisation as being tantamount to feminisation. These complex gender effects are part of what we might call the 'double logic of modern civilisation', which promotes the interests of patriarchal culture while creating conditions that may weaken the bodily foundations of masculinity.

A number of key historical developments characterise the concept of modernity. Far more than a simple reference to the 'new', 'modernity' refers to the rise of secular forms of political authority, large-scale monetary economies, the decline of religious worldviews and the emergence of a secular, materialist and individualist ethos. With the end of the feudal order, traditional societies with fixed hierarchies gave way to more dynamic social relationships organised around class- and sex-based divisions of labour, particularly in countries where capitalism dominated (Hall 1996). This transition from the medieval to early modern periods also entailed a reformation of the behaviour of elite males. European Renaissance humanists (1350–1600) found in culture and learning an alternative form of virtue that they claimed was superior to the kind that demanded valour on the battlefield. Around the time that European monarchs began to consolidate power over their states (c. 1500–1700), their court societies required the softening of the rough, aggressive and potentially divisive tendencies of knights, thus fostering an emphasis on refinement and manners that would later be adopted by the middle classes (Elias [1939] 1994). A further alteration of noble identities occurred on the level of increased attention to education and culture, which became more desirable upper-class male attributes as military experience became less essential for elite male identity. From the seventeenth century onward, European scientific and technological developments not only advanced colonial projects but also created exclusively male domains that were emblems of Western global superiority (Bryson 1990).

The rising power of bourgeois groups, who valued education and commercial acumen over military valour, accelerated many developments that are integral to our ideas of modernity. The eighteenth-century emergence of a political 'public sphere', where hitherto private individuals could come together to discuss matters pertaining to society as a whole, has been rightly viewed as an implicitly gendered ideal: in most cases it was white, propertied men who were admitted into this purportedly universal domain, while women, proletarians and non-whites were typically excluded. Rationality lay at the heart of this privileging of elite white men as political subjects, the implication being that women and non-white/non-elite men were less capable of mastering their instincts and emotions and were thus biologically unqualified to contribute to the public world. The consolidation of the public sphere simultaneously created a complementary 'private' sphere of the hearth and home considered to be 'naturally' suited to women. By the late eighteenth century new medical knowledge about sexual difference deemed women 'naturally' fit for motherhood and incapable of muscular prowess, emotional control or higher mental powers (Laqueur 1990). Although this idea of 'separate spheres' was more an ideal than a reality, by the mid-nineteenth century evolutionary biology would view sexual polarisation as a 'natural' consequence of modernisation. Finally, these same medical discourses also generated the taxonomies that would characterise most non-reproductive forms of sexuality as pathological, thus scientifically reinforcing the heteronormative notions of masculinity that have characterised Western society for centuries.

Most of these developments enshrined the power and prestige of upper-class white men across the Western world and thus implicitly promoted the desirability of certain masculine models. Yet patriarchy and masculinity are not identical constructions. Ample evidence suggests that modernity has contradictory effects that support male domination while paradoxically undermining masculinity. 'To be modern,' Berman writes, 'is to find ourselves in an environment that promises us adventure, power, joy, growth, transformation of ourselves and the world – and, at the same time, that threatens to destroy everything we have, everything we know, everything we are' ([1982] 1992: 62). Berman's definition includes many conventionally 'masculine' activities and experiences (reason, development, etc.) that suggest a divide between male and female encounters with modernity, and his account largely ignores the perspective of women. However if we keep in mind the *simultaneity* and *reflexivity* upon which Berman's definition clearly insists, we see that masculinity too is profoundly affected by the energies and developments unleashed by modernity.

Many of the developments that marked elite masculinity since the sixteenth century were viewed as deeply problematic for men. In Germany, Britain, France and Russia, the refined manners of noble sociability were frequently contrasted to the supposedly direct and authentic expressions of simpler times, a perception that encouraged bourgeois elites to criticise these manners even as they imitated them (Cohen 2005). The intellectual regimens of most modern professions were counterposed (both morally and medically) to more physically active male occupations, thus contributing to the long-standing opinion that males who study too much are less than masculine. Moreover, the luxuries that accompanied industrial production and spurred industry were frequently blamed for fostering an 'effeminate' submission to appetite, appearances and vices. The sedentary existence implied by the polite, cerebral and consumer-oriented society was condemned as the opposite of manly action and health and as the root cause of obesity and muscular atrophy, which could best be 'cured' through sports and military training. Similarly, the mechanical technologies that extended the power of the male body also threatened to diminish those powers through the physical inactivity they permitted, for example as horseback riding gave way to riding trains and automobiles.

Misgivings about the relationship between modernity and masculinity recur in numerous contexts. In the eighteenth century, the critique of the over-refined (and female-dominated) 'effeminacy' of king and aristocracy lent a considerable gender spin to the anxieties that erupted in the French Revolution (de Baecque [1993] 1997). Just as medical specialists pathologised the 'unmanly' practices of masturbation and sodomy/homosexuality, most admitted that these activities were bound up with the physical and moral corruptions of modern urban life (especially excessive study, stimulating diets, sedentary habits and luxurious lifestyles) and that they increased in frequency as society became more civilised (Laqueur 2003; Oosterhuis 2000). While evolutionary biologists contended that civilisation and sexual polarisation marched together as signs of biological progress, they also conceded that modern trends generated the opposite effect. The liberal sexologist Ellis was not alone when he observed that tendencies towards sexual democratisation (evident in the rise of women's movements) threatened to *diminish* sexual dimorphism and return Western humanity to a 'primitive' level (Birkin 1988).

As other critics noted towards the end of the nineteenth century, civilised life generated other dubious effects for masculinity. It promoted mental superiority at the expense of muscular development, thus producing nervous weaklings incapable of physical effort; a combination of increasingly refined sensibilities and an expanding consumer economy created men who were pampered, overfed, and unable to endure pain and hardships; and the associated problem of modern charity encouraged the dysgenic proliferation of the 'unfit', thus weakening the nation as a whole. Many of these misgivings about the effect of modern civilisation upon male bodies were crystallised around 1900, when middle-class men were widely viewed as weak and unfit for military service (Bederman 1995; Forth 2004). Movements aiming at the consolidation of national identities thus often insisted upon the need to rebuild masculinity through rigorous physical practices like boxing, bodybuilding, team sports, hunting, hiking and mountaineering, activities that Bederman (1995) likens to 'inoculations' of primitivity in order to stave off the feminising effects of modernity. Most of these rejuvenating practices were also praised by fascist movements across Europe, for whom a return to corporeal toughness was central to the creation of the 'new man' (Bellassai 2005).

Many of these tensions have been exacerbated by the shift in many Western countries towards consumer-oriented societies since the Second World War. With the medical connection of coronary heart disease (CHD) to the recently minted 'Type A Personality', the 1950s gave rise to what Riska (2004) has dubbed 'the victimisation view of men's health', which in many respects extended and reworked earlier explanatory models of the poor health of men in white-collar professions. Considered an 'epidemic' by some health experts, for others CHD was nothing less than 'the scourge of Western civilisation' (quoted in Ehrenreich 1983). When coupled with post-1960s discourses of the negative effects of patriarchy on men's as well as women's lives (whether rightist or left-liberal in leaning), one has the ingredients for a broader discourse of male victimisation continuing to the present (Robinson 2000). The mythopoetic fascination with the 'wild man' as an antidote to the woes of modern manhood is just one recent example of how representations of the 'primitive' continue to fulfil an 'inoculating' role in Western society. Contemporary misgivings about the 'metrosexual' as a 'soft', consumer-oriented and appearance-obsessed male represent variations on this durable Western theme.

Modernity is thus very much a Janus-faced phenomenon, especially when it comes to gender identities and practices. Aside from the fact that gender identity is a dynamic and always incomplete process, one may conclude that the historical recurrence of 'crisis' as a means of describing the predicament of masculinity since the sixteenth century also reflects the internal contradictions of modernity itself.

References and further reading

Bederman, G. (1995) *Manliness and Civilization*, Chicago, IL: University of Chicago Press.

Bellassai, S. (2005) 'The masculine mystique', *Journal of Modern Italian Studies*, 10 (3): 314–35.

Berman, M. [1982] (1992) *All That is Solid Melts into Air*, London: Verso.

Birkin, L. (1988) *Consuming Desire*, Ithaca, NY: Cornell University Press.

Bryson, A. (1990) 'The rhetoric of status: gesture, demeanour and the image of the gentleman in sixteenth- and seventeenth-century England', in L. Gent and N. Llewellyn (eds) *Renaissance Bodies*, London: Reaktion.

Cohen, M. (2005) '"Manners" make the man', *Journal of British Studies*, 44 (April): 312–29.

de Baecque, A. [1993] (1997) *The Body Politic*, translated by C. Mandell, Stanford, CA: Stanford University Press.

Ehrenreich, B. (1983) *The Hearts of Men*, New York: Anchor.

Elias, N. [1939] (1994) *The Civilizing Process*, translated by E. Jephcott, Oxford: Blackwell.

Forth, C. (2004) *The Dreyfus Affair and the Crisis of French Manhood*, Baltimore, MD: Johns Hopkins University Press.

Hall, S. (1996) 'Introduction', in S. Hall, D. Held, D. Hubert and K. Thompson (eds) *Modernity*, Oxford: Blackwell.

Laqueur, T. (1990) *Making Sex*, Cambridge, MA: Harvard University Press.

—— (2003) *Solitary Sex*, New York: Zone.

Oosterhuis, H. (2000) *Stepchildren of Nature: Krafft-Ebing, Psychiatry, and the Making of Sexual Identity*, Chicago, IL: University of Chicago Press.

Riska, E. (2004) *Masculinity and Men's Health*, Lanham, MD: Rowman and Littlefield.

Robinson, S. (2000) *Marked Men*, New York: Columbia University Press.

See also: consumption; Fascism and Nazism; masculinity politics; patriarchy

CHRISTOPHER E. FORTH

HISTORY, NORTH AMERICA

The history of men and masculinities emerged in North America as an academic specialty in the 1980s and has gained increasing momentum since the mid-1990s. It has two main origins. The first was the accumulating work of women's historians, who identified gender as a distinct principle of social organisation with major ramifications for large-scale historical change and individual identity formation. In reaction to conventional history's neglect of women, the new wave of women's historians who began producing major work in the late 1970s concentrated at first mainly on recovering the lives of women and rendering them visible as historical actors. Still, an underlying principle that animated their work from the outset is that the gender order embraces both men and women. A second impetus for the launching of men's history was the felt contemporary crisis in masculinity. A series of men's movements arose in North America during the 1980s in response to economic and demographic changes that were producing (and continue to produce) realignments in family dynamics and the economic division of labour between men and women. Coupled with feminist demands for economic and political equality, these changes have eroded men's sense of prerogative in the workplace and at home. Academic men's history is in part a response to this sense of manhood in crisis.

One obvious question to ask is, 'Why do we need men's history?' Prior to the establishment of women's history as a specialty in the late 1970s, conventional history had been, after all, virtually nothing but the history of men and their doings. Still, these conventional histories tended to view men not as persons who were gendered in culturally specific ways, but as people who acted as political leaders, peasants and farmers, warriors and captives, and so forth. By and large, conventional academic historians simply did not notice that men had genders and that their gender structured their subjectivity and social behaviour in all the arenas in which they acted. Nor were conventional historians prior to the 1980s especially interested in identifying the privileges and power accruing to those men who successfully embodied culturally approved forms of manhood.

In alliance with women's history, men's history seeks to change all that. It has had a dramatic impact on the history of North America, and perhaps the best place to illustrate this impact is in the domain of political history. Prior to the 1980s, historians thought about the principles of political freedom and participation championed by the political leaders of the American Revolution and the new United States in gender-neutral terms. The unwillingness of the founding fathers to apply these principles to women and non-whites was, scholars agreed, a kind of historical accident – the consequence of a cultural bias that would erode slowly in the nineteenth and early twentieth centuries. Following the lead established by intellectual historians examining late eighteenth-century republican ideology, scholars of men's history have shown that these exclusions were not simple failures of political nerve among otherwise farsighted men. Instead, early American political institutions and ideology were by design masculinist. The culturally sanctioned definition of adult manhood, including its political privileges, was tightly coupled to achieving the status of married, property-owning household head: only patriarchal masters were entitled to full citizenship rights precisely in virtue of their property and authority over others. Wives, children, servants and slaves, all of whom were household dependents, lacked by definition the independence necessary for active political citizenship (Kann 1998; Nelson 1998). As the legislation and policies governing marriage, immigration and the treatment of freedmen after the Civil War show, a marked masculinist streak in the nation's understanding of citizenship would endure throughout the nineteenth century. Men's history has shaped other fields of inquiry as well. In the field of labour history, to take another example, workplace struggles over the family wage and the advantage accruing to male wage earners similarly underscore the tight coupling between adult manhood and attaining the status of head of household (Cott 2000; Stanley 1998).

Like scholars in other disciplines who study manhood, men's historians take it as axiomatic that several types of masculinity coexist and mutually inform one another in any given society and culture. Taking their cue from Connell (1995) and other social theorists, historians have been especially interested in the relationships among hegemonic or culturally dominant forms of masculinity, and complicit or marginal forms of masculinity. So, for example, eighteenth-century planter elites subscribed to a dominant code of masculinity that melded gentility with martial skill and a preoccupation with honour; meanwhile, evangelical Christians in the South forged a sentimental, emotionally demonstrative style of masculinity that appealed to men and women who were vying with planter elites for cultural and social authority (Lindman 2000). Similarly, the sailors and fishermen who travelled and worked in all parts of the Atlantic world participated in a culture of masculinity that emphasised independence, physical prowess and courage. Their languages and practices of manhood were in tension with dominant norms that associated adult manhood with the settled life of marriage and the family (Norling and Creighton 1996). Taken together, one overarching theme of such studies is that the gender order includes a series of linked masculinities that structure relationships among men as well as between men and women.

As these lines of inquiry might suggest, men's historians are especially interested in how social class and the cultural construction of 'race' intersect with gender norms to produce variant models of manhood. So, for example, historians of the eras of Reconstruction and Jim Crow in the United States have shown that white political leaders in the South promoted a code of masculine chivalry that consolidated a political alliance among white men of different classes that was designed to exclude black men from politics. This code emphasised the defence of white women's sexual purity and the superiority of white men's rationality and capacity to moderate their passions. By the same token, this racialised gender ideology viewed black men as uncivilised, irrational and unable to control their passions, especially their sexuality. Combined with the complementary sexual stereotyping of middle-class white women as naturally modest and black women as sexually seductive, these representations of white and black masculinity reinforced a particularly virulent form of racism that helped to justify the legislation and extra-legal violence that supported segregation. Meanwhile, African-American men and women developed alternative gender codes that sustained them in the face of institutionalised racism (Gilmore 1996, Carby 1986). The irony is that in the early twentieth century, a new dominant ideal of muscular masculinity associated with the imperial exploits of the United States in Cuba, the Philippines and elsewhere incorporated some elements of once stigmatised masculinity, especially the emphasis on physical vigour and robust sexuality (Bederman 1995). What especially interests the historian of masculinity in this case and others is how these linked sets of dominant, alternative and stigmatised masculinities work to distribute economic resources and political power among different groups of men.

No short introduction to men's history in North America would be complete without mention of its close affinities with the history of sexuality. Historians of homosexuality and transgender/transsexuality are foremost contributors to our understanding of the social and cultural practices that go into the making and transformation of gender identities. Scholarship on, for example, homoeroticism in nineteenth-century female friendships (Smith-Rosenberg 1975) and on the men of different classes and ethnicities who had sex with other men in early twentieth-century New York City (Chauncey 1994) have alerted us to the historical variability in the cultural constructions of sex and its relationship to gender. They also highlight the wide variety of gender/sexual practices that can emerge despite the power dynamics that reinforce dominant gender expectations about marriage, reproduction, and sexuality. A closely related set of inquiries concerns individuals and groups who transgress dominant gender codes by melding masculinity and femininity in culturally proscribed ways. These range from people in the colonial era who lived as men and alternately as women during different phases of their lives to mid-twentieth-century transsexuals who pursued their desire for bodily transformation (Meyrowitz 2002). These studies highlight the tremendous cultural and political labour that goes into the construction and policing of everyone's gender identities, whether culturally sanctioned or otherwise.

More generally – and in line with larger theoretical trends associated with social constructionism and even with postmodernism – men's historians tend to take a processual view of gender identity and its formation. In this view, masculinity, like femininity, is a set of complex and provisional identifications, not a fixed or monolithic condition. It is the consequence of myriad daily social practices and their determinants. Among men's historians this understanding of gender formation has produced a methodological commitment to examining the micro-processes that consolidate and alter the gendered subjectivity of groups and individuals. This processual approach has also contributed to the current interest in historical studies of the gendered body, which include attention to fashion, manners and comportment, and standards of fitness and beauty. All of these cultural standards and related social practices contribute to a gendered stylisation of the body that helps to consolidate and also to rework our sense of ourselves as gendered beings.

To look ahead, two exciting new directions in the history of manhood and masculinity in North America are taking shape. The first concerns the alignment of men's history with global studies. This line of inquiry is especially valuable because it attends to the dynamics of gendered power in colonial and postcolonial settings. Historians of early America emphasise what they call 'cultural encounters' between Europeans, Africans and the indigenous populations of North America as these encounters occur both on the American continent and on the sea lanes and in the trading centres that connected Europe with Africa and the Americas. Historians of gender and manhood in the nineteenth and twentieth centuries are now starting to draw upon theoretical insights associated with postcolonial studies, especially when they examine US territorial expansion and imperial ventures abroad. Whether studying the early modern or contemporary eras, these historians focus on cultural hybridity or the emergence of culturally mixed norms of masculinity and femininity out of the social interactions – both peaceable and violent – that crossed cultural and political boundaries and created empires (Stoler 2001).

The second new direction concerns the effort to create greater integration between men's history and women's history. One of the founding premises of men's history is that the gender order structures relations between men and women. By the same token, most scholars assume that masculinity and femininity are co-articulated aspects of the larger gender order. Even so, men's history, especially the history of the nineteenth- and twentieth-century United States, has tended to focus largely on men alone. Preoccupied with the question of how norms of manliness and masculinity structure alliances and competition between men, it has neglected the unequal distribution of resources and power relations between men and women (Ditz 2004). But there are signs of a fruitful reintegration of men's with women's history that is likely to yield a more robust history of gender and, with it, an enhanced understanding of manhood and masculinity.

References and further reading

Bederman, G. (1995) *Manliness and Civilization*, Chicago, IL and London: University of Chicago Press.

Carby, H.V. (1986) 'On the threshold of the woman's era', in H.L. Gates, Jr (ed.) *'Race,' Writing, and Difference*, Chicago, IL: University of Chicago Press, pp. 301–17.

Chauncey, G. (1994) *Gay New York*, New York: Basic Books.

Connell, R. (1995) *Masculinities*. Berkeley and Los Angeles, CA: University of California Press.

Cott, N.F. (2000) *Public Vows*, Cambridge, MA: Harvard University Press.

Ditz, T.L. (2004) 'The new men's history and the peculiar absence of gendered power', *Gender and History*, 16 (1): 1–35.

Gilmore, G. (1996) *Gender and Jim Crow*, Chapel Hill, NC: University of North Carolina Press.

Kann, M.E. (1998) *A Republic of Men*, New York: New York University Press.

Lindman, J.M. (2000) 'Acting the manly Christian', *William and Mary Quarterly*, 3rd series, 57 (2): 393–416.

Meyrowitz, J. (2002) *How Sex Changed*, Cambridge, MA: Harvard University Press.

Nelson, D. (1998) *National Manhood*, Durham, NC: Duke University Press.

Norling, L. and Creighton, M.S. (eds) (1996) *Iron Men, Wooden Women*, Baltimore, MD: Johns Hopkins University Press.

Smith-Rosenberg, C. (1975) 'Female world of love and ritual', *Signs*, 1: 1–29.

Stanley, A.D. (1998) *From Bondage to Contract*, Cambridge: Cambridge University Press.

Stoler, A.J. (ed.) (2001) 'Empires and intimacies', Special Issue of *Journal of American History*, 88 (3).

See also: colonial and imperial masculinities; cultural formations, North America; global masculinities; history, colonisation;

TOBY L. DITZ

HISTORY, PACIFIC

In the nineteenth century Indigenous Pacific masculinity was, like the untamed countryside, something to be conquered and civilised; in the twentieth century it was harnessed to provide manual labour for developing colonial nations; in the twenty-first century it became a historical vestige played out by Pacific men on the sports field.

Contemporary Pacific masculinity stems from historical colonial construction. From a poststructural analysis, colonisation's legacy of control does not remain through military intervention but rather through the power to define – that is, to create normal representations of Pacific masculinity through racist historical notions. European colonial expansion was partially validated on the grounds that colonisation would enable lesser societies to come into contact with a more mature, moral and just civilisation. Accordingly, the savages to be saved were represented as living in pre-philosophical dream-worlds. Laclau (1990) argued Indigenous peoples were essentially history-less and incapable of universal thought. Pacific worldviews were described by eighteenth- and nineteenth-century Western translators as irrational fairytales and unconscious history (Nandy 1983). Hegel suggested primitive Indigenous cultures possessed a 'character of spirit in a state of dream', incapable of action and, therefore, 'pre-historical' (1956: 204–25).

As opposed to the reasoned intellect of the enlightened European man, Pacific men were ruled by passion. Descartes's claim that the mind was divorced from the extended material or mechanics of the body created Cartesian Dualism; a concept later employed to cast the physicality of Indigenous peoples as unenlightened, and thus as uncivilised. Pacific men were described as savage, emotionally impulsive, aggressive and violent. Their masculinity was located somewhere between the civilised European and the ape: deceptive, delusional and childlike (Hokowhitu 2004; Smith 1999). The missionary, for example, with little propensity to understand the complexities of Pacific culture, simply described cultural practices as barbaric. Similarly, European travellers sowed the seeds for future representations of Pacific male savagery. New migrants to the Pacific colonies, subsequently, brought with them preconceived misinformation regarding Pacific men (Smith 1999). At times, Pacific men were depicted as having seemingly positive qualities such as physical prowess, nobility and a warrior-like nature. Yet, such representations were always tempered through a discourse of colonial benevolence.

Social Darwinism validated the commonsense claims that Pacific peoples were less intelligent than the advanced settlers. European political, military and economic superiority resonated with Darwinian notions of the survival of the fittest. An early traveller to New Zealand, Thomson (1859), for example, employed craniometry to quantify Pacific intellect:

> It was ascertained by weighing the quantity of millet seed skulls contained . . . that New Zealanders' heads are smaller than the heads of Englishmen, consequently the New Zealanders are inferior to the English in mental capacity . . . The memory they possess is the memory of boyhood; and their minds may be compared to mirrors . . . incapable of retaining any trace of the past . . . The faculty of imagination is not strongly developed among them, although they permitted it to run wild in believing absurd superstitions . . . This analysis shows that the New Zealanders have the minds of children.
>
> (Thomson 1859: 81–4)

The early representations of Pacific men as unintelligent later came to mean practical-mindedness when the need for a manual workforce to work crops and livestock became necessary. The colonial education of Mäori boys, for instance, demanded a corresponding emphasis on manual, technical and agriculture skills. From the 1860s through to the 1940s, colonial educational policies channelled Mäori boys into non-academic areas, preventing them from gaining intellectual qualifications and subsequent white-collar employment.

The sporting arena was an obvious realm where Pacific men could gain colonial kudos. The success of Pacific sportsmen perpetuated stereotypes of Pacific male savagery; he was the disciplined brute – his aggression and savagery confined to the sporting arena. He also provided evidence that the various colonial systems had accomplished the assimilation of its savages. Colonial rugby and cricket, described as 'Britain's gift to the world', signalled the success of imperialism (Beynon 2002: 42). Vestiges of historical constructions of Pacific men remain within contemporary Pacific societies. Quasi-Social Darwinism is currently being used to explain the dominance of Polynesian men within physically robust sports such as rugby union and league. Similar to the discourse surrounding African–American men, Pacific men are described as descendents of a physically superior gene-pool:

> The ancestors of today's [elite Pacific Athletes] voyaged into the Pacific thousands of years ago. It wasn't an easy trip, so the survivors who made landfall in Samoa and Tonga . . . were tough . . . The process of natural selection left the strongest and fittest ones alive to start this new race . . . to actually live there and survive off the land required strength and adaptability and toughness . . . which added to our modern day physique.
>
> (New Zealand television host Oscar Kightley, cited in Matheson 2001: 36)

As opposed to white sportsmen who achieve through human endeavour, Pacific men are said to succeed because of innate physical attributes, and thus their achievements lack moral integrity. The Pacific sportsman represents a historical vestige that remains operative in the contemporary Pacific.

References and further reading

Beynon, J. (2002) *Masculinities and Culture*, Buckingham: Open University Press.

Descartes, R. (1996) *Meditations on First Philosophy*, Melbourne: Cambridge University Press.

Hegel, G. [1899] (1956) *The Philosophy of History*, translated by J. Sibree, New York: Colonial Press.

Hokowhitu, B. (2004) 'Tackling Mäori masculinity: a colonial genealogy of savagery and sport', *The Contemporary Pacific*, 16 (2): 259–84.

Laclau, E. (1990) *New Reflections on the Revolution of Our Time*, translated by J. Barnes, New York: Verso.

Matheson, J. (2001) 'So what's the white answer?' *NZ Rugby World*, 47: 36.

Nandy, A. (1983) *The Intimate Enemy*, Oxford: Oxford University Press.

Smith, L. (1999) *Decolonizing Methodologies: Research and Indigenous Peoples*, Dunedin: University of Otago Press.

Thomson, A. (1859) *The Story of New Zealand: Past and Present, Savage and Civilised, Vol. 1*, London: John Murray.

See also: African–American masculinities, colonial and imperial masculinities; critical race studies; cultural formations, Asia and Pacific; history, colonisation; Indigenous and First Nations masculinities; postcolonial masculinities

BRENDAN HOKOWHITU

HISTORY, SOUTH ASIA

The paucity of attention towards South Asian masculinity as an object of analysis has a direct bearing on the historiography of the subject. While geographically cohesive, South Asia is culturally diverse. However, it is possible to discern core values, norms and structures that bind the region into a culture – not just geographical – area. Core values of maleness also position certain forms of masculinity as marginalised.

Colonial history, particularly the British control of the sub-continent from the seventeenth to the mid-twentieth centuries, is definitive in constructing masculinity in the region and is the best-documented (although the Dutch in Sri Lanka and the Portuguese in the west coast of India left significant cultural traces as well). The 'femininity' of colonised territories and subjects provided colonial Orientalist discourse with a metaphor for racial tropes of white manly Englishmen sent out to the East to establish order and morality. As Sinha in *Colonial Masculinity* (1995) and Krishnaswamy in *Effeminism: The Economy of Colonial Desire* (1999) clarify, emasculation and effeminisation were the most enduring tropes that created the frontiers between 'effeminised natives' and the core hegemonic masculinity embodied by white colonialists, creating a link between physical prowess, moral fibre and the power to rule.

In the eyes of the British, Nawab Wajid Ali Shah, the ruler of the eastern kingdom of Oudh from 1847 until his exile after the Mutiny of 1857, epitomised the effeteness of the East. An accomplished poet, dancer and composer, Wajid Shah was given to an elaborate aesthetic. He bestowed his cavalry with names that drew on a poetic rather than a military tradition and conferred honours on his pigeon keeper who bred birds of two colours, actions the British could only classify as wildly extravagant. To them his poetic temperament was unsuited to the weighty and very masculine sense of responsibility that exemplified enlightened rule.

Almost a century later the nationalist movements that sought independence from colonial rule absorbed the trope of enlightened manliness. Swami Vivekananda, founder of the Ramakrishna Movement, preached the path to realisation as a combination of spiritual worship and intellectual and physical action. The British interpreted this as a call to terrorist, not bodily, action. Perhaps the best-known and most enduring opposition to colonial rule came from Mohandas Karamchand Gandhi, a lawyer, whose *ahimsa* philosophy of non-violence gave the world a new form of political resistance. His own crafting of his image as a celibate sage drew on the Hindu ideas of renunciation. He forswore English mill-made cloth in preference to Indian handloom, most famously appearing before the immaculately attired Viceroy Lord Irvine at the peace talks dressed in the simplicity of a hand-woven loincloth. His attire roused Winston Churchill to call him a half-naked fakir striding up the steps of the vice-regal palace inappropriately dressed. Gandhi's valorisation of an emaciated rib-showing body embodied the idea of spiritual suffering, countering the trope of physical weakness that the British disavowed and which Vivekananda tried to overcome.

Gandhi's celibate renunciation – and Vivekananda's insistence on physically healthy bodies – are two sides of a single deeply rooted idea of semen control and spiritual attainment that runs through Buddhist and Hindu philosophies and Islamic humeral medicine of South Asia. The virtues of continence and non-ejaculation are countered by the anxiety of wasted or spilled semen and a consequent weakening of the male body and the masculine self. Seminal control and loss is a trope that epitomises notions of health and spiritual well-being and runs through the somatic practices of yoga, wrestling and medicine that pay detailed attention to the development of the male body and the male self. Foods and sexuality are closely linked, classified as heating and aphrodisiacal or cooling and purifying.

Masculine body politics has a long history in the subcontinent. The princely states and royal lineages of Rajasthan represent a particular formation of chivalry and male honour that distinguishes a whole swathe of territory stretching from western India towards Pakistan and Afghanistan. Male honour as the bastion of community and clan identity is the basis of political authority and anchored in the political institution of the feud. Male codes of honour dictate the public display of heroic deeds and male valour, rooted in the ability to lead a charge in battle as much as in a display of hospitality. Interestingly, the aura of honour and charisma could be inherited through blood as well as through the performance of meritorious acts that were narrated in ballads of praise or performed in epics. The valour of the exemplar king became part of travelling theatres and epic dramas, such as the story of the divine King Ram that runs from Nepal to southern India, with some interesting variations of kingly virtue and meritorious piety.

The heroic exemplary man is a significant focus of South Asian cinema. Popular commercial cinema, better known as Bollywood cinema, binds South Asia as a cultural region, drawing on archetypes of playful lovers and powerful patriarchs. Variations on these formations of masculinity run through the subregional cinemas of South Asia. Equally important is the figure of the hero fighting to save the nation from threat, a theme of some significance at the turn of the twenty-first century given the increase in separatist movements that have troubled the different national polities of South Asia. Embodiments of the state in masculine portrayals of police and army men are countered by cinematic images of downtrodden men in search of justice and turning towards violence to fight repression. The fierce anti-state movements in Sri Lanka, Bangladesh and Kashmir have harnessed the idea of men saving national and community honour. The South Asian representation of male honour has entered the political domain and is simultaneously harnessed to signify political resistance and the protective patriarchal state.

References and further reading

Krishnaswamy, R. (1999) *Effeminism: The Economy of Colonial Desire*, Ann Arbor, MI: University of Michigan Press.

Sinha, M. (1995) *Colonial Masculinity: The 'Manly Englishman' and the 'Effeminate Bengali' in the Late Nineteenth Century*, New York: Manchester University Press.

See also: cultural formations, Asia and Pacific; South Asian masculinities

RADHIKA CHOPRA

HISTORY, WESTERN

The history of 'the West' provides a fertile arena for exploring the various ways in which what we might now call masculinity (Connell 1987) has been constructed in diverse social, historical and cultural contexts. It is important to realise that, even for 'the West', which prides itself on a certain continuity of 'civilised' culture, there is no essential or transcendental masculinity that stands above or outside the historical process. Rather, it is necessary to appreciate the extent to which in 'the West' the construction of masculinity has varied in accordance with shifts in the way in which power is organised and distributed in society. The result is that the many different social formations that make up the history of 'the West' each furnish their own idea of masculinity – or set of masculinities – aspects of which might survive into later formations, while other attributes will be discarded with the passage of time. The history of 'the West' can thus be read as a series of successive, parallel and overlapping masculinities, all of which inform, to some extent, the construction of contemporary Western masculinity.

Premodern masculinities

The first instance of a recognisably 'Western' form of masculinity appears in ancient Greece, where the definition of the 'citizen' as a rational, autonomous, self-governing subject first emerges (Rhodes 1986; Foucault 1985). Here, the definition of masculinity depended upon exercising control over the self in order to assert control over others, specifically, social inferiors such as women, children and slaves.

The Romans added to the Stoic ideal of the Greeks the idea of empire, which defined masculinity in terms of the ability to dominate other cultures. This entailed asserting the cultural superiority of 'civilisation' over so-called 'barbaric' peoples (Halsall 2004: 21). These two attributes – citizenship and imperialism – constitute the two major contributions of the ancient world to the historical construction of Western manhood. Other aspects of ancient masculinity, however, such as the valorisation of homoeroticism, and the pedagogical pederasty that regulated entry into manhood, would be discarded with the rise of Christianity, which excoriated such pagan 'excesses'.

The medieval world created by the spread of Christianity and the rise of feudalism gave rise to a whole new range of masculinities. Christianity promulgated an ascetic ideal – embodied most clearly in the monks, priests and other churchmen – that urged strict abstinence from worldly involvement (including celibacy) in order to gain access to the divine essence. Through control of the Word and the spiritual 'capital' of Christianity, the ascetic masculinity of the male theocracy wielded considerable power (Leyser 1999; Nelson 1999).

Another predominant masculinity of the medieval period is the knightly or chivalric ideal that governed the behaviour of the feudal elite. Prowess in battle, strong homosocial bonding, the practice of 'courtly love' and the ability to sire (preferably male) offspring were key aspects of this type. For many aristocratic men, the chivalric ideal was a model they were expected to follow in order to serve their kingdom and glorify their family line (Bennett 1999).

Little is known about the nature of masculinity among the medieval peasantry, due to a lack of detailed sources concerned with recording the practices of peasant society. What is known, however, is that peasant culture was made up of a mixture of pagan and Christian values, and that manhood was defined by kinship ties, ritual ceremonies and marriage strategies, all of which aimed at preserving and increasing the common weal of the kinship network. However, because the peasantry were subject to the authority of the feudal lords, the definition of peasant masculinity was generally quite unstable. Indeed, the compromised masculinity of the peasant is indicated by the custom of *jus primae noctis*, which entitled the feudal lord to spend the first night with the brides of his male serfs.

Early modern masculinities

The early modern period is marked by the incursion of an expanding commercial economy into the hierarchical world of feudalism (Braudel 1982). This led to the creation of a new class of masculinity, that of the merchant or middle classes, which was defined by what Sidney Pollard calls the 'capitalist spirit' – the desire for personal gain – and associated attributes of rational calculation and possessive individualism (1968: 28).

The rise of this middle-class masculinity inflected existing categories of masculinity, as these were repositioned in relation to the growing influence of commerce and trade. Some noblemen ventured outside the field of military endeavour to dabble in science, agriculture or trade; peasants uprooted by land enclosures took up work as carriers or deckhands in the commercial economy. Currents of economic change were subtly altering the complexion of society, as the divisions of social rank were blurred by the levelling medium of the market.

However, this blurring of rank actually led to an exaggerated investment in the notion of 'honour' as a marker of male social distinction. Noblemen whose livelihoods were threatened by economic forces stoutly clung to ideas of lineage and 'blue blood'; bourgeois upstarts seeking to make their way in society were particularly anxious to guard their reputation and 'good name'. As a result of this heightened status anxiety, we see in the early modern period a veritable explosion in the practice of duelling as a way of proving one's honour (Foyster 1999: 179–81; Stone 1977: 234). This phenomenon is observable in the literature of the time – i.e. the plays of Shakespeare and Beaumarchais, Spanish Golden Age literature – where the 'point of honour' (the challenge of a duel) is frequently invoked.

The expansion of the secular state in the sixteenth and seventeenth centuries also contributed to the decline of feudalism, as monarchs such as Louis XIV and Henry VIII sought to restrict the power of the nobility and centralise authority in the hands of the Crown. As state bureaucracies replaced the feudal lords, obedience to the sovereign replaced loyalty to kin, clientage and factions. This is what Lawrence Stone calls the shift from lineage society to civil society (1977: 134). As part of this process, we see the emergence of the 'restricted nuclear family' as the dominant social unit, an institution in which power was increasingly invested in the husband and father over wife and children. The Protestant Reformation also contributed to this transformation in masculinity, as the Lutheran revaluation of matrimony as a 'holy' state transferred to the male head of household much of the religious authority previously monopolised by the priest (Stone 1977: 135–6).

Modern masculinities

A recognisably 'modern' type of masculinity emerged during the Enlightenment, when the economic, social and religious reforms of the early modern period coalesced to create a new social order that nominated 'man' – specifically the educated, propertied 'white' man – as the subject of history (Foucault 1970). According to Enlightenment thinkers, 'man' could use his reason to understand and control the natural world, and thereby bring about a continual increase in human happiness and well-being.

The reorganisation of knowledge around the concept of 'nature' enabled gender to be redefined along biological lines: men and women became anatomically categorised as belonging to one of two mutually exclusive biological sexes. This was a new development, as Thomas Laqueur argues: previously, to be a man or woman was to hold a social rank, not to belong to a biological category (1992: 8). At the same time, as industrialisation began to take hold, operations of scientific classification were applied to the natural and social world as a whole, creating a new discourse of power that installed the middle-class European male as the sole legitimate agent of knowledge and power. Operating under the guise of scientific disinterestedness, this new regime of 'bio-power' sought to legitimate the emerging social structures of industrial capitalism (Foucault 1978), including the Victorian 'separation of spheres' which excluded women from participation in public, productive life. Women's exclusion was justified on the basis of their 'biological' infirmity. Likewise, the exploitation of the working classes was justified on the basis of their hereditary predisposition to labour; and the colonisation of the New World was explained away as the result of evolutionary processes and the 'survival of the fittest' (McClintock 1995: 40).

In this context, masculinity was identified with the agents of this apparatus of knowledge-power: in other words, the educated, middle-class white men who administered and put into effect the imperatives of the industrial-imperial regime. At the same time, the regime of 'bio-power' created a whole range of subordinate masculinities: the bucolic lower-class male; the primitive black man; the unruly half-caste; and later in the nineteenth century, the degenerate homosexual. The new industrial regime also produced its share of self-proclaimed cultural 'misfits', such as the Romantics, the Pre-Raphaelites and the dandies, all of whom broadcast resistant forms of masculinity that sought to define themselves in opposition to the means–ends mentality of the scientific–industrial complex.

By the turn of the twentieth century, the progress of the natural and human sciences – coupled with the expansion of industrial capitalism – had produced a new global order of Western masculine hegemony. This order would find extreme manifestation in the science of eugenics, which sought to eradicate racial and sexual 'deviants' from society and create an ideal race free from the dreaded taint of 'degeneration' that haunted the limits of industrial society: in the ghettoes, the shanty towns, the colonial backwaters. The

Western masculine dream of a scientifically engineered society was mirrored by the increasing artificiality of everyday life, where technology was invading more and more aspects of existence: electric lights, automobiles, telephones, elevators, etc. In this context, Western masculinity was increasingly identified with the making of technological progress, an association often celebrated, and sometimes parodied, in the modernist movements of the early twentieth century. Perhaps the most fitting monument to the technological progress of 'Western man', however, is the two world wars which provided the coda to both the Enlightenment belief in historical progress through science, and the 'modernist' identification of Western masculinity with technological advancement. As science enabled war to reach ever-greater levels of technological destructiveness, the dark side of the Enlightenment dream of scientific progress became apparent. At the same time, the potential inadequacy of the Western male subject was glimpsed, in the form of mutilated, shell-shocked and traumatised soldiers, whose wounds carried not the prestige of honour but the stigma of inadequacy (Silverman 1992: 53). The historical trauma of the world wars, and further shifts in economic and social structure, would stimulate a new phase in the history of Western masculinity.

Postmodern masculinities

The industrial-imperial ideals of Western masculinity began to tarnish in the postwar period, as the economy shifted away from manufacturing towards services and information, creating a 'postindustrial' economy, and the imperial project entered a 'postcolonial' phase of 'imperialism without colonies' (McClintock 1995: 13). The protest and counter-culture movements of the Sixties reinforced the fact that the social authority of the gender order was in jeopardy. Thousands of young men in North America avoided the draft for the Vietnam war, underscoring that traditional definitions of masculinity were being challenged by younger generations. Indeed, after Vietnam, general conscription quickly became a thing of the past. Readiness to fight was no longer an assumed prerequisite for masculinity. Expanding consumerism throughout the West led to the reconceptualisation of gender identity along the lines of consumption and 'lifestyle'. Masculinity was increasingly equated with the consumption of certain types of commodities – cars, motorcycles, televisions, hi-fi systems, yachts, watches, etc. – deflecting attention away from women's incursion into the workplace in the wake of feminist struggles for economic equality. Work was no longer an adequate site for the construction of masculinity; the Victorian 'separation of spheres' was starting to blur. As a consequence of upsetting the 'natural' boundaries between men's and women's spheres, in the latter part of the twentieth century we see gender difference itself perhaps beginning to blur in certain settings, as the emergence of gay and lesbian minorities challenges the mutually exclusive definition of 'masculinity' and 'femininity' in some social contexts. The increasing presence of 'queer' identity in mainstream culture – particularly in film, television and radio – suggests that the blurring of gender definition in response to the social transformations of late capitalism may continue to partly mark Western culture for some time. However, in spite of the challenges posed by the postmodern era, the structure of male hegemony remains intact throughout the West, due to the fact that the key strongholds of masculine power – politics and business – remain male-dominated, even if they do appear increasingly subject to contestation. The question for the future will be whether the alleged crisis of 'postmodern man' has any substantial effect upon the overall distribution of power in the West – not only between men and women, but also other disenfranchised groups: racial and ethnic minorities, the working classes, sexual minorities – or whether the postmodern represents merely another stage in the ongoing reproduction of masculine hegemony.

References and further reading

Bennett, M. (1999) 'Military masculinity in England and Northern France c.1050–c.1225', in D.M. Hadley (ed.) *Masculinity in Medieval Europe*, London and New York: Longman, pp. 71–88.

Braudel, F. [1979] (1982) *The Wheels of Commerce: Civilisation and Capitalism 15th–18th Century, Vol. II*, London and Sydney: William Collins Sons.

Connell, R. (1987) *Gender and Power*, Stanford, CA: Stanford University Press.

Foucault, M. (1970) *The Order of Things: An Archaeology of the Human Sciences*, New York: Random House.

—— [1976] (1978) *The Will to Knowledge: The History of Sexuality Volume 1*, London and New York: Penguin.

—— [1984] (1985) *The Use of Pleasure: The History of Sexuality Volume 2*, London and New York: Penguin.

Foyster, E.A. (1999) *Manhood in Early Modern England: Honour, Sex and Marriage*, London and New York: Longman.

Halsall, G. (2004) 'Gender and the end of empire', *Journal of Medieval and Early Modern Studies*, 34 (1): 17–39.

Laqueur, T. (1992) *Making Sex: Body and Gender from the Greeks to Freud*, Cambridge, MA, and London: Harvard University Press.

Leyser, C. (1999) 'Masculinity in flux: nocturnal emission and the limits of celibacy in the early Middle Ages', in D.M. Hadley (ed.) *Masculinity in Medieval Europe*, London and New York: Longman, pp. 103–20.

McClintock, A. (1995) *Imperial Leather: Race, Gender and Sexuality in the Colonial Contest*, New York: Routledge.

Nelson, J.L. (1999) 'Monks, secular men and masculinity, c. 900', in D.M. Hadley (ed.) *Masculinity in Medieval Europe*, London and New York: Longman, pp. 121–42.

Pollard, S. (1968) *The Idea of Progress: History and Society*, Harmondsworth and Baltimore, MD: Penguin.

Rhodes, P.J. (1986) *The Greek City States: A Source Book*, London and Sydney: Croom Helm.

Silverman, K. (1992) *Male Subjectivity at the Margins*, New York and London: Routledge.

Stone, L. (1977) *The Family, Sex and Marriage in England 1500–1800*, London: Weidenfeld and Nicholson.

See also: slavery

JADE M. NOBBS

HIV/AIDS

The transmission of HIV and other sexually transmitted infections (STIs) by and to men (including sexually active boys) is determined by several factors. These include the number of sexual partners, the extent to which men are aware of HIV/STIs, and whether they have access to the means of preventing transmission. Each factor is influenced to a certain extent by concepts of masculinity.

The risk of contracting HIV/STIs is proportional to the number of partners with whom individuals have unprotected sexual intercourse. Cross-cultural studies confirm that men tend to have more sexual partners than women and therefore more opportunity to contract and transmit infections. Their dominant status also frequently allows them to decide the form of sexual intercourse, including whether a condom is used or non-penetrative sex is practised and therefore whether the risk of transmission is reduced. In sex between men the partner who is larger, older, wealthier, more knowledgeable and/or possesses other markers of status is also likely to determine whether safer sex is practised.

Men's reluctance to use condoms is often attributed to culturally determined norms that encourage men to take risks and imply that strong men are not vulnerable to infection. It is also attributable to the reduction in sensation that many men experience when wearing a condom. Reluctance to practise non-penetrative intercourse is commonly attributed to a need to prove dominance through penetration. It may also reflect the wish to give one's partner pleasure through penetration, and the more intense pleasure experienced by many men in penetrative than in non-penetrative intercourse.

The impact of HIV/AIDS is also affected by norms of masculinity. In societies where the virus is primarily transmitted between men, and more men than women are living with HIV, services for men appear more widespread than for women, and men appear to live longer after diagnosis than women.

Where HIV is primarily transmitted heterosexually and more women than men are living with HIV, services for women appear more widespread and women live longer after diagnosis than men. In these societies, particularly in sub-Saharan Africa and parts of Asia, masculinity is often seen as a barrier to acceptance of one's HIV status, while women are motivated to live longer by the need to look after their children (Foreman 1999).

References and further reading

Foreman, M. (1999) *AIDS and Men*, London: Panos/Zed Books.

Scalway, T. (2001) *Young Men and HIV: Culture, Poverty and Sexual Risk*, London: Joint United Nations Programme on HIV/AIDS (UNAIDS)/The Panos Institute.

See also: condoms; sexuality; sexually transmitted infections

MARTIN FOREMAN

HOMBRE

Hombre means 'man' in Spanish. Depending on social class, generation and local cultures, the concept has nuanced meanings in an increasingly urban and globalised Mexican society. For men who migrate to the United States, migration and settlement experiences alter meanings of manhood. For some, *ser hombre* means surviving a harsh migration journey as an undocumented person. It may also mean being tough enough to put up with long hours of underpaid work in the midst of rhetoric celebrating ethnic diversity and xenophobic immigration laws.

In the United States, *un hombre de verdad* – a real man – works hard to survive in a decent and honest way. He is responsible, aware and sensitive to the financial needs of those he loves in Mexico, deciphering the world of inequality while sending money to the family he left behind, and also subsidising the Mexican economy.

The concept of 'macho' has promoted the misrepresentation of US Latino and Latin American men in academic and popular publications. However, Mexican women and men may use this concept to identify a sexist man. Some immigrant men use the expression *un buen padre es hombre pero no macho* (a good father is a man but not macho) to describe the good father who is promoting equal rights in the sex education and academic opportunities he provides for both daughters and sons. Paradoxically, some of these men may resent women who use US laws to challenge gender inequality (i.e. domestic violence).

In the United States and Mexico, *los hombres* are incessantly and creatively redefining their gender identities. Men's groups organised by the Colectivo de Hombres por Relaciones Igualitarias in Mexico City (CORIAC), Los Forkados in Monterrey, Mexico, and the men's circles in the western United States (Mena 2000) illustrate what men are doing to disrupt violent expressions of masculinity. They nurture gender egalitarian expressions of manhood that are transforming their relationships and families.

References and further reading

González-López, G. (2004) 'Fathering Latina sexualities', *Journal of Marriage and Family*, 66: 1118–30.

—— (2005) *Erotic Journeys*, Berkeley, CA: University of California Press.

González-López, G. and Gutmann, M.C. (2005) 'Machismo', in *New Dictionary of the History of Ideas*, Vol. 4, New York: Scribner's, pp. 1328–30.

Gutmann, M.C. (1996) *The Meanings of Macho*, Berkeley, CA: University of California Press.

Mena, J. (2000) 'Creating the new macho man', *Los Angeles Times*, 12 December, Section E: 1, 3.

See also: cultural formations, Latin America

GLORIA GONZÁLEZ-LÓPEZ

HOMOEROTICISM

Relations between men can be placed on a hypothetical scale ranging from the purely homosocial (non-sexual but nonetheless strong emotional bonds between men) to the purely homosexual (involving sexual attraction, arousal and genital activity). Within modern Western societies homosocial and homosexual are meant to be kept strictly separate, a separation enforced by homophobic policing of any signs of sexual interest between men. Where, then, does this leave homoeroticism?

According to the *Oxford English Dictionary*, homoeroticism is 'pertaining to or characterised by a tendency for erotic emotions to be centred on a person of the same sex; or pertaining to a homo-erotic person'. The definition is interesting because while it refers to emotions it says nothing about physical acts. It also mentions a 'homo-erotic person' who, if we accept the first definition, may be homoerotic emotionally but not necessarily in deeds. Yet the *OED* also includes the following entry under 'eroticise': 'To transform an emotion into a sexual feeling', and 'To make erotic, to stimulate sexually'. In Webster's dictionary, we find a similar progression towards a more sexualised definition in the following entry: 'Erotic: pertaining to, or prompted by love; treating of love; amorous; tending to excite sexual desire.' In the Webster entry, the shift is from 'love', which need not immediately suggest sex, to 'amorous', which has stronger sexual connotations, to the explicit 'sexual desire'. In all the above entries the relationship between erotic emotions and sexual acts is ambiguous. Both are clearly related to each other but the exact nature of the relationship between them and which has priority is unclear.

Given the ambiguous combination of the emotional and sexual in definitions of homoeroticism, we might expect it to emerge where homosocial and homosexual relations overlap to produce social ties between men that are informed by an unstable emotional–sexual amalgam.

The instability of homoeroticism reflects the instability of the categories created by the polarisation of men into either heterosexual or homosexual. The dichotomy is relatively recent and is constantly produced and enforced through a range of cultural and social practices including homophobia and the psychic and cultural disavowal of any form of sexual interest between men. The concept of homoeroticism illustrates well the poststructural argument that meaning is achieved through exclusion and that what is excluded in order to create a cultural category both maintains but also inhabits and therefore destabilises that category. Having been expelled from the Western cultural definition of normative male heterosexuality, sexual interest between men, however diffuse and implicit it may be, is a continual 'absent presence' that threatens to undermine its integrity. Indeed, the stronger the repression and denial, the more strenuous the efforts put into recognising and eradicating all signs of homoeroticism in order to strengthen the bulwark against homosexuality. Freud was of the opinion that the boundary between homosexual and heterosexual is unclear when he argued that we are all capable of making a homosexual object choice and have all done so in our unconscious. He argued that polymorphous perversity, which is the starting point for everyone's sexuality and which includes homoeroticism, is the bedrock on which later oedipalised heterosexuality is built (Freud 1905). Consequently, homoerotic emotions and identifications are present in the unconscious of everyone.

Homoeroticism is therefore an unstable concept that attempts to signify relations between men that are poised precariously between homosexuality, which is socially and culturally recognised and fixed within dominant discursive frameworks, and heterosexuality, in which the homosocial ties of male bonding and friendship are strong but expected to exclude and disavow all forms of sexual interest between men.

In Freud's view, some apparently nonsexual human activities are in fact driven by the force of sexual instinct. Within heteronormative regimes, forms of sexual attraction between men are desexualised and displaced into non-sexual activities that are socially valued. Freud's point is that the force of this sexual attraction can be sublimated into social and cultural ends without losing its intensity (Laplanche and Pontalis 1988). These include relations between men that are central to the creation of society as a whole. On this account, homoeroticism is a repressed but inescapable dimension of male bonds that permeates all relations between men – the more effectively, the more it is sublimated and concealed – and through them, all the central institutions of society including politics, industry and commerce, and not least single-sex organisations, like the military, and activities like sport. Thus, rather than being a matter only for a minority of men who identify as homosexual or gay, homoeroticism is a part of the very formation of all men as human subjects and social actors.

On occasion, the eroticism that is a subtext in relations between men appears to surface under controlled conditions. The initiation ceremonies that are common in all-male institutions, such as the armed forces, are a case in point. Rituals intended to faze new recruits may include inserting objects into the anus of the young men, simulated anal intercourse and analingus. To an outsider these actions strongly suggest sexuality, however burlesque in form. Yet those taking part normally dismiss any suggestions that these actions have any sexual dimension whatsoever (Zeeland 1995). The possibility of a sexual subtext in male relations is 'recognised' in these ritual practices but not explicitly named as such. Explicit comment, to the extent that it occurs, involves denial. In short, there is the usual combination of recognition and misrecognition at work which is a leitmotif of the homoerotic.

In contexts where there is a prohibition on homosexual practices and emotions, cultural references to them may often be oblique (Woods 1987). The poems of Walt Whitman and their intense celebration of male bodies and 'friendships' are well-known examples. Such is the cultural imperative to deny the possibility of sexual interest that many examples are denied, go unremarked or are subjected to a heterosexual interpretation even to the extent of making alterations to texts in translation. The literature of ancient Greece provides numerous examples which have been systematically subjected to censorship of any homoerotic dimension, including the works of Plato (for an example, see Tripp 1987: 217–19). This has not always been the case. Literary traditions in the West and elsewhere contain many examples of explicit homosexual interest, such as in the works of ancient Greece, and also in works of Arab literature in which authors praise the beauty of male youths, as well as in Chinese literature stretching back many centuries (Hinsch 1990). In present day male 'buddy' films, strong friendships between male protagonists are sometimes referred to as homoerotic. The level of concern, attentiveness and the obvious love of the male characters for each other are of an intensity normally expected within heterosexual relationships.

However, the term 'homoerotic' is often confined to relationships that appear to be platonic. This raises a question: Why call them homoerotic? Does the willingness to use the term to refer to relations between men signal a greater awareness or belief that there is a strong erotic dimension to close male friendships? Or is the term simply a shorthand device for intense male bonds? To label something as homoerotic is, then, immediately to become embroiled in questions of interpretation. When do male bodies become homoerotic objects that arouse homoerotic feelings and even sexual feelings? Is it enough to have several attractive men, nude or semi-nude for example, in close physical contact with each other to signify homoeroticism? Or must the image provoke a sexual response in the viewer such that (s)he reads the image as signifying some kind of erotic relationship between the men, or at least the potential for such a relationship? Or is it the experience of the men themselves which decides whether their relationship to each other contains a sexual, that is to say homoerotic, dimension?

Different historical periods and different cultures have prescribed or tended to favour certain male–male relations over others. Homoerotic attraction has been expected to follow differences in class or age, and to reflect local ideals of male physical beauty. Differences in power between men may also be eroticised. Cultural icons such as sportsmen and entertainers are all the objects of homoerotic interest. Forms of masculinity that are perceived to be unattainable for gay men have often become erotic objects, including soldiers, police, fire-fighters and men from traditional working-class occupations that are regarded as the preserve of heterosexual men, such as construction workers. These 'forbidden' masculinities are eroticised and made available for sexual fantasies; they are the staples of gay pornography.

For men who do not identify as homosexual or gay, interest in other men, not least an appreciation of their bodies, is only permissible in certain contexts, sport in particular. In sports, men are free to be in physical contact with and to stare at other men as much as they wish as long as the stares are ostensibly engaged in judging skills whether with the ball or the cricket or baseball bat, or admiring the stamina of a swimmer or the force of a rugby tackle. The intense admiration, even hero-worship, of men for sportsmen may be interpreted as stemming from unconscious and unacknowledged homoerotic feelings.

The male body has increasingly become an object to be admired within Western consumer culture beyond the bounds of sport. Whereas previously only the female body was an erotic and sexualised object in advertising, pin-ups and pornography, nowadays the male body – usually young, physically attractive, able-bodied and ostensibly heterosexual – is a common sight in advertising and a range of other media (Mort 1996; Nixon 1996).

However, most advertisers still wish to avoid having their advertisements and the products they sell interpreted explicitly and unambiguously as 'gay' or 'homosexual', especially when the product is meant to appeal to and bolster traditional male gender. The possibility is foreclosed by various devices, of which the commonest is to introduce a supernumerary woman into the advertisement. Her presence, usually alluring and obviously displaying heterosexual interest in the man or providing him with a heterosexual object, guarantees his heterosexuality and confirms that the product has made him heterosexually attractive while excluding homosexual attractiveness and homoerotic narcissism. The device is particularly obvious in advertisements for male grooming, such as shaving products, shampoo, soap and skin creams where the male body is nude or semi-nude and an object of beauty to be admired. The ubiquity and frequency of this device suggests strongly that advertisers are well aware of these possible interpretations. At the same time, there is an increasing number of advertisements that play on sexual ambiguity and allow both a heterosexual and homosexual interpretation which does not exclude any potential buyers. As we have repeatedly seen, it is this ambiguity which is at the centre of much homoeroticism.

When attempting to identify the homoerotic, we would do well to recall that Freud had reservations about the term 'erotic' itself, because he recognised that it could be used to camouflage sexual phenomena in favour of its sublimated forms by means of a less sexually explicit term (Laplanche and Pontalis 1988: 153). There is considerable merit in Freud's reservation. If homoeroticism involves sexual desires, why not simply call it homosexual? If the term 'homoeroticism' must be employed, then it might be best to use it to refer to the sublimated and unacknowledged forms of homosexuality that inform all male relations, while using 'homosexual' to refer to explicit sexual interest in other men.

Homoeroticism, as a concept and label for a form of sexuality, ought perhaps to be seen as the product of the strict heterosexual–

homosexual binary that pervades Western culture and which demands that homosexual feelings be confined to and associated with a particular sexual type, homosexual men who are thereby clearly differentiated from heterosexual men. The term 'homoeroticism' is, then, often used to refer to a border or transition zone where neither of these two master categories can enforce an uncontested claim. If it were not so vital to maintain the two as mutually exclusive sexual types, then it might be possible to admit that the sexuality of all men includes a homosexual (and heterosexual) dimension without recourse to the slippery and ambiguous term 'homoeroticism'.

References and further reading

Freud, S. [1905] (1953–74) 'Three essays on the theory of sexuality', *The Standard Edition, VII, of the Complete Psychological Works of Sigmund Freud*, edited and translated by J. Strachey, London: The Hogarth Press and The Institute for Psychoanalysis.

Hinsch, B. (1990) *Passions of the Cut Sleeve: The Male Homosexual Tradition in China*, Berkeley, CA: University of California Press.

Laplanche, J. and Pontalis, J.-B. (1988) *The Language of Psycho-analysis*, translated by D. Nicholson-Smith, London: Karnac Institute and the Institute of Psychoanalysis.

Mort, F. (1996) *Cultures of Consumption: Masculinities and Social Space in Late Twentieth-Century Britain*, London: Routledge.

Nixon, S. (1996) *Hard Looks: Masculinities, Spectatorship and Contemporary Consumption*, New York: St Martin's Press.

Simpson, M. (1994) *Male Impersonators: Men Performing Masculinity*, London: Routledge.

Tripp, C.A. (1987) *The Homosexual Matrix*, 2nd edn, New York: Meridian.

Woods, G. (1987) *Articulate Flesh: Male Homoeroticism and Modern Poetry*, New Haven, CT and London: Yale University Press.

Zeeland, S. (1995) *Sailors and Sexual Identity: Crossing the Line Between 'Straight' and 'Gay' in the US Navy*, New York: Harrington Park Press.

See also: homophobia and heterosexism; homosexuality; sexuality

MARK GRAHAM

HOMOPHOBIA AND HETEROSEXISM

Since its introduction in the early 1970s, the term 'homophobia' has attracted a steady flow of academic argument about what the term actually means (Weinberg 1972). The standard dictionary definition refers to a 'hatred or fear of homosexuals' (Brown 1993), but rather than resolving the debate, this definition leaves many paradoxical aspects of this complex phenomenon unaddressed.

First, the term has lexical problems. The use of the word 'hatred' in the standard definition reveals that this term is not confined to being a true phobia. Moreover, there are ambiguities in the use of the prefix 'homo-' which can be taken both as a reference to the Greek root *homos*, meaning the same, and the Latin *homo*, meaning man (Herek 2004; Haaga 1991). While these semantic issues can be largely resolved by agreeing on certain conventions of use, the deeper academic debates are much more complex and relate to the relationships between gender and sexuality and the deployment of homophobic words and meanings in everyday life.

While there is no argument that homophobia at least refers to negative biases against homosexuality in the contemporary Western world, research has repeatedly revealed broader definitional problems, not least of which is the omnipresence of gender references in homophobic dynamics (Plummer 1999). The paradox here which challenges the conventional definitions is that while references to 'appropriate' masculine and feminine roles appear to be a universal feature of homophobic dynamics, explicit references to sexuality are not invariable. Take, for example, the homophobic abuse a boy experiences if he makes the grave error of wearing a pink jumper or prefers reading books to playing football.

Perhaps it is not so surprising that gender is an invariable feature of homophobia. After all, both homosexuality and prejudices against homosexuality are inextricably gendered by their very definitions – because they specifically refer to the gender configurations of sexual partnering. In short, without this gender configuration, there is no homosexuality. On the other hand, how should the regular absence of sexual references in homophobic dynamics be interpreted, given that the conventional definition of homophobia relies so heavily on sex?

Differing schools of thought

Since the early 1970s, academics and activists have followed several distinct lines of argument in response to these conceptual problems (Herek 2004; Haaga 1991; Plummer 2005).

One approach involves advocating for restricting the use of the term 'homophobia' to fairly narrow definitions such as its literal sense or to those phenomena that exhibit unequivocal anti-homosexual bias (Haaga 1991). This is probably motivated by a wish to preserve the original intentions of those who introduced the term. This approach helps to maintain a focus on the harmful impact on homosexual men and women – clearly a key issue that must not be allowed to get buried in the debate. However, as we have already seen, restricting the term to its literal sense is semantically problematic; it is out-of-step with the general use of the term, which is rarely used to refer to a true phobia. Moreover, even in his original milestone work, Weinberg used the term 'homophobia' imprecisely, variously referring to it as a 'hostility', a 'revulsion towards homosexuals', 'the desire to inflict punishment as retribution', a 'prejudice', a 'pattern of attitudes' and 'part of the conventional American attitude' among others (Weinberg 1972: 3, 4, 8, 18, 132). Moreover, limiting the term in this way still fails to address the more intractable theoretical issues, such as when homophobia seems to be active in the absence of any overtly sexual scenarios – typically in response to stereotypical gender transgressions (see below).

Another approach is to advocate for broadening the field by arguing that the current definition of homophobia is quite inadequate for describing the complex social and behavioural phenomena to which the term is currently being used to refer in the literature and in everyday life. This argument opens the way for two possibilities: to extend the definition of homophobia so that it embraces the phenomena it is actually being applied to more adequately; or to introduce new words to complement and extend the term and to locate it in a broader, more meaningful vocabulary. To this end, a range of new terms have been coined in the last two decades in an attempt to better respond to the inadequacies of homophobia. These include: 'homoerotophobia', 'anti-homosexual prejudice', 'homonegativism', 'homosexism', 'homosexual taboo', 'homosexual bias' and 'heterosexism' among others (Plummer 1999; Herek 2004).

However, with the exception perhaps of 'heterosexism', none of these terms appears to have survived the test of time. Instead, what is apparent from this contested field is that homophobia is a highly complex phenomenon, presided over by a problematic term, and that both the terminology and the theoretical frameworks that underpin it are inadequate. In short, there is a growing consensus that these issues can only be resolved by thoughtfully and comprehensively re-theorising the field.

Heterosexism?

The term 'heterosexism' has been in currency for about the same period of time as 'homophobia', and as with 'homophobia', there have been notable inconsistencies in its use. In particular, heterosexism often has been conflated with homophobia, while at other times heterosexism has served to make the distinction between a socio-cultural ideology (heterosexism) and the derivative individual attitudes, beliefs and behaviours (homophobia). In either case, there is clearly a close linkage between homophobia and heterosexism in the frameworks people use to navigate and understand gender roles and sexual relationships. In Herek's (2004) words, 'the dichotomy between homosexuality and heterosexuality is at the heart of heterosexism'.

It is now generally held that heterosexism is an ideology that privileges heterosexual people, relationships, behaviours and attitudes and in so doing subordinates non-heterosexual forms (Herek 2004). In addition, the concept of heterosexism has been used as the basis for further theorising about the links between gender and sex. For example, during the 1990s cultural theorists introduced the term 'heteronormativity'. This concept added to the idea of heterosexism by arguing that privileging heterosexuality created a set of normative standards against which alternative sexualities are judged. In so doing, these standards have become 'normalised' or 'naturalised' in such a way that they play a taken-for-granted role in everyday relations. The result is that the normative ideological content of heterosexist attitudes is rendered second nature and is usually invisible.

Heterosexism has also been used as the basis for improving our understanding of biases about sexual difference in other ways. Recently, Herek (2004) used the concept as the centrepiece of an attempt to move beyond the theoretical problems inherent in homophobia. For him, heterosexism offered a promising basis for re-theorising homophobia while, as important as it is, homophobia has outlived its usefulness. Herek introduced three new concepts as the basis for a framework for better understanding attitudes towards sexual difference. First, he defines *sexual stigma* to mean 'the shared knowledge of society's negative regard for any non-heterosexual behaviour, identity, relationship or community'; second, *heterosexism* specifies 'the cultural ideology that perpetuates sexual stigma'; and finally, *sexual prejudice* refers to the negative attitudes of individuals based on sexual orientation.

In suggesting this framework, Herek is trying to supersede homophobia with a more sophisticated approach in which heterosexism takes centre stage. However, in order to succeed, this manoeuvre, like previous attempts to introduce new words and concepts, needs to offer an explanatory framework which researchers and activists find productive and which passes the test of time. Is homophobia entirely explained as a manifestation of heterosexist ideologies in individual people or is there more to the story?

Beyond heterosexism

Further critical insights into the meanings that underwrite homophobia can be found in the way in which homophobic words are deployed in everyday settings.

Among the homophobic terms most frequently used against males in the English-speaking world are words like 'poofter' and 'faggot' (Plummer 1999, 2005). These terms can be mapped according to the settings in which they are used, the characteristics that trigger their use, and the meanings they invoke. Far from being random terms of abuse, these terms have specific (albeit very complex) meanings from their first appearance during childhood. These meanings fall into four broad classes, providing valuable clues as to what underpins and drives homophobia in everyday life. These classes of homophobic meaning are:

Feminisation: Boys are prone to attracting homophobic abuse if they demonstrate characteristics that are culturally associated with being female. Examples include cross-dressing, playing girls' games, displaying feminine mannerisms or taking a receptive/submissive role in sex. The common thread in this class of meanings is the *acquisition* of (culturally constructed) feminine characteristics. Male peers who typically enforce the homophobic response under these circumstances appear to be preoccupied with the polluting role of femininity and the prevention of masculinity's contamination by feminine features.

Emasculation: The second set of meanings that readily provokes homophobic abuse, the preoccupation instead is with a *deficit or lack of masculinity*. This set of meanings includes delayed puberty, under-developed physical stature, insufficient secondary sexual characteristics such as muscle or body hair, impotence, lack of courage and aggressiveness, a failure to adhere to stereotypical masculine roles and so on. These meanings closely accord with the classic psychoanalytic taboos known as 'castration anxiety'.

Inter-gender relationships: This third set of meanings associated with homophobic abuse focuses on the relationships between males and females. Interestingly, these meanings demonstrate how the triggers for homophobia are socially constructed and can change as boys mature: initially young boys are prone to attracting homophobia if they are too close to girls; later, from puberty onwards, boys who do not associate with girls enough or who do not objectify women are vulnerable to homophobic criticism. For adults, this set of meanings accords best with Adrienne Rich's famous dictum of 'compulsory heterosexuality'. The taboos that are active in this class of meanings include classic (anti-gay) homophobia and the obligations of heterosexism.

Intra-gender relations: The final class of meanings that are prone to provoking homophobic abuse relates to the rules governing same-gender relations, especially peer-group solidarity. Boys who betray peer-group solidarity; who are loners; who avoid team sports; who place external authority (e.g. to parents, teachers, the police) above loyalty to the peer group; and who fail to demonstrate what I call 'compulsory homosociality' are also at risk of attracting homophobia (Plummer 2005).

It is clear that homophobia that is neither heterosexist nor antigay is also not random. Instead, this content constitutes a highly patterned, regular feature of homophobic abuse that extends well beyond the conventional definitions of homosexuality and heterosexism and much more deeply into culture. Second, the homophobic content that is neither heterosexist nor antigay is also not a minor aspect of homophobic abuse that can be easily dismissed, but a major, if not fundamental preoccupation. It would therefore seem that any framework that aims to account for homophobia, but which confines itself to the antigay and heterosexist elements and does not adequately account for these additional meanings, runs the risk of not providing adequate explanations.

Re-theorising homophobia

The meanings associated with the homophobic archetypes of 'poofter' and 'faggot' are rich and multilayered and they offer insights into the wider significance of homophobia (Plummer 2005). First, it is notable that the complex layers of meaning associated with homophobia appear to collectively define a virtual male 'other': the limp-wristed, effete, lonely, sexual pervert. These meanings systematically specify not only his sexual transgressions but also his betrayal of his peers, his personal inadequacies and his shameful feminisation.

Second, the meanings that contribute to the construction of this 'virtual male other' are derived from binaries and they have their counterpoints. By way of contrast, these counterpoints collectively describe masculine archetypes that conform to 'hegemonic masculinity' (Connell 1995). In effect these two elaborate systems of meaning themselves exist as a binary which consists of hegemonic masculinity and its antithesis, what I call the 'virtual male other' or the 'hegemonemesis' and what everyday culture refers to as 'poofters' and 'faggots' (Plummer 2005).

Importantly, while many theories about sexuality and homophobia focus on the masculine/feminine gender binary, there is a subtle but important difference at work here in that the operative binary that underwrites homophobia appears to be between idealised masculinity and failed masculinity. Of course, this antithesis of idealised masculinity includes, but is not confined to, femininity and heterosexuality. In other words, homophobia actively invokes *everything a 'real man' should not be.*

Homophobia clearly has central significance for how masculine archetypes are defined and is deeply implicated in policing them (Kimmel 1994; Plummer 1999, 2005). It is here, in the realm of gender rather than sexuality, that we start to see why male homophobia is so deeply cathected and so resilient: homophobia is masculinity's henchman.

References and further reading

Brown, L. (ed.) (1993) *The New Shorter Oxford English Dictionary*, Oxford: Clarendon Press.
Connell, R. (1995) *Masculinities*, Sydney: Allen and Unwin.
Haaga, D.A.F. (1991) 'Homophobia?' *Journal of Social Behaviour and Personality*, 6 (1): 171–4.
Herek, G.M. (2004) 'Beyond "homophobia": thinking about sexual prejudice and stigma in the twenty-first century', *Sexuality Research and Social Policy*, 1 (2): 6–24.
Kimmel, M.S. (1994) 'Masculinity as homophobia: fear, shame and silence in the construction of gender identity', in H. Brod and M.K. Kaufman (eds) *Theorising Masculinities*, Thousand Oaks, CA: Sage, pp. 119–41.
Neisen, J.H. (1990) 'Heterosexism: redefining homophobia for the 1990s', *Journal of Gay and Lesbian Psychotherapy*, 1 (3): 21–35.
Plummer, D. (1999) *One of the Boys: Masculinity, Homophobia and Modern Manhood*, New York: Haworth.
—— (2005) 'Crimes against manhood: homophobia as the penalty for betraying hegemonic masculinity', in G. Hawkes and J. Scott (eds) *Perspectives in Human Sexuality*, Melbourne and Oxford: Oxford University Press, pp. 218–32.
Rich, A. (1980) 'Compulsory heterosexuality and lesbian existence', *Signs*, 5 (4): 631–60.
Weinberg, G. (1972) *Society and the Healthy Homosexual*, Boston, MA: Alyson Publications.

See also: sexuality; homoeroticism; homosexuality

DAVID PLUMMER

HOMOSEXUALITY

'Homosexuality' and 'homosexual' are terms of relatively recent vintage. It would have been meaningless for a man to claim 'I am a homosexual' prior to 1869 as the term did not exist. This is not to say that sexual relations between men – what will hereafter simply be called homosexuality – did not occur before this date; they did and have probably done so throughout human history (Greenberg 1988). But prior to the entry of the term into the languages of Western countries in the late nineteenth and early twentieth century it was not possible to classify a person or to classify oneself as a homosexual. Scholars are divided over whether the term 'homosexual' ought to be confined to men who *identify* themselves as members of a separate sexual category on the basis of their sexual orientation/preference in contrast to a heterosexual majority. Those who argue that it should be confined in this way are often indebted to Michel Foucault's claim that the homosexual was invented as a sexual species in the second half of the nineteenth century and had a specific childhood, clinical history and personality (Foucault 1978).

Yet some kind of recognition that sexual preference is not always exclusively for the other sex has a history much longer than that of the term 'homosexual'. Witness, for example, the famous myth of Aristophanes in which the world was once filled with people who were two-sexed – male and female, male and male, or female and female. Zeus split them all in two and since then people have searched for their other half, whether male or female.

The term 'sodomy' was used in Europe for centuries to refer to illegal forms of sexuality. It has often been conflated with homosexuality, but was used to refer to a wide range of sexual practices, not only homosexual relations between men. Neither does the term 'sodomite' seem to have denoted a specific type of person or identity, as 'homosexual' came to do. That said, it may have been the case that some men did recognise themselves to be different on the basis of their sexual preferences even if not to the same extent as today's gay men. There is, for example, some evidence of this from the Molly subculture of eighteenth-century urban England (Norton 1992).

In the light of the complexity of historical and ethnographic evidence, perhaps it is reasonable to conclude that no clear or abrupt emergence of a 'homosexual' can be detected and that there are continuities between the modern category and identity of homosexual, which emerged in the latter half of the nineteenth century as an object of medical and legal intervention, and earlier forms of homosexuality

Homosexual relations between men can be classified in different ways on the basis of whether they conform to class-stratified, age-stratified, gender-stratified, or egalitarian systems (see Murray 2000). For the ancient Greeks, the distinction between the active and passive (penetrator–penetrated) roles in intercourse was of great importance. The passive role was only acceptable for social 'inferiors', women, slaves and male youths, but not adult male citizens. The ideal was a relationship between an adult male in his twenties or thirties and a youth (Halperin 1990; Dover 1978). Age-stratified homosexual relations are known from ancient Greece, Aboriginal Australian cultures and the samurai of Japan. Often, these relations were seen as masculinising boys and young men. Gender stratified relations have been recorded among the plains Indians of North America, in the Middle East (for example the Xanith of Oman), as well as the Mahu of Tahiti, and in the Mediterranean and parts of Latin American cultures. In gender-stratified systems it is often the case that the man adopting the role of penetrator in anal intercourse is expected to be conventionally masculine while the man who is penetrated is 'feminised' and expected to display elements of conventional feminine behaviour. He is also sometimes derided and ascribed lower social standing. Egalitarian systems involve sexual relations between men of the same age and social standing, either during certain periods of life or as part of lifelong relationships. Egalitarian homosexuality has been reported from Dahomey (Benin) in Africa, and most famously, perhaps, at least in the West, in the fabled relations between mythic heroes such as Achilles and Patroclus, and, less mythic, Alexander the Great and Hephaestion. Modern-day western gay masculinities are the most widespread and recognisable expression of egalitarian homosexuality. Although these relationships are sometimes marked by inequalities of age and wealth, there is no cultural expectation or demand that they be so. However, none of the above categories is watertight even in their respective historical and cultural settings (Murray 2000; Herdt 1994). In some cases, homosexual relations are associated with specific cultural and social niches, such as shamanic traditions in Siberia and the berdaches or two-spirit people among first nations of North America.

The category of homosexual, like that of heterosexual, took some time to develop. It did so in the context of nineteenth-century sexology which witnessed an explosion of works on forms of human sexual behaviour and an eagerness to classify them. For example, Richard Krafft-Ebing, in 1886, described homosexuality as a perversion among many others and an indicator of social degeneration. More positive in his appraisal was Karl Ulrichs, who considered homosexuality to be the result of a woman's soul trapped in a man's body. Homosexual men were 'inverts' who displayed the typical gender characteristics of the other sex, including their sexual preference. After his conviction in 1895, the 'effeminate' and dandified Oscar Wilde was, perhaps, the best known representative of the newly emerged sexual type. The British reformer Edward Carpenter took a slightly different position, arguing in his *The Intermediate Sex* (1908) that 'uranism', as he termed homosexuality, was not only on the increase but heralded the dawn of a new age of sexual liberation. In Germany, Magnus Hirschfeld campaigned for the rights of homosexuals. The Nazis destroyed his Institute for Sexology in 1933.

The emerging psychiatric profession in the late nineteenth century and onwards played a central role in the construction of the homosexual category. Freud, for one, argued that everyone has homosexual fantasies and dreams. However, he also claimed that these were sublimated into solidarity with persons of the same gender. In his view, it was pointless to try and cordon off homosexuality from heterosexuality, as both develop out of a universal polymorphous perversity or 'bisexuality'. Not surprisingly, perhaps, Freud opposed the punishment and criminalisation of homosexuality. However, Freud's teleological view of sexual development, which ought always to lead to genital heterosexuality, inevitably cast homosexuality as an example of arrested development, and hence a 'perversion'. It was this aspect of Freud's thinking that many of his more conservative followers were to emphasise.

Homosexuality was increasingly seen not as a deliberate choice, as in the acts of the sodomite, but as the result of involuntary characteristics over which the individual had little or no control. It became possible to speak of latent homosexuality: that is to say, a man with homosexual inclinations caused by his biological or psychological makeup who did not act on them.

While the terms 'homosexuality' and 'homosexual' originated as medical labels to denote a perversion or sickness and had stigmatising consequences, they also made it possible for the men so labelled to recognise themselves in the term, to realise that they were not alone, and eventually to organise on the basis of a homosexual identity, however stigmatised. The existence of large cities with a sufficiently large 'homosexual' population was an important prerequisite for this development. The first homosexual rights organisation appeared in Germany at the very end of the nineteenth century, and was followed by, for example, the British Society for the Study of Sex Psychology (1914), the Mattachine Society in the USA (1950–1) and the Dutch COC (Cultur-en Ontspannings-Centrum (The Culture and Recreation Centre) (1966). Homosexual activists and academics eventually came to question or reject outright many of the theories and medical 'truths' about homosexuality and provide alternatives of their own.

The categorisation into predominantly two sexual populations of men, either homosexual or heterosexual, became dominant in Euro-American societies. However, the common belief that homosexual acts were confined to a small minority of exclusively homosexual men was challenged when the American sexologist Alfred Kinsey published the results of his studies into the sexuality of American men in 1948. In it, he reported that 37 per cent of men had been involved in homosexual sex to the point of orgasm. Kinsey's findings cast doubt over the assumption that men can be neatly divided into a heterosexual majority and a homosexual minority. On the contrary, he devised his famous scale of 0 to 6 to illustrate that sexuality has the character of a continuum rather than clear-cut divisions into sexual types. A score of 0 on the scale denotes exclusive heterosexuality and a score of 6, exclusive homosexuality.

In a groundbreaking article published in 1968, Mary McIntosh argued against seeing homosexuality as a specific condition which you either do or do not have. In her view, the assumption generates an overly dichotomised view of sexuality. It also tends to focus attention on the aetiology of homosexuality. The 'causes' of homosexuality have been extensively debated. Explanations included seeing it as a choice, the result of faulty upbringing by dominant mothers or distant fathers, the consequence of being 'recruited' or 'seduced' into homosexuality at an early age by an older homosexual man, medical theories of hormone imbalance, and most recently the result of a homosexual gene or brain. The claims of these more recent medical searches for the aetiology of homosexuality are hotly debated and considerable doubt has been expressed as to the reliability of their findings (Murray 2000). One obvious difficulty with this research is that it takes as given the homosexual–heterosexual dichotomy and assumes that it refers to two distinct types of men and that the distinction is biologically generated. Situational homosexuality – in the military, in prisons or during certain periods of life (e.g. boarding schools) – casts doubt on this neat division, as do the different ways in which homosexual relations are institutionalised in cultures outside the Euro-American West, as well as the historical variability in homosexual relations found within the same cultural tradition. Another difficulty is that the research only looks for the causes of homosexuality, while viewing heterosexuality as a given in need of no explanation.

Those who believe in a biological cause may do so for very different reasons. Some advocates of homosexual rights argue that it proves the naturalness of homosexuality and therefore refutes the moralists who condemn it as sinful. Other advocates are more cautious and warn that a biological cause can easily be interpreted by the opponents of homosexual rights as a medical 'fault' or 'abnormality' that ought to be treated or eradicated altogether, either by the abortion of a 'homosexual' foetus or the removal of a 'gay gene' through genetic engineering.

One of the attractions of a biological explanation also lies in its function as a guarantee that heterosexuality is distinct from and cannot become homosexuality. A biological cause for homosexuality provides heterosexuality with a stable and permanent counterfoil against which to define and stabilise itself. The assumption that male homosexuality always coincides with gender nonconformity (i.e. that all homosexual men are effeminate), and that effeminacy is an accurate predictor of homosexuality, has served the same function of maintaining a clear boundary between homosexual and heterosexual men. The appearance of urban gay subcultures and distinctive gay masculinities in the 1970s to some extent reinforced the notion that two mutually exclusive sexual categories of men exist at the same time as it has helped to undermine the assumption that, with the exception of sexual object choice, homosexuality is always associated with gender non-conformity. Ironically, it was early gay liberation that frequently questioned the validity of the dichotomy. Indeed, in 1971 Dennis Altman looked forward to the day when there were no homosexuals and no heterosexuals either (cf. Hocquenghem 1978: 36). This is unlikely to happen as long as sexual preference remains a primary means of categorising people and is expected to predict sex, gender and a host of other characteristics.

References and further reading

Altman, D. [1971] (1993) *Homosexual Oppression and Liberation*, New York: New York University Press.

Dover, K. (1978) *Greek Homosexuality*, London: Duckworth.

Foucault, M. (1978) *The History of Sexuality: An Introduction*, New York: Pantheon.

Greenberg, D. (1988) *The Construction of Homosexuality*, Chicago, IL: University of Chicago Press.

Halperin, D. (1990) *One Hundred Years of Homosexuality, and Other Essays on Greek Love*, New York: Routledge.

Herdt, G. (1994) *Third Sex, Third Gender: Beyond Sexual Dimorphism in Culture and History*, New York: Zone Books.

Hocquenghem, G. (1978) *Homosexual Desire*, translated by Daniella Dangoor, London: Allison and Busby.

McIntosh, M. (1968) 'The homosexual role', *Social Problems*, 16 (Fall): 182–92.

Murphy, T. (1997) *Gay Science: The Ethics of Sexual Orientation Research*, New York: Columbia University Press.

Murray, S. (2000) *Homosexualities*, Chicago, IL: University of Chicago Press.

Norton, R. (1992) *Mother Clap's Molly House: The Gay Subculture in England 1700–1830*, London: The Gay Men's Press.

Plummer, K. (ed.) (1981) *The Making of the Modern Homosexual*, London: Hutchinson

See also: gay and lesbian studies; gay liberation; gay literature; gay masculinities; homoeroticism; homophobia and heterosexism; men who have sex with men; sexuality; working with gay men

MARK GRAHAM

HONOUR

Honour is one of the most basic social codes for prompting and regulating men's competition for status. A mode of social control as well as self-control, it helps to stabilise male hierarchies, especially in small social groups beset by internal instabilities and external threats. Typically, the code praises manly valour, independence and self-control, while blaming and shaming men who seem weak, vulnerable or dependent. A man of honour would rather die than know that other men see him as cowardly or humiliated. Such codes, which apparently arose in cultures around the Mediterranean Sea, function most intensely in small villages or kinship units. Honour–shame societies tend to devalue compromise and negotiation, while highly valuing confrontation and rituals of public self-display.

Honour cannot be separated from the social uses of shaming. In larger groups, shaming also disciplined elites. From 1200 to 1500 in northern Italy, cities commissioned paintings of aristocratic men who had fled the city as accused criminals or traitors, and hung those portraits upside down on the city walls to deface their names (Egerton 1985). The spectre of family dishonour lured many fugitives back to face trial and even death. In the antebellum American South, nose-pulling constituted instant shaming, often prompting duels among the elite (Greenberg 1996). In many US urban areas, to be 'dissed' (disrespected) requires assault to avenge the shaming. In post-industrial countries, the quest for honour through controlled violence may also be outsourced to spectator sports.

In many small patriarchal societies, a dutiful daughter can serve as a prime gift to secure her father's honour, while an independent or sexually active daughter becomes a prime signifier of her father's, and therefore her family's, shame. Fathers or brothers may kill an unchaste daughter. The reciprocal expectations that significantly constrain young women's autonomy help to secure family alliances and clans in conditions of threat and scarcity. In the Bosnia conflict in the mid-1990s, as repeatedly throughout history, armies have used rape to destroy the honour of enemy fathers or brothers, whose inability to protect a kinswoman's virtue brings lifelong shame to the family.

References and further reading

Egerton, S. (1985) *Pictures and Punishment*, Ithaca, NY: Cornell University Press.

Freeman, J. (2001) *Affairs of Honour*, New Haven, CT: Yale University Press.

Greenberg, K. (1996) *Honour and Slavery*, Princeton, NJ: Princeton University Press.

Peristiany, J.G. (ed.) (1966) *Honour and Shame*, Chicago, IL: University of Chicago Press.

Wyatt-Brown, B. (1982) *Southern Honour*, Oxford: Oxford University Press.

DAVID LEVERENZ

HONOUR KILLINGS

Honour killings are socially sanctioned premeditated murders of women by male kin because of an alleged or real infraction of social and/or sexual behaviour. Victims are always women. They may be married or unmarried, adolescent or mature women. Perpetrators of these murders are always men. The perpetrator believes that, by his action, he is protecting the honour of his family and community.

Pressured by patriarchal norms, most families and communities carefully cover up this horrible crime to protect the criminal from the law. The United Nations Population Fund reports that more than five thousand women are murdered in honour killings every year.

In most societies, women have been subjected to various forms of violence. The violence results from ingrained patriarchal practices that are generally attributed to cultural and religious norms. Historically, Romans, Babylonians and Assyrians, Aztecs and Incas, the Germanic tribes, Chinese, Japanese and other Asian cultures have sanctioned the killing of adulterous wives to protect the honour of their families (Goldstein 2002). The books of Leviticus and Deuteronomy in the Old Testament and also the New Testament sanction the killing of adulterous wives by men.

The ancient legal and religious codes that prescribe violence against women continue to exist (Spierenburg 1998). The object of the violence is the control of women's sexuality within patriarchal power relations of a family or a community (Coomaraswamy and Kois 1999). In the twenty-first century, honour killings still occur in Bangladesh, Egypt, India, Iran, Iraq, Israel, Jordan, Lebanon, Nigeria, Pakistan, Palestine, Morocco, Saudi Arabia, Turkey and Uganda. Honour killings have also been reported in various European countries such as Great Britain, Germany, Italy, Sweden and in the United States. Because of the large number of honour killings that occur in the Middle Eastern countries, there is a strong tendency to link honour killings to Islam. However, the sacred texts of Islam, the Koran and the Hadith, do not prescribe honour killings. While Muslim sacred books prohibit adultery, they sanction non-capital punishment for both adulterous men and women (Arberry 1955).

Gender-sensitive approaches locate honour killings within particular patriarchal practices that prescribe violence against women. In the Middle East and in Mediterranean countries, the patriarchal concept of honour and shame is considered the basis of a moral code (Bourdieu 1996). In the Middle East, the concept of honour is closely related to honour killings (Araji 2000). The concept is conceived as the honour of the family, kinship group or community, which is represented by men. It is directly linked to women's chastity. In order to protect the honour of men, women's mobility, sexual behaviour and sexuality must be strictly controlled. The linking of honour to women's chastity established the right to kill women if they are considered to have transgressed men's honour. This applies even in the case of rape.

While some honour killings may be the acts of individual men, the majority come as the result of a patriarchal council whose male head consults, judges and organises extra-judicial executions. In most cases, the husband or the husband's younger brother, or the brother of the victim herself, is ordered to carry out the murder, knowing that they will receive a reduction of penalty as a result of their age. Often the victim may predict the outcome of her case. Many times, however, the patriarchy purposefully lulls her into the hope of clemency in order to prevent her trying to escape from their grasp and turning to the authorities. The murder may take place almost anywhere – in an urban location, in the family compound, in an abandoned lot, in a deserted rural area. The victim may be forced to commit suicide, or she may be drowned, shot, burned, stabbed or strangled with a rope or a cable.

The state is often directly linked to and plays a role in perpetuating these killings. It remains indifferent to what happens or merely fails to intervene. The authorities frequently return a woman who has escaped back to the family. Courts rule that 'extenuating circumstances' or 'unjust provocation' in committing the crime provide a basis for rendering lenient punishments. This occurs in both Western and non-Western countries.

The gender-sensitive campaigns of the non-governmental women's organisations across the Middle East about honour killings resulted in the international commitment to end this most heinous form of violence against women (Asamoah 1999). The United Nations' landmark declaration on the Elimination of Violence Against Women, along with the International Bill of Rights for Women, known as the Convention on the Elimination of Discrimination Against Women (CEDAW), calls states to establish necessary mechanisms to combat abuses of women's human rights and to eliminate honour killings and to punish perpetrators. The convention also obliges states to address the practice of honour killings in the criminal justice system.

Signatory states are responsible for implementing educational programmes in line with international and regional standards of human rights law to prevent and end honour killings.

References and further reading

Araji, S.K. (2000) *Crimes of Honor and Shame*, Anchorage, AK: University of Alaska Press.

Arberry, A.J. (1955) *The Koran Interpreted*, New York: Macmillan, 2, 4, pp. 2–4.

Asamoah, Y. (1999) 'Women's human rights and "honor killings" in Islamic cultures', *Buffalo Women's Law Journal*, 8: 21–2.

Bourdieu, P. [1966] (1996) 'The sentiment of honor in Kabyle society', in J.G. Peristiany (ed.) *Honor and Shame*, Chicago, IL: University of Chicago Press.

Coomaraswamy, R. and Kois, L. (1999) 'Violence against women', in K.D. Askin and D.M. Koening (eds) *Women and International Human Rights Law*, New York: Transnational, 1, pp. 177–286.

Friedrich, P. (1977) 'Sanity and the myth of honor', *Ethos*, 5: 281–305.

Goldstein, M.A. (2002) 'The biological roots of heat-of-passions crimes and honor killings', *Politics and the Life Sciences*, 21 (2): 28–37.

Spierenburg, P. (1998) *Men and Violence*, Columbus, OH: Ohio University Press.

See also: aggression; domestic violence; honour; patriarchy

MIHRI INAL CAKIR

HUMOUR

Humour is imbued with social significance, despite its seemingly non-serious intent. In interactions among men, humour plays a significant part in the ways they relate to each other and can be seen to serve a variety of purposes in male peer group cultures beyond the obvious sharing of a joke. Humour provides men with a repertoire for conveying masculine identities. An obvious feature of this repertoire is the spirit of camaraderie that pervades everyday social interactions between men. These exchanges are commonly punctuated by moments of humour, often expressed in an exchange of banter resembling verbal tennis. Such exchanges can be seen as an expression of friendship, signalling support for one another and commonality – the recognition of a shared world-view.

Like other social practices, humour is context-specific and inevitably shaped by dynamics of social class, gender and ethnicity. In the academic field of masculinities, humour is most apparent in studies that focus upon adolescent males and young men. School-based researchers noted the importance of humour to young men. Peter Woods (1976) described laughter as an 'antidote to schooling', claiming that it provided students with a form of escapism and a coping strategy that mitigated against the harsh realities of life within educational institutions. Paul Willis (1977), in a famous ethnography of working-class young men, indicated that 'having a laff' was the most important feature of school life for the 'lads', giving them status and authority within their peer group. Willis argued that the counter-culture of resistance and humour developed by the 'lads' was a form of preparation for working-class jobs. The rough humour and horseplay of the lads was also a feature of shop-floor culture in the factories and manual trades that the lads moved into after school. From this perspective, having a 'laff' was instrumental and purposeful; a way of *learning to labour* that remained an important point of class-cultural reproduction. A further study elaborating upon some of Willis' themes (Dubberley 1993) suggests that students use humour to resist the dominant culture of the school through forms of parody and subversion.

In a study of schoolboy humour carried out with Anoop Nayak (Kehily and Nayak 1997), we argued that humour is not an outcome or effect of working-class masculinity, but, rather, is constitutive of these very identities. Our study suggested that heterosexual masculinities were organised and regulated through humour. We observed humour as a style drawn upon by young men to consolidate heterosexual masculinities through game-playing, story-telling and the practice of insults. We noted that although male peer group humour may contain moments of subversion (aimed at teachers, bourgeois values or compulsory education), it can also be seen as a compelling mode of gender conformity. While humour involved resistance to the authority of teachers and the school system, young men's humorous performances had oppressive effects upon other students. Significantly, young women were targets for male humorous insults, while young men who did not conform to dominant heterosexual codes of masculinity were also subject to adverse consequences.

The regulatory effects of humour among young men were most evident in relation to homosexuality. A rich vein of homophobic humour and accompanying gestures were used to enact a hyper-masculine identity that treated homosexuals as both fearful and laughable. Many features of homophobic humour were ritualistically rehearsed and performed, sometimes several times a day. We argued that these homophobic performances suggested the instability of gender categories wherein masculinity was asserted through repeated struggle. Our study concluded that masculine identities were sustained through fraught exhibition, in which the highly dramatised performance is, in itself, evidence of the insecurity and splittings within the male psyche.

The potential of humour to emphasise the power of dominant versions of masculinity has been explored in a number of studies. A striking feature of these studies is the overlap between the use of humour and verbal abuse leading to highly competitive forms of denigration. Lyman's (1987) study of a US male fraternity focused upon the practice of 'dozens' – the ritual exchange of insults. Lyman argued that 'dozens' served a range of functions. In particular, the battery of sexist jokes consolidated the bonds of the 'in-group' through mutual hostility against an 'out-group'. In these exchanges the ability to keep control of one's emotions in the face of sustained abuse is seen as essential for group membership and the demonstration of a competent, socially validated masculinity. A similar practice can be found in Labov's (1972) study of black vernacular among young men in urban USA. Labov describes 'sounding' as a form of verbal duelling involving the trading of ritualistic insults for prestige within the peer group. Those most skilled at employing sophisticated insults achieved higher status in the group. Significantly, most insults were based around the verbal abuse of an opponent's mother. The invocation of a boy's mother in the male peer group taps into the contradictory 'private' emotions of maternal affection and the public disavowal of the feminine. Despite the importance of humour to masculine identities, little attention has been paid to the humorous practices of subordinate males.

References and further reading

Dubberley, W.S. (1993) 'Humour as resistance', in P. Woods and M. Hammersley (eds) *Gender and Ethnicity in Schools: Ethnographic Accounts*, London: Routledge.

Kehily, M.J. and Nayak, A. (1997) '"Lads and laughter": humour and the production of heterosexual hierarchies', *Gender and Education*, 9 (1): 69–87.

Labov, W. (1972) *Language in the Inner City: Studies in Black English Vernacular*, Pennsylvania, PA: University of Pennsylvania Press.

Lyman, P. (1987) 'The fraternal bond as a joking relationship: a case study of sexist jokes in male group bonding', in M. Kimmel (ed.) *Changing Men*, London: Sage.

Willis, P. (1977) *Learning to Labour: How Working-class Kids Get Working-class Jobs*, Farnborough: Saxon House.

Woods, P. (1976) 'Having a laugh: an antidote to schooling', in M. Hammersley and P. Woods (eds) *The Process of Schooling*, London: Routledge.

See also: boys and boyhood; male youth cultures; men's relations with men

MARY JANE KEHILY

HUNTING

'Man the hunter' is a central metaphor in the construction of masculinities – both symbolically and practically. It serves to explore, explain and justify patriarchal social dynamics, in particular to justify the 'naturally' predatory instincts of men in relation to animals and women, both of whom are seen as prey in both private and public contexts (Bergman 1996). Historically men have served as hunters and soldiers since ancient times. In modern nuclear families, however, the metaphor naturalises the male breadwinner/female dependent model of relationships which ultimately privileges men. It re-emerges in contexts as diverse as 1950s scientific discourse in which 'Man the Hunter' was codified by the United Nations as the basis of a universal human experience supported by the new physical anthropology (Haraway 1992) and contemporary 'wild men' movements, in which urban middle-class men are seen to reclaim their essential masculinity as hunters.

Sports hunting has always been male dominated and serves as a resource for men to construct a masculinity based on militarism and to 'bond' in ways that continuously demonstrate men's superiority to women, immigrants and nature, i.e. the 'Other' (Herman 2003). Kalof *et al.* (2004) point out that the sexualisation of animals, women and weapons which occurs in such contexts is a form of sexual objectification used to construct traditional masculinities. Kalof and Fitzgerald (2003) reiterate this with their discussion of the othering of animals which takes place in hunting magazines and serves to posit animals as objects that confirm the hunter's place as a 'real man' via the display of animal bodies as trophies. Competing feminist perspectives on women hunters show how masculine practices have been contested by women, though with limited effects (Fitzgerald 2005). Hunting both practically and discursively reaffirms a 'man's' right of unfettered access to nature and to women.

References and further reading

Bergman, C. (1996) *Orion's Legacy*, New York: Penguin.

Fitzgerald, A. (2005) 'The emergence of the figure of "woman-the-hunter"', *Women's Studies Quarterly*, 33: 1–2.

Haraway, D. (1992) *Primate Visions*, London: Verso.

Herman, D. (2003) 'The hunter's aim', *Journal of Leisure Research*, 35 (4).

Kalof, L. and Fitzgerald, A. (2003) 'Reading the trophy', *Visual Studies*, 18 (2): 112–22.

Kalof, L., Fitzgerald, A. and Baralt, L. (2004) 'Animals, women, and weapons', *Society and Animals*, 12 (3): 237–51.

SHANE HOPKINSON

HUSBANDS

The term 'husband' denotes marriage status: a man who has entered into a legally or religiously sanctioned commitment with a woman within a heterosexual relationship.

In European and North American cultures, husbands have historically been associated with certain kinds of masculine identities and roles in relation to family and work. To enter into marriage is traditionally viewed as transition into adult masculine status and identity, and as linked to the taking up of power and responsibility with respect to one's female partner, children and household. This is underscored in legal and popular notions of the male 'head of household', and by the idea of the husband as 'breadwinner'.

Despite the economic, legislative and social changes said to be transforming gender relations within 'Western' cultures over the past four decades, sociological studies continue to suggest role specialisation between husbands and wives within the home, with the latter performing the bulk of domestic work like cleaning, food preparation, childcare and caring work. Even where both partners are in full-time paid work, men generally undertake less domestic and caring work than their wives. Where they do contribute to work around the home, husbands tend to take up tasks traditionally deemed 'masculine'. Despite the decline of the household wage, which implies that both partners' earnings are essential for supporting families, men's and women's perception of husbands' status and domestic practices tends to conform to a 'head of household' model. Even where husbands are eager to share domestic work and childcare, or where both members of a couple are retired, studies suggest that the balance of domestic and caring work remains with the female partner across the life course (see Arber and Ginn 1995).

A number of studies have explored the subtle qualities of husband and wife relationships, and the place of masculinities in this, by focusing on 'intimacy' and the division of 'emotional labour'. A landmark British study by Mansfield and Collard (1988) suggested that in heterosexual married relationships, husbands and wives tended to operate as 'intimate strangers': following the demise of initial romantic notions associated with falling in love, men and women sought incompatible emotional goals in marriage. This led to a kind of emotional distance, which men largely put down to the demands work made on them. In later work Duncombe and Marsden (1993) claim that a key feature of marriage is gender difference in husbands' and wives' emotional behaviour. This study reports the different approaches that husbands and wives adopt to emotional participation within relationships, with women feeling that they undertake the majority of emotional work. While the women were critical of their partners' emotional distance, the husbands themselves argued they did have feelings, but that they were theirs and not to be disclosed. Husbands, the research suggests, often felt pulled apart by the competing demands of coupledom and work.

The research outlined so far provides a sense of limited change with respect to how husbands and wives 'do' gender relations in the 'West'. This is at odds with post-war expert discourse and popular conceptions that posit marriage as a relationship between equals. Such an interpretation of modern marriage relationships is also evident in sociological accounts of 'the symmetrical family' where husbands and wives' roles are said to be equal and interchangeable, and with contemporary media representations of 'new men' such as stay-at-home husbands and fathers. A number of influential European social theorists have also touched on the consequences for men of what they suggest is a new economic and emotional gender equality that is reshaping married relationships. Beck and Beck-Gernsheim (1995), for example, claim that husbands and wives must now engage 'battles' to maintain do-it-yourself equal relationships that have no historical precedents. Giddens (1992) similarly argues that husbands and wives are increasingly involved in equal relationships. For Giddens, economic, social and cultural changes mean that husbands and wives must negotiate for the first time in history as equals. While this has profound implications for relationships between husbands and wives (in making them more fragile and in encouraging partners to be more open about what they want from the relationship), Giddens theorises that it also has potentially profound implications for heterosexual masculinities: they are likely to be transformed in reflexively responding to the changes in gender relations that women are demanding.

Despite Giddens' obvious concern with gender developments in Western cultures, his argument implies that democratic gender relationships, and their implications for reflexive masculinities, could become universalised in the global world. Against this argument, feminist and other critics point out the continuing importance of economic, institutional and socio-cultural contexts in shaping the *different* kinds of power and roles that husbands have – and how these are related to different configurations of masculinity and gender power – both *within* the West (see Jamieson 1998) and elsewhere in the world (see, for example, Charsley 2005; Connell 2005; Magazine 2004; Peletz 1994).

References and further reading

Arber, S. and Ginn, J. (1995) *Connecting Gender and Age*, Buckingham: Open University Press.

Beck, U. and Beck-Gernsheim, E. (1995) *The Normal Chaos of Love*, Cambridge: Polity.
Charsley, K. (2005) 'Unhappy husbands', *Journal of the Royal Anthropological Institute*, 11 (1): 85–105.
Connell, R. (2005) 'A really good husband', *Australian Journal of Social Issues*, 40 (3): 369–83.
Duncombe, J. and Marsden, D. (1993) 'Love and intimacy', *Sociology*, 27 (2): 21–41.
Giddens, A. (1992) *The Transformation of Intimacy*, Cambridge: Polity.
Jamieson, L. (1998) *Intimacy*, Cambridge: Polity.
Magazine, R. (2004) 'Both husbands and banda (gang) members', *Men and Masculinities*, 7 (2): 144–65.
Mansfield, P. and Collard, J. (1988) *The Beginning of the Rest of Your Life*, London: Macmillan.
Peletz, M.G. (1994) 'Neither reasonable nor responsible', *Cultural Anthropology*, 9 (2): 135–78.

See also: divorce and separation; heterosexuality; intimacy; marriage

BRIAN HEAPHY

HYBRID/THIRD GENDER/THIRD SEX

These terms refer to gender roles other than the two typical for male- and female-bodied people within a culture. The term 'third gender' is used as an alternative to the absolute contrast of binary genders (Herdt 1994a). A third gender may include body modification and/or cross-dressing. It may involve taking on the role of the 'opposite' gender completely or being a hybrid of both. A third gender may also be a completely different role, involving behaviours expected of neither men nor women in a culture.

The 'third gender' designation is used almost interchangeably with the idea of a 'third sex', and there is little consistency in the application of each term as it distinguishes between gender variance on the one hand and embodied variance on the other. 'Third sex' has been used to describe an identity defined by atypical or 'opposite' gender traits, even when no bodily difference from a typical sexed morphology is visible. In Europe, during the nineteenth century, Karl Heinrich Ulrichs coined the term 'third sex' to refer to people who harboured a female soul in a male body and desired other men (Van der Meer 1994), while the term 'third gender' has been applied in situations where physical differences such as sterility or castration determine entry into the 'alternative' category. In the Byzantine Empire people who were born, or became, sterile could serve a distinct social and political role at court. Some men were castrated specifically in order to qualify for this role (Ringrose 1994). The *hijras* of India, similarly, serve a particular religious and ceremonial role and are defined by their inability to procreate, but the category is also open to men who do not desire women or who feel feminine (Nanda 1994). Thus a strict distinction between sex and gender does not necessarily exist in 'third gender' categories.

Third genders do not operate as universal categories encompassing every unusual body or gender behaviour. The roles are highly circumscribed and are often associated with a specific social or religious function, as the examples of the *hijras* and the Byzantine eunuchs show. A third gender category may be available only to male or female persons, or to both. There may be more than one alternate gender category in a given context, as in Native American cultures, where the *berdache* or 'two-spirit' person was sometimes a shaman, but in other cases merely a person who lived as the opposite sex with no necessary religious role (Roscoe 1994). In Reche society, in southern Chile during the seventeenth century, at least three alternate gender categories were available, depending on age and status, and varying in permanence as well as social and religious function (Bacigalupo 2004). A third gender category may deal with a specific intersexual condition, as in the case of the Sambia of Papua New Guinea, where the condition called 5-alpha reductase deficiency occurs with some frequency. Men with this condition are often mistaken for female and raised as girls until the physical changes of puberty make the mistake apparent. They are excluded from some male initiation rituals and sometimes continue to live as women. (Herdt 1994b).

A third gender identity may or may not persist throughout an individual's lifetime. Among the Gaddhi, who live in the foothills of the Himalayas, there is the *sadhin*, a category for women who commit to living a celibate life, and who dress and work as men, but retain female names and some female roles. If they give up their *sadhin* position by having sex with a man, they are cast out of their community (Penrose 2001). In the Polynesian islands, on the other hand, the intermediate or third gender categories of the Tahitian *mahu*, the Samoan *fa'afafine* and the Tongan *fakaleiti* do not involve permanent cross-dressing or require a life-long identification. In some cultures, categories that can be considered third genders constitute a typical life stage for all men or all women. In ancient Athenian society, older men of status could penetrate boys, women, slaves and foreigners, and in seventeenth-century Japan men and boys were differentiated through dress and hairstyles, with older men taking the youths as sexual partners. Some Japanese men did, however, choose to retain the 'boy' role into adulthood (Rupp 2001). It is debatable whether these two instances provide examples of a third gender or of a two-gender system based on age or status, rather than biological sex. Towle and Morgan caution against assuming that the third gender is an unproblematic correlative of Western identity categories such as transgender or transsexual.

References and further reading

Bacigalupo, A.M. (2004) 'The struggle for Mapuche shamans' masculinity', *Ethnohistory*, 51 (3): 489–533.

Herdt, G. (1994a) 'Introduction', in G. Herdt (ed.) *Third Sex, Third Gender*, New York: Zone, pp. 21–81.

—— (1994b) 'Mistaken sex', in G. Herdt (ed.) *Third Sex, Third Gender*, New York: Zone, pp. 419–46.

Nanda, S. (1994) 'Hijras', in G. Herdt (ed.) *Third Sex, Third Gender*, New York: Zone, pp. 373–418.

Penrose, W. (2001) 'Hidden in history', *Journal of the History of Sexuality*, 10 (1): 3–39.

Ringrose, K.M. (1994) 'Living in the shadows', in G. Herdt (ed.) *Third Sex, Third Gender*, New York: Zone, pp. 85–110.

Roscoe, W. (1994) 'How to become a berdache', in G. Herdt (ed.) *Third Sex, Third Gender*, New York: Zone, pp. 329–72.

Rupp, L.J. (2001) 'Toward a global history of same-sex sexuality', *Journal of the History of Sexuality*, 10 (2): 287–302.

Towle, E.B. and Morgan, L.M. (2002) 'Romancing the transgender native', *GLQ*, 8 (4): 469–97.

Van der Meer, T. (1994) 'Sodomy and the pursuit of a third sex in the early modern period', in G. Herdt (ed.) *Third Sex, Third Gender*, New York: Zone, pp. 137–212.

SUSANNAH BREDENKAMP

HYPERMASCULINITY

Hypermasculinity is an exaggerated expression of traits, beliefs, actions and embodiment considered to be masculine. Central to hypermasculinity is an understanding of normative or ideal masculinity. Traditional conceptions of masculinity including independence, instrumentality, aggressiveness, decisiveness and physical strength (David and Brannon 1976) have been measured at times, as well as theorised as normal (Parsons 1956). Enactments of masculinity in which these traits, most especially aggression and physical strength, are accentuated, can be seen as hypermasculine.

Still, given the work of scholars in the 1980s and 1990s (Connell 1995; Kimmel 1996), few continue to argue in support of a single masculinity but rather recognise multiple masculinities. In fact, these scholars have shown that masculinity and masculinities are relational, not absolute. In other words, being masculine is more often an expression of not being feminine.

Hypermasculinity is an attempt actively to demonstrate masculinity in opposition to femininity. Common expressions include focusing on the male body, style of dress, conversation and actions. Unfortunately, hypermasculinity has become linked to sexism, homophobia, and self-destructive behaviours

(Kaufman 1987). Since aggression is often considered a masculine trait, hypermasculinity has been connected to violence, gang activity, domestic violence and attacks on gays. In that others have associated sexual prowess with masculinity (MacKinnon 1996), hypermasculinity has also been tied to both promiscuity and sexual abuse. While some see hypermasculinity as pathological or at least deviant, sociologists of gender argue that so long as being masculine is understood primarily as demonstrating that one is not feminine, hypermasculinity will often involve exaggerated, dangerous and destructive behaviours.

References and further reading

Connell, R. (1995) *Masculinities*, Berkeley, CA: University of California Press.

David, D.S. and Brannon, R. (1976) *The Forty-Nine Percent Majority*, Reading, MA: Addison-Wesley.

Kaufman, M. (1987) 'The construction of masculinity and the triad of men's violence', in M. Kaufman (ed.) *Beyond Patriarchy*, Toronto: Oxford University Press.

Kimmel, M. (1996) *Manhood in America*, New York: Free Press.

MacKinnon, C. (1996) *Only Words*, Cambridge, MA: Harvard University Press.

Parsons, T. (1956) *Family Socialization and Interaction Process*, London: Routledge.

DONALD P. LEVY

I

IDENTITY

Many men profess and practise an essentialist understanding of self. Man is who he is; masculine is what he is. Such certainty of identity ensures that established frameworks of knowledge – and the normalised practices that result – remain unchallenged. Men are permitted to maintain their position of dominance in society because their masculine identities and corresponding behaviours are deemed natural.

Simone de Beauvoir's assertion that 'One is not born, but rather becomes, woman' has not remained exclusively a critique of the female identity and female behaviour. This attack on the essentialism of 'woman' has been turned against the identity of man. Where the masculine identity relies on an absolute heterosexuality, queer theory exposes the proximity of this masculine ideal to homosociability and homosexual desire. Similarly, in response to power imbalances produced and sustained by a naturalised masculine identity, feminist theory introduces an equally powerful female identity while also engaging in attacks against established masculinised systems of knowledges that allow hegemonic identities to exist and remain.

In the poststructuralist critique, identification with the masculine is not a birthright, but a learned and performed habit. The notion of a natural masculine identity has been exposed for failing to recognise the privileged status of its white, heterosexual self. The naturalness of the masculine identity is secured only through silencing and punishing those bodies that exist outside the hegemonic imaginary of what the culture deems it means to be a man.

While traditionally women and femininity have been the major focus of investigations within 'women's studies', the recent move towards 'gender studies' accounts for, accommodates and encourages an increasing interest in deconstructing the naturalised masculine identity. Moreover, the identity of man is no longer assumed as the base from which all investigations into gender must proceed. Indeed, as Judith Halberstam asserts, the masculine identity is not the domain simply of those bodies born as male. It is a social and corporeal component of all kinds of bodies in the culture.

In the everyday practices of gender, men are learning to take on board new identifications with the masculine as they are influenced by the changing status of women, queer cultures and consumerism.

References and further reading

Badinter, E. (1995) *XY: On Masculine Identity*, New York: Columbia University Press.

de Beauvoir, S. (1949) *The Second Sex*, New York: Vintage Books.

Halberstam, J. (1998) *Female Masculinities*, Durham, NC: Duke University Press.

DEAN DURBER

IMPOTENCE AND SEXUAL DYSFUNCTION

Impotence is a type of sexual dysfunction that is associated with problems maintaining an erection, ejaculating or reaching orgasm. The term traditionally implies that a man is unable to achieve an erect penis. Impotence also connotes that a man who does not have an erect penis is considered weak or feeble. The term 'impotence' has been largely replaced with 'erectile dysfunction' or 'sexual dysfunction' when referring to a person's physical body. 'Impotence' remains, however, a loaded word in terms of defining men and masculinity; it refers to a man who lacks political power and, by inference, also lacks sexual power.

'Sexual dysfunction' is a broad term that encompasses problems relating to a person's sexual performance. It describes the various ways in which a person is not able to experience and perform desire – in a man's case, through erection, ejaculation and orgasm. As such, sexual dysfunction connotes a medical condition, defined as the inability to achieve an erection that is adequate for satisfactory sexual performance. This broader medical descriptor moves impotence under the medical heading of sexual dysfunction. Importantly, this linguistic turn shifts responsibility for a flaccid penis away from the man and places fault with the organ – now called the 'dysfunctional' organ. Nevertheless, sexual dysfunction may be evidence of a man's emotional well-being, his physical health, his relationships with a partner, or even with the culture at large (Bordo 1999).

Sexual dysfunction, also called erectile dysfunction, is often the result of illness or aging. Sexual dysfunction may be caused by a number of physiological and psychological conditions. Physiological antecedents include diabetes, depression, prostate cancer, spinal cord injury, multiple sclerosis, artherosclerosis and heart disease. Injuries to the penis that cause nerve, tissue or vascular damage can also trigger sexual dysfunction. It is also a common side effect of some prescription medications, including antihistamines, antidepressants, antihypertensives, antipsychotics, beta blockers, diuretics and tranquillisers. Psychological antecedents include sexual performance anxiety, stress and relationship difficulties.

Since its publication, Masters and Johnson's *Human Sexual Inadequacy* (1970) has served as the prototype for research done in the area. This work was influential in moving the discourse of sexual relations from relationships to sexual physiology. The categories of sexual dysfunction defined by Masters and Johnson were subsequently included in the *Diagnostic and Statistical Manual of Mental Disorders* (DSM-III-R; APA 1987) and are now considered 'mental disorders' that can be measured and treated. In the context of the DSM, sexual dysfunction is defined exclusively in terms of heterosexual sex – the inability to reach orgasm in a vagina (APA 1987) – and thus also represents a major area of critique for its heterosexist assumptions.

At one time, psychotherapy and sex therapy were considered the only ways in which men could treat sexual dysfunction. However, the use of physiological and psychological measures, such as the International Index of Erectile Function (IIEF; Rosen 1997), shifted the way in which sexual dysfunction was assessed and treated. Brief assessments, like the IIEF, ushered in a new model of sexual health for men that emphasised medical treatment of sexual dysfunction over psychological interventions. These have mainly included pharmaceutical options, including phentolamine which causes blood vessels to expand, thereby increasing blood flow, which results in an erection, and sildenafil citrate (sold under various brand names, such as Viagra and Cialis), a vasodilator that dilates the blood vessels. These medications work through improving blood circulation to the penis, which relaxes the smooth muscle of the penis and regulates blood vessels during sexual stimulation, allowing the penis to become engorged, leading to an erection.

The present-day implications of this medical model are that sexual dysfunction is now treated solely as a problem concerning the lack of adequate blood flow to the penis. Critics argue (Tiefer 2004) that physicians' use of diagnostic tools regarding sexual dysfunction reduces a man's sexual health to whether or not he has a functioning penis and that other layers of his health – both physical and psychological – are overlooked in order to treat the 'dysfunctional' organ. This perspective states that without attention to the relationship in which the sex occurs, medications may produce erections, but a discussion of pleasure for either partner remains silent and therefore remains untreated.

No doubt, developments in the late twentieth century concerning the diagnosis and treatment of sexual dysfunction have allowed more men to speak more openly about health issues that affect their sexuality, thereby combating stigma. However, all of the talk about the male anatomy, not to mention 'four-hour erections', has created a host of new expectations and normativising pressures on erect men and their partners. First, the 'Viagra phenomenon' often assumes a model of sexuality in which intercourse is the only method of appropriate sexual activity. Second, the resultant definition of sexual dysfunction emphasises functionality irrespective of pleasure. It is essential to keep sexual desire as a component of how functioning is imagined, discussed and sought. If sexual desire is the sum of the forces that lean us towards and away from sexual behaviour, then it is essential for sexual function to be defined in terms of this sum of desires, not merely the desire to adequately penetrate another person.

References and further reading

American Psychiatric Association (APA) (1987) *Diagnostic and Statistical Manual of Mental Disorders*, 3rd revised edn, Washington, DC: APA.
Bordo, S. (1999) *The Male Body*, New York: Farrar, Straus and Giroux.
Irvine, J.M. (1990) *Disorders of Desire*, Philadelphia, PA: Temple University Press.
Mamo, L. and Fishman, J. (2001) 'Potency in all the right places', *Body and Society*, 7 (4): 13–35.
Masters, W.H. and Johnson, V.E. (1970) *Human Sexual Inadequacy*, Boston, MA: Little, Brown.
Rosen, R.C. (1997) The international index of erectile function (IIEF)', *Urology*, 49 (6): 822–30.
Tiefer, L. [1995] (2004) *Sex is Not a Natural Act*, Boulder, CO: Westview.

See also: male sex drive; penetration; penis; sex; sexuality; Viagra; virility

SARA I. MCCLELLAND
JONATHAN M. METZEL

INDIAN MASCULINITIES

'Indian masculinities' are the concomitant of the varied histories of the pre-colonial, colonial and post-colonial eras, and caste and religious identities. A key theme during colonialism concerns the 'masculinisation' of European identity, and the 'feminisation' of its native counterpart. However, while some natives were feminised, others – such as Sikhs and Gurkhas – were declared to be 'martial races' (Omissi 1991). This concept was particularly deployed in the aftermath of the 1857 mutiny in light of the subsequent reorganisation of the Indian army. Concurrently, there emerged the figure of the effeminate Indian, of whom the educated Bengali (Sinha 1995) was only the best known of a number of such stereotypes. However, this does not imply that the British simply 'invented' certain types of masculine cultures and imposed them upon Indian culture. 'Martial masculinity' (O'Hanlon 1997) was also an important aspect of *pre-colonial* life, one which the colonisers built upon and incorporated into the discourses of colonial masculinity.

The colonial period also witnessed a stigmatisation of non-heterosexual masculinity. Section 377 of the Indian Penal Code, prohibiting 'unnatural sex', was enacted in 1861 and continues to be law in contemporary India. The relative lack of censure regarding (male) homosexual relationships that characterised the pre-colonial period eventually gave way to the *public* and legal heteronormativity that later came to pass. Hence, groups such as *Hijras* became both legally and socially stigmatised. Colonialism did not, however, completely overwrite those indigenous contexts where gender identities continued to be ambiguously inflected. The example of a number of celebrated transvestite performers of the Parsi, Gujarati and Marathi theatres during the late nineteenth and early twentieth centuries is a case in point (Hansen 2004).

Ironically, perhaps the most salient context within which the colonial discourse on masculinity became codified was that of nationalism, with Mahatma Gandhi being the exception in as much as he questioned the dominant discourses on masculinity. Many among nineteenth-century Indian (Hindu) intelligentsia came to believe that in addition to colonial rule, 'emasculation' was also attributable to Muslim rule. As well, in the wake of several anti-Brahmanical movements during the early twentieth century, the 'barbarity' of lower-caste masculinity became an explicitly articulated position. The Hindu–Muslin angle finds play in the contemporary politics of 'Hindutva' (or Hindu-ness), where a 'depleted' Hindu masculinity is seen to confront an aggressive Muslim one which, in turn, must be countered.

One response to the colonial characterisation of Indian effeminacy was the attempt to become more 'scientific', as well as seek evidence for 'scientific rationality' in the 'ancient' Indian past. So, while on the one hand religious ideologues scoured religious texts for signs of manliness and 'rationality' in ancient texts, on the other, secular nationalist educational institutions aimed at producing an 'epistemological masculinity' (Srivastava 1998) based on modern science. There were also concurrent efforts at instituting new regimes of physical education through which the Indian male body was sought to be restored to its lost masculinity. Some of these built upon existing indigenous traditions such as wrestling (Alter 1992), while others looked to prevalent European ideas on the male body. Within the former context, a recurring theme is that of 'semen anxiety', where semen 'wastage' and the loss of masculine vigour are seen to be linked.

An important adjunct to the consolidation of ideas of colonial masculinity and modernity among the Indian intelligentsia was, unsurprisingly, the concurrent worsening of women's position in society. Hence, feminist scholars have argued that the imposition of English law upon an indigenous system, though it was commonly seen as a sign of 'progress', may, in fact, have worsened the situation for women who enjoyed certain rights and freedoms under customary law.

One of the most striking ways in which the valorisation of masculinity is expressed in the contemporary period is through the persistence of preferences for male children, as manifested in the worsening male–female ratios across a number of states in India. The social privileging of masculinity also finds play in the pervasiveness of the linkage between men's 'honour' and women's propriety. This expresses the idea that the integrity of masculine identity is dependent not merely on male behaviour but also on that of women. Hence, in India a great deal of violence towards women occurs in those contexts where women are seen to have violated the norms of female behaviour, which in turn has consequences for male honour. In many instances, the control of female sexuality is explicitly at issue.

With respect to contemporary non-heterosexual practice, gay masculine identities seem largely to be confined to urban middle-class contexts. Hence, many men who may take part in homosexual acts continue to view their identity as a heterosexual male one.

In twentieth-century filmic culture, 'Indian masculinity' has been represented through the nation-building hero, the 'sensitive' creative genius and the working-class antihero who loses faith in justness of the law. With the economic liberalisation of the Indian economy, and the greater incursion of globalisation into Indian society, consumption practices and transnational flows have emerged as major influences on masculine identity. So, for example, both the cultures of muscularity and cosmetics have, at least in urban India, found an often overlapping male audience. The conjoining of muscularity and masculinity, in particular, is something that appears to be a by-product of transnational cultural flows and the major impact of the latter appears to be in terms of body image.

References and further reading

Alter, J. (1992) *The Wrestler's Body*, Chicago, IL: University of Chicago Press

Hansen, K. (2004) 'Theatrical transvestism in the Parsi, Gujarati and Marathi theatres (1850–1940)', in S. Srivastava (ed.) *Sexual Sites, Seminal Attitudes. Sexualities, Masculinities and Culture in South Asia*, New Delhi: Sage, pp. 99–122.

O'Hanlon, R. (1997) 'Issues of masculinity in North Indian history: the Bangash Nawabs of Farrukhabad', *Indian Journal of Gender Studies*, 4 (1): 1–19.

Omissi, D. (1991) '"Martial races": ethnicity and security in colonial India 1858–1939', *War and Society*, 9 (1): 1–27.

Sinha, M. (1995) *The 'Manly Englishman' and the 'Effeminate Bengali' in the Late Nineteenth Century*, Manchester: Manchester University Press.

Srivastava, S. (1998) *Constructing Postcolonial India. National Character and the Doon School*, London: Routledge.

See also: cultural formations, Asia and Pacific; South Asian masculinities; history, South Asia

SANJAY SRIVASTAVA

INDIGENOUS AND FIRST NATIONS MASCULINITIES

Multiple Indigenous tribal definitions of masculinity remain within Indigenous communities and cultures throughout the world. While such definitions are pluralistic and it is largely impossible to generically define Indigenous and First Nations masculinity, a connection to a particular land area as a cultural and spiritual space, and as a cultural determinant typically informs how Indigenous and First Nations men defined themselves in the past and how some continue to define themselves in the present. Colonisation, however, ripped asunder tribal life and worldviews, meaning that most Indigenous and First Nations men have come to define themselves or rather have come to be defined through an allegorical relationship with the white man. Indeed, the very notion of Indigenous and First Nations masculinity cuts across tribal definitions, yet has political uses for Indigenous and First Nations communities within a neo-colonial political context.

Indigenous and First Nations men are tied to a commonsense discourse that links them to a savage physiology and biological approach to gender, which suggests men's persona and behaviour are natural outcomes of their physiological make-up (hooks 2004). The compounding of commonsense gender and racial stereotypes produces a strongly coded masculinity that serves to represent and confine Indigenous men as the 'Other'. Moreover, the socially constructed behaviours that align with these narratives are highlighted by the dominant discourse to provide examples of 'truthful' representations.

Early colonial representations

The representation of Indigenous and First Nations masculinity was needed to contrast emerging notions of Western masculinity. That is, descriptions of European men were constantly reinforced by counter-images of the masculine Other. Racist representations of Indigenous men emerged because of a mentality that denoted the Western man as normal and the Indigenous and First Nations man as abnormal. When defining Indigenous men as barbaric, inferior and/or childlike, European men were implicitly defining themselves as civilised, superior and advanced (Smith 1999).

The eighteenth-century notion of the primitive Other was based upon the idea of the 'Great Chain of Being', the belief that God had created all living things and organised them into a hierarchy of existence with white men at the top. As the nineteenth century approached, evolutionary theories supported the fragmentation of the universal human body into a hierarchy of racialised bodies. Western science validated arbitrary differences between the body of the European and that of the Other by providing objective evidence that races were real and based on inherent and unalterable biological and natural differences (Miles 1989). Depictions of amoral savages gave Europeans moral authority to free first peoples from their heathen state, culture, language and, most importantly, lands and resources. For instance, Locke's notion of *terra nullius* suggested that if land was not under 'human' control (i.e. not cultivated or employed for profit) then it was 'empty' or uninhabited land and, therefore, free to be usurped. The Indigenous Other resided within an unconscious body, and thus did not have the same rights as conscious citizens.

In relation to masculinity, early colonial accounts of the exotic masculine Other provided an increasingly literate European public with an image of Indigenous masculinity in a primitive state. Early representations portrayed Indigenous and First Nations men as lacking the qualities of civilised European men, who were the epitome of manliness; they were protectors, stoic of character and in control of their passions (Bederman 1995). Aboriginal men, on the other hand, were physical, whimsical, unsophisticated, childlike and ruled by passion and, therefore, in need of civilised enlightenment (Hokowhitu 2003). Racism in the colonies did not develop because of simple ignorance of or hatred for an alien culture. Rather, it emerged because colonisation was justified through discourses of race and the coloniser's right to rule. The white man had a humanistic 'burden' to conquer the world, civilise it and then provide enlightened leadership into the twentieth century; only he possessed the mental fortitude to tackle such a task. He was individually free to assert his own will, virtuous, secular, liberated in thought and autonomous. Conversely, the savage Indigenous man was immoral and sinful (Bederman 1995; Hokowhitu 2004a). It must also be recognised that some commentators, such as Jean-Jacques Rousseau, believed savage men to be noble possessors of innocent moral superiority because they lived closer to nature and uncorrupted by civilisation. Hence, they were at times romanticised as part of the natural physical world. Regardless, early depictions of Indigenous and First Nations men served to limit their access to the privileges enjoyed by their colonial brethren, and became iconic representations that invariably led to colonial stereotypes.

While there are numerous representations of Indigenous and First Nations men that one can see daily, the dominant discourse accents but a few of these representations in the creation of a regime of truth (Bhabha 1994). The formation of such stereotypes was necessary in the colonial context because if Indigenous and First Nations men were afforded self-determination and self-definition, then there would be no justification for colonial rule: 'The object of colonial discourse is to construe the colonised as a population of degenerate types on the basis of racial origin, in order to justify conquest and to establish systems of administration and instruction' (Bhabha 1994: 70).

Colonial education

Early settlers portrayed education as an evangelical duty to advance Indigenous and First Nations people away from their heathen culture and into modern civilisation. Settlers and embryonic colonial governments hoped by educating native peoples that they would avoid what would ultimately occur if all else failed – extermination. Similarly guided by righteous intent, missionary schools replaced first peoples' cultural institutions with 'civilised' European faculties. Assimilationist policies encouraged first peoples to adopt European customary, moral and commercial practices as preparation for receiving Christianity (Simon 1998).

Colonial education was also viewed as a way of creating a cultural rupture between one generation of Aboriginal people and the next. Successful colonisation required Indigenous students to be assimilated through an educational system that encouraged the acceptance of European values while undermining the validity of Indigenous knowledges and fragmenting communities. In Canadian Indian residential schools, for example, for over a century First Nations children were taken from their parents and placed into environments where physical and sexual violence and other atrocities were common (Haig-Brown 1988). Similarly, in Australia the 'stolen generations' of children resulted from 'half- or semi-caste' children being forcibly removed from their families and communities by state officials (Bird 1998). The colonial education of Indigenous and First Nations people also meant confinement to the lower classes. Often the education supplied to first peoples was based on curricula that channelled them into non-academic areas and away from access to academic qualifications (and subsequent white-collar employment). Later, the failure of Indigenous and First Nations people to gain academic qualifications was blamed on parents and the environment of the traditional home (Hokowhitu 2004b).

The violent cultural disruption caused by colonial education, combined with colonisation's devastating effect on the ability of Indigenous and First Nations men to access colonised forms of masculinity, in terms of colonial employment and power, and even basic human rights, has had profound effects on the self-determination and social consciousness of Indigenous men. Social problems such as domestic violence, sexual abuse, suicide, drug and alcohol addiction, health problems, poverty, unemployment and illiteracy are common among many Indigenous and First Nations communities. The alienation of Indigenous and First Nations men from their culture, while also limiting the right to be self-determining in the wider colonial societies, led many Indigenous men to assert themselves dysfunctionally. A recourse to violence and abuse against themselves and others has been one way in which some Indigenous and First Nations men have confronted their powerlessness.

Traditional Indigenous masculinity

For most Indigenous and First Nations communities, colonisation decimated the very fabric of tribal life and the threads of culture that held their communities together. Indeed, many Indigenous cultures and peoples came perilously close to extinction following colonisation. Indigenous and First Nations men were forced to assert themselves within the developing colonial states, even when those masculine qualities they assumed aligned more with the culture of the coloniser than with their own. The consumption of Western masculinity by Indigenous men served to assimilate them into the patriarchal and hypermasculine world of the coloniser. Yet this assimilation did not include indoctrination into the full gamut of colonial masculinities. The Indigenous and First Nations male, like various Othered groups, had only conditional access to the white man's world.

An effective colonial policy to create a cultural divide between one generation and the next involved the creation of an elite group of Indigenous men who embraced and then advocated among their communities for the Western way of life. To this end, a select few Indigenous boys were educated within elite European-style colonial institutions. Such an education promoted European forms of self-determination but also loyalty and obedience: that is, the self-assurance to lead united with the impulse to follow (Mangan 1986). Many of the Indigenous gentlemen who came out of such instructional institutions formed a colonised Indigenous masculine elite who held merely approximated power. They became leaders in their communities, strong, competent and eloquent, yet they also acted as conduits for the indoctrination of colonial culture. For their communities, they became symbols for the path to survival within a chaotic postcolonial world. These elitist forms of colonised Indigenous masculinity remain deeply imbedded within what has, ironically, now come to be thought of as 'traditional' Indigenous masculinity. In reality, these forms of elitist masculinity are not traditional – rather, they mimic the dominant forms of colonial masculinity (Hokowhitu 2003). Coupled with the above generic policy was an imperial tactic to present the colonised man as traditional and fixed and, thus, as unable to evolve totally to be a modern European man. The notion of traditional Indigenous masculinity is bound to the idea that the cultures of first peoples were and are stagnant. Supposedly, pre-European Indigenous societies were culturally inferior, torpid, and had failed to evolve into a civilised state.

Such stagnation is evident in the contemporary representation of traditional Indigenous masculinities as patriarchal and hypermasculine. While some Western masculinities have, in the last three to four decades, moved away from such patriarchal constrictions, the construction of Indigenous masculinity as both traditional and patriarchal serves to fix Indigenous men into hypermasculine roles. Indeed, the depiction of Other cultures as hegemonically male is a common contemporary signifier that the culture is unevolved or, at least, that it has not reached the civilised echelons of Western culture. Ironically, androgyny used to be the marker of uncivilised cultures. Until the second half of the twentieth century, Western masculinity and femininity were commonly referred to as stable, biologically dichotomous categories (Beynon 2002). The androgynous savage provided the civilised self with examples of the exotic and outlandish Other, where women performed masculine duties and men had womanlike qualities. Currently, while some Western masculinities are increasingly enjoying an androgynous fluidity, the ability of Indigenous and First Nations men to transform their identity is limited by notions of tradition and patriarchy. The Indigenous man, as Other, struggles to reside in the world of the 'new age man' because he embodies the antithesis of the new man; he is economically, culturally and physiologically tied to the patriarchal masculine prototype. These traits may reproduce masculine power over women and children at the micro-level (i.e. in terms of base physical power) but ultimately they limit Indigenous men to hypermasculine roles.

Indigenous and First Nations men need to be self-determining by constructing hybridised versions of global/indigenous masculinity that will benefit themselves and their communities within both their local contexts and the broader socio-cultural milieu. To enable this, Indigenous and First Nations men must break away from notions of colonial tradition that serve to fix them within unalterable states. History indicates, however, that Indigenous and First Nations men have struggled to throw off the shackles of the Other, and will continue to face a number of difficulties and barriers within the neo-colonial context. First, Indigenous men are located within a discursive genealogical representation that ties them to their physical, violent and savage past. Second, the continuous emergence and construction of dominant white masculinities requires the counter-image and stagnation of Indigenous and other minority masculinities. Third, the confinement of the majority of Indigenous and First Nations men to the working and lower classes, and often to poverty, limits their ability to be self-determining.

References and further reading

Bederman, G. (1995) *Manliness and Civilization. A Cultural History of Gender and Race in the United States, 1880–1917*, Chicago, IL: University of Chicago Press.

Beynon, J. (2002) *Masculinities and Culture*, Buckingham: Open University Press.

Bhabha, H.K. (1994) *The Location of Culture*, New York: Routledge.

Bird, C. (1998) *The Stolen Children: Their Stories*, Sydney: Random House.
Haig-Brown, C. (1988) *Resistance and Renewal: Surviving the Indian Residential School*, Vancouver: Tillacum Library, Arsenal Pulp Press.
Hokowhitu, B. (2003) 'Mäori masculinity, post-structuralism, and the emerging Self', *New Zealand Sociology*, 18 (2): 179–201.
—— (2004a) 'Tackling Mäori masculinity: a colonial genealogy of savagery and sport', *The Contemporary Pacific*, 16 (2): 259–84.
—— (2004b) 'Te Täminga o te mätauranga Mäori: colonisation in education', in T. Ka'ai, J. Moorfield, M. Reilly and S. Mosley (eds) *Ki te Whaiao: An Introduction to Mäori Culture and Society*, Auckland: Pearson, pp. 190–200.
hooks, b. (2004) *We Real Cool: Black Men and Masculinity*, New York: Routledge.
Mangan, J. (1986) *The Games Ethic and Imperialism: Aspects of the Diffusion of an Ideal*, Harmondsworth: Viking.
Miles, R. (1989) *Racism*, London: Routledge.
Simon, J. (1998) *Ngä Kura Mäori: The Native Schools System 1867–1969*, Auckland: Auckland University Press.
Smith, L. (1999) *Decolonizing Methodologies: Research and Indigenous Peoples*, Dunedin: University of Otago Press.

See also: colonial and imperial masculinities; critical race studies; diasporic and migrant masculinities; ethnography; history, colonisation; marginalised masculinity; postcolonial masculinities; race and ethnicity; racism; white men; working with marginalised and minority men

BRENDAN HOKOWHITU

INFERTILITY

Infertility, or the inability to conceive after a year or more of trying, affects approximately 8 to 14 per cent of all couples worldwide. Male infertility, involving primarily low sperm count, poor sperm motility, defects of sperm morphology and total absence of sperm in the ejaculate, contributes to more than half of these cases, with its etiology largely unknown (Irvine 1998).

Male infertility is a health and social problem that remains deeply hidden, including in the West. Studies have shown male infertility to be among the most stigmatising of all male health conditions (Becker 2000), perhaps because male infertility is mistakenly conflated with impotency and the inability to prove one's virility, paternity and manhood (Inhorn 2004; Webb and Daniluk 1999).

For example, emerging social science research from the Middle East suggests that male infertility is an emasculating condition, with infertile men's secretive behaviour reflecting a high degree of social stigmatisation (Inhorn 2003). Furthermore, the actual or suspected use of donor sperm, which is prohibited in the Muslim world, may create suspicions about paternity.

However, a new reproductive technology called intracytoplasmic sperm injection (ICSI) is helping to bring this still hidden condition from behind its veil of secrecy. Developed in Belgium in 1992, ICSI has allowed thousands of severely infertile men to father children with their own gametes, through direct injection of 'weak' spermatozoa into ova (thereby forcing fertilisation to occur). A variant of in vitro fertilisation, ICSI is still expensive and unsuccessful in many cases. Nonetheless, ICSI is clearly a new 'hope technology' for infertile men, whose condition is usually untreatable by any other means.

References and further reading

Becker, G. (2000) *The Elusive Embryo*, Berkeley, CA: University of California Press.
Inhorn, M.C. (2003) *Local Babies, Global Science*, New York: Routledge.
—— (2004) 'Middle Eastern masculinities in the age of new reproductive technologies', *Medical Anthropology Quarterly*, 18 (2): 162–82.
Irvine, D.S. (1998) 'Epidemiology and aetiology of male infertility', *Human Reproduction*, 13 (suppl. 1): 33–44.
Webb, R.E. and Daniluk, J.C. (1999) 'The end of the line', *Men and Masculinities*, 2: 6–25.

See also: contraception, male; reproductive issues and technologies

MARCIA C. INHORN

INFIDELITY

Infidelity is stereotypically regarded as a nearly universal attribute of masculine identity. Infidelity has been a part of human culture, arts, mores, and morality since the beginning of sociality, and it is difficult to find a sustained cultural text where love is not paired with infidelity or its specter. Even in polyamorous communities, notions of infidelity exist. Most often referring to a breach of a sexual or emotional commitment in an ostensibly monogamous relationship, infidelity is subject to many meanings: extramarital sex, extramarital emotional attachment, or even dating or flirtation outside the sanctioned couple. An inclusive definition treats infidelity as a breach of a trust based on expectations rather than an explicit promise (Abrahms Spring and Spring 1997). In contrast, most sociological and psychological research on infidelity focuses on extramarital sex, which is also called adultery.

With regard to the association of masculinity with infidelity, we encounter a range of cultural and social contingencies, including those based on race and ethnicity (Bassett 2005). A partner's infidelity in some cultures affronts a man's masculine identity (Wiederman and Kendall 1999), while committing adultery may affirm masculinity.

The prevalence of cultural stereotypes does not necessarily correspond to real behaviors: the rate of reported extramarital sex in the United States, for example, has changed markedly over time. As the first major statistical study, Kinsey's research on rates of reported extramarital sex suggested half of the American male population (Kinsey 1948) and one in five American women (Kinsey 1953) engaged in sexual infidelities in their lifetimes. Moreover, Kinsey's work suggests the rate of reported extramarital sex remains relatively stable with age. Subsequent research emphasizes factors other than gender in predicting extramarital sex, such as residing in urban or rural community (Weis and Jurich 1985), or the high correlation between infidelity and divorce or separation. Limitation of such studies include disregard of the unmarried population and data collection methods that do not offer anonymity or have non-representative population samples.

Research from the 1990s and 2000s points to age and class as predictors of infidelity independent of culture (Wiederman 1997). Wiederman's work accounts for ethnicity, gender, and age as independent variables and points to several elements apart from gender playing a role in infidelity. These include (1) no significant difference in rates of reported extramarital sex for men and women under forty years of age, (2) a lifetime increase in the rate of reported extramarital sex for men as opposed to a peak for women between 40–60 years of age, and (3) close alignment for both men and women between beliefs about infidelity and the propensity for it. Furthermore, Wiederman found a comparable ratio to Kinsey for men compared to women engaging in extramarital sex, although smaller percentages for both: 22 percent of men and 11 percent of women. Age and gender play a greater role than ethnicity, as is further evidenced by international comparisons.

These changes from Kinsey to Wiederman point to shifting social mores, although Wiederman emphasizes several environmental factors that could skew such interpretations: the gender imbalance in a population as age increases, the scarcity of female reports of extramarital sex from the eldest reporting group, and the greater opportunities for male extramarital sex among some populations based on ethnicity and cultural contexts. These relate to the cross-cultural relationship between infidelity and opportunity, rather than gender. Supporting Wiederman's position are studies of infidelity in other cultural contexts, which generally show factors such as wealth and place of residence playing an important role, although rates of reported extramarital sex vary widely, such as 19 percent reporting extramarital sex in the past year in Zambia but only 4 percent in the United States (Kimuna and Djamba 2005;

Wiederman 1997). Such comparisons, however, are not sufficiently controlled to account for opportunity and cultural variables, the former appearing to be the most significant. No systematic cross-cultural comparisons are yet complete on rates of extramarital sex, although Wiederman (1997) does account for ethnicity, pointing out that environmental factors likely account for small variations. However, studies of the relationship between sexual jealousy and infidelity point to evolutionary commonalities for which cultural variations in notions of masculinity between the USA, Japan, Korea, and Sweden cannot fully account (Bennett 1999; Wiederman and Kendall 1999).

Given the lack of significant statistical difference between men and women in reporting extramarital sex for those under the age of forty (Wiederman 1995), it is important to note that infidelity during dating, in the form of dating or kissing others, likewise shows no significant distinction between men and women, although men still report extradyadic sex at a higher rate than women (Wiederman and Hurd 1999). These factors all trouble a reductive understanding of infidelity based primarily on masculinity.

References and further reading

Abrahms Spring, J. and Spring, M. (1997) *After the Affair*, New York: HarperCollins.

Bassett, J.F. (19) 'Sex Differences in Jealousy in Response to a Partner's Imagined Sexual or Emotional Infidelity with a Same or Different Race Other', *North American Journal of Psychology*, 7 (1), pp. 71–84.

Bennett, K. *et al.* (1999) 'Jealousy and the Nature of Beliefs About Infidelity', *Personal Relationships*, 6 (1), pp. 125–50.

Kinsey, A.C. [1948](1998) *Sexual Behavior in the Human Male*, Bloomington, IN: Indiana UP.

—— [1953](1998) *Sexual Behavior in the Human Female* Bloomington, IN: Indiana UP.

Kimuna, S. and Djamba, Y. (2005) 'Wealth and Extramarital Sex Among Men in Zambia', *International Family Planning Perspectives*, 31 (2), pp. 83–89.

Weis, D.L. and Jurich, J. (1985) 'Size of Community of Residence as a Predictor of Attitudes Toward Extramarital Sex', *Journal of Marriage and the Family*, 47, pp. 173–78.

Wiederman, M.W. (1997) 'Extramarital Sex', *The Journal of Sex Research*, 34 (2), pp. 167–74.

Wiederman, M.W. and Hurd, C. (1999) 'Extradyadic Involvement During Dating', *Journal of Social and Personal Relationships*, 16 (2), pp. 265–75.

Wiederman, M.W. and Kendall, E. (1999) 'Evolution, Sex, and Jealousy'. *Evolution and Human Behavior*, 20, pp. 121–28.

JAMES GIFFORD

INITIATION

Initiation involves incorporating individuals as members of a community or into successive life cycle stages. Accomplishing gender identity and distinct social roles lie at the core of initiation rituals. Circumcision, a paradigm for male initiation rituals, is extensively documented among Islamic and Jewish communities but is also prevalent among other societies including Filipino, Australian Aboriginal, Kenyan and Madagascar cultures. Unlike female gender identity which is biologically apparent and celebrated usually at the first menstruation, the symbolism of male initiation rituals suggests that masculinity must be compelled to emerge and acknowledged by a witnessing community, critically composed of men. A central concern of such initiations is literally wresting the boy away from female worlds and feminine attributes and incorporating him into male spheres. Initiations may focus on a single individual or on a group of young initiates collectively.

Circumcision highlights the idea of masculinity emerging from an androgynous body. In other initiations, biological symbolism stresses the materialisation of the reproductive male body. Caste rituals in India such as the *yagyopaveet* – donning the sacred thread – are publicly performed to simultaneously establish high caste status and entry into domesticated, mature sexuality. There is no single age for performing *yagyopaveet*; a young man may be initiated just before marriage when he enters the life cycle stage of householder. The imprecise age of initiation underlines the fact that masculine gender identity or male sexuality cannot be biologically assumed and needs ritual affirmation.

Initiation by violence and violence-as-initiation is another critical frame for initiations into masculine identity. In movements of resistance, young men as recipients of violent beatings or torture are catapulted into adulthood. Peteet (2002) identifies beatings in the street and prison as disruptive of age hierarchies in the Palestinian Intifada. Elders defer to young men who sit at the centre or head at public gatherings and play a pivotal advisory role in community affairs. Feldman's (1991) study of imprisonment and resistance in Northern Ireland suggests similar understandings of incarceration-as-initiation.

References and further reading

Feldman, A. (1991) *Formations of Violence: The Narratives of the Body and Political Terror in Northern Ireland*, Chicago, IL: University of Chicago Press.

Peteet, J. (2002) 'Male gender and rituals of resistance in the Palestinian intifada', in R. Adams and D. Savran (eds) *The Masculinities Studies Reader*, Oxford: Blackwell, pp. 318–35.

See also: rites of passage

RADHIKA CHOPRA

INTELLECTUALS

In most cultures literacy and literary work have been principally the domain of men. Women have frequently been excluded from formal education or denied respect as authors. This aspect of gender relations has had important consequences for ideas about masculinity. In European modernity, for instance, there has been a widespread belief that intellectuality and rationality are inherent in masculinity, while femininity is associated with the irrational and emotional.

It follows that in Western culture the bearers of intellectuality are culturally understood to be men (or 'masculinised' women). The Canadian sociologist Dorothy Smith has developed this insight, proposing that the realm of state policy debates, academic life, science and research are part of a system of power, the 'relations of ruling', to which women are subordinated. Intellectuals as a collectivity are here seen as the bearers of patriarchal power.

But intellectuals have also been bearers of change in men's lives. Alongside feminist women, prominent male intellectuals such as the Norwegian dramatist Henrik Ibsen and the British philosopher John Stuart Mill have articulated powerful critiques of patriarchy, making arguments for gender equality. In the 1960s a movement of young intellectuals, the 'new left', engaged in debates about sexuality and personal life which led to dramatic changes in gender awareness – and to some extent in gender practice – through the women's liberation movement of the 1970s. Intellectual leaders in the women's movement, such as Juliet Mitchell in Britain and Nancy Chodorow in the United States, have had a powerful influence on modern thinking about men and masculinity.

With the short-lived 'men's liberation' movement of the early 1970s, the longer-lasting gay liberation movement and a growing diversity of 'men's movements' around the world, a new role for male intellectuals has emerged – that of reflecting on, and strategising for, changes in men's lives. Prominent examples are the Australian gay theorist Dennis Altman and the US poet Robert Bly. Research on men's movements suggests that all have 'organic intellectuals' articulating their ideologies and goals for change.

References and further reading

Altman, D. (2001) *Global Sex*, Chicago, IL: University of Chicago Press.

Connell, R. (2002) 'Gender and the intellectuals', in R. Connell, *Gender*, Cambridge: Polity Press, pp. 115–35.

Newton, J. (2005) *From Panthers to Promise Keepers*, Lanham, MD: Rowman and Littlefield.

Seidler, V. (1989) *Rediscovering Masculinity*, London: Routledge.

Smith, D. (1990) *The Conceptual Practices of Power*, Boston, MA: Northeastern University Press.

See also: epistemology

RAEWYN CONNELL

INTERNATIONAL RELATIONS

International Relations was established as a discipline separate from Political Science and political theory in Britain and North America beginning in the 1920s. Its traditional objects of study are states in political relationships in the first instance, rather than individuals, humanity or human nature as a 'political animal'. By convention International Relations (with initial capitals, or 'IR') is the study, whereas international relations (with no capitals) represents the social phenomena that are studied. While conceptions of international politics and its practice can be traced back to ancient times, modern studies of international relations as a self-conscious academic practice are a twentieth-century phenomenon. States are typically (though not exclusively) identified with the 'system' of territorial nation-states (whether ordered or anarchic), and concepts of balance, power, diplomacy, foreign policy, international society and international law are foundational to the discipline (Goldstein and Pevehouse 2006).

In most mainstream theoretical perspectives in International Relations the state is said to be irreducible to the actions of human individuals, though in practice this methodological constraint is seldom strictly observed. States are of course represented by human individuals, and have interrelations only in virtue of what people do. Compared with Political Science and political theory, however, International Relations is at the outset one step removed from the human subject, simply because in most of its theoretical perspectives, its initial engagement is with states as objects of study. Political Science and political theory, by contrast, have an initial engagement with the human subject and so have self-conscious conceptualisations of the human individual. Since the 1970s Political Science and political theory have been critiqued by feminists on precisely this point, using the 'gender lens'. This has revealed that the human subject in Political Science and political theory was not generically human, and thus of either sex indifferently, or equal between the two sexes, as had generally (though not exclusively) been supposed. While there have been overtly misogynistic conceptualisations in political theory, which specifically excluded women from politics or demoted them to a lower class of citizenship than men, the most common modes of theorising since the seventeenth century have been expressed in terms of 'man' as an abstraction that supposedly operates over and above the particular properties of sex and gender.

However, as well as 'man', theorisations in Political Science and political theory also typically mentioned women, but almost always only in relation to social reproduction, family and household, marriage and the like. Sex itself in these theorisations was almost always conceived not just physically but socially in terms of its presumed purpose and practice, namely heterosexual reproduction. In particular 'woman' was conceptually and indissolubly linked to conceptions of motherhood, child-rearing and domesticity, which were differentiated from the impulses and obligations of males (insofar as these were mentioned at all). Feminist analysis characterised this as an exclusion and demotion of women to a 'private' and supposedly apolitical sphere of life, thus revealing that generic 'man' acting as a political subject 'in public' was in fact not a woman. According to the binary logic of gender, then, this non-woman but still human subject must therefore be a man. On this feminist view traditional Political Science and political theory both reflected and constituted the supposedly unchanging and unchangeable realities and norms of 'public man' and 'private woman'.

Because International Relations is conceptualised as one step removed from the human subject, it is therefore one step removed from the feminist critique that reveals the existence and operation of gender.

Moreover, International Relations has been insulated from feminist critique in another way, because its subject matter – inter-state politics – typically involves concepts and practices that are heavily and sometimes exclusively associated with males and with masculine or even hyper-masculine behaviour. These include statecraft, war and weaponry, national and international security, diplomacy, geo-politics, international political economy and the like. Over the last 150 years women have forced their way into the public realm within the nation-state by wresting civil rights for themselves as individuals, in particular the rights of property ownership, legal personhood, equal suffrage and office-holding. Correspondingly Political Science and political theory, particularly under feminist criticism, have come to an engagement with the female political subject, both as a theoretical equal to the male subject, and as different from the male subject, but in ways to be explored, rather than merely assumed. International Relations has not been subject to similar incentives, since few states are represented by females, and even fewer defence and military establishments are under female command, nor are women at the top of the most important economic and business organisations on the global stage. It is no longer credible to conceive of the national 'public' realm in many countries as wholly a male preserve, precisely because of large-scale female participation in politics (at least as voters, in most states). However, this is not quite the case with International Relations, where the subject-matter is not conceived as a mass but rather as an elite phenomenon, namely the state (in so far as the human subject is invoked at all), and where there is so little direct female representation and participation.

Since the 1980s feminist critique has nonetheless significantly changed the discipline of International Relations by gendering the concept 'man'. By invoking the gendered human subject in every substantive study and theoretical critique, feminists have exposed the gendered character of its traditional conceptions at every level as masculine. Feminist critique has thus worked to redefine traditional conceptions within the discipline by including women as significant objects of study and so revitalising a number of subject areas (Enloe 1989). These include statecraft and diplomacy, which was redefined to include a previously dismissed or downgraded 'social' or 'personal' side to the male representation of states in inter-state relations (e.g. the role of wives, of sexual dynamics, of women in supporting roles). Feminists have also redefined military engagements to include the generally hidden and denigrated service economies and societies surrounding soldiers (e.g. the role of sex-workers and other working females inside and outside military bases). And they have reconceptualised acts of warfare to include previously sidelined or understudied victimisation strategies directed at women in wars and conflict zones (e.g. rape, forced labour including sexual slavery, ritualised violations, and humiliations including forced pregnancy) (Tickner 2001).

Feminist critique has focused on concepts and definitions previously unexamined by men, precisely because they were presumed by men to be male-exclusive or male-dominated areas of activity by nature, history, culture or tradition. Or men presumed that if these areas were extended in the ways that feminists suggested, then they would no longer be part of the discipline of International Relations, and so would belong to some other study instead. Or men presumed that these areas would not be worthy of academic study at all, or at least not in the overtly politicised way that feminist critique implied or declared. Indeed, International Relations was already being done by a minority of female scholars who were not feminists, thus apparently validating traditional claims to gender-neutrality, value-objectivity and disciplinary boundary lines. Men had little interest in putting their concepts and activities under the 'gender lens' in the first place, since it might raise unwelcome questions about women's participation, interests and views. In the absence of women's and gender issues, men could easily feel that their subjectivities coincided with the generically human in an uncontroversial way, and so their interests and views would not face challenges from outside their own perspectives. Feminist critique and research has perforce generated a picture of men and their masculinities that many male practitioners of International Relations do not recognise as relevant, or as a reflection of their own being in the world, academic or otherwise. Feminists have thus challenged the scope of International Relations as traditionally conceived. This has in turn produced a critique of International Relations as itself 'masculinised' in both its theoretical conceptions and its professional practices, and moreover as a field which itself helps to sustain international politics in its masculinised modes (Hooper 2001).

There are a range of theoretical perspectives commonly identified within International Relations itself. It is variously conceptualised as a social science (realism), as a realm of strategic interaction (rational-choice and game-theoretical approaches), as inductive explanation (neo-realism and neo-liberalism) or as a practice of critical enquiry (Marxist and hermeneutic or 'constructivist' modes of analysis) (Baylis and Smith 2001). While the last mode, that of critical enquiry, is generally more open to the challenges of feminist critique (and much feminist critique also shares a critical orientation and similar set of methodologies), not all critical International Relations work is aligned with feminist approaches to inter-state politics by any means. Conversely, there are some women arguing for the incorporation of a 'gender variable' into the other research paradigms, albeit on what they say are 'non-feminist' terms, and some men following a similar strategy, marking men with their gender, and descriptively exploring the varieties of masculinity through which inter-state politics is pursued, without framing their inquiries in feminist terms (Goldstein 2001; Carpenter 2002; Jones 2004).

Feminist-inspired, or at least feminist friendly, men's studies, gender studies and queer theory all bear on concepts of and practices involving masculinities. Scholars within those areas have made varying efforts to enrich the character of International Relations as a discipline by making it self-conscious of its gendering and so re-engaging with basic tenets of professionalism, methodology and subject-matter. This would necessarily include the human subject as a gendered presumption within any account of social phenomena, such as states and their political relations. Some of the most important studies that have gendered International Relations with specific reference to men and masculinity have examined conflicts and wars, including Vietnam and the first Gulf War. These emerge as large-scale efforts to validate militarised masculinities as a national ideal, followed by revalidation of 'peacetime' foreign policies in somewhat different but still compatible 'manly' terms. Other studies have engaged in close analysis of the gay-men-in-the-military debates and conflicts, revealing the interlinkage of 'macho' masculinity with heteronormativity, and the exact operation of masculine practice in relation to femininity as it is projected on to denigrated men (Zalewski and Parpart 1998). The 'manly' terms of security discourse, as employed in a 'defence' establishment generating scenarios and strategies of mass destruction and death, have themselves been subjected to an intense analysis (Cohn 1987). Further discourse research has juxtaposed the 'combatant/non-combatant' distinction to contemporary exceptions, evasions and practices which derive from the gendered assumptions built into the original distinction and its documentary revisions. These researches have revealed the selective and discriminatory operation of gendered norms in inter-state and inter-agency politics in international activities such as conflict management and peace-keeping (Kinsella 2004).

Feminists have rather painfully explored 'difference' among women, and consequently exposed hierarchies of advantage and disadvantage that complicate any overly simplistic view of gender oppression along the sexual binary. Masculinity studies have similarly exposed the importance of 'race'/ethnicity, class, language, religion, political status and other factors in generating hierarchies among men, as well as their power over women (Connell 1995). Considerations of non-national participation in imperial or multi-national armies, international migrations of predominantly male workers impacting on local cultures and politics, the sexual politics involved in the deployment of overwhelmingly male forces in conflict zones, and inter-male relationships and strategies at the state level are all areas where men's studies meets International Relations productively (Pease 2002). As men have so much more power, wealth and advantage – as a group – than women – it follows that there is more for men to play for in terms of individual advantage through competition with each other, and that gender and sexuality play a distinct role in providing markers or counters in competitive struggle among men themselves, in myriad international activities ranging from business to sport to warfare (Connell 2002).

Since its foundation, International Relations has become much more thoroughly engaged with the human subject, because it has engaged with gender. 'Man' is therefore no longer quite so generally and unproblematically regarded as a sufficient marker for some assumed generic humanity, and state-centric 'IR' has to some extent devolved into wider-ranging conceptions of world politics (Smith and Little 2005).

References and further reading

Baylis, J. and Smith, S. (2001) *The Globalization of World Politics*, 3rd edn, Oxford: Oxford University Press.

Carpenter, R.C. (2002) 'Gender theory in world politics', *International Studies Review*, 4: 153–65.

Cohn, C. (1987) 'Sex and death in the rational world of defense intellectuals', *Signs*, 12: 687–718.

Connell, R. (1995) *Masculinities*, Cambridge: Polity.

—— (2002) *Gender*, Cambridge: Polity.

Enloe, C. (1989) *Bananas, Beaches and Bases*, London: Pandora.

Goldstein, J.S. (2001) *War and Gender*, New York: Cambridge University Press.

Goldstein, J.S. and Pevehouse, J.C. (2006) *International Relations*, 7th edn, New York: Pearson Longman.

Hooper, C. (2001) *Manly States*, New York: Columbia University Press.

Jones, A. (ed.) (2004) *Gendercide and Genocide*, Nashville, TN: Vanderbilt University Press.

Kinsella, H. (2004) 'Securing the civilian', in M. Barnett and B. Duvall (eds) *Power and Global Governance*, Cambridge: Cambridge University Press.

Pease, B. (2002) *Men and Gender Relations*, Melbourne: Tertiary.

Smith, M. and Little, R. (eds) (2005) *Perspectives on World Politics*, 3rd edn, London: Routledge.

Tickner, J.A. (2001) *Gendering World Politics*, New York: Columbia University Press.

Zalewski, M. and Parpart, J. (eds) (1998) *The 'Man' Question in International Relations*, Boulder, CO: Westview.

See also: colonial and imperial masculinities; political science

TERRELL CARVER

INTERSEX

Intersex is a condition in which an individual is born with genitalia and/or reproductive system not fitting conventional descriptions of female or male physiology, resulting from various causes (e.g. hormonal, genetic). Intersex conditions vary widely, and sometimes individuals with atypical chromosomal makeup (such as XXX or XYY) but no outwardly visible variance are termed intersexed. Frequency estimates range from

0.06 per cent (ISNA) to 1.7 per cent (Fausto-Sterling 2000) of births, depending upon defining criteria. While Western physicians consider intersex a medical emergency, some cultures consider intersexed individuals a third gender (sex), often holding specific ritual powers and practices not open to others.

Intersex and gender activists cite difficulties in defining intersex as proof that the categories 'male' and 'female' are not clear-cut and stable. Challenging both the conceptualisation of intersexuality and conventional treatments, the Intersex Society of North America (ISNA) targets surgeries performed on infants to make their genitalia conform to medically determined, gender-dependent standards. Though such surgeries are claimed vital to ensure development of a healthy gender identity, activists say this approach is concerned more with the comfort of parents, doctors and society. They point out that 'normal' genitalia vary tremendously in size and shape; further, surgical treatments reify both the naturalness of two polarised sexes and the primacy of genitalia – rather than other aspects of body and mind – in sex/gender assignment and personal identity (Dreger 1998, 1999).

Male sex assignment for an intersexed infant has generally been based upon doctors' assessment of the penis: will the penis be capable of performing vaginal penetration (heterosex) and standing urination? Thus a chromosomally male (XY) intersexed infant with a 'micropenis' traditionally has been assigned female and undergoes penis 'reconstruction' to form a (nonfunctional) clitoris. Similarly, a chromosomally female infant with atypically large labia and clitoris is often surgically altered to provide her with more 'feminine' and less 'obtrusive' genitalia. Kessler (1998) asserts that these treatment protocols reinforce a phallocentric perception of manhood and masculinity grounded in size and assertive action, juxtaposed against dainty and passive womanhood or femininity.

References and further reading

Dreger, A.D. (1998) *Hermaphrodites and the Medical Invention of Sex*, Cambridge, MA: Harvard University Press.

—— (ed.) (1999) *Intersex in the Age of Ethics*, Hagerstown, MD: University Publishing Group.

Fausto-Sterling, A. (2000) *Sexing the Body*, New York: Basic Books.

Intersex Society of North America (ISNA) at http://www.isna.org

Kessler, S. (1998). *Lessons from the Intersexed*, Rutgers, NJ: Rutgers University Press.

See also: bodies and biology, male; hijras

ELIZABETH RENFRO

INTIMACY

Seen from a historical perspective, masculinity as a social construct has been largely associated in many cultures with the public sphere, work, career and discipline. In many respects, the masculine sphere has constituted a contrast to the intimate, feminine and private sphere. This has been manifested, among other things, in a specific division of roles between the sexes, such that intimacy, emotions and longing for closeness have been viewed as feminine features and qualities, while the features of instrumental rationality, distance and incapacity for achieving closeness have similarly been seen as masculine. In this review, the current situation and future trends are surveyed from a predominantly 'Western' perspective, but with an 'eye' to, and an awareness of, variability across the globe.

British sociologist Anthony Giddens (1992) considers that the struggle for equality between the sexes has contributed to the growth of what he calls *pure relations*. By this he means that a more individualised attitude towards intimate relations has been created. Relations are evaluated and scrutinised. The individual chooses to stay with or leave his/her partner. According to Giddens, this development means two things: that women, to an increasing extent, are leaving men who are not interested in achieving gender equality and that new demands are being placed on men's capacity for intimacy. Consequently, this leads to a situation in which men are forced to work through and transform their view of intimacy and masculinity. In several of his books, British sociologist Victor Seidler has analysed the demands often more or less explicitly placed on men to disregard their emotions (Seidler 1994).

This process of change has also resulted in the growth of a more *plastic sexuality*. Sexuality and intimacy are now tied, to a decreasing extent, to the biological body or to gender. This implies, among other things, that it is conceivable and possible to develop several different types of sexual identities and attitudes. Here, Giddens highlights the importance of the struggle by gay and lesbian persons for equal status and the efforts made towards equal rights for all, regardless of sexual orientation.

Giddens' thesis on the transformation of intimacy has met with some criticism, but has also received support. The critics consider that Giddens tends to overestimate the extent of these changes. They argue that the traditional distribution of power between men and women largely still remains (Jamieson 1998). Most scholars, however, agree that certain shifts in the balance of power between the genders have occurred in many societies in the world. This is perhaps most evident in the context of the family. The question is: how great are these changes?

There is considerable empirical support for the observation that the fathers of today are more family-oriented. Compared with the fathers of previous generations, today's fathers spend more time with their children and participate to a greater extent in household work. At the same time, however, we may establish that, compared to women, men still carry out a much smaller proportion of unpaid housework and unpaid work caring for children and elderly relatives (Johansson and Kuosmanen 2003). Yet in contrast to the situation in the recent past, this problem is now receiving a great deal of attention. The family sphere is also marked, to an increasing degree, by transformation and by an ongoing process of democratisation. That more men are choosing to participate actively in housework and childcare would seem to imply changes in how men view intimate relations and care. For instance, in Sweden today, discussions are ongoing concerning the opportunities for parents to share equally the parental leave allowance allotted during the child's first year of life. This would entail, in practice, that fathers and mothers share equally the responsibly for the home and the care of infants and small children. On the other hand, it should be noted that such a trend – and the current policy in Sweden of allotting two specific 'daddy-only' months of parental leave – is partly a response to the fact that Swedish fathers still take a relatively small proportion of parental leave available compared to the very large proportion taken by mothers, despite the very considerable social policy supports already available in Sweden to fathers.

Hence, while we do find some support for the thesis that a new ideal of fatherhood and masculinity is now growing, such a development is far from applicable to all men. There is great variation across countries, social strata and social environments. All men are not affected in the same way by the new ideal of equality. It is still the case that the majority of men leave most of the responsibility for the children to the mother. This dismal picture becomes clearer when we study European statistics on men's violence against women. Several quantitative studies reveal that men's violence against women constitutes a substantial social problem, including in societies famous for 'gender equality' such as Finland and Sweden. Many men show a tendency towards ignoring, depreciating and toning down this problem. It is obvious that such violence cannot be understood solely in terms of mental disturbance on the part of men, but that it must be seen mainly in relation to the overall power structures found in society. While we can establish a connection between the prevailing system of power and men's violence against women, we can also see today a growing social mobilisation among men to challenge men's violence to women. For instance, men's networks are being created, in which men actively work to prevent violence and severely criticise the web of gendered power relations associated with it.

Men have a complicated relationship to intimacy. This is seen clearly when we approach the different spheres of intimacy in society. If we study the new generations of young men, in many societies we see to a greater or lesser extent several tendencies towards a changed form of intimacy and we see how traditional patterns counteract more radical transformations of male intimacy. Today, the opportunities to break free from a stereotyped image of male sexuality have increased in some cultures. In a growing number of countries there is also growing criticism of how men are portrayed and of the demands placed on male sexuality. But, at the same time, the idea still exists that men should be virile, potent and strong and that they should function as conquerors. In reality, however, many men find it difficult to relate to this hegemonic and demanding image of male sexuality (Plummer 2005).

A major Swedish study of young people's sexuality shows that young men are generally positive towards equality and sexuality on equal terms (Hammarén and Johansson forthcoming). The young men felt, for example, that they and young women have the same need for sexuality and that it is good that women recognise their own sexuality. In many respects, we see how efforts towards equality have percolated through to everyday life, at least with respect to men's attitudes. But the picture is more complicated. The study also shows that young men are more positive towards pornography than young women are. Moreover, a great proportion of young men have a negative attitude towards homosexuality. At the same time, it is important to note that one in four young men are opposed to pornography and that the same proportion also have more positive attitudes towards homosexuality. This would seem to indicate that there are a number of possible positions that young men may occupy.

A great number of studies from different European countries have shown a strong relationship between homophobia, sexism, repudiation of the feminine and the construction of masculinity. This does not mean, however, that all young men are characterised by this cultural matrix. We find, naturally enough, great variation in how young men choose to relate to these issues. Thus, it is important that we focus not only on more regressive forms of masculinity, but also that we point out the growth of 'new forms'. Scandinavian research finds significant numbers of young men who choose to call themselves feminists – who seek equal relations and who wish to develop a new form of male intimacy (Johansson and Lalander, forthcoming). Moreover, in some countries increasing numbers of young people are now interested in experimenting with different sexual lifestyles. Their tolerance for bisexuality and homosexuality seems to have increased, at least among certain strata of young men. At the same time, however, we can observe a considerable amount of violence against homosexual men.

Male intimacy has long been formed and defined in opposition to 'the feminine' and to homosexuality. Yet, at the same time, it has become increasingly difficult to maintain any fixed and distinct lines of demarcation. Danish sociologist Henning Bech talks about an *absent homosexuality*. By this he means that, despite the fact that heterosexual men often repudiate homosexuality, it is possible to trace many influences and connections between these two different sexual identities (Bech 1997).

These connections, according to Bech, may be manifested in several ways. The very prohibition against great intimacy and closeness that marks many male relations emerges from the charged relationship to homosexuality. This explains why men often have difficulty showing tenderness, closeness and care for other men. The risk is ever present that such expressions may be misinterpreted. Today, however, we see several tendencies indicating that these 'prohibitions' against intimacy are undergoing a change towards a more open-minded attitude. Moreover, we can see how men, to increasing degrees, are being influenced by a gay lifestyle. This is especially noticeable in relation to the considerable *aesthetisation* that characterises much of contemporary masculinity in many Western countries (Edwards 2005). Men wear make-up, use perfume, are more conscious of their clothing and show a completely new interest in caring for their bodies. At the same time, however, we still see more or less explicit limits to what is viewed as manly versus unmanly.

We find support, therefore, for our current observations of transformations of the sphere of intimacy. In particular, men have been forced to take a stand on and adapt to the increasing demands placed on them for equality, emotional closeness and a new fatherhood. Significant attitude changes have occurred among fathers. There is an increased willingness on the part of men to present themselves as and to actually be more attentive and available fathers. Similar ambitions are evident among many young men who wish to develop relations of equality with young women. Yet, at the same time, there is a great variation in how different men relate to this new horizon of demands and possibilities. As previously mentioned, there are still many men who prioritise their own careers and development over their family and children. For many men, the sphere of intimacy is primarily a sphere of power and dominance, from which they control and commit violence against women and children.

In the 'study of gender and men's practices' the concept of *homosociality* is frequently used when discussing men's attitudes towards and relation to intimacy and closeness. This concept has largely been used to point out the connection between male friendship, intimacy and power. When men seek out other men, the motive is often to establish alliances, form associations and make pacts. But such an interpretation of male friendship, intimacy and closeness excludes the possibility that men may actually seek out other men in order to cultivate real friendship relations, not necessarily tied to a longing for power. It is reasonable, therefore, that the concept be broadened to include the complexity and inconsistency that characterise men's desire for intimacy.

Today, in some societies, associating masculinity with the public sphere and femininity with the private sphere is not quite as self-evident as it once was – to a greater or lesser extent. For although this polarised gender division has proved to be robust – even in allegedly gender-equal societies such as Denmark and Sweden – it is becoming increasingly problematic in some cultural contexts to use simple classifications such as these. At the same rate as masculinity is being charged with aspects of intimacy, closeness and caring, we see that it is slowly but significantly being transformed to a greater or lesser extent in a growing number of societies around the world. With respect to the global arena, however, we must maintain that there is considerable opposition to such changes in many parts of the world. Moreover, we should not forget that in certain parts of the world it even seems that the balance of power between women and men is being turned further in favour of men. Equality between the sexes is still a highly controversial issue.

References and further reading

Bech, H. (1997) *When Men Meet. Homosexuality and Modernity*, Cambridge: Polity Press.

Edwards, T. (2005) 'Queering the pitch? Gay masculinities', in M. Kimmel, J. Hearn and R. Connell (eds) *Handbook of Studies on Men and Masculinities*, London: Sage.

Giddens, A. (1992) *The Transformation of Intimacy. Sexuality, Love and Eroticism in Modern Societies*, Cambridge: Polity Press.

Hammarén, N. and Johansson, T. (forthcoming) 'Gender order or disorder?' in T. Johansson and P. Lalander (eds) *The Transformation of Sexuality*, Aldershot: Ashgate.

Jamieson, L. (1998) *Intimacy. Personal Relationships in Modern Societies*, Cambridge: Polity Press.

Johansson, T. and Kuosmanen, J. (2003) *Manlighetens många ansikten – fäder, feminister, frisörer och andra män* (English version: The Many Faces of Masculinity – Fathers, Hair-dressers and Other Men), Stockholm: Liber förlag.

Johansson, T. and Lalander, P. (forthcoming) *The Transformation of Sexuality*, Aldershot: Ashgate.

Plummer, K. (2005) 'Male sexualities', in M. Kimmel, J. Hearn and R. Connell (eds) *Handbook of Studies on Men and Masculinities*, London: Sage.

Seidler, V. (1994) *Unreasonable Men. Masculinity and Social Theory*, London: Routledge.

See also: emotions; heterosexuality; love; metrosexual

THOMAS JOHANSSON

J

JAPANESE MASCULINITIES

'Japanese masculinity' is often described with symbols referring to the samurai or military class which was dominant from the eighth to the seventeenth centuries. Numerous books, even today, describe the *bushido*, or samurai ethics. This moral code includes values such as loyalty, self-sacrifice, courtesy and honour. It develops a sense of shame and requires a modest lifestyle, but its hallmark is fearlessness in the face of death. Although men of the samurai class represented only a small percentage of the whole population, idealisation of the 'samurai' image developed from the Tokugawa shogunate through the relatively peaceful period until the nineteenth century. On the other hand, Norinaga Motoori, a famous Japanese thinker in the eighteenth century, described pre-modern Japanese culture as feminine (Taoyameburi) compared with the more masculine (Masuraoburi) China.

Only in the second half of the nineteenth century did the 'warrior masculine' image of the bushido spirit spread throughout the society, following nation-state building efforts after the Meiji Restoration of the Emperor (1866–69). The Japanese–Chinese War (1894–5) and the Japanese–Russian War (1904–5) contributed to Japanese men identifying with the tough and self-sacrificing soldier. Moreover, education and a patriarchal legal system accelerated the development of gender differences.

After World War II, the gender structure of Japanese society changed dramatically. The new constitution emphasised gender equality and undermined the patriarchal family system. At the same time, rapid economic recovery and industrialisation facilitated the cultural dominance of the breadwinner–husband family in which the wife stayed at home, taking care of the housework and child-rearing. Despite this image, 54.4 per cent of Japanese women worked outside the home.

However, after 1970 Japan diverged from other countries which developed policies to increase gender equity. Instead, Japan limited the social opportunities of women while extending the working hours of men. Thus in 2000, women's labour participation was 59.6 per cent, only 5 per cent higher than in 1970.

The long working hours of Japanese men bolstered Japan's economic success, but at a significant social price. Women's social opportunities remained restricted and being 'closed' within their houses increased their stress. Meanwhile, men became deprived of their family life by being forced to lead a workaholic lifestyle.

The word *karôshi*, meaning 'death from overwork', became well known internationally to describe the sudden deaths of men who were assumed to be suffering from work pressures and the silent repression of their feelings. Estimates at the beginning of the century suggest that 10,000 Japanese men may die of *karôshi* each year.

The collapse of the bubble economy in the 1990s further stressed Japanese men. Around 2000, the suicide rate of Japanese men around the age of fifty rapidly increased. Apparently men's fears of looking weak and inhibitions about seeking professional help for personal problems remain strong. As in other countries, some academic masculinity research and some gender-sensitive men's movements started developing under feminist influence in Japan in the 1970s. The Group for Discussing Men's Role in Child-rearing (Otokono-kosodatewo-kangaeru-kai) and the Group Demanding Time for Child-rearing Men and Women (Otokomo onnamo ikuji jikanwo! renrakukaigi) first appeared during the 1980s. Two pioneering studies are Ito's 'The breakdown of masculinity'([1984], in Ito 1993), which connected Japanese masculinity issues with those of Italian fascism, and Watanabe's *Datu-dansei-no-jidai* (The Age of Post-masculinity), which studied transvestite men (1987).

In 1991 Japanese Men's Liberation movements began seriously with the Research Group for Men's Liberation (Menzuribu-kenkyuukai), with members mainly from Osaka and Kyoto. This group organised workshops and meetings, indebted to but separate from feminist movements, in order to discuss and solve men's gender issues.

Men's Liberation movements have now spread throughout the country, but especially in Tokyo and Osaka. Some of these independent groups allow women to become members, while some do not. These groups all over the country communicate with each other and since 1996 have held an annual nationwide meeting called the Men's Festival. Workshops in this festival discuss matters such as job problems, domestic violence and gay liberation.

Even the Japanese government has now become involved in efforts for gender equality, passing the 1999 Basic Law for Gender Equal Society. Both the national government and local authorities are also paying increasing attention to the role of men. While recognising the necessity of changing men's consciousness and working style in order to improve women's position, these efforts also raise social recognition of the importance of gender equality for saving men for values other than those of the workaholic-like lifestyle. Although the men's movements in Japan today are small compared with those internationally, they are beginning to affect Japanese society.

References and further reading

Ito, K. (1993) *Otokorashisa-no-yue* (The Whereabouts of Masculinities), Tokyo: Shinyosha.

—— (2005) '*Danseigakunyn* (an introduction to Men's Studies)', in M. McLelland and R. Dasgupta (eds) *Genders, Transgenders and Sexualities in Japan*, London: Routledge.

Louie, K. (ed.) (2003) *Asian Masculinities*, London: Routledge.

Robertson, J. and Suzuki, N. (2002) *Men and Masculinities in Contemporary Japan*, London: Routledge.

Watanabe, T. (1987) *Datu-dansei-no-jidai* (The Age of Post-masculinity), Tokyo: Keisoshobo.

See also: karôshi

KIMIO ITO

JEWISH MASCULINITIES

Judaism, as codified in the Torah or Hebrew Scriptures, is one of the primary sources for the historical construction of masculinity. The creation story of Adam and Eve; the Jewish patriarchs' relationship with their monotheistic God, the Father; and the behavioural laws set down in the books of Leviticus and Numbers have virtually defined acceptable male behaviour in every aspect of life – from marriage practices to fathering to conduct in war. Abraham's willingness to sacrifice his son Isaac is a defining narrative of Judaism that continues to affect Jewish fathers and sons. Contemporary Jewish feminist scholars, following the historic practice of rabbinic exegesis, have questioned and modified the male gender bias inherent in the foundational scriptural texts.

Recent scholarship (Biale, Gilman, Boyarin) describes the ideal Jewish male during the Rabbinic/Diasporic period, from the destruction of the Temple in Jerusalem (70 CE) to the founding of the State of Israel, as a counter-image to the hegemonic Western masculine ideal of the warrior/knight. With no nation-state to defend, the ideal Jewish male became a biblical scholar, a congregant, and a loving husband and father who rejected violence. As Jews were subject to anti-Semitic attacks and expulsions throughout the Diasporic period, a code of *menschlichkeit* (Howe 1976) evolved that located Jewish superiority in the refusal to share the aggressive values of their oppressors. Yet also in response to persecution, the seventeenth-century Jewish mystic Sabbatai Zevi longed for the return of a messianic warrior figure like Simon Bar Kokhba, who had fought against the Romans in the second century CE (Breines 1990).

The Enlightenment and the rise of nationalism, culminating in Zionism, undermined the ideal of the gentle, scholarly Jewish mensch, or good Jewish man. In response to a discourse that saw the Jewish male as effeminate, Zionists such as Max Nordau proposed that Jewish men become 'muscle Jews' so that they could take their prophetic place among the nations of men (Gilman 1991). Even Sigmund Freud, in a famous passage in *The Interpretation of Dreams*, saw his own father's passivity in response to an anti-Semitic act 'as unheroic conduct'.

Early twentieth-century migrations to the United States exposed European Jews to American gender norms. Old-world Jewish fathers often lost the respect of sons attracted to a more aggressive American male model. Life in urban ghettos led to the rise of Jewish entrepreneurs and gangsters, as well as to an interest in sports, especially boxing (Levine 1992). A tradition that held learning in high esteem resulted in a second generation of professionals and intellectuals. Socialist and anarchist movements attracted many Jewish men, who constituted a majority of the Abraham Lincoln brigade fighting fascism in Spain. The Holocaust, in addition to threatening the survival of all European Jews, exacerbated the tensions surrounding Jewish masculinity, as the very passivity that had characterised the ideal of Jewish manhood was now seen as contributing to its extinction. The post-World War II years were dominated by psychic and political responses to the Holocaust, culminating in the founding of the State of Israel in 1948.

With their own nation, Jewish men had at last entered the historical mainstream. The founding, along with the victories of the 1967 and 1973 wars, and later the rescue of hostages at Entebbe by Jewish Special Forces, changed the international perception of the Jewish male from non-violent 'schlemiel' to savvy warrior. While the mensch remained a Jewish ideal in American life and culture, as evidenced by the Yiddish stories of Isaac Bashevis Singer and the novels of Bernard Malamud, Philip Roth rebelled against the 'good Jew' image. In his novels he contrasts the neurotic diasporic Jewish male with the self-possessed Israeli citizen-soldier. Yet writers like Tony Kushner and Michael Chabon have questioned the hyper-masculine Jewish male image, opening a space for gay Jews and more multifaceted incarnations of Jewish masculinity (Boyarin 2003).

Jewish-American men have had a marked influence on American popular culture, most powerfully in Hollywood film and television. From the first sound film, *The Jazz Singer* (1927), with Al Jolson, a cantor's son, emoting in black face, to the antics of Jerry Lewis and Mel Brooks, to Woody Allen's urbane nebbishes, to Steven Spielberg's erudite action hero Indiana Jones, American film has had a distinctly Jewish male inflection. Comedians like Lenny Bruce and Jerry Seinfeld established a coolly ironic and transgressive sensibility, and a postmodern image of Jewish masculinity can be seen in the films of Adam Sandler and Ben Stiller, in Jon Stewart's political satire, and in the magazine *Heeb*.

The nightly news across the world shows Israeli soldiers fighting street battles with Palestinians and Jewish settlers, reinforcing the militant image of the Jewish male and recalling the scriptural patriarchs. In America and Europe, however, a renewed interest in Jewish religious practice has led to a re-evaluation of what it means to be a Jewish man in light of Jewish feminism, men's studies and rabbinic teachings (Salkin 1999).

References and further reading

Biale, D. (1992) *Eros and the Jews*, New York: Basic Books.

Boyarin, D. (ed.) (1997) *Unheroic Conduct*, Berkeley, CA: University of California Press.

—— (2003) *Queer Theory and the Jewish Question*, New York: Columbia University Press.

Breines, P. (1990) *Tough Jews*, New York: Basic Books.

Brod, H. (1988) *A Mensch Among Men*, Freedom, CA: Crossing.

—— (1995) 'Of mice and supermen', in T.M. Rudavsky (ed.) *Gender and Judaism*, New York: New York University Press, pp. 279–93.

Eilberg-Schwartz, H. (1994) *God's Phallus*, Boston, MA: Beacon.

Gilman, S. (1991) *The Jew's Body*, New York: Routledge.

Howe, I. (1976) *World of Our Fathers*, New York: Simon and Schuster.

Levine, P. (1992) *Ellis Island to Ebbets*, New York: Oxford University Press.

Rosenberg, W. (2001) *Legacy of Rage*, Amherst, MA: University of Massachusetts Press.

Salkin, J.K. (1999) *Searching for My Brothers*, New York: G.P. Putnam's Sons.

See also: world religions, Judaism

WARREN ROSENBERG

JOURNALISM AND THE NEWS

Objectivity is hailed as an industry virtue for journalism and news media. Reporters and readers alike tend to think that daily newspapers, TV, radio and cable news broadcasts and internet news websites are unbiased and accurate representations. Yet journalism and news do much more than merely reflect the issues and events of the day. Increasingly, theorists point out that news and journalism shape public opinion, bolster cultural values and shore up political leaders as well as deliver messages about gender: journalism and news serve the interests of men and masculinity.

Men – particularly white, Western, wealthy and powerful men – dominate global news media as its producers, owners and subjects (Crouteau and Hoynes 1992). White heterosexual men are over-represented and often depicted flatteringly in news stories, photographs, headlines and as expert sources quoted in articles, compared to women, men of colour, and gays and lesbians, who are especially absent from politics, international affairs, science and technology and military coverage. Men also control media mergers, formulate telecommunications policy and define what is considered newsworthy. Men not only determine what qualifies as news, but also place themselves at the centre of that definition and representation. Most of the presumably 'alternative' voices to straight news are also men, as in the satirists posing as newscasters in US programmes such as *The Daily Show* or *The Colbert Report*.

Early examinations of how news and journalism function in society did not consider gender in their assessment, nor do more recent criticisms of news and journalism such as *The Problem of the Media* (2004) by McChesney. Often men who advocate for media reform overlook male dominance and the culture of masculinity within journalism. And, while there are many content analyses of news stories for their depiction of women, many legally adjudicated allegations of sexist bias against women in the journalism industry, and a number of organisations that take up representation issues as they concern women, comparatively little work examines men and masculinity in news and journalism (Crouteau and Hoynes 1992).

Journalism gets gendered with a pro-male bias in four main ways:

He-said, he-said: pale male news media

First, news media reflects the men who mostly produce it. News media's voice of authority and face of the people is most often that of a middle-aged white male from a Western country, particularly the US or UK, where most international mainstream news outlets, such as CNN or BBC World, are based. These men dominate the opinion-shaping forums of talk radio, newspaper and television news, and editorials and commentary. '[N]ews is mostly written about men,' comments BIA, a Turkish media monitoring organisation: 'more news is reported about rich men than about poor men, but the news gives even less weight to poor women than to poor men' (BIA 2006). According to FAIR (Fairness and Accuracy in Reporting), of all US sources interviewed on national nightly news broadcasts on ABC, NBC and CBS in 2001, 92 per cent were white and 85 per cent were male; corporate representatives were regular guests, but public interest voices were absent. Such coverage presents Western white masculinity as the social and cultural norm.

Content analysis shows the dominance of men's coverage in mainstream news. News media 'can help constitute an "ideal" male identity' while preserving the *status quo* (Crouteau and Hoynes 1992: 157). One study found that men appear more frequently than women by a ratio of four to one in news stories and a ratio of two to one in photographs (Len-Rios *et al.* 2005). Another study found that a news anchor's gender influenced audience evaluation of the news report, because male anchors were considered to be more credible and more professional than women (Smee 2004). 'Journalists think more often of male experts – doctors, academics, psychiatrists, engineers, and so forth-as sources,' describes a Turkish media monitoring group, (BIA 2006). Furthermore, the male voices and faces depicted as newsworthy or as respectable commentators tend also to reflect politically conservative points of view favouring the interests of corporations, politicians and powerful religious groups.

Content is king: gendered news stories

Second, news stories are told in ways that reflect dominant gender norms. In the age of the Internet a familiar phrase – 'content is king' – refers to the power acquired by determining news coverage. Some communications theorists claim that news and journalism are based on a masculine communication style, such as the demand that news 'hooks' establish competing sides and present stories as conflict rather than consensus. Another well-known motto, 'if it bleeds, it leads', promotes values often praised in patriarchal culture, like danger, violence and hierarchy. Many propose that news coverage that emphasises spectacle and power must be overhauled with different values (Lynggard 2002). The placement of front page news stories considered important to men also reinforces the idea that coverage is about male power. 'Hard news' – war, business, politics, the economy and sports – is typically men's beat and considered of particular interest to men, whereas 'soft news' – 'human interest stories' like arts and entertainment, profiles and features, and community and local news – is still seen as women's areas. Thus stories about rape, childcare, healthcare, welfare and the family are considered irrelevant to men and therefore as trivial issues. 'The paradoxical fact that rape, a crime that happens overwhelmingly to women, is usually covered by men, may partly explain why the press has been so slow to change its approach to sex crimes,' claims Benedict, arguing that news coverage of sex crimes legitimates male violence and blames women victims (Benedict 1992: 5). Mainstream news discredits topics such as welfare, labour, global trade and nuclear proliferation as unconnected to gender and race politics around the world. Furthermore, rarely do gender critiques of the news make the news.

Sexist newsroom culture: boys' club and men's locker rooms

Third, structural biases in media industries contribute to the perpetuation of men's dominance. Despite a few prominent women before the cameras, institutional structures keep men in most news-making positions of power. The poor retention rates of women indicate that pursuing a tough lead for a breaking story as a deadline-driven journalist is an inflexible, burnout job primarily suitable for childless young people with high sleep-deprivation thresholds. As in many other professions, women in news media leave the job earlier, get promoted less and earn less. Despite widespread gender equity in journalism educational programmes in many countries, after graduation men and women enter different jobs and are treated differently. Men more frequently become foreign correspondents, crime beat reporters, sportscasters, senior-level managing editors, editors-in-chief and owners. More men are employed as working reporters – 62 per cent in TV, 63 per cent in newspapers, and nearly 80 per cent for radio and wire services – and advance more quickly (Poynter Institute, 2004). In contrast, women have traditionally been seen as selling, not producing, the news, and judged on their physical appearance. Critics also point to the labelling of women in the field as 'female journalists' – noted first for their gender and then sidelined to less serious beats typically considered 'women's issues'. 'I don't mind being a token,' said one of the first black women at *The Washington Post*. 'The real issue for me and for workers in general is: are we allowed and encouraged to do the work we can do and are hired to do once we're in the institution?' (Flanders 1997: 214–15).

Some maintain that there is a sexist newsroom culture, especially in sports journalism: 'There might not be a less diversified group of paunchy, balding, middle-aged white guys anywhere in America,' said Chad (2006). And nothing highlights men's global dominance of news industries more than debates over where women do or do not belong in the business, particularly as sports reporters on the athletic field or in men's locker rooms. Alleged to be husband-hunting, there just to gawk, or ignorant of sports, women sportswriters have faced intimidation and harassment from male athletes, coaches and even colleagues. Some argue that enforcement of gender-equality guidelines for news broadcasting is the only way to alleviate injustice and inequality in news media and journalism (Fuller 1992).

Newsman as hero – popular culture's image of the journalist

Lois Lane and Clark Kent are both reporters, but only one is Superman. In fact, both comic-book heroes Superman and Spiderman work in the news media. Popular culture's representation of newsmakers as *newsmen* is another way in which journalism gets gendered as masculine. Hollywood especially glorifies journalists as Western heroes – white men in pursuit of truth, justice and the American way. Journalistic lore and best-selling biographies tend to elevate early media moguls like Pulitzer or Hearst. Many Hollywood films from the 1940s to the present bolster the image of reporters as daring men willing to forsake personal safety to ask tough questions.

Ending male-dominance of news and journalism is essential for gender equity and democracy. Today there is international recognition of the need to examine gender equity in news and journalism. At the recent Beijing Plus Ten meeting, a number of women's media and communication organisations submitted a resolution calling on governments to ensure that women and media issues would receive critical attention. Section J of the Beijing Platform for Action (1995) signed by representatives of 189 countries claimed the media play a fundamental role in the perpetuation of unequal gender relations at all levels of society globally, thereby undermining many citizens' participation in public dialogue.

Media monitors and alternative media makers, in contrast, use the media to dismantle gendered power systems and empower women, and they also characterise access to media, communications technologies and free press as fundamental human rights. Many media monitoring organisations, such as the Center for Media and Public Affairs, the Global Media Monitoring Project, the Pew Charitable Trust, NewsWatch Canada, Media Awareness Network, Media Watch, FAIR (Fairness and Accuracy In Reporting), WIMN (Women In Media and News), the Annenberg Public Policy Center, We Interrupt This Message, and Women, Men and Media, founded by former feminist pioneer Friedan, were established to ensure greater democratic access to the press and offer to train reporters and editors to achieve higher, non gender-biased standards in the field. The Countrywide Network in Turkey for Monitoring and Covering Media Freedom and Independent Journalism (known as BIA2) was founded in 2000 to train news professionals in 'rights-based journalism'. In addition, alternative news outlets are often antidotes to mainstream male-dominated news media. The Center for International Media Action, ReclaimTheMedia.org and Media-Alliance.org all support legislation for diverse, local, independent and uncensored media, and may eventually combat male dominance of media concentration. It remains to be seen if Web blogs, as novel technological and democratic approaches to news gathering and media representation, will level the gender hierarchies in traditional forms of news and journalism. For example 'Riverbend's' blog, 'Baghdad Burning', reports an anonymous young woman's experience of being under bombardment in Iraq (Riverbend 2006). Only when more gender-egalitarian will news and journalism accurately reflect the events of the day that concern all people.

References and further reading

Benedict, H. (1992) *Virgin or Vamp*, New York: Oxford University Press.

BIA (Bagnsiz Iletsim Agi) (2006) www.Bianet.org

Burkhart, F.N. and Sigelman, C.K. (1999) 'Byline bias?' *Journalism Quarterly*, 67 (3): 492.

Chad, N. (2006) 'I'm in the white business', *Washington Post*, available at http://www.washingtonpost.com/wp-dyn/content/article/2006/07/02/AR2006070200565_pf.html

Croteau, D. and Hoynes, W. (1992) 'Men and the news media', in S. Craig (ed.) *Men, Masculinity, and the Media*, Newbury Park, CA: Sage, pp. 158–64.

Flanders, L. (1997) *Real Majority, Media Minority*, Monroe, ME: Common Courage.

Fuller, C. (1992) 'Our pale male media', *Canadian Forum*, 71 (809): 5–8.

Hanke, R. (1998) 'Theorizing masculinity with/in the media', *Communication Theory*, 8 (2): 183–203.

Len-Ríos, M., Rodgers, S., Thorson, E. and Yoon, D. (2005) 'Representation of women in news and photographs', *Journal of Communication*, 55 (1): 152–68.

Lynggard, T. (2002) 'Gender representations in the Nordic news media', paper presented at Women's Worlds 2002, the 8th International Interdisciplinary Congress on Women, Makarere University, Kampala, Uganda.

McChesney, R.W. (2004) *The Problem of the Media*, New York: Monthly Review.

Poynter Institute. (2004) 'The face and mind of the American journalist', Poynter Online, available at www.pointer.org

Ricchiardi, S. (2004/5) 'Offensive interference', *American Journalism Review*, December–January: 54–62.

'Riverbend' (2006) 'Baghdad burning', at www.riverbendblog.blogspot.com

Smee, T.W. (2004) 'Does a news anchor's gender influence audience evaluations of the anchor?' *Media Report to Women*, 32 (4): 13–21.

SARAH L. RASMUSSON

JUNGIAN PERSPECTIVES

Carl Jung understood 'masculinity' as a form of consciousness – an essential, instinctive way of assessing and relating that he defined intuitively through the term 'Logos', by which he meant discrimination, judgment and insight into the meaning of the situation to be met. This interpretation of the 'masculine principle' assumes an underlying archetypal predisposition built up by the behaviour of males within civilisations across the millennia. Since for Jung the guiding principle of a woman's consciousness is the less separative feminine Eros, masculine consciousness tends to be more unconscious for her and achieved through the archetype of the animus, which has the peculiarity of using the Logos in a more dogmatic, approximate, off-the-point way. With consciousness, however, the animus can enable a woman to discriminate her psychic depths with insight and judgment. Emma Jung suggested four ways in which the animus presents Logos to women: as word, as deed, as meaning and as power. Like the anima (the archetype carrying the man's more unconscious Eros) the animus is seen by Jung to function as a bridge to the inner authority of the Self.

Jung recognised disadvantages to this model. When Logos is postulated as the conscious cultural achievement of men (and Eros as the consciousness emerging in women), the implication is that the other gender is inherently deficient in the principle that is contrasexual to it. In his work on alchemy, Jung attempted to rectify this restrictiveness by developing archetypal images for the masculine and feminine 'principles'. He chose the alchemical Sol and Luna, which were personifications of the (masculine) Sun and the (feminine) Moon as conceived by Renaissance astrology. When applied, by analogy, to depth psychology, these archetypal 'lights' could become conjoined in the consciousness of the same person, through the alchemical *coniunctio*, symbolising the inner union of masculine and feminine consciousness in the mature person. Even more important, room was allowed for the construction of these gendered principles, rather than fixing their natures *a priori*. Sol, in the understanding of the alchemists who were trying to forge in the laboratories earthly representatives of the astrological powers, was created by bringing sulphur in relation to mercury, and this implied both chemical and spiritual effort.

This symbolism implies that mature masculinity requires both a direct and forceful emotional expression (the explosive sulphur) and a capacity for irony and conscious ambivalence (the elusive, paradoxical mercury, which qualifies masculine emotional and behavioural decisiveness). Sol, the constructed masculine principle that results from the combination of mercury and sulphur, has the capacity to illuminate a situation with insight rather than simply react to it explosively. The ur-masculine quality of 'sulphur' is itself a product of uniting white and red sulphurs, the colours referring to the moon and the sun, implying that there is a lunar as well as solar component of masculinity that must be combined to construct this basic element of masculine consciousness. The 'union of sames' in constructing sulphur points to the importance of homosexual fantasy and relationships to the building up of masculine confidence. This is a theme pursued by Jung and other Jungians with the aid of anthropological observations of initiation practices, which often require boys to be receptive to older men.

On the other hand, Jung's close associate von Franz exposed the resistance to initiation into maturity in studies of the 'puer aeternus' (eternal boy) archetype, as found in such literary works as St Exupery's *The Little Prince* and Apuleius' *The Golden Ass*. Other Jungians have simply emphasised a range of archetypal masculine roles, such as king, magician, warrior and lover; *senex* and *puer*; trickster, hero and initiate; the 'gods in everyman'; and the father, whose nature has to be configured anew with each generation. Zoja's historical study pointed to the insecurity of the father in maintaining his position as guide to the effective use of masculine consciousness. Collins emphasised that father and son represent, intrapsychically, a fused selfobject relationship that he calls 'fatherson'. Father and son transmit and split persona, ego, shadow and anima attributes, and fathers affect their daughters by projecting archetypal attributes on to them. The child's experience of the father's body helps to internalise masculine consciousness. The role of father can be played by either sex, and masculinity itself can be expressed in both holding and penetrating ways.

In the United States, the mythopoetic men's movement, drawing on Jungian ideas, led to a resurgence of initiation practices in the late twentieth century and debate on what men should be, want and become. Moving beyond simple notions of heroism, a number of Jungian authors offered a range of models for the self-construction of masculine consciousness, from the individuating Arthurian knight Parsifal to the triad of constructors from Greek mythology – the inventive Daedalus, the brooding, introverted Hephaistos and the tricksterish Hermes – and the destructive *senex*-god Saturn. More human images of masculinity, such as phallic and priapic preoccupations, fantasies of rape, and the roles men play within heterosexual and homosexual couples, were also addressed by Jungian authors, drawing upon novels and films to elucidate the archetypal patterns. The goal by the end of the first century of Jungian thought was not to pathologise so much as to contextualise contemporary expressions of maleness within a range of archetypal and cultural options for what masculinity can be.

References and further reading

Collins, A. (1994) *Fatherson*, Wilmette, IL: Chiron.
Henderson, J. (2005) *Thresholds of Initiation*, Wilmette, IL: Chiron.
Hill, G. (1992) *Masculine and Feminine*, Boston, MA: Shambhala.
Hillman, J. (1989) *Puer Papers*, Dallas, TX: Spring Publications.
Hopcke, R., Carrington, K.L. and Wirth, S. (eds) (1993) *Same Sex Love*, Boston, MA: Shambhala.
Jung, C.G. (1989) *Aspects of the Masculine*, edited J. Beebe, Princeton, NJ: Princeton University Press.
Jung, E. (1969) *Animus and Anima*, New York: Spring Publications.
Moore, R. and Gillette, D. (1990) *King, Warrior, Magician, Lover*, San Francisco, CA: HarperCollins.
Samuels, A. (ed.) (1985) *The Father*, London: Free Association Books.
Tacey, D. (1997) *Remaking Men*, London: Routledge.
Von Franz, M.L. (1970) *The Problem of the Puer Aeternus*, New York: Spring.
Zoja, L. (2001) *The Father*, East Sussex: Brunner-Routledge.

See also: psychoanalysis

JOHN BEEBE

KARÔSHI

The literal English translation for this Japanese term is 'death from excessive work'. It is a term that since the late 1980s has come to be associated with Japanese corporate culture. However, it should be noted that similar phenomena have also been reported in corporate organisations in other industrialised countries.

Karôshi refers to situations where victims collapse and die, often from cardiac arrest or stroke, as a consequence of work-related stress and fatigue. Underlying this stress and fatigue are often excessively long working hours coupled with intense work responsibilities. Features of Japanese corporate culture such as after-work socialising and difficulty in taking extended holidays also play a role. Moreover, structural readjustments to the workplace since the 1990s, forcing many employees to work harder and longer, have further aggravated the situation. Although victims of *karôshi* include women and younger male employees, the typical victim is often constructed as a middle-aged male, generally occupying a middle-management position. In this sense, the construction of *karôshi* is connected to the dominant ideal of masculinity in post-World War II Japan of the husband/father/provider white-collar 'salaryman', responsible both for the continued prosperity of his corporate organisation and for the sustenance of his family.

Although *karôshi* is not a new phenomenon (the first recorded case dates back to the late 1960s), it only started receiving widespread media attention in the 1980s in Japan and overseas. This publicity and media attention continued through the 1990s, as concerned legal and medical groups took up the cause of compensation for families of victims. Despite widespread publicity and numerous litigations for compensation, corporations and the government have been slow to recognise *karôshi* in itself, as an identifiable cause of death. Although Japan's Ministry of Health, Labour and Welfare did subsequently recognise cases of death from 'cerebro-vascular' or 'cardio-vascular' disease, and even acknowledged a few instances of suicide as linked to *karôshi*, the actual number of cases recognised (and hence eligible for compensation) over the years has been a very small proportion of the total number of cases reported.

References and further reading

National Defence Council for Victims of Karoshi, 'Karoshi Hotline': National Network, at http://www.bekkoame.ne.jp/i/karoshi/index.htm

Zenkoku Karôshi o Kangaeru Kazoku no Kai (National Association of Families Concerned about *Karôshi*) (ed.) (1997) *Shinu hodo Taisestsuna Shigoto-tte nan desu ka: Risutora, Shokuba-ijime jidai ni Karôshi o Kangaeru* (What Job is Important Enough to Die For? Thinking about *Karôshi* in an Age of Restructuring and Workplace Bullying), Tokyo: Kyôiku Shiryô Shuppan-kai.

See also: Japanese masculinities

ROMIT DASGUPTA

L

LADDISM

'The Lads' – white working-class boys, defined through their defiant and humorous opposition to the work ethic and middle-class respectability – were central figures in Willis' school-based ethnography in Britain in the 1970s. Laddish values such as '"having a laugh", alcohol consumption, disruptive behaviour, [and] objectifying women' have been attributed, more recently, to boys generally and implicated in popular and academic explanations for boys' presumed under-achievement and bad behaviour (Francis 1999).

Similar hedonistic values were celebrated in the 'new' laddism popularised in the British media in the 1990s. With new magazines aimed at heterosexual men adopting a laddish tone and addressing 'readers as mates' (Gill 2004), chat and quiz show hosts making laddish jokes and TV sitcoms featuring older men 'behaving badly', not only was laddism milked for entertainment but middle-class and middle-aged men were made (potential) lads.

New Laddism represents a backlash against feminism, which it associates with political correctness, and against male responsibilities linked with traditional breadwinning roles. It is celebrated as self-reflexive and free in opposition to 'older' less narcissistic forms of masculinity, and, in opposition to 'new' more nurturing and caring ways of being men, as refreshingly honest, sexual and smart.

Gill (2004) argues that new laddism counterposed to the 'new man' was a media construction, and that empirical studies have not shown boys straightforwardly inhabiting either identity. There is evidence, however, of laddish values becoming 'hegemonic' although boys' and girls' relationships with these are complex. For example, boys may negotiate a 'middle way' between laddism and their school's academic demands (Frosh *et al.* 2002), white boys may both admire and criticise black laddism (reflecting associations of black masculinities, in contemporary Britain, with laddish values) (Frosh *et al.* 2002), and girls, derided as boring, may complain about boys' 'immaturity' and 'loudness', yet find 'laddish boys' 'appealing and amusing' (Francis 1999).

Laddish humour is a key medium, as recent school-based studies have shown, through which boys establish gendered hierarchies, with boys constructing themselves as funny by feminising seriousness and maturity (Francis 1999; Frosh *et al.* 2002; Kehily and Nayak 1997). The media has elevated laddish humour and males 'behaving badly' to an art form, and the appeal of this to both males and females poses particular problems for feminism. For 'laddism' in the media is presented not only as funny but also as 'ironic', with its male exponents reflexively playing with immaturity and boorishness. Feminist criticisms are deflected by portraying the critics not only as humourless but as too strait-laced to understand the irony.

References and further reading

Francis, B. (1999) 'Lads, lasses and (new) Labour: 14–16 year-old students' responses to the "laddish" behaviour and boys' underachievement debate', *British Journal of Sociology of Education*, 20: 357–73.

Frosh, S., Phoenix, A. and Pattman R. (2002) *Young Masculinities*, Basingstoke: Palgrave.

Gill, R. (2004) 'Power and the production of subjects: a genealogy of the New Man and the New Lad', in B. Benwell (ed.) *Masculinity and Men's Lifestyle Magazines*, Oxford: Blackwell.

Kehily, M. and Nayak, A. (1997) '"Lads and laughter": humour and the production of heterosexual hierarchies', *Gender and Education*, 9 (1): 69–88.

Willis, P. (1977) *Learning to Labour*, Aldershot: Gower.

See also: class, work and masculinity

ROB PATTMAN

LANGUAGE

Contemporary research on language and gender takes into account an awareness of culture, multilingualism and gender, on language performance, preference and development. Notions of language as performance have transformed the Saussurian perspective of language as structure (text-based and linear). Linguistic accounts of language use and acquisition, whether generative or socio-cultural, presuppose that the complexity of language, as a means of positioning, is always made most evident in the interaction between people. Recent debates suggest that interaction is understood as a constructed engagement, not only in terms of the elaboration or restriction of codes deployed by speakers or writers, but also in terms of the subject's positioning *vis-à-vis* the discourse performed by (Coates 1986) or enacted upon subjects (see Bernstein 1975). Gender is a fundamental feature of positioning. Subjectivity and subject positioning have been well interrogated and elaborated in literary studies which, perforce, focus closely on language use. Yet linguistic and educational accounts of language learning and signification appear not to have taken advantage of these insights. Those accounts that do exist draw upon existing structural or constructivist accounts of the construction of knowledge, identity and power.

Typically three broad areas of research are apposite in understanding language and its implications for gender: language and cultural studies, education, and sociology. Even surveys of literacy have begun to interrogate more carefully the relation between gender, literacy acquisition and academic performance (see Wilson and Pillay 1995, for example). Broad sociological surveys are often complemented by smaller studies (situated mostly in schools) that indicate how these findings come to be manifested in day-to-day practice. Wing (1997), for example, discusses the relationship between gender roles, boys' and girls' language, and classroom behaviour, while Balfour analyses boys' and girls' reading and interpretation strategies. Jones *et al.* (1997) have explored gender roles and typing in educational and literary texts, while Stokoe (1997) explores the methodological difficulties associated with research on gender and language.

In general such studies suggest that boys' and men's talk deploys syntax, vocabulary and meaning in ways qualitatively different to the ways girls' and women's talk is deployed. Further, the language reserved for interaction within gender groups has been shown to differ, qualitatively, from the language employed by either group for interaction between gender groups. Finally, the deployment of language to delimit gender roles and typing is is accompanied by behavioural patterns that serve to mark and maintain patriarchal hegemony through a complex process of positioning and signification.

It is clear that the role of gender in language is regarded, unsurprisingly, as part of any agenda in which the deconstruction of power is central. Thus within the research community the study of language and gender tends to derive from feminist theories and/or post-colonial theories in which language is seen as the most generalised means used to (dis)empower or (dis)possess subjects regarded as deviant from predetermined and seemingly natural configurations of normativity (whether as sexual, political or economic) (see Spender 1980). Thus de Klerk's (1997) study of the role of expletives in the construction of masculinity explores the connections between the use of expletives (not far from the concept of 'symbolic violence' defined by Bourdieu and Passeron 1990) and class, suggesting that language, aggression and violence are enacted simultaneously but in different ways depending on the social class and gender of the subject. With respect to the study of language education, genre theorists, critical pedagogues and socio-linguists (see Cameron 1997), all regard learning language from infancy onwards as the primary means by which knowledge, values and normative behaviour come to be constructed. Thus language is the primary means through which (gender) difference and identity is constructed, reinforced, maintained and policed. This has been well documented in relation to language, class and power (see Honey 1997). Philosophers point to a similar trend regarding the enlightenment legacy of rationalism, the language of which is revealed to be masculine and patriarchal.

While many studies focus on the relationship between gender and education, or identity, or race, there are still relatively few studies that have addressed the relationship between language and masculinity (especially from a masculinities studies perspective) per se. There is some scepticism among scholars regarding the necessity of a 'masculinities' perspective on language performance, given the richness of research already undertaken by feminists and linguists who have studied both boys'/men and girls'/women's talk (see Lakoff 1975; Poynton 1985).

References and further reading

Balfour, R. (2003) 'Between the lines: gender and the reception of texts in a rural KwaZulu-Natal school', *Gender and Education*, 15 (2): 183–200.

Bernstein, B. (1975) *Class, Codes and Control: Towards a Theory of Educational Transmission*, Vol. 3, London: Routledge and Kegan Paul.

Bourdieu, P. and Passeron, J.-C. (1990) *Reproduction in Education, Society and Culture*, translated by R. Nice, London: Sage.

Cameron, D. (1997) 'Performing gender identity: young men's talk . . . ', in S. Johnson and U.H. Meinhoff (eds) *Language and Masculinity*, Oxford: Blackwell, pp. 8–26.

Coates, J. (1986) *Women, Men, and Language*, 2nd edn, London: Longman.

de Klerk, V. (1997) 'The role of expletives in the construction of masculinity', in S. Johnson and U.H. Meinhoff (eds) *Language and Masculinity*, Oxford: Blackwell, pp. 144–8.

Honey, J. (1997) *Language is Power: The Story of Standard English and its Enemies*, London: Faber & Faber.

Jones, M.A., Kitetu, C. and Sunderland, J. (1997) 'Discourse roles, gender, and language textbook dialogues: who learns what from John and Sally?' *Gender and Education*, 9 (4): 469–90.

Lakoff, R. (1975) *Language and Women's Place*, New York: Harper and Row.

Poynton, C. (1985) *Language and Gender*, Oxford: Oxford University Press.

Spender, D. (1980) *Man Made Language*, London: Routledge.

Stokoe, E. (1997) 'The evaluation of two studies of gender and language in educational contexts: some problems of analysis', *Gender and Education*, 9 (2): 233–44.

Wilson, F. and Pillay, P. (eds) (1995) *Project for Statistics on Living Standards and Development*, Cape Town: University of Cape Town Press.

Wing, A. (1997) 'How can children be taught to read differently: *Bill's New Frock* and the "hidden curriculum"', *Gender and Education*, 9 (4): 491–504.

See also: culture and representation

ROBERT JOHN BALFOUR

LEISURE

The subject of men and leisure has received scant attention in comparison to the growing literature about women and leisure. Examining men, masculinity and leisure provides insight into how leisure is gendered as well as how leisure can contribute to the quality of life for all individuals.

Leisure is often misunderstood. It has been defined as free time, unobligated time and time away from work. Leisure is used as a noun to mean activity such as playing or watching football, reading, woodworking or hunting. Leisure also is defined as a psychological experience of enjoyment, pleasure or satisfaction, which occurs within the context of time or activity. Further, leisure is an expression of identity and culture regarding what individuals or groups choose, or are socialised, to do in their unobligated time. Leisure can be gendered because some activities, such as team sports, fishing or drinking, are more often associated with boys and men than with women.

Traditionally the study of leisure has been about men's leisure (Henderson *et al.* 1996). Some focus has been placed on men, masculinity and sports (McKay *et al.* 2000), but few efforts have examined leisure related to gender construction and reproduction. Although gender is an important organising principle of society, its influence on boys and men in leisure studies generally has been ignored. Using a gender lens to understand men's leisure requires an analysis of social change related to hegemonic masculinity and men's power over women.

Hegemonic masculinity disadvantages men in their leisure in several ways. For example, men's life expectancy is shorter than women's. This difference is usually the result of lifestyle rather than genetics (Sabo 1998). Unhealthy lifestyle practices associated with some men include drinking, risk-taking or failing to take care of physical and emotional health. Another disadvantage is to boys and men who do not fit the ideal image of masculinity – who are not competitive, tough, successful and heterosexual. They may face problems especially with the hypermasculinity associated with sports (Kimmel and Messner 1998; Messner 1992, 1998). The compulsory nature of sports for boys and men may also constrain opportunities for other leisure activities or constrain the quality of the sports experience for boys. Further, boys' and men's (leisure) participation in some activities such as violent video games and their consumption of pornographic movies and magazines contributes to the reproduction of particular notions of masculinity (Shaw 1999).

The analysis of men's leisure as well as of male scholars doing this research is missing in the leisure literature. Many researchers have not thought about leisure in gendered terms, and some do not see a 'problem' surrounding men and leisure. Most men have more leisure time than most women (Schor 1991), but that apparent difference may or may not mean that men's leisure is more meaningful. Some men may unconsciously believe that gender does not make any difference and discrimination should no longer exist. Without specific research, however, the value of leisure cannot be fully analysed for men, and the status quo will remain.

Researchers ought to ask what leisure would resemble if gender, including both femininity and masculinity, was moved to the centre of analysis. The gendered leisure opportunities and constraints of boys and men would be apparent. The contradiction between the way men are supposed to feel and the way many of them do feel in their daily lives (and leisure) would be evident (Brod and Kaufman 1994). They might try new activities and enjoy their free time more if the opportunities were compatible with their interests and not just with the desire to appear masculine.

Changes are occurring in choices surrounding leisure. New activities such as windsurfing, extreme skiing, snowboarding and skateboarding have evolved in opposition to dominant sporting cultures (e.g. soccer, rugby, American football) because they have fewer rules with less formal restrictions and exclusion policies (Wheaton 2000). These sports also combine the (feminine) aesthetic with (masculine) adventure and danger.

Men's resistance to hegemonic masculinity through leisure needs examination. Leisure participation should be understood not only in factors that reduce or prevent participation (i.e. constraints from participation), but also as factors that cause some activities to become obligatory, and thus act as constraints *into* participation (Shaw 2001). Examining leisure for men might focus on men's emotions and personal identity, men in groups, placing men's experience in structural context, and examining power interactions with one another and with women.

Issues of social identity such as race/ethnic inequalities, social class, sexual orientation and disability status must also be considered since the experiences of leisure are anything but monolithic (McKay *et al.* 2000). Leisure is related to diverse social contexts and individual subjectivities. In other words, examining how a variety of men 'do gender' in relation to how they 'do leisure' will provide insights about leisure experiences among men as well as among women, the role of gender as a leisure enabler, the gendered nature of leisure constraints, and the need to examine hegemonic dimensions of leisure for both women and men.

References and further reading

Brod, H. and Kaufman, M. (eds) (1994) *Theorizing Masculinities*, Thousand Oaks, CA: Sage.

Henderson, K.A., Bialeschki, M.D., Shaw, S.M. and Freysinger, V.J. (1996) *Both Gains and Gaps*, College Park, PA: Venture.

Kimmel, M.S. and Messner, M.A. (ed.) (1998) *Men's Lives*, 4th edn, Boston, MA: Allyn and Bacon.

McKay, J., Messner, M.A. and Sabo, D. (eds) (2000) *Masculinities, Gender Relations, and Sport*, Thousand Oaks, CA: Sage.

Messner, M. (1992) *Power at Play*, Boston: Beacon.

—— (1998) 'Boyhood, organized sports, and the construction of masculinities', in M.S. Kimmel and M.A. Messner (eds) *Men's Lives*, 4th edn, Boston: Allyn and Bacon, pp. 109–21.

Sabo, D. (1998) 'Masculinities and men's health', in M.S. Kimmel and M.A. Messner (eds) *Men's Lives*, 4th edn, Boston, MA: Allyn and Bacon, pp. 347–61.

Schor, J.B. (1991) *The Overworked American*, New York: Basic Books.

Shaw, S.M. (1999) 'Men's leisure and women's lives', *Leisure Studies*, 18: 197–212.

—— (2001) 'Conceptualizing resistance', *Journal of Leisure Research*, 33: 186–201.

Wheaton, B. (2000) 'New lads?' *Men and Masculinities*, 2: 434–56.

See also: sport, athletes and athletic training

KARLA A. HENDERSON

LITERARY THEORY

Literary theory is a generic term usually modified by a specific emphasis (for example, Marxist, feminist, poststructuralist) that refers to theories of reading and of what constitutes the literary.

Although reading has never been unmediated by theory, it was only in the second half of the twentieth century that literary criticism was gradually replaced by the highly contested discourses of critical theory. Literary criticism – which begins with Aristotle's *Poetics* – up until the 1960s was largely regarded as an adjunct to reading, an academic enhancement of a transparent process. Beginning in the 1960s, Anglo-American literary theory shifted from a formalist preoccupation with literary works as discrete objects of study to a contentious debate about the production of meaning, about what difference it makes who is writing or who is reading, and about the effects of various axes of difference, including race, class, gender, sexuality and history. This radical shift was due to two major factors: the critique of the university and its practices of knowledge-formation launched by the US New Left and women's movements; and the translation into English of a wave of European critical theorising that included work by Althusser, Bakhtin, Barthes, Derrida, Foucault, Jauss, Lacan and Lévi-Strauss. In relation to men and masculinity, feminist literary theory is most relevant. Literary theory at the beginning of the twenty-first century draws upon a vast array of disciplines and discourses, including linguistics, philosophy, psychoanalysis, psychology, sociology, anthropology and history. Furthermore, literary theory is now more commonly identified as critical theory to indicate that the notion of the 'literary' has been superseded by the 'textual' and now encompasses a much broader range of cultural artefacts (e.g. film, advertising, mass media, popular culture as well as elite literature).

In the United States, women's studies instigated a re-thinking, or what Rich called a re-visioning, of the literary canon. Among several possible candidates for the ur-text of feminist literary theory, Millett's *Sexual Politics* is most frequently identified. Millett's readings of male authors (Lawrence, Miller, Mailer, Genet) established a political reading of their fiction that sharply differed from the received ideas of the dominant New Critical ways of reading, which bracketed off literary works from considerations of context, class, race or gender. Millett analysed instances of sexual description to reveal the power dynamics in texts that she argued were reproduced in social institutions that maintained men's dominance over women.

This first stage of feminist literary theory focused on the recovery of a neglected female literary tradition with the aim of adding women writers to curricula and anthologies. Biographies and critical works on women writers were produced as context for the republication of many neglected female-authored works. An inevitable concomitant of this emphasis on sexual difference was the identification as masculine of norms that the dominant critical tradition had represented as 'universal'. Initially, an essentialist notion of sexual difference became a lens for reading, and so attention was devoted to the study of women's representations of men and men's representations of women, as well as to the gendered nature of reading (see Flynn and Schweickart 1986). As the essentialist model of opposed male and female natures was discredited, critical work began to be undertaken on the construction and representation of masculinity in literary texts. The canon of American fiction, in particular, was criticised as equating Americanness with being male (Fetterley 1978; Baym 1981) and with excluding women as both proper subjects of fiction and as its creators. Women as readers were said to be 'immasculated', i.e. trained to read as men (Fetterley 1978). In contrast to prevailing theories such as Bloom's 'anxiety of influence', writers like Baym, Fetterley, Gubar and Gilbert and many others argued that literature and literary theory privileged men by creating narratives of creativity that excluded women.

During the same period when women's studies research was establishing the relevance and necessity of female-authored texts, a cluster of French theoretical writings from a variety of disciplinary perspectives were being translated into English and disseminated to profound effect in the Anglo-American academy. Several influential European thinkers drew on the structural linguistics of Saussure to argue that language is a closed system and that meaning cannot be 'authorised' by reference to anything outside a text. The work of adding female-signed texts to the canon was challenged by, for example, Barthes's notion of the 'death of the author', and Foucault's question, 'What difference does it make who is speaking?' (Foucault 1984: 120). The question of reading *as* or *like* a man or woman became central in debates about literary theory in the US during the 1980s as the hitherto parallel tracks of feminist theory and French poststructuralism began to crisscross one another (see Culler 1982; Miller 1986). Some feminist critics (notably Showalter) were wary of what they saw as male critics' opportunistic appropriation of feminist literary theory as it became a successful area of study and publication. The question of men's relation to feminism was often argued in the context of literary theory in the 1980s as male critics began to produce feminist works, often prefaced by anxious justifications for their doing so.

Concurrent with these high-profile intellectual disputes, the work of feminist literary theory continued to revolutionise both what was considered worth reading and how that reading should produce interpretations. Many articles and books argued that critical approaches to canonical works were partial, at best, once the insights of feminist theory were applied; when the difference of experience of female readers was privileged, previously settled interpretations were refashioned. Duyfhuizen's critique of a popular textbook's account of Andrew Marvell's widely taught poem 'To His Coy Mistress' is a paradigmatic example of the kind of work done by both men and women in the 1980s as the canon was revised and expanded. Duyfhuizen revealed the cultural bias in the critical tradition that assumes a poet is a man speaking to men. He described a widely used and representative student handbook as 'an allegory of initiation to masculine criticism' (Duyfhuizen 1988: 416). By positing a female student as the reader of Marvell's poem, Duyfhuizen demonstrated the exclusion of her perspective in commonly accepted interpretations.

The encounter between what was in the 1980s often termed in the US 'French' theory and 'American' feminism (a distinction that was not tenable for long) resulted in a shift away from a focus on sex difference per se in favour of an analysis of gender as a social construction and of the complex interplay between texts and the interpretive choices involved in the reading process. In a landmark collection of essays, Abel wrote that the 'analysis of female talent grappling with a male tradition translates sexual difference into literary difference of genre, structure, voice, and plot' (Abel 1982 :2). As women's studies gradually shifted to gender studies throughout the 1990s, so feminist literary theory widened its scope to a consideration of the functioning of gender in both literary creation and literary history.

Existing on a continuum with feminist literary theory, gender criticism has been particularly significant to masculinity and the study of men in a literary context (see Greenblatt and Gunn 1992: 271–302). Sedgwick's (1985) study of male homosocial bonding and its consequences for women as encountered in the triangles of desire in eighteenth- and nineteenth-century English fiction demonstrates how masculinity studies can enrich literary theory by using the insights of feminist theory to investigate men as gendered subjects. By the end of the twentieth century, gender as a category of analysis dominated literary theory, producing readings of texts in every genre and from every period that highlighted the way in which literature has at once contributed to and reflected the construction and performance of masculinities. Men are now common objects of inquiry *as men* in literary critical works, as is attested to by the large number of studies that link an author's name with the word 'masculinity' (*Conrad and Masculinity*, *Shakespeare and Masculinity* are but two examples, both published in 2000). Gender criticism on literature published since the 1990s is highly diverse. Many of these literary studies of masculinity employ a 'new historical' approach, a corrective to the last two decades of the twentieth century's dominance by ahistorical deconstructive approaches that obscured an account of specific masculinities' cultural effects.

For the generation of male literary scholars who came to feminism not via the women's movement but via late twentieth-century cultural theories, writing about men and masculinity in a feminist framework poses no contradiction of the kind their precursors often struggled with. As Claridge and Langland note, '"Universality" is no gender for either sex' (1990: 8). In their important anthology, the eclecticism of literary critical interest in masculinity is reflected both in the contributors' range of approaches and in the variety of time periods and authors they focus on. The first 'full-length feminist study written by a man' for the prestigious Women in Culture and Society series was published in 1987 (Boone 1987), and its author has also co-edited a collection of essays by male critics who think through the male position in culture in feminism's wake (Boone and Cadden 1990). By 1990, it was no longer necessary for men to be defensive about their right to be feminist literary critics, but Claridge and

Langland also noted in that year that male critics writing against the confines of patriarchal definitions of masculinity were not necessarily feminist (Claridge and Langland 1990). Each historical field of literary study now prominently features work on the representation of men and masculinity as the feminist work of re-vision has expanded from its initial concern with recovery to a current emphasis on the ways identities are structured by language and how gender is performed and understood at different times and in different places. The influence of queer theory, gay and lesbian studies, postcolonial studies (see Edmondson 1999) and new historicism on the broader field of literary theory has had transformative effects on how canonical texts are read and what constitutes notions of the literary, and also has marked out new areas for investigating the dialectical relations between aesthetics and gender formation.

References and further reading

Abel, E. (ed.) (1982). *Writing and Sexual Difference*, Chicago, IL: University of Chicago Press.

Baym, N. (1981) 'Melodramas of beset manhood', *American Quarterly*, 33 (2): 123–39.

Boone, J.A. (1987) *Tradition Counter Tradition*, Chicago, IL: University of Chicago Press.

Boone, J.A. and Cadden, M. (eds) (1990) *Engendering Men*, New York: Routledge.

Claridge, L. and Langland, E. (eds) (1990) *Male Writers and Gender(ed) Criticism*, Amherst, MA: University of Massachusetts Press.

Culler, J. (1982) *On Deconstruction*, Ithaca, NY: Cornell.

Duyfhuizen, B. (1988) 'Textual harassment of Marvell's Coy Mistress', *College English*, 50 (4): 411–23.

Edmondson, B. (1999) *Making Men*, Durham, NC: Duke University Press.

Fetterley, J. (1978) *The Resisting Reader*, Bloomington, IN: Indiana University Press.

Flynn, E.A. and Schweickart, P. (eds) (1986) *Gender and Reading*, Baltimore, MD: Johns Hopkins University Press.

Foucault, M. (1984) 'What is an author?' in P. Rabinow (ed.) *The Foucault Reader*, New York: Pantheon.

Greenblatt, S. and Gunn, G. (eds) (1992) *Redrawing the Boundaries*, New York: MLA.

Miller, N.K. (1986) 'Changing the subject', in T. de Lauretis (ed.) *Feminist Studies/Critical Studies*, Bloomington, IN: Indiana University Press.

Millett, K. (1969) *Sexual Politics*, London: Virago.

Sedgwick, E.K. (1985) *Between Men*, New York: Columbia University Press.

MARK HUSSEY

LITERATURE

Via Old French, from the Latin *litteratura*, 'learning', 'writing' – itself derived from *litteratus*, 'knowledgeable', 'lettered', 'literate' – 'literature' has, until the second half of the twentieth century, signified a body of creative writing, in verse or prose, intended to be differentiated from other, more workaday forms. More recently, however, 'literature' has also included critical or theoretical writing (not only about literary works but also about other, broader topics, such as the nature of art itself), essays and even works of philosophical or historical interest. It has even been expanded to include any writing of a certain length and substance. Thus, for instance, one can read the medical 'literature' on a particular ailment, or one can collect from one's travel agent the 'literature' on one's holiday destination.

The uses or functions of literature

A written literary tradition emerges historically as a consequence of the rise of literacy. If, following a number of historians, we take the modern period to have begun in or around the fifteenth to sixteenth centuries, then in pre-modernity literacy was generally limited to members of the upper classes, who could afford to acquire and had the leisure to read books, in whatever form (scrolls, illuminated manuscripts, etc.). Even so, not all members of the upper classes were literate.

In traditional societies with an oral rather than a written literary tradition, the bard – the poet or troubadour who recited in verse and sometimes in song literary renditions of the culture's history, legends or mythology –

made it possible for a broad range of people to hear, at least, if not to read for themselves the literature of their people, even if this was limited chiefly to the deeds of the noble classes. One of the earliest representations of this kind of oral literary tradition is to be found in the Greek poet Homer's two epic verse narratives, *Iliad* and *Odyssey*, thought to have been composed around the eighth century BC. Homer, himself believed to have been a bard, describes bardic recitations to audiences that, in addition to landowners, often included servants or slaves.

Literature and the literary text have historically invoked and provoked a range of responses in their relevant cultural contexts. One of the earliest debates on the value and function of literature, at least in the West, turned ostensibly on moral and ethical issues. In his *Republic*, the Greek philosopher Plato in the fifth century BC argued for the exclusion of poets (by which he meant writers of all sorts) from his ideal republic because the work they produced affected the audience/reader by heightening the emotions and addling reason, something anathema to Plato's notion that the world could be known through natural reason and through a process of simple investigations leading to a complex conclusion. Many readers of Plato's work, however, have questioned the purity of the moral issue he invokes, because he does permit into his republic those poets who are adept at working the citizens up into the proper state of mind for heroic deeds, nationalist pride and so on – in other words, propagandists.

Aristotle, Plato's contemporary, implicitly challenged this moral question in his *Poetics* by arguing that literature – specifically, tragic drama – actually had a morally and emotionally purging effect (which he called *catharsis*) on the audience, leaving it cleansed, morally uplifted and devoid of 'negative' emotions. Plato and Aristotle thus established a key theme for future critics and defenders of literature, for the debate has continued over the centuries since the fifth century BC about whether literature's capacity to create imaginary worlds, characters and actions, and to sway the reader's emotions, is a positive or negative quality. (There are many anthologies of critical writing on literature and art that present a broad historical sweep from Plato to the present; see, for instance, Gilbert 1962; Allen and Clark 1962; Smith and Parks 1951.)

Indeed, as literary forms have emerged or gained popularity, they have often been stigmatised as leading innocent readers or audiences into dangerous states of mind. For instance, the Puritans in England in the earlier seventeenth century regarded the theatre, a dominant art form at the time, as a sink of iniquity, encouraging vice and immorality in the audiences that attended plays, while the authorities of the time often also regarded the theatre as dangerous, because it encouraged sedition and treason against the government and the monarch. In the late eighteenth and early nineteenth centuries, critics inveighed against the new literary form of narrative fiction, the novel, claiming that it invited idleness and stirred up the emotions. Some even advised against allowing young women and girls to read novels, since such publications could induce hysteria and cause prolapsing of the uterus! In the past half-century, we have seen the same arguments adduced against film, television and pornography: all of these have been named as producing antisocial behaviours, summoning forth inappropriate emotions and practices, and so on.

In addition to indirectly addressing Plato's complaints against literature, Aristotle's *Poetics* sought also to analyse tragedy into its component parts, and to show how it was typically structured. This too has remained a central approach in reading and understanding literary texts, and has led to the distinguishing of various *genres* or types of text, based on common features, structures or purposes, as well as explorations of language use. While from about 1980 onwards these generic distinctions have been called into question – whether because they were felt to be too restrictive, or because in fact most texts draw on a range of sets of generic structures and features, thereby becoming cross-generic or generic hybrids – genre categories remain important in the publishing industry and in the ways in which booksellers set up their businesses, identifying the kinds of work (romance, science fiction, etc.) available.

'Classics' versus contemporary and/or popular literature

The term 'classics' in relation to literature has developed two key meanings. The first distinguishes between the work of the classical Greek and Roman writers and material written since classical times, while the second distinguishes between canonical literature (that is, works officially and institutionally sanctioned as great writing or good literature, and therefore often taught in the schools and universities, as well as being held up as a key cultural text; for instance, Shakespeare's plays, Tolstoy's *War and Peace*) and popular literature, a category that includes what booksellers sometimes call 'contemporary' – that is, writing intended as serious literary work but not (yet) canonised as 'classic'.

The distinction between Greco-Roman classics and vernacular literatures has a long history, dating back to the later Middle Ages and the emergence of vernacular literature as part of a developing sense of national identity. Accorded value because of its antiquity and its integral association with what the nineteenth-century American poet Edgar Allan Poe called 'the glory that was Greece, and the grandeur that was Rome' ('To Helen'), classical writing was deemed by many to have said all that there was to say, and to have said it as fluently and persuasively as possible. All subsequent writing could be only variations on that classical original. There was, inevitably, a groundswell of dissent against the pressure to use classical works and themes as the only worthwhile models for contemporary writing, a dissent that became manifest, for instance, in late seventeenth-century France in the so-called Quarrel of the Ancients and the Moderns, its English equivalent satirically reflected in Jonathan Swift's 1697 *Battle of the Books*.

Classical literature, however, remained ascendant until the end of the nineteenth century in the universities, where it was thought to provide an essential training in logic, criticism, history and rhetoric. The introduction of vernacular literature as a legitimate object of academic study was the result of a struggle that sought to undo the mindset which held that Classics (the capital indicating the academic field of study) was appropriate for the 'more able' student, whereas the study of the vernacular literature ('English,' as it came to be called in Britain and the US) was dismissed as appropriate only to the 'less able', a group which included women and working-class men, as well as those middle- and upper-class males who could not cope with Classics. One effect of the legitimation of vernacular literature as the object of academic/educational study was the canonisation of some works over the rest as 'great literature' or part of a national tradition. (For one account of this history of struggle, see Mathieson 1975.)

The social and cultural upheaval during and following World War I saw the foregrounding of vernacular literatures as part of the process of rebuilding the idea of the nation in the minds of the people. At the same time, given the ascendancy in the culture of science from the mid-nineteenth century onward, there was in addition an attempt to make the reading and study of literature more 'scientific', in opposition to the more impressionistic approach of the later nineteenth century, which assumed that the cultivated person had a natural affinity for and 'appreciation' of literature. I.A. Richards's important 1929 publication *Practical Criticism*, for instance, sought to establish the terms by which anyone could learn to read poetry (Richards 1964). The school of criticism that came to be called the New Criticism included such figures as F.R. and Q.D. Leavis in Britain and Cleanth Brooks in the US, the British critics tending to emphasise the moral and ethical dimensions of literature (its capacity to 'improve' the reader), the American ones the formal aspects (structure, rhetoric and so on).

Though there were other important theories of art and literature, such as Marxist criticism, New Criticism held sway in the English-speaking literary worlds until the late 1960s, when theories of art and literature based on different sets of assumptions and approaches began to rise in importance. These included semiotic and structuralist theories, guided initially by the work of thinkers such as Roland Barthes; new Marxist theories, inspired by Louis Althusser, Antonio Gramsci and others; and Russian formalism (sometimes also called Russian semiotics or structuralism), propounded by figures such as Viktor Shklovsky, Mikhail Bakhtin and Roman Jakobson.

Literature, genre and gender

Some categories of literature are gendered by their intended readership. Thus, for example, romance fiction is assumed to be feminine because it is largely written for female readers, whereas science fiction, now often read also by women, was until recently thought of as literary material for male readers, and hence masculine literature. It is also the case that, at different moments in a culture's literary history, certain genres come to be dominant, and are often therefore assumed to be in some way 'masculine', while the remainder are distributed along a conceptual axis between masculinity and femininity. Thus, for instance, today prose fiction is the dominant literary form, and tends to be considered 'masculine' – at any rate, male writers in the genre are not derided as feminine, which is not the case with, say, male poets, many of whom, operating within the legacy of the image of the nineteenth-century Romantic poet, are often deemed to be highly sensitive, emotionally vulnerable and therefore in some way feminised. By contrast, playwrights now appear to occupy a fairly neutral position, though of course individual plays and the work of particular playwrights may well be strongly gendered.

Indeed, nowadays the study of literature itself is sometimes seen, especially in high schools both by some students and by teaching staff, as inappropriate to aggressively masculine ('real') boys, so that, while literature may be thought innocuous for girls, boys who elect to study literature may be subject to derision and ridicule. At the same time, some educational systems consider literature difficult, and ironically reverse nineteenth-century practice by making the study of literature available only to the 'more able' student, which implicitly creates an elite (though one which, for many excluded from it, remains feminised).

For other systems in former European colonies the study of the colonial power's literature may be seen as a nostalgic attachment to the past, which in turn may be read as a feminisation of the nation or its intelligentsia, or as an attempt to acquire mastery over the former power's culture, which by contrast would be read as a move towards (re-)masculinisation of the nation.

Literature and the masculine

It has been argued forcefully by a number of feminist critics that, given the historical dominance by men in the culture, most literary works will tend almost inevitably to represent the masculine point of view. To counter this, many scholars have set themselves the task of uncovering and publishing works by hitherto unknown and neglected women writers.

However, the literary representation of masculinity is by no means a simple issue. Today, few readers and critics would accept the view that the literary text unproblematically reflects a prior social reality. More subtle approaches to the literary text today explore not only what the text explicitly says, but also what it *fails* to say – its silences and suppressions, its indirections and implications. What emerges from this is a more complex understanding of the text that is able, as is the case with a queer reading, to expose the contradictions, uncertainties and anxieties that may underlie the representation and/or construction of gender – and specifically of masculinity – in a work of literature.

References and further reading

Allen, G.W. and Clark, H.H. (eds) (1962) *Literary Criticism*, Detroit, MI: Wayne State University Press.

Gilbert, A.H. (ed.) (1962) *Literary Criticism*, Detroit, MI: Wayne State University Press.

Mathieson, M. (1975) *The Preachers of Culture*, London: George Allen and Unwin.

Richards, I.A. (1964) *Practical Criticism*, London: Routledge and Kegan Paul.

Smith, J.H. and Parks, E.W. (eds) [1951] (1977) *The Great Critics*, New York: W.W. Norton.

See also: culture and representation; detective novel, crime fiction; literary theory; science fiction; sports literature, sportscasting

DAVID BUCHBINDER

LOVE

'The stage is more beholding to Love than the life of man,' wrote Shakespeare's contemporary Bacon (1625), confirming the prevalence of heterosexual romantic love in literature. Bacon distinguishes three sorts of love: marital love, which 'maketh mankind' through sexual reproduction; 'wanton love', presumably including romance; and 'friendly love', the highest human form, to be found only between equals, which for most centuries and most cultures meant love between men.

In monotheistic religions, God's love for humanity and the believer's love for God are often held up as examples for the most selfless human love, which aspires only to the beloved's good, while polytheisms may feature deities of earthly love like the Roman Venus, Hindu Parvati or Voodoo Erzulie. In Plato's *Symposium* (early fourth century BCE), Aristophanes defines love as a longing for completion by one's 'other half', preferably both being men, whereas Socrates defines love as the quest for the good and the beautiful, beginning with desire for a beautiful young man though ultimately transcending the body for eternal philosophic ideals.

Although it has been allegorically interpreted as signifying divine love, the Judeo-Christian Bible includes a great poem of heterosexual love, the Song of Solomon, which claims that 'love is strong as death' (Solomon 8: 6). The New Testament uses the language of homosocial love to describe Jesus's mission and sacrifice: 'This is my commandment, That ye love one another, as I have loved you. Greater love hath no man than this, that a man lay down his life for his friends' (John 15: 12–13).

Thus simultaneously love is seen as a rare, peak and enobling experience and as a virtually universal feeling. Rare and pitied is the person who claims he is not loved or cannot love. The love of parents for children and of children for parents is assumed to be natural, if not instinctive, though mothers' love is often considered stronger than fathers' love. In the literature of romantic love, men are usually the ideal lovers, devoted and constant. In Persian and Arabic medieval poetry, the beloved may be a woman or young man. In European medieval literature, she may be a married or marriageable woman whose love inspires the man's heroic deeds. In classical Japanese and Chinese poetry, the lover may be a spouse of either sex longing for an absent partner.

The belief in idealising love as primarily male continues into the present, although women in love become the staple of novels and popular culture from the eighteenth century onward. Goethe's sorrowful hero Werther (1774) committed suicide from unrequited love for a married woman, supposedly inspiring real suicides. Men's treatises on love from Stendahl's in 1822 to Freud's writings in the early twentieth century describe romantic love as an exciting fantasy in which a man idealises and pursues a woman, often to be disillusioned after sexual consummation. According to Freud, erotic attachments are all based on the child's early love of the caregiving mother. The Oedipus complex describes normal male heterosexual development: the boy loves and wants sole possession of his mother, but because he is frightened of his powerful rival, his father, he represses this incestuous early love and instead after puberty turns his affection towards another adult woman. However, since idealising love is connected with the mother, Freud theorises that many men split their affections between devotion to a maternal wife and sexual passion for women unlike the wife/mother, like prostitutes or mistresses.

Although romantic love is supposed to ennoble the lover, its derangement or perversion includes harmful passions, such as sadism and masochism, both predominantly male, in which the desire to hurt and dominate or be hurt and dominated by the beloved fuses with sexual satisfaction. Jealousy and behaviours now characterised as harassment were previously accepted as normal for men in love – like following the beloved everywhere and not taking 'no' for an answer. Men's feelings of possession and entitlement reach a negative extreme against wives and girlfriends who leave or reject them. Even honour killings, in which men murder wives, daughters or sisters for alleged unchastity, can be seen as partly springing from feelings that the beloved is the property of the lover, her behaviour reflecting on his, so that he would rather destroy her than allow another man to possess her.

In contemporary popular culture, unmarried men are frequently portrayed as fearing love, commitment and monogamy, while women are assumed to be more interested in, and more susceptible to, romantic love. Some twentieth-century feminists have therefore attacked romantic love as a masculine strategy for persuading free women to become subordinated wives (Greer 1971). Although popular culture is based on fantasies, it shapes people's expectations and actions, and Hollywood images of romantic love are now circulated globally. Fed by popular culture and merchandising, occasions like anniversaries, a woman's birthday and Valentine's day are supposed to bring forth gifts and expressions of love from male partners. This influence can also be seen in some US men's formal marriage proposals, even to women with whom they have had sustained sexual relationships – for example, with surprise diamond rings presented on cakes at fancy restaurants or during hikes to mountain peaks. Homosexual as well as heterosexual relationships are now also sometimes represented by romantic language and symbolism.

References and further reading

Bacon, F. (1986) 'On Love', *Essays*, New York: Penguin.

Freud, S. (1997). *Sexuality and the Psychology of Love*, New York: Touchstone/Simon and Schuster.

Goethe, W. (1989) *The Sorrows of Young Werther*, New York: Penguin.

Greer, G. (1971) *The Female Eunuch*, New York: McGraw Hill.

Hippocrene Books (eds) (1999) *Love Poems from Around the World*, New York: Hippocrene.

Plato (2001) *Plato's Symposium*, translated by S. Benerdete, Chicago, IL: University of Chicago Press.

Stendhal (Beyle, H.) (1957) *On Love*, translated by T. Talbot, New York: Meridian.

See also: emotions; intimacy; marriage

JUDITH KEGAN GARDINER

LYNCHING

Lynching involves acting outside the legal system to inflict punishment, often fatal, against individuals perceived as committing some offence against social order. Beyond tarring and feathering in the English mode, lynching in the US has comprised acts of beating, hanging, dragging, torture, mutilation and burning, and has occurred in every region during social, economic and political crises. Although sometimes attacking alleged criminals, lynchers usually targeted members of stigmatised groups, including immigrants, political radicals, religious, sexual and racial minorities. Lynching also was identified with the frontier as a form of Wild West vigilantism. The lynch mob, lynch law and the legendary 'Judge Lynch' have become defining figures of US culture.

After the Civil War, white men, often organised through terrorist groups like the Ku Klux Klan, used lynching to reassert their rule over newly emancipated blacks and prevent their assuming the traditional masculine roles of provider, protector and property-owner. During the peak of lynching violence, the 1880s to the 1930s in the deep South, at least one lynching a week was recorded, including of women and children (Tolnay and Beck 1995). White crowds celebrated in a carnival atmosphere. This state-sanctioned terror was justified by an ideology of southern chivalry, predicated on superior white men protecting fragile white women from beastly black men, as in the D.W. Griffith film *Birth of a Nation* (1915). Anti-lynching crusader Ida B. Wells-Barnett pointed out that this sexual rationale cast African Americans as unworthy of political rights and economic gains (1997). Lynching thus exposes the violence needed to sustain racial patriarchy based in notions of Anglo-Saxon manhood supremacy.

When possible, African Americans fought the lynchers. From its 1909 founding, the National Association for the Advancement of Colored People published annual lynching statistics, lobbied for federal laws, and organised mass protests (Zangrando 1980).

Currently, police brutality and the death penalty can be seen as forms of 'legal lynching' that perpetuate the myth of the dangerous black male.

References and further reading

Allen, J., Hilton, A., Lewis, J. and Litwack, L.F. (2000) *Without Sanctuary*, Santa Fe, NM: Twin Palms.

Brown, M.J. (2000) *Eradicating This Evil*, New York and London: Garland.

Tolnay, S.E. and Beck, E.M. (1995) *A Festival of Violence*, Urbana and Chicago, IL: University of Illinois Press.

Wells-Barnett, I.B. (1997) *Southern Horrors and Other Writings*, edited J.J. Royster, Boston, MA and New York: Bedford.

Zangrando, R.L. (1980) *The NAACP Crusade Against Lynching, 1909–1950*, Philadelphia, PA: Temple University Press.

MARLON B. ROSS

M

MACHISMO (AND MACHO)

As synonyms for sexism, 'machismo' and 'macho' have a very short history. 'Macho', for example, first appeared in Mexico in the late 1930s and in the United States about a decade later. In Latin America today, the term 'machismo' still has a social science and journalistic ring for many people, and is less commonly used in everyday speech than is the case north of the border, despite the fact that many people in the United States assume that 'machismo' has a uniform and long sociolinguistic lineage in Latin America. On the contrary, within Latin America, the terms 'macho' and 'machismo' have far more divergent meanings for different people than is the case in the United States.

'Machismo' must be viewed as describing more than simply sexist ideas: in most usages the expression refers to a whole network of (generally unequal) social relations between men and women and between men and men – relations that involve far more than mental constructs alone.

The semantic roots of the word 'macho' relate in part to what is genetically male in animals and plants, not cultural values. Some scholars trace the sexist notion of macho to the Spanish who conquered the Indigenous peoples of Mesoamerica 500 years ago. Others claim that the Spanish encountered a sexist, macho Indigenous tradition upon their arrival. A brilliant essay by Américo Paredes (1967) demonstrates the clear connections between the advent of machismo and nationalism, racism and international affairs, between the peculiar history of US–Mexican relations in the nineteenth century and the individualist and self-sacrificing *vaquero*-cowboy. Américo chides those who let their imaginations dwell on the rape of Indian women and asks how Mexican is machismo and to what degree is it a Hispanic, a New World, or a universal manifestation.

References and further reading

González López, G. (2005) *Erotic Journeys*, Berkeley, CA: University of California Press.

Gutmann, M.C. (1996) *The Meanings of Macho*, Berkeley, CA: University of California Press.

Lancaster, R.N. (1992) *Life is Hard*, Berkeley, CA: University of California Press.

Núñez Noriega, G. (1994) *Sexo entre varones*, Mexico City: UNAM/Porrúa/El Colegio de Sonora.

Paredes, A. [1967] (1993) 'The United States, Mexico, and machismo', in A. Paredes, *Folklore and Culture on the Texas–Mexican Border*, Austin, TX: University of Texas Press, pp. 215–34.

Zinn, M.B. (2001) 'Chicano men and masculinity', in M.A. Messner and M.S. Kimmel (eds) *Men's Lives*, Boston, MA: Allyn and Bacon, pp. 24–32.

See also: cultural formations, Latin America; history, Latin America

MATTHEW C. GUTMANN

MALE

Although commonly understood to relate to a biological sex distinction from female, the term 'male' is heavily implicated in cultural notions of manliness, masculinities and maleness.

Arguably the most powerful identification on all human subjects is that of sex. 'Is it a boy or a girl?' is invariably the first question asked of the newborn child. This seemingly apolitical question is, however, invested with powerful signifiers and expectations which will surround and inform the child from that moment on and throughout its life. In that respect, while it might be socially necessary, and not least welcomed by the parents, identifying a newborn child as male or female is also a political act for the reason that such naming imposes gendered expectations, limitations and conditions upon that child, even if that is not the intention. How the individual child, and subsequent adult, copes with, negotiates, overcomes and responds to such expectations can be seen to be evidence of the unique artistry that goes into each discursive subject's (individual's) self creation (Foucault 1991).

Biology is, then, never far from discussions around men, masculinities and maleness; indeed, it is the desire to critique the essentialist assumptions underpinning patriarchal ideologies and gendered discourses that motivates most contributors to the sociology of masculinity (Whitehead and Barrett 2001). However, 'male' is one of those points at which biology and culture powerfully connect and confuse. The child can legitimately be pronounced 'male', if only on account of its genitalia. Indeed, clearly identifying their sex as male or female can be seen to be a necessary process for all children, not least because at that point their positioning within the social web is, apparently, guaranteed and legitimised. But is this labelling 'male' so uncorrupted by the cultural values which actually prefigure and constitute the social web? Poststructuralist writers such as Judith Butler would argue not. For Butler (1993), the terms 'male' and 'female' are not pre-given truths about the human subject, but correspond to performative acts or 'practices of self-signification' that serve to locate the discursive subject in associated regimes of power/knowledge. The child is, at birth and through the subsequent act of naming it male (or female), posited in a discursive power regime which will, from that moment on and in culturally specific ways, configure and influence its process of self-identification.

Similarly drawing on feminist poststructuralist understandings, Whitehead (2002) argues that concepts such as 'male' and 'female', while having a biological presence, remain foremost ontological locations for the ungrounded discursive subject. In other words, prior to the naming of the child as 'male' (or female) it has potentially little or no legitimate presence in the social world and therefore is denied access to the gendered discourses that provide one of the primary identification signifiers for the human subject. As Whitehead argues, being male is, then, more than a biological identification based on physique, appearance, body structure, genitalia: it is a social naming that enables the discursive subject to pursue a masculine ontology – 'to be and become' male/man/masculine, thereby mitigating any potential existentialist disruption that might accrue from otherwise being 'nameless' (also McNay 2000).

The persuasiveness of this masculine ontological quest is given added force by the commonly held assumptions and expectations that surround the word 'male'. Such expectations were subject to examination in some of the earliest writings within the sociology of masculinity. Theorists such as Joseph Pleck (1981) explored the concept of the 'male sex role' and the pressures on males to conform to predetermined, socially prescribed models of masculine behaviour. Pleck was highly influential in promoting the 'male sex role' concept as a means to explain the social constructionist and psychological dynamics of gender. He argued that contemporary changes in work and relationships, coupled with pressures on men to demonstrate more feminine traits such as emotional expression, were creating a tension for many males. Masculine ideology was recognised as fundamentally incompatible with these new and powerful social pressures on men to change, one consequence being a 'male role strain' as men attempted to negotiate a shift from 'traditional' to 'modern' gender roles. However, Brittan (1989) was one of those who noted that male role theory was based on an essentialist assumption, whereby 'roles are added to biology to give us gender' and that the roles under discussion were far too simplistic and limiting to cover the diversity apparent across the category of males (see also Connell 1987).

Similarly, if the work of influential psychologists such as Sigmund Freud and Carl Jung has any grounded assumptions, they are that male and female are essentially different and will remain so, the only variables being the familial, social and cultural experiences that may impact on the male and female through childhood and adulthood. Convenient as this assumption may be for some psychologists, there is a clear risk that it will inevitably influence their ability to apply a depth analysis to complex social and psychological phenomena, not least because the inevitability of male and maleness, as they assume it, becomes its own predictor of behaviour.

A similar position can be adopted in respect of the male body. The male body is inevitably inscribed with masculinities, and masculinities, by definition, speak to and of the male body (Morgan 1993). Therefore, even to speak of the male body is to some extent serving to reify the male–female dualism at the heart of sex/gender discourses and ideologies. In our everyday lived lives we exist within, alongside and in relationship to male and female bodies, even though we have the intellectual means to dismiss the male, and its body, to recognise it as not given but as a contested terrain, the ultimate surface upon which power and resistance operate (Foucault 1984). Indeed, we draw on such gendered embodiment in our own self-identification work. There seems no escape from the male–female dualism. The best we can hope for, then, is to constantly work at questioning, critiquing and disrupting those dominant, powerful understandings which surround and are invested in the term 'male' and that serve to make it appear fixed, unchanging and real.

So what comes with the term 'male' – beyond, that is, the material body? At this point we move into the epistemological dimensions of gender. For example, can we identify a male way of thinking and relating to the world, a form of masculine subjectivity which is particularly male? Certainly there is a strong argument to be made that the experience of living in a sexed/gendered body, and its location in a gendered social web, has the distinct potential to create a gendered subjectivity, in this case male. In other words, the fact that I am male and am discursively positioned within the category of males strongly suggests that I am highly likely to see the world through a subjective 'male gaze' (Middleton 1992). Feminist writer Alison Assiter (1996) makes exactly this case for women, who, she argues, exist in a political categorisation as an 'epistemic community'. Assiter suggests that women develop a feminine subjectivity, a set of knowledges and understandings that are the direct consequence of their social experiences in the political community of women (see also Stanley and Wise 1993).

At this point we can see that there is nothing that is male which is preordained at birth: knowledge, body, roles, behaviour, all are subject to that tantalisingly powerful variable called culture, be it mediated through ideology or discourse. Yet maybe there is something which is undeniably predicted by being male, something fixed and unchanging, at least at its core, throughout the male's life. This is the political place of the male. To be born a male is to be born into a gendered political category which exists primarily, if not only, in relation to the political category of female. To be sure, these categories are macro and not predictors of individual subjectivity or behaviour, but they do exist. That fact would seem self-evident to any feminist or profeminist contributor to these debates. So when a male speaks, he speaks not only for himself, he speaks as a member of the category of males, and in many social and cultural settings males are not only heard first, they are heard loudest, and expect to be. Being male brings with it a gendered presence, and whatever its individual manifestation might be, it is not female. Indeed, it is this dualist distinction which renders male 'real' in the first place, for without the female male cannot exist: it would have no political place, no political purpose, no political platform from which to measure its worth, identity, status – manliness.

Always the aim of the critical gender theorist is, then, to look beyond, or behind, the given commonsense assumptions that come with powerful terms such as 'male'. It is too easy to merely locate male as the biological essence from which all else – roles, masculinities, manliness, sexuality – flows. If we succumb to this thinking then we merely reinforce the very determinism that must be challenged and overcome if we are to fully recognise the diversity and contrasts existing across the social and political category that is 'male'. Also, the social understandings which come with 'male' can be seen to be historically specific, changing and unpredictable. What it means to be male in one social setting is not inevitably translated into another. Likewise, throughout history we can see that being male carries different expectations dependent on the cultural context. However, as is argued above, if there is one uniform characteristic of male it is that it brings with it benefits in respect of power, influence, possibilities, though these are heavily mitigated by factors such as race, ethnicity, sexuality and class.

Yet to fall back on a wholly ideological account of the term 'male' is similarly problematic. For example, should we consider 'male' to be a blank page upon which are subsequently written the scripts of culture, ideology, discourse, and from which emerge the social constructs 'boy', man', 'masculinity'? Certainly this was the direction of early theorising within the genre of the sociology of masculinity, but as Whitehead (2002), Petersen (1998) and others have noted, not only did this theoretical position serve to deny the agentic possibilities among men (and women), it gives little or no account of male power, male identity work or male subjectivity. Do all males think the same? Are all males invested with the same predictors of behaviour from conception? Are all males prone to violence? Is men's power merely, and only, a consequence of being male? Are males biologically incapable of changing? If a child is male can I – indeed, should I – make any assumptions about how he will fare at school, with girls, with his mates, in a future career? For sociologists the answer to all these questions must be 'no', and in that respect as feminist and profeminist theorists we undertake our exploration of men and masculinities somewhat separated from everyday, commonsense, understandings surrounding male and female which tend to view male and female as ultimately biological, and therefore unchanging, constructs. For sociologists there is no inevitability to the gender order or any particular male/female status quo: all is open to question and to change.

So, in the final analysis, what can we say of males? Are they a social/cultural illusion or are they a concrete, embodied reality? The answer is they are neither simply illusion nor reality. Rather, males are a complex mix of biology and culture, though let us place more emphasis on the culture than the biology, for that would recognise the diversity, the changeability, the fluidity of the male while steering us away from a reductionist, essentialist perspective. What we do know is that there is nothing predictable about individual males, other than their social positioning in a gendered political category, and even that is heavily mitigated by factors such as class, race, ethnicity and age. Male is one half of a primary social dualism and as such it provides a powerful and universal identification on those who are born into its category. Understanding how individual and particular social groups of males subsequently experience and construct this identity is a key objective within the sociology of masculinity.

References and further reading

Assiter, A. (1996) *Enlightened Women: Modernist Feminism in a Post-Modern Age*, London: Routledge.
Brittan, A. (1989) *Masculinity and Power*, Oxford: Blackwell.
Butler, J. (1993) *Bodies that Matter: On the Discursive Limits of 'Sex'*, New York: Routledge.
Connell, R. (1987) *Gender and Power*, Cambridge: Polity.
Foucault, M. (1984) 'Nietzsche, genealogy, history', in P. Rabinow (ed.) *The Foucault Reader*, London: Penguin.
—— (1991) 'On the genealogy of ethics: an overview of work in progress', in P. Rabinow (ed.) *Technologies of Self: A Seminar with Michel Foucault*, London: Tavistock.
McNay. L. (2000) *Gender and Agency*, Cambridge: Polity.
Middleton, P. (1992) *The Inward Gaze: Masculinity and Subjectivity in Modern Culture*, London: Routledge.
Morgan, D.H. (1993) 'You too can have a body like mine: reflections on the male body and masculinities', in S. Scott and D. Morgan (eds) *Body Matters*, London: Falmer Press.
Petersen, A. (1998) *Unmasking the Masculine: 'Men' and 'Identity' in a Sceptical Age*, London: Sage.
Pleck, J.H. (1981) *The Myth of Masculinity*, Cambridge, MA: MIT Press.
Stanley, L. and Wise, S. (1993) *Breaking Out Again: Feminist Ontology and Epistemology*, London: Routledge.
Whitehead, S.M. (2002) *Men and Masculinities: Key Themes and New Directions*, Cambridge: Polity.
Whitehead, S.M. and Barrett, F.J. (eds) (2001) *The Masculinities Reader*, Cambridge: Polity.

See also: bodies and biology, male; feminist theory; gender role strain; manhood; masculinity/masculinities; masculinity politics; men; power relations; sex role theory

STEPHEN M. WHITEHEAD

MALE GAZE

The term, describing a cinema-viewing mechanism, was coined by Laura Mulvey in a 1975 essay. Using psychoanalytic and semiological theories, Mulvey delves into a complex relationship between spectator and film text. She studies a number of classical Hollywood films in order to unveil a viewing apparatus whereby the male gaze, equipped with political, economic, social and sexual power, consigns women to silence, marginality and absence. In conventional narrative films – argues Mulvey – men are 'bearers of the look' whereas women connote 'to-be-looked-at-ness'. This is accomplished in a three-step process: the look of the camera involved in recording the pre-filmic event, that of the male characters within the narrative, and that of the spectator who identifies with a male protagonist on screen. In the essay, Mulvey consistently uses the masculine pronoun to refer to the spectator. Criticised for neglecting female spectators, Mulvey wrote 'afterthoughts' to the original article, arguing that the spectator was not necessarily male but adopted a masculine subject position.

The essentialist binarism of Mulvey's argument was challenged by a number of critics who pointed out that, in the signifying practices of the text, masculinity is not always aligned with activity. Nor is femininity permanently equated with passivity. Neale (1983) questions Mulvey's assertion that men are never sexually objectified within the space of the film, noting a voyeuristic gaze directed at male characters by other men in Westerns and epic films. Stacey (1987) makes a similar contention regarding women and explores erotic exchanges of looks between female characters in contemporary, as well as classical, Hollywood films. Other commentators suggest that gender is not the only factor in determining subject positions in spectatorship. Race, ethnicity, class, nationality, sexuality, etc., are also key factors. hooks (1992) politicises looking relations by actively proposing a viewing strategy, an 'oppositional gaze', that would negotiate hegemonic norms and values both in spectatorship and film-making. The option of an interrogating gaze, of looking back, of appropriating a visual space, of naming what is seen – in other words, creating a space for agency – became a key issue of the debate on looking relations in the 1990s.

References and further reading

hooks, b. (1992) 'Oppositional gaze', in b. hooks, *Black Looks. Race and Representation*, Boston, MA: South End Press.

Mulvey, L. (1975) 'Visual pleasure and narrative cinema', *Screen*, 16 (3): 6–18.

—— (1981) 'Afterthoughts on "Visual pleasure and narrative cinema" inspired by King Vidor's *Duel in the Sun* (1946)', *Framework*, 10: 3–10.

Neale, S. (1983) 'Masculinity as spectacle', *Screen*, 24 (6): 2–16.

Stacey, J. (1987) 'Desperately seeking difference', *Screen*, 28 (1): 48–61.

ELŻBIETA H. OLEKSY

MALE LESBIAN

A male lesbian is a biological male who claims to be a lesbian. The term 'male lesbian' was first used by Thais E. Morgan in a 1992 article entitled 'Male lesbian bodies: the construction of alternative masculinities in Courbet, Baudelaire, and Swinburne'. Morgan argues that a male lesbian identification allows men to occupy both gender positions, thereby retaining male privilege. Elizabeth Ladenson (1999) and Kaja Silverman (1992) discuss Marcel Proust as a lesbian from a psychoanalytic perspective. Silverman describes the male lesbian as someone whose sexuality is oral rather than phallogocentric. She reads Proust as a homosexual man who can love men as well as lesbian women, and who occupies a feminine psychic position. Ladenson, on the other hand, believes that the immutability of the body means that male lesbianism involves a male's identification with his female lover. Naomi Schor argues that the nineteenth-century term 'a feminine', used by Gustave Flaubert and Paul Verlaine to describe themselves, designates the category today understood as the male lesbian. According to Schor, male lesbianism allows men to identify with passivity and to withdraw from the demands of masculinity.

Jacquelyn Zita argues against the immutability of the body, suggesting that biological sex is itself constructed by discourse. She disputes the 'realness' of any given sex, gender or sexuality category and suggests that men who happen to be lesbians (socially, politically or sexually) can be included, despite male embodiment, in the category 'lesbian' through a de-essentialising strategy which would allow for 'passage from one sex to the other through the meanings given to sex-specific sex acts' (Zita 1992: 120). A male can have sex as a female, through a kind of erotic encounter that de-centres the penis and intercourse, and can thereby engage in lesbian sex. The idea of the male lesbian serves not only as a point of inquiry into the self-evidence of biological sex, but also as a category which unsettles the idea of what constitutes sexual activity for male-bodied people.

References and further reading

Ladenson, E. (1999) *Proust's Lesbianism*, Ithaca, NY: Cornell University Press.

Morgan, T.E. (1992) 'Male lesbian bodies', *Genders*, 15: 37–57.

Schor, N. (2001) 'Male lesbianism', *GLQ*, 7 (3): 391–99.

Silverman, K. (1992) *Male Subjectivity at the Margins*, New York: Routledge.

Zita, J. (1992) 'Male lesbians and the postmodernist body', *Hypatia*, 7 (4): 106–27.

SUSANNAH BREDENKAMP

MALE SEX DRIVE

The construction of sexuality by sexologists in the late nineteenth century was premised on the notion of hydraulic sexual instinct (Weeks 1986). Through the use of metaphors such as 'overpowering forces, engulfing drives, gushing streams and uncontrollable spasms' (Weeks 1986: 46), sexologists figured sexuality as an instinctual force. The male body and the body part of the penis were at the centre of this figuring of sexuality, and were referenced as an unstoppable biological force. This social construction of the male sex drive has proliferated and dominated Western discourse on sex (Weeks 1986).

Wood (1985) suggests what is key in this normative constitution of sexuality as an instinctual force is the discourse on heterosexual sex. This contention is borne out in Smart's (1989) investigation of the legal trial of rape whereby the discourse of the male sex drive was found to be utilised by male defendants as a technique to legitimise and neutralise (hetero)sexual acts of sexual violence. While such interpretations have challenged the social construction of male sexuality as 'biological sex drive', Hollway (1984) argues that feminist writers concerned with the configuration of gender relations often substitute an analysis of hydraulic sexuality with corporeal male power, a substitution which problematically emphasises the social power of the body, and mainly the penis.

In a reconsideration of Hollway's concerns, Vitellone (2002) has pointed out that there has indeed been a tendency to conflate the male sex drive discourse with the literal male body. Such a narrow focus, she suggests, negates the ways in which sexuality – and especially a male heterosexual sex drive – may have other sources than that of the body part of the penis. In particular, Vitellone argues that, post-AIDS, the figuring of the male sex drive is linked to the performativity of cultural objects and more specifically the performativity of the condom.

References and further reading

Hollway, W. (1984) 'Women's power in heterosexual sex', *Women's Studies International Forum*, 7 (1): 63–8.

Smart, C. (1989) *Feminism and the Power of the Law*, New York: Routledge.

Vitellone, N. (2002) 'Without or with condoms? AIDS and the male sex drive', *Critical Psychology V: Embodiment*, 5: 30–50.

Weeks, J. (1986) *Sexuality*, London: Ellis Horwood/ Tavistock Publications.

Wood, N. (1985) 'Foucault on the history of sexuality: and introduction', in V. Beechey and J. Donald (eds) *Subjectivity and Social Relations*, Milton Keynes: Open University Press, pp. 156–75.

See also: sexuality

NICOLE VITELLONE

MALE YOUTH CULTURES

Since ancient times, elders have expressed worries and complaints about young people, their behaviour, their manners, their lack of respect and responsibility. Most of this concern, including its more recent social-scientific forms, has been about young men.

The nineteenth century saw the rise of the concept of adolescence, along with a number of state measures and organisations designed to keep young working-class men healthily and gainfully occupied while developing respectable habits in their leisure time. Between the two world wars, social scientists turned their attention to problems of adolescence, notably in connection with deviancy and juvenile delinquency. A central argument was that the adolescent peer group was a key milieu for the transition from childhood to adulthood; when this transition became deviant, the clique could become a 'gang' in the negative sense. Displays of adolescent masculine toughness, competition and heterosexual experience and prowess were seen as central in Western societies to 'gangs' of either the functional or deviant sort.

Only after World War II did the concept of youth culture come into focus. The term 'teenager' had been invented in the USA in the 1930s and soon circulated in popular culture. Sociologists saw the new category as connected with the advent of the youth market. Muncie (2004: 56) cites the first notable sociological study of youth culture in Britain as being Abrams' (1959) *The Teenage Consumer*, which observes that 'the consumer habits of youth were dominated by the interests of working-class males'. When W.B. Miller (1958) noted that working-class youth is intent on 'toughness, trouble, smartness, excitement, fate and autonomy' (cited in Brake 1985: 7), he meant male youth. Well into the 1970s, studies of youth cultures often referred, by default, to *male* youth cultures.

Research associated with the Centre for Contemporary Cultural Studies at the University of Birmingham in the 1970s attempted to grasp a series of successive youth 'subcultures' in post-war Britain as 'magical' ideological resolutions of real contradictions in the experience of working-class youth. Accompanying the breakdown of tightly knit geographical working-class communities, these contradictions involved the restructuring of the labour market that particularly disadvantaged working-class young men: 'Looking for opportunities in their father's trades, and lacking the qualifications for the new industries, they were relegated to jobs as van boys, office boys, packers, warehousemen, etc., and long spells out of work' (Cohen 1972, cited in Clarke 1976: 32). From the appropriation and adaptation of the style of Edwardian dandies by the Teds in the 1950s to the exaggeratedly working-class braces and workboots style of the Skinheads in the 1970s, these working-class men's styles worked their imagined solutions by performing new modes of masculinity.

Fighting, along with other displays of physical prowess and violence, was important to all these white British male youth 'subcultures', from the Teds, through the Mods and Rockers, to the Skinheads. The Teds were very 'touchy' about 'real or imagined' insults, especially about their clothes or style, often leading to fights (Jefferson 1976: 82). Fights with other groups of Teds cemented the group and emphasised loyalty to it. Fights also involved asserting control over particular territory. Racism was often involved in targeting those who did not 'belong'. The Skinheads likewise connected their various 'mobs' to their localities, expressing solidarity, especially in the face of 'trouble', violently exercising their resentments on 'outsiders' such as immigrants through 'Paki-bashing', and celebrating a 'hard' masculinity policed through 'queer-bashing' (Clarke 1976).

Willis (1977) showed how both misogyny and racism were bound up in the white working-class male youth culture which he studied in the British Midlands in the 1970s. This culture was tied to the reproduction of the very class relations which exploited working-class youth and which they resented. 'Having a laff' and 'doing nothing' became earmarks of masculinity (Corrigan 1979). Displays of physical prowess and sexual success, bravado, risk-taking, and winning and defence of respect are all crucial to the male youth culture of subaltern strata. The celebration of physical prowess is related to traditional labour processes for working-class men (Willis 1977), and the emphasis on respect compensates for the lack of it for the marginalised in class society (Bourgois 1995). Bourgois shows how the male youth culture which maintains a feeling of dignity among crack dealers in the US Puerto Rican *barrio* is profoundly patriarchal and riven by contradictions. Status in this youth culture is derived from masculine violence, sexual exploits and substance abuse, yet these behaviours undermine the basis of adult masculine status, which depends on heading and providing for families.

Relatively little has been written about ruling-class male youth cultures, since they cause less concern. Yet 'gangs' are equally central to male youth culture in the ruling class, above all in the elite private boarding school. These male youth cultures split emotion from friendship and devalorise affection and caring. Interpersonal relations are instrumental, and trust is seen as weakness. Ruling-class young men who express feelings are mistrusted; their masculinity depends upon separating rationality and emotion. The expression of feelings other than anger, jubilation, scorn and jocularity is considered feminine, and homosexual relationships are despised. Bullying is endemic, institutionalised in the hierarchy and indeed celebrated. Competitive individualism rules, and ruthlessness is inculcated (Donaldson and Poynting 2006).

In men whose work and familial relations are undergoing profound change we may now find new and distinct male youth cultures emerging.

References and further reading

Abrams, M. (1959) *The Teenage Consumer*, London: Press Exchange.
Bourgois, P. (1995) *In Search of Respect*, Cambridge: Cambridge University Press.
Brake, M. (1985) *Comparative Youth Culture*, London and New York: Routledge and Kegan Paul.
Clarke, J. (1976) 'The Skinheads and the magical recovery of community', in S. Hall and T. Jefferson (eds) *Resistance through Rituals*, London: Hutchinson/Centre for Contemporary Cultural Studies, pp. 99–102.
Corrigan, P. (1979) *Schooling the Smash Street Kids*, London: Macmillan.
Donaldson, M. and Poynting, S. (2006) *Ruling Class Men*, Bern: Peter Lang.
Jefferson, T. (1976) 'Cultural responses of the teds: the defence of space and status', in S. Hall and T. Jefferson (eds) *Resistance through Rituals*, London: Hutchinson/Centre for Contemporary Cultural Studies, pp. 81–6.
Muncie, J. (2004) *Youth and Crime*, 2nd edn, London: Sage.
Willis P. (1977) *Learning to Labour,* London: Saxon House.

See also: boys and boyhood; young men

SCOTT POYNTING

MANHOOD

Manhood is the period in a male's life from when he is socially recognised as a man.

There is no predicted, universally accepted age when males are deemed to have become men, as this is dependent upon the cultural and social norms prevailing in specific locales. However, what is common within both industrial and non-industrial cultures, and appears to have been for much of history, is that the transition from boy to man is invariably invested in some form of male-dominated ritual and initiation practice. Examples may include circumcision, sexual activity, male bonding rites and various tests of strength, prowess and endurance. The rites of passage into manhood can be further characterised by a symbolic, and in many instances spatial, separation of the male from the female, thereby serving to reinforce the patriarchal intent which can underpin these practices while simultaneously weakening the boy's dependence on, and association with, the maternal, the feminine (see Chodorow 1978). Such rites of passage and their accompanying male bonding are apparent in work organisations (e.g. the armed forces), street gangs, male clubs, sporting fraternities and brotherhoods.

While manhood does correspond with the maturing male and related bodily changes, its significance transcends the biological. A male's journey into manhood is a gendered political moment during which his emergent adult masculinity is subjected to examination and validation by peers and adult men. Manhood must not only be attained, it must be seen to have been attained by others – men, for it is men who are its ultimate judges and arbiters, not women. Men's hegemonic influence upon this transitional stage serves to present them as exemplars of the masculinity to be achieved by the boy, while simultaneously perpetuating a dominant masculine discourse.

As Kimmel (1995) illustrates, manhood is a culturally sanctioned stage in a male's life which purports to connect to a deeper, if not mythological, male essence, thereby reinforcing men's status. Despite the cultural ambiguities that surround it, manhood constitutes a highly significant identification upon males and in so doing provides a powerful ontological connection for the otherwise transient masculine subject.

References and further reading

Chodorow, N. (1978) *The Reproduction of Mothering: Psychoanalysis and the Sociology of Gender*, Berkeley, CA: University of California Press.
Kimmel, M.S. (ed.) (1995) *The Politics of Manhood*, Philadelphia, PA: Temple University Press.

See also: initiation, male; male youth cultures; masculinity/masculinities; mythopoetic movement; rites of passage; young men

STEPHEN M. WHITEHEAD

MARGINALISED MASCULINITY

Marginalised masculinities do not represent a fixed character type but configurations of practice produced in certain situations and in a fluid structure of relationships (Connell 1995). The formation of masculinities is not just through specific gender configurations of practice but also through differences in structures external to gender such as race, ethnicity and class and their interaction with gender (Connell 1995). These differences exist between the hegemonic masculine group and the groups of men located within particular subordinated classes, ethnic or racial minorities, as well as disabled and aged groups. Their subordination within these structures ensures their social de-authorisation (Connell 2000) or marginalisation from the central principles of the hegemonic masculine group. The types of differences that produce marginalisation are depicted in films such as *The Full Monty*. This presents the gendered nature of a deindustrialising economy: that is, where working-class masculinity is made marginal through unemployment (Pearce 2000), driven by changes in technology, education and work practices. The effect is that traditional hegemonic masculine ideals, based on hard work, toughness and a carefree homosocial existence, are displaced. Traditional working-class men thus become confused about their own sense of masculine identity and place.

The level and severity of the marginalisation of masculinities is always relative to authorisation: that is, to the acceptance or rejection by the hegemonic group of certain marginalised configurations of practice or identities as representative of the hegemonic masculine ideal (Connell 1995). For example, in the United States the efficacy of the marginalisation of black masculinities is blurred through the enabling of black athletes and popular music personalities to assume the exemplar status of hegemonic masculinity. However, the success of these individuals does not ensure the emancipation of the broader group of racially marginalised black men. In effect, authorisation acts as a release valve that controls challenges to hegemonic masculinity from the many subordinated groups of men but, in the final analysis, stops short of allowing the hegemonic masculine ideal to be jeopardised.

References and further reading

Connell, R. (1995) *Masculinities*, St Leonards, NSW: Allen and Unwin.

—— (2000) *The Men and the Boys*, St Leonards, NSW: Allen and Unwin.

Pearce, S. (2000) 'Performance anxiety: the interaction of gender and power in *The Full Monty*', *Australian Feminist Studies*, 15 (32): 227–36.

See also: working with marginalised and minority men

RICHARD HOWSON

MARRIAGE

Marriage is generally understood to be a more or less formal, conventional intimate couple relationship. Typically, marriage is celebrated as the exclusive and permanent union of one man and one woman as husband and wife. Marriage is often presented as the 'natural' or 'proper' way to couple. While marriage is certainly a popular and enduring social arrangement, assuming that it is *natural* is troublesome on two counts. First, while marriage exists across time and cultures, it is by no means uniform. Rather, marriage is constituted in widely divergent forms. The couple marrying in van Eyck's famous 1434 painting, *Giovanni Arnolfini and His Wife*, for example, would have entered into a very different set of obligations and expectations than a couple marrying in the Netherlands today. Similarly, marriage in contemporary Lebanon comes with a different set of threats and promises than its counterpart in South Africa. As a social practice marriage is robust and resilient, but its nature and effects vary. In this sense, marriage is not one institution but many; as a social regulation it endures even as it is renovated and rebuilt. Second, appeals to the naturalness of marriage conceal the social, legal, religious and political means through which it is constructed. As Hunter explains, unlike parenthood (but like the related concept of illegitimacy), marriage does not exist *as such* in the absence of socio-legal (or other forms of) authority. Without social conventions, people may form lasting relationships, but to *marry* one needs a pronouncement, a certificate, a moment of cultural transformation (Hunter 1995). Marriage requires some form of underpinning social-conventional authority, whether religious, cultural or legal.

The study of marriage forms part of many disciplinary areas, including anthropology, theology, history, sociology, psychology, social work and law. Traversing and criticising these studies are feminist analyses, focusing on marriage as emblematic of relations between men and women. Very few studies, however, focus on the experience of men as husbands. The general impression left by countless studies is that marriage is, fundamentally, an arena which plays a crucial role in shaping *women's* lives. As Friedan puts it, for men marriage is like a station on life's journey, whereas for women it is more often understood as a destination (Friedan 1963). It is not difficult, however, to extrapolate theorisations of men and marriage from feminist analyses.

Even in feminist studies not directly concerned with marriage, questions about the relationship between husbands and wives often arise. This is not surprising, given that feminism examines relations between the sexes while marriage represents a formal and structural aspect of sex/gender relations. While feminists generally agree that marriage serves husbands better than it does wives, speculation on the nature and design of this relationship varies widely. Historically, two views have dominated feminist debates. The view that marriage is recuperable competes against the idea that marriage inherently and perhaps deliberately oppresses women and is thus irredeemably patriarchal.

The first view – that marriage is not necessarily antithetical to gender equality – has prompted feminists to identify and seek to remove double standards in matrimonial law and to argue that spouses should have the opportunity to stand in a structurally symmetrical relationship to each other. In many jurisdictions, husbands and wives are treated differently in the eyes of the law. Some matrimonial codes have allowed a husband to divorce his wife on the grounds of her commission of a single instance of adultery, for example, while requiring that a wife prove repeated instances of adultery or grounds in addition to adultery on the part of the husband before she might seek a divorce. In Thailand, for example, a man cannot be divorced on the ground of his adultery unless he 'keeps' a mistress – that is, unless he offers continuing economic support to a woman other than his wife. Thai wives, however, commit adultery as soon as they have sexual intercourse with a man other than their husband, regardless of whether or not the relationship endures (Ekachai 1997). Responding to this sort of double standard, some feminists have argued that until husbands and wives are granted identical status and rights, marriage will continue to operate at women's expense.

Others argue that reforming matrimonial law is unlikely to solve marriage's problems for women. Given that marriage assumes sexual difference – and is perhaps thus, by definition, a coalition of unequal elements – efforts to render husbands and wives equivalent in law may be doomed from the start. Analyses adopting this point of view have sought to explain the part marriage plays in establishing the gendered social order, arguing that marriage does not *reflect* gender inequality so much as create it. The most influential of such accounts is Pateman's *The Sexual Contract* (1988), which argues that an origin-myth of marriage as endogamous and monogamous operates alongside (and carries similar explanatory weight to) the political myth forming the basis of social contract theory. According to Pateman, the 'sexual contract' – that is, the sum of these myths – disguises coercion and subordination as 'contract', incorporating women into the body politic as it simultaneously enslaves them.

Accounts such as Pateman's leave several questions unresolved. If marriage is inherently and irredeemably patriarchal, it is unlikely ever to serve women well, no matter how it is reformed. However, the alternative and (arguably) less contractual arrangement of cohabitation in lieu of marriage seems to present the same range of problems – particularly in those jurisdictions where the two forms are treated identically. It follows, then, that marriage as such may not be the oppressive heart of intimate relationships. Further, if cohabitation (sometimes also referred to as 'de facto' or 'common-law' marriage) offers a range of male privileges identical to bona fide marriage, perhaps the problem with marriage is symptomatic of 'compulsory heterosexuality' and its institutions more generally. In any case, with the advent of poststructural explanations of power, feminist advocacy of the simple abolition of marriage is dwindling. Attention is now more likely to focus on any of several intersections of marriage, gender and privilege. Here, marriage has often served as a site at which feminism's broadest political concerns have been refracted. Indeed, marriage continues to operate as a sort of theoretical pivot for a range of key feminist concerns, including labour, wealth and violence. In these analyses, marriage is rarely characterised as the single cause of women's oppression, but as an institutional facilitator of women's subordination through exploitative economic exchange, male violence, and so on.

For example, the subordination of women both in unpaid household labour and in the paid workforce is at least partly premised on their being actual or potential wives. Indeed, whether or not an individual woman is married or unmarried, her life's opportunities and experiences will be coloured by social regimes linking marriage and the institutionalised sexual division of labour. Women are disciplined, from an early age, to comply with social expectations that housework is women's work. Certainly until the mid-1970s, wives' contributions both to their household and husband's prosperity were routinely ignored by society at large and by judges settling property in divorce cases in particular. Even with the enactment of law reforms designed to redress this failure, it has been argued that women continue to be routinely short-changed upon divorce. Moreover, feminist analyses of the sexual division of domestic labour in marriage are by no means limited to household applications. As Okin points out, the 'public' and 'private' realms work to buttress male privilege and exacerbate women's subordination in each arena (Okin 1989: 146). In the (paid) labour market, women's job opportunities are constrained by social expectations that they will also labour at home, as a wife. In the public realm, women are typically clustered in certain occupations and industries, reinforcing the notion that some kinds of work are inherently more suitable for women than others. These 'women's' jobs tend to be cast in service roles and industries, conforming to a domestic model that places wives at the service of their husbands (Delphy and Leonard 1992). Along with the sexual divisions of labour and wealth, violence has been theorised by feminists as intrinsically linked to the institution of marriage. Of particular concern has been the incidence of domestic violence and rape in marriage. The majority of female homicide victims in the United Kingdom, Canada and Australia are murdered not by strangers but by their husband or de facto husband (Mouzos and Rushforth 2003). The situation is no better in the majority world, where brutal punishments against a wife's adultery (or other matrimonial 'offence') include death by stoning, acid attacks and 'honour killings'. The situation regarding sexual assault is similar: despite popular misconceptions, women are more likely to be raped at home than outside it, and by a husband (or other sexual intimate) than a stranger (Easteal 1994: 5–6).

And again, like domestic violence laws, sanctions against rape are historically linked to matrimonial law – where, for example, the husband of a raped woman could sue her attacker for damaging his 'property' (that is, his wife) (Miller and Biele 1993: 50). The repeal of such laws, and even the criminalisation of rape in marriage, has not remedied the problem: if rape in general is notoriously difficult to prosecute, marital rape is even more difficult to prove. Similarly, while formal regulations governing the dissolution of marriage in developed industrial nations might lead us to infer that it is now easy for women in such places to leave a violent relationship, the reality is different.

It is well known that marriage has at various times endowed husbands with tremendous power over their wives. The eighteenth-century English doctrine of coverture – that is, the idea that, in marriage, husband and wife become as one, that one being the husband – is frequently cited to illustrate the legal privileges of marriage afforded to husbands. The doctrine meant, in effect, that upon marriage women entered into a strikingly subordinate relationship: their property, and to a certain extent their liberty, became subject to their husband's direction. Under coverture, husbands were permitted to beat their wives 'within reason', and could forbid them from going to certain places or associating with certain people. If a wife murdered her husband, she could be charged with treason as well as homicide, having killed her husband and ruler (Yalom 2001).

The role of marriage in implementing various racist programmes is less frequently acknowledged. However, inscriptions of race have been regulated through marriage, particularly in the historical prohibition of marriage between 'mixed race' couples. As recently as 1960 in Australia, for example, marriage served as a model of racial and cultural assimilation whose coherence depended on governmental links connecting white privilege and male privilege (Brook 1997). That the repeal of racist prohibitions on 'inter-racial' unions is now being cited as an analogous precedent for the legal recognition of gay and lesbian relationships suggests that the matrimonial landscape is continuing to shift – and for some, quake. Recent debates concerning 'same-sex marriage' have brought feminist theorisations of marriage back into the spotlight as an arena in which sex, gender and sexualities are tightly intermeshed (Calhoun 2000). And, just as there has never been any straightforward feminist consensus on marriage, opinions as to the usefulness of marriage as a vehicle which might challenge homophobia are mixed (Baird and Rosenbaum 1997).

While most of marriage's more obvious racist and sexist double standards have been removed from the legal codes of Western societies, and in some places efforts have been made to divest marriage of its homophobic and heteronormative trappings, problems concerning labour, domestic and sexual violence remain hinged to marriage. Feminist analyses have thoroughly debunked the belief that marriage serves women or that it exists to 'protect' women. While some of the masculine power and privileges of marriage have gradually eroded, in many places marriage is now understood to be a relationship of equals. In their study of contemporary families, Bittman and Pixley (1997) adopt the useful term 'pseudomutuality' to describe a preference for 'equal' sharing of housework. They report that while most of the people they studied described their own relationship as 'equal' by design, very few reflected equality in fact. For household labour, as in domestic-sexual violence, the rhetoric of formal equality may disguise ongoing problems. There is no doubt, however, that in places like the United States, divorce is less difficult and painful than it once was. Childrearing and housework are now recognised as contributions to marital prosperity, and assault between spouses has been criminalised. The price of some of these improvements has been an angry backlash (Flood 2004). In other places, however, women continue to struggle against the heinous effects of deeply misogynist marriage systems.

The gradual removal of legal ties binding women to the service of their husbands, coupled with increased opportunities for women's economic and personal independence, has seen the popularity of marriage – particularly as a life-long commitment – wane in developed nations. This is evidence, perhaps, that marriage is becoming less compulsory and less necessary to those social orders in which women's participation as workers and citizens is recognised. Whether this signals the rise of more egalitarian or perhaps self-centred relationships is debatable. What does seem clear is that completely just systems for regulating intimate relationships remain an ideal – but an ideal well worth women's and men's continuing attention.

References and further reading

Baird, R.M. and Rosenbaum, S.E. (eds) (1997) *Same-Sex Marriage*, New York: Prometheus.

Bittman, M. and Pixley, J. (1997) *The Double Life of the Family*, St Leonards, NSW: Allen and Unwin.

Brook, H. (1997) 'The troubled courtship of Gladys and Mick', *Australian Journal of Political Science*, 32 (3): 419–36.

Calhoun, C. (2000) *Feminism, the Family, and the Politics of the Closet*, Oxford: Oxford University Press.

Delphy, C. and Leonard, D. (1992) *Familiar Exploitation*, Cambridge: Polity.

Easteal, P. (1994) *Voices of the Survivors*, North Melbourne: Spinifex Press.

Ekachai, S. (1997) 'Adultery is for women only', *Bangkok Post*, 19 March. Reprinted in *Women's Studies Center Annual 2002*, vol. 2, p. 79.

Flood, M. (2004) 'Backlash', in S.E. Rossi (ed.) *The Battle and Backlash Rage on*, Philadelphia, PA: Xlibris.

Friedan, B. (1963) *The Feminine Mystique*, London: Victor Gollancz.

Hunter, N.D. (1995) 'Marriage, law and gender', in L. Duggan and N.D. Hunter (eds) *Sex Wars*, New York: Routledge.

Miller, P. and Biele, N. (1993) 'Twenty years later: the unfinished revolution', in E. Buchwald, P. Fletcher and M. Roth (eds) *Transforming a Rape Culture*, Minneapolis, MN: Milkweed Editions.

Mouzos, J. and Rushforth, C. (2003) *Family Homicide in Australia*, Trends and Issues in Crime and Criminal Justice, 255, Canberra: Australian Institute of Criminology.

Okin, S.M. (1989) *Justice, Gender and the Family*, New York: Basic.

Pateman, C. (1988) *The Sexual Contract*, Cambridge: Polity.

Yalom, M. (2001) *A History of the Wife*, New York: HarperCollins.

See also: child custody; divorce and separation; family law; heterosexuality; husbands; intimacy; men's relations with women

HEATHER BROOK

MARTIAL RACES

The term 'martial race' refers to the belief that some groups of men, for cultural or biological reasons, make better soldiers than others. Although the idea that some populations produce superior soldiers was quite old (dating at least from the Enlightenment), martial race ideology was at its most influential in the years between 1880 and 1914. In this period, proponents of martial race ideology consciously and systematically sought to construct recruiting policies geared towards the enlistment of groups of men thought to possess martial qualities.

A variety of peoples all over the world found the idea of martial races convincing by the late nineteenth century, but it was most influential in European countries that possessed overseas colonies such as Britain, France and the Netherlands. Some of the populations Europeans believed possessed martial qualities were the Bedouin, the Zulu, Scottish Highlanders, the Irish, Punjabi Sikhs, Nepalese Gurkhas, Afghan Afridis and the Ambonese. Yet while many believed in the purchase of martial race ideology, nowhere was the ideology translated more successfully into practice and policy than in British India.

In India, army commanders and imperial administrators who believed in the idea of martial races inaugurated policies that radically shifted the recruiting base of the Indian

Army. Whereas in 1857 the vast majority of the Indian Army hailed from Bengal and lower India (later thought to be non-martial populations), by 1893 almost 44 per cent of the army was recruited from populations thought to produce martial races – especially Sikhs and Gurkhas. By 1904 the proportion of 'martial races' in the Indian Army had risen to 57 per cent, and by 1914 that number reached a stunning 75 per cent.

In India and elsewhere, 'martial races' were frequently targeted because they had previously demonstrated loyalty to Europeans, whereas 'non-martial' groups often hailed from politically suspect populations. However, this reality was often disguised by the 'scientific' conventions of late Victorian notions about race and masculinity. Thus, discussions of the martial qualities of particular populations were couched in terms of scientific fact and biological proclivities rather than opinion or experience. Similarly, advocates argued that martial races were inherently more manly than non-martial races, and that their rough-and-ready warrior masculinity was far more trustworthy than the supposedly effeminate masculinity displayed by other groups. Indeed, martial race ideology came to be one of the markers by which Europeans judged both the racial and gendered worthiness of colonised populations. As such, it was used both to articulate ideal characteristics of colonial populations and as a tool of exclusion.

References and further reading

Caplan, L. (1995) *Warrior Gentlemen: 'Gurkhas' in the Western Imagination*, Providence, RI: Berghahn Books.

Omissi, D. (1994) *The Sepoy and the Raj: The Indian Army, 1860–1940*, London: Macmillan.

Sinha, M. (1995) *Colonial Masculinity: The 'Manly Englishman' and the 'Effeminate Bengali' in the Late Nineteenth Century*, Manchester: Manchester University Press.

Streets, H. (2004) *Martial Races: The Military, Race, and Masculinity in British Imperial Culture, 1857–1914*, Manchester: Manchester University Press.

HEATHER STREETS

MARXISM

Marxism is an approach to the study of society (also called 'historical materialism') in which analysis of the totality of social relations of production and reproduction is central. At the same time Marxism is a political movement that aims at transforming society so as to eliminate all exploitation and oppression through the conscious, self-organised activity of the working class in alliance with other oppressed groups. Its founders, Karl Marx and Friedrich Engels, first approached the issue of gender by way of the concept of the 'natural division of labour existing in the family', which they saw as the starting point in the development of property (Marx and Engels 1976: 33). Later Marxists have developed their analysis of masculine identities and behaviour in interaction with other paradigms: psychoanalysis, feminism and gay liberation.

The Marxist emphasis on the agency of oppressed people has particular implications for the study of men and masculinities. Attitudes towards masculinity in classical Marxism, with its predominant focus on class, must often be read between the lines in discussions of workers, whom early Marxists tended to view implicitly as male. More recently Marxist feminists have considered men mainly as oppressors of women, who to a lesser extent themselves suffer from this oppression and can contribute to ending it. They also analyse men through the lenses of homosexuality, bisexuality and transgender and transsexuality; gay, bisexual and transgendered men are seen to varying degrees as beneficiaries of sexism yet also as women's allies in the struggle against it.

All this helps explain why Marxists stress the importance of analysing society as a complexly structured, contradictory whole. It means that 'intersectionality', the ways in which identities and power relations based on class, gender, race and ethnicity, disability, religion and other identities overlap and interact (Brenner 2000), is crucial to a Marxist analysis of masculinities. Marxism cannot have a 'men's theory' parallel to and separate from 'women's theory', or oppose a materialism based on reproduction to one based on production (cf. Hearn 1987). A Marxist politics of masculinity is necessarily a rainbow politics: working-class, feminist and sexually liberating.

Engels

While several of Marx and Engels's works contain scattered comments on how capitalism distorts relations between men and women, the classical Marxist reference on gender is Engels's 1884 work *The Origin of the Family, Private Property and the State*. The book emphasises that the development of social institutions is conditioned not only by relations of production but also by relations of reproduction in the family – including physical reproduction of human beings, the ideological reproduction required for children to become workers, and the nurturance workers need to keep on working. Drawing on the anthropology of his time (critically re-examined later by Marxist feminist anthropologists, e.g. Coontz and Henderson 1986), Engels describes the replacement of a supposed original matrilinealism by a still existing patrilinealism, an event he describes as 'one of the most decisive [revolutions] ever experienced by mankind . . . the *world-historic defeat of the female sex*' (Engels 1972: 67–8). While economic interest still prevails in bourgeois family life, he argues, mutual affection is the main factor in relations between working-class men and women. Failing to question the sexual division of labour in the home, Engels sees women's full integration into the waged labour force and the elimination of capitalism as preconditions for fully free and equal relations between men and women.

Engels's analysis went largely unchallenged and underdeveloped during the period of the Second International (1889–1914). During the 1917 Russian Revolution Marxist ideas about women's emancipation were initially put into practice to a limited extent and further radicalised. Alexandra Kollontai, the first Bolshevik commissar for social affairs, argued (1977) in a series of articles between 1919 and 1923 that mothers' specific responsibilities included giving birth, breastfeeding and nothing more – not even changing nappies, washing the baby or rocking the cradle. Men can share equally in children's education, she says, as well as take part in collective cleaning teams. Kollontai's influence declined rapidly, and most attempts to collectivise domestic labour were abandoned after early 1921. Stalinism, while increasing women's participation in waged labour, involved in most respects a return to a more traditional conception of masculinity, a pattern characteristic of later Communist regimes as well.

Bolsheviks' initial radicalism on gender issues did stimulate some innovative thinking, however, first in early Communist parties and later among dissident Marxists. The Sex-Pol movement sponsored by the mass Communist Party in pre-Nazi Germany was particularly noteworthy. Its leading figure, psychoanalyst Wilhelm Reich, warned that a sense of family responsibility, all-male clubs, sports, militarism and particularly bourgeois sexual morality and men's power over their wives and children helped depoliticise men (Reich 1972). But he had an orthodox Freudian conception of healthy male sexuality as active and dominant, and was less nuanced than Freud in seeing homosexuality as pathological. The Frankfurt School's synthesis of psychoanalysis and Marxism was in some ways more radical, particularly Herbert Marcuse's portrayal of a paternal authority diffused throughout society, his plea for a reconciliation of 'man' and 'nature', and his championing of play and 'polymorphous perversity' (Marcuse 1966).

Feminism

The second wave of feminism in the 1960s and 1970s, more than anything else, has stimulated Marxists to integrate gender and reproduction into their analysis, however incomplete and unhappy the marriage of Marxism and feminism has remained. Socialist feminists have in particular gone beyond earlier Marxist–Freudian accounts of male personality formation. They have analysed marriage's positive effect on men's mental health and negative effect on women's, and how mothering and later distancing stimulate boys' thirst for achievement and hunger for authority (Chodorow 1979).

Socialist feminists have produced many studies of the economics of gender relations, based on the premise that 'the working class has two sexes'. They have described the still profound though shifting gender segmentation of the global labour force and its role in keeping men's wages higher than women's. They have also illuminated historical processes of economic restructuring, as in the industrial revolution – when men's craft labour (often organised in exclusively male guilds) was often devalued by capitalists employing women and children at low wages in factories – and later when male workers in developed countries helped push women out of the industrial work force as they laid claim to a 'family wage'. African–American women even appealed to this ideology to claim higher wages for their husbands (Mullings 1997). The result was a working-class paternalism in which 'the man must be the sole provider for the family, pass on his trade to his son and keep a stern eye on his apprentice' (Rowbotham 1979: 123). Waged work, particularly work seen as 'conquest of nature', has been key to ideas of masculinity (Hearn 1987).

Now, under neoliberal globalisation, gender is again being used for purposes of economic restructuring. A crisis of masculinity arose as men were laid off from their jobs in steel plants, left unemployed and feeling useless at home, and then perhaps worked for a lower wage at McDonald's while their wives often kept primary responsibility for home and children and became primary breadwinners as well. Socialist feminists have analysed how capitalists deploy masculine imagery and competitiveness to raise levels of productivity among male workers, in dependent as well as developed countries.

Male bonding through drinking, hunting and sports can be a specifically working-class male response to the perceived stifling constraints of both work and home. This working-class masculinity contrasts with other masculine styles characteristic of owning/governing and managerial/professional classes, in which men tend to value wives and families more as career assets. Eroticisms of male power and wealth come into competition with an eroticism of male strength, and inter-male rivalry intersects with class and racial conflict. This rivalry spurs men to consume more products in the 'masculinity market' (Burstyn 1999). Yet these patterns are changing as profits are increasingly drawn less from manufacturing and more from reproductive labour, increasingly done by men as well as women, in restaurants, shops, hospitals and schools (Brown 1981). The growth of the male market for perfumes and cosmetics may reflect class-linked shifts in masculinities, as well as advancing consumerism, feminism and increased attention to female and gay male desire.

Families

Shifts in the economy have an impact on changing families. Marxist feminists have intervened cogently in debates between conservatives claiming to defend the 'traditional' family and feminists and gays seeking to push on with their emancipation. They have analysed the phenomenon of men fleeing their marriages and deserting their children, as children have changed from an asset that men wish to control to a burden that men wish to avoid. The paradoxical result, despite studies showing that men increasingly draw gratification from family life, is a system of male domination in which fathers are more often absent, a system once condescendingly identified with the 'black family' but now more widespread. The exceptional Swedish model, which increased fathers' role in childcare through parental leave and other benefits, is being eroded by neoliberal austerity – leaving aside questions like mothers' resistance to fathering and whether more fathering can in some ways reinforce paternal power (Hearn 1987).

In examining male domestic violence, socialist feminists combine a feminist understanding of the role of violence in perpetuating male privilege with an understanding of the helplessness and pent-up aggression that working-class male batterers and battered women sometimes share.

Abandoning the insistence of earlier Marxists that capitalism alone is responsible for women's oppression, socialist feminists have concluded that working-class men too (contrary to their own long-term best interests, but in keeping with their immediate interests) help perpetuate women's inferior position at work and at home. Some have argued, however, that men tend increasingly to defend their superior position less as individuals, by asserting their power over their individual wives at home, and more collectively through the state, professions like medicine and social work, and the market – a change sometimes defined (controversially) as a shift from 'private' to 'public patriarchy' (Brown 1981). Working-class men in particular may pay a high psychological and practical toll in the process, which joins male power to male pain. The shift to a more diffuse system of male domination makes men's attractiveness, once of little concern to married working-class men, more important, for example.

Socialist feminist challenges to male chauvinism caused a wave of debate and upheaval in Marxist organisations beginning in the late 1970s. Women have battled against rejection of women's caucuses as 'anti-Leninist', but also against persistent, subtler mechanisms that marginalise women. In the words of one wickedly astute observation, leaders of Leninist groups tend to look 'over your head when they talk to you', either 'taking a long objective view' or 'looking for more prestigious "contacts" in the shape of a shop steward or so' (Rowbotham 1979: 130). Black socialist feminists have challenged black nationalist insistence on male leadership in black freedom struggles (Mullings 1997), although engagement in a common struggle sometimes gives women a more positive view of men as allies.

Sexuality

Marxist feminist study of male sexuality can be divided into analyses of male heterosexuality, which have mostly considered its role in limiting women's reproductive freedom or in rape and other forms of sexual violence, and analyses of gay masculinities. There has been little work as yet on class factors in gay masculinities – studies suggest that gay men are underrepresented both among blue-collar workers and in top management – although black gay men have expressed alienation from the masculinities prevalent among white gay men. Marxists have paid some attention to the development of gay 'hyper-masculinities' (Burstyn 1999) and some have even defined male homosexuality as such as a fetishisation of maleness.

But Marxist theorists of gay liberation have been more inclined to portray modern gay male identity as a challenge to the sex/gender system and male power and as a symptom of their breakdown, even going so far as to call for the total abolition of gender, seen as linked to growing threats of ecocide and warfare (Fernbach 1981). Analysing the latent homoeroticism in male bonding among straight men and the misogyny implicit in their homophobia, Marxist gays have insisted on the radical potential of open gay and gender-bending behaviour: 'There is more to be learned from wearing a dress for a day, than there is from wearing a suit for life' (Mieli 1980: 193). Studies of male homosexuality in dependent countries, particularly since the late 1990s, have analysed sexual relationships – particularly among working-class and poor men – between men who have sex with men and transgendered people as class-linked forms of resistance to a Western, consumerist, gender-conformist gay model (Drucker 2000).

Overall Marxist approaches to male sexuality are broadly compatible with widely accepted social constructionist approaches but tend to reject queer theory's view of sexuality as performance and instead to stress material, social, ideological and psychological factors that contribute to shaping sexuality. Unfortunately the relative eclipse of Marxism since the 1980s has held back a potentially fruitful dialogue between Marxist feminists and queer theorists.

References and further reading

Brenner, J. (2000) *Women and the Politics of Class*, New York: Monthly Review.

Brown, C. (1981) 'Mothers, fathers and children', in L. Sargent (ed.) *Women and Revolution*, London: Pluto, pp. 239–67.

Burstyn, V. (1999) *The Rites of Men*, Toronto: Toronto University Press.

Chodorow, N. (1979) 'Mothering, male dominance, and capitalism', in Z. Eisenstein (ed.) *Capitalist Patriarchy and the Case for Socialist Feminism*, New York: Monthly Review, pp. 83–106.

Coontz, S. and Henderson, P. (eds) (1986) *Women's Work, Men's Property*, London: Verso.

Drucker, P. (2000) 'Introduction', in P. Drucker (ed.) *Different Rainbows*, London: Gay Men's Press, pp. 9–41.

Engels, F. (1972) *The Origin of the Family, Private Property and the State*, New York: Pathfinder.

Fernbach, D. (1981) *The Spiral Path*, Boston, MA and London: Alyson/Gay Men's Press.

Hearn, J. (1987) *The Gender of Oppression*, Brighton: Wheatsheaf.

Kollontai, A. (1977) *Selected Writings*, translated and edited by A. Holt, London: Allison and Busby.

Marcuse, H. (1966) *Eros and Civilization*, Boston, MA: Beacon.

Marx, K. and Engels, F. (1976) 'The German ideology', in K. Marx and F. Engels, *Collected Works*, vol. 5, New York: International Publishers, pp. 19–539.

Mieli, M. (1980) *Homosexuality and Liberation*, translated by F. Fernbach, London: Gay Men's Press.

Mullings, L. (1997) *On Our Own Terms*, New York: Routledge.

Reich, W. (1972) 'What is class consciousness?' in L. Baxandall (ed.) *Sex-Pol*, New York: Vintage, pp. 275–358.

Rowbotham, S. (1979) 'The women's movement and organizing for socialism', in S. Rowbotham, L. Segal and H. Wainwright (eds), *Beyond the Fragments*, London: Merlin, pp. 21–155.

See also: class, work and masculinity; unions/organised labour movements

PETER DRUCKER

MASCULINITY/MASCULINITIES

The concept of masculinity is well established; the concept of masculinities is much more recent, dating from the late 1970s. The word 'masculinity' derives from the Middle English *masculin,* from Middle French and from Latin *masculinus* ('male, of masculine gender', 'male person, male') and *masculus* (male). Recorded uses of 'masculine' date from the late fourteenth century, as 'belonging to' or 'of the male sex'. The grammatical use of 'masculine' is from the same period. More specific meanings of having 'appropriate' qualities of the male sex, such as 'powerfulness', 'manliness' and 'virility', date from the early seventeenth century. These have been elaborated to refer to characteristics traditionally thought to be suitable for men; traits of behaving in ways considered typical for men; or properties characteristic of the male sex. The concept links closely with concepts of manhood and manliness (Mangan and Walvin 1987).

The first steps towards the modern analysis of masculinity are found in the pioneering psychologies of Freud and Adler. These demonstrated that adult character was not biologically predetermined but constructed through emotional attachments to others in a turbulent growth process (Connell 1994). Anthropologists such as Malinowski and Mead went on to emphasise cultural differences in such processes, structures and norms. By the mid-twentieth century, these ideas had crystallised into the associated concepts of masculinity and the male sex role. The concept of masculinity has also been used in analysing literary and other texts.

In the 1960s and 1970s masculinity was understood mainly as an internalised role, identity or (social) psychological disposition, reflecting a particular (often US or Western) cluster of cultural norms or values acquired by learning from socialisation agents. This was represented in various formulations of masculinity in learning and socialisation theories. In masculinity–femininity (m–f) scales, certain items were scored as 'masculine' (such as 'aggressive', 'ambitious', analytical', assertive' and 'athletic') compared with other items scored as 'feminine' (such as 'affectionate', 'cheerful', 'childlike', 'compassionate' and 'flatterable'). The best known are various formulations of the Bem Sex Role Inventory (BSRI). Such notions of masculinity were subject to substantive and conceptual criticism in the 1970s and 1980s. Such m–f scales were criticised for obscuring differences between cultural ideals and practices, ignoring which gender assesses which, showing bias in using them on students to construct scales, lacking a power perspective and being ethnocentric, especially US-centric (Eichler 1980). Since then, masculinity scales have been refined, in terms of gender orientation and gender ideology (Thompson and Pleck 1995; Luyt 2005).

At the same time as sex role theory and m–f scales were being critiqued, in theories of patriarchy men were analysed societally, structurally and collectively. Different theories of patriarchy have emphasised men's structural social relations to women, in terms of biology, reproduction, politics and culture, family, state, sexuality, economy and combinations thereof. By the late 1970s, however, a number of feminist and profeminist critics were suggesting that the concept of 'patriarchy' was too monolithic, ahistorical, biologically determined and dismissive of women's resistance and agency.

These twin debates and critiques around masculinity/male sex role and patriarchy in many ways laid the conceptual and political foundations for a more differentiated approach to masculinities. Building on both social psychological and social structural accounts, social constructionist perspectives of various kinds highlighting complexities of men's social power have emerged. Increasingly, different masculinities are interrogated in the plural, not the singular, in discussions of hegemonic, complicit, subordinated, marginalised and resistant masculinities. Masculinities, hegemonic or not, can be understood as signs and practices obscuring contradictions. The concept of masculinities has been extremely important in widening the social analysis of men and gender relations (Brod 1987; Carrigan *et al.* 1985; Brod and Kaufman 1993; Connell 1995). Key features include: critique and supplanting of sex role theory; understanding masculinities as power-laden, in unequal relations between women and men and between men and men; highlighting the implications of gay liberation/scholarship and sexual hierarchies; acknowledgement of socio-historical transformation, contradictions, resistance and interrelations of institutional/social, interpersonal and intra-psychic dimensions.

The construction of masculinities has been explored in many different arenas, including: global, regional, institutional, interactional and individual men's gendered performance and identity constructions. Masculinities do not exist in socio-cultural vacuums but are constructed within specific institutional settings (Kimmel *et al.* 2005). They vary and change across time (history) and space (culture), within societies and through life courses and biographies.

The first substantial discussion of 'hegemonic masculinity' was in the paper 'Men's bodies', written by R. Connell in 1979 and published in *Which Way Is Up?* in 1983. Its background was debates on patriarchy; the Gramscian hegemony at issue in relation to masculinities was hegemony in the patriarchal system of gender relations. The social construction of the body in boys' and men's practices is analysed. In discussing 'the physical sense of maleness', Connell (1983: 18) notes the importance of sport as 'the central experience of the school years for many boys', emphasising taking and occupying space, holding the body tense, skill, size, power, force, strength, physical development and sexuality. Regarding men's bodies, she highlights physicality within work, sexuality and fatherhood. Connell stresses

> the embedding of masculinity in the body is very much a social process, full of tensions and contradiction; that even physical masculinity is historical, rather than a biological fact ... constantly in process, constantly being constituted in actions and relations, constantly implicated in historical change.
>
> (Connell 1983: 30)

The notion of hegemonic masculinity was reformulated in the early 1980s, in the light of gay activism, thus articulating analyses of oppression from both feminism and gay liberation. Accordingly, it is not men in general who are oppressed in patriarchal sexual relations, but particular groups, such as homosexual men, whose situations are related differentially to the 'logic' of women's subordination to men (Carrigan *et al.* 1985: 586).

In *Masculinities*, Connell (1995) discusses hegemonic masculinity in more depth. She reaffirms the link with Gramscian analysis of economic class relations through the operation of cultural dynamics. Hegemonic masculinity is now defined as: 'the configuration of gender practice which embodies the currently accepted answer to the problem of legitimacy of patriarchy, which guarantees (or is taken to guarantee) the dominant position of men and the subordination of women' (p. 77).

Though rather stable, hegemonic masculinity is contested and subject to struggle and change. Connell notes that the most powerful bearers of the cultural ideal of hegemonic masculinity are not necessarily the most powerful individuals. Indeed, the individual holders of power may be very different from those who represent hegemonic masculinity as a cultural ideal. Even so, there is some correspondence between the cultural ideal and institutional power, as in state and corporate power. There are also complex interplays of hegemonic, subordinated, complicit and marginalised forms of masculinity, for example when some black men or gay men adopt or accept aspects of hegemonic masculinity but remain marginalised.

In identifying forms of domination by men, both of women and of other men, the concept of hegemonic masculinity has been notably successful. The reformulation of masculinity to masculinities is not, however, without problems. The term 'masculinities' has been applied in very different, sometimes confusing ways; this can be a conceptual and empirical difficulty (Clatterbaugh 1998). There is growing debate and critique on the very concepts of masculinities and hegemonic masculinity from various methodological positions, including historical, materialist and poststructuralist (Whitehead 2002; Howson 2006).

Several other unresolved issues remain. First, are we talking about cultural representations, everyday practices or institutional structures? Second, how exactly do the various dominant and dominating ways that men are – tough/aggressive/violent; respectable/corporate; controlling of resources; controlling of images; and so on – connect with each other? Third, the concept of hegemonic masculinity may carry contradictions and, arguably, has failed to demonstrate the autonomy of the gender system from class and other social systems. Mike Donaldson (1993) has pointed out that the concept of hegemonic masculinity is unclear, may carry contradictions and fails to demonstrate the autonomy of the gender system. For example, does men's greater involvement in fathering indicate an intensification of hegemonic masculinity or not? For him, in foregrounding (hegemonic) masculinity, economic class remains crucially important, politically and analytically. Fourth, why is it necessary to hang on to the concept of masculinity, rather than being more specific by referring to, say, men's practices or men's identities (Hearn 1996)?

Detailed discursive and ethnographic researches have provided close-grained descriptions of multiple, internally complex masculinities. Margaret Wetherell and Nigel Edley (1999) have identified three specific 'imaginary positions and psycho-discursive practices' in negotiating hegemonic masculinity and identification with the masculine positions: heroic, 'ordinary' and rebellious. The first in fact conforms more closely with the notion of complicit masculinity: 'it could be read as an attempt to actually *instantiate* hegemonic masculinity since, here, men align themselves strongly with conventional ideals' (emphasis in original) (p. 340). The second seeks distance from certain conventional or ideal notions of the masculine; instead, 'ordinariness of the self; the self as normal, moderate or average' (p. 343) is emphasised. The third is characterised by its unconventionality, with the imaginary position involving flouting social expectations (p. 347). With all these self-positionings, especially the last two, ambiguity and subtlety, even contradiction, are present in self-constructions of masculinity, hegemonic or not. Indeed, one feature of the hegemonic may be its elusiveness: the difficulty of reducing it to a set of fixed positions and practices.

More generally, Stephen Whitehead (1999) argues that:

> the concept of hegemonic masculinity goes little way towards revealing the complex patterns of inculcation and resistance which constitute everyday social interaction . . . it is unable to explain the variant meanings attached to the concept of masculinity at this particular moment in the social history of Euro/American/Australasian countries.
>
> (Stephen Whitehead 1999: 58)

While this may be a harsh verdict, it points to possible empirical limitations, as well as the need to subject concepts to scrutiny in changing historical contexts.

Recent work has emphasised multiple masculinities in terms of ways of being men and forms of men's structural, collective and individual practices, their interrelations, and complex interweavings of masculinities, powers, other social statuses and, indeed, violences. There has been strong emphasis on the interconnections of gender with other social divisions, such as age, class, disability, ethnicity, nationality, occupation, racialisation, religion and sexuality. For example, relations of gender and class can demonstrate how different class-based masculinities may both challenge and reproduce gender relations among men and between women and men. Masculinities are placed in cooperative and conflictual relations with each other: – in organisational, occupational and class relations – and in terms defined more explicitly in relation to gender, such as family, kinship and sexuality. Such relations are complicated by contradictions, ambiguities and paradoxes that persist intrapersonally, inter-personally, collectively and structurally. Such intersectional perspectives link with current research on global, (neo-) imperialist and (post)colonial relations.

The range of conceptual and empirical debates points to more fundamental problematics. Both masculinity and masculinities have been used in a wide variety of ways, often rather imprecisely and serving as shorthands for various social phenomena. Sometimes their use may reinforce a psychological model of gender relations located in the individual, or represent masculinity/ies as a primary or underlying cause of other social effects. The concepts can lead to an antimaterialism that may not reflect historical, cultural, (post)colonial and transnational differences. They can reproduce heterosexual dichotomies. There is also increasing scholarship on the separation of masculinity/ies from men, as in female masculinity (Halberstam 1998), within queer studies. Such various critiques provide the ground for the deconstruction of the social taken-for-grantedness of the category of 'men' and its own hegemony. Critique of the hegemony of men can bring together feminist materialist theory and cultural queer theory, as well as modernist theories of hegemony and poststructuralist discourse theory (Hearn 2004).

References and further reading

Brod, H. (ed.) (1987) *The Making of Masculinities*, London: Unwin Hyman.

Brod, H. and Kaufman, M. (eds) (1993) *Theorizing Masculinities*, Newbury Park, CA: Sage.

Carrigan, T., Connell, R. and Lee, J. (1985) 'Toward a new sociology of masculinity', *Theory and Society*, 14 (5): 551–604.

Clatterbaugh, K. (1998) 'What is problematic about "masculinities"?' *Men and Masculinities*, 1 (1): 24–45.

Connell, R. (1983) *Which Way Is Up?* Boston, MA: Allen and Unwin.

—— (1994) 'Psychoanalysis on masculinity', in H. Brod and M. Kaufman (eds) *Theorizing Masculinities*, Thousand Oaks, CA: Sage.

—— (1995) *Masculinities*, Cambridge: Polity Press.

Donaldson, M. (1993) 'What is hegemonic masculinity?' *Theory and Society*, 22 (5): 643–57.

Eichler, M. (1980) *The Double Standard: A Feminist Critique of Feminist Social Science*, London: Croom Helm.

Halberstam, J. (1998) *Female Masculinity*, Durham, NC, and London: Duke University Press.

Hearn, J. (1996) '"Is masculinity dead?" A critical account of the concepts of masculinity and masculinities', in M. Mac an Ghaill (ed.) *Understanding Masculinities: Social Relations and Cultural Arenas*, Milton Keynes: Open University Press, pp. 202–17.

—— (2004) 'From hegemonic masculinity to the hegemony of men', *Feminist Theory*, 5 (1): 97–120.

Howson, R. (2006) *Challenging Hegemonic Masculinity*, London: Routledge.

Kimmel, M., Hearn, J. and Connell, R. (eds) (2005) *Handbook of Studies on Men and Masculinities*, Thousand Oaks, CA: Sage.

Luyt, R. (2005) 'The male attitude norms inventory – II: A measure of masculinity ideology in South Africa', *Men and Masculinities*, 8 (2): 208–29.

Mangan, J.A. and Walvin, J. (1987) (eds) *Manliness and Morality: Middle Class Masculinity in Britain and America, 1800–1940*, Manchester: Manchester University Press.

Thompson, E.H. and Pleck, J.H. (1995) 'Masculinity ideologies. A review of research instrumentation on men and masculinities', in R.F. Levant and W.S. Pollock (eds) *A New Psychology of Men*, New York: Basic Books, pp. 129–63.

Wetherell, M. and Edley, N. (1999) 'Negotiating hegemonic masculinity: imaginary positions and psycho-discursive practices', *Feminism and Psychology*, 9 (3): 335–56.

Whitehead, S.M. (1999) 'Hegemonic masculinity revisited', *Gender, Work and Organization*, 6 (1): 58–62.

—— (2002) *Men and Masculinities: Key Themes and New Directions*, Cambridge: Polity.

See also: complicit masculinity; hegemonic masculinity; hypermasculinity; male; men; marginalised masculinity; protest masculinity; subordinate masculinity

JEFF HEARN

MASCULINITY POLITICS

Since the inception of the modern women's movement in the 1960s there have been a great many social/political responses that address the place of men and masculinity with respect to this movement. Of course, the women's movement itself was extremely diverse; for example, some sought gender equality – that is, opportunities for women to pursue traditionally male roles and occupations – whereas others took it upon themselves to transform society and the gender roles that it embodied. This essay attempts to trace in outline form the social/political perspectives or masculinity politics that achieved enough momentum to become movements. In fact, there have been only four major social movements that focus on men and masculinity, namely profeminist, men's rights, mythopoetic and the Promise Keepers. But each of these is a complex mix of sometimes incompatible views that hang together more because of an ideological commitment to what they oppose than what they defend.

Before turning to the complexities of each of these four points of view it is worth saying what components are required to make a social/political point of view into a social movement. First, each perspective must have an account of the social/political reality that it confronts. Thus, for example, the women's movement stressed the kind of systemic inequality that women face in work, law and almost every area of society. Second, a movement must offer an analysis of that reality, what is right or wrong about it. This analysis goes well beyond the description of reality in that it identifies causal factors that explain the reality. Thus, the women's movement often identified sexism, an undervaluing of women's activities and an overvaluing of men's, as the cause of the systemic inequality. Finally, a movement must offer some social/political agenda for removing what is wrong with the social reality or reinforcing what is right. This agenda must be both politically viable and morally acceptable to those who offer it. Thus a national Equal Rights Amendment seemed to many in the early women's movement to be the appropriate mechanism for undoing the inequalities brought about by sexism. Some social critics might argue that a fourth condition for having a social movement is that there exist a critical mass of individuals who share this ideological perspective. In this essay the size of the groups engaged in masculinity politics is ignored because they all at one time had such a critical mass.

Of the four major movements concerned with men and masculinity only the profeminist men's movement has been generally positive towards feminism. Initially this movement was deeply personal. Its founders were men whose lives had been greatly influenced by women. They were asked to confront their own sexism and to become reliable allies of feminism. They accepted the analysis of social/political reality that feminism offered and because there were multiple feminist analyses there were divisions within the profeminist men's groups from the beginning. Some men following the lead of liberal feminism sought to create greater equality under the law and to ban discrimination against women. Other men, following a radical feminist perspective, focused on ending violence against women. Groups who called themselves 'men against rape' or 'men's antiviolence networks' appeared in every country with a reasonably strong feminist movement. The two sides of profeminism were hardly incompatible except as a matter of emphasis. Typically men who favoured antiviolence work became impatient with men whose focus was on equal opportunity and equal wages. Conversely, liberal profeminists often argued that perhaps the best way to confront violence was to help women gain equal social and political status. In the United States and Canada this split led to a significant number of radical profeminist men leaving the coalitions of profeminist men and forming their own antiviolence organisations.

In the late 1960s and early 1970s the primary opponents of profeminist men were conservatives who sought to hold on to the traditional male roles. These conservatives believed that men were better suited to be protectors and providers and that efforts to transform men from playing these traditional roles would be devastating to the social order. Sometimes these conservatives based their views in biology, but more often it was simply grounded in a vague concept of 'male nature'. However, profeminist men soon encountered another political conflict with an emerging movement that called itself the men's rights movement. This movement, like the profeminist men's movement, enjoyed the support of some prominent feminist writers and activists. The men's rights movement was premised on an agreement with the profeminists, namely that men were severely damaged by having to play the traditional male gender role. But they departed from the profeminists by arguing that this damage was so extensive that it was a mistake to view men as the privileged sex. They attacked feminists and profeminists from this vantage point and accused them of overlooking the oppression of men. They further charged that feminists and profeminists were actually contributing to that oppression by denouncing men as violent rapists and oppressors of women. The antifeminist rhetoric of the men's rights perspective quickly resonated with the more traditional conservatives and fathers' rights groups who felt that they were victims at the mercy of a feminist judicial system. By the 1980s there were men's rights publications in most countries where feminism was strong and there was a growing alliance between the men's rights perspective, the fathers' rights groups and conservatives. Profeminist groups after a brief attempt to create a dialogue with men's rights activists banned presentations from a men's rights perspective from their national and international conferences. Of course, a counter exclusion came from the men's rights coalitions.

By 1990 the extensive and repetitive political infighting between profeminists and men's rights advocates had made many men tired of sectarian political agendas. Men were looking for an alternative ideology. The publication of *Iron John* by Robert Bly provided the occasion for the third major social movement. The central thesis of Bly's book was that men had been deprived of a proper initiation into masculinity. They were denied this by the industrial revolution that removed fathers (and uncles) from the home and left the nurturing of boys to their mothers and women schoolteachers. For various reasons Bly thought that women would misrepresent men and give sons an unfair and prejudicial view of their fathers. As adults these young men would feel this father loss in ways that would make them uncomfortable with their lives. As a remedy Bly helped to organise all-male gatherings where men could speak freely of the loss of their fathers and perhaps their anger at their mothers. The hope was to offer men a belated initiation into masculinity. Bly borrowed from Jungian psychology that talked about archetypes in the collective unconscious; he invented rituals that were followed at these gatherings such as passing a talking stick from speaker to speaker, he encouraged men to write their feelings out in poetry, and he criticised the image of men that in his mind women had helped to create. He saw the liberation of men as a spiritual/psychological journey that could only be led by other men. These men identified themselves as the mythopoetic men's movement.

Obviously this movement contained something for everyone who was active on the politics of masculinity stage. Many profeminists picked up on the gentle side of Bly's message that men needed to learn to express their feelings, and poetry and ritual were seen as a way to do this. They also liked the friendship and trust among men that Bly was trying to create. Men's rights advocates picked up on Bly's distrust of women and the clear suggestion that women make men look bad. They liked the atmosphere at gatherings where they could vent against women and feminism – there was always a confusion between the two within men's rights rhetoric – and not have profeminists criticise them. Bly's message was of course intercepted and transformed. Other groups were created who developed different rituals: for example, they would go on outdoor retreats, build large fires, talk and make spears. Bly was increasingly critical of such spin-offs, and he became alarmed at what he saw as anti-woman rhetoric based upon his ideas. By the late 1990s this movement had spread widely, especially into Canada, Australia and Great Britain. There were multiple magazines and newsletters, the largest being *Wingspan* in the United States and Canada, written from this point of view; some were strongly profeminist, but most were a mix of mythopoetic and men's rights writings.

The 1990s, however, saw a new development in the politics of masculinity. Christian men's groups have been around since the early 1980s. They often focused on sexual purity, fidelity and avoidance of pornography. However, in the early 1990s a major evangelical movement called the Promise Keepers, founded by University of Colorado football coach Bill McCartney, made a huge debut on the stage of masculinity politics. Starting with the premise that men were divinely mandated to be head of the family, church and community, the Promise Keepers held a series of gigantic rallies in the United States, Canada, Australia and the United Kingdom. These rallies (attended by 60,000 and more) were fairly typical of Billy Graham-type rallies with songs, music, witnessing and conversions. Men were asked to sign a pledge to honour

Jesus, to pursue vital relationships with men, to live moral and sexually pure lives, to support their church, to reach beyond racial and denominational boundaries, and to influence the world by loving their neighbours and spreading the gospel. Women were discouraged from attending these gatherings, although women were present as organisers and workers. Men were encouraged to take back their traditional roles as head of the family, and women were encouraged to submit to their husbands. Similar dynamics were advocated for their individual congregations. Women, sometimes referred to as 'the weaker vessels', were encouraged to support the Promise Keepers' agenda because they were told their husbands would be better providers, more sober and faithful husbands.

The Promise Keepers found few allies among the members of the three earlier men's movements. Leaders of the earlier movements all rejected the religious fundamentalism of the Promise Keepers. But, some fathers' rights groups embraced the idea that men should be head of the household and they were sympathetic to the theme that women and children needed a man in their lives. Generally, the Promise Keepers were not friendly to feminism or to profeminism, and they did not like what they saw as the paganism of Robert Bly or the secular nature of men's rights. And although they agreed with social conservatives that men were better equipped to be leaders and heads of families, they rejected most biological or political assumptions that underlay these secular conservative views. The Promise Keepers read the Bible as literally true and took biblical passages such as Ephesians 5: 22–33 at face value. The Promise Keepers overreached, however, and by the twenty-first century were cutting back on the number and size of the rallies. There were extensive staff layoffs that greatly reduced the size of the organisation.

The early years of the twenty-first century find the politics of masculinity in free fall. The profeminist men's movement is very small; courses taught at universities are becoming rarer; mythopoetic groups are small and most publications have disappeared; men's rights groups have been increasing captured by the fathers' rights movement that mainly opposes current divorce and custody practices; and the Promise Keepers still hold a few small gatherings, mostly in the United States. At the same time there has been a resurgence of political language favouring the role of fathers in the family. There is a general drift, especially in the United States, towards encouragement of marriage and traditional family values. But such a drift is also present in conservative governments in Australia, Italy and the United Kingdom.

References and further reading

Astrachan, A. (1986) *How Men Feel*, New York: Doubleday.

Baumli, F. (ed.) (1985) *Men Freeing Men*, Jersey City, NJ: New Atlantis.

Blankenhorn, D. (1995) *Fatherless America*, New York: HarperCollins.

Bly, R. (1990) *Iron John*, New York: Addison-Wesley.

Clatterbaugh, K. (1997) *Contemporary Perspectives on Masculinity, Men, Women, and Politics in Modern Society*, Boulder, CO: Westview.

Doyle, R. (1976) *The Rape of the Male*, St Paul, MN: Poor Richard's Press.

Farrell, W. (1975) *The Liberated Man*, New York: Bantam.

—— (1993) *The Myth of Male Power*, New York: Simon and Schuster.

Fasteau, M.F. (1974) *The Male Machine*, New York: McGraw-Hill.

Friedan, B. (1963) *The Feminine Mystique*, New York: Dell.

Gilder, G. (1986) *Men and Marriage*, London: Pelican.

Goldberg, H. (1976) *The Hazards of Being Male*, New York: Signet.

Harding, C. (ed.) (1992) *Wingspan*, New York: St Martin's Press.

Hicks, R. (1993) *The Masculine Journey: Understanding the Six Stages of Manhood*, Colorado Springs, CO: Navpress.

McCartney, B. (ed.) (1992) *What Makes a Man? Twelve Promises That Will Change Your Life*, Colorado Springs, CO: Navpress.

See also: Christian men's movements; fathers' rights; men's groups; men's movement; men's rights; mythopoetic movement; profeminism

KENNETH CLATTERBAUGH

MASOCHISM

What does the male masochist want? In psychoanalytic theory, masochism is regarded as a perversion in which the individual achieves satisfaction from being subjected to painful experiences. In film and literature, the (heterosexual) male masochist is usually subjected to pain (flagellation, pricking, burning) by a dominatrix who chastises her victim for his degrading desires. Fantasies play a key role in scenarios between masochist and sadist. It is argued, however, that the dominatrix is not necessarily a genuine sadist because she has been engaged (often paid money) to carry out the masochist's desires. A genuine sadist would not derive pleasure from doing what is wanted. Similarly, insofar as the masochist has an agreement with his tormentor, he is ironically 'in control'.

The German physician Krafft-Ebing was the first to present a detailed account of masochism in his book *Psychopathia Sexualis* (1886). He named masochism after Leopold von Sacher-Masoch, who wrote the controversial novel, *Venus in Furs* (1870) based on his own experiences. At one point, Venus explains that if a woman is submissive: 'the more readily man recovers his self possession and becomes domineering', but if she is 'cruel and faithless' and 'ill-treats him', 'the more she quickens his desire and secures his love and admiration' (Sacher-Masoch 1971: 121–2).

There is a sub-genre of pornography that is addressed to the male masochist in which the protagonist is usually tied up and sexually humiliated by a dominatrix. The image of male as victim is pushed to extremes in the art-house film *Maîtresse* (1976) directed by Barbet Schroeder. The sub-plot features a group of mainly male masochists who pay the dominatrix to humiliate and torture them. In one scene a character experiences extreme pleasure from having a nail driven through his penis. In his essay, 'The economic problem of masochism' (1924) Sigmund Freud distinguished between three types of masochism. These were: erotogenic, in which sexual pleasure is linked with pain; feminine masochism in which the male (or female) adopts a so-called feminine position of subservience; and moral masochism related to the desire of the individual to experience a sense of guilt. Sado-masochistic encounters exist in heterosexual, homosexual and all other forms of relationships.

References and further reading

Freud, S. [1924] (1984) 'The economic problem of masochism', in *Pelican Freud Library*, vol. 11, Harmondsworth: Penguin Books.

Krafft-Ebing, R. (1959) *Psychopathia Sexualis*, London: Staples.

Sacher-Masoch, L. (1971) *Venus in Furs*, London: Faber & Faber.

BARBARA CREED

MASTURBATION

The advent of masturbation as a putative medical and moral problem can be dated with a precision rare in cultural history; 'onanism', as it came to be understood by doctors and moralists of all sorts, came into being in London around 1712. Before then silence largely reigned. There was relatively little discussion of it among the doctors of antiquity; among playwrights and poets it was treated largely as a joke. As for the Church, masturbation was regarded as begin of little consequence until the twelfth century and even after that, when it came to be classified as a mortal sin – an unnatural act – it received almost no pastoral attention.

After 1712 the topic became nearly inexhaustible. It became of consequence as a result of the writings of the progressive secular authorities of the eighteenth century, medical and lay. The beginnings of this vice are humble, and its rise to the highest reaches of the Enlightenment represents a remarkable episode of intellectual upward mobility.

Sometime around 1712 there appeared an 88-page tract named *Onania* after Onan, the biblical son of Judah who refused to sire a child by his dead brother Er's wife, instead 'spilling his seed on the ground' (Genesis 38: 9–10). This was interpreted by the Church as *coitus interruptus*, and not until the eighteenth century was the boy's name associated with masturbation. The book grew from edition to edition, from translation to translation. Using only their hands and their 'filthy imaginations', the author proclaimed, anyone could procure the pleasures of orgasmic intercourse. If the sternest of warnings failed to stop masturbation, then at least the medicines he offered would cure its ill effects.

The success of *Onania* and of the new association of Onan's name to a very old practice that no one before had accused him of was almost immediate. The best known and most translated of eighteenth-century doctors, Samuel August Tissot from Lausanne, wrote *Le Onanisme* in 1759 and gave still more publicity to the new vice; a vast range of physical and mental ills were now authoritatively blamed on it. His book was still being sold in the late nineteenth century all through Europe and much of the rest of the world. Major Enlightenment thinkers and encyclopedias bewailed the rampant deadly practice.

Three aspects of masturbation were especially troubling. First was the fact that it was secret, practised alone by groups of schoolboys and girls beyond the reach of civilisation. Second, it was by its nature excessive. In sex alone there seemed to be always one more time. And finally, and perhaps most dangerously, onanism was understood to be the product of the imagination. Masturbation, said that monument of the Enlightenment, the *Encyclopédie*, was born of a 'fiery and voluptuous imagination'.

These features of solitary sex became suddenly so threatening because they stood the virtues of the age on their heads. Privacy and solitude were newly discovered virtues; they were the essence of humanity and the basis of public life. Economists thinking about a nascent consumer society argued that desire was good for society. And the imagination went from being a relatively obscure faculty of the mind to being at the core of aesthetics, economics and morality. This was the great age of fiction, of the novel; it was the age of the romantics. So we might think of onanism as the evil doppelgänger of the Enlightenment. Masturbation was the arena on which the battle for self-control was fought; guilt about doing it became a new kind of interior self-generated guilt.

The nineteenth century added little new except more and more horrible consequences and more guilt. The spread of European medicine and European fiction carried the anxiety to Japan, China and India. (Indigenous medicine had regarded seminal loss as dangerous, but masturbation was not regarded as its most likely cause.)

Sigmund Freud changed how we think about the subject. No longer an abyss to be avoided, it became a crossroads to be successfully traversed. Auto-erotocism was the primary sexuality, the testing grounds for what was to come. It had to be outgrown in both sexes, but more was demanded of women: they had to give up not only masturbation but the site of infantile pleasure – the clitoris – in favour of the vagina.

Kinsey's research and much that followed after it argued against this view. Male masturbation was shown to be almost universal, learned when young by almost all men and continued on and off throughout life. Female masturbation seemed less prevalent; it was often learned later in life through self-exploration.

Feminists, beginning in the 1970s, endorsed masturbation as a way of asserting the right to sexual pleasure and more generally of reclaiming the female body from a male medical establishment. *Our Bodies Ourselves*, for example, makes the case for a right to female sexual pleasure and for solitary sex as the first and primary exercise of that right. More recently masturbation has become an aspect of men's sexual radicalism. Even before the AIDS crisis, group masturbation clubs had been founded in major cities as a part of the creation of a new, anti-heterosexual, male culture. In the

United States the putative vice born around 1712 has become a weapon in the culture wars. Bill Clinton fired his progressive Surgeon General, Joyce Elder, because she said that perhaps teaching about masturbation should be part of sex education. Performance artists like Vito Acconci and radical porn stars like Annie Sprinkle did it in public.

And yet, masturbation remains difficult to talk about, the most embarrassing form of sexuality in a world that tolerates almost anything. It is the ultimately private act; to speak about it is to confess to it; to confess is tantamount to doing it in public. We are at an interesting moment in the history of sexuality when the new sexual vice of modernity may be slowly being transformed into something else.

References and further reading

Boston Women's Health Book Collective (2005) *Our Bodies, Ourselves*, New York: Touchstone/Simon and Schuster.

Laqueur, T.W. (2003) *Solitary Sex*, New York: Zone Books.

See also: sexuality

THOMAS LAQUEUR

MATESHIP

'Mateship' is homosocial bonding between Australian men, traditionally stressing equality, fraternity and solidarity, which operates at the individual level of men as 'mates' and at the level of the institution of 'mateship', mythologised as a core element of Australian national identity. Attempts to locate historical origins emphasise the importance of British working-class traditions of male solidarity in colonial Australia and the experience of rural workers in the 'hostile' Australian bush. Ward (1965) also argued that an absence of women in the Australian bush led to the primacy of male bonds, but this argument ignored the existence of relationships between white men and Aboriginal women. Instead, a deep antipathy to women may have been at the heart of mateship's male homosociality (Thompson 1994).

Moore has categorised 'exclusive' formations of mateship, where male solidarity was directed against another group and 'inclusive' formations directed towards a higher ideal, such as 'the brotherhood of man' (1967). Even in the latter instance, however, mateship has historically been a defensive formation on the basis of gender, race and sexuality. Mateship was elevated to the level of national mythology following Australian involvement in the First World War and remains a core idea about Australian national identity.

Mateship is central to dominant notions of masculinity in Australia. Through bonding and rituals within homosocial groups (white, heterosexual) Australian men acknowledge and affirm each other as men. Even applied to strangers, the term 'mate' carries this implicit recognition and acknowledgement. Since the 1970s, mateship has been critiqued by feminists as masculinist and by male critics as severely limiting. Colling argues that, in the absence of an external threat, mateship is a dysfunctional model for contemporary men, which privileges an imagined male solidarity over relationships with women and children (1992). Partly in response to feminist criticism, attempts have been made to re-configure mateship beyond its masculinist and homosocial origins to encompass an all-inclusive notion of community solidarity and equality. Contemporary images of mateship, however, remain largely reliant on soldiers and sporting heroes.

References and further reading

Altman, D. (1987) 'The myth of mateship', *Meanjin*, 46: 165–72.

Colling, T. (1992) *Beyond Mateship: Understanding Australian Men*, Sydney: Simon and Schuster.

Moore, T.I. (1967) 'The meanings of mateship', in C.B. Christesen (ed.) *On Native Grounds: Australian Writing from Meanjin Quarterly*, Sydney: Angus and Robertson, pp. 223–31.

Thompson, E. (1994) *Fair Enough: Egalitarianism in Australia*, Sydney: University of New South Wales Press.

Ward, R. [1954] (1965) *The Australian Legend*, Melbourne: Oxford University Press.

See also: friendship; men's relations with men

LINZI MURRIE

MEDICINE

In recent years medicine has faced significant challenges to its authority and some decline in its dominance in Western capitalist societies (Coburn 2001). Nevertheless, it remains a foundational social institution. Medicine shapes the *kinds* of health services most commonly available, and people's *access* to them. It is also influential in determining nation states' health priorities. These have focused on hospital-based curative services, often involving 'hi-tech' interventions for individual illness and disease. Yet such an approach has not advanced the health of nations (Navarro and Shi 2002). Nor has it addressed the single most pressing health-service priority – care for chronic illness and disability and palliative care (Lewis and Leeder 2001).

According to critics, these limitations stem from medicine's gendered character and the role it plays in the production of gendered social relations (Schofield 2004). While women's entry into the profession since the 1970s has increased, this has not been accompanied by gender parity in its more privileged echelons (Pringle 1998). Women are simply not present in equal numbers alongside men in decision-making processes in medical education and training, planning, administration and service delivery. Just as significantly, medicine fails to recognise what women, as the *major users of health services*, regard as health priorities, and what kinds of health services *they* identify as important in addressing them. Medicine's hierarchical practices in health policy and service organisations render it the male-dominated 'subject' and women the excluded or marginalised 'other'. Accordingly, medicine is a gendered and gendering institution that secures the privilege of a predominantly elite group of men at the expense of a large majority of women.

References and further reading

Coburn, D. (2001) 'Health, health care and neoliberalism', in P. Armstrong, H. Armstrong and D. Coburn (eds) *The Political Economy of Health and Health Care in Canada*, Toronto: Oxford University Press.

Lewis, M. and Leeder, S. (2001) *Where to from Here? The Need to Construct a Comprehensive National Health Policy*, Australian Health Policy Institute Commissioned Paper Series 2001/01, Sydney: University of Sydney.

Navarro, V. and Shi, L. (2002) 'Health and equity in the world in the era of globalization', in V. Navarro (ed.) *The Political Economy of Social Inequalities*, Amityville, NY: Baywood Publishing.

Pringle, R. (1998) *Sex and Medicine: Gender, Power and Authority in the Medical Profession*, Cambridge: Cambridge University Press.

Schofield, T. (2004) *Boutique Health? Gender and Equity in Health Policy*, Australian Health Policy Institute Commissioned Paper Series 2004/08, Sydney: University of Sydney.

TONI SCHOFIELD

MEN

In biological terms men are adult males; in sociological terms men are a socially constituted political category informing a gender arrangement or order. Within this category there is, however, a complex and shifting diversity.

The sociology of masculinity is primarily concerned with men in so much as such studies are informed by feminist questions concerned with men's power, men's identity, men's practices and men's futures. Indeed, the very notion of masculinities is without meaning or importance unless connected to men, for it is primarily through men's subjectivities and behaviours that masculinities become reified. Yet despite the dominance of men across most social spheres, and men's powerful influence on the writing of history and production of knowledge itself (O'Brien 1983), there has, certainly until relatively recently, been an invisibility to them. For too long a 'silence' has surrounded men (Collinson and Hearn 2001). Not until the development of modern feminist thought did discussions of men and their practices turn into a globally informed critical gaze, a process enhanced through writings within the sociology of masculinity.

One of the key dynamics serving to render men 'invisible', not least unto themselves, has been the dualities at the heart of gender. For example, if one takes women and men as a defining social dualism then from this emerge equally significant binaries serving to provide opportunity and/or restraint upon the gendered individual. Dominant notions of what is included within and defining of, for example, the public/private, nature/nurture and feminine/masculine remain powerful even at this postmodern turn in human history (Nicholson 1990). Such gendered binaries serve to suggest or 'tell truths' about women and men and their capacities as gendered beings. These notions are invariably reinforced through a narrative of women and men as functional, pre-gendered individuals. The gender order which informs or arises from such narratives and associated practices identifies men as a (discursive) political category, following which one can see that without the feminist inspired interventions of recent decades, the circularity of men, masculinities, power and identity would remain largely invisible and unquestioned.

The aim of critical studies of men and masculinities is, then, to turn attention to men in a way that renders them and their practices visible, apparent and subject to question, and to undertake this examination with an explicit political intent. This feminist and profeminist naming of men is now further informed by gay and queer scholarships, though as Hearn (2004) points out, the relationship of such writings to feminism can and does vary. It is apparent from critical gender writings that men are diverse, often unpredictable and creative, both as individuals and in alliance with others. These political and contrasting dimensions to men are made explicit by, for example, their differing responses to feminism, which range from the 'essentialist retreats' of conservatives to the radical and socialist feminist men's movements (Messner 1997)

Fundamental to all critical studies of men is the issue of power – that is, how is men's power experienced, manifested, exercised, resisted and produced? Furthermore, to what extent is this power patriarchal, hegemonic, discursive, socially constructed or functional? The debates which arise from concerns with this key aspect of men and masculinities initially derived from feminist notions of patriarchy (Walby 1989), though more recently there has been a substantial engagement with feminist poststructuralist thought which seeks to explore power at the level of the subject without, however, omitting sight of its macro dimensions (see, for example, Weedon 1991). Arguably the concept most persistently and widely used by theorists to interrogate men's power remains that of 'hegemonic masculinity', introduced initially by Carrigan *et al.* (1985) (see also Connell 1987), but since taken up by numerous feminist and profeminist writers, though not without critique (for example, Jefferson 2001, Whitehead 2002).

Whatever theoretical position one draws on to explore and critically interrogate the relationship between men and power, and there are several, what is not in question is that power exists between and within the political categories of women and men. Indeed, these categories cannot exist without a power dimension, though it is important to recognise that the origin and character of this power remains subject to continuing debate.

It can be argued that compared to notions of the public and private, the concept of power is relatively substantive and concrete. For example, there remains a powerful mythology attached to men and the public world of work which is not so apparent in respect of men and power. The idea that men actually live out their lives within distinctly compartmentalised public and private spaces is largely myth, while the idea that men can exercise power (over women and other men) as a consequence of their position within the (discursive) category of men, is not. At the very least there is seepage between the dominant discourses of the public and those of the private. More likely there is overflow; emotional selves, organisation, intimacies, relationships, friendships, families, parenting, sexuality are just a few of the dimensions of gender and identity which, while often understood to be positioned in either the public or private, are more realistically configured and experienced across and within both spheres. For example, are men's violences confined to the public or the private spheres? Clearly men have historically expressed violent behaviour in all spheres, and not just in the contexts of organised, militaristic, violence or criminal activity (Hearn 1998). Yet while as individuals we may experience these aspects of our being in a discontinuous if not often unsettling manner, in terms of subjectivity and narrative we invariably seek to position them as either part of our public, or private, worlds.

One way to understand this apparent reluctance of many men, especially, to embrace the multiple dimensional aspects of their being is to recognise that in so doing they would undermine a central mythology of masculinity; which is that men can only become men through their achievement of a particular expression of masculine performance, one traditionally exercised in the public world of work and often reinforced through the male family breadwinner role. While the latter aspect is now not so common among Western men especially, the relationship between men and work appears as strong as ever. So while the traditional family model may well have given way to a looser, even fragmented familial arrangement for many men, work remains one of those gendered sites wherein men still expect to acquire some sense of masculine validation. Indeed, any site where men predominate (e.g. sport, prisons, fraternities, clubs) is likely to provide rich research data that illuminates the practices of masculine validation in which men may engage. While such practices may be limited and limiting for men, they remain powerful for that very reason. They are effective in reinforcing men's sense of themselves as men through the apparatus of a dominant cultural (hegemonic or discursive) process.

Many critical gender theorists consider that it would be to men's advantage if they were to invest less of themselves in a control-focused, work-oriented subjectivity, thereby enabling the creation of a different, possibly less instrumental intimacy between them and others (for example, Kerfoot 2001). This raises questions regarding the degree to which men can manage their gendered subjectivity in ways which are, ultimately, more beneficial to them as individuals and to others, and less invested in traditional, if not damaging, forms of masculinity. At this point we need to consider how processes of gender identity correspond to the structure–agency dichotomy. Is there a case for arguing that men's masculinity, being more a process than a fixed outcome, remains highly contingent, fragile and ungrounded?

Certainly this is the argument put forward by writers across the spectrum of critical gender studies, a claim strengthened by increasingly influential poststructuralist perspectives which highlight the discursive character of identity (McNay 1992). But this being so would suggest that many men will find it hard to change their masculine subjectivity, not least because in so doing they take an ontological risk. That is, by virtue of not being men, or indeed an individual, in any biologically grounded way, their discursive identity work is always in process and, ultimately, highly reliant on the gaze of the other for validation (see Sarup 1993 for discussion). So for many men, especially those located in more traditional masculine sites formed, for example, around particular race, class and ethnic spaces, it is neither realistic nor, indeed, reasonable to expect an opening up of their epistemological framework to more feminist, and liberating, subjectivities. For whatever agency they may have at their disposal that might facilitate such an ontological shift remains problematised by the structural conditions which have hitherto reinforced their sense of masculinity. In other words, for many men the act of changing their masculine subjectivity is not one they can readily undertake or accept, for even if they have the intent and agency to do exactly this, the outcome would be to render their previous (masculine) identity nigh worthless, a highly threatening condition if the man remains situated in a traditional masculine site. In addition to the identity issues at stake here, there is the issue of power. As Hearn argues, why would men want to change if in so doing it reduces their access to a gendered order? Nevertheless, many men have changed and many more will. The current gender arrangement is markedly different from even two decades ago, never mind ten, and men are inevitably part of that shift.

Those men who do become sensitive and sympathetic to gender, even feminism, invariably come to this (self) awareness of themselves as gendered subjects as a result of being confronted and subsequently disrupted by the inherent contingency of their masculine assumptions. They come to recognise that the way they have been living as men is not the way they wish to continue to live. From this, many have gone on to become highly active in seeking to challenge the gender injustices of which they had become newly aware (for example, Tolson 1977; Stoltenberg 1990).

Yet vital as this process is, it is not in any way straightforward and nor is it predictable. As critical gender theorists, and despite our political concerns, we must remain sensitive to the powerful identity investment that most men have in 'stable' masculine formations, be they discursively formed or ideological. Still, feminism undoubtedly offers a positive counter-discourse to traditional masculine codes, and one which many men appear increasingly comfortable to engage with.

It is important to recognise that the dimensions to men are multiple and contrasting. There is no single over-arching position that men adopt or that can be adopted on behalf of men. Similarly, any definition of men must be loose and flexible enough to encapsulate their diversity. Class, sexuality, race, ethnicity, age, education and health are just some of the variables that contribute to this diversity which is men. The key strengths of post-structuralist and postmodernist feminist thought are in emphasising precisely this contingency and fluidity which surrounds both women and men, while providing a nuanced exploration of the identity work being undertaken by individuals. There is nothing inevitable to men, other than arguably the one fixed aspect which is their location, like women, within a gendered political category, itself rooted in an apparently fixed dualism.

Feminist and profeminist social constructionist approaches to the study of men have provided valuable insights into men and their experiences within the public (e.g. work) and private (e.g. family) spheres. More recently, and in contributing to the sociology of masculinity, there has been a surge of writings on men from previously neglected social and cultural locations covering virtually every part of the globe (see Whitehead 2006). So, in a relatively few short decades, men have gone from being historically 'invisible' to being exposed. The driver for this powerful shift in the gaze on men has been feminism. While the precise impact of this gaze is difficult to quantify, one can expect it to illuminate an increasing number of gendered sites and lead to changes in the gendered subjectivities of many men.

References and further reading

Carrigan, T., Connell, R. and Lee, J. (1985) 'Toward a new sociology of masculinity', *Theory and Society*, 5 (2): 551–604.

Collinson, D.L. and Hearn, J. (2001) 'Naming men as men: implications for work, organizations and management', in: S.M. Whitehead and F.J. Barrett (eds) *The Masculinities Reader*, Cambridge: Polity.

Connell, R. (1987) *Gender and Power*, Cambridge: Polity.

Hearn, J. (1998) *The Violences of Men*, London: Sage.
—— (2004) 'From hegemonic masculinity to the hegemony of men', *Feminist Theory*, 5 (1): 49–72.
Jefferson, T. (2001) 'Subordinating hegemonic masculinity', *Theoretical Criminology*, 6 (1): 63–88.
Kerfoot, D. (2001) 'The organization of intimacy: managerialism, masculinity and the masculine subject', in S.M. Whitehead and F.J. Barrett (eds) *The Masculinities Reader*, Cambridge: Polity.
McNay, L. (1992) *Foucault and Feminism*, Cambridge: Polity.
Messner, M.A. (1997) *The Politics of Masculinities: Men in Movements*, Thousand Oaks, CA: Sage.
Nicholson, L.J. (ed.) (1990) *Feminist/Postmodernism*, New York: Routledge.
O'Brien, M. (1983) *The Politics of Reproduction*, London: Routledge and Kegan Paul.
Sarup, M. (1993) *Post-Structuralism and Postmodernism*, 2nd edn, New York: Harvester Wheatsheaf.
Stoltenberg, J. (1990) *Refusing to be a Man*, Glasgow: Fontana/Collins.
Tolson, A. (1977) *The Limits of Masculinity*, London: Tavistock.
Walby, S. (1989) 'Theorizing patriarchy', *Sociology*. 23 (2): 213–34.
Weedon, C. (1991) *Feminist Practice and Poststructuralist Theory*, Oxford: Blackwell.
Whitehead, S.M. (2002) *Men and Masculinities: Key Themes and New Directions*, Cambridge: Polity.
—— (ed.) (2006) *Men and Masculinities: Critical Studies in Sociology* (Volume 5: *Global Masculinities*), London: Routledge.

See also: epistemology; feminism; gender order; identity; male; manhood; masculinity/masculinities; men's practices, individual and collective

STEPHEN M. WHITEHEAD

MEN IN WOMEN'S/FEMINISED OCCUPATIONS

While there is growing evidence of some desegregation of occupations in terms of gender, gender segregation remains a significant aspect of most labour markets. Segregation includes both vertical (location in the organisational hierarchy) and horizontal gender segregation (specialisation at the same organisation or in particular occupations). In feminised occupations, the majority of employees are women and the occupations are viewed as requiring workers with 'feminine' characteristics. The work is frequently defined as 'passive' and often involves caring for individuals who are vulnerable in relation to their age and/or ability. Typical feminised occupations include nursing, primary school teaching, social work and librarianship. Men have been able to maintain a dominant position in gender relations by representing masculinity as the valued norm, resulting in men's practices and masculinity being 'taken for granted, hidden and unexamined' from analysis (Collinson and Hearn 1994: 3).

The study of men in feminised occupations provides one site where masculinities, privilege and transgression are more exposed and potentially open to critique (Christie 2006). Explanations for men's employment in these occupations are varied. They range from theories that highlight broad changes in the labour market and the changing definitions of particular jobs, to theories that focus on the attributes of individual men and the psychological and social construction of masculinities. There may be particular advantages for men working in feminised occupations. As men are assumed to be technically competent and have leadership skills, they tend to rise to the top of occupations more quickly, 'riding a glass escalator', adopting particular high-status specialities, and being encouraged into administration or management roles (Williams 1995). Men's 'difference' is rewarded with higher levels of pay and better working conditions. These gender dynamics often result in men distancing themselves from women colleagues and from feminine aspects of the occupation.

Work in feminised occupations may also create tensions for men with regard to their gender and professional identities. These tensions can arise when men work alongside women and undertake roles that are regarded as traditionally undertaken by women (e.g. caring for children). Although employment in feminised professions may lead to increased job satisfaction for individual men, men who work in feminised occupations are sometimes fearful of being defined as not 'real men', effeminate, homosexual, eccentric and/or failures within the 'male world' of work.

Some argue that employment within these occupations limits men's opportunities to reinforce their own sense of masculinity (Lupton 2000). To reduce/obscure some of the these tensions and consequent discomfort, men and women often negotiate to (re)produce men's gendered and professional identities. This may involve processes such as the relabelling and redefinition of jobs. Particular discursive strategies may also be employed to justify men's choice of employment and emphasise the particular masculine qualities that they bring to their work. However, attempts to (re)assert these men's masculinity will be incomplete and fragmentary as hegemonic masculinity in itself is ambiguous and inconsistent (Simpson 2004).

While caring occupations are described as a feminised profession, other types of work and professions are becoming increasingly feminised. Values that are associated with femininity, such as effective communication skills and working with emotions, are now more valued within organisations. This change may be related to the management of emotions as an increasingly important mode of regulating society. However, as men gain new opportunities within work to express particular feminine qualities and to be rewarded for doing so, opportunities for women to adopt more masculine characteristics remain restricted (Adkins 2002). This generalised feminisation of the workplace and the increasing role of management of emotions as a form of social control open up possibilities for change in men's relationships to and locations within feminised occupations in the future.

References and further reading

Adkins, L. (2002) *Revisions*, Buckingham: Open University Press.

Christie, A. (2006) 'Negotiating the uncomfortable intersections between gender and professional identities in social work', *Critical Social Policy*, 26 (2): 390–411.

Collinson, D. and Hearn, J. (1994) 'Naming men as men', *Gender, Work and Organization*, 1 (1): 2–22.

Lupton, B. (2000) 'Maintaining masculinity', *British Journal of Management*, 11 (Special Issue): S33–S48.

Simpson, R. (2004) 'Masculinity at work', *Work, Employment and Society*, 18 (2): 349–68.

Williams, C.L. (1995) *Still a Man's World: Men Who Do Women's Work*, Berkeley, CA and London: University of California Press.

See also: class, work and masculinity; men working with children

ALASTAIR CHRISTIE

MEN WHO HAVE SEX WITH MEN

In the late 1980s, increasing understanding of sexual activity between men – particularly among researchers working in HIV/AIDS – led to recognition that many men are sexually active with other men in a wide range of situations and contexts and for diverse motives. These motives include: desire – when the individual's primary sexual interest is other men; reward – when his primary sexual interest may be women or men but at least some of his sexual activity is with men for financial or other reward; lack of available women – when the individual prefers women but has sex with men where women are not available, in situations such as prison or conservative Muslim societies; curiosity or pleasure – where the individual wishes to explore and enjoy his own sexual response and that of other men; and violence – where he asserts his power over another man, or is the victim of such assertion.

The term 'men who have sex with men' therefore encompasses all men who have sex with men at least once, irrespective of the identity they give themselves and the motive or motives underlying their behaviour. The term contrasts strongly with 'gay/queer', which generally refers to men (and women) who seek social and legal acceptance of individuals who practise same-sex behaviour, and 'homosexual', which is usually interpreted as preference for same-sex behaviour.

Statistics are not available for the number of men who have sex with men in any society.

The United Nations suggests a figure of 2 to 5 per cent, but there is circumstantial evidence that the percentage is much higher among men under thirty years old (Foreman 2004).

Although the phrase 'men who have sex with men' refers only to behaviour, the acronym MSM is increasingly used as an identity by men in non-Western societies who reject the term 'gay' but who nonetheless wish to distinguish themselves from men who have sex with women. Use of the acronym as an identity is not universally agreed and may lead to confusion.

Some activists and researchers, particularly in South Asia, prefer the term 'males who have sex with males'. This is partly because such sex may involve adolescent or pre-pubescent boys – often without their full consent – and partly because some males who identify as women or an intermediate sex reject the term 'men' because of its associations with masculinity.

References and further reading

Foreman, M. (2004) 'Unknown men', unpublished manuscript.

Khan, S. (2001) 'Culture, sexualities, and identities: men who have sex with men in India', in G. Sullivan and P.A. Jackson (eds) *Gay and Lesbian Asia: Culture, Identity, Community*, Binghamton, NY: Harrington Park Press, pp. 99–115.

See also: gay masculinities; HIV/AIDS; homophobia and heterosexism; homosexuality; working with gay men

MARTIN FOREMAN

MEN WORKING WITH CHILDREN

In most educations systems in English-speaking countries there are fewer men than women working in the primary sector, and in particular in early childhood. Over the last decade this situation has been constructed as a crisis in the teaching profession prompting government inquiries, policies and working parties (Education Queensland 2002; Teacher Training Agency 1999). The topic has also attracted much media interest (Murray 2003), often driven by sections of the men's lobby (Kindlon and Thompson 1999). Concerns about the lack of male teachers have often paralleled and intersected with concerns about boys' education (House of Representatives Standing Committee on Education and Training 2002).

The dominant argument for more male teachers goes something like this: boys are currently underperforming academically in relation to girls, and they are also more badly behaved than girls. The reasons for this, the argument continues, are a lack of boy-friendly curricula, assessment and pedagogical practices and a lack of male teachers who can employ such practices. The suggestion is that male teachers will understand boys better than female teachers and will be able to connect with them in ways in which women teachers cannot. These claims rest upon shaky ground and can have quite negative effects upon the teaching profession.

The argument that boys are currently the new disadvantaged in school is a contested claim (Francis and Skelton, 2005). Many of those claiming that boys are the new disadvantaged fail: to disaggregate data based upon school performance; to consider post-school options; to raise issues of sexual harassment of girls; and/or to take into account patterns of enrolment in high-status subjects. Thus, basing the call for more male teachers on the grounds of improving boys' education is a reasonably tenuous one. However, even in some situations where groups of girls are outperforming certain groups of boys, there is no research evidence to indicate that male teachers, because they are male teachers, can improve such boys' academic results. Indeed, the research evidence suggests that it is not the sex of the teacher that makes a difference to underachieving boys' results, but the quality of the classroom pedagogies (Lingard *et al.* 2002).

Ironically the push for more male teachers may well have a negative impact upon some boys' academic success. In some communities and some classrooms there has been identified an anti-learning culture on the part of some boys. This anti-learning culture can be identified with dominant constructions of masculinity. However, the argument for more male role models often suggests that it is such dominant masculine constructs that are needed in the classroom in order to control and to appeal to boys. The employment of more male teachers who demonstrate such masculinities is only likely to further legitimise those behaviours that are a problem in schools.

There is also a way in which the current debate around male teachers is having a negative impact upon the teaching profession. The claim that boys are failing at school and that the remedy for this is fewer female and more male teachers serves to blame female teachers for the supposed poor state of boys' education. The misogynist tone of this is often an extension of the attacks on single mothers' parenting strategies with young boys. Indeed, a popular argument for more male teachers is that given the current proliferation of single-mother families and lack of male teachers, boys often grow up with no male role models in their lives. The resentment that some women are likely to feel as male teachers are constructed as a valued commodity is wonderfully captured in the ironically titled Murray (1996) article '"We all love Charles": men in childcare and the social construction of gender'.

However, for many men being loved like 'Charles' is not particularly attractive. Many of the backlash lobby have suggested that this is because men feel alienated by such things as the 'feminised' culture of schools, by the poor wages and lack of career advancement, and by the prevalence of supposed false sexual harassment claims by students against male teachers. Again these are all problematic claims. It is difficult to suggest that simply because there are more female teachers than male teachers, school cultures are feminised. As Skelton (2002) indicates, the curriculum is still largely about men, and male teachers often experience a very rapid career advancement, in what Williams (1992) refers to as the 'glass escalator effect', so much so that there are disproportionate numbers of men in senior positions in most education systems. Encouraging schools and education systems to take the sexual harassment and physical and sexual abuse of students by teachers seriously has been a difficult task. That some systems may undermine structures put in place to address these issues is a worrying consequence of the male teacher debate.

Some of the reasons rarely considered in the popular press, texts, government reports and policies as to why men are not attracted to teaching are homophobia and misogyny. These two very powerful discourses clearly impact upon men's decisions to enter or not enter the teaching profession (King 1998). These discourses operate to suggest that working with children is women's work. This positions men who want to work with children as suspect, as gay or as wanting to be women. The sanctions against men labelled as such are so severe that many young men shun the teaching profession.

While many of the claims for more male teachers are grounded within an anti-feminist framework, there can be feminist and profeminist claims for more male teachers (see, for example, Mills 2000; King 1998). Working with children is a critical and highly responsible task, but many men have avoided this by constructing teaching as women's work; a more gender-just society would be one where men share this responsibility. However, this responsibility should not solely relate to boys nor should it involve denigrating the work of women teachers. A gender-just approach to the issue of male teachers also needs to take into account the ways in which misogyny and homophobia police the boundaries of the teaching profession with the effect of devaluing teaching, keeping downward pressure on teachers' wages and privileging male career advancement over that of women. Similar issues are evident too in child care.

References and further reading

Education Queensland, (2002) *Male Teachers' Strategy*, Brisbane: Queensland Government.

Francis, B. and Skelton, C. (2005) *Reassessing Gender and Achievement*, London: Routledge.

House of Representatives Standing Committee on Education and Training (2002) *Boys*, Canberra: Commonwealth of Australia.

Kindlon, D. and Thompson, M. (1999) *Raising Cain*, London: Michael Joseph.

King, J. (1998) *Uncommon Caring*, New York: Teachers' College.

Lingard, B., Martino, W., Mills, M. and Bahr, M. (2002) *Addressing the Educational Needs of Boys*, Canberra: DEST.

Mills, M. (2000) 'Issues in implementing boys' programmes in schools', *Gender and Education*, 12 (2): 221–38.

Murray, J. (2003) 'Man in a girls' world', *Times Educational Supplement*, 21 March.

Murray, S. (1996) '"We all love Charles": men in childcare and the social construction of gender', *Gender and Society*, 10 (4): 368–85.

Skelton, C. (2002) 'The "feminisation of schooling" or "re-masculinising" primary education', *International Studies in the Sociology of Education*, 12 (1): 77–96.

Teacher Training Agency (1999) *Teacher Training Agency Annual Review*, UK: TTA.

Williams, C. (1992) 'The glass escalator', *Social Problems*, 39: 253–67.

MARTIN MILLS

MENOPAUSE, MALE

Male menopause (or 'andropause') is a multidimensional change of life with hormonal, physical, psychological, interpersonal, social, sexual and spiritual aspects. Male menopause occurs in all men, generally between the ages of 40 and 55, although it can occur as early as 35 or as late as 65. It signals the end of the first part of a man's life and prepares him for the second half.

The term 'male menopause' is, of course, a misnomer. Men do not have menstrual periods and so they do not stop having them. Unlike women, men can continue to have children late into their lives. But in terms of other life changes, women's and men's experiences are quite similar, and so the term is still useful. In 1944 Heller and Myers identified symptoms they labelled the 'male climacteric', including loss of libido and potency, nervousness, depression, impaired memory and concentration, fatigue, insomnia, hot flushes and sweating. They found that their subjects had below normal levels of testosterone and that symptoms improved dramatically when patients were given replacement doses. This early recognition has been extended in contemporary biomedical research. At present, the concept of male menopause is more widely accepted in Britain, Australia and Europe than it is in the United States, where many clinicians believe that it is synonymous with hypogonadism (low testosterone levels).

Morley (2000) developed a ten-item screening for male menopause, but emphasised testosterone loss as the primary cause. Mintz *et al.* (2001) believe that other hormones, diet and exercise are equally important. Depression is one of the most common problems of men going through male menopause, yet it is greatly underdiagnosed in men and can be deadly.

Several effective intervention strategies (Diamond 1998) include: hormone replacement therapy; exercise, dietary changes, stress reduction; acupuncture, herbal treatments; couple counselling, career refocusing and spiritual support; chemical dependency treatment; sexual compulsivity treatment; treatment for depression; and finding and engaging one's 'calling' in the second half of life.

References and further reading

Diamond, J. (1998) *Male Menopause*, Naperville, IL: Sourcebooks.

Heller, C.G. and Myers, G.B. (1944) 'The male climacteric', *JAMA*, 126: 472–7.

Mintz, A.P., Dotson, A. and Mukai, J. (2001) 'Hormone modulation, low glycemic nutrition, and exercise instruction', *Journal of Anti-Aging Medicine*, 4: 357–71.

Morley, J.E. (2000) 'Clinical diagnosis of age-related testosterone deficiency', *The Aging Male*, 3 (1, February): 55.

JED DIAMOND

MEN'S CONSCIOUSNESS RAISING

Consciousness raising is the process of becoming aware of broader social or political issues or, alternatively, developing an understanding and awareness of personal motivations, experiences, behaviours or actions and how these are related to larger social forces. Consciousness raising is typically a facilitated process, taking place in specially convened groups. Consciousness raising is used to effect personal, political and social change, for both group participants and society writ large.

Consciousness-raising groups first emerged as part of the second-wave feminist movement in the 1960s, and it is in this context that the term was first coined. These early groups were facilitated by women (usually radical feminists) for women, with the express aim of enabling participants to see that personal issues facing women were not individual problems but part of a larger structure of oppression.

The first men's consciousness-raising groups were founded in the 1970s in the UK, Canada, the US and Australia. These early groups either sought to achieve profeminist consciousness among men or encouraged men to see that their lives are also affected by gender issues, including the 'male sex role' (Pease 2002). Unlike women's consciousness raising, which is a response to their oppressed social position, men's consciousness raising, particularly of the profeminist kind, must begin with a recognition of men's complicity in women's oppression. Male participants are therefore usually required to engage in introspection and self-analysis, much of which can be confronting or difficult.

Purposely convened men's consciousness-raising groups have appeared less frequently since the late 1980s; most of the newer groups are devoted to exploring the meaning of manhood and how men's lives are gendered, rather than seeking to create an awareness of and response to issues of gender inequality. Several contemporary men's groups, notably those organised around divorced fathers' rights and anger management, also engage in consciousness-raising activities, even if this is not their explicit or declared purpose.

Group-facilitated consciousness raising for men is achieved in a number of ways, including regular meetings in a men-only space, personal reflection, structured exercises, intimate sharing, and reading key books (Flood 1994; Pease 1997).

References and further reading

Clatterbaugh, K. (1997) *Contemporary Perspectives on Masculinity*, 2nd edn, Boulder, CO: Westview.

Flood, M. (1994) 'Men's groups', *XY: Men, Sex, Politics*, 4 (2), available at http://www.xyonline.net/groups.shtml

Messner, M. (1997) *Politics of Masculinities*, Thousand Oaks, CA: Sage.

Pease, B. (1997) *Men and Sexual Politics*, Adelaide: Dulwich Centre Publications.

—— (2000) *Recreating Men*, London: Sage.

—— (2002) *Men and Gender Relations*, Melbourne: Tertiary Press.

See also: masculinity politics; men's groups; men's movement

ANDREW SINGLETON

MEN'S GROUPS

A men's group is a small collective of men who meet on a regular, ongoing basis or who commit to a structured programme which runs over a set period of time. Long-established examples include fraternal orders like the Freemasons and the Odd Fellows (Messner 1997). Since the emergence of the first profeminist groups in the early 1970s, many different kinds of men's groups have appeared, facilitating or exploring new age spirituality, men's rights, divorced fathers' rights, Christian men's issues, anger management, male peer support, cancer treatment, first-time fatherhood or mythopoetic men's activities (see Bartkowski 2000; Guilliatt 2000; Flood 1998; Maddison 1999; Pease 2000; Reddin and Sonn 2003; Schwalbe 1996; Singleton 2003). More contemporary, offbeat examples include 'shed clubs', where members meet in one another's garden sheds for male-related discussion, and a New York-based support group for gay men with small penises. Men's groups have been organised by psychologists and psychotherapists, social workers, academics, religious professionals, political activists and non-specialist members of the community.

Many men's groups are a key practical component of wider men's movements (e.g. groups organised to further the goals of the fathers' rights movement or the Christian men's movement). While broader men's movements seek to effect political, structural or cultural change, not all men's groups have a larger political agenda. Some simply act as a support group for men in similar circumstances. Irrespective of why a group is formed, most groups have the tacit or expressed goal of empowering or transforming men. Participation might produce self-transformation (e.g. learning to control one's anger) or feelings of camaraderie and support among individual participants (e.g. a testicular cancer sufferer understands that he is not alone) or galvanising men to campaign against divorce laws. Almost all men's groups operate on the premise that it is men who are best equipped to assist other men to achieve self-transformation, not because men are necessarily more self-aware than women but, rather, because men are bonded together by the experience of being male and thus are assumed to share an intimate understanding of each other's issues.

The emergence of groups which seek to assist men to achieve personal transformation or empowerment is indicative of a larger societal trend towards self-improvement. Sociologist Anthony Giddens (1991: 75) suggests that in late modern Western society 'the self is seen as a reflexive project, for which the individual is responsible . . . We are, not what we are, but what we make of ourselves.' Doing something to address one's situation or circumstances is deeply enmeshed in Western culture. This late modern concern with self-reflexivity is reflected in the widespread growth of self-help literature, diets and fitness programmes and various therapeutic or self-help groups.

To be successful in achieving their goals, it is necessary that men's groups participants are emotionally open, vulnerable and intimate with one another. However, many men believe that they are not as proficient at articulating their emotions as women; indeed, such behaviour goes against the prevailing way most Western men are socialised. Men's groups provide a context for men to transcend traditional masculine modes of relating and form intimate and trusting relationships with other participants (Bartkowski 2000; Reddin and Sonn 2003; Singleton 2003). For example, in his study of a Promise Keepers accountability group Bartkowski (2000) found that the spatial arrangement of the group's meeting space, including the close circular arrangement of the chairs, facilitated 'intense brotherly intimacy'. In another study of two Christian men's groups, Singleton (2003) found that the groups replicated traditional modes of male bonding: participants gathered in a 'female-free' environment, with time and space set aside so that participants could properly relax in each other's company.

A common theme in the scholarly literature on men's groups is the perception that most of those who become involved in men's groups have experienced some form of difficulty associated with being a man or reached a crisis point in their lives, often in relation to their gender roles (Collier 1996; Faludi 1999; Flood 1998; Schwalbe 1996; Singleton 2003). Other research suggests that men also have pragmatic reasons for becoming involved: a group is recommended by a friend or, in the case of the common religious men's groups, because this is an extension of their usual religious practice (Singleton 2003).

References and further reading

Bartkowski, J. (2000) 'Breaking walls, raising fences: masculinity, intimacy, and accountability among the Promise Keepers', *Sociology of Religion*, 61: 33–53.

Collier, R. (1996) 'Coming together', *Feminist Legal Studies*, 4: 3–48.
Faludi, S. (1999) *Stiffed*, London: Chatto and Windus.
Flood, M. (1998) 'Men's movements', *Community Quarterly*, 46: 63–71.
Giddens, A. (1991) *Modernity and Self-identity*, Oxford: Polity Press.
Guilliatt, R. (2000) 'The Y front', *Good Weekend*, 26 August: 18–26.
Maddison, S. (1999) 'Private men, public anger', *Journal of Interdisciplinary Gender Studies*, 4: 39–51.
Messner, M.A. (1997) *Politics of Masculinities*, Thousand Oaks, CA: Sage.
Pease, B. (2000) *Recreating Men*, London: Sage.
Reddin, J.A. and Soon, C.C. (2003) 'Masculinity, social support and a sense of community', *Journal of Men's Studies*, 11: 207–24.
Schwalbe, M. (1996) *Unlocking the Iron Cage*, Oxford: Oxford University Press.
Singleton, A. (2003) 'Men getting real?' *Journal of Sociology*, 39: 131–47.

See also: Christian men's movements; masculinity politics; men's consciousness raising; men's movement; mythopoetic movement

ANDREW SINGLETON

MEN'S HEALTH STUDIES

Men and their health have emerged as the target of population health policy in the last ten to twenty years. There are three ways in which men's health can be understood: as a cultural site of unmarked health practice, as a site of a targeted population health focus, as a political concern within the field of gender change and, critically, as an evolving site of cultural practice.

In the first instance men's health has been the standard by which health studies and health service provision have been conceived and practised. Critical research into men's health studies argues that bio-medical research and health service programmes have operated within a health system where the male body and men's health needs are the implicit universal which guides their ideals and practices (Petersen and Lupton 1996). Research by Dresser (1992), for example, explains how early studies into breast cancer, (a predominantly but not exclusively female disease) were conducted on men, and the findings extrapolated to women. Other discussions of gender and health describe how the health system and health care have been established upon the character of male anatomy. Many public health campaigns – for example, drink driving, vehicle speeding or occupational health and safety – fail to acknowledge the gendered status of these health concerns. It is men who predominantly have motor vehicle accidents, who smoke and drink excessively and who work in occupations that are dangerous to their health (Mathers 1995). These general population campaigns, that have no explicit subject for their concerns, are implicitly focusing on men.

The marked 'men's health' has developed alongside increasing interest in the links between masculinity and health status. In 1978, Harrison (65–86) wrote an article entitled 'Warning, the male sex role may be dangerous to your health', discussing the implications of being male for a person's health. This title highlights the influence of broader cultural change (namely the effects of feminism) on men, their health and the development of specific men's health services. It also signals the emergence of targeted 'men's health' programmes. State-wide health policies have only emerged in the last ten or so years in the West.

Specific men's health programmes have grown over this time both in 'developing' and 'developed' national contexts. Bio-medical, nursing, allied health and health promotion discourse has increasingly focused upon men as a specific group. Their concern lies with specific studies of men's health needs including prostate cancer, testicular injuries, workplace and sporting accidents, cardiovascular disease, men's sexually transmitted diseases and men's attendance at health services. Men's health has become an issue of concern on the global stage as well, for supra-state organisations like the World Bank Group, the World Health Organisation and various non-government AIF agencies. These studies and programmes have focused upon men's sexuality and safe-sex practice, homophobia and

AIDs transmission, men and violence prevention, and relationship building.

Political men's health claims are deployed through arguments about gender equality and health care resourcing. Arguments about men's health in this context are largely made in relation to ideas about women and women's health. Men's health lobbyists and researchers in Western nations like Australia, North America or the United Kingdom have made the case for men's health in reference to ideas about women in two key ways. First, it has been argued that women have had their turn through the development of women-specific health services and a women's health philosophy over the past thirty or so years. Second, men's health concerns are conceived in comparison to and competition with women's health concerns. Health status data is used in comparisons to make claims about equality of health resourcing. The prevailing rationality in men's health uses the higher rates of men's cancer, heart disease, injuries and lower rates of general practitioner attendance as the basis for legitimising studies of and service provision to and for men (Fletcher 1996).

The breast cancer vs prostate cancer health service resourcing is a clear example. It has been argued that men's prostate cancer diagnosis, prevention and treatment should be considered equally with women's breast cancer servicing. However, prostate and breast cancer are qualitatively different diseases with significantly different treatment regimes. Breast cancer is more virulent than prostate cancer, women are diagnosed with breast cancer earlier than men with prostate cancer, more men die with prostate cancer than from it, the methods of diagnosis are extremely different – breast cancer diagnostics are more effective than the digital rectal examination or the prostate specific antigen blood test.

Critical studies of men's health focus upon the cultural context within which men's health concerns are arising. The focus of critical men's health studies is on how men make sense of their lives and the types of practices they engage in, within local and global contexts. These studies pay attention to the economic and social environment of men, the cultural meanings of masculinities and gender relations and place of men and women in their local environments. These studies are concerned with men and their use of violence, the relationship between masculinity and men's health practices, including youth and risk taking, sexual health and men's political subject positions within men's health discourse.

References and further reading

Dresser, R. (1992) 'Wanted: single white male for medical research', *Hastings Centre Report*, January–February: 24–8.

Fletcher, R. (1996) *Testosterone Poisoning or Terminal Neglect: The Men's Health Issue*, Research Paper No. 22, Parliamentary Research Service AGPS, Canberra: ACT.

Harrison, J. (1978) 'Warning, the male sex role may be dangerous to your health', *Journal of Social Issues*, 34: 65–86

Mathers, C. (1995) 'Health differentials between Australian males and females: a statistical profile', in *Proceedings from the National Men's Health Conference*, AGPS, Canberra: ACT.

Petersen, A. and Lupton, D. (1996) *The New Public Health: Health and Self in the Age of Risk*, St Leonard's, NSW: Allen and Unwin.

Wadham, B. (2000) 'Global men's health and the crisis in Western masculinity', in B. Pease and K. Pringle (eds) *A Man's World?* London: Zed Books, pp. 69–82.

See also: health and illness, men's

BEN WADHAM

MEN'S INTERESTS

It is uncontroversial to observe that men share with women an interest in countless public goods which affect the health, wealth, safety, happiness and well-being of themselves, their social group and the species as a whole. Moreover, individual men, through bonds of affection and family, and other kinds of affiliation, have an interest in promoting the interests of certain women, at least. Two significant questions about men's interests, as a sex, are these:

Do men inevitably have some interests different from those of women? Those who believe in strong innate sex differences necessarily believe that nature directs each sex towards the pursuit of distinct interests, in the ultimate interest of the species as a whole. For example, hard evolutionary psychology holds that men's interests include the achievement of power, status and access to multiple sexual partners, while those of women include the achievement of strong relationships and the support and protection of a reliable high-status male provider (Goldberg 1993). At the other extreme is the view that since sex differences are largely, or indeed entirely, socially constructed, no significant differences exist between the innate interests of men and women (Pease 2002).

Are the interests of men privileged over those of women? Those who argue for innate sex differences usually hold that this is not the case, and that while social life may or may not involve considerable struggle between (and among) the sexes, neither sex is advantaged, with the overall outcome being beneficial for the group, and indeed the species as a whole, through an efficient specialisation of sex roles and the achievement of maximal genetic fitness. However, many difference theory feminists argue that men use their greater power to privilege specifically masculine interests so that, for example, nurturance is given less value than competitiveness (Chodorow 1991).

Those who argue against significant innate sex differences, at least with respect to interests, often hold that the interests of men are privileged in existing societies, with men the beneficiaries of what Connell (2000) has called the 'patriarchal dividend', namely the manifestly greater access of men to resources such as wealth, power, authority and status, which allows individual men to pursue their specific interests, whatever they may be. Here the argument may characterise men as a social group acting to protect their interests, rather like other social groups organised by economic class or by race (McMahon 1999). Aspects of sexual difference such as male physical strength and women's vulnerability through motherhood are usually relied on in such arguments, at least implicitly, even though the arguments may be couched in a seemingly sexually neutral discourse of social structure.

However, it has been argued that this takes too narrow a view of men's interests, based on traditional masculine preoccupations. Accordingly, it may be claimed that neither men nor women have their (similar) interests markedly privileged: thus, for example, men in existing societies gain in connection with the pursuit of wealth and power but, as a result, have less time, and less skill, in connection with human relationships.

A further issue is the context of the analysis. Thus it could be granted that men benefit from the current situation, but that both men and women would fare better in an achievable non-patriarchal alternative which exhibits lower competitiveness and aggression (Pease 2002). This view is the most optimistic about men's interest in, and willingness to support, gender equity. Unlike the preceding view in which men benefit from patriarchy, it requires no ethical appeal to men to support change, but rather a project of the education of men concerning their ultimate interests.

The following three brief cases may demonstrate the complexities of the issues:

For a particular man, affirmative action for women may disadvantage his career prospects, weaken his status as a man, and weaken his desirability as a husband and family provider, but at the same time may advance the prospects of the women in whose welfare he has an interest, and may be an aspect of a wider political programme which supports his values and interests in a more productive, humane and democratic society.

For a particular man, resistance to active participation in child-rearing affords him more time for employment and other activities in the public sphere, along with greater opportunities for leisure, but may have the effect of compromising his marriage, and his enjoyment of his children both now and in the future, reduce the opportunity for his wife to participate in employment (see above), and contribute to the reproduction of the problematic culture of masculinity (see below).

A culture of masculinity celebrating manly virtues such as virility, independence and competitiveness supports male domination, with its attendant benefits for men. However, this culture provides differential advantages, and for less successful or less assertive men, and for many homosexual men, it may be at least partially detrimental. The incitement of men, the young and those of low social status in particular, to displays of masculine prowess and risk-taking can lead to incarceration and death. And for men as a whole, the culture may be linked to practices inimical to health, ranging from participation in war to inattention to diet, and practices inimical to beneficial and supportive relationships both within the family and outside it. Nevertheless, some would suggest that such is the price men must pay in order to maintain and defend a strong social system able to hold its own in a globally competitive world.

Thus the issue of men's interests raises questions in philosophical anthropology, concerning the existence or otherwise of innate differences in interests between men and women; in politics, concerning the achievability of greater gender equity, the relation between the anti-patriarchal project and other political issues, and the long-term viability of a non-patriarchal society; and a host of empirical questions, such as whether men who embody the dominant culture of masculinity actually do have diminished satisfactions from relationships and family life.

References and further reading

Chodorow, N. (1991) *Feminism and Psychoanalytic Theory*, New Haven, CT: Yale University Press.

Connell, R. (2000) *The Men and the Boys*, Sydney: Allen and Unwin.

Goldberg, S. (1993) *Why Men Rule*, Chicago, IL: Open Court Publishing.

McMahon, A. (1999) *Taking Care of Men*, Melbourne: Cambridge University Press.

Pease, B. (2002) '(Re)Constructing men's interests', *Men and Masculinities*, 5 (2): 165–77.

See also: oppression; patriarchal dividend; patriarchy; power relations

ANTHONY MCMAHON

MEN'S LIBERATION

In the broadest sense men's liberation is a concept that is synonymous with the men's movement. The index in Clatterbaugh (1997) identifies most of the men's movements under the name 'men's liberation'. But there is a narrower concept of men's liberation that played an important role in the politics of masculinity at the outset of the profeminist men's movement in the early 1970s. The narrower concept is the subject of this entry. Briefly stated, this view holds that the social roles for men have allowed them to be only half human. Many early feminist writings decried the fact that women were socialised for (and punished for not displaying) certain characteristics such as being passive, dependent, non-assertive, soft, afraid of science and mathematics, overly emotional, and whose goal in life should be to bear children and comfort a man. Men's liberation, taking a cue from this critique, argued that men were socialised for (and punished for not displaying) certain opposite characteristics such as aggression, independence, toughness, love of science and mathematics, being unemotional, and whose life goal should be to succeed (be breadwinners) in whatever profession or work life they undertake. Thus, women were to become secretaries, schoolteachers and nurses, men were to become lawyers and doctors or, in working-class masculinities, labourers and machine operators. Both Jack Sawyer's essay 'On male liberation' (1974) and Warren Farrell's *The Liberated Man* (1975) are classic expressions of the men's liberation point of view in the narrower sense. Similarly the Berkeley Men's Center Manifesto

(1973) is written from a men's liberation point of view.

There was no shortage of social science research to back up these observations. Studies were done to show that boys were severely punished for failing to display appropriately masculine behaviour. Advocates for men's liberation criticised the old masculinity/femininity scales that put masculinity at one end and femininity at the other so that it was impossible for anyone to be both high masculine and high feminine. They defended a different way of seeing human nature that claimed each person had a need or at least the capacity to be all of these things, emotional at times and unemotional at times, passive in some situations and aggressive in others, and so on. Men were told to get in touch with the woman inside of them and conversely women were encouraged to contact their inner male. Thus the social roles, because they were limiting, were seen as stultifying a natural androgyny that was inherent in human nature.

There were two political liabilities to such a view of masculinity. First, it was directly at odds with the theme in liberal feminism that took liberation for women as being able to do the things that men are expected and encouraged to do. Thus, for feminists of this perspective, men's liberation was an oxymoron: men had what women wanted. The second political liability to the men's liberation perspective was the danger that if men are being oppressed, then men should be engaged in a struggle to liberate themselves. Some feminists welcomed this attention to the other side of the coin, as Gloria Steinem argues in her introduction to *The Male Machine*. But other critics were wary that this line of argument would come to be at odds with the feminist movement itself. In a patriarchal society, if men claim that they are being harmed, resources and attention will naturally flow towards men.

Social scientists also criticised the men's liberation analysis of gender. They argued that the concept of human nature upon which it was built was unrealistic. Sociobiologists argued that there are deep biological differences between men and women and that these differences are reflected in their different social roles. It is naïve to think that we are at bottom the same and that everyone is capable of androgyny. Accordingly, new scales of masculinity and femininity were constructed in which individuals could test out high masculine *and* high feminine or high masculine *and* low feminine or high feminine *and* low masculine or low in both. Thus a new concept of androgyny appeared in which an androgynous society was not a society in which everyone held a full complement of masculine and feminine traits, but a society in which individuals could choose without cost how to live their lives. Thus androgyny was replaced by a kind of gender autonomy.

The narrower concept of men's liberation today is viewed as an idealistic prototype of contemporary gender movements. Its somewhat simplistic solution of creating a whole person based on a mixture of traditionally masculine and feminine traits is perceived as both naïve and unattainable. But the struggle to give people more control over how they live and such issues as how emotional men can be or how assertive women can be are still very much alive. Male political candidates who cry are still perceived as weak. Men who do not want to go to war are still treated as 'girlie men'. Women who frequently speak out are still treated as too aggressive. The ideal of the 1970s, however it is rearticulated, has proved to be an illusive goal, but for many it is still a goal worth pursuing.

References and further reading

Clatterbaugh, K. (1997) *Contemporary Perspectives on Masculinity*, Boulder, CO: Westview.

Farrell, W. (1975) *The Liberated Man*, New York: Bantam.

Fasteau, M.F. (1974) *The Male Machine*, New York: McGraw-Hill.

Pleck, J.H. (1981) *The Myth of Masculinity*, Cambridge, MA: MIT Press.

Pleck, J.H. and Sawyer, J. (eds) *Men and Masculinity*, New York: Prentice Hall.

Sawyer, J. (1974) 'On male liberation', in J.H. Pleck and J. Sawyer (eds) *Men and Masculinity*, New York: Prentice Hall, pp. 170–73.

See also: masculinity politics; men's movement

KENNETH CLATTERBAUGH

MEN'S MAGAZINES

Magazines hold a central place in popular print culture and the commercial nature of magazines helps to maintain dominant ideologies and ensure that there is little space for resistance to these ideologies (Gilbert and Taylor 1991). In the 1980s there was a rise of new men's magazines. This rise was strongly linked to the influence of second-wave feminism and its perceived attack on men and masculinity that called for a new, more sensitive and caring form of masculinity. The rise and style of these magazines was also due to the historical specificity of the period and increased uncertainties within work cultures, which included a decrease in job security and in manual employment (Jackson *et al.* 2001). However, the new men's magazines were not completely new. The 1950s and 1960s magazines were precursors to these new men's lifestyle magazines, and the success of magazines such as *Arena* can be seen as a development of the 1950s magazine *Playboy*. Although the new men's magazines professed to be at the 'cutting edge' of culture (Mort 1996), they have generally adhered to and reinforced traditional and hegemonic forms of masculinity.

Before the 1980s, male magazines tended to be based on hobbies and leisure activities. The 1980s initially saw a rise of men's magazines in the United States and Europe that was linked to advertising and young males as consumers (Mort 1996). As a response to feminism and a perceived crisis in masculinity, a need was felt for men to reinvent themselves and, for example, to find their 'feminine' side. The increased anxiety led to interpretations of masculinities in terms of the 'new man'. The new men images provided a new form of visual language linked to the cultural market and to changing perceptions of masculinity (Nixon 1996). However, despite fragmentations in hegemonic masculinity, the new man image represented merely a modification of dominant masculinity. The rise of this new man image effectively reinforced existing power structures through a construction of a hybrid masculinity more suitable to retaining power (Chapman 1988).

The changing and internationalised nature of masculinities is reflected in the rapid success of men's magazines, which, by the mid-1990s, focused primarily on lifestyles. These new men's magazines became a site for (re)negotiating masculinities. Magazines such as *Loaded* and *FHM* increased their sales as images of the new man were taken over by images of laddish masculinity. In Britain, with lad culture at its height in the late 1990s, laddish masculinity legitimised behaviour that would otherwise have been criticised (Jackson *et al.* 2001). Laddism powerfully signified a specific kind of homosociality, that magazines such as *FHM* and *Loaded* helped secure (Tincknell *et al.* 2003). In Australia, the mid-1990s changed images of Australian men to move to a 'cooler' masculinity that reflected both physical fitness and rationality (Cook 2000). However, magazines such as *Ralph* continue simultaneously both to celebrate and distance themselves from a masculinity promoted by mateship/ockerism (Schirato and Yell 1999) and hegemonic masculinity.

Advertising images in the new men's lifestyle magazines resulted in an inversion of traditional interpretations of the male gaze, so that by the 1990s some male narcissism was socially approved (Edwards 1997; Patterson and Elliott 2002). Irony and ambivalence are significant features of these magazines. The often ironic and humorous tone of advice offered to readers enables men safely to experience the ambivalence of the magazines, and hence the contradictory nature of masculinity. However, the maturity of males is represented in respect to their link to consumerism rather than to emotional responsibilities. Indeed, as Tincknell *et al.* (2003) suggest, the form of masculinity encouraged in these magazines is of a prolonged adolescence which advocates hedonism, irresponsibility and heterosexual lubricity, particularly when faced with relationship demands from women. Absence of friendship possibilities with women is evident with the new men's magazines positioning females in stereotypical ways, as sexual objects and as essentially different from men (Nixon 1996).

The rise of the new lifestyle magazines for men became possible as a consequence of the 'gendering' of masculinity provoked by feminism and the growth of consumer culture in the 1970s and 1980s. However, while the new men images were recognised as cultural construction, the new laddish forms of masculinity, although also social constructions, were perceived as 'natural' and thus needed no defence of their expression (Jackson *et al.* 2001). Thus, despite significant sociological shifts in the 1980s and 1990s, hegemonic masculinity remains securely intact with the new men's magazines generally representing a white heterosexual male culture. With few exceptions, for example, *Attitude*, which explicitly appeals to both gay and heterosexual male readers, the men's lifestyle magazines all affirm male readers' heterosexuality (Edwards 1997; Nixon 1996). However, they also reveal the instabilities and ambivalences of dominant forms of masculinities (Jackson *et al.* 2001). It is through these ambiguities, which may disrupt hegemonic masculinity, that these magazines offer alternative ways of perceiving masculinity and provide access to multiple masculinities.

References and further reading

Chapman, R. (1988) 'The great pretender: variations on the new man theme', in R. Chapman and J. Rutherford (eds) *Male Order*, London: Lawrence and Wishart.

Cook, J. (2000) 'Men's magazines at the millennium', *Continuum*, 14 (2): 171–86.

Edwards, T. (1997) *Men in the Mirror*, London: Cassell.

Gilbert, P. and Taylor, S. (1991) *Fashioning the Feminine*, Sydney: Allen and Unwin.

Jackson, P., Stevenson, N. and Brooks, K. (2001) *Making Sense of Men's Magazines*, Cambridge: Polity.

Mort, F. (1996) *Cultures of Consumption*, London: Routledge.

Nixon, S. (1996) *Hard Looks*, London: UCL Press.

Patterson, M. and Elliott, R. (2002) 'Negotiating masculinities', *Consumption, Markets and Culture*, 5 (3): 231–46.

Schirato, T. and Yell, S. (1999) 'The "new" men's magazines and the performance of masculinity', *Media International Australia*, 92: 81–90.

Tincknell, E., Chambers, D., Van Loon, J. and Hudson, N. (2003) 'Begging for it', *Feminist Media Studies*, 3 (1): 47–63.

See also: culture and representation

HELEN HATCHELL

MEN'S MOVEMENT

The men's movement is made up of networks of men self-consciously involved in activities related to men and gender. It emerged in the late 1960s and 1970s in Western countries, alongside and often in response to the women's movement and feminism. The men's movement, comprised of groups, networks, organisations and events, engages in a variety of activities from self-help and support to political lobbying and activism.

The men's movement is distinct from other mobilisations comprised largely of men, such as the gun lobby or early trade unions, by its self-conscious orientation towards gender issues. Twentieth-century men's movements have historical precedents such as organised male support for women's suffrage in the eighteenth and nineteenth centuries (John and Eustance 1997). While the term 'men's movement' is useful in capturing the array of activities and organisations through which men have explored and contested gender relations, the term is problematic in several ways. In contrast to most other social movements, the men's movement has had a largely therapeutic focus, is internally contradictory, and is composed of members of a privileged group.

The men's movement has been preoccupied with therapeutic goals, showing stronger affinities with self-help movements than with movements centred on social change. Much men's movement activity, and that in men's groups in particular, is oriented towards personal growth and healing. This reflects the intertwined influences of therapy and counselling on the one hand and spiritual and 'New Age' cultures on the other. Common goals among men's movement participants include finding support and intimacy among other men in a community of men, healing from past hurts and injustices, and developing positive identities 'as men'. Some participants are also involved in or have come from twelve-step programmes, counselling groups and psychology, and some participate also in alternative spiritual events and communities.

However, recognition is growing that personal growth and the reconstruction of individual masculinities are useless without an accompanying shift in the social relations and ideologies that support or marginalise different ways of being men. One wing of the men's movement engages in increasingly politicised and often anti-feminist campaigns on such issues as family law and domestic violence. In some men, the men's movement has always been a tool for social and political change, whether through anti-violence activism or radical cross-dressing to confuse gender boundaries.

The men's movement shares with many other social movements a preoccupation with identity. The women's, black and gay and lesbian movements which erupted in the late twentieth century were characterised by 'identity politics', the articulation of social identities as the basis of collective mobilisation and resistance to oppression. The profound phrase 'the personal is political', coined by early second-wave feminists, embodied the recognition that women's everyday and personal lives are shaped by power relations, often unjust and oppressive, and therefore are a necessary part of the terrain of political activism (hooks 1997).

The men's movement's engagement with identity and personal experience has been less politicised than that of these other movements. For many participants, examining one's personal life is a means to personal growth and interpersonal intimacy rather than to radical political consciousness. At the same time, the more politicised wings of the men's movement, both pro- and anti-feminist, have taken up differing forms of identity politics. In the early 1970s, anti-sexist men's groups, inspired directly by the women's movement, adopted consciousness-raising in small all-male groups to reflect critically on their involvements in sexism and to build non- or anti-sexist identities (Hornacek 1977). Contemporary profeminist men's groups continue this tradition, using group discussion, education and social marketing. From a very different political direction, men's and fathers' rights groups draw on their members' experiences to articulate a public vision of men and/or fathers as the victims of a man-hating social and legal system.

Nor has the men's movement followed the same trajectory as other movements centred on identity politics, in which there has been an increasing questioning and destabilisation of the identities on which mobilisation was first based. Identity politics involves potentially contradictory impulses, essentialist and deconstructionist (West 1990). However, only the more feminist-informed strands of the men's movement have paid much attention to deconstructing male identities and masculinities. This draws on feminist scholarship on the social construction of gender, although less so on recent and more philosophical feminist debates regarding the category 'woman' and its deployment. Elsewhere, essentialist tendencies are more apparent, whether in Jungian-inspired accounts of transcultural masculine archetypes, ahistorical accounts of men's 'natural' place at the head of the family, or biologically determinist defences of male aggression. More widely, the crude stereotypes of male and female psychology offered by pop-psychological authors hold sway among many men's movement participants.

The men's movement's agendas and understandings can be understood in terms of five overlapping strands: men's liberation, anti-sexist or profeminist, men's rights and fathers' rights, spiritual and mythopoetic, and Christian. The men's liberation strand argues that men are hurt by the male 'sex role' and that men's lives are alienating, unhealthy and impoverished. This perspective, perhaps the dominant one, focuses on the damage, isolation and suffering inflicted on boys and men through their socialisation into manhood. While the anti-sexist strand acknowledges men's pain, it gives greater emphasis to male privilege and gender inequalities. Clatterbaugh (1990) describes the first of these tendencies as 'liberal profeminism' and the second as 'radical profeminism'. Liberal profeminist men stress that both men and women are constricted by gender roles, and some say that men, like women, are 'oppressed'. And in saying this, some versions of men's liberation slide into men's rights.

Men's rights and fathers' rights advocates also argue that men's roles are damaging to men, but blame women or feminism for the harm done to men, deny any idea of men's power, and argue that men are now the real victims. For some advocates, feminism has largely achieved its goals and women have more choices, while men are still stuck in traditional masculine roles. For others, 'feminazis' are involved in a conspiracy to discriminate against men and cover up violence against them (Flood 2004).

Mythopoetic men derive their thinking from Jungian psychology, especially through the work of Bly (1990). Masculinity is seen as based on deep unconscious patterns and archetypes that are revealed through myths, stories and rituals. By exploring these, men can 'heal' and restore their psychospiritual health.

Another strand of men's movement activity with a spiritual focus is Christian, with the best-known example being the Promise Keepers. This network defines itself as a Christ-centred ministry dedicated to uniting men through vital relationships to become godly influences in their world (Claussen 2000). Such groups are primarily evangelical and fundamentalist and favour a return to traditional gender relations.

The most feminist and politically progressive wing of the men's movement is also the smallest. Profeminist men emphasise that men must take responsibility for their own sexist behaviours and attitudes and work to change those of men in general. Many advocates distance themselves from the men's movement, which they see as defending men's privilege. While they often work in all-male groups, they also build alliances and coalitions with other progressive movements such as feminism and anti-racism.

The most unusual aspect of the men's movement is that it represents a movement by members of a dominant or privileged group. It is more typical for people on the subordinate side of a set of power relations to generate social movements. The men's movement involves groups and activities aimed at both the defence of men's privilege and its abolition. The term 'men's movement' invites the misleading assumption that this movement is the male equivalent of the women's movement. Given the reality of pervasive gender inequalities which benefit men as a group, collective mobilisations among men cannot have the same meaning or trajectory as mobilisations among women.

The experience of personal crisis, and especially of separation and divorce, is a common path to men's participation in the men's movement. Having gone through deeply painful marriage break-ups, men join men's groups in search of solace, support or justice. Other men join out of realisations that they have no close male friends, they lack intimacy and community, their working lives are meaningless and soul-destroying, or the traditionally masculine lives they have tried to lead are hollow and corrupt. Some men find their way to the men's movement in dealing with substance abuse and addiction, violence, anger or sexuality. While the men's movement is largely heterosexual, small numbers of gay men participate.

Second-wave feminism tapped into a widespread frustration and resentment among women, speaking to the domestic isolation, dependency and abuse they suffered. Women continue to join the women's movement through realising the ways in which their lives are constrained by gender. While some men's paths to the men's movement are broadly similar, men's and women's contrasting social positions mean that these paths also are different. There are certainly areas of male suffering to which the men's movement speaks, but there is not the same potential for an explosion of consciousness or social catharsis among men. Many men experience their involvement in gender relations as normal, natural and invisible, and many experience privileges and benefits under the current gender order.

Because men in general are privileged in relation to gender, their collective mobilisation involves the danger of enhancing this privilege (Flood 2003). This is apparent in the energetic and masculinist activism being conducted by men's rights and fathers' rights groups. At the same time, men have other interests that can be mobilised in more egalitarian directions, such as their concerns for personal health and well-being, investments in their intimate, familial and social relations with women and girls, collective interests in community well-being, and their ethical, political or spiritual commitments.

Over the past decade, men's movements have undergone proliferation, professionalisation and institutionalisation. Men's groups and networks have spread across the globe. While their preoccupations are shaped by local and regional formations of gender, Western and especially US understandings have a global influence, reflecting patterns of Western political and intellectual hegemony in both publishing and internet communication.

Issues of men and gender have been taken up by community and social sectors and to a lesser extent articulated in government policy. This trend is most apparent in three areas: fathering, men's health and boys' education. For example, in Western countries since the late 1990s, policy interest has been growing concerning the need to promote fathers' involvement in families. In the US there is bipartisan support for new fatherhood initiatives promoting 'responsible fatherhood' through increasing fathers' contact and co-residence with their children and strengthening marriage. Nevertheless, compared with most other social movements, men's movements have had relatively little direct involvement in policy-making.

Community and social sectors also have taken up 'men's issues'. Men's movement activity, including men's groups and male practitioners within workplaces, has been influential in shaping overt attention to men among health and welfare agencies. However, in Australia and elsewhere, it is often women who have advocated for and initiated programmes on men's health, fathering, and so on. And there has been growing demand for such services from men and fathers themselves (Russell *et al.* 1999).

Considerable controversy surrounds the attention to men and gender being shown by governments and community sectors. Some initiatives are criticised for reinstating or reinforcing patterns of male advantage, treating males as an homogenous and disadvantaged group, or taking away fresources from women.

There is also growing professionalisation. Community courses, training programmes and university curricula focused on men's issues have proliferated, such as those concerning men's health or work with male perpetrators of violence. Such trends have both advantages and disadvantages. On the one hand, they signal the establishment of men's issues as legitimate areas of government and public concern, and they involve the development of 'best practice' standards in working with men. On the other, such trends can deradicalise and de-politicise men's movement activism (to the extent that this activity was radical to begin with), and their corporatist and entrepreneurial emphases diverge from potential emphases on community development and grassroots mobilisation.

References and further reading

Bly, R. (1990) *Iron John*, Dorset: Addison-Wesley.
Clatterbaugh, K. (1990) *Contemporary Perspectives on Masculinity*, Boulder, CO and Oxford: Westview.
Claussen, D.S. (2000) *The Promise Keepers*, Jefferson, NC: McFarland.
Flood, M. (2003) 'Men's collective struggles for gender justice', in M. Kimmel, J. Hearn and R. Connell (eds) *The Handbook of Studies on Men and Masculinities*, Thousand Oaks, CA: Sage.
—— (2004) 'Backlash', in S.E. Rossi (ed.) *The Battle and Backlash Rage on*, Philadelphia, PA: Xlibris Press, pp. 261–78.
hooks, b. (1997) 'Feminism,' in S. Kemp and J. Squires (eds) *Feminisms*, Oxford and New York: Oxford University Press.
Hornacek, P. (1977) 'Anti-sexist consciousness raising groups for men,' in J. Snodgrass (ed.) *A Book of Readings*, Albion, CA: Times Change.
John, A.V. and Eustance, C. (eds) (1997) *The Men's Share?* London: Routledge
Messner, M.A. (1997) *Politics of Masculinities*, Thousand Oaks, CA: Sage.
Russell, G., Barclay, L., Edgecombe, G., Donovan, J., Habib, G., Callaghan, H. and Pawson, Q. (1999) *Fitting Fathers into Families*, Canberra: Commonwealth Dept of Family and Community Services.
West, D. (1990) *Authenticity and Empowerment*, London: Harvester Wheatsheaf.

See also: masculinity politics; men's groups; men's rights; mythopoetic movement; profeminism

MICHAEL FLOOD

MEN'S PRACTICES, INDIVIDUAL AND COLLECTIVE

'Men's practices' includes the critical examination of men's actions and practices, both individually and as a gender political category.

While masculinity may not be real in any fixed, discernible form, its consequences as men's practices certainly are. The myths, illusions, stereotypes which surround masculinity – indeed, serve to invest it with meaning – are not in themselves grounded in any fundamental order, in which case we can recognise their transient state, their impermanence and contingency. However, masculinity's power lies in its potency as a male signifier thereby offering the masculine subject, man, a means of identification within the social world. Man cannot achieve this identification, it is a process, an expression of identity work which men must engage with constantly, albeit largely unknowingly, and within the social milieu. It is from such engagements that men's practices emerge. Put simply, from this perspective the search for identity informs, if not drives, the practice and not vice versa.

The critical study of men and masculinity arises from this concern with men's practices and how such practices, individually and collectively, inform or constitute a gender order, hegemonic condition (Connell 1995) or discursive framework (Whitehead 2002). So it is important to note that men's practices are political. That is, they are enacted by individuals who are themselves located in a political category, and not by choice but by gender. The implications for this in respect of understanding men are profound. For example, male violence can be seen as a dimension of masculinity, but at the same time it is a form of male practice with powerful political overtones. The history of men has many dimensions, but violence is arguably one of the most important, not least because male violence often sustains men's dominance. So men's individual violences connect directly and irrevocably to the gender category of men (see Hearn 1998). Individual men may not recognise this connection, but at a social level it is there. As individual men, we represent the male species or political category of men. So our practices as men are political and influential, whether such practices are positive or negative. For example, when individual or groups of men espouse non-violence and respond in such a way, that response, as practice, signals the potential for all men to be non-violent. In this way the practices of individual men connect directly or indirectly to political movements within the category of men, thereby illustrating the potential for change or a rejection of change within men.

Men are always more than simply men. We cannot attach any clear meaning to an individual simply by identifying them as a man. We must go beyond that and into the realms of the social web from which, individuals come to be and represent 'themselves'. So dimensions of class, ethnicity, age, race, nationhood, religion, sexuality, health, are some of the key effects, which individually and together, conspire to produce the individual that is 'man'. Each of these areas has investment in and is given meaning through specific practices which in turn serve to reinforce their cultural significance and meaning. So the health, sexuality or religion of individual men manifests itself through the practices of those men. In this we can see the direct, if not seamless, connection between the individual and the collective. This connection is given added poignancy once we recognise the fragility of masculinity. For it can be argued that it is only through the practices of men that masculinity is made real.

This connection between men's practices and the collective that is 'men' offers us a glimpse of the circularity that continues to sustain gender. Men's practices emerge from the conditions of possibility that are offered to them through powerful ideological or discursive regimes (e.g. sexuality, ethnicity, class, work) and which are central to their life course and experience. In taking up these gendered practices individual men practise masculinity while simultaneously contributing to the identification of a collective that is men. There seems little chance of breaking this circularity, not least because arguably the key driver behind this process is the desire to be (a man). So all men's practices are, at base, related to some form of gender signification, or masculine identification, process. To be sure, there may well be the more instrumental pursuit of power, control, dominance or material accumulation, also driving these practices. However, to posit all men's practices as a drive for dominance is to slip back into a biological determinism which assumes all men have an inner urge to dominate women and other men. Self-evidently this is not the case, so we have to look beyond the pursuit of power to the pursuit of identity to understand how men's practices are sustained, while recognising that male power may well be reinforced through exactly these same practices. For to be sure, all men must have an identity, not least because such identities are not offered them through biology but through engagement with the social (see McNay 2000).

Recognising men's practices in this way takes us towards a recognition that men can change. There is nothing inevitable about men and their maleness which requires men to always behave and respond in a certain way. So men's practices should be seen as indicative of their possibilities, not indicative of their limits. This makes the critical study of men and masculinity all the more significant, not least because the sheer contingency of men and masculinity requires us to constantly examine and interrogate their actions and behaviours. In other words, there is no final answer to men, and indeed no finite, closed definition of them. As with their practices, all is open to possibility.

References and further reading

Connell, R. (1995) *Masculinities*, Cambridge: Polity.
Hearn, J. (1998) *The Violences of Men*, London: Sage.
McNay, L. (2000) *Gender and Agency*, Cambridge: Polity.
Whitehead, S.M. (2002) *Men and Masculinities: Key Themes and New Directions*, Cambridge: Polity.

See also: gender order; identity; masculinity/masculinities; masculinity politics; men

STEPHEN M. WHITEHEAD

MEN'S RELATIONS WITH MEN

Men's relations with men structure the practices, processes and cultures of a wide variety of social contexts. Homosocial bonds have a profound influence on men's friendships with other men and their social and sexual relations with women. Various institutional contexts, from schools and workplaces to militaries and governments, are dominated by males and shaped by the relations between them. Male–male relations define important kinship and familial connections. Finally, sexual relations between men have been documented across the world and throughout history, although their meanings and their associations with sexual identities and communities are diverse.

Scholarship on men and gender has emphasised that masculinity is highly homosocial – that men's lives are highly organised by relations between men. Homosociality refers to social bonds between persons of the same sex, and more broadly to same-sex-focused social relations. Men's performances of gender often represent homosocial enactments, undertaken in front of and in search of approval from other men (Kimmel 1994). Dynamics of bonding and solidarity, as well as hierarchies of power and status, characterise male–male relations in many social contexts. Men's homosocial bonds are central to the organisation and maintenance of women's subordination. However, male homosociality does not necessarily involve the subordination of women or of particular groups of men.

Homosociality plays a central role in boys' and men's performances of gender. Proper masculine status often is granted by other males. In front of male audiences, men demonstrate their gendered status by accumulating key markers of manhood: interpersonal power, dominance, physical and sexual prowess (Kimmel 1994). While other males can grant masculine status, they can also take it away. Male collectivities, especially informal male peer groups among boys and young men, police and reward or punish males' performances of gender.

Gender inequalities disadvantaging women are sustained in part by male homosocial relations. Early feminist work emphasised that patriarchy, the social system of male domination, was built on relations between men 'which, though hierarchical, establish or create interdependence and solidarity among men that enable them to dominate women' (Hartmann 1981: 14). Men's dominance of political and economic hierarchies is sustained in part through informal male bonds or 'boys' clubs'. Men may maintain women's exclusion from or subordination in workplaces and institutions through male-focused work networks, bonding, and investment in and pursuit of other men's attention, company and approval (Flood and Pease 2006). Processes of male bonding in workplaces also construct men's privilege by emphasising men's difference from and superiority to women.

Male homosociality is implicated too in some of the bluntest expressions of sexism and gender inequality, in men's violence against women. Participation in homosocial male peer groups can intensify men's tolerance for violence against women, and male peer support is a critical factor in men's perpetration of physical and sexual violence (Reitzel-Jaffe and Wolfe 2001). The cultures and collective rituals of male bonding among closely knit male fraternities and male athletes on college campuses foster leniency towards or even perpetration of sexual assault against women. Rape is more likely in fraternities showing greater gender segregation, less non-sexual male–female interaction, and local cultures of sexism, sexual boasting and sexual harassment. Rape may be both a means to and an expression of male bonding.

Similar dynamics are evident in violence against gay, lesbian, bisexual and transgender persons in public spaces, typically carried out by groups of young men and expressing homosocial and heterosexist bonds (Herek 1992). Male bonding is also associated with the solidarity between men expressed in and maintained through military combat. Mateship fosters the dehumanising of the enemy as Other and enables individuals to endure war and maintain the killing process. The sense of loyalty and commitment to one's fellow soldiers sustains military conflict (Page 2002).

Male homosocial bonds and desire have been widely documented in literary and cultural contexts. Sedgwick (1985) argues that an erotic triangle between two men and one woman, based on homosocial relays of desire between rival heterosexual males, is found throughout British literature. Other scholarship has examined bonds between men in such diverse texts as ancient Greek poetry, Western films and science fiction. Homosocial relations were central to the fraternal organisations that proliferated in nineteenth-century Europe and the sworn brotherhoods of imperial China, based on secrecy, authority and male–male or brotherly solidarity (Nye 2000).

Homosocial bonding can support or oppose homosexual sex. Anthropological research notes examples where homosociality and homosexuality overlap, in which sexual practices between older and younger men or boys establish masculinity. Homoerotic homosociality has characterised some cultural and institutional contexts, for example in Nazi Germany, in which intense and eroticised male bonding was intertwined with misogyny (Nye 2000).

Male–male sexual relations have been documented in a wide variety of historical and cultural contexts. Such sexual involvements do not necessarily involve discrete homosexual or gay identities. The relationships between sexual identity and sexual practice are complex and contradictory, as the category 'men who have sex with men' (MSM) in AIDS education recognises. The term 'MSM' itself risks masking diversities and fluidities. As Dowsett *et al.* (2003) note in a review of male–male sexual relations in Bangladesh, India, Indonesia and Thailand, men who have sex with men may not fit into any socially or self-defined group of MSM. While some male–male sexual practices express 'traditional' sexual relations and categories, others result from modernisation and urbanisation, and while some male–male sexual networks are dense and stable, others are scattered and intermittent.

In male-dominated and highly homosocial contexts such as military institutions, male–male relations may also structure men's sexual and social relations with women. Flood (2006) reports that some young heterosexual Australian men give top priority to their male–male friendships and find platonic friendships with women dangerously feminising. For them heterosexual activity confers masculine status and is an important medium for male bonding.

There have been historical shifts in the dominant bonds of male–male friendships. Nye (2000) describes a democratisation of friendship, from an orientation towards vertical ties and the advancement of personal or family interest to an orientation towards horizontal ties. In some historical moments male friendship has been contained through associations with homosexuality and effeminacy, while in others it has been affirmed through associations with virility and manhood. Intimate male friendships, secret male societies and brotherly bonds have posed various challenges to established social orders, by undermining the patriarchal authority of fathers or rulers or destabilising the traditional solidarities and processes of kinship. Nevertheless, most male bonds have been premised on men's domination and the rejection of femininity (Nye 2000).

Male–male relations define the kinship and familial connections between fathers and sons, brothers, uncles, nephews, grandfathers and others. Other than scholarship on fathers and sons, there has been relatively little research on the gendered character of kin and family relations among men. Nye (2000) describes historical examinations of fraternal bonds in Europe and late imperial China and the ways in which brothers' competition or closeness was shaped by wider social and political forces. Contemporary qualitative research in New Zealand and the USA documents diverse relationships among uncles and nephews and finds evidence that (some) uncles act as mentors, family historians and intergenerational buffers in conflicts between parents and children, while nephews provide uncles with companionship and support (Milardo 2005).

While male homosociability is implicated in various patriarchal practices, it may also be neutral or desirable. Men may bond as friends, comrades, family members or lovers in ways that do not subordinate women or other men. Indeed, intimate friendships between men are valuable correctives to men's emotional stoicism and reliance on women's emotional labour.

It is a robust finding in Western scholarship that men's same-sex friendships are less intimate than women's (Bank and Hansford 2000). Bank and Hansford reject the idea that intimacy and support have different meanings for men and women, noting that these do not vary by gender. They also reject the idea that intimacy is less crucial to men's enjoyment of their friendships than to women's. For both men and women, greater enjoyment is associated with greater self-disclosure and expressive behaviours. Instead, intimacy in male–male friendships is constrained by masculine emotional restraint (emotional repression, stoicism and insensitivity) and homophobia. While overt expressions of affection were common in young men's close friendships in nineteenth-century America, they are largely prohibited by contemporary American social norms (Morman and Floyd 1998). There are strong cultural proscriptions against the expression of verbal and non-verbal male–male affection, although these are relaxed when men are related (as there is less danger of being seen as homosexual), the situation is emotionally charged, or it is in public.

Men's groups and men's movements have attempted to break down men's emotional isolation, foster male intimacies and support, and build communities of men. Such efforts may involve personal sharing, critical consciousness-raising or rituals of male bonding and initiation.

Male–male relations in many cultures have been seen as central in inducting or initiating boys into manhood. The most visible contemporary incarnation of this in Western countries is the emphasis on the importance of 'male role models', and especially fathers, in aiding boys' transition into proper adult male status. Children in general, and boys in particular, are seen to require the presence of a biological father to ensure their healthy development. However, empirical examinations of parental influence find that fathers' masculinity and other individual characteristics are far less important formatively than the warmth and closeness of fathers' relationships with their sons. In other words, it is the characteristics of fathers as parents rather than their characteristics as men that influence child development. Nor is there evidence that boys raised only by women (including by lesbian mothers) are any more likely than other boys to become homosexual, adopt an unconventional gender identity or orientation, or experience other kinds of behavioural and social maladjustment and dysfunction (Flood 2003). Indeed, why do unconventional gender or sexual orientations necessarily count as adverse outcomes? At the same time, men's involvement with children is desirable because it expands the practical, emotional and social resources available for parenting and because of the distinctive, but not unique, contribution to parenting made by male parents.

References and further reading

Bank, B.J. and Hansford, S.L. (2000) 'Gender and friendship', *Personal Relationships*, 7: 63–78.

Dowsett, G.W., Grierson, J. and McNally, S. (2003) *A Review of Knowledge about the Sexual Networks and Behaviours of Men who have Sex with Men in Asia*, Melbourne: Australian Research Centre in Sex, Health and Society, La Trobe University.

Flood, M. (2003) *Fatherhood and Fatherlessness*, Canberra: The Australia Institute, Discussion Paper No. 59.

—— (2007) 'Men, sex, and homosociality', *Men and Masculinities*.

Flood, M. and Pease, B. (2006) 'Undoing men's privilege and advancing gender equality in public sector institutions', *Policy and Society*, 24 (4): 119–38.

Hartmann, H. (1981) 'The unhappy marriage of Marxism and feminism', in L. Sargent (ed.) *Women and Revolution*, Boston, MA: South End, pp. 1–41.

Herdt, G.H. (1982) *Rituals of Manhood*, Beverley Hills, CA: University of California Press.
Herek, G.M. (1992) 'Psychological heterosexism and antigay violence', in G.M. Herek and K.T. Berrill (eds) *Hate Crimes*, Thousand Oaks, CA: Sage, pp. 149–69.
Kimmel, M.S. (1994) 'Masculinity as homophobia', in H. Brod and M. Kaufman (eds) *Theorizing Masculinities*, London: Sage, pp. 119–41.
Milardo, R.M. (2005) 'Generative uncle and nephew relationships', *Journal of Marriage and Family*, 67: 1226–36.
Morman, M.T. and Floyd, K. (1998) 'I love you, man', *Sex Roles*, 38 (9/10): 871–81.
Nye, R.A. (2000) 'Kinship, male bonds, and masculinity in comparative perspective', *American Historical Review*, 105 (5): 1656–66.
Page, J. (2002) 'Is mateship a virtue?' *Australian Journal of Social Issues*, 37 (2): 193–200.
Reitzel-Jaffe, D. and Wolfe, D. (2001) 'Predictors of relationship abuse among young men', *Journal of Interpersonal Violence*, 6 (2): 99–115.
Sedgwick, E.K. (1985) *Between Men*, New York: Columbia University Press.

See also: friendship; mateship

MICHAEL FLOOD

MEN'S RELATIONS WITH WOMEN

'Ways in which to be a man are shaped through relationships with other men' (Bredesen 2004). This sentiment characterises to a large extent the key interests of many researchers on men and masculinities (for a critical reflection, see Hearn 2004; Connell and Messerschmidt 2005). Does it make sense to make men's relations with women (MRWW) a topic at all? This question indicates that MRWW, far from being an easy topic, are rather comprehensive: they include men's relation to feminism as politics and as research; to women as partners, mothers, sisters, daughters, friends, colleagues, competitors and adversaries; but also as a gender category.

This entry has four foci. First, the analytical levels of MRWW. Then, the various fields and topics that have been covered by research, an issue which can itself be further subdivided into two: men's *accounts* concerning their relations with women; and their *practices* in relations with women. Fourth and finally, some areas of tension and public discourse are discussed, and a utopian horizon of possible relations with women is outlined.

Analytical levels

As gender is relational, 'men' can only be conceptualised as 'men' in relation to 'women'. While this is widely accepted in masculinities scholarship, the ways of doing theory are diverse. In addition, MRWW may be understood as a task for empirical description and analysis. Again, a variety of perspectives can be considered.

MRWW may be articulated on a 'macro'-level, at the level of society. Gender relations appear as a structure that is characterised by the positioning of gender groups in society, for instance in the economic realm, according to a line of gendered segmentation. 'Patriarchy', 'gender system' and 'gender-hierarchical division of labour' are concepts that underline the structural aspects of MRWW. Relations of exploitation and appropriation, domination and oppression, represent important features of MRWW; continuous gendered inequality, for instance gendered wage-gaps, may provide an important empirical clue regarding the structural relevance of gender. Debates about what principle is predominant – capitalism or patriarchy – have been central in the 1970s and 1980s and important attempts have been made to transfer the concept of patriarchy into an analytically useful concept for present societies. Nowadays, structural perspectives in the West have mainly abandoned or transformed the concept of patriarchy (Walby 1997), whereas international organisations like WHO still use it, with good reasons, as a concept to name problematical and stable structural relations of MRWW, such as violence, sexual exploitation and gender-linked oppression (WHO 2002).

At the 'meso'-level, organisations and institutions are under consideration. Institutions (such as those of the law, social politics, family and schooling), and organisations in the market and non-market sectors of society, frame

MRWW in such a way that they either are themselves gendered, and/or produce and reproduce gendered outcomes. Recent analysis shows that gender segregation on the level of organisations may be significantly higher than in the labour market as a whole (Hinz and Schuebel 2001 for West Germany). Homosocial work situations in which MRWW are characterised by the absence of women may be more frequent than they appear on the macro-level. This may contribute to constructing 'women' as a distant group. Legal institutions may explicitly treat men differently to women, or create different outcomes because they are 'gender-blind'. Family, social policy, educational and employment organisations may intersect in such a way that, on average, men's biographies cumulate in an advantageous way with regard to power and income, whereas women's cumulate to their disadvantage. But institutions and organisations may be modified to convey more equality in men's and women's biographies, for example through measures in education and health (United Nations 2003), or parental leave (Nordic Council 2006).

A third level is the 'micro'-level, of personal, everyday interaction. Here, MRWW seem direct, individual and emotional. While personal authenticity may be analysed as an ideology and mode of dominance, men's accounts of their relations with women constitute an important sphere of reality in their own right as they provide an insight into the development of male subjectivities, providing a potential basis for change towards gender democracy (United Nations 2003).

Men's accounts about their relations with women

In Western societies, men and women agree in surveys upon many issues of life. There are gender gaps with reference to the distribution of housework (women are more in favour of equal shares than men), 'work–life balance' models (men are more reluctant to reduce their own working time) and political measures aimed at gender equality (both genders agree on their necessity, but men support them to a smaller extent). Consensus prevails about child education values, how to spend money, the importance of interesting jobs for both genders, and a satisfying sexual life for both partners; both genders tend to come closer to each other referring to questions of general interest, such as politics. Surveys repeatedly find that about 20 per cent of men are 'traditionalists', 20 per cent are gender-democratic progressives, and the majority oscillate between those poles: liberals (gender equality evolves over time, no special measures are necessary) or pragmatics, and irritated, uncertain men (Pringle *et al.* 2006). All these findings differ, though, in their extent between countries (Pringle *et al.* 2006).

Qualitative methodology provides information about men's difficulties and potentials in approaching women, and building up relationships with them. German men report that women seem difficult to understand (Meuser 1998). Is this a gendered inevitability or more a construction in itself? Meuser (1998) supports the argument for it being constructed: various groups of men construct a 'man's' and a 'woman's' world, the latter remaining a planet unknowable to men. Men with experience in men's groups, however, manage to articulate irritations and embarrassment towards women's challenges without constructing binary oppositions.

Men's practices in their relations with women

Studies agree on discrepancies between men's accounts of their relations with women and their practices. Although Western men support the norm of equality, their participation in housework and childcare contradicts this (Hearn and Pringle 2006). There are also differences between countries, with the Scandinavian countries showing more male participation, whereas in some East European countries, men's avoidance is reinforced through new family ideologies

(Novikova and Kambourov 2003). Men may overestimate their participation; on the other hand, there are some hints from qualitative studies that egalitarian women abandon the integration of love and equality, and prefer to compare their non-egalitarian partners with other more traditional men in order to maintain the relationship (Hearn and Pringle 2006). Social class or milieu is reported in some studies to play a role, whereas others find no convincing connection. Academic men's egalitarian accounts may differ from their practices, whereas the practices of working-class men may be against (or with) traditional values. Marriage seems to promote unequal shares of housework (Hearn and Pringle 2006). Time utilisation creates considerable differences between men and women, partially against men's accounts of their wishes, and time negotiations between men and women become more frequent (Hearn and Pringle 2006).

Western men support a shared responsibility for sexual pleasure and contraception, but mostly leave the use of contraceptives to their female partners. This dimension is different in a worldwide scope (WHO 2002), where analysis often reveals asymmetrical power to a large extent, with women having more children than they wish, and men still wanting more than they have got; furthermore, in many areas, men seem to know very little about female corporality, maternal morbidity, etc.

Nothing but problems?

Today's men seem to have two possible ways of reacting to women's challenges, expressing themselves as an acquisition of new rights, a shaking of the basic premises of patriarchal structures, an expansion of the socio-symbolic representation of the 'feminine', and a politicisation of the asymmetry between the genders in society. First, men may acknowledge the situation voluntarily or reluctantly as a potential, and engage in attempts to exploit this potential for themselves. Second, they may give way to a feeling of being threatened and reject the new potential through destructive devaluation. The majority of men seem located on a continuum between these two poles (Hearn and Pringle 2006; Pringle *et al.* 2006).

While Giddens (1992) writes that the transformation of intimacy as a result of modernity is leading to gender democracy, feminist literature is cautious about the chances of positive change (Evans 2003); this may well ameliorate when anti-sexist and profeminist accounts from men have more impact in scholarly as well as in public discourses. Public discourses, as represented in newspapers in ten European countries (Hearn and Pringle 2006), tend to either make masculinity invisible or to reproduce traditional views. Scandalisation and individualisation of irresponsible, dangerous and/or violent behaviour are rather widespread as media strategies (Hearn and Pringle 2006). More serious newspapers often spread the idea of a feminist hegemony that is threatening the freedom of thought and the creative development of culture. Metaphors from other realms are used to denounce feminist fights against sexual violence as victim cult, feminist paternalism and interdiction, thus preparing the ground for refusing any claims that victims might express for compensation and shelter. Therefore, daily newspapers do not represent and support male self-reflection and the diversification of masculinities in MRWW, but petrify traditional gender features. Violence against female partners appears as a regrettable, but foreseeable 'side-effect' of men in despair, in situations of separation and divorce – or when feeling provoked. As a mode of constructing gendered femininities, these findings indicate that women – and in popular literature, particularly mothers – are assigned responsibility for the internal processes of men, and promote references to an imaginary female, and not to the 'real' and diverse women men encounter.

Delegating responsibility for men's internal processes to women does work because women may shoulder this responsibility within the traditional division of labour, which is also an asymmetric division of emotional commitment and moral responsibility. The culturally dominant pattern for emotional commitments and happiness – normative heterosexuality and traditional marriage, based on gender dichotomy – keeps an asymmetric type of gender relationship alive, and with it traditional patterns of MRWW. A gender-egalitarian division of labour and power would also impact on the constraints of the prevailing structures of emotional commitment and thus 'pull the rug out' from underneath the male inclination for violence against women – at least in the long term.

To understand the difference between women and men as an egalitarian and therefore erotically attractive 'differentness', in which each person is viewed as complete rather than in terms of a reciprocal attribution of deficits, is to propose an alternative model that seems still utopian. This model provides a 'critical horizon', a reciprocal conception of gender in which 'gender' is not used to define one's social 'place', difference is not construed through devaluation, and the male inclination for violence is not viewed as the 'normal case' in society, but as a developmental failure.

References and further reading

Bredesen, O. (2004) 'Global masculinities', *Kvinneforskning* (Journal of Gender Research in Norway), Special Edition: 'North South. Gendered views from Norway'.

Connell, R. and Messerschmidt, J.W. (2005) 'Hegemonic masculinity – rethinking the concept', *Gender and Society*, 19 (6): 829–59.

Evans, M. (2003) *Love: An Unromantic Discussion*, Oxford: Polity.

Giddens, A. (1992) *The Transformation of Intimacy*, Cambridge: Polity.

Hearn, J. (2004) 'From hegemonic masculinity to the hegemony of men', *Feminist Theory*, 5 (1): 49–72.

Hearn, J. and Pringle, K., with members of Critical Research on Men in Europe (2006) *European Perspectives on Men and Masculinities*, Houndmills: Palgrave.

Hinz, T. and Schuebel, T. (2001) 'Geschlechtersegregation in Westdeutschen Betrieben' (Gender Segregation in West German Work Organizations), *MittAB*, 34 (1): 286–301.

Kimmel, M., Hearn, J. and Connell, R. (eds) (2006) *Handbook of Studies on Men and Masculinities*, Thousand Oaks, CA: Sage.

Meuser, M. (1998) *Geschlecht und Männlichkeit* (Gender and Masculinity), Opladen: Leske and Budrich.

Nordic Council of Ministers (ed.) (2006) *Possibilities and Challenges? – Men's Reconciliation of Work and Family Life*, Conference Report, Copenhagen: Nordic Council of Ministers.

Novikova, I. and Kambourov, D. (eds) (2003) *Men in the Global World. Integrating Post-Socialist Perspectives*, Helsinki: Kikimora Publications.

Pringle, K., Hearn, J., Ferguson, H., Kambourov, D., Kolga, V. *et al.* (2006) *Men and Masculinities in Europe*, London: Whiting and Birch.

United Nations (2003) *The Role of Men and Boys in Achieving Gender Equality*, Expert Group organised by DAW in collaboration with ILO and UNAIDS, Reports prepared by R. Connell, EGM/Men-Boys-GE/2003/WP.2, October, Brasilia, Brazil, available at http://www.un.org/womenwatch/daw/egm/men-boys2003/index.html

Walby, S. (1997) *Gender Transformations*, London, Routledge.

WHO (2002) *World Report on Violence and Health*. Geneva: WHO.

See also: divorce and separation; heterosexuality; husbands; intimacy; mother–son relationships

URSULA MÜLLER

MEN'S RIGHTS

The concept of men's rights generally embraces a variety of points of view that are overwhelmingly hostile to feminism or profeminism. As Astrachan (1986) and Clatterbaugh (1997) argue, these points of view range from groups of men who began as feminists, rejected traditional masculinity, and came to find fault with the women's movement to groups of men whose whole reason for being is to attack feminism and to shore up traditional masculinity to groups of men (father's rights groups) who focus narrowly on questions of divorce and custody. The story of how these groups evolved and are evolving and how the various ideologies bleed into one another is one of the most complex and politically interesting stories about contemporary men's movements.

Early feminist writers such as Betty Friedan noticed that the imbalance of gender roles included some costs to men. Being the breadwinner put heavy burdens on the male head of family in the 1950s and 1960s. Friedan believed that men would be better off in a more gender-equal family arrangement. Similarly, those who supported the Equal Rights Amendment in the 1970s argued that men would benefit from a more equal society particularly because they would no longer be exclusively responsible for paying child support or excluded from benefits that went to widows but not to widowers. Men would be perceived as both caregivers and breadwinners, and so would women. Thus men could divorce with fewer financial obligations and gain greater access to the custody of their children. Many of these early writers saw a strong parallel between the kind of gender role oppression that women suffered and the gender role oppression that men suffered. Following a men's liberation line, both men and women were said to be dehumanised by the roles that society expected them to play. And both men and women paid dearly for this rigid gender stereotyping. In the 1970s some of the earliest men's rights groups worked on behalf of women and men to secure an Equal Rights Amendment to the United States Constitution.

However, tensions soon developed between feminist and profeminist ideologies on the one hand and the men's rights ideologies on the other. In the 1970s two issues in particular appeared that drove a wedge between men's rights ideologies and feminist perspectives. The first was that men began to organise around the idea that men were at least as oppressed as women or even more disadvantaged than women by their gender roles. They directly attacked the concept of male privilege and the claim that modern society is a patriarchy. Men's groups sprang up calling themselves 'free men' or 'men's rights associations'. They argued that men's lives were shorter, that men and not women are subject to the draft during times of war, that men have a higher successful suicide rate, and that men lack the many tax benefits that go to widows. Book titles like *The Hazards of Being Male: Surviving the Myth of Masculine Privilege* (1976) and *The Rape of the Male* (1976) reflected the gender role bitterness of these men. Second, consistent with the denial of male privilege these groups demanded that men have an equal say in deciding on abortion, automatic joint custody in the event of divorce, men's studies departments at colleges and universities and men's commissions at the level of both state and national governments. They denied that the women's movement was ever interested in the harms done to men; in fact, they claimed that feminists sought to perpetuate male oppression by devaluing men and their role in the family.

During this same decade men's rights groups reached out to fathers' rights groups and conservatives. All three came together under the umbrella organisation The National Congress for Men in 1980. Ideological differences were hard to overcome. All of these groups were anti feminist. But men's rights groups generally agreed with the early profeminist idea that the traditional role of man as breadwinner and protector of the family was injurious to men. Fathers' rights groups and conservatives disagreed. They saw value in the traditional role, and they sought to preserve it. And conservatives, unlike both fathers' rights groups and men's rights groups, argued that men are essentially barbarians who require the civilising effect of the traditional family.

The 1970s wave of men's rights groups maintained its strength throughout the 1980s and into the 1990s, although new grievances against the women's movement began to appear. The new theme was the powerlessness of men. Warren Farrell produced two books that stressed the power of women relative to men, namely, *Why Men Are the Way They Are* (1986) and *The Myth of Male Power: Why Men Are the Disposable Sex* (1993). In addition to the usual concerns about men being subject to the draft and the impact of stressful careers on male health, these books and other writing began to cite studies that showed that men are equally victims of domestic violence and that women are the initiators of that violence. They took up the cause of male circumcision as another bit of evidence of the male mutilation. Concern about what they call 'male bashing' is a constant theme in this literature. They claimed that 'male' was a four-letter word in feminist discourse and that men were exposed to mean mockery and categorical denunciation as abusers, oppressors, exploiters and chauvinist sexist pigs. Men do bad things, they admitted, but these bad behaviours are explained in terms of the powerlessness of men rather than their power. Thus, unlike many conservative authors, they see men not as uncivilised by nature but as good people who are badly treated by women, especially by feminist women.

Conservative men had always argued that the role of the traditional male as head of household was critical to the health of the family and indeed to civilisation itself. Thus much conservative literature tries to argue that by pushing men out of their traditional roles the women's movement was creating greater dysfunction in the family and throughout society. Teen pregnancy, drug use, crime, school drop-out rates, poor work performance and many other social problems are attributed to the rise of feminism and the decline of the traditional male. George Gilder argued in *Sexual Suicide* (1973) that it is civilisation itself that is at stake if feminism succeeds in its agenda of revolutionising gender roles. Gilder's message was motivated by the assumption that men are barbarians by nature who need civilising by being required to play the traditional male role of breadwinner and father. Women, church and community act as a buffer between this male nature and the values of nurturance and civil life.

Such a view of male nature was obviously unacceptable to the men's rights perspective, and for a time it kept the two groups apart. These two groups were able to find a common ground in the 1990s by embracing the biological/social assumption that children and women need a traditional father figure. This traditional father contrasts with the new father who is promoted by the women's movement. Children who grow up without a provider and protector or women who try to turn the father into an androgynous caregiver will find that their family fails and society becomes subject to youth violence, teen pregnancy and social turmoil. Such was the message of David Blankenhorn's book *Fatherless America: Confronting Our Most Urgent Social Problem* (1995) as well as Gilder's 1986 rewrite of *Sexual Suicide, Men and Marriage*. Thus men, in the revised men's rights ideology, can find value in traditional masculinity with the emphasis upon fathering. The National Congress for Men in the United States became The National Congress for Men and Children and took as part of its platform the right of men to choose to be a traditional or nontraditional man. It has in the twenty-first century transformed again into The National Congress for Fathers and Children dedicated to preserving and promoting the father/child relationship. Internationally there are parallel men's rights groups in every country that has been touched by a strong feminist movement. The International Men's Network is a twenty-first-century coalition that boasts of having men's rights groups throughout Europe, Israel and Australia. These groups demand ministries of men to match the ministries of women; they offer divorce counselling; they object to inferior social security provisions for men; they protest 'male bashing' in the media; and they monitor the feminist lobby in the political arena.

Two other men's movements assisted this push towards a reinstatement of the value of men in the traditional family. The first was the neo-Jungian, mythopoetic movement of the 1990s. Beginning with the publication of Robert Bly's *Iron John* (1990) men began to come together to celebrate being a man, to acknowledge the loss of their fathers, and to initiate younger men into manhood. Bly's critique of men's lives stressed that fathers (and other male figures) were taken away from the family by the industrial revolution; boys were then raised by their mothers and women schoolteachers. This change, together with the Freudian theme that women lie to their sons about their fathers in order to compete for the boys' affection, suggested to Bly that fathers (and other male figures) were what was missing from men's lives. Men's rights advocates seized this rhetoric (much to Bly's dismay), and mythopoetic essay collections such as *Wingspan: Inside the Men's Movement* (1992) were often divided between the new age neo-Jungian articles and bitter essays by men's rights proponents.

The 1990s also saw the growth of a large conservative evangelical religious movement, the Promise Keepers. This movement too stressed the absolute need for a father and the need for traditional masculinity. Grounding their view in biblical passages that suggest that women should follow men's lead in the family and in the church and that women should pledge subservience to their husbands, this movement sought to restore men to their rightful place in church, community and family. The movement grew from a few hundred in the early 1990s to rallies around the world involving tens of thousands of men. The Promise Keepers began with the premise that men had not fulfilled their divinely mandated responsibilities to women and to each other. Thus they asked men to renew their religious vows, pursue vital relationships with other men, especially men of colour, seek moral and sexual purity, build strong marriages, support their churches, and spread the word. Throughout their all-male meetings, there is no doubt that the man is head of the household and that women are the weaker vessels.

Given the huge push towards traditional roles and the ascendancy of conservative governments that support policies that reject feminist values, it is small wonder that the men's rights movement would bleed into conservatism. Conservatism offers a way to critique feminism – think of right-wing radio's vehement attacks on feminists – and to value men as fathers, providers and protectors. Thus the key goals of the men's rights movement – namely, antifeminism and respect for men – were better achieved by conservative ideologies that transformed this movement or in some cases simply superseded it.

References and further reading

Astrachan, A. (1986) *How Men Feel*, New York: Doubleday.

Baumli, F. (ed.) (1985) *Men Freeing Men*, Jersey City, NJ: New Atlantis.

Blankenhorn, D. (1995) *Fatherless America*, New York: HarperCollins.

Bly, R. (1990) *Iron John*, New York: Addison-Wesley.

Clatterbaugh, K. (1997) *Contemporary Perspectives on Masculinity*, Boulder, CO: Westview.

Doyle, R. (1976) *The Rape of the Male*, St Paul, MN: Poor Richard's Press.

Farrell, W. (1986) *Why Men Are the Way They Are*, New York: McGraw-Hill.

—— (1993) *The Myth of Male Power*, New York: Simon and Schuster.

Friedan, B. (1963) *The Feminine Mystique*, New York: Dell.

Gilder, G. (1973) *Sexual Suicide*, New York: Bantam.

—— (1986) *Men and Marriage*, London: Pelican.

Goldberg, H. (1976) *The Hazards of Being Male*, New York: Signet.

Harding, C. (ed.) (1992) *Wingspan*, New York: St Martin's Press.

Hicks, R. (1993) *The Masculine Journey*, Colorado Springs, CO: Navpress.

McCartney, B. (ed.) (1992) *What Makes a Man?* Colorado Springs, CO: Navpress.

See also: fathers' rights; masculinity politics; men's movement

KENNETH CLATTERBAUGH

METHODS, METHODOLOGY AND RESEARCH

Studying men raises recurring issues of methods, methodology and theory. Methods here refer to how research information on men is gathered, analysed and written about.

Methodology refers to the framework of or logic of or relations between different elements in the research process. It can be seen as the link between research methods and broader theoretical questions.

Many research methods have been used in studies of men and masculinities, including: social surveys; statistical analyses; ethnographies; interviews; qualitative, discursive, deconstructive, textual and visual analyses; as well as various mixed methods. An explicitly gendered focus on men and masculinities within the frame of Critical Studies on Men can mean rethinking how research methods are done, as, for example, when interviewing men (Schwalbe and Wolkomir 2002). Feminist research has made clear the possibilities of women interviewing women with empathy, solidarity, even friendship. Subsequent feminist debates have noted some difficulties in too simple an approach to women interviewing women: for example, divisions rather than commonalities between women. Women interviewing men complicates such questions still further. With women interviewing men there may be a range of additional questions: for example, threat and safety, and heterosexual definitions of the situation. There is also the question of to whom the interviewer owes allegiance. Interviewing the powerful is not one-dimensional. Women interviewers may be subject to gender power from men interviewees but may themselves be more powerfully placed in terms of, say, race, disability, class and education.

Men interviewing men again raises some similar and some different questions – for example, should men interviewing men seek equality, even empathy, or critical distance? When interviewing men, it is necessary to draw on several models of interviewing, including feminist, peer and profeminist. Men interviewers also need to be aware of differences, of, for example, class and race, and of how both parties being men may mean shared assumptions, even collusion. This is especially important in researching men's dominance and oppression: for example, men's violence to women and children. For men to critically interview men is likely to be a contradictory process – necessitating politeness and respect, avoidance of collusion, and use of firmness and authority in the interview. A relevant comparison may be feminist researchers interviewing anti-feminist women.

A novel example of research methods used in researching men stems from Frigga Haug (1987) and colleagues' memory-work approach. This approach has been applied by Bob Pease (2000) to a group of self-identified profeminist men of which he was part over eighteen months. Participants reported their memorised experiences on particular themes that were relevant to the formation of their profeminism. This raised several methodological issues: participants' long-term commitment, placing the researcher both inside and outside the group, the status of memories. To address the relation of men's subjectivities to others who might not agree with them, Pease adopted the method of interlocutors, in which others, ranging from men's rightists to feminists, came to the group, as critics, reference points and clarifiers. Another approach to studying 'men who either identified themselves with the profeminist, anti-sexist men's movement, or were identified by others as being relatively non-sexist' has been used by Martin Acker (interview, 1996). He began interviews with the question. 'How do you know you are emerging towards non-sexism?' A third method is David Jackson's (1990, 2003) critical autobiography and critical life history work, using his own life as a resource to theorise his male selfhood and gendered constructions of boys and men more generally.

Textual analyses of novels, film and other representations have made the gendering of men, as authors and as characters, explicit (Schwenger 1984; Middleton 1992). Academic texts, including 'classics', can be re-read in order to understand how 'men' are constructed (Morgan 1992). This method can be applied to empirical and other research material, as that gathered earlier for one purpose can be *reviewed* in terms of what it says about men (McKegany and Bloor 1991).

Methodologies can be retheorised and repractised, with a more explicit recognition of their gendering, and this applies especially to researching men (Hearn 1998a). Feminist research has highlighted the importance of gendered power *throughout* the research process and all of its 'stages', as well as in relation to particular aspects of doing research. These include questions of epistemology, ethics, collaborative working, reflexivity, power relations between researchers and researched, and emotions in research. Critically studying men presents a somewhat similar set of both continuities and discontinuities with other research approaches, both non-feminist and feminist. For example, in research about men who have been violent to known women, all 'stages' of research needed to be rethought critically (Hearn 1998b). Confidentiality and anonymity may be given unconditionally in much research, but, for the sake of women's, children's, men's and indeed interviewers' safety, unconditional confidentiality may be inappropriate when interviewing men who have been violent to known others, usually women and children. Instead it is important to explain to interviewees that confidential esearch interviews still have to operate within the limits of the law. For example, if in a research interview a man confesses to an unsolved murder or affirms that he was going to attack his woman partner that evening, it is possible for researchers to report this (Cowburn 2005).

There are various approaches to methodology, epistemology and ontology, both generally and in studying men – rationalist, empiricist, critical, standpoint, postmodernist, and so on. Rationalists believe that there are innate ideas that are not found in experience: ideas exist independently of experience, and may in some way derive from the structure of the human mind, or exist independently of the mind. We might know, for example, the 'deep essence' of 'deep masculinity', as in the work of the mythopoetics. It is very difficult to prove or disprove such knowledge. In this view, men, or women, may *know* what men are like, even if evidence appears otherwise. Empiricists deny that concepts exist prior to experience: all knowledge is a product of human learning, based on human perception. In this, men need to be studied by sense perceptions, through one's own perceptions or more systematic study of the perception of others, as indicative of the way men are. This perspective can be seen as the basis of much mainstream social science on men. The focus on perception, however, brings its own causes for concern, since illusions, misunderstandings and hallucinations show that perception does not always depict the world as it 'really is'.

Problems remain with both these epistemologies, and certainly so in pure or extreme forms. Kant, and subsequently many other critical thinkers, attempted to develop some synthesis between these views. According to such more critical views, people do have knowledge that is prior to experience – for example, the principle of causality – and Kant held that there are *a priori* synthetic concepts, but empirical knowledge is also important. Many have expanded this insight and developed forms of knowledge that mix elements of rationalism, empiricism and critical reflection, whether through emphasis on meaning and interpretation, as in hermeneutics, or more societally grounded analysis of knowledge, as in the Hegelian–Marxist tradition. Standpoint traditions, the view that knowledge is shaped by social position, inform much feminist and profeminist critical standpoints and studies on men.

A contrast can be drawn between more individually defined standpoint theory which prioritises knowledge from the individual's identity politics claims, and more socially contextualised standpoint theory that sees knowledge as a more collective endeavour and production linked to historical and organisational political positions and circumstances, not necessarily rooted in individual identity politics, and less still to deterministic validations. Differentiations in the positioning of the researcher in relation to the topic of men are partly a matter of individual political choices and decisions, but increasingly the importance of the more structural, geopolitical positioning is being recognised. More collective understanding of standpoint theory can inform research designs, highlighting gendered power relations in both the research focus and the research process. It can assist the production of more explicitly gendered and grounded knowledge about men, masculinities and gender relations.

Standpoint and related positions have been challenged by postmodernist approaches, including postmodernist feminist positions. Postmodernist approaches can themselves be more or less anti-foundational, so producing possible multiple accounts and realities – including of and about men. Postcolonial and other critical epistemologies, including those that do not necessarily prioritise gender, may serve to show that men are not just men, but are aged, classed, ethnicised, racialised, embodied as disabled/able-bodied, and so on (Haywood and Mac an Ghaill 2003).

There are also key questions of ontology, including the gendering of the researcher, of social reality, and of their interrelations. In its simplest form one view would suggest that it does not matter *who* it is studying men – a woman or a man, a feminist, profeminist or anti-feminist. On the other hand, the empirical is not so transparent. This counter view complicates, for example, what is seen, data gathered, modes of analysis, interpretation. Such non-transparency is clear from, for example, gay re-readings of film and other media. It is not that gay men necessarily read films in 'gay ways', rather that there are probabilities or tendencies for certain gay men to read film in ways that most straight men might not see. Emphasising the researcher is not to suggest a deterministic account of their impact; rather, researchers' social positionality is *relevant*, especially in researching certain topics and sites, but not all-encompassing. The 'topic' of 'men' ranges from broad theoretical analyses to specific social situations, which might be individual, 'men-only', mixed-gender, and so on. Studying men cannot be left to only men, or to non-feminists. Men's knowledge of men is at best limited and partial, at worst violently patriarchal. Subject positions are different for women and men: women are researching/writing in relation to another object, 'men'; men are in relation to a similar object, a category of which they are part. Women's studies of men can name men as men, study men as other than women, and 'know' men through their effects upon women (Willott 1998; Campbell 2003).

Standpoint traditions inform much feminist and profeminist studies on men. The positioning of the author in relation to the topic of men, as a personal, gendered, epistemological and geopolitical relation, shapes the object of research and the topic of men and masculinities in a variety of ways. One might argue that different knowledge is available to men than to women, or to feminists, profeminists or anti-feminists. There are various relations of the researcher and the researched, the relation of the author and the topic/object (men):

- *Absence, fixed presence, and avoidance*: in which either topic (men) or author are absent, avoided or present yet non-problematic. One major way of studying, or not studying, men has been through ignoring the category of men or of making any gendering of men implicit.
- *Alliance and attachment*: in which both topic and author are present, yet both or either remain non-problematic. There is an alliance/attachment between author and topic.
- *Subversion and separation*: in which both topic and author are problematic and subverted.
- *Ambivalence*: in which topic and/or author are problematic and ambivalent.
- *Alterity*: in which topic and/or author are problematic and made other.
- *Critique*: in which authors critically and reflexively engage with both themselves and the topic, within an emancipatory context.

(Hearn 1998a)

Critique entails: a critical relation to the topic, encompassing a self-reflexivity of the author, an awareness of social location of both author and topic, and consideration of the social bases of knowledge; commitment to the political emancipation of women and men; and, where appropriate, empirical inquiry and not just assertion and speculation. For men to develop a critical relation to men rests partly on the possibility of a profeminist, anti-patriarchal standpoint and praxis. This rests on developing profeminist, anti-patriarchal actions, activities, research and organising, and positive relations with feminist theory and practice. Needless to say, plural or hybrid discourses often operate in particular researches on men.

Another implication of the relations of researcher and researched concerns the very constitution of social theory. Conventional social theory has usually ignored gender relations and reproduced patriarchal social relations through its own practices. There is silence in most social theory about the gendered reflexivity of the author and constitution of that theory. Changing this involves problematising silences on the category of men in social theory and men's practices of theorising. Linked questions are: how can the silences that there are about men's reflexive gendered presence in social theory be countered, including the silence on itself, and how to reconstitute the silences around the relation of men and social theory? Problematisation and reconstitution of objectivity and subjectivities through situated knowledges may assist the process of providing some provisional answers.

Patriarchal society provides the context, data and norms of research, including studies on men. Men dominate research and the social contexts of research on men. Men perform gendered practices in universities, university management, research and science, with inclusions and exclusions of particular people, priorities and theories. We may ask: to what extent does dominant 'scientific' knowledge rely on *particular* forms of academic men's subjectivity? To what extent is 'objectivity' in research a form of subjectivity, often made possible by invisible labour, unspoken powers, exclusions and marginalisations, and a thousand and one ways in which malestream science has been and is done?

The gendering of academic organisations has tremendous implications for rethinking the position and historical dominance of men in academia and how that structures what counts as knowledge. Developing critical, less pre-scientific methodologies and epistemologies for studying men means changing men and recognising the importance of breaking paradigms, not just doing 'normal science'. Studying men remains political – when such studies exist in societies that historically and epistemologically continue to privilege men.

References and further reading

Acker, M. (1996) 'The good guys', *The IASOM Newsletter*, 3 (1): 11–17.

Campbell, E. (2003) 'Interviewing men in uniform: a feminist approach?' *International Journal of Social Research Methodology*, 6 (4): 285–304.

Cowburn, M. (2005) 'Confidentiality and public protection: ethical dilemmas in qualitative research with adult male sex offenders', *Journal of Sexual Aggression,* 11 (1): 49–63.

Haug, F. [1987] (1999) *Female Sexualization. A Collective Work of Memory*, London: Verso.

Haywood, C. and Mac an Ghaill, M. (2003) *A Sociology of Men and Masculinities*, Buckingham: Open University Press.

Hearn, J. (1998a) 'Theorizing men and men's theorizing: men's discursive practices in theorizing men', *Theory and Society*, 27 (6): 781–816.

—— (1998b) *The Violences of Men. How Men Talk About and How Agencies Respond to Men's Violence to Women*, London: Sage.

Jackson, D. (1990) *Unmasking Masculinity: A Critical Autobiography*, London: Unwin Hyman and Routledge.

—— (2003) 'Beyond one-dimensional models of masculinity: a life-course perspective on the processes of becoming masculine', *Auto/Biography*, 11 (1 and 2): 71–87.

McKegany, N. and Bloor, M. (1991) 'Spotting the invisible man: the influence of male gender on fieldwork relations', *British Journal of Sociology*, 42 (2): 195–210.

Middleton, P. (1992) *The Inward Gaze*, London: Routledge.

Morgan, D. (1992) *Discovering Men*, London: Routledge.
Pease, B. (2000) *Recreating Men: Postmodern Masculinity Politics*, London: Sage.
Schwalbe, M.L. and Wolkomir, M. (2002) 'Interviewing men', in J.F. Gubrium and J.A. Holstein (eds) *Handbook of Interview Research*, Thousand Oaks, CA: Sage.
Schwenger, P. (1984) *Phallic Critiques*, London: Routledge and Kegan Paul.
Willott, S. (1998) 'An outsider within: a feminist doing research with men', in K. Henwood, C. Griffin and A. Phoenix (eds) *Standpoints and Differences. Essays in the Practice of Feminist Psychology*, London: Sage.

See also: epistemology

JEFF HEARN

METROSEXUAL

A metrosexual is a heterosexual man with an interest in personal style and grooming traditionally considered 'feminine'. The term, originating with British journalist Mark Simpson in the mid-1990s, combines 'metropolitan' and 'heterosexual' to identify the key demographic of single young men, living or working in urban centres and having a high disposable income. It must also be distinguished from homosexual men, who form a similar demographic, though the 'gay lifestyle' of the 1980s is in many ways the model for the metrosexual 'new man'. Icons such as football player David Beckham show a mingling of 'male' sport and 'female' fashion, seeking admiration from both men and women; ultimately, the metrosexual himself is his own best audience. The term carries negative associations of vanity and narcissism, characterising one who is self-obsessed and self-indulgent.

The metrosexual image is largely a creation of the market, designed to fill a gap in consumer capitalism. The emphasis laid on outer appearance and exhibitionism creates a demand for fashion, accessories, personal care services and cosmetics aimed specifically at men, and changing the way time as well as money is spent. The uncertain identity of the metrosexual leaves him vulnerable to the collection of fantasies about maleness sold to him through advertising. Indeed, metrosexuality can be seen as corresponding to an emasculation of men through the increasing aestheticisation and eroticisation of the male body in advertising and popular culture. This lifestyle exerts a new set of pressures on men related to body image and physical expectations, as well as the professional competitive edge gained by such grooming.

Though the metrosexual is primarily a social phenomenon, the term has entered the realm of geopolitics as an analogy for the 'soft power' of the European Union. The progressive diplomacy and peace strategies of 'metrosexual' Europe are contrasted to the 'macho' and militant politics of conservative America. Just as metrosexuals are redefining metrosexuality, new political orientations are redefining old notions of power and influence.

References and further reading

Anon (2003) 'Metrosexuality', *The Economist*, 3 July 2003.
Dodds, P. (2003) 'Metrosexual machismo all the rage', *CBS News*, 25 November.
Khanna, P. (2004) 'The metrosexual superpower', *Foreign Policy*: 143.
Simpson, M. (1994) 'Here come the mirror men', *Independent*, 15 November: 22.
—— (2002) *Sex Terror*, New York: Harrington Park.

See also: new man

ANDREA HASENBANK

MEXICAN MASCULINITIES

Many references in the sordid history of the term 'Mexican masculinity' carry the implicit assumptions that, first, this concept is best understood in the singular; second, Mexican masculinity is heterosexual; and third, Mexican male sexuality represents a fixed entity and something entirely distinct from Mexican female sexuality.

Attention to Mexican masculinities by scholars in Mexico as well as the United States originates as a result of several intellectual urges. The first political impulse came from the second-wave feminist movement of the 1970s and 1980s in Mexico, as well as later feminist organisations in the 1990s among men, such as the Laboratorio de la Masculinidad. What it meant to be a man, what men-as-men do (to be men, to not be less-manly-men, and to not act and think like women) was called into question in Mexico as never before, including in terms of men's sexualities. In a sense the notion of heterosexuality as a constructed component of male homosociality – and not something preordained – has been easier in Mexico than the United States because of involvement from the beginning by feminist scholars.

The second major source of attention to Mexican masculinities has been AIDS, from the first diagnosed case in 1983 to the belated but eventually widespread public health campaigns for safe sex, condom use and the general coming out of the closet in Mexico City, Guadalajara and other urban areas. A third factor contributing to the rise of studies of Mexican masculinities has to do with the perverse, often racist preoccupation (especially in the United States) with machismo in Mexico. Not only is machismo hardly original or essential to Mexico in any narrow sense, but in fact macho male metaphors in the United States predate such imagery in Mexico. Machismo, it seems, is far from a 'national' character trait in Mexico alone.

The construction of Mexican masculinities in relation to male homosociality has been intimately tied to the notion of a Greater Mexico. More than 23 million Mexicans live in the United States today; one in seven Mexicans will live and work in the United States. The implications of this transnational social and cultural context are subsequently profound, because in the twenty-first century, migratory flows, communications and political economies less than ever restrict their activities to neatly bounded geopolitical borders. An example is found in the development of the AIDS epidemic among Mexicans: what was originally (and incorrectly) labelled as a homosexual, elite disease has become increasingly a problem for poor, rural migrant men who become infected in the United States and return home to Mexico, where they in turn infect their sexual *compañeras* and *compañeros*.

In part as a result of these public health issues, questions of heterosexuality, homosexuality and bisexuality among Mexican men are being examined more carefully, and cultural stereotypes about Mexican masculinities are being increasingly shown as hindrances to prevention and treatment campaigns. The Mexican anthropologist Guillermo Núñez (2001) offers a penetrating critique of what he terms the dominant model for understanding homoeroticism in Mexico. In particular he challenges us to move beyond standard dichotomies of penetrator–penetrated, active–passive, dominant–dominated. Gutmann's (2005) work on the totemic illusion of male sexuality, which treats male sexuality as naturalised, fixed and entirely distinct from female sexuality, similarly aims to dislodge such manly dichotomies.

Whereas scholarship prior to 1980 treated Mexico as intrinsically more sexist than the US, this recent scholarship has consequently led to a more holistic study south of the Rio Grande border. Our understanding of Mexican masculinities has developed in the context of demographic developments such as women working outside the home for money, birthrates plummeting, and rough parity in education levels attained (at least through secondary schooling) by men and women, as well as powerful social movements, including feminist struggles to legalise abortion and gay liberation struggles throughout the country. Consequently, work on fathering, work, sexuality, violence, machismo, health (especially AIDS and alcohol use and abuse) are among the important topics explored by social scientists, literary critics and historians of Mexico.

With respect to fathering, for example, until recently assumptions were common and studies were few as to what fathers actually do and or do not do with children of various ages. Do they wash little ones? What is their role in disciplining children? How accurate is the stereotype that Mexican men wish to sire many children (especially male children) to prove their virility? Gutmann (1996) found that class is a major factor in understanding what constitutes a good father. Although there is great diversity in what working-class men are willing and able to do with children, the higher the class the less men appear to want and have to play an active part in parenting, and the less active fathering is linked to men's and women's definitions of who is a manly man.

References and further reading

Brandes, S. (2002) *Staying Sober in Mexico City*, Austin, TX: University of Texas Press.

Carrillo, H. (2002) *The Night is Young*, Chicago, IL: University of Chicago Press.

González López, G. (2005) *Erotic Journeys*, Berkeley, CA: University of California Press.

Gutmann, M.C. (1996) *The Meanings of Macho*, Berkeley, CA: University of California Press.

—— (2005) 'Scoring men', *Culture, Medicine and Psychiatry*, 29: 79–101.

Herta Rojas, F. (1999) *El juego del hombre*, Puebla, Mexico: Benemérita Universidad Autónoma de Puebla/Plaza y Valdés.

Irwin, R.M. (2003) *Mexican Masculinities*, Minneapolis, MN: University of Minnesota Press.

Monsiváis, C. (1981) *Escenas de pudor y liviandad*, Mexico City: Era.

Núñez Noriega, G. (1994) *Sexo entre varones*, Mexico City: UNAM/Porrúa/El Colegio de Sonora.

—— (2001) 'Reconociendo los placers, desconstruyendo las identidades', *Desacatos*, 6: 15–34.

Prieur, A. (1998) *Mema's House, Mexico City*. Chicago, IL: University of Chicago Press.

Stern, S. (1995) *The Secret History of Gender*, Chapel Hill, NC: University of North Carolina Press.

See also: cultural formations, Latin America; machismo (and macho)

MATTHEW C. GUTMANN

MID-LIFE CRISIS

A mid-life crisis is a developmental stage that people go through characterised by erratic behaviour as they transition from adulthood to middle age. The idea of a mid-life crisis was popularised by Sheehy (1976), building upon stage models of human development, such as those popularised by Erikson (1980). Supposedly, mid-life crises spring from the desire to reinvigorate lost youth in response to declining physical and sexual functioning and unsatisfying jobs or marriages. Although the idea of a mid-life crisis continues to remain a popular idea, scientific research fails to find evidence for the mid-life crisis as a normal stage in male adult development.

The failure to find evidence that most men go through a period that can be termed a crisis does not mean that men do not experience difficulties accepting the aging process. Culturally held portrayals of masculinity tend to define masculinity in terms of the abilities and accomplishments of younger men. Specifically, masculinity in Western societies is typically defined by the achievement of power and control. Mass media and advertising tend to reinforce the idea that older men should reproduce young men's forms of masculinity. For example, ads for Viagra equate sexual functioning and happiness with the ability to achieve erection. Moreover, stereotypes about elderly men associate them with attributes typically considered unmasculine (e.g. declining physical, mental and sexual abilities, as well as impaired mental functioning). The lack of realistic and positive social constructions of masculinity for elderly men can have adverse implications for men's self-concept.

More recently, scholarship on the intersection between masculinity and aging has started to recognise that the multiple ways to define and present masculinity can and should change across the lifespan. In other words, rather than view a mid-life crisis as a medical problem within a man, it might be better to see the subjective experience of a mid-life crisis as evidence that culturally held masculinity scripts need to be redefined. Mental health professionals should be ready to assist men experiencing distress associated with aging to construct legitimate personal identities, informed by culturally hegemonic definitions of masculinity, but not a strict reproduction of them.

References and further reading

Erikson, E.H. (1980) *Identity and the Life Cycle*, New York: Norton.
Newberger, E.H. (2001) 'Treating this heavy midlife of men', *American Journal of Orthopsychiatry*, 70: 278–80.
Sheehy, G. (1976) *Passages*, New York: Dutton.
Spector-Mersel, G. (2006) 'Never-aging stories', *Journal of Gender Studies*, 15: 67–82.

See also: age and ageing; menopause, male; retirement

JAMES K. BEGGAN

MILITARY INSTITUTIONS

Military institutions deal explicitly in life, death and warfare. Their primary function is 'to organise legitimate violence and supervise its use' (Gerth and Mills 1954: 26–30). In fulfilling these obligations, military institutions may be required to protect the state by repelling external threats, or to maintain the power of the state against possible internal threats.

The military has been referred to variously as a total institution (Goffman 1961), a social institution (Janowitz 1971) and a masculine institution (Higate 2003). In his book *Asylums* (1961), the sociologist Erving Goffman highlights the strictly regimented and disciplined organisation of personnel within a number of total institutions including military barracks. During training, military recruits are denied 'offstage' areas, and are subject to intense secondary socialisation through which attempts are made to supplant civilian with military identities. Military institutions tend to be isolated from their civilian host communities, both physically (behind the wire) and culturally in terms of military personnel's investment into ideologies of militarism (Enloe 2000).

In the late 1980s scholars began to explore the masculinised culture of military institutions (Morgan 1987). Militaries are dominated by men and heavily influenced by hypermasculine values. As such, their traditional and conservative culture turns on the formal and informal othering of marginal masculinities, women and homosexuals. The archetypal warrior figure, embodied in the mythologised *Special Forces* troop, or alternatively in the decorated combat pilot, represents two examples of hegemonic military masculinity. Importantly, the ways in which generals are socialised is different to that of privates, pointing to the complexity of a gender order in which a plurality of military masculinities co-exist.

From the mid-1990s, a combination of external juridical pressure and recruiting crises for military institutions in the developed nations has seen the implementation of more 'enlightened' equal opportunities and diversity policies, leading to an increase in the proportion of females in the armed services. However, changes in informal military culture in terms of attitudes, values and beliefs continue to be wedded to the superiority of the masculine over the feminine. Armies remain synonymous with essentialist understandings of men with regard to their 'controlled' use of aggression and violence against stated enemies.

References and further reading

Enloe, C. (2000) *Maneuvers*, Berkeley, CA: University of California Press.
Gerth, H.H. and Mills, C.W. (1954) *Character and Social Structure*, London: Routledge and Kegan Paul.
Goffman, E. (1961) *Asylums*, New York: Doubleday.
Higate, P.R. (ed.) (2003) *Military Masculinities*, New York: Praeger.
Janowitz, M. (1971) *The Professional Soldier*, New York: Free Press.
Morgan, D. (1987) *'It Will Make a Man of You.' Notes on National Service, Masculinity and Autobiography*, Studies in Sexual Politics No. 17, Manchester: Department of Sociology, University of Manchester.

See also: armies; military masculinities; war

PAUL HIGATE

MILITARY MASCULINITIES

The study of military masculinities brings together two principal theoretical fields: critical masculinity studies and military studies. Military studies typically address issues including war, armies, conflicts and studies that enquire into the relationship between the military, the nation-state and national citizenship. Critical masculinity studies encompass the ways in which gender and masculinities are socially constructed across space, time and place. Studies of military masculinities observe the relations between the state and citizen, state and military and military and citizen.

Critical studies of military masculinities take the position that war and the military organisation are hegemonic masculine practices. War is predominantly, but not exclusively, the business of men, from soldiers to the elites who command their lives. Men as a group, in a structural sense, and often in an individual sense also, are the principal progenitors of violence, both state-sanctioned and individual and community violence (Connell 1985).

A particular insight of critical military masculinity studies is that there is a principal connection between masculine dominance, class relations, social inequality and militarism (Lee and Daly 1987). Critical analysis of military masculinities, and the military and masculinities, has been prompted or informed by feminist studies. Feminist studies of men, masculinity, armies and war have focused upon questions of political economy, social organisation, gendered division of labour, sexuality and violence (see Enloe 1989).

Studies of military masculinities consider the multiple locations and forms of masculinity that are constructed within, or in relation to, the military. These include studies of different types of soldiers, within diverse military institutions, or research into the political and cultural movements of powerful elites and their preoccupation with war and conflict or studies of the construction of soldier identity (Theweleit 1989). Paul Higate (2003) has produced an edited collection entitled *Military Masculinities: Identity and the State*. This is the most comprehensive collection of current research into the field of military masculinities.

References and further reading

Connell, R. (1985) 'Masculinity, violence and war', in P. Patton and R. Poole (eds) *War/Masculinity*, NSW: Intervention.

Enloe, C. (1989) *Bananas, Beaches and Bases: Making Feminist Sense of International Politics*, London: Pandora.

Higate, P. (ed.) (2003) *Military Masculinities: Identity and the State*, Westport, CN: Praeger.

Lee, R. and Daly, R. (1987) 'Man's domination and Woman's oppression: the question of origins', in M. Kaufman (ed.) *Beyond Patriarchy: Essays on Pleasure, Power and Change*, New York: Oxford University Press, pp. 1–27.

Theweleit, K. (1989) *Male Fantasies Vol. 2*, Minneapolis, MN: University of Minnesota Press.

See also: armies; military institutions; war

BEN WADHAM

MISANDRY

Generally, 'misandry' refers to the hatred and oppression of men on a genotypic basis. Paul Nathanson and Katherine Young's *Spreading Misandry* (2001) describes man-hating in contemporary popular culture, especially the tropes of absent, insensitive and/or abusive males, as representing a cultural shift towards a gynocentric order. They conclude that misandry results from a feminist project to privilege gender as the principal site of identity and power and to redress traditional androcentrism through legitimised forms of dehumanising and demonising men. Curiously, they contend that misandry is gender oppression since it requires a polarised gender order.

Despite contrary claims, misandry lacks the systemic, transhistoric, institutionalised and legislated antipathy of misogyny. Nevertheless, the notion is gaining in currency among 'masculists' and 'men's rights' groups seeking to redress supposedly discriminatory divorce, domestic violence and rape shield laws. But as Naomi Schor (1987) cautions, assuming that misandry mirrors misogyny reduces questions of gender and power to a male/female binary and ignores within-gender hierarchies. Thus, Nancy Kang (2003) recognises a misandric tendency in the dominant culture's interactions with marginalised masculinities.

Examples of racialised misandric impulses occur both in canonical works and in literatures of the margins. Famously, Shakespeare's Shylock calls on his manhood to plead his humanity. Echoing W.E.B. du Bois, James Baldwin (1985) observes that the African–American male is infantilised to salve the dominant order's insecurities. bell hooks cautions in *Black Looks* (1992) that there has never been a time when African–American men have not been represented fantastically and stereotypically. These are exemplified by the simultaneous attraction–repulsion of popular depictions of the eroticised and hypermasculine African-American of entertainment and of professional sports.

References and further reading

Baldwin, J. (1985) 'The black boy who looks like a white boy', in J. Baldwin, *The Price of the Ticket: Collected Non-fiction 1948–1985*, New York: St Martin's Press, pp. 289–303.

du Bois, W.E.B. (1995) *The Souls of Black Folk*, New York: Signet.

hooks, b. (1992) *Black Looks: Race and Representation*, Boston, MA: South End Press.

Kang, N. (2003) 'To love and be loved: considering black masculinity and the misandric impulse in T. Morrison's *Beloved*', *Callaloo*, 26 (3): 836–54.

Nathanson, P. and Young, K. (2001) *Spreading Misandry: The Teaching of Contempt for Men in Popular Culture*, Kingston and Montreal: Queen's-McGill University Press.

Schor, N. (1987) 'The portrait of a gentleman: representing men in (French) women's writing', *Representations*, 20: 1–23.

See also: fathers' rights; men's rights; sexism

MARC OUELLETTE

MISOGYNY

Misogyny is the hatred of women. Though most common in men, misogyny also exists in and is practised by women against other women or even themselves. Misogyny functions as an ideology or belief system that has accompanied patriarchal, or male-dominated, societies for thousands of years and continues to place women in subordinate positions with limited access to power and decision-making. This hatred of women most often focuses on their bodies, objectifying and commodifying them and constructing women metonymically as body parts, or at most amalgamations of parts. Aristotle contended that women exist as naturally occurring deformities or imperfect males (even seeing menses as impure sperm, missing the constituent part of soul). Ever since, women in Western cultures have internalised their role as societal scapegoats, influenced in the twenty-first century by the multimedia objectification of women with its culturally sanctioned self-loathing and fixations on plastic surgery, anorexia and bulimia.

Misogyny historically has been justified and has arisen from women's essentialised roles, limited to childbearing and other domestic duties. Though some feminist theorists continue to search for 'original' matriarchal societies, evidence remains scarce and problematic. Western cultures, in particular, have legitimised and institutionalised the hatred of women, justifying women's lower position via religious doctrine, blaming the biblical 'Mother Eve' as the Pandora who introduced Sin and Evil into the world. This stance often normalised the mistreatment of women, and the pain of menstruation and childbirth become God's judgment on Eve's daughters.

Medieval misogyny focused on women's voracious and insatiable sexuality, pointing to women's capacity for multiple orgasms as a threat to men's masculinity. Through the Early Modern period, women were seen as being too unstable, unclean and emotional – situated in their essentialised bodies and associated with passions and bodily functions – to make either effective rulers or thinkers.

In the Early Modern period, Petrarchan love poetry idealised the dead woman as being perfect (beloved, beautiful, dead woman as motif would surface again in the works of Romantic writers like Poe). The fifteenth century in Europe witnessed the beginnings of a literary debate, the *Querelle des femmes* ('debate over women') which raged for two centuries and included the very popular pamphlet by Swetnam, who claimed that even beating a woman to death could not assure her obedience.

Meanwhile, the image of the hag or shrew, popularised in the English mystery plays, survived as a source of humour in Shakespeare's *The Taming of the Shrew* and into the twentieth century as the musical and film *Kiss Me, Kate* and the teen films *10 Things I Hate About You* and *Deliver Us from Eva*. The image of the outspoken, aggressive woman who must be beaten, physically and/or mentally, into happy submission continues to resonate with audiences in the twenty-first century.

Though women were expected throughout the history of US expansion to domesticate the frontier, in US literature women's civilising influence was often rendered as petticoat despotism – as in the work of Irving and Twain – and the cause of flight by beset males into the freedom of the wilderness.

Freud's revolutionary work on the human psyche explained women as being neurotic creatures suffering from their own sense of lack, which he named penis envy. Subsequent psychoanalysts including Lacan furthered this notion with the discussion of woman as formed by absence, void and gap. The lesbian, the woman who attempts to exist and be defined outside of a relationship with a man, has also drawn much misogynist ire, condemned as a woman who cannot attract or keep a male.

Misogynistic views coupled with their secondary legal status prevented women from attaining the right to vote until the twentieth century, with women in Kuwait in the twenty-first century still denied the right to vote.

Even positive representations of women have traditionally had misogynistic overtones as expectations for woman's purity, obedience, chastity and fecundity have all been used to evaluate her social, moral and physical worth. Most major world religions contain within their dogma or practices some form of misogyny. Women have often been limited to the role of mother or prostitute, caught in the Eve–Mary or Whore–Virgin dichotomy.

Many scholars argue that the cultures of pornography and rape both grow out of and feed the hatred of women. The reification of women's bodies allows them to be dehumanised and tortured.

Misogyny has been traced through most cultures' literature and art, culminating in discussions in twenty-first-century Women's Studies classes over issues ranging from female genital circumcision/mutilation to considerations of those 'Lipstick' or 'Do Me' young women who claim to embrace a sexuality like that of men. Twenty-first-century misogyny appears prominently in much rap and hip-hop music and popular culture and advertising. Beginning with the othering, objectification and dehumanisation of women, misogyny is manifest when the desire for and fascination with women's bodies combines with loathing and contempt to produce representations of women as consumable goods and as obstacles to male bonding. Meanwhile, honour killings, son-preference abortions, rapes and sexual harassment still persist in most areas of the world.

References and further reading

Ackley, K.A. (ed.) (1992) *Misogyny in Literature*, New York: Garland.

Bloch, R.H. (1991) *Medieval Misogyny and the Invention of Western Romantic Love*, Chicago, IL: University of Chicago Press.

Bloch, R.H. and Ferguson, F. (eds) (1989) *Misogyny, Misandry, and Misanthropy*, Berkeley, CA: University of California Press.

Daileader, C.R. (2005) *Racism, Misogyny, and the Othello Myth*, Cambridge: Cambridge University Press.

Gilmore, D.D. (2001) *Misogyny*, Philadelphia, PA: University of Pennsylvania Press.

Haskell, M. [1974] (1987) *From Reverence to Rape*, Chicago, IL: University of Chicago Press.

hooks, b. (2003) *We Real Cool*, New York and London: Routledge.

Jeffreys, S. (2005) *Beauty and Misogyny*, London: Psychology.

Smith, J. [1989] (1993) *Misogynies*, London: Faber & Faber.

See also: oppression; patriarchy; sexism

SAMANTHA A. MORGAN-CURTIS

MOTHER–SON RELATIONSHIPS

'Mothers and Sons' is a relatively new field of study in feminist scholarship. As compared to the far more popular topic of Mothers and Daughters, only a handful of publications have examined mother and son relationships, and most of these have been published recently. The feminist scholarship on mothers and sons may be organised under two interrelated themes: a call for greater mother–son connection and a challenge to traditional masculine socialisation (O'Reilly 2001a). Central to both perspectives is the belief that feminist practices of mothering modelled on connection and concerned with the creation of new modes of masculinity will dismantle patriarchal gender roles and male power and privilege. While most of this scholarship has been Anglo-American in focus, recent research has looked at more diverse populations, in particular African American (O'Reilly 2001b; Lee and Williams 2001; Bernard 2004) and lesbian (Wells 2001).

A central theme in contemporary feminist thought on the mother–son relationship is a celebration of mother–son connection and a challenge to the belief that mother–son separation is normal, inevitable and good for our sons. Since the early 1990s, feminist writers have called for greater mother–son connection and have positioned it as central to the reconfiguration of traditional masculinity (Dooley and Fedele 2001). In particular, they challenge the hegemonic narrative of mother and son attachment – as scripted in parenting books, psychoanalytic theory and popular wisdom – which assumes that sons must separate from their mothers in order to acquire a 'normal' masculine identity. A close and caring relationship between a mother and her son is pathologised, while a relationship structured upon separation is naturalised as the real and normal way to experience mother–son attachment. Silverstein and Rashbaum (1994) write 'the love of a mother – both the son's for her, and hers for him – is believed to "feminise" the boy, make him soft, weak, dependent, homebound ... only through renunciation of the loving mother does the boy become a man' (11). Feminist theorists question the patriarchally mandated mother–son separation as both natural – hence inevitable – and 'good' for our sons, arguing that this process is culturally scripted and orchestrated (Rich 1986). Whether or not the son is fully cognisant of this sudden or subtle detachment, he nonetheless experiences it as a profound and inexplicable loss that leaves him feeling vulnerable and alone. To save her sons from becoming detached and wounded men and to change the patriarchal world in which we all live, a mother must foreground her presence in the life of her son. She must also maintain a close and caring connection with her sons throughout their lives.

Feminist literature on masculinity argues that while men learn that they are beneficiaries of power and privilege, they pay a high price for this status. Kaufman, for example, describes masculinity as 'an idealised version of what it means to be male ... a collective hallucination ... a state of mind and a story of how to behave' (1994: 25, 32, 29). Having been socialised to repress and deny emotions associated with the feminine – empathy, vulnerability, compassion, gentleness – and having been taught to tough it out on their own through our culture's valorisation of an independent, individualistic (and fully individuated) masculinity, men grow into manhood deeply wounded and isolated. Masculinity then becomes a façade or a place of refuge where men seek to convince themselves and others that they are as brave and strong as the idealised version of masculinity purports them to be. Feminist mothers seek new socialisation for boys wherein traditionally feminine characteristics such as gentleness, vulnerability and compassion are emphasised, and the more harmful aspects of macho masculinity are eliminated. In addition, feminist mothers practise anti-sexist childrearing wherein male privilege is challenged and gender equality is insisted upon (Epp and Cooke 2004; O'Reilly 2004). However, the work of raising anti-sexist sons has proven to be more difficult and daunting than the task of rearing feminist daughters. The task of raising a new 'generation of men' is seldom supported by fathers or the world at large. Furthermore, many mothers worry that their feminine/feminist sons may find themselves misfits in a patriarchal society (Thomas, 2001).

By way of a close mother–son relationship and feminist childrearing, mothers seek to destabilise and deconstruct normative patterns of male socialisation and traditional definitions of masculinity that are harmful to men and the society at large.

References and further reading

Bernard, W. (2004) 'Bringing out boyz to men', in A. O'Reilly (ed.) *Mother Outlaws*, Toronto: Women's Press, pp. 329–40.

Dooley C. and Fedele, N. (2001) 'Raising relational boys' in A. O'Reilly (ed.) *Mothers and Sons*, New York: Routledge, pp. 185–216.

Epp, J.R. and Cook, S. (2004) 'The (male) advantage of a feminist mother', in A. O'Reilly (ed.) *Mother Outlaws*, Toronto: Women's Press, pp. 75–94.

Kaufman, M. (1994) *Theorizing Masculinities*, Thousand Oaks, CA: Sage.

Lee, C. and Williams, E.H. (2001) 'Masculinity, matriarchy, and myth', in A. O'Reilly (ed.) *Mothers and Sons*, New York: Routledge, pp. 56–70.

O'Reilly, A. (2001a) 'Introduction', in A. O'Reilly (ed.) *Mothers and Sons*, New York: Routledge, pp. 1–21.

—— (2001b) 'In black and white', in A. O'Reilly (ed.) *Mothers and Sons*, New York: Routledge, pp. 91–118.

—— (2004) 'A mom and her son', in A. O'Reilly (ed.) *Mother Outlaws*, Toronto: Women's Press, pp. 387–99.

Rich, A. [1976] (1986) *Of Woman Born*, New York: Norton.

Silverstein, O. and Rashbaum, B. (1994) *The Courage to Raise Good Men*, New York: Viking.

Thomas, A. (2001) 'Swimming against the tide', in A. O'Reilly (ed.) *Mothers and Sons*, New York: Routledge, pp. 121–40.

Wells, J. (2001) 'Lesbians raising sons', in A. O'Reilly (ed.) *Mothers and Sons*, New York: Routledge, pp. 141–56.

See also: families; father–son relationships

ANDREA O'REILLY

MUSCLES AND MUSCULARITY

Muscularity plays a critical role in the construction of masculine identity for many Western males. Size, particularly muscularity, has long been regarded as a major signifier of masculinity (Pope *et al.* 2000). This notion is further historically linked to men's bodies being a product of (manual) labour. Connell (1983), in his groundbreaking article, discusses men's bodies in terms of 'doing' and 'being'. Until recently the archetypal male body has largely been perceived as one which has been created through manual labour (Tolson 1987). Working in traditional 'blue-collar' professions, which demand a degree of physicality, traditionally has been perceived as the expected and accepted way of achieving a desirable masculine physique. However, the advent of the feminist movement and the rise of industrialisation have eroded traditional sites of masculine labour where men once attained their masculinised physiques. Therefore, the way in which many males now attain their archetypal masculine physique is largely through conscious forms of exercise such as bodybuilding, specifically designed to build and sculpt culturally defined exemplars of masculinity.

Size and muscularity are not the only factors to be taken into consideration for contemporary males to achieve an archetypal masculine aesthetic. The archetypal male body of today is not only muscular, but also devoid of fat, symmetrical and well groomed (Drummond 2005). It is arguable that much of the pressure to attain this 'look' is being directed from external commercial influences such as media, film and television, which in turn impact on contemporary Western cultural views and expectations.

Importantly, the archetypal male body now requires a good deal more attention, and control, to be achieved. As a consequence, contemporary Western culture is witnessing an increase in young men's concerns regarding body image (Drummond 2002).

References and further reading

Connell, R. (1983) 'Men's bodies', *Australian Society* 2 (9): 33–9.

Drummond, M. (2002) 'Men, body image and eating disorders', *International Journal of Men's Health*, 1 (1): 79–93.

—— (2005) 'Men's bodies: listening to the voices of young gay men', *Journal of Men and Masculinities*, 7 (3): 270–90.

Pope, H., Phillips, K. and Olivardia, R. (2000) *The Adonis Complex. The Secret Crisis of Male Body Obsession*, New York: The Free Press.

Tolson, A. (1987) *The Limits of Masculinity*, London: Routledge.

See also: bodies and biology, male; body image; bodybuilding

MURRAY DRUMMOND

MUSIC

Music impacts issues of masculinity in terms of varying – and, in multicultural contexts, destabilising – culture-specific gender roles and identities, as well as affecting such roles and identities' ties to social performances of masculinity.

Music has been a topic of cultural debate primarily through the conflict over its universality as a medium of expression as opposed to the particularities of its manifestations. Regardless of the genre, cultural context, time period or class affiliation, music is closely aligned with the cultural worldview of the group that performs or consumes it, and the conventions of its performance often overlap with gendered domains of this group.

In vocal music, performance creates a number of complexities. At the macro level, dramatic performances in Western cultures (opera, semi-opera, musical theatre, music videos and most stage performances of popular music) are frequently tied to social issues bound to notions of masculinity: love, sex, infidelity, political tensions, and so forth. This macro level of vocal performance is tied to the narrative of the text being sung, and as such addresses issues more typically aligned with drama. Apart from the narrative, the exigencies of performance raise other tensions.

Performance and stage practices have frequently challenged typical notions of masculinity, such as the cross-dressing of Elizabethan theatre where young men typically played female roles. This practice also existed for dramatic musical performances, such as in 'breeches' roles where women dress in men's clothing (as in the popular film and stage production *Victor/Victoria* but beginning in the Restoration theatre for English works, and earlier in Continental Europe). Cultural requirements for exclusively male performers also necessitated men taking female roles, as in church music across most of Europe. This is a practice that continued after women were allowed to perform in theatres following the Restoration of the monarchy in Britain in 1660, since women were still not permitted to take part in the performance of sacred music. Performers of female roles in sacred dramas, typically without any form of staging (the Oratorio being a dramatic but unstaged sacred work), could range from boy sopranos and altos to adult countertenors or falsettists. The latter begins to illustrate the flexibility of specific notions of masculinity in musical performance, such that the countertenor (a male voice higher than the tenor and different in timbre, more closely resembling the female alto though with a less robust resonance) can take on both male and female roles. On the Restoration stage, a countertenor could appear in drag, but invariably in a comic role. For sacred music, however, countertenors and boy sopranos would frequently perform vocal music associated with a female character. Confusion arises from the more typical North American anachronism of performing such music with female singers. In dramatic performances, the countertenor has also been associated with homosexuality, although this appears to be changing in modern contexts. Moreover, this is not a typical association for the eighteenth century and preceding periods, where the countertenor was associated with roles ranging from the ethereal (as in Purcell's setting of Shakespeare's *The Tempest*, where Ariel is sung by a countertenor) to the heroic (as in Rameau's *Platée*). This vocal type is further confused by ongoing debates over distinctions between countertenors and adult male altos (falsettists), though the legitimacy of this distinction is still contested (DeMarco 2002).

A further issue arises from the now-defunct vocal type of the castrato, a castrated boy who retained the extended upper register while developing the 'masculinity' of a resonating adult body. Castrati performed both secular and sacred music, the last dying in the Vatican in 1921. Roles written for castrati are now typically performed by female altos or mezzo-sopranos or male countertenors, and are occasionally transposed by an octave for male baritones in order to match gender with the character (such as in Handel's *Giulio Ceasare*). Perhaps most famously, Gluck's *Orfeo* was initially written for a castrato in the titular role, but Gluck transposed the role for a male tenor in order to retain the gender of the performer when a castrato was not available.

Nonetheless, the castrati could perform roles of both genders, especially in sacred music where women were not permitted to perform. For instance, the first performance of Handel's *La Resurrezione* (in Rome, 8 April 1708) featured a soprano as Mary Magdalen, but the second performance the next day cast a castrato in the role. Perhaps the most striking feature of the castrati, which has been extensively explored in scholarship, is the combination of androgyny, castration and contemporary erotic appeal. In this era, the castrato appears erotic, both as a personality and in the preponderance of repertoire written for the voice type, in contrast to the modern sense of the castrato being an asexual creature (Scholz 2001; Wassersug 2004). Instead, the castrati were typically cast as heroic, desirable, erotically charged and noble male leads more in line with the typical domain of the modern tenor from the late eighteenth century onward (Freitas 2003).

These are only a few of the instances of versions of masculinity represented in vocal performance in classical music. Modern popular music reflects many of the same tensions. The countertenor is typically an accepted extension of the male vocal range in popular music and has no associations with effeminacy, most often being very much the opposite, especially given the prevalence of the falsetto in rock and pop music. Throughout the jazz era, 'crooners' typically mixed head voice and falsetto in the ballad genre; early rock singers used falsetto as a natural extension of their range rather than using it as a distinct register typifying the singer; and in contemporary pop and rock music it is used by nearly all male vocalists, irrespective of genre. Importantly, these otherwise contextually effeminate vocal practices lose this association in the arena of popular music, pointing to the arbitrary nature of the construction in light of the otherwise masculine image of the male rock star (Young 2004; Nehring 1997). In modern musical theatre, however, the countertenor or any male's extended use of the falsetto is typically a comic role or an extension of a comic character's range, showing that some associations with effeminacy still persist within the same cultural group. Hence, the association is context-sensitive in addition to being culturally specific. Moreover, these distinctions tend to vary cross-culturally as well as within classes and sub-cultures (Magrini 2003; McClary 1991).

In addition to these elements of male vocalisation, the serious study of music (vocal and instrumental) has also been surrounded by questions regarding the role of masculinities. In Western societies, musical training since the eighteenth century has typically been construed as a feminine pursuit, emasculating, and illegitimate in terms of serious academic attention.

This conflicts with the ancient Greek view, where Plato espouses musical education as among the highest pursuits, though later philosophers such as Locke shifted the popular mindset. Musical study has often been denigrated as ephemeral and better suited for women, foreigners and the lower classes (Ahlquist 2004), though this view is by no means universal or independent of class and other social markers. Enjoyment of 'refined' music, such as opera or classical music in general, has also been frequently associated with emasculation or feminisation (Campbell 2003), at least in the North American popular perspective. While these concerns are less pressing before adolescence, music education during and after puberty is notably charged with the increasing demands of gender roles. Pre-adolescents, however, are not exempt from the impact of hegemonic masculinity and its divergence from the biological facts of the early childhood body and voice (Hall 2005). In particular, choral instruction (a mainstay of the education system in the West) reflects the development of perceptions of masculinity and effeminacy, the former being negatively and the latter positively associated with vocal music instruction (Harrison 2004; Koza 1994). Unlike instrumental instruction, such as stage band, where some gender associations are tied to instrument choice, vocal pedagogy also faces the challenges of the physical male body during puberty. As with the challenges to vocal gender norms troubled by the castrati and countertenor, the changing male voice confronts the heteronormative, adult associations of masculine identities (Adler 1999). As a public marker of puberty, the change in voice signals other changes in masculine identity, not the least of which is sexual maturation, leading to the tension over continued singing in this upper register or in the developing falsetto that resembles the pre-pubescent voice.

There is also a smaller body of work that examines gendered representations in musical works (Ford 2000). However, since a given musical trait may be arbitrarily associated negatively or positively with a specific community's notions of masculinities, it is problematic to add the further complexity of musical meaning and aesthetics, which do not enjoy the benefits of explicit reference to real-world objects or ideas. Apart from programmatic music, musical texts are usually non-referential or at least non-representational when divorced from literary texts, though even this varies greatly across cultural groups and time. Therefore, discussions of gender and music generally focus attention on narrative, text, cultural associations with specific practices, the performer as a public figure and potential role, pedagogy and the taboos tied to traditional or counter-normative musical forms. The overarching trend is to see masculinities in musical practices as flexible, subject to change across time, specific to musical genres, culturally embedded and capable of internal contradictions. Stable notions of masculinity are not reliably tied to any specific cross-cultural musical practices or forms, nor do they appear to be stable within cultural groups over time.

References and further reading

Adler, A. (1999) 'A survey of teacher practices in working with male singers before and during the voice change', *Canadian Journal of Research in Music Education*, 40 (4): 29–33.

Ahlquist, K. (2004) 'Masculinity and legitimacy on the English musical stage', *Women and Music*, 8: 1–21.

Campbell, G.J. (2003) 'Classical music and the politics of gender in America, 1900–1925', *American Music*, 21 (3): 446–73.

DeMarco, L.E. (2002) 'The fact of the castrato and the myth of the countertenor', *The Musical Quarterly*, 86 (1): 174–85.

Ford, C. (2000) 'On music and masculinity', in D. B. Scott (ed.) *Music, Culture, and Society*, New York: Oxford University Press, pp. 77–82.

Freitas, R. (2003) 'The eroticism of emasculation', *Journal of Musicology*, 20 (2): 196–249.

Hall, C. (2005) 'Gender and boys' singing in early childhood', *British Journal of Music Education*, 22 (1): 5–20.

Harrison, S.D. (2004) 'Engaging boys, overcoming stereotypes', *Choral Journal*, 2: 24–9.

Koza, J. (1994) 'Big boys don't cry (or sing)', *Quarterly Journal of Music Teaching and Learning*, 4–5 (4–1): pp. 48–63.

McClary, S. [1991] (2002) *Feminine Endings*, Minneapolis, MN: University of Minnesota Press.
Magrini, T. (ed.) (2003) *Music and Gender*, Chicago, IL: University of Chicago Press.
Nehring, N. (1997) *Popular Music, Gender and Postmodernism*, Thousand Oaks, CA: Sage.
Scholz, P.O. (2001) *Eunuchs and Castrati*, translated by J.A. Broadwin and S.L. Frisch, Princeton, NJ: Marcus Weiner.
Wassersug, R. (2004) 'Eunuch power in Old Byzantium', *Gay and Lesbian Review Worldwide*, 11 (3): 18–20.
Young, G. (2004) 'So slide over here', *Popular Music*, 23 (2): 173–93.

See also: culture and representation

JAMES GIFFORD

MYTHOPOETIC MOVEMENT

The mythopoetic men's movement emerged in the United States in the early 1980s. After years of doing New Age spiritualist retreats for groups of women and men, the poet Robert Bly (b. 1926) held his first all-male retreat at the Lama Foundation community in New Mexico in 1980. A similar retreat was held near Mendocino, California, in 1982. A key feature of these gatherings, in addition to being all male, was the use of myth and poetry as tools for self-discovery and personal growth. Less than ten years later, Bly's book *Iron John*, an extended example of using a fairy tale to interpret men's lives, was a national bestseller, and, by one insider estimate, over 100,000 men had attended a mythopoetic event of some kind.

Bly and other leaders of the mythopoetic movement – most notably the archetypal psychologist James Hillman (b. 1926) and the storyteller Michael Meade (b. 1944) – as well as many of the men involved, resisted using the term 'movement' to describe what they were doing. While numerous mythopoetic men's groups sprang up around the United States between the mid-1980s and mid-1990s, there was no national organisation, no uniform doctrine, and no effort to change public policy. The mythopoetic movement thus was not a social movement in the usual sense. It was, more accurately, a collective therapeutic activity that drew men seeking self-change, not social change. What made it of special interest were its Jungian basis, its colourful practices and its implicit gender politics.

The movement received a great deal of media attention in the 1990–1 period, owing largely to Bly's exuberant and charismatic persona. But media were also drawn to the spectacle of mythopoetic activity. Mythopoetic gatherings included not only poetry and the telling of myths and fairy tales, but also drumming, dancing, chanting, mask-making, talking circles, sweat lodges and initiation rituals. What made this all the more curious was that the participants were mostly middle-aged, middle-class, heterosexual white men. This made mythopoetic activity ripe for mockery, as sceptical journalists wondered why participants were whining about their privileged lives and cavorting in the woods like primitive tribesmen.

Sympathetic portrayals of mythopoetic gatherings credited participants with seeking new insight into their lives as men. Participants were said to be exploring the emotions that traditional manhood had forced them to repress and learning how to benefit from connecting emotionally with other men. The men were also portrayed as trying to understand how they had been affected by relationships with their fathers. Seemingly odd mythopoetic practices were then explained as necessary to help men overcome ingrained barriers to emotional exploration and expression. This account of mythopoetic activity was largely correct, though incomplete.

Missing from most popular media accounts of mythopoetic activity was an explanation of its Jungian basis. The Swiss psychologist Carl Jung (1875–1961), once a student of Freud, held that human thought, feeling and behaviour are shaped by psychic energies that take archetypal forms. Insight into individuals, Jung argued, comes from understanding which archetypes are activated and how they are balanced as parts of an integrated Self. Archetypes themselves are not directly observable, but are manifested in recognisable patterns of feeling and behaviour and are given imagistic representation in myths and fairy tales. Examples of the latter are the archetypes of king, warrior, magician, lover and wildman.

According to Jung, when these characters appear in myths, they represent not real people but archetypes that are part of the collective unconscious. The figure of the wise, powerful, generous, protective king thus represents a form that psychic energy can take in any human individual, if the king archetype is activated. Likewise with other named archetypes: each refers to a potentiality that is part of our common evolutionary heritage. By studying myths and fairy tales in which these archetypes are personified, we can begin to understand and realise these potentialities in ourselves. What myths and fairy tales also offer is a dramatic representation of how archetypes relate to each other and the dangers that arise when they are out of balance.

At mythopoetic gatherings it was common for a leader (or 'teacher', as participants preferred to say) to tell a mythological story and ask the men to pay special attention to images that struck a strong emotional chord in them. The idea, based on Jung's psychology, was that a man could gain insight into his own psyche by exploring the emotions evoked by an image. Poetry and poetic images were used in a similar way: to tap into currents of emotion that were otherwise inaccessible to the rational ego. The value of psychic energies discovered through myth and poetry might then be affirmed through initiation rituals. With an understanding of the Jungian theory behind these practices, the practices made a great deal more sense.

Jungian theory, though rarely discussed at mythopoetic gatherings, also gave the mythopoetic movement much of its ideological and therapeutic appeal. Men drawn to mythopoetic activity often complained of emotional numbness, of feeling dispirited and of being 'one-sided' (i.e. overly rational). What the mythopoetic movement promised them, based on Jungian theory, was a path to the complex strengths and energies that were already inside them. The idea that the archetypes of the king, warrior, magician, lover and wildman were present in every man – and just needed activation – was appealing to men experiencing mid-life doldrums.

Another part of the movement's appeal stemmed from its revaluing of the identity 'man'. Many college-educated American men who were in mid-life in the 1980s and 1990s had grown up with the women's movement and were familiar with feminist criticism of patriarchy. This was true of the mythopoetic men, most of whom were sympathetic to liberal feminism. But many of the men had come to feel morally indicted by feminist criticism that seemed, to them, to hold that all men were, by their basic nature, emotionally inept, brutish, violent and dominating. The Jungian basis of mythopoetic activity helped the men deflect this indictment.

One thing that men learned through involvement in the mythopoetic movement was that there is, in all people, the potential for good and evil. Women thus had no monopoly on good, nor men a monopoly on evil. In fact, as Jungian theory had it, there was in all men the potential for enormous good, if only they could activate the positive masculine archetypes that impel constructive behaviour. Men who felt dispirited by meaningless work and beleaguered by feminist criticism found this idea appealing. Through mythopoetic practice, men could discover and realise their essential goodness, thereby revaluing and reinvigorating themselves as men.

Jungian theory also offered appealing ideas about gender. As suggested above, Jungian theory defines some archetypes as masculine, others as feminine. The king, warrior, magician and wildman archetypes represent distinctly masculine psychic energies. While both masculine and feminine psychic energies are found in all people, according to Jungian theory, the masculine archetypes predominate in men, while the feminine archetypes predominate in women. The message men could thus take from mythopoetic philosophy was that all men – no matter how unmacho they appear – are endowed with socially valuable masculine energies.

Most of the mythopoetic men were not in the macho mould. They were indeed critical of 'John Wayne-style' masculinity, which they associated with relentless competition, striving for domination, emotional isolation and ruthless rationalism. They were also men who were gentle and, despite the one-dimensionality imposed on them by their jobs, wanted to be more emotionally alive and connected to others. The problem was that without a sufficiently valued alternative to hegemonic masculinity the mythopoetic men felt unsure of themselves as men. Jungian theory offered the redemptive message that deep inside all men was a noble, constructive masculinity.

Based on Jungian theory, the movement also taught men that the desire to explore and express emotion was not a feminine or womanly desire. Rather, this was said to be part of 'deep masculinity'. The men thus learned that their concerns for emotion did not make them lesser men, but rather men who were further along a path of development. Mythopoetic activities that might otherwise have seemed unmanly – hugging, crying, sharing feelings – were defined as means to cultivate deep masculinity. The mythopoetic movement and its guiding theory thereby allowed men who rejected hegemonic masculinity, largely because of its emotional costs, to feel better about themselves as men for having found, deep in their own psyches, a better form of masculinity. Some Jungians were wary, however, of the form of masculinity nurtured by what they saw as Bly's muddled psychology. Most notably, David Tacey (1997) criticised Bly for engaging in 'patriarchal nostalgia' and for naively idealising the wildman archetype, the inherent primitivity of which, Tacey argued, had 'led to patriarchal excess and compulsiveness in the first place'. Tacey also accused Bly of teaching a distorted Jungianism that led men to dissociate from, rather than to embrace and fully integrate with, the feminine. Most movement participants ignored these backstage disputes, preferring to focus on the entertainment and therapeutic value they could derive from mythopoetic teachers and activities, rather than on doctrinal correctness.

Feminist critics of the mythopoetic movement had several major concerns (Hagan 1992; Kimmel 1995). One was with the movement's theory of gender. Women and men, according to Jungian theory, are different because each sex is naturally endowed with archetypes of different strengths. To feminist critics, this sounded like old-fashioned biological essentialism that ignored the inequalities in power that may lead women and men to think, feel and behave differently. Ignoring these inequalities in power, feminist critics argued, was akin to denying the existence of sexism.

A second concern was with the masculinist imagery vaunted by the movement. The warrior archetype/image was particularly suspect. While mythopoetic teachers and participants argued that this archetype had to do with being resolute and fierce in defence of community – and should not be confused with the soldier archetype – critics saw it as reflecting a typical male desire for power achieved through violence. Other valued archetypes – king, magician, wildman – were also suspect, as they seemed to imply that men were naturally endowed with qualities that specially fitted them to be rulers, rather than equal partners. Conversely, in many of the myths and fairy tales favoured by the movement, women and 'the feminine' were disturbingly represented by images of witches, hags, beautiful princesses and embosoming mothers.

Profeminist men who criticised the mythopoetic movement pointed to the movement's failure to see women's demands for justice as more pressing than the desire of middle-class, heterosexual white men to find psychic comfort within a system that privileged them. They also criticised the mythopoetic men for attributing women's and men's gender troubles to 'sex roles' or to industrialism, rather than to a system of exploitation that disproportionately benefited elite white men. As critics saw it, by failing to challenge capitalist patriarchy, the mythopoetic men failed to confront the system that caused their troubles in the first place, and were doing no better than practising an entertaining form of masculinity therapy.

Despite its small size, the mythopoetic movement dominated national discourse about gender and gender politics in the early 1990s. Millions of people who had never attended a mythopoetic gathering were exposed to the movement's ideas. Bly's *Iron John*, other bestselling books in the mythopoetic genre (e.g. Moore and Gillette's *King, Warrior, Magician, Lover;* Sam Keen's *Fire in the Belly*) and the media coverage given to the movement, raised popular awareness of the emotional costs of traditional masculinity. This in turn evoked debate about how, and whether, men could shed these costs without being part of the anti-feminist backlash. Although mythopoetic practices were often mocked, the movement's claim that even privileged white men had legitimate grievances was taken seriously by proponents of the reactionary men's rights position, by cultural pundits and by some academic feminists.

By the mid-1990s the mythopoetic movement had peaked. Attendance at large gatherings declined after *Iron John* ended its run on the bestseller list and media exhausted their interest in the movement. Efforts to widen the ethnic appeal of the movement by bringing in men of colour to teach at workshops met with marginal success. Still, many veterans of the movement continued to participate in men's groups and attend all-male retreats that used mythopoetic ideas and practices. Though the movement never achieved the same success outside the US, mythopoetic men's groups sprang up in Canada, the United Kingdom, Australia and New Zealand. Halfway through the first decade of the twenty-first century, mythopoetic groups and gatherings still exist, though much less visibly than in the movement's heyday.

References and further reading

Bly, R. (1990) *Iron John*, Reading, MA: Addison-Wesley.

Hagan, K.L. (1992) *Women Respond to the Men's Movement*, San Francisco, CA: HarperCollins.

Harding, C. (ed.) (1992) *Wingspan*, New York: St Martin's.

Hillman, J. (1983) *Archetypal Psychology*, Dallas, TX: Spring.

Keen, S. (1991) *Fire in the Belly*, New York: Bantam.

Kimmel, M. (ed.) (1995) *The Politics of Manhood*, Philadelphia, PA: Temple University Press.

Meade, M. (1993) *Men and the Water of Life*, San Francisco, CA: HarperCollins.

Messner, M. (1997) *Politics of Masculinities*, Thousand Oaks, CA: Sage.

Moore, R. and Gillette, D. (1990) *King, Warrior, Magician, Lover*, New York: HarperCollins.

Newton, J. (2005) *From Panthers to Promise Keepers*, Lanham, MD: Rowman and Littlefield.

Schwalbe, M. (1996) *Unlocking the Iron Cage*, New York: Oxford University Press.

Storr, A. (ed.) (1983) *The Essential Jung*, Princeton, NJ: Princeton University Press.

Tacey, D. (1997) *Remaking Men*, London: Routledge.

Thompson, K. (1982) 'What men really want', *New Age Journal* (May): 30–7, 50–1.

See also: archetypes; Jungian perspectives; masculinity politics; men's groups; men's movement

MICHAEL SCHWALBE

MYTHOPOETIC SUPPORT GROUPS

Mythopoetic groups mainly provide emotional social support to their members, which the members are not receiving from the other institutions in their lives such as family of origin (Barton 2003). These mythopoetic groups provide this support through the use of ritual, sharing myths, writing poetry, psychodrama, guided imagery and drumming (Barton 2000). Men develop a sense of community plus fulfilment of needs (Reddin and Sonn 2003). A second aspect of membership was development of a common set of symbols such as rituals, sharing circles and talking sticks. Third, through these common rituals, emotional safety resulted, creating an environment in which it was safe to be vulnerable, to share, take risks of truth-telling and self-disclosing of personal, often painful, secrets and stories (Reddin and Sonn 2003).

These activities contain experiential educational and psycho-educational aspects and may have an initiatory component such as the New Warrior Training Adventure of the ManKind Project (Pentz 2000) and follow-up support groups, called I-Groups (Mankowski *et al.* 2000). Social supports in these mythopoetic/psycho-educational activities have an important function in supporting change and transformation.

Men benefit from participating in mythopoetic groups by improved relationships with partners and children, increased ability to feel and express emotions, deeper sense of spirituality, developing a sense of community and a willingness to redefine their masculinity, acting differently in the group than the patriarchal macho norm, moving away from patriarchy, and incorporating these changes in their lives. These activities may be easier than traditional therapy for men to participate in and can be effective adjuncts to traditional therapy.

References and further reading

Barton, E.R. (2000) 'Parallels between mythopoetic men's work/men's peer mutual support groups and selected feminist theories', in E.R. Barton (ed.) *Mythopoetic Perspectives of Men's Healing Work*, Westport, CT: Bergin and Garvey, pp. 3–20.

—— (2003) 'A qualitative exploration of participation in men's peer mutual support groups', unpublished doctoral dissertation, Michigan State University.

Mankowski, E.S., Maton, K.I., Burke, C.K., Hoover, S.A. and Anderson, C.W. (2000) 'Collaborative research with a men's organization', in E.R. Barton (ed.) *Mythopoetic Perspectives of Men's Healing Work*, Westport, CT: Bergin and Garvey, pp. 184–203.

Pentz, M. (2000) 'Heuristic and ethnographic study of the ManKind Project', in E.R. Barton (ed.) *Mythopoetic Perspectives of Men's Healing Work*, Westport, CT: Bergin and Garvey, pp. 204–25.

Reddin, J.A. and Sonn, C.A. (2003) 'Masculinity, social support, and sense of community', *Journal of Men's Studies*, 11 (2, Winter): 207–23.

EDWARD READ BARTON

N

NEW MAN

A new man is a male figure characterised in the Western media of the 1980s and 1990s as an emotionally expressive and sensitive man who questioned the traditional gender division of labour and was committed to fatherhood (Messner 1993: 724). Although the exact origins of the term are disputable, the new man was the product of social changes that occurred during the 1970s and 1980s such as second wave feminism, the gay liberation movement, and the rise of the lifestyle press.

In addition to the social vision of the new man, this figure was aligned with consumerism. In North America, the UK and Australia, the media-driven new man was an avid consumer who embodied a narcissistic concern with the body and fashion. Denoting a shift in the representation of the male body, the iconic image of the new man combined strong masculine features with elements of softness, such as developed chest, arm and upper-body muscles with full lips and highly groomed hair and skin (Nixon 1996).

The new man was challenged in the 1990s by the new lad, a reactionary figure largely disseminated through men's lifestyle magazines, such as *Loaded*. Although younger than the new man, the new lad marked a nostalgic revival of old patriarchy, defined by sexism and homophobia. The new lad's pleasure-seeking, hedonistic attitude can be understood as a rebellion against traditional adult male responsibilities such as employment and fatherhood (Gill 2003).

Although not as widespread, a discourse on the new man also emerged a century earlier, in the 1890s. The creation of the New Woman, a radical feminist figure, caused writers to question the possible evolution of a new man. While the new man of the 1890s was an object of satire in the periodical press, many late Victorian feminists, such as Olive Schreiner (1911), optimistically imagined the emergence of this figure.

References and further reading

Gill, R. (2003) 'Power and the production of subjects', in B. Bethan (ed.) *Masculinity and Men's Lifestyle Magazines*, Oxford: Blackwell, pp. 34–56.

Messner, M.A. (1993) '"Changing men" and feminist politics in the United States', *Theory and Society*, 22: 723–37.

Nixon, S. (1996) *Hard Looks*, New York: St Martin's.

Schreiner, O. (1911) *Woman and Labour*, New York: Frederick A. Stokes.

See also: metrosexual; laddism

TARA MACDONALD

NOVEL, THE

The novel, as a literary form, has been closely tied to cultural mores and contemporary social anxieties since its formal inception in the seventeenth century, although it was preceded by the romance genre, which can be regarded in much the same way. Having become a major literary form, and perhaps the most prominent since the eighteenth century, the novel both reflects and is a vehicle for discussing the social and cultural contexts of its own production. Not surprisingly, then, the novel reflects the tensions surrounding normative forms of masculinity, especially during periods of change and conflict.

History

Often regarded as the first modern novel, Cervantes's *Don Quixote de la Mancha* was published in 1605 and satirises the preceding romance genre's courtly ideals – epitomised in the gallant knight, rescuer of ladies in distress – while reinforcing normative masculine identities through the emasculation of its protagonist (Cartegena-Calderón 2000). An important distinction here is the work's rejection of the stylised masculinity of earlier courtly and chivalric romances while concurrently satirising undue attachments to masculine ideals inappropriate on the grounds of age, class, race and social position. In line with this propitious opening to the genre, one of the earliest novels in the English language is Aphra Behn's *Oroonoko*, first published in 1688. With its hero an African slave in the new world, this work reflects the challenges of reconciling contemporary male privilege to racial difference and female authorship (Gruber 2003). This is particularly significant since the work is set and was printed during the politically contentious period of religious and imperial strife that followed the restoration of the monarchy, with its abjected slave hero also reflecting royalist ideals. This combination is indicative of the social pressures often examined in the novel by scholars. Daniel Defoe's *Robinson Crusoe* (1719) explores the same nexus of tensions revolving around relations between men across racial divisions (Haggerty 2005). In this work, Crusoe, a white Englishman, must manage his self-identity when abandoned on an island with only a black male companion, thus anticipating the later interaction between theoretical studies of masculinity, race and postcolonialism. Significantly, these issues, which dominate critical approaches to masculinities in the novel in the 1990s and 2000s, have been with the genre since its inception.

Given the relative voyeurism and sense of transgression in Restoration English literature (1660 to approximately 1700), this focus on the shifting ground of masculine identities is not surprising. However, this contrasts with the English novel in the eighteenth century, where the genre is frequently taken up as a morally didactic medium suitable for feminine pursuits, in terms of both readership and authorship. Richardson's *Pamela: or, Virtue Rewarded* exemplifies this turn well with the subtitle: *Now first published in order to cultivate the Principles of Virtue and Religion in the Minds of the Youth of Both Sexes*. With the novel increasingly seen as a conduct manual, typically for women but also for men, its tone shifts away from the sexual titillation found in some earlier French and English fictions. Nonetheless, the representation and struggle with masculine identities and notions of masculinity remain constant. In the same pattern as *Pamela* (1740) and as the most popular novel of its time, Richardson's *Clarissa* (1747–8) draws a negative example of unsuccessful masculinity in the aristocratic seducer/rapist who violates the pure heroine (Spacks 1995). In contrast, Fielding resists Richardson's didacticism and offers a more ribald though still morally virtuous masculine ideal in the lusty yet generous heroes of *The History of Tom Jones* (1749) and *Joseph Andrews* (1742) (Potter 1998; Bartolomeo 2002). More dramatically, the Marquis de Sade responded to these texts with sexually promiscuous and perverse characters in his novels of the late eighteenth-century.

However, the dominant mode of the eighteenth-century novel was sentimentalism, as seen in Goethe's *The Sorrows of Young Werther* (1774), where the male protagonist, after anguished self-examination, commits suicide, contrary to dominant notions of masculinity

(Brodey 1999). Contrary to the idea that novels simply reflect social anxieties, however, this text prompted imitations in both life and art.

Whereas Gothic novels of the late eighteenth and nineteenth centuries like Radcliffe's *The Mysteries of Udolpho* (1794) and Mary Shelley's *Frankenstein* (1818) featured mysterious or tortured male characters, the nineteenth-century comedy of manners more realistically portrayed men as subjects of economic calculation and as objects seen from the perspective of women seeking appropriate husbands. For example, Austen's most famous novel, *Pride and Prejudice* (1813), excludes private conversations between men that were not readily observed by a woman and thus approaches notions of masculinity only through the public face of male characters (Brinks 2003; Frantz 2003).

The later nineteenth century saw the rise of the popular serial novel, its prime exemplars being Dickens in England and Dumas in France, with their various masculine ideals of a poor boy who goes from rags to riches and swashbuckling comrades wielding their swords to fight side by side.

In the twentieth century, there is an increasing shift to the psychological study of the male subject, such as in the male-centred existentialism of Camus, Dostoyevsky and Kafka, whose male characters brood about the meaning of life, guilt and responsibility. The modernist novel is particularly rich in ties to the predominant social anxieties and predilections of the period and continues to express developing notions of masculinity (Boone 1998; McKracken 2001). The quintessential exemplars of modernism are expressly concerned with gender and the social construction of normative masculine and feminine roles (McKracken 2001). For instance, the change from male to female experienced by the protagonist in Woolf's *Orlando* (1928) requires the reader to examine the role of gender and the behaviours expected of each sex in life and in literature. Lawrence likewise challenges received notions of masculinity through the homoerotic male bonding of the ostensibly heterosexual male protagonists of such novels as *Women in Love* (1920). Miller's *Tropic of Cancer* (1934) became one of the most famously banned books of the twentieth century, prompting a legal battle of greater intensity than either Lawrence's *Lady Chatterley's Lover* (1928) or Joyce's *Ulysses* (1922) (Boheemen-Saaf and Lamos 2001), primarily owing to his satirical representations of American and European masculinity performed through misogyny and sexual conquest. The sexist, apparently unconscious male-centred tendencies of the early modernist novel have been much discussed, while the high modernist novels of the 1940s and 1950s explore the social construction of gender roles more explicitly.

In late colonial and postcolonial novels, race, class, gender and other intercultural points of conflict are shown to intersect with masculinities, and critics have focused upon the connections between sexualities and identity politics that are produced or maintained in hybrid postcolonial societies (Ouzgane and Coleman 1998). In Conrad's *Heart of Darkness* (1902), for example, Kurtz and Marlowe show competing modes of British masculine identity that contrast with the simultaneously denigrated and idealised men of the Belgian Congo. In Gide's *L'Immoraliste* (1902) the feminised French protagonist rediscovers his masculine identity through interactions in Algeria, whereas in Durrell's *The Alexandria Quartet* (1957–60), the recovery of masculinity ironically becomes an express concern of the emasculated narrator although its essential or constructed nature is questioned by homosexual and bisexual male and powerful female characters as well as by gender-indeterminate passages (Boone 1998). Achebe's *Things Fall Apart* (1958) closely examines male and female relationships among the Igbo in pre- and post-contact Africa, as well as gendered constructions of selfhood and colonial relations between men of competing nationality. Ondaatje compares competing interracial conceptualisations about able-bodied and disabled forms of masculinity in *The English Patient*

(1992), while Rushdie's *Fury* (2001) explores the emasculation of middle age from the perspective of male–female relations and the postcolonial migrant's experience in urban and rural societies. All of these novels have been studied with regard to the relationship between postcoloniality and masculinities.

Critical approaches

Studies of the forms of masculinity represented in novels began to seek prominence in the 1980s, most notably with Sedgwick's *Between Men* (1985) and *Epistemology of the Closet* (1992). This points to the emergence of literary studies of masculinities developing within academic gay and lesbian studies and feminist approaches to the novel as a genre. This trend continued through the 1990s and early 2000s. The overlap between literary studies of masculinities with gay and lesbian studies, queer theory and feminism remains significant, as does the generally interdisciplinary nature of masculinities studies based in the arts. Other approaches within literary criticism about masculinities in the novel include single author studies (Boheemen-Saaf and Lamos 2001), those relating to postcolonial masculinities (Ouzgane and Coleman 1998), and studies of modernism as a literary movement (Boone 1998).

The general recent trend in studying masculinities in the novel has been to focus on masculinities and the queer male protagonist or to decipher queer readings of the ostensibly heterosexual male protagonist. Particularly important novels in this trend, apart from pornographic or erotic texts with homoerotic or homosexual materials, such as *Fanny Hill* (1749) and *Teleny* (1890), begin with Wilde's *The Picture of Dorian Gray* (1890). This work ties the protagonist's close bonds with other male characters to Wilde's aestheticism and dandyism, challenging the stereotypical notions of male identity and behaviour of his time (Sedgwick 1992). In the same vein, Mann's novella *Death in Venice* (1912) depicts a similar aesthete also struggling not only with the relationship between masculinity and aging, but also with his late-blooming homoeroticism. Melville's posthumously published novella *Billy Budd* (1924) and Forster's similarly posthumous novel *Maurice* (1971) have also attracted criticism from the joint directions of masculinities studies and of gay and lesbian studies (Sedgwick 1992). Operating against the social taboos that still surround such subjects, such studies have only begun to explore the ties between male bonds generally and men's homoeroticism.

References and further reading

Bartolomeo, J. (2002) *Matched Pairs*, Newark, NJ: University of Delaware Press.

Boheemen-Saaf, C. van and Lamos, C. (eds) (2001) *Masculinities in Joyce*, Amsterdam: Rodolpi.

Boone, J. (1998) *Libidinal Currents*, Chicago, IL: University of Chicago Press.

Brinks, E. (2003) *Gothic Masculinity*, Lewisburg, PA: Bucknell University Press.

Brodey, I.S. (1999) 'Masculinity, sensibility, and the "man of feeling"', *Papers on Language and Literature*, 35 (2): 115–41.

Cartegena-Calderón, J.R. (2000) 'Entre telones masculinos', dissertation, Harvard University.

Frantz, S. (2003) 'Jane Austen's heroes and the great masculine renunciation', *Persuasions*, 25: 165–75.

Gruber, E.D. (2003) 'Dead girls do it better', *Literature, Interpretation, Theory*, 14 (2): 99–117.

Haggerty, G.E. (2005) 'Thank God it's Friday', in M.E. Novak and C. Fisher (eds) *Approaches to Teaching Defoe's Robinson Crusoe*, New York: Modern Language Association, pp. 78–87.

McKracken, S. (2001) 'From performance to public sphere', *Textual Practice*, 15 (1): 47–65.

Ouzgane, L. and Coleman, D. (1998) 'Postcolonial masculinities', Special Issue of *Jouvert*, 2 (1).

Potter, T. (1998) *Honest Sins*, Montréal: McGill-Queen's University Press.

Sedgwick, E.K. (1985) *Between Men*, New York: Columbia University Press.

—— (1992) *Epistemology of the Closet*, Berkeley, CA: University of California Press.

Spacks, P.M. (1995) 'The grand misleader', *Studies in the Literary Imagination*, 28 (1): 7–22.

See also: literature; literary theory

JAMES GIFFORD

O

OBJECT RELATIONS PERSPECTIVES

The first and simplest thing to say about men and object relations theory is that whereas Freud made the father and the Oedipus complex central, object relations theory makes mother and the quality of attachment central. Not only that, but for at least some in the object relations tradition, the young boy's developmental path to manhood is more arduous than the young girl's to womanhood (Chodorow 1978).

Object relations theory is not just one theory, but a range of theories. Leading figures in its development include Melanie Klein, D.W. Winnicott and, more recently, Stephen Mitchell. What this short list plays down is the centrality of women in the founding of object relations theory.

Object relations theory should probably be called simply 'relations theory', for its thesis, shared by all of the above, is that what humans seek is relationships with other humans, at first with parts of other humans, which is one reason it is called 'object' relations theory. The other reason is in deference to Freud's notion of the object of a drive, by which he meant either the real, tangible physical person or thing, or the internal representation, the idea of the object. That the 'object' can be both is the source of almost all of the richness, and much of the confusion, surrounding psychoanalysis in general, and object relations theory in particular.

What does it mean, as far as men and masculinity are concerned, to put women and the quality of mother, rather than father and the Oedipal conflict, at the centre of psychoanalytic theory? For Freud, it is the task of the father to come between the little boy and his mother, so that the little boy might give up his infatuation with his mother until one day he is old enough to marry a girl 'just like the girl who married dear old Dad', as the old song puts it.

For object relations theory the task of the father is to care for the mother, so the mother can care for the child. This view is, of course, terribly old-fashioned, and much can and should be done to bring it up to date. Nevertheless, the key point remains: the father is the second parent, the parent without breasts. This applies primarily to the first twelve to eighteen months of life, a period of time which Freud largely ignored, and which object relations theorists believe is essential. What happens during this time? What happens is the laying down of a psychic foundation that is remarkably subtle and built on paradox.

The ordinary devoted mother, as Winnicott calls her, is with her child so her child can be alone. The process is called attunement, in which a type of emotional mirroring takes place, as the child is comforted when the parent reflects and modulates the child's mood and feeling, often in another modality. For example, mother coos when baby smiles. Attunement is how humans are comforted, their emotional extremes contained, as mother calmly rocks a crying baby. Attunement is comfort beyond, or beneath, words, the first comfort, the first communication. It is through attunement that we learn we are not emotionally isolated in the world.

How, according to object relations theory, does the little boy separate from his mother? By not having had to devote himself to thinking about her all the time, not having to anticipate her moods, whims and desires, so that during this precious time he can just be, imagining that he is the world, that the world is made for him, that there really is no difference, no boundary, between himself and mother. In a flash, this limitless state may become terrifying, and so it is up to mother to neither intrude upon nor abandon her child. Indeed, that is the definition of what Winnicott calls the 'good enough mother'.

Growth, separation, individuation, the little boy becoming a man, and eventually a father who will care for his own wife and child, is from an object relations perspective normal and natural, requiring neither forced separation nor harsh 'make a man out of him' upbringing. Quite the opposite. If the little boy can be one with his mother, while not even having to know that he is 'one with his mother', just that he is 'one', then all the rest will come naturally.

To all this one should add that just as Winnicott talks about the 'good enough mother', perhaps it is time to talk about the 'good enough man', good enough to love his partner man or woman, and perhaps that is enough. If not, then to be a good enough man may include, for some men, becoming that new species, the man who is a 'good enough mother' for his children.

Chodorow argues that because girls physically resemble mothers, they may identify with them rather than separate from them and take the easy path of social conformity and undeveloped identities. In contrast, little boys must struggle painfully, manfully to separate from mother. Perhaps this is so, though this view may reflect a Protestant Ethic of sexual and emotional development, in which not care but pain and hard work are the signs of one's election to maturity. The primary contribution of object relations theory is to remind us that the development of boys to men depends more on love and care than on anything else, including strict fathers, or even the much vaunted male role model.

References and further reading

Alford, C.F. (2005) *Melanie Klein and Critical Social Theory*, reprinted edn, New Haven, CT: Yale University Press.

Chodorow, N. (1978) *The Reproduction of Mothering*, Berkeley, CA: University of California Press.

Dinnerstein, D. (1999) *The Mermaid and the Minotaur*, New York: Other Press.

Greenberg, J. and Mitchell, S. (1983) *Object Relations in Psychoanalytic Theory*, Cambridge, MA: Harvard University Press.

Klein, M. and Riviere, J. (1964) *Love, Hate and Reparation*, New York: W.W. Norton.

Winnicott, D.W. (1971) *Playing and Reality*, London: Routledge.

See also: psychoanalysis

C. FRED ALFORD

OCCUPATIONAL SEGREGATION

'Occupational segregation' (OS) is the distribution of occupations by gender, ethnicity or any other demographic group. Horizontal occupational segregation refers to the concentration of women or minorities into lower-paid 'less prestigious' occupations, and vertical OS to their restriction to lower positions in the hierarchy. Blaxall and Reagan's (1976) seminal work discusses the stratified nature of work, as well as the history and theoretical underpinnings of OS, including Marxist–Feminist and labour market perspectives.

Men's sense of masculinity is deeply related to their participation in paid work; the 'breadwinner' image and its accompanying socio-economic power is iconic to many men. Hegemonic masculinities (elite/white/heterosexual/Western) seek to retain this power for themselves, using the division of labour to relegate women and minorities to lower-paying positions and occupations. This organisational gendering and polarisation is achieved and reified by: (1) valuing hegemonic 'masculine' traits (e.g. rationality and aggression) and associated labour over all others; and (2) devaluing the work done by women and marginalised groups by allocating to it lower remuneration and prestige. Such differential channelling despite similar skills and experience leads to wage gaps, and has provoked arguments for comparable worth, i.e. equal pay for *similar* work (Collinson and Hearn 2005; Kimmel 2000; Acker 1990).

Workplace segregation into 'male' and 'female' professions also creates the following differential experiences. Women in predominantly male professions face the 'glass ceiling', the invisible barrier preventing them from rising beyond a particular professional level. Men in women's occupations experience the 'glass escalator', the invisible track that carries them upwards, pressured by social norms to participate in appropriately 'masculine' roles such as administration or supervision (Williams 1995).

As greater numbers of women and minorities progress up the ranks and enter previously white male domains, desegregation is bound to occur. However, resistance to such change is still visible in many societies, leaving much scope for progress. In this endeavour, we would do well to also promote the egalitarian division of unpaid labour (Kimmel 2000; Acker 1990).

References and further reading

Acker, J. (1990) 'Hierarchies, jobs, bodies', *Gender and Society*, 4 (2): 139–58.

Blaxall, M. and Reagan, B. (1976) *Women and the Workplace*, Chicago, IL: University of Chicago Press.

Collinson, D. and Hearn, J. (2005) 'Men and masculinities in work, organizations, and management', in M. Kimmel, J. Hearn and R. Connell (eds) *Handbook of Studies on Men and Masculinities*, Thousand Oaks, CA: Sage.

Kimmel, M. (2000) *The Gendered Society*, Oxford: Oxford University Press.

Williams, C. (1995) *Still a Man's World*, Berkeley, CA: University of California Press.

See also: class, work and masculinity

VANDANA WADHWA

OEDIPUS COMPLEX

An Oedipus complex (OC) is a constellation of loving and hostile thoughts and feelings that the young child experiences towards his parents as a consequence of his psychosexual development. It was named by Sigmund Freud after the mythical figure Oedipus, who committed patricide and incest when he unwittingly killed his father and married his mother; whether the child resolves or fails to resolve his OC will determine his personality, sexual orientation and masculine identity.

Children experience both sexual and aggressive feelings, and how these manifest in the relationship with their parents will shape the specific form of the OC. Freud identified various forms that the complex may assume. In its so-called *positive* form, the child wishes to have exclusive emotional and physical possession of his mother, displays jealousy towards his father, and wishes to exterminate this paternal rival for mother's affection. The second, *negative*, variation is the inverse, with father being the homosexual object of the son's affectionate longings, and mother the hated rival. The third, most common, variation is the *complete* OC. This comprises both negative and positive attitudes towards both parents, based on the child's *constitutional bisexuality*. He experiences sexual desire for both mother and father and, during the course of his development, sets up both parents as antagonistic rivals at different times.

Resolution of the OC is typically motivated by fear that his father will punish his sexual and aggressive wishes by castrating him, and/or concern that his rivalrous antagonism towards his father will result in the loss of an ambivalent, but valued, relationship with a needed paternal figure.

Resolution is accomplished by the child renouncing his desire for his mother, while simultaneously internalising and *identifying* with his father. In this way the child's masculine identity is formed through the installation of father as a prohibitive, but also loving, internal authority. The important consequence of this identification is a psychic structure called the *super-ego*, which is the moral agency that serves as the source of self-observation, values, conscience and guilt feelings. Failure to resolve the OC results in intrapsychic conflict, and the OC's mere *repression* and subsequent pathological unconscious manifestation in later life.

References and further reading

Freud, S. [1923a] (1961) 'The ego and the id', *Standard Edition of the Complete Psychological Works of Sigmund Freud* (*SE*), Vol. 19, London: Hogarth, pp. 3–66.

—— [1923b] (1961) 'The infantile genital organization', *SE*, Vol. 19, London: Hogarth, pp. 141–5.

—— [1924] (1961) 'The dissolution of the Oedipus complex', *SE*, Vol. 19, London: Hogarth, pp. 173–9.

See also: Jungian perspectives; object relations perspectives; psychoanalysis

GAVIN IVEY

OPPRESSION

The essence of oppression is an asymmetrical dynamic between oppressors or structures of oppression that exercise unjust power, on the one hand, and those who suffer oppression, on the other. Oppression is often presented as a systematic, overarching force that subjugates groups and dehumanises or even demonises people. Some also refer to 'internalised oppression' whereby individuals or targeted groups incorporate hateful or demeaning images as part of their identities. Oppression is pervasive in society, disguised and distorted through ideologies of social advancement that claim discrimination is the exception, not the norm (Thompson 2003). Oppressive practices include activities associated with injustice, cruelty and subservience, often involving large institutions such as government, culture and education, and affecting groups of people more than individuals. Oppression has been defined as 'a social dynamic in which certain ways of being in this world – including certain ways of identifying or being identified – are normalised or privileged while other ways are disadvantaged or marginalised. Oppression includes 'racism, classism, sexism, heterosexism, anti-Semitism, ableism, colonialism . . .' (Center for Anti-Oppressive Education 2006). Young (1990) lists exploitation, marginalisation, powerlessness, systematic violence and cultural imperialism as five kinds of oppression, and presents women's oppression as 'a systematic and unreciprocated transfer of powers from women to men' (1990: 51).

The concept of oppression is central to masculinities theory and many other critical perspectives in contemporary scholarship and activism. In masculinities theory, the specific concept of oppression is often missing or implicit although it has been addressed at length by Hearn (1987). The men's movement has grappled with a legacy of misogynistic norms, policies and laws that explicitly or implicitly condone violent and hateful actions against women (Pease 2000). This pro-feminist view involves a recognition of patriarchal power and privilege exercised by many, if not all, men. There is a growing body of work about how masculinities theory can complement feminist theories and practices and how men's and women's rights and needed reforms could be realised through pro-feminist strategies (Young 1993).

Patriarchal power is seen as so ubiquitous in society that one feminist fiction writer, Marilyn French (1977), caricatured a feminist position as follows: 'All men are rapists . . . They rape us with their eyes, their laws, and their codes.' A counterpoint to the men-as-oppressors approach involves the viewpoint that men are oppressed and suggests how men might resist various forms of oppression to achieve men's liberation (Nichols 1975). Some scholars credit the women's movement for challenging and changing some aspects of our androcentric world yet argue that popular feminism promotes contempt for and suspicion of men (Nathanson and Young 2001: 6–8).

Ongoing work in masculinities theory has, however, moved well beyond a point-counterpoint approach. Researchers and activists concerned with how men or women are oppressed in given situations draw on more nuanced analyses of complex 'intersectionalities' played out within hierarchies of power. The social construction of 'hegemonic masculinity' can be both empowering and limiting for men, and men can act as agents of oppression against other men and against women. Others concentrate on men at particular risk of oppressive practices. Oppression may be directed towards sexual orientation, disability, race or ethno-cultural groupings, social class or a host of other factors (Hearn 1992). Tolerance of 'gay bashing' can be reflected in inadequate police, prosecutorial and judicial responses (Janoff 2005). Oppression may take the form of fathers belittling or attacking their sons (Pease 2000) or 'fat oppression' where morbidly obese men are subject to ostracism and discrimination (Longhurst 2005).

Some fathers' rights groups criticise family law as an institutionalised form of oppression, claiming systemic bias against fathers in divorce situations. Much of the work in masculinities theory cautions against insupportable claims of discrimination against men and explicitly warns against thinly disguised anti-feminist efforts designed to dismantle feminist gains in law, social policy and society in general. Critics of a men-as-victims motif point out how spousal violence and intimidation continue to be exercised by males against women in the family law sphere and other contexts. Moreover, loss of power or privilege is not necessarily a sign of oppression.

In summary, oppression is best understood as an expression of structural power that serves to exploit and demean targeted populations. Anti-oppression initiatives are fundamental to liberation efforts linked with gender, sexuality, race, social class and other factors. In masculinities theory, recognition of men's oppressive practices is essential in early consciousness-raising work and in ongoing studies of hierarchies of oppression and intersections of factors in men's experience of – and possible resistance to – oppressive forces.

References and further reading

Center for Anti-Oppressive Education http://www.antioppressiveeducation.org/index.html (accessed 27 July 2006; definition adapted from writing by K. Kumashiro).

French, M. (1977) *The Women's Room*, New York: Summit.

Hearn, J. (1987) *The Gender of Oppression*, Sussex: Wheatsheaf.

—— (1992) *Men in the Public Eye*, New York: Routledge.

Janoff, D.V. (2005) *Pink Blood*, Toronto: University of Toronto Press.

Longhurst, R. (2005) '"Man-breasts"', in B. van Hoven and K. Hörschelmann (eds) *Spaces of Masculinity*, New York: Routledge, pp. 165–78.

Nathanson, P. and Young, K. (2001) *Spreading Misandry*, Montreal/Kingston: McGill-Queen's University Press.

Nichols, J. (1975) *Men's Liberation*, Harmondsworth: Penguin.

Pease, B. (2000) *Recreating Men*, London: Sage.

Thompson, N. (2003) *Promoting Equality*, 2nd edn, New York: Palgrave Macmillan.

Young, B. (1993) 'Feminism and masculinities', in T. Haddad (ed.) *Men and Masculinities*, Toronto: Canadian Scholars' Press, pp. 315–32.

Young, I.M. (1990) *Justice and the Politics of Difference*, Princeton, NJ: Princeton University Press.

See also: patriarchy; privilege; sexism

BRIAN BURTCH

ORGANISATIONS, GENDERED

In the USA, Australasian countries and western Europe, research has been concerned to locate women's experience in the context of the paid labour market and to advance our understanding of women's continued differential status in terms of pay and employment opportunities. Women's shattering the 'glass ceiling' is seen as an outcrop of this move into the workplace and of their increased presence in decision-making, although the extent to which women now occupy positions of seniority differs across organisations and between countries. From a liberal perspective, the assumption has been twofold: that women's presence may facilitate a shift in organisational cultures and level the playing field upon which men and women compete for posts in the paid labour market; that in using women's hitherto untapped talent, a 'business case' can be made where managerial interests to reduce costs and improve efficiency can equate with equity and fairness. Liberal arguments dominate within management literature. Here, access to jobs in the capitalist marketplace and to positions of management is regarded as desirable, and the overarching aim is to remove the barriers to women's fuller economic participation. The underlying economic argument is that lost talent equates with lost business. Liberal arguments are criticised because they focus on hierarchically senior women; issues of class, race, ethnicity, sexual orientation, age and disability are overlooked; the outcomes tend to 'tokenism' not substantive change; organisational cultures are less amenable to change than is assumed by liberal commentators; and notions of competitiveness within existing structures are merely downplayed or denied rather than rendered inherently problematic.

In the Anglo-American context, the transformation in management theory and practices towards greater entrepreneurialism on the part of managers and employees has signalled the demise of the manager as a rule-bound, hierarchically driven and controlled 'organisation man'. The philosophy of 'modern' management in the developed West has shifted from a preoccupation with regulating aspects of the employment relationship in large bureaucracies towards practices seen as enhancing the commitment and co-operation of managerial and other employees in the direction of the consumer. For managers, the drive to apprehend the ultimate 'value-added' of employees by means of harnessing their creative potential has led to the call for managers to access what are held to be their so-called feminine qualities in the name of 'better' management under the rubric of 'modernisation, marketisation and managerialism'. The study of the gendered organisation has thus been sustained partly by managerial and practitioner interest in finding ways of feminising organisations and their managements.

Despite successive waves of legislation across nations (it is over thirty years since the Sex Discrimination Act in the UK, for example), organisations remain gendered in that the type of jobs women do varies within and between different sectors, across different industries. Women remain employed in large numbers in lower-hierarchy jobs: the status of women's work is such that many occupy low-status work, and remain associated with service or support functions such as cleaning or care work. Their work is frequently part-time, contract or unregistered work. Moreover, women's work role and status is often an expression of underlying power relations surrounding particular jobs, where the definition of work is unclear. Nursing and even secretarial work embody specific, and often themselves gendered, understandings of 'caring', for instance, which combine to affect women and men differently and affect the very definition of what counts as work. This distinction alerts us to the differing definitions of work across the public and private spheres. Housework goes unpaid and is seldom defined as work, whereas the (broadly similar) activities in the public sphere of employment, such as office cleaning, take place in the paid economy and are defined as 'work'.

The shifting definition of work alerts us to the concept of work as a gendered construct. From this perspective, gender is not biologically determined but socially constructed. Contemporary analysis of the gendered organisation thus provides a way of exploring the processes of how gender difference in organisations is reproduced and sustained. A recent turn is the study of identity. Although not confined solely to the analysis of gender, the work on identity has implications for the way in which commentators and theorists have come to explore the everyday dynamics of organisational life. The study of identity challenges the theoretical and methodological accounts developed by liberals, rather than merely reproducing essentialist and positivist understandings of gender.

Of particular concern is the operation of 'femininity' and 'masculinity' and their relationship to gender and gendering in organisations. Associated with poststructuralism, the theorisation of Michel Foucault on subjectivity and identity, of Judith Butler on gender identity and, more latterly, Gherardi on gender and organisational culture, this theoretical turn suggests identity is not fixed but performed. Here, identity is conceived of as a 'structure in formation', always in dynamic process and having no essential unity outside of the particular locale in which meanings and behaviours are constituted. From this perspective, identities are performed in work and 'masculinity' and 'femininity' have no core or essence but exist in the everyday interactions of organisations. This development has triggered reflection on narrow, essentialist, binary understandings of gender, and advanced the study of 'diversity' and how 'difference' is experienced by organisational members (people) themselves. From this perspective, organisations are gendered in that identities must be made and remade as an ongoing project of the self where people attempt to build identities to avoid insecurity. The search for a secure identity extends beyond the organisation to encompass discourses – ways of thinking and behaving – surrounding the way we consume goods and services, our behaviour in relationships, the way we dress, drink, eat, form friendships and relationships and so on. The extent to which this process is all-embracing is contested: some academic writers argue that the debate turns on the extent to which employees as human beings resist and transform the very processes of identity formation (see Hatch 1997 for discussion) within which they are embedded and embodied as subjects in, and subjects of, the gendered organisation.

References and further reading

Butler, J. (1990) *Gender Trouble*, London: Routledge.

Foucault, M. (1980) *Power/Knowledge*, edited by C. Gordon, Brighton: Harvester Wheatsheaf.

Gherardi, S. (1995) *Gender, Symbolism and Organisational Cultures*, London: Sage.

Hatch, M.J. (1997) *Organization Theory*, Oxford: Oxford University Press.

See also: class, work and masculinity

DEBORAH KERFOOT

ORGASM

Orgasm is the climax of sexual pleasure (coming, ecstasy), from Greek *orgaô*, 'swell, radiate with desire'. Masters and Johnson established a four-phase cycle of human sexual response: excitement, plateau, orgasm and resolution. During plateau, women's outer third of the vagina swells ('orgasmic platform'). During both male and female orgasm, diverse genital parts contract rhythmically at intervals of 0.8 seconds (three to fifteen times); cramping, moaning, crying or laughing is mostly more uninhibited in women due to stronger expectations of male self-control. Since antiquity, women's experience has been held to be more intense (Ovid, *Metamorphoses* III: 320–39).

Male orgasm usually occurs with ejaculation. First vas deferens, prostate, seminal vesicles and anal sphincter contract; seminal fluid is pumped into the urethra, experienced as the inevitable imminence of ejaculation. In the second phase, rhythmic contractions of prostate, anal sphincter, urethra and penis propel the semen to external ejaculation. The bladder's internal sphincter is shut to prevent the semen from entering ('retrograde ejaculation'). Orgasm without ejaculation ('dry orgasm') is normal in boys before puberty, and may happen among adult men in cases of a diseased or operated prostate or as an intended effect of certain techniques. Present pornography and male imagery are often centred on ejaculation as the goal of sexual activity. On the contrary, sexual therapies stress the subjective experience of non-orgasmic and orgasmic pleasure, potentially without ejaculation. Anal penetration of a man may cause his instant ejaculation due to the prostate's stimulation or the rectal sphincter's relaxation.

According to the Hite report, many women experience the plateau as a goal in itself and need to stay there longer in order to orgasm, with most men but only 13–16 per cent of women experiencing orgasm during heterosexual intercourse. After ejaculation, men inevitably enter the 'refractory period' while women may stay on the plateau and have orgasms repeatedly. Male multi-orgasmic potential needs training to avoid the second phase of orgasm or external ejaculation. Spiritual and therapeutic schools addressing sexuality frequently integrate Eastern spiritualities (Taoism, Tantrism), recommending complete abstention from the 'loss of semen' and multiple orgasms in order to reach a wider 'transcendental' consciousness.

References and further reading

Masters, W.H., Johnson, V.E., and Kolodny, R.C. (1988) *Masters and Johnson on Sex and Human Loving*, Boston, MA, Toronto and London: Little, Brown.

Hite, S. (2000) *The New Hite Report*, London: Hamlyn.

See also: impotence and sexual dysfunction; male sex drive; phallocentrism; semen anxiety

MICHAEL GRONEBERG

P

PATRIARCHAL DIVIDEND

Patriarchal dividend is the notion that patriarchy privileges most men, regardless of their particular location within, or support for, the hegemonic system of male domination.

The concept of patriarchy became prominent within the social sciences and beyond from the early 1970s, from when it was popularly used to describe men's domination over women across all aspects of the social world. Promoted especially within the second wave of feminism, the concept of patriarchy was adopted as a theoretical tool within most of the key strands of feminist thought at that time (see Tong 1993). From these beginnings, the concept became widely taken up within the developing critical study of men (for example, Hearn 1987). Although since subjected to significant critique as a theoretical tool by both feminist and pro-feminist writers (for example, Pollert 1996; Whitehead 2002), the concept of patriarchy continues to be of use in describing and critiquing male domination.

One of the most important and compelling arguments for continuing to use the notion of patriarchy is that its presence signals that most men are advantaged over most women as a result of their gender. Being a man brings with it certain privileges. Connell highlighted this condition of patriarchy in her groundbreaking work *Masculinities* (1995) in which she explores the patriarchal dividend. Connell recognises that while not all men relate to hegemonic ways of being a man in exactly the same ways, 'the majority of men gain from its [masculinity] hegemony, since they benefit from the patriarchal dividend, the advantage men in general gain from the overall subordination of women' (1995: 79).

For Connell, individual men do not necessarily have to consciously or actively support patriarchy or its practices: it is enough that they are men for them reap the benefits that patriarchy bestows on them as members of this gender group. Therefore, to some degree, all men may be complicit in sustaining patriarchy, not least because there is a benefit to them in doing so. As Connell puts it, not all men need be 'frontline troops for patriarchy', though many may be. Likewise, while some men may indeed be marginalised, both economically and socially, their embodiment as males/men triggers for them a potential advantage over women. This advantage may usually be material, but it is also underpinned by violence or its threat, the reason being that violence is almost always a male practice and as such most men carry that threat with them of being rapists, abusers, assaulters of women (and other men). So whatever material advantages men may reap, such benefits are, to some degree, underpinned by the threat, overt or covert, of male violence, whether it is organised and premeditated, or individual and random.

The patriarchal dividend is most visible in the fact of men's dominance across the public world. For example, men are more likely than women to be senior executives of multinational corporations, leading politicians and heads of state, army and police force commanders, and self-employed entrepreneurs. Being a man clearly carries an advantage in respect of them being perceived to be 'natural' leaders, managers and authority figures. A further material advantage to being a man manifests itself in the fact that whether in full or part-time work, men continue to be paid more than women for doing the same jobs as them.

So while some individual men may experience severe social and economic marginalisation, and others may be actively against women's oppression and relate to women in equitable ways, the concept of the patriarchal dividend alerts us to the macro conditions which continue to inform women's and men's experiences as members of distinct political gendered categories.

However, the concept of a patriarchal dividend is only really effective if we explore gender at a macro level and if we ignore the costs to men of certain forms of masculinity. For example, the patriarchal dividend tends to reinforce, if inadvertently, a notion of gender as ultimately a zero-sum game, one which can only be won by either men or women, not both. This approach works best if we are emphasising the material disadvantages which women experience as a result of their gender and recognise that there are finite resources available, e.g. material wealth or time, to both genders. For this there is compelling evidence. However, the material is only one aspect of gendered realities: the other is the emotional, and at this level the patriarchal dividend appears less helpful. For example, men are more likely to commit suicide than women, more likely to be living alone and socially isolated than women, and more likely to die younger than their female counterparts. So if one stays with the idea of patriarchy, which one must do in order to use the term 'patriarchal dividend', then one must respond to the evidence that even on its own terms, patriarchy is not overwhelmingly successful in advantaging all men (Faludi 1999). Not only that, but women increasingly challenge assumed male dominance wherever it is manifest, and resist its imposition. This critique becomes even stronger once we move away from a macro and to a micro perspective. There can be little arguing against the idea that men and women occupy distinct gendered political categories, but the ways in which individual women and men experience and negotiate whatever dividends/penalties may arise from location in these categories cannot be assumed. In other words, we might wish to continue to use terms such as 'patriarchy' and 'patriarchal dividend' to highlight men's oppression of women, but at a qualitative, subjective level, the terms may be considered too crude to offer insights into an individual's lived experience.

References and further reading

Connell, R. (1995) *Masculinities*, Cambridge: Polity

Faludi, S. (1999) *Stiffed: The Betrayal of the Modern Man*, London: Chatto and Windus.

Hearn, J. (1987) *The Gender of Oppression*, Brighton: Wheatsheaf.

Pollert, A. (1996) 'Gender and class revisited: or, the poverty of "patriarchy"', *Sociology*, 30 (4): 639–60.

Tong, R. (1993) *Feminist Thought*, London: Routledge.

Whitehead, S.M. (2002) *Men and Masculinities: Key Themes and New Directions*, Cambridge: Polity.

See also: complicit masculinity; men's interests; oppression; patriarchy; power relations; privilege.

STEPHEN M. WHITEHEAD

PATRIARCHY

Literally the rule of the law of the father, patriarchy designates structural dominance of women by men in all aspects of life, including the political, social, economic and legal realms. The early critical work on patriarchy has been largely the effort of feminist critics, who traced its origins to social constructions of masculinity and femininity, a division based upon biological differences that valorised male physical strength. Since the family is considered patriarchy's main paradigm, feminist theories have especially relied on the contributions of Sigmund Freud, in whose work paternity is at the centre of a power axis.

More recently, studies of masculinity also consider patriarchy as a power structure, calling attention to the limitations of the concept in defining masculinity and in defining patriarchal male identity as dominant masculinity. While patriarchy presents male dominance as historical, the idea of the father as a powerful cultural symbol and site of contestation has remained throughout historical and social conflicts and textual productions. This idea is already present in myth and religious tradition. Abraham's story in the Bible centres on paternity, on Abraham's desire to have a son. Even the name of Abraham etymologically denotes fatherhood ('father of a multitude') to a varied (and conflicting) collectivity (Genesis 17: 5). This religious myth has been significant in the construction of patriarchal masculinity in the Judeo-Christian and Islamic traditions.

Writers and critics – from Kafka to Darwish, and from Benjamin to Schwartz – have expressed the need to textually re-envision the inherited figure of Abraham, since his story combines nationalist and religious constructions of identity and forges collective identity by way of submission to the authority of the father and exclusion of the other. In the Old Testament, paternity guarantees inheritance of home and identity, but through the dispossession of others (Genesis 12: 1–7). The critics suggest that this long literary heritage speaks of dispossession and exclusion and enacts those predicaments historically through repeated readings of such inherited myths. According to Schwartz, Abraham ultimately promotes dissension rather than community (Schwartz 1997). The critics reconsider early forms of these monotheistic myths in order to explore new ways of thinking about identity. Some, like Djebar, invoke the memory of Abraham to recall Hagar's repudiation and the overall exclusion of women, while others such as Darwish invoke the father who exiles, who sacrifices the future for the past.

Abraham is henceforth seen as a figure of the double bind who marks the conflict between divine commands and communal duties. His paternity is already in question in the biblical story, even as it is being consolidated. Abraham furthermore emerges as a figure of ambivalence – as father and as rebelling son destroying the idols worshipped by his forefathers – who will become in Islamic readings the father of submission to divine will (The Koran 37: 109).

As the Abraham story and studies on masculinities illustrate, the foundation upon which the claim to paternity is made is never secure. The valorisation of paternity creates a certain family order out of unstable elements: the father's claim to paternity has to be shared with another being; the mother is rendered absent; and the future of the son is offered to the past – that is, to God. This is the heritage of paternity received as social (and political order) from the myth of Abraham filtered through various traditional accounts.

Lacan, in his lecture 'Les noms du père', reconsiders the father as origin. Instead, the father is revealed as both absent and plural: the absence of the father is ultimately an indication of an absence of authority. The father is incapable of preventing the sacrifice of the son, which is the source of the son's trauma. The invocation of the father will henceforth be an attribution of responsibility. The father is also plural, where alongside Abraham other fathers of the Old Testament continue to live. It is noteworthy that the ending of Genesis 22 establishes the patriarchal lineage through Abraham's brother Nahor, 'as if Isaac had ceased to exist' (Delaney 1998: 124).

While patriarchy as a cultural system is contradictory and far from monolithic, as recent masculinity (and feminist) studies suggest, historically it has represented for many feminist theorists the systematic dominance of men over women. Such an approach, critics such as Shepard contend, does not place enough emphasis on other dimensions of patriarchy, such as generational domination.

While some critics have posed the question as to whether patriarchy is still relevant, others consider patriarchy useful in revealing 'the masculine intent to dominate through the creation of law, the military, marriage, family, and other institutions' (Petergrew 2003: 141).

Recent work by anthropologist Joseph has called into question even the primacy of the father–son power axis in patriarchy, arguing instead that 'the real foundation of patriarchy in Arab societies comes not from the relationship of children to their parents, but from the socialisation of brothers and sisters, in which siblings of the opposite sex learn their sexual roles by 'rehearsing' for each other' (cited in Armburst 2000: 214).

References and further reading

Armburst, W. (2000) 'Farid Shauqi', in M. Ghassoub and E. Sinclair-Webb (eds) *Imagined Masculinities*, London: Saqi.

Delaney, C. (1998) *Abraham on Trial*, Princeton, NJ: Princeton University Press.

Joseph, S. (1994) 'Brother/sister relationships', *American Ethnologist*, 21 (1): 50–73.

Lacan, J. (1963) (Séance) 'Les noms du père', 20 Novembre, Montréal: École Lacanienne de Montréal; available at http://www.elm.qc.ca

Petergrew, J. (2003) 'Deepening the history of masculinity and the sexes', *American History* 31 (1): 135–42.

Schwartz, R.M. (1997) *The Curse of Cain*, Chicago, IL: University of Chicago Press.

Schwenger, P. (1994) 'Barthelme, Freud, and the killing of Kafka's father', in P.F. Murphy (ed.) *Fictions of Masculinity*, New York: New York University Press.

Shepard, A. (2003) *Meaning of Manhood in Early Modern England*, Oxford: Oxford University Press.

Walby, S. (1990) *Theorizing Patriarchy*, Oxford: Oxford University Press.

See also: oppression; power relations; privilege

NAJAT RAHMAN

PEDAGOGY

College and university courses on men and masculinity have found their home within three institutional locations: men's studies, women's studies and gender studies programmes. Even though men's studies has developed on the feminist model of women's studies programmes, there has been some concern about the politics of mounting courses on men and masculinity. Hasn't the general university curriculum always been focused on men and masculinity, with an interest in women pushed into an interdisciplinary enclave, critics ask. This objection can be met rather easily by noting that, while traditional disciplinary curricula have emphasised the contributions, history and theories of men, little attention has been devoted to an analysis of men as men and of social constructions of masculinity. Men's studies programmes, especially in the United States, typically offer an interdisciplinary range of courses, most geared towards disrupting the seamless equation between men and 'mankind'. Such courses have been welcomed by feminist scholars and by all scholars interested in tracing the causes and effects of a gender system that distributes power unevenly. Men's studies programmes often pay a great deal of attention to marginalised men, to masculinities (as opposed to masculinity), and to the social, cultural and political effects of gender ideologies. Harry Brod has been the scholar most responsible for theorising the importance of men's studies to the larger feminist project. Most recently, Brod has made the argument that thinking of men's studies as 'superordinate studies' enables us to think more cogently about the social construction of group identities and the ways in which privileges attach to particular groups. For example, noting that much has been said about the feminisation of poverty, but nothing about the masculinisation of wealth, Brod suggests that a slight change in perspective can help to denaturalise gender categories and to work towards real social change.

In settings where men's studies programmes do not exist, courses on men and masculinity can be taught within women's studies programmes, an arrangement not without its own complicated theoretical and political challenges.

Women's studies programmes originally arose to reverse a history of absence; women's studies was necessary precisely because traditional disciplinary curricula focused on men. Given this mandate, it is perhaps not surprising that women's studies developed a politics dependent on the linkage between men and patriarchy. Women's studies needed men, not so much to complicate and enrich its own analysis of gender, but as the force against which to fight, the enemy, as it were. While it is certainly true that women's studies programmes have moved far away from a simplistic accounting of the power of patriarchy as it affects individuals and groups, it is still the case that women's studies pedagogy often remains indebted to an oppressor/oppressed paradigm. In the classroom, the oppressor/oppressed paradigm limits what can be learned about men and masculinity, because it sets up a binary relation between the empowered and the disempowered that causes sceptical students and faculty to wonder how the study of men fits into a discipline that has focused its energy on remedying historical absences and theorising the effects of patriarchy on those most obviously disempowered or victimised by it. Teaching courses on men and masculinity within women's studies programmes makes visible the fact that men's studies and women's studies are not, and should not, be complementary; men and women have, quite simply, enjoyed vastly different relationships to male power and dominance. This insight is a useful starting point for anyone interested in offering courses on men and masculinity within women's studies programmes.

The most common institutional home for courses on men and masculinity is the gender studies programme, a relatively recent mutation of women's studies, and sometimes expressly designed to accommodate the study of men and masculinity alongside the study of women. Far more controversial than the simple adding on of men's studies to already existing women's studies curricula, the move to replace women's studies with gender studies has occasioned a lively and sometimes rancorous debate among feminist scholars. Bryce Traister wonders whether the new interest in masculinity is another example of men trying to remain centre stage, while Tania Modleski worries that the move away from women and to gender obscures the asymmetry of power within patriarchal systems. Robyn Wiegman notes that, in the US at the turn of the century, the move from Women's to gender studies must also be understood as part of a larger climate of anti-affirmative action; from this perspective, gender studies ameliorates the 'exclusion' of men from women's studies. But the move to gender studies, some would argue, makes it possible to expand the field of study to include not only men and masculinity, but also queer theory, transgender and transsexual studies. Thinking about gender as something more than an identity – as something other than the individual qualities that comprise masculinity and femininity – enables us to focus on the institutionalisation of gender as a system of meaning that intersects with other systems of meaning. The question of where the study of men and masculinity fits into the overall production of knowledge about gender is not yet settled, and perhaps this instability is a measure of the field's vitality.

References and further reading

Brod, H. (1987) 'The case for Men's Studies', in H. Brod (ed.) *The Making of Masculinities*, Boston and London: Unwin Hyman.

—— (2002) 'Studying masculinities as superordinate studies', in J.K. Gardiner (ed.) *Masculinity Studies and Feminist Theory: New Directions*, New York: Columbia University Press.

Modleski, T. (1991) *Feminism without Women*, New York and London: Routledge.

Wiegman, R. (2002) 'The progress of gender', in R. Wiegman (ed.) *Women's Studies on its Own: A Next Wave Reader*, Durham, NC and London: Duke University Press.

See also: women's studies/gender studies/feminist studies

SALLY ROBINSON

PEDERASTY

Pederasty refers to homosexual desire or love between an adult male and a boy who is usually aged between twelve and seventeen. Pederasty has been a very common mode of homosexual interaction across time and cultures. Dover's book *Greek Homosexuality* describes how ancient Greek civilisation was notable for its acceptance of homosexual love between an adult male known as an *erastes* and a *paides*, or a boy in the early stages of puberty. Leupp's book *Male Colors* demonstrates that Japan, too, had a well-attested tradition of pederasty between adult samurai known as *nenja* and their youthful retainers or *wakashu* in the early modern period (1600 to 1856). In some tribal societies, such as the Sambia studied by Herdt (1997), pederastic relationships between men and boys were an obligatory part of male initiation rites. All these examples involved ongoing relationships which generally lasted until the boy was accorded adult status and either married or took a boy lover of his own. The relationships between the adults and the youths were frequently acknowledged by the wider society but, unlike marriage, were considered temporary, albeit an integral part of growing up. Such pederastic relationships did not confer a fixed 'homosexual' status on either party but were entered into by men and boys in general.

Unlike in some ancient and tribal societies where pederasty was an acceptable relationship with its own strict etiquette and rules of conduct, in the modern world it has come to be almost universally despised as one of the most serious of sexual crimes. Organisations such as the North American Man/Boy Love Association (NAMBLA), while condemning child sexual abuse, have tried to rehabilitate the practice through appeal to its widespread popularity over time and across cultures. Gay organisations, however, tend to distance themselves from NAMBLA because of the extreme stigma now associated with both pederasty and paedophilia (sex between adults and children of either sex). Discussion of pederasty has become almost impossible in the public sphere although there are books such as Eglinton's *Greek Love* and movies such as Kerbosch's *For a Lost Soldier* which portray love between adult men and male youths as mutual and beneficial for both parties.

References and further reading

Dover, K. (1979) *Greek Homosexuality*, London: Gerald Duckworth.

Eglinton, J. (1971) *Greek Love*, London: Spearman.

Herdt, G. (1997) *Same Sex, Different Cultures*, Boulder, CO: Westview.

Leupp, G. (1995) *Male Colors*, Berkeley, CA: University of California Press.

See also: child abuse; commercial sexual exploitation of children; homosexuality; violence

MARK MCLELLAND

PENETRATION

Penetration is widely accepted as evidence of the accomplishment of sex. In Freudian terms, normative sex is the joining of the male and female genitalia. Penetration of the woman by the man must be the end result of any sexual foreplay. Sexual pleasure that deviates from this becomes a perversion, the practitioner a pervert.

A critical feminist reading, however, views penetration as an act of power. For Irigaray, penetration is a 'violent intrusion' that forces open the connectedness of the woman for the purpose of male sexual gratification. The man's right to penetrate the woman at will has been a major focus of the feminist critique of traditional masculinity and its oppression of women. Because traditional masculinity also regards the penetrated man as weak, the right of the man to be penetrated has been the foundation of the gay liberation movement's battle against traditional (hetero)sexual mores and heterosexist demands for the impenetrable man.

Within gay culture, attempts to de-effeminise the 'passive' insertee involved in anal penetration have been extremely loud. For a man to be penetrated, it is claimed, is not to become (like) woman. On the contrary, the reality of man remains throughout and beyond the act: one should 'take it like a man'. For Rubin, this re-masculinisation of the penetrated male signifies a shift in understandings regarding gender identities of male homosexuals. In Bersani's assessment, however, the reclamation of macho masculinity in gay culture does nothing to undermine traditional masculinity that sustains heterosexual male dominance.

More recently, anal penetration has been discussed alongside shifts in male heterosexuality. Acts of unwanted anal penetration have been exposed in professional sporting competitions. The 'metrosexual' image speaks proudly about the pleasures of being anally penetrated, thereby revealing his ability to engage in traditionally non-masculine desires and practices while maintaining a heterosexual identity.

References and further reading

Bersani, L. (1997) 'Is the rectum a grave?' in R. Krauss, A. Michelson, Y.-A. Bois, B.H.D. Buchloh, H. Foster, D. Hollier and S. Kolbowski (eds) *October: The Second Decade 1989–1996*, Cambridge, MA: MIT Press, pp. 303–28.

Freud, S. [1905] (1977) 'The sexual aberrations', in A. Richards (ed.) *Sigmund Freud on Sexuality*, London: Penguin, pp. 45–87.

Irigaray, L. (1981) 'This sex which is not one', in E. Marks and I. de Courtivron (eds) *New French Feminisms: An Anthology*, New York: Schocken Books, pp. 99–106.

Rubin, G. (1998) 'Sexual traffic', in M. Merck, N. Segal and E. Wright (eds) *Coming out of Feminism?* Malden, MA: Blackwell, pp. 36–73.

See also: heterosexuality; penis; phallocentrism; phallus; sexuality

DEAN DURBER

PENIS

It is conventional to view the possession of a penis as what defines one as male, and so as the key marker of sexual difference. Many commentators argue that a sexually functioning penis is central to a man's sense of masculinity. Though rarely seen in popular culture, the penis is centre stage in hardcore pornography, with repeated imagery of it as always hard, improbably sized and never failing. The penis is also central to representations of sexual expertise, where it is the means for producing women's sexual satisfaction (Mooney-Somers 2005). While it is women's sexual satisfaction which is explicitly depicted in most representations of heterosexual sex – proving a man's sexual skill – in hardcore pornography the penis signifies the successful culmination of sex through the 'money' shot, when the man withdraws his penis and ejaculates on the woman's breasts or face. In contrast to the dominant characterisation of a driven unstoppable male sex drive – enacted by the penis – are representations of a temperamental penis, failing to enact a man's sexual desires, which have emerged from the public discussion of erectile difficulties generated by the advent of sexuopharmaceuticals such as Viagra. Sexual health education materials focused on condom use not only reinforce coitus as the dominant practice in heterosexual sex, but also construct the penis as the site of a man's vulnerability to disease. A related representation of vulnerability evident in men's talk around condom use is of the power of the condom to render a hard penis flaccid (Flood 2003). Within representations of the penis as vulnerable, the penis is easily toppled, be it through aging, illness, a latex sheath or the sexual demands of an insatiable woman. However, these representations simultaneously reinforce the ideal of an effortlessly erect, hard, large and reliable penis, exaggerating men's common anxieties about penis size.

The penis is central to sexual science's models of heterosexual sex. Feminist critics have demonstrated how models of sexual dysfunction privilege biological and reproductive aspects of sex, articulating both a coital imperative, which positions penile–vaginal sex as the most natural and therefore fundamental sexual practice, and an orgasmic imperative, which sees the goal of sexual practice as orgasm (Potts 2002). The penis is also fundamental to cultural understandings of heterosexual sex, such that 'having sex' is commonly taken to mean penile–vaginal intercourse. In men's and women's accounts, sex without intercourse is often positioned as unimaginable (Gavey *et al.* 1999).

The penis symbolises the apparent simplicity of male sexuality – one sexual organ which is visible and active, functioning as both an indicator of desire and a means for the satisfaction of that desire. This construction enacts the prevailing discourse of male sexuality as something produced by a natural biological drive oriented to reproduction of the species (Hollway 1984). Indeed, analysis of men's and women's accounts of sex demonstrates that an erect penis is often read as a request for sex and, in some accounts, sufficient to create feelings of obligation in women. Within the prevailing discourses of male sexuality, once activated, a man's desire – embodied by the penis – is seen as unstoppable; this is a common theme in accounts of sexual coercion.

An implication of prevailing constructions of male sexuality and heterosexual sex is that a penis not capable of erection and penetration is dysfunctional. The consequences of not 'fixing' the ill-performing penis are made clear in promotional material for both sexuopharmaceuticals and over-the-counter remedies. One commonly used image is a middle-aged heterosexual couple, sharing a bed but facing in different directions; the message is that their relationship has been torn apart by the failing penis. A functioning penis is construed as vital not only for a man's wellbeing but also for a healthy heterosexual relationship.

In the prevailing models of male sexuality, the penis is taken out of the contexts of the body and of the relationship between the man and his partner; male sexuality becomes the performance of fragmented body parts (Tiefer 1991). In cultural representations, there is a recurring theme of man as separate from his penis, evoking the common mind–body dichotomy. Further, the penis is repeatedly represented as having a will of its own (Potts 2002). We see this in men's accounts of erectile difficulties and in sexual humour featuring a man at the mercy of his penis. Thus, 'problems' of the penis are, by and large, an issue of control.

Research has repeatedly demonstrated the significance of an erection to men's understandings of their sexuality and masculinity. For many, erectile dysfunction is a deeply humiliating experience (Frachner and Kimmel 1998), with an 'ill-performing' penis perceived as a failure of masculinity (Symonds *et al.* 2003). The ability to control the penis signifies the ability of a man – or rather his mind – to exert control over his sexual nature and sexual body. The loss of control over the penis can be experienced as a loss of rationality and of mastery over the body, principles central to hegemonic masculinity (Frosh 1995).

References and further reading

Flood, M. (2003) 'Lust, trust and latex', *Culture, Health and Sexuality*, 5 (4): 353–69.

Frachner, J. and Kimmel, M.S. (1998) 'Hard issues and soft spots', in M.S. Kimmel and M. Messner (eds) *Men's Lives*, Boston, MA: Allyn and Bacon.

Frosh, S. (1995) 'Unpacking masculinity', in C. Burch and B. Speed (eds) *Gender, Power and Relationships*, London: Routledge.

Gavey, N., McPhillips, K. and Braun, V. (1999) 'Interruptus coitus', *Sexualities*, 2 (1): 35–68.

Hollway, W. (1984) 'Women's power in heterosexual sex', *Women's Studies International Forum*, 7 (1): 63–8.

Mooney-Somers, J. (2005) 'Heterosexual male sexuality', unpublished PhD thesis, University of Western Sydney, Sydney.

Potts, A. (2002) *The Science/Fiction of Sex*, London: Routledge.

Symonds, T., Roblin, D., Hart, K. and Althof, S. (2003) 'How does premature ejaculation impact a man's life?' *Journal of Sex and Marital Therapy*, 29 (5): 361–70.

Tiefer, L. (1991) 'Historical, scientific, clinical and feminist criticisms of "The Human Sexual Response Cycle" model', *Annual Review of Sex Research*, 2: 1–23.

See also: bodies and biology, male; phallocentrism; phallus; sexuality

JULIE MOONEY-SOMERS

PHALLOCENTRISM

Phallocentrism is the condition where the phallus, signifier of the symbolic order of masculine power, is privileged as the dominant perspective. A term arising out of Freudian psychoanalysis, the phallus is not the physical or biological penis, but rather an external representation of the penis that symbolically stands in for the power and patriarchal authority of men and masculinity. Feminist theory has employed the term 'phallocentrism' across disciplines from literary criticism to architecture to critique the taken-for-granted presence and supremacy of hegemonic masculinity in social, gendered and cultural relations.

Psychoanalytic theory argues that the phallus represents an external symbol of *lack* which men and women attempt to resolve or address in different ways as a part of ordinary psychological development. Some feminist psychoanalytical theorists such as Kristeva and Irigaray have challenged the way phallocentrism inevitably constructs women as outside of the privileged relation to the phallus. Individual men need not actively enforce patriarchy, or even be present, under the shadow of the ever-present phallus. However, not all men share in the power and privilege of the phallus equally. There are material consequences for those who are excluded from the phallic regime.

Lacanian psychoanalytic theorists focus on the importance of language. They argue that human subjectivity involves an unconscious process constituted in the symbolic order through language. Identifying the ways phallocentrism is a part of the language we use offers an escape from the assumed stability and inevitability of phallic dominance and control by some men over women and other marginalised men. Transgender and lesbian theorists such as Butler and Halberstam have further challenged the exclusivity of privilege residing solely in the penis of a biologically male body and have suggested the possibility of the 'lesbian phallus', which offers women a more direct connection to power and privilege. The advent of drag king performances that mock and parody masculinities has also acted to subvert phallocentrism and phallocentric assumptions about gender and power.

References and further reading

Brennan, T. (1989) *Between Feminism and Psychoanalysis*, New York: Routledge.

Butler, J. (1993) *Bodies That Matter*, New York: Routledge.

Friedan, B. (1963) *The Feminine Mystique*, London: Gollancz.

Grosz, E. (1995) *Space, Time and Perversion*, New York: Routledge.

Halberstam, J. (1998) *Female Masculinity*, Durham, NC: Duke University Press.

Jaggar, A.M. (1983) *Feminist Politics and Human Nature*, Totowa, NJ: Harvester.

See also: penis; phallus; sexuality

KEVIN G. DAVISON

PHALLUS

A phallus is a figurative representation of masculinity that is not reducible to the anatomical penis, but serves instead as a universal symbol of power, authority and fertility. It thus transcends anatomical sexual differences even as it represents qualities traditionally designated masculine.

The psychoanalyst Lacan (1901–81) posited the influential reconceptualisation of the phallus as an unattainable signifier of *desire*. Desire, unlike a specific wish, can never be fulfilled because it is what remains inevitably lacking in each specific experience of fulfilment. Lack originates from the loss of maternal union in the act of birth, but later becomes associated with sexual difference because the penis is visibly absent in women. The phallus thus designates something longed for but inevitably missing in both sexes.

This lack, moreover, cannot be adequately expressed because of a self-alienation that is a condition of language. To articulate desire presupposes speaking a language that precedes us and determines us as social subjects. As speaking subjects we can never be fully present to ourselves because the symbolic expression of our identities and desires through language automatically severs us from our preverbal experiences.

To overcome this experience of loss and self-alienation each child wishes to become the *mother's* phallus, to be the complete object of her desire. This is impossible, however, because there is always something beyond the child, beyond any experience, possession or accomplishment, to which desire points. Thus, even though the male child may have a penis, he can never possess or become the phallus, which remains an eternal signifier of something lacking in oneself. In this sense both men and women necessarily experience *symbolic castration*, an ineffable lack of something that, if present, would render one complete. The crucial developmental challenge of negotiating the Oedipus complex by renouncing one's incestuous wishes thus takes on a new meaning, namely accepting a more primal loss symbolised by the phallus.

In patriarchal culture the *illusion* that the penis is the phallus leads to the production of gendered subjectivities, in which masculinity is privileged over 'castrated' femininity. In this way the phallus, a valorised, but empty signifier, comes to symbolise power and gendered authority.

References and further reading

Frosch, S. (1994) *Sexual Difference*, London and New York: Routledge.

Grosz, E. (1990) *Jacques Lacan*, London and New York: Routledge.

Lacan, J. [1958] (1982) 'The meaning of the phallus', in J. Mitchell and J. Rose (eds) *Feminine Sexuality*, London: Macmillan.

See also: bodies and biology, male; penis

GAVIN IVEY

PHILOSOPHY

The canonical texts in Western philosophy have been written by men and have inscribed male experiences and perspectives into that philosophy.

Clack's *Misogyny in the Western Philosophical Tradition* offers selections from the writings of major philosophers which provide the evidence for what its title describes, including founding figures Plato and Aristotle and the two nineteenth-century philosophers often considered to be the field's most notorious misogynists, Nietzsche and Schopenhauer. Such evidence has been a foundation on which analysts have been able to piece together what philosophers thought about masculinity because, as is true of most traditional intellectual life, assumptions about masculinity have been so deeply embedded and unconsciously taken for granted in the Western philosophical tradition that most philosophers have said very little explicitly about it, despite philosophy's claims to be able to probe to the deepest foundations of knowledge and reality. In fact, most of what philosophers have had to say about the gendered aspects of men's lives emerges only in contrast to what they have had to say about women.

While feminist criticism has focused primarily on philosophy's images and exclusion of women, it has also critically questioned the nature of philosophy's masculinity. Two books that exemplify an early wave of such scholarship looking specifically at political philosophy, where the male bias was conspicuously pronounced, were Wendy Brown's *Manhood and Politics: A Feminist Reading in Political Theory* and Di Stefano's *Configurations of Masculinity: A Feminist Perspective on Modern Political Theory*.

At the time of their publication in the late 1980s and early 1990s attention to masculinity was still so suspect in academia that both authors seem to have felt compelled to specifically name their books as 'feminist' in their subtitles, and both begin with a defence of the project, almost an apologia. Brown's primary subjects are Aristotle, Machiavelli and Weber, while Di Stefano's are Hobbes, Marx and Mill. In a recapitulation of the trajectory of early feminist theorising about women, the earlier book, Brown's, tends to discuss masculinity in a more monolithic manner, while Di Stefano begins to move the question from masculinity to masculinities.

Di Stefano explicitly situates her treatment in the tradition of psychoanalytic feminism, synthesising Anglo-American 'object relations' and Continental Lacanian schools. What these perspectives share is a move away from the Freudian paradigm wherein gender identity formation takes place in the patricentric Oedipal phase to place it in the earlier matricentric phase, designated as 'pre-Oedipal' by the Freudian euphemism invented precisely to avoid naming the mother's importance. A decisive result of this shift is that masculinity appears as a defensive reaction formation against earlier maternal identification, rather than as a primary ground of identity. Emphasis is placed on the difficulty and pain of the male's rejection of and by the mother, so that female rather than male development emerges as a more continuous and secure process, with the result that masculinity is always fragile, requiring strong defensive mechanisms against re-engulfment within the feminine. The violence that accompanies male domination is therefore in this new conceptualisation not evidence of some deep aggressive instinct constituting some essence of masculinity, but rather evidence of the fragility of masculine identity, of precisely the lack of depth to which it can be internalised. Masculine identity is at best a temporary achievement, standing always under the threat of regressive dissolution. Hence the need to marshal and deploy massive resources of aggression in its defence.

Brown argues that our concept of the political is determined by the need to satisfy male developmental needs. Freedom becomes defined as autonomy from and domination over anything associated with the early experience of the feminine in the body of the mother: the body itself, nature, birth, dependence, necessity, desire and, ultimately, life itself. For Brown discerns 'a traceable genealogy' whereby masculinity, as well as humanity, ultimately finds itself entrapped in an 'iron cage' forged by its very successes:

> Freedom cast as freedom from the body, need and necessity is therefore inherently oppressive as well as ultimately impossible – living things cannot transcend or overcome themselves, the fact of their lives. This construction of freedom breeds a politics against life, dooms the activities and persons involved with necessity [i.e. women] to organization under domination, and renders life an instrument rather than a cause of freedom. The utter bankruptcy of this approach to freedom was revealed by Weber: under modern systems of power, the quest for freedom as control of necessity has utterly subverted itself and man appears dominated by and trapped within the cogs of his own machinery of freedom.
>
> (Brown 1988: 194)

Rather than seeing the figures she analyses as part of a single trajectory as does Brown, Di Stefano sees Hobbes, Marx and Mill as embodying three types: 'heroic, productive, and disciplinary metaphors of modern masculine selfhood' (Di Stefano 1991: 201). Di Stefano sees the theme of men's denial of women's birthing powers and childrearing work as central to a myth of 'autogeneration' essential to all the ideals of modern manhood provided by these philosophers, whether it be in Hobbes' injunction in his classic work of political philosophy *De Cive* ('The citizen') to 'consider men as if but even now sprung out of the earth, and suddenly, like mushrooms, come to full maturity, without all kind of engagement with each other', Mill's embrace of an individualist code of self-discipline, or Marx's dictum that 'man makes himself'. Contingencies of nature and fate – or, in Machiavellian terms, the feminine *fortuna* – must be conquered by masculine control and virtue (*virtu*). The masculinist taboo against theorising reproduction as central to political theory is one of the foundations of the public/private split and all of its gendered connotations which have so thoroughly redounded to the detriment of women.

Consider further how many of the founding myths of our culture contain crucial instances of the founding fathers committing or permitting violence against their sons, whether it be Laius against Oedipus, Abraham against Isaac, or the Christian God the Father against Jesus. (Many feminist theorists have argued that Freud's seduction theory covers up the violence of the fathers against the daughters as well.) What emerges here is that the Freudian tale placing the origins of civilisation in the revolt of the sons against the father in the primal horde similarly covers up the prior violence of the fathers against the sons, motivated by the Laius rather than the Oedipal complex, i.e. by the father's fear of the son's impending ascension to power.

Some theorists have argued that modern patriarchy is more correctly conceptualised as the rule of the brothers rather than the fathers. This theme emerges, for example, in Pateman's *The Sexual Contract* (1988) and Kann's *On the Man Question* (1991).It is implicit in Carol Brown's (1981) oft-cited distinction between private and public patriarchy, and led me to suggest that 'fratriarchy' might be a more descriptive term for the more advanced patriarchy that developed after this shift from private patriarchy, in which men hold power as individual heads of families, to public patriarchy, in which men collectively hold power through the state, and whose philosophical expression lies in all that followed in the wake of the death of God the Father in the nineteenth century.

Also in the nineteenth century, the paradigm shift documented by Foucault of the rise of the concept of homosexuality as a distinct identity transformed the public/private split so central to liberal political theory into not only a male/female divide but also a straight/gay one. The assignment of sexuality to the private sphere became not merely a relegation of an aspect of everyone's life to a place out of the public eye, but also a consignment to public and political invisibility of those whose sexuality now marked them as essentially 'other', i.e. both women and gay men.

The critique of philosophy's masculinity extends well beyond the parameters of political philosophy. Lloyd's *The Man of Reason: 'Male' and 'Female' in Western Philosophy* (1984) argued that the supposedly neutral, objective standard of reason on which philosophy as a whole prides itself actually privileges those qualities of thought and habits of mind usually associated with men. This has led to the identification of the field's perspective as 'phallogocentric' by contemporary French philosopher and psychoanalyst Irigaray, who analyses the philosopher's ascent to knowledge in Plato's famous 'Allegory of the cave' in the *Republic* as an allegory of men's escape from the clutches of the womb of the feminine. The dualisms embedded in Western philosophical thought are profoundly gendered, which is why so many of the dominant and dominating hierarchical dichotomies which pervade our culture and establish the philosophical foundations of patriarchal thought map on to each other, privileging the 'male' side of the marked pair to the overall benefit of men: man:woman = culture:nature = mind:body = reason:emotion = subject:object = active:passive = spirit:matter = essence:appearance = order:chaos = adult:child = discipline:wantonness = permanence:malleability = transcendence:immanence=universality:particularily = public: private = work:home = reality:illusion = light/white:dark/black(bothmetaphoricallyandracially)=knowledge/enlightenment: ignorance/superstition = independence/separation: dependence/connection=freedom/liberty:necessity/enslavement.

Bordo's *The Flight to Objectivity* finds tendencies towards historically masculine ways of defining the self as radically individualist and separated from its world to be embedded in the foundations of the deeply influential metaphysical dualism of Descartes, the 'Father' of modern philosophy, including the mind–body dichotomy that empowers men by associating them with the powers of the intellect while at the same time objectifying women. Many analyses, including those typically found in ecofeminist philosophy, argue that the opposition between a sky 'father' and 'Mother' Earth found in much religious imagery resurfaces in modern science, where the manly domination of nature mirrors men's domination of women.

Nineteenth-century German philosopher G.W.F. Hegel infamously wrote that 'The difference between man and woman is the difference between animal and plant', men being animated by thought and finding their natural spheres of activity in such areas as work, government and warfare, while women naturally found an outlet for their instinctual and sentimental nature in the domestic sphere of home, family and love. The Hegelian dialectic of lordship and bondage (or master and servant) has been deeply influential in philosophy, nowhere more so than in Beauvoir's founding feminist paradigm in *The Second Sex* that woman has been 'other' to man's 'self', giving rise to her famous statement, which this encyclopedia and the entire field of masculinity studies are now happily contributing towards correcting, that 'a man would never set out to write a book on the peculiar situation of the human male'. Italian feminist theorist Lonzi's response to Hegel and the entire mainstream (what radical feminist theologian Daly called 'malestream') intellectual tradition of which she takes him as an exemplar is expressed in the title of her essay 'Let's spit on Hegel'.

Nye's *Words of Power: A Feminist Critique of the History of Ideas* extends the critique of philosophy's masculine bias into the sacrosanct precincts of logic itself, from ancient Greek pre-Socratic philosopher Parmenides to modern German philosopher, mathematician and logician Frege, often called the father of modern logic. Moulton's 'Duelism in philosophy' sees the performance of masculinity in the adversarial, competitive way philosophy is practised, to the discipline's detriment because it blocks other more cooperative and productive ways of philosophising, dubbing it not 'dualism' but 'duelism'.

Kittay and Meyers' *Women and Moral Theory* analyses the male standpoint of traditional moral theory, highlighting its impersonal and overly abstract nature, and May's *Masculinity and Morality* provides 'a progressive male standpoint' from which men may counter it.

References and further reading

Beauvoir, S. [1949] (1991) *The Second Sex*, New York: Knopf.

Bordo, S. (1987) *The Flight to Objectivity*, Albany, NY: SUNY.

Brod, H. (1992) 'Pornography and the alienation of male sexuality', in L. May and R. A. Strikwerda (eds) *Rethinking Masculinity*, Totowa, NJ: Rowman and Littlefield, pp. 149–65. Originally in *Social Theory and Practice* (1988) 14 (3): 265–84.

Brown, C. (1981) 'Mothers, fathers, and children', in L. Sargent (ed.) *Women and Revolution*, Boston, MA: South End.

Brown, W. (1988) *Manhood and Politics*, Totowa, NJ: Rowman and Littlefield.

Clack, B. (1999) *Misogyny in the Western Philosophical Tradition*, New York: Routledge,

Di Stefano, C. (1991) *Configurations of Masculinity*, Ithaca, NY: Cornell University Press.

Kann, M. (1991) *On the Man Question*, Philadelphia, PA: Temple University Press.

Kittay, E.F. and Meyers, D.T. (eds) (1987) *Women and Moral Theory*, Totowa, NJ: Rowman and Littlefield.

Lloyd, G. (1984) *The Man of Reason*, Minneapolis, MN: University of Minnesota Press.

Lonzi, C. [1970] (1991) 'Let's spit on Hegel', in P. Bono and S. Kemp (eds) *Italian Feminist Thought*, Cambridge, MA: Blackwell, pp. 40–59. The quote from Hegel is from the Addition to §166 of his *Elements of the Philosophy of Right* [1821] (1991) ed. Allen W. Wood. trans. H.B. Nisbet. New York: Cambridge University Press, p. 207.

May, L. (1998) *Masculinity and Morality*, Ithaca, NY: Cornell University Press.

Moulton, J. (1980) 'Duelism in philosophy', *Teaching Philosophy*: 419–33.

Nye, A. (1990) *Words of Power*, New York: Routledge.

Pateman, C. (1988) *The Sexual Contract*, Cambridge: Polity.

See also: psychoanalysis

HARRY BROD

PHOTOGRAPHY

Photography is a technology that facilitates documentation of the visible world by manipulating light with a mechanical device. It is also a subjective medium capable of challenging stereotypical constructions of masculinity in art and culture, given the power through the relationships established between the photographer and the photographed subject.

Influenced by idealisations of the Greco-Roman male form dominant in Western art of the nineteenth century, early photographers of the male body also wished to represent its perfectibility, beauty and poise. During the late nineteenth century, interest in the photographed male body grew extensively because of the perceived links between men's physical fitness and disciplined behaviour and national well-being. The photography of Koch and Rieth, particularly their *Der Akt* (The Nude) series of 1894–5, resurrected the importance of *Gymnastik*, the Classical art of physical training. By depicting the male nude interacting with, even serving as, architectural structures, Koch and Rieth photographically fashioned masculinity as a literal cornerstone of German society. In Britain during the 1890s, interest in the well-proportioned muscular male body culminated in the frequent photographing of the bodybuilder Sandow by artists such as Steckel. Circulation of these photographs produced a cult following of the hyper-muscular male body, known as 'Sandowism', and illustrated what the Sandow Society called a 'crying need for a fitter race'. Photographs of Sandow anticipated the popularity of nude male photography in the 1950s and 1960s, a genre known as 'Beefcake' (Leddick 2005).

In Germany, other photographers such as von Gloeden relied upon Classical and Orientalist motifs in the imaging of nude male youths; nevertheless, his work, especially *Two Young Men with Grecian Urns* (c. 1890s), illustrated a different idealisation of the male body as younger, more feminine and subject to homoerotic desires. Because of the homoerotic overtones present in von Gloeden's oeuvre, Mussolini's Fascist police destroyed much of his work, illustrating the photograph's potent ability to subvert social and political norms imposed on the male body and its representation.

Interest in photography as a documentation of the healthy virile male body continued into the 1920s and 1930s, in the Naturist Movement. During this period in Germany, photographs of males exercising and engaged in outdoor activities served as an increasingly agitprop art form, reflecting Aryanism as a corporeal and social ideal. Photographic tableaux by Riebicke and Holmes Nicholls represented masculinity as perfectible through physical exertion, a process aestheticised by its situation within idyllic landscapes.

In the United States, wartime photography of the 1940s illustrated that the male body, joined with themes of violence and valour, could also propagandise and mythologise history, as well as complicate photography's usual association with 'truth'. Rosenthal's *The Raising of the Flag on Iwo Jima* (1945) seemingly depicted six men asserting victory following intense battle on the Pacific island. Yet, considering that the island was not completely secured until a month following the photograph's publication, the image served as a staged spectacle of heroic masculinity that performed as a patriotic icon. Just as Rosenthal's photograph immortalised the male-as-hero, Franklin's photograph of firemen raising the United States flag over the rubble of the World Trade Center on 11 September 2001 similarly became symbolic of the nation's resilience following the terrorist attacks. The firemen's stances in Franklin's photograph, as well as the overall composition of the photograph, maintain an uncanny resemblance to Rosenthal's image.

In contrast to photography's tendency in the early to mid-twentieth century to illustrate an idealised masculinity, more recent photography has explored the contentiousness, complexity and instability of masculinity as a visual paradigm. In his work *Portrait (Twin)* (1988), Morimura plays the roles taken in the famous Impressionist painting by both Manet's nude white Olympia and her African maidservant. In so doing, Morimura demonstrates that clear representations of masculinity can be problematised by gender, sexuality, class and race. For Morimura, photography serves as an act of translation in which familiar images from art history can be unsettled and questioned using the artist's shifting understandings of his masculine identity. Other artists, notably Mapplethorpe, believed that viewing the male body had become regimented and routine. Rather than using photography to establish a standardised vision of masculinity, Mapplethorpe's photographs openly showcased masculinity as a function of the body's uncensored desires. In so doing, Mapplethorpe forced viewers to confront stereotypes such as racism and homophobia that have frequently governed visualisations of the male body. One of Mapplethorpe's most famous works, *Self Portrait* (1978), depicts the artist's leather-clad body with a bullwhip inserted in his anus. Resistant to portraiture conventions, the work unabashedly displays the artist's self-determinations of masculine identity and sexual desire. Such forthright renderings of the male body would not only fuel the 'Culture Wars' of the 1990s, but would also prompt other artists, such as Wojnarowicz, Hujar and Serrano, to use photography as a means of addressing the myriad social, cultural and political dimensions of contemporary masculinity.

References and further reading

Bright, D. (ed.) (1998) *The Passionate Camera*, London and New York: Routledge.

Davis, M.D. (1991) *The Male Nude in Contemporary Photography*, Philadelphia, PA: Temple University Press.

Ellenzweig, A. (1992) *The Homoerotic Photograph*, New York: Columbia University Press.

Ewing, W.A. (1994) *The Body*, San Francisco, CA: Chronicle.

Goldstein, L. (ed.) (1995) *The Male Body*, Ann Arbor, MI: University of Michigan Press.

Leddick, D.W. (2005) *The Male Nude*, New York: Taschen.

Lehman, P. (1993) *Running Scared*, Philadelphia, PA: Temple University Press.

Meyer, R. (1993) 'Robert Mapplethorpe and the discipline of photography', in H. Abelove, M.A. Barale and D.M. Halperin (eds) *The Lesbian and Gay Studies Reader*, London and New York: Routledge, pp. 360–80.

Stern, W. (1996) 'Aestheticising masculinity', *Thresholds*, 9: 40–4.

Vettel-Becker, P. (2005) *Shooting from the Hip*, Minneapolis, MN: University of Minnesota Press.

Weiermair, P. (ed.) (1987) *The Hidden Image*, Cambridge: MIT Press.

See also: art; bodybuilding; heroes; homophobia and heterosexism; racism; terrorism; young men

ROYCE W. SMITH

PICTURE BOOKS

Generally considered for children between two and five years old, picture books are literacy primers that feature entertaining graphics with large and simple text. Concerned that picture books also teach children gender socialisation, researchers and children's advocates for the past few decades have criticised stereotypical and sexist storylines and illustrations that seem to prescribe outdated standards for boys' and girls' behaviour. As a result, authors and illustrators are creating a new generation of picture books in order to address a range of gender roles, family relationships, racial identities and multicultural heritages.

Historically, picture books for children have represented conformity to traditional gender dichotomies: boys and girls are featured unequally and as complementary opposites – masculinity is active and adventurous, while femininity is passive and pretty. Initially concerned with picture books' depiction of girls, content analyses found that girls were underrepresented in the titles, central roles and illustrations and, when depicted, were shown in domestic roles (Weitzman *et al.* 1972). Critics then turned their attention to boys and masculinity. Boys are depicted more often, with higher status, as confident and in control, athletic and daring, and often dominant over and independent from other characters. Many book titles feature boys' names, such as *Harold and the Purple Crayon*, *Curious George* and *Oliver Button is a Sissy*.

Picture books are often framed from the perspective of white boys, assume they will be the readers, and encourage all children to sympathise with this dominant point of view and to dismiss the perspectives of boys of colour and girls.

New picture books promote both more accurate representations of all children and gender and racial fairness. They feature boys in a range of non-traditional activities and emotions, for example in feminist scholar bell hooks' *Be Boy Buzz*. New non-sexist and anti-racist picture books are thought to produce positive changes in how children think of themselves and others, help to raise better young men who can conceive of multiple possibilities for their future and positively impact individual behaviour and social problems.

References and further reading

Jackson, S. and S. Gee. (2005) '"Look Janet," "No you look John"', *Gender and Education*, 17 (2): 115–28.

Stephens, J. (ed.) (2002) *Ways of Being Male*, New York and London: Routledge.

Turner-Bowker, D.M. (1996) 'Gender stereotyped descriptors in children's picture books', *Sex Roles*, 35: 461–88.

Weitzman, L.J., Eifer, D., Hokada, E. and Ross, C. (1972) 'Sex-role socialization in picture books for preschool children', *American Journal of Sociology*, 77 (6): 1125–50.

SARAH L. RASMUSSON

PIMPS AND TRAFFICKERS

In the academic literature a pimp is defined as 'one who controls the actions and lives off the proceeds of one or more women who work the streets' (Williamson and Cluse-Tolar 2002). But this gender-neutral language belies the gender and racial stereotypes usually applied to the figure of the pimp. Pimps are almost always seen to be *men* who exploit female sex workers; in film and popular literature, pimps are often African–American men. Clearly, however, pimping can be performed on and off the street; it can be conducted by women (who may be called 'madams' or 'escort managers' instead of pimps) and by men of all nationalities. Pimps may also simply be the partners of sex workers, perhaps offering protection and support on the street or during an escort call, or (like other partners) just sharing income. In many jurisdictions (for example, in the USA and UK), living off the earnings of the prostitution of another is always illegal. In other jurisdictions (for example, in parts of Australia), 'living off earnings' is only illegal if it has been achieved via coercion. This latter approach allows for sex workers to share their income in the way they see fit and thus gives sex workers the same rights as other workers.

It is likely that pimp-controlled prostitution is more common in countries where prostitution is illegal; in jurisdictions where prostitution is legal sex workers have more agency and are generally less vulnerable to coercion. It is clear from the literature that pimp-controlled prostitution is both gendered and dangerous. Pimp-controlled prostitutes are more likely to be female than male; they are also more likely to be drug-addicted and to experience violence (from clients and pimps). Pimp-controlled prostitutes are certainly less able than other sex workers to plan for their own safety or to exit prostitution. Traffickers are usually regarded as pimps who operate in the international domain, bringing vulnerable women from third world and developing countries to places where they are forced into prostitution. Traffickers may indeed be members of organised criminal gangs who *coerce* women into prostitution. Others are called 'traffickers' if they simply facilitate and/or employ migrant sex workers (where there is no coercion or where this is similar to other forms of paid employment). So it is important to look at what definition of 'trafficking' is being used in debate. In the last decade a world-wide campaign against trafficking has emerged and new national and international laws have been developed (Sullivan 2003). This campaign has often been driven by a simplistic radical feminism that regards all prostitution (and trafficking for the purposes of prostitution) as forced and as one of the worst violations of women's human rights. Other feminists, however, argue that anti-trafficking laws are frequently used against migrant women workers; attention needs then to be re-focused on eliminating all coerced labour (including in prostitution) and also maximising women's labour rights.

References and further reading

May, T., Harocopos, A. and Hough, M. (2000) *For Love or Money: Pimps and the Management of Sex Work*, Police Research Series Paper 134, London: The Home Office.

Norton-Hawk, M. (2004) 'A comparison of pimp- and non-pimp-controlled women', *Violence Against Women*, 10 (2): 189–94.

Sullivan, B. (2003) 'Trafficking in women. Feminism and new international law', *International Feminist Journal of Politics*, 5 (1): 67–91.

Williamson, C. and Cluse-Tolar, T. (2002) 'Pimp-controlled prostitution. Still an integral part of street life', *Violence Against Women*, 8 (9): 1074–92.

See also: prostitution

BARBARA SULLIVAN

PLAYBOYS

Playboys are men who aspire to live an affluent, hedonistic and sexually extravagant lifestyle. Typically, playboys resist perceived restrictions society places on a maturing man, seeking instead to enjoy their adulthood while perpetuating wild and youthful ways. Playboys may also be characterised by a certain suave international sophistication, of which the fictional James Bond is an exemplar, and playboy characters often appear in popular romantic novels.

The playboy lifestyle is synonymous with *Playboy* magazine, founded in 1953 by Hugh Hefner. Although the magazine is often sexually explicit, it has successfully established itself as a mainstream publication by using 'tasteful' nude photographs of (often famous) women and publishing articles by reputable writers. The magazine's logo, a rabbit wearing a tuxedo, is emblematic of its mythic lifestyle, which combines pseudo upper-class sophistication, constant sexual success and a material indulgence also displayed in various media and mass merchandising. *Playboy* magazine has sought to legitimise being a playboy, suggesting it is a playful and light-hearted way of life.

However, under the superficial glamour lie more sinister and pathological traits. Hefner's famous sexual indulgences highlight that playboys can be subject to what is described as the Don Juan Syndrome, where a man has excessive urges to have sex with multiple partners, devoid of any emotional involvement. These Don Juans, also known as 'players' or 'Lotharios', go to elaborate and predatory lengths to seduce as many women as possible in order to satisfy their need for thrill and conquest. The Don Juan Syndrome is underscored by a distinct hostility towards women who, with each successful seduction, repeatedly reinforce the player's perception that women are bad and whorish. Ultimately, then, playboys are far from playful and light-hearted, but rather proponents of manipulative misogyny masked by wealth and power.

References and further reading

Beggan, J.K. and Allison, S.T. (2001) 'The Playboy rabbit is soft, furry, and cute', *Journal of Men's Studies*, 9: pp. 341–70.

Ehrenreich, B. (1983) *The Hearts of Men*, Garden City, NY: Anchor.

Kimmel, M. (1995) *Manhood in America*, New York: Free Press.

Novellino, M. (2006) 'The Don Juan Syndrome', *Transactional Analysis Journal*, 36: 33–43.

Osgerby, B. (2001) *Playboys in Paradise*, Oxford: Berg.

See also: infidelity; laddism; male sex drive; men's magazines; misogyny; pornography; sexuality

JOSEPH GELFER

POETRY

Poetry has a long history of being critically dissociated from considerations of gender, although it is inevitably entangled in it. Examining it in relation to gender issues illuminates important but missing ideological dimensions in poetic texts. Feminists have already signalled the need for a feminist history of poetry (DuPlessis). Poetry, which has been deemed, since Plato's time, to be either too dangerous or hardly useful, has since the Renaissance been suspected of being 'effeminising' in its offers of pleasure. Such anxiety reveals how closely attached discussions of poetry and gender have been (Lamb 1994).

Current studies of poetry that focus on gender find Adorno's work on lyric an important point of departure, since he argues that every lyric expresses 'social antagonism' (Adorno 1957: 45). Adorno challenges formalist visions of the poetic text that dissociate it from social reality. Instead, as DuPlessis emphasises, the social dimension of the poem is evident in its very nature and structure, and not necessarily in its themes, for the poem encapsulates 'negative relationships between issue and statement, mediated by subjectivity' (DuPlessis 2004: 95).

Considerations of the poetics of masculinity have tended to focus on particular poets, such as Frank O'Hara or Walt Whitman; or particular periods, such as the Renaissance, Romanticism, Modernism, etc. (Elledge 1994; Felluga 2004). For example, DuPlessis notes a transformation of gender configurations in modernity, where the figure of the inspirational female muse can no longer be fully sustained in poetry (DuPlessis 2004: 125, 126). She argues that the use of the female muse overshadows actual female work depicted, whether economic or cultural. 'But this female work breaks through', revealing an increasing contradiction 'between the growing autonomy of historical women as workers and the poetic convention of the muse' (DuPlessis 2004: 126).

While the focus has often been on the role of poetry in constructions of masculinity, recent work has also analysed the role of gender perceptions in determining the status of poetry. The history of poetry's marginalisation, argues Felluga, is tied to nineteenth-century reaction to such poets as Lord Byron, whose poetry was viewed as nothing less than pathological. Poetry nonetheless plays an important political role, as evidenced by the work of American writers of the 1950s and 1960s who attempted to oppose a stultifying politics of consensus in anticommunist America by offering alternative visions of masculinity, and thus offering a counter-rhetoric of masculinity in community. It is poetry's possibility of 'naming the unnameable' that allows for its resistance to large-scale misinformation in political and social institutions (Davidson 2003: 225). In fact, Davidson privileges poetry as a cultural site of contestation against dominant ideologies.

Some critics question claims about poetry's presumed femininity (or masculinity). Lamb, for example, considers Sir Philip Sidney's 'Apology for Poetry' in the sixteenth century and sees an anxious vision of poetry, where men, under the influence of its pleasures, are reduced to passivity and regression. Sidney sees poetry as having an effect not unlike that of female domination, where males are at risk of regressing to infancy and childish femininity.

> This rejection of ... sensual pleasures for a ... world of intellectual accomplishments created a problem within an institution designed to transform androgynous boys into virile leaders of men. Poetry remained essential ... as a repository of eloquence, but because of its pleasures, poetry became a site of conflict.
>
> (Lamb 1994: 32)

Other studies consider masculinity as a mode in the form of poetry. For instance, the sonnet has been examined in terms of masculine subjectivity; whereas in the female complaint poem a male poet like Donne or Shakespeare speaks in the female voice. One could further point to epic as traditionally a form that valorises the male quest for identity, in the tradition of Homer and Virgil. Such themes as feminisation, male impotence and homosexuality are also currently explored in poetry of different periods.

Most studies of masculinity and poetry have been situated within a 'Western' tradition. Little work has been done, for instance, on Arabic poetry, whether pre-Islamic, medieval or modern, in which a complex and rich rendition of this problematic can be found. See, for instance, the poetic work of Darwish, which is a long inquiry into the paternal – whether that of a poetic, mythic or historical heritage. The work of Ouzgane on Middle Eastern, Islamic and African masculinities has greatly contributed to closing this gap, both by calling attention to the need for such studies and by calling into question the opposition of femininity–masculinity as the primary foundation for the definition of male identity in these regions. He argues instead that masculinity is founded on homosocial stratifications and relations, the effects of which are often violent acts against women.

References and further reading

Adorno, T. (1957) 'On lyric poetry and society', *Notes to Literature*, 1: 37–54.

Davidson, M. (2003) *Guys Like Us*, Chicago, IL: University of Chicago Press.

DuPlessis, R.B. (2004) 'Marble paper', *Modern Language Quarterly*, 65 (1): 93–129.

Elledge, J. (1994) 'The lack of gender in Frank O'Hara's love poems to Vincent Warren', in Peter F. Murphy (ed.) *Fictions of Masculinity*, New York: New York University Press.

Felluga, D.F. (2004) *Perversity of Poetry*, Albany, NY: SUNY Press.

Lamb, M.E. (1994) 'Apologizing for pleasure in Sidney's "Apology for Poetry"', *Criticism*, 36: 5–36.

Ouzgane, L. (1997) 'Masculinity as virility in Taher Ben Jelloun's work', *Contagion*, 4: 1–13.

—— (ed.) (2003) 'Islamic masculinities', Special Issue of *Men and Masculinities*, 5 (3).

See also: aesthetics

NAJAT RAHMAN

POLICE

Policing remains dominantly masculine: some politically progressive states (such as Norway and Sweden) have reflexively pursued the incorporation of women and of feminised understandings of policing practice. Others (such as Australia, South Africa, USA and the UK) have pursued newly gender-sensitive policies while preserving traditionally masculinist structures and operational practices in which hegemonic masculinity is embedded systemically and self-consciously reproduced at every stage of a policeman's career, from training, through the essential credibility of having worked on the streets, to command. In functioning as cultural interpreters, enforcers of often unpopular laws, social workers, bureaucrats, priests and 'hard men', police continually negotiate role ambiguities. Structurally inherent in 'the job', these mirror the ambiguities of the self-conscious cultures of masculinity which many police take with them on to the streets. The brief (and, for many police, comparatively rare) episodes of violence which punctuate the routine banalities of policing are described by many police as representing intense confrontations with a heightened awareness of hyper-reality, as a person, but most particularly as 'a man'. In endemically violent policing environments (e.g. Colombia, South Africa), physical and psychological violence envelop the culture as primary criminal tactics, and police responses articulate whether or not a man can be known as 'a good policeman'.

Popular images derived from media reporting or from the fictions of film, television or crime novels focus on dramatic, photogenic, elemental moments which exemplify and magnify a culture of violence, often portrayed as testosterone-charged, militarised and hypermasculinist. In such threat-filled representations, policemen are imaged as operating collectively as coercive bodies and individually as entities in constant psychological arousal: attentive to, reacting to and eliminating threats both to the body politic and to the individual police body, with extreme violence. But the realities of cultures of violence mitigate against popular obsessions with reactive or irrational violence. Police understandings of violence and the performance of masculinity differ markedly from popular stereotypes. While many police adopt superficial external markers of these stereotypes (a taste for high-speed driving and high-performance vehicles, physical fitness or participation in extreme sports), almost all operate through nuanced understandings that the more violent the culture, the less possible displays of individual braggadocio or overtly masculinist postures by police become. Police in such cultures are trained (formally and unofficially) to recognise the dangers of psychological or performative engagement with crowd or individual violence, and to negotiate alternative notions of masculinities which focus on restrained and tactical uses of responsive violence.

References and further reading

Herbert, S. (2001) '"Hard charger" or "station queen"? Policing and the masculinist state', *Gender, Place and Culture*, 8: 55–71.

Prokos, A. and Padavic, I. (2002) '"There oughtta be a law against bitches": masculinity lessons in police academy training', *Gender, Work and Organisation*, 9: 439–59.

Wardrop, J. (2001) '"Simply the best": the Soweto Flying Squad, professional masculinities and the rejection of *machismo*', in R. Morrell (ed.) *Changing Men in Southern Africa*, Pietermaritzburg: University of Natal Press, pp. 255–70.

Westmarland, L. (2001) 'Gender and policing: sex, power and police culture', Cullompton: Willan.

See also: crime, criminality and the law

JOAN WARDROP

POLITICAL SCIENCE

What useful insights do male political theorists offer to men? Can we understand how theorists approach men and masculinities by viewing what they have to say about women? (Okin 1979). I argue that the status of men in the historical canon of political theory needs to be examined through the perceptions and attitudes the theorists had towards women. Manliness in the views of political theorists well into the nineteenth century was the opposite of being a woman, feminine or possessing traits theorists attributed to women. Women were tangential to the interests of men and occupied the status of onlookers, property, commodities and sexual objects.

Plato's *Republic* (1961) is a notable exception to this view. Men stand, at least in terms of political rule, on the same level as women. But men represent virtue and possess traits that set them apart from all women, save the 'guardian' women. Breeding future guardians becomes woman's primary contribution in Plato's community of rulers; but men and women share identical values regarding political judgment and rule. Plato refuses to relinquish the concept of male superiority, which casts some doubt on the integrity of his moral claims for women. 'Do you know,' he asks Glaucon, 'of anything practised by mankind in which the masculine sex does not surpass the female?' although he grants that in private matters, in household activities, women may indeed be superior to men.

Subsequent political theory had little sympathy for Plato's visionary world, particularly its inclusion of women in the activities of political rule. In the cultured world of Periclean Athens, Greek men kept their wives largely invisible, confined to the household, while the Athenian male citizen appeared in public with an imported mistress; or he might enjoy himself with slaves or with young boys. For Aristotle men serve as citizens and uphold the political virtue of the polis. Theorists from Aristotle through Rousseau argued that men controlled the public domain and political power. Renaissance Europe, ruled by men, was firmly grounded in the economics and politics of the market, in the exchange value of women (Shanley 1989).

In the canon of political theory, men know themselves by what they are not; and what they are not are traits associated with women, for example being unreasonable, uncertain, unpredictable, disruptive, subject to sexual corruption and passionate outbursts, inconstant, fickle and 'effeminate'. Masculinity brought power and opposed conceptions of femininity. In Machiavelli's *Prince* (1515) men dominate a world of violence, action and uncertainty. Successful Princes need to be strong and wily, like the lion and the fox, both metaphors for male prowess, intelligence and strength. Boldness, strength, 'reason' are qualities that seventeenth- and eighteenth-century political theory associates with male prowess.

Machiavelli writes: 'It is better to be impetuous than cautious because Fortune is a woman and it is necessary, in order to keep her under, to cuff and maul her.' Women favour strong men and desire to submit to the bold. Men therefore know their strength through their ability in battle and through their impact on women.

> [Fortuna] more often lets herself be overcome by men using such methods than by those who proceed coldly; therefore always, like a woman, she is the friend of young men, because they are less cautious, more spirited and with more boldness master her.
> (Machiavelli 1965: 92)

Thus men in Machiavelli's view are the true heroes of the public space, not women (Pitkin 1984). Real Princes subdue Fortuna; if Fortuna overcomes the Prince, then the Prince ceases to be master of the political universe, with consequences that end in failure, defeat and death. For Machiavelli as for other political theorists in the tradition, succumbing to femininity meant death. The line between male/female is maintained without any possibility of a breach.

The theme of men being the only fit persons to rule received further theoretical justification in social contract theory. The patriarchal family, the propertied value of women to men, placed the moral and political status of women in a secondary, inferior relationship to men. Social contract theorists like Thomas Hobbes, John Locke and Jean-Jacques Rousseau insist on protecting male prerogative. Men set up the legal order defining inheritance, the distribution of wealth and power. Women could not lay claim to the idea of contract as an inclusionary dynamic, because morally, in the view of men, women possessed no standing in the prevailing political concepts conferring legitimacy on competing claims. How could women consent to a social contract when, the theorists argued, they lacked that special male ability to make informed judgments on matters political and could not summon sufficient reason (which men excelled at) to make an intelligent contractual decision? Men enforced what Carole Pateman (1988) calls the 'sexual contract'. In this ideological and perceptual universe constructed by men to protect their patrilinear and propertied interests, the values of tradition, male dominance, the superiority of male reasoning, the camaraderie of male togetherness defined the political environment (Spelman 1988). Men in the contract tradition stripped women of rights that today we take for granted.

In *Leviathan* (1660) Hobbes' sovereign is composed of men, its unity enforced by men. In the new world of legitimacy established by Hobbes' social contract, 'a multitude of men, are made one person, when they are by one man, or one person represented' (107). And even if that one person is not the King, the representer is an assembly of men, and in seventeenth-century England, political assemblies of men rigorously excluded women.

John Locke criticises the argument that patriarchal authority should be the model for political rule. Men, he argues (1690), exist in a world of brothers as well as fathers and sons; therefore, the distribution of power within patrilinear lines needs to be broader, taking into account the needs of all the brothers rather than just the eldest son. Families conceptually bear little relationship to commonwealths; therefore Locke rejects the authoritarian Hobbesian view that all power should be held by a single (masculine) sovereign. Instead he locates power in the sovereignty, the people and the male holders of property. Men were the sole possessors of property. And in Locke's view the 'people' refers to male property holders. Men hold property rights in the bodies of their women; ownership remains a male prerogative. The masculine notion of property in self could not be transferred to a broader social concept where women possessed an equal right to self ownership and therefore were free of patriarchal power. Only men could claim the right to be free of medieval and royalist concepts of ownership in others' bodies. In both household and civil society, males remain the sole owners of property.

While Rousseau dissociates sovereignty from property and grounds sovereignty in a community of political equals, he embraces the masculine values of simplicity, austerity, strength and integrity. The pursuit of liberty is a male prerogative; Rousseau's misogyny, hatred of sexual decadence, and proclamations of moral decline forge a political position that radically distinguishes not only between 'good' women and 'bad' women, but more generally between the power of men and the weakness of women, even good women. He finds the impact of women on masculine value to be poisonous, since 'feminine' practices arise in morally corrupt environments like cities. The ideal male will avoid such places and focus attention on the rough pleasures of 'nature'. Men, if they are to be authentically masculine, must avoid women who offer them respite from the rigors of a masculine life. Besides, woman's focus on the sensuality of the body and its pleasures enervates masculine will and corrodes masculine reason. Modern men, Rousseau maintains, have allowed their values, habits and sensibilities to be corrupted by wanton, sexual women. Furthermore, Rousseau believed that men, not women, should vote, and the constitutions he wrote for Poland and Corsica drew close associations between the practice of citizenship and masculine virtues.

In the mid-nineteenth century Karl Marx and John Stuart Mill initiated the first real questioning of the canon on how men should understand themselves and politics in terms of their relationship to women. For Marx, capitalism transformed both women and men into objects, alienated not only from themselves but placed in an antagonistic relationship with the community itself. Women in the world of property were regarded as marketable commodities who sold themselves, because of necessity, into 'universal prostitution', marriage being one of these prostituted relationships. Men regard themselves as commodities in the world of markets; capitalism then places both men and women on an equal level: exploited and dominated by mechanisms of production and exchange. Marriage in capitalism degenerates to a system of possession, 'a form of exclusive private property'. Such a relation debases men, because it denies men the enjoyment of women based on individuality and instead causes men to see women only as product or instrument through which to achieve gratification. And because they lack power, women become 'the prey and the handmaid of communal lust', to be possessed by whichever male buys them (1964: 154). Clearly for Marx, the way men see themselves has a great deal to do with how they treat others, including women.

John Stuart Mill, interested not in revolution but in reform, begins the first modern dialogue about men, women and the political system. For Mill, masculine consciousness at least historically had a great deal to do with how men treated women as property and possession. In Mill's view, women, in becoming freer, also have a hand in liberating men from archaic and tyrannical forms of political argument. Men, by refusing to subject women to domination, also expand their own liberty and human possibilities. Mill believes that political and juridical remedies for women will improve the relations between men and women and enrich society by bringing a class formerly excluded more directly into the political process. Mill's essay on *The Subjection of Women* (1869) provoked many men into thinking differently about themselves and their masculine prerogatives. Although in Mill's time many men rejected the idea that women could be politically informed and exercise rational political judgment equal to that of men, today we take his argument for granted. His essay can also be considered to be a forerunner to much in modern political liberal theory, including the ideas of John Dewey and John Rawls.

The late nineteenth-century philosopher Friedrich Nietzsche, who has been very influential in the movement called postmodernism, understood male values in terms of discipline, responsibility and psychological distance. Nietzsche's hero is a male prophetic figure who stands apart from society and culture and from the corruption of 'feminine' values, democrats, socialists and so on. Although postmodernist thinkers accept aspects of Nietszsche's philosophy, particularly regarding the multiplicity of personality, they have discarded his notion of the strong masculine philosopher, uncontaminated by the weakness of feminine will.

It would be fair to say that our modern concept of masculinities as it regards the organisation of the public space owes as much to the influence of women as it does to historically inherited ideas of male political domination. For example, global capitalism, the role of multinational corporations, women's movements in non-Western environments, have given feminist theory new and unprecedented challenges in their relationship to concepts that historically have been the province of men (Nussbaum 1999; Okin 1979). And political theory written by men cannot today ignore the lessons of modern feminism.

References and further reading

Hobbes, T. [1660] (1957) *Leviathan*, London: Basil Blackwell

Locke, J. [1690] (1963) *Two Treaties on Government*, edited by Peter Laslett, New York: New American Library.

Machiavelli, N. [1515] (1965) *The Prince*, in *Machiavelli*, vol. 1, edited by A. Gilbert, Durham, NC: Duke University Press.

Marx, K. (1964) *Karl Marx*, edited by T.B. Bottomore, New York: McGraw Hill.

Mill, J.S. (2002) *The Basic Writings of John Stuart Mill*, New York: Modern Library.

Nietzsche, F. (1992) *Basic Writings of Nietzsche*, New York: Modern Library.

Nussbaum, M.C. (1999) *Sex and Social Justice*, Oxford: Oxford University Press.

Okin, S.M. (1979) *Women in Western Political Thought*, Princeton, NJ: Princeton University Press.

Pateman, C. (1988) *The Sexual Contract*, Stanford, CA: Stanford University Press.

Pitkin, H. (1984) *Fortune is a Woman*, Berkeley, CA: University of California Press.

Plato (1961) *The Republic*, in *Collected Dialogues of Plato*, edited by E. Hamilton and H. Cairns, Princeton, NJ: Princeton University Press.

Rousseau, J.J. [1762] (1993) *Emile*, New York: J.M. Dent.

Shanley, M.L. (1989) *Feminism, Marriage and the Law in Victorian England 1850–1895*, Princeton, NJ: Princeton University Press.

Spelman, E.V. (1988) *Inessential Woman*, Boston, MA: Beacon.

See also: elite culture; Fascism and Nazism; philosophy

JAMES M. GLASS

PORNOGRAPHY

There is a wide range of (contested) definitions of pornography, ranging from the etymological through the sociological to the psychological. Moreover, there is also the issue of what particular (political/epistemological) standpoint underpins particular definitions. Definitions or understandings of pornography inevitably carry with them not only an outline of what pornography 'is' but also what pornography 'does' (to whom). We will consider, in turn, issues that emerge out of attempts to define pornography – in particular, notions of obscenity and censorship. We will then consider pornography and sexual coercion.

At the basic etymological level pornography means the depiction of the activities of female slaves (Cox 2000). More widely, pornography can be defined as sexually explicit media that are primarily intended to sexually arouse the audience (Malamuth 2001). Pornography includes any media that can be viewed, read or heard. Apart from the well-established areas of magazines, books and films, there is now also the (vast) area of Internet pornography. There are three areas of discourse that have variously influenced attempts to define or classify pornography: law, psychology and (with a small 'p') politics.

Although legal discourse has centrally concerned itself with issues pertaining to pornography, it has not, in any country, provided a definition of what constitutes pornography. Legal attention has, rather, concentrated on issues of obscenity and censorship (Grace 1996). In her comparative study of international laws relating to the control of obscene material, Grace identifies two distinct approaches to this issue: the proactive and the reactive. Both are concerned with the possible affects of obscene material on target audiences. However, in the countries where a proactive approach is taken (Australia, Canada, Germany, New Zealand and the Republic of Ireland), obscenity is more clearly defined and obscene material is classified. In countries where a reactive approach is dominant (England and Wales, Scotland, the Netherlands and the USA), whether an item is obscene or not has to be proved in the courts and often one of the key features in making the decision is the current community standards where the material circulates. However, countries adopting either a reactive or a proactive approach share a strict standpoint in relation to the manufacture and consumption of child pornography.

Pornography and censorship

A consequence of an item being deemed to be obscene may be that it is censored; that it is either given a limited circulation or taken out of circulation altogether. The various classifications, in most countries, of films and videos are a clear example of this (Grace 1996). However, the issue of censorship is immediately juxtaposed to whether people have freedom of expression. Particularly in the countries where a reactive approach to obscenity is taken, the issue of freedom of speech is considered simultaneously with deciding on whether an item is obscene or not. This most often occurs in countries that have a written constitution guaranteeing certain civic rights, including freedom of speech. In the USA, for example, the First Amendment states that 'Congress shall make no law . . . abridging the freedom of speech or of the press.' (Grace 1996: 11). Feminists have highlighted the issue of relative freedoms – freedom of speech versus freedom from discrimination. Perhaps the most illustrious attempt to pursue this argument through the courts was that of Catherine MacKinnon and Andrea Dworkin (Everywoman 1988) who in 1983 drafted an amendment to the Minneapolis Civil Rights Ordinance stating that pornography was 'a form of discrimination on the basis of sex' and therefore an infringement of the civil rights of women (cited in Grace 1996: 12). Although the amendment to the Ordinance was initially accepted in local courts, it was eventually overruled in the US Supreme Court in favour of the US Constitution's First Amendment. (See Chester and Dickey (1988) for contributions on both sides of this debate.)

Pornography and sexual coercion

Robin Morgan, in an essay written in 1974, made explicit links between pornography and rape. For anti-pornography feminist writers, pornography 'sexualises and normalises inequalities' and 'makes violence sexy' (Russo 1998). What is objectionable is not pornography's sexual explicitness, but its abusive, hierarchical, objectifying and degrading portrayal of females and female sexuality (Jensen and Dines 1998: 65–6). Feminists' initial linking of pornography and rape stimulated much empirical exploration, not to ascertain whether pornography depraved and corrupted but to find out whether it was causally linked to acts of sexual coercion.

Empirical research regarding the relationship between pornography and sexual violence typically is either experimental or quasi-experimental. In the case of research into the effects of pornography in stimulating sexual violence, the experimenter is, inevitably, ethically constrained from including rape or other violation in the experiment and thus has explored either attitudinal or physiological change. Experimental studies have exposed sample populations (generally men) to various types of pornography, and have then endeavoured to measure either changes in expressed propensities to commit acts of aggression or expressed attitudes related to gender, sexuality and violence. However, empirical literature does not consider pornographic material to be homogenous and has attempted to distinguish different types of pornography. Clinical research (see, for example, Linz *et al.* 1987) differentiates between types of pornography and identifies differential impacts on consumers.

Meta-analyses of the experimental evidence find a clear association between the consumption of violent pornography and pro-rape attitudes and behaviours (Malamuth *et al.* 2000). In laboratory studies, adults show significant strengthening of attitudes supportive of sexual aggression following exposure to pornography, especially sexually violent material. They have less empathy for victims and diminished emotional response to the violence. Participants also show an increase in behavioural aggression following exposure.

Much of this literature lacks consistency in how it classifies the nature and type of the material. Laboratory-based studies have been criticised for being too artificial (in excluding masturbation, for example), neglecting the long-term impacts of exposure, and imposing patterns of pornography usage upon the subjects. In the real world, a user of the material can choose what, when, where and how he will use the material (Check 1992).

Other studies in the general population find correlations between the use of pornography and sexual violence. Males who use pornography frequently, and males who use more violent pornography, are also more likely to report an attraction to or involvement in sexual violence (Malamuth *et al.* 2000). Finally, other research has attempted to correlate the amount of recorded sexual crime with the prevalence of pornographic materials within a specific geographic area. Such studies involve immensely complex social situations and attempt to describe relationships between diverse variables within these settings, and generally they find no positive correlation between pornography and violence.

There are three caveats to this argument for a causal relationship between pornography and sexual violence. First, pornography is not the sole determinant of men's violence against women, and many other social factors are relevant. Second, pornography is not the only important source of sexist and violence-supportive representations. Third, the relationship between representations and behaviour is complex, and the impact of pornography exposure is mediated by the viewer, their interpretations and the contexts of consumption.

However, other feminist and non-feminist authors argue that the vast range of sexual images in pornography should not be characterised solely in terms of sexism or violence. They also argue that male and female viewers interpret representations in complex, selective and ambiguous ways (Strossen 1995), diverse meanings may be attributed to the same scenes and sexual acts, and the usual criticisms of pornography cannot be applied simply to gay male pornography (Thomas 2000).

Recent feminist and profeminist scholarship has asserted the importance of not seeing pornography as isolated pieces of media devoid of social context. This has insisted on considering how the material is made, how such production relates to the larger sex industry, and how this industry is linked to economic, ethnic, racial and gender inequalities across the world which disadvantage vulnerable populations of poor migrant women and children in particular (Forna 1992; Hughes 2000; Kelly and Regan 2000). Pornography is thus construed as violent, coercive and harmful to the children, women and men who participate in making it

Pornography as education, therapy, pleasure or politics

There are those who believe that, in three ways at least, pornography consumption can have positive effects and meanings. First, some feminist commentators argue that while pornography does exaggerate sexism, it has also challenged sexual repression and restrictive sexual norms and thus benefited women. Pornography has served to flout conventional sexual mores, ridicule sexual hypocrisy and promote sexual pleasure (Duggan *et al.* 1988). Pornography has been identified as sexually and thus socially transgressive in its exploration of taboo sexual desires and fantasies. Women can and do use pornography to explore their sexualities and desires (McNair 1996).

Second, gay male and lesbian pornographies are defended as important positive expressions of non-heterosexual sexualities, as an element in gay and lesbian struggles for social recognition and legitimation and as educational tools in eroticising safe sex (McNair 1996). Third, some men argue that pornography has played a therapeutic role in helping them develop healthier sexualities (Kimmel 1990). Pornography has allowed men to learn about female and male bodies and sexual techniques, to feel less shame about ejaculation and semen, and to accept themselves as sexual beings. Others argue instead that while pornography harms women, it harms men as well: pornography has helped to homogenise men's sexual tastes, narrow the range of male sexual satisfaction, channel all men's intimate needs into genital sexual activity, and promote myths of perpetual male sexual readiness and penis size (Brod 1990).

While there certainly is pornographic diversity, there is also a dominant form of pornography, a cluster of repetitive themes characteristic of mass-marketed heterosexual pornography. This hegemonic pornography is in part the product of men's control of economic, political and cultural power, so that much pornography caters more to heterosexual men's desires and fantasies than it does to women's (Chancer 1998). In other words, social inequalities are the context for the particular passions of much heterosexual pornography. Of course, heterosexual pornography does not cater for all men's desires, nor are its appeals exclusive to men, but it works in a symbiotic relationship with common constructions of masculine heterosexual sexuality.

Pornography and the hegemony of men

To conclude this essay, we offer some reflections and questions on both the individual and global presence of pornography and how this relates to the dominance of men across the world. Hearn (2004) has suggested that to understand how men maintain their dominance in most global societies attention should be focused on the personal and political practices that sustain the hegemony of men. Thinking about pornography provides a perfect case study for contemplating these issues. At the personal level, do men use pornography to develop and sustain oppressive and humiliating (hetero)sexual practices with non-consenting partners? How does the individual use of pornography affect a man's sense of (sexual) self and his subsequent sexual practices? How do these practices impinge on other areas of coexistence with women and children and other men?

At a political level detailed exploration into the means of production of pornography is essential. Is coercion used in the manufacture and dissemination of pornography? Does the pornography embody racist, sexist and heterosexist stereotypes?

Thus, to understand and respond to pornography requires more than experimental reassurance (or not) that men consuming it may go on to develop (or not) harsh(er) attitudes to women and children or commit sexual offences. It requires more than assertions that if it does not cause sex crime it is ethically acceptable. It requires a detailed analysis on a personal and political level as to what pornography is representing – in terms of gendered and racial sexual dynamics – and it requires consideration of the conditions of the manufacture and dissemination of the product.

References and further reading

Brod, H. (1990) 'Eros thanatized', in Michael Kimmel (ed.) *Men Confront Pornography*, New York: Crown, pp. 190–206.

Chancer, L. (1998) *Reconcilable Differences*, Berkeley, CA: University of California Press.

Check, J.V.P. (1992) 'The effects of violent pornography, nonviolent dehumanizing pornography, and erotica', in C. Itzin (ed.) *Pornography*, Oxford: Oxford University Press, pp. 350–8.

Chester, G. and Dickey, J. (eds) (1988) *Feminism and Censorship*, Bridport: Prism Press.

Cox, P. (2000) 'Pornography', *Journal of Sexual Aggression*, 6 (1–2): 128–49.

Duggan, L., Hunter, N. and Vance, C.S. (1988) 'False promises', in K. Ellis, B. Jaker, N. Hunter, B. O'Dair and A. Talmer (eds) *Caught Looking*, Seattle, WA: Real Comet Press, pp. 72–85.

Dworkin, A. (1981) *Pornography*, London: The Women's Press.

Everywoman (1988) *Pornography and Sexual Violence*, London: Everywoman.

Forna, A. (1992) 'Pornography and racism', in C. Itzin (ed.) *Pornography*, Oxford: Oxford University Press, pp. 102–12.

Grace, S. (1996) *Testing Obscenity*, London, Home Office.

Harding, S. (1991) *Whose Science? Whose Knowledge?* Milton Keynes: Open University Press.

Hearn, J. (2004) 'From hegemonic masculinity to the hegemony of men', *Feminist Theory*, 5 (1): 49–72.

Hughes, D.M. (2000) 'Welcome to the Rape Camp', *Journal of Sexual Aggression*, 6 (1–2): 29–51.

Jensen, R. and Dines, G. (1998) 'The content of mass-marketed pornography', in G. Dines, R. Jensen and A. Russo (eds) *Pornography*, New York: Routledge, pp. 65–100.

Kelly, L. and Regan, L. (2000) 'Sexual exploitation of children in Europe', *Journal of Sexual Aggression*, 6 (1–2): 6–28.

Kimmel, M. (ed.) *Men Confront Pornography*, New York: Crown.

Linz, D., Donnerstein, E. and Penrose, S. (1987) 'Sexual violence in the mass media', in P. Shaver and C. Hendrick, *Sex and Gender*, London: Sage.

McNair, B. (1996) *Mediated Sex*, London and New York. Arnold.

Malamuth, N. (2001) 'Pornography', in N.J. Smelser and P.B. Baltes (ed.) *International Encyclopedia of Social and Behavioral Sciences*, 17, Elsevier: Amsterdam, New York, pp. 11816–21.

Malamuth, N., Addison, T. and Koss, M. (2000) 'Pornography and sexual aggression', *Annual Review of Sex Research*, 11, Allentown, PA: Society for the Scientific Study of Sexuality.

Morgan, R. (1980) 'Theory and practice', in L. Lederer (ed.) *Take Back the Night*, New York: Morrow, pp. 134–40.

Russo, A. (1998) 'Feminists confront pornography's subordinating practices', in G. Dines, R. Jensen and A. Russo (eds) *Pornography*, New York: Routledge, pp. 9–35.

Strossen, N. (1995) *Defending Pornography*, London: Simon and Schuster.

Thomas, J. A. (2000) 'Gay male video pornography', in R. Weitzer (ed.) *Sex for Sale*, New York: Routledge, pp. 49–66.

See also: child pornography

MALCOLM COWBURN
MICHAEL FLOOD

POSTCOLONIAL MASCULINITIES

Postcolonial theory, emerging in recent years out of debates within literary theory and anti-colonial literature and discourse theory, has come to play an increasingly important role in an ever-expanding range of intellectual pursuits, including discussions of gender and of masculinity. Postcolonial theory itself refers to a heterogeneous set of theories and discursive practices aimed at theorising and explicating the texts, cultures and politics arising out of Third World contexts after their hard-won independence from colonial rule. These postcolonial theories are often very closely associated and allied with the 'posts' of postmodernism and poststructuralism as well. Sometimes the hyphenated term 'post-colonial' is used to designate and specify the historical moment of decolonisation and to separate it from the more expansive use of 'postcolonial' which also tends to encompass these additional theoretical attachments, commitments and tendencies (Ashcroft *et al.* 1995). The discussion below will focus on the uses of the broadest notion of postcolonial theory in helping to understand and theorise the enormous variety of currently existing masculinities, both heterosexual and homosexual, through examinations of masculinities not just as they are produced and experienced in First World contexts, but also by looking transnationally and considering masculinities as they are produced and experienced in various Third World contexts as well as in the hybrid masculinities created through the cultural fusions of global diasporas.

Some of the earliest and most influential writings in what would later transform itself into postcolonial theory come from the works of Fanon. Drawing on his upbringing in Martinique, his education in France and his experiences in Algeria, Fanon's works are both results of colonialism and anti-colonial struggles as well as a critique of those histories. His writings are equally important for their keen insights into the production of gender and, in particular, to the distortions of masculinities produced in those oppressed by colonisation as well as in the masculinities experienced by the colonisers themselves. In his book *The Wretched of the Earth*, Fanon writes: 'At whatever level we study it ... decolonisation is quite simply the replacing of a certain "species" of men by another "species" of men' (Fanon 1961: 35). These changed men are brought about by and through the violent crucible of decolonisation itself. Both the circumstances of colonisation, as well as the overthrow of that colonisation, impact the production of consciousness. The gendered nature of consciousness is something always highlighted in Fanon's psychoanalytically framed arguments, as is the reciprocal influence the colonised and the coloniser exercise on each other in the formation of their respective gendered identities.

> The need for this change exists in its crude state, impetuous and compelling, in the consciousness and in the lives of the men and women who are colonised. But the possibility of this change is equally experienced in the form of a terrifying future in the consciousness of another 'species' of men and women: the colonizers.
>
> (Fanon 1961: 35–6)

In his earlier book *Black Skin, White Masks*, Fanon explores the psychopathology of colonialism and racism as they manifest in both the colonised and the coloniser. In particular, he shows how this pathology expresses itself in sexualised identifications and fantasies of rape and aggression that become internalised by the colonised native (Fanon 1952).

The principal inspiration for postcolonial theory, however, lies in the work of Palestinian-American literary critic Edward Said. In his extraordinarily influential book, *Orientalism,* Said employs a Foucauldian notion of discourse as a means not simply of representing, but also of controlling and disciplining the 'other' that lies outside of the West. At the same time, this discourse helps to constitute and create the West by way of the boundaries and contrasts supplied by Orientalist discourse. The issue for Said is not the accuracy, or lack thereof, of these Western representations of the Orient, but rather the function of these representations in the West in helping produce and sustain imperialism and colonialism, and in the reiteration and recirculation of these representations in the East itself. This politics of representation lies at the heart of Said's project. Glossing Marx's line in *The Eighteenth Brumaire of Louis Bonaparte*, that since 'they cannot represent themselves, they must be represented', Said holds that the Orient becomes not a representing subject in its own right, but a subject represented by the West (Said 1978: 21). Representation thus becomes an arena for the dissemination of colonial control as well as for indigenous resistance to these Western discourses and representations.

Bhabha's work further elaborates on these issues raised by both Fanon and Said and explores the ways in which strategies such as mimicry and hybridity can often function as moments of resistance for subaltern subjects inhabiting the peripheries of Western culture and Western discourse (Bhabha 1994). Spivak's writings have also been central to the development of postcolonial theory. Her insightful and influential article 'Can the subaltern speak?' has provoked enormous amounts of critical attention. Arguing not only that the exclusion of subaltern speech and representation happens within Western discourse, Spivak also asserts the impossibility of any such subaltern speech occurring and being heard within the confines and constraints imposed, created and maintained by Western discourse (Spivak 1988).

These questions of representation are central to the study of postcolonial masculinities. First World discourses about Third World masculinities often produce and maintain representations that serve to create, perpetuate and reinforce First World norms of masculinity and heterosexuality by way of the boundaries and contrasts provided by these 'other' Third World masculinities and sexualities. For instance, Western representations of 'native' men as dangerously hypersexual beasts who pose an immanent threat to the safety, security and virtue of white women have been used as mechanisms to help mobilise and justify the use of force against native populations in the Third World as well as immigrant populations in the West. At the same time, these representations of 'native' men also work to create and bolster violently repressive martial masculinities in the First World. Perceived threats to 'native' women from these same presumptively predatory 'native' men can also serve as justifications for colonial and neocolonial violence. Practices shocking to Western sensibilities, such as polygyny, widow sacrifice, burqas or infibulation, can function as pretexts for First World intercessions. Spivak describes these as instances of 'White men saving brown women from brown men' (Spivak 1988: 297). These myths of postcolonial masculinities can be construed as yet another form of subaltern consciousness that does not speak and represent itself and so becomes represented through Western eyes and through Western discourse for Western purposes. Postcolonial masculinities thus run a similar risk of being essentialised and appropriated as the constitutive periphery of a central First World masculinity in much the way that Mohanty argues that 'Third World Difference' has served as an imaginary backdrop for First World feminism (Mohanty 1991: 54). This essentialising and homogenising of postcolonial masculinity serves to obscure the actual diversity and plurality of lived postcolonial masculinities around the globe.

Postcolonial theories of masculinity can also find connections and affinities with queer theory. For instance, Butler writes: 'It seems crucial to resist the model of power that would set up racism and homophobia and misogyny as parallel or analogical relations' (Butler 1993: 18). That is, it is an illegitimate shortcut to construe the constructions of race and of masculinity as being the results of separate and disconnected systems of power, and it is also illegitimate to see them as necessarily following the same trajectories. Instead, it is the interlocking and mutual articulation of race by sex and sex by race that works to create and produce the subject of postcolonial masculinity. Using Butler, postcolonial masculinities, not unlike queer identities, may be construed as being produced and regulated by the performative citation and repetition of pre-existing cultural scripts that surround and enable the categories of race, sex and compulsory heterosexuality (Butler 1993). This starting point also provides possibilities for resistance to these First World norms. Butler writes: 'That this reiteration is necessary is a sign that materialisation is never quite complete, that bodies never quite comply with the norms by which their materialisation is impelled' (Butler 1993: 2). For Butler, the dissonances and incongruities surrounding the cultural circulation and reception of representations of postcolonial masculinities may provide one method of contesting and resisting the always tentative hold exercised by the dominant culture on the meaning of these discourses.

Other approaches to postcolonial masculinities can be found in works ranging from those of R. Connell and other sociologists, who originally focused on ethnographic case studies, to recent works in the literature on gender and development and postdevelopment (Connell 2005; Pease and Pringle 2001; Morrell and Swart 2005; Lind and Share 2003). These works overlap and explore in new ways many of the same terrains that have been traversed by postcolonial theory. These alternative explorations of the sociological and economic dimensions of transnational masculinities cut across some of the same boundaries of nationality and ethnicity breached by postcolonial theory. They provide new concrete accounts of the varieties of these lived postcolonial masculinities. However, the meta-theoretical issues that occupy much of postcolonial theory concerning the always-vexed relationship of any First World discourse to the Third World experiences it seeks to represent, continue to sound a salient, useful and perhaps inescapable cautionary note for all such enquiries.

References and further reading

Ashcroft, B., Griffiths, G. and Tiffin, H. (eds) (1995) *The Post-Colonial Studies Reader*, New York: Routledge.

Bhabha, H. (1994) *The Location of Culture*, New York: Routledge.

Butler, J. (1993) *Bodies That Matter*, New York: Routledge.

Connell, R. (2005) 'Globalization, imperialism, and masculinities', in M. Kimmel, J. Hearn and R.W. Connell (eds) *Handbook on Studies of Men and Masculinities*, London: Sage.

Fanon, F. [1952] (1967) *Black Skin, White Masks*, New York: Grove.

—— ([1961] (1963) *The Wretched of the Earth*, New York: Grove.

Lind, A. and Share, J. (2003) 'Queering development', in K. Bhavnani, J. Foran and P. Kurian (eds) *Feminist Futures*, London: Zed Books, pp. 55–73.

Mohanty, C.T. (1991) 'Under western eyes', in C.T. Mohanty, A. Russo and L. Torres (eds) *Third World Women and the Politics of Feminism*, Bloomington, IN: Indiana University Press.

Morrell, R. and Swart, S. (2005) 'Men in the Third World', in M. Kimmel, J. Hearn and R. Connell (eds) *Handbook on Studies of Men and Masculinities*, London: Sage.

Ouzgane, L. and Coleman, D. (eds) (1998) 'Postcolonial masculinities', *Jouvert*, 2 (1), available at http://social.chass.ncsu.edu/jouvert/v2i1/con21.htm

Pease, B. and Pringle, K. (eds) (2001) *A Man's World?* London: Zed Books.

Said, E. (1978) *Orientalism*, New York: Vintage.

Spivak, G.C. (1988) 'Can the subaltern speak?' in C. Nelson and L. Grossberg (eds) *Marxism and the Interpretation of Culture*, Urbana, IL: University of Illinois Press.

—— (1999) *A Critique of Postcolonial Reason*, Cambridge, MA: Harvard University Press.

DEREK STANOVSKY

POSTMODERNISM

'Postmodernism' is used to name at least three things of interest to the critical study of men and masculinities: (1) a new global context of contention in the wake of the 1960s (often distinguished as 'postmodernity'); (2) the writings of a set of predominantly French philosophers of the political Left who came to prominence in connection with the events of the 1960s and 1970s (often distinguished as 'poststructuralism'); and (3) a problematic position within feminist debate that emerged during the 1980s and became dominant during the 1990s (under the name 'postmodernist feminism'). Conflict over gender and sexuality, in feminism, gay liberation and antifeminism, is one of the defining features of postmodernity. Post-structuralist philosophies have proven valuable in rethinking the modern and premodern, including their use of gender. 'Men's studies' itself is based, in part, in the rise and institutionalisation of postmodernist feminism.

While these three things can be distinguished, discussion of 'postmodernism' commonly elides their differences. One of the French philosophers (sense 2) played a key role in promoting the interpretation of the post-1960s period as 'postmodern' (sense 1), while the feminist position (sense 3) drew explicitly on arguments from that philosopher and the other 'poststructuralists' (sense 2). More generally, what holds the three together is the claim that a prevailing set of distinctions is no longer valid (or, at least, not in the way those distinctions are usually understood). What permits their distinction is differences in *which* distinctions are challenged, by *whom* and *how*.

Metanarratives and the two modernities

A 'post-' modernism or 'post-' modernity implies a relationship to something called 'modernity' or 'modernism'. One can think of 'modernity' as the political economy and 'modernism' as the dominant cultural framework of the period 1848 to 1968. (These dates – marking two periods of revolutionary uprisings across the modern world-system – should be taken as symbols, rather than as hard and fast.) During this period, the main axis of contention was between liberalism and socialism, representing two solutions to the problem of 'class'.

Today, after ('post') modernity, the differences between these two seem less important. There has been a proliferation of new struggles around crisscrossing axes of oppression. In this new context, both 'modernist' parties face a host of attacks *together* – sometimes both being decried as 'secularist' or 'socialist', sometimes as 'neocolonialist', 'patriarchal', 'state capitalist' or 'anthropocentric'. Postmodern contention is often called 'cultural politics'. In it the distinctions between 'the political', 'the economic', 'the social', 'the cultural' and even 'the natural', have increasingly broken down, taking with them familiar distinctions between 'the public' and 'the private', between 'facts' and 'values'. The nation-state, the individual and the revolutionary subject have been displaced in favour of the global, the local and problems of 'identity' and 'difference'.

Interpretation of these developments in terms of 'postmodernism' began in the early 1970s with the efforts of such critics as Ihab Hassan (literature), Robert Venturi (architecture) and Daniel Bell (sociology). But critical categories can be said to 'arrive' when controversy about them explodes. In the case of postmodernism, this explosion can be dated to Lyotard's *The Postmodern Condition* (1979, English 1984) and to Habermas's 1980 response, originally titled 'Modernity versus postmodernity' and later re-published as 'Modernity – an incomplete project'. Lyotard defined postmodernism as 'incredulity towards metanarratives' (Lyotard 1984: xxiv), and this has served as its most common definition ever since.

A 'narrative' is just a story, and stories are the traditional way of laying claim to legitimacy (truth, justice). By a 'metanarrative', however, Lyotard meant a legitimacy claim in a discourse (science) that *specifically denied* the validity of recourse to stories (hence, 'meta', meaning 'beyond'). Modern metanarratives are most familiar as stories of *progress* – the progressive 'modernisation' and 'development' of our culture, knowledge, politics, economy and morals. 'Progress' was appealed to equally by the US/NATO and the USSR/Warsaw Pact, liberalism and Marxism. Whatever differences they had, both sides took themselves to be justified by both science and the promise of freedom and fulfilment, to be progressively achieved under the guidance of technocrats.

Narratives of progress take it for granted that technology, capital accumulation and technocratic administration go along naturally with liberation and fulfilment. It is this assumption that has lost credibility, hence postmodern 'incredulity' (disbelief). Even in modernist authors one now finds a split between these two sets of objectives, these two *modernities*. Habermas distinguishes administrative-economic 'societal modernisation' from anti-authoritarian 'cultural modernity' just as Lyotard distinguishes the 'speculative' from the 'humanist' narratives of legitimation. These different formulations matter. Habermas defends modernism in the name of its anti-authoritarian currents, while Lyotard promotes the postmodern 'search for instabilities' on the grounds that both of modernity's narratives are authoritarian. But such differences are arguably less important than recognition of the split. For the point is that, under modernism, these two objectives were presumed to go together, while today this unity can no longer be presumed.

Language, power and the threat of 'relativism'

This leads to one of the most characteristic difficulties of postmodern discourse: language becomes a problem. Consider, as an example, the meanings of key words like 'man' and 'woman'. If we reject what they have been used to mean, or take such meanings as arbitrary, how are we to dispose ourselves to them? Should we allow that 'woman' is dependent on 'man', and reject the category, perhaps promoting 'womyn' or 'lesbian' instead? Or, is the goal a 'positive category of women' (Frye)? What, if anything, would 'femininity' mean in either case? Is 'man' defined by oppression, whether of 'woman' or otherwise? What could it mean to accuse gay men of 'effeminacy'? Can one speak of a 'gay masculinity', and how would it relate to the 'real masculinity' of 'real men'? One could go on.

The problems of language are the special purview of 'poststructuralist' philosophies (taken to include such authors as Foucault, Derrida, Kristeva, Deleuze, Irigaray and Lacan, among numerous others). Speaking generally, what a word means is not something merely given, neutral or uncontroversial. Despite modernist orthodoxy, 'reality' and 'truth' will not tell us what categories we 'ought' to use. Instead, words are 'essentially contested' (Gallie): they emerge from social practice and embody social choices That a choice is 'social' does not imply that it is universal or unanimous, much less that it is fixed once and for all. Precisely because it is a choice, different choices are always possible, with different implications. Social choice is an active and ongoing process, a matter of *politics*.

One consequence of this is that it matters *what* collectivity is at issue when a word is being defined or debated. Within a given collectivity, a word may mean very different – even opposite – things to what it means in other collectivities, including the predominant ones. Perhaps the most glaring example of this is the inversion of the meaning of 'bad' successfully brought about by young black men in North America in the late 1980s. If someone said of something, 'Oooh ... that's bad,' an outside observer would be reduced to asking, 'Is that "bad" as in bad, or "bad" as in good?'

This recognition of the contingency, contestability and non-universality of language gives rise to the characteristic charge that postmodernism is nothing but relativism (scepticism, nihilism, cynicism, irrationalism, etc.). Supposedly, for postmodernists 'anything goes'. They have no way to distinguish between right and wrong, so all things, no matter how horrific, must be permissible and – *poof* – here come the Nazis and the death camps (as exemplars of ultimate evil). This shows the significance of the modern framework to modernists. Either their preferred distinctions are accepted or the world dissolves into Hobbes' hypothetical 'war of all against all' – despite the fact that Nazism and death camps, 'total war' and Weapons of Mass Destruction are *products* of modernism.

Sadly, many 'introductions', and other books about postmodernism, treat postmodernism exclusively in this manner. While such a move actually demonstrates the postmodern point ('postmodernism' is itself a contested term), readers new to the literature should be wary of such introductions. Keep in mind that the charge of 'relativism' means only 'does not treat my preferred distinctions as the only possible ones, or in the manner in which I prefer them treated' and is not terribly helpful to the student.

Feminism, gender and postmodernism

Feminism was postmodern before the term. Feminist theorists' efforts to articulate 'the problem that has no name' (sexism, misogyny, patriarchy) and to work out the terms of their relation to Marxism played a key role in shaping postmodern discourse. Indeed, the idea of 'postmodernity' specifically cites feminism in its reading of a 'crisis' of modernity. Despite this, 'postmodernism' has been a controversial and polemical word in feminist debate. This is owing to the emergence of a self-described 'postmodernist feminism' in the 1980s.

Postmodernist feminism can be seen as a product of three earlier critiques:

1 a critique of institutionalised feminism in the US by feminists of colour, embodied particularly in the book *This Bridge Called My Back* (1981);
2 a critique of feminist theories growing out of the Anglo-American 'analytic' philosophical tradition by feminist theorists working within the 'Continental' (European) phenomenological philosophical tradition, embodied first in the volume *New French Feminisms* (1980) and later especially associated with Judith Butler; and,
3 an all-out attack on radical feminism by some socialist feminists, most notably Alice Echols and the other contributors to the volume *Pleasure and Danger* (1984).

The politics of these three critiques are very different. For feminists, the first is presumptively just. It can be rebutted, but the burden of proof lies on the criticised. The second is presumptively indifferent. While such differences of philosophical vocabulary make a difference, there is no reason why it must be a *feminist* difference. The third, however, is a specifically feminist controversy. Given these different politics, there is no reason why the three critiques need be taken as one, nor are they always. However, the 'postmodernist feminist' position is precisely about eliding their differences, in effect using the presumptive justice of the first to sell the indifferent second and the controversial third.

The controversy over this third critique came to be known as the 'sex wars'. Fought over the politics of lesbianism and the appropriate feminist approach to heterosexuality, gay men's culture and movements, pornography, prostitution, sadomasochism, fetishism, body mutilation and transsexualism, these 'wars' coincided with the anti-feminist backlash. The anti-radical feminists in these debates (not exclusively socialist, but by no means everyone associated with the other two critiques) claimed to be 'sex-positive', and accused radical feminists of practising an 'essentialist' 'identity politics' and 'cultural feminism' that suppressed 'difference'. This is where 'postmodernism' entered in.

Stated briefly, the critique of 'essentialism' is that there is no way to define a word without leaving something out. Taken from the poststructuralist critique of metaphysics, anti-radical feminists used it to argue that radical feminism offered a 'white, middle-class' analysis of 'women' that succumbed to biological determinism. While calling, uncontroversially, for more detailed studies of and by women in different social locations (i.e. women of different races, classes, sexualities, (dis)abilities, nationalities, etc.), they also argued that the radical feminist project of building a movement around women's oppression as *women* had to be abandoned, since this supposedly got in the way of building movements against women's oppression as workers, or as people of colour, or what have you. Their project was institutionalised, in part, by a move away from women's studies to gay and lesbian and/or gender studies, and by the emergence of queer theory and so-called 'third wave feminism'.

This has had direct consequences for the critical study of men, starting with the fact that the study of men as *men* has been a crucial part of this project (predictably, once again decentring women). It is now commonly considered proper to study 'masculinities', a differentiated field of people and practices marked as 'male' in differing ways, variously privileged and oppressed, rather than to study 'masculinity', an axis of domination. This has meant, in particular, an increased attention to 'hybrid' or 'border' categories, like intersexuality and so-called 'male lesbians' and 'female masculinity'. While these developments have done wonders to promote 'men's studies', why masculinity/masculinities should be an 'either/or' choice has not been well answered.

'Postmodernism' continues to incite controversy. In that respect, it is worth keeping in mind that 'category' comes from the ancient Greek word for prosecuting someone in a court of law. Nonetheless, for all who see the limits and presumptions of modernity as a problem, 'postmodernism' is at least suggestive of possibilities – a presentiment of a future still in formation.

References and further reading

Bell, D. and Klein, R. (eds) (1996) *Radically Speaking*, North Melbourne: Spinifex.

Benhabib, S., Fraser, N. and Cornell, D. (1995) *Feminist Contentions*, London: Routledge.

Braidotti, R. (1994) *Nomadic Subjects*, New York: Columbia University Press.

Butler, J. (1990) *Gender Trouble*, London: Routledge.

Butler, J. and Scott, J. (eds) (1992) *Feminists Theorize the Political*, London: Routledge.

Drolet, M. (ed.) (2003) *The Postmodernism Reader*, London: Routledge.

Habermas, J. [1985] (1990) *The Philosophical Discourse of Modernity*, Cambridge, MA: MIT.

Lyotard, J.-F. [1979] (1984) *The Postmodern Condition*, Minneapolis, MN: University of Minnesota Press.

Marks, E. and de Courtivron, I. (eds) (1980) *New French Feminisms*, Amherst, MA: University of Massachusetts Press.

Moraga, C. and Anzaldúa, G. (eds) (1981) *This Bridge Called My Back*, Watertown, MA: Persephone.

Nicholson, L. (ed.) (1990) *Feminism/Postmodernism*, London: Routledge.

Ross, A. (ed.) (1988) *Universal Abandon?* Minneapolis, MN: University of Minnesota Press.

Sim, S. (ed.) (1998) *Post-Marxism*, Edinburgh: Edinburgh University Press.

Vance, C. (ed.) (1984) *Pleasure and Danger*, London: Routledge.

Waugh, P. (ed.) (1992) *Postmodernism*, London: Edward Arnold.

See also: cultural studies; culture and representation; epistemology; literary theory; phallocentrism; social construction

CHRIS BORST

POWER RELATIONS

Power relations involve interconnected contexts, often associated with dominance and control, through which individuals and groups achieve certain ends. Although it is important not to contextualise men and masculinities exclusively in terms of power relations, Seidler (1997: 3) argues that through modernity a dominant patriarchal masculinity formed that set contemporary terms of relationships of power between men, women and children. Feminist analysis tracks the ways in which patriarchy defines the terms for control of processes of production, reproduction and consumption globally and locally. In addition, feminist theorising analyses individual contexts of power by elaborating the insight that the 'personal is political', thus challenging assumptions that the politics of oppression and injustice are manifest only in the public realm.

Contemporary studies on men suggest that although some groups of men gain power from the marginalisation of men displaying other forms of masculinity, most individual men and groups of men are limited by dominant white, heterosexual masculinities (Connell 2000; Whitehead and Barrett 2001). Also, individual men's lives at present are impoverished through disconnections with their bodies and emotions and through their marginalisation from familial social relations. McDowell (2000) argues that as the role of women in society has changed, younger generations of men and boys do not easily fit into so-called traditional gender power relations.

However, Bourdieu (2001) notes that the increase of women in the workplace does not necessarily herald a redress of power imbalances. He claims that new occupational fields and subfields differentiate but nevertheless reproduce and continue old structures of patriarchy. Bourdieu's work is noteworthy in stressing the specificity of masculine domination and the enduring spaces of patriarchy. Within this framework, recent research suggests the importance of finding ways of validating the diversity of men's experiences, rather than simply identifying men with oppressive power relations.

References and further reading

Bourdieu, P. (2001) *Masculine Domination*, Stanford, CA: Stanford University Press.

Connell, R. (2000) *The Men and the Boys*, Cambridge: Polity.

McDowell, L. (2000) 'The trouble with men?' *International Journal of Urban and Regional Research*, 24: 201–9.

Seidler, V.J. (1997) *Man Enough*, Thousand Oaks, CA: Sage

Whitehead, S.M. and Barrett, F.J. (2001) *The Masculinities Reader*, Cambridge: Polity.

See also: oppression; philosophy; privilege

STUART C. AITKEN

PRISONS

Prisons offer one of the most illuminating sites for those seeking to understand men and masculinities. Gender theorists argue that the social construction of dominant ideals of masculinity can explain not only why males constitute the majority within most prison populations but also why imprisonment and harsh punishment are viewed as acceptable responses to antisocial behaviour. Messerschmidt (2001) claims that for some males who may be poor or otherwise disadvantaged and thus do not have access to socially acceptable means to demonstrate manhood, crime is one avenue by which they can perform their masculine gender role.

According to Sabo *et al.* (2001), white-collar crimes are also perpetrated predominantly by males and exhibit a type of egoism and depersonalisation of their victims that is characteristic of dominant forms of masculinity. The 'get tough on crime' rhetoric and 'wars' on drugs and crime, which according to Maur and Chesney-Lind (2002) began to replace American ideals of rehabilitation in the 1980s, can be seen to represent patriarchal attitudes towards solving social problems. Moreover, it has been suggested that class hierarchies in society are maintained in part because middle- and working-class males, though relatively disempowered in relation to the ruling elite, are made to feel powerful when they compare themselves against a criminal class of 'weaker' males who are stigmatised through the prison system.

Donaldson (2001), a male prisoner rape survivor and founder of Stop Prisoner Rape (www.spr.org), reveals how prison culture creates a hierarchy, maintained by sexual assaults and modelled on the race, class and gender-based power structures found outside of prison. Among male prisoners, those with the most status will fight or are at least willing to fight, even to the point of death, and those with the least status are gentle, nonviolent, gay, bisexual, transgender or appear 'soft' in any way. The hypermasculinity present in prison environments dictates that either one is a 'real man' who rapes and victimises or one is a 'punk' who has suffered emasculation by assuming the 'female role' in voluntary or involuntary sexual acts. After being penetrated, male prisoners must accept a permanently lower status within the prison hierarchy and either risk repeated sexual assaults or find a 'man' for protection in exchange for a kind of sexual servitude that borders on sexual slavery.

Although both the rapist and the 'man' (in the protective relationship) are engaging in homosexuality or homosexual acts, their masculinity is nevertheless preserved, in accordance with the norms of prison life, because they do not experience penetration or adopt the stereotypically defined roles of women. Donaldson believes that these sexual practices sanctioned in male prisons, though obviously expanding traditional notions of masculinity, ultimately demonstrate the pervasiveness of sexism and homophobia in male prisons and within society as a whole. Davis (2003), a feminist prison abolitionist, also argues that the state of unaccountability found in many female prisons creates a similar culture of fear in which male correctional officers may sexually assault with few worries of repercussion.

As Paczensky (2001) notes, most people in prison will one day be released back into society, and many of the men who have (often out of necessity for survival) learned to become more violent and sexist while incarcerated will act out these destructive behaviours in the form of domestic violence and child abuse. Masters (2001) similarly argues that until prisons are restructured to include at a minimum anti-violence programmes and other opportunities for education to help men rethink their masculinity and abusive behaviour, prisons will continue to reproduce the cycles of crime, violence and oppression that exist in society.

Lastly, Sabo *et al.* argue that by focusing attention on the sensationalistic acts of violence in prison and defining prison violence as an unusual spectacle unconnected with the gender relations of mainstream society, the continuing epidemic of male violence occurring in all aspects of society is either rendered invisible or normalised. Furthermore, failing to politicise prisons and the plight of prisoners also prevents an appreciation of the ways in which particular types of male bodies have become criminalised. For example, the terms 'black male' and 'criminal' have become closely identified in the media and in the popular imagination, which inevitably perpetuates racism against communities of colour and contributes to the high rate of incarceration for African–American males (Davis 2001).

References and further reading

Carrabine, E. and Longhurst, B. (1998) 'Gender and prison organization', *The Howard Journal*, 37: 161–76.

Davis, A. (2001) 'Race, gender, and prison history: from the convict lease system to the supermax prison', in D. Sabo, T. Kupers and W. London (eds) *Prison Masculinities*, Philadelphia, PA: Temple University Press, pp. 35–45.

——(2003) *Are Prisons Obsolete?* New York: Seven Stories.

Donaldson, S.D. (2001) 'A million jockers, punks, and queens', in D. Sabo, T. Kupers and W. London (eds) *Prison Masculinities*, Philadelphia, PA: Temple University Press, pp. 118–26.

Masters, J. (2001) 'Scars', in D. Sabo, T. Kupers and W. London (eds) *Prison Masculinities*, Philadelphia, PA: Temple University Press, pp. 203–6.

Maur, M. and Chesney-Lind, M. (2002) 'Introduction', in M. Maur and M. Chesney-Lind (eds) *Invisible Punishment*, New York: New Press.

Messerschmidt, J.W. (1993) *Masculinities and Crime*, Lanham, MD: Rowman and Littlefield.

—— (2001) 'Masculinities, crime, and prison', in D. Sabo, T. Kupers and W. London (eds) *Prison Masculinities*, Philadelphia, PA: Temple University Press, pp. 67–72.

Paczensky, S.V. (2001) 'The wall of silence', in D. Sabo, T. Kupers and W. London (eds) *Prison Masculinities*, Philadelphia, PA: Temple University Press, pp. 133–6.

Sabo, D., Kupers, T. and London, W. (2001) 'Gender and the politics of punishment', in D. Sabo, T. Kupers and W. London (eds) *Prison Masculinities*, Philadelphia, PA: Temple University Press, pp. 3–18.

See also: crime, criminality and law; working with men in prison; working with perpetrators or offenders

JASON L. MALLORY

PRIVILEGE

Bailey (1998: 109) describes privilege as 'systematically conferred advantages individuals enjoy by virtue of their membership in dominant groups with access to resources and institutional power that are beyond the common advantages of marginalised citizens'. The main benefits that accrue from privilege include a disproportionate share of political authority and power, high social status, wealth and affluence (Sidanius and Pratto 1999). Individuals come to possess these benefits as a result of their membership in, for example, particular gender, class, race and ethnic groups. An individual's privilege is thus more a product of membership in privileged groups than it is of individual capabilities.

McIntosh (1992), one of the first writers to relate the concept of privilege to the specific benefits individuals receive, distinguishes between 'earned strength and unearned power conferred systematically' (1992: 78). In this classic article, McIntosh constructed a list of forty-six advantages that were available to her as a white person that were not available to people of colour under racism. Schacht (2003) similarly lists the ways in which he as a man is privileged: he has a better chance of getting a job than a woman; the majority of news reports he reads will be about the accomplishments of men; he can rely on his wife to do most of the housework; he feels safe from sexual harassment and sexual assault in public places and so on.

To explore the concept of privilege critically, we need to identify its key characteristics: the invisibility of privilege to those who have it; the power of the privileged group to determine the social norm; the naturalisation of privilege and the sense of entitlement that accompanies it.

Most privilege is not recognised as such by those who have it (Bailey 1998). So not being aware of privilege is an important aspect of privilege. Johnson (2001) refers to this lack of awareness as 'epistemic privilege'. He observes how members of privileged groups either do not understand what others mean when they refer to them as privileged or they tend to get angry and defensive. Because privilege does not necessarily bring happiness and fulfilment, this will sometimes be used to deny the existence of privilege. These responses represent significant obstacles to the struggle for equality.

Privileged groups have become the model for normative human relations and this explains in part why they do not want to know about the experiences of the oppressed. The privileged group thus comes to represent the hegemonic norm whereby, for example in the US and Europe, male white heterosexual young financially secure Christians come to represent what it means to be considered normal (Perry 2001). Perry (2001) observes that through the positioning of self and other, various dualisms are established in which forms of difference are devalued because they are seen as inferior, weak or subordinate in relation to the normal, which is presented as superior, strong and dominant. The normativity of privilege means that this becomes the basis for measuring success and failure. Thus, those who are not privileged are potentially regarded as deviant. The negative valuation of difference is thus reproduced by the establishment of the normative standard. Because the privileged are regarded as 'normal', they are less likely to be studied or researched because the norm does not have to be 'marked'.

The social divisions between the privileged and the oppressed are further reproduced through their attributed naturalness. Rather than seeing difference as being socially constructed, gender, race, sexuality and class are regarded as flowing from nature. Beliefs about social hierarchy as being natural provide a rationale for social dominance and absolve dominant groups from responsibility for addressing social inequalities. Belief in the 'God-given' or biological basis of dominance reproduces social inequality. Members of privileged groups either believe that they have inherited the characteristics which give them advantages or they consciously set out to cover up the socially constructed basis of their dominance (Wonders 2000).

Another aspect of privilege is the sense of entitlement that members of privileged groups feel about their status. They believe that they have a right to be acknowledged, respected and rewarded, and they often become angry when their sense of entitlement is thwarted (Rosenblum and Travis 1996). Members of privileged groups also believe that they deserve the benefits and status they hold and are often unable to recognise how these benefits are derived from their membership of particular groups.

Bailey (2000) argues that members of dominant groups can develop what she calls 'traitorous identities'. She differentiates between those who are unaware of their privilege and those who are critically cognisant of their privilege. Traitors are those who refuse to reproduce their privilege and who challenge the worldviews that dominant groups are expected to adhere to. These dominant group members are able to identify with the experiences of oppressed groups. It is from this basis that white people will challenge racism and that men will challenge patriarchy. From this premise, while it is difficult for members of privileged groups to appraise their own position critically, it is not impossible.

References and further reading

Bailey, A. (1998) 'Privilege', *Journal of Social Philosophy*, 29 (3): 104–19.

—— (2000) 'Locating traitorous identities', in U. Narayan and S. Harding (eds) *Decentering the Center*, Bloomington, IN: Indiana University Press.

Johnson, A. (2001) *Privilege, Power and Difference*, Mountain View, CA: Mayfield.

McIntosh, P. (1992) 'White privilege and male privilege', in M. Anderson, and P. Collins (eds) *Race, Class and Gender*, Belmont: CA: Wadsworth.

Perry, B. (2001) *In the Name of Hate*, New York: Routledge.

Rosenblum, K. and Travis, T. (1996) 'Experiencing difference', in K. Rosenblum and T. Travis (eds) *The Meaning of Difference*, New York: McGraw-Hill.

Schacht, S. (2003) 'Teaching about being an oppressor', in M. Kimmel and A. Ferber (eds) *Privilege*, Boulder, CO: Westview.

Sidanius, J. and Pratto, F. (1999) *Social Dominance*, Cambridge: Cambridge University Press.

Wonders, N. (2000) 'Conceptualising difference', in Criminal Justice Collective of Northern Arizona University (eds) *Investigating Difference*, Boston, MA: Allyn and Bacon.

See also: oppression; power relations; white privilege

BOB PEASE

PROCREATION

From a male perspective, procreation refers to the conception and begetting of human life through the use of sperm. In the United States, males first produce viable sperm around age fourteen. Heterosexual intercourse is by far the most common means by which the procreative process is initiated, although men increasingly procreate using various forms of assisted reproductive technologies (ART), including in-vitro fertilisation, microepididmal sperm aspiration and direct testicular aspiration (Marsiglio and Hinojosa, forthcoming). The relationship between biological procreation, social fathering and legal paternity has become more complex due to developments in ART (Marsiglio 1998). One man's contribution to procreation may or may not result in his legal or informal establishment of paternity – the recognition of a specific man as a child's father (Hubin 2003).

Worldwide, most men report wanting to have a biological child at some point in their life, and most do so. In the United States, roughly 87 per cent of men aged forty to forty-nine report having offspring (Alan Guttmacher Institute 2002). Estimates of male procreation based on self-reports understate men's procreative experiences because some men are unaware that a conception due to sexual intercourse or sperm donation resulted in a birth, and some are unwilling to acknowledge paternity.

Although procreation is commonly associated with the physiological processes of conception and birth, social psychologists also focus on how men develop and express a procreative consciousness and identity (Marsiglio and Hutchinson 2002). Procreative consciousness represents men's (and women's) various forms of procreative knowledge and emotional experiences when they are aware of their potential to create human life. One form of knowledge, paternity confirmation, is affected by diverse cultural norms. The emergence of DNA fingerprinting technology in industrialised societies during the late twentieth century affords men a novel and more objective way to determine their biological paternity status and refute their sexual partner's verbal claims.

Typically, procreation and paternity are viewed as a singular event: one man is responsible for begetting one child. But the Indians of the lowland regions of South America provide intriguing examples of partible paternity (multiple fatherhood) that demonstrate the plasticity of these notions (Beckerman and Valentine 2002). These peoples believe that children are often the product of primary as well as secondary or contributing fathers who have had sexual intercourse with the mother immediately prior to conception and during her pregnancy. Sometimes women are encouraged to have multiple partners to enhance the prenatal child's well-being and development.

References and further reading

Alan Guttmacher Institute (2002) *In Their Own Right: Addressing the Sexual and Reproductive Health Needs of American Men*, New York: New York University Press.

Beckerman, S. and Valentine, P. (2002) *Cultures of Multiple Fathers. The Theory and Practice of Paritable Paternity in Lowland South America*, Gainesville, FL: University of Florida Press.

Hubin, D.C. (2003) 'Daddy dilemmas: untangling the puzzles of paternity', *Cornell Journal of Law and Public Policy*, 13: 29–80.

Marsiglio, W. (1998) *Procreative Man*, New York: New York University Press.

Marsiglio, W. and Hinojosa, R. (forthcoming) 'Social and psychological influences on male reproductive function', in R. Swerdloff and J. Pryor (eds) *Male Reproductive Dysfunction: Pathophysiology and Treatment*, New York: Marcel Dekker.

Marsiglio, W. and Hutchinson, S. (2002) *Sex, Men, and Babies: Stories of Awareness and Responsibility*, New York: New York University Press.

See also: infertility; reproductive issues and technologies; sexuality

WILLIAM MARSIGLIO

PROFEMINISM

Profeminism is a development of the men's movement that originated in the late 1960s as small groups of men under the influence of the women's liberation movement began to challenge existing sexist practices.

In the US, the meetings of these groups of men led to yearly conferences and then to the formation of a national organisation originally called the Men's National Organization, then later the National Organization for Changing Men and now called the National Organization of Men Against Sexism (NOMAS). From 1979, this organisation published a magazine *Changing Men: Issues in Gender, Sex and Politics* (originally *M.: Gentle Men for Gender Justice*). However, this magazine ceased publication in 1996 and was replaced by a quarterly journal entitled *Brother* in 1999 (Goldrick-Jones 2002). NOMAS describes itself as an activist organisation of men and women advocating a perspective for enhancing men's lives that is profeminist, gay-affirmative, anti-racist and committed to justice on a broad range of social issues including class, age, religion and physical abilities (NOMAS homepage 2005). In Australia, Men against Sexual Assault (MASA) was formed in the late 1970s and has sponsored a range of events and projects, including the profeminist magazine, *XY*. In Europe, the European Profeminist Men's Network maintains an extensive website of activities and publications.

At early profeminist men's conferences, there was a strong challenge from gay men arguing that men should make the political choice to be gay because otherwise they would be supporting oppressive heterosexist norms. Similar challenges were made at women's feminist conferences as well. Nevertheless, while these feminist and profeminist groups strongly supported gay and lesbian rights, most of their members did not feel compelled to make the political choice to adopt a gay or lesbian life style themselves.

Men who describe themselves as profeminists usually choose not to call themselves feminists. They take feminism to involve the empirical claim that women and men are not equal in the public or the private sphere and the moral claim that such inequality is wrong and should be eliminated. While they endorse both of these claims, they also hold that to be a feminist one must, in addition, have experienced sexist oppression. This, they claim, men cannot have experienced because they are privileged rather than oppressed by sexism. Men benefit from educational, professional, political and economic advantages over women and, to be sure, they are oppressed, but they are not oppressed as men. Men are oppressed because of their race, class, age, ethnicity or sexual orientation, but not because of their sex. To be a feminist, profeminist men maintain, one needs not only to share the feminist analysis and vision but also to experience that oppression as well.

But this distinction between feminists and profeminists is difficult to maintain in all cases. Surely men generally benefit from sexist institutions just as women generally are harmed by them. But some men are significantly harmed by sexist institutions, particularly those who deeply value and work for gender equality in their lives, just as some women are significantly benefited by sexist institutions, particularly those women who are served well by existing gender roles. For example, some men are significantly harmed by sexist institutions either because they do not live up to them or because they openly flaunt the sexist standards of their society. So even if suffering from sexist institutions were required to be a feminist, it wouldn't follow that only women could be feminists. Accordingly, it would seem best to only require of feminists and profeminists alike that they be supportive of the cause of feminism.

But how can men be supportive of the cause of feminism? From the beginning of the women's movement, men have found ways to make contributions to the cause of feminism. In the US, at the Seneca Falls Convention in 1848, Fredrick Douglass made a speech that helped the resolution proposed by Elizabeth Cady Stanton to pass. Thirty-nine other men attended this convention and James Mott chaired all its sessions. Later, men who participated in suffrage demonstrations were seen as traitors to their sex; they were labelled 'Aunt Nancy men', or 'miss-Nancys' or 'man-milliners'. Playwright George Middleton recounts one demonstration where,

> while the women were gazed upon with respect and frequent applause, the men every step of the two-mile walk had to submit to jeers, whistles, 'me-a-ows', and such cries as 'Take that handkerchief out of your cuff', 'Oh, you gay deceiver' . . . None of these men 'deserted the ranks' [Middleton reported proudly].
>
> (Middleton 1947)

This role for feminist or profeminist men continues today in academia and elsewhere when feminist views are widely attacked and particularly when there are few women committed to feminism around to respond to such attacks. For example, many departments in colleges and universities still have no senior women and few, if any, junior women, and the areas of expertise of these women may or may not include feminism. So, in these contexts, if feminist views are not defended by men, then they may not be defended at all.

There is also an enriching effect that comes from women and men defending feminist views together. Sexists have come to expect that women might endorse feminist views, but when women and men endorses such views together, it is particularly effective, given the advantages that accrue to men in a sexist society.

In the field of philosophy, it is unsettling to sexists to see those who are trained and recognised as competent in mainline areas of the discipline, particularly the areas of ethics and social and political philosophy, demanding the inclusion and infusion of feminist views in these areas of philosophy. Accordingly, this is another context where men can be particularly useful to the cause of feminism.

In 1991, during the week of 1–6 December (the second anniversary of the Montreal massacre of fourteen women by a man enraged against feminists), a group of men in the Canadian cities of Toronto, Kingston and Ottawa distributed white ribbons to passers-by as a expression of opposition to violence against women. The event was highly successful, with even the prime minister and members of parliament choosing to join the demonstration and wear a white ribbon. The idea has now spread to a number of other countries.

In addition, there are contexts where men because of their past involvement with sexist practices and institutions can be helpful in exposing and critiquing those same practices and institutions. One such practice is that of hard-core pornography, which MacKinnon has argued causes harm to women by increasing discriminatory attitudes and behaviour in men towards women that take both violent and nonviolent forms (MacKinnon 1987). Now men who participate in this practice learn through the pleasures of masturbation to enjoy depictions of the forceful subordination of women. Accordingly, those who think that the practice of hard-core pornography does not harm women must think that it is possible to enjoy depictions of the forceful subordination of women without in any way desiring to actually forcefully subordinate women in real life. But given that the enjoyment of hard-core pornography comes from vicariously experiencing and identifying with the activity of forcefully subordinating women, it is difficult to see how men can experience such enjoyment, culminating in orgasm, without desiring to forcefully subordinate women in real life.

Moreover, some women may underestimate the harmfulness of hard-core pornography. They may sample hard-core pornography and find that they have little difficulty renouncing the submissive and degraded images of the women that it displays. They may then mistakenly infer from their own reactions to hard-core pornography that men should have little difficulty doing the same.

Here it would be helpful if men were to explain how their reactions to hard-core pornography are typically different from those of women. Men should explain how hard-core pornography when combined with the pleasures of masturbation can enter their psyches and structure their sexual tastes in ways that can be quite difficult to resist. This happens whenever the sexual images drawn from hard-core pornography impose themselves on men's real-life encounters, demanding to be re-enacted as the price of sexual pleasure. Men can easily find themselves in a situation where they cannot easily achieve orgasm without somehow incorporating the sexual images of hard-core pornography, leading them either to impose or to try to impose hard-core pornographic roles on the women who come into their lives, with more or less harmful effects. It is just in this regard that men can testify to the destructive impact hard-core pornography can have on their relations with women and thereby help demonstrate the necessity for banning it.

In so many contexts, women are in a much better position than men to expose and argue against the harmful effects of sexist practices. Generally, nothing succeeds better at sharpening one's perception of unjust practices or at developing one's argumentative skills to oppose such practices than actually having suffered from them oneself. That is why women's subjection to the injustice of sexist practices makes them the obvious leaders in the fight to rid society of those practices. Nevertheless, there are a number of contexts where men are in a particularly good position to contribute to women's liberation, and one of these is the role they can play in exposing the harmful effects that hard-core pornography can have on their own lives and on the lives of the women with whom they come in contact.

Feminist or profeminist men have been involved in the women's movement from its very beginning. They have been particularly helpful in defending feminism when no women can or will defend it, and by contributing their own special insights to overturning sexist practices and institutions. This collaboration of men and women in the cause of feminism can only be expected to increase and intensify in the future as feminism is able to achieve more and more of its goals.

References and further reading

Clatterbaugh, K. (1997) *Contemporary Perspectives on Masculinity: Men, Women and Politics in Modern Society*, 2nd edn, Boulder, CO: Westview.

Digby, T. (ed.) (1998) *Men Doing Feminism*, New York: Routledge.

Goldrick-Jones, A. (2002) *Men Who Believe in Feminism*, Westport, CN: Praeger.

Kimmel, M.S. (2004) *Gendered Society*, 2nd edn, New York: Oxford University Press.

Kimmel, M.S. and Mosmiller, T.E. (eds) (1992) *Against the Tide*, Boston, MA: Beacon.

Kimmel, M.S., Hearn, J. and Connell, R. (eds) (2005) *Handbook of Studies on Men and Masculinities*, London: Sage.

Lingard, B. and Douglas, P. (1999) *Men Engaging Feminism*, Philadelphia, PA: Open University Press.

MacKinnon, C. (1987) *Feminism Unmodified*, Cambridge, MA: Harvard University Press.

May, L. (1998) *Masculinity and Morality*, Ithaca, NY: Cornell University Press.

May, L., Strikwerda, R. and Hopkins, P. (eds) (1996) *Rethinking Masculinity*, Lanham, MD: Rowman and Littlefield.

Messner, M.A. (2000) *Politics of Masculinities*, Lanham, MD: Rowman and Littlefield.

Middleton, G. (1947) *These Things are Mine*, New York: Harcourt, Brace.

National Organization of Men Against Sexism (NOMAS) (2005) http://www.nomas.org/sys-tmpl/door

See also: feminism; feminist theory; homosexuality; masculinity politics; pornography; privilege; sexual violence; women's studies/gender studies/feminist studies

JAMES P. STERBA

PROSTITUTES, MEN AS

Despite recent attempts to study male sex workers, within the overall literature on the sex industry they remain an understudied group. Yet evidence suggests that male sex work is a growing enterprise and the male body is increasingly seen as a commodified product. The expansion of men's participation as sex workers is complemented by the growing eroticisation of men's bodies in popular culture. For example, male-to-male pornography constitutes a sizeable segment of the US pornography market, about one third to one half of the $2.4 billion adult industry (Watson 2000). In recent years, masculinity and male bodies have been openly represented in eroticised cultural terms within the context of art, fashion and film (Kay *et al.* 2000). Porn films, but particularly gay videos of the 1990s, have focused on 'handsome, beefy masculine men', and give more emphasis to muscularity. Pornography websites now show the erotic predominance of male sexuality through the visual display of the erect penis and 'gangbang' group activity with one or two female characters interacting with a group of naked men together. The 1990s also saw the growing display of male bodies in mainstream magazines and newspapers, including in sexually oriented commercial and classified advertisements. These developments confront and challenge heterosexual culture head on. They also validate male-to-male sex by seeing it played out in the public domain.

Not surprisingly, there has been a shift in the discourse about male sex work. The discourses of criminology, deviance and social control have been used as conceptual frameworks to explain male prostitution, and, as a result, the negative and pathological aspects of male prostitution were the exclusive focus of such research. Within this broad literature, researchers have reported that male sex workers tend to have multiple problems, including running away from home and leaving school early, which results in a lack of educational, social and employable skills (Coombs 1974). These foci have led to stereotyping of the male sex worker as a psychopathological social misfit and as a public health risk in spreading HIV. Recent work suggests that such views are outdated and incorrect. This also shows that the intrinsic nature of sex work is not all oppressive and that there are different kinds of worker and client experiences and varying degrees of victimisation, exploitation, agency and choice (Parsons 2005). While male sex workers have been portrayed as contributing to HIV infection, the evidence is that having a legalised, professionalised and state-controlled industry results in lower risk of HIV transmission (Minichiello *et al.* 2000).

Although male sex workers fitting the popular negative stereotypes do exist, these descriptions do not recognise the diversity of lifestyles and experience that constitute the wider male sex worker population. Furthermore, such representations ignore broader structural understandings of the sex industry and portray male sex workers as oppressed victims who are incapable of rational choice. Entering into sex work can be seen as the outcome of a rational choice for financial gain and lifestyle and the worker's choice can be as free, or indeed as constrained, as the choice to enter other forms of wage labour. Furthermore, conditions vary among male sex workers. For example, there is a perception of drug dependency and low education level among sex workers, but in a recent study, independent sex workers who self-advertise were about two times less likely to report heroin consumption but were twice as likely to report using ecstasy than street sex workers. They were also more likely to have completed secondary education (Minichiello *et al.* 2001). Cyberspace has extended sex work beyond the streets, and the last decade has witnessed a growth in the number of men who sell sexual services on the Internet. There is evidence to suggest that men are entering sex work and taking advantage of the sexual appeal of the male body to sell to both female and male clients.

Research on male prostitutes demonstrates the complexity of the meanings and practices associated with sexuality, gender, power and social life. Non-gay identifying men who sell sex to other men provide us with an opportunity to interrogate how they link 'masculinities' to their sex and work, and how this is experienced and enacted within the particular social and sub-cultural space of the sex industry. Homophobia is also relevant here because despite increasing political and legal reforms, more liberal attitudes and greater tolerance of gay 'lifestyles', it is still true that there is a powerful link between homophobia and manliness in many countries (Plummer 2000). A recent study on male sex workers shows how it is possible for them to manage their sexual work experiences such that they can preserve a masculine image and identity, while having paid sex with other men. This work challenges a potent stereotype that heterosexual masculinity and engaging in male–male sexual activity cannot co-exist (Caceres and Jimenez 1999). It is difficult to conduct research that fully informs us of the thinking and fantasies behind men's sexualities because of their reluctance to openly reveal aspects about their sexualities through interviews or questionnaires, although understanding the sexual interactions of sex workers or conducting a content analysis of contemporary pornography may offer some new insights into this topic.

The notion that male sex work is a clandestine activity that occurs on the streets is no longer accurate. In most Western countries, male sex work increasingly is becoming a legalised business operating through escort agencies and advertisements. Increasingly, men are entering the business with more positive and professional attitudes towards their work. For example, in the US and Australia, many workers continue to work in this industry over a long period of time and find the work rewarding. Lower levels of unsafe sex practices and of alcohol and drug use occur in a professionalised male sex-work industry (Parsons 2005). It is important to understand that different cultures have somewhat different ways of conceptualising sexuality and gender, and this impacts on how the male sex industry is organised at a social level and personally experienced. This may also explain differences between the male and female sex industry.

References and further reading

Caceres, C. and Jiminez, O. (1999) 'Sexual cultures among young men who sell sex to other men in Lima', in P. Aggleton (ed.) *Men Who Sell Sex*, London: UCL Press, pp. 179–94.

Coombs, N. (1974) 'Male prostitution: a psychosocial view of behaviour', *American Journal of Orthopsychiatry*, 44: 78–89.

Kay, K., Nagle, J. and Gould, B. (eds) (2000) *Male Lust: Pleasure, Power and Transformation*, New York: Harrington Park Press.

Marino, R., Minichiello, V. and Disorga, C. (2003) 'Male sex workers in Cordoba, Argentina', *Pan American Journal of Public Health*, 5: 311–19.

Minichiello, V., Marino, R., Browne, J., Jamieson, M., Peterson, K. and Reuter, B. (2000) 'Commercial sex between men: a prospective diary based study', *Journal of Sex Research*, 37: 151–60.

—— (2001) 'Male sex workers in three Australian cities: sociodemographic and sex work characteristics', *Journal of Homosexuality*, 1: 29–51.

Parsons, J. (ed.) (2005) *Contemporary Research in Sex Work*, New York: Haworth Press.

Plummer, D. (2000) *One of the Boys: Masculinity, Homophobia and Modern Manhood*, New York: Haworth Press.

Watson, J. (ed.) (2000) *Male Bodies: Health, Culture and Identity*, Buckingham: Open University Press.

See also: prostitution

VICTOR MINICHIELLO
GLENN P. HARVEY

PROSTITUTION

There are wildly varying estimates available about the scale of the prostitution industry in the world today, although most of these are not obtained by any scientific method. There is, however, general agreement that prostitution is widespread, even in places where it is illegal, and that gender and other inequalities are fundamental factors in the structuring of prostitution. The vast majority of those who obtain their daily needs via sex work are female and poor. Some feminists argue that prostitution is always forced and thus the same as rape; prostitution needs to be seen, then, as a basic violation of women's human rights and to be subject to strong criminal penalties. Other feminists, however, argue that prostitution should be seen as a form of work; attention then is focused on maximising the labour and human rights of sex workers, including the decriminalisation of prostitution (see Sullivan 2003).

Men are the main participants in prostitution. They are the vast majority of prostitution clients world-wide (although women may also be clients, especially in sex tourism destinations). Men also participate in prostitution as *sex workers* (mostly seeing male clients) and are major actors in the *organisation and management of prostitution*.

In 1948 Kinsey and his co-authors reported that two-thirds of all American men had been to a prostitute at least once in their lives. Close to 9 per cent of men in London aged sixteen to forty-four, and 4.3 per cent nationally, have paid for sex in the past five years (Erens *et al.* 2001), representing approximately 2.5 million commercial sex transactions. Yet remarkably little research has focused on the reasons why men go to prostitutes and what they believe they are purchasing. The vast majority of sex industry research is focused on female sex workers. Research on clients is often seen as difficult to conduct, but perhaps the main obstacle to research on clients is pervasive cultural beliefs about the fixed and biological nature of the male heterosexual 'drive'; so men who go to prostitutes are seen to be engaged in a largely natural activity (unlike women who are prostitutes). Indeed, if this sexual outlet is not available to men – particularly men without wives – then they are sometimes regarded as more likely to resort to the rape of 'innocent' women (i.e. those who are not sex workers).

In the last decade a small but focused literature has appeared regarding men's motivations and sexual behaviour with prostitutes (Jordan 1997; Monto 2000). Researchers have found that 'clients sought sex workers not so much for different types of sexual activity as for different sexual partners' (Perkins 1999: 42), and that most clients wanted the same sexual activities they sought in their non-prostitution relations. Most men, whether married or unmarried, said they went to sex workers because they wanted 'uncomplicated' sex and because they 'liked sex with a variety of women/men' (Perkins 1999: 43). In their more psychological study, Plumridge *et al.* found that all the clients interviewed 'explained their motivation in paying for sex in terms of pleasure'. This pleasure involved a clear relaxation of the normal duties and obligations associated with sexual activity in our society, in which the clients 'rejoiced in feeling free to utilise commercial sex according to their own unilateral needs and convenience'. Perversely, they also endowed their commercial sex transactions with notions of sexual reciprocity and mutuality. So an essential part of the pleasure of paying for sex was a perceived emotional and sexual mutuality (Plumridge *et al.* 1997: 173). The physical and emotional labour of sex workers was clearly invisible to clients.

References and further reading

Erens, R., McManus, S., Prescott, A. and Field, J. (2001) *National Survey of Sexual Attitudes and Lifestyles II, 2000–2001*, London: National Centre for Social Research.

Jordan, J. (1997) 'User pays: why men buy sex', *Australian and New Zealand Journal of Criminology*, 30 (1): 55–71.

Monto, M.A. (2000) 'Why men seek out prostitutes', in R. Weitzer (ed.) *Sex for Sale. Prostitution, Pornography and the Sex Industry*, New York: Routledge, pp. 67–83.

Perkins, R. (1999) '"How much are you, love?" The customer in the Australian sex industry', *Social Alternatives*, 18 (3): 38–47.

Plumridge, E.W., Chetwynd, S.J., Reed, A. and Gifford, S.J. (1997) 'Discourses of emotionality in commercial sex: the missing client voice', *Feminism and Psychology*, 7 (2): 165–81.

Sullivan, B. (2003) 'Trafficking in women. Feminism and new international law', *International Feminist Journal of Politics*, 5 (1): 67–91.

See also: pimps and traffickers; prostitutes, men as; commercial sexual exploitation of children

BARBARA SULLIVAN

PROTEST MASCULINITY

Protest masculinity advanced by Connell (1995), based on Adler's psychoanalytic notion of the 'masculine protest', is a form of over-compensation for childhood weakness or inferiority, resulting in aggressiveness and unremitting pursuit of triumphs as an adult. Connell's sociological deployment of the concept refers to collective practice rather than patterns internalised in the individual psyche. It involves compensatory claims to imagined powerfulness on the part of marginalised young men experiencing social injury at their lack of real power, expressed through a hypermasculine style.

Such forms of practice can be found among those working-class men most disadvantaged by the restructured labour market, 'gangs' of young men from racialised minorities (Messerschmidt 1993; Bourgois 1995), diasporic and migrant men, and formerly colonised men who have engaged in armed struggle for liberation in a context of poverty structured by racism (Xaba 2001). Protest masculinity can be characterised by school resistance, violence, occasional crime, substance abuse, obsession with motor vehicles, or often short-lived and exploitative heterosexual relationships (Connell 1995: 110).

Willis's ethnography (1977) shows the ideological effect of the sexism and racism of the working-class, anti-school 'lads' in the British Midlands, compensating through what could be seen as protest masculinity for their put-downs in schooling and at work. The crucial paradox is that their own cultural resistance leads to the reproduction of their class subordination; their masculinity is integral to this process. Two decades later, in different labour market circumstances, Mac an Ghaill (1994) identified an oppositional culture of working-class masculinity among English 'macho lads', where the gendered rejection of the official school culture registers a protest against the very class-determined world of unemployment or fraudulent work-for-the-dole 'training' programmes for which they are likely destined.

As the globalised 'new world order' is disrupted by a 'war on terror' of indefinite duration, attention is turning to the global reaction of those who experience in religious terms the marginalisation and humiliation that is the legacy of colonialism and imperialism. To what extent, it may be asked (Kimmel 2003), is the male suicide bomber practising an ultimate form of protest masculinity?

References and further reading

Bourgois, P. (1995) *In Search of Respect*, Cambridge: Cambridge University Press.

Connell, R. (1995) *Masculinities*, Sydney: Allen and Unwin.

Kimmel, M.S. (2003) 'Globalisation and its (mal(e) contents', *International Sociology*, 18 (3): 603–20.

Mac an Ghaill, M. (1994) *The Making of Men*, Buckingham: Open University Press.

Messerschmidt, J.W. (1993) *Masculinities and Crime*, Lanham, MD: Rowman and Littlefield.

Willis, P. (1977) *Learning to Labour*, London: Saxon House.

Xaba, T. (2001) 'Masculinity and its malcontents', in R. Morrell (ed.) *Changing Men in Southern Africa*, Pietermaritzburg: University of Natal.

SCOTT POYNTING

PSYCHOANALYSIS

From the perspective of critical masculinity studies, psychoanalytic accounts of gender formation offer one great benefit, which is that they are indeed *accounts*. Despite Freud's easily misconstrued assertions equating anatomy with destiny, in fact neither he nor his follower Jacques Lacan view gender or sexuality as biologically determined or as proceeding from instinctual nature. Rather, both insist upon gender and sexuation as psychic formations, socio-symbolic organisations for which accounts are precisely what need to be given, even if the accounts themselves are inevitably imprecise. Although patriarchal and misogynist assumptions are demonstrably at work in their accounts, Freud and Lacan also provide critical strategies for questioning, or at least de-naturalising, those very assumptions. Even at their most normative, both remain discernibly ambivalent towards the norm. Both see psychic and sexual normativity as essentially fictional, emerging not from a determining nature but as part of the complex representational structure that is human reality itself. Norms, such as those that regulate the performance of masculinity, are for psychoanalysis not innately given but socially produced, enforced through structures of repression and orders of symbolisation. Complete conformity to those norms is thus never a matter of happy organic development but remains rather only a fragile and tenuous achievement that always leaves a residue of dissatisfaction and unconscious desire. Psychoanalysis is concerned with exactly this residue. It addresses the failure of normal human beings ever to simply be normal human beings.

For psychoanalysis, then, failure to 'be a man' is all it can ever finally mean to 'be a man'. As psychoanalysis conceives it, all it can ever mean to be a man, or to be human in the first place, is the all too human failure to have been an animal. I refer to a 'first place', because in describing psychoanalytic accounts of gendered subjectivity it is best to begin there, not exactly in the womb, but from the hard fact that we leave that 'first place' too soon. Lacan speaks of our species' prematurity at birth, while Freud emphasises its consequence: a prolonged period of helpless dependency for human offspring compared with other animal neonates. A conjectural evolutionary explanation for this deficiency is that premature birthing developed as a strategy of adaptation when our primate ancestors' assumption of an upright gait precipitated a contraction of the pelvic cavity in females such that heads of fully formed foetuses were suddenly too big to be born. But whatever the speculative prehistorical cause, the ongoing effect is that, unlike the animal, we are not born human but have to be made that way. While any other animal that survives its neonativity will grow to become an adult of its species, the infant of our species, congenitally inadequate to its own animality, requires extensive assistance and training if it is actually going to become a human being – accede to the symbolic order, become a speaking subject, enjoy (or endure) a meaningful (if discontented) existence as a recognised participant in a specifically human, socio-symbolic reality.

Forget gender for a moment: for psychoanalysis, humanness itself is an acquisition, the result of various processes of humanisation/socialisation. For psychoanalysis the human subject is the anthropomorphised animal, the organism that must sacrifice an already inadequate animality to accede to an anthropomorphic status that – because it is constitutionally representational – must mean, must be meaningful, but is itself never finally settled or secured in its being or its meanings. The processes of humanisation (which vary culturally and historically but are universal and transhistorical in their necessity) require us to give up or renounce what was impossible for us anyway – an immediate, purely natural, animal existence – in order to live in an inherently unstable social network of signs. If the unconscious is structured like a language, as Lacan has it, then language is the slippery foundation of psychoanalysis as the 'talking cure'. But if there is a biological 'bedrock' in psychoanalytic theory, it can only be these always already crumbling grounds of human natal prematurity, a biological determination that seems the very failure of biological determination and which allows psychoanalysis its vision of a primordial discord – a radical rupture or gap – at the heart of our organic, subjective and sexual existence. For psychoanalysis, humanness is itself the compensatory symptom of failed and sacrificed animality. It is a substitute satisfaction, a consolation prize not only for not having succeeded as animals but also for the symbolic scission that, installing us in language, separates us from what little real animality we ever briefly enjoyed. And yet, since the permanently real animal can never act to transform the terms of its existence, this sacrifice of impossible animality becomes the very condition of possibility for human freedom. Such potentiating failure helps account for the fact that human sexuality always exceeds the imperatives of mere species reproduction as well as for the fact that we are never only physically, chromosomally male or female but must always live subjectively in some relation to the fictions of masculinity and femininity that prevail (fictions that, as fictions, are conceivably open to revision, historical transformation). As physical bodies, we are of course prey to biology: we are anatomically destined or driven to die. But as psychical entities we are subject to representation, and it is only as decentred representational structures that we live in our bodies or have relations with the bodies of others.

Freud conveys his understanding of the fundamental antagonism – between deficient organic existence and the overarching structures of representation and socialisation that constrain and sustain it – in various terms throughout the course of his career: as the conflict between primary and secondary processes; as the negotiation between the pleasure and reality principles; as the distinction between free and bound libidinal cathexes; as the developmental organisation of infantile 'polymorphous perversity' into Oedipalised normality; as (for the early Freud) the topography of the unconscious, preconscious and conscious; as (for the later Freud) the intricate agons among the ego, the superego and the id; even, finally, as the radical tension between Eros and Thanatos, the representatives of the drives of life and death.

Here I will focus on the pleasure/reality negotiation. By 'pleasure', Freud means the reduction of unpleasurable tension. By 'pleasure principle' he means a principle of psychic functioning that demands unpleasure's immediate reduction. Under the pleasure principle's dominance, the infant experiencing unpleasure attempts to reduce it by immediately hallucinating the object of gratification (say, the breast). But since the instant image fails to satisfy, the pleasure principle must give way to the mediations of the reality principle: the infant must articulate a demand, cry out for a real object that may only eventually appear, may appear in altered or diminished form (pacifier instead of breast) or may never appear again at all. Crucial here is the way the reality principle impels the infant's accession to temporality and exchange, the way the infant must renounce the immediate pleasures of hallucinated images in order to accept not only the delayed, partial, substitutive or withdrawn gratifications that reality offers but the fact that human reality is itself delay, partiality, substitution, withdrawal – is itself language, which must always unfold in time and involve delay and deferral, the endless substitution of words for missing, withdrawn or prohibited things. The displacement of pleasure by reality is the sacrifice of being for meaning (*l'etre pour la lettre*), and without this exchange the infant won't become a 'meaningfully' human being, much less a properly gendered subject. If it prefers its own internally conjured image of the breast to the point of refusing the externally real thing, it will starve to death. If it refuses the reality principle altogether, refuses to swap its demand for immediate gratification for its desire for the other's recognition, refuses to renounce the present pleasure for the promise of a more significant, more culturally important pleasure in the future, then it will fail to absorb linguistic training, much less the social processes of gendered ego-ideal formation. It will not accede to the symbolic order. Freud's thesis is that in reality no one ever seamlessly exchanges pleasure for reality: there is always an incommensurable leftover, unconscious but unceasingly productive of symptoms, dreams, slips of the tongue, perversions, literature, art, philosophy, religion and other substitutive satisfactions or signs of our discontent.

The 'symbolic order' mentioned above is in Lacan's view the order of language and culture, an order of symbols, a grammatically organised concatenation of words. But it also involves an order to symbolise, the social imperative to mean. Lacan's insight intimately links this symbolic imperative with the taboo against incest that founds and structures the exogamic social order. Oedipalising the 'extimate' acquisition of language, Lacan recasts the line that joins the signifier and the signified in structural linguistics as a bar of prohibition separating the infant from the mother, alienating the subject from the real. Just as language cannot completely 'coincide' with the real (signification depends upon dividing rather than uniting signifier and signified, sign and referent, word and thing), so the infant cannot completely 'coincide' with the mother, nor can the subject be 'at one' with the real. Lacan conflates the mythical 'no to the real' that initiates language with the structurating 'no of the father' that prohibits incest: both prevent impossible mergers. Because the infant enters the symbolic order by acceding to the father's law and agreeing to symbolise the mother rather than be (with) or 'possess' her, symbolisation entails sacrifice of the fantasised merger with the mother (and, beyond her, the oceanic, unsymbolisable totality of the real). This sacrifice opens up language as a structure of desire. Because desire is the presence of the absence of a reality in the same way that a word is the presence of the absence of a thing, language and desire are co(in)substantial. The speaking subject is a subject of desire.

For Lacan, desire always entails lack, always means something is missing. This conflation of language with desire as lack allows him to characterise accession to the signifier as symbolic castration: in language, as in castration, the subject is always missing something, missing (from) the mother, missing (from) the real. In Freud's interpretation, castration anxiety precipitates the dissolution of the 'simple' Oedipus complex for boys: seeing a female body, misinterpreting absence as loss, fearing castration as punishment for his own desire, the boy gives up on his mother in order to save his penis (though he may still dream about penetrating chrysanthemums) and represses aggression against the father in favour of identification (though he may still dream about sawing off the nozzle of a bottle of pop). Lacan revises the Oedipal scenario to focus not on the child's repressed desire for the mother but on the child's desire to ascertain and be the mother's desire. This desire presupposes that the mother in fact desires, lacks something, and Lacan joins Freud in having the child interpret the mother's lack as castration. Hence the child, in wanting to be what the mother wants, wants to 'complete' the mother by being the phallus he thinks she lacks. But the father's putative possession of the phallus prohibits this fantasy of completion. Thus, in the Lacanian account, the disappointed child must attempt to install itself into the fantasised position of either having the phallus (masculine) or being the phallus for another (feminine). But because the phallus is not a real organ but the signifier of lack, both 'sexuated' positions are impostures, masquerades: the phallus is what no one can fully have or be (hence Lacan asserts that there is no sexual relation and that genital activity involves the attempt to give what one doesn't have to someone who doesn't exist). No one has or is the phallus, and yet everyone must continue to speak, to symbolise, as the phallic function dictates. In Lacan's account, the phallus is what makes signification possible because its function is not only to separate infant from mother, but also to divide symbolic from real, signifier from signified. Any word is thus always an emblem of unconscious desire, of prohibited merger – not because of what it means, but because it means at all – and any completed sentence is only the nostalgic echo of a lost mythic plenitude, a dissatisfying substitute for the phantasmatically 'completed' mother restored to phallic wholeness.

Psychoanalytic accounts of gender formation are obviously problematic, but they are at least accounts. Psychoanalytic accounts are also necessarily prolonged and complicated, imprecise and incomplete, but mainly because they attempt to describe formations that are themselves prolonged, complicated, imprecise and incomplete. There are countless ways to get gender wrong but no way to get it fully and happily right. This is why the 'talking cure' is in one sense interminable: no one is ever one; no one is ever done; no one can ever finally say or be enough. There is no cure for talking. The constitutive failure of psychoanalysis is thus the exact source of its value.

References and further reading

Freud, S. (1953) *The Standard Edition of the Complete Psychological Works*, 24 vols, London: Hogarth.

Frosh, S. (1994) *Sexual Difference*, New York: Routledge.

Lacan, J. [1966] (2002) *Écrits*, New York, Norton.

Moi, T. (2000) 'Is anatomy destiny? Freud and biological determinism', in P. Brooks and A. Woloch (eds) *Whose Freud?* New Haven, CT: Yale University Press, pp. 71–92.

Shepherdson, C. (2000) *Vital Signs*, New York: Routledge.

Van Haute, P. (2002) *Against Adaptation*, New York: Other Press.

See also: Jungian perspectives; object relations perspectives; psychology

CALVIN THOMAS

PSYCHOLOGY

Psychology is focused on first observing and describing, and then trying to explain, causes of individuals' thoughts, feelings and behaviour. The scope of psychology is broad, with researchers investigating topics as diverse as perception, learning, motivation, personality, social behaviour and mental health. Some psychologists adopt a biological perspective that focuses on the relationship between brain function and behaviour. Others focus on social processes, such as the role of peers, family members and school as influences on behaviour.

Historically, psychologists used the words 'sex' and 'gender' interchangeably. It was widely assumed that there were two mutually exclusive sexes (male and female) which corresponded to two mutually exclusive genders (masculine and feminine). Moreover, in traditional viewpoints, men were sexually attracted to women, whereas women were sexually attracted to men. In other words, there was an assumed correspondence among sex, gender and desire.

In the early 1970s, psychologists (Bem 1974; Spence *et al.* 1974) recognised that gender was not an automatic expression of being born male or female. Gender was seen as the expression of masculine and feminine traits, often but not automatically associated with biological sex. In other words, masculinity and femininity were two separate dimensions rather than opposite endpoints on a single dimension of gender. An individual who displayed both masculinity and femininity was conceptualised as androgynous. In contrast, someone who scored low on both masculinity and femininity was classed as undifferentiated. Gender is conceptualised as a routine performance by approaches that emphasise the way that social reality is created through social interactions (Goffman 1976; West and Zimmerman 1987).

Sexual orientation represents another challenge to simple views of gender and sexuality. Sexual orientation has been conceptualised by researchers as a continuum rather than as a dichotomy (Kinsey *et al.* 1948). Although many people would define themselves as exclusively heterosexual or homosexual, some individuals view their orientation as sexual desire for both men and women, i.e. bisexual. As with gender, scholars have argued that heterosexuality and homosexuality should not be thought of as opposite ends of a single dimension but rather as two separate dimensions. People may engage in situationally driven sexual actions. For example, men who view their sexual identities as heterosexual will sometimes perform sexual acts with other men for economic reasons (e.g. male prostitutes) or because they lack access to available women (e.g. prisoners).

Available evidence indicates very small psychological differences as a function of biological sex. One landmark analysis of gender differences was the book *The Psychology of Gender Differences* (1974). In their review of over 2,000 studies, Maccoby and Jacklin found fewer significant differences than might be expected between men and women. For example, sex differences were not found in self-esteem, sociability or achievement motivation. Findings were mixed regarding nurturance and competitive dominance. One gender difference was that women had greater verbal ability than men. In contrast, men were more visual-spatial and mathematical than women. Men were also more aggressive than women.

Meta-analysis is a statistical technique to combine the results from many studies on a particular topic, such as gender differences. Consistent with Maccoby and Jacklin, and in contrast to lay intuition, the magnitude of sex differences obtained from meta-analysis is almost always small. Some differences between men and women seem consistent with gender role stereotypes. For example, women tend to smile more than men. Compared to women, men tend to be more risk-taking and indicate higher global self-esteem. Although unprovoked men are more aggressive than women, provocation reduces this difference. Men and women differ in preferences for mates, with women assigning greater weight than men to socioeconomic status, ambitiousness and status. Job attribute preferences of men and women tend to be consistent with gender roles and stereotypes. Men and women do not differ in personality traits such as social anxiety, impulsiveness, orderliness or locus of control. Differences in verbal ability, long considered an important distinction, are so small it has been argued that the difference no longer exists. Sex differences in spatial abilities and mathematical performance are also small.

One area where there do seem to be reliable and large differences between men and women is in the domain of sex (Baumeister 2000). Men think about sex more, desire sex more, and desire to have a greater number of sex partners than women. Men have more permissive attitudes towards sexual practices. For example, men report a greater interest and more enjoyment in pornography than women. Men, to a much greater degree than women, are willing to report masturbating.

Although psychological differences between men and women are thought to be relatively small, psychologists have tried to determine the extent to which differences reflect biological or learned processes. Several psychological traditions interpret differences in terms of innate, biologically based tendencies. Other perspectives focus on how socialisation creates gender differences. Not surprisingly, some approaches incorporate both a biological and learned component

Psychoanalysis, founded by Sigmund Freud (1924) in the late nineteenth century, is the most famous theory in psychology. Although discredited in many ways, psychoanalysis has had a profound effect on how both scientists and lay individuals conceptualise human beings. The most important contribution of psychoanalysis was the concept that an individual's behaviour was governed by unconscious forces. According to Freud, the transition from childhood to adulthood was characterised by several developmental stages. An adult's behaviour could be understood in terms of how he or she resolved conflict at each psychosexual stage. The phallic stage around age three to six was the key psychosexual stage in understanding the child's transition to adulthood. Moreover, the phallic stage has a strong gendered component. The central element of the phallic stage is the Oedipal complex, named for the Greek myth of Oedipus, who was doomed to unknowingly murder his father and marry his mother. For a boy, the Oedipal complex involves the simultaneous experience of a desire to murder his father and incestuous sexual desire for his mother.

Evolutionary psychology, which has its roots in sociobiology, focuses on how biological factors can be seen as core contributors to complex social behaviours (Buss and Schmitt 1993). Evolutionary psychologists assume that evolutionary processes of natural selection have affected how people think, feel and behave in complex ways. The underlying logic of evolutionary psychology rests with the obvious differences in the way that men and women reproduce. The male contribution of sperm is low cost, whereas the female contribution of the egg carries much higher costs. First, women produce only one egg per month after reaching puberty and prior to menopause. In contrast, men produce millions of sperm in a single day. In addition, the act of carrying an unborn child for nine months, not to mention the physical stresses of childbirth, adds considerably to the cost for women of having children. Moreover, once a child is born, women do more than half of active parenting. The advantage to women for their heavy investment in having and taking care of children is that they are certain that a child is theirs, whereas for men there may be uncertainty associated with paternity.

Evolutionary psychologists assert that basic biological differences between men and women, which lead to different costs and benefits of having children, produce important differences with regard to mate preferences. The fact that men have a higher sex drive, on average, can be understood as a result of the evolutionary benefit to men associated with having multiple partners with whom to reproduce. Women's desire to secure a mate to provide for her and her children manifest themselves in women's greater willingness to have partners older than themselves. Older men, presumably, have more time to collect resources and develop skills that assist them in accumulating resources. In contrast, men's preferences for younger women are seen as stemming from the desire to mate with reproductively viable females.

Social structural theory (Eagly 1987) posits that in historical hunter-gatherer societies physical sex differences (e.g. size, upper body strength) encouraged men and women to take on different activities to maximise the likelihood of their joint survival. These initial differences in activities became institutionalised as sex-appropriate roles as society grew more complex. Moreover, the tendency of men and women to strive to develop skills associated with appropriate role performance further reified what characteristics were associated with masculinity and femininity. Because what came to be known as men's roles were associated with greater status and resource acquisition, relative to women's roles, men developed a more dominant orientation, whereas women developed a more cooperative, conciliatory orientation. According to this perspective, what might be thought of as major differences between men and women came about because of social processes that emerged from relatively small biological differences between the sexes.

Social structural theory and evolutionary psychology both agree that men and women have different preferences for mate selection and sexuality. The important difference between the two approaches is how they explain these differences. Social structural theorists view the differences as resulting from the way that social institutions reward men and women. In contrast, evolutionary psychologists see differences as reflecting innate biological differences between men and women. Part of the controversy between these two approaches is that evolutionary psychology legitimises stereotypic beliefs about gender (e.g. women innately desire to be cared for by men, whereas men innately desire to be sexually promiscuous) that reinforce patriarchal views of gender.

The socialisation process begins at birth with adults treating boys and girls in accord with gender stereotypes as a function of sex. Descriptively, stereotypes portray men as strong, confident, aggressive and sexually motivated. Women, in contrast, are characterised as communicative and emotional, nurturant and less sexually oriented than men (Deaux and Lewis 1984). In addition, the proscriptive element informs men and women how they should behave. Unlike other categories, such as race or religion, gender stereotypes can be seen as positive. It is therefore often the case that both men and women adhere to stereotypic roles.

Gender role strain refers to stress that people experience as a result of trying to live up to societal standards of gender (Pleck 1995). One form of gender role strain is discrepancy strain, where people experience a conflict between how they see themselves and society's view of how they should behave. Discrepancy strain occurs, for example, with the conflict a man might experience between expressing emotional connection to other men and appearing effeminate. Dysfunction strain occurs when living out a stereotypically gendered role produces conflict with others. For example, a man's unwillingness to communicate his emotions might lead to his wife feeling ignored or unloved. Finally, trauma strain results when living out a gendered identity leads to physical harm. Typically, men are expected to be strong and uncomplaining. Hence, they may delay seeking medical attention for injuries.

Transgenderism refers to the idea that a person of one biological sex will adopt the appearance or behaviours of the opposite gender (Tewksbury and Gagne 1996). Although not universally true, transgenderism tends to involve men expressing an interest in adopting the presentation of women rather than women who seek to emulate masculine conventions. Transgenderism ranges in the intensity to which it is expressed. Lower levels of intensity include female impersonators, drag queens and cross-dressers. There are a variety of possible motives for these forms of transgenderism, including economic gain, amusement and sexual arousal. For example, transvestitism is a form of cross-dressing where the individual achieves sexual pleasure from wearing the clothing of the opposite gender.

Given the importance society places on gender, it is not surprising that people may experience a great deal of psychological distress when their gender identity conflicts with their biological sex. Gender identity disorder is a diagnosis that psychologists and psychiatrists give to an individual who expresses a strong and long-lasting cross-gender identification. Transsexuals represent a small proportion of individuals whose response to cross-gender identification includes seeking out medical interventions such as hormone treatments and surgery to bring their physical body more into congruence with their gendered self-concept.

References and further reading

Baumeister, R.F. (2000) 'Gender differences in erotic plasticity', *Psychological Bulletin*, 126: 347–72.

Bem, S.L. (1974) 'The measurement of psychological androgyny', *Journal of Consulting and Clinical Psychology*, 42: 155–62.

Buss, D.M. and Schmitt, D.P. (1993) 'Sexual strategies theory', *Psychological Review*, 100: 204–32.

Deaux, K. and Lewis, L.L. (1984) 'Structure of gender stereotypes', *Journal of Personality and Social Psychology*, 46: 991–1004.

Eagly, A.H. (1987) *Sex Differences in Social Behavior*, Hillsdale, MI: Earlbaum.

Freud, S. (1924) 'The dissolution of the Oedipus complex', *The Standard Edition of the Complete Psychological Works*, 24 vols, London: Hogarth, vol. 19, pp. 172–79.

Goffman, E. (1976) 'Gender display', *Studies in the Anthropology of Visual Communication*, 3: 69–77.

Kinsey, A., Pomeroy, W. and Martin, C. (1948) *Sexual Behavior in the Human Male*, Philadelphia, PA: Saunders.

Maccoby, E.E. and Jacklin, C.N. (1974) *The Psychology of Sex Differences*, Stanford, CA: Stanford University Press.

Pleck, J.H. (1995) 'The gender role strain paradigm', in R.F. Levant and W.S. Pollack (eds) *A New Psychology of Men*, New York: Basic Books, pp. 11–32.

Spence, J.T., Helmreich, R.L. and Stapp, J. (1974) 'The personal attributes Questionnaire', *JSAS Catalog of Selected Documents in Psychology*, 43: 617.

Tewksbury, R. and Gagne, P. (1996) 'Transgenderists', *Journal of Men's Studies*, 5: 105–29.

West, C. and Zimmerman, D.H. (1987) 'Doing gender', *Gender and Society*, 1: 125–51.

See also: Jungian perspectives; object relations perspectives; psychoanalisis; transgender; transsexual

JAMES K. BEGGAN
JILL M. HARBISON

Q

QUEER MASCULINITIES

Queer masculinities encompass traditionally masculine traits of character and/or appearance occurring in people other than heterosexual males, specifically gay men and lesbians. One of the tenets of queer theory is the notion that gender is socially constructed and not a naturally occurring phenomenon. Related to this, Judith Butler (1990) argues that an individual must achieve a gender identity via constant, repeated performances of socially sanctioned acts that signify as 'masculine' and 'feminine', and thus 'male' and 'female'. Social norms in dominant society require masculine gender performance by males and feminine gender performance by females. Moreover, the common assumption is that individuals who adhere to these guidelines are heterosexual.

When women perform traditionally masculine character traits, they divorce sex from gender and illustrate how the first is biological while the latter is culturally constructed. While not all women who perform masculinity are lesbians, lesbians often perform masculine character traits to deliberately contest the erroneously naturalised relationship between sex and gender. Examples of this range from refusals to shave legs and underarms to assuming the fashion and posturing of men via 'drag king' performances. Society associates particular modes of physical presentation and personal demeanour with hegemonic masculinity, and performances of masculinity by gay men highlight how society assumes that male homosexuals are necessarily effeminate. Gay male athletic leagues and the fashion and posturing of gay men involved in leather culture demonstrate how gay men associate themselves with the power and assertiveness implied by performances of masculinity.

Because so many gay men and lesbians present themselves using means frequently associated with masculinity, there is some debate as to whether or not performances of masculinity by queer people actually denaturalise the relationship between heterosexuality and masculinity. Some critics charge that these representations and practices reinforce dominant heterosexual norms that privilege masculinity over femininity, while others highlight the liberatory potential of gay men and lesbians who manipulate appearances to challenge the heterocentrist status quo.

References and further reading

Adams, R. and Savran, D. (eds) (2002) *The Masculinity Studies Reader*, Malden, MA: Blackwell.

Butler, J. [1990] (1999) *Gender Trouble*, London and New York: Routledge.

—— (1993) *Bodies That Matter*, London and New York: Routledge.

Case, S. (1993) 'Toward a butch/femme aesthetic', in H. Abelove, M. Barala and D. Halperin (eds) *The Lesbian and Gay Studies Reader*, London and New York: Routledge, pp. 294–306.

Connell, R. (1995) *Masculinities*, Cambridge: Polity.

Halberstam, J. (1998) *Female Masculinity*, Durham, NC and London: Duke University Press.

See also: queer theory

HOLLIS GRIFFIN

QUEER THEORY

Queer theory begins from the premise that gender and sexuality are culturally constructed (understood, lived and experienced) in historically and culturally specific ways. Queer theory emerged in the late 1980s in response to the various problems associated with gay and lesbian theory and (identity) politics, and as a result of the popularisation of the work of Michel Foucault and of feminist and poststructuralist accounts of subjectivity and social relations.

Post-structuralism is most often associated with a radical rethinking of 'truth', 'subjectivity', 'freedom', 'power' and so on. Post-structuralist theorists argue that there are no objective and universal truths but, rather, that particular forms of knowledge and the ways of being they engender, become 'naturalised' in culturally and historically specific ways. For example, it has been claimed that heterosexuality is a complex matrix of discourses, practices and institutions which has become normalised in our culture, thus making particular relationships, lifestyles, desires and identities seem natural, ahistorical and universal. Heterosexuality, far from being a biologically determined identity, is, according to this way of thinking, a truth-effect of hegemonic systems of power/knowledge whose dominant position and current configuration is contestable and open to change. This being the case, the liberationist understanding of sex as an instinctual drive that has been repressed by oppressive institutions and thus is in need of being freed, is, according to theorists such as Foucault, misguided to say the least. Besides the fact that it embraces a notion of subjectivity and sexuality as somehow pre-cultural, the 'repressive hypothesis', as Foucault calls it, is founded on an understanding of power as negative, dis-enabling and belonging solely to the ruling elite. It is now commonly accepted among critical theorists that power is productive rather than simply oppressive, that it functions as a network of relations rather than being something one group exerts over another, and that as subjects we are all agents and effects of systems of power/knowledge. Rather than there being some place outside of systems of power to which we can escape in order to become our true selves and/or from which we can objectively formulate the correct revolutionary response to the dominant order of things, Foucault argues that resistance is inseparable from power (rather than opposed to it). Moreover, he shares with other post-structuralist theorists a commitment to a plurality of heterogeneous and localised resistances, the effects of which can never be entirely predicted in advance. It is this sort of focus on the constructed, contingent, unstable and heterogeneous character of subjectivity, social relations, power, knowledge and resistance that has paved the way for queer theory.

Despite, or perhaps because of, this, over the last decade or two queer theorists have produced diverse examples of queer scholarship and have been embroiled in important debates and disagreements. Nevertheless, it is possible to identify similarities in the ways in which queer theory has been characterised and practised by those involved in its ongoing (re)formulation. Perhaps the most common point of agreement is that queer is inextricably bound up with contestation. Rather than having an identity fundamental to itself, queer is more often than not characterised as a radical questioning of identity, a strategic and provisional position that can potentially be inhabited by anyone. In this sense, queer differs significantly from the terms 'homosexual', 'gay' or 'lesbian', all which have historically been associated with identity and identity politics.

Having said this, it is important to note that queer sometimes functions quite differently in counter-cultural communities than it allegedly does in the hallowed halls of the academy. It is not uncommon, for example, for queer to be used as an umbrella term for gays, lesbians, bisexuals, drag queens, transsexuals, the intersexed and in fact any number of individuals or groups who see themselves as marginalised on the basis of their sexuality and/or gender. The obvious problem with this particular use of the term 'queer' is that it tends to reproduce, rather than challenge, heteronormative notions of subjectivity; to veil the differences between, for example, lesbianism and gayness (as these 'identities' are currently lived and experienced), between 'women', between transsexualism and cross-dressing, and so on; and to ignore differences of class, race, age, (dis)-ability, once again positing sexuality as a unified and unifying phenomenon. In implying the existence of some sort of queer solidarity which has triumphed over the kinds of political divisions historically associated with the homophile movement, gay liberation, political lesbianism, sex radicalism and feminism(s), this particular use of the term 'queer' both homogenises and misrepresents a diverse range of positions, practices, 'identities', bodies, knowledges, life-styles, desires and commitments.

Rather than functioning as an empty signifier of subversion, 'queer' is sometimes employed in an antithetical way to refer to an identifiable and allegedly unambiguous counter-hegemonic identity, one that is ideologically opposed to gay and lesbian identity (whatever that might mean). This is apparent in the fierce opposition of the Chicago-based activist group Queers United Against Straight Acting Homosexuals (QUASH) to what they regard as the assimilationism of gay and lesbian lifestyles, politics and activism. Ironically, the anti-assimilationist queer identity claimed by members of QUASH has the politically questionable affect of restigmatising and essentialising gayness and lesbianism, and of reproducing the hierarchical dichotomous logic long associated by queer theorists with heteronormativity. On a more positive note, what this virulent attack on assimilationism brings to the fore is the potentially problematic effects of the refusal to define queer theory.

As I said earlier, it is commonly assumed that queer's transgressive potential is firmly tied to its ephemerality. This often goes hand in glove with the assumption that the 'naming' of queer, the identification of its characteristics, would assimilate it into the logic of heteronormativity and circumscribe its radical potential. However, as Alan McKee has noted, the claim that queer theory is indefinable belies the fact that queer theory courses are taught in academia, and that some articles are chosen over others for inclusion in such courses, and for publication in queer theory journals and books. In other words, some sort of sense of what queer is (or is not) is at work in the judgments being made in these institutional situations. This being the case, it seems clear that queer is not an empty signifier. Moreover, insofar as queer does operate in particular (unacknowledged) ways, it inevitably tends to validate, even if inadvertently, specific knowledges, identities, texts, practices and interests at the expense of others. Steven Seidman shares McKee's concern that if exclusory praxis is allowed to go unchecked in the name of some sort of ideal of indefinability and non-assimilation, queer theory will ultimately (re)produce the logic and the effects of the (heteronormative) system that it claims to be working to deconstruct.

A range of unacknowledged (prejudicial) assumptions underpinning queer theory have been identified by those who have felt the effects of its exclusory practice. It has been claimed, for example, that queer theory is the province of gay men (Jeffreys 2003), is white-centred (Anzaldúa 1991; Barnard 2004), middle-class (Cohen 1997) and assumes able-bodiedness (McRuer 2002). Whether or not one agrees with these criticisms, it is clear that queer functions in contradictory ways and that at times overly simplistic distinctions are made (at least implicitly) between what or who is deemed to be queer, and what or who is not: for example, heterosexual/queer or gay and lesbian/queer. This exclusory tendency stems, at least in part, from queer theory's primary focus on the sexual. As a result, theorists such as Ian Barnard, Gloria Anzaldúa and Cathy Cohen have called for a broader understanding of queerness informed by a theoretical knowledge of intersectionality. This, they argue, would enable a recognition of, and a critical engagement with, the ways in which interlocking systems of power/knowledge function to constitute subject positions in specific yet complex ways. It would also allow nuanced theoretical analyses of the significantly different ways in which differently marked bodies are able (or not) to take up and mobilise queer positionalities. This is crucial, as Elizabeth Grosz notes, because of the ease with which dominant groups (re)produce their interests and define others in relation to them.

One way of avoiding the problems associated with the notion of queer as a position equally accessible to all, an identity (albeit a non-essential, provisional and fragmented one) that anyone can choose to inhabit, is, as Janet R. Jakobsen suggests, to think of queer as a verb (a set of actions), rather than as a noun (an identity, or even a nameable positionality associated with the practice of particular actions). In keeping with the logic of anti-identity associated with the work of Foucault, queer, as Jakobsen envisages it, involves a shift from being to doing.

Here queer (theory) constitutes a deconstructive practice that is not undertaken by an already constituted subject, and does not, in turn, furnish the subject with a nameable identity. The term 'deconstruction' is often associated with the French philosopher Jacques Derrida. Deconstruction works away at the very foundation of western metaphysics (a historically and culturally specific binary system of meaning-making) by destabilising the notion of polarised essences. It is important to note, however, that deconstruction is not synonymous with destruction: it does not involve the obliteration and replacement of what is erroneous with that which is held to be true. In other words, a deconstructive approach to the hierarchised binary opposition heterosexuality/homosexuality would not consist of reversing the terms or of attempting to somehow annihilate the concepts altogether. Rather, a deconstructive analysis would highlight the inherent instability of the terms, as well as enabling an analysis of the culturally and historically specific ways in which the terms and the relation between them have developed, and the (social, political, ethical) effects they have produced. So, for example, a deconstructive reading of heterosexuality would show that it is dependent on its so-called opposite (homosexuality) for its identity, that rather than being discrete (id)entities, the latter is internal to the former (and vice versa), it haunts it and is haunted by it.

Deconstructing the alleged opposition between homosexuality and heterosexuality, the 'unnatural' and the 'natural', is important because it highlights the constructedness of meaning and identity and allows us to begin to imagine alternative ways of thinking and of living. At the same time, a deconstructive analysis or a queering of heterosexuality, homosexuality and the relations between them enables a critical interrogation of the arbitrary ways in which being is divided up in and through specific epistemic regimes, and to ask who it is that benefits from the cultural logic that (re)produces these kinds of ontological divisions, and how.

It is this understanding of queer theory as a deconstructive practice that Sue-Ellen Case has in mind when she says that queer theory works at the site of ontology to shift the ground of being itself, thus challenging the most fundamental distinction of all, the distinction between life and death. According to Case, this dichotomy is central to the denigration of homosexuality on the grounds that, unlike heterosexuality, it is a sterile or non-reproductive, and therefore unnatural, relationship. Queer theory, she argues, has the potential to destabilise this ontology and the being(s) to which it gives life, to perform a vampiric assault on the (allegedly unified) body politic and all that it holds dear.

As well as being opposed to and disruptive of the logic of identity, the logic of fracture that Case articulates, also queers a (problematic) model of sociality inextricably bound up with identity politics. According to this homogenising model, community consists of a group of (already constituted) autonomous individuals with shared characteristics. An example of this is the idea that the lesbian community is a unified social body made up of women who share a singular, fixed, self-evident and mutually exclusive gender and sexual identity. In contrast to this, Linnell Secomb argues that if subjectivity is constituted in and through relations with others and with specific historic-cultural contexts, then being is always already a being-with, an affect of community. But being-with, as it is envisaged here, has nothing to do with shared characteristics, and community does not (and cannot) refer to an identifiable group or to a project of fusion. Rather, community, in this sense, queers the logic of identity, or, as Secomb notes, it is nothing but this undoing. Queer community, then, as a being-with animated by disagreement, discord, resistance, not only destabilises the logic of identity, but simultaneously invokes multiplicity, heterogeneity and the transgression of boundaries, identities and ontological categories.

References and further reading

Anzaldúa, G. (1991) 'To(o) queer the writer: loca, escrita y chicana', in Betsy Warland (ed.) *Inversions: Writing by Dykes, Queers and Lesbians*, Vancouver: Press Gang, pp. 249–63.

Barnard, I. (2004) *Queer Race: Critical Interventions in the Racial Politics of Queer Theory*, New York: Peter Lang Publishing.

Case, S.-E. (1991) 'Tracking the vampire', *Differences: A Journal of Feminist Cultural Studies*, 3 (2): 1–20.

Cohen, C.J. (1997) 'Punks, bulldaggers and welfare queens', *GLQ: A Journal of Lesbian and Gay Studies*, 3: 437–65.

Duggan, L. (1992) 'Making it perfectly queer', *Socialist Review*, 22 (1): 11–31.

Foucault, M. (1980) *The History of Sexuality Volume One: An Introduction*, New York: Vintage Books.

Grosz, E. (1995) 'Experimental desire: rethinking queer subjectivity', in E. Grosz, *Space, Time and Perversion: The Politics of Bodies*, Sydney: Allen and Unwin, pp. 207–27.

Jagose, A. (1996) *Queer Theory*, Melbourne: Melbourne University Press.

Jakobsen, J.R. (1998) 'Queer is? Queer does? Normativity and the problem of resistance', *GLQ: A Journal of Gay and Lesbian Studies*, 4 (4): 511–36.

Jeffreys, S. (2003) *Unpacking Queer Politics: A Lesbian Feminist Perspective*, Cambridge: Polity Press.

McKee, A. (1999) '"Resistance is hopeless": assimilating queer theory', *Social Semiotics*, 9 (2): 235–50.

McRuer, R. (2002) 'Compulsory able-bodiedness and queer/disabled existence', in S.L. Snyder, B.J. Brueggmann and R. Garland-Thomson (eds) *Disability Studies: Enabling the Humanities*, New York: MLA, pp. 88–99.

Secomb, L. (2000) 'Fractured community', *Hypatia*, 15 (2): 133–50.

Seidman, S. (1995) 'Deconstructing queer theory or the under-theorization of the social and the ethical', in L. Nicholson and S. Seidman (eds) *Social Postmodernism: Beyond Identity Politics*, Cambridge: Cambridge University Press, pp. 116–41.

Sullivan, N. (2003) *A Critical Introduction to Queer Theory*, Edinburgh: Edinburgh University Press.

See also: queer masculinities

NIKKI SULLIVAN

R

RACE AND ETHNICITY

We typically associate cultural images of masculinity with racial and ethnic categories. The cowboy is almost always assumed to be white, the jungle native black or brown. Yet we rarely consider how or why such stereotypes emerge and whose interests they serve. The frequency with which we comment on questions of sex and gender on the on one hand and questions of race on the other does not obtain when it comes to the politics of male identity. This gap has much to do with the fact that the dominant Western public culture has little interest in acknowledging how the popular image of the hegemonic male – white, heterosexual – stands in opposition not only to women and queers, but also to racial and ethnic others, particularly men of colour. The West, invested in popular fantasies of democracy, does not like to discuss openly how, for example, the heroic American cowboy stands in deliberate contrast to the savage and uncivilised Native American or how the British colonialist seems civilised and purposeful when compared to the effeminate or brutal Indian (Drinnon 1980; Sharpe 1993). The West's belief that the exemplary white male subject represents the antithesis of the animalistic or infantile man of colour exists as an open secret – assumed but not spoken.

What undoubtedly proves all the more troubling to our public culture is the fact that such exemplary images of the white man are in fact reliant upon such negative stereotypes of the black man. The former does not exist without the latter. They require one another's presence, a presence often both physical and cultural, in order to emerge as legible. While this interrelationship of the two males may be theorised in many different ways, perhaps the most compelling understanding of the dynamic has arisen out of psychoanalysis. Drawing loosely on Freudian and Lacanian thought, scholars from postcolonial and American literary studies have each posited what we might dub the projection thesis: the argument that white men have at least since the Enlightenment, if not before, constructed their own identities by projecting on to men of colour all of those urges, needs and desires Western Christian culture deemed unacceptable. Once those impulses had been disavowed and associated with men of colour, then white men could revel in their superiority (Fanon 1967; Bhabha 1994). Scholars also have argued that the dominant white culture has rendered ethnic and religious minorities crucial players in this longstanding psychocultural process. At various times, white European Christians rendered the Irish, the Jews, the Gypsies and other disadvantaged groups and minorities as demonised groups whose feared and desired presence enabled the construction of an idealised white male.

The Western domination of the world-system over the past few centuries has ensured that such a process has taken a particularly heavy toll on men of colour who have been conquered, enslaved and otherwise dominated. The fact that white European and European colonial cultures have for centuries insisted on representing men of colour as insufficiently masculine or overly animalistic has meant that the subaltern male has found subject formation difficult, to say the least. As Baldwin puts it with respect to the African–American context,

> To become a Negro male ... one had to make up oneself as one went along. This had to be done in the not-at-all metaphorical teeth of the world's determination to destroy you. The world had prepared no place for you and if the world had its way, no place would ever exist.
>
> (Baldwin 1998: 279)

What renders Baldwin's insight so striking is that even as he acknowledges the tremendous challenge confronting males of colour in a white-dominated world, he also registers the fact that strategies of self-invention and social performance offer some recourse to the dispossessed. Modern culture offers countless examples of and commentaries on men of colour who made themselves up as they went along, often by engaging in a complicated relationship to the oppressive dominant culture. To take only one example, in his famous memoir *Breaking the Boundary*, West Indian writer C.L.R. James argues that a passion for cricket allowed him to both learn from and work against the British colonial apparatus. James's understanding of himself as a black Caribbean man cannot be separated from a vexed, but intense, relationship to Englishness.

To the Martiniquan-born psychiatrist and activist Fanon, James's cathexis to cricket no doubt would have appeared disempowering. In *Black Skin/White Masks*, Fanon warns his fellow black men against acts of colonial mimicry, arguing that to imitate the oppressive culture was to undercut a sense of subaltern masculinity and breed self-hatred. Indeed, at times Fanon links the threatening seductiveness of the colonising culture with the emasculating dangers of femininity and homosexuality. He is hardly alone among male intellectuals of colour in using misogyny and homophobia to shore up the ideal of an empowered minority male subject. From the nineteenth century onward, a range of anti-colonialist and anti-racist intellectuals have maintained that only a heroic and heteronormative male identity can provide the bedrock needed to liberate people of colour from the yoke of white oppression. African–American leader Douglass suggests as much when he informs readers of his 1845 *Autobiography* that in getting the better of a white overseer in a fight, he had 'rekindled the few expiring embers of freedom, and revived ... a sense of his [his] own manhood' (50). By besting his white master, Douglass relegates him to the subordinate and implicitly feminine position, however briefly, thereby claiming for himself the rights associated with autonomous manhood.

Over the past thirty years, feminist and queer theorists have combated such a strategy. In claiming a stereotypical white notion of superlative male identity as their own, men of colour run the risk of replicating the dominant society's crimes.

Contemporary literary critic Eng makes this abundantly clear in his analysis of how pioneering Asian–American activist intellectuals such as Chin worried openly about the effeminate image of Asian men in the West and proclaimed the need to remasculinise Asian–American culture. Eng points out, rightly, that Chin's 'cultural nationalist tenets mirrored the mainstream heterosexist and racist structures by which stereotypical conceptions of Asian American as "efficient housewives" ... were produced in the first place' (Eng 2001: 210). African Americans have often endured a countervailing image of black animalistic savagery in US culture, but resistance to this stereotype has often convinced black male intellectuals that an equally uncritical embrace of what we might call nationalist macho would serve the community well. As famed activist and scholar Angela Davis argues in a dialogue with rapper Ice Cube, such strategies do little but perpetuate the gender and sexual divisions that weaken black America. In response to Ice Cube's comment, 'the black woman can't look up to the black man until we get up,' Davis offers the riposte, 'Well, why should we look *up* to the black man? Why can't we look at each other as equals?' (quoted in McDowell 1997: 376).

That men of colour have found it difficult to imagine a way of engaging in the utopian exchange called for by Davis is hardly surprising. Combating racism, sexism and homophobia simultaneously can prove daunting. If male intellectuals of colour often slipped into the habit of replicating the dominant patriarchal order, profeminist and queer white men tended to emphasise counterhegemonic approaches to the sex/gender system while ignoring completely the politics of race. At present, the most visible work on the nexus of race, ethnicity and masculinity has emerged in the academy, particularly in the boom areas of queer studies of colour and whiteness studies. The former area first undertook a critical analysis of the dominant culture's fear of and desire for the black male body. Black British scholar Mercer's essay on Mapplethorpe's *Black Book* thus takes issue with the white gay photographer's fetishistic exploitation of the black male body and explores the polyvalent meanings of such a fantasy in the context of contemporary Western culture (Mercer 1994). More recent work in the field has argued for various strategies of resistance on the part of male queers of colour, whether through aesthetic and political disidentifications with the status quo or through personal essays (Munoz 1999; Reid-Pharr 2001).

Whiteness studies approach the problem of race, ethnicity and masculinity from the converse perspective – by taking issue with the assumption that all white men either desire or achieve full identification with the hegemonic order. Important scholarship on working-class, ethnic and queer identities has emphasised how many putatively white men hardly feel that their lived experience qualifies as hegemonic. Indeed, these scholars have suggested that the vast majority of such subjects feel alienated from the white male power structure. Such feelings of alienation can lead to direct expressions of anger towards minorities, as manifest in some poor southern US whites' violent hostility towards their black neighbours, or in more complicated feelings of desire and hate, as witnessed in such cultural phenomena as blackface minstrelsy or the idea of going native (Lott 1993; Silverman 1992). That many of the subjects engaged in the latter strategy have been white ethnics is hardly incidental, for the Irish in the UK and the Jews and Italians in the United States often have found themselves in a not quite/not white position that breeds a vexed relationship to powerful whites and disenfranchised people of colour (Rogin 1994).

References and further reading

Baldwin, J. (1998) 'The black boy looks at the white boy', in J. Baldwin, *Collected Essays*, New York: Library of America, pp. 269–85.

Bhabha, H. (1994) *The Location of Culture*, London: Routledge.

Douglass, F. [1845] (2001) *Narrative of the Life of Frederick Douglass*, New Haven, CT: Yale University Press.

Drinnon, R. (1980) *Facing West*, Minneapolis, MN: Minnesota University Press.

Eng, D. (2001) *Racial Castration*, Durham, NC: Duke University Press.

Fanon, F. [1952] (1967) *Black Skin, White Masks*, New York: Grove.

James, C.L.R. [1963] (1983) *Beyond a Boundary*, Durham, NC: Duke University Press.

Lott, E. (1993) *Love and Theft*, New York: Oxford University Press.

McDowell, D. (1997) 'Pecs and reps', in H. Stecopoulos and M. Uebel (eds) *Race and the Subject of Masculinities*, Durham, NC: Duke University Press.

Mercer, K. (1994) *Welcome to the Jungle*, London: Routledge.

Munoz, J. (1999) *Disidentifications*, Minneapolis, MN: Minnesota University Press.

Reid-Pharr, R. (2001) *Black Gay Man*, New York: New York University Press.

Rogin, M. (1994) *Blackface, White Noise*, Berkeley, CA: University of California Press.
Sharpe, J. (1993) *Allegories of Empire*, Minneapolis, MN: Minnesota University Press.
Silverman, K. (1992) *Male Subjectivity at the Margins*, London: Routledge.

See also: lynching; racialised masculinity politics

HARRY STECOPOULOS

RACIALISED MASCULINITY POLITICS

Race is a social and political construct that varies from culture to culture. Early human classification into races was solely dependent upon the physical characteristics (appearance, skin colour, hair texture) of a subset of the human species. While the United States has historically had a binary racial scheme, Brazil has more than 500 different racial labels. Inherent in racial categorisation has been the prescribed assumption that certain racial groups are superior to others. Class-based societies have perpetuated racial myths to ensure domination. One of the primary political issues in many societies has been the assertion by those that have been dominated that they are equal to their oppressors.

Conceptualisations of racial differences among groups of men lie at the heart of racialised masculinity politics. The widespread nature of slavery in the Western world framed much of the debate over racialised differences among men. Slave traders and slave masters throughout the Americas argued that those they enslaved were inferior based upon biological, intellectual and religious differences. Those that opposed slavery contested this notion. For Douglass, manhood, freedom and identity were connected: being a man meant not being a slave (Douglass 2001).

In Western slavery, the enslavers attempted to dismantle the roles of warrior, father and protector from the male slave's notion of self. Within the institution was a binary scheme of attributes that defined the slave master and his male slave. These attributes included human/subhuman, owner/owned, adult/child and master/servant. This binary system attempted to racially define white/man, black/non-man despite numerous ruptures in the institution including slave rebellions, maroon communities and runaways. Therefore, to assert one's independence by escaping into freedom or committing violence against one's oppressor was deemed an assertion of one's manhood.

Toussaint L'Ouverture emerged as an important figure in the nineteenth century as an example of revolutionary black male consciousness. L'Ouverture led the most significant slave rebellion in the western world and created the first black nation in the Americas. Freedom within a racialised masculine discourse implied the freedom from and the freedom to do certain things. Within the period 1890–1955, African–American men attempted to obtain judicial and federal protection from lynching, a barbarous form of vigilante justice in the American South in which victims were hanged, tortured and castrated. Freedom has also meant the ability for marginalised men to be able to obtain certain rights that were taken for granted within the dominant culture. These included the right to live where one wanted, obtain an education, work at a profession for which one was qualified and marry whoever one chose.

The ending of the slave trade and the emancipation of the slaves did not eradicate racism. The destruction of slavery did not end the notion of black inferiority in the minds of the dominant culture. Science, philosophy and popular culture in the Western world all designated non-white men as subaltern. Pseudo-scientific racism, which flourished in the late nineteenth and early twentieth centuries, offered evolutionary 'proof' that non-white individuals were the most primitive on the earth. The eugenics movement warned that racial interbreeding would destroy the white race and that anti-miscegenation laws were proper and biologically appropriate. During the same period, Social Darwinism was a theory of natural selection that argued weak societies would give way to strong societies. Western man, according to

Social Darwinian, stressed aggressive masculine individualism, which allowed the West to dominate non-Western cultures (and men). Popular culture of the late nineteenth and early twentieth century was highly predicated upon stereotypical imagery of non-Western cultures. Lithographs, pottery, sheet music, children's books and early motion pictures stressed the abnormality, exoticism and primitivism of non-white men, while blackface minstrels utilised the black male caricature as a mouthpiece to comment on non-white masculinity.

Whiteness was deemed the normality of Western manhood and its designation allowed certain political rights, freedoms and privileges that were not available to men of colour. The right to vote was denied millions of men, even in nations with non-white majorities. Most of the independence movements of the Third World in the nineteenth and twentieth centuries were built upon the premise that all men, regardless of race, be guaranteed the right to vote and run for political office. One such example was South Africa. Under the system of apartheid, black South Africans were denied the right to vote despite the fact that they were the majority of the population. In April 1994, nearly 23 million male and female citizens voted; 17 million of them were black South Africans voting for the first time. On the first day of voting Nelson Mandela remarked, 'Today marks the dawn of our freedom.' In the United States, Native Americans were denied citizenship until 1924. Even with citizenship, however, full political participation was not guaranteed. Many Western states continued to deny Native Americans the right to vote and basic civil liberties.

The connection between economic opportunity and racialised masculinity is apparent around the globe. Within Japanese society, Korean, Okinawan and Ainu men have had limited access to employment and vocational training; therefore, they have suffered from low income. Within Canadian and American auto manufacturing plants, minority men were often excluded from all but the most menial positions before World War II. Within Indonesia, Papau men have claimed that they are denied positions within the civil service because the government openly discriminates against them.

A number of resistance movements fought against this lack of economic opportunity. In 1905, W.E.B. Du Bois helped organise the Niagara Movement which demanded 'full manhood rights' for African-Americans. Malcolm X stressed the importance of black people economically controlling the areas in which they lived. As a proponent of black nationalism, Malcolm stressed, 'Once you control the economy of your own community, then you don't have to picket and boycott and beg some cracker downtown for a job in his business.' Black working men on strike during the American Civil Rights Movement held placards proclaiming 'I AM A MAN' (Memphis Sanitation Workers' Strike 1968).

Economic globalisation has helped to create a gendered world order. Current world systems of power, investment, trade and communication have brought disparate nations in frequent contact with each other. Within transnational and multinational corporations are gendered divisions of labour and a racialised hierarchy of positions. Globalisation has often disrupted traditional notions of masculinity. But public and domestic patriarchies have been reconfigured as market conditions replace localised economies. While globalisation has often placed men of colour into low-paying positions it has also increasingly made the non-Western male worker a threat to hegemonic European/American economic patriarchy. The fear of outsourcing in the early twenty-first century has been the fear that the highly educated, cooperative non-Western man might take one's position of employment.

The direct colonial rule and indirect economic domination that Western men imposed around the globe in the period 1450–1950 was predicated on the belief that Western man was superior, and therefore should rule over non-Western and non-white men. The colonising force, be it economic, political or military, was overwhelmingly male. Defenders of colonialism argued that Western men were bringing civilisation to non-Western men. To justify this practice, colonised men were ordained with a number of negative labels including primitive, savage, sexually uncontrollable, effete and untrustworthy. The conquest, settlement and economic domination of colonised regions disrupted indigenous ways of life. Many colonised men were drawn into what R. Connell describes as 'the masculinising practices and hierarchies of colonial society' (Connell 1995: 75). To associate with the colonial state, in terms of learning the language of the dominating culture, working for the colonial administration or even serving in social functions such as in the Boy Scouts, made one more of a man. Imperialism and masculinity were inextricably linked in the nineteenth and twentieth centuries.

The gendered subjectivities of Third World men are still marked by the remnants of colonialism. The post-colonial Third World is still 'othered'. Poverty, warfare and violence are far too common in these regions. Boys as young as ten years old have been recruited militarily in Africa. Many post-independence nations have not found suitable economic roles for young men; therefore, they have often found other alternatives to support their families and assert their masculinity.

Fanon has been the pre-eminent theorist on the psychological impact of racism on both the coloniser and the colonised. His two major works, *Black Skin, White Masks* (1952) and *The Wretched of the Earth* (1961), challenged colonised men to liberate themselves from psychological domination. After examining political development in the Third World, Fanon advocated liberation rooted in violence, claiming, 'At the level of individuals, violence is a cleansing force. It frees the native from his inferiority complex and from his despair and inaction; it makes him fearless and restores his self-respect' (Fanon 1963: 73). For a generation of activists around the world, Fanon's advocacy served as a rationale for the assertion of one's masculinity through violent means and the fighting for one's nation/tribe/race.

The relationship between racialised masculinity politics and feminism is often one of contrasting loyalties and identification. In liberation struggles globally, male advocates have often asked their female compatriots to place their primary loyalty to the race, submerging their own unique issues as women, or they have asked women to take a supporting role in the struggle. Carmichael infamously told participants at the 1964 Student Non-Violent Coordinating Committee, 'The only position for women in SNCC is prone.' Michele Wallace in *Black Macho and the Myth of Superwoman* argued that African–American men embraced a misogynist macho ethic that put black men and women on a collision course. While traditional gender roles were unquestioned by many men in colonial or independence struggles, women around the world recognised the unique circumstances that Third World women and children faced. Even in nations with rampant male unemployment, many professions that are associated with cleaning or childcare are defined as feminine due to stereotypical conventions of masculinity or femininity.

Sexuality has been significantly racialised globally. One of the major components for a defence of imperialism was the contention that non-white men could not control their own sexuality; therefore, they must be civilised. Non-white men were often portrayed as hypersexualised (African American), effete or asexual (Asian) or deviant (Middle Eastern). Within contemporary global culture, HIV/AIDS, first perceived as a disease of Western gay white men, has become a plague ravaging people of colour around the world. Racialised gender stereotyping is used to 'sell' Asian women to Western male travellers. The connection between sexuality and racialised masculinity is still a pre-eminent feature in eroticised and pornographic materials. Such materials explicitly capitalise on the exoticised attributes of the non-white sexual creature.

Homophobia has prominently factored into masculine racial identification. Within many contemporary African societies, homosexuality is deemed an immoral 'disease' of the Western white man even though social scientists have proven that homosexuality is present in almost every culture. Homosexuals are vilified in much of Africa as the scapegoat for AIDS. They are denounced as remnants of colonialism and as symbols of Western decadence. In the Middle East, homosexuality has been associated with being non-Islamic. Al-Qaradawi described homosexuality as 'illicit', a 'sexual deviation', 'perverted' and a 'corruption of man's sexuality' (2004: 1–4). Being gay has been deemed unacceptable for a male member of society by much of the leadership of Western and non-Western societies.

Within the last few decades an international mass media has emerged based upon the Western model. Gendered imagery figures prominently within this media, which sells motion pictures, music and commercial products. The globalisation of hip-hop has reintroduced questionable racial stereotypes of African Americans to a world market.

The recognition of racial divisions among men complicates the notion of patriarchal power. Earlier feminist analysis of the equation of men with violence, as a way to prove their manhood, is problematic when many other avenues of expressing such manhood are closed off. Economic, political and social barriers have often restricted non-white and non-Western men from fulfilling their full potential. But the use of violence, homophobia and misogyny is equally problematic.

References and further reading

al-Qaradawi, Y. (2004) 'Cleric says it's right to fight US civilians in Iraq', available at www.bad thinking.com/study/files/qqaradawiyusufal.shtml

Black, E. (2003) *War Against the Weak*, New York: Four Walls Eight Windows.

Carmichael, S. (n.d.) 'The revolution is happening in our minds', available at http/www.jofreeman.com/feminism/happening.htm

Connell, R. (1995) *Masculinities* Cambridge: Polity.

—— (2005) 'Globalization, imperialism and masculinities,' in M.S. Kimmel, J. Hearn and R.W. Connell (eds) *Handbook of Studies on Men and Masculinities*, Thousand Oaks, CA: Sage.

Douglass, F. (2001) *Narrative of the Life of Frederick Douglass*, New Haven, CT: Yale University Press.

Equiano, O. (2004) *The Interesting Narrative of the Life of Olaudah Equinao or Gustavus Equiano*, New York: Modern Library.

Fanon, F. [1952] (1991) *Black Skins, White Masks*, New York: Grove.

—— [1961] (1963) *The Wretched of the Earth*, New York: Grove.

Hawkins, M. (1993) *Social Darwinism in European and American Thought, 1860–1940*, Cambridge: Cambridge University Press.

Kondo, D. (1999) 'Fabricating masculinity', in C. Kaplan, N. Alarcon and M. Moallam (eds) *Between Women and Nation*, Durham, NC: Duke University Press.

Malcolm X (2002–3) 'The ballot or the bullet', available at www.blackleadershipforum.org/articles/ballott-or-bullet.htm

Mandela, N. (1996) 'Speech from first day of voting, 1994', available at www.crf-usa.org/bria/bria12_2.html

Memphis Sanitation Workers' Strike (1968) at www.reuther.wayne.edu/man/1intro.htm

Stecopoulos, H. and Uebel, M. (eds) (1997) *Race and the Subject of Masculinities*, Durham, NC: Duke University Press.

Wallace, M. (1979) *Black Macho and the Myth of the Superwoman*, New York: Dial.

GERALD R. BUTTERS

RACISM

Racism is the belief that the perceived superiority, whether physical, intellectual or cultural, of one group over another is attributable to the inherent quality of race. Such a belief has, throughout history, served as justification for the domination, oppression and extermination of groups designated as in some way inferior, usually due to their possession of different genetically transmitted physical characteristics such as skin colour.

Since the early 1930s, when the term originated, racism has become an increasingly capacious concept, now often used to signify a system of oppression. That is, it refers to the intersection of racist beliefs, whether avowed or unconscious, cultural practices and social institutions that discriminate against a class of persons possessing a common racial identity.

Globally, racism has produced deep tension across the social fabric. The former colonies of European states, including the US, are sites of racial violence, extending beyond its usual form of white against black to include indigenous genocide (e.g. Rwanda). Anti-colonialist thinkers point to the seamless continuity between colonialism, racism and patriarchy to account for racism's remarkable intransigence (Fanon 1967). The privilege attached to white masculinity often goes unquestioned; indeed, as a marker of cultural dominance, it becomes 'natural' (Frankenburg 1993).

Under the surface of colonialism and racism resides masculinism. The term 'White Man's Burden', the title of an 1899 poem by Kipling, refers to the notion that white European colonists had the responsibility of civilising the so-called primitive and heathen masses of the globe. As a way of rendering noble an imperial mission founded upon racism, the 'White Man's Burden' was a cultural lens through which Europeans saw other cultures as child-like and feminine as well as demonic.

Fascism, like the anti-Semitic racism at its core, is animated by beliefs about masculinity and the repudiation of femininity, softness and indulgence (Theweleit 1989). The fascist warrior, 'a man of steel', is armoured against the femininity of his racial others. The association of Jewishness with femininity can be traced back to medieval anti-Semitism, and it received one of its sharpest modern articulations in Weininger's *Sex and Character* (1903).

References and further reading

Fanon, F. (1967) *Black Skin, White Masks*, translated by C.L. Markmann, New York: Grove Weidenfeld.

Frankenburg, R. (1993) *White Women, Race Matters*, Minneapolis, MN: University of Minnesota Press.

Theweleit, K. (1989) *Male Fantasies, Volume 2: Male Bodies*, Minneapolis, MN: University of Minnesota Press.

Weininger, O. [1903] (2005) *Sex and Character*, translated by L. Löb, edited by D. Steuer, Bloomington and Indianapolis, IN: Indiana University Press.

See also: race and ethnicity

MICHAEL UEBEL

RADICAL FAERIES

The Radical Faerie movement emerged as a distinct feature of the queer cultural landscape in the United States during the 1980s (Timmons 1990; Thompson 1987). Influenced by such diverse cultural strands as environmentalism, Marxism, feminism, paganism, new age spirituality, radical individualism, the psychology of self-actualisation, camp and drag, Faeries challenge binary gender conceptions by encouraging gender fluidity and hybridity, sometimes expressed in terms of a 'third gender'. Today there are at least a dozen such communities across the United States, as well as several Faerie communities in Canada, Europe and Australia. Faerie 'gatherings' are typically held in rural or wilderness areas to foster a deep connection with the land and nature. The Radical Faeries can be seen as a reaction to the culture of sexual objectification, commodification and hypermasculinity that developed in gay male urban enclaves in the wake of gay liberation. Most Faeries are men with same-sex interests, but anyone may be 'called' to the community. Faerie identity is a fascinating mix of essentialism (emanating from an internally stable 'fae spirit') and fluidity (Faeries change their names to acknowledge personal and spiritual transformation). The Radical Faeries are perhaps best characterised by their playful rejection of the heteronormative masculinity that characterises other communities of gay men (e.g. traditionally masculine 'Bears' and gay leathermen). This is exhibited in the community's innovative deployment of drag. Typically, the emphasis is less on creating gender illusion than on sowing gender confusion, as the outrageous mix of masculine and feminine attributes in the typical Faerie's self-presentation parodies both traditional genders (Pickett 2000). In terms of gender politics, this radical critique is tempered by an emphasis within Faerie culture on retreat. Those communities lucky enough to own their own land refer to these spaces as 'sanctuaries', sacred spaces where fae spirits may thrive, safe from the hostile elements of a disenchanted world. However, the strong emphasis on collective introspection and consciousness-raising within these communities suggests that Radical Faeries may one day adopt a more aggressive political profile and become more actively engaged in resistant gender politics (Hennen 2004).

References and further reading

Hennen, P. (2004) 'Fae spirits and gender trouble', *Journal of Contemporary Ethnography*, 33 (5): 499–533.

Pickett, K. (2000) *Faeries*, New York: Aperture.

Thompson, M. (1987) 'This gay tribe', in M. Thompson (ed.) *Gay Spirit*, New York: St Martin's, pp. 260–78.

Timmons, S. (1990) *The Trouble with Harry Hay*, Boston, MA: Alyson.

PETER HENNEN

RAPE

Rape is many things: a sexually violent and degrading act perpetrated by one or more persons against a victim or victims, a ferociously symbolic violation of boundaries, and a representation of patriarchal domination enacted through physical and psychological harm. Rape has been customarily defined as forced or coerced penetration of a bodily orifice by a body part or object. Rape is typically thought of as the rape of a woman by a man, though rape can be and is perpetrated (as well as survived) by people of all genders. Sexual violence has a very long history. In the Code of Hammurabi (c. 2000 BC) women were officially declared the property of men, and sanctions for women who experienced rape were deemed the proper purview of men. Depictions of rape are featured prominently in the Bible and in the Talmud, as well as in the earliest preserved literature, art, poetry and music of ancient Greece, Rome and Egypt. Rape has been used as a tool of war in every modern conflict, culminating in atrocities such as rape camps set up for the purpose of terrorising Bosnian Muslim women during the Bosnian–Croatian–Serbian war of the 1990s (Barstow 2001).

Analysis of rape as an act with both individual and social /contextual causes and consequences began in the early 1970s, with Brownmiller's seminal work, *Against Our Will*. Brownmiller and other feminist theorists argued that rape is both an act of violence and a paradigmatic representation of torture located in a specific power nexus (male dominant, female subordinate) and that, like lynching, its meaning upholds group subordination (Brownmiller 1975; MacKinnon 1989). They also argued that because rape laws and enforcement of these laws have been conceived of and created almost entirely by men, absence of consent is frequently disputed when a woman's relationship to the male perpetrator implies past or present intimacy. For many centuries, the notion of rape in the context of marriage was considered to be an oxymoron and this act was not in fact officially criminalised in all fifty United States until 2004. Feminist analyses of rape emanating from the late twentieth-century women's movement have been criticised for lack of attention to the voices and experiences of women of colour (Davis 1990) and for neglecting the crucial leadership of activist women of colour in the anti-rape movement (Smith 2000).

Men's role in rape has historically been subsumed under the role of perpetrator. Data in the 2003 Department of Justice crime statistics suggest that 70 per cent of all rapes are committed by someone the victim knows; 96.5 per cent of all rape perpetrators are men, while approximately 7 per cent of victims are men (US Department of Justice 2004). No studies exist that have comprehensively measured the rape victimisation prevalence of men and boys in any society. Estimates of victimisation among males range from 5 to 10 per cent (Scarce 1997). Recent attention to the plight of male rape victims in the US has resulted from revelations starting in 1992 of sexual abuse within the Roman Catholic Archdiocese of Boston, resulting in greater awareness of male survivors and the unique aspects of their recovery. Male rape survivors, much like female survivors, are frequently silenced through shame, self-blame and unsupportive social norms that tend to attribute responsibility to the actions or choices of the victim. Rape has also been a racist social phenomenon. Black men during the Reconstruction period in the United States were conveniently demonised: the Ku Klux Klan often conducted their hate-filled crusades on a platform of 'protecting' white women from the imaginary menace of rape by black men (Davis 1990).

Feminist analyses of rape have identified complex social forces which contribute to what has been termed a 'rape culture'. These forces include the prevalence of eroticised violence in mainstream popular culture, the ubiquitous nature of pornography (particularly that which features violent and degrading images of women and children), legal standards which serve to regulate rape rather than prohibiting it, and adherence to a hegemonic masculinity steeped in power, violence and control. The masculinity implicated in the perpetuation of rape is of a very specific Western formulation: man as master of his domain, exerting control over women's (and children's) bodies, in both a socially and legally sanctioned framework where women's choice and consent hold relatively little weight.

Beginning in the early 1980s, and at the impassioned urging of prominent anti-rape activists such as Dworkin (1993), men began to join the anti-rape movement. Sharing feminists' commitment to prevent individual rapes and to unseat what theorist Gavey (2005) deems the 'cultural scaffolding of rape', organisations such as Men Can Stop Rape (USA), Instituto Promundo (Brazil), Men As Partners (South Africa) and many others engage in anti-rape activism and education. Focusing on men's change and accountability, they challenge images that encourage or condone rape in popular culture and the media and shift norms among young men by modelling inclusive, gay and feminist-affirming ideals of masculinity.

References and further reading

Barstow, A.L. (2001) *War's Dirty Secret*, New York: Pilgrim.

Brownmiller, S. (1975) *Against Our Will*, New York: Bantam.

US Department of Justice (2004) *Criminal Victimization in the United States, 2003 Statistical Tables*, Washington, DC: US Department of Justice, Office of Justice Programs, Bureau of Justice Statistics.

Davis, A.Y. (1990) *Women, Culture and Politics*, New York: Vintage.

Dworkin, A. (1993) *Letters from a War Zone*, Brooklyn, NY: Lawrence Hill.

Gavey, Nicola (2005) *Just Sex?* London: Routledge.

MacKinnon, C.A. (1989) *Toward a Feminist Theory of the State*, Cambridge, MA: Harvard University Press.

Scarce, M. (1997) *Male on Male Rape*, New York: Plenum.

Smith, A. (2000) 'Colors of violence', *ColorLines*, 3 (4): 1–5.

See also: aggression; child abuse; crime, criminality and law; domestic violence; sexual violence; violence; White Ribbon Campaign; working with perpetrators or offenders; working with victims and survivors

SUSAN MARINE

RECOVERY AND SELF-HELP

Recovery is the main goal of the self-help movement, which has grown in popularity since the late 1940s. According to Heidi

Rimke (2000: 62) 'Self-help is . . . an undertaking to alter, reform or transform the self, or some "intrinsic" aspect of it, which is contingent upon a person seeking some form of authoritative assistance.' This assistance can take the form of a self-help programme, group or book.

Self-help programmes are usually designed to target a specific, often addictive, behaviour. Well-known recovery-oriented programmes include Alcoholics Anonymous (AA), Narcotics Anonymous (NA) and CoDependents Anonymous (CoDA) (see Denzin 1990; Rimke 2000). Self-help literature comes in many forms, but typically encourages readers to address some lifestyle issue, including their sex lives, parenting styles or relationships. Self-help literature for men – seeking to address the loss of an authentic manhood – has grown in popularity since the early 1990s, and important titles include Robert Bly's *Iron John* (1990), Steve Biddulph's *Manhood* (1995) and Sam Keen's *Fire in the Belly* (1992). Self-help is an extremely popular genre: Americans spent $563 million on self-help books in 2000 (Paul 2001: 60). The self-help movement is primarily about *personal* problem-solving, presenting diagnoses, analysis and solutions to issues that an individual desires to change.

Recovery, as an aspect of the self-help movement, requires several steps (popularised through AA's twelve-step programme). It is achieved through the admission that one has a problem, the recognition that specific assistance is required to overcome the problem or addiction (in the case of AA, that a person is powerless to triumph over their addiction), and the adoption of a specified course of action prescribed by an external expert or experts (Denzin 1993; Rimke 2000). This usually involves some form of behaviour modification, such as the cessation of drinking.

References and further reading

Biddulph, S. (1995) *Manhood: An Action Plan for Changing Men's Lives*, Sydney: Finch Publishing.

Bly, R. (1990) *Iron John*, New York: Vintage Books.

Denzin, N. (1990) 'The sociological imagination revisited', *Sociological Quarterly*, 31: 1–22.

—— (1993) *The Alcoholic Society: Addiction and Recovery of the Self*, New Brunswick, NJ: Transaction Books.

Keen, S. (1992) *Fire in the Belly*, New York: Bantam Books.

Paul, A.N. (2001) 'Self-help: shattering the myths', *Psychology Today*, 34: 60–8.

Rimke, H. (2000) 'Governing citizens through self-help literature', *Cultural Studies*, 14: 61–78.

See also: counselling and therapy; men's groups; men's movement; working with men

ANDREW SINGLETON

REDNECK MASCULINITY

In Australia, as in the USA, 'redneck' is a popular term for the ignorant white rural male whose sunburned neck is associated with a body of reactionary opinion. The imagery is founded in the white supremacist masculinity allegedly characteristic of white pioneers who 'opened up' these lands. Living versions of an ideology asserting that true males are tough, white and racist are deployed in various organisations (Lattas 2001; Ferber 2000), but the term itself is eschewed as derogatory. 'Redneck' opinion is a favourite target of progressive urban thought but has been defended (Murray 1996). The mythic dimension of such imagery is now familiar (Schaffer 1988), but the intertwining of gender and race in Australia's 'outback' in the early twentieth century generated more ambiguous meanings.

There was courage and toughness needed in the isolated, remote and potentially dangerous outback where white men established farms and pastoral stations and, with white women, civilisation. Self-denial was an intrinsic part of the asceticism of bush life; a 1955 magazine asserted that, in addition to the four staples, 'potatoes and onions are carried by such men as consider that their reputations for robust manhood will stand the possible implications' (Cowlishaw 1999: 72). Rough conditions may nurture rough opinions, and explicit racism, sexism and xenophobia are more candidly expressed in rural areas where white supremacist masculinity is still celebrated (Rose 1997). Racial or evolutionary inequality was assumed, and harsh laws tried to enforce racial separation. But neither the laws against 'consorting' nor the shame and contempt it brought prevented intimate companionships forming. Some Aboriginal women actively sought relationships with white men (McGrath 1987). Masculinist myths have erased not only women but the feminine, the tears, the warmth and the nurturing from the outback. Love which emerged between black and white people, and the love of brown children, gave way to accounts of men's brave adventures on the frontiers or, more recently, to exposing the grim reality behind the pioneer myths.

References and further reading

Cowlishaw, G. (1999) *Rednecks, Eggheads and Blackfellas*, Ann Harbor, MI: Michigan University Press.

Ferber, A.L. (2000) 'Racial warriors and weekend warriors,' *Men and Masculinities*, 3 (1): 30–56.

Lattas, A. (2001) 'Redneck thought', *UTS Review* 7 (1): 106–24.

McGrath, A. (1987) *Born in the Cattle*, Sydney: Allen and Unwin.

Murray, L. (1996) *Subhuman Redneck Poems*, Manchester: Carcanet Press.

Rose, D. (1997) 'Australia Felix rules OK?' in G. Cowlishaw and B. Morris (eds) *Race Matters*, Canberra: Aboriginal Studies Press, pp. 121–38.

Schaffer, K. (1988) *Women and the Bush*, Melbourne: Cambridge University Press.

GILLIAN COWLISHAW

REPRODUCTIVE ISSUES AND TECHNOLOGIES

Reproductive issues include a broad collection of topics related to human fertility, conception, pregnancy and parturition. Reproductive technologies address specific applications of human knowledge through techniques, artefacts and practices which seek to control, regulate and alter reproductive processes, often emphasising advances in contraceptive and infertility technologies in the twentieth and twenty-first centuries. Because of the complexity of human social interaction, reproductive issues typically extend beyond procreation to include social, political, personal and religious dimensions of sex, sexuality, parenthood and childhood. Globally many men and women are increasingly aware that, while women bear children and play central roles in their rearing in many societies, (1) reproductive issues are not synonymous with women's issues and (2) many key aspects of masculinity and men's lives relate directly and indirectly to reproduction. Contraceptive and infertility technologies and the reproductive issues surrounding them thus play important roles in men's lives around the world.

Long characterised primarily as barriers to or facilitators of women's contraceptive use, men themselves use contraceptives and negotiate their use with partners. Despite recent contraceptive technologies such as hormone-based alternatives to the contraceptive pill (such as injections, implants and vaginal rings), spermicides and female condoms, contraceptive options specifically for men are limited. Apart from withdrawal and ovulation calculation with periodic abstinence, men's contraceptive choices are limited to surgical sterilisation and condoms. Men do not currently have access to a reliable male hormonal contraceptive (MHC), although MHCs are currently in clinical trial in ten countries. In MHC, testosterone is administered (via injection, implant, patch, oral pill and/or gel) to interfere with the hypothalamus–pituitary–gonadal axis. Gonadotropin production (hormones which regulate sperm and testicular testosterone) is reduced, reversibly interrupting sperm production. The only uniquely male-centred contraceptive that does not require some measure of partner cooperation is the vasectomy, or tubal ligation of the vas deferens, which is used by over 40 million men globally. In developed countries vasectomy prevalence declined and levelled in the 1990s. With increasing rates of divorce and re-marriage, vasectomy reversal rates have also risen, and failure of vasectomy reversal may place stresses on couples similar to non-surgical infertility.

Condom use continues to be an important male-centred contraceptive as well as an effective prophylaxis in the prevention of sexually transmitted infections. Relatively inexpensive and low-technology, but requiring some degree of negotiation between two partners, condom use varies greatly regionally, with more developed countries having around three times the prevalence of condom use relative to less developed countries. Since the advent of HIV (Human Immunodeficiency Virus), men's condom use has become intimately associated with strategies to prevent HIV infection. Globally, women infected with HIV by male partners are the fastest growing group of infected individuals. Moreover, the large percentage of adults of both sexes infected with HIV in many sub-Saharan African nations has meant an increase in the number of children losing one or both parents to the illness. In many more developed countries, access to effective antiretroviral therapy may have produced so-called 'condom fatigue', with men foregoing condom use because of diminished fear of the consequences of HIV infection.

Assisted reproductive technologies (ARTs), or new reproductive technologies (NRTs), include a growing list of techniques for the treatment of male infertility. Male factor infertility may contribute to half of all cases of infertility globally and may directly account for one third of cases, and sperm counts in many industrialised nations have shown declines in the twentieth century. Intracytoplasmic Sperm Injection (ICSI) allows for the fertilisation of an egg with collection of a single viable sperm. Like other ARTs, ICSI may be difficult for both partners, however, with painful sperm retrieval and the possibility of expensive treatment without achieving pregnancy. Moreover, ICSI and other ARTs can produce multiple fertilised embryos, some of which may be reserved for later attempts at pregnancy. Such ARTs thus directly contribute to ongoing debate on scientific research with unused embryonic stems cells. Insofar as impotence contributes to infertility, new drugs which treat erectile dysfunction may also treat infertility. Sperm donation is another option for infertile couples as well as single women and lesbians who choose to reproduce without male partners. Sperm donation has encountered cultural prohibitions on sex and procreation between unmarried men and women, and use of donor sperm may also be clandestine to conceal the perceived shame of male infertility. Sperm donation also offers new procreative options for donors, but with the increasing awareness that children of donation may wish to know their biological fathers.

Men's participation in pregnancy and parenting has changed with greater gender equality. Early pregnancy tests and foetal imaging technologies provide new possibilities for men's participation, increasing a sense of foetal personhood and connection to the developing child. With such participation, men may risk increased loss in the event of miscarriage. Worldwide, over one third of pregnancies do not end in a live birth, with men playing varying roles in both pregnancy loss and induced abortion. In induced abortion decision-making, men may range from primary deciders to equal partners to uninformed or absent impregnators; moreover, men and women may differ concerning abortion decisions. Finally, in many countries, increasing tolerance of diverse sexual orientations has led to more reproduction and parenting by gay male couples via children from previous heterosexual relationships, adoption or 'surrogate' mothers. Such alternative family structures broaden the context of men's reproductive experiences.

References and further reading

Anawalt, B.D. and Armory, J.K. (2001) 'Advances in male hormonal contraception', *Annals of Medicine*, 33: 587–95.

Guttmacher Institute (1999) 'Facts in brief: induced abortion worldwide', New York: Guttmacher Institute; available at http://www.guttmacher.org/pubs/fb_0599.html

Inhorn, M.C. and van Balen, F. (eds) (2002) *Infertility Around the Globe*, Berkeley, CA: University of California Press.

UNAIDS (2006) *UNAIDS 2006 Report on the Global AIDS Epidemic*, WHO Library Cataloguing-in-Publication Data, available at http://www.unaids.org/en/HIV_data/2006GlobalReport/default.asp

US Census Bureau. (2004) 'International population reports WP/02', *Global Population Profile: 2002*, Washington, DC: US Government Printing Office; available at http://census.gov/ipc/prod/wp02/wp-02.pdf

World Health Organization (2006) *The World Health Report 2005*, available at http://www.who.int/whr/2005/en/index.htm

See also: contraception, male; infertility; procreation

MATTHEW R. DUDGEON

RETIREMENT

Retirement represents a key life transition in the lives of older men. This life change from a focus on work and career to leaving paid labour often involves a contradictory mixture of perceived loss and potential growth and reconstruction. Some men view retirement constructively: they are hopeful about new beginning; open to fresh approaches to their health and well-being; and look forward to more time for playful exploration, travel and enjoyment. Other men perceive retirement as mainly about loss: loss of positive social recognition and support from work colleagues and loss of an arena within which they can demonstrate masculine competence and build status.

Retirement can be threatening for many men in gendered terms. They can be anxious about losing the work activities and social relations that have primarily defined their masculine identities. In western societies, being workless in the public sphere can undermine a man's sense of being masculine, especially when he is then more household-defined.

Men's experiences of retirement are extremely diverse, depending on their work histories, social and economic circumstances and emotional and physical well-being. Those men who experienced fulfilment, self-worth and stability in their working lives are more likely to view retirement positively. Other men who have confronted poverty, insecure and subordinating work conditions and poor health often view retirement with fear and anxiety. Indeed, some men cannot afford to view themselves as retired at all, and economic necessity keeps some men working for their entire lives.

Another key social factor that affects men's retirement experiences is partnership status. The problems of loneliness and social isolation after retirement are urgently real for some heterosexual men who are widowed or divorced, gay men living alone and men who have never married. Marriages or partnerships, and the informal social networks often associated with such relationships, often protect many men from mental health problems, illness or a lack of social embeddedness.

Giving up restricted work conditions, in retirement, can lead to the exploration of new forms of masculinity. This breaking out of narrow and rigid models of masculinity can prompt older men to reintegrate earlier, excluded masculinities, such as more tender, creative, self-reflexive and socially connected masculine identities, but again this is partly dependent on the quality of men's earlier experiences in boyhood and the middle years.

See also: age and ageing; men's relations with men; men's relations with women; mid-life crisis

DAVID JACKSON

RISK-TAKING

It is often stated that men participate in risk behaviours to a much greater extent than women. Waldron (1995), using figures from the United States, suggests that males drink more heavily, are more likely to drive while under the influence of alcohol, have higher rates of HIV and have a higher prevalence of intravenous drug use than females. Similarly, Morrell and Swart (2005), discussing African societies, highlight men's lack of regard for safety in sexual transactions and Heidensohn (1997) illustrates how, within England and Wales, nearly all weapon-related offences are perpetrated by males.

These risk-taking behaviours cannot be explained through recourse to reductionist arguments which emphasise hormones or the male role. Rather, the argument is that men use these behaviours in order to define themselves as masculine (Connell 2000), in the context of cultural associations between bravery, aggression, stoicism and manliness. For example, Connell (2000) suggests that in Australia the 'Marlboro Man' campaign connected cigarette smoking with frontier masculinities and that the smoking jacket, smoking room and after-dinner cigar are all constructed as male, and thus as a way of achieving masculinities.

However, two caveats need to be entered. First, there is diversity among males and females as well as between them (Carpenter 2000). Second, there has been a tendency to pick a defining feature of masculinities and 'hang an account of men's lives on that' (Connell 1995: 68). Risk-taking may well be one of these defining features, but to hang an account solely on this would be both arbitrary and essentialist (Connell 1995).

References and further reading

Carpenter, M. (2000) 'Reinforcing the pillars: rethinking gender, social divisions and health', in E. Annandale and K. Hunt (eds) *Gender Inequalities in Health*, Buckingham: Open University Press, pp. 36–63.

Connell, R. (1995) *Masculinities*, Cambridge: Polity Press.

—— (2000) *The Men and the Boys*, Berkeley, CA: University of California Press.

Heidensohn, F. (1997) 'Gender and crime', in M. Maguire, R. Morgan and R. Reiner (eds) *The Oxford Handbook of Criminology*, 2nd edn, Oxford: Oxford University Press, pp. 761–98.

Morrell, R. and Swart, S. (2005) 'Men in the Third World: postcolonial perspectives on masculinity', in M.S. Kimmel, J. Hearn and R. Connell (eds) *Handbook of Studies on Men and Masculinities*, London: Sage, pp. 90–113.

Waldron, I. (1995) 'Contributions of changing gender differences in behaviour and social roles to changing gender differences in mortality', in D. Sabo and D.F. Gordon (eds) *Men's Health and Illness: Gender, Power and the Body*, London: Sage, pp. 22–45.

See also: health and illness, men's

ROBERT MEADOWS

RITES OF PASSAGE

Rites of passage are the constitutive moments of ritual transformation of an individual or collective subject from one culturally defined status to another mode of life. Through this process subjects break with one element of their identity and assume another position in the social system more adequately befitting their age, gender, experience, skills, education or professional status. The gendered component of this universal practice is a major driving force in the confirmation of society's cultural values and gender regime.

The classical formulation of the concept in Van Gennep's *Rites de Passage* (1909) and its later theoretical elaboration by Turner (1969) identify three stages to this process: separation, transition and incorporation. In the first stage, designated participants are removed from the structure of everyday life in the social order. In the second phase, they undergo ordeals that mark their transitional otherness. The third stage completes the cycle, repositions the participants in their new status, and identifies them as members of the appropriate target group.

Rites of passage include birth rites, marriage rites, death rites and initiation rites. All of these are gendered. However, this essay focuses on a few examples of initiation rites that socialise males into normative masculinity: rites in the context of religious systems that transform young males into duty-bearing adult moral subjects; rites in the context of social systems that transform young males into tribal warriors; rites in the context of the modern military that transforms young males into field fighters; and rites in the political context of national conflicts that transform young males into freedom fighters.

Religious rites of passage are nexuses of communication between the realms of the sacred and the profane (Eliade 1957). Among the three monotheistic religious traditions, Christianity features baptism, Judaism emphasises male circumcision and the Bar Mitzvah, while Islam features male circumcision. A heavily ritualised culture, traditional Judaism endowed the boy's Bar Mitzvah ceremony with the status of a founding rite of passage in which thirteen-year-old Jewish boys assume adult religious responsibilities and moral duties. The Bar Mitzvah boy commonly reads portions of the Bible and delivers a sermon, thus symbolising his initiation into the adult male religious community of duty-bearing individuals.

A prominent example of social rites concerns the Sambia of eastern New Guinea (Herdt 1994). Born genderless, through mothers' milk Sambia men become more female. The Sambia initiatory cycle starts when the boy is between the ages of six and ten and proceeds through six stages until he becomes a father some ten to fifteen years later. At puberty males receive semen ('men's milk'), regarded as the essence of all life and power, through fellatio. This ingestion was largely a preparation for war, which was endemic in New Guinea. The men later often combined this activity with heterosexual relations and marriage. This ritualised homosexuality was not a feminising ritual, as conceived in the West, but rather a socialisation into fierce and brutal warrior identity.

Modern states have historically been founded on ideas of normative masculinity and have utilised young men to serve their security interests in the name of their hegemonic ideologies (Mosse 1996). The modern military is a particularly salient institutional vehicle for this process, as it requires the uniform formation and training of large groups of men. Through soldiership and combat, these men not only learn to become good citizens and patriots, but they also learn valorised forms of manhood.

Historical Zionism had a profoundly gendered agenda, which aimed at re-masculinising the supposedly effeminate diasporic Jew. In contemporary Israeli society, military service, although compulsory for both men and women, is directly linked to patriarchal hegemonic notions of citizenship (Sasson-Levy 2002). Military service is composed of rites that differentiate men from women, heterosexuals from homosexuals, elite-unit soldiers from regular infantry combatants, and field fighters from blue-collar soldiers (Kaplan 2003). In basic training, Israeli infantry recruits go through an 'infantilisation' stage *vis-à-vis* their superiors; the second phase is aimed at their becoming fighters; finally, after advanced training, the fighters are redefined as 'real men' (Si'on 1997). For elite units on dangerous missions, military conditioning through violence, control and pleasure produces a distinct hypermasculine 'violent body' (Samimian-Darash 2004).

Patterns of masculinity are particularly implicated in personal and collective political agency during national conflicts and colonial occupation. In the West Bank and Gaza, life under Israeli occupation has pushed young Palestinians to an unprecedented social role as organisers of popular resistance. Traditionally subordinated to the patriarchal authority of the family elderly, young Palestinian men have assumed, during the two Palestinian Uprisings (*Intifada*), the role of their parents in mobilising both peaceful and violent collective protest. Rather than a sign of humiliation and submission, beating and detention of Palestinians by Israeli soldiers during the First *Intifada* (1987–93) was construed by Palestinians as a rite of passage into manhood (Peteet 1994). Common sayings such as 'prison is for men' foreground a political agency designed to reverse relations of domination between occupied and occupier. This symbolic inversion presents the Palestinian unarmed male facing the armed soldier as the 'real man' in the true moral sense.

References and further reading

Eliade, M. (1957) *Birth and Rebirth*, New York: Harper.

Herdt, G. (1994) *Guardians of the Flutes*, Chicago, IL: University of Chicago Press.

Kaplan, D. (2003) 'The military as a second Bar Mitzvah', in G. Mai, and E. Sinclair-Webb (eds) *Imagined Masculinities*, London: Saqi.

Mosse, G. (1996) *The Image of Man*, New York: Oxford University Press.

Peteet, J. (1994) 'Male gender and rituals of resistance in the Palestinian "Intifada"', *American Ethnologist*, 21 (1): 31–49.

Samimian-Darash, L. (2004) *Violence, Control and Enjoyment*, Jerusalem: Shaine Centre, Hebrew University (in Hebrew).

Sasson-Levy, O. (2002) 'Constructing identities at the margins', *Sociological Quarterly*, 43 (3): 110–30.

Si'on, L. (1997) *Images of Masculinity among Combat Soldiers*, Jerusalem: Shaine Centre, Hebrew University (in Hebrew).

Turner, V. (1969) *The Ritual Process*, Chicago, IL: Aldine.

Van Gennep, A. [1909] (1960) *The Rites of Passage*, Chicago, IL: University of Chicago Press.

See also: initiation; Jewish masculinities; military masculinities, sperm, semen

DANIEL MONTERESCU

S

SADISM

The term 'sadism' was coined by Krafft-Ebing in his *Psychopathia Sexualis* (1886). For Krafft-Ebing, sadism was a degenerate category of male sexual cruelty that reflected the violence in the Marquis de Sade's eighteenth-century works. Ellis disputed Krafft-Ebing's definition of sadism, arguing for its redefinition as a type of sexual play that heightened sensual feelings and depended on empathy instead of antipathy. Although Ellis concluded that sadism was not exclusively a male category, Freud not only realigned it with aggressive masculinity but reinstated Krafft-Ebing's notion of antipathetic cruelty.

The Krafft-Ebing/Freud definition of sadism informed twentieth-century American, Australian, British and Canadian radical feminist movements' notion of 'cultural sadism'. In *Female Sexual Slavery* (1979), Barry described cultural sadism as male sexual violence against women that is elevated to the level of a cultural norm. Radical feminists formed two main camps regarding the origins of male sadism: one who saw it as an extension of the male aggression demonstrated in penetrative heterosexual intercourse and another who conceived it as the learned expression of a cultural ideology that normalised violence against women. This version of sadism, however, did not remain unchallenged. Ellis's de-gendered idea of sadism as sexual play re-emerged in groups such as the San Francisco lesbian S/M organisation Samois and in the gay and queer movements hailed by Halperin as incarnating the sensual enjoyment of the body.

Outside the confines of this sexological paradigm, what radical feminists called sadism could be explained as a Machiavellian approach to the world where the rational deployment of cruelty is both accepted and celebrated as a means to successfully gain or retain power. Sadism in this sense is a strategic mode of securing male supremacy in every sphere of life from the sexual to the political. Its logic is that the end always justifies the means and that the use of force yields power, respect and awe. This definition of sadism explains not only male sexual violence against women, but also men's cruelty against other men.

References and further reading

Barry, K. (1979) *Female Sexual Slavery*, Englewood Cliffs, NJ: Prentice-Hall.

Ellis, H. [1897] (1941) 'Love and pain', in H. Ellis, *Studies in the Psychology of Sex*, Vol. 1, New York: Random House.

Freud, S. [1919] (1941) 'A child is being beaten', in *The Standard Edition of the Complete Psychological Works of Sigmund Freud*, Vol. 17, London: Hogarth.

Halperin, D. (1995) *Saint Foucault*, New York: Oxford University.

Krafft-Ebing, R. [1886] (1965) *Psychopathia Sexualis*, New York: Bantam.

LINDA D. WAYNE

SCIENCE

Science is a continuous, bi-directional process that relates empirical facts to theoretical formulations. The modern scientific method was first described by Sir Francis Bacon (1561–1626) shortly after the end of the Renaissance (1450–1600) in *The Advancement of Learning*. The goal of the scientific method is to develop theories, derived from empirical evidence, that explain phenomena and allow for the prediction and control of the external world. Valuable theories explain a broad, rather than narrow, range of facts. A theory must be refutable: that is, be able to be shown to be incorrect. The scientific method valorises objectivity, replicability, logical thought, linear thinking and empirical evidence. It is assumed that the scientific method operates in the absence of emotion and rejects intuitive means of knowing. All scientific knowledge is tentative in that at some future point, someone may put forward data or theoretical formulations that require the reinterpretation or revision of generally accepted beliefs (Kuhn 1962).

Since its development, the scientific method has been remarkably effective in transforming the way we examine and interact with our physical world. One of the greatest scientists of all time, Sir Isaac Newton (1643–1727), illustrated the power of science in two incredibly productive years when he began revolutionary advances in mathematics, physics, optics and astronomy. His *Principia*, considered the most important scientific book ever produced, presented laws that applied to falling objects on earth as well as the motion of the planets and comets. These principles are essential to understanding applications ranging from the firing of cannon balls to the orbits of rockets in space. Working in a different domain, Gregor Johann Mendell (1822–84) examined how traits are passed from one generation to the next. Although he was unable to explain the mechanism of genetic transmission, his identification of dominant and recessive traits could be seen as the basis for current research on cloning and genetic testing. Modern medical miracles such as heart transplants and life-saving drugs like antibiotics have been made possible by the exercise of the scientific method.

Although the methodologies of different branches of science might vary, depending on the phenomenon under consideration, it is typically assumed there is one unitary method of performing science. The scientific method is thought to reflect an objective means of analysis that operates independently of values or personal bias. Despite the unequivocal successes of science, this conventional view of science has been challenged on a number of fronts, notably by feminist-based scholars (e.g. Keller 1985; Schiebinger 1999), who have argued that science actually reflects a masculine bias as a means of collecting knowledge. Rather than being completely objective and value-free, the scientific method, as typically defined, reflects hegemonic masculinity and the subordination of femininity. The masculine bias in science is expressed in its sexist language, masculinist structure and methodologies, and androcentric epistemology (Letts 2001).

There is a correspondence between stereotypical masculine traits and the definition of the scientific method. Masculinity is associated with competitiveness, dominance hierarchies and logical, as opposed to emotionally driven, thought. The scientific method can be seen as the valuation of the same attributes.

An important part of the scientific method is that theories are in direct competition with each other for dominance. A theory is defined as dominant when it better explains empirical evidence. The scientific method can be seen in this light as a process where theories are pitted against each other until a dominant theory emerges. In other words, science is performed under the assumption that there is an inherent competition among theories, just as a defining feature of masculinity is competitiveness among males.

Another important characteristic of science is that theories are developed and evaluated in an objective manner devoid of emotion. An essential component of hegemonic masculinity is the valuing of emotional control. Thus, just as masculinity is performed without emotion, it is assumed that scientific truth will be obtained without reference to emotionality. In reality, emotional and non-objective criteria do enter the process of science. For example, it is difficult to publish articles that contain findings that contradict dominant paradigms or go against the tide of popular opinion. Kuhn (1962) argued that paradigm shifts occur when proponents of outmoded theories die out and leave room for a new generation to propose alternative interpretations.

Basic science is a theory-based enterprise where the goal is to develop a better understanding of the world without necessarily having a clear application in mind. In contrast, applied science is problem-focused. Science occupies a favoured position in Western cultures because it serves as a basis for problem-solving. For example, engineering can be seen as the application of principles involving physics, chemistry and biology. The ability of basic scientific discoveries to have far-reaching practical applications corresponds to task-oriented masculine values that focus on problem-solving.

Scientists often look for differences. What makes one metal stronger than another? Why are some stars brighter than others? Why do some people get sick and die whereas others can weather an illness and recover quickly? A kind of scientific decision-making known as null hypothesis significance testing is based on the quest for differences. Though subject to extensive criticism (e.g. Howson and Urbach 1989), null hypothesis significance testing is the cornerstone of research in most of the social sciences. This approach uses statistical methods to determine whether an observed difference reflects the operation of random chance or the influence of real factors. When applied to gender, null hypothesis significance testing addresses whether an observed difference, such as different scores on a questionnaire, represents a real difference between men and women, such as a different level of intelligence.

The reproductive differences between males and females are assumed to correspond with personality and character differences. There is a huge body of research on what is known as sex (or sometimes gender) differences. In 1974, Maccoby and Jacklin published *The Psychology of Sex Differences* that reviewed the findings of over 1,400 studies. The search for gender differences includes topics as diverse as religious beliefs, intellectual abilities, temperament, motor skills, mental health and dysfunction, and emotionality. Despite the common-sense belief that men and women should greatly differ, research has shown that there are relatively few reliable differences between men and women. Even when differences exist, they tend to be rather small in magnitude. In other words, there tends to be greater variation of individuals around their gender's group mean than there is between the means of men and women. Rather than focus on gender differences, Connell (2002) has noted that researchers should redefine their field of inquiry as gender similarity research.

Although gender differences in intellectual ability are nonexistent (Halpern and LaMay 2000), small differences in mathematical ability favour men (Hyde *et al.* 1990). However, the magnitude of these differences does not explain the gender gap in science and mathematics education that privileges men over women (Greenfield 1996). Although women receive 55 per cent of both bachelor's and master's degrees, this ratio is reversed in engineering, mathematics and the natural sciences. One explanation for this pattern is that boys tend to be more confident than girls in their ability to perform in mathematics and science (Ma and Kishor 1997).

Differences in the rates at which men and women enter the fields of science and mathematics reflect societal factors. Right from birth, boys and girls are socialised differently, with boys being treated more roughly and at a relatively early age being encouraged to distance themselves from their emotions. Boys are more likely than girls to play with tools and building kits. Gender stereotypes that involve activity and achievement orientation tend to encourage boys to become more active in science, whereas stereotypes about girls as emotional and intuitive tend to demote the importance of science and emphasise nurturing components. As boys get older, they tend to attribute success in science and mathematics to internal attributes such as ability and failure to external factors such as bad luck. In contrast, as girls get older, they tend to attribute success in mathematics and science to good luck and failure to a lack of ability. Parents and teachers also encourage boys to pursue careers in science and mathematics to a greater degree than girls.

The exclusion of women from a science and mathematics curriculum reflects the operation of many large-scale social processes, such as stereotypes, roles, parental expectations, mass media and the influence of peers. It is difficult to produce lasting change on these social institutions. Moreover, there is evidence that the influence of these factors may operate in a complex and subtle fashion. For example, Felson and Trudeau (1991) failed to find evidence that level of parental encouragement was associated with females' difficulties with mathematics, suggesting that parental socialisation of females is more difficult to model than typically believed. In keeping with this argument, Smith (1992) reported that the female disadvantage in science achievement is stronger for females living outside a nuclear family, a finding he explained in terms of separated mothers becoming role models for more conventional feminine roles.

One area where improvement might occur more readily is through the influence of elementary and secondary school teachers (Tindall and Hamil 2004). During their training, teachers can be made aware of these gender disparities. Moreover, they can use a variety of tools to minimise bias in their classrooms and promote more egalitarian models of science education for boys and girls.

One technique would be to establish norms that promote greater levels of verbal classroom participation among girls. Because girls tend to raise their hand before speaking, whereas boys are more likely to shout out answers, girls should be encouraged to speak out, even without being formally recognised by the teacher. Another technique is to make classroom participation mandatory rather than voluntary.

Another means of encouraging girls to become more interested in science is to promote a conceptualisation of science more consistent with how girls and women approach learning. Rather than always emphasise the principles of rational analysis and logic that are assumed to form the basis of the scientific method, teachers could also point out how science also includes processes related to cooperation and communication. In the modern research world, the image of the lone scientist in the laboratory has been replaced by the concept of teams of scientists working collaboratively on large projects they would be unable to solve individually. The process of science would cease if research findings were not disseminated through public venues such as conferences, journals and electronic media.

By promoting supportive environments that build confidence, teachers could help girls could become more comfortable about their potential abilities in the natural sciences, mathematics and engineering. Another way to help girls recognise their potential is to provide girls with positive role models. Women scientists and engineers who visit the class as a point of contact could show girls that women can succeed in those fields. It is important to note that these examples could also help boys understand that the girls in class may also have potential as scientists. If a teacher is female, she can also serve as a role model for students. An important caution when using role models is that to be effective as a change agent, the role model has to be appealing to the target. Thus, role models that are closer in age to the students and who have upbeat and outgoing personalities would be most likely to be effective influence agents.

Another approach for creating a less biased representation of gender in the sciences would be to promote policies that encourage boys and men to enter careers typically associated with women. One place where bias exists is in nursing. Although becoming a nurse requires an extensive background in science, especially biology and chemistry, it is a field dominated by women. The failure of the nursing profession to recruit men has contributed to the significant shortage of skilled nurses and can be explained, in part, by the disadvantage in nurses' salaries in comparison to the salaries of other health care professionals.

References and further reading

Connell, R. (2002) *Gender*, Malden, MA: Blackwell.

Felson, R.B. and Trudeau, L. (1991) 'Gender differences in mathematics performance', *Social Psychology Quarterly*, 54: 113–26.

Greenfield, T.A. (1996) 'Gender, ethnicity, science achievement, and attitudes', *Journal of Research in Science Teaching*, 33: 901–34.

Halpern, D.F. and LaMay, M.L. (2000) 'The smarter sex', *Educational Psychology Review*, 12: 229–46.

Howson, C., and Urbach, P. (1989) *Scientific Reasoning*, La Salle, IL: Open Court.

Hyde, J.S., Fennema, E. and Lamon, S.J. (1990) 'Gender differences in mathematics performance', *Psychological Bulletin*, 107: 139–55.

Keller, E.F. (1985) *Reflections on Gender and Science*, New Haven, CT: Yale University Press.

Kuhn, T.S. (1962) *The Structure of Scientific Revolutions*, Chicago, IL: University of Chicago Press.

Letts, W. (2001) 'When science is strangely alluring', *Gender and Education*, 13: 261–74.

Ma, X. and Kishor, N. (1997) 'Attitude toward self, social factors, and achievement in mathematics', *Educational Psychology Review*, 9: 89–120.

Maccoby, E.E., and Jacklin, C.N. (1974) *The Psychology of Sex Differences*, Stanford, CA: Stanford University Press.

Schiebinger, L. (1999) *Has Feminism Changed Science?* Cambridge, MA: Harvard University Press.

Smith, T.E. (1992) 'Gender differences in the scientific achievement of adolescences', *Social Forces*, 71: 469–84.

Tindall, T. and Hamil, B. (2004) 'Gender disparity in science education', *Education*, 125: 282–95.

JAMES K. BEGGAN

SCIENCE FICTION

Science fiction is a broad category including anything from low-budget monster movies to the sophisticated speculative fiction of Samuel R. Delany or Ursula K. Le Guin. The genre's ability to investigate social roles and identities was formally marked in 1991 by the creation of the James Tiptree, Jr, Award, honouring fiction that explores and expands ideas about gender. The Tiptree Award took its name from the pen-name of Alice Sheldon, whose own work throws considerable light on the subject and who successfully masqueraded as a male for ten years. It called attention to a tradition begun by Mary Shelley, who wrote what is arguably the first science fiction novel, *Frankenstein*. While feminist writers such as Le Guin and Joanna Russ have received more attention for their fictional explorations of women's roles, SF has also been in the forefront in investigating images of masculinity.

Many science fiction stories offer two versions of the male hero: the man of action and the man of science. Hollywood's simplified form of the genre usually favours the action hero. Flash Gordon gets the girl and the screen time, while Dr Zarkov remains a semi-trustworthy, secondary figure. Glasses-wearing scientists are revealed as hopelessly naive in a universe full of monsters. SF's men of action are mostly interchangeable with heroic males from other popular forms such as the Western. However, the tension between the fighting hero and his brainier counterpart is specific to science fiction and is one reason this genre has become a particularly powerful tool for questioning gender.

Within print SF, the macho hero is much less likely to triumph over the scientist. Even in the early days of science fiction magazines, when such character types as the square-jawed space captain were first developed, writers tended to take an ironic view of the masculine ideal he represented. In a 1937 story called 'Forgetfulness', John W. Campbell, Jr, created versions of both the scientist and the action hero. The latter is typically 'tall and powerful, his muscular figure in trim Interstellar Expedition uniform' (22). He dismisses his scientist colleague as having no part to play in conquering the pastoral world of Rhth. Yet it is the astronomer who figures out that the gentle people of Rhth are, in reality, far more powerful than their would-be invaders. The aggressive Commander comes across as a blustering fool, while the quiet scientist salvages at least a bit of knowledge from the disastrous campaign.

The same masculine roles reappear in more exaggerated form in R.A. Lafferty's 1966 story 'Nine hundred grandmothers'. The scientist hero's commander complains that 'Nobody can be a hero with a name like Ceran Swicegood!' (142) and suggests he copy his redubbed colleague George Blood: 'Though the hair on George's chest was a graft job, yet that and his new name has turned him from a boy to a man' (142).

Such parodic self-awareness is a function of the way SF story ideas are traded around and elaborated like jazz tunes. It also reflects the genre's combination of high-level intellectual content with more-or-less formulaic storytelling. One source of intellectual infusions is the scientific study of gender. From Darwinian sexual competition to computer-simulated sex, SF has frequently drawn on current thinking about sexual difference. The investigation of masculinity, in particular, has generated a number of fictional tropes, including the superman story, the single-sex utopia (or dystopia), the world of androgynes, and the post-human future.

In the typical superman story, a mutant hero struggles against human rivals, using superior intellect to gain power and win the girl. Philip K. Dick's story 'The Golden Man' (1954) tweaks this scenario by positing a superman with strength, agility, preternatural beauty – and few brains. The implication is that a hypermale is not necessarily a superior human being.

All-female societies have been a useful tool for feminist writers, starting with Charlotte Perkins Gilman's *Herland* (1915). Fewer writers have used the single-sex trope to explore masculinity, but Katherine Burdekin (*Swastika Night*, 1937), Lois McMaster Bujold (*Ethan of Athos*, 1986), Ursula K. Le Guin (the Tiptree-winning 'The matter of Seggri', 1994), and Eleanor Arnason (*Ring of Swords*, 1993) extrapolate societies based on a wide range of male behaviours, from Burdekin's erotically charged violence to Bujold's pair-bonding and nurturing.

The best-known SF treatment of androgyny is Le Guin's *The Left Hand of Darkness* (1969). She was anticipated by Theodore Sturgeon, in *Venus Plus X* (1960), which not only imagines a society with no sexual difference and no resulting imbalance of power or opportunity, but also depicts the resistance of a male observer to what he perceives as loss of phallic prerogatives. Samuel R. Delany's *Triton* (1976) and John Varley's 'Options' (1986) posit a kind of androgyny in the form of easy and complete sexual change.

Gender is entirely elective for computer-simulated beings like those in Greg Egan's *Permutation City* (1994). In the post-human world of cyborgs, bioengineered bodies and virtual reality, one's sexuality is no more fixed than one's form. Writers who have led the exploration of post-human existence include William Gibson (whose cyber-cowboys can be read either as simple retreads of or ironic commentaries on older masculine ideals), Raphael Carter, Gwyneth Jones and Geoff Ryman.

References and further reading

Attebery, B. (2002) *Decoding Gender in Science Fiction*, New York: Routledge.

Campbell, J. (as Stuart, D.) [1937] (1946) 'Forgetfulness', in R. Healy and J. McComas (eds) *Adventures in Time and Space*, New York: Random House, pp. 21–46.

Delany, S. (1994) *Silent Interviews*, Middletown, CT: Wesleyan Press.

Garber, E. and Paleo, L. (1990) *Uranian Worlds*, Boston, MA: Hall.

Lafferty, R. [1966] (1993) 'Nine hundred grandmothers', in Ursula L. Le Guin and Brian Attebery (eds) *The Norton Book of Science Fiction*, New York: Norton, pp. 142–50.

Larbalestier, J. (2002) *The Battle of the Sexes in Science Fiction*, Middletown, CT: Wesleyan Press.

Roberts, R. (1993) *A New Species: Gender and Science in Science Fiction*, Urbana, IL: University of Illinois Press.

See also: heroes; hypermasculinity; literature

BRIAN ATTEBERY

SCULPTURE

If stabilised masculinities depend for their survival on a limited range of conventional types transmitted and maintained through various forms of cultural production, then sculpture, being historically one of the most physically enduring, publicly viewed and icongraphically significant art forms, plays a vital role in constructing, reflecting and at times undermining dominant gender ideologies, especially as they are written on the body. Because of its priveleged position in Western aesthetics, the sculpted male body in particular has been essential in shaping our perception of what it means for a male body to be properly 'masculine'. Sculpture is doubly influential on visualised masculinities when considering its role in monuments and memorials, those essential landmarks of urban space that often employ idealised male bodies to commemorate soldiers, athletes, civic leaders, politicians and other hero- or god-like figures.

For the Western tradition, classical Greek sculpture marks a key development in the theoretical and cultural relationship between sculpture and the male body. Until the fifth century BCE, Egyptian sculpture provided the prototypical model: males were depicted with linear, striding postures, clenched fists and v-shaped torsos, common types in both Egyptian tomb sculpture and archaic Greek *kouroi* (commemorative sculptures celebrating the dead). Classical Greek sculptors, believing the youthful male body epitomised aesthetic beauty, still idealised the male form, but created more naturalistic and detailed figures. This model is exemplified by Polykleitos's *Doryphoros* or 'Spear-Bearer' (c. fifth century BCE), the Apollo Belvedere (c. fourth century BCE), and the fragmented Belvedere Torso (c. first century BCE), all youthful, muscular depictions wrought according to canons observing harmony, proportion and balance.

Though the Greek influence has proven significant, its influence has not been uniform. Within the Italian Renaissance, a period that produced Michelangelo's marble *David* (1504), which continues to represent the apotheosis of neo-classical heroic masculinity, there also springs Michelangelo's sensuous, rounded *Bacchus* (1499) and Donatello's adolescent, nearly androgynous *David* (1432), both of which depict highly eroticised and feminised male bodies. But it isn't until the nineteenth century that the classically formulated male body is seriously threatened. Auguste Rodin, for example, continues to depict male bodies, but a statue like *The Age of Bronze* (1876), and his fragmented bodies like *Walking Man* (1878) portray realistic, less heroic male forms. The New Sculpture movement in Britain, represented by Frederic Leighton's *Athlete Wrestling with a Python* (1877), enthusiastically embraced the heroic male nude, but James Havard Thomas's *Lycidas* (1905), a product of the same movement, depicts a tall, lanky male whose shrugging pose suggests a helplessness reflective of the modern condition.

Twentieth-century sculptural depictions of the male body continue within the tradition, but two important developments challenge it in unprecedented ways: the machine aesthetic and the objectification of the sculpted body. Douglas Tilden's *Mechanics Fountain*, a prominent public monument to industrialised labour in San Francisco, California, depicts an optimistic balance between man – represented by nude males draped over a giant punch press – and the machines they operate. Umberto Boccioni's Futurist *Unique Forms of Continuity in Space* (1913) is a proto-cyborg whose formidable, flame-like limbs transform flesh into pure metal, an embodiment of the Futurist paradigm that celebrates the machine's potential for fashioning new supermen. Yet these more Utopian fusions of man and machine are contrasted by Constantin Brancusi's *Male Torso* (1917). While Brancusi's sculpture, consisting of smooth, tubular planes representing the abdomen and two legs, recalls the ancient *Belvedere Torso*, its radical objectification of the male body presents a very different type of masculine subject – one that is devoid of any essentially male qualities.

Twentieth-century public monuments provide a useful contrast to the objectification and machinisation of the male body. Serguiz Michalski notes that while the 'cult of the great man seems to have lost . . . much of its normative appeal' in twentieth-century figuration, the 'archetypal vivacity' of conventional monuments continues to retain their symbolic power (Michalski 1998: 8). Theorising the sculpted male body, then, begins with establishing the extent of its public function, which is inseparable from such other theoretical matters as aesthetics, erotics and the gaze. Melissa Dabakis, for example, contends that *Mechanics Fountain*, as well as other male nudes that exist in public space, 'both allows and refutes homosocial desire' (Dabakis 1999: 93). Michael Hatt's important studies on sculpture and masculinity call attention to the complicated racial, national, sexual and gender politics involved in constructing and viewing the sculpted male body in public. In general, critics tend to agree that sculpture remains an important site for tracing, across different eras and cultures, the shifting status of masculinity as representation.

References and further reading

Chard, C. (1999) 'Effeminacy, pleasure and the classical body', in G. Perry and M. Rossington (eds) *Femininity and Masculinity in Eighteenth Century Art and Culture*, Manchester: Manchester University Press, pp. 142–61.

Dabakis, M. (1999) *Visualizing Labor in American Sculpture*, Cambridge: Cambridge University Press.

Dressler, R. (2004) *Of Armor and Men in Medieval England*, Burlington, VT: Ashgate.

Getsy, D. (ed.) (2004) *Sculpture and the Pursuit of a Modern Ideal in Britain c. 1880–1930*, Burlington, VT: Ashgate.

Hatt, M. (1992) 'Making a man of him', *Oxford Art Journal*, 15 (1): 21–35.

—— (1999) 'Physical culture', in E. Prettejohn (ed.) *After the Pre-Raphaelites*, New Brunswick, NJ: Rutgers University Press, pp. 240–56.

Michalski, S. (1998) *Public Monuments*, London: Reaktion Books.

Poggi, C. (1997) 'Dreams of metallized flesh', *Modernism/Modernity*, 4 (3): 19–43.

Potts, A. (1992) 'Male phantasy and modern sculpture', *Oxford Art Journal*, 15 (2): 38–47.

Saslow, J. (1998) 'Michelangelo', in S. McHam (ed.) *Looking at Italian Renaissance Sculpture*, Cambridge: Cambridge University Press, pp. 223–45.

Sherman, D. (1996) 'Monuments, mourning and masculinity in France after World War I', *Gender and History*, 8 (1): 82–107.

See also: aesthetics; art; body image; bodybuilding; culture and representation; heroes; male gaze

SAMUEL SCHWARTZ

SECURITY SERVICES

An association between masculinities and military service is familiar in many parts of the world. In some cultures military heroism has been valorised as the highest form of masculinity. In the formation of the modern European nation-state, military service was virtually equated with citizenship, and during the nineteenth century state security thus became the basis of official definitions of manhood. This fed into the terrible slaughter of 1914–18 in Europe.

In the same cultures, however, there have always been dissident traditions, mocking military masculinity – represented in great works of European literature from *Don Quixote* through *Simplicissimus* to *The Good Soldier Schweik*. And in other cultures, military masculinity has been subordinate to, or at best an alternative to, hegemonic civilian masculinities

Research on police, military forces and prisons has shown how particular patterns of masculinity are institutionalised, becoming part of the organisational culture. These patterns vary between different parts of security services. This institutionalisation is functional, in the sense of making possible the social practices of confrontation and violence that are inherent in what security forces do. But it may also produce chronic and oppressive violence that is very difficult to limit, as seen in military dictatorships and both military and civilian prisons.

In recent decades, the security services of rich western countries have changed. Mass conscript armies have been replaced with professional mercenary armies. Under equal opportunity laws, a minority of women have entered military and police forces, creating pressure to change institutionalised masculinities. At the same time, private security forces have expanded rapidly, and now in many countries outnumber official police services. Private forces are less subject to equal opportunity and civil rights pressures, and consequently may be helping a shift back towards older patterns of masculinity.

In recent years the role of security services in peacemaking has come under scrutiny, especially in United Nations interventions. There is an obvious paradox in military masculinity, oriented to confrontation and violence, being a vehicle of peacemaking. The role of women in peacemaking processes and the need to combine security operations with positive reconciliation and rebuilding post-conflict societies are increasingly emphasised.

References and further reading

Barrett, F.J. (1996) 'The organizational construction of hegemonic masculinity', *Gender, Work and Organization*, 3: 129–42.

Breines, I., Connell, R. and Eide, I. (ed.) (2000) *Male Roles, Masculinities and Violence*, Paris: UNESCO.

Seifert, R. (1993) *Individualisierungsprozesse, Geschlechterverhältnisse und die soziale Konstruktion des Soldaten*, München: Sozialwissenschaftliches Institut der Bundeswehr.

Tickner, J.A. (1999) 'Feminist perspectives on security in a global economy', in C. Thomas and P. Wilkin (eds) *Globalization, Human Security and the African Experience*, Boulder, CO: Lynne Rienner, pp. 41–58.

See also: armies; military institutions; military masculinities; war

RAEWYN CONNELL

SELF-HARM

Self-harm (SH) is the deliberate, non-suicidal destruction of one's own body tissue. Self-harm spread dramatically as a behaviour among adolescents in the 1990s. Self-harm has gone by several names, including deliberate self-harm syndrome, self-mutilation, self-cutting, self-injurious behaviour, self-wounding and self-injury. Although many behaviours may be considered self-harming, the psychiatric community defines this syndrome as: self-cutting, burning, branding, scratching, picking at skin or re-opening wounds, biting, head-banging, hair-pulling, hitting (with a hammer or other object) and bone-breaking.

Self-harm, long considered a suicidal gesture, is recognised today as offering short-term release from anxiety, depersonalisation and rapidly fluctuating emotions leading to euphoria, reduced anger and tension, satisfaction of self-punishment urges, and relief from depression, loneliness, loss and alienation. As an emotion regulation strategy, it provides a sense of control, reconfirming the presence of one's body, dulling feelings and converting unbearable emotional pain into manageable physical pain.

The psycho-medical community considers self-harm an impulse disorder, often starting in early adolescence, with most practitioners still adolescent (Favazza 1998). Girls are regarded as more frequent practitioners than boys, although some assert that there are more, or nearly equal, male practitioners (Suyemoto and MacDonald 1995). Like eating disorders, SH has been thought to originate and remain located primarily among a Caucasian, intelligent, middle- or upper-class population (Ross and Heath 2002).

Research in the twentieth century suggests that the practice has become more widespread, including among prisoners, especially juveniles; homeless street youth; boys and men; people of colour; those from lower socio-economic statuses; members of alternative youth subcultures; and youth suffering typical adolescent stress. A growing group of older hard-core users begin the practice to seek relief but settle into a lifetime pattern of chronic SH. Many of these people operate as loner deviants (Adler and Adler 2005), hiding their behaviour, but the rise of Internet SH chat rooms, websites and groups has created cyber-subcultures and cyber-relationships where communities of SHers flourish.

References and further reading

Adler, P.A. and Adler, P. (2005) 'Self-injurers as loners', *Deviant Behavior*, 26: 345–78.

Favazza, A.R. (1998) 'The coming of age of self-mutilation', *Journal of Nervous and Mental Disease*, 186: 259–68.

Ross, S. and Heath, N. (2002) 'A study of the frequency of self-mutilation in a community sample of adolescents', *Journal of Youth and Adolescence*, 31: 67–77.

Suyemoto, K.L. and MacDonald, M.L. (1995) 'Self-cutting in female adolescents', *Psychotherapy*, 32: 162–71.

PATRICIA A. ADLER
PETER ADLER

SEMEN ANXIETY

'Semen anxiety' has been an important theme in the study of male sexuality in India. It refers to a widely held perception – irrespective of caste and religious differences – that 'loss' of semen equates to a loss of masculine strength and 'life-force'. It is *not*, however, connected with concerns over 'premature' ejaculation. There are folkloric measures of equivalence between a quantum of semen wasted and the amounts of energy expended. These are usually expressed in terms of precious materials such as *ghee* (clarified butter) and blood. The conservation-of-semen perspective is also linked – in certain contexts – to the valorisation of *Brahmacharya*, or celibacy, which is said to engender spiritual masculine energy. Semen has considerable significance in Hindu religious texts, and its 'spilling' by the gods is often represented as an act of creation. Scholars – who regard semen anxiety as a culturally specific syndrome – argue that religious texts provide the most significant basis for the belief. Hence, it is suggested that Indian popular sexological practice and advice condemns masturbation as an act that leads to weak men with inadequate sex lives as well as diminished capacity to function as men. The 'syndrome' has been the object of considerable, anthropological, psychological and public health-orientated analysis. In public health work, in particular, it has taken on the form of an 'essential' aspect of Indian culture that, say, strategies against HIV/AIDS must take into account. However, more recently, others have questioned the centrality of the concept in understandings of male sexuality in the Indian subcontinent. It has been suggested that while 'semen anxiety' may well be of considerable cultural significance, it is not clear that it has as definitive a status in the lives of men as is often suggested. An understanding of masculine sexuality also requires the positioning of 'semen anxiety' alongside the cultures of consumption, globalisation and the shifting identities of manhood.

References and further reading

Carstairs, M. (1957) *The Twice Born. A Study of a Community of High Caste Hindus*, London: Hogarth Press.

Lal, V. (1999) 'Nakedness, non-violence, and the negation of negation: Gandhi's experiments in *Brahmacharya* and celibate sexuality', *South Asia* (NS), XXII, (2): 63–94.

Osella, F. and Osella, C. (2002) 'Contextualising sexuality: young men in Kerala, South India', in L. Manderson and P. Liamputtong (eds) *Coming of Age in South Asia and South-East*

Asia. Youth, Courtship and Sexuality, London: Curzon Press.

See also: Indian masculinities; sexuality

SANJAY SRIVASTAVA

SEX

Sex has two broad meanings. Sex refers to the basic biological difference of whether an individual possesses the reproductive organs associated with being female or male. Although sex is thought of as a dichotomous category, individuals can be defined as hermaphrodites because they possess sex organs of both sexes. Asexuals lack sexual organs of any kind. Sex also refers to using sex organs to engage in sexual behaviour. In addition to reproduction, there is also a strong element of pleasure associated with sex. Among humans, sexual behaviour is related to self-concept and self-esteem. Culture applies a great deal of socially constructed meaning to the act of sex.

The most basic image of sex is intercourse between a man and a woman. As such, penile-vaginal penetration might be considered the defining element of sex. This definition is limited, however, because it fails to recognise activities that would be defined as sexual behaviour between same-sex individuals. Moreover, forms of sexually gratifying behaviour occur between men and women without penile-vaginal penetration, including oral-genital contact and anal penetration. Even as simple a phenomenon as masturbation challenges a conventional definition of what constitutes sex, given that masturbation cannot serve in the goal of reproduction and takes place without a partner. The results of a random sample of students in a United States college illustrate ambiguity associated with the meaning of sex (Sanders and Reinisch 1999). Virtually everyone agreed that penile-vaginal intercourse qualified as 'having sex'. In contrast, 20 per cent did not consider penile-anal intercourse and about 60 per cent did not consider oral-genital contact to fit the definition.

Modern media and communication have created new forms of social interaction that can be defined as sexual behaviour, even though participants may not even be in each other's presence, let alone have physical contact. Telephone conversation can be used by romantic partners as a means of sexual stimulation. Through commercial phone-sex lines, customers can call professional sex workers and obtain physical gratification through masturbation (Flowers 1998). Whereas phone sex is legal, telephone scatologia refers to a criminal form of exhibitionism associated with making obscene phone calls.

The development of the Internet has created new forms of sexual activity (Cooper 2002). Cybersex refers to a particular form of online sexual activity where participants obtain sexual gratification by looking at images or communicating with others in forums such as chat rooms or by instant messaging. Research has shown that there are people who report using the Internet for sexually related reasons to a degree that they might be classified as 'addicted' to online sexual activity (Cooper *et al.* 1999). Tentative evidence (Griffiths 2001) indicates that men and women differ in their use of the Internet for sexual purposes, with men being less interested than women in experiencing sexual gratification in the context of an Internet relationship.

Men experience concerns about a number of aspects related to their sexual performance. Most of these concerns are rooted in a view of masculinity as accomplishment-oriented and skills-based. Perhaps most basic is the worry that their penis is sufficiently large. Although at minor levels this concern is considered normal, it has been known to reach pathological levels with a cross-cultural mental disorder known as koro, an irrational fear that the penis is shrinking or being absorbed by the abdomen. Although predominantly reported in Chinese culture, it began to appear in western men in the 1970s (Chowdhury 1998).

The ability to achieve an erection is considered an essential component of masculinity in the United States (Tiefer 1999).

Representative samples from Japan and the Netherlands indicate that men in those cultures report less distress with a failure to achieve erection than men in the United States. Addressing concerns about erectile dysfunction has become big business, with medical interventions that include the insertion of a penile prosthesis and injecting vasodilator drugs directly into the penis. Other treatment approaches have focused on non-invasive drug therapies such as Viagra.

Another way that men's sexual performance is evaluated is in terms of ejaculation timing. It is difficult to generate an adequate definition of premature ejaculation because the appropriate time for ejaculation is dependent upon culturally derived scripts regarding sexual behaviour. For example, premature ejaculation could be defined in terms of number of penile thrusts, minutes to ejaculation after penetration, or minutes prior to a partner's orgasm. Given these difficulties, premature ejaculation is often limited to ejaculation either prior to or immediately following vaginal penetration (which would impede the reproductive component of sexual behaviour). According to a national probability sample of the United States (Laumann *et al.* 1994), approximately 30 per cent of men reported experiencing premature ejaculation in the past year. Sometimes men report the opposite difficulty of being unable to achieve ejaculation, a problem often termed 'inhibited ejaculation' or 'anejaculation'.

References and further reading

Chowdhury, A.N. (1998) 'Hundred years of koro', *International Journal of Social Psychiatry*, 44: 181–8.

Cooper, A. (ed.) (2002) *Sex and the Internet*, New York: Brunner-Routledge.

Cooper, A., Scherer, C., Boies, S. and Gordon, B. (1999) 'Sexuality on the Internet: from sexual exploration to pathological expression', *Professional Psychology Research and Practice*, 30 (2): 154–64.

Flowers, A. (1998) *The Fantasy Factory*, Philadelphia, PA: University of Pennsylvania Press.

Griffiths, M. (2001) 'Sex on the Internet', *Journal of Sex Research*, 38: 333–42.

Laumann, E.O., Gagnon, J., Michael, R. and Michaels, S. (1994) *The Social Organization of Sexuality*, Chicago, IL: University of Chicago Press.

Sanders, S.A. and Reinisch, J.M. (1999) 'Would you say you "had sex" if . . . ?' *Journal of the American Medical Association*, 281: 275–7.

Schover, L.R. and Thomas, A.J. (2000) *Overcoming Male Infertility*, New York: Wiley.

Tiefer, L. (1999) 'In pursuit of the perfect penis', in K. Lebacqz and D. Sinacore-Guinn (eds) *Sexuality*, Cleveland, OH: Pilgrim Press.

See also: infertility; penetration; penis; procreation; sex/gender system; Viagra

JAMES K. BEGGAN
JILL M. HARBISON

SEX/GENDER SYSTEM

A sex/gender system refers to a society's norms and institutionalised patterns of everyday interactions based on biological differences between men and women. Although most cultures assume there are two sexes and two corresponding genders, the biological reality of dimorphic sex categories has been challenged. Anne Fausto-Sterling (2000) argued that humans cannot be dichotomised as male or female because intersexuals possess both male and female sex organs. Moreover, transsexuals represent a challenge by using hormone therapy and surgical intervention to alter their external sex organs.

Connell (2002) analysed sex/gender systems using four dimensions: power, production, emotion and symbolism. Power relations between men and women tend to be patriarchal and contain gender-biased laws and values that favour men. For example, Rubin (1975) interpreted sex/gender systems in terms of kinship patterns where women are treated as objects of exchange.

The division of labour can be used to understand how sex/gender systems are involved in economic production. Men's work is more valued than women's work in most societies. Consistent with gender stereotypes, men tend to perform tasks that involve physical strength, ambitiousness and competitiveness. Women are viewed as well suited for tasks involving nurturing and caregiving. A significant proportion of labour contributed by women is unpaid and unrecognised work that occurs in the home.

Emotions are involved in sex/gender systems by helping to define boundaries of appropriate sexual behaviour. Marriage legitimises both sexual behaviour and reproduction. Even in the absence of marriage, emotional involvement plays a part in defining an appropriate sex partner. Western sex/gender systems associate sexual acts with a correspondent sexual identity. Thus, people who engage in same-sex acts are now frequently seen as having a homosexual sexual identity. This correspondence is relatively recent given that the concept of a homosexual person was not defined in Western culture until the late 1800s.

The sex/gender system can also be understood as operating on a symbolic level. Symbols of masculinity and femininity are culturally constructed rather than reflected purely in biology. The distinction between men and women is created through language, gestures, dress, art and even discourses on gender.

References and further reading

Connell, R. (2002) *Gender*, Malden, MA: Blackwell.
Fausto-Sterling, A. (2000) *Sexing the Body*, New York: Basic Books.
Rubin, G. (1975) 'The traffic in women', in R.R. Reiter (ed.) *Toward an Anthropology of Women*, New York: Monthly Review, pp. 157–210.

JILL M. HARBISON
JAMES K. BEGGAN

SEX ROLE THEORY

Sex role theory has been important in the study of masculinity since the 1970s. It has its origins in the work of Parsons (Parsons and Bales 1953), who argued that all societies needed to fulfil the functions of production and reproduction. In his view, these social activities required separate 'instrumental' and 'expressive' roles. He believed that men were more suited to perform the instrumental activities such as competition and rational action, while women were most suited to undertake expressive activities such as nurturing, caring and creative work. Parsons regarded these culturally prescribed roles as complementary to each other and as meeting the functions required by society. Consequently, men and women needed to be socialised into the 'appropriate' sex roles. Boys and girls learn the social expectations conveyed by family, peer groups, education and the media to guide appropriate behaviours for men and women. Men and women were thus socialised into dominant and submissive behaviours respectively (Clatterbaugh 1990).

Brannon's (1976) influential article on the male sex role in the 1970s outlined what he saw as the four main rules that men needed to adhere to. They were: no sissy stuff – avoid all feminine behaviour traits; be a big wheel – acquire success and status in the breadwinning role; be a sturdy oak – develop strength and confidence; and give 'em hell – be daring, aggressive and violent. He argued that this role was harmful to men as well as being oppressive to women. In this view, boys see models of men who seek material success, physical and psychological strength, independence, toughness, leadership and invulnerability. They suppress their fear and control their emotions. Sex role theorists argue that this stereotype of masculinity is imposed on boys from birth and is reinforced through pre-school and school (see Farrell 1975).

The sex role approach to masculinity parallels the theoretical ideas underlying liberal feminism, wherein women's disadvantages are said to result from stereotyped customary expectations, internalised by both men and women. Inequalities between men and women can then be eliminated by giving girls better training and more varied role models (Connell 1987). Because it is compatible with liberal feminism, sex role theory has been influential in shaping government programmes concerned with discrimination against girls and women, particularly non-sexist school curricular, assertiveness training for women, anti-discrimination legislation, equal opportunity policies and affirmative action programmes.

In spite of the implicit social determinism, sex role theory promised the possibility of social change in gender roles because if masculinity was not biologically determined, it could be changed by setting up more positive role models. As Connell (1995) pointed out, it was simply a matter of transmitting new expectations through the family, school and media. Men's dominance, aggression and emotional stoicism could be challenged by teaching them to be more egalitarian, gentle and expressive.

Sex role theory informed the early men's liberation movement of the 1970s, whose theorists maintained that freeing sex role conventions might be good for men as well as for women. Men were thus encouraged to break free of the stereotypes and restrictions of traditional male sex roles. Through this popular discourse, the liberation of men was linked with expanding the role options available to them. By implication, men's transformation was envisaged without reference to wider social processes, as the male role was seen to be a constraint that could be discarded, allowing the human being in the man to emerge. These ideas promoted the view of men's liberationists that men were also oppressed by traditional sex roles (see Messner 1997): since symmetrical sex roles hurt men and women equally, there was no hierarchy of oppression between women and men.

Pleck, an important theorist of male sex roles in the 1970s, constructed what he called the Male Sex Role Identity (MSRI) (Pleck 1976). He believed that the male sex role was contradictory and that this thwarted the successful attainment of male sex role identity (Pleck 1987). He consequently developed an alternative model, which he called the Male Sex Role Strain (MSRS), where the tensions inherent in the role were openly acknowledged and addressed. However, his models did not adequately explain men's social power.

A major criticism of sex role theory is that it under-emphasises the economic and political power that men exercise over women and cannot explain male domination or gender inequality. Nor is it able to explain men's resistance to change. A number of critics have also pointed out that by focusing on one normative standard of masculinity that is white, middle class and heterosexual, sex role theory is unable to account for diversity and difference in men's lives (see Edley and Wetherell 1995). Because of its inability to theorise power and interests, and its assumption that a normative standard exists throughout history, many theorists argue that sex role theory is inadequate for explaining masculinity. Consequently, this approach has been overtaken by other theoretical accounts of masculinity.

References and further reading

Brannon, R. (1976) 'The male sex role', in D. David and R. Brannon (eds) *The Forty-Nine Percent Majority*, Reading, MA: Addison-Wesley.

Clatterbaugh, K. (1990) *Contemporary Perspectives on Masculinity*, Boulder, CO: West View.

Connell, R. (1987) *Gender and Power*, Cambridge: Polity.

—— (1995) *Masculinities*, Sydney: Allen and Unwin.

Edley, N. and Wetherell, M. (1995) *Men in Perspective*, London: Prentice Hall.

Farrell, W. (1975) *The Liberated Man*, New York: Bantam.

Messner, M. (1997) *Politics of Masculinities*, Thousand Oaks, CA: Sage.

Parsons, T. and Bales, R. (1953) *Family, Socialisation and the Interaction Process*, Glencoe, IL: Free Press.

Pleck, J. (1976) 'The male sex role', *Journal of Social Issues*, 32: 155–64.

—— (1987) 'The theory of the male sex role identity', in H. Brod (ed.) *The Making of Masculinities*, Boston, MA: Allen and Unwin.

See also: masculinity/masculinities

BOB PEASE

SEXISM

Sexism has been defined (Humm 1989) as 'a social relationship in which males denigrate females'. Like racism, on which the word is based, it is a form of prejudice.

Sexism is deeply engrained, and hard to get at. It often requires a real change in the whole attitude structure of the person before it can shift. So this is more long-term work. Sexism is often based on low self-esteem, so that the man in question is able to boost himself up by putting women down, or so it seems to him. So the whole pattern of low self-esteem has to change before sexism can go, and this is a long-term therapeutic operation.

However, all these things are kept in place by social assumptions about the male ego and how it should be. It is often stated in articles and books (Connell 1987) that because of hegemonic masculinity the male ego needs a lot of support and boosting (and this job is of course mainly done by women) in order to keep it functioning at all. This seems to be the case. One of the most striking statements I came across in the early days of the men's movement was a quote from Keith Paton (later Mothersson) in a newsletter which said – 'The healthy male ego is oppressive and wrong.' This insight sounds condemnatory, but unless we see how normal (in the statistical sense) sexism is, we can never deal with it.

A substantial body of feminist research has documented sexism in the media, for example in the use of sex-role stereotyping where women are always mothers and domestic workers. Feminism is always anti-sexist, but the anti-sexist men's movement, which appeared to be growing in the 1970s and early 1980s, has now almost disappeared in the West (Rowan 2004), although there have been anti-violence movements in other countries. The reason for this may be that we all underestimated the importance of the Patripsych – an internal constellation of patriarchal patterns. This is a structure inside, which corresponds to oppressive structures outside, each supporting the other. The internal structure arises out of a set of movements towards, against and away from a symbolic patriarchal figure or set of figures, and is held out of consciousness by the usual defence mechanisms, this time in the cultural unconscious. The tendency for men is to have unconscious 'against' patterns, with idealised glorified images of aggressive mastery; and the tendency for women is to have unconscious 'towards' patterns, with the glorification of morbid dependency as love, motherhood, etc.; while the tendency for both may be to have unconscious 'away from' patterns, glorified as private living, religions of withdrawal, etc. All these unconscious patterns would then be seen as defences against messages coming from the Patripsych (Rowan 1997).

Now if we see one of the key political issues as patriarchy (or to put it more generally, dominance cultures), and one of the key psychological issues as the Patripsych, anything we do on one level will feed into whatever we do on another. Patriarchy forms a good lead in to all the problems of domination and submission in our social system; I have spelt this out in some detail elsewhere (Rowan 1987). And the Patripsych forms a good lead in to all the problems of internal self-oppression which affect us most inwardly. This is similar to what Hogie Wyckoff (1975) has called the Pig Parent – an internalised form of cultural oppression. Most importantly, the insights we get on one level can be applied directly to the other level.

We can do serious work on the Patripsych using the group workshop methods of psychotherapy as outlined by Hogie Wyckoff (1975), Sheila Ernst and Lucy Goodison (1981) and others, and in this way can get a lot of feeling for the kind of work we are going to have to do to change patriarchy on a large scale. We shall get a much better sense of what is possible, what is important, what works and what doesn't. And as we do this, we can start to find new ways of working, which do more justice to the fact that the person within the person *is* the person behind the person. Rowan has done a lot of work with men on male consciousness, which bears directly on these points (Rowan 1997). And there is no reason why we can't think of many new ways of working, once we have the basic insight. The whole thing opens up. As the feminist Laura Brown succinctly puts it: 'I do not see it as either a- or anti-political to attend to internal, nonconscious manifestations of oppressive phenomena' (Brown 1992: 244)

Similarly, we can start to look at other things in the same way. We can look at situations, and see from a dialectical point of view that in order to understand the situation, we have to look at the situation behind the situation – history, class interests, alliances, power structures, economic resources, etc. – and at the situation within the situation – interpersonal relations, norms, shared experience, attitudes, etc. – and then see that the situation behind the situation *is* the situation within the situation. But this would take us too far away from our central concerns here.

References and further reading

Brown, L.S. (1992) 'While waiting for the revolution: the case for a lesbian feminist psychotherapy', *Feminism and Psychology*, 2 (2): 239–53.

Connell, R. (1987) *Gender and Power*, Cambridge: Polity.

Ernst, S. and Goodison, L. (1981) *In Our Own Hands*, London: The Women's Press.

Humm. M. (1989) *The Dictionary of Feminist Theory*, Hemel Hempstead: Harvester Wheatsheaf.

Rowan, J. (1987) *The Horned God: Feminism and Men as Wounding and Healing*, London: Routledge.

—— (1997) *Healing the Male Psyche: Therapy as Initiation*, London: Routledge.

——(2004) '*Achilles Heel* and the anti-sexist men's movement', *Psychotherapy and Politics International*, 3 (1): 58–71.

Wyckoff, H. (1975) 'Problem-solving groups for women', in C. Steiner (ed.) *Readings in Radical Psychiatry*, New York: Grove Press.

See also: oppression; privilege

JOHN ROWAN

SEXUAL ANXIETY, MALE

Male sexual anxiety (MSA) is a term that we use to describe the thoughts, feelings and faulty ideations that many men come to experience from their childhood and lifelong socialisation in stifling, limiting patriarchal masculine arrangements, in alienating industrial and post-industrial economies. Although an individual male psychosexual and psychoemotional condition, MSA has its origin as a historical, social and cultural by-product of structured patriarchal arrangements within prevailing masculine environments differentiating, and according preference to, masculine vs feminine gender identities (Beck *et al.*, 1995; Connell 1987).

MSA may be conceptualised as the sexual counterpart of generalised anxiety disorder (GAD) operating as background noise in those men who come to see their masculine self-concept and self-esteem as falling considerably short of the prescribed sociocultural masculine standards of manhood (Philaretou 2004; Philaretou and Allen, 2003). Drawing on the symptomatology of GAD, outlined in the fourth edition of the *Diagnostic and Statistical Manual of Mental Disorders* (DSM IV) (APA 1994), MSA may be manifested as:

- restlessness from constant sexual fantasising and the haunting of atypical sexual thoughts;
- guilt for purchasing pornography, soliciting sex workers, forcing oneself upon a partner, or manipulating a partner into sex;
- tiredness from expending considerable physical and mental energy in the pursuit of sex;
- inability to concentrate on social, occupational and interpersonal tasks as a result of getting easily distracted from everyday sexual stimuli;
- irritability from failing to live up to one's unrealistic and exaggerated sexual goals.

For those men experiencing MSA, their personal sexual arena becomes the last resort in their battle to regain their masculine worth amid limited patriarchal arrangements. Casual sexual relations and ideations are erroneously perceived as viable avenues for the reinstatement of their masculine worth.

References and further reading

American Psychiatric Association (1994) *Diagnostic and Statistical Manual of Mental Disorders*, 4th edn, Washington, DC: American Psychiatric Association.

Beck, J., Gayle, B. and Bozman, A. (1995) 'Gender differences in sexual desire', *Archives of Sexual Behavior*, 24: 595–612.

Connell, R. (1987) *Gender and Power*, Stanford, CA: Stanford University Press.

Philaretou, A. (2004) *The Perils of Masculinity*, Lanham, MD: University Press of America.

Philaretou, A. and Allen, K. (2003) 'Macro and micro dynamics of male sexual anxiety', *International Journal of Men's Health*, 2: 201–20.

See also: masculinity/masculinities; patriarchy

ANDREAS G. PHILARETOU
KATHERINE R. ALLEN

SEXUAL VIOLENCE

Sexual violence is not innate but learned. It originates in social processes of gender and sexuality, themselves conditioned by male supremacy. The term 'sexual violence' encompasses a range of violent, coercive and intimidating behaviours, chiefly performed by men, from voyeurism and flashing through sexual assault (varying from stranger rape to rape in marriage), child sexual abuse, sexual slavery, sexual mutilation and sexual murder. It also includes organised systems of violence and violation such as the pornography and prostitution industries and sexual violence as a military and political tactic. Sexual violence is both pan-historical and cross-cultural and its objects overwhelmingly women and girls, though some boys are also victimised by adult male predators, becoming thereby feminised males. The perpetrators of sexual violence may be individual men, small informal groups such as fraternity brothers, or organised units such as militias.

Inasmuch as sexual violence is targeted, it can be viewed as a practice of group-based discrimination in which crimes are committed not against individuals per se, but against an entire gender. This conceptualisation conforms to lived experience in which the rights and freedoms of all women and girls are diminished by, for example, the threat of stranger rape. Thus it is appropriate to describe the targeting of women as 'sex violence'. Analogous to sex discrimination, sex violence summarises the pattern of women and girls becoming the objects of male violence because they are female. Socially, being female means being vulnerable, being subordinate and, at least sometimes, being the object of hate. Adding to this notion the understanding that much of men's violence is sexual, whether overtly or not, the subject may be identified as 'men's sex/sexual violence' (Price 2005: 22).

There is nothing inherent in men that makes them violent. Rather, men learn particular ways in which it is socially and culturally legitimate to direct violence against women. Learned violence is inextricably entwined with learned sexuality: that is, sexuality which is socially constructed, gendered and revolves around the eroticisation of relations of dominance and submission. This eroticisation encapsulates two mutually reinforcing constructs. The first is that 'real sex' requires dominance, aggression, conquest, violation. The 'best sex' for some men is that which involves the least consent or mutuality. This construct is reciprocated by one in which dominance is experienced as sexy. For example, Caputi cites research indicating that depictions of gendered violence devoid of explicit sexual content provoke arousal in a significant portion of men. Caputi calls such depictions 'gorenography' (Caputi 1992: 210). Thus the eroticisation of dominance and submission may be summarised in shorthand as 'sex as violence plus violence as sex' (cf. MacKinnon 1987).

Stoltenberg maintains that dominance and submission have become so culturally eroticised as to be almost physically addictive. Pornography plays a central role in this, to the extent that, in Stoltenberg's view, it makes sexism '*necessary* for some people to have sexual feelings' (Stoltenberg 1993: 69). The purpose of pornography is to give its consumers sexual excitement including but not limited to erection and ejaculation. In both commercial and homegrown settings, women and children are harmed in the production of pornography – beaten, raped, threatened with weapons or drugged. Other women and children are harmed by being forced to replicate the postures of submission found in pornographic magazines and videos. Still other women and children are harmed by rapists who consume pornography prior to attacking their victims. Finally, women and children are harmed when pornography is put on public display so as to make the school, workplace, shop, or larger environment a more dangerous and alienated place for them. Similarly, the institution of prostitution damages not just the women and children trapped in it – through HIV/AIDS, physical and sexual assault, sexual mutilation and sexual murder – but all women and children in a society. To characterise pornography and prostitution as 'victimless crimes' is to mask their true nature, as practices of sex/sexual violence.

One of the underpinnings of male sexuality, and hence sex/sexual violence, is a sense of entitlement. This sense pervades all aspects of gender relations and, as Kimmel observes, is offered to boys as part of their birthright (Kimmel 1990). Within the realm of sexuality, men learn to feel entitled to unrestricted sexual access to women, sometimes especially against women's will. More extremely, some men feel entitled to kill when women thwart them. Social supports for men's experience of entitlement go beyond boyhood lessons, incorporating law, 'common sense' and cultural beliefs such as religion. Relative degrees of entitlement, however, vary. In the West, hegemonic men – white, middle-class, able-bodied, heterosexual – feel and are encouraged to feel greater entitlement than other men. Similarly, entitlement may vary depending upon a man's relationship to a particular female: the incestuous father may feel he has the right to impose sexual demands on his own daughter but not on another man's child.

At the same time as feeling sexually entitled, many men also hate and fear women's sexuality. This leads some men to seek to control female sexuality by both physical and psychological means. Women involved in prostitution may seem especially threatening, putting them at particular risk. Thus Hollway claims that serial killer Sutcliffe used (and killed) prostitutes rather than acknowledge his wife as a sexual being (Hollway 1981: 39). For many men, sexual violence is a means of proving their masculinity, a way of assuring themselves of their power and potency. In short, for some men masculine identity requires evidence in the form of hurt or dead women.

Gender is a constructed social relation. Its content is changeable in response to historic, cultural and material conditions and in response to other social relations such as race and class. Sexism interacts synergistically with other hierarchies such that, for example, gender hatred and racial hatred fuse to create complex intersectional harms. Thus for black women in the West, sometimes racism exacerbates sexism and sexism exacerbates racism. This dynamic interaction generates violence as a complex fusion in which the two elements cannot be separated. Such violence may be of an intensity far in excess of the additive value of the two elements and may be qualitatively different from single-axis oppression. One is assaulted not just as a woman and not just as a Bosnian Muslim but specifically as a Bosnian woman. Again, the content of pornography is illustrative, for in it can be seen that race is sexualised and that racism conforms to the familiar pattern of the eroticisation of inequality. The black woman in chains, the Asian woman so passive as to appear dead, the Jewish woman posed in a concentration camp are all pornographic tropes in which what is done to each racial category is specific, the abuses qualitatively different. So too in war, soldiers may rape only 'enemy' women and may accompany their sexual assaults with racist invective or acts of racial humiliation such as forcing a Muslim woman to eat pork. A whole industry has developed catering to 'sex tourists', chiefly North American, European and Japanese men who travel to the developing world for the specific purpose of sexually abusing women and children deemed racially inferior. In the Rwandan genocide, Hutu men mutilated not only the sexual organs of Tutsi women (breasts cut off, vaginas slashed) but also features considered to be representative of Tutsi beauty – noses and fingers.

Sexual violence does not just happen. Neither is it inevitable. At base, all violence, including sexual violence, is intentional and is engaged in by choice. Notwithstanding childhood socialisation, cultural supports, male bonding and the ethos of male comradeship, both individually and collectively men opt to be sexually violent towards women and children. Individually and collectively men have agency. Consider the evidence of similarly located men – subject to the same ideological forces, intragroup pressures, etc., as perpetrators – who do not sexually abuse women. Not all soldiers rape in war; indeed, some try to protect women from the sexual violence of their comrades. Not all boys who witness their fathers beating their mothers grow up to be batterers. (The reverse is also true: not all batterers had violent fathers.) The existence of such men suggests that the nexus of environmental factors and behaviour does not entirely abolish individual agency. And where there is agency there must be responsibility.

Itzin offers a simple formula for ending men's sex/sexual violence. First we must address the 'men thing' of it: that men are overwhelmingly the perpetrators and that little is done to stop them. Then the men who choose to be sexually violent must decide to stop, and the men who are not violent must decide to stop the men who are (Itzin 2000: 448). The 'men thing' speaks to incidence, that the vast majority of perpetrators are male. That little is done to stop them is a commentary on a cultural norm of acceptance of male sexuality (at least in its heterosexual mode) regardless of how abusive its expression. Accordingly, it is men who must change: abusers must stop abusing, and other men must stop condoning them.

In any process of violence there are three players: the perpetrator, the victim and society at large. We are all affected by the perpetrator's actions. This understanding leads to three conclusions. First, women should have a special say in what social actions would protect them and what kind of reparation is due the individual victim and women in general. Second, state censuring of men's sex/sexual violence should fulfil a social purpose beyond the perpetrator/victim dyad, that of communicating to all citizens that such behaviour is an intolerable violation of fundamental social values. Third, recognising that leaving a violent man in a cell alone with his thoughts will not bring about attitudinal change: the point of punishment should be both repentance and reconnection with the community. Taken together, these conclusions suggest that we must develop principles of accountability that require men to face up to their responsibility and that tell the perpetrator, the victim and society that his actions were wrong and that harming women is harming society at large (c.f. Lamb 1996).

If we are serious about ending men's sex/sexual violence, we must begin where the violence begins – with the perpetrators themselves. We must challenge at every turn their attempts at diversion, including victim blaming and their attempts to cast themselves as victims. We must also expose and critique male supremacy and its prescribed gender relations. Crucially, we need male exemplars for boys, men who can model relations with women based on respect for themselves and for women's full humanity. For this reason, it is imperative that the lives of nonviolent men, as seen through the prism of profeminism, be made available to boys as they struggle to understand what it means to be a man.

Feminist activism and research have produced a wealth of understandings regarding the meanings and consequences of men's sex/sexual violence. Conceptualisations such as socially constructed gender and sexuality have been pivotal in providing an analytical framework by which specific instances of violence may be understood. Some areas remain under-theorised. We need to know more about men who are not sexually violent and women who are. Intersectionality is an important preliminary model, but more analysis is needed to capture the complex dynamics among social statuses and their relation to violence. We also need to generate more sophisticated analyses of sex/sexual violence that is organised and centrally coordinated, as when sexual violation is used as a tactic of 'ethnic cleansing'. These reservations notwithstanding, we have available ways of perceiving and making sense of men's sex/sexual violence that earlier generations did not. And with knowledge comes a force for change.

References and further reading

Caputi, J. (1992) 'Advertising femicide', in J. Radford and D. Russell (eds) *Femicide*, Buckingham: Open University Press, pp. 203–21.

Crenshaw, K. (1995) 'Mapping the margins', in D. Danielsen and K. Engle (eds) *After Identity*, New York: Routledge, pp. 332–54.

Hearn, J. (1998) *The Violences of Men*, London: Sage.

Hollway, W. (1981) '"I just wanted to kill a woman"', *Feminist Review*, 9: 33–40.

Itzin, C. (2000) 'Child protection and child sexual abuse prevention', in C. Itzin (ed.) *Home Truths about Child Sexual Abuse*, London: Routledge, pp. 405–45.

Kaufman, M. (1997) 'The construction of masculinity and the triad of men's violence', in L. O'Toole and J. Sciffmen (eds) *Gender Violence*, New York: New York University Press, pp. 30–51.

Kimmel, M. (1990) 'Clarence, William, Iron Mike, Tailhook, Senator Packwood, Spur Posses, Magic . . . and us', in E. Buchwald, P. Fletcher and M. Roth (eds) *Transforming a Rape Culture*, Minneapolis: Milkweed, pp. 119–38.

Lamb, S. (1996) *The Trouble with Blame*, Cambridge, MA: Harvard University Press.

MacKinnon, C. (1987) *Feminism Unmodified*, Cambridge, MA: Harvard University Press.

May, L. and Strikwerda, R. (1994) 'Men in groups: collective responsibility for rape', *Hypatia*, 9 (2): 134–51.

Price, L. (2001) 'Finding the man in the soldier-rapist', *Women's Studies International Forum*, 24 (2): 211–27.

—— (2005) *Feminist Frameworks*, Halifax, NS: Fernwood.

Sanday, P. (1990) *Fraternity Gang Rape*, New York: New York University Press.

Stoltenberg, J. (1993) 'Pornography and freedom', in D. Russell (ed.) *Making Violence Sexy*, Buckingham: Open University Press, pp. 65–77.

See also: aggression; prisons; rape; violence

LISA S. PRICE

SEXUALITY

Sexuality refers to beliefs, practices and feelings regarding sexual behaviour. As such, it encompasses a range of sexually intimate behaviours that include masturbation, kissing, fondling, vaginal intercourse and anal intercourse, as well as related practices (e.g. masochism) and aids (e.g. aphrodisiacs). Sexuality also includes emotional reactions, fantasies and attitudes regarding these behaviours.

Many authors have argued that conceptions of sexuality are socially constructed, and cross national data generally support this position. Hofstede (1998) described two broad types of sexual cultures, although there are certainly variations within these categories. In 'masculine' cultures (e.g. Japan, Mexico, UK, US), sexuality research focuses on frequencies and numbers of partners; bridal chastity is emphasised (and male promiscuity is allowed, if not encouraged); sexual attitudes are moralistic (and thus have limited the availability of contraceptive information and the options for fighting AIDS); and women are positioned as sexually passive. In 'feminine' cultures (e.g., Sweden, Denmark, Thailand, South

Korea), people place minimal importance on chastity; view premarital sex as socially acceptable; endorse a matter-of-fact attitude towards sexuality (which has allowed taboos to be set aside to address AIDS); focus research on personal feelings and interpretations of sex; view sex as relational; and position both men and women as active (vs passive). Although the constructed nature of sexual belief is apparent when making cross-national comparisons, sexuality may be understood to be natural and normal by members of a culture.

In Finland, an egalitarian perspective with a matter-of-fact approach dominates and has allowed research to focus on topics such as sexual satisfaction. Researchers have found that women and men reported nearly identical levels of pleasure from sexual intercourse, including similar rates of pleasure from the most recent intercourse. This was the result of a general increase in women's pleasure from 1971 to 1992; men's ratings were nearly constant across time periods. Moreover, Finnish studies of sexual satisfaction move beyond orgasm to include emotional satisfaction, the use of a variety of sexual techniques and practices, the importance partners assign to sex, the frequency of intercourse, and the use of pornographic imagery. Results indicate that each of these factors directly influences sexual satisfaction (Haavio-Mannila and Kontula 1997).

In English-speaking countries, a moralistic approach dominates and researchers have focused on readily quantifiable constructs. Examination of differences between men and women is common. One meta-analysis of research from 1966 through 1990 revealed that men, when compared to women, were more accepting of nonmarital sex (especially premarital sex outside of committed or engaged relationships), were more sexually permissive, reported greater levels of sexual interest, reported greater frequency and variety of sexual behaviours, and reported greater numbers of sexual partners. They also reported lower levels of anxiety, fear and guilt and were less supportive of the sexual double standard (Oliver and Hyde 1993). These male–female differences are well known in the United States, and lay conceptions of men's sexuality position sexual desire as ever present, easily aroused, and very difficult to control. As a result, men are expected to be oriented towards sex but not relationships, and men's social behaviour towards women is readily explained as efforts to increase the likelihood of sex. This perspective on men's sexuality is sufficiently widespread that it not only appears regularly on US television (Ward 1995), but also in sexual education curricula (Fine 1988).

Theories

Researchers have adopted several approaches to understanding the manner in which individuals come to enact (or reject) their culture's prescribed sexual script. The masculinity ideology (MI) approach, derived from feminist theory and reliant on cultural analyses, positions masculinity as a belief system that dictates what boys and men *should* and *should not* do. These principles are learned and reinforced during childhood and throughout adulthood. In the US, MI directs adolescent boys and adult men to engage in promiscuous sexuality and emphasise the sexual, but not interpersonal, aspects of relationships. MI also directs men to avoid being perceived as feminine and to pursue status (David and Brannon 1976). In a series of studies conducted with nationwide samples of American adolescents aged 15–19, Pleck and his colleagues found that adolescent boys who offered greater endorsement of MI also reported greater numbers of sexual partners, more adversarial relations with women, and lower levels of emotional intimacy. High MI boys also viewed condoms more negatively, did not believe their partner wanted them to use condoms, thought women had primary responsibility for preventing pregnancy, and believed that impregnating a woman validates masculinity (Pleck *et al.* 2004).

Other social scientific approaches rely on modelling of sexuality by important others. Researchers have repeatedly observed that adolescents acquire much of their knowledge regarding sexuality from peers and the media (Haggstrom-Nordin *et al.* 2002), who tend to portray sex positively and encourage premarital heterosexual intercourse. By adolescence, parents have become a less available source, likely the result of discomfort, their focus on undesirable outcomes (e.g. disease, pregnancy) and their discouragement of their children's sexuality (Sutton *et al.* 2002). Researchers have repeatedly demonstrated the effect of non-familial sources and find, for example, that associating with peers who have experienced coitus is related to a greater probability that an adolescent has experienced intercourse himself (Selvan *et al.* 2001). Moreover, US adolescents who view television with greater proportions of sexual content engage in heretofore unexperienced sexual behaviours more quickly than adolescents who view less sexual content. Those who view greater levels of sexual content, in comparison with those who view lower levels, engaged in heterosexual intercourse approximately nine months earlier. The computed age differential was approximately seventeen months for noncoital behaviours (Collins *et al.* 2004).

Sexual development

Sexual development refers to the shift from being asexual in childhood (i.e. not thinking about and not engaging in sexual behaviour) to being sexual during adulthood. Nearly all adults experience this transition. Specification of 'milestone' behaviours, as well as the timing and responses to these milestones, varies across cultures. First heterosexual intercourse, for example, is a common milestone whose rates vary. The percentage of adolescents who report having experienced intercourse ranges from 4 per cent in Mumbai, India (Selvan *et al.* 2001) to almost 50 per cent of Swedish (Haggstrom-Nordin *et al.* 2002) and US high school students (Pleck *et al.* 2004). Variations within subcultures and across time have been documented in Sweden, where the percentage of adolescents who reported intercourse rose from the late 1970s into the 1980s and remained constant throughout the 1990s. Adolescents in vocational schools were more likely to report sex than their peers in college preparatory schools (Haggstrom-Nordin *et al.* 2002). Historical and subnational variations are also present in the US, where intercourse rates increased from the late 1970s until the late 1980s and fell in the first half of the 1990s. The decrease in the early 1990s was due primarily to delays in first intercourse among white adolescents; black and Hispanic adolescents' reports of intercourse were relatively constant during this time (Pleck *et al.* 2004).

Sexual development includes changes during adulthood. Although results from nonclinical samples are rare, one longitudinal study of men aged between forty and sixty-nine (Time 1) revealed a pattern of decreased sexuality nine years later. More specifically, men reported less frequent intercourse, fewer frequent erections, lower levels of sexual desire, lower levels of satisfaction and greater levels of orgasmic difficulty. Ability to ejaculate by masturbating, which reflects continued ability to achieve orgasm, was unchanged. Rates of change suggested a curvilinear pattern, with men between sixty and sixty-nine reporting greater declines than men between fifty and fifty-nine, who mostly reported greater declines than men between forty and forty-nine (at Time 1). Although this study did not examine causes of dysfunction such as overall health or the effects of medication and has other sampling limitations, it suggests a pattern of decreased sexuality with advanced age (Araujo *et al.* 2004).

Issues and omissions

One important issue facing sexuality researchers today is an issue of definition. In this essay, sexuality was intentionally and broadly defined as 'beliefs, practices, and feelings regarding sexual behaviour'. This definition is ambivalent about behaviours such as nocturnal emissions and public nudity (which is considered sexual in the US). Definitional concerns also exist at the measurement level. In their review, Oliver and Hyde (1993) identified four distinct questions regarding premarital sex (any, casual, committed, engaged) and their analyses revealed different strengths of effect for these questions. Researchers have noted that a minority of self-identified 'heterosexual' men also engage in sexual behaviour with other men (Pleck *et al.* 2004), which suggests a disjunction between terminology and behaviour. Of greater concern is evidence that 'virgin' and 'sex' may have different meanings among research participants. One examination found that individuals routinely accepted penile-vaginal intercourse as sufficient for virginity loss, with fewer accepting anal sex and even fewer accepting oral sex as sufficient. Approximately half of the sample held different criteria for virginity loss as a function of sexual orientation, and a small minority believed it was impossible to lose one's virginity through same-sex practices (Carpenter 2001).

In English-speaking countries, the research has focused primarily on numerical markers such as age of first intercourse and number of sexual partners, and rarely addresses topics such as men's subjective experiences (Hofstede 1998). As a result, there is little research in these countries that examines men's subjective interpretation of their sexual experiences. One study found that young adult men described their first experience of intercourse as positive, empowered, loving and negative, respectively. More positive ratings were also associated with the possession of more masculine ('instrumental') traits and greater satisfaction with one's upper body strength (Smiler *et al.* in press), characteristics typical of the national stereotype of men. Examination of first ejaculation, a milestone indicative of men's sexual development, is very limited. American adolescents typically report curiosity and excitement, whereas Nigerian adolescents report feeling grown up and excited (Frankel 2002). Studies of this sort suggest that men's experiences are not well described by focusing on (assumed) pleasure from orgasm or number of partners.

Political factors also influence the questions that researchers ask. In the 1970s, US policymakers began to emphasise preventing pregnancy and reducing disease transmission among adolescents, but focused their efforts on girls. When the AIDS epidemic emerged in the 1980s, policymakers began to include men, but this effort was slowed by cultural taboos regarding male homosexuality. In the mid-1990s, American policymakers began emphasising abstinence and downplaying the role of contraceptives. In each case, research support followed political objectives. In the early 2000s, US lawmakers threatened to withhold funding for a small number of sexuality studies they deemed inappropriate *after* these studies had been approved by the requisite peer review committees. Recognition of the constructed nature of sexuality, combined with a broader definition of sexuality, would produce a better understanding of this important aspect of life.

References and further reading

Araujo, A.B., Mohr, B.A. and McKinlay, J.B. (2004) 'Changes in sexual function in middle-aged and older men', *Journal of the American Geriatrics Society*, 52: 1502–9.

Carpenter, L.M. (2001) 'The ambiguity of "having sex"', *Journal of Sex Research*, 38: 127–39.

Collins, R.L., Elliott, M.N. and Berry, S.H. (2004) 'Watching sex on television predicts adolescent initiation of sexual behavior', *Pediatrics*, 114: e280–e289.

David, D. and Brannon, R. (1976) 'The male sex role', in D. David and R. Brannon (eds) *The Forty-nine Percent Majority*, Reading, MA: Addison-Wesley, pp. 1–48.

Fine, M. (1988) 'Sexuality, schooling, and adolescent females', *Harvard Educational Review*, 58: 29–53.

Frankel, L. (2002) 'I've never thought about it', *Journal of Men's Studies*, 11: 37–54.

Haavio-Mannila, E. and Kontula, O. (1997) 'Correlates of increased sexual satisfaction', *Archives of Sexual Behavior*, 26: 399–419.

Haggstrom-Nordin, E., Hanson, U. and Tyden, T. (2002) 'Sex behavior among high school students in Sweden', *Journal of Adolescent Health*, 30: 288–95.

Hofstede, G. (1998) 'Comparative studies of sexual behavior', in G. Hofstede (ed.) *Masculinity and Femininity*, Thousand Oaks, CA: Sage, pp. 153–78.

Oliver, M.B. and Hyde, J.S. (1993) 'Gender differences in sexuality', *Psychological Bulletin*, 114: 29–51.

Pleck, J.H., Sonenstein, F.L. and Ku, L. (2004) 'Adolescent boys' heterosexual behavior', in N. Way and J.Y. Chu (eds) *Adolescent Boys*, New York: New York University Press, pp. 256–70.

Selvan, M.S., Ross, M.W., Kapadia, A.S., Mathai, R. and Hira, S. (2001) 'Study of perceived norms, beliefs and intended sexual behaviour among higher secondary school students in India', *AIDS Care*, 13: 779–88.

Smiler, A.P., Ward, L.M., Caruthers, A. and Merriwether, A. (under review) 'Pleasure, power, and passion'.

Sutton, M.J., Brown, J.D., Wilson, K.M. and Klein, J.D. (2002) 'Shaking the tree of knowledge for forbidden fruit', in J.D. Brown, J.R. Steele and K. Walsh-Childers (eds) *Sexual Teens, Sexual Media*, Mahwah, NJ: Lawrence Erlbaum, pp. 25–55.

Ward, L.M. (1995) 'Talking about sex', *Journal of Youth and Adolescence*, 24: 595–615.

ANDREW SMILER

SEXUALLY TRANSMITTED INFECTIONS

Sexually transmitted infections (STIs) are infections transmitted mainly through sexual contact, also called venereal diseases in the past. Infected syringes, blood products and mother-to-child transmissions also contribute towards STIs. Worldwide, chlamydia, gonorrhoea and syphilis are the most commonly occurring treatable STIs, primarily affecting South and Southeast Asia, followed by Africa. Bacteria, viruses and parasites can all cause STIs; bacterial infections are treated by antibiotics, and others are controlled by alternative pharmacological regimens. However, there is no definitive cure for many STIs, making surveillance, screening and education the best disease management options (WHO 2001).

HIV/AIDS is the world's third most common STI, and has become a lethal pandemic, particularly affecting sub-Saharan Africa. Globally, 3 million people died of AIDS and almost 5 million new HIV infections were reported in 2004. An estimated 40 million people are living with HIV/AIDS (UNAIDS/WHO 2004).

The links between masculinity, sexuality and risk behaviour are central to any discussion on men's health. Hegemonic masculinities (elite/male/white/heterosexual) emphasise sexualities of aggression and entitlement (frequent sex with multiple partners, sometimes involving force). These ideologies often result in substance abuse or unprotected sex, exposing men and their partners to risk of STIs. A larger network of STI exposure is developing as the demand for 'exotic' sexualities by hegemonic 'transnational business masculinities' creates a globalising sex trade (Sabo 2005).

Marginalised masculinities construct their own sexualities, such as Hispanic machismo and related risk behaviour, safe-sex adaptations in behaviour by HIV+ gay communities, or backlash against such practices by men who have sex with men by unprotected anal intercourse (Ferri 2004; Kimmel and Messner 2001).

STIs affect more women than men, reflecting their differential sexual activity and vulnerability. Men's frequent control over women's sexual choices increases women's STI risk, and that of neo-natal infections (MTCTs). Men's frequent control over women's sexual choices increases STI risk among both women and neonates. Therefore, men are uniquely positioned to play a critical role in STI prevention and control.

References and further reading

Ferri, R. (2004) 'Issues in gay men's health', *Men's Health*, 39 (2): 403–10.

Kimmel, M. and Messner, M. (eds) (2001) *Men's Lives*, 5th edn, Oxford: Oxford University Press.

Sabo, D. (2005) 'The study of masculinity and men's health', in M. Kimmel, J. Hearn and R. Connell (eds) *Handbook of Studies on Men and*

Masculinities, Thousand Oaks, CA: Sage, pp. 326–52.
UNAIDS/WHO (2004) *AIDS Epidemic Update 2004*, Geneva: UNAIDS/WHO.WHO (2001) *Global Prevalence and Incidence of Selected Curable Sexually Transmitted Infections*, Geneva: WHO.

VANDANA WADHWA

SLAVERY

The intersection of men, masculinity and slavery provides a site for examining the formation of male subjectivities within slavery. Slavery, a social relation in which people own other people as legal property, has been practised in all of the world's civilisations and cultures. Prisoners of war, victims of raids, criminals, debtors and foreigners have been enslaved by ancient, classical, medieval and modern societies.

Slavery in classical Greece, Rome and medieval Islam was patriarchal and paternalistic. Rodriguez (1997) notes that the Greeks perceived slavery as a natural relationship that required inferiors – wives and slaves – to obey their superior – husbands and masters. The Judeo-Christian belief in the natural inequalities in human relations served as a justification for slavery in Brazil and the antebellum Southern United States (Pleck 2004). Unlike modern slavery, early societies scarcely employed race or ethnicity to distinguish between slave and master. Race hierarchy coded white middle-class heterosexual Protestant and northern European men as innately superior to Negroid and Mongoloid races and therefore suited for self-government (Kimmel 1994).

Slave societies maintained differing attitudes towards slaves' rights. Nevertheless, bondage exerts undue control over slaves and their maleness. Slave codes seldom legitimise slaves' rights to marry, maintain a family, testify in court, own property, read and write. In the Americas, slave laws reduced Negroes and Amerindian men to chattels of their masters and not as owners of their own bodies and souls. Slaves were forced to perform traditionally female tasks and occasionally castrated either to serve as eunuchs for the emperor's court, as in the Chinese and Ottoman empires, or to deny their manhood and kinship ties, as in the United States (Rodriguez 1997). In classical Greece, enslaved men were compelled to engage in the submissive role in homosexual intercourse.

Despite the constraints that curtailed their masculine privilege, enslaved men developed their own modifications of masculinity in order to claim and preserve their manhood within the economies of slavery.

References and further reading

Kimmel, M.S. (1994) 'Masculinity as homophobia', in H. Brod and M. Kaufman (eds) *Theorizing Masculinities*, Thousand Oaks, CA: Sage, pp. 119–41.
Pleck, J.H. (2004) 'Men's power with women, other men and society', in P.F. Murphy (ed.) *Feminism and Masculinities*, Oxford: Oxford University Press, pp. 57–68.
Rodriguez, J.P. (1997) 'Gender', in J.P. Rodriguez (ed.) *The Historical Encyclopedia of World Slavery*, Santa Barbara, CA: ABC-CLIO, pp. 298–301.

See also: racism; subordinate masculinity; violence

SAMUEL ADU-POKU

SOCIAL CONSTRUCTION

Social construction refers, in its most basic articulation, to the idea that external reality is meaningful only to the extent that it is apprehended as a condition of its social embeddedness. Initial understanding is thus local and individual, not global or objective. Opposed to this view of reality is a positivist one wherein facts are objectively knowable, immune, for example, to the political choices that motivated their pursuit. A social constructionist viewpoint holds that the material world of communicative-instrumental social relations, and exclusively this world, builds the categories of thought. Once thought is constructed in this manner, the person projects these socially instilled categories back on to the world and, in this sense, constructs the known world. Thus a social constructionist view of reality ascribes meaning to concepts usually taken for granted, like masculinity, from a foundation in social reality and relations.

Ideas described as social constructs include race, class, gender, nature, mental illness, death, time, space and reality. Thus, the claim that gender is socially constructed means that gender, understood to be the division of all people into male and female persons, is not an inevitable result of biology, but highly contingent on social relations and historical processes. Indeed, the school of thought known as social constructionism, now dominant in gender and queer studies, holds that categories of gender and sexuality like masculine/feminine and hetero/homo derive from cultural influences, not from inherent or innate features of an individual's biology or psychology as essentialists believe. Although influenced by anthropological cultural relativism and phenomenology, contemporary social constructionists trace the genealogy of their theoretical viewpoints to postmodern philosophy, especially to Foucault and Derrida.

After Marx, the position that only from the foundation of social reality is it possible to construct the known world was elaborated by the pragmatist Mead under the rubric of 'social behaviourism'. The Russian psychologist Vygotsky has come to be viewed as the forefather of the social constructionist movement, largely because some progressive Marxists viewed his work as providing a critique of the prevailing tendency to attribute personal success or failure to genetic endowment.

With the structuralist linguistics of Saussure and its poststructuralist elaborations, the late constructionist notion that one knows the world not on its own terms but only through the conceptual and linguistic structures of one's own culture became firmly established. Language functions not as a transparent medium for conveying thought but as that which actually constructs the world and the self through the course of its use. Constructionism is interested, then, in culture as a set of structures (of meaning and power, for example). Constructionists and poststructuralists share a postmodern interrogation of such concepts as objectivity, reality and truth. They hold, for example, that the reality of masculinity is not inherently or essentially tied to such traditional attributes as rationality or aggression but rather is dynamic, contingent upon the cultural moment of its construction.

As part of the title of a major theoretical statement, 'social construction' was first used in Berger and Luckmann's *The Social Construction of Reality* (1966). Since then, the term has entered the mainstream of the social sciences, even to become something of a buzzword. Berger and Luckmann offer rich insights into the way society organises itself and the ways its members make sense of themselves and of their social experience.

Philosopher and historian of science Hacking claims the status of the term 'social construction' as a buzzword has emptied it of useful meaning. The favourable use of the term, he suggests, has become nothing more than a shorthand way of declaring one's radicalism.

However, the legitimate radicalism of social construction theory resides in its use as a political critique of modern identity formation. One central idea here is that the contemporary self is, as Gergen puts it, 'saturated'; that is, individuals are socially stimulated – by TV, cell phones, computers, satellite images, etc. – to such a degree that self-coherence is shattered. Agreement is now more difficult, with beliefs thrown into radical question by multiple and multiplying points of view. The extent to which individuals are controlled by institutions such as advertising becomes then a question about the workings of power and inevitably raises the question of how much freedom individuals have to formulate their identities according to their own terms, their own histories. Social constructions, in this view, are the ways by which dominant discourses describe us.

Social construction is not only something that a person endures passively; it can also be part of an active, political meaning-making. For example, on 16 October 1995, African-American men from across the US gathered on Washington DC's National Mall for a massive Million Man March advocating 'unity, atonement and brotherhood'. The march is an example of how to reconstruct the reality of black masculinity as portrayed in dominant (white) discourse. In this sense, part of its political force derives from its anti-essentialist stance.

The implications of social construction for social justice are potentially profound. Given, for example, that the status of white men is inscribed in the dominant discourse primarily on the basis of the racial group to which they belong, the Million Man March was one way of demonstrating, as Burr has argued in another context, that knowledge and social action merge to the extent to which reality is socially constructed by interconnected patterns of communicative behaviour. Reality is defined less by individual acts than by complex, collective and organised patterns of ongoing actions. If the construction with which the dominant group is satisfied can be dismantled, then it can perhaps be reconstructed in new, more just terms.

References and further reading

Berger, P. and Luckmann, T. (1966) *The Social Construction of Reality*, New York: Doubleday.

Burr, V. (1995) *An Introduction to Social Constructionism*, London: Routledge.

Gergen, K.J. (1991) *The Saturated Self*, New York: Basic.

Hacking, I. (1999) *The Social Construction of What?* Cambridge, MA: Harvard University Press.

Mead, G.H. (1934) *Mind, Self, and Society*, Chicago, IL: University of Chicago Press.

See also: power relations

MICHAEL UEBEL

SOCIAL WORK

Social work is a profession in which men are numerically under-represented as workers and service users/clients. The main focus of the profession is on the feminised work of care, welfare and intervention in the private sphere. However, social workers increasingly carry out the more masculinised function of control. Men working in this profession tend to be viewed as either challenging or promoting hegemonic constructions of masculinity and often as both (Christie 2001). Men's locations as social work service users, workers, students and academics are discussed below with reference to data drawn largely, but not exclusively, from the UK.

Men are numerically under-represented as social work service users. The majority of social work service users are women and children and the majority of issues that social workers address are gender-related, in particular the care of children and 'vulnerable' adults. Women's over-representation as service users can be explained by factors such as women undertaking most of the care work in society, the feminisation of poverty, the gendered/patriarchal nature of society and the extent of men's violence to women (Pringle 1995; Dominelli 2002). The focus on some social work practice is on men's violence against women and other men, but this area of practice is generally poorly resourced. Men are most likely to come into contact with social workers in the areas of criminal justice and mental health services. In both of these areas, men service users tend to be involuntarily allocated a social worker. In other areas, such as child welfare, men both appear to avoid contact with social workers, and tend to be excluded by social workers (Milner 1996).

Men are numerically under-represented as social workers. The majority of social workers are women. While men are present in all aspects of social work practice, there are clear patterns of vertical and horizontal job segregation within the profession. Men are over-represented in senior management and specialist positions and under-represented in areas of social work where there is more direct contact with service users, in particular services for older people. The gendered hierarchical structure of the profession results in men social workers gaining advantage over women colleagues in relation to pay, career progression and access to particular types of work. While men are likely to gain particular career advantages in social work, 'gender contradictions' for men within feminised professions are sometimes partly resolved by movement between feminised professions, such as nursing, primary school teaching and social work.

In line with the under-representation of men as social workers, men are also under-represented as social work students. As in the employment patterns of social workers, the distribution of men on social work programmes follows particular gendered patterns. Men tend to be over-represented on higher academic programmes, higher status programmes and on employer-sponsored routes to professional qualification. Yet the motivations of individual men entering social work are varied (Cree 1996). Although under-represented as students, men are over-represented as social work academics, and in particular in tenured, full-time and senior academic positions. Despite the promotion of anti-sexist practice in education and training, employment patterns in social work education largely reinforce dominant gendered occupational patterns.

References and further reading

Christie, A. (ed.) (2001) *Men and Social Work*, Basingstoke: Palgrave.

Cree, V.E. (1996) 'Why do men care?', in K. Cavanagh and V.E. Cree (eds) *Working with Men*, London: Routledge, pp. 64–86.

Dominelli, L. (2002) *Feminist Social Work Theory and Practice*, Basingstoke: Palgrave.

Milner, J. (1996) 'Men's resistance to social workers', in B. Fawcett, B. Featherstone, J. Hearn and C. Toft (eds) *Violence and Gender Relations*, London: Sage, pp. 115–29.

Pringle, K. (1995) *Men, Masculinities and Social Welfare*, London: UCL Press.

See also: men in women's/feminised occupations

ALASTAIR CHRISTIE

SOCIOBIOLOGY

Classical biologists defined the sexes in terms of differences in gamete (the reproductive cells) sizes, with females having large, relatively immobile, nutrient-rich eggs and males having motile small sperm. This definition describes an essential sex difference in humans and most other sexual organisms. However, even this criterion for maleness in non-human organisms is no longer universal: in some *Drosophila* species (fruit flies), males have giant sperm, in which a single sperm is as large as a single egg, blurring the classical defining characteristic of the sexes. Thus, the relative size of the reproductive cells defines the sex *male* in relation to the sex *female* for most biologists to this day.

Classical biologists, including Darwin (1871), defined male behaviour in contrast to female behaviour. Gene-centric sociobiologists (Wilson 1975) took off from there and posited that genes determined fundamental sex differences; that ancient selection pressures favoured these genes for sex-differentiated behaviour; and that these genetically determined traits are invariant (fixed) within sex (so that differences between the sexes are strict). Evolutionary psychologists, who took inspiration from the gene-centrist sociobiologists (Buss 1989) argue that genes determine that men are competitive, indiscriminate and profligate in their mating psychology and females are 'coy', discriminating, and passive. They argue that genes favouring these sex-differentiated psychologies accumulated because of the environments experienced by our Pleistocene ancestors, 'the environment of evolutionary adaptiveness'. Thus, they say, the ancient environments of human ancestors favoured genes that determine sex-differentiated reproductive psychology and behaviour, some of which is now associated with 'masculinity' in human societies.

Contemporary with the gene-centrists of the last thirty years were other sociobiologists interested in the origins and maintenance of flexible traits due to developmental plasticity. Their view of how phenotypes arise is considerably more sophisticated than the ideas of the gene-centrist evolutionary psychologists. The ideas of sociobiologists interested in developmental plasticity are based on genes and environmental effects – inextricably intertwined through development. While their ideas have been around for as long as those of gene-centrists, it is only recently that ideas about adaptive, induced, developmentally flexible sex-associated traits are coming into their own (e.g. West-Eberhard 2003). These sociobiologists hypothesise that environmental and social variation coupled with mechanisms of developmental plasticity induce masculinity (and femininity). Thus, these sociobiologists hypothesise that 'masculinity' – behavioural and psychological traits that are stereotypically associated with men – is context specific, induced and flexible, rather than invariantly determined by genes.

An early selection argument about the origins of sex differences is from anisogamy (Parker *et al.* 1972). This idea provides a selection scenario for the evolution of two sexes; i.e. it explains how two gamete sizes (anisogamy) may have evolved from an ancestral population of gametes of the same size (isogamy). The anisogamy hypothesis says that disruptive selection on gametes with a normal size distribution favoured large gametes (eggs) that emphasised accumulation of resources and smaller, more mobile gametes (sperm) able to successfully compete over access to the larger, resource-rich eggs. In this scenario, what is emphasised is that the energetic cost of producing an egg is larger than the energetic cost of a sperm, a differential that results in selection with different effects on the behaviour of egg-bearers and sperm-bearers. Evolutionary biologists (Williams 1966) argued that these cost differentials would favour the evolution of choosy egg-bearers but competitive and indiscriminate sperm-bearers. Thus, anisogamy theory says that profligate, competitive males and choosy females arose early in the history of sexually reproducing organisms. 'Masculinity' in this context refers to males that compete among themselves for access to females or resources (a surrogate variable that increases the access of males to females) and to males that mate profligately as opportunities arise, in contrast to females that are 'coy' and discriminating about those with whom they mate.

In mammals, including humans, sex differences in investment continue after insemination and fertilisation. In contrast to the huge energetic burden of reproduction in female mammals, the cost of reproduction for most male mammals is small, being the cost of spermatogenesis and insemination (Williams 1966). Because of pregnancy and lactation, mothers invest heavily in offspring up through the end of weaning, and, in many cases, as in humans, throughout an extended period of continued offspring dependence. Many, but not all, sociobiologists emphasise the notion that ancestral human mothers, unlike females in most other mammals including most other primates species, were universally less capable of raising their offspring without the help and support of fathers or others. They argue that women are dependent on men and paternal investment for successful reproduction. Parental investment theory (Trivers 1972) says that in species with substantial paternal post-zygotic offspring care, selection will have favoured competitive and promiscuous but simultaneously choosy and caring males. As applied to humans, Trivers's parental investment argument added considerable subtlety to sociobiological discussion of sex essentialisms. Trivers argued that in socially monogamous organisms, selection would favour genes in males for cooperation with one female in raising their offspring, as well as genes for competing over access to females and for seeking copulations with as many other females as possible, most of whom he would not collaborate with in offspring care. Applied to humans, this means that masculine men are competitive and choosy over whom they marry, if not with whom they copulate. Note that this idea assumes that the selective value of male parental care arises because of the neediness of mothers that only fathers can fill. If this assumption is false, another explanation is required for the evolution of male post-zygotic parental care and for the behavioural traits associated with masculinity that supposedly depend on a species-specific requirement of paternal care. With other explanations, changes in sociobiological concepts of masculinity have followed.

Evolutionary psychologists seized on the parental investment hypothesis to characterise human bonding and mating behaviour as short and long term. For long-term mateships, they argue that men prefer young women with 'high reproductive value', a stringent criterion that is relaxed for short-term mateships. Reproductive value is a concept associated with demographic analyses of fitness (survival and reproductive success). Reproductive value is a relative term referring to the age-specific likelihood of future reproduction given parameters of average age of first reproduction and age-specific mortality rate. In populations that are increasing, younger breeding individuals have higher reproductive value than older individuals. In declining populations, reproductive value of older individuals is often equal to that of younger individuals. They melded this view with classic sociobiological ones of selection acting on our ancient ancestors, so they assumed that human females are universally dependent on male help in raising offspring: thus, double-standard views of sex differences (dependent, choosy females and profligate, competitive but paternally helpful males) determined by genes gained primacy in sociobiology. Masculinity in this context suggests that men are competitively dominant to one another and compete among themselves for access to resources, because of women's dependence on men for resources essential for reproduction.

Masculinity also refers to the dominance of men over women, which sociobiologists explain as arising primarily as a by-product of male–male combat, which is thought to favour genes for large males. In as much as size is a determinant of dominance, men thus can physically dominate women.

Criticism of the narrow characterisation of sex differences and their phenotypic origins that define 'men and masculinities' began in 1875, three years after Darwin's (1871) volume, and has continued ever since. Yet few are aware of this long history of criticism, perhaps because mainstream sociobiological ideas fit intuitive expectations of what makes men masculine and women feminine. Modern criticisms focus on the facts from experimental tests. Observations often fail to fit the predictions of universally indiscriminate males. Observations of competitive females are common. The best-known experimental tests used species with male-biased parental investment, in which females were predicted to be the competitive, profligate sex and the males the choosy sex. Results indicated less sex differentiation than predicted, in that both sexes are competitive and both sexes choosy. In fact, in broad-scale testing of nonhuman species, males are often as choosy as females, and females are often as indiscriminate as males.

Thus, these tests, which investigators usually cite as consistent with parental investment theory, because of so-called 'reversed sex roles', suggest that sex differentiation is not as invariant as once thought. Such experiments challenge the idea that sex differences are fixed genetically. Under observational controls that levelled the ecological playing fields of females and males, sex differences in behaviour associated with 'masculinity' and 'femininity' often disappear, raising questions anew about the origins of sex differences in behaviour. Rather than being genetically determined, it appears as though 'sex typical' pre-mating behaviour may be similar in males and females, when environmental variation is controlled. In the face of these data, one must wonder if masculinity is induced by the environments males typically experience. If masculinity is environmentally contingent in nonhumans, it is likely that similar processes also account for masculinity in humans.

Roughgarden's recent critique of sexual selection theory, *Evolution's Rainbow* (2004), focuses also on biologists' often narrow characterisation of male and female. She argues that within each sex there are many genders and that theories that emphasise gender binaries, rather than gender continua, obscure the underlying variation in male-associated and female-associated traits.

An alternative to sexual selection is a new predictive theory of environmentally induced variation in choosy and indiscriminate behaviour (Gowaty and Hubbell 2005). The theory is symmetric in that the inducing factors work the same way in males and females; what determines differences in individual behaviour is variation in the environments they experience. According to this theory, if there is gender-associated variation in the inducing factors, gender-associated variation in choosy versus indiscriminate behaviour will occur. What makes the sexes different or similar in this theory is variation in the inducing factors. The inducing factors are completely specified by two things: first, cues to the amount of time an individual has left for mating during a season and over a lifetime; and second, the fitness variation that would result from mating with alternative potential mates. The hypothesis assumes that all individuals, irrespective of sex, were fixed genetically through very ancient selection to express flexible and adaptive behaviour – specifically tuned to the real-time environments that individuals inhabit. The model predicts quantitatively when females will express competitive, indiscriminate mating behaviour (usually associated with males) and when males will express choosy, 'coy' mating behaviour (usually associated with females). The new hypothesis calls for re-evaluation of sex differences under strong experimental controls that level the ecological playing fields of males and females, i.e. under experimental conditions that would inform the mechanisms determining phenotypes.

Sociobiological ideas about masculinity include gene-centric hypotheses, such as those of the evolutionary psychologists, that predict stereotypically masculine behaviour, as well as environmentally contingent, induced, developmentally flexible and adaptive hypotheses that predict considerable within-population variation in male-typical (masculine) behaviour. Modern sociobiology thus accommodates more than one idea about the determination of sex roles, including masculinity. Yet most sociobiological hypotheses predict that masculinity is associated with fitness, either in ancestral environments, as claimed by gene-centric evolutionary psychologists, or in current environments, as claimed by those interested in genes and environments, inextricably entwined during development.

References and further reading

Buss, D.M. (1989) 'Sex differences in human mate preferences', *Behavioral and Brain Sciences*, 12: 1–14.

Darwin, C. (1871) *The Descent of Man and Selection in Relation to Sex*, London: John Murray.

Gowaty, P.A. and Hubbell, S.P. (2005) 'Chance, time allocation, and the evolution of adaptively flexible sex roles', *Journal of Integrative and Comparative Biology*, 45 (5): 931–44.

Parker, G.A., Baker, R.R. and Smith, V.G.F. (1972) 'The origin and evolution of gamete dimorphism and the male–female phenomenon', *Journal of Theoretical Biology*, 36: 529–53.

Roughgarden, J. (2004) *Evolution's Rainbow*, Berkeley, CA: University of California Press.

Trivers, R.L. (1972) 'Parental investment and sexual selection', in B. Campbell (ed.) *Sexual Selection and the Descent of Man*, Chicago, IL: Aldine, pp. 136–79.

West-Eberhard, M.J. (2003) *Developmental Plasticity and Evolution*, New York: Oxford University Press.

Williams, G.C. (1966) *Adaptation and Natural Selection*, Princeton, NJ: Princeton University Press.

Wilson, E.O. (1975) *Sociobiology*, Cambridge, MA: Harvard University Press.

See also: bodies and biology, male; sex/gender system; sexuality

PATRICIA ADAIR GOWATY

SOCIOLOGY

Sociology was involved in debates about gender relations from the time it was conceived as a branch of human knowledge, in Europe in the mid-nineteenth century. The position of women was often considered a touchstone of social 'progress' – itself the main theoretical concern of the first two generations of sociologists. Many of the early sociologists believed in gender reform, for instance in ending the barriers to women's education. But the perspective was limited. Evolutionary sociologists, themselves almost exclusively men, had little to say about men as a topic in sociology – except to arrange men in racial or cultural hierarchies. Men were the point of reference, the taken-for-granted norm of humanity, so masculinity in itself was not subject to close examination.

This situation began to change with the breakdown of evolutionary sociology in the early twentieth century, the creation of depth psychology, the trauma of the Great War, the rise of first wave feminism and the broad impact of cultural modernism. The first genuinely social theory of gender, which deduced masculinity and femininity not from biological imperatives but from institutionalised power structures, was proposed by the German educationist Mathilde Vaerting. Masculine character, in her view, developed in whatever group was socially dominant.

In the following generation a more conservative, but equally social, view of gender developed in the United States in the form of 'role theory'. This was the view of social process that saw the key determinant of behaviour in social expectations, or 'norms'. Conformity to norms was thought to be enforced by social sanctions or punishments – more often informal than formal – applied to anyone who deviated from the norm.

Role theory was initially formulated by anthropologists, seeking to explain non-Western social systems, but it was soon adopted by sociologists discussing industrialised societies. The most important theorist of the period was the US academic Talcott Parsons, who combined role theory with a functionalist view of society, analysing every institution in terms of the 'function' it performed for society as a whole. In the early 1950s Parsons applied this theoretical framework to the family and to the 'sex roles' that he detected within it. Masculine and feminine roles were seen as reciprocal – one was instrumental, the other was expressive – and allowed the family to function as an institution and to perform its social function of reproducing social relations and raising the young.

The idea of two linked 'sex roles' became very widespread, eventually spreading beyond academia and entering mass media and everyday language. Sociologists from the 1940s to the 1960s used this idea uncritically, conducting research on what the role norms were, how the roles were learnt, how some people deviated from them, etc. The usual idea was that deviance from the conventional sex roles was dangerous to society, and might lead to psychological disturbance, criminality or other dysfunctions. This was, for instance, a common view of male homosexuality at the time.

It was in this context that the first empirical investigations of the 'male role' were conducted by sociologists. This soon led to a modification of the conservative functionalist view, as it became clear that role norms were subject to change. The US sociologist Helen Hacker was one of the first to emphasise what she called 'the new burdens of masculinity', produced by the changing demands on men in the context of North American consumer capitalism and suburban life. It remained the conventional view that sex roles were necessary to society and that successfully acquiring them was, therefore, in the interest of the individual too.

The new feminism, picking up momentum at the end of the 1960s, turned sex role theory upside down. Far from being the proper destiny of women, the 'female role' was now regarded as the source of oppression. Sex role expectations were seen as a disabling miasma that prevented women being full citizens.

Almost as soon as this criticism of the female role was articulated, a parallel critique of the 'male role' began to circulate. In the early 1970s a small 'men's liberation' movement formed, mainly in the USA, and began to criticise sex role expectations as putting oppressive demands on men, too. The conventional male role was pictured as narrow, constraining, anti-humane and also dangerous in terms of its impact on men's health and psychological well-being. Conformity to the male sex role, rather than deviance from it, was now seen as the source of trouble.

Role theory as a framework for social analysis has significant weaknesses, and was falling out of favour in sociology just as it was being applied to gender politics. One of the key problems is that role theory has no very convincing way of understanding power relations in society; it tends to assume all roles are equal. Critiques of the 'male role' therefore tended to assume that men were oppressed in the same way, and to the same extent, as women were via the 'female role'. This was inconsistent with the mounting evidence of large-scale social inequalities as a continuing feature of gender systems.

In place of role theory, therefore, the radical wing of the women's liberation movement developed a view of gender which made inequalities of power the centre. Men and women were seen as two discrete categories, linked by a relation of domination. This pattern was often called 'patriarchy', and debates arose about the origins of patriarchy, the universality of patriarchy, and the possibilities of overthrowing it as a social system. By 1980 socialist feminists often saw patriarchy and capitalism as 'dual systems' of oppression and exploitation, which intersected to produce the gender inequalities of everyday life.

The view of gender or class as a system of social relations posed the question of how this system was reproduced over time. The question of 'social reproduction' became important in social theory about the same time as feminist theories of gender were being formulated, and for some thinkers these issues merged. The British feminist and psychoanalyst Juliet Mitchell analysed patriarchy as the means by which the economic class structure was reproduced. The French sociologist Pierre Bourdieu developed a cyclical theory of social reproduction which emphasised the habitus (system of dispositions for action) of the individual. Much later, Bourdieu applied this to gender in the form of a theory of the reproduction of patriarchy, which has led other sociologists to fresh investigations of masculine habitus and particularly embodiment.

Apart from this, theories of patriarchy had no very clear account of masculinity. They generally saw men simply as the group who occupied the position of power in a patriarchal system, though there was also some attention to the ways men defended their privilege. The more sophisticated theorists of patriarchy, especially those with a Marxist background, also emphasised how institutions such as the capitalist state worked impersonally to reproduce men's privileges.

The debates about theories of patriarchy were, however, crucial in pushing understandings of men in new directions. Socialist feminists drew a clear distinction between the economic roles of working-class men and bourgeois men, and this led to pioneering work on different cultural patterns of men's lives by investigators such as the British activist Andrew Tolson. Critiques of theories of universal patriarchy, by black feminists in the metropole and feminists from the third world, called attention to the diverse situations of women in different parts of the world. In due course this led to recognition of the diverse situations of men, as well. Attempts to improve on over-simple theories of patriarchy led to more sophisticated uses of the concept of 'social structure' in theorising gender, and this also led to better theorisation of gender patterns such as masculinities.

When a new generation of research on masculinity picked up steam in the mid and late 1980s, it mostly relied on a broad 'social constructionist' perspective. In some ways this still resembled the 'sex role' perspective.

It denied biological determination of gender, it was interested in norms and stereotypes of masculinity, and it was interested in how patterns of masculinity were learned, as boys grew into men. But the social constructionist approach was more directly concerned with power – both power that men exercised over women and power some men exercised over other men. It paid attention to the institutional contexts of masculinity and the embedding of gender patterns in workplaces and organisations. It was also much more attuned to historical change and cultural specificity in conceptions of the masculine.

Above all, the social constructionist approach took a different view of normative definitions of masculinity. Where the sex role approach had usually seen just one 'male role' in a given society, social constructionism identified multiple masculinities within the same culture or the same institution. Here it was strongly influenced by gay liberation theory, which since the 1970s had identified power differences and patterns of oppression among men, and had often seen gay identity as offering an alternative way of being a man. The concept of 'hegemony' was adapted from Gramsci's version of Marxist theory and applied to gender. The result was a picture of multiple masculinities ordered in relation to a dominant or hegemonic pattern of masculinity at any particular moment of history.

One group of theorists developed these insights into theories of masculinity in the context of a structural theory of gender. The idea of gender as itself a social structure (and not just a side-effect of other structures such as capitalism) had been implicit in women's liberation thought in the 1970s. From the 1980s on this idea was reformulated by gender theorists using the more flexible conceptions of structure and agency that had been emerging in general sociology. The Australian sociologist R. Connell formulated a model of gender as a multi-dimensional social structure. This yielded a model of masculinity (and femininity) as a 'configuration of practice' that was related simultaneously to all the dimensions of gender.

The Norwegian sociologist Øystein Holter took a somewhat different approach, distinguishing gender, as a distinctively modern system of social exchange and identity, from the underlying (and much older) structure of patriarchy. To Holter, the decisive fact was the historically developed division between the capitalist economy, as a sphere of paid work and economic rationality identified with the masculine, and the household, as a sphere of unpaid work and gift exchange identified with the feminine. The structural subordination of the household to the economy provided the basis for modern gender hierarchy and for the social definitions of masculinity and femininity.

In strong contrast with these structural analyses are approaches to masculinity based on discourse analysis and poststructuralist theory, influenced by Foucault. Post-structuralism is a complex intellectual movement, and there has been no unanimity in the way it has been applied to gender questions. Broadly, however, poststructuralists have questioned ideas of liberation and traditional models of the subject; have emphasised the fluidity of gender identities, and have concerned themselves with how discourses (including frames of thought and patterns of language) construct identities.

The most effective applications of post-structuralist ideas to issues about masculinity have been in psychology rather than in sociology. Discursive psychologists have investigated in fine detail how conceptions of masculinity are brought into play in conversations, and how individuals can move strategically between different positions in discourse or even between different discourses. In the social sciences, poststructuralist principles have been used to question social-constructionist ideas about the relationship between crime and masculinity. Poststructuralist critics have charged masculinity research with suffering from essentialist ideas of the masculine – a criticism that misses both the anti-essentialist bases of social constructionism and its empirical documentation of diverse masculinities.

Sociological theory is now generally agreed to be in a 'multi-paradigm' state. There is no common framework to which all, or most, sociologists subscribe. Rather, there are multiple points of view in theory, and many attempts at reformulation or synthesis. It is not surprising that this plurality is also found in sociological work on men and masculinities. This should be a source of invention and energy – provided that the pursuit of different theories does not lead researchers away from a concern with the social realities of gender.

References and further reading

Barrett, M. (1980) *Women's Oppression Today*, London: Verso.

Bourdieu, P. (2001) *Masculine Domination*, Stanford, CA: Stanford University Press.

Carrigan, T., Connell, R. and Lee, J. (1985) 'Toward a new sociology of masculinity', *Theory and Society*, 14: 551–604.

Collier, R. (1998) *Masculinities, Crime and Criminology*, London: Sage.

Connell, R. (1987) *Gender and Power*, Sydney: Allen and Unwin.

David, D.S. and Brannon, R. (ed.) (1976) *The Forty-nine Percent Majority: The Male Sex Role*, Reading, MA: Addison-Wesley.

Hacker, H. (1957) 'The new burdens of masculinity', *Marriage and Family Living*, 19: 227–33.

Holter, Ø. G. (1997) *Gender, Patriarchy and Capitalism: A Social Forms Analysis*, Oslo: University of Oslo Press.

Mitchell, J. (1974) *Psychoanalysis and Feminism*, New York: Pantheon.

Parsons, T. and Bales, R.F. (1956) *Family Socialization and Interaction Process*, London: Routledge and Kegan Paul.

Tolson, A. (1977) *The Limits of Masculinity*, London: Tavistock.

Vaerting, M. [1921] (1981) *The Dominant Sex*, Westport, CN: Hyperion.

RAEWYN CONNELL

SODOMY

The meaning of the term has changed over time, referring first to fornication 'against nature', then to anal penetration, (male) homosexuality and bestiality. The term derives from the biblical story about the city of Sodom (Genesis 19) where Lot hosted two angels under his roof. The town's men demand to send them out in order to know, i.e. to rape, them. Trying to enter his house by force, they violate hospitality and confirm God's anger about the city, which He then destroys. Hence 'sodomy' meant the violation of God's will by sexual behaviour; from the late Roman Empire on, every sexual behaviour except marital and procreative intercourse was 'sodomy'. The nineteenth century termed this 'perversion'; 'sodomy' came to denote 'bestiality' (sex with animals; the constant inclination is 'zooerasty') and 'pederasty', defined as anal penetration (buggery; Latin *pedicatio = immissio penis in anum*), often associated with male-to-male sex. The latter sense differs from ancient Greek *paederastia*, the relation between an adult and a young man, and from *paedophilia*, an adult's erotic preference for children before puberty. Same-sex sexuality was also called 'inversion', 'uranism', 'homosexuality' and 'contrary sexual feeling'. Since the 1920s, 'homosexuality' has dominated, 'pederasty' denotes male sexual preference for young men and 'sodomy' has been narrowed down to sex between distinct species. In the USA, former usages of 'sodomy' are still present. In Arabic, the 'sin of Lut' meant the violation of boys; *lutti* now means homosexual.

The Roman Empire introduced the death sentence on fornication against nature in 326. The Church punished it by burning. In 1769, Austria added masturbation as a kind of sodomy, to be punished by death in case of ejaculation. Christian countries abolished death sentences shortly afterwards, the last being England (1861), Scotland (1889) and some parts of Australia. Some Islamic countries still knew the death sentence on homosexuality in 2000. Decriminalisation of sodomy was mostly followed by its pathologisation.

Anal penetration of any sort was criminalised by many laws until the twentieth century. On a moral level, being anally penetrated was and sometimes still is interpreted as submission or humiliation; radical feminism tends to read it as being dominated. A certain de-stigmatisation was achieved by anti-HIV safe-sex advertising.

References and further reading

Coogan, M.D. (ed.) (2001) *The New Oxford Annotated Bible*, Oxford: Oxford University Press.
Hirschfeld, M. [1914] (2000) *The Homosexuality of Men and Women*, Buffalo, NY: Prometheus.
Krafft-Ebing, R. von [1886, 1912] (1965) *Psychopathia Sexualis*, London: Staples.
MacKay, J. (ed.) (2000) *The Penguin Atlas of Human Sexual Behaviour*, Brighton: Myriad.

See also: homophobia and heterosexism; homosexuality; phallocentrism; violence

MICHAEL GRONEBERG

SOUTH ASIAN MASCULINITIES

The study of south Asian masculinities is an emerging field growing out of three main analytical foci: gender and nation; semen loss anxiety ('*dhat* syndrome'); MSM (males who have sex with males). Meanwhile, several classic and recent ethnographies take men and men's world's as their focus. As with other themes in south Asian research, work on India dominates.

Debates on gender and nation offer excellent examples of ways in which 'race' and 'gender' become entwined in social hierarchies and work to produce and reinforce each other. Studies split into two major sub-themes: colonial masculinity – where historical and post-colonial studies of the effects of British dominance lead the way; and ethnicity and minorities, focused on relationships between the dominant majority Hindu community and the minority Muslim community.

The common argument is that the British in India carefully presented themselves as hyper-masculine: rational, scientific, progressive, active, martial and even bloodthirsty. They then derided Indian men as effeminate: superstitious and irrational, lacking in self-control, weak and passive, unable to defend or govern themselves. A series of oppositions supporting these constructions – such as beef-eater versus vegetarian, Christian versus Hindu – were troped through idioms of gender. Gendered ways of viewing relative power became a plank of British justifications – to self and other – for colonialism. Indians were seen, like women, as needing direction and governance, discipline and rule by middle- and upper-class British men. The latter claimed to be shaped into superior persons by the twin highly masculine and masculinising institutions of public school and army (Nandy 1983; Sinha 1995). Mutual attraction and homosocial/homosexual desire crept, perforce, into this gendered relationship (Krishnaswamy 1998). Certain groups among the colonised were exempted from effeminacy and encouraged – through stereotypes produced in missionary and administrative writing, employment policies and so on – to think of themselves as outside of the 'unmanly native' category but as martial or rational – allies of empire and of the British (Caplan 1995; Luhrmann 1996).

Many writers have explored similar processes of identity formation within India itself across the nineteenth and twentieth centuries, trooped through progressively intensifying and congealing metaphors of race and gender in the post-independence period, after the partition of India and Pakistan (1947). Distinctions between Hindu and Muslim have sharpened, with the position of Muslims within the Indian nation becoming increasingly precarious. Historical and ethnographic studies trace how Muslim masculinity becomes demonised as rapaciously sexual, violence-prone and even criminal (Gupta 2001). Meanwhile, Hindu masculinity, self-perceived as inadequate and effeminate (whether measured against colonial or Muslim others) becomes subject, post-independence, to aggressive recuperations, in the form of militant and often violent and anti-Muslim Hindu nationalism (Banerjee 2005).

Literature on 'semen loss anxiety' by contrast takes an ahistorical and psychological (generally Freudian) direction. From the 1950s to date, Indian male sexuality has been conventionally portrayed as immature and deviant, warped by south Asian patterns of family and gender relationships. These, it is alleged, prompt men to avoid Oedipal competition with the father and instead submit to his authority, in a latent/implicitly homosexual move. Mothers are portrayed as involved in inordinately intense and inappropriately sensual relationships with their sons and as exerting ambivalent and sexualised power over boys. The result, it is claimed, is that all sexual activity for Indian men is fraught with apprehension and negativity, with mature women provoking especial anxiety. These pathologies are argued to be part of a deep mytho-cultural structure, evident in: the Hindu goddess complex – notably the fierce (castrating) mother-goddess; ambivalent portrayals of women, such as beliefs around women's qualities as carriers of pollution and inauspiciousness; widespread male anxieties about losing bodily and mental strength through ejaculation (Caldwell 1999). Despite the focus on Hindu goddesses and so on, this literature is often unclear about whether the negative complex is supposed to exist among Hindu men alone or south Asian men generally, since male anxieties about loss of semen are pervasive.

Two recent ethnographic studies focused on masculinities and heterosexuality argue both against the tendency to paint 'deep structures' of culture rooted in timeless bedrocks such as myth or religious texts, and against the wholesale pathologisation of Indian male sexualities. These are part of contemporary moves to explore ways in which contemporary sexuality is produced and enjoyed. Both books point towards ways in which men may experience (especially hetero) sexuality as part of contemporary cultures of self-making and as connected to participation in regimes of consumption, which may sometimes be drawn into domesticity and conjugality (Srivastava in press; Osella and Osella 2006).

Interesting work emerging on male sexuality shifts from policy-oriented studies (focused on HIV prevention strategies) through depth anthropological monographs and into queer theory (e.g. Vanita 2001; Boyce 2006). The category of *hijra* has long drawn much attention beyond south Asia as a possible example of third gender/third sex. Recently, this has been considerably complicated by Reddy, who draws out the complex and variable ways in which sex, operative status (i.e. castrated or not), gender, class and religious affiliation are woven together in *hijra* circles (2005). Debate is currently raging around whether 'sexuality' is or is not an identity in south Asia; whether it makes sense or not to speak of a 'homosexual' /heterosexual' distinction; and whether homosociality and homosexuality are related or form a continuum. Some argue that 'sexuality' – as an identity, or understood as part of one's 'inner self' – does not exist in south Asia outside narrow sections of the metropolitan middle classes. Sexual behaviour is focused not on an object of desire but on one's own need for 'discharge'; sexual behaviour, rather than identity, is what we find. Homosexual activity is framed not as sex but as 'play' and 'fun' (*maasti*) and sexual acts do not necessarily gender a person. Married men who seek male commercial sex workers in no way compromise their masculine status. Male sexual behaviours among MSM exist either quite distinctly from gendered identities or linked to gender in highly specific ways, and not through the terms of familiar European binaries. Instead, gendering is tied into sexuality through complex taxonomies of 'real men', 'effeminate men', 'penetrable men' and so on, within a clearly hierarchical structure in which the most salient gendered pair is the *kothi:panthi* – the effeminised male and the 'real man'.

Others deny outright the relevance of the *kothi:panthi* or 'effeminised male:real man', 'penetrated:penetrator' models, either across the region or as the main authentically local way in which sexuality is organised. They suggest a vast range of gendered and sexual positionings among men who enjoy homosexual activities, way beyond any *kothi:panthi* binary. At the same time, they also argue for the local recognition (albeit often latent or emerging) of a homosexual–heterosexual distinction and a local concept of 'gay'. Such claims are generally linked in to activism and to programmes (claimed as emancipatory) which promote coming out and urge self-identification of men as gay within a broad homosexual-heterosexual framework (Cohen 2005). Explorations of queerness seem to support some claims made by the first group, which refuses to tie homosexuality to gay or to identity, but instead recognises a link between homosocial structures of intimacy and affection and homosexual activity. We might then predict a greater prevalence and tacit tolerance of same-sex sexual activity in south Asia, albeit concealed under stringent heteronormativity in the form of compulsory heterosexuality via arranged marriage and parenthood. Some writers do indeed suggest this to be so. Yet the second group may also be correct to insist that neither the figure of the *kothi*, the effeminate man who takes other men as sexual partners, nor the *kothi:panthi* distinction is necessarily the most salient local configuration of male homosexuality. Research has hardly begun in this highly contested field and we may expect significant shifts as more studies unfold.

Recent scholarship highlights the historical contingency and regional/ethnic variability of styles of masculinity across south Asia. Srivastava (2004) argues that existing tropes of 'south Asian sexuality' fail to capture the complex ways in which a variety of muted discourses shape and produce a range of gendered subjectivities, and a highly uneven array of knowledge and techniques of sex. In certain subaltern modern spaces at least, sexuality is not mere behaviour but is becoming a site for identity production, albeit in ways quite different from the modern sexual imagined by Foucault (Srivastava 2004).

A more general volume explores configurations of masculinities across ethnography and cultural representations (Chopra *et al.* 2004). Sexuality figures as a theme alongside broader questions: men and work; gendering of social spaces; men's negotiations of 'honour' and dominance; interrogations of the putative Hindu 'crisis of masculinity'. Contributions discussing Sri Lanka, Bangladesh and Pakistan mark a useful beginning to a wider regional discussion of masculinities.

Finally, a few ethnographers have examined the production of masculinities in particular contexts. Using interviews with men in the city of Banaras/Varanasi, Derné claims that Indian men prefer to live in joint families and to have arranged marriages, while working to restrict contact between husband and wife and control women's activities. He suggests four masculine types, depending upon their expressed attitude towards cultural norms: 'true believers, cowed conformists, innovative mimetists and unapologetic rebels' (1995). More recently, Derné (2000) traces some ways in which men view Hindi films. Men enjoy films breaking conventional social boundaries, as in celebrations of individualism and romance. Movies embracing the emergence of ideas about 'love' between men and women may even re-shape certain social structures. But film also works to bolster existing structures of male dominance and even to magnify male sexualised aggression towards women. Ultimately, male power and even violence form the bedrock of men's expectations of their relationships to women. While men enjoy watching rebellion and signs of the modern on screen, they are also antagonistic to what is perceived as negative and decadent Western modernity.

Alter's study of one popular south Asian men's practice – wrestling – engages both with micro-ethnography of men's daily lives and regimes of masculinity and with wider debates about the Hindu male body and sexuality. Wrestlers, typically youthful and unmarried, build virility through diet and training to produce a body which is specifically coded as both powerful and moral through stringent semen build-up and retention. Here indeed is one social arena where the loss of semen is deplored and checked, but in a wider somatic and less neurotic (and of course highly circumscribed) context than that suggested by the wholesale generalisations and accusations made in the 'semen loss anxiety' literature. Alter's book also provides an intimate portrait of one of south Asia's segregated spaces – the masculine homosocial world of the *akhara*, or wrestling pit.

The field of masculinity studies within the south Asia region is only now beginning to develop and is significantly skewed towards the foci mentioned here. It seems likely that significant insights will continue to grow out of the already rich and complex literatures relating to sexuality and ethnicity. Men's economic behaviours and the relations of globalisation to masculinity are also emerging as future arenas of study.

References and further reading

Alter, J.S. (1992) *The Wrestler's Body*, Berkeley, CA: University of California Press.

Banerjee, S. (2005) *Make Me a Man!* New York: SUNY Press.

Boyce, P. (2006) 'Ambiguous practices', in B. Bose and S. Bhattacharyya (eds) *The Phobic and the Erotic*, Oxford: Berg.

Caldwell, S. (1999) *Oh Terrifying Mother!* Delhi: Oxford University Press.

Caplan, L. (1995) *Warrior Gentlemen*, Oxford: Berghahn Books.

Chopra, R., Osella, C. and Osella, F. (eds) (2004) *South Asian Masculinities*, Delhi: Women Unlimited.

Cohen, L. (2005) 'Kothi wars', in V. Adams and S. Leigh Pigg (eds) *Sex in Development*, Durham, NC: Duke University Press.

Derné, S. (1995) *Culture in Action*, New York: SUNY Press.

—— (2000) *Movies, Masculinity, and Modernity*, Westport, CN: Greenwood.

Gupta, C. (2001) *Sexuality, Obscenity and Community*, New York: Palgrave Macmillan.

Krishnaswamy, R. (1998) *Effeminism*, Ann Arbor: Michigan University Press.

Luhrmann, T. (1996) *The Good Parsi*, Cambridge, MA: Harvard University Press.

Nandy, A. (1983) 'The psychology of colonialism', in A. Nandy, *The Intimate Enemy*, Delhi: Oxford University Press.

Osella, C. and Osella, F. (2006) *The Production of Masculinity in south India*, London: Anthem Press.

Reddy, G. (2005) *With Respect to Sex: Negotiating Hijra Identity in South India*, Chicago, IL: University of Chicago Press.

Sinha, M. (1995) *Colonial Masculinity*, Manchester: Manchester University Press.

Srivastava, S. (ed.) (2004) *Sexual Sites, Seminal Attitudes*, Delhi: Sage.

—— (2007) *Passionate Modernity: Sexuality, Class, and Consumption in India*, London: Routledge.

Vanita, R (ed.) (2001) *Queering India*, London: Routledge.

See also: cultural formations, Asia and Pacific; history, South Asia; semen anxiety

CAROLINE OSELLA
FILIPPO OSELLA

SPERM, SEMEN

Biologically, semen is fluid discharged from the penis typically at the time of orgasm. Semen is whitish and slightly viscous. The most important component of semen is sperm, the male cellular contribution to reproduction. The sperm cell, with twenty-three chromosomes, contains half the genetic material required to produce a human being. The sperm cell is tiny (about 0.05 millimetre or 0.002 inch) and consists of three distinct parts. The head contains the chromosomes. The midpiece separates the head from the tail and contains structures that provide energy for swimming. The tail permits the sperm to move forward by creating a whiplike motion. Although an average ejaculation contains between 200 million and 500 million sperm cells, they make up only about 2 per cent of the volume of semen. The majority of semen consists of seminal fluid, a mix of prostaglandin, fructose and fatty acids that serves as the medium in which sperm travels during heterosexual intercourse from the vagina, through the cervix and uterus, and into the fallopian tubes. Although biologically complex, the reproductive function of sperm is simple. Socially constructed views of sperm and semen add additional layers of meaning that both reflect and reify cultural beliefs about gender, especially masculinity.

Cultural accounts view semen and the production of semen in ways consistent with stereotypes of masculinity. These cultural interpretations are so powerful that they influence the thinking of supposedly objective biomedical researchers (Martin 1991; Moore 2002). Sperm cells are conceptualised as aggressive and hardworking agents of reproduction that accomplish fertilisation through heroic efforts of swimming through the internal passages of a woman's body to arrive at the waiting and passive egg. This metaphor is reinforced by the fact that the acidic vaginal environment is hostile to sperm. The slightly alkaline nature of semen is necessary for sperm to function optimally. The egg, in contrast, is presented as passively waiting for the arrival of sperm, just as women are characterised in society as waiting for men to approach them. In fact, the transmission of sperm to the egg is facilitated by several elements of a woman's physiology. During ovulation, the cervix is primed for sperm transport. The walls of the cervical canal contain cilia that help move the sperm through it. Research on fertilisation has shown that the egg has an active role in fertilisation. For example, proteins on the surface of the egg capture and hold sperm that make contact.

Conflicting metaphors regarding competition and cooperation have been applied to sperm. One interpretation focuses on the competition inherent among the sperm contained in a single ejaculation of semen. A Darwinian perspective would assign the greatest competency to the winner of the race for the egg. By extension, it would be assumed that the most competent sperm will transform into the most competent human being. Sperm competition theory (Gallop and Burch 2004) focuses on the competition among sperm from different males that might coexist in one woman's vagina. According to this perspective, the male reproductive system has evolved elements to displace other males' sperm. For example, the shape of the glans (the head of the penis) and the coronal ridge may pull rival semen away from the cervix as the penis is thrust repeatedly into the vagina. Likewise, post-ejaculatory penis hypersensitivity will discourage a male from thrusting after ejaculation (and prevent him from displacing his own semen). Although sperm competition theory has been in existence since the 1970s, one more recent and controversial interpretation suggests that cooperation exists among sperm from the same individual. According to this approach, only a tiny number of sperm actually possess the potential to fertilise an egg. The 'Kamikaze Sperm Hypothesis' (Baker and Bellis 1995) states that remaining sperm exist in a cooperative relationship with viable sperm by providing interference for sperm from rival males. Criticisms focus on the conceptualisation of the actions of sperm in terms of team or sports metaphors.

Although seminal fluid can be a medium for the spread of sexually transmitted diseases, including HIV, the virus that causes AIDS, semen itself is harmless if swallowed or put in contact with the skin. Societies have applied complex meanings to the consumption of semen. The Etoro people of Papua New Guinea believe that boys must fellate adult males and ingest their semen in order to achieve sexual maturity. Semen is also thought to provide beneficial cosmetic properties. The pop song 'H.W.C.' (Hot White Cum) by Liz Phair expresses the belief that semen can clear up a woman's skin, make her hair more shiny and make her look younger.

One important sexual practice is the consumption of semen at the conclusion of fellatio. Among hetereosexual men, the distinction between women who 'spit' versus 'swallow' is important, with women who enjoy consuming, or at least are willing to consume, semen being seen as more sexually desirable. One of the defining features of hard core pornography is the inclusion of external ejaculation (often called the 'cum shot' or 'money shot') (Williams 1989). External ejaculation is necessary to demonstrate to the viewer that the sex is real rather than simulated. Typically, ejaculation occurs on a woman's chest, back or face. One controversial specialty in pornography is known as bukkake, which refers to the scenario of a large number of men ejaculating on to a woman's face. The external cum shot is often cited by feminists and antipornography advocates as evidence that pornography is degrading to women.

References and further reading

Baker, R.R. and Bellis, M. (1995) *Human Sperm Competition*, London: Chapman and Hall.

Gallop, G.G., Jr and Burch, R.L. (2004) 'Semen displacement as a sperm competition strategy in humans', *Evolutionary Psychology*, 2: 12–23.

Martin, E. (1991) 'The egg and the sperm', *Signs*, 16: 485–501.

Moore, L.J. (2002) 'Extracting men from semen', *Social Texts*, 20: 91–119.

Williams, L. (1989) *Hard Core*, Berkeley, CA: University of California Press.

See also: bodies and biology, male; penis; reproductive issues and technologies; procreation; rites of passage; virility

JAMES K. BEGGAN

SPIRITUALITY

Spirituality has to do with the extension of humanity into the divine realms in one way or another. But it has been pointed out in recent years (Wilber 2000) that there are different levels of understanding of what spirituality is all about.

At level one, spirituality is seen as having to do with the supernatural. There is often a high degree of fear associated with this level of consciousness. Often no distinction is made between what is genuinely divine and what is merely paranormal. And at this level there is often a great deal of fear of other groups with rival definitions and there may be a great deal of prejudice and narrowness about one's view of spirituality. There may also be a high degree of reliance on ritual and ceremony as keeping the purity of the doctrine. Gender is taken for granted as divided into masculine and feminine domains, in a conventional way.

At level two, spirituality is seen as nothing to do with the supernatural, but everything to do with authenticity. To be fully human, to be a fully functioning person, to be a *mensch* – these are the highest we can aspire to. At this level we have an existential approach to life, seeing it as something we have to create from moment to moment, and where we are personally responsible for our own destiny. This can even sometimes be a completely atheistic position, but it does not have to be. Its definition of spirituality is anything to do with ultimate concerns. At this level gender is not taken for granted, and may be radically questioned. It is more important to be a self-actualised person than to be a man or a woman.

At level three, which Wilber calls the Subtle, spirituality is seen as an approach to the divine through symbols and images. To be contacted by the divine in some shape or form is desirable and achievable. Intuition can be cultivated, and so can creativity, but in both cases it is a surrendered form which looks to outside inspiration rather than personal achievement. Archetypes may be encountered and valued. We are now in the realm of mysticism considered as a personal quest. Here gender runs right through everything, and it is common to refer to gods and goddesses for inspiration and guidance.

At level four, which Wilber calls the Causal, spirituality is seen as identification with the divine. All the symbols and images, all the intermediaries, are not needed. There is a direct contact with the divine without signposts or landmarks. We see things as they are, not as we are, without definitions and without categories. No longer do we look for meaning. We may talk in terms of God, or we may talk in terms of Emptiness, but in both cases it is not a limited definition. Here gender is not an issue worth considering, because it defines us too narrowly.

These distinctions help us to keep separate and distinct what kind of spirituality we are talking about. Some have argued – and I am one of them – that it is better to use the word 'transpersonal', which clearly refers to levels three and four, rather than using a broad word like 'spirituality', which means so many different things to so many different people.

In recent years it has become much more respectable to talk about spirituality, because the above definitions make it clear that there is more to spirituality than superstition and god-fear.

It is also clear that there can be a downside to spirituality. Fukuyama and Sevig (1999) have an interesting chapter on positive and negative expressions of spirituality. It is important to recognise, they say, that there are unhealthy expressions of spirituality as well as the more healthy ones which are often mentioned to the exclusion of anything else. Spirituality, like anything else, can be defensive as well as transformative. Some examples:

- when anger is suppressed on the grounds that to do so is morally superior: this is called the 'spiritual bypass';
- submission to others, rationalised as being loving, but actually being much more like co-dependency;
- failure to ask for support and nurturance, rationalised by such views as 'God is all I need';
- failure to deal with interpersonal or sexual needs, rationalised as ascetic practice;
- failure to deal with interpersonal problems, rationalised as 'It's all a spiritual lesson';
- claiming special treatment, because of spiritual superiority, known as 'narcissistic spirituality';
- offensive spirituality, which consists often in criticising others for not being spiritual enough – often this goes with spiritual perfectionism;
- spiritual avoidance, such as refusing to go in for counselling because it might involve criticising parents, which is forbidden;
- compulsive religiosity, which puts correct observances before healthy and productive personal relationships;
- resorting to dangerous practices such as exorcism instead of more modest means, such as counselling.

It is important, they say, to recognise that not everything that goes by the name of spirituality is positive or worthwhile. Other people have said this too: for example, John Battista (1996) has an entire chapter on 'Offensive spirituality and spiritual defences'. And Weinhold and Hendricks (1993) say: 'As one of my clients put it, "As soon as my ex-husband started meditating and doing The Course in Miracles, he stopped sending his child support payments"' (p. 80)

Spirituality is perhaps particularly important for men to understand, since in the past they have been the guardians of religion but their spirituality has been rare and sparse. Of course spirituality and religion are not the same thing. If we ignore the distinctions mentioned above, we are condemned to life in Flatland, where the divine is not even considered.

References and further reading

Battista, J.R. (1996) 'Offensive spirituality and spiritual defences', in B.W. Scotton, A.B. Chinen and J.R. Battista (eds) *Textbook of Transpersonal Psychiatry and Psychology*, New York: Basic Books.

Fukuyama, M.A. and Sevig, T.D. (1999) *Integrating Spirituality into Multicultural Counselling*, Thousand Oaks, CA: Sage.

Weinhold, B.K. and Hendricks, G. (1993) *Counselling and Psychotherapy: A Transpersonal Approach*, 2nd edn, Denver, CO: Love Publishing.

Wilber, K. (2000) *Integral Psychology*, Boston, MA: Shambhala.

See also: Christian men's movements; world religions, Buddhism; world religions, Christianity; world religions, Hinduism; world religions, Islam; world religions, Judaism

JOHN ROWAN

SPORT, ATHLETES AND ATHLETIC TRAINING

Modern sport originated in elite British schools like Eton around the middle of the nineteenth century, when masters transformed the brutal and chaotic football contests that had existed since medieval times into organised competitions in order to discipline their unruly boy pupils. The 'old boys' who graduated from these privileged schools established sporting clubs at the prestigious British universities and also governed most of the important national sporting organisations. The perceived civilising potential of sport was also applied to wider contexts, with team games acclaimed as an essential forum for 'building character' in white heterosexual males. During the second half of the nineteenth century this middle-class male ethos – embodied by the amateur-gentleman who played sport purely for its own sake – became dominant throughout the British Empire and eventually the entire world. However, it was also modified by a host of interlacing social movements, ideologies and local conditions: muscular Christianity, eugenics, racism, social Darwinism, nationalism, imperialism, government-sponsored physical education, public health and hygiene programmes, myriad religious, youth, educational, police, military and immigrant sports leagues, and neo-classical romanticism (epitomised by the 'revival' of the ancient Olympics as an international festival of male corporeality and diplomacy). During the twentieth century, this white, male, middle-class, amateur form of sport gradually became more *formally* democratic, while also being eroded by the entwined processes of commercialisation, commodification, bureaucratisation, globalisation, professionalisation and governmentalisation (Gruneau and Whitson 2001; Ingham 2005; Miller *et al.* 2001). Consequently, present-day sport is a multibillion-dollar industry that directly and indirectly involves people from nearly every nation in the world.

People participate in sport at various levels and for many reasons. However, following Coakley (2004: 98–100) it is possible to delineate two ideal-types of sporting practices: the 'pleasure and participation' and 'power and performance' models. The former approach stresses: (1) accommodating differences in physical skills; (2) maximising well-being; (3) democratic relations among athletes, coaches and administrators; (4) holistic connections among mind, body, people and the environment; and (5) support and mutual concern among participants. The latter model has the following characteristics: (1) using strength, speed and power to push limits and set records; (2) putting well-being at risk in the quest for success; (3) treating opponents as enemies to be dominated; (4) obedience to owners, coaches and administrators; and (5) viewing the body as a machine. The bodily capital required for the power and performance mode has been central to sustaining myths about men's inherent superiority to women. Whereas physical strength has lost much of its importance in bolstering ideologies of masculine superiority in most institutions, the sheer brute power demanded by some sports is still hailed as both material and symbolic 'proof' of men's biological ascendancy. This valorisation of men's corporeal power is evident in constant claims that their athletic performances will always be faster, higher, further and stronger than those of women.

The mass media has also been implicated in naturalising masculine supremacy via sport. For instance, Morse (1983) notes that sport is one of the few spheres in the mainstream media where men's bodies are on display more frequently and in a wider range of activities than are women's bodies. However, she also observes that since looking at objects is both a privilege and an instrument of power, there has been a deep-seated reluctance to make (the assumed heterosexual) male body an object of homoerotism and scopophilia (the pleasure of gazing). Morse argues that the media minimise the potential for male athletes to be read in homoerotic and scopophilic ways by constructing their bodies as scientific objects involved in extending the limits of human performance. Thus, the image of man-as-machine supersedes that of man-as-exhibitionist by surrounding male athletes in an 'aura of scientificity' and sustaining a 'phantasmatic image of male perfection'.

Treating the male sporting body as a machine is unmistakable in combative sports. For instance, boxers derive prestige and power from knowing they belong to a minuscule number of men who literally embody hegemonic masculinity. According to Wacquant (1995: 72), it takes about four years just to produce a 'seasoned amateur' and another three to develop a competent professional. In order to produce the requisite pugilistic capital, boxers must commit themselves to an arduous routine of daily training. This gruelling regimen involves 'ringwork', 'floorwork' and 'roadwork' (Wacquant 2001: 8), as well as adherence to the 'trinity of pugilistic sacrifice' (Wacquant 1995: 76), consisting of a strict nutritional regime, the severe truncation of social and family life, and the cessation of sexual intercourse for an extended time before matches (Wacquant 1998: 341–2). The terms Wacquant uses to describe the career of a prize-fighter are also instructive: 'modern-day gladiator', 'ring warrior', 'torture', 'monastic devotion' and 'wilful Spartanism'. Wacquant notes that such somatic practices eventually produce a body that is 'both the weapon of assault and the target to be destroyed', and 'the focus of unremitting attention' in a gym that is 'a social factory for remaking human bodies into virtual "fighting machines"' (Wacquant 1995: 67, 68, 70). This system of pugilistic pedagogy constitutes 'a *quasi-panoptical apparatus* [emphasis in original] that ideally subjects the boxer to constant surveillance fit to perform the maximal accumulation of bodily capital for the bout' (Wacquant 1995: 81).

Although extreme, the training regime of prize-fighters effectively resembles that of all athletes involved in the power and performance model. In a curious epilogue to the Cold War, most Western nations have adopted training methods from the old Soviet regime that were once decried as 'totalitarian' for producing 'robots'. Hence, masses of children around the world now train in both private and government-funded sports academies up to eight hours a day for six or seven days a week under the watchful eyes of professional coaches obsessed with developing world champions. This is a striking example of governmentalisation, the process by which capitalist states have steadily calibrated and managed the conduct of their citizens. Whereas health tended to be targeted at the population in general during the early stage of governmentalisation in the eighteenth and nineteenth centuries, citizens are now the objects of myriad private and public strategies that frame health, wellbeing, lifestyle, fitness, quality of life and 'at risk' behaviour as a matter of individual responsibility (Rose 2001: 5–7). In tandem with the processes of commercialisation, commodification, professionalisation and bureaucratisation, this increasing governmentalisation of everyday life has resulted in what Hoberman (1992: 29) terms a 'Frankenstein procedure' that pervades high-performance sport virtually worldwide: Thus athletes subject their bodies to a multitude of legal and illegal performance-enhancing techniques in attempting to improve athletic performance by minuscule amounts: using aerodynamic bicycles and aquadynamic swimsuits; simulating the altitude, temperature and humidity of venues; employing hypnosis, stress reduction and relaxation strategies; engaging in blood-packing; recovering in hyperbaric chambers; and taking amino acids, vitamins, glucose, electrolytes, diuretics, hormones, beta-blockers, nandrolone, erythropoietin and tetrahydrogestrinone.

The power and performance model is neither even nor uncontested – it constantly must be defended from a variety of sources, including some of the very processes that constructed it. For instance, commodification, narcissism, the emergence of the celebrity-athlete, women's entry into traditionally all-male sports, and the 'coming out' of gay athletes have all destabilised hegemonic masculinity in sport in various ways (Miller *et al.* 2001). English football captain David Beckham wears a sarong in public and is applauded as the quintessential 'metrosexual'; African American professional basketball player Denis Rodman – an archetypal 'hard man' – is a cross-dresser; Ian Roberts, one of Australia's toughest rugby league footballers, proudly declares his homosexuality, as does Samoan-Hawaiian and former American professional football player Esera Tuaolo; Australia's multiple Olympic gold medal-winning swimmer Ian Thorpe is a global fashion icon, who advertises his line of underwear and deliberately cultivates an ambiguous sexual persona. While it is important not to over-generalise from emerging practices like these, they nevertheless indicate that even elite sport is no longer the domain of only heterosexual white men.

As mentioned, there also is a pleasure and participation approach to sport, which is evident, for instance, in youth leagues, physical education curricula, community recreation programmes, Masters sport (for those over age forty), sportswomen advocacy groups, anti-racist groups, indigenous sports movements and sporting organisations run by and for sexual minorities. Despite having a marginal status and always being susceptible to co-optation by the power and performance model, such alternatives provide a basis for extending sporting practices that are egalitarian, prosocial and promote an ethic of care (Burstyn 1999; Markula 2004; Sabo 2005; Van Ingen 2004).

References and further reading

Burstyn, V. (1999) *The Rites of Men*, Toronto: University of Toronto Press.

Coakley, J. (2004) *Sport in Society*, 8th edn, Boston, MA and New York: McGraw-Hill.

Gruneau, R.S. and Whitson, D. (2001) 'Upmarket continentalism', in V. Mosco and D. Schiller (eds) *Continental Order?* New York: Rowman and Littlefield.

Hoberman, J. (1992) *Mortal Engines*, New York: The Free Press.

Ingham, A.G. (2005) 'The sportification process', in R. Giulianotti (ed.) *Sport and Modern Social Theorists*, Houndmills: Palgrave Macmillan.

Markula, P. (2004) 'Tuning into oneself', *Sociology of Sport Journal*, 21: 302–21.

Miller, T. (2001) *Sportsex*, Philadelphia, PA: Temple University Press.

Miller, T., McKay, J., Lawrence, G. and Rowe, D. (2001) *Globalization and Sport*, Thousand Oaks, CA: Sage.

Morse, M. (1983) 'Sport on television', in E.A. Kaplan (ed.) *Regarding Television*, Frederick, MD: University Publications of America.

Rose, N. (2001) 'The politics of life itself', *Theory, Culture and Society*, 18: 1–30.

Sabo, D. (2005) 'The study of masculinities and men's health', in M.S. Kimmel, J. Hearn and R. Connell (eds) *Handbook on Studies of Men and Masculinities*, Thousand Oaks, CA: Sage.

Van Ingen, C. (2004) 'Therapeutic landscapes and the regulated body in the Toronto Front Runners', *Sociology of Sport Journal*, 21: 253–69.

Wacquant, L. (1995) 'Pugs at work', *Body and Society*, 1 (1): 65–93.

—— (1998) 'The prizefighter's three bodies', *Ethnos: Journal of Anthropology*, 63 (3): 325–52.

—— (2001) 'Whores, slaves, and stallions', *Body and Society*, 7 (2–3): 181–94.

See also: football

JIM MCKAY

SPORTS LITERATURE, SPORTSCASTING

As a nearly total male domain, modern sport operates to establish and validate a hegemonic masculinity that emphasises misogyny and homophobia. First-hand tales of how boys and men are validated as important citizens through sporting achievements are commonly told through sports literature, including novels, short stories and poems as well as sports journalism found in magazines and daily papers, and sportscasting of sporting events on television and radio. Sports channels in the US such as ESPN and SkySports recount such tales on numerous live and tape-delayed sporting events and all-sports news programming. All-sport radio stations, daily newspapers and sporting journals, print and internet, carry reports, descriptions and stories about the events. While boys and men often participate directly in sports, it is through these media that the discourses validating hegemonic masculinity through sport are most prominently, albeit vicariously, experienced.

Sport literature, particularly novels and short stories, often deconstructs the myth of the athletic male figure as the ideal masculine subject. Chris Messenger's readings of authors such as Ernest Hemingway, F. Scott Fitzgerald and Norman Mailer (1981, 1990) analyse the contradictions in the idealised masculinity of the athletic male figure. Yet, as Michael Oriard demonstrates (1993 and 2001), other less canonical forms of sport literature, including pulp fiction, serialised stories for adolescent boys, and sports journalism, repeatedly perpetuate the hegemonic masculinity of the idealised athletic male.

The language used to describe the hegemonic masculinity of idealised athletic males, identified by authors Michael A. Messner (1992) and Donald F. Sabo (Sabo and Runfola 1980), finds its way into all forms of sports literature and sportscasting. The broadcasters continually inform their audience what qualities determine whether or not a man is a worthy. The words 'man' and 'men' become positive qualifiers in and of themselves. To be something less than a man misogynistically implies that being something closer to a woman renders one a second-class citizen. For men to become 'men', according to the discursive logic of sports literature and sportscasting, they must be 'tough', 'warriors', 'gladiators', unafraid of physical pain and willing to sacrifice their bodies. Aggression, even when it spills over into unsanctioned violent behaviour, is always lauded as an appropriate and admirable quality. Writers and broadcasters are more often critical of a lack of restraint in displaying such behaviour than they are of over-aggressive and violent behaviour itself.

The language used in sports literature and sportscasting also pays particular attention to the physiques of the athletes and is often accompanied by visual portrayals of the idealised athletes. The bodies thus celebrated are 'hard', 'chiselled' and presented as flawless. Descriptions of aggressive, gladiatorial athletes are commonly linked with presentations of large men with well defined musculature, and athletic feats are attributed to accomplished male physiques. While readers and viewers are inundated with discourses describing this hegemonic masculinity, they are simultaneously presented with the image of the male body that should accompany the values lauded by the literature and broadcasting. Moreover, such bodies become representative of phallic and sexual power.

The compliments paid to the idealised male body highlight what Brian Pronger (1990) identifies as the masculine paradox, where the need to celebrate the athletic body immediately conflicts with the necessity to establish that hegemonic masculinity as heterosexual. The praises that broadcasters lavish on both the athletes' physical accomplishments and their physical bodies are necessary to establish this particular masculine model as one to be admired, but such praise immediately and simultaneously gives rise to Pronger's paradox. The bodies and men that the writers and broadcasters encourage their mostly male viewing audience to emulate also become bodies to be erotically desired.

Sports literature and sportscasting attempt to alleviate this paradox through constant emphasis on the heterosexuality of the athletes. They refer to wives and girlfriends watching from the stands and spotlight highly feminised and sexualised female cheerleaders as appropriate objects of erotic desire. Such attempts to reinforce heterosexuality also reinforce sports literature's and broadcasting's role in asserting that a homosexual man, much like a woman, can never occupy the pedestal on which the idealised male athlete rests.

While there are a few instances in which sports literature and broadcasting deconstruct the myth of the idealised male athlete, the vast majority of it promotes the myth and establishes the male athlete as the prime example of hegemonic masculinity. Yet even in its promotion, it still struggles with the paradox that the desire to emulate the idealised male athlete must not become a desire for the idealised male athlete.

References and further reading

Messenger, C.K. (1981) *Sport and the Spirit of Play in American Fiction*, New York: Columbia University Press.

—— (1990) *Sport and the Spirit of Play in Contemporary American Fiction*, New York: Columbia University Press.

Messner, M.A. (1992) *Power at Play*, Boston, MA: Beacon.

Messner, M.A. and Sabo, D.F. (eds) (1990) *Sport, Men, and the Gender Order*, Champaign, IL: Human Kinetics Books.

Oriard, M. (1993) *Reading Football*, Chapel Hill, NC: University of North Carolina Press.

—— (2001) *King Football*, Chapel Hill, NC: University of North Carolina Press.

Pronger, B. (1990) *Arena of Masculinity*, New York: St Martin's Press.

Sabo, D.F. and Runfola, R. (1980) *Sports and Male Identity*, Englewood Cliffs, NJ: Prentice-Hall.

See also: football; literature; muscles and muscularity; sport, athletes and athletic training

TODD STARKWEATHER

STATE

The concept of the state is generally non-gendered in most social science debates. The presupposition that the state is 'gender-neutral' is a legacy of mainstream political science. The 'man question' is almost always present implicitly when talking of the state but rarely made explicit. Such conceptualisations of the state have been criticised by feminist and related gender scholarship.

State theory and social contract theory, as developed by Hobbes, Locke, Rousseau and others, was constructed as a male-dominated process (Pateman 1979, 1988). The founding principles of the state are based on the idea that free individuals ('political man') give consent or contract with each other to move from the 'state of nature'. Women were excluded from this process, from the beginning of emerging 'political spheres', while men were (represented as) active. The public political sphere was created to better (certain) men and their life chances (O'Brien 1981). The presumed framework for the political being (man) was the sovereign state, with Western political institutions generally created for and by men. Law(s) can be seen as the rules of the male-dominated, masculine, patriarchal sovereign state (Burstyn 1983; MacKinnon 1989).

Carver (2004) has shown, however, that it is very particular kinds of political men that state rules and structures are designed for, and that the founding texts that lie behind modern states are deeply creative of a dichotomy between men and women:

> Male fantasies about men are potent. They marginalise women and subordinate some men to others through symbolic oppressions, institutional disciplines and systematic violence. They are not pictures of what is 'natural' nor even if they were, should they have the political force that they currently evoke.
>
> (Carver 2004: 199)

State theory has been dominated by two major traditions – liberal and Marxist:

> In the first the state is a social accumulation of powers, rights, duties and obligations from the previously unfettered individual of civil society – the personal freedom of the individual is lost to the contract of collective benefit; in the second the state is a social structural form which contributes, sometimes determinedly, to the social constitution of classes, including individuals within them – collective freedom is gained or lost according to the particular domination of class relations within and indeed outside the state.
>
> (Hearn 1990: 57–8)

Neither approach has traditionally taken gender into consideration. The state has a dual meaning: state actions and decisions, and their consequences, for its citizens within the state, and for others outside it. The state has traditionally been seen as protecting its citizens from outside threat and from each other through the sovereign power invested in it. Sovereignty means a state has a right to speak for all its citizens even if not all within the given state would recognise the state's legitimacy (C. Weber 1992). Sovereignty provides the grounds for citizenship and nationality, whether in terms of positive belonging/inclusion or negative not belonging/exclusion, and the rights and duties an individual does or does not thus receive. These processes are gendered: with suffrage, it has been men who originally voted and then allowed women to do so (Hearn 1992); in states' foreign policy and international relations, patriarchal, militaristic norms are frequently enacted (Zalewski and Palpart 1998).

States display their power and enforce different ideologies through different sectors and services. The state has been seen as the dominant legitimate controller of violence – 'a human community that (successfully) claims the *monopoly of the legitimate use of physical force* within a given territory' (M. Weber [1919] 1946) – as in the military, the police and repressive forces. This has brought huge collective violence and associated constructions of men and masculinities. The state also often structures and provides education, welfare and many other services. These are also gendered – whether through men's direct domination, constructions of specific masculinities and sexualities, different categories of men or forms of boyhood, uneven gendered service delivery, welfare state forms, and so on (Hearn 1998). They are generally organised through formal structures, typically in male-dominated bureaucracies but increasingly through various regulatory forms. The state can also be more contradictory, establishing a 'woman-friendly' set of structures and practices and promoting measures that support women's emancipation directly or indirectly (Hernes 1987).

Finally, the gendered nature of the state cannot be reduced only to the structuring of 'men' and 'women'; rather, the gendering of the state intersects with other social divisions (Pettman 1998).

References and further reading

Burstyn, V. (1983) 'Masculine dominance and the state', in R. Miliband and J. Savile (eds) *The Socialist Register*, London: Merlin, pp. 45–89.

Carver, T. (2004) *Men in Political Theory*, Manchester: Manchester University Press.

Hearn, J. (1990) 'State organisations and men's sexuality in the public domain 1870–1920', in L. Jamieson and H. Corr (eds) *The State, Private Life and Political Change*, London: Macmillan, pp. 50–72.

—— (1992) *Men in the Public Eye*, London and New York: Routledge.

—— (1998) 'The welfare of men?' in J. Popay, J. Hearn and J. Edwards (eds) *Men, Gender Divisions and Welfare*, London: Routledge, pp. 11–36.

Hernes, H.M. (1987) *Welfare State and Woman Power*, Oslo: Norwegian University Press.

MacKinnon, C.A. (1989) *Toward a Feminist Theory of the State*, Cambridge, MA: Harvard University Press.

O'Brien, M. (1981) *The Politics of Reproduction*, London: Routledge and Kegan Paul.

Pateman, C. (1979) *The Problem of Political Obligation*, New York: John Wiley.

—— (1988) *The Sexual Contract*, Cambridge: Polity.

Pettman, R. (1998) 'Sex, power, and the grail of positive collaboration', in M. Zalewski and J. Palpart (eds) *The 'Man' Question in International Relations*, Oxford; Westview, pp. 169–84.

Weber, C. (1992) *Simulating Sovereignty: Intervention, the State and Symbolic Exchange*, Cambridge: Cambridge University Press.

Weber, M. [1919] (1946) 'Politics as a vocation', in H.H. Gerth and C.W. Mills (trans and eds) *From Max Weber*, New York: Oxford University Press, pp. 77–128.

Zalewski, M. and Palpart, J. (eds) (1998) *The 'Man' Question in International Relations*, Oxford: Westview.

JEFF HEARN
HERTTA NIEMI

SUBORDINATE MASCULINITY

Subordinated masculinities encompass beliefs, values, behaviours and attitudes that fall outside the prevailing meaning of what it means to be masculine in a given society. Subordinate masculinity is defined by and in opposition to hegemonic masculinity in a society. Hegemonic masculinities are culturally honoured, glorified and praised forms of masculinities. For example, in American and European societies hegemonic masculinity encompasses such valued characteristics as achievement, aggression, toughness and domination over women. Males inhabiting less appreciated traits such as compassion, nurturance, sensitivity, softness and empathy are likely to be denigrated in those societies.

In *Masculinities* (1995) Connell cites male homosexuality as a common example of a subordinated masculinity. Homosexual men are culturally viewed as inferior, discriminated against economically, physically subject to hate crimes and other violence, and politically oppressed. These forms of harm illustrate societal disapproval for those who exhibit non-typical male behaviour. A hierarchy exists in masculinity within which subordinated masculinities serve to bolster dominant forms of masculinity.

Subordinated masculinities are socially constructed, and views on subordinated masculinity may vary from culture to culture. Subordinated masculinities may also vary within a given society or environment. In prison culture the dominant form of masculinity ('Men') is categorised in relation to subordinated masculinities such as queens, punks, intellectuals, jailhouse lawyers and religious leaders (Donaldson 2001). Subordination can occur to males during certain periods of their lives, i.e. the low social position of apprentices in London printing shops to tradesmen (Cockburn 1986). Dominant and subordinate masculinities can also be defined culturally: for example, in American college fraternities where accepted male behaviour is defined through aggressive drinking, challenges to this behaviour can cast males as inferior to other members of the group (West 2001).

Race and class can serve as categories of subordinated masculinities. The historic oppression of black males in United States society is manifest in physical (lynching), cultural (segregation) and economic (professional discrimination) abuse.

References and further reading

Cockburn, C. (1986) *Machinery of Dominance*, London: Pluto Press.

Connell, R. (1995) *Masculinities*, Berkeley, CA: University of California Press.

Donaldson, S. (2001) 'A million jockers, punks and queens', in D. Sabo, T.A. Kupers and W. James (eds) *Prison Masculinities*, Philadelphia, PA and London: Temple University Press.

West, L.A. (2001) 'Negotiating masculinities in American drinking subcultures', *Journal of Men's Studies*, 9 (3, 30 April): 371–86.

See also: gay masculinities; hegemonic masculinity; lunching

MANUEL TORRES

SUICIDE

Suicide – intentional, self-inflicted death – is markedly patterned by gender, with the number of males killing themselves several times greater than that of females in most countries. Men talk and think about suicide (suicidal ideation) and attempt it less often than women. But when they engage in suicidal behaviour, they are more likely to die.

Suicide rates are higher among males than females in almost all countries, according to World Health Organization data (WHO 2003). Male rates typically are two to four times higher than female rates, and men also suffer higher rates of other forms of premature death (Möller-Leimkühler 2003).

Males' greater vulnerability to (completed) suicide increasingly has been explained in terms of constructions and practices of masculinity. As Hunt *et al.* (2003: 642) summarise, men choose more lethal methods; may be less resilient to stressful life events, such as marriage breakdown; may have more psychopathology and a greater propensity to violence and substance abuse; and may 'be more reluctant to seek help or less able to articulate emotional distress; and suicide may be seen as more acceptable for men'.

Other social circumstances, such as the presence of poverty, crime, divorce and family breakdown, and licit and illicit drug abuse, also are influential (Sabo 2005). Gay and bisexual males, especially among adolescents, have higher rates of suicidal ideation, attempts and completions than heterosexual males, presumably because of homophobic social contexts and resulting depression, lack of social support, family dysfunction and substance abuse (Sabo 2005).

Rising suicide rates particularly among young men may be influenced by shifts in employment, intensified gender-role conflict and excessive norms of individualism in industrialised nations and rapid social change in post-communist countries (Möller-Leimkühler 2003; Smalley *et al.* 2005).

References and further reading

Hunt, K., Sweeting, H., Keoghan M. and Platt, S. (2003) 'Sex, gender role orientation, gender role attitudes and suicidal thoughts in three generations', *Social Psychiatry and Psychiatric Epidemiology*, 41 (8): 373–81.

Möller-Leimkühler, A.M. (2003) 'The gender gap in suicide and premature death', *European Archives of Psychiatry and Clinical Neuroscience*, 253 (1): 1–8.

Sabo, D. (2005) 'The study of masculinities and men's health', in M. Kimmel, J. Hearn and R. Connell (eds) *The Handbook of Studies on Men and Masculinities*, Thousand Oaks, CA: Sage.

Smalley, N., Scourfield, J. and Greenland, K. (2005) 'Young people, gender and suicide', *Journal of Social Work*, 5 (2): 133–54.

WHO (2003) Suicide rates (per 100,000) by country, year and gender at http://www.who.int/mental_health/prevention/suicide/suicide rates/en/print.html (accessed 15 September 2006).

See also: depression; health and illness, men's; men's health studies

MICHAEL FLOOD

T

TANTRIC AND TAOIST SEXUALITIES

Although Tantra and Taoism (Daoism) emerged from different cultural backgrounds (the former Hindu and Buddhist and the latter Chinese), these Eastern philosophies share key ideas on masculinity and sexuality. Both seek spiritual enlightenment by developing one's mind and body according to prescribed principles and practices such as yoga and meditation. These practices include detailed instructions on how to engage in sexual unions. Such unions are elevated to cosmic male–female principles (*shiva–shakti* in Tantra and *yin–yang* in Taoism). Even though the sexual dimension is only one among many in these philosophies, it is the one that has been emphasised and popularised in the West, mainly due to interest in Eastern spirituality in the 1960s and 1970s and New-Age eclectic religions in the 1980s and 1990s.

In Taoist *yin–yang* philosophy, every woman and man embodies both *yin* and *yang* essences (*qi*), and during sexual intercourse these essences are exchanged. For the male the ideal is to absorb *yin* which predominates in women without losing the precious *yang* that predominates in men. For the woman the reverse is true. This sexual vampirism implies a form of expanding capabilities wherein an individual maintains his/her original essence and yet also can potentially absorb additional essences that expand vitality and natural powers. 'Real men' are supposed to have plenty of the *yang* essence – materially concentrated in the semen. Thus, to retain one's peak masculinity and ideal balance in life forces, it is important to maintain self-control so as to delay or avoid ejaculation during sexual intercourse.

It is this 'self-control' that has resonance in Tantric sexuality. Intercourse in Tantra is regarded as a means to pleasure and procreation, but also, when practised correctly, as a path for couples to reach a transcendental state of consciousness. For men, the Tantric sexual ritual follows a strict set of rules including the ideal time of the day and day of the month for sex, and the ideal appearance and health of the sexual partner (the *asana*). Self-control can be so mentally and physically demanding that postures and movements in the sex act are carefully described in terms of cosmic forces. Tantric ecstasy is thus regarded as a state reached when the couple have achieved a Shiva–Shakti consciousness during which they are so deeply joined that they become one entity.

References and further reading

Rawson, P. (1973) *Tantra: The Indian Cult of Ecstasy*, London: Thames and Hudson.

Van Gulik, R.H. (1974) *Sexual Life in Ancient China*, Leiden: E.J. Brill.

KAM LOUIE

TATTOOS

Of the various motives for tattooing, the quest for personal identity is central. Tattoos are inextricably connected to 'body projects':

tattooing is one means by which gendered subjects (re)construct and represent themselves. Traditionally women in the West have been actively discouraged from participating in this form of self-inscription because of its long-standing association with masculinity and male-dominated subcultures such as the military, street gangs, bikers and prisoners. Among these groups tattooing has functioned as a sort of voluntary stigma, a mechanism for creating and confirming machismo (Atkinson; DeMello). Historically, then, in the West at least, tattoos were less a form of decorative art than an announcement and an affirmation of strength, endurance, courage, virility, domination, aggressiveness, non-conformity and a commitment to other men. Hence Clinton Sanders' claim that tattoos represent masculinity.

Tattoos continue to be associated with resistance. However, the philosophies that inform the use of body art as a sign of cultural dissent vary somewhat. For example, individuals who identify with Modern Primitivism often describe tattooing as a rite of passage associated with the values of so-called 'primitive' cultures in which bodies, nature and spirituality are not only esteemed, but inextricably connected (see Atkinson; Pitts; Sullivan). 'Straight-edgers', on the other hand, have adopted tattooing as a means by which to signify their contempt for what they regard as the physical excesses endemic in contemporary culture, and to promote physical purity, personal pacification and control (see Atkinson 2003). At the same time, it has been argued that for counter-cultural figures such as Tupac Shakur, tattoos function as narratives of the flesh that not only articulate the struggles of young African–American men, but also situate them within a history of violent corporeal inscription (see Tucker). Female tattooing is also increasingly popular and is often regarded as a radical violation of gender norms, a reclaiming of the body, and a form of self-(re)narrativisation (see Pitts). While in the contemporary context tattooing seems less clearly tied to masculinity than it has been in the past, it nevertheless continues to be a gendered practice.

References and further reading

Atkinson, M. (2001) 'Flesh journeys', *Deviant Behaviour: An Interdisciplinary Journal*, 22: 117–46.

—— (2002) 'Pretty in ink', *Sex Roles*, 47 (5–6): 219–33.

—— (2003) 'The civilizing of resistance', *Deviant Behaviour*, 24: 197–220.

DeMello, M. (2000) *Bodies of Inscription*, Durham, NC: Duke University Press.

Pitts, V. (2003) *In the Flesh*, New York: Palgrave Macmillan.

Sanders, C. (1989) *Customizing the Body*, Philadelphia, PA: Temple University Press.

Sullivan, N. (2001) *Tattooed Bodies*, Westport, CT: Praeger.

Tucker, L. (2001) 'Holler if ya hear me', *Canadian Review of American Studies*, 31 (2): pp. 57–8.

NIKKI SULLIVAN

TELEVISION

There has been a surprising paucity of research into the term 'televisual masculinity', namely the broadcast media's representations of masculinity. The primary focus to date has fallen upon masculinity as depicted in film (for example, Spicer 2001) and work on televisual masculinity continues to lag behind that on televisual femininity.

Historical overview: from the 1950s to the 1980s

Gunter (1995) demonstrates that from the inception of television in the United Kingdom as a means of mass entertainment from the mid-1950s up to the 1980s, the depiction of gender was highly stereotypical. Men were generally presented as dominant, aggressive, rational and competent, whereas women were the opposite and featured mostly in comedies and soap operas. Throughout the late 1960s and 1970s feminists attacked these narrow stereotypes, but as late as 1978 it was still possible for a commentator to refer to the 'symbolic annihilation' of women on television while, at the same time, male displays of any feminine characteristics were extremely rare. However, throughout the 1980s there was an accelerating move towards gender equalisation on television as narrow stereotypes were attacked. Glamorised representations of muscular male bodies were still used to sell products, but male leads started to combine toughness with a degree of sensitivity, even vulnerability, while female ones became far less dependent on men. The change was particularly noticeable in advertisements, the arena where masculinity could be most easily changed. Meanwhile, homosocial 'buddy relationships' between men became increasingly popular on prime time television, best epitomised by the American series *Starsky & Hutch*, with its display of male bonding and even a degree of emotional disclosure, albeit strictly in the line of work. In other popular series (for example, *Thirty Something*), male friendships became more intimate and thereby more ambiguous. Meanwhile, Fiske (1987) points to the elegant clothing of the two male leads in *Miami Vice* as an example of the male appropriation of the pleasures of appearance and style, but without any loss of male power.

By the late 1980s the mask of toughness and emotional restraint had undoubtedly been lowered, if not finally discarded, as macho masculinity began to be viewed as more of a problem than a strength. Traditional masculine qualities were interjected with those previously reserved for women on television, such as a caring, sensitive nature. A notable instance of this was the somewhat melancholic lead character in *Inspector Morse* who, Brunsdon (1998) argues, was to be admired by men (for his dogged quest for justice) and attractive to women (as a paternalistic individual who would make both an ideal father and a mature lover). At the same time increasing numbers of women were appearing in more and more 'masculine' roles, especially in crime and police series.

Historical overview: from the 1990s

The period since the 1990s has witnessed the further 'repackaging' of masculinity on television with the result that its representation has become far less straightforward, with Hearn and Melechi (1992) pointing to television's role in 'assisting the fragmentation of (traditional) masculinity' (p. 231). Indeed, Gauntlett (2002) concludes that 'modern media has a more complex view of gender and sexuality than ever before' (p. 90), a view to which not everyone would subscribe. In support he lists programmes he believes have been particularly influential in transforming gender representations during this period, amongst them *Ally McBeal*, *Buffy the Vampire Slayer*, *NYPD Blues*, *Friends*, *Frasier*, *ER*, *Dawson's Creek* and *The West Wing*. In the groundbreaking UK police series *Prime Suspect*, a woman (Detective Chief Inspector Jane Tennison) wins through in the masculinist police culture while still managing to retain important aspects of her femininity, albeit perhaps sacrificing others (Creeber 2004). Meanwhile, previously stigmatised formations (such as gay masculinities) have appeared on the screen, for example, in *Queer as Folk*, *Will & Grace* and *Gimme, Gimme, Gimme*. However, 'gayness' in sitcoms has become synonymous with 'campness', television finding it difficult to depict homosexuality in any other way (Mills 2005).

Whannel (2000) highlights another significant aspect of British mainstream television from the 1990s to date, namely its enthusiastic embracing of anti-feminist, laddish masculinity (in, for example, *Men Behaving Badly*, *Fantasy Football League* and *They Think It's All Over*). To be accepted in these programmes, women had either to be Barbie doll-like 'babes' or surrogate 'lads' (even, ideally, a combination of both) and be happy to be the butt of irreverent male humour. The anti-intellectual, juvenile and sexist joking was, as Whannel points out, placed in inverted commas as 'ironic' and, thereby, rendered clever and acceptable. His thesis is that such 'postmodern television' is based on depthless parody and pastiche and characterised by a 'high degree of intertextuality and self-referentiality' (2000: 300).

Researching televisual masculinity

This section reviews a small number of selected analytical concepts I believe to be useful in 'reading' televisual masculinity. Fiske (1987) usefully distinguishes between masculine and feminine narrative forms. 'Masculine narratives' celebrate machismo and the uncommunicative man of action. The emphasis is upon physical performance and heroic achievements so that these male characters only truly 'live' in their moments of performance. Meanwhile, 'masculine intensifiers' (like low camera angles, slow motion action shots, a celebration of the male body's power, pounding music, etc.) heighten the drama of the action in cop, thriller and adventure stories, including Westerns, especially when they conclude with a successful resolution like the triumph of good over evil. Moreover, any hint of the feminine is excluded from masculine narratives, where male bonding carefully circumnavigates real intimacy. He analyses an archetypal masculine narrative, namely the 1980s American series *The A-Team*, in which 'the determination to succeed replaces feelings; mechanical ingenuity replaces insight into real people; and success in problem-solving replaces process' (Fiske 1987: 215) in a celebratory, masculinist 'carnival' of male violence. Masculinity is portrayed differently in 'feminine narratives' (such as soap operas), which are predominantly aimed at a female audience. The brutal and exploitative male villains therein are usually handsome and loved, hated, admired and despised in equal measure, while the weak are unattractive and despicable. If goal-centredness and aggression are employed to characterise the villain, the good, feminised, self-disclosing man is presented positively and invariably possesses the good looks associated with virile heterosexuality. He is 'caring, nurturing and verbal ... [and] will talk about feelings and people and rarely expresses his masculinity in direct action' (Fiske 1987: 186). Although he retains his masculine identity, he imbues it with what Fiske terms a 'feminine inflection'.

Hearn and Melechi (1992) are insightful on the study of televisual masculinities when they distinguish between the 'imaging' and 'imagining' of American men on television. They comment that they 'are shown to be bigger, stronger, fitter, younger, healthier, better-looking, sexier, more tanned, more famous ... American men are "hyper-real". We are moving from imaging to the imaginary' (p. 218). They shift the discussion from the 'image-as-text' to the 'dialectic of the gaze and the process of identification' (p. 228). Given the pervasiveness of American programmes worldwide, the role of the 'trans/atlantic gaze' is worthy of closer attention in our global age and its role in the construction of 'phantasy masculinities'.

Finally, the influence of television on people's attitudes is more often than not assumed rather than substantiated. Viewers do not passively absorb television, which is, after all, only one of many influences upon the sense of selfhood and gendered identity. Neither can we assume that the programme-maker's intended meanings are the ones necessarily picked up by the viewer. Fiske (1987) talks of 'producerly texts' that encourage viewers to participate in the meaning-making and exploit television's 'semiotic potential' at the moment of reception. Meanwhile, Morley (1986), for example, demonstrates that reception itself is gendered in that men tend to prefer knowledge-based programmes, documentaries, news and sport, whereas women generally favour programmes containing the sensitive and expressive, including dramas and soaps. More recent ethnographies of 'media reception' (for example, Mackay and Ivey 2004) continue to support this finding.

Masculinity, television and social change

Representations of gender on television have clearly diversified considerably over the past fifty years, gathering momentum since the 1980s. The earlier, relatively uniform and stereotypical representation of masculinity (and femininity) on television has today been replaced by a wider range. It is helpful to introduce the concept of 'hegemonic masculinity' (Connell 1987) at this point. Hegemonic masculinity retains its primacy by being flexible and by selectively incorporating oppositional definitions for its own purposes. In the case of television the widened representations of masculinity function to win over the ideological consent of both male and female viewers and thereby safeguard its hegemony. Today a new generation of 'gender literate' television writers and directors are more prepared to experiment with non-traditional and subversive gender representations. This is in line with many academic voices who have repeatedly called for television to become more proactively involved in articulating new masculinities based on personal qualities and relationships rather than power, action, achievement and possessions. British television today is, it would at first appear, more open than ever to alternative depictions of gender. New channels (whether terrestrial, cable or satellite), along with DVDs and the Internet, are providing additional opportunities for both stereotyping and its subversion. It is to the paradoxical and ambivalent representation of 'masculinities', whether in dramas, advertisements or pop music, that commentators have repeatedly been drawn. The case for contemporary masculinity being 'in crisis' has certainly been widely asserted by both the print and broadcast media (Beynon 2002). An aspect of this 'crisis creation' is articulated by MacKinnon (2003), who sees the medium not so much 'reflecting' masculinity as 'teaching' it by persisting to trade on idealised images that place an impossible set of demands on men, but to which they nevertheless have to aspire if they are to be designated 'real men'. The narrow equating of masculinity with machismo in the scores of sentimental 'telenovas' ever-popular across Latin America is a case in point. Also, competitive, young and athletic men are constantly celebrated in television's now worldwide coverage of sport, especially in contact sports, particularly boxing, kick-boxing and, in hyper form, wrestling.

In spite of this, Gauntlett (2002) confidently asserts that television is 'full of information about being a man in the here and now' (p. 7), mirroring our 'postmodern times' in which the enactments and depictions of gender are increasingly mobile. Against this can be set Wood (2003), who suggests that most changes that have taken place are superficial: in fact, all that has really happened is that a new set of stereotypes has been substituted for the old, so much so that 'underneath what appear to be radically different images of women and men are some very familiar, very traditional themes' (p. 262). An apt illustration of this might be the British police drama *Prime Suspect*, referred to earlier. Although previous police/cop series had featured women in leading roles, it took things a stage further in that Jane Tennison (memorably played by Helen Mirren and subsequently syndicated worldwide) drew upon her feminism to erode the masculinist 'canteen culture' surrounding her (Creeber 2004). However, in order to earn respect and credibility she had to take on many of the attributes of the misogynistic detectives she led. For this reason Brunsdon (1998) concludes that *Prime Suspect* still preserved intact and extolled the virtues of the traditional masculine narrative.

To conclude, perhaps we ought to be wary of what might at first appear to be radical changes in television's representations of masculinity and continue to question the medium's capacity to reflect social change adequately, let alone orchestrate change.

References and further reading

Beynon, J. (2002) *Masculinities and Culture*, Buckingham: Open University.

Brunsdon, C. (1998) 'Structure of anxiety', *Screen*, 39 (3): 223–43.

Connell, R. (1987) *Gender and Power*, Cambridge, MA and Oxford: Blackwell.

Creeber, G. (2004) 'Prime suspect', in G. Creeber (ed.) *Fifty Key Television Programmes*, London: Arnold, pp. 159–63.
Fiske, J. (1987) *Television Culture*, London: Routledge.
Gauntlett, D. (2002) *Media, Gender and Identity*, London: Routledge.
Gunter, B. (1995) *Television and Gender Representation*, London: John Libbey.
Hearn, J. and Melechi, A. (1992) 'The trans/atlantic gaze', in S. Craig (ed.) *Men, Masculinity and the Media*, London: Sage, pp. 215–32.
Mackay, H. and Ivey, D. (2004) *Modern Media in the Home*, Rome: John Libbey.
MacKinnon, K. (2003) *Representing Men*, London: Arnold.
Mills, B. (2005) *Television Sitcom*, London: British Film Institute.
Morley, D. (1986) *Family Television*, London: Comedia.
Spicer, A. (2001) *Typical Men*, London: I.B. Tauris.
Whannel, G. (2000) 'The lads and the gladiators', in E. Buscombe (ed.) *British Television*, Oxford: Clarendon Press, pp. 290–302.
Wood, J.T. (2003) *Gendered Lives*, Belmont, CA: Thomson Wadsworth.

See also: hegemonic masculinity

JOHN BEYNON

TERRORISM

Most terrorists are men, points out Morgan in *The Demon Lover: On the Sexuality of Terrorism* (1989). Even though the stock image of a terrorist is a man in a ski mask, considerations of terrorists *as men* are often ignored, and discussions of terrorism as a political strategy *about masculinity* are typically overlooked. Terrorism – that act most explicit in its violent aggression, most obvious in its destructive aims and most hideously spectacular in its headlines – in fact makes men invisible. Terrorist manifestos, media representations of terrorists and current policy debates over the causes and consequences of terrorism all typically de-gender terrorism.

The connections between men, masculinity and terrorism are beginning to be examined. Scholars argue that all terrorist acts should be seen as connected, understood in a global context of shrinking economies, shifting gender roles, increased militarisation and expansive media, and defined as extreme forms of men's violence ranging from abuse to bombings. War has traditionally been a male initiation rite and proving ground where men battle with one another over the ideals of masculinity like courage and strength. Yet, unlike traditional wars over national borders or natural resources, terrorism may be a war over the symbolic meanings of who men are, how they should behave and what they think they deserve. These theorists claim terrorist men use hyper-aggressive and ultra-violent means to maintain the sense of entitlement and privilege that gender dominance has historically bestowed.

Media images: men, women and de-gendered terrorism

Portrayed in news coverage as psychotic, barbaric or unexplainable, terrorism gets de-gendered. For example, since the bombing of the World Trade Center and Pentagon in the United States on 11 September 2001, there has yet to be one full exploration of men and masculinity in relation to terrorism (Rasmusson 2005). So nearly exclusive is the connection between gender and terrorism that it goes unmentioned except when terrorists are women, who are then explicitly named, as in 'female suicide bomber'. Rare in comparison, attacks by women are treated in accounts that typically begin with the expectation that terrorists are men, then skipping over that original story to relay a story of alarming gender-equality in terrorist activity. Shocking and titillating, these accounts channel an analysis of gender away from the centre of the story – men and masculinity.

The media-driven, American-led 'War on Terror' was presented as the theatre in which men and masculinity were staged. After 9/11, Western manhood was put to the test, Lorber claims, as men were called upon to avenge the brutality against the US and assert both their own manhood and a national and international alliance among men as brethren (Lorber 2002). Journalism highlighted the courage of macho men in uniform – fire-fighters, police officers, rescue workers – yet never discussed the ever-present issue of men and masculinity.

First, media's focus on women as new terrorists, weeping widows, mourning mothers, wives of soldiers, or oppressed victims under fundamentalist regimes privileges masculine norms of authority, rationality, strength and decision-making. Many scholars have criticised the discussions of Muslim women's veiling as signs of their degradation and their culture's atavism (Sarikakis 2002). Furthermore, both Lorber and Sarikakis argue that anti-terror protectionist rhetoric and patriotic propaganda invoke gendered notions of fear to increase public suspicion and state power to fight terrorist activity.

Second, masculinity is bolstered by media images that pit the presumably savage and backwards manliness of terrorists against that of the clean-cut and civilised elected leaders charged with stopping them. The good masculinity of Western men was hailed over the bad masculinity of terrorists – non-Western men of colour from developing nations, religious zealots, fanatic ideologues and oppressors of women. Gendered images and news stories erased the contributions of women, people of colour and the reality of working-class labour in New York City. Furthermore, this simple segregation of 'good guys' from 'evil doers' rendered other forms of masculinity invisible. 'Forgotten in this picture of heroes and victims were the poor, non-White, working-class men, the cooks, dishwashers, and busboys of the World Trade Center restaurant, the mail handlers and maintenance personnel of the building – many of whom were immigrants,' writes Lorber. 'Their masculinity was not valued enough to be called heroic' (Lorber 2002: 385). In addition, rarely does the public see gay men, men with disabilities or men who weep for their loved ones in media representations of terrorism.

Dying to be a man: domestic and international terrorism

It is too simple to assert that terrorists are either lone wolf psychopaths or pathetic chaps with low-self esteem. Essentialist and stereotypical explanations that men are driven 'naturally' to war and violence due to aggression-inducing testosterone or because they have 'always been the hunters' must also be eschewed. Instead, some theorists maintain that an analysis is necessary of terrorists' own masculine identity and experiences of manhood, on the one hand, and of the power imbalances and inequities between the world's men, on the other. Terrorism should be framed, they say, as an ideological re-investment in strict gender roles, especially in a masculinity rooted in aggression, violence and domination. Ideologies of strict sexual difference through gender segregation in social practice, and often law, also nurture terrorists. Furthermore, terrorism may bolster masculinity that is perceived to be in danger or lost. Braudy, in *From Chivalry to Terrorism* (2003), recounts how perceptions of masculinity are based on the perceived need for war. In a historical examination, he claims that the nostalgic appeal of 'warrior masculinity' inspires men to take up terrorism as a route back to the ancient virtues of the brave hero. Whether they call themselves soldiers of God, or keepers of traditional values, or protectors of racial purity, according to Braudy, all these men are gender militants (Braudy 2003: 543). Terrorism, then, is a new occupation that calls men forth to define themselves as manly. And, as more young boys are taught that the way to be a real man is to prepare to die for one's cause, terrorism cyclically continues to exploit men's fears and anxieties about masculinity.

As ideals of masculinity are increasingly unattainable – fierce independence, physical toughness, moral resolution, emotional asceticism and decisive manliness – incidents of domestic and international terrorism increase. Shor (2002) describes 'militarised masculinity' as a cultural, political and industrial enterprise that contributes to terrorism. When men are trained to kill as instruments of their nation's military and are disillusioned by the dwindling prospects of making it in civilian life, they may become terrorists. Examining their writings, Kimmel shows that Oklahoma bomber and white supremacist McVeigh and al-Quaeda member Atta similarly complained about the erosion of masculine ideals. McVeigh wrote two years before he bombed the federal building in Oklahoma City, decrying the difficulty of being a breadwinner and achieving the American Dream. Atta, the suspected strategist and pilot of the first plane to hit the World Trade Center, left carnally obsessed burial plans that stipulated that no women should attend his funeral. Kimmel concludes, 'It is from such gendered shame that mass murderers are made' (Kimmel 2002: 12).

Terrorists, then, appear dissatisfied *as men*. They perceive themselves to be struggling and are striving to achieve dominance *as men*. Personal feelings of loss, desperation and disenfranchisement at a time of material, moral and political uncertainty may conduce to terrorism. In addition to stringent ideals of masculinity, terrorist men are compellingly aware of relationships of power and domination. Kimmel theorises that terrorism can be viewed as a showdown between dominant men with economic, educational and other institutional advantages, and subordinated men of minoritised masculinities where each 'side' depicts the other as the wrong kind of man. Subordinate men 'as martyrs' may believe they can become dominant men. What unites all terrorists, according to these theorists, is their acceptance of strict codes of masculinity, their sense of entitlement, their anger at thwarted ambitions and their desperate need to blame others for failure. 'Central to their political ideology is the recovery of manhood from the emasculating politics of globalisation' (Kimmel 2002: 11).

Gender war and global backlash

These theorists write about terrorism as a gender war involving men's struggle for power and control. Terrorist men often report that their people have been sidelined by global shifts in power, capital and opportunity or that their 'traditional culture' has been corrupted by contemporary values, mass media or moral degradation. And, as other citizens who were once disadvantaged gain greater social recognition and legal rights, terrorists may be resentful against women, homosexuals and racial and ethnic minorities because they are believed to have stolen men's rightful place at the head of the world's table. Thus, some theorists discuss, terrorist men may be exacting revenge on a society they think has betrayed them even as they crusade as righteous avengers. They use terrorism as a repressive and regressive route back to an imagined bygone era of prosperity and certainty when men knew they were men and women needed to be saved by them. Thus terrorism may be a form of global backlash. As such, it always plays catch-up to reclaim manhood when traditional routes to it are perceived as lost.

As men define it: terrorism and men's violence

Who is a terrorist? Who is most likely to be the target of terrorist attack? Who responds to terrorism? Who decides what qualifies as a terrorist attack? Mostly, the answer to all these questions is: men. Just as men have the most to gain by using terror for the acquisition of political power and control, it is men who define terrorism. Certainly, defining terrorism has always depended on perspective. For example, one man's terrorist is another man's freedom fighter. Differentiating liberationist struggles for self-determination from terrorism, or civil rights clashes from terrorism, or revolutionary activism from terrorism depends on who commands the context. Furthermore, the words 'terrorist' and 'terrorism' are often invoked as a rhetorical strategy for certain political and social purposes. To be sure, if those who are the object of attack are also the ones who control the language and access to the media, then 'terrorism' is likely the term to be used. Simply said: terrorism is a discourse controlled by men, a meaning-making imagery system intended to matter to men, and political violence perpetrated mostly by men against a backdrop of dominating forces such as globalisation, capitalism, consolidating multi-national corporations, new postcolonial governments and transnational media, which are also mostly ruled by men (Rasmusson 2005).

Working to redefine terrorism, some theorists expand common representations and understandings of political violence to include a wide range of men's violence based on intimidation. A lot of what men do could, subsequently, be considered terrorist activity: schoolyard bullying, school shootings, fraternity hazing, stalking and sexual harassment, rape, child abuse and domestic violence, racist profiling and white supremacy, gang violence, anti-gay hate crimes, threatening reproductive health clinics and assassinating abortion providers, militias, foreign occupation, ethnic cleansing and genocide, holocausts and the torture of prisoners of war and detainees in military prisons. Lutz (2004), for instance, in 'Living room terrorists' refers to domestic violence as a form of *domestic* terrorism by pointing out the increasing rates of abuse within American military families since 9/11. Similarly concerned with sexualised violence against women, Sheffield's 'Sexual terrorism' (1987) identifies any use of violence and fear that helps maintain male control and domination of females. In fact, the sensationalised images of hostage-taking, weapon-wielding insurgents may work to normalise the far more prevalent everyday but less newsworthy campaign of terror that many men lead on their families, loved ones, children and marginalised 'others' such as women, racial and ethnic and sexual minorities. Terrorism should be added to the list of 'isms' – racism, sexism, heterosexism, ethnocentrism, imperialism, etc. – as a hate-based form of oppression perpetuated by those who desire to maintain dominance over others.

Unmask terrorism and make men visible

The recent rush to follow developments in terrorism around the world is accompanied by the hope that defining, identifying and isolating terrorism's origins can prevent it. Yet terrorism's connections to men and masculinity are often overlooked and ignored. And this oversight deflects analytical attention, policy formulation and political action. Some social historians and cultural theorists unmask terrorist men and make the gendered nature of terrorism visible. If terrorism continues, and continues mostly at the hands of men, then men and masculinity should be at the root of all discussions about, analyses of, policies for and reactions to terrorism, they argue. Future analysis of terrorists and terrorism should also continue complicated and thorough discussions of gender and rightly pose relevant questions of geopolitics, nationalism, natural resources like oil, racial and ethnic strife, religion and fundamentalism, imperialism, poverty and military technology. Ultimately, seeing terrorism through a lens of masculinity may aid prospects for non-violence, peace and global stability.

References and further reading

Braudy, L. (2003) *From Chivalry to Terrorism*, New York: Knopf.

Kimmel, M. (2002) 'Gender, class, and terrorism', *The Chronicle of Higher Education*, 8 February: B11–12.

Lorber, J. (2002) 'Heroes, warriors, and burqas', *Sociological Forum*, 17 (3): 377–96.

Lutz, C. (2004) 'Living room terrorists', *The Women's Review of Books*, 5 (February): 17–18.

Morgan, R. [1989] (2001) *The Demon Lover*, New York: Washington Square.

Rasmusson, S.L. (2005) 'Masculinity and *Fahrenheit 9/11*', *International Feminist Journal of Politics*, 7 (1): 137–41.

Sarikakis, K. (2002) 'Violence, militarism, terrorism', *Feminist Media Studies*, 2 (1): 151–4.

Sheffield, C. (1987) 'Sexual terrorism', in B.B. Hess and M.M. Ferree (eds) *Analysing Gender*, London: Sage, pp. 171–89.

Shor, F. (2002) 'Militarized masculinity and home-grown terrorists', CounterPunch.org (2 November), http://www.counterpunch.org/shor1102.html

See also: military institutions; military masculinities; oppression; state; violence

SARAH L. RASMUSSON

TESTOSTERONE

Testosterone is an organic steroid compound that is commonly referred to as the male hormone. It is produced naturally both in men and (in much smaller quantities) in women. Testosterone is the principal masculinising hormone that produces the secondary male characteristics, which include the development of the male sexual organs, facial hair, the deepening of the voice, sebaceous gland development, skeletal bone growth and skeletal muscle growth. Administration of testosterone or other androgenic hormones to females can result in the deepening of the voice, facial hair growth, hypertrophy of the clitoris and hair loss. Many of the differences between male and female physical and psychological characteristics are due to the higher levels of testosterone in males during the developmental period.

Testosterone was first isolated in crystalline form in 1935. The availability of synthetic testosterone made possible the production of the many modified versions of the testosterone molecule that are known as anabolic-androgenic steroids, or simply androgens, and that mimic the actions of naturally occurring testosterone.

Anabolic-androgenic steroids include hundreds of possible variations. These hormone drugs have both anabolic (protein synthesising) and androgenic (masculinising) properties, although the relative effects differ according to which version is administered. The effects of testosterone and its derivatives are achieved by these molecules binding to anabolic steroid receptors in various types of cells throughout the body.

Clinical uses of androgenic drugs date from the late 1930s. The most common therapeutic application has been as a replacement therapy for hypogonadal men who do not produce enough natural testosterone. Androgens have also been used to treat wasting conditions resulting from chronic debilitating illnesses, trauma, burns, surgery and radiation therapy. Because androgens stimulate red blood cell production (erythropoiesis) they were once used to treat various anaemias.

The use of androgenic drugs as an 'anti-aging' therapy has become increasingly common since the mid-1990s. The popularity of these drugs as a largely cosmetic hormone replacement therapy for older people, and their use as (illicit) performance-enhancing drugs by many elite athletes, which dates from the 1950s, represent the non-medical or quasi-medical careers of drugs which originated as therapeutic medications.

References and further reading

De Kruif, P. (1945) *The Male Hormone*, New York: Harcourt, Brace.

Hoberman, J. (2005) *Testosterone Dreams*, Berkeley and Los Angeles, CA: University of California Press.

Hoberman, J. and Yesalis, C.E. (1995) 'The history of synthetic testosterone', *Scientific American*, pp. 60–6.

See also: bodies and biology, male; sport, athletes and athletic trining

JOHN HOBERMAN

THEATRE AND MUSICALS

The primary task for contemporary scholars of theatre and musicals who study men and masculinities is to critically interpret how such identities are learned, created, performed and understood as iterations of self and other that are simultaneously aesthetic and mundane.

In contrast, scholars of earlier theatrical traditions often focus on the contradictions of masculine codes that lead to tragic outcomes, for example in the competing demands of honour and vengeance in the drama of the Spanish 'Golden Age' of the seventeenth century or in Macbeth's quandary about whether ambitious murder can be considered 'manly'. When Macbeth says, 'I dare do all that may become a man;/Who dares do more is none', the taunting Lady Macbeth replies, 'What beast was't, then/That made you break this enterprise to me?/When you durst do it, then you were a man;/And, to be more than what you were, you would/Be so much more the man' (Shakespeare, *Macbeth* I.7.46–51). Furthermore, critics debate the effects on the audience of all male performers from the ritual and metaphysical quandaries posed by ancient Greek dramas like Sophocles' *Oedipus the King* (fifth century BCE) to the stylised class and gender roles of classical Japanese Kabuki theatre of the seventeenth century to the present. Callaghan controversially argues that Shakespeare's transvestite actors were not meant to represent women, while the plays are shaped by the absence and exclusion not only of female bodies but of those of men of colour (Callaghan 1999).

Rodgers and Hammerstein's *Oklahoma!* (1943) is a particularly rich example of the conventions of the classical Broadway musical. The characters of the rustic Curly and Jud are exemplars of a traditional white American manhood and masculinity, yet the actors who play Curly and Jud sing and dance about the stage in a manner commonly understood to be 'unmanly'. The character of the 'Persian' peddler Ali Hakim participates in a problematic, although not historically unprecedented, performance of identity; the body of the actor who plays this role suffers the colonisation of his race and ethnicity in a manner that nevertheless reveals the invisibility of whiteness in much of theatre and musicals in contrast to the over-emphasised racialisation of blackface characters like Al Jolson in *The Jazz Singer* (1927). The nuanced identities of the mainstream white characters and the men who play them help create the norms of American men's identities both on and off stage.

At the turn of the twenty-first century, theatre and musicals countenance a broad range of representations of gay and straight masculinity, from the tragic courage of those who face the AIDS epidemic and an array of bigotries in Kushner's *Angels in America* (1993) to the conflicts between authority, patriotism, integrity and history that divide the atomic scientists Bohr and Heisenberg in Frayn's *Copenhagen* (2000).

The significance of men's roles in theatre and musicals is not limited to elite and professional stage performances. The experiences of men and boys who perform in theatre and musicals at the amateur level (e.g. community theatre, secondary schools) influence how ideas of masculinity come to be understood in our lives. The creation of theatre and musicals continues to occur in contexts dominated by men in the roles of author, producer, director and designer and mediated by social class.

Contemporary scholars have studied gender in theatre and musicals from a number of perspectives. Wolf (2002) identifies a way of making meaning from performances outside traditional gender norms. Her case studies of Ethel Merman, Mary Martin, Julie Andrews and Barbra Streisand from the position of 'lesbian spectator' serve as an example of performance studies theorising in traditional theatre. Ramanathan (1996) offers a feminist criticism of the portrayal of women in modernist Eurocentric works by male playwrights. Dickinson (1999) makes use of queer theory to consider the role of (other-gendered) Trickster in the work of Canadian First Nations playwright Tomson Highway. Roberts (2006) critiques post-Maoist analyses of gender erasure in Maoist theatre by arguing for a renewed understanding of the importance of women heroines in that genre.

The topic of single-gender (all-male) casting as a historical practice even came to be the subject of an Oscar-winning film in Norman and Stoppard's *Shakespeare in Love* (1998).

References and further reading

Callaghan, D. (1999) *Shakespeare Without Women*, New York: Routledge.
Dickinson, P. (1999) *Here is Queer*, Toronto: University of Toronto Press.
Frayn, M. (2000) *Copenhagen*, New York: Anchor.
Kushner, T. (2002) *Angels in America*, New York: Theatre Communication Group.
Norman, M. and Stoppard, T. (1998) *Shakespeare in Love*, New York: Hyperion.
Ramanathan, G. (1996) *Sexual Politics and the Male Playwright*, London: McFarland.
Roberts, R. (2006) 'From Zheng Qiang to Jiang Shuiying', *Asian Theatre*, 23 (2): 265–91.
Wolf, S. (2002) *A Problem Like Maria*, Ann Arbor, MI: University of Michigan Press.

See also: theatre and performance studies

SCOTT WILLIAM GUST

THEATRE AND PERFORMANCE STUDIES

Performance studies and theatre, as disciplines, have commented on gender and sexuality since the field's inception, offering ways of seeing self and others in both traditional and subversive ways.

Performance studies and theatre have been investigating gender and sexuality (directly or indirectly) since their inception. From Plato to Shakespeare, the roles of performance and performer have been gendered, cultured and historically marked. The field today is as diverse and comprehensive as the members who work within the theatre and/or academy. Performance studies today is built from more than one discipline. Scholars such as Schechner (1988) built performance studies from theatre, using the theatrical metaphor as an analytic tool for seeing performance across genres. Street theatre and political protest, within this logic, can be seen as acts in the presence of an audience, fulfilling the theatrical functions of performer and witness. In the field of anthropology, Turner (1982) used performance as both a lens of analysis to see human action and a method for studying ethnographic texts. Turner examined customs and rituals as culturally specific acts and considered how gender is produced through repeated and stylised human actions. Other scholars such as Pelias and VanOosting (1987) worked within oral interpretation and communication studies to argue that 'performance studies takes as its domain the practice of aesthetic communication' (Pelias and VanOosting 1987: 220).

This framework is especially hopeful for the study of masculinity and gender, as it shifts from marked performance acts (i.e. plays and/or street theatre) to more everyday enactments of identity. In this manner, we can see the utility of the performance lens on human action, both on stage and in everyday settings. In their description of this 'new paradigm', Pelias and VanOosting (1987) organise performance studies into several levels: *texts* expand beyond the canons of literature; *events* are broadly conceived; *performers* stretch beyond the artist to everyday social actors; and the *audience* is approached not only as witnesses but also as possible participants. In this new way of seeing, Pelias and VanOosting (1987) reconfigure the power of performance. These multidisciplinary scholars have generated a complex field of study, opening questions for performance across sites, methods and actors.

To examine performance studies and theatre, one might consider three trends in the conceptualisation of performance. Here, the field opens towards advanced questions on culture and gender. First, performance is analysed as a site of investigation, calling forth critical studies that examine both traditional performance spaces and non-traditional contexts. For instance, Schechner (1988) asks multiple questions about the cultural productivity of staged art. Román (1998) reads 'interventions' like candlelight vigils and Broadway plays such as *Rent* as complex responses by gay male culture to the AIDS crisis. In these examples, staged and mundane performances become vehicles to understand both culture and the high and everyday art that produces culture.

Second, performance is offered as a metaphor for all human action, a way of seeing human actors within everyday contexts in which they are essentially performing creatures. Turner (1982) treated performance as ritual, examining weddings and other cultural acts as repeated and socially constituted enactments. Through performance scholarship, he demonstrated how culture is produced through social enactments. Johnson's (2003) writings on black queer masculinity as a performance are a powerful example of the potential of this approach. He shows how blackness as a gendered performance is enacted and thus produced within everyday contexts. By applying performance as a lens, he is able to see how social actors make their lives meaningful, producing gender and other cultural identifiers in the process.

Third, performance is examined as an epistemological practice, a method of coming to know the world around the actor. Bacon (1987) noted, '[Performance] is a form of knowing – not just a *skill* for knowing, but a *knowing*' (73). Here, we see the potential of recognising performance as an engagement that generates knowledge, not just a tool to express some idea in a text. Nowhere has this been more examined than in work on performative pedagogy, where teachers and scholars have used the doing of performance to generate knowledge, arguing that reading and listening produce different (and less complicated) ways of knowing than the acts of doing or becoming that embodiment makes possible – a shift that happens within performance (see Madison and Hamera 2006). Creating performance (like Boal's forum theatre) has generated much productive work, allowing men and women to come to understand issues of gender and power through their bodies. Embodied knowledge can make spaces for subversion and hope by imagining different possibilities and methods of theorising, in and through bodily knowing.

Current essays on gender and performance cross these analytical frames and contexts (Dailey 1998; Goodman 1998; Lengel and Warren 2005; Madison and Hamera 2006).

Movement towards these three trends has been building since the late 1970s, when many disciplines, including theatre and oral interpretation, began to take seriously the question of culture. Theatre scholars like Schechner and Dolan were prominent in making the shift, broadening the view of theatre studies to encompass culture writ large. For instance, Schechner (1993) examined the Tiananmen Square protest and massacre in 1989 as a form of street theatre, using performance, theatre and cultural studies to analyse how these events transformed cultural imagination. Theatre was profoundly changed by this turn in focus, moving political and educational theatre to the centre as more and more theatre scholars and artists used the stage (and street) as a space of activism. Oral interpretation also was affected by this movement, emphasising the power of embodiment. For example, in his essay 'Performance as a moral act' Conquergood (1985) focused on the ethical imperatives involved in working with texts produced by cultures other than one's own. While frequently applied to literary texts and performances, Conquergood's ideas have been widely used in ethnographic and cultural studies. They portray the everyday cultural interactions of marginal and/or oppressed communities in a mode that he called 'dialogic performance' – a way of being and speaking with others that is ethically and morally sound. Conquergood lived these principles in his work on Hmong refugee camps and street gangs. For instance, he noted how Chicago gangs create and sustain racial and gendered identities through repeating embodied gestures. Through coding the body, a male gang member can properly perform being a 'man' and his gang affiliation (Conquergood 1994).

The most influential scholar on performance studies and theatre since the 1990s is philosopher Judith Butler, whose pioneering book *Gender Trouble* (1990) has led to innumerable texts and analyses. Specifically, she contests the idea that masculinity and femininity are deep internal essences in each individual. Instead, she argues that gender and sex are social performances, creating identities constituted in and through our everyday communicative acts. Butler disrupts sex as a biological certainty, arguing that gender defines and naturalises sex, not the other way round. Butler's proposition that our cultural and gendered baggage precedes any analysis of gender shows that the category of sex is a product of the social.

Similarly, Lengel and Warren (2005) and Goodman (1998) show that notions of femininity and masculinity, male and female, as well as of man and woman, are enacted, performed accomplishments. Within this logic a simple binary conception of gender is displaced in favour of a more complicated picture of how, within the everyday enactments of self, we produce the naturalised categories of self and other. Analyses of men and masculinity have grown as a result of this new theoretical frame. Instead of seeing maleness as a cause for the misuse and abuse of power, this analysis considers that relations of power are themselves productive of identities, including gender. Thus agency is not seen as inherent in individual identity, but rather as made in and through our everyday enactments. Change is possible because identities are not static and fixed but contingent on the reproduction of norms, and each repetition of a norm may vary from the former instance, producing something new.

The future of performance studies and theatre within the frame of gender is rich indeed. New volumes are being published each year that feature innovative work on gender and performance (Lengel and Warren 2005; Madison and Hamera 2006; Goodman 1998). However, much remains to be done along the line of masculinity studies. While many innovative writings touch on masculinity in relation to the study of race (e.g. Johnson 2003) and other markers of difference, no work to date has fully analysed men's lives within the frame of performance. Whether on stage or in everyday life, much is left unspoken and under-theorised. As scholars begin to analyse the centre of power (i.e. straight studies and whiteness studies), more work in masculinity studies would enrich the fields of theatre and performance. In particular, few studies that are written or staged within a performance frame centre on the lives of gay men. So far this important research fails to understand the breadth of men's experience (and privilege) generally. As it is, the field remains ready for more advanced and varied questions on the role of performance in/as/of masculinity in the lives of men.

References and further reading

Bacon, W.A. (1987) 'Afterword', in W.A. Bacon (ed.) *Festschrift for Isabel Crouch*, Las Cruces: New Mexico State University Press, pp. 71–80.

Butler, J. (1990) *Gender Trouble*, New York: Routledge.

Conquergood, D. (1985) 'Performing as a moral act', *Literature in Performance*, 5 (2): 1–13.

—— (1994) 'Homeboys and hoods', in L.R. Grey (ed.) *Communication in Context*. Hillsdale, NJ: LEA, pp. 23–55.

Dailey, S.J. (1998) *The Future of Performance Studies*, Annandale, VA: National Communication Association.

Goodman, L. (ed.) (1998) *The Routledge Reader in Gender and Performance*, New York: Routledge.

Johnson, E.P. (2003) *Appropriating Blackness*, Durham, NC: Duke University Press.

Lengel, L. and Warren, J.T. (eds) (2005) *Casting Gender*, New York: Peter Lang.

Madison, D.S. and Hamera, J. (2006) *The SAGE Handbook of Performance Studies*, Thousand Oaks, CA: Sage.

Pelias, R.J. and VanOosting, J. (1987) 'A paradigm for performance studies', *Quarterly Journal of Speech*, 73: 219–31.

Román, D. (1998) *Acts of Intervention*, Bloomington, IN: Indiana University Press.

Schechner, R. (1988) *Performance Theory*, New York: Routledge.

—— (1993) *The Future of Ritual*, New York: Routledge.

Turner, V. (1982) *From Ritual to Theatre*, New York: PAJ.

See also: theatre and musicals

JOHN T. WARREN

TORTURE

Torture, a form of gender-related violence, can be seen to reflect and reinforce the power imbalances of patriarchal society (El-Bushra and Piza Lopez 1993: 1). The use of rape and other forms of forced sexual penetration in times of warfare, for example, is culturally ingrained misogyny and racism acted out and legitimated by conflict (Seifert 1993: 6, 12; Card 1997). Rape is a deliberate weapon of humiliation and destruction and its usage in conflict reinforces cultural beliefs about the dirtiness or cleanliness of sexuality and ethnic identity (Olujic 1998: 39).

During the 1960s, 1970s and 1980s in the military dictatorships of the Southern Cone of Latin America, torture consisted, across the board, of violent sexual attacks on the bodies of women and men, reflecting cultural constructions of masculinity and femininity in Latin American society.

Hollander (1996: 53) has suggested that male violence against women relates to men's need to combat feelings, experienced since early infancy, of engulfment by the omnipotent mother. Hence, women are constructed through cultural myths in terms of polar opposites. The glorification and debasement of women enables men to neutralise woman's power by placing her 'either above or below male fear' (ibid.). From time to time, however, men must reassure themselves of their domination by violently abusing that which is potentially powerful.

As the military state enforced an ideology of adoration of the dominant and aggressive male sex (Hollander 1996: 67), it became necessary for men who opposed the state to be transformed into something other than this adulated sex. To feminise subversiveness, men's bodies were transformed into penetrable bodies. Jokes were made about the size of their penises, they were taunted about their manhood and their genitalia, and other orifices became the subject of prodding and poking by various torturous devices (Franco 1992: 107). Thus, the Latin American military also used psychological torture in the form of forcing men to witness the torture and rape of female relatives: being powerless to prevent this represented an attack on the masculine role of men. (Hollander 1996: 60).

Suffering these forms of torture forced male prisoners, as Franco says (1992: 109), 'to live like women'. It was here, often for the first time, that men became aware of what it meant to be objectified, to be battered and ridiculed and to be constantly aware of their bodies. And it was also here, often for the first time, that men learnt the comfort found in everyday activities and the strength gained from talking to friends (ibid.).

References and further reading

Card, C. (1997) 'Addendum to "Rape as a weapon of war"', *Hypatia*, 12 (2): 216–18.

El Bushra, J. and Piza Lopez, E. (1993) 'Gender-related violence', in H. Connell (ed.) *Women and Conflict*, Vol. 1, Oxford: Oxfam, pp. 1–9.

Franco, J. (1992) 'Gender, death and resistance', in J. Corradi, E.P. Weiss Fagen and M.A. Garreton (eds) *Fear at the Edge*, Berkeley, CA: University of California Press, pp. 104–18.

Hollander, N.C. (1996) 'The gendering of human rights', *Feminist Studies*, 22 (1): 41–80.

Olujic, M.B. (1998) 'Embodiment of terror', *Medical Anthropology Quarterly*, 12 (1): 31–50.

Seifert, R. (1993) *Women and Rape*, Geneva: Women's International League for Peace and Freedom.

See also: violence; war

HELEN LESLIE

TRANSGENDER

'Transgender' has emerged as a term to describe the phenomenon and identity of individuals who transgress normative aspects of the Western sex/gender system. Earlier use of the term referred to those who cross gender boundaries without recourse to transsexual surgeries. However, it has now developed into an umbrella term to designate what Kate Bornstein describes as gender outlaws, including transsexuals, transgenderists, gender liminal persons, Two-Spirit people (former colonial term: 'berdache'), transvestites, drag queens/kings, gender benders, intersexed persons (formerly: 'hermaphrodites') and queer identified people who resist the binary of being women/men.

The term gained its present currency through works such as Judith Butler's *Gender Trouble* (drawing on theories of performativity) and Leslie Feinberg's novel *Stone Butch Blues* (showing transgender as political resistance). Transgender is a celebrated constituent of queer theory, which draws on postmodernism and poststructuralism to unpack gendered subject positions. 'Trans' implies movement, flux, fluidity and crossing. Critics point out that a focus on transgender may underestimate the intersectionality of gender with other identity configurations based on race, age and culture. In some societies (Polynesia, for example), prevalent cultural identities include gender variations that do not fit Western queer theory or a transgender umbrella. Other critics point out that the transgender umbrella masks deep differences among those whom it claims to shelter. Transsexuals, for example, may be committed to the sex/gender binary in embodied ways that challenge the performative play and indeterminacy of transgender. Moreover, the disdain that some transgenderists express towards transsexual 'passing', as well as the postmodern suspicion of essentialism, may run contrary to the lived and embodied experiences of some transsexuals and intersexed people.

Transgender is central to the emergence of 'trans studies', an area of scholarship that also includes transdisciplinary, transnational and transcultural realms. Trans studies challenge the institutions and pervasive binaries of Western cultures. Trans, in its short form, can also be conceptualised as an identity referent for all those individuals (including some transsexuals) who embrace the umbrella aspect of transgender inclusiveness. This includes a consensus regarding the need to deal with the oppression of trans people made manifest in transphobia.

References and further reading

Bornstein, K. (1994) *Gender Outlaw*, London: Routledge.

Butler, J. (1990) *Gender Trouble*, London: Routledge.

Feinberg, L. (1993) *Stone Butch Blues*, New York: Firebrand.

Roen, K. (2001) 'Transgender theory and embodiment', *Journal of Gender Studies*, 10 (3): 253–63.

See also: postmodernism; queer masculinities; transsexual

CHRIS SHELLEY

TRANSSEXUAL

A transsexual is an individual who medically changes his or her embodied sexual characteristics in order to address a chronic incongruity between gender identity and the sexed body (male to female – MtF – or female to male – FtM). Transsexuals argue that without medically, legally and socially transitioning from one side of the sexed binary to the other, they will be doomed to live a life of embodied alienation with negative social, psychological and emotional consequences. Some transsexuals repress their gender incongruency for periods of their life, yet after transitioning they describe their previous existence as inauthentic, unhappy and unsustainable.

Transsexuals make use of surgeries and hormones to heal the (mis)sexed body. Critics of transsexuality, such as Sheila Jeffreys (2002) who draws on the earlier anti-transsexual writing of Janice Raymond, argue that transsexual people are victims of the patriarchal medical system. They claim that transsexuality is 'produced' solely through a false consciousness based on liberal conceptions of consumer choice. Such a view, however, repudiates the agency of transsexuals, disavowing their lived experience as well as the historical fact that transsexuals existed well before transsexual surgeries began in the 1920s. Other critics draw attention to the rare cases where individuals regret their transition and revert to living in their originally assigned sex/gender. Longitudinal studies in fact consistently demonstrate that most people who undergo sexual reassignment surgery experience no regrets and report feeling relieved from their long-standing *gender dysphoria* (the clinical term for their previous condition). Medical science did not produce the transsexual.

Rather, it responded to the chronic suffering of individuals whose sex/gender incongruity pre-existed surgical and hormonal innovations and was not healed through psychiatry and psychology (including psychoanalysis). Before the term 'transsexual' was coined in the 1940s, individuals who presented chronic gender incongruency were subsumed under problematic categories, as in the nineteenth-century discourse of the *invert*, which encompassed various manifestations of homosexuality.

In recent years the number of FtM transsexuals has increased, challenging the assumption that most transsexuals are MtF, which resulted from sensationalism surrounding some cases in the 1950s, such as that of Christine Jorgensen. Wide disparities still exist in the West regarding what treatments are considered medically necessary and therefore covered by health insurance.

References and further reading

Jeffreys, S. (2002) *Unpacking Queer Politics*, Cambridge: Polity.

Meyerowitz, J. (2002) *How Sex Changed*, Cambridge, MA: Harvard University Press.

Prosser, J. (1998) *Second Skins*, New York: Columbia University Press.

See also: transgender

CHRIS SHELLEY

TYRANNY AND DICTATORSHIP

Tyranny in its standard meaning designates a situation of extreme social inequality and repressive rule. Tyranny takes different forms across time and place, but a dictatorship that rules via terrible means is popularly thought to be typical. The paradigm of tyranny in the modern world is Nazi Germany, led by charismatic dictator Adolf Hitler. However, because most societies fall short of the extreme form yet manifest various degrees of hierarchy, inequity and oppression, it is useful to conceptualise social orders as lying along a continuum, with democracy at one end and tyranny at the other.

In a second sense, tyranny is a metaphor for situations wherein certain ideas and practices trump other ideas and practices. In the field of gender studies, Connell (1995) theorises that hegemonic masculinity defines women's roles while at the same time suppressing subordinate masculinities. By creating a situation in which prevailing gender relations seem normal, and by checking challenges to the status quo, heterosexual males impose a tyranny of masculinity over women, homosexuals and children. State and non-state actors using legal and extra-legal strategies and tactics (marriage, bullying, rape, etc.) reproduce hegemonic masculinity. (The major challenges to sociological explanations of male dominance emanate from sociobiology and evolutionary psychology, which hold that traditional masculinity and men's dominance have a biological-evolutionary basis. Upon closer inspection, this view is found to be an element of hegemonic masculinity and not an objective scientific position.)

What is of particular relevance to the present essay is the relationship between dominant ideologies of masculinity and tyrannies of various stripes. It is here that both meanings of tyranny, the literal and the metaphorical, come together in the intersection of gendered interpersonal relations and the larger societal structure. Values attendant to prescribed male-dominant gender roles predispose a population to acceptance of political tyranny in the first sense. In other words, people's ideological acceptance of hegemonic masculinity also encourages their assent to dictatorial political regimes. Societal tyranny in turn exaggerates group differences and intensifies oppressive gender relations, at the extreme generating hypermasculinities. It is no accident, then, that tyrannies should possess and emphasise such 'virtues' as aggression, competition and violence.

These associations are evident in the coercive methods with which oppressors achieve tyranny, methods that fall broadly under the category of warfare, chiefly police and military machinery. Collins (1975) theorises the empirical link between warfare and men's domination: conversely, men do not organise into military units, and approximate conditions of equality exist between men and women in societies in which military threats are few and the means of destruction are limited. In turn, military organisation emphasises aggression and violence, which are associated with the intensity of men's domination. More broadly, Connell (1997) documents that in the modern world violence is culturally masculinised, and men are its main agents.

The intersection of prescribed gender roles and political-military tyranny is readily found in fascist dictatorships. For example, in what Burleigh and Wippermann (1991) call the 'barbarous utopia', subordination of women and glorification of masculine images and values reflect the centrality of patriarchal relations in Nazi constructions of the state. In 1933, prominent anti-fascist Wilhelm Reich theorised that authoritarian society is reproduced by the authoritarian family, a conclusion later confirmed by Nazi actions that removed women from the workplace and sharply limited their numbers entering college. The regime established the Reich Mothers' Service to promote a eugenic vision of a 'New Germany', criminalising abortion for healthy 'Aryan' women and sterilising and euthanising the 'unfit'. The patriarchal-tyrannical rule of Fascism thus reached into the womb. In turn, warrior men became the subjects of adulation, especially Hitler, with propaganda depicting the Führer as the ideal type of male virility. Theweleit concluded that fascist writings 'revolve around the same central axes: the community of the male society [and escape] from a world that is rotten and sinking (from the morass of femaleness)' ([1987] 1989: II, 361).

The fascist vision of the 'healthy' family also affected homosexuals. Hitler's violent purge of leading associates was in part justified by alleging 'sexual deviance' among its members, most notably Staff Chief Röhm, an openly homosexual Nazi. Homosexuals were labelled 'sexual subversives' and 'sexual saboteurs', and after Röhm the Nazis registered all persons engaged in homosexual activities (the so-called 'pink lists'). The regime focused on high-profile homosexuals both to eliminate opposition and to draw attention to the Nazi campaign to portray hegemonic masculinity as central to the rebirth of the German nation as a pure biological and moral entity.

Oppressive gender relations occur in a matrix of domination that includes class and race. For example, the tyranny of masculinity reinforces violent practices of white supremacy, namely the extra-legal practice of the lynching of black people – often justified as retribution for the alleged crime of interracial rape and including ritual emasculation of the accused. While the affirmation of whiteness is explicit in these crimes, less obvious is the affirmation of men's dominance over women. Such moments channel and concentrate the masculinity inherent in patriarchal societies, even those with a presumably democratic and liberal character, reminding us that tyranny is an ever present threat in segmented societies.

References and further reading

Bowker, L.H. (ed.) (1998) *Masculinities and Violence*, Thousand Oaks, CA: Sage.

Burleigh, M. and Wippermann, W. (1991) *The Racial State*, Cambridge: Cambridge University Press.

Collins, R. (1975) *Conflict Sociology*, New York: Academic Press.

Connell, R. (1987) *Gender and Power*, Sydney: Allen and Unwin.

—— (1995) *Masculinities*, Sydney: Allen and Unwin.

—— (1997) 'Arms and the man', Expert Group Meeting on Male Roles and Masculinities in the Perspective of a Culture of Peace, UNESCO, Oslo, Norway, 24–28 September.

Griffin, R. (ed.) (1995) *Fascism*, Oxford: Oxford University Press.

Reich, W. (1946) *The Mass Psychology of Fascism*, New York: Orgone Institute.

Theweleit, K. [1987] (1989) *Male Fantasies*, 2 vols, Cambridge: Polity.

See also: aggression; armies; bullying; families; Fascism and Nazism; hegemonic masculinity; lynching; patriarchy; power relations; rape; subordinate masculinity; violence, organisational and collective; war

ANDREW AUSTIN

U

UNIONS/ORGANISED LABOUR MOVEMENTS

Feminist research reveals that many unions remain dominated by men and are still characterised by highly masculine policies, structures, cultures and practices. Trade unions were originally established as a collective response by working people designed to counter employer practices that were deemed unfair, exploitative or discriminatory. A key strength of the union movement has always been its collectivity, typically expressed in the motto 'unity is strength'. It is somewhat ironic, then, that organisations set up with the expressed aim to improve workplace equity and fairness should themselves be criticised for reinforcing various inequities (such as status, gender and ethnicity).

Within Western capitalist economies, unions were most influential in the middle of the twentieth century. The influence of UK unions and the extent of their membership began to decline after the election of Margaret Thatcher in 1979 (although they still tend to retain more power than their US counterparts). It may be partly because of this reducing influence that the male dominance of unions has been neglected by critical studies of men and masculinity, an area of research that has grown during this same period.

Most of the research on gender within trade unions has been conducted by feminist women writers. In particular, they have examined the ways in which male-dominated unions have maintained a policy of either excluding women altogether or ensuring their segregation into subordinated, low-paid and insecure forms of employment (Walby 1986). Union officials have often seen women as a threat to male employment levels and pay because employers often use women as 'cheap labour'. In certain jobs and industries women's entry is also seen as a challenge to the gendered view of specific skills being the exclusive province of men. Cockburn (1983) examined the exclusionary labour market practices of the UK print unions. She revealed how the National Graphical Association (NGA), as a male-dominated craft union, historically sustained its members' wages by resisting women's entry into printing.

Feminist researchers have also explored the internal dynamics of unions, revealing how their masculine cultures often constitute an important barrier to women's participation. They document women's historical and contemporary struggles to be recognised and heard within union cultures that are predominantly male, white and working-class. Studies reveal the masculine governance of unions, how men remain dominant in terms of union participation rates, hierarchy profiles, activism rates and membership (Rees 1992). Although there has been a growth in women's labour market participation and union membership, this has not been matched by proportionate increases in female representation in lay or full-time union positions.

Men's numerical dominance can also shape union policies and strategies. For example, unions have often neglected important 'women's issues' such as equal pay, maternity leave, job segregation and job sex-typing, part-time work, childcare, maternity leave and sexual harassment. Quinn (2004) examines trade union activity in representing claimants at equality officer investigations in the Irish Republic. She found that union use of the Equality Act over twenty-five years had been mainly reactive rather than strategic. At best, unions merely followed members who had initiated claims. At worst, they supported discriminatory agreements with employers against members' claims. She concludes that the patriarchal trade union tradition is continuing in Ireland.

Cunnison and Stageman (1995) show how different unions are characterised by various mechanisms of male control. Parker (2003) examines the reasons for unions' 'under-engagement' with women. Comparing the proportion of women union members in the ten largest UK unions with the proportion of women in key posts within union hierarchies, she argues that paid union official posts remain disproportionately dominated by men. Those women who have progressed within union hierarchies tended to be older, single and without dependent children, typically conforming to the 'masculine' job model of a union official with a long unbroken record of activism and full-time employment. Roby and Uttal (1993) found that Canadian female stewards with children tended to reduce their union work outside work time in order to prioritise family commitments. In contrast, their male counterparts often allowed union work to spill over into non-work time and relied heavily on the support of their wives.

This male dominance of the union movement can also facilitate the emergence of aggressive forms of (men's) sexuality and of sexual harassment within trade unions (Collinson and Collinson 1989). It may also inform a tendency for union officials to mismanage members' claims of sexual harassment, especially by seeking to 'keep the lid' on these issues through highly informal mechanisms (Collinson and Collinson 1992).

References and further reading

Cockburn C. (1983) *Brothers*, London: Pluto Press.

Collinson, D. and Collinson, M. (1989) 'Sexuality in the workplace: the domination of men's sexuality', in J. Hearn, D. Sheppard, P. Tancred-Sheriff and G. Burrell (eds) *The Sexuality of Organization*, London: Sage, pp. 91–109.

—— (1992) 'Mismanaging sexual harassment: blaming the victim and protecting the perpetrator', *Women and Management Review*, 7, 7: 11–17.

Cunnison, S. and Stageman, J. (1995) *Feminizing the Unions*, Aldershot: Avebury.

Parker J. (2003) *Women's Groups and Equality in British Trade Unions*, Lampeter: Edwin Mellen Press.

Quinn, M. (2004) 'Trade unions, gender and claims under Irish employment equality legislation', *Gender Work and Organization*, 11 (6): 648–67.

Rees, T. (1992) *Women and the Labour Market*, London: Routledge.

Roby, P. and Uttal, L. (1993) 'Putting it all together: the dilemmas of rank-and-file union leaders', in D. Cobble (ed.) *Women and Unions*, New York: ILR Press, pp. 365–77.

Walby, S. (1986) *Patriarchy at Work*, Cambridge: Polity Press.

See also: class, work and masculinity

MARGARET COLLINSON

V

VIAGRA

Viagra is a prescription drug designed to treat erection difficulties; sildenafil citrate increases blood flow to the penis during sexual arousal. Made available by the Pfizer Corporation in 1998, the 'little blue pill' is advertised to improve sex lives of men with erectile dysfunction (ED). Viagra continues the medicalisation of masculinity, sexuality and the penis. Impotent becomes what the man is, not a condition he has, and Viagra claims to be the solution to this crisis. Sexuality and masculinity require that the penis penetrate and remain erect.

Pfizer has successfully medicalised the penis and sexuality by constructing ED as an epidemic that needs fixing. In 2005, Viagra's advertising told men to 'get back to mischief', which is equated with the ability to keep an erection and have sexual intercourse. That this is equated with naughtiness further fuels the correlation between masculinity and being a 'bad boy' or even violent. This phallocentrism equates a man's ability to be confident and powerful with the functioning of his penis. Men experiencing impotence are encouraged, through the discourse surrounding Viagra, to feel unworthy, self-conscious and unvalued: at most, unmanly.

Viagra is paid for by many insurance companies in the United States, demonstrating that it is a problem worthy of compensation and attention. To not tend to ED when hegemonically masculine men do (in advertising featuring sports stars, for instance) and insurance companies cover the drug is the ultimate betrayal of one's masculinity. Flexibility in masculinities and variation in displays of sexualities are not allowed under Viagra's rule. This implicates how we envision ageing, masculinity, sexuality and 'sexual performance'. Viagra and related drugs send the message that broken masculinity can and should be fixed with biotechnology.

References and further reading

Bordo, S. (1998) 'Penis and power tools', *Men and Masculinities*, 1: 87–90.

—— (2000) *The Male Body*, New York: Farrar, Straus and Giroux.

Loe, M. (2004) *The Rise of Viagra*, New York: New York University Press.

Morgantaler, A. (2003) *The Viagra Myth*, San Francisco, CA: Jossey-Bass.

Rubin, R. (2004) 'Men talking about Viagra', *Men and Masculinities*, 7: 22–30.

Tiefer, L. (2004) *Sex is Not a Natural Act and Other Essays*, Boulder, CO: Westview.

See also: age and ageing; aphrodisiacs; impotence and sexual dysfunction; penetration; penis; phallocentrism; sperm, semen; testosterone; virility

AMI LYNCH

VIOLENCE

This entry does not provide an overview of the whole range of men's violences (Hearn 1998). Many of the relevant issues are already addressed in a broad range of other entries noted at the end of this entry. This present essay partly responds to the task of bringing together analyses of different kinds of violence, including organisational and collective violence, military violence, rape and violence to women in the home. It also addresses another key question (Hearn and Pringle 2006): how do men's gendered practices intersect with other oppressive power relations around sexuality, cultural difference/ethnicity, age, disability and class, and what are the implications of such analyses for challenging those practices and assisting those abused?

Whilst acknowledging that some women engage in acts of violence and that clearly not all men are violent (Hearn 1998), this entry starts from a recognition that

> in modern Western and many other societies, men are the experts, the specialists, in the doing of violence. There are a multitude of connections and associations between the way violence is perpetuated in society and the ways men socially construct themselves/ourselves and are socially constructed.
>
> (Hearn 1996: 99)

This essay is also premised upon the understanding that men's violence represents a huge problem world-wide. In concluding their edited collection that surveys men's practices across the world, Pease and Pringle consider the commonalities across men's practices – some of them very negative – in various countries:

> The most important of these is the broad and global extent of men's violence towards women, children and other men . . . Thus the material in this book contributes in a major way to our awareness of an often neglected but absolutely essential fact: men's violence represents one of the most massive global social problems.
>
> (Pringle and Pease 2001: 246)

Moreover, a recent large-scale and systematic re-evaluation of data on men's practices across fourteen European countries highlighted that violence against known women is becoming recognised as a major social problem in most of the fourteen countries. Hearn and Pringle (2006) also add that a recent Council of Europe report has noted that for women between fifteen and forty-four years old, domestic violence is considered the major cause of death and injury. The fourteen-country European review concluded (Hearn and Pringle 2006):

> first, that men's violences to women, children and to some extent other men represent a massive form of social exclusion themselves; and, second, men's violences, together with dominant and dominating ways of being a man, are intimately connected with the dynamics of racism – another profound form of social exclusion.

The review also confirmed the pervasiveness of men's violences insofar as they clearly interconnected in complex ways with a very wide range of men's practices associated with issues such as home and work or health.

This present essay seeks to conceptualise the huge and diverse problem of men's violences within some broader theoretical understandings of men's practices and masculinities. It is clear that a whole series of frames of understanding are available, and indeed have been used at various times in various places. These range from the biological and genetic through various psychological (including psychoanalytic) perspectives; through role theory and a variety of socialisation approaches as well as cultural/sub-cultural explanations; and, more recently, to more multi-causal and/or power-oriented and/or postmodern frames (Hearn 1998, and see also Archer 1994). The more recent recognition of the need for multi-causal explanations of men's violences only partly arises from the fact that such violences are themselves diverse. In fact, multi-causality also reflects a growing awareness that the processes underpinning the generation of men's violences are immensely complex and therefore a multi-dimensional analysis is necessary.

In the space available here, we examine only two of a number of suggested conceptual frames for analysing the complexity of men's violence. They are in many ways complementary and closely related. For instance, both partly build on the theoretical model of *masculinity/masculinities* developed by R. Connell (1987, 2002) and both make explicit use of 'intersectionality' and 'mutual constitution' perspectives on power relations (West and Fenstermaker 1995).

The first frame is that developed by Messerschmidt (1997) as part of his broader approach to men and crime. In summarising Messerschmidt's frame as it relates to violence, we focus on his classic study of lynching in the post-Civil War United States (1998). Messerschmidt locates men's violences within the dynamics of gender, race and class oppression 'viewed as *structured action* – what people do under specific social structural constraints' (1998: 128). Echoing West and Fenstermaker, Connell and Giddens (1984), he concludes that 'the accomplishment of gender, race and class occurs simultaneously through social interaction, and ... social actors perpetuate and transform these social structures within the same interaction; simultaneously these structures constrain and enable gender, race and class social action' (1998: 128–9).

As a point of clarification, Messerschmidt adds: 'the salience of each social relation to *influencing crime* varies by social situation. Although gender, race and class are ubiquitous, the significance of each relation shifts with a changing context' (1998: 129). The meanings of this for the generation of violent crime are clear: 'This perspective permits us to conceptualise masculinities and violence more realistically and completely, enables us to explore how and in what respects masculinity is constituted in certain settings at certain times, and how that construct relates to crime' (1998: 131).

The second conceptual frame for analysing the complexity of men's violences that is explored here builds, in a sense, on Messerschmidt's and is to be found in the work of the present author (Pringle 1995, 2005). As noted earlier, Messerschmidt drew heavily on Connell's broader theoretical model regarding masculinities and, in particular, hegemonic forms of masculinity. Interestingly, Connell herself has never really applied her model of gender relations to the specific issue of men's violences in any depth. Pringle's 1995 study of men and social welfare explicitly sought to test out Connell's model in relation to the empirical evidence we possessed about the potential dynamics of men's violences, especially social psychological evidence (Archer 1994; Pringle 1995: 94–8). In fact, the primary focus at that time was on men's sexual violences, but the conclusions may well be valid for men's violences more broadly.

Drawing partly on the earlier work of Liddle (1993), Pringle demonstrated how Connell's (1987) three-fold structures – labour, power and, in particular, cathexis – can be used very effectively to illuminate the complex dynamics of men's violences and to assist in developing strategies for challenging such violences (Pringle 1995: 177–80). More recently of course, Connell (2002) has also recognised a fourth, symbolic dimension underpinning the development of hegemonic configurations of men's practices. This symbolic dimension can certainly also be applied to the processes associated with the generation of men's violences. For instance, in Messerschmidt's analysis of lynching, there is a clear recognition of the symbolic force and meaning of that phenomenon (Messerschmidt 1998: 148).

At that time, Pringle also highlighted the clear potential within Connell's explanatory model for incorporating the concept of complex interconnecting power relations within the processes generating the violences of men. In later work (for example, Pringle 2005), Pringle explicitly related such interconnections to the concepts of intersectionality and mutual constitution of power relations (West and Fenstermaker 1995). In 1995 (Pringle 1995: 175) Pringle had already suggested that men's violences cannot be explained adequately only by reference to gendered power relations: instead, one needed to consider the complex and shifting interconnections of a range of power dimensions including those associated with gender, ethnicity, age, sexuality, disability and class.

It is important to acknowledge that both the conceptual frames outlined here for exploring the complex dynamics of men's violences have several major limitations. First, each of them uses a series of conceptual tools, almost all of which derive from one, albeit rather broad, cultural context: the so-called 'English-speaking' world. One therefore has to keep an open mind about the extent to which such tools may or may not be applicable in other cultural contexts. For instance, even in a context which is relatively close, such as the Nordic countries, care must be exercised. As Eriksson (2003) has pointed out, West and Fenstermaker's concept of 'doing difference' as a means to inequality may often be very useful in analysing social situations in the Nordic countries, but it needs to be supplemented by a recognition that 'doing sameness' can also be a powerful strategy for promoting inequality in that particular cultural context. For example, it has been suggested (Pringle 2005) that the extremely visible profile of gender equality discourses – and indeed social collectivist discourses more generally – in the Nordic countries has partly hindered acknowledgement of the high level in men's violence to women in Finland and Sweden. Moreover, it may be partly for the same reason that Norway and Sweden have hitherto failed to play an important European role in the researching of men's violences while they have been key European players in researching the topic of gender relations and work (Hearn and Pringle 2006). It has also been argued (Eriksson 2003) that the process of 'doing sameness' through gender equality discourses has played a central role in the previous tendency of Swedish courts to sometimes award joint custody of children to fathers who had a clear record of violence to their relationship partners. If one has to be so careful even when dealing with contexts relatively close, in cultural terms, to those of the 'English-speaking' world, then clearly considerable caution must be exercised when addressing contexts that are even more culturally diverse.

However, a further, perhaps even more salient, limitation of the Messerschmidt and Pringle frames exists – and this applies to most work in the field. The two frames may well assist us in exploring the complex dynamics of how and why men's violences do occur. Yet they both seem relatively silent when it comes to helping us understand the complex dynamics of why some men do not engage in violent behaviours. This question is of great importance for the future well-being of all of us – and yet we are relatively ignorant about the potential answers. It may be that ongoing research elaborating the intersecting or mutually constituting relations of power will assist us more with that question in the future. Similarly, another key to the issue may be further and more detailed studies of both men's violences and their non-violences in specific interstices of time and space.

More broadly, despite considerable research in many parts of the world on numerous aspects of the topic, the fact remains that the problem of men's violences is still a disturbingly closed book with many gaps awaiting further research – and action (Hearn and Pringle 2006).

References and further reading

Archer, J. (1994) *Male Violence*, London: Routledge.

Connell, R. (1987) *Gender and Power*, Cambridge: Polity.

—— (2002) *Gender*, Cambridge: Polity.

Hearn, J. (1996) 'Men's violence to known women', in B. Fawcett, B. Featherstone, J. Hearn and C. Toft (eds) *Violence and Gender Relations*, London: Sage, pp. 99–114.

—— (1998) *The Violences of Men*, London: Sage.

Eriksson, M. (2003) *I skuggan av Pappa* (In the Shadow of Daddy), Stehag: Förlags AB Gondolin.

Giddens, A. (1984) *The Constitution of Society*, Cambridge: Polity.

Hearn, J. (1998) *The Violences of Men*, London: Sage.

Hearn, J. and Pringle, K. (2006) 'Men's violences', in J. Hearn and K. Pringle, with members of Critical Research on Men in Europe, *European Perspectives on Men and Masculinities*, Houndmills: Palgrave Macmillan.

Liddle, A.M. (1993) 'Gender, desire and child sexual abuse', *Theory, Culture and Society*, 10: 103–26.

Messerschmidt, J.W. (1997) *Crime as Structured Action*, Thousand Oaks, CA: Sage.

—— (1998) 'Men victimising men', in L.H. Bowker (ed.) *Masculinities and Violence*, Thousand Oaks, CA: Sage.

Pringle, K. (1995) *Men, Masculinities and Social Welfare*, London: UCL Press.

—— (2005) 'Neglected issues in Swedish child protection policy and practice', in M. Eriksson, M. Hester, S. Keskinen and K. Pringle (eds) *Tackling Men's Violence in Families*, Bristol: Policy, pp. 155–71.

Pringle, K. and Pease, B. (2001) 'Afterword', in B. Pease and K. Pringle (eds) *A Man's World?* London: Zed Books, pp. 245–52.

West, C. and Fenstermaker, S. (1995) 'Doing difference', *Gender and Society*, 9 (1): 8–37.

See also: child abuse; crime, criminality and law; domestic violence; fatherhood and violence; military institutions; military masculinities; sexual violence; torture; violence, men as victims of; violence, organisational and collective; violence, sport; violence, workplace

KEITH PRINGLE

VIOLENCE, MEN AS VICTIMS OF

The victims of violence often are male. This is true in particular of collective, public forms of violence (in wars, political conflicts, street and gang violence). For example, in areas of political conflict such as Palestine or Northern Ireland, young men have a greater exposure to and participation in violence than young women (Reilly *et al.* 2004). However, males also comprise a significant proportion of the victims of violence in relationships and families. The perpetrators of these diverse forms of violence also are predominantly male. Boys and men are most at risk from other boys and men, and much violence is male-to-male. At the same time, males also are subjected to violence by female perpetrators.

The gendered character of men's subjection to violence often has gone unremarked. Scholars and policy-makers have neglected the ways in which this violence is shaped by and itself helps to constitute social codes and relations of masculinity. However, there is now growing scholarship on the gendered character of male victimisation, in such settings as wars and civil conflicts, gangs and street violence, prisons, schools, workplaces and other institutional contexts, and relationships and families.

The high incidence and typical dynamics of male–male violence reflect and themselves define the norms and relations of manhood. In contexts where dominant constructions of masculinity emphasise aggressiveness, entitlement to power and emotional callousness, males are more likely both to use violence and to be subjected to violence. Men's subjection to violence in many cultures often represents performances of masculinity by other men. For example, gay men and those perceived to be gay are assaulted by young men intent on proving their masculinity and heterosexuality. Violence may be used as a resource in achieving masculinity – as part of a repertoire of behaviours that define and emphasise particular forms of masculinity (Messerschmidt 1997). For some young men, violent behaviour is perceived as inevitable, compulsory, an appropriately masculine and heterosexual response to conflict, as having substantial rewards, and as respected by young women who are attracted to 'hard' men (Reilly *et al.* 2004). Such social codes take their toll on many men in terms of physical injury, ill health and death.

Male-on-male violence is the most common form of public violence, and men comprise the majority of victims of homicide and public assaults. Assaults in public venues are often the result of contests over male honour (Polk 1994). Minor incidents can set off lethal violence. Men may swap insults, argue, challenge each other's strength or manhood, or defend their honour in front of their male peers. Group drinking, rowdiness, arguing and fighting are pleasurable forms of entertainment for some men, as are power struggles with authority figures such as the police. Male victimisation is the outcome too of ritualised forms of male–male violence in the initiation and participation rituals of university fraternities, workplaces and other contexts.

Sex-selective mass killings of males are a gendered component of political and military conflicts (Carpenter 2002). Abuses and atrocities have been systematically perpetrated against non-combatant men, from the Stalinist purges in the 1930s and 1940s to more recent conflicts in Indonesia, Bangladesh, Cambodia and East Timor. There is growing recognition of the sexual torture of men. During the war in the former Yugoslavia in the early 1990s, substantial numbers of men were subjected to forced sexual acts, castration, genital beatings and electroshock. One study found that three-quarters of male political prisoners in El Salvador had been subjected to sexual torture (Oosterhoff *et al.* 2004).

Other forms of male subjection to violence are almost entirely socially legitimate. On-field aggression is routine in male-dominated contact sports such as American football, ice hockey and rugby, and may even constitute the sport itself, as is the case in boxing, wrestling and other martial arts. In these contexts, violence to men and by men is normative, codified (albeit bound by certain rules) and celebrated.

Where there has been public debate in Western countries regarding violence to men, it has often focused on violence by female partners. Yet this represents only a tiny proportion of the physical abuse to which men are subjected. For example, in a four-year study of admissions to the Emergency Department of an American hospital, over 8,000 men had been assaulted and injured. Of these, only forty-five men were injured by their intimate female partners or ex-partners, representing 0.55 per cent of male assault visits (Muelleman and Burgess 1998). While some studies find apparent gender symmetries in subjection to domestic violence, others suggest that in heterosexual relationships men are far less likely than women to experience frequent, prolonged, and extreme violence, sustain injuries, fear for their lives, be sexually assaulted or experience post-separation violence (Flood 2005).

Gender norms and relations also shape males' responses to victimisation. Being able to respond aggressively and heroically to other men's physical aggression often is a marker of manhood. Stories of withstanding aggression, and the scars which accompany these, can be badges of manliness, which embody courage, adventure and street toughness. Men who show pain or weakness risk being seen as feminised and homosexualised. Males' ability to admit to, recover from, and seek help for their abuse is constrained by masculine stoicism, homophobic taboos and laws (in cases involving male–male sexual assault), and stereotypical views in health care and other institutions of men as aggressors and women as victims.

References and further reading

Carpenter, R.C. (2002) 'Beyond "gendercide"', *International Journal of Human Rights*, 6: 77–101.

Flood, M. (2005) 'Domestic violence', in M. Kimmel and A. Aronson (eds) *Encyclopedia of Men and Masculinities*, Santa Barbara, CA: ABC-Clio, pp. 234–9.

Messerschmidt, J.W. (1997) *Crime as Structured Action*, Thousand Oaks, CA: Sage.

Oosterhoff, P., Zwanikken, P. and Ketting, E. (2004) 'Sexual torture of men in Croatia and other conflict situations', *Reproductive Health Matters*, 12: 68–77.

Muelleman, R.L. and Burgess, P. (1998) 'Male victims of domestic violence and their history of perpetrating violence', *Academic Emergency Medicine*, September, 5 (9): 866–70.

Polk, K. (1994) *When Men Kill*, Cambridge and New York: Cambridge University Press.

Reilly, J., Muldoon, O.T. and Byrne, C. (2004) 'Young men as victims and perpetrators of violence in Northern Ireland', *Journal of Social Issues*, 60: 469–84.

MICHAEL FLOOD

VIOLENCE, ORGANISATIONAL AND COLLECTIVE

The recognition of the importance of gender and sexuality in organisations in feminist theory and practice has provided the groundwork for analysing organisations through the perspective of violence. Violence can be *in, by* or *around* organisations and collectivities (Hearn and Parkin 2001). This contribution focuses on the second and third elements, as the first is discussed in the entry on violence, workplace. In addition, organisations and collectivities can respond to violence elsewhere. Collectivities can be more or less organised, ranging from established social movements to political groupings and networks – for the status quo, revolutionary or some other agenda – to less organised crowds and mobs, in both national and international contexts (Zalewski and Parpart 1998). Collective violence can also be considered in terms of societal structural explanations of men's individually orientated violence, for example, to (ex-)wives or partners, but this aspect of collectivity is not specifically addressed in this entry.

In a broad, socially contextualised understanding of violence as violation, violence can be defined as structures, actions, events and experiences that violate or cause violation or are considered as violating. Violence can include physical violence, harassment and bullying, intimidation, interrogation, surveillance, persecution, subjugation, discrimination and exclusion that lead to experiences of violation (Hearn 1998). Violations include use of force or potential force; structured oppression; harassment, bullying and physical violences; and mundane, everyday violations within organisations and collectivities. Bringing together analyses of different kinds of violence, such as organisational and collective violence, military violence, rape and violence to women in the home is a key challenge

Men's violence, organisational and collective, is a major element in the perpetuation of men's power and a necessary object of analysis and intervention in feminist and profeminist theory and practice. Domination by men is characteristically associated with violence. Dominant forms of violence as violation by organisations involve violence by men to women, children and other men. They range across physical, sexual, verbal, emotional, psychological and representational attacks, threats and degradations; use of weapons and other objects; destruction of property; rape; and murder. Homicide and most other violence is mainly perpetrated by men.

Violence and violation figure in relation to organisations and collectivities in many ways. At the macro, collective extra-organisational level, there is the impact of structural violations. Violence and violations are closely linked, but not totally determined, by structural power differences, including patriarchal social structural relations; systems of capitalist and imperialist exploitation; and national and cultural exclusions, structural racism and xenophobia. The very existence of organisations and collectivities can be violating. Violation also figures in the contexts and formation of organisations. This may involve the reproduction of institutional violations, even of whole societies, including the creation of the conditions for violence.

This links to how men's violence is organised in different societies. Howell and Willis (1989) found that different societal definitions of masculinity had a significant impact on men's propensity for violence. In societies where men were permitted to acknowledge fear, levels of violence tended to be low. In those where masculine bravado and denial of fear were defining features of masculinity, violence was likely to be high. Societies where such bravado is prescribed for men tended to be those in which the definitions of masculinity and femininity are very highly differentiated. Generally, the less gender differentiation between women and men, the more men are nurturing and caring, or can express fear, and the more women are seen as capable, rational and competent in the public sphere, the less likely is men's violence. To diminish different societal levels of men's violence means reducing that violence done in the name of mythic entities of nation, religion or blood, along with strict control of men's use of guns, weapons and organised violences.

At the meso level, organisations and collectivities can be seen as sites of violence and violation, and constellations of violent/violating, potentially or threatened violent/violating actions, behaviours, intentions and experiences. A key set of questions concerns specific organisational orientations to violation: the place of violence and violation in the aims and tasks of organisations, and collectivities too. One way of conceptualising this is the recognition that organisations can have *explicit* or *implicit* orientations to violation. Explicit relations include: (a) legitimated use of violence and violation by organisations (e.g. state, sport, schools); (b) organisations created to respond to violence and violation (e.g. criminal justice system, anti-violence/peace organisations); (c) organisations explicitly responding to violence and violation in other ways. Implicit relations include: (d) illegitimated use of and violation by managers/owners (e.g. capitalist, counter-state); (e) organisations where other violence and violation is used (e.g. resistance organisations); (f) organisations where violence and violation are not overt issues (Hearn and Parkin 2001).

At the level of micro processes and practices, violence and violations by organisations and collectivities can be ways of reinforcing relations of domination and subordination; developing resistance; refining gradations of status and power; facilitating alliances, coalitions, inclusions, exclusions and scapegoating; and forming identities. Violation can be dramatic or subtle, occasional or continuous, chronic and endemic (as in slave workplaces), generally invisible and 'unnecessary' (as inequalities are so entrenched), normalised and naturalised (as in acceptance of sexual harassment as part of some jobs), an indication of changing power relations (through challenging previous power relations) or a reassertion of power by dominant groups (as in men's responses to women's power).

Men can relate to all these various forms of violence and violations, organisational and collective, as the sole or main or more random doers and/or the receivers or targets of violence. Violence may be done mainly to other men, mainly to women and children, or more randomly to people, regardless of gender. In some cases men are specifically targeted by men, including using boys and younger men to harm older men of their own ethnic or other category, as in gendercide (Jones 2004). Indeed, the collective, historical power of men may be understood as maintained by the dispensability of some men, as with soldiers in war, even with the violence to women and children, usually as non-combatants.

The interconnections of men, violences, organisations and collectivities are perhaps clearest in the case of the military and paramilitary (Higate 2003; Higate and Hopton 2005). They are among the obvious arenas of men's violence and killing. Military matters are urgent and powerful; how 'war and peace' proceed, and how armies and their members are organised and act, are literally questions of life and death. This applies in 'wars of resistance', 'just wars', 'terrorism', 'peacekeeping' or simply 'peacetime'. The organisation of war has become more complex in recent years, with UN peacekeepers, military outsourcing, counter-terrorism, and private security, policing and mercenary organisations. Many are transnational in their interests, most intensely male-dominated.

Despite this, discussions of men, masculinities, the military, militarism and other collective political violence, such as revolutions, insurrections, state and non-state terrorism, have generally not been put together. The connections have often either been taken for granted or gone unnoticed for other reasons. Men, militarism and political violence are historically, profoundly and blatantly interconnected. Many armies and other fighting forces have been composed exclusively of men, young men and boys. Yet already there are some complications.

First, it is important not to presume that all armies consist of men. The historical interrelations of men and militarism should not obscure the significance of women's military activity at particular times and places. For example, in the mid-nineteenth century it was estimated that out of the king of Dahomey's 12,000 strong army, 5,000 were women. In the 1941 Yugoslav Liberation War about 100,000 women carried arms as active fighters, 25,000 were killed in action, 40,000 were wounded (Oakley 1972: 145). Over 10,000 women took part in the Algerian Liberation War armed struggle, of whom a fifth suffered imprisonment or death. Women's involvement in nation-formation, as in struggles against colonial and imperialist powers, has often been formidable, only to be later undermined with the move to 'peace' (Knauss 1987). Second, even armies and other military institutions formally made up of men often have women in servicing or administrative positions. Third, the impact of such military masculinities upon those outside the military – women, men and children – is often huge. Fourth, the exact nature of the connections between men and the military are themselves various and plural – hence there are military masculinities, and not just military masculinity.

As is clear from feminist scholarship, these are matters of politics and social organisation, gender and sexuality, rather than biology. Future work needs to attend to dominant constructions of military masculinities, to deconstruct and question those often naturalised military masculinities. Such complicating issues need to be taken up in terms of the complex and variable relation of identities and the state. The growth of the modern military state has been very closely associated with the formation, organisation and modernisation and management of national armies. The modern state has become a major controller of violence, and a major producer of violence, injury, fear, torture and death. The scale of very largely manmade (*sic*) death, often organised quite specifically by states, para-states and counter-states, is difficult to appreciate. Men have dominated these individual and collective actions.

The extreme case might appear to be the destructive machinery of the state under the Nazi regime of the Third Reich. However, there are many other examples of mass persecutions by states, para-states and counter-states in recent history, in the Soviet Union, China, South East Asia, East and Central Africa, the Balkans and elsewhere. One of the greatest state violences in the 'postwar' period is the US bombing of Cambodia (Kampuchea). In order to destroy sanctuaries where Vietnamese had fled for safety, the US began secret bombing in 1970–3, killing an estimated 150,000 Cambodians with more than 500,000 tons of bombs, more than three times the tonnage used against Japan in the Second World War, and creating over a million refugees. Following this, Pol Pot and the Khmer Rouge took over in 1975, with the 'killing fields' over the next four years claiming an estimated 1.7 million people.

The relation of the military and identities is complex. The making of 'military male gender' is a practical, continuous, social accomplishment. Mundane military processes, such as military training, can have major impacts upon individuals and groups. Military organisations provide social and psychological resources for the reproduction and changing of individual psychologies (Dixon 1976), often around violence. These include the processes of rationalisation, distancing, 'role' following, obeying orders and trivialisation. Bomber crews may adopt trivialising, casual, ironic and supposedly humorous phrases, such as 'There goes the cookie', in continuing their bombing without too much direct thought for their bombs' impact upon others (Johnson 1986; Smith 1993).

Relations of states and identities are subject to historical change. The construction of men and masculinities in and around state and nation has often been very closely allied to the development of complex, sometimes contradictory, military identities. Morgan (1994) has examined interconnections between militarism and dominant, and occasionally counter, masculinities. He stressed how both the 'boundedness' and 'pervasiveness' of militarism seem strongly linked to its coding as masculine. There are also intense contradictions to be observed – between hypermasculinity and misogyny on one hand, and 'softer', more tender masculinities on the other, not least in the throes of military survival. The recognition of contradiction and plurality should not obscure the persistence and immensity of military violence and violation. There may appear to be a contemporary weakening of the links of dominant, violent masculinity and militarism, within current politics of war, peacekeeping and human rights. However, more likely is that new associations between militarism and masculinism may arise in so-called 'post-militarist' societies.

In making sense of all these matters, questions of space and place, ground and land, domain and terrain, whether the personal space of the body or the extended domain of the nation, are persistently important. Much militarism, especially nation-based militarism, is 'international' or 'transnational' by definition and ambition. The geographies of military, organisational and collective violences are often plain to see, if not always to decipher.

References and further reading

Dixon, N. (1976) *On the Psychology of Military Incompetence*, London: Jonathan Cape.

Hearn, J. (1998) *The Violences of Men*, London: Sage.

Hearn, J. and Parkin, W. (2001) *Gender, Sexuality and Violence in Organizations: The Unspoken Forces of Organization Violations*, London: Sage.

Higate, P. (2003) *Military Masculinities: Identity and the State*, Westport, CT: Praeger.

Higate, P. and Hopton, J. (2005) 'War, militarism, and masculinities', in M. Kimmel, J. Hearn and R. Connell (eds) *Handbook of Studies on Men and Masculinities*, Thousand Oaks, CA: Sage, pp. 432–47.

Howell, S. and Willis, R. (eds) (1989) *Societies at Peace: Anthropological Perspectives*, Boston, MA: Routledge.

Johnson, R. (1986) 'Institutions and the promotion of violence', in A. Campbell and J.J. Gibbs (eds) *Violent Transactions*, Oxford: Blackwell, pp. 181–205.

Jones, A. (ed.) (2004) *Gendercide and Genocide*, Nashville, TN: Vanderbilt University Press.

Knauss, P.R. (1987) *The Persistence of Patriarchy: Class, Gender, and Ideology in Twentieth Century Algeria*, New York: Praeger.

Morgan, D. (1994) 'Theater of war: combat, the military and masculinities', in H. Brod and M. Kaufman (eds) *Theorizing Masculinities*, Thousand Oaks, CA: Sage, pp. 165–82.

Oakley, A. (1972) *Sex, Gender and Society*, London: Temple Smith.

Smith, J. (1993) *Misogynies*, London: Faber & Faber.

Zalewski, M. and Parpart, J.L. (eds) (1998) *The 'Man' Question in International Relations*, Boulder, CO: Westview.

See also: domestic violence; men's relations with women; military institutions; violence; war

JEFF HEARN

VIOLENCE, SPORT

Messner (2005) has usefully situated the normalisation of violence in sport in the 'triad' of men's violence against themselves, other men, and women and children. Men have been encouraged to validate their masculinity in sport by treating their bodies as machines and weapons with scant regard for deleterious outcomes (Sabo 2005). Thus male athletes perpetrate violence against themselves by overtraining, using steroids to enhance performance, suppressing mental and physical pain, and competing while injured (often with pain-killing drugs). Men's violence against other men in sport is evident in myriad ways: the pervasive gladiatorial aspect of competitions, the sadistic rituals by which novices are initiated into sports teams, and fan violence in terms of both 'spontaneous' riots at games and the ritualised aggression of soccer hooligans. Violence against women and children in sport has received increasing attention following a series of assault, rape and murder trials involving high-profile American athletes, the laying of sexual assault charges against members of Australian and English football clubs, and prison sentences being handed out to coaches for sexual assault. Messner (2005: 318) argues that sexual assault in sport cannot be explained by a 'single factor'. Rather, he points to a matrix of causes, such as the 'bonding' activities of certain team sports, the consumption of alcohol, men's incapacity to empathise, and the rewards that male athletes obtain through direct involvement in and complicity with homophobic, misogynist and violent practices.

This triad of men's violence simultaneously constitutes and is constituted by the 'sports manhood formula' of the mass media, which encourages males to prove their masculinity by taking risks, behaving violently, enduring pain and injury, and treating females as sex objects (Messner *et al.* 2000). Male athletes are frequently described as 'young guns', 'top guns' and 'hit men' engaged in a 'blitzkrieg', 'battle' or 'shootout' in which they 'blow away' and 'take out' their opponents. Exalting violence by male athletes in the media also means that instead of assaults, injuries and deaths being defined as antisocial, they are excused, even lauded, as 'part of the game', the 'price to be paid' or 'what a man's gotta do'. The alcohol industry, which is one of the largest sponsors of sport, often uses advertisements depicting groups of heterosexual men consuming alcohol while watching women in sexually objectified settings. The media are also implicated in exonerating violence against women by male athletes. This usually takes the forms of victim-blaming by attributing men's violent behaviour to personal and external forces which they allegedly cannot control and constructing perpetrators as pathologically disturbed aberrations or victims themselves – the prey of 'groupies' who consent to group sex and then file bogus complaints (Messner 2002).

Men can help to dismantle this triad of violence in sport by alerting people to the individual and social costs involved in the power and performance model, as well as to the alternative 'pleasure and participation' model of sport (Coakley 2004). They also can provide alternative pedagogical techniques for physical education teachers, coaches, journalists, administrators and athletes (McKay 2002; Tough Guise). Finally, men can support women's attempts to attain equity in sport (McKay 1997) and participate in violence prevention initiatives (Brackenridge 2001; Messner and Stevens 2002; The Mentors in Violence Prevention Program).

References and further reading

Brackenridge, C. (2001) *Spoilsports*, London: Routledge.

Coakley, J. (2004) *Sport in Society*, 8th edn, Boston, MA and New York: McGraw-Hill.

Kaufman, M. (1998) 'The construction of masculinity and the triad of men's violence', in M.S. Kimmel and M.A. Messner (eds) *Men's Lives*, Boston, MA: Allyn and Bacon.

McKay, J. (1997) *Managing Gender*, Albany, NY: State University of New York Press.

—— (2002) 'Against the grain', in S. Ball-Rokeach, M. Ganz and M.A. Messner (eds) *Paradoxes of Youth and Sport*, Albany, NY: State University of New York Press.

Messner, M.A. (2002) *Taking the Field*, Minneapolis, MN: University of Minnesota Press.

—— (2005) 'Still a man's world', in M.S. Kimmel, J. Hearn and R. Connell (eds) *Handbook on Studies of Men and Masculinities*, Thousand Oaks, CA: Sage.

Messner, M.A., Dunbar, M. and Hunt, D. (2000) 'The televised sports manhood formula', *Journal of Sport and Social Issues*, 24: 380–94.

Messner, M.A. and Stevens, M. (2002) 'Scoring without consent', in S. Ball-Rokeach, M. Ganz, and M.A. Messner (eds) *Paradoxes of Youth and Sport*, Albany, NY: State University of New York Press.

Sabo, D.S. (2005) 'The study of masculinities and men's health', in M.S. Kimmel, J. Hearn and R. Connell (eds) *Handbook on Studies of Men and Masculinities*, Thousand Oaks, CA: Sage.

The Mentors in Violence Prevention (MVP) Program, at www.sportinsociety.org/mv

Tough Guise, at http://mediaed.org/videos

JIM MCKAY

VIOLENCE, WORKPLACE

Workplace violence is one of several concepts that address negative actions and behaviour involving mistreatment in places of work, employment or other working activity. Sometimes the concept is applied strictly to physical violence and threats thereof, but often what is addressed within the term overlaps with harassment (sexual, racial, personal), bullying, employee abuse, destructive leadership, workplace aggression or incivility, social undermining, interpersonal conflict, corporate abuse and organisation violations (Hearn and Parkin 2001). Bullying is one of the most commonly identified forms of workplace violence.

Certain work sectors and factors have been presented as making for particular or greater risks of physical violence: handling money, valuable goods and goods with street value; being in authority; working alone; providing care, advice, education and service; and those working with people who have been or are potentially violent people. While this may be so by some definitions, it fails to address the wider picture of organisation violations that are generated structurally and occur routinely.

Various forms of violence and violation in and around work organisations are relatively common. There have been rapid increases in reports of violence at work in recent years. In the UK the annual rate of reported violent assaults doubled over 1981–91 and represented 13 per cent of all reported assaults. The 2002–3 British Crime Survey estimated about 850,000 incidents classified as 'violence at work', with over half of these beign assaults. Homicide is the second most common cause of death in US workplaces (Vanden Bos and Bulutao 1996). According to the International Labour Organization, 1.1 million people, including 12,000 children, are killed at work every year, mainly in workplace accidents. The figures are especially high in developing countries, where the death rate in the construction industry is more than ten times that in industrialised countries. The ILO estimates that 160 million people develop occupational diseases and 250 million suffer workplace injuries every year (Di Martino 2000).

Many studies confirm the continuing significance, and indeed complexity, of gender relations in workplace violence. While men are the main perpetrators of workplace violence, clearly men can also be subjected to harassment, bullying and physical violence (Einarsen and Raknes 1997; Gerrity 2000). Some studies indicate that more men than women suffer from workplace assaults, largely from other men, as in some initiation rituals (Kenway *et al.* 2000). At the same time, women often seem more willing than men to report some forms of workplace violence, such as bullying, perhaps as reporting as a victim may be contradictory to some men's identity and masculine norms (Salin 2003). Finnish and Swedish official victim statistics indicate that more women report 'job-related violence' than men. Statistics Finland's surveys have indicated violence at work as the most common form of violence against women, and the most rapidly increasing category of violence. The UK Trades Union Congress (1999) report, *Violent Times: Preventing Violence at Work*, found that nearly a quarter of women aged twenty-five to thirty-four had been threatened with violence at work, and 11 per cent had been attacked, as against 6 per cent of men of this age.

There are several ways in which men's domination of workplace violence operates. First, there is the perpetration of sexual harassment, bullying and physical violence by men, individually, in groups or more collectively, to women and other men.

Second is men's dominant presence throughout organisations and their hierarchies, such as business, governments, the judiciary and the church, and especially in predominantly male organisations, such as fire-fighting, police and armed services, where bullying, harassment and violence can be common.

Third, men predominate in the bodies and processes intended to respond to sexual harassment, bullying and physical violence, and men's domination is evident too in their collusion, avoidance or other responses.

Fourth, there are many organisations and professions seen as predominantly 'women's work' which still have men's management directly or at a distance. There are clear gendered hierarchies of occupations, professions and whole or parts of organisations, such as doctors over nurses, lawyers over social workers, which may act as the context for harassment, bullying and physical violence, facilitating some forms of behaviour and constraining others.

Fifth, there are powerful assumptions about what constitutes management with the emphasis on 'strong' 'macho' environments still seen as desirable, providing institutional support for workplace violence and abuse. Such management cultures are imposed on personnel regardless of gender but with women having to comply in order to progress and men having to comply to avoid being seen as 'soft' or 'feminine'. Men's reluctance to complain about bullying can affirm the unwillingness of men to present other than a strongly masculine image. Some men accept 'all's fair in business' thinking, suppressing their reactions and refusing to label negative experiences as bullying or violation. Wright and Syme (1997) identify three kinds of 'corporate abuse': extremely competitive win/lose corporate cultures in which people strive against their colleagues rather than work with them; blaming cultures in which people are frightened to step out of line; and sacrifice and overwork cultures which involve people putting their jobs and their work above their personal and social lives and well-being to the extent that they become ill. On the other hand, emphasis on 'strong management' contrasts with 'weak management' and leadership regimes, where harassment, bullying and violence may not be intervened against.

In this context, the idea of violation-free organisations or workplaces may seem utopian. Nevertheless, this is a necessary state to work towards. The concept allows violation to be voiced and dealt with explicitly. There is a need for policies and practices for violation-free organisations, comparable with equal opportunities. This wider societal perspective is important given the increasing presence of interlocking organisations and institutional networks in people's working lives.

References and further reading

Di Martino, V. (2000) *Violence at the Workplace: The Global Challenge*, Geneva: ILO.

Einarsen, S. and Raknes, B.I. (1997) 'Harassment in the workplace and the victimization of men', *Violence and Victims*, 12 (3): 247–63.

Gerrity, D.A. (2000) 'Male university employees' experiences of sexual harassment-related behaviors', *Psychology of Men and Masculinity*, 1 (2): 140–51.

Gruber, J. and Morgan, P. (eds) (2004) *In the Company of Men: Sexual Harassment and Male Domination*, Boston, MA: Northeastern University Press.

Hearn, J. (1994) 'The organisation(s) of violence: men, gender relations, organisations and violences', *Human Relations*, 47 (6): 731–54.

Hearn, J. and Parkin, W. (2001) *Gender, Sexuality and Violence in Organizations: The Unspoken Forces of Organization Violations*, London: Sage.

Kenway, J,, Fitzclarence, L. and Hasluck, L. (2000) 'Toxic shock: understanding violence against young males in the workplace', *Journal of Men's Studies*, 8 (2): 131–51.

Salin, D. (2003) 'The significance of gender in the prevalence, forms and perceptions of bullying', *Nordiske Organisasjonsstudier*, 5 (3): 30–50.

Vanden Bos, G. and Bulutao, E.Q. (eds) (1996) *Violence on the Job: Identifying Risks and Developing Solutions*, Washington, DC: American Psychological Association.

Wright, L. and Syme, M. (1997) *Corporate Abuse*, New York: Simon and Schuster.

JEFF HEARN
WENDY PARKIN

VIRILITY

The central sense of 'virility' is 'being sexually potent'. Much research has documented the variety of conceptions of manhood in different societies, and in different classes within Western societies. But virility – the ability to have a firm erection for penetrating a woman's vagina until orgasm – is a central component of many different conceptions of manhood. However else they think of their manhood, most men want to be 'sexually potent' and are panicked about losing that potency, of becoming impotent.

Men who learn that medicines to lower blood pressure may affect their virility are prepared to risk early strokes and death rather than take the medication. Psychologists report that men afflicted with impotence feel completely worthless. Virility is central in the men's world of Ernest Hemingway and D.H. Lawrence. A large and profitable industry exists to repair damaged virility through medications, penile implants and various mechanical devices. An extensive literature reports on the functioning of these contrivances; the effect on men's sexual partners is rarely studied. The search to rejuvenate flagging sexual powers is not motivated by the desire to increase the sexual satisfaction of one's sexual partner.

Why then is virility so important in otherwise different conceptions of manhood? Men are thought to regard sexual acts as performances. But the underlying analogy with the great athlete or the violin virtuoso is unconvincing. The man with rock-hard erections that last has not worked to perfect that sexual power. It is a purely physiological matter for which he can take no more credit than for his digestion.

Men, it is often said, sexually dominate women. The ideology of virility eventuates in the culture of rape or gang-rape in which women are injured, frightened and humiliated. That is true, but is only one half of the story. Women also are loved and adored by men. Men profess to be inspired by women; women are their solace. To the women they love, men show themselves as weak and needy. But as long as they can retain sexual control, they can still regain control after letting go for a moment. Virility allows men to dominate the women they love.

References and further reading

Candib, L. and Schmitt, R. (1996) 'About losing it', in L. May, R. Strikwerda and P.D. Hopkins (eds) *Rethinking Masculinity*, 2nd edn, Langham, MD: Rowman and Littlefield, pp. 211–34.

See also: impotence and sexual dysfunction; manhood; penetration; penis; sperm, semen; Viagra

LUCY M. CANDIB
RICHARD SCHMITT

W

WAR

It is hard to imagine men without war, masculinity without military, male without (chain) mail. This is not to say that all men love war, make war or advocate war. It is to say that the imagining and enterprise of war are deep constructs embedded in virtually all masculine cultures and reflected in widely held conceptions of masculinity. The intimate connection between war and manhood is longstanding and ubiquitous. Attributes of hegemonic masculinities across time and space mirror the cultural components of warrior traditions: bravery, toughness, daring, honour, strength, courage (Cuordileone 2005).

Given the allure and defining power of militarised notions of masculinity, it is an ironic fact that most men do not serve in the military. This is especially true of privileged and powerful men: those who send others to war seldom serve themselves, but in their calls for others to serve, they speak in a language rich with images of manly honour and bravery. In most societies, and certainly in the United States, despite the loss and folly associated with many military campaigns, definitions of manhood remain imbued with militarised meanings and admonitions: don't be a wimp, don't be a traitor, don't be afraid, serve your country, defend your honour, take it like a man (Savran 1998). These calls to duty do their mobilising work by portraying war as an attractive and exciting opportunity for men to prove themselves.

The intersection between manhood and war is a space that is occupied not only by men. Women are partners in the 'men at/as war' project. Men depend on women to provide a logic for war, a purpose for fighting, a gender foil against which manliness is animated and contrasted. If men are the battlefront, women are the homefront. They are also the fans: fervent femininity embracing muscular masculinity. Women affirm manly mettle by their attraction to and admiration for men displaying these traits and by their disdain for cowards and weaklings. Although they historically have been absent as active agents on the battlefield, women are crucial characters in military productions of masculinity, albeit cast in primarily supporting roles. On the homefront, women serve as men's mothers and sisters and daughters and lovers and as their temporary replacements in the labour force; on the battlefield women are enlisted as enemy men's property to be threatened and violated, and during lulls and leaves as pinups, prostitutes and providers of aid and comfort. Both women and men are spectators and consumers of war and the opportunities it provides to exhibit heroism and patriotism, to display pride and loyalty, and to perform duty and sacrifice.

Men do not depend only on women as partners in wartime enactments of manliness. Men also collaborate with other men – both friends and foes. Men join forces with comrades as bands of brothers, as men in arms, as buddies bound together fighting the good fight. Men also rely on enemy men to serve as credible and admirable adversaries. Men reach across battle lines to hold close their mortal foes, inviting their opponents to join in conflict's deadly embrace. Men rely on both allies and antagonists in combat theatres; they are teammates in the martial arts, co-stars in military spectacles of manhood.

War is not only hell, it can be costly and dangerous for those who participate as well as for those who resist. Men who answer the call to war risk losing their lives; men who refuse to listen risk losing their honour. Women supporters of war risk losing their men and perpetuating martial masculinity; women detractors face charges of dishonouring their men and abetting the enemy. The close cultural fit between war and conceptions of manly honour and power makes it difficult for many men and women to envision manhood in the absence of military symbolism. The historical interdependence of war and hegemonic masculinity buttresses making war as essential to making men out of boys, legitimates war as the only true crucible of manhood, and exploits men's desires and anxieties about successfully enacting masculinity (Ducat 2004).

Images of man as warrior in traditional societies have become wedded to notions of nationalism in contemporary societies and welded into the massive military machinery that is the pride of most modern states. The anti-colonial and nationalist movements that swept aside empires in the twentieth century have overturned some aspects of those colonial economic and political relationships, but little change has occurred in the structure and operation of national gender orders. Post-colonial patriarchies have replaced colonial patriarchal structures, and masculinism remains entrenched as an organising principle in contemporary states. Enloe notes that to the extent that nationalist movements are based on male pride and privilege, an increase in the number of states in the global system will not result in a transformation of the system or of the states populating it: 'A dozen new patriarchal nation-states may make the international bargaining table a bit more crowded, but it won't change the international game being played at that table' (Enloe 1990: 64).

It is important to note that the international game being played is militarised. Men at the helm of modern states back up their martial posturing by spending often limited national funds on military hardware, manpower and missions. Contemporary international relations take the form of contests among national manhoods engaged in economic competition, geopolitical compacts and military conflicts. The most cursory survey of military discourse exposes the man in the state. Many researchers have noted the use of the masculine imagery of sexual potency, rape, penetration and sexual conquest to depict military weaponry and offensives. Goldstein (2001: 349) cites one US Vietnam-era veteran's description of his intimate relationship with his weapon: '[t]o some people carrying a gun was like having a permanent hard-on. It was a pure sexual trip every time you got to pull the trigger.' A commonly reported phrase alleged to have been written on US missiles targeted on Iraq during the 1990 Gulf War and again in the 2003 Iraq War was 'Bend over, Saddam.' There is a tendency in national defence discourse to personify and sexually characterise the actions of states and armies. Cohn (1993: 236) reports that during the Cold War one well-known academic security advisor was quoted as saying that 'under Jimmy Carter the United States is spreading its legs for the Soviet Union', and she quotes another US defence analyst referring to former West German politicians concerned about popular opposition to the deployment of nuclear Euromissiles in the 1980s: 'Those Krauts are a bunch of limp-dicked wimps.'

It is no secret that one weapon in wartime's masculinist arsenal is sexual assault. Rapes of women and sexual humiliation and torture of both women and men in wars are widespread and well-documented (Enloe 2000). Because rape and sexual assault seem to fly in the face of many more elevated masculinist values, such as honour, dignity and self-discipline, sexual violence in war seems always to be a surprise when it is 'discovered'. In fact, virtually all military conflicts involve rape, either as relatively informal 'opportunity' assaults or as organised campaigns of intimidation or 'ethnocide' through forced impregnation. One way to think about wartime sexual assaults is as transactions between enemy men, with the women as the currency in the exchange. Another way to think about rape in war is as a homosocial bonding exercise – part of the pressure and pull of men to prove to one another their loyalty, steadfastness and sangfroid.

The widespread rape and sexual exploitation that occurred during twentieth-century military operations have been increasingly the subject of scholarly investigation, including, but not limited to, studies of the Japanese Imperial Army's rape of thousands of Chinese women (the 'Rape of Nanking') and enslavement of thousands more Asian women during the Second World War, the Soviet Army's rape of German women during the same period, the Indian Army's large-scale rape of Bengali women in Bangladesh in the 1970s, the militarisation of Southeast Asian women's sexuality in the form of survival sex in war zones, rapes by troops, and the development of large-scale commercial prostitution for US soldiers on 'R&R' during the Korean and Vietnam Wars (Chang 1997; Moon 1997; Mookherjee 2003; Epp 1997; Bishop and Robinson 1998). Despite the scale and infamy of these and other military sexual exploits, towards the end of the century the world once again was shocked by the magnitude of mass rape in the former Yugoslavia and in Rwanda in the 1990s and by sexual intimidation and violence used by US troops in the Iraq War in the 2000s. The latter was most notoriously exposed in Iraq's Abu Ghraib prison and resulted in a scandal that revealed a new twist in the relationship between men and war: the participation of women as partners in the historically masculine domain of sexual abuse.

Just as women can be enlisted as sexual aggressors in war, men can be damaged by sexualised warfare – both as targets of sexual assault and in their role as soldiers. Watanabe argues that men are trapped in masculinist roles and forced to act out patriarchal and sexual scripts that commodify and endanger them as well as the women they victimise. During the Second World War, 'male soldiers were dehumanised to make them good fighters then stimulated by sexual desire that was fulfilled by comfort women' (Watanabe 1995: 506–7). Watanabe's analysis suggests that although they are perpetrators of the rapes and sexual abuse of women and other men in times of war, men pay a psychological, social and physical price for their complicity in patriarchal masculinist systems of sexual violence. As Kimmel (1996) reports, many soldiers display varying degrees of post-traumatic stress or 'shell shock' following combat. The extent of these psychological and physical costs of militarised manhood remains to be fully estimated in calculations of the cost of war.

Certainly there are wars that men resist, and there are men who resist all wars. However, once a war is widely defined as a matter of 'duty', 'honour', 'patriotism' or as a defence of 'freedom' and 'the American way of life', etc., then resistance for many men (and for some women) becomes a matter of cowardice and dishonour. For men confronted with the unpalatable and humiliating labels associated with resisting war, there are added some sweeteners: the allure of adventure, the promise of masculine camaraderie, the opportunity to test and prove oneself, the chance to participate in an historic, larger-than-life, generation-defining event. Given this stick and these carrots, for many men the attraction of war is as irresistible as it is deadly.

References and further reading

Bishop, R. and Robinson, L.S. (1998) *Night Market*, New York: Routledge.

Cohn, C. (1993) 'Wars, wimps, and women', in M. Cooke and A. Woollacott (eds) *Gendering War Talk*, Princeton, NJ: Princeton University Press, pp. 227–46.

Chang, I. (1997) *The Rape of Nanking*, New York: Basic Books.
Cuordileone, K.A. (2005) *Manhood and American Political Culture in the Cold War*, New York: Routledge.
Ducat, S.J. (2004) *The Wimp Factor*, Boston, MA: Beacon.
Enloe, C. (1990) *Bananas, Beaches, and Bases*, Berkeley, CA: University of California Press.
—— (2000) *Maneuvers*, Berkeley, CA: University of California Press.
Epp, M. (1997) 'The memory of violence', *Journal of Women's History*, 9: 58–87.
Goldstein, J. (2001) *War and Gender*, Cambridge: Cambridge University Press.
Kimmel, M. (1996) *Manhood in America*, New York: Basic Books.
Mookherjee, N. (2003) 'Gendered embodiments', in N. Puwar and P. Raghuram (eds) *Critical Reflections on Gender and the South Asian Diaspora*, Oxford: Berg, pp. 157–77.
Moon, K.H.S. (1997) *Sex among Allies*, New York: Columbia University Press.
Mosse, G.L. (1996) *The Image of Man*, New York and Oxford: Oxford University Press.
Savran, D. (1998) *Taking it Like a Man*, Princeton, NJ: Princeton University Press.
Watanabe, K. (1995) 'Trafficking in women's bodies, then and now', *Peace and Change*, 20: 501–14.

See also: military institutions; military masculinities

JOANE NAGEL

WAR LITERATURE

Much of early Indo-European literature is preoccupied with war. Canonical accounts of the Western literary tradition typically begin with the epic of the Trojan War, the *Iliad*, continue with the postwar epic of warrior returns, the *Odyssey*, and often include the *Aeneid*, in which Virgil conflates Homer's two long poems into a tale of the founding of Rome. In such works, along with the Indian epics the Mahabharata and the Ramayana, the tales of the Norse gods and heroes collected in the Elder Edda and the Younger Edda, as well as the later Icelandic sagas, collective war and personal violence are the settings for stories that often evoke a distant heroic past and delineate traditions of religion and statecraft, along with social customs.

Similarly, the first historians in the West, Herodotus and Thucydides, take as their subjects the Persian Wars and the Peloponnesian Wars respectively. It will not be until the end of the eighteenth century, almost 2,500 years later, that historiography will move beyond war as its central subject.

In Asia, the emphasis of early literature is not so chiefly military. With a few exceptions, like Sun Tzu's *The Art of War*, it is only in the era of the Japanese shogunate, in the years akin to the European Late Middle Ages, that a widespread literature of war and a focus on the samurai warrior begin to appear. Meanwhile, in Europe, a revival of classical literary themes coupled with a newly articulated nationalism produced such military epics as the French *Song of Roland*, the German *Die Nibelungenlied*, the Italian *Orlando Furioso* and the Portuguese *Lusiads*.

For the most part, the heroes of these works, when they weren't gods or demigods, came from the upper classes of society. They were celebrated for their physical prowess and sense of honour, almost exclusively displayed in battle, that would make their names last through eternity. But with the introduction of gunpowder weaponry in the late Middle Ages, the literature of war, along with the concepts of honour, chivalry and military *virtú* that nurtured it, shifted decisively.

When faced with cannon balls and bullets, noble genealogy and prowess at arms made little impact. Soldiers and war hardly vanished from literature, but the perspective on their profession and the experience of war itself was definitely changing. Shakespeare's soldiers, for example, include the hot-blooded Hotspur, the cool Henry V, the love-besotted Troilus, the cowardly Bardolph, and the mama's boy Coriolanus.

Most previous epics had been written from a poetic God's-eye-view above the battle, picking out the heroes and serenely describing the mayhem. But when guns rearranged the ancient equation of prowess and heroism, the foot soldier began to impose a point of view all his own. In Grimmelhausen's novel

Simplicissimus and in the engravings of Callot, the indiscriminate slaughter and brutality of the seventeenth-century Thirty Years War in Europe is depicted without sentimentality or uplifting heroics.

In the eighteenth century, with more non-professionals joining battle in the American and French revolutions, the volume of war memoirs and war scenes in literature again increased, but often with the same anti-epic edge. Byron's poem *Don Juan* is epic in length, but when its hero is fighting to win honour in battle, the scene is a bewildering chaos of noise and smoke, dead and dying. As in Stendhal's *The Charterhouse of Parma*, which includes scenes of the Napoleonic War, instead of the clarity of the older epic vision, these soldiers fight amid a world of what the military theorist Clausewitz described as absolute confusion.

Advances in weapons technology might convince the policy-makers of European nations bent on carving up the rest of the world to still believe in war as the only decisive way to determine questions of power and authority. But the historiography that chronicled war above all was beginning to give way to a more complex analysis of social, political and economic issues.

In many ways the inescapable result of a decades-long arms race between the English and the Germans, the First World War also became the first truly bookish war because so many of the men who served on all sides had a good literary education. Poetry, short stories, novels and memoirs poured from the presses, often posthumously because the author had already been killed crossing no-man's land. The more democratic the war, the more literary it would be, especially in the literature of personal witness. An expanded literacy among citizen-soldiers met an expanded literacy among the reading audience, eager to experience, even vicariously, the pain of war, and perhaps even more eager for someone to make literary and artistic sense of its turmoil and confusion. In works like Barbusse's *Under Fire*, Remarque's *All Quiet on the Western Front* and Hemingway's *A Farewell to Arms*, the old stories of epic heroism were swallowed up in the muddy reality of the trenches.

The wake of the Second World War, with its even greater mobilisation of manpower and materiel, brought more literary efforts to understand the immediate effects of war through the lens of personal experience, while historians laboured to construct a coherent overview of its causes and unfolding. But the increasingly limited wars of the end of the twentieth century, with their generally professional armies, seemed to engender more memoirs than fiction and even less poetry. The effort of centuries of war literature to understand violence in the name of a tribe or a religious cause or a political idea seems to ring more hollowly in an age of devastating nuclear weapons and a globalism that erodes national borders. From its early grandeur as the heart of much literature, war has become one subject among many.

References and further reading

Blomberg, C. (1994) *The Heart of the Warrior*, Sandgate, VT: Japan Library.

Duby, G. (1977) *The Chivalrous Society*, Berkeley, CA: University of California Press.

Fussell, P. (1975) *The Great War and Modern Memory*, New York: Oxford University Press.

Hynes, S.A. (1990) *War Imagined*, New York: Atheneum.

Parker, G. (1988) *The Military Revolution*, Cambridge: Cambridge University Press.

See also: military institutions, military masculinities

LEO BRAUDY

WESTERN, THE

The Western first emerged in the late nineteenth century, when the closing of the American frontier coincided with full-scale industrial and urban development, domestically and abroad. Nostalgia for the presumed individualism of frontier life led to a celebration of the independent cowboy hero, astride a horse, gun at his hip, master of his destiny. Owen Wister introduced the figure in his best-selling *The Virginian* (1902), and Zane Grey established the genre with *Riders of the Purple Sage* (1912), followed by other titles set during the western cattle drives (1867–87). The emergence of cinema fuelled the genre's new popularity, with countless Westerns churned out by Hollywood over the next half-century. The best film Westerns appeared at the height of the genre's popularity in the 1950s, cementing their lead actors' reputations as stars: Alan Ladd in George Stevens' *Shane* (1952), Gary Cooper in Fred Zinnemann's *High Noon* (1952), and John Wayne in John Ford's *The Searchers* (1955). Thereafter, Sergio Leone's spaghetti Westerns starring Clint Eastwood registered a turn to parody that also signalled the genre's declining popularity.

No other popular text asks as assiduously as the Western what it means to be a man, and the eruption of violence that occurs so often is meant to test not only a distinctively masculine body (tall in the saddle, quick on the draw) but also certain learned male virtues (restraint, taciturnity, endurance). Violence in the Western begins with the hero's body, which is where close attention is paid to physical features, costumed appearance and upright stance. The frequency with which the body is celebrated, then punished, only to convalesce, suggests the paradox involved in making true men out of biological men, taking their male bodies and distorting them beyond the power of self-control so that in the course of recuperation, a masculinity can be revealed that is at once physical yet based on performance. From the beginning, observers have delighted in the picturesqueness of the cowboy, who depends more on specialised garb than any other modern worker. His dress is so conventional, in fact, that it has become a sort of language, signalling moral and emotional stature (the excess of two guns versus the restraint of one, or the contrasting claims made by fringe, silk, leather and silver). Yet the cowboy hero's self-presentation often seems at odds with his inexpressive persona. Self-preening vies with self-effacement, exhibitionism with restraint, as the visual 'busyness' of his demeanour is balanced by vocal inactivity so complete that he seems to exist beyond the everyday commonplaces of talk and explanation, of persuasion, argument, indeed beyond conversation altogether.

The restraint worn by the Western hero as part of his sign-laden costume sharply distinguishes him from other men – indeed, requires others whose lack of restraint provides a foil to the true man's achieved coherence. Talking too much or laughing easily or expressing fear too readily are more than signs of bad form; they reveal an inability to maintain composure under the pressure of vivid sensation. The irony is that restraint can only be demonstrated through narratives of excess. Without plots in which restraint can be displayed, the blankness of the hero's countenance expresses only blankness, not the deliberateness of prudent intention or the saving power of self-control.

Despite its celebration of the male physique, then, the Western constantly threatens that body with violence, offering recurrent scenes of men being beaten, allowing us to see men recover, regaining their strength in the process of once again making themselves into men. The paradox lies in the fact that we watch them become what they already are, as we exult in the confirmation of a man again becoming a man. On the one hand, the genre advertises itself as committed to essentialism, showing how men are always already there, biologically fixed by the accident of genitals. On the other hand, Westerns depend upon means that expose this ideology, relying on plots that demand the creation of manhood, then its re-creation.

Violence in the Western never exists for itself but rather as a means of raising the question of whether a man's face and body constitute little more than a gendered mask, in need of being destroyed and reshaped to confirm that manhood exists beneath. Westerns treat the hero as a rubber doll to be wrenched and contorted so that we can then watch him magically recover his shape. The process reveals how the cherished image of masculinity we had dismissed as simply learned behaviour is in fact a resilient, biological process. Stretching the body proves its natural essence, and all the leather, spurs, chaps, pistols, handkerchiefs and hats may now be excused as dead talismans.

Yet the contradiction of the Western is that masculinity is always more than physical, and that in favouring an ideal of restraint it reveals how manhood is as much learned as found. Since restraint is not apparent on the surface, it needs to be exacerbated by the threat of violence, which explains the recurrent narrative pattern of imperilling the body to watch it convalesce, a pattern reinforcing our ambivalent sense that masculinity is as much a cultural effect as a natural cause or biological imperative. Whenever a man is being beaten in the Western, it is to prepare us for the process by which he becomes what he already is. We find ourselves, male and female, identifying with the subject of suffering and in that moment also identifying with the masculinising process itself as one of American culture's most powerful (and powerfully confused) imaginative constructions. For the Western hero – unlike the leading men in any other genre – is placed before us to be looked at. And in that long, oscillating look, we watch men still at work in the unfinished process of making themselves, even as we are encouraged to believe that manhood doesn't need to be made.

References and further reading

Bold, C. (1987) *Selling the Wild West*, Bloomington, IN: Indiana University Press.

Cawelti, J. (1984) *The Six-Gun Mystique*, 2nd edn, Bowling Green, OH: Bowling Green Popular Press.

Mitchell, L.C. (1996) *Westerns*, Chicago, IL: University of Chicago Press.

Tompkins, J. (1992) *West of Everything*, New York: Oxford University Press.

Warshow, R. [1954] (1962) 'Movie chronicle', reprinted in R. Warshow, *The Immediate Experience*, Garden City, NY: Doubleday, pp. 135–54.

Wright, W. (1975) *Six Guns and Society*, Berkeley, CA: University of California Press.

See also: manhood

LEE CLARK MITCHELL

WHITE MEN

To be white and male is a standard of global privilege and power. Critical masculinity studies, feminism and postcolonial studies have all in some way described the ways in which white men embody hegemonic cultural relations. However, while the notion of 'white men' expresses structural hegemony, the specific and localised embodiment of white masculinities is very diverse, existing within a hierarchy of cultural relations.

It is useful to understand the notion of 'white men' in both a general and a specific sense. Specifically, the notion of 'white men' refers to groups of white men who have achieved global dominance. It was predominantly white men who established the basis of Western imperialism and dominance since the seventeenth century. It was

> white men who took to their ships and travelled the globe in search of trade, resources and adventure, white men who oversaw the establishment of mines, factories and plantations and white men who commanded the global flows of wealth and resources, who established the regulations and bureaucracies, who dispossessed the native inhabitants and who owned and administrated around 85 per cent of the earth's surface.
>
> (McClintock 1995: 5–6)

White men continue to have a possessive investment in these global acquisitions and racialised privileges.

In the early twenty-first century it remains that being white and male is a strong indicator of authority and privilege. The majority of the world's politicians are men, and in Western nations like the United States, Britain or Australia it is predominantly men who fill positions of power and influence more generally. They make up the chief executive officers and managers of large powerful corporations, the heads of media organisations, the judges, solicitors and barristers, and the politicians who oversee the governance of the populations. In the United States white men constitute around 40 per cent of the population although they disproportionately constitute 92 per cent of state governors, 90 per cent of daily newspaper editors, 83 per cent of people earning over $265 million per annum, 77 per cent of members of Congress and 70 per cent of tenured university lecturers. In 2002 eight of the ten richest people in the world were white men. To be white and male means that one literally has a greater access to power and privilege within both Western and global social relations.

On the other hand, to speak of white men generally draws attention to the relations of power that constitute this cultural phenomenon. It is to recognise that to be white and male does not always confer power and privilege. Instead, it is generally a particular class of white men who hold these positions of power and dominance within global relations. White men from lower socioeconomic areas or 'developing' nations, for example, exercise relatively little power and authority, whereas some white women, and some non-white men and women, may individually occupy positions of significant power and influence. The important issue is their location within particular economies of culture and power and their participation in relationships of global power and patronage, which are overwhelmingly shaped and dominated by 'white men'.

Queer theorist Eve Kosofsky Sedgewick argues this point succinctly: 'when something is about masculinity, it is not always about "men"' (1995: 12). Subsequently, to speak of whiteness and masculinity is not always to speak of the white man. Whiteness and masculinity refer to the relations of meaning and practice that constitute the field of gender and race relations. These concepts refer to the discourses and practices that are accessible to all, albeit in highly differentiated ways, and within highly variable contexts.

Globalisation is a cultural phenomenon that highlights the way whiteness and masculinities are challenged and reasserted on the world stage. It involves and affects all social groups, from cultural elites, through the bourgeoisie to local proletariats and peasantries. This is played out in different ways, namely through complicity, resistance, reactionary responses and the reassertion of hegemonic cultural relations.

Globalisation, based upon a particular cultural ideal of a world order, is a dynamic process but in significant ways it can be seen as the white masculinist corporatisation of global relations (i.e. Americanisation, Coca-Colonisation). It is an ongoing form of cultural and economic colonisation of largely black and Asian poor nations. The impact of globalisation upon developing nations includes the proletarianisation of local peasantries, the reassertion of, or resistance to, local elites, coerced labour and cultural migrations, colonisation and decolonisation, genocide and cultural violence.

Resistance to the ongoing cultural influence of white men is evident in movements such as 'terrorism' and religious fundamentalism (i.e. McWorld vs Jihad, 'the clash of fundamentalisms'). Movements of resistance involve both struggle against 'hegemonic white masculinities' (e.g. Al Qaeda) and the reassertion of white masculinities (e.g. white supremacy organisations like National Action, Posse Comitatus). In developed and largely Western nations, groups like the Ku Klux Klan, American Nazi Party, National Action in Australia, Posse Comitatus and the radical militias like the group that enacted the bombing of a government building in Oklahoma City are constituted by marginalised white men who feel their birthright has been taken away through burgeoning government bureaucracy, 'rabid' feminism or liberal immigration policies, or indigenous rights movements (see Ferber 1995, 2000; Kimmel and Ferber 2000).

In other ways the cultural challenges to the hegemony of white men through social movements such as feminism, indigenous movements, forms of civil disobedience and the burgeoning of the welfare state and its incorporation of difference into civic machinery generate a mobilisation of hegemonic interests. These reactions involve the reassertion of hegemonic white masculinities. In the last three decades reactions to the cultural challenges of the new social movements have included middle-class men's rights groups like men's rights and fathers' rights groups, the mythopoetic movement, the Promise Keepers and muscular Christianity movements in Western nations (see Robinson 2000; Savran 1998; Kusz 2001).

In late industrial societies, and in global culture more generally, the 'institution' of white men has become challenged, marked by many with scepticism and resistance to their cultural power and white race privilege. However, this cultural formation remains an enduring and entrenched phenomenon of privilege also generating resistance from marginalised white and non-white populations.

References and further reading

Ferber, A.L. (1995) 'Shame of white men', *Masculinities*, 3 (2, Summer): 1–24.

—— (2000) 'Racial warriors and weekend warriors', *Men and Masculinities*, 3 (1, July): 30–56.

Kimmel, M. (2001) 'Global masculinities', in B. Pease and K. Pringle (eds) *A Man's World?* London: Zed Books, pp. 21–38.

Kimmel, M. and Ferber, A.L. (2000) 'White men are this nation', *Rural Sociology*, 65 (4, December): 582–604.

Kusz, K.W. (2001) 'I want to be the minority', *Journal of Sport and Social Issues*, 25 (4, November): 390–416.

McClintock, A. (1995) *Imperial Leather*, London: Routledge.

Sedgewick, E.K. (1995) 'Gosh, Boy George, you must be awfully secure in your masculinity!' in M. Berger, B. Wallis and S. Watson (eds) *Constructing Masculinity*, New York: Routledge.

Robinson, S. (2000) *Marked Men*, New York: Columbia University Press.

Savran, D. (1998) *Taking It Like a Man*, Princeton, NJ: Princeton University Press.

BEN WADHAM

WHITE PRIVILEGE

White privilege is the set of advantages that accrue to individuals, frequently without their conscious awareness, from being perceived as members of the dominant 'white' or 'Caucasian' racial category, especially in Europe, North America and countries formerly colonised by Europeans or Americans. In many societies' racial hierarchies, whiteness is connected with power, status, beauty and authority. The concept of white privilege has become useful to masculinity studies in two overlapping ways: as an analogy to help explain male privilege and as an essential concept for intersectional analyses of power, gender and status, such that masculine, white, heterosexual and middle-class privileges reinforce one another in hegemonic masculinity and the institutions that uphold it.

Ignatiev (1995) shows how the Irish, discriminated against in Great Britain, 'became white' in the nineteenth-century United States by discriminating against black people and by rising in the white power structure through big city political organisations, labour unions and the Roman Catholic Church. These positions of power and privilege were overwhelmingly male, consolidating the interdependent social construction of whiteness and masculinity, with privileged white men holding advantages even over privileged white women.

McIntosh (1988) describes white privilege as, like male privilege, an invisible bundle of unearned advantages like being treated courteously by shopkeepers and police officers or speaking in public without fearing that failures will be attributed to one's race rather than to oneself. Brod (2002) coins the term 'superordinate studies' to expose the usually invisible privileges that accrue to the dominant group. Thus, for him the 'feminisation of poverty' has its corollary in the 'masculinisation of wealth', which operates synergistically with the economic advantages that white people accumulate in comparison to those of people of colour. Brod disputes the myth of social neutrality or the 'level playing field'; instead, he describes society as like a stream in whose uneven currents white men advance with less effort than people of colour and white women, although they perceive their success as due solely to their own efforts and do not see the currents that holds others back.

References and further reading

Brod, H. (2002) 'Studying masculinities as superordinate studies', in J.K. Gardiner (ed.) *Masculinity Studies and Feminist Theory*, New York: Columbia University Press, pp. 161–75.

Ignatiev, N. (1995) *How the Irish Became White*, New York: Routledge.

Kendall, F. (2006) *Understanding White Privilege*, New York: Routledge.

McIntosh, P. (1988) *White Privilege and Male Privilege*, Wellesley, MA: Centers for Women Working Papers.

See also: privilege; race and ethnicity; racism; white men

JUDITH KEGAN GARDINER

WHITE RIBBON CAMPAIGN

The White Ribbon Campaign (WRC) is a grassroots activist campaign created by men and dedicated to ending men's violence against women. Founded in Canada in 1991 in response to the killing of fourteen women by an armed man in Montreal, WRC has expanded internationally to over forty countries and is now the largest global effort of its kind. While the campaign is not centrally organised – each local group takes responsibility for its own agenda and activities – the Canadian effort does have a small staff in Toronto, an elected board of directors, and a website with information, announcements and educational materials. Some of WRC's typical activities include the development and distribution of curricular materials for teachers, public awareness campaigns, participation and cooperation with both academic and activist feminist initiatives, and fund-raising for women's organisations. In Canada each year for one week, from 25 November (the International Day for the Elimination of Violence Against Women) to 6 December (the anniversary of the tragedy in Montreal), men wear a white ribbon to express their commitment to never engage in, condone or remain silent about men's violence against women.

WRC is one among many anti-violence men's organisations active in the world today. As such, it forms part of a much larger history of influence, collaboration and tension between profeminist men and men's organisations and feminism since the 1970s. WRC's particular campaign is based on the idea that a mass movement of men from across a broad spectrum of political perspectives and backgrounds can be mobilised around the single purpose of ending violence against women. Like other men's groups that have sought to contribute to, and collaborate with, feminist activism, WRC seeks a delicate balance between raising men's awareness and mobilising them against a gender order that gives them privilege, and at the same time not displacing the role of women in that effort.

References and further reading

Flood, M. (2003) 'Men's collective struggles for gender justice', in M. Kimmel, J. Hearn and R. Connell (eds) *The Handbook of Studies of Men and Masculinities*, Thousand Oaks, CA: Sage.

Goldrick-Jones, A. (2002) *Men Who Believe in Feminism*, New York: Praeger.

Kauffman, M. (2001) 'The White Ribbon Campaign', in B. Pease and K. Pringle (eds) *A Man's World?* London: Zed Books, pp. 38–51.

Messner, M. (1997) *Politics of Masculinities*, Thousand Oaks, CA: Sage.

See also: masculinity politics; men's groups; profeminism

JOHN C. LANDREAU

WOMEN'S STUDIES/GENDER STUDIES/ FEMINIST STUDIES

Women's studies, gender studies and feminist studies are terms used to describe areas of academic study relating to the social rights and roles of men and women. Research, teaching and activist/advocacy work are done in these fields in a variety of disciplines, and some universities have departments devoted to them, usually under the title of women's or gender studies.

History of women's studies

Women's studies, also known as feminist studies, came out of the changes brought about by the feminist movement of the 1960s. The feminist movement raised awareness about the inequalities women faced in Western society, including such factors as lower wages, discriminatory laws and reduced access to education and other opportunities. Notions of men and masculinity were used as a standard of normality around which society was based, setting up women as inferior others. With the increased awareness of such bias, academic feminists also began to point out the extent to which women and women's issues were excluded from university studies and from the content of curricula. Women's accomplishments and their roles in history were rarely acknowledged in humanities classrooms; scientific research was based on men and men's health needs; and female students often had trouble gaining recognition for their academic accomplishments. Female students were generally encouraged to study in areas deemed appropriate for women, fields like the humanities and nursing, because of the prevailing belief that most of the women would be focusing on marriage and motherhood after college, rather than on careers. Female teachers, as well, were often limited in academia to the lowest-level professorial jobs and were frequently passed over for promotions and research funding. Feminist teachers and students, therefore, sought a way to make women a legitimate and valued part of the education system.

In order to do this, courses focusing on women started to be taught in the 1960s, eventually leading to the creation of the first official Women's Studies Department in the United States at San Diego State University in 1970. Later the same year, Cornell University became the second American school to authorise a department. Prior to receiving approval for a department at San Diego State, faculty had to teach women's studies classes on a voluntary overload basis, a situation that was also happening at other institutions. Taking on extra teaching duties was necessary because of the difficulty in convincing university administrators that women's studies was an important and justifiable teaching area. Officials were reluctant to dedicate university resources to the field and had to be shown that there was enough interest on the part of students. Women's studies programmes were being similarly developed in Europe, particularly in Britain, and in Australia and Canada. In England, the first women's studies courses were taught at the University of North London, in Australia at Adelaide and Flinders Universities, and in Canada at the University of British Columbia. Over the last thirty years women's studies programmes have expanded to many other parts of the world.

The development of women's studies programmes started off slowly, with schools first offering related courses; then some beginning to develop undergraduate certificates and minors, majors and eventually graduate degrees. As the field grew, women's studies periodicals started being published, such as *Feminist Studies* (1972), *Women's Studies* (1972), *Radical Teacher* (1975), *Frontiers* (1975), *Hecate* (1975), *Al-Raida* (1976), *Feminist Review* (1979), *Signs* (1980), *Australian Feminist Studies* (1985) and the *Nordic Journal of Women's Studies*. Since the 1990s, journals in the field have increased exponentially, in terms of both subject matter and geographic origins. Some examples include the *Journal of South Asian Women Studies* (1995), the *Asian Journal of Women's Studies* (1995), *Nashim: A Journal of Jewish Women's Studies and Gender Issues* (1998) and the *Journal of Cultural and African Women Studies* (2000). Hundreds of professional organisations have also been established. Some of the prominent ones include the National Women's Studies Association in the United

States (www.nwsa.org), formed in 1977, the Institute for Women's Studies in the Arab World, in 1973, the Feminist and Women's Studies Association in the United Kingdom (www.fwsa.org.uk), the Australian Women's Studies Association in 1989, the New Zealand Women's Studies Association in 1984 (www.womenz.org/wsa/journal.htm), the World-wide Organisation for Women's Studies, in 1996 (www.fss.uu.nl/wows/start.html) and Women's International Studies Europe, in 1990 (http://www.wise.medinstgenderstudies.org/).

Development and diversification of women's studies

Women's studies helped to initiate widespread academic changes both in what is taught and in how universities include and encourage women. Issues of women and gender are now addressed, in varying degrees, in almost every discipline. In literary studies, for example, work by feminist scholars has brought about the recovery of many forgotten women's texts. As well, the rewriting of literary and other histories to recognise women's cultural contributions has given many female students more confidence in their own abilities. Women's studies forced the remembering of many who had been forgotten or dismissed by history.

Significantly, the dialogues of remembering and revaluing both sexes that were opened by women's studies led to expanded dialogues on differences based on factors such as 'race' and ethnicity, religion, nationality, sexual orientation and gender. However, it is important to note that these dialogues often came about through cultural moments of great tension similar to those producing and produced by the women's movement. Initially the project of women's studies was to acknowledge women's place in society and to analyse and redress systems of sexual inequality. However, the strategies used to combat inequalities sometimes involved essentialising women and femininity. What came to represent the essence of womanhood was often based on white, heterosexual women. In the late 1970s, women's studies and the feminist movements were criticised for focusing primarily on the needs and concerns of these white, heterosexual women and setting them up as a norm for femininity. Black and lesbian scholars and activists pointed out the ways in which this essentialisation excluded them from much of the discourse surrounding feminism. Their courage helped to diversify the field of women's studies. International feminists have also built on their ideas since that time to reprove the overemphasis on women of North America and Europe and the assumptions made by women in these areas about women and their roles in the rest of the world.

As women's studies and women's rights organisations have been formed around the world, women in Asia, Africa, Latin America, Eastern Europe and other marginalised areas have been better able to express their own needs and adapt women's studies towards them. In these areas educational work is often intrinsically tied to community advocacy work.

So beyond gender inequality, therefore, women's studies has delved into disparities based in many other factors. The field has, for the most part, moved away from essentialised or overly simplistic ideas about women and men to value instead the differences within and between genders and to look at the ways in which those differences are often used as a rationale for oppression. Furthermore, a crucial part of what women's studies has accomplished is to give women a voice, or a place of power in society from which to speak and be recognised despite their differences from dominant ideals.

Challenges of women's studies

A popular misconception about women's studies is that it ignores men or that it is anti-men. This idea has grown out of a backlash against feminism, part of the reason that the label of women's studies has been more popular than feminist studies, as a means of protecting the field from the backlash. Men have always been a factor in women's studies, though women have generally been foregrounded as a counterbalance to the historically routine emphasis on men in academia. One of the key goals of women's studies has been to create a system that balances the needs of men and women, rather than privileging one over the other. A stereotype of man-hating feminists wanting to dominate men nevertheless persists, which has caused women's studies to be viewed with suspicion by some. It has been condemned by some people as being too political or too woman-centred. The tolerance for and encouragement of multiple perspectives in the field also make it difficult to unify women's studies scholars because they have different beliefs and are focusing on many different causes. As well, the diversity and interdisciplinary basis of women's studies make the field difficult to define easily and render it vulnerable to simplistic misunderstandings about its purposes. The stigma attached to the field has limited its potential for growth at some schools and has kept some students, including many men, away from studying it. Despite the stigma, increasing numbers of courageous men have enrolled in women's studies.

Men's studies and women's studies

Some critics have responded to the contentiousness of women's studies by calling for and developing men's studies programmes. Notions of men's studies have come out of two opposing beliefs. On one side, some argue for men's studies because of their mistrust of or discomfort with women's studies and its ideas of female empowerment. They suggest that there is a need to counteract feminist voices that they deem too influential. On the other side, others argue that having formal men's studies programmes will allow for a productive space of dialogue with women's studies because both would be able to look at the construction of men and women in society. This side of the men's studies debate sees value in what feminism has done for women and wants to develop further that potential for social change involving men. Still others reject the term men's studies as colonising and suggesting a false complementary, arguing instead for 'Critical Studies of Men'.

Development of gender studies

One of the more popular and recent developments in the field to reduce the misconceptions about women's studies is the move towards the label of gender studies. Some schools have changed the names of their women's studies programmes, while others developing new programmes have chosen to take the newer name. Gender studies focuses on the social construction of masculine and feminine roles in society and the effects of such roles on individual and collective development. The term 'gender studies' has become increasingly popular for a number of reasons. Some scholars believe that it is a more accurate title than women's studies, because women are not studied exclusively or in isolation from men. Another argument for the term 'gender' is that it moves beyond the limiting categories of male/female, feminine/masculine, man/woman, which exclude people who cannot be classified in those ways, such as transgender persons. It also reflects a belief that the field is no longer as singularly focused on sexual inequality as it started out to be. In addition, the word 'gender' is, in some people's minds, even further removed from the word 'feminist', a distance that would give greater protection from the backlash against feminism.

Critics against the adoption of gender studies over women's studies argue that the trend may lead to a re-erasure of women in the curriculum and that the project of balancing the sexual and gender roles in academia and society is not yet done. With the persistence of sexual inequality, they suggest, the need for acknowledging women still exists.

The debate over the names of women's studies versus gender studies is unlikely to be resolved nationally or internationally, but rather it is decided by individual schools based on the needs of their student populations and on university and community pressures. There are feminists and non-feminists on both sides of the debate and powerful arguments can be made for the use of either term.

Regardless of the label used, work is now being done in women's and gender studies at universities around the world, and hundreds of schools now have formal programmes in these areas.

References and further reading

Auslander, L. (1997) 'Do women's + feminist + men's + lesbian and gay + queer studies = gender studies?' *Differences*, 9 (3): 1–30.

Boxer, M. (1998) 'Remapping the university', *Feminist Studies*, 24 (2): 389–404.

Brod, H. (1987) 'The new Men's Studies', *Hypatia*, 2 (1): 179–96.

Dolling, I. and Hark, S. (2000) 'She who speaks shadow speaks truth', *Signs*, 25 (4): 1195–9.

Feminist and Women's Association in the United Kingdom, homepage at www.fwsa.org.uk

Institute for Women's Studies in the Arab World, homepage at www.lau.edu.lb/centers-institutes/iwsaw/programs.html

Libertin, M. (1987) 'The politics of Women's Studies and Men's Studies', *Hypatia*, 2 (2): 143–52.

National Women's Studies Association, homepage at www.nwsa.org

New Zealand Women's Studies Association, home page at www.womenz.org/wsa/journal.htm

San Diego State University Women's Studies Department (2005) 'SDSU Women's Studies timeline', 20 April, available at http://www.rohan.sdsu.edu/dept/wsweb/timeline.htm

Women's International Studies Europe, homepage at http://www.wise.medinstgenderstudies.org/

Worldwide Organisation for Women's Studies, homepage at www.fss.uu.nl/wows/start.html

Yee, S. (1997) 'The "women" in Women's Studies', *Differences*, 9 (3): 46–62.

—— (1998) 'Establishing an international doctoral program in women studies at the University of Washington', *Feminist Studies*, 24 (2): 366–73.

See also: academia; masculinity politics; men's practices, individual and collective; methods, methodology and research

SHELLEY MARTIN

WORKING WITH BOYS

In the West, interest in 'working with boys' has been provoked by contemporary concerns (and moral panics) about boys and young men which have focused on their disproportionate representation among, for example, suicide victims, perpetrators of theft and violence, those posing behavioural problems, those suspended and expelled from schools, and school leavers with few or no qualifications. Working with boys implies that boys, or some boys, are creating or experiencing problems which stem from being boys, and a wide range of initiatives targeting boys and young men have been developed in Western countries. These include mentoring schemes, programmes for fathers and sons, educational programmes addressing sexual and other forms of violence, adventure schemes, and programmes designed to improve academic achievement.

What sorts of interventions are considered appropriate depends on *how* boys or masculinity/ies are constructed as troublesome, and this is informed by key assumptions about gender and identity. Boys become troublesome, according to one popular view, because their masculine energies and inclinations are not being channelled in appropriate ways. Based on this view, intervention programmes have been proposed, with mainly working-class and black boys in mind, focusing on boys alone, promoting apparently 'natural' activities for boys like football and boxing (British Home Secretary, *Guardian*, 27 September 2004) and using 'strong' male role models (Biddulph 2000). Another opposing view, influenced by feminisms, argues that certain boys become troublesome – monopolising space, being disruptive, sexually harassing – not because they fail to express masculinity appropriately but because of how they position themselves in opposition to 'femininity'. Work with boys, according to this view, should not encourage this, and should concentrate on girls as well, or boys' views of femininity.

One version of feminism assumes that boys and girls enact socially prescribed and, in the case of boys, problematic scripts or sex roles. This has informed well-intentioned anti-sexist programmes which have sought to break down gender polarities but which have often alienated boys and precipitated a backlash, with boys reasserting themselves in relation to girls. Such programmes have addressed boys and girls as passive and unitary gendered subjects (Holland 2003).

Another version proposes that there are different ways of being male and female negotiated and performed (Butler 1990) by boys and girls, and that certain masculinities become 'hegemonic', and are asserted through the subordination not only of girls but of other boys (Connell 1995). Recent studies focusing on boys' constructions of masculinities suggest that it is precisely *through* activities like football, which boys associate with toughness, that they subordinate girls and feminise other boys, including, in Britain, South Asians (Frosh *et al.* 2002). This version implies an empathetic approach to working with boys which helps them to explore the different ways they construct masculinities, and raises possibilities of being boys which do not depend on subordinating girls and feminising boys (MacNaughton 1998).

Rather than problematising boys in general, the emphasis in this approach is on engaging with, respecting and validating boys and encouraging them to become more reflexive and critical. There is evidence, indeed, that the very process of addressing boys as active agents, whether in classes (Raey 1990) or research interviews (Frosh *et al.* 2002), promotes self-reflection and emotional articulacy – qualities normally construed by the boys themselves as feminine. When offered opportunities to explore their multiple identities, cracks start to appear in the simple binary model of gender power, with boys themselves highlighting the costs and limitations of being tough boys. Possibilities then emerge of appealing to boys' self-interest to 'disempower themselves' (Redman 1996) or become less fixated with chasing the constantly elusive hegemonic ideal. Frosh *et al.* found that boys were most critical of hegemonic forms of masculinity when interviewed individually, and also more likely to praise (or less likely to deride) girls and perform in 'softer' and less raucous ways than in the single-sex group interviews. Rather than authenticating boys' 'individual' voices, as teachers tended to do by constructing boys as inauthentic and problematic in groups, Frosh *et al.* argue that such contradictory performances may characterise the lives of boys seduced by hegemonic ideals but also troubled by the competition, violence, anti-intellectualism and homophobic policing which these engender, and that boys should be encouraged, in non-accusatory ways, to reflect on these contradictions.

Encouraging boys to be less invested in defining themselves in opposition to girls may mean affirming boys when they talk in ways normally constructed as feminine (Raey 1990), or providing images of caring men (Salisbury and Jackson 1996), or male facilitators/researchers exemplifying such models, and, in contrast to the strong role models advocated by writers like Biddulph, subverting gender polarities (Frosh *et al.* 2002). Significant adults, like black teachers and parents, can provide key role models for black boys, who, in countries like Britain and the US, may embody forms of hegemonic masculinity as a way of deriving power and self-esteem denied to them in a racist culture. Treating them with respect and validating their experiences of racism may help them to deal with this less destructively and reflect on the costs to them and others of living up to hegemonic male ideals (Sewell 1997; Frosh *et al.* 2002).

In southern Africa, in the light of HIV/AIDS, concerns about violence, sexual violence and the limitations of educational initiatives targeting mainly females, working reflexively with boys has become critical (Bujira 2000). On the basis of a qualitative study of black young people in the region, Pattman (2005) argues for reflective activities requiring cross-gender participation to encourage boy–girl friendships (combined with elements of single-sex work to encourage girls' voices). This study identified as major problems for girls sexual harassment, restrictions imposed on movements and expressions of desire, and for boys, fears of heterosexual rejection, heterosexual competition with older males, and difficulties expressing intimacy. These problems were understood as stemming from the polarised ways in which boys and girls identified and related to each other, with sexuality, unmediated by friendship and structured by male desire, becoming the main source of attraction between them. Like Frosh *et al.*, Pattman found contradictory performances by boys involving idealisations and denigrations of girls in individual and group research activities, and argues for sex educational exercises, like improvised role play, to allow young people to create different contexts and explore their different and contradictory identities.

References and further reading

Biddulph, S. (2000) *Raising Boys*, London: HarperCollins.

Bujira, J. (2000) 'Targeting men for a change: AIDS discourse and activism in Africa', *Agenda*, 44.

Butler, J. (1990) *Gender Trouble*, Cambridge: Polity Press.

Connell, R. (1995) *Masculinities*, Cambridge: Polity.

Frosh, S., Phoenix, A. and Pattman, R. (2002) *Young Masculinities*, Basingstoke: Palgrave

Holland, P. (2003) *We Don't Play with Guns Here*, Maidenhead: Open University Press.

MacNaughton, G. (1998) 'Improving our gender equity "tools": a case for discourse analysis', in N. Yelland (ed.) *Gender in Early Childhood*, London: Routledge, pp. 149–74.

Pattman, R. (2005) 'Boys and girls should not get too close: sexuality, the identities of African boys and girls and HIV/AIDS education', *Sexuality*, 8 (4): 501–20.

Raey, D. (1990) 'Working with boys', *Gender and Education*, 2 (3).

Redman, P. (1996) 'Empowering men to disempower themselves', in M. Mac an Ghaill (ed.) *Understanding Masculinities*, Buckingham: Open University Press.

Salisbury, J. and Jackson, D. (1996) *Challenging Macho Values*, Bristol: Falmer Press.

Sewell, T. (1997) *Black Masculinities and Schooling*, Stoke on Trent: Trentham Books.

See also: counselling and therapy; recovery and self-help; working with men; working with young men

ROB PATTMAN

WORKING WITH GAY MEN

Working with gay men in a counselling context is both similar and different to counselling with other populations. Like many individuals, gay men experience depression, anxiety and other psychological disturbances for which they seek counselling. They also have distressing life events that cut across sexual orientation, gender, race and culture such as relational problems, death of family and friends, physical illness and loss of direction and meaning in life. However, counselling with gay men also warrants special consideration given their status as a largely invisible minority living in cultures where family and relationships are generally defined through heterosexuality. Moreover, gay men may have a conflicted relationship with a mental health system that purports on the one hand to offer assistance and support but on the other is rooted in a history in which gay men were frequently diagnosed as 'sick' and 'abnormal'.

Although many Western mental health groups have formally declared that homosexuality is not a mental illness and therefore not in need of 'repair' (Haldeman 2002) this has been the case only for the last few decades of the twentieth century. Formerly, handbooks of psychological disorders such as the *Diagnostic and Statistical Manual of Mental Disorders* (American Psychiatric Association 1994) and the *International Statistical Classification of Diseases and Related Health Problems* (World Health Organization 2003) deemed homosexuality a distinct form of mental illness. Thus, treatment focused on decreasing homosexual attraction, increasing heterosexual attraction, and forming lasting heterosexual partnerships (Davison 2001). This approach is referred to as 'conversion' or 'reorientation' therapy, and although its practice has substantially decreased, it has a solid following especially within cultures and religious faiths that deem homosexuality to be aberrant and sinful. Groups such as the American Psychological Association and the American Psychiatric Association have called into question the ethicality of conversion therapy on the grounds that it has not been proven effective and has the potential to harm those who undergo it (Haldeman 2002).

Since the late twentieth century, counsellors in areas of the world such as North America, Europe and Australia often adopt a 'gay affirmative' approach to working with gay men (Cochran 2001). From this vantage point, counsellors can address homosexuality as one of the many diverse aspects of a person to be respected and, when relevant, to be examined in a supportive, non-judgemental and non-pathologising manner. In particular, counsellors are encouraged to examine their own heterosexist and homophobic biases, to not assume that psychological distress is related to sexual orientation, and to consider the impact of environmental factors like discrimination and stigmatisation with regard to an individual's presenting symptoms (Izzard 2000). Documents such as the *Guidelines for Psychotherapy with Lesbian, Gay, and Bisexual Clients* adopted by the American Psychological Association (Division 44/Committee on Lesbian, Gay, and Bisexual Concerns Joint Taskforce on Guidelines 2000) offer counselling professionals needed direction for providing culturally competent care to this population.

Gay men have a distinct set of issues that may be of particular focus in treatment. Some common issues directly related to sexual orientation include identity development, coming out to friends and family, episodes of discrimination, harassment and violence, and internalised homophobia. Coming out or disclosing one's sexual orientation is not achieved in a single episode but is repeated throughout one's life. With each coming out, one risks family rejection and marginalisation. Additionally, gay men may become targets of harassment and violence by individuals who are intolerant or fearful of transgressions of the heterosexual norm. Gay men are also not immune to the socialisation process that occurs from early childhood, reinforcing men to play out the role of provider and patriarch within a traditional heterosexual family. The result can be feelings of internalised homophobia and conflict regarding sexual orientation identity. Counselling can be a useful vehicle for exploring these issues, getting support, and strengthening coping and relationships. When gay men do not get assistance for these issues and instead either hold in their distress or act out towards others, the consequences may be low self-esteem, relationship and intimacy problems, mood and anxiety disorders, substance abuse and even suicide (Mays and Cochran 2001). Gay youth often experience profuse isolation from family and peers and may be at particular risk. Furthermore, many of these problems (e.g. active substance abuse, untreated mental health problems) are also risk factors for exposure to HIV, the virus that causes AIDS, which has wreaked havoc on gay male communities throughout the world. Substance abuse and mental health counselling, safe sex and substance abuse prevention, and 'gay affirmative' approaches are essential interventions. However, increasing legal equality and societal tolerance for gay men (and other sexual and gender minorities) may prove to be the most powerful intervention of all.

References and further reading

American Psychiatric Association (1994) *Diagnostic and Statistical Manual of Mental Disorders*, 4th edn, Washington, DC: APA.

Cochran, S.D. (2001) 'Emerging issues in research on lesbian and gay men's mental health', *American Psychologist*, 56 (11): 932–47.

Davison, G.C. (2001) 'Conceptual and ethical issues in therapy for the psychological problems of gay men, lesbians, and bisexuals' *JCLP/In Session: Psychotherapy in Practice*, 57 (5): 695–706.

Division 44/Committee on Lesbian, Gay, and Bisexual Concerns Joint Taskforce on Guidelines (2000) 'Guidelines for psychotherapy with

lesbian, gay, and bisexual clients', *American Psychologist*, 55: 1440–51.
Haldeman, D.C. (2002) 'Gay rights, patient rights', *Professional Psychology: Research and Practice*, 33 (3): 260–64.
Izzard, S.A. (2000) 'Psychoanalytic psychotherapy', in D. Davis and C. Neal (eds) *Therapeutic Perspectives on Working with Lesbian, Gay, and Bisexual Clients* (*Pink Therapy* Vol. 2), Buckingham: Open University Press.
Mays, V.M. and Cochran, S.D. (2001) 'Mental health correlates of perceived discrimination among lesbian, gay, and bisexual adults in the United States', *American Journal of Public Health*, 91 (11): 1869–76.
World Health Organization (2003) *International Statistical Classification of Diseases and Related Health Problems*, Geneva: WHO.

See also: counselling and therapy; recovery and self-help; working with men

LARA M. STEPLEMAN

WORKING WITH MALE PATIENTS

Men's experiences of their masculinised bodies and gendered selves are central to understanding how their sense of maleness and masculinity and their participation in gender relations are shaped by illness. Most literature on men's illness is contextualised in autobiographical and biographical accounts of specific illnesses (read autopathographical and pathographical, see Hawkins 1993). For example, Frank (1991), Sparkes (1996) and Watt (1997) have provided unprecedented accounts of illness experiences and through them we can identify an association between the illness experience and men's feelings, frustrations and frailty.

Work with male patients is a relatively new field in the health care literature, emanating essentially from the psycho-social disciplines, which have heightened consciousness regarding the need to focus on working with males, for example in families (James 2001) or with victims of sexual abuse (O'Leary 2001). The focus of this work is principally on the establishment and maintenance of therapeutic relationships in the counselling milieu. This literature offers enormous insight into issues for male and female therapists: for example, the impact of entrenched and embodied power dynamics, the impact of traditional gender roles, and the problems of countertransference. While these issues are central to how practitioners engage with males in this type of therapeutic relationship, for many health care disciplines working with male patients involves dealing with their bodies and providing body care. The extent to which gender is central to the way in which men experience what is done to them by health professionals and how this might be constructed in the context of masculinity has not been systematically explored and the discourse has not extended to how practitioners might engage with male patients while providing this arguably most intimate type of care. Even the more recent literature on men's physical illnesses such as testicular cancer, prostate cancer and cardiac disease remains primarily focused on illness experience, embodiment and issues related to masculinity and does not translate this to practice in the sense of what health professionals do to patients and how they might construct these activities. However, this literature provides insight into the way an altered body impacts on gender relations and the ways men reconstruct or renegotiate their masculinity.

In this way, the discourse(s) surrounding the practice of health professionals in relation to body care are fundamentally genderless, even though disciplines such as nursing claim to have the person and holistic care as their principal focus. This does not mean that the practice of health professionals is genderless. There is evidence to suggest that the practice of experienced health professionals and their engagement with male patients is constructed with regard to gender. Curiously, it is these aspects of practice that are silent in the literature and reflect the taboo nature of body care.

While men experience threats to their masculinity and male identities as a feature of their illness experience, there is not a strong case to see these experiences as essentially gendered – rather, gender becomes an additional feature

(Newman 2000). However, there may be individuals whose sense of self is so centrally gendered that for them a threat to their gendered embodied being can be the dominant if not overwhelming quality of the experience. Charmaz (1995: 281) notes that men attempt to make sense of their altered selves and the situations in which they find themselves by drawing on the existing cultural logic that currently defines masculinity. This raises the question of how men from different cultural backgrounds experience illness and clinicians might practise patient care in this context. These types of questions fall outside the cultural safety parameters and subsequently have not been addressed. Clearly, this sort of investigation offers great benefits for clinicians in providing greater understanding about men's embodied experiences and improving our practice to take into account these experiences.

The lack of investigation of masculinities and embodiment in the health literature reflects the primacy of the economically based models used to describe patient care in health care systems in developed countries. These models only allow for concepts located inside directly observable and quantifiable domains, and there is no evidence that any of the compelling literature on men's socially constructed or embodied experiences is considered formally or informally in these systems (Newman 2000). What remains problematic is the extent to which the concepts of care and caring have been de-emphasised by economic models of health care delivery, and subsequently the relationship of masculinities and male embodiment to men's experiences of what is done to them and for them as patients and how these experiences might inform practice within the disciplinary domains in health care. Consequently, if health care practitioners are concerned with truly therapeutic care, there is a need to consider how care is provided to male patients and how their experiences of that care are influenced by the interplay between masculine ideology, identity and illness experience.

References and further reading

Charmaz, K. (1995) 'Identity dilemmas of chronically ill men', in D. Sabo and D.F. Gordon (eds) *Men's Health and Illness*, Thousand Oaks, CA: Sage, pp. 266–91.

Frank, A.W. (1991) *At the Will of the Body*, Boston, MA: Houghton Mifflin.

Hawkins, A. (1993) *Reconstructing Illness*, West Lafayette: Purdue University Press.

James, K. (2001) 'Making the connections', in B. Pease and P. Camilleri (eds) *Working with Men in the Human Services*, Sydney: Allen and Unwin, pp. 37–53.

Lawler, J. (1991) *Behind the Screens*, Melbourne: Churchill Livingstone.

Newman, S. (2000) 'Masculinities and men's bodies', paper presented at the Qualitative Research in Health and Social Care Conference, Bournemouth University, 25–27 August.

O'Leary, P. (2001) 'Working with males who have experienced childhood sexual abuse', in B. Pease and P. Camilleri (eds) *Working with Men in the Human Services*, Sydney: Allen and Unwin, pp. 80–92.

Sparkes, A.C. (1996) 'The fatal flaw', *Qualitative Inquiry*, 2: 463–94.

Watt, B. (1997) *Patient*, London: Penguin.

See also: counselling and therapy; recovery and self-help; working with men

STUART NEWMAN
MURRAY FISHER

WORKING WITH MARGINALISED AND MINORITY MEN

Often racial and ethnic minorities become socially invisible unless they make their presence known in active confrontation with the majority society. Such confrontations may result in surveillance by the majority culture, which assesses the needs of minorities based on its own standards. These contradictions complicate examining minority men's marginalisation in family and health service provision.

In their roles as husbands and fathers across racial and socioeconomic statuses, men are socialised to embrace the provider role as demonstrating paternal commitment and responsibility. Cazenave (1979) contended that for African–American men, provider role success leads to their undertaking nurturing and other paternal roles. Cazenave's contention raises legitimate concern because African–American husbands and fathers are less likely than their white peers to experience provider role success, through racial discrimination and an out-migration of labour force opportunities. Structural barriers to paternal role success include unemployment, underemployment and educational, vocational and developmental unpreparedness, specifically among young fathers. These problems contribute to psychological role strain, common among African American fathers and induced by their inability to uphold paternal expectations (Bowman 1989).

Provider role failure among racial and ethnic minority men resulting in father absenteeism and irregular material support may appear as non-commitment to parenthood and family headship (Johnson 1995; Ehrenreich 1983). Clearly, some fathers shirk all responsibility for their children. However, provider role failure among poor urban nonresident and unwed fathers may reflect the pressures of structural and demographic changes in family formation patterns and paternal role behaviours as well as incarceration, broken relationships with their children's mothers, and even unknown paternity (Johnson 1998). Many minority men experience intergenerational absence of fathers and few other male models on whom they can develop parenting roles. Many men, often unwed fathers, assume paternal responsibility after making poor choices regarding formal and vocational education. They seek employment in an era when the human capital necessary to sustain family headship has increased. Older men in intact married families are often better prepared for sustaining themselves in the labour force, chiefly due to their advanced age, human capital development and work experience. Their wages are more likely to support a family, thus making them more attractive as husbands and fathers. These men, however, are not immune to job losses due to deindustrialisation. In contrast, adolescent and young adult men who become fathers before they are fully prepared educationally, vocationally and developmentally to assume the economic and other challenges of family life are less likely to sustain themselves in intact families (Johnson 2000).

Paternal engagement, however, encompasses far more than the provision of financial support. When examined solely from an instrumental perspective, our understanding of paternal involvement is limited. The assumption of multiple, interactive paternal roles is particularly crucial for poor, unmarried and nonresident fathers, given the developmental and socioeconomic statuses that often truncate their effectiveness as financial providers. In addition, many of these fathers are noncustodial parents. Assessing paternal involvement among nonresident fathers using indicators developed for intact, co-resident families is inappropriate and yields weak results. Without needed parenting supports, poor fathers, like poor mothers, experience great difficulty in meeting their children's emotional needs. Because parenting support services are generally tied to child custody, unwed fathers who neither reside with their children nor have established legal paternity are at risk of being ignored and marginalised (Salter and Johnson 1997).

Clearly, broader, integrative perspectives of paternal involvement that include and value nurturing as well as financial contributions are needed. Practitioners who work with poor nonresident fathers can empower them by helping them to enlarge their conception of fatherhood and paternal involvement. Given these fathers' limited labour force participation, recognising and embracing affective as well as instrumental paternal roles is crucial to realising more fulfilling paternal relationships with their children.

Men's health is an underdeveloped area of medical and public health research and practice. Across a broad range of indicators, men report poorer health than women. Although men in all socioeconomic groups are doing poorly in terms of health, some especially high-risk groups include men of low socioeconomic status (SES) of all racial/ethnic backgrounds, low-SES minority men and middle-class African–American men (Williams 2003). Poor economic circumstances can create a feeling of powerlessness in individuals. Limited income and opportunity may be viewed as barriers to achieving life goals. Personal responsibility and self-direction may not develop, leading to negative effects on health behaviours. Perceptions that failure is inevitable can have direct physiological effects.

Lack of attention to men's health increases gaps in health status, health care access and quality. More emphasis should be placed on addressing men's negative health behaviours, particularly focused on improving the health of racial and ethnic minority, low-income, gay and older men. In addition, all men need better health-related resources. Increased attention to men's health will dispel myths, positively change health care and health behaviours and improve men's health status (Williams 2003). Though African–American males are chiefly referenced here, these contentions should be considered for other marginalised males and men.

References and further reading

Bowman, P. (1989) 'Research perspectives on black men', in R. Jones (ed.) *Black Adult Development and Aging*, Berkeley, CA: Cobbs and Henry, pp. 117–50.

Cazenave, N. (1979) 'Middle-income black fathers', *Family Coordinator*, 28 (4): 645–53.

Ehrenreich, B. (1983) *The Hearts of Men*, Garden City, NY: Anchor/Doubleday.

Johnson, W. (1995) 'Paternal identity among urban, adolescent males', *African American Research Perspectives*, 2 (1): 82–6.

—— (1998) 'Paternal involvement in fragile, African American families', *Smith College Studies in Social Work*, 68 (2): 215–32.

—— (2000) 'Work preparation and labor market experiences among urban, poor, nonresident fathers', in S. Danziger and A. Lin (eds) *Coping with Poverty*, Ann Arbor, MI: University of Michigan Press.

Salter, W. and Johnson, W. (1997) 'Paternal involvement among poor, nonresident fathers', invited presentation at the School of Social Service Administration Friends' Luncheon.

Williams, D. (2003) 'The health of men', *American Journal of Public Health*, 93 (5): 724–31.

See also: counselling and therapy; recovery and self-help; working with men

WALDO E. JOHNSON, JR

WORKING WITH MEN

Work with men on gender issues is now evident in most countries of the world and growing in both sophistication and mainstream appeal. Yet this work is still controversial and often poorly understood.

Work with men has activist beginnings rooted in a commitment to social justice and human rights. In the late 1970s in response to requests from battered women's movement activists and in support of the women's liberation movement, men in cities across the United States began to set up activist projects. Michael Radetsky, one of the founding members of Men Overcoming Violence (MOVE) in San Francisco, captures the mood of the times: 'It was a chance to do the sort of exciting things women were doing, a way to take the stuff men's groups were dealing with and make it about social change and justice and political struggle, not just about ourselves' (Yurman 1995).

Typically linked to other social justice movements, the early men's programmes were dedicated to ending men's violence against women and argued that men had a particular responsibility to end men's violence. These organisations often described themselves as pro-feminist. Pro-feminist men seek to work in support of feminism and feminist goals, adopting processes of partnership rather than colonisation and espousing an activist sensibility oriented towards social change and gender justice (Flood 2002).

Central to pro-feminist work has been a belief that men can, and often do, have a personal investment in challenging the current gender order. For example, many men have suffered directly as a result of violence done to them or to their female loved ones (Katz 2003). Another core feature of most profeminist men's organisations, especially following the publication of scholarship on masculinities, has been the recognition that men are not monolithic and that their experiences, understandings and embodiments of manhood are shaped by diverse life experiences. As Greig (2002: 5) emphasises, the term 'masculinities'

> recognizes the heterogeneity of the group of people referred to by the term 'men' and suggests that the links between gender identity and ... men's lives are complicated by relations of power between men, along lines of economic class, social status, race/ethnicity, sexuality and age.

Reflecting these origins, men across the world have begun to work creatively to end men's violence against women and children, prevent HIV/AIDS and foster gender equity. Launched by a small group of men in Toronto in 1991, the White Ribbon Campaign now provides tools and strategies to a loose network of mostly male gender activists in more than fifty countries who work to end men's violence. In Nicaragua, the Men's Group of Managua launched a national campaign making the connection between Hurricane Mitch and increased male violence against women, based on the theme 'Violence against women: a disaster that men CAN do something about' (Peacock 2000). In South Africa, the Men as Partners Network uses workshops, community education and activism to engage men in reducing the spread and impact of HIV and AIDS (Peacock and Levack 2004). And in Brazil, Instituto Promundo works with young men in the urban slums surrounding Rio de Janeiro and Sao Paulo to promote gender-equitable values and practices.

Alongside community-based efforts to work with men, a number of international conferences and campaigns have promoted efforts to reach and engage men in working towards gender equality. The 1994 International Cairo Conference on Population and Development (ICPD) Programme of Action affirms the need to 'encourage and enable men to take responsibility for their sexual and reproductive behavior and their social and family roles'. Emphases on male involvement are evident too in the 1995 Fourth World Conference on Women in Beijing and the 2000–1 World AIDS Campaign by UNAIDS.

As work with men has grown in scope and scale an evidence base has begun to emerge. Research conducted by Horizons and Instituto Promundo in Brazil has shown that young men who participated in Programme H activities demonstrated significant positive shifts in gender norms at six and twelve months, were more likely to use condoms, and were less likely to report symptoms of sexually transmitted infection (Pulerwitz *et al.* 2004). Evaluations of the Men as Partners Network in South Africa found that 71 per cent of past MAP workshop participants believed that women should have the same rights as men, whereas only 25 per cent of men in the control group felt this way, and that 82 per cent of the participants thought that it was not normal for men to sometimes beat their wives, whereas only 38 per cent of the control group felt that way (Kruger 2000).

Gender-conscious work with men and boys is an increasingly visible aspect of the activities of community, health, social service and government sectors, as well as voluntary networks in men's movements. This includes work with particular categories of men such as fathers, male prisoners, gay men, and so on, and efforts to introduce an awareness of issues of men and gender in areas of practice in health, education, development, conflict reduction and other fields. While some efforts are supportive of feminism and oriented towards gender equality, others are ignorant of feminism and risk entrenching gender inequalities. Much work with men works within narrow psychological and sex role understandings of men's issues, ignores men's privilege and power, and is often anti-feminist.

Work with men to promote gender equality is relatively new but it appears to be growing fast. As it expands across the globe it will be important that it remain informed by the work of women's rights activists and that it stays consistent with its origins in social justice movements.

References and further reading

Flood, M. (2002) 'Frequently asked questions about pro-feminist men and pro-feminist men's politics', *XY Online*.

Greig, A. (2002) *Political Connections. Virtual Seminar Series on Men's Roles and Responsibilities in Ending Gender-based Violence*, United Nations International Research and Training Institute for the Advancement of Women (INSTRAW), Santo Domingo: United Nations.

Katz, J. (2003) 'Building a big tent approach to ending men's violence', *Building Partnerships Initiative*, available at www.endabuse.org/bpi

Kruger, V. (2000) *Evaluation Report: Men as Partners Program*, Project Evaluation and Research Service, September.

Peacock, D. (2000) 'Que no nos separen fronteras', *Movement*, Summer.

Peacock, D. and Levack, A. (2004) 'The Men as Partners Program in South Africa', *International Journal of Men's Health*, 3 (3): 173–88.

Pulerwitz, J., Barker, G. and Segundo, M. (2004) *Promoting Healthy Relationships and HIV/STI Prevention for Young Men. Horizons Research Update*, Washington, DC: Population Council, available at http://www.promundo.org.br/controlPanel/materia/view/380

Yurman, R. (1995) 'A bit of history', unpublished.

See also: counselling and therapy; recovery and self-help

DEAN PEACOCK

WORKING WITH MEN IN PRISON

Prison is a dark mirror of society-wide gender relations. There is a very clear, unspoken prison code for men: act tough, never appear weak or vulnerable, don't snitch (don't inform on others to the staff), stand up for yourself if disrespected or challenged to fight, win the fight and humiliate or destroy your opponent in any way you can, do not cooperate with the authorities, don't depend on anyone for anything, and above all else don't do anything that might appear feminine – that could lead to victimisation, even rape. Thus the successful male prisoner must hone the very qualities that add up to toxic masculinity, the concomitants of patriarchy that constrict men's lives and lead to abuse and violence on the outside (Sabo *et al.* 2001). One of the most difficult tasks for men who have spent time in prison, when adjusting immediately after being released, is re-learning how to express tenderness and how to gain objectives in some way other than proving one's manliness in battle. Working with men in prison involves helping them work through complicated and conflicting needs and feelings so they can do their time successfully and then be successful again as free men in the community.

The first step in the work is connecting, forming a trusting and mutually respectful relationship with someone who can be intent on posturing in hyper-masculine fashion in order to survive. The worker must first gain the respect of the prisoner in a tough environment. There is a lot of testing. Prisoners want to see if the one offering the help is tough enough or smart enough to really help. Passing the test requires an in-depth familiarity with prison culture.

Since prisoners typically feel disrespected at every step in the criminal justice process, respect is a very big issue. The clinician can begin to demonstrate respect for the prisoner by respecting his reasons for remaining silent in certain contexts, and by carefully spelling out what the ground rules are for the helping relationship – for example, will there be absolute confidentiality, or what will the worker report to the authorities (Kupers 1999)? The worker must understand the reality-based fears that lie behind the question about confidentiality, and, in this and many other ways, the more the clinician can demonstrate to the prisoner that he or she understands the prisoner's plight, the more the prisoner will feel respected and heard, and the more effective the work that can be accomplished.

If a prisoner is experiencing emotional difficulties but refuses to seek mental health treatment lest he be labelled a weakling or a 'bug', the worker needs to help him figure out how to proceed with dignity. If a man is repeatedly getting angry at officers and consequently spends inordinate periods of time in segregation (where his mental condition deteriorates), he needs help figuring out a more constructive way to express indignation when those in charge of him seem to be abusing and disrespecting him. When a man has been assaulted or raped the worker needs to help him decide whether to report the incident and risk retaliation.

Prisons' objective conditions matter (Haney 2006). In recent years, in the USA, crowding has accelerated rapidly while rehabilitation programmes have been cut. There has been an influx of prisoners suffering from serious mental illness. And prison systems have resorted to punitive segregation for a growing proportion of their wards (including supermax or supermaximum security facilities where men are kept isolated and idle in their cells for months or years). All of these dreadful realities serve to intensify toxic masculinity.

When the prisoner is able to convince the worker that an injustice is being done, the worker must on certain occasions be willing to 'take the heat' and stand up to security staff or administration for the rights or needs of the prisoner. To the extent non-security staff entirely succumb to the culture of security and, for example, become as singularly punitive as security staff in their approach to prisoners, the less they are inclined to advocate for prisoners' legitimate needs, and the less likely they are to accomplish the work.

Prisoners who successfully maintain contact with loved ones throughout a prison term, and those who participate in educational and rehabilitative pursuits in prison, have a stunningly lower recidivism rate than those who lose contact with the outside world and are not able to prepare themselves for a life after prison. This is because, the more one is able to 'keep one's head outside of prison' while doing time, the better one's chances for post-release success at 'going straight'. On the other hand, the more one lets 'prison get into your head', the more difficult it is to succeed in the community after release. The human connection the worker forms with the prisoner is critical in this regard, including the refreshing reminder that the prisoner still deserves to be treated as a human being even though he is behind bars.

Of course, there are aspects of prison reality that clinicians are not capable of directly changing. Prison crowding will be a reality of prison life until the public, the government and the courts decide to change sentencing guidelines and parole requirements. And rehabilitation resources will be inadequate until the public and the legislators evolve more compassion for prisoners. The current tendency within prison systems to rely increasingly on harsh punishment, and ultimately long-term segregation, as a means of controlling prisoners, can only be changed at a higher level of administration. But work with prisoners can accomplish great gains, especially in ameliorating some of the worst pitfalls of the toxic masculinity that is exacerbated by prison deprivations and cruelties.

References and further reading

Haney, C. (2006) *Reforming Punishment*, Washington, DC: American Psychological Association.
Kupers, T. (1999) *Prison Madness*, New York: Wiley/Jossey-Bass.
Sabo, D., London, H. and Kupers, T. (eds) (2001) *Prison Masculinities*, Philadelphia, PA: Temple University.

See also: crime, criminality and law; criminal justice system; prisons

TERRY A. KUPERS

WORKING WITH OLDER MEN

While older men remain understudied in gerontological research and work with older populations, there has been a recent shift towards exploring their vulnerabilities and life situations (Arber *et al.* 2003). These explorations focus on examining both the new possibilities of extended life expectancy and the reasons for their continuing low longevity compared to women (Mathers *et al.* 1999). Contemporary studies consider the diversity of men's lives, especially their particular vulnerabilities and those circumstances which put them at risk (Kosberg and Kaye 1997). Attention has also been placed on understanding their help-seeking behaviours, needs with regard to social service provision, and engagement in social and community programmes (Kosberg and Kaye 1997).

The health facts on men's late life vulnerability are clear. They predecease women by about five to seven years, although this may be improving. They have higher rates of cardiovascular disease and cancer than women, and their diseases are comparatively more often lethal than disabling. They are less likely than women to use health services, especially in relation to preventive services and early intervention; the quality of their mental health appears more compromised as a result of their gendered roles.

Older men more at risk are the never-married, the homeless, aboriginal men, prisoners and veterans (Arber *et al.* 2003; Eckert and Repaci 1997; Cotter *et al.* 2006). The vulnerability of these groups appears to relate to the lack of protective intimate relationships across the lifecourse and/or to these groups' specific disadvantages and trauma.

In general, however, men's socioeconomic status in late life is superior to women's. The majority of men reach late life in a protective marital relationship. They are more likely to predecease their wives, hence tend to be well cared for in later years (Hooyman and Rubenstein 1996).

The long-term downward trend in older males' employment since 1900 due to early exit (Magnum 1997) poses major individual and societal challenges as countries seek to restructure their workforce in a globalising world. Although some countries recognise the cost of this practice in major skill shortages, remedial policies and programmes are yet to prove effective (Kohli *et al.* 1991).

Recent debate highlights distinct handicaps various men experience in entering late life. For example, some men will be more prone to poverty, loneliness, physical and mental health problems. However, men also have the potential for more experimentation in later life as they live longer.

Work with older men and women is informed by ongoing scholarship in ageing studies (Thompson 1994). Kosberg and Kaye's work (1997) marked a major turning point in focusing specifically on the vulnerabilities of older men, prompting major feminist writers like Arber, Davidson and Ginn (2003) to acknowledge that older men face particular challenges.

In the last decade conferences have increased on men's general health and health service relatedness, as well as on utilisation of services across the life course. Older men figure centrally in efforts related both to health and employment/retirement status. Older men's self-help groups have burgeoned, including older gay men's groups. The internet hosts many men's groups focused around mid and late life issues.

According to Barusch and Peak (1997), effective intervention design with older men follows guidelines that are responsive to both masculine identity and age characteristics. Such tailored interventions utilise an educational rather than therapeutic orientation, maximising opportunity for peer feedback and support. In addition, several major research studies are currently underway in relation to men's health in late life, for example the Florey Adelaide Male Aging Study (AIHW 2004).

References and further reading

Arber, S. (2004) 'Gender trajectories', in S. Svain, O. Daatland and S. Biggs (eds) *Ageing and Diversity Policy*, Bristol: Policy Press.

Arber, S., Davidson, K. and Ginn, J. (eds) (2003) *Gender and Ageing*, Maidenhead: Open University Press.

Australian Institute of Health and Welfare (AIHW) (2004) *Longitudinal Studies of Ageing*, Canberra: AIHW, Cat. No. AGE 42 Appendix L, p. 132, Florey Adelaide Male Aging Study.

Barusch, A.S. and Peak, T. (1997) 'Support groups for older men', in J. Kosberg and L.W. Kaye (eds) *Elderly Men*, New York: Springer.

Cotter, P., Anderson, I. and Smith, L. (2006) *Indigenous Australians*, Sydney: University of New South Wales Press.

Eckert, J. K. and Repaci, L.G. (1997) 'Elderly men of the inner city', in J. Kosberg and L.W. Kaye (eds) *Elderly Men*, New York: Springer.

Hooyman, N.R. and Rubenstein, R.L. (1996) 'Is aging more problematic for women than men?' in A.E. Scharlach and L. Kaye (eds) *Controversial Issues in Aging*, Needham Heights, MA: Allyn and Bacon, pp. 125–35.

Kohli, M., Rein, M., Guillenare, A.-M. and Van Gunsteren, H. (1991) *Time for Retirement*, Cambridge: Cambridge University Press.

Kosberg, J. and Kaye, L.W. (1997) 'The status of older men', in J. Kosberg and L.W. Kaye (eds) *Elderly Men*, New York: Springer.

Magnum, W.P. (1997) 'A demographic overview of elderly men', in J. Kosberg and L.W. Kaye (eds) *Elderly Men*, New York: Springer.

Mathers, C.D., Vos, T. and Stevenson, C. (1999) *The Burden of Disease and Injury in Australia*, Canberra: Australian Institute of Health and Welfare.

Thompson, E. (ed.) (1994) *Older Men's Lives*, Sage, Thousand Oaks, CA: Sage.

See also: counselling and therapy; recovery and self-help; working with men

FIONA MCDERMOTT
ELIZABETH OZANNE

WORKING WITH PERPETRATORS OR OFFENDERS

The terms 'perpetrators' (of crime) and 'offenders' are problematic insofar as they obscure the fact that they are people. And in most cases they are likely to be men. Trends in social and penal policy in the UK and USA and Australasia have objectified men who have practised or been convicted of criminal offences as 'offenders' and 'perpetrators'. Both terms de-humanise the individuals concerned, obscure from consideration their various social identities, and distract attention from wider criminogenic factors such as poverty and gender. Many scholars now prefer to use phrases such as 'men who commit crime' or 'use violence', drawing attention to both sex and agency.

Work with offenders aims to reduce the likelihood of them committing further offences and to reduce the amount of crime committed in a given community (Cavadino and Dignan 2002; Hollin 2002). Underpinning most approaches is the desire to change the person who has committed the offences and thereby change their behaviour. In the late nineteenth and early twentieth century in Europe, North America and Australasia the dominant means for seeking change was moral reform. The offender or 'sinner' was enabled through spiritual guidance to tread the 'straight and narrow path' of moral rectitude. The early–middle part of the twentieth century, in the West, saw the focus move from the spiritual to the medical/psychiatric (Foucault 1977). The concern was still to help the individual gain insight into their behaviour, but now the insight related to the psychological origins of their criminal behaviour. Attention focused on the influence of childhood in the aetiology of crime. It was assumed that insight into criminal behaviour would lead to its cessation. However, there was little evidence to support this secular act of faith. Martinson (1974) reviewed studies of work with offenders and, famously, concluded 'nothing works'. Although this paper has subsequently been subject to methodological critique, it did undermine therapeutic confidence in working with men who commit offences (McGuire 1995). However, by the early 1980s a body of empirical evidence indicated that one approach did appear to work in reducing reconviction rates (Gendreau and Ross 1987): cognitive-behavioural therapy (CBT).

CBT is used with groups (and individuals) who have committed a wide range of offences or failed to manage their consumption of alcohol or drugs. The programmes aim to change the ways men think and consequently behave. CBT is the dominant approach to working with offenders in the UK, North America and Australasia. Generally, men who have committed offences are required to attend a groupwork programme and failure to do so may result in imprisonment. CBT groups are also common in prisons.

A wide body of empirical evidence suggests that CBT is effective in reducing reconviction rates (Hollin 2002). However, a number of commentators question the long-term effect of these programmes, asking if they teach men to 'walk the walk' or merely help them to 'talk the talk' (Kendall 2004).

Although CBT is construed as 'therapy', in the context of work with men who have committed offences, it is generally mandated therapy. Those so mandated have limited options: either consent or go to gaol. In prison, they either consent or harm their chances of early release. Coerced consent does not occur in other forms of therapy where members of the non-convicted population make informed, free, choices about undergoing therapy. Locating therapy within a mandated criminal justice setting fundamentally changes the nature of the 'therapeutic' relationship and process. CBT is used as a key part of a 'tougher' community penalty. This raises questions as to whether mandated CBT is therapy or compulsory (re)education

CBT assumes a relationship between feelings, thoughts and behaviours. Among offenders, the therapeutic process helps men identify the feelings and the thoughts that prompt behaviours which lead to offences. The therapy identifies thoughts that facilitate men committing offences (for example, they deny responsibility for the offence or minimise its consequences) and replaces them with thoughts that inhibit the commission of offences. Central to this process is the notion of cognitive distortion: statements that deny, minimise or justify offending behaviour (Murphy 1990).

However, in CBT the concept of a distortion is based on the problematic assumption that there is a norm that can be clearly identified, and is common across cultures, gender, class and ethnicities (Cowburn 2006). Linked to this is the apparent failure of CBT to incorporate issues of gendered identity into therapeutic programmes. Most 'offenders' are men. Given this, the aetiology of offending behaviour cannot only be viewed within a framework predicated on the notion of failures of cognition, neglecting issues relating to what sustains male identities.

Work with male offenders needs attention at a social policy level – where issues relating to harmful aspects of male behaviour can be addressed through education and health policies – but also at a therapeutic programme level where the feelings, thoughts and actions of men who have committed criminal offences are considered in the wider context of the behaviours and attitudes of men in general. This may then draw attention to the possibility that some so-called 'cognitive distortions' are, in fact, common to many men.

References and further reading

Cavadino, M. and Dignan, J. (2002) *The Penal System*, London, Sage.

Cowburn, M. (2006) 'Constructive work with male sex offenders', in N. Parton, P. O'Byrne, K. Gorman and M. Gregory (eds) *Constructive Probation Work*, London: Jessica Kingsley.

Foucault, M. (1977) *Discipline and Punish*, London: Allen Lane.

Gendreau, P. and Ross R. R. (1987) 'Revivication of rehabilitation', *Justice Quarterly*, 4: 349–407.

Hollin, C. R. (2002) 'An overview of offender rehabilitation', *Australian Psychologist*, 37 (3): 159–64.

Kendall, K. (2004) 'Dangerous thinking', in G. Mair (ed.) *What Matters in Probation*, Cullompton, Devon: Willan Publishing.

McGuire, J. (ed.) (1995) *What Works: Reducing Reoffending*, Chichester: John Wiley.

Martinson, R. (1974) 'What works? Questions and answers about prison reform', *The Public Interest*, 23: 22–54.

Murphy, W.D. (1990) 'Assessment and modification of cognitive distortions', in W.L. Marshall, D.R. Laws and H.E. Barbaree (eds) *Handbook of Sexual Assault*, New York and London: Plenum.

See also: counselling and therapy; recovery and self-help; working with men

MALCOLM COWBURN

WORKING WITH VICTIMS AND SURVIVORS

Violence and abuse are significant gendered issues in that most perpetrators are male. However, a significant proportion of child and adolescent victims also are males. Therefore, it is important that there are some specific considerations for working with male victims and survivors. It is widely acknowledged that acts of abuse and violence can have lasting effects for individuals, families and the community. The World Health Organization (Krug *et al.* 2002) acknowledges that violence is a significant public health issue. Surveys of males in psychiatric, prison and substance abuse populations show much higher rates of childhood abuse than is found in community samples (Fondacaro *et al.* 1999). Abuse can impact on males' psychosocial functioning in a variety of ways, and it is important to view effects in the context of a response to trauma. Psychiatric diagnoses such as Post Traumatic Stress Disorder occur at much higher rates among survivors of child sexual abuse than in the general population (Fondacaro *et al.* 1999). When professionals are responding to individuals showing various psychosocial problems, they should be cognisant of a possible history of childhood victimisation.

The impact of abuse on males needs to be conceptualised in the context of the dominant constructions of masculinity, gender and sexuality. Hegemonic masculinity has encouraged a perception that 'real men' do not get sexually assaulted; this has resulted in secrecy and community silence regarding the issue. Male victims of sexual violence are often silenced by being stigmatised, trivialised or seen in jest. It can often be decades later that males come forward to discuss their experiences (O'Leary 2005). This is evident in inquiries into institutional abuse (in churches, orphanages, state wards and juvenile training centres) that often involves incidences of abuse that have occurred many years earlier. As a result, it is important that professionals work to create environments that make it easier for men to talk about experiences of violence. This can occur at an individual and community level. Raising community consciousness about male victimisation is important and education should focus on dispelling common myths and providing accurate information to male victims and their potential supporters.

When working with males who have been abused, it is important to consider the impact of language, myths and dominant gender stereotypes. There is debate about the terms 'victim' and 'survivor' (Scott 2001). This entry uses these terms interchangeably with the acknowledgement that neither adequately encapsulates the experiences and identities of those individuals who have experienced abuse and violence. However, it is important to acknowledge that acts of abuse and violence often constitute a crime, which has victims who, in most cases, endure pain and struggle because of these acts.

It is popularly assumed that male victims themselves become perpetrators of abuse. In fact, this is an unlikely outcome (Salter *et al.* 2003). There is no simple causal link between being victimised and becoming a perpetrator. While victimisation does increase one's risk of becoming a perpetrator, numerous other factors shape the relationship between the two (Salter *et al.* 2003). The critique of the hypothesis of 'victim to perpetrator' highlights the absence of an adequate account of gender and power, especially when it is considered that a large number of females are abused yet many fewer females are represented in offender populations, especially among those who sexually abuse (Cossins 2000; O'Leary 2001).

Many male survivors of sexual abuse report a fear of offending, but this is no indication that they actually go on to abuse. Indeed, this fear can be an important foundation in working to prevent the reproduction of abuse. Adding to the complexity is the widespread belief that paedophiles are homosexual. This serves to collapse sexual offending and non-heterosexual sexualities, despite evidence indicating that the majority of male offenders identify as heterosexual (Cossins 2000).

Male survivors suffer a great degree of self-blame, gender shame, guilt, aggression, sexual identity concerns, identification with the perpetrator, and fear of becoming a perpetrator themselves. They also experience responses that are similar to those among females, such as depression, anxiety, denial, relationship difficulties, lack of trust, a sense of betrayal, inappropriate sexual behaviours, anger and grief (O'Leary 2001). Constructions of masculinity and sexuality shape males' distinct responses to abuse. In the majority of cases of sexual abuse the perpetrator is an adult male. Prevailing prescriptions for manhood tend to stigmatise experiences of victimisation, especially same sex sexual abuse. To be victimised often results in both an internalised and external questioning of masculine legitimacy, because hegemonic masculinity positions non-heterosexual sexualities as abnormal. These specific reactions are often a central consideration for working with the effects of abuse and violence on males.

In any work with boys and men, professionals in a variety of fields should be mindful of a hidden population of male victims of abuse and violence. Dominant constructions of masculinity, sexuality and deviance shape the ways in which males experience the effects of abuse. In order to work with male survivors, there is a need to find ways to help negate the negative and restraining influence of hegemonic masculinity.

References and further reading

Cossins, A. (2000) *Masculinities, Sexualities and Child Sexual Abuse*, The Hague, Boston, MA: Kluwer Law International.

Durham, A. (2003) *Young Men Surviving Child Sexual Abuse*, West Sussex: John Wiley.

Fondacaro, K.M., Holt, J.C. and Powell, T.A. (1999) 'Psychological impact of childhood sexual abuse on male inmates', *Child Abuse and Neglect*, 23 (4): 361–9.

Krug, E.G., Dahlberg, L.L., Mercy, J.A., Zwi, A.B. and Lozano, R. (2002) *World Report on Violence and Health*, Geneva: World Health Organization.

O'Leary, P. (2001) 'Working with males who have experienced childhood sexual abuse', in B. Pease and P. Camilleri (eds) *Working with Men in the Human Services*, Sydney: Allen and Unwin, pp. 80–92.

—— (2005) 'Integrating a narrative approach to men who have been sexually abused in childhood', *Journal of Brief Therapy*, 4 (1).

Salter, D., Macmillan, D., Richards, M., Talbot, T., Hodges, J., Bentovim, A., Hastings, R., Stevenson, J. and Skuse, D. (2003) 'Development of sexually abusive behaviour in sexually victimised males', *Lancet*, 361 (9356).

Scott, S. (2001) 'Surviving selves', *Feminist Theory*, 2 (3): 349–61.

See also: counselling and therapy; recovery and self-help; working with men

PATRICK O'LEARY

WORKING WITH YOUNG MEN

Despite various attempts to articulate work with young men there still appears to be considerable confusion as to the focus of this work and how it should be delivered. Also missing is a clear theoretical framework and context in which work with young men has evolved. Yet, as work in Northern Ireland demonstrates, there is growing awareness of what constitutes effective practice in this field.

While it could be argued that the majority of young people in Northern Ireland display resilience and have very successful outcomes, Harland's study (2000) revealed that young men aged fourteen to sixteen living in inner-city Belfast were fearful of young men from different traditions and backgrounds and wary of certain young men within their own community. Paramilitary attacks were a constant threat that made them feel intimidated, suspicious and confused. Increases in male alcohol abuse, drug dependency, violence, suicide, mental illness, academic underachievement and involvement in crime caused these young men concern, and they struggled to live up to unrealistic masculine expectations.

Historically, work with young men in Northern Ireland has tended to focus on recreational needs and diversionary responses to aggressive and anti-social male behaviour with little concern for young men's emotional, mental and sexual health. In Harland's (2000) study, young men learned to use public settings as opportunities to 'perform' and 'prove' themselves to others. Fear of being 'put down' or shamed among their peers shaped their understanding of masculinity and inhibited their ability to talk openly and honestly about their thoughts and feelings.

Since the mid 1990s programmes have been developed to help young men acquire new skills and confidence and more realistically prepare them for the future. Through an 'advocacy approach' (Harland and Morgan 2003), young men are encouraged to address a range of issues they rarely can discuss elsewhere, such as self-esteem, relationships, risk-taking behaviour, mental health, transitions from boy to man, and fatherhood. Programmes combine reflective discussion with activities such as teambuilding, adventure, interactive games and role-playing that harness young men's natural energy and help them recognise important links between feelings and movement. Importantly, this approach helps lay a solid foundation for addressing more challenging work around young men's attitudes and behaviour in regard to issues such as sectarianism, sexism, homophobia and violence.

Creating environments where young men can think, reflect, talk openly and honestly, explore values and consider other viewpoints crucially depends on ensuring that young men feel valued and safe from threat and judgement. Skilled engagement by practitioners encouraged the young men in Harland's (1997) study to talk in a more purposeful way about what was important to young men and helped them better appreciate the impact of wider social, political and economic developments upon their lives. In work on the theme of violence with young men aged sixteen to twenty-five, Harland (2002) found that, through increased self-reflection and learning appropriate skills, practitioners were more effective at engaging young men and experienced increased empathy in regard to young men's issues. Experience in Northern Ireland suggests that the following factors are fundamental to successful work with young men:

- a proactive approach that focuses on developing young men's self-confidence;
- an appreciation of masculinity and how this impacts upon young men's behaviour;
- identification of issues affecting young men and the use of creative ways to address these;
- establishing appropriate learning environments in which young men feel safe and valued;
- combination of reflection and activity;
- the practitioner's skills, knowledge and empathy towards young men;
- the practitioner's commitment to building meaningful relationships with young men;
- appreciation of the qualities that young men look for in a practitioner – trust, genuineness, respect, humour, support and acceptance.

Work with young men has also proven to be successful in other parts of the world. Barwick's (2004) comprehensive review of best international practice reveals that 'strengths-based and male-focused' approaches are highly effective in working with young men. These intensive and prolonged programmes are diverse in their focus and location and acknowledge that strengths exist in individuals, families, schools, peer groups and communities. In the UK a developmental model underpinned by practice principles and an appreciation of masculine socialisation has been developed by Lloyd (1997).

It is increasingly recognised that developmental work with young men should facilitate expression of their thoughts, feelings and expectations. Adopting a proactive approach where the voice, needs and interests of young men are central to the process helps unlock their natural energy, talents and creativity. This approach also helps free young men from their perceived need to hide behind 'masculine masks' that prevent them from recognising and accepting that men can be sensitive, caring and at times vulnerable, without believing they are somehow compromising what it means to be a man.

References and further reading

Barwick, B. (2004) *Young Males: Strengths-Based Male-Focused Approaches*, New Zealand: Ministry of Youth Development.

Harland, K. (1997) *Young Men Talking – Voices from Belfast*, London: Working with Men Publications.

—— (2000) 'Men and masculinity: the construction of masculine identities in inner-city Belfast', PhD thesis submitted to the University of Ulster.

—— (2002) 'Everyday life: developing youth work practice with young men in Northern Ireland around the theme of violence', *Working with Young Men Journal*, 1: 7–12.

Harland, K. and Morgan, S. (2003) 'Youth work with young men in Northern Ireland: an advocacy approach', *Journal of Youth and Policy*, 81.

Lloyd, T. (1997) *Let's Get Changed, Lads: Developing Work with Boys and Young Men*, London: Working with Men Publications.

See also: boy and boyhood; counselling and therapy; recovery and self-help; working with men

KEN HARLAND
SAM MCCREADY

WORLD RELIGIONS, BUDDHISM

Buddhism is one of the world's major religious traditions, with an estimated 350 million followers worldwide. More than 98 per cent of the world's Buddhists live in Asia (Esposito *et al.* 2002); it is the most followed religion in many countries including Sri Lanka, Myanmar, Thailand, Cambodia, Laos, Japan and Vietnam (Harvey 1990). There is a significant number of Buddhists in China, Taiwan, Singapore and Hong Kong, but it is difficult to provide precise figures for these countries, given the overlap between Buddhism and traditional Chinese Folk religion. Buddhism has an ever-increasing number of adherents in Western nations, including the US and Australia. This is mostly due to immigration and, to a lesser extent, Westerners converting to Buddhism. For example, Buddhists now represent approximately 2 per cent of the Australian population and it is one of the fastest growing religions there. Western interest in Buddhism also extends beyond those who specifically identify as Buddhists, as evidenced by the popularity of figures such as the Dalai Lama and the proportion of the population who believe in reincarnation.

Most contemporary Buddhists follow one of two major traditions, Theravada (approximately 38 per cent of followers) or Mahayana (62 per cent of followers) (Esposito *et al.* 2002). Theravada is the major tradition in Thailand, Laos, Cambodia and Myanmar, while the Mahayana tradition is practised in China, Japan, Singapore, Taiwan and Vietnam.

The origins of Buddhism can be traced to the teachings of Siddhârtha Gautama (c. 556 – 486 BCE), a prince from a kingdom in north-east India, whose story is central to Buddhist doctrine and teaching. As his story is traditionally told, Prince Siddhârtha grew up in cloistered surroundings. As an adult he accompanied his chariot driver on several trips around his city, where he witnessed great suffering. Disillusioned, he left the palace at the age of twenty-nine and took up with the various ascetic groups, or *shramanas*, common in the region at this time, with a view to finding an end to suffering in this world (Esposito *et al.* 2002: 359).

Legend has it that while sitting under a bodhi tree, and having fallen out with his fellow mendicants, Siddhârtha achieved a state of enlightenment (*nirvana*), recognising that freedom from suffering can be achieved not through extreme asceticism or gross hedonism, but a 'middle way' (Carrette and King 2005: 95). Following his enlightenment, Siddhârtha was known as the 'Buddha', although he never thought of himself as a deity. Inspiring others, Buddha's teachings soon spread throughout the region, then further north and east.

Unlike other major world religions, Buddhism proffers no central deity or deities which humans ought to worship and follow (although many Buddhists accept the existence of the supernatural). Rather, Buddhists are encouraged to end life's cycle of suffering and continual rebirth through achieving a state of *nirvana*. Meditation is central to achieving this aim and is a very significant part of Buddhist religious practice. Buddhism has no universal religious text analogous to the Koran, Torah or Christian Bible, although various writings are canonised. There is an extremely strong monastic tradition in Buddhism, known as the *sangha*, the first of which was founded by the Buddha.

The central Buddhist doctrines are the Four Noble Truths and the Eightfold Path. The Four Truths are: life is characterised by suffering; the cause of suffering is ignorance and desire; ignorance and suffering are removed when desire is taken away; and following the Eightfold Path will remove suffering and desire. The Eightfold Path is: right views, right thought, right speech, right action, right livelihood, right effort, right mindfulness and right concentration (for a full description, see Harvey 1990).

Like all the world's major religions, Buddhism first emerged from a patriarchal culture and men continue to dominate Buddhism at an institutional and administrative level (Esposito *et al.* 2002). Feminist commentator Rita Gross argues that although Buddhist teaching posits no abiding or essential self, 'Buddhist texts, institutions, and individuals are just as likely to believe in gender as a fixed, rigid, determinative, and limiting trait as anyone else' (Gross 2004: 6). Within the Theravada tradition, for example, women cannot become official members of a *sangha*, or fully ordained, and although some women do become 'unofficial' nuns, they are not accorded the same privileges as their male counterparts (Bartholomeusz 1992: 37). (Women are ordained in some communities.) In the late twentieth century, however, various Buddhist feminist movements have emerged, campaigning for female ordination or offering feminist reconstructions of Buddhist teachings (see Gross 1993).

Although very little has been written about masculinity and Buddhism, some recent scholarship suggests that Buddhism both supports and contradicts prevailing ideals of masculinity in major Buddhist societies, including Vietnam and Thailand. Klunkin and Greenwood (2005) note that Thai society has two dominant constructions of masculinity: the traditional mendicant image associated with Buddhism and hegemonic ideal, valuing traditional masculine traits such as 'authority, courage, self-assurance, physical and emotional strength, and sexual prowess' (Klunkin and Greenwood 2005: 50). Despite these apparent contradictions, Thai men are expected, upon reaching the age of twenty, to enter the priesthood for three months, and this 'temporary ordination is seen as a rite of passage from raw or immature man to ripe or wise man' (Klunkin and Greenwood 2005: 50). Soucy (1999) notes that in Vietnam, young men are generally not expected to be religious because many Buddhist temple practices are associated with the 'feminine'. This pattern is typical of many religions, especially Christianity; men dominate institutionally, but more women are adherents. Less is known about how Buddhism might be implicated in the gendered behaviours of Western converts.

References and further reading

Bartholomeusz, T. (1992) 'The female mendicant in Buddhist Sri Lanka', in J.I. Cabezon (ed.) *Buddhism, Sexuality and Gender*, Albany, NY: SUNY Press, pp. 37–64.

Carrette, J. and King, R. (2005) *Selling Spirituality: The Silent Takeover of Religion*, London: Routledge.

Esposito, J.L., Fasching, D.J. and Lewis, T. (2002) *World Religions Today*, New York: Open University Press.
Gross, R. (1993) *Buddhism after Patriarchy: A Feminist History, Analysis and Reconstruction of Buddhism*, Albany, NY: SUNY Press.
—— (2004) 'The dharma of gender', *Contemporary Buddhism*, 5: 3–13.
Harvey, P. (1990) *An Introduction to Buddhism: Teachings, History and Practices*, Cambridge: Cambridge University Press.
Klunkin, A. and Greenwood, J. (2005) 'Buddhism, the status of women and the spread of HIV/AIDS in Thailand', *Health Care for Women International*, 26: 46–61.
Soucy, A. (1999) 'Masculinities and Buddhist symbolism in Vietnam', in K. Biber, T. Sear and D. Trudinger (eds) *Playing the Man: New Approaches to Masculinity*, Sydney: Pluto Press, pp. 123–34.

See also: world religions, Christianity; world religions, Hinduism; world religions, Islam

ANDREW SINGLETON

WORLD RELIGIONS, CHRISTIANITY

Two moments in the origins and development of Christianity have significantly shaped Christian notions of masculinity: the belief in the incarnation and the virtue of chastity. They have provided men with a rationale for securing male privilege within hierarchical institutions, but have also allowed them to experiment with alternatives to hegemonic masculinities.

As told in the New Testament, the disciples and early followers of Jesus of Nazareth, a Jewish-born man, believed him to be the Messiah, the son of God. After his crucifixion and resurrection, the Greek title 'Christ' (*khristos)* for Messiah was added to his name. More than a Jewish teacher and prophet, Jesus Christ was seen as God himself: God incarnate. The biblical God became flesh, embodied in the human Jesus. The church fathers wrestled with the mystery of incarnation in increasingly abstract theological debates about the Trinity (Father–Son–Spirit) and Christology (the nature of Christ), but affirmed in the Nicene Creed (325 CE) that Jesus Christ was of the substance of God, at once fully divine and fully human.

For Christians, incarnational faith opens the possibility of experiencing the divine presence at work in the human body. For Christian men, the fact that God became incarnate in a male saviour figure (rather than a female body) had two lasting consequences: first, men could argue theologically for their privileged position within the emerging church, rationalising the exclusivity of the male clergy and papacy on the grounds of Christ's maleness. Second, they disciplined their male bodies and passions through asceticism, monasticism and an ethics of chastity in the hope of imitating the sinless Christ, who was seen as the embodiment of an ideal masculinity.

As Christianity spread, the blending of the prophetic Hebrew traditions with the Greco-Roman ethos enabled men to live against the prevailing expectations of the Roman empire. Instead of free statesmen, soldiers or Roman householders, they became 'slaves of Christ' in the form of nomadic wanderers, martyrs, eunuchs (castration), hermits (desert dwellers), monks, urbanised Gnostic teachers and soldiers for Christ. Christian ascetics went beyond Greco-Roman ideas of controlling one's passions through temperate eating and sexuality. Probing the body at its limits, they pushed for life-long celibacy and extended fasts in order to overcome the sinful human condition and end human dependency on the fallen, material world. Imitating Christ meant to live in a male body without masculine desires – a struggle that, according to Christian hagiographies, only a few saints accomplished.

Concurrent with asceticism, the lives of Christian male householders, who had no desire to break out of secure social structures, were regulated by moral codes. Grafted upon the Roman *pater familias*, the Christian householder was not expected to be celibate or ascetic but to moderate his behaviour. Licit sexuality for laity was channelled into marriage and reproduction, whereas clergy were urged to celibacy and humility. At the waning of the Roman empire, the virtues of ascetic and chaste behaviour of a once marginalised masculinity became dominant.

While Eastern Christianity (Greek and Russian Orthodox traditions) never required clergy to be celibate, except for bishops and monks, the medieval Western Catholic Church settled on three pathways for Christian men: the domestication of the ascetic spirit into monastic orders; a non-celibate laity following rules of chastity; and a celibate clergy.

As the medieval Catholic Church gained power, it enforced celibacy among its priests after the Gregorian reform and the Second Lateran Council in the eleventh and twelfth centuries. This era also saw the emergence of devotional chivalry and of militant defenders of faith as new Christian masculine ideals. Crusaders and Knights of God battled perceived external threats (infidels); the inquisitor, internal enemies (heresy). Monastic orders proliferated, some dedicated to active ministry (*vita activa*), others to a secluded life (*vita contemplativa*). Furthermore, scholastic theology posited reason as the highest form of faith, and man, within the natural order, as the most rational being.

The Protestant Reformation no longer required clergy or laity to be celibate, ascetic or monastic. Monasteries and convents were disassembled in Protestant countries, thus disabling a spiritual and communal alternative for men and women alike. The clerical monopoly was replaced by a focus on family ruled by a male head. The ideal Protestant man submitted to a marital code of chastity and to the virtue of moderation. The Reformation as harbinger of modernity also led to church–state separation and a privatisation of religion. As a result, men shifted their quest for power and authority from ecclesiastical circles of male celibates to secular spheres of influence (e.g. nation states, science, economy). Christianity became perceived as a feminised realm, and various nineteenth- and twentieth-century Christian men's movements tried to counteract this trend by re-masculinising the church.

Despite the dominance of androcentric theologies and patriarchal practices, the belief in the incarnation as the possibility of divine presence embodied in humans has always provided liberating, non-hegemonic and sometimes queer trajectories for Christian men (and women). Modern sensitivities concerning questions of human rights, equality and diversity as well as the women's movement and world-wide ecumenical efforts have deepened such liberating visions.

In North America, men's studies in Religion has emerged as a new field of scholarly inquiry. Informed by feminist and queer theory as well as gay studies, it investigates the effects of gender and sexuality upon faith and religious practice. However, a sustained analysis of global Christianity from a consciously male-gendered perspective is still in its infancy. Missing still is an assessment of Christian masculinities as lived, embodied and articulated in specific localities, especially postcolonial masculinities in non-Western countries.

References and further reading

Boswell, J. (1980) *Christianity, Social Tolerance, and Homosexuality*, Chicago, IL: University of Chicago Press.

Boyd, S., Longwood, M. and Muesse, M. (1996) *Redeeming Men*, Louisville, KY: Westminster/John Knox.

Brown, P. (1988) *The Body and Society*, New York: Columbia University Press.

Burrus, V. (2000) *Begotten, Not Made*, Stanford, CA: Stanford University Press.

Jordan M. (2000) *The Silence of Sodom*, Chicago, IL: University of Chicago Press.

Krondorfer, B. (ed.) (1996) *Men's Bodies, Men's Gods*, New York: New York University Press.

Kuefler, M. (2001) *Manly Eunuchs*, Chicago, IL: Chicago University Press.

Moore, S. and Anderson J. (2003) *New Testament Masculinities*, Atlanta, GA: SBL.

Nelson, J. (1992) *Body Theology*, LouisvilleKY: Westminster/John Knox.

Noble, D. (1992) *A World Without Women*, New York: Oxford University Press.

Ranke-Heineman, U. [1988] (1990) *Eunuchs for the Kingdom of Heaven*, New York: Doubleday.

See also: Christian men's movements; history, colonisation; history, Europe, early modern to 1917; history, European Middle Ages; history, western

BJÖRN KRONDORFER

WORLD RELIGIONS, HINDUISM

The dominant religion of ancient India, prior to the rise of classical Hinduism around the beginning of the Common Era, was a sacrificial religion geared towards creating 'twice-born' men. Jay (1992) suggests that, in patrilineal societies, the ritual of sacrifice serves to ensure the continuity and purity of patrilineal succession. Presiding over the 'birth' of new men, priests chanted Sanskrit mantras while placing liquid offerings in the womb of the fire altar. The liturgically inseminated altar gave birth to the new self of the sacrificer. No one could doubt the paternity of this ritually engendered new man, a pure offspring of his father's line, whereas a child born of a woman might always be another man's son. After living a long life and fathering many sons of his own, a twice-born man who had sponsored sacrifices would at death join his male ancestors in post-mortem felicity in 'the world of the fathers', there to be maintained by rituals performed by his/their male descendants on earth. This religion required a married man as sacrificer and could not be performed without the sacrificer's wife or ritual stand-in (Jamison 1996). Her spiritual duty was to give birth to sons and facilitate the priestly process whereby new men emerged from the fire through the midwifery of priests, thus vouchsafing an eternal paternal line.

Three millennia later, the rituals that many Hindus perform use vegetarian rather than animal offerings, are directed to different deities, and take place in temples rather than in the open air. Some women learn the liturgical language of Sanskrit; a few even serve as priests. But maintaining the social order through controlling the purity of the male line still ranks as a cardinal objective for many Hindus today, especially in rural India. This concern with descent accounts for much of the pressure put on young women to select a spouse of the proper caste, to marry as soon as they have acquired the education necessary to secure a professional spouse, and to have sons who will carry on the ancestral rites to ensure the well-being of the paternal line.

The requirement of deference to patriarchal order weighs equally heavily on men. To know and to show your place in relation to the male head of the house constitutes the essence of moral probity (Carstairs 1970; Kakar 1978). Carefully arranged matrimony contributes to the purity of the male line and transmission of wealth from patriarch to his patrilineage. Both purity of pedigree (caste identity) and purity of conduct must be guarded. But after giving birth to a healthy son and nurturing him to adulthood, a woman's duty is more or less done. A man's responsibility to the patrilineage never ends, even in death. He should show deference to his father and elder brothers at all times, and in their presence he must not show physical affection for his wife.

In many Western cultures, marriage makes a boy a man. For Hindus, marriage makes a boy a potential father. But proper conduct of men towards one another, as mediated through women, makes a boy a man. Fidelity to one's elder brothers is a crucial virtue, especially in north India. Fraternal treachery is one of the greatest taboos. The two classic epics of Indian literature narrate crises over the ownership of women that threaten the bonds between brothers. When the epic hero Rama must protect his father's honour by going into exile, his younger brother accompanies him. Likewise Bharata, the brother appointed to rule, places Rama's sandals on the throne and rules reluctantly in his stead, indicating the legitimacy of his elder brother's right to the throne.

Rama's story illustrates how a model eldest son should behave in a world of chaos and disorder. Poor urban Hindus especially find comfort in visions of the fair-minded king

Rama riding in his war-chariot, vanquishing evildoers. Hindu kings began to build Rama temples and style themselves as his incarnations when Muslim invasions began to threaten Hindu hegemony (Pollock 1993). With the rise of political Hinduism in the 1990s, Rama now enjoys immense popularity. Visions of a theocracy where righteous men like Rama hold sway bring voters to the polls, especially in areas blighted by poverty and urbanisation. Politicians on the Hindu right (belonging to political parties collectively known as Hindutva, or 'Hinduness') fulminate against the decline of Hindu values, particularly the confusion of gender roles, the loss of respect for elders, and the breakdown of authority in the family. They claim that past values can be restored and that India's problems are attributable to the new ways brought by Muslim and Christian outsiders.

Images of hyper-masculine warrior gods such as Rama appeal to those who seek a righteous protector of the poor, the elderly and the disenfranchised. Rhetoricians soothe the fearful with images of Rama winning his wife through bravery, while whipping up indignation for political purposes by positioning Hindus as victims from whom manhood has been stolen by outsiders (Sinha 1995; Nandy 1983; Alter 1994).

In a country where the accomplishments of many male deities and human statesmen have been attributed to the *shakti* or divine energy of the great goddess flowing through them, perhaps the justice that Rama represents to many Hindus will be achieved through a more balanced repertoire of religio-political icons in the future.

References and further reading

Alter, J. (1994) 'Celibacy, sexuality, and transformation of gender into nationalism in north India', *Journal of Asian Studies*, 53 (1): 45–66.

Carstairs, M. (1970) *The Twice-Born*, Bloomington, IN: Indiana University Press.

Jamison, S.W. (1996) *Sacrificed Wife/Sacrificer's Wife*, Oxford: Oxford University Press.

Jay, N. (1992) *Throughout Your Generations Forever*, Chicago, IL: University of Chicago Press.

Kakar, S. (1978) *The Inner World*, Delhi: Oxford University Press.

Nandy, A. (1983) *The Intimate Enemy*, New York: Oxford University Press.

Pollock, S. (1993) 'The Ramayana and political imagination in India', *Journal of Asian Studies*, 52 (2): 216–97.

Sinha, M. (1995) *Colonial Masculinity*, Manchester: Manchester University Press.

See also: history, South Asia; Indian masculinities

LIZ WILSON

WORLD RELIGIONS, ISLAM

While masculinity serves Islamic communities as a key political and legal concept, there is no single, comprehensive or unitary Muslim masculinity: rather, Muslim masculinity is plural in terms of language and the law. Of the world's thirty largest language communities, eleven – Arabic, Bengali, Malay, Farsi, Urdu, Punjabi, Javanese, Turkish, Telugu, Marathi and Gujarati – include significant populations of Muslim men. While 'masculinity' may be so fundamental to Islam as to be invisible (those responsible for successive editions of the *Encyclopedia of Islam* have overlooked it and affiliated topics), masculinity is a concept which differs among Muslims. While the Qur'an – source of Islamic law – contains numerous references to men in their capacity as believers in Allah, schools of jurisprudence interpret these references differently. Nation-states then codify social practices, providing fresh expression for such legal masculinities (Choueiri 2002: 651–2). Such differences are particularly evident in issues of men's rights as women's legal sex partners. Muslim men in Iran, for example, enjoy far greater legal powers over their wives than men in Tunisia.

The Qur'an's second chapter – Al-Baqara – identifies men's masculinity in terms of their legal responsibilities: 'men have a degree (of advantage) over them', i.e. women (002.228, Yusufali). Referring to child support after divorce, the Qur'an advises, 'he shall bear the cost of their food and clothing on equitable terms. No soul shall have a burden laid on it greater than it can bear' (002.233, Yusufali). Sunni Islam is currently restricted to four schools of legal interpretation, or *madahab*: Hanafi, Hanbali, Malaki and Shafa'I. Each school of jurisprudence, or *usul al-fiqh*, grants men different rights (see Makdisi 1979, 1984; Meron 1969); Shi'a Islam offers an alternative institution, the Ja'fari school of jurisprudence, to guarantee Muslims' legal rights.

While their specific rights have differed from one school to another, 'masculinity' remains a central concept. As Roded points out, the Prophet Mohammed's reported virility was an important model Muslims sought to emulate; colonists used the same reports to vilify his historical personage and his contemporary followers (2006: 58, 62). All four schools of Sunni law give husbands the privilege of breaking their marital bonds at will and the right to marry more than one woman, and they differentiate men's greater shares in inheritance from women's lesser shares.

Contemporary men's legal status is specific, dependent and situated. Among Muslims, Ouzgane points out: 'the opposite of masculinity is not necessarily femininity and . . . even misogyny is not the core of masculinity' (1997). While modern states' laws establish normative citizenship for male Muslims, these same men's rights and obligations before the law depend on their mental soundness and sexual performance. As Anderson argues, even among marginal Islamic communities such as the Druze, believers follow mainstream Hanafi interpretations of Islamic law. Men are only guaranteed exclusive legal access to their wives on the condition of the husbands' sexual potency. If a man suffers incurable impotence, his wife may seek dissolution of marriage (Anderson 1950, 1952). Sexual performance doesn't necessarily remain a private issue between husbands and wives, but it also refers to such public issues as regional market and civic hegemonies, as Rothenberg demonstrates (2006: 102).

Nation-states' claims to secular law point up the flexibility of men's rights in the Islamic world. Charrad points out that while most explanations of change in Muslim men's experience of normative citizenship in post-colonial states 'emphasize factors such as economic development or revolutionary ideology', neither is a determining characteristic in North Africa, where men's rights 'are also shaped by the political requirements of state stability or consolidation' (1990: 19–20). Among predominantly Muslim residents of *maghribi* states, Tunisian husbands are denied the right to verbal repudiation and must seek a court date; if they take multiple wives, they can be punished with imprisonment and a fine. Tunisian men are denied legal guardianship over adult women.

Following Iran's revolution, Aghajanian (1986) noted structural changes in Shi'a men's experience of divorce. Like all law governing Muslims, Shi'ite interpretation in Iran is mediated by modern nation-states' administrative forms. The 1967 law accepted divorce only through a court; such public proceedings were time-consuming, tedious and embarrassing, but the 1979 law allows couples divorcing by mutual consent to sidestep these courts and register a change in personal status before a notary public (*mahzai*) and two witnesses. That said, Iranian men report different experiences after a divorce than their partners. Shi'i Muslim men begin to enjoy legal protections after the divorce, since fathers have custody of boys over the age of two and girls over the age of seven. Men's masculinity also enjoys extra-legal structural protections, since divorced mothers are vulnerable to poverty. Aghajanian noted that 73 per cent of divorcing fathers agree to pay child support to their ex-wives, even though the law does not require a man to support children's living expenses outside his home after the age at which he enjoys custody (1986).

References and further reading

Aghajanian, A. (1986) 'Some notes on divorce in Iran', *Journal of Marriage and the Family*, 48: 4.

Anderson, J.N.D. (1950) 'Invalid and void marriages in Hanafi law', *Bulletin of the School of Oriental and African Studies*, 13 (2): 357–66.
—— (1952) 'Personal law of the Druze community', *Die Welt des Islams*, 2 (2): 83–94.
Charrad, M. (1990) 'State and gender in the Maghrib', *Middle East Report*, 163: 19–24.
Choueiri, Y. (2002) 'The Middle East', *Journal of Contemporary History*, 37 (4): 649–63.
Makdisi, G. (1979) 'Significance of Sunni schools of law in Islamic religious history', *International Journal of Middle East Studies*, 10 (1): 1–8.
—— (1984) 'Juridical theology of Shafi'i', *Studia Islamica*, 59: 5–47.
Meron, Y. (1969) 'Development of legal thought in Hanafi texts', *Studia Islamica*, 30: 197–203.
Ouzgane, L. (1997) 'The rape continuum', *Queen*, 1 (1) [n.p.].
Roded, R. (2006) 'Alternate images of the Prophet Muhammad's virility', in L. Ouzgane (ed.) *Islamic Masculinities*, London: Zed Books, pp. 57–71.
Rothenberg, C. (2006) 'My wife is from the jinn', in L. Ouzgane (ed.) *Islamic Masculinities*, London: Zed Books, pp. 89–104.

See also: history, colonization; history, Middle east; history, South Asia

ELIZABETH BISHOP

WORLD RELIGIONS, JUDAISM

Judaism is a religious civilisation of the Jewish people. The term 'Judaism' (Hebrew, *Yahadut*) was first used among Greek-speaking Jews in the first century of the Common Era (see II Macabees 2:21) and is unknown in the Bible and rabbinic literature. The word 'Jew' (Hebrew, *Yehudi*), is biblical and refers to both someone who originates from the tribe of Judah, and one who lived in the Southern Kingdom of Judah (in the land of Israel), no matter what their tribal origin. Today a Jew is considered to be one who is born to a Jewish mother or has converted to Judaism and accepts the obligation to observe its religious commandments. The written language of the Bible is Hebrew (Hebrew, *ivrit*), but Aramaic is also an ancient Jewish language which has found its way into the Talmud and other sacred books. Modern Hebrew is spoken by Jews in Israel. Another language associated with Jewish people is Yiddish, which is spoken by many Jews of European origin and is still a common language among ultra-Orthodox Jews.

Jewish law, which has continued to develop and change since biblical times, is called *halakha*. Jewish society is fashioned and ruled by *halakha*, a legal system that pervades all aspects of life, with judicial and legislative functions, both of which are performed by rabbis whose authority is recognised by the Jewish community. *Halakha* is also a religious system and, as such, its influence is much more pervasive than an ordinary legal system, for it prescribes norms not only of legal behaviour, but also of ethical behaviour and standards. It has moulded the major institutions of Jewish life, including marriage and the family. It is based not only on interpretation of the words of the Biblical texts according to rabbinic religious tradition, but also on the understanding of its intentions and values as transmitted throughout Jewish history.

Judaism is based on the doctrine that there are two sacred Torahs – the Written Torah (the Bible) and the Oral Torah (the traditions, including the rabbinic ones) – out of which the *halakha* develops. Eventually the Oral Torah was written down as part of Jewish sacred literature. But it was never monolithic in its decisions. Just as in any legal system there can be different legal decisions based on similar cases, so it is in *halakha*. *Halakha* has shown amazing flexibility and staying power by being able to accommodate disagreement.

Treatment of women in halakha

The plurality of opinion and interpretation that constitutes *halakha* also applies to its treatment of women. The attitude of *halakha* towards women can be characterised as ambivalent rather than monolithic. The input of women into the halakhic process is rare, and it is almost always men who have the authority to make halakhic decisions. In addition, social and cultural needs are major factors in determining the stance of *halakha*. The status of women is caused in part by the worldview of the males who have created *halakha*, whose modes of thought have led to a mind-set which is unfavourable to women. This may stem from the fact that the deity is usually expressed in masculine terms, with God often described metaphorically as a husband or male parent.

Place of men in Judaism

The husband has control over his wife, and Jewish law objectifies that control in legislation. In biblical law man is master over woman and women are perceived as chattels. The husband is the master (*ba'al*), whose permission to rule over his wife originates in Genesis 3: 16, where God tells the first woman that her husband shall rule over her. The word *ba'al* implies ownership as well as lordship. A man gets his wife by taking and possessing her, and if she fails to please him, he can divorce her (Deuteronomy 24: 1). In post-biblical times, a woman is acquired in three ways: with money or something of nominal value, with a marriage contract, or by sexual intercourse (Mishnah Kiddushin 1: 1). In marriage, the man is responsible for his wife's physical (food, clothing and housing) and emotional needs. It is the man, not the woman, who is commanded to procreate. He is the agent, and she the receiver.

Often the referent of person and personhood is Man (*adam* or *ish*). Since Hebrew is a gendered language, the plural men (*anashim*) can be construed to include women, but very often is not. A man daily recites in the Morning Prayer (*shaharit*), 'We thank you for not being created a woman', whereas a woman says, 'We thank you for creating us in your will.'

Masculinity in Judaism

'The heroic man (*gibor*) is the one who conquers his urges (*kovesh et yitzro*)' (Ethics of the Fathers 4: 1). This repudiation of brute strength can be applied to the classic role model of the husband who spends years of studying in the academy (*beit midrash* or *yeshiva*). Sacrifice of family life for the sake of learning is normative. Intellectual and spiritual pursuits, not physical prowess, are the cultural ideals.

References and further reading

Biale, R. (1984) *Women and Jewish Law*, New York: Shocken.
Cantor, A. (1995) *Jewish Women/Jewish Men*, San Francisco, CA: HarperCollins.
Dorff, E.N. and Rossett, A. (1988) *The Living Tree*, Albany, NY: SUNY Press.
Hyman, P. (1983) 'The Jewish family', in S. Heschel (ed.) *On Being a Jewish Feminist*, New York: Schocken, pp. 19–26.
Sigal, P. (1975) 'Elements of male chauvinism in classical Halakha', *Judaism*, 24: 226–44.
Wegner, J.R. (1988) *Chattel or Person?* New York: Oxford University Press.

See also: history, Europe; history, Middle East; Jewish masculinities

NAOMI GRAETZ

Y

YOUNG MEN

In certain world cultures transitions into manhood are celebrated through rituals and often painful ordeals that signal the advent of adulthood (Gilmore 1990). In industrial societies, going to work was a traditional 'rite of passage' for young men and male socialisation essentially prepared young men for the world of work. In post-industrial Western societies transitions from boy to man have become much more blurred, leaving many young men facing paradoxes, contradictions and tensions for which they are not mentally or emotionally prepared (Pollack 2001).

Issues surrounding masculinity and what it means to be a man have also become increasingly complex and contradictory. Contexts where this can be seen particularly clearly are those where the transition from boy to manhood takes place in societies in – or emerging from – conflict situations such as present-day Northern Ireland.

In many working-class areas of Northern Ireland, living up to local traditions of masculinity has placed particular pressures on young men. Males comprised 91 per cent of all victims of sectarian homicides over the period from 1969 to 2001. More than a third of victims were in their twenties and one in six was aged nineteen or less (Smyth and Hamilton 2003). This highlights a complex phenomenon related to being young and male in a society emerging from a period of prolonged violence. While young men are caught up in the transition from conflict to peace, they have not been equipped with the skills to manage this change. Since 1969 many young men have experienced a sense of place and significance as defenders and protectors of their community. They have defended against 'invasion' from other communities and unwanted intrusion by security forces. Their aggression, as these defenders, afforded them status among peers and other community members. Within a post-conflict society the need for the defender and protector has become virtually redundant. The behaviour of young men, once lauded and feted, has now become a focus for criticism, violent assault and/or expulsion from that community. As in many other contexts, young men's experiences of violence in Northern Ireland influence their understanding of masculinity and what it means to be a man.

References and further reading

Gilmore, D. (1990) *Manhood in the Making; Cultural Concepts of Masculinity*, New Haven, CT: Yale University Press.

Pollack, W. (2001) *Real Boys' Voices*, Harmondsworth: Penguin Books.

Smyth, M. and Hamilton, J. (2003) 'The human costs of the Troubles', in O. Hargie and D. Dickson (eds) *Researching the Troubles: Social Science Perspectives on the Northern Ireland Conflict*, London: Mainstream.

See also: boys and boyhood; male youth cultures; working with young men; youth movements

KEN HARLAND
SAM MCCREADY

YOUTH MOVEMENTS

In the twenty-first century, much is made of young people's apparent apathy. Even when they are protesting, accusations abound that youth are merely filling time by imitating 1960s activism (Borosage 2000). In reality, such claims are merely symptomatic of efforts to belittle youth, as, across the globe, numerous young people are involved in movements that challenge human rights, social and environmental injustices.

Although since criticised for ignoring female cultural activities, as well as hiding influences of family and the domestic sphere, academic interest in youth movements first focused largely on male sub-cultures and practices in the public arena. Granted 'youth' is a difficult category to define, but scholars tend to agree that it refers to a transitional period between childhood and adulthood, this being between about the ages of sixteen and twenty-five. The sub-cultural 'classics' of the 1970s focused on this subordinate age group, using Gramsci's theory of hegemony to argue that young people negotiate or oppose society's dominant ideology by actively appropriating and transforming its meanings. Chiefly associated with the Centre for Contemporary Cultural Studies at Birmingham University (UK), researchers like Phil Cohen, Paul Willis and Dick Hebdige maintained that oppositional lifestyles were evidence of young people's cultural struggle for control over their lives, specifically in the case of working-class white males such as punks (see Skelton and Valentine 1998; Leblanc 1999).

Male youth cultures used dress to play on mainstream ideas of masculinity. Combat boots, typically associated with military discipline, became part of the anti-authoritarian and anarchistic punk outfit. Punk attire like safety-pins worn as piercings, tattoos, hair shaved and glued into mohawks, and subversively worn traditional garments like kilts displayed society's rejection of punks as well as punks' rejection of society. Indeed, the punk movement is a very male-dominated scene, not only in terms of the ratio of males to females but also with regard to punk behaviours and attitudes. Early punk zines claimed that 'punks are not girls' (Laing 1985 cited in Leblanc 1999: 108), and today the majority of punk bands remain all male, their song lyrics misogynistic and the thrash pit, where they perform, male territory (see Leblanc 1999).

Giroux (1983) argued that individual acts of resistance are as politically significant as large-scale subcultures and that such resistance is not deviant but should be recognised as political protest by members of disenfranchised groups. Rather than position individuals as passive victims of oppression, this perspective gave greater recognition to people's own agency.

During the 1960s, university students in the USA advocated for direct action to change university and government policy. Influenced by Marxism, students questioned the role of universities in the political economy, as evidenced by government contracts, military research and corporate investments. Aided by predominantly male-led organisations such as Students for a Democratic Society (SDS), they requested input into tenure decisions, demanded courses more aligned to their agendas, and expressed their hatred of the Vietnam War. In fact, university became something of a male safe haven for those avoiding the draft, resulting in an 8 per cent increase in the enrolment rate of college-age men between 1963 and 1968 (Card and Lemieux 2001). The end of the draft and downsizing of the war after 1969 meant students no longer instigated large-scale protests; however, students, together with other civil rights groups in the 1960s, were nevertheless instrumental in shaping the New Left Movement (see Horowitz 1986).

Today activism has changed somewhat. Rather than build an exclusive youth movement, grassroots organisations and non-governmental organisations disperse power among global networks, mobilising a multinational, multiethnic, multigendered, multigenerational and multiclass fight against global capitalism (Klein 2003). And the anti-globalisation movement now tends to have not leaders but celebrities, most of whom are women (Bygrave 2002).

Youth have not, however, simply been subsumed into some broader movement, but also remain active in their own right. Zimbabwe's SHAPE (Sustainability, Hope, Action, Prevention, Education) operates on a for-youth-by-youth premise, educating young people about HIV/AIDS. One of its programmes, Gender Equality, aims to empower females and help males redefine their masculinity, thereby encouraging condom use (Taking ITGlobal website). The Australian-based International Youth and Public Space Network advocates for youth-inclusive policy and practice in the design and management of public and community accessible spaces, and, in doing so, highlights the role gender can play in space. Other youth-based organisations include the Club of Youth Working for the Environment (India), the Environmental Youth Network of Yucatan (Mexico), the Native Youth Movement (North America) and the Anarchist Youth Network (UK), to list but a few. Students also continue to organise, evidenced by the 1989 Beijing Student Movement. Less directly youth-led, the men's rights movement targets unequal treatment of boys and girls in areas like education and the law, as well as fathers' rights to see their offspring (Men's Activism News Network).

Youth movements remain significant, although they are perhaps more integrated with other groups than in previous decades. With organisations like the Ruckus Society offering its (often youth-age) participants training in nonviolent direct action techniques to help further environmental, human rights and social justice causes, there is little reason to buy media hype that today's youth are apathetic.

References and further reading

Borosage, R. (2000) 'Mixing '60s activism and anti-globalization', *Los Angeles Times*, 23 April.

Bygrave, M. (2002) 'Where did all the protesters go?' *Observer* (London), 14 July.

Card, D. and Lemieux, T. (2001) 'Going to college to avoid the draft', *American Economic Review*, 91 (2): 97–102.

Giroux, H. (1983) *Theory and Resistance in Education*, Westport, CN: Bergin and Garvey.

Horowitz, H. (1986) 'The 1960s and the transformation of campus cultures', *History of Education Quarterly*, 26 (1): 1–38.

International Youth and Public Space Network, at www.yspace.net

Klein, N. (2003) 'Demonstrated ideals', *Los Angeles Times*, 20 April.

Leblanc, L. (1999) *Pretty in Punk*, Piscataway, NJ: Rutgers University Press.

Men's Activism News Network, at www.mensactivism.org

Skelton, T. and Valentine, G. (1998) *Cool Places*, London: Routledge

TakingITGlobal, at www.takingitglobal.org

The Ruckus Society, at http://www.ruckus.org/

See also: boys and boyhood; male youth cultures; working with young men; young men

CARO HARPER

index